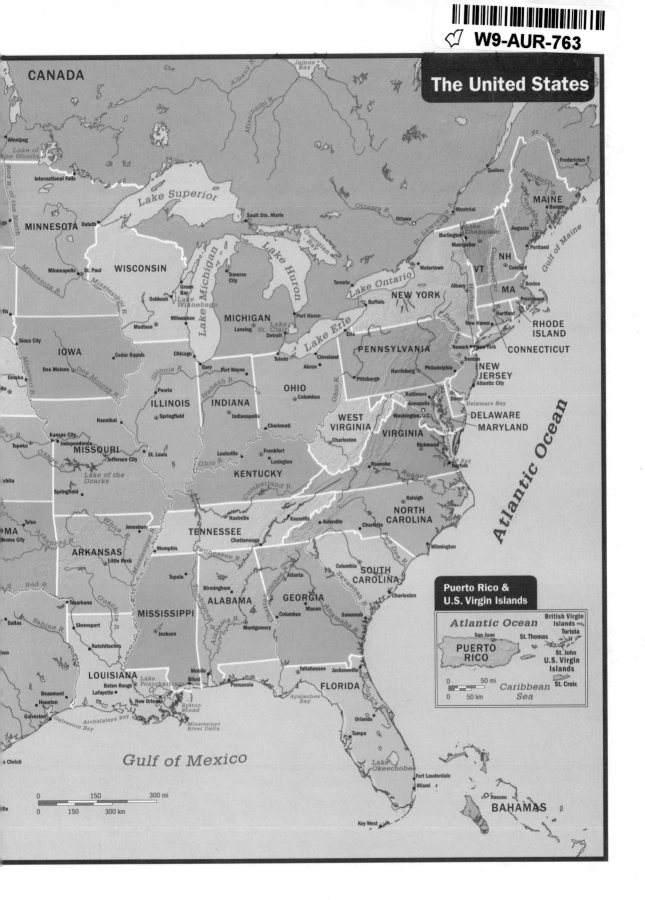

The United States

CANADA

MINNESOTA
Winnipeg
Lake of the Woods
International Falls
Duluth
Minneapolis
St. Paul
WISCONSIN
Oshkosh
Madison
Milwaukee
Green Bay
Lake Winnebago
Lake Superior
Sault Ste. Marie
MICHIGAN
Lansing
Traverse City
Lake Michigan
Lake Huron
Georgian Bay
Albany R.
Missinaibi R.
James Bay
Ottawa R.
Lake St. Clair
Detroit
Port Huron
Toronto
Lake Erie
Cleveland
Akron
Toledo
Lake Ontario
Buffalo
Erie
NEW YORK
Watertown
Albany
St. Lawrence R.
Ottawa
Montréal
Québec
Burlington
Montpelier
Lake Champlain
VT
NH
Concord
MAINE
Bangor
Augusta
Portland
Gulf of Maine
Fredericton
St. John R.
Penobscot R.
Kennebec R.
Connecticut R.

IOWA
Sioux City
Cedar Rapids
Des Moines
Omaha
Missouri R.
Des Moines R.
Chicago
Gary
Fort Wayne
ILLINOIS
Peoria
Springfield
Hannibal
Illinois R.
Wabash R.
INDIANA
Indianapolis
Cincinnati
OHIO
Columbus
PENNSYLVANIA
Pittsburgh
Harrisburg
Philadelphia
Ohio R.
Allegheny R.
Newark
New York
Trenton
NEW JERSEY
Atlantic City
Boston
Providence
Hartford
New Haven
MA
RHODE ISLAND
CONNECTICUT
Hudson R.
Delaware R.
Baltimore
Annapolis
Washington, D.C.
Dover
DELAWARE
MARYLAND
Delaware Bay

MISSOURI
Kansas City
Independence
Jefferson City
St. Louis
Topeka
Osage R.
Lake of the Ozarks
Springfield
Tulsa
wichita
Little Rock
ARKANSAS
White R.
Arkansas R.
Jonesboro
Memphis
MA
oklahoma City
Louisville
Frankfort
Lexington
KENTUCKY
Ohio R.
Cumberland R.
Nashville
Knoxville
Chattanooga
TENNESSEE
Tennessee R.
WEST VIRGINIA
Charleston
VIRGINIA
Richmond
Roanoke
Norfolk
Roanoke R.
Chesapeake Bay
Raleigh
Asheville
Charlotte
NORTH CAROLINA
Wilmington
Pee Dee R.
Columbia
SOUTH CAROLINA
Charleston
Savannah R.

Dallas
Texarkana
Shreveport
Natchitoches
Red R.
Sabine R.
Ouachita R.
MISSISSIPPI
Jackson
Tupelo
Birmingham
ALABAMA
Montgomery
Tombigbee R.
Alabama R.
LOUISIANA
Baton Rouge
Lafayette
Beaumont
Houston
Galveston
Galveston Bay
New Orleans
Atchafalaya Bay
Mississippi River Delta
Lake Pontchartrain
Breton Sound
Mobile
Biloxi
Pensacola
Apalachee Bay
GEORGIA
Columbus
Macon
Atlanta
Savannah
Chattahoochee R.
Altamaha R.
Tallahassee
Jacksonville
St. Johns R.
FLORIDA
Orlando
Tampa
Lake Okeechobee
Fort Lauderdale
Miami
Key West
Nassau
BAHAMAS

Atlantic Ocean

Gulf of Mexico

Corpus Christi
ville

Puerto Rico & U.S. Virgin Islands

Atlantic Ocean
San Juan
PUERTO RICO
St. Thomas
British Virgin Islands
Tortola
St. John
U.S. Virgin Islands
St. Croix
Caribbean Sea
0   50 mi
0   50 km

0   150   300 mi
0   150   300 km

EIGHTH TEXAS EDITION

We the People

AN INTRODUCTION TO AMERICAN POLITICS

Benjamin Ginsberg
THE JOHNS HOPKINS UNIVERSITY

Theodore J. Lowi
CORNELL UNIVERSITY

Margaret Weir
UNIVERSITY OF CALIFORNIA AT BERKELEY

Anthony Champagne
UNIVERSITY OF TEXAS AT DALLAS

Edward J. Harpham
UNIVERSITY OF TEXAS AT DALLAS

 W. W. NORTON & COMPANY
NEW YORK   LONDON

To Sandy, Cindy, and Alex Ginsberg
Angele, Anna, and Jason Lowi
Nicholas Ziegler

W. W. Norton & Company has been independent since its founding in 1923, when William Warder Norton and Mary D. Herter Norton first published lectures delivered at the People's Institute, the adult education division of New York City's Cooper Union. The Nortons soon expanded their program beyond the Institute, publishing books by celebrated academics from America and abroad. By mid-century, the two major pillars of Norton's publishing program—trade books and college texts—were firmly established. In the 1950s, the Norton family transferred control of the company to its employees, and today—with a staff of four hundred and a comparable number of trade, college, and professional titles published each year—W. W. Norton & Company stands as the largest and oldest publishing house owned wholly by its employees.

Editor: Ann Shin
Assistant editor: Jake Schindel
Project editor: Melissa Atkin
Senior production manager: Benjamin Reynolds
Book design: Lissi Sigillo
Information Graphics Design: Kiss Me I'm Polish LLC, New York
Design director: Rubina Yeh
Managing editor, College: Marian Johnson
Composition: Jouve
Manufacturing: R. R. Donnelley & Sons—Jefferson City, MO
Photo editor: Junenoire Mitchell
Photo researcher: Susan Buschhorn
E-media editor: Peter Lesser
Marketing manager: Nicole Netherton

Library of Congress Cataloging-in-Publication Data

We the people : an introduction to American politics / Benjamin Ginsberg . . . [et. al.]. — 8th Texas ed.
    p. cm.
Includes bibliographical references and index.

ISBN 978-0-393-93525-7 (hardcover)

1. United States—Politics and government—Textbooks.   2. Texas—Politics and government—Textbooks.   I. Ginsberg, Benjamin.
  JK276.W4 2011
  320.473—dc22

                                                2010041072

W. W. Norton & Company, Inc., 500 Fifth Avenue, New York, N. Y. 10110
www.wwnorton.com

W. W. Norton & Company Ltd., Castle House, 75/76 Wells Street, London W1T 3QT

3 4 5 6 7 8 9 0

contents

2 ● The Founding and the Constitution 36

5 ● Civil Rights 150

PART II Politics

10 ● Campaigns and Elections   346

11 ● Groups and Interests   400

PART III Institutions

12 ● Congress 434

15 ● The Federal Courts   562

PART IV Policy

16 ● Government and the Economy   602

17 ● Social Policy   650

18 ● Foreign Policy and Democracy   684

PART V   Texas Politics

19 ● The Political Culture, People, and Economy of Texas   720

20 ● The Texas Constitution   754

21 ● Parties and Elections in Texas   **786**

22 ● Interest Groups, Lobbying and Lobbyists   816

23 ● The Texas Legislature   834

24 ● The Texas Executive Branch   862

preface

This book has been and continues to be dedicated to developing a satisfactory response to the question more and more Americans are asking: Why should we be engaged with government and politics? Through the first seven editions, we sought to answer this question by making the text directly relevant to the lives of the students who would be reading it. As a result, we tried to make politics interesting by demonstrating that students' interests are at stake and that they therefore need to take a personal, even selfish, interest in the outcomes of government. At the same time, we realized that students needed guidance in how to become politically engaged. Beyond providing students with a core of political knowledge, we needed to show them how they could apply that knowledge as participants in the political process. The "Get Involved" sections in each chapter help achieve that goal.

As events from the last several years have reminded us, "what government does" can be a matter of life and death. Recent events have reinforced the centrality of government in citizens' lives. The U.S. government has fought two wars abroad, while claiming sweeping new powers at home that could compromise the liberties of its citizens. America's role in the world is discussed daily both inside and outside the classroom. Moreover, students and younger Americans have become more aware of and involved in politics, as the 2008 elections illustrated. Reflecting all of these trends, this new Eighth Edition shows more than any other book on the market (1) how students are connected to government; (2) how American government is connected to the world; and (3) why students should think critically about government and politics. These themes are incorporated in the following ways:

- **New "Who Are Americans?" units ask students to think critically about how Americans from different backgrounds experience politics.** These sections use bold, engaging graphics to present a statistical snapshot of the nation related to each chapter's topic. Critical-thinking questions in each unit and related exercises on the StudySpace Web site give students a chance to compare their own views and experiences and consider the political implications. The Who Are Americans? PowerPoint slides include enhanced versions of the graphics for use in lectures.

- **"Get Involved" units show students how they can make a difference in politics.** The 2008 elections produced a surge in political participation among young Americans, as well as changes in the ways that they participated. These full-page boxes use contemporary examples to explain how young people (even those with busy lives!) can get involved in politics. Specific, step-by-step instructions guide students through a range of possible political activities related to each chapter's topic.

- **"Politics and Popular Culture" boxes connect politics to topics students are interested in.** In each chapter "Politics and Popular Culture" boxes ask students to look critically at how politics intersects with television, film, music, cartoons, and the Internet. Drawing on a range of social science research, these boxes engage students in questions such as "Do non-news TV shows that include political content, like *The Daily Show with Jon Stewart*, have an effect on political knowledge?" "Is there a culture war?" and "Why do candidates sometimes prefer to be interviewed on talk shows rather than traditional news programs?"

- **Chapter introductions focus on "What Government Does and Why It Matters."** In recent decades, cynicism about "big government" has dominated the political zeitgeist. But critics of government often forget that governments do a great deal for citizens. Every year, Americans are the beneficiaries of billions of dollars of goods and services from government programs. Government "does" a lot, and what it does matters a great deal to everyone, including college students. At the start of each chapter, this theme is introduced and applied to the chapter's topic. The goal is to show students that government and politics mean something to their daily lives.

- **"America in the World" boxes show students how American government is connected to the world.** These one-page boxes in every chapter illustrate the important political role the United States plays abroad. Topics include "Should America Export Democracy?" "Human Rights and International Politics," "The American Health Care System in Comparison," and "What Is Congress's Role in Foreign Policy?" These boxes exemplify the critical-analytical approach that characterizes the text and include "For Critical Analysis" questions.

- **"For Critical Analysis" questions are incorporated throughout the text.** "For Critical Analysis" questions in the margins of every chapter prompt students' own critical thinking about the material in the chapter, encouraging them to engage with the topic. The two "For Critical Analysis" questions that conclude each "America in the World" box get students to think more deeply about America's role in the world. The questions at the end of each "Politics and Popular Culture" box ask students to think critically about the intersection of politics and mass media. And the questions that accompany each "Who Are Americans?" unit ask students to consider how Americans from various backgrounds experience politics.

We continue to hope that our book will itself be accepted as a form of enlightened political action. This Eighth Edition is another chance. It is an advancement toward our goal. We promise to keep trying.

acknowledgments

W e are pleased to acknowledge the many colleagues who had an active role in criticism and preparation of the manuscript. Our thanks go to:

First Edition Reviewers

Sarah Binder, Brookings Institution
Kathleen Gille, Office of Representative David Bonior
Rodney Hero, University of Colorado at Boulder
Robert Katzmann, Brookings Institution
Kathleen Knight, University of Houston
Robin Kolodny, Temple University
Nancy Kral, Tomball College
Robert C. Lieberman, Columbia University
David A. Marcum, University of Wyoming
Laura R. Winsky Mattei, State University of New York at Buffalo
Marilyn S. Mertens, Midwestern State University
Barbara Suhay, Henry Ford Community College
Carolyn Wong, Stanford University
Julian Zelizer, State University of New York at Albany

Second Edition Reviewers

Lydia Andrade, University of North Texas
John Coleman, University of Wisconsin at Madison
Daphne Eastman, Odessa College
Otto Feinstein, Wayne State University
Elizabeth Flores, Delmar College
James Gimpel, University of Maryland at College Park
Jill Glaathar, Southwest Missouri State University
Shaun Herness, University of Florida
William Lyons, University of Tennessee at Knoxville
Andrew Polsky, Hunter College, City University of New York
Grant Reeher, Syracuse University
Richard Rich, Virginia Polytechnic
Bartholomew Sparrow, University of Texas at Austin

Third Edition Reviewers

Bruce R. Drury, Lamar University
Andrew I. E. Ewoh, Prairie View A&M University
Amy Jasperson, University of Texas at San Antonio
Loch Johnson, University of Georgia

Mark Kann, University of Southern California
Robert L. Perry, University of Texas of the Permian Basin
Wayne Pryor, Brazosport College
Elizabeth A. Rexford, Wharton County Junior College
Andrea Simpson, University of Washington
Brian Smentkowski, Southeast Missouri State University
Nelson Wikstrom, Virginia Commonwealth University

Fourth Edition Reviewers

M. E. Banks, Virginia Commonwealth University
Lynn Brink, North Lake College
Mark Cichock, University of Texas at Arlington
Del Fields, St. Petersburg College
Nancy Kinney, Washtenaw Community College
William Klein, St. Petersburg College
Dana Morales, Montgomery College
Christopher Muste, Louisiana State University
Larry Norris, South Plains College
David Rankin, State University of New York at Fredonia
Paul Roesler, St. Charles Community College
J. Philip Rogers, San Antonio College
Greg Shaw, Illinois Wesleyan University
Tracy Skopek, Stephen F. Austin State University
Don Smith, University of North Texas
Terri Wright, Cal State, Fullerton

Fifth Edition Reviewers

Annie Benifield, Tomball College
Denise Dutton, Southwest Missouri State University
Rick Kurtz, Central Michigan University
Kelly McDaniel, Three Rivers Community College
Eric Plutzer, Pennsylvania State University
Daniel Smith, Northwest Missouri State University
Dara Strolovitch, University of Minnesota
Dennis Toombs, San Jacinto College–North
Stacy Ulbig, Southwest Missouri State University

Sixth Edition Reviewers

Janet Adamski, University of Mary Hardin–Baylor
Greg Andrews, St. Petersburg College
Louis Bolce, Baruch College
Darin Combs, Tulsa Community College
Sean Conroy, University of New Orleans
Paul Cooke, Cy Fair College
Vida Davoudi, Kingwood College
Robert DiClerico, West Virginia University
Corey Ditslear, University of North Texas
Kathy Dolan, University of Wisconsin, Milwaukee
Randy Glean, Midwestern State University
Nancy Kral, Tomball College
Mark Logas, Valencia Community College
Scott MacDougall, Diablo Valley College
David Mann, College of Charleston
Christopher Muste, University of Montana
Richard Pacelle, Georgia Southern University
Sarah Poggione, Florida International University
Richard Rich, Virginia Tech
Thomas Schmeling, Rhode Island College
Scott Spitzer, California State University–Fullerton
Dennis Toombs, San Jacinto College–North
John Vento, Antelope Valley College
Robert Wood, University of North Dakota

Seventh Edition Reviewers

Molly Andolina, DePaul University
Nancy Bednar, Antelope Valley College
Paul Blakelock, Kingwood College
Amy Brandon, San Jacinto College
Jim Cauthen, John Jay College
Kevin Davis, North Central Texas College
Louis DeSipio, University of California–Irvine
Brandon Franke, Blinn College
Steve Garrison, Midwestern State University
Joseph Howard, University of Central Arkansas
Aaron Knight, Houston Community College
Paul Labedz, Valencia Community College
Elise Langan, John Jay College
Mark Logas, Valencia Community College
Eric Miller, Blinn College
Anthony O'Regan, Los Angeles Valley College
David Putz, Kingwood College
Chis Soper, Pepperdine University
Kevin Wagner, Florida Atlantic University
Laura Wood, Tarrant County College

Eighth Edition Reviewers

Andrea Aleman, University of Texas at San Antonio
Stephen Amberg, University of Texas at San Antonio
Steve Anthony, Georgia State University
Brian Arbour, John Jay College, CUNY
Greg Arey, Cape Fear Community College
Ellen Baik, University of Texas–Pan American
David Birch, Lone Star College–Tomball

Bill Carroll, Sam Houston State University
Ed Chervenak, University of New Orleans
Gary Church, Mountain View College
Adrian Stefan Clark, Del Mar College
Casey Clofstad, University of Miami
Annie Cole, Los Angeles City College
Greg Combs, University of Texas at Dallas
Cassandra Cookson, Lee College
Brian Cravens, Blinn College
John Crosby, California State University–Chico
Scott Crosby, Valencia Community College
Courtenay Daum, Colorado State University, Fort Collins
Paul Davis, Truckee Meadows Community College
Peter Doas, University of Texas–Pan American
Vida Davoudi, Lone Star College–Kingwood
John Domino, Sam Houston State University
Doug Dow, University of Texas–Dallas
Jeremy Duff, Midwestern State University
Heather Evans, Sam Houston State University
Hyacinth Ezeamii, Albany State University
Bob Fitrakis, Columbus State Community College
Brian Fletcher, Truckee Meadows Community College
Paul Foote, Eastern Kentucky University
Frank Garrahan, Austin Community College
Jimmy Gleason, Purdue University
Steven Greene, North Carolina State University
Jeannie Grussendorf, Georgia State University
M. Ahad Hayaud-Din, Brookhaven College
Virginia Haysley, Lone Star College–Tomball
Alexander Hogan, Lone Star College–CyFair
Glen Hunt, Austin Community College
Mark Jendrysik, University of North Dakota
Krista Jenkins, Fairleigh Dickinson University
Carlos Juárez, Hawaii Pacific University
Melinda Kovács, Sam Houston State University
Paul Labedz, Valencia Community College
Boyd Lanier, Lamar University
Jeff Lazarus, Georgia State University
Jeffrey Lee, Blinn College
Alan Lehmann, Blinn College
Julie Lester, Macon State College
Steven Lichtman, Shippensburg University
Mark Logas, Valencia Community College
Fred Lokken, Truckee Meadows Community College
Shari MacLachlan, Palm Beach Community College
Guy Martin, Winston-Salem State University
Fred Monardi, College of Southern Nevada
Vincent Moscardelli, University of Connecticut
Jason Mycoff, University of Delaware
Sugmaran Narayanan, Midwestern State University
Adam Newmark, Appalachian State University
Larry Norris, South Plains College
Anthony Nownes, University of Tennessee, Knoxville
Elizabeth Oldmixon, University of North Texas
Anthony O'Regan, Los Angeles Valley College

John Osterman, San Jacinto College–Central
Mark Peplowski, College of Southern Nevada
Maria Victoria Perez-Rios, John Jay College, CUNY
Sara Rinfret, University of Wisconsin, Green Bay
Andre Robinson, Pulaski Technical College
Paul Roesler, St. Charles Community College
Susan Roomberg, University of Texas at San Antonio
Ryan Rynbrandt, Collin County Community College
Mario Salas, Northwest Vista College
Michael Sanchez, San Antonio College
Mary Schander, Pasadena City College
Laura Schneider, Grand Valley State University

Ronnee Schreiber, San Diego State University
Subash Shah, Winston-Salem State University
Mark Shomaker, Blinn College
Roy Slater, St. Petersburg College
Scott Spitzer, California State University–Fullerton
Debra St. John, Collin College
John Vento, Antelope Valley College
Eric Whitaker, Western Washington University
Clay Wiegand, Cisco College
Walter Wilson, University of Texas at San Antonio
Kevan Yenerall, Clarion University
Rogerio Zapata, South Texas College

Students at several schools around the country participated in small focus groups that helped shape the Eighth Edition's new pedagogical program. They included Brittany Boyle, Luan Do, Brent Harvey, Jorge Hernandez, Tiara Jackson, Josh Jacobs, Jimmy Johnson, Laura Konisek, Gabriela Maddox, Taylor Marcantel, Anna Mearidy, Lori Mendel, Jacob Minter, Mayela Montano, Diana Ortega, Natalie Pereira, Michael Rocca, Christine Sanders, Kirk Sharma, Andrea Soto-Innes, Mary Storey, Joe Street, Jamie Sula, and Mia Williams. We are grateful for their smart and candid feedback.

We also must pay thanks to the many collaborators we have had on this project: Dannagal Young of the University of Delaware, who contributed the "Politics and Popular Culture" boxes; Molly Andolina of DePaul University and Krista Jenkins of Fairleigh Dickinson University, who together contributed the new "Get Involved" boxes, and Erin Ackerman and Brian Arbour, both of John Jay College, who contributed "Who Are Americans?" boxes. Brian also wrote all of the new "Who Are Texans?" boxes.

We are also grateful for the talents and hard work of several research assistants, whose contributions can never be adequately compensated. In particular, for their work on this Eighth Edition, we thank Ali Charania, Lisa Holmes, Josh Payne, and Peter Ryan.

Perhaps above all, we wish to thank those at W. W. Norton. For its first five editions, editor Steve Dunn helped us shape the book in countless ways. Our current editor, Ann Shin, has carried on the Norton tradition of splendid editorial work. We thank Junenoire Mitchell and Susan Buschhorn for devoting an enormous amount of time to finding new photos. For our student Web site and other media resources for the book, Peter Lesser has been an energetic and visionary editor, and Lorraine Klimowich has efficiently managed the test bank and instructor's manual. Patterson Lamb copyedited the manuscript with Marian Johnson's superb direction, and project editor Melissa Atkin devoted countless hours keeping on top of myriad details. Ben Reynolds has been dedicated in managing production. Finally, we wish to thank Roby Harrington, the head of Norton's college department.

Benjamin Ginsberg
Theodore J. Lowi
Margaret Weir
Anthony Champagne
Edward J. Harpham

November 2010

EIGHTH TEXAS EDITION

We the People

AN INTRODUCTION TO AMERICAN POLITICS

Most Americans share the core political values of liberty, equality, and democracy and want their government and its policies to reflect these values. However, people often disagree on the meaning of these values and what government should do to protect them.

American Political Culture

WHAT GOVERNMENT DOES AND WHY IT MATTERS Americans sometimes appear to believe that the government is an institution that does things *to* them and from which they need protection. Business owners complain that federal health and safety regulations threaten their ability to make a profit. Farmers and ranchers complain that federal and state environmental rules intrude on their property rights. Motorists allege that municipal "red light" cameras, designed to photograph traffic violators, represent the intrusion of "Big Brother" into their lives. Civil libertarians express concern over what they view as sometimes overly aggressive police and prosecutorial practices. And, almost everyone complains about federal, state, and local taxes.

Yet many of the same individuals who complain about what the government does *to* them also want the government to do a great deal *for* them. When the mortgage and banking crisis that began in 2008 threatened to throw the world economy into depression, all eyes turned to the federal government for help. The Treasury Department and the Federal Reserve

focusquestions

- Do Americans trust their government?
- Why should we pay attention to politics?
- What type of government do we have?
- How have the American people changed over time?
- Does the system uphold American political values?

responded with an unprecedented $787 billion rescue plan that they hoped would restore confidence in financial institutions and prevent a major economic downturn.

In a similar vein, after the September 11 terrorist attacks on the World Trade Center and the Pentagon, Americans demanded government action. President George W. Bush responded by mobilizing powerful military forces and creating an Office of Homeland Security (later reorganized as a cabinet department). Congress authorized tens of billions of dollars in new federal expenditures to combat terrorism and to repair the damage already caused by terrorists. The states mobilized their own police and national guard forces, and local police and public safety departments were placed on high alert.

Americans also look to government for assistance with more routine matters. Farmers are the beneficiaries of billions in federal subsidies and research programs. Motorists would have no roads on which to be photographed by those hated cameras if not for the tens of billions of dollars spent each year on road construction and maintenance by federal, state, and municipal authorities. Individuals accused of crimes benefit from procedural safeguards and state-funded defense attorneys. Most Americans would not be here at all if it were not for federal immigration policies, which set the terms for entry into the United States and for obtaining citizenship. And, as for those detested taxes, without them there would be no government benefits at all.

As the government seeks to help and protect its citizens, it faces the challenge of doing so in ways that are true to American values. Liberty, equality, and democracy are key American political values. Most Americans find it easy to affirm all three values in principle. In practice, however, matters are not always so clear. As we will see in this chapter and throughout the text, policies and practices that seem to affirm one of these values may contradict another.

chaptercontents

● What Americans Think about Government

Since the United States was established as a nation, Americans have been reluctant to grant government too much power, and they have often been suspicious of politicians. But over the course of the nation's history, Americans have also turned to government for assistance in times of need and have strongly supported the government in periods of war. In 1933, the power of the government began to expand to meet the crises created by the stock market crash of 1929, the Great Depression, and the run on banks of 1933. Congress passed legislation that brought the government into the businesses of home mortgages, farm mortgages, credit, and relief of personal distress. More recently, when the economy threatened to fall into a deep recession in 2008 and 2009, the federal government stepped in to shore up the financial system, oversee the restructuring of the ailing auto companies, and inject hundreds of billions of dollars into the faltering economy. Today, the national government is an enormous institution with programs and policies reaching into every corner of American life. It oversees the nation's economy; it is the nation's largest employer; it provides citizens with a host of services; it controls the world's most formidable military establishment; and it regulates a wide range of social and commercial activities in which Americans engage.

Citizens are so dependent on government today that much of what they have come to take for granted—as, somehow, part of the natural environment—is in fact created by government. Take the example of a typical college student's day. Throughout the day, every student relies on a host of services and activities organized by national, state, and local government agencies. The extent of this dependence on government is illustrated by Box 1.1 on the following page.

Trust in Government

Ironically, even as popular dependence on it has grown, the American public's view of government has turned more sour. Public trust in government has declined, and Americans are now more likely to feel that they can do little to influence the government's actions. The decline in public trust among Americans is striking. In the early 1960s, three-quarters of Americans said they trusted government most of the time. By 1994, only one-quarter of Americans expressed trust in government; three-quarters stated that they did not trust government most of the time.[1] Different groups vary somewhat in their levels of trust: African Americans and Latinos express more confidence in the federal government than do whites. But even among the most supportive groups, more than half do not trust the government.[2] These developments are important because politically engaged citizens and public confidence in government are vital for the health of a democracy.

In the aftermath of the September 11 terrorist attacks, a number of studies reported a substantial increase in popular trust in government. For example, in October 2001, 60 percent of American college students surveyed said they trusted the government to "do the right thing" all or most of the time. Before September 11, only 36 percent expressed a similar view. In addition, 75 percent said they trusted the military,

Americans looked to the government to address the recession that began in 2008 and to prevent a similar crisis in the future. In 2010, President Obama described the government's ongoing efforts toward economic recovery, with Treasury Secretary Timothy Geithner and economic advisor Christina Roemer by his side.

BOX 1.1

The Presence of Government in the Daily Life of a Student at "State University"

TIME OF DAY	SCHEDULE
7:00 am	Wake up. Standard time set by the national government.
7:10 am	Shower. Water courtesy of local government, either a public entity or a regulated private company. Brush your teeth with toothpaste whose cavity-fighting claims have been verified by a federal agency. Dry your hair with an electric dryer, manufactured according to federal government agency guidelines.
7:30 am	Have a bowl of cereal with milk for breakfast. "Nutrition Facts" on food labels are a federal requirement, pasteurization of milk required by state law, freshness dating on milk based on state and federal standards, recycling the empty cereal box and milk carton enabled by state or local laws.
8:30 am	Drive or take public transportation to campus. Air bags and seat belts required by federal and state laws. Roads and bridges paid for by state and local governments, speed and traffic laws set by state and local governments, public transportation subsidized by all levels of government.
8:45 am	Arrive on campus of large public university. Buildings are 70 percent financed by state taxpayers.
9:00 am	First class: Chemistry 101. Tuition partially paid by a federal loan (more than half the cost of university instruction is paid for by taxpayers), chemistry lab paid for with grants from the National Science Foundation (a federal agency) and smaller grants from business corporations made possible by federal income tax deductions for charitable contributions.
Noon	Eat lunch. College cafeteria financed by state dormitory authority on land grant from federal Department of Agriculture.
2:00 pm	Second class: American Government 101 (your favorite class!). You may be taking this class because it is required by the state legislature or because it fulfills a university requirement.
4:00 pm	Third class: Computer lab. Free computers, software, and Internet access courtesy of state subsidies plus grants and discounts from IBM and Microsoft, the costs of which are deducted from their corporate income taxes; Internet built in part by federal government. Duplication of software protected by federal copyright laws.
6:00 pm	Eat dinner: hamburger and french fries. Meat inspected for bacteria by federal agencies.
7:00 pm	Work at part-time job at the campus library. Minimum wage set by federal government, books and journals in library paid for by state taxpayers.
10:00 pm	Go home. Street lighting paid for by county and city governments, police patrols by city government.
10:15 pm	Watch TV. Networks regulated by federal government, cable public-access channels required by city law. Weather forecast provided to broadcasters by a federal agency.
Midnight	Put out the garbage before going to bed. Garbage collected by city sanitation department, financed by "user charges."

69 percent expressed trust in the president, and 62 percent trusted Congress.[3] These views, expressed during a period of national crisis, may have been indicative less of a renewed *trust* in government to do the right thing than of a fervent *hope* that it would. And, indeed, by July 2003, trust in government had returned to its pre–September 11 level, with only 36 percent of Americans indicating that they trusted the government most or all of the time (see Figure 1.1).[4]

By 2010, trust in government had dropped even lower, with only 25 percent trusting the government in Washington "to do what is right" all or most of the time.[5] Several factors contributed to the decline in trust. Revelations about the faulty information that led up to the war in Iraq and ongoing concern about the war had increased Americans' mistrust of government. In March 2007, 54 percent of those surveyed believed that the Bush administration had deliberately misled the American public about whether Iraq had weapons of mass destruction. In 2003, only 31 percent of Americans believed that the administration had misled the public. By 2009, government's growing role in the economy began to arouse public doubts. Six months after Congress approved an emergency bailout for the banking industry, just 37 percent of Americans approved of the federal government providing money to financial institutions. The same poll found that 48 percent of Americans reported feeling "mostly resentful" that the government's policies could benefit irresponsible managers and bankers; just 41 percent felt "mostly relieved" that those institutions might start lending to homebuyers and businesses again.[6] The majority of Americans were also unhappy with the government's decision to provide emergency federal loans to automobile manufacturers General Motors and Chrysler. One poll found that just 22 percent of Americans approved of the government intervention, while an overwhelming 76 percent of people favored allowing the two companies to go bankrupt.[7]

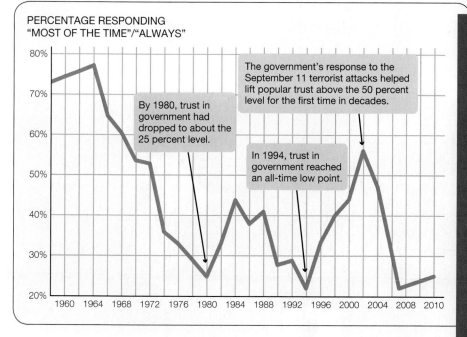

PERCENTAGE RESPONDING "MOST OF THE TIME"/"ALWAYS"

By 1980, trust in government had dropped to about the 25 percent level.

The government's response to the September 11 terrorist attacks helped lift popular trust above the 50 percent level for the first time in decades.

In 1994, trust in government reached an all-time low point.

FIGURE 1.1

Trust in Government, 1958–2010

Participants in these polls were asked if they trusted the government to "do the right thing" always, most of the time, or only some of the time.

Since the 1960s, general levels of public trust in government have declined. What factors might help to account for changes in the public's trust in government? Why has confidence in government dropped again since September 11, 2001?

SOURCES: *The National Election Studies*, 1958–2004; and NBC News / Wall Street Journal Poll, May 2010, iPoll Databank, www.ropercenter.uconn.edu (accessed 6/17/10).

forcriticalanalysis

What recent events have affected Americans' trust in government? Did the federal government's efforts to save the financial system in 2008 and 2009 increase the public's trust in government?

Does it matter if Americans trust their government? For the most part, the answer is yes. As we have seen, most Americans rely on government for a wide range of services and laws that they simply take for granted. But long-term distrust in government can result in public refusal to pay taxes adequate to support such widely approved public activities. Low levels of confidence may also make it difficult for government to attract talented and effective workers to public service.[8] The weakening of government as a result of prolonged levels of distrust may ultimately harm our capacity to defend our national interest in the world economy and may jeopardize our national security. Likewise, a weak government can do little to assist citizens who need help in weathering periods of sharp economic or technological change.

Political Efficacy

political efficacy the ability to influence government and politics

Another important trend in American views about government has been a declining sense of **political efficacy**, the belief that citizens can affect what government does, that they can take action to make government listen to them. In recent decades, the public belief that government is responsive to ordinary citizens has declined. In 2009, 59 percent of Americans said that elected officials don't care what people like them think; in 1960, only 25 percent felt so shut out of government. Accompanying this sense that ordinary people can't get heard is a growing belief

In response to the terrorist attacks of September 11, 2001, Americans rallied around government officials and offered unprecedented support. Is support for the government during times of crisis at odds with Americans' distrust of government at other times?

that government is not run for the benefit of all the people. In 2009, 48 percent of the public disagreed with the idea that the "government is really run for the benefit of all the people."[9] These views are widely shared across the age spectrum.

This widely felt loss of political efficacy is bad news for American democracy. The feeling that you can't affect government decisions can lead to a self-perpetuating cycle of apathy, declining political participation, and withdrawal from political life. Why bother to participate if you believe it makes no difference? Yet the belief that you can be effective is the first step needed to influence government. Not every effort of ordinary citizens to influence government will succeed, but without any such efforts, government decisions will be made by a smaller and smaller circle of powerful people. Such loss of broad popular influence over government actions undermines the key feature of American democracy—government by the people.

Citizenship: Knowledge and Participation

The first prerequisite for achieving an increased sense of political efficacy is knowledge. Political indifference is often simply a habit that stems from a lack of knowledge about how your interests are affected by politics and from a sense that you can do nothing to affect politics. But political efficacy is a self-fulfilling prophecy: if you think you cannot be effective, chances are you will never try. Most research suggests that people active in politics have a high sense of their efficacy. This means they believe they can make a difference—even if they do not win all the time. Most people do not want to be politically active every day of their lives, but it is essential to our political ideals that all citizens be informed and able to act.

The state of political knowledge in the United States today is spotty. Most Americans know little about current issues or debates. Numerous surveys indicate that the majority of Americans have significant gaps in their political knowledge.

Following the 2003 Iraq war and the ongoing fighting in Afghanistan, Americans' trust in government declined sharply. Why do you think so many Americans were critical of the government's handling of these conflicts?

TABLE 1.1

What Americans Know about Government

RESPONDENTS WHO	PERCENTAGE
Knew that only citizens can vote in federal elections	48
Could identify two members of the president's cabinet and name their department	46
Knew how much of a majority is required for the U.S. Senate and House to override a presidential veto	38
Knew that Chief Justice John Roberts, Jr., is generally considered a conservative	37*
Felt that the government spends more on social security than foreign aid	18
Could identify Secretary of State Hillary Clinton	85**
Could identify (former) House Speaker Nancy Pelosi	72
Knew Federal Reserve Chairman Ben Bernanke	45**

SOURCES: Center for Information and Research on Civic Learning and Engagement, www.civicyouth.org (accessed 2/4/08); and Pew Research Center for People and the Press, http://people-press.org (accessed 2/4/08).

*Pew Research Center for the People and the Press, "Hillary's New Job Better Known Than Dow Jones Average," news release December 15, 2008, http://people-press.org (accessed 9/26/09).

**Pew Research Center for the People and the Press, "Public Knows Basic Facts about Financial Crisis," news release April 2, 2009, http://people-press.org (accessed 9/26/09).

For example, in 2009 only 45 percent of those surveyed could identity Federal Reserve Chairman Ben Bernanke and only 37 percent knew that Chief Justice John Roberts, Jr., is generally considered a conservative. On the other hand, the public is more knowledgeable about politicians who have been prominent in national politics. For example in 2008, 72 percent could identify Nancy Pelosi, the first female Speaker of the House, and 85 percent could identify Secretary of State Hillary Clinton (see Table 1.1). But rather than dwell on the widespread political ignorance of many Americans, we prefer to view this as an opportunity for the readers of this book. Those of you who make the effort to become more knowledgeable will be much better prepared to influence the political system regarding the issues and concerns that you care most about.

After September 11, many commentators noted a revival in Americans' sense of citizenship, as manifested by ubiquitous flag displays and other demonstrations of patriotic sentiment. There seems to be little doubt that millions of Americans experienced a renewed sense of identification with their nation. Citizenship, however, has a broader meaning than just patriotism.

Beginning with the ancient Greeks, citizenship has meant membership in one's community. To the Greeks, citizenship entailed involvement in public discussion, debate, and activity designed to improve the welfare of the community. Our meaning for **citizenship** derives from the Greek ideal: enlightened political engagement.[10] To be politically engaged in a meaningful way, citizens require resources, especially political knowledge and information. Democracy functions best when

citizenship informed and active membership in a political community

citizens are informed. But to be a citizen in the full sense, as understood first by the ancient Greeks, requires more than an occasional visit to a voting booth. A good citizen must have the knowledge needed to participate in political debate.

The Necessity of Political Knowledge

Political knowledge means more than having a few opinions to offer the pollster or to guide your decisions in a voting booth. It is important to know the rules and strategies that govern political institutions and the principles on which they are based, but it is more important to know them in ways that relate to your own interests. Citizens need knowledge in order to assess their interests and to know when to act on them. Knowledgeable citizens are more attentive to and more engaged in politics because they understand how and why politics is relevant to their lives.

Without political knowledge, no citizen can be aware of her interests or stake in a political dispute. In the year preceding the 2008 presidential election, for example, many of the prospective Democratic candidates presented rather detailed proposals on ways to change the current American health care system. How many voters paid enough attention to the discussion to be able to distinguish meaningfully among the various proposals and their implications? Did you attempt to ascertain whether you and your family would be better off under the health care system envisioned by Clinton, Obama, or Edwards rather than the system favored by Giuliani, Romney, or McCain? How could you participate intelligently without this knowledge? Various public and private interest groups devote enormous time and energy to understanding alternative policy proposals and their implications so they will know whom to support. Interest groups understand something that every citizen should also understand: effective participation requires knowledge.

Citizens also need political knowledge to identify the best ways to act on their interests. If your street is rendered impassable by snow, what can you do? Is snow removal the responsibility of the federal government? Is it a state or municipal responsibility? Knowing that you have a stake in a clear road does not help much if you do not know that snow removal is a city or a county responsibility and you cannot identify the municipal agency that deals with the problem. Americans are fond of complaining that government is not responsive to their needs, but in some cases, it is possible that citizens simply lack the information they need to present their problems to the appropriate government officials.

Citizens need political knowledge, as well, to ascertain what they cannot or should not ask of politicians and the government. We need to balance our need for protection and service with our equally pressing need for liberty. Particularly during periods when the nation's safety is threatened, Americans may be inclined to accept increased governmental intrusion into their lives in the name of national security. Since 2001, for example, Americans have accepted unprecedented levels of governmental surveillance and the erosion of some traditional restrictions on police powers in the name of preventing terrorism. It remains to be seen whether this exchange of liberty for the promise of security was a wise choice. Political knowledge includes knowing the limits on, as well as the possibilities for, pursuing one's own individual interests through political action. This is, perhaps, the most difficult form of political knowledge to acquire.

The rest of this chapter will look at the forms of political knowledge that we believe are most critical for a citizen to possess. In the next section, we will examine the principles of government and politics. Following that, we will review the democratic principles on which the United States is based and assess how well

for critical analysis

Many studies seem to show that most Americans know very little about government and politics. Can we have democratic government without knowledgeable and aware citizens?

Political Knowledge and Comedy Television

Political knowledge is at the core of a healthy democracy. Historically, newspapers, news magazines, television news programs, and speeches and debates have been the most common sources of political information. However, in recent years more Americans—especially young Americans—report receiving political information from entertainment programs such as late-night comedy shows.

A report released by the Pew Research Center in 2007 showed that 26 percent of young people (aged eighteen to twenty-nine) reported regularly learning about politics from comedy shows such as *The Daily Show with Jon Stewart* and *The Colbert Report*. When similar findings first caught the public's attention in 2004, many journalists were openly critical of the apparent trend. News anchor Ted Koppel stated, "A lot of television viewers, more, quite frankly, than I'm comfortable with, get their news from the comedy channel on a program called *The Daily Show*."

Many critics of the trend are concerned that the information conveyed through late-night comedy shows is not a good basis for political decision making. Although one-liners by Jay Leno and David Letterman do cover politics, these jokes tend to focus on the personal weaknesses of public officials rather than on complex issues of public policy.[a]

But could political content on comedy shows provide at least some information to viewers who are not receiving political news elsewhere? Scholars such as Matthew Baum argue that this "piggybacking" of politics on top of entertainment content does have the effect of informing typically apolitical viewers. Some research has shown that for late-night comedy viewers without a lot of political knowledge, watching these comedy shows can shape their impressions of the candidates. For example, one study found that viewers of late-night comedy shows who did not know a lot about politics rated Al Gore as less inspiring over the course of the 2000 campaign in keeping with his cardboard caricature from late-night jokes.[b]

Another way of assessing learning from late-night comedy is by testing the political knowledge of people who watch late-night comedy shows. The 2007 study by the Pew Research Center found that the audiences of *The Daily Show with Jon Stewart* and *The Colbert Report* tied with the audiences of major newspaper Web sites as the most knowledgeable about politics and world affairs, with 54 percent of their audiences falling into a "high knowledge group." This compares with 34 percent for network morning shows, 38 percent for network evening news audiences, and 43 percent for local daily newspaper audiences.

The question of whether late-night comedy shows inform and influence viewers is illustrative of a larger phenomenon in the political-information environment—the blurring of the lines between entertainment and information. Popular culture has always been a part of political life, from political cartoons to movies about war. But in today's complex media environment, popular culture and politics are more intertwined than ever. From *South Park* to *The West Wing*, Rush Limbaugh to Michael Moore, YouTube to Facebook, a discussion about contemporary American politics would be incomplete without considering the role played by popular culture.

[a]D. Niven, S. R. Lichter, and D. Amundson, "The Political Content of Late Night Comedy," *Press/Politics* 8 (2003): 118–33.
[b]Dannagal Goldthwaite Young, "Late Night Comedy in Election 2000: Its Influence on Candidate Trait Ratings and the Moderating Effects of Political Knowledge and Partisanship," *Journal of Broadcasting and Electronic Media* 48, no. 1 (2004): 1–22.

for critical analysis

1. Could the political content on late-night comedy television have a beneficial effect on political knowledge?

2. Does the blurring of the line between news and entertainment mean Americans are less politically engaged or more so?

American government fulfills these principles. We will conclude with suggestions of what you and other ordinary citizens can do to become more knowledgeable and more engaged.

● Government

Government is the term generally used to describe the formal institutions through which a land and its people are ruled. To govern is to rule. A government may be as simple as a tribal council that meets occasionally to advise the chief, or as complex as its elaborate vast establishment, with procedures, laws, and bureaucracies. In the history of civilization, governments have not been difficult to establish. There have been thousands of them. The hard part is establishing a government that lasts. Even more difficult is developing a stable government that is compatible with liberty, equality, and democracy.

> **government** institutions and procedures through which a territory and its people are ruled

Is Government Needed?

Americans have always harbored some suspicion of government and have wondered how extensive a role it should play in their lives. Thomas Jefferson famously observed that the best government was one that "governed least." Generally speaking, a government is needed to provide those services, sometimes called "public goods," that all citizens need but are not likely to be able to provide adequately for themselves. These might include defense against foreign aggression, maintenance of public order, enforcement of contractual obligations and property rights, and a guarantee of some measure of social justice. The precise extent to which government involvement in our society is needed has been debated throughout our history and will continue to be a central focus of political contention.

Forms of Government

Governments vary in their structure, in their size, and in the way they operate. Two questions are of special importance in determining how governments differ: Who governs? And how much government control is permitted?

Some nations are governed by a single individual—a king or dictator, for example. This state of affairs is called **autocracy**. Where a small group—perhaps landowners, military officers, or wealthy merchants—controls most of the governing decisions, that government is said to be an **oligarchy**. If more people participate and have some influence over decision making, that government is a **democracy**.

Governments also vary considerably in terms of how they govern. In the United States and a small number of other nations, governments are limited as to what they are permitted to control (substantive limits), as well as how they go about it (procedural limits). Governments that are limited in this way are called **constitutional governments**, or liberal governments. In other nations, including many in Latin America, Asia, and Africa, though the law imposes few real limits, the government is nevertheless kept in check by other political and social institutions that it is unable to control and must come to terms with—such as autonomous territories, an organized religion, organized business groups, or organized labor unions. Such governments are generally called **authoritarian**. In a third group of nations, including the Soviet Union under Joseph Stalin, Nazi Germany, perhaps prewar Japan and Italy, and North Korea today, governments not only are free of legal limits but also seek to

> **autocracy** a form of government in which a single individual—a king, queen, or dictator—rules

> **oligarchy** a form of government in which a small group—landowners, military officers, or wealthy merchants—controls most of the governing decisions

> **democracy** a system of rule that permits citizens to play a significant part in the governmental process, usually through the election of key public officials

> **constitutional government** a system of rule in which formal and effective limits are placed on the powers of the government

> **authoritarian government** a system of rule in which the government recognizes no formal limits but may nevertheless be restrained by the power of other social institutions

eliminate those organized social groups that might challenge or limit their authority. These governments typically attempt to dominate or control every sphere of political, economic, and social life and, as a result, are called **totalitarian**.

Americans have the good fortune to live in a nation in which limits are placed on what governments can do and how they can do it. Much of the world's population does not live in a constitutional democracy. By one measure, just 46 percent of the world's population (those living in eighty-nine countries) enjoy sufficient levels of political and personal freedom to be classified as living in a constitutional democracy.[11] And constitutional democracies were unheard of before the modern era. Prior to the eighteenth and nineteenth centuries, governments seldom sought—and rarely received—the support of their ordinary subjects. The available evidence strongly suggests that the ordinary people had little love for the government or for the social order. After all, they had no stake in it. They equated government with the police officer, the bailiff, and the tax collector.[12]

Beginning in the seventeenth century, in a handful of Western nations, two important changes began to take place in the character and conduct of government. First, governments began to acknowledge formal limits on their power. Second, a small number of governments began to provide ordinary citizens with a formal voice in public affairs—through the vote. Obviously, the desirability of limits on government and the expansion of popular influence were at the heart of the American Revolution in 1776. "No taxation without representation," as we shall see in Chapter 2, was hotly debated from the beginning of the Revolution through the Founding in 1789. But even before the Revolution, a tradition of limiting government and expanding participation in the political process had developed throughout western Europe.

America's founders were influenced by the English thinker John Locke (1632–1704). Locke argued that governments need the consent of the people.

Limiting Government

The key force behind the imposition of limits on government power was a new social class, the bourgeoisie, which became an important political force in the sixteenth and seventeenth centuries. *Bourgeois* is a French word for "freeman of the city," or *bourg*. Being part of the bourgeoisie later became associated with being "middle class" and with being in commerce or industry. In order to gain a share of control of government, joining or even displacing the kings, aristocrats, and gentry who had dominated government for centuries, the bourgeoisie sought to change existing institutions—especially parliaments—into instruments of real political participation. Parliaments had existed for centuries, but were generally aristocratic institutions. The bourgeoisie embraced parliaments as means by which they could exert the weight of their superior numbers and growing economic advantage against their aristocratic rivals. At the same time, the bourgeoisie sought to place restraints on the capacity of governments to threaten these economic and political interests by placing formal or constitutional limits on governmental power.

John Stuart Mill (1806–1873) presented a ringing defense of individual freedom in his famous treatise On Liberty. *Mill's work influenced Americans' evolving ideas about the relationship between government and the individual.*

Although motivated primarily by the need to protect and defend their own interests, the bourgeoisie advanced many of the principles that became the central underpinnings of individual liberty for all citizens—freedom of speech, freedom of assembly, freedom of conscience, and freedom from arbitrary search and seizure. The work of political theorists such as John Locke (1632–1704) and, later, John Stuart Mill (1806–1873) helped shape these evolving ideas about liberty and political rights. However, it is important to note that the bourgeoisie generally did not favor democracy as we know it. They were advocates of electoral and representative institutions, but they favored property requirements and other restrictions so as to limit participation to the middle and upper classes. Yet once these institutions of politics and the protection of the right to engage in politics were established, it was difficult to limit them to the bourgeoisie.

Access to Government: The Expansion of Participation

The expansion of participation from the bourgeoisie to ever-larger segments of society took two paths. In some nations, popular participation was expanded by the crown or the aristocracy, which ironically saw common people as potential political allies against the bourgeoisie. Thus in nineteenth-century Prussia, for example, it was the emperor and his great minister Otto von Bismarck who expanded popular participation in order to build political support among the lower orders.

In other nations, participation expanded because competing segments of the bourgeoisie sought to gain political advantage by reaching out and mobilizing the support of working- and lower-class groups that craved the opportunity to take part in politics—"lining up the unwashed," as one American historian put it.[13] To be sure, excluded groups often agitated for greater participation. But seldom was such agitation, by itself, enough to secure the right to participate. Usually, expansion of voting rights resulted from a combination of pressure from below and help from above.

The gradual expansion of voting rights by groups hoping to derive some political advantage has been typical of American history. After the Civil War, one of the chief reasons that Republicans moved to enfranchise newly freed slaves was to use the support of the former slaves to maintain Republican control over the defeated southern states. Similarly, in the early twentieth century, upper-middle-class Progressives advocated women's suffrage because they believed that women were likely to support the reforms espoused by the Progressive movement.

Influencing the Government through Participation: Politics

Expansion of participation means that more and more people have a legal right to take part in politics. *Politics* is an important term. In its broadest sense, "politics" refers to conflicts over the character, membership, and policies of any organization to which people belong. As Harold Lasswell, a famous political scientist, once put it, politics is the struggle over "who gets what, when, how."[14] Although politics is a phenomenon that can be found in any organization, our concern in this book is narrower. Here, **politics** will be used to refer only to conflicts and struggles over the leadership, structure, and policies of governments. The goal of politics, as we define it, is to have a share or a say in the composition of the government's leadership, how the government is organized, or what its policies are going to be. Having a share is called having **power** or influence.

Politics can take many forms, including everything from sending letters to government officials to voting, lobbying legislators on behalf of particular programs, and participating in protest marches and even violent demonstrations. A system of government that gives citizens a regular opportunity to elect the top government officials is usually called a **representative democracy** or **republic**. A system that permits citizens to vote directly on laws and policies is often called a **direct democracy**. At the national level, America is a representative democracy in which citizens select government officials but do not vote on legislation. Some states and cities, however, have provisions for direct legislation through popular initiative and ballot referendum. These procedures allow citizens to collect petitions requiring an issue to be brought directly to the voters for a decision. In 2010, more than

politics conflict over the leadership, structure, and policies of governments

power influence over a government's leadership, organization, or policies

representative democracy/ republic a system of government in which the populace selects representatives, who play a significant role in governmental decision making

direct democracy a system of rule that permits citizens to vote directly on laws and policies

184 initiatives appeared on state ballots. Recent initiatives have dealt with matters ranging from taxes and education to animal cruelty and affirmative action. Many hot-button issues are decided by initiatives. For example, Michigan voters approved a measure that prohibits public institutions such as the University of Michigan from giving preferential treatment on the basis of race; in Colorado, voters passed a referendum that called on the state to sue the federal government to enforce immigration laws. Often, broad public campaigns promote controversial referenda, attempting to persuade voters to change existing laws. For example, a campaign by the American Civil Liberties Union and other groups helped persuade Rhode Island voters to support a measure allowing people with a felony conviction to vote as soon as they are released from prison. The initiative changed the existing law, which barred those with a felony conviction from voting until they had completed probation or parole. Other measures, such as animal-rights proposals, reach the ballot due to a small but dedicated set of activists. One example occurred in Arizona in 2008, when voters approved an initiative guaranteeing a minimum living space for pregnant pigs and cows.

Groups and organized interests do not vote (although their members do), but they certainly do participate in politics. Their political activities usually consist of such endeavors as providing funds for candidates, lobbying, and trying to influence public opinion. The pattern of struggles among interests is called group politics, or **pluralism**. Americans have always been ambivalent about pluralist politics. On the one hand, the right of groups to press their views and compete for influence in the government is the essence of liberty. On the other hand, Americans often fear that organized groups may sometimes exert too much influence, advancing special interests at the expense of larger public interests. We will return to this problem in Chapter 11.

Sometimes, of course, politics does not take place through formal channels at all but instead involves direct action. Direct-action politics can include either violent politics or civil disobedience, both of which attempt to shock rulers into behaving more responsibly. Direct action can also be a form of revolutionary politics, which rejects the system entirely and attempts to replace it with a new ruling group and a new set of rules. In recent years in the United States, groups ranging from animal-rights activists to right-to-life advocates to protesters against the war in Iraq have used direct action to underline their demands. Direct political action is protected by the U.S. Constitution. The country's Founders knew that the right to protest is essential to the maintenance of political freedom, even where the ballot box is available.

pluralism the theory that all interests are and should be free to compete for influence in the government. The outcome of this competition is compromise and moderation.

● Who Are Americans?

While American democracy aims to give the people a voice in government, the meaning of "we the people" has changed over time. Who are Americans? Through the course of American history, politicians, religious leaders, prominent scholars, and ordinary Americans have puzzled over and fought about the answer to this fundamental question. Since the Founding, the American population has been a moving target, growing from 3.9 million in 1790, the year of the first official census, to 310 million in 2010. As the American population has grown, it has become more diverse on nearly every dimension imaginable.[15]

At the time of the Founding, when the United States consisted of thirteen states arrayed along the Eastern Seaboard, 81 percent of Americans counted by the census

An Increasingly Diverse Nation

Since the Founding, the American people have become increasingly diverse. This diversity and the changes in the population have frequently raised challenging questions in American politics.

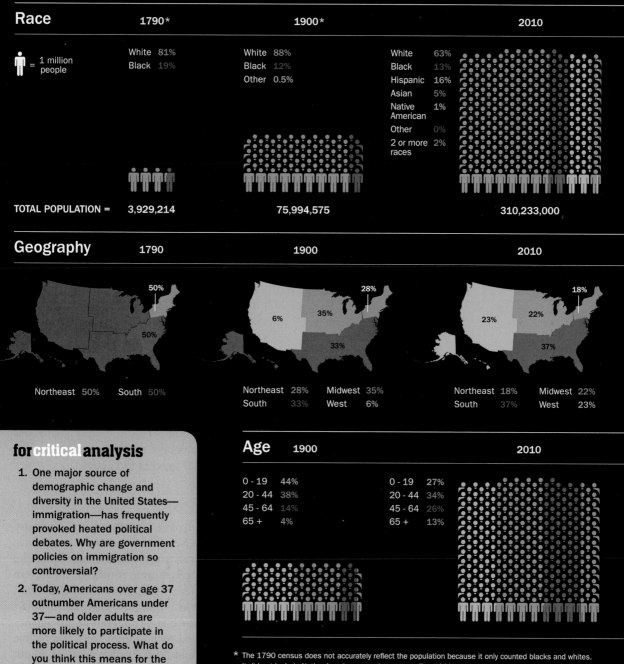

Race

	1790*	1900*	2010
= 1 million people	White 81%	White 88%	White 63%
	Black 19%	Black 12%	Black 13%
		Other 0.5%	Hispanic 16%
			Asian 5%
			Native American 1%
			Other 0%
			2 or more races 2%

TOTAL POPULATION = 3,929,214   75,994,575   310,233,000

Geography

1790	1900	2010
50% / 50%	28% / 35% / 6% / 33%	18% / 22% / 23% / 37%
Northeast 50% South 50%	Northeast 28% Midwest 35% South 33% West 6%	Northeast 18% Midwest 22% South 37% West 23%

Age

	1900		2010
0 - 19	44%	0 - 19	27%
20 - 44	38%	20 - 44	34%
45 - 64	14%	45 - 64	26%
65 +	4%	65 +	13%

for critical analysis

1. One major source of demographic change and diversity in the United States—immigration—has frequently provoked heated political debates. Why are government policies on immigration so controversial?

2. Today, Americans over age 37 outnumber Americans under 37—and older adults are more likely to participate in the political process. What do you think this means for the kinds of issues and policies taken up by the government?

* The 1790 census does not accurately reflect the population because it only counted blacks and whites. It did not include Native Americans or other groups. The 1900 census did not count Hispanic Americans.

SOURCE: U.S. Census Bureau, www.census.gov (accessed 3/5/10).

Native American societies, with their own forms of government, had existed for thousands of years before the first European settlers arrived. By the time this photo of Red Cloud and other Sioux warriors was taken around 1870, Native Americans made up about 1 percent of the American population.

traced their roots to Europe, mostly England and northern Europe; nearly one in five were of African origin, the vast majority of whom had been brought to the United States against their will to work as slaves.[16] Only 1.5 percent of the black population was free. There was also an unknown number of Native Americans, the original inhabitants of the land, not counted by the census because the government did not consider them Americans. The first estimates of Native Americans and Hispanics in the mid-1800s showed that each group made up less than 1 percent of the total population.[17]

Flash forward to 1900. The country now stretched out across the continent, and waves of immigrants, mainly from Europe, boosted the population to 76 million. In 1900, the United States was predominantly composed of whites of European ancestry, but this number now included many from southern and eastern as well as northern Europe; the black population stood at 12 percent. Residents who traced their origin to Latin America or Asia each accounted for less than 1 percent of the entire population (see Figure 1.2).[18] The large number of new immigrants was reflected in the high proportion of foreign-born people in the United States: the foreign-born population reached its height at 14.7 percent in 1910.[19]

Immigration and Ethnic Diversity

As the European-origin population grew more diverse, anxiety about Americans' ethnic identity mounted. In 1900, the author of a *New York Times* front-page article answered his own question—"Are the Americans an Anglo-Saxon People?"—in the affirmative.[20] But the growing numbers of immigrants from southern and eastern Europe who were crowding into American cities spurred heated debates about how long Anglo-Saxons could dominate. Much as today, politicians and scholars argued about whether the country could absorb such large numbers of immigrants. Concerns ranged from whether their political and social values were compatible with American democracy, to whether they would learn English, to alarm about the diseases they might bring into the United States.

● How have the
American people
changed over time?

Millions of immigrants from Europe came to the United States in the early 1900s. Most passed through New York's Ellis Island, where they were checked for diseases before being admitted. Today, many Americans trace their ancestry to immigrants who passed through Ellis Island.

The distinct ethnic backgrounds and language differences of the new immigrants were not the only characteristics that worried the Anglo-Saxon natives; immigrant religious affiliations also aroused concern. The first immigrants to the United States were overwhelmingly Protestant, many of them fleeing religious persecution. The arrival of Germans and Irish in the mid-1800s began to shift that balance with increasing numbers of Catholics. Even so, in 1900, four in five Americans were still Protestants. The large-scale immigration of the early twentieth century threatened to reduce the ranks of Protestants significantly. The eastern European immigrants pouring into the country, especially those from Russia, were heavily Jewish; the southern Europeans, especially Italians, were Catholic. A more religiously diverse country challenged the implicit Protestantism embedded in many aspects of American public life. For example, religious diversity introduced new conflicts into public schooling, as Catholics sought public funding for parochial schools and dissident Protestant sects lobbied to eliminate Bible reading and prayer in the schools.

Anxieties about immigration sparked intense debate about whether the numbers of immigrants entering the country should be limited and whether restrictions should be placed on which types of immigrants should be granted entry. After World War I, Congress responded to the fears swirling around immigration with new laws that sharply limited the number who could enter the country each year. Congress not only limited the number of new immigrants, it also established a new National Origins Quota System, based on the nation's population in 1890 before the wave of immigrants from eastern and southern Europe arrived.[21] Supporters

Are the Americans an Anglo=Saxon People?

Written for THE NEW YORK TIMES

By EDWARD E. CORNWALL, M. D.

THE question, Are the Americans an Anglo-Saxon people? is usually answered in the affirmative. Most of the world takes it for granted as a universally accepted fact that they are Anglo-Saxon. But occasionally we hear a protest against taking this for granted, or a denial that it is so. In a recent number of The Forum an Irish writer insists that one-half of the American people have Irish blood; and in recent English newspapers have appeared the following statements: "The fact is, that the people of the United States are a mixed race, and are no more related to us than the Germans." "All the chatter about cousinship, brotherhood, and blood is the merest cant. There may be about 5 to 10 per cent. of the Americans of English descent, and as a Nation they use the English language, but the masses are of Irish and foreign extraction." Of course such statements as these are absurd, but the

000 in 1890. These are divided racially as follows:

Anglo-Saxon	1,900,000
Continental Teutonic	4,100,000
Celtic	2,000,000
Miscellaneous	1,200,000

The native-born whites both of whose parents were of foreign birth numbered 8,100,000 in 1890. These are racially divided as follows:

Anglo-Saxon	1,200,000
Continental Teutonic	3,800,000
Celtic	2,400,000
Miscellaneous	700,000

The native-born whites of mixed native and foreign parentage numbered 8,300,000 in 1890. Dividing these according to the race divisions of the foreign-born parent, (which is at least one-half correct, and probably much more than one-half correct,) we get the following proportions:

Anglo-Saxon	1,100,000
Continental Teutonic	1,200,000
Celtic	800,000
Miscellaneous	200,000

The influx of immigrants from southern and eastern Europe set off debates about Americans' ethnic identity and social and political values. This New York Times article from 1900 argued that Americans were an Anglo-Saxon people, and in the 1920s strict quotas were placed on immigration from areas other than northern Europe.

of ethnic quotas hoped to turn back the clock and revert to an earlier America in which northern Europeans dominated. The new system set up a hierarchy of admissions: northern European countries received generous quotas for new immigrants, whereas eastern and southern European countries were granted very small quotas. These restrictions ratcheted down the numbers of immigrants so that by 1970, the foreign-born population in the United States reached an all-time low of 5 percent.

Immigration and Race

Official efforts to use racial and ethnic criteria to restrict the American population were not new but had been used to draw boundaries around the American community from the start. The very first census, as we have seen, did not count Native Americans; in fact, Native Americans were not granted the right to vote until 1924. Although the Constitution infamously declared that each slave would count as three-fifths of a person for purposes of apportioning representation among the states, most people of African descent were not officially citizens until the Fourteenth Amendment to the Constitution conferred citizenship on the freed slaves.

Over half a century earlier, the federal government had sought to limit the non-white population with a 1790 law stipulating that only free whites could become naturalized citizens. Not until 1870 did Congress lift the ban on the naturalization of nonwhites. In addition to the restrictions on blacks and Native Americans, restrictions applied to Asians as well. The Chinese Exclusion Act of 1882 outlawed the entry of Chinese laborers to the United States. These provisions were not lifted until 1943, when China became America's ally during World War II. Additional barriers enacted after World War I meant that virtually no Asians entered the country as immigrants until the 1940s. People of Hispanic origin do not fit simply into the American system of racial classification. In 1930, for example, the census

● How have the
American people
changed over time?

counted people of Mexican origin as nonwhite but reversed this decision a decade later—after protests by the Mexican-origin population and the Mexican government. Only in 1970 did the census officially begin counting persons of Hispanic origin, noting that they could be any race.[22]

Twenty-First-Century Americans

By 2000, immigration had profoundly transformed the nation's racial and ethnic profile once again. The primary cause was Congress's decision in 1965 to lift the tight restrictions of the 1920s, allowing for much expanded immigration from Asia and Latin America. One consequence of the shift has been the growth in the Hispanic, or Latino, population. Census estimates for 2008 show that the total Hispanic proportion of the population is now 15 percent; the black, or African American, population is under 13 percent of the total population. Asians made up 4 percent of the population. European Americans accounted for only two-thirds of the population in 2008—their lowest share ever. Moreover, 1.6 percent of the population now identified itself as of "two or more races," a new category that the census added in 2000.[23] Although it is only a small percentage of the population, the biracial category points toward a future in which the traditional labels of racial identification may be blurring, marking a major shift in the long-standing American tradition of strict racial categorization. The blurring of racial categories poses challenges to a host of policies—many of them put in place to remedy past discrimination—that rely on racial counts of the population.

Large-scale immigration means that many more residents are foreign born. In 2005, 12 percent of the population was born outside the United States, a figure comparable to foreign-born rates at the turn of the previous century. Over half of the foreign born came from Latin America: one in ten from the Caribbean, nearly four in ten from Central America (including Mexico), and 6 percent from South America. Those born in Asia constituted the next-largest group, making up one-quarter of foreign-born residents. In sharp contrast to the immigration patterns of a century earlier, fewer immigrants came from Europe (see Figure 1.2). By 2004, only 14 percent of those born outside the United States came from Europe.[24]

These figures represent only legally authorized immigrants. One new feature of American society in recent years is the very large number of immigrants who live in the country without legal authorization. Estimates put the number of unauthorized immigrants at 11.5 to 12 million, the majority of whom are from Mexico and Central America.[25] The large unauthorized population has become a flashpoint for controversy as states and cities have passed a variety of conflicting laws. Some states have offered driver's licenses to undocumented immigrants, while others have sought to bar them from public services, such as education and emergency health care, both of which are constitutionally guaranteed to unauthorized immigrants.[26] In 1982, the Supreme Court ensured access to education when it ruled in *Plyler v. Doe* that Texas could not deny funding for undocumented students. In 1986, Congress guaranteed emergency medical care to all people regardless of immigration status when it passed the Emergency Medical Treatment and Active Labor Act (EMTALA).

The new patterns of immigration combined with differences in birth rates and underlying social changes to alter the religious affiliations of Americans. In 1900, 80 percent of the American population was Protestant; by 2000 only a little over half of Americans identified themselves as Protestants.[27] Catholics now made up a quarter of the population, and Jews accounted for close to 2 percent. A small Muslim population had also grown, with nearly one-half of 1 percent of the population.

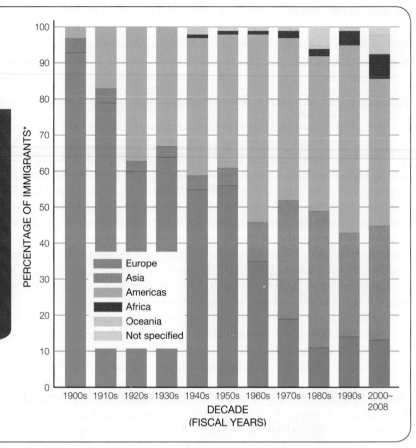

FIGURE 1.2

Immigration by Continent of Origin

Where did most immigrants come from at the start of the twentieth century? How does that compare with immigration in the twenty-first century?

*Less than 1 percent not shown.
SOURCE: Department of Homeland Security, "Yearbook of Immigration Statistics, 2008: Persons Obtaining Legal Permanent Resident Status by State of Residence: Fiscal Years 1999 to 2008," www .dhs.gov (accessed 9/28/09).

One of the most important shifts in religious affiliation during the latter half of the twentieth century was the percentage of people who professed no organized religion. In 2008, 16 percent of the population was not affiliated with an organized church. These changes suggest an important shift in American religious identity: although the United States thinks of itself as a "Judeo-Christian" nation—and indeed was 95 percent Protestant, Catholic, or Jewish from 1900 to 1968—by 2008, this number had fallen to only 80 percent of the population.[28] The presence of such religious diversity and a growing secular population sets the stage for deep conflicts over policy. For example, many religious groups welcomed former president George W. Bush's faith-based initiative, which sought to channel more funds to religious groups to administer social services. Secularists viewed the policy as abrogating the division between church and state.

As America grew and its population expanded and diversified, the country's age profile shifted with it. In 1900 only 4 percent of the population was over sixty-five. As life expectancy increased, the number of older Americans grew with it: by 2008, 13 percent of the population was over sixty-five. The percentage of children under the age of eighteen also changed; in 1900 this group comprised 43 percent of the American population; by 2008, children eighteen and under had fallen to just under a quarter of the population.[29] Another way to think about the age of Americans is that in 1800, the median age of the population was 16 years; by 1900, it was 22.9 years, and by 2000 it was 35.3 years. Even though the average age of Americans has increased, Americans tend to be younger than citizens of many

In 1965, Congress loosened restrictions on immigration, allowing millions of people from Latin America and Asia to enter the country in the decades that followed. By 2002, Hispanics were the largest minority group in the United States. Here, Antonio Villaraigosa campaigns to become the first Latino mayor of Los Angeles in 130 years.

industrialized countries, mainly because of the large immigrant population in the United States. In most European countries, the median age was above forty in 2000.[30] But an aging population poses challenges to the United States as well. As the elderly population grows and the working-age population shrinks, questions arise about how we will fund programs for the elderly, such as Social Security.

Over the nation's history, Americans have changed in other ways as well, moving from mostly rural settings and small towns to large urban areas. The idealization of country life in American culture traces its roots to the long period in which the majority of Americans lived in rural areas. Before 1920 less than half the population lived in urban areas; today three-quarters of Americans do.[31] Critics charge that the American political system—created when America was a largely rural society—underrepresents urban areas. The constitutional provision allocating each state two senators, for example, overrepresents sparsely populated rural states and underrepresents urban states, where the population is far more concentrated. In addition to becoming more urban over time, the American population has shifted regionally. During the past fifty years especially, many Americans left the Northeast and Midwest and moved to the South and Southwest. As congressional seats have been reapportioned to reflect the population shift, many problems that particularly plague the Midwest and Northeast—such as the decline of manufacturing jobs—receive less attention in national politics.

The shifting contours of the American people have regularly raised challenging questions about our politics and governing arrangements. Population growth has spurred politically charged debates about how the population should be apportioned among congressional districts. These conflicts have major implications for the representation of different regions of the country and for the balance of representation between urban and rural areas. Population growth has also transformed the close democratic relationship between congressional representatives and their constituents envisioned by the framers. For example, the framers stipulated that the number of representatives in the House of Representatives "shall not exceed one for every thirty Thousand . . ." constituents; today the average member of Congress represents 646,952 constituents.[32] Immigration and the cultural and religious changes it entails provoked heated disputes a hundred years ago and sparks passionate debate today. The different languages and customs that immigrants bring to the United States trigger fears that the country is changing in ways that may undermine American values and alter fundamental identities. The large number of unauthorized immigrants in the country today makes these anxieties even more acute. Yet a changing population has been one of the constants of American history. Indeed, each generation has confronted the myriad political challenges associated with answering anew "Who are Americans?"

● Thinking Critically about American Political Culture

Underlying and framing political life in the United States are agreements on basic political values but disagreements over the ends or goals of government. Most Americans share the values of liberty, equality, and democracy. Values shape citizens' views of the world and define their sense of what is right and wrong, just and unjust, possible and impossible. If Americans shared no values, they would have difficulty communicating, much less agreeing on a common system of government and politics. On the other hand, sharing broad values does not guarantee political consensus. We can agree on principles but disagree over their application.

For example, some critics claim that measures such as affirmative action have not promoted political inclusion and instead have condoned reverse discrimination and a segmented society. Far from fulfilling American ideals, they argue, these policies represent a movement away from our most fundamental values. An opposing perspective questions the progress that has been made in promoting equality. Pointing to the disproportionately high rates of poverty among women and minorities and continuing evidence of discrimination against these groups, this side questions whether Americans are serious about equality. Much of the debate over the role of government has been over what government should do and how far it should go to reduce the inequalities within our society and political system.

Even though Americans have disagreed over the meaning of such political ideals as equality, they still agree on the importance of these ideals. The shared values, beliefs, and attitudes that form our **political culture** and hold the United States and its people together date back to the time of the founding of the Union.

The essential documents of the American Founding—the Declaration of Independence and the Constitution—enunciated a set of political principles about the purposes of the new republic. In contrast with many other democracies, in the United States these political ideals did not just remain words on dusty documents. Americans actively embraced the principles of the Founders and made them central to the national identity. Let us look more closely at three of these ideals: liberty, equality, and democracy.

Liberty

No ideal is more central to American values than liberty. The Declaration of Independence defined three inalienable rights: "life, liberty and the pursuit of happiness." The preamble of the Constitution likewise identified the need to secure "the blessings of liberty" as one of the key reasons for drawing up the Constitution. For

political culture broadly shared values, beliefs, and attitudes about how the government should function. American political culture emphasizes the values of liberty, equality, and democracy.

Patrick Henry's famous "Give me liberty, or give me death" speech demanded freedom at any cost and has resonated with Americans throughout the nation's history.

Americans, **liberty** means both personal freedom and economic freedom. Both are closely linked to the idea of **limited government**.

The Constitution's first ten amendments, known collectively as the Bill of Rights, above all preserve individual personal liberties and rights. In fact, liberty has come to mean many of the freedoms guaranteed in the Bill of Rights: freedom of speech and writing, the right to assemble freely, and the right to practice religious beliefs without interference from the government. Over the course of American history, the scope of personal liberties has expanded, as laws have become more tolerant and as individuals have successfully used the courts to challenge restrictions on their individual freedoms. Far fewer restrictions exist today on the press, political speech, and individual moral behavior than in the early years of the nation. Even so, conflicts persist over how personal liberties should be extended and when personal liberties violate community norms. For example, one of the most contentious issues in the last forty years has been that of abortion. Whereas defenders of the right to choose abortion view it as an essential personal freedom for women, opponents view it as murder—something that no society should allow.

In addition to personal freedom, the American concept of liberty means economic freedom. Since the Founding, economic freedom has been linked to capitalism, free markets, and the protection of private property. Free competition, unfettered movement of goods, and the right to enjoy the fruits of one's labor are all essential aspects of economic freedom and American capitalism.[33] In the first century of the Republic, support for capitalism often meant support for the doctrine of *laissez-faire* (translated literally as to "leave alone"). **Laissez-faire capitalism** allowed very little room for the national government to regulate trade or restrict the use of private property, even in the public interest. Americans still strongly support capitalism and economic liberty, but they now also endorse some restrictions on economic freedoms to protect the public. Federal and state governments now deploy a wide array of regulations in the name of public protection. These include health and safety laws, environmental rules, and workplace regulations. Not surprisingly, fierce disagreements often erupt over what the proper scope of government regulation should be. What some people regard as protecting the public, others see as an infringement on their own freedom to run their businesses and use their property as they see fit.

Equality

The Declaration of Independence declares as its first "self-evident" truth that "all men are created equal." As central as it is to the American political creed, however, equality has been a less well-defined ideal than liberty because people interpret "equality" in different ways. Few Americans have wholeheartedly embraced full equality of results, but most Americans share the ideal of **equality of opportunity**—that is, the notion that each person should be given a fair chance to go as far as his or her talents will allow. Yet it is hard for Americans to reach agreement about what constitutes equality of opportunity. Must *past* inequalities be remedied in order to ensure equal opportunity in the *present*? Should inequalities in the legal, political, and economic spheres be given the same weight? In contrast to liberty, which requires limits on the role of government, equality implies an *obligation* of the government to the people.[34]

Americans do make clear distinctions between political equality and social or economic equality. **Political equality** means that members of the American political community have the right to participate in politics on equal terms. Beginning from

liberty freedom from governmental control

limited government a principle of constitutional government; a government whose powers are defined and limited by a constitution

laissez-faire capitalism an economic system in which the means of production and distribution are privately owned and operated for profit with minimal or no government interference

equality of opportunity a widely shared American ideal that all people should have the freedom to use whatever talents and wealth they have to reach their fullest potential

political equality the right to participate in politics equally, based on the principle of "one person, one vote"

a very restricted definition of political community, which originally included only propertied white men, the United States has moved much closer to an ideal of political equality that can be summed up as "one person, one vote." Broad support for the ideal of political equality has helped expand the American political community and extend the right to participate to all. Although considerable conflict remains over whether the political system makes it harder for some people to participate and easier for others and whether the role of money in politics has drowned out the public voice, Americans agree that all citizens should have an equal right to participate and that government should enforce that right.

In part because Americans believe that individuals are free to work as hard as they choose, they have always been less concerned about social or economic inequality. Many Americans regard economic differences as the consequence of individual choices, virtues, or failures. Because of this, Americans tend to be less supportive than most Europeans of government action to ensure equality. Yet when major economic forces, such as the Great Depression of the 1930s, affect many people or when systematic barriers appear to block equality of opportunity, Americans support government action to promote equality. Even then, however, Americans have endorsed only a limited government role designed to help people get back on their feet or to open up opportunity.

Democracy

The essence of democracy is the participation of the people in choosing their rulers and the people's ability to influence what those rulers do. In a democracy, political power ultimately comes from the people. The idea of placing power in the hands of the people is known as **popular sovereignty**. In the United States, popular sovereignty and political equality make politicians accountable to the people. Ideally, democracy envisions an engaged citizenry prepared to exercise its power over rulers. As we saw earlier, the United States is a representative democracy, meaning that the people do not rule directly but instead exercise power through elected representatives. Forms of participation in a democracy vary greatly, but voting is a key element of the representative democracy that the American Founders established.

American democracy rests on the principle of **majority rule** with **minority rights**. Majority rule means that the wishes of the majority determine what government does. The House of Representatives—a large body elected directly by the people— was designed in particular to ensure majority rule. But the Founders feared that popular majorities could turn government into a "tyranny of the majority" in which individual liberties would be violated. Concern for individual rights has thus been a part of American democracy from the beginning. The rights enumerated in the Bill of Rights and enforced through the courts provide an important check on the power of the majority.

popular sovereignty a principle of democracy in which political authority rests ultimately in the hands of the people

majority rule, minority rights the democratic principle that a government follows the preferences of the majority of voters but protects the interests of the minority

Liberty, Equality, and Democracy in Practice

Liberty, equality, and democracy are core American ideals. But like many abstract ideals, they are not always easy to put into practice. Americans have always hotly debated the meaning and implications of each ideal as well as the proper balance among them.

Liberty The central historical conflict regarding liberty in the United States was about the enslavement of blacks. The facts of slavery and the differential treatment of the races have cast a long shadow over all of American history. In fact, scholars today note that the American definition of freedom has been formed in relation to the concept of slavery. The right to control one's labor and the right to receive rewards for that labor have been central elements of our definition of freedom precisely because these freedoms were denied to slaves.[35]

Concerns about the meaning of liberty also arise in connection with government regulation of economic and social activity. Economic regulations imposed to ensure public health and safety are often decried by the affected businesses as infringements on their freedom. For example, in September 2009, the Food and Drug Administration banned the sale of flavored cigarettes under the terms of the Family Smoking Prevention and Tobacco Control Act passed by Congress three months earlier. The FDA and health care professionals argue that such cigarettes are manufactured primarily to lure children and teenagers into smoking; by banning these cigarettes the agency hopes to reduce the 3,600 children and teenagers who are estimated to start smoking each day. Manufacturers of these products, however, are wary of such regulations, feeling that the government is limiting their freedom and their ability to make a profit.[36]

Social regulations prompt similar disputes. Some citizens believe that government should enforce certain standards of behavior or instill particular values in citizens. Examples of such activity abound: welfare rules that once denied benefits

Political participation was greatest during the nineteenth century. But as this 1854 painting indicates, white men were virtually the only people who could vote at the time.

to women who were found with a "man in the house," the practice of saying prayers in school, and laws that require citizens to wear seat belts are just a few examples. Deciding the proper scope of economic and social regulation is a topic of great concern and much conflict among Americans today.

More recently, concerns about liberty have arisen in relation to the government's efforts to combat terrorism. In the months following September 11, hundreds of individuals—mainly of Middle Eastern origin—were arrested by federal authorities and held on immigration charges or by material witness warrants that allowed the government to incarcerate them without having to show any evidence they were linked to terrorist activities. Also in the immediate aftermath of September 11, President George W. Bush issued secret orders to the National Security Agency, authorizing the agency to monitor domestic phone traffic in search of possible communications among terrorist groups. This program meant that the calls of millions of Americans were secretly intercepted without a court warrant. Concerns about terrorism leave us with an extraordinary dilemma. On the one hand, we treasure liberty, but on the other hand, we recognize that the lives of thousands of Americans have already been lost and countless others are threatened by terrorism. Can we reconcile liberty and security? Liberty and order? In previous national emergencies, Americans accepted restrictions on liberty with the understanding that these would be temporary. Because the threat of terrorism has no clear end point, doubts have grown about whether special government powers that infringe on liberties should be continued.

Equality Because equality is such an elusive concept, many conflicts have arisen over what it should mean in practice. Americans have engaged in three kinds of controversies about the public role in addressing inequality. The first is determining what constitutes equality of access to public institutions. In 1896, the Supreme Court ruled in *Plessy v. Ferguson* that "separate but equal" accommodations for blacks and whites were constitutional. In 1954, in a major legal victory for the civil rights movement, the Supreme Court overturned the "separate but equal" doctrine in *Brown v. Board of Education* (see Chapter 5). Today, new questions have been raised about what constitutes equal access to public institutions. Some argue that the unequal financing of public schools in cities, suburbs, and rural districts is a violation of the right to equal education. To date, these claims have not been supported by the federal courts, which have rejected the notion that the unequal economic impacts of public policy outcomes are a constitutional matter.[37] Lawsuits arguing a right to "economic equal protection" stalled in 1973 when the Supreme Court ruled that a Texas school-financing law did not violate the Constitution even though the law affected rich and poor students differently.[38]

A second debate concerns the public role in ensuring equality of opportunity in private life. Although Americans generally agree that discrimination should not be tolerated, people disagree over what should be done to ensure equality of opportunity (see Table 1.2). Controversies about affirmative action programs reflect these disputes. Supporters of affirmative action claim that such programs are necessary to compensate for past discrimination in order to establish true equality of opportunity today. Opponents maintain that affirmative action amounts to reverse discrimination and that a society that espouses true equality should not acknowledge gender or racial differences. The question of the public responsibility

In political terms, the abortion debate hinges on the extent of government control over personal liberty.

Should America Export Democracy?

Americans are justifiably proud of their democratic political institutions and often believe that the people of all nations would benefit from living under American-style democratic rule. Indeed, on a number of occasions Americans have sought to transform other nations into democracies—a policy called "democratization." In the aftermath of World War II, American military forces occupied Japan and the western portion of Germany, imposing new democratic governments to replace the dictatorial regimes blamed for launching the war. More recently, after successful American military campaigns to overthrow the governments of Afghanistan and Iraq, the United States has undertaken an effort to build democratic governments in those nations.

Exporting democracy might be seen as a desirable goal for three reasons. The first of these is humanitarian. Generally speaking, individuals are better off when they possess civil liberties and political rights. Indeed, former president George W. Bush asserted that one of the main purposes of American policy in the Middle East was to bring democracy to the people of the region. "It is the calling of our country," Bush said.

A second reason sometimes given in support of American efforts to export democracy is the promotion of political stability. In a democracy, competing economic and social forces have a chance to work out their differences through lawful political struggle. Dictatorial regimes, by contrast, seldom provide opportunities for lawful political activity and usually seek to quash expressions of political dissent or opposition. Lacking lawful channels, political grievances in nations ruled by dictatorships usually manifest themselves in such forms as public protest, political violence, and terrorism. Instability and violence in one country can easily spread beyond borders to pose threats elsewhere. As Bush put it, "As long as the Middle East remains a place where freedom does not flourish, it will remain a place of stagnation, resentment and violence ready for export."

A third reason Americans might wish to support policies of democratization is that the spread of democracy may promote world peace. In his famous 1795 essay "Toward Perpetual Peace," the German philosopher Immanuel Kant observed that democratic regimes seldom made war on each other. Thus, he argued, the expansion of democracy would enhance the prospects for world peace. In recent years, a good deal of empirical research has supported Kant's hypothesis.

Although a more democratic world might, indeed, be more humane, stable, and peaceful, a policy of democratization faces daunting prospects. First, a huge percentage of the world's population lives in nations that are not democracies. It seems unlikely that America could actually democratize so much of the globe. Second, many nations might not be capable of sustaining democratic regimes even if they were established. Democracy is most likely to flourish where there are vigorous social institutions and a stable economy—conditions that do not exist in many regions of the world. Finally, the process of democratization can, itself, be dangerous for American interests because it may lead to political instability or the election of hostile governments. By 2009, some observers were questioning whether it would be possible to build democracies in Iraq and Afghanistan, where corruption and security challenges were undermining government stability. With the threat from the Taliban mounting in Afghanistan, the British ambassador there went so far as to suggest that it would take "an acceptable dictator" to unite the country.

for critical analysis

1. What are some of the factors that might help to determine whether democratic politics can take root in a country that has not previously experienced democracy?

2. Is it appropriate for America to try to shape the governments and political arrangements of other countries?

TABLE 1.2

Equality and Public Opinion

Americans believe in some forms of equality more than others. How do these survey results reflect disagreement about what equality means in practice?

STATEMENT	PERCENTAGE WHO AGREE
Male and female citizens of the United States have equal rights.	97
Our society should do what is necessary to make sure that everyone has an equal opportunity to succeed.	87
Homosexuals should have equal rights in terms of job opportunities.	89
Marriages between same-sex couples should be recognized by the law as valid, with the same rights as traditional marriages.	40
It's OK to have a country where the races are basically separate from one another, as long as they have equal opportunity.	36
The opportunity for equal justice under the law is equal for blacks and whites (according to whites).	53
The opportunity for equal justice under the law is equal for blacks and whites (according to blacks).	21

SOURCES: Opinion Research Corporation, 2001; Pew, 2009; Gallup, 2009; Foundation for Ethnic Understanding, 2005; and National Conference for Community and Justice, 2005.

for private inequalities is central to gender issues. The traditional view, still held by many today, sees the special responsibilities of women in the family as falling outside the range of public concern. Indeed, from this perspective, the role of women within families is essential to the functioning of a democratic society. In the past thirty years especially, these traditional views have come under fire, as advocates for women have argued that women occupy a subordinate place within the family and that such private inequalities *are* a topic of public concern.[39]

A third debate about equality concerns differences in income and wealth. Unlike in other countries, income inequality has not been an enduring topic of political controversy in the United States, which currently has the largest gap in income and wealth between rich and poor citizens of any developed nation. But Americans have generally tolerated great differences among rich and poor citizens, in part because of a pervasive belief that mobility is possible and that economic success is the product of individual effort.[40] This tolerance for inequality is reflected in America's tax code, which is more advantageous to wealthy taxpayers than that of almost any other Western nation. Indeed, tax changes enacted in recent years have sharply reduced the tax burdens of upper-income Americans. Debate about taxes dominated the closing days of the 2008 presidential race. John McCain promised to enact no new taxes and accused Barack Obama of being a socialist for commenting that he wanted to "spread the wealth around." President Obama signed tax reductions into law as part of the American Recovery and Reinvestment Act that he claimed would provide relief for up to 95 percent of Americans.[41] He has, however, defended the need to raise the tax rate of Americans earning more than $250,000 a year to support programs that benefit the middle class; in early 2009 he signaled that he would allow the 2001 tax cuts for these upper-income Americans to expire in 2010.[42]

for critical analysis

Economic inequality among Americans is now as high as it was a hundred years ago. Many politicians and news commentators say that inequality is threatening the middle class. Is there any evidence that the American public is worried about the growth in inequality?

Honing Your Political Radar

Numerous surveys have shown that the vast majority of college students view the world of government as a remote, far-off land dominated by "old white guys in suits." For many people politics seems like something that doesn't really have an impact on their lives, largely because the political system does so little to help younger Americans recognize how important government can be.

As you'll see throughout this book, the political decisions that government officials make can have a real impact on your life. Whom you can and cannot marry, how clean the environment is where you live—these are just two of many examples.

Even though you may never become a politician or a full-time activist, it's important to spend some time thinking through where you fit into the broader political debates that may affect your life. Doing so requires you to recognize that even core American political values—liberty, equality, and democracy—mean different things to different people. After all,

it's one thing to say that everyone should be entitled to equal treatment under the law, but as the current debate over gay marriage and civil unions demonstrates, equality doesn't always mean the same thing to everyone.

The same thing can be said regarding government and the environment. Even though most Americans believe government has a role to play in protecting the environment, many also fear that their personal liberties are at stake if the government starts passing legislation that penalizes people for the kinds of cars they drive.

The following are a few steps you can take to better understand where you fit into policy debates today and how core political values play out in the real world.

- Investigate a political or social issue that you have an opinion on yet know little about. This sounds odd at first, but we are often asked to offer opinions on things that we haven't had time to examine carefully, simply because our lives are already consumed with

work, school, family, and friends. Try doing an Internet search of the issue of your choice and reading up on it. Be sure to read things that both contradict and reinforce your opinion. As you do this, think about how your interpretation of one or more core political values (liberty, equality, or democracy) shapes your understanding of this issue. Did thinking through other people's opinions change yours?

- Talk to friends and family about a political or social issue that tends to promote a variety of opinions, such as abortion laws, the environment, health care, or the "right to die." Ask questions about their positions and listen to what differences of opinion emerge in your conversations. Do the differences have anything to do with disagreements over liberty and equality?

- Watch a TV show with political content, like *The Daily Show with Jon Stewart* or *The O'Reilly Factor*, and examine an issue that's covered in the broadcast. What you hear may be just one side of the issue, but a good place to explore other sides to many controversial issues is the Public Agenda Foundation Web site (www.publicagenda.org). If you click on the "Issue Guides" link at the top of the page, you can see what others say about an issue and how political values are interpreted differently when applied to this issue.

- Read the other "Get Involved" sections in this book for specific ways that you can influence government and politics at the national level, the state level, on your campus, and in your community. As you consider getting involved in a particular issue, think about how it relates to core values such as liberty, equality, and democracy, and why government should (or should not) assume more responsibility in addressing this issue.

Voting rights expanded dramatically during the civil rights movement, which forced the government to allow people to vote regardless of their race. Here, residents of Wilcox County, Alabama, line up to vote in 1966. Prior to the passage of the Voting Rights Act of 1965, Wilcox County had no registered black voters.

Democracy Despite Americans' deep attachment to the *ideal* of democracy, many questions can be raised about our *practice* of democracy. The first is the restricted definition of the political community during much of American history. The United States was not a full democracy until the 1960s, when African Americans were at last guaranteed the right to vote. Property restrictions on the right to vote were eliminated by 1828; in 1870, the Fifteenth Amendment to the Constitution granted African Americans the vote, although later exclusionary practices denied them that right; in 1920, the Nineteenth Amendment guaranteed women the right to vote; and in 1965, the Voting Rights Act finally secured the right of African Americans to vote.

Although Americans are no longer legally barred from voting on the basis of gender or race, many people do not participate. In the 2008 election, only 62 percent of eligible voters came to the polls.

Just securing the right to vote does not end concerns about democracy, however. The organization of electoral institutions can have a significant impact on access to elections and on who can get elected. During the first two decades of the twentieth century, states and cities enacted many reforms that made it harder to vote, including strict registration requirements and scheduling of elections. The aim was to rid politics of corruption, but the consequence was to reduce participation. Other institutional decisions affect which candidates stand the best chance of getting elected (see Chapter 10).

A further consideration about democracy concerns the relationship between economic power and political power. Money has always played an important role in elections and governing in the United States. Many argue that the pervasive influence of money in American electoral campaigns today undermines democracy. With the decline of locally based political parties that depended on party loyalists to turn out the vote, and the rise of political action committees, political consultants, and expensive media campaigns, money has become the central fact of life in American politics. Money often determines who runs for office; it can exert a heavy influence on who wins; and, some argue, money affects what politicians do once they are in office.[43]

Low turnout for elections and a pervasive sense of apathy and cynicism characterized American politics for much of the past half-century. The widespread interest in the 2008 election and the near-record levels of voter turnout, which, at 61.7 percent was the highest voter turnout since 1980, reversed this trend.[44] Nine million voters registered and voted for the first time in 2008, including near-record numbers of voters under the age of 24.[45] Volunteers found ways to become personally involved in politics. These developments are a hopeful sign for those wishing to revitalize American democracy.

for critical analysis

Think of some examples that demonstrate the gaps between the ideals of America's core political values and the practice of American politics. How might these discrepancies be reconciled?

studyguide

Practice Quiz

Find a diagnostic Web Quiz with 33 additional questions on the StudySpace Web site: www.wwnorton.com/we-the-people

What Americans Think about Government

1. Political efficacy is the belief that *(p. 8)*
   a) government operates efficiently.
   b) government has grown too large.
   c) government cannot be trusted.
   d) one can influence what government does.

2. American's trust in their government *(pp. 5–8)*
   a) rose significantly between 1964 and 1980.
   b) increased immediately following September 11, 2001, but declined shortly thereafter.
   c) declined immediately after the September 11th attacks but has risen dramatically since 2004.
   d) has remained the same over the last fifty years.

Citizenship: Knowledge and Participation

3. Generally speaking, Americans know *(p. 9)*
   a) very little about current political issues but are able to identify high-profile political leaders.
   b) a great deal about current political issues but are not able to identify high-profile political leaders.
   c) very little about current political issues and are not able to identify high-profile political leaders.
   d) a great deal about current political issues and are able to identify high-profile political leaders.

4. According to the authors, good citizenship requires *(pp. 10–11)*
   a) political knowledge.
   b) political engagement.
   c) a good education.
   d) both a and b

Government

5. What is the basic difference between autocracy and oligarchy? *(p. 13)*
   a) the extent to which the average citizen has a say in government affairs
   b) the means of collecting taxes and conscripting soldiers
   c) the number of people who control governing decisions
   d) They are fundamentally the same thing.

6. The famous political scientist Harold Lasswell defined politics as the struggle over *(p. 15)*
   a) who gets elected.
   b) who gets what, when, how.
   c) who protests.
   d) who gets to vote.

7. Although not present at the national level, a number of states and cities permit citizens to vote directly on laws and policies. What is this form of rule called? *(p. 15)*
   a) representative democracy
   b) direct democracy
   c) pluralism
   d) laissez-faire capitalism

8. Pluralism is a theory that says: *(p. 16)*
   a) The means of economic production should be privately owned and operated without interference from the government.
   b) All interests in a society should be free to compete for influence over governmental decisions.
   c) Government should always follow the preferences of the majority while also protecting the rights of those in the minority.
   d) American political culture should emphasize the values of liberty, equality, and democracy.

Who Are Americans?

9. Since 1900, which of the following groups has increased as a percentage of the overall population in the United States? *(p. 18)*
   a) black
   b) Hispanic
   c) Asian
   d) All of the above have increased as a percentage of the overall population.

10. The percentage of foreign-born individuals living in the United States *(pp. 20–21)*
    a) has increased significantly since reaching its low point in 1970.
    b) has decreased significantly since reaching its high point in 1970.
    c) has remained the same since 1970.
    d) has not been studied since 1970.

Thinking Critically about American Political Culture

11. The principle of political equality can be best summed up as *(p. 26)*
    a) "equality of results."
    b) "equality of opportunity."
    c) "one person, one vote."
    d) "equality between the sexes."

12. Which of the following is an important principle of American democracy? *(pp. 25–26)*
    a) popular sovereignty
    b) majority rule, minority rights
    c) limited government
    d) All of the above are important principles of American democracy.

13. Which of the following is *not* related to the American conception of liberty? *(pp. 26–28)*
    a) freedom of speech
    b) free enterprise
    c) freedom of religion
    d) All of the above are related to liberty.

14. Which of the following is *not* part of American political culture? *(p. 28)*
    a) belief in equality of results
    b) belief in equality of opportunity
    c) belief in individual liberty
    d) belief in free competition

15. Which of the following restrictions on voting have been repealed over the last 182 years of American history? *(p. 32)*
    a) property
    b) gender
    c) race
    d) all of the above

Chapter Outline

Find a detailed Chapter Outline on the StudySpace Web site: www.wwnorton.com/we-the-people

Key Terms

Find Flashcards to help you study these terms on the StudySpace Web site: www.wwnorton.com/we-the-people

authoritarian government *(p. 13)*
autocracy *(p. 13)*
citizenship *(p. 10)*
constitutional government *(p. 13)*

democracy *(p. 13)*
direct democracy *(p. 15)*
equality of opportunity *(p. 25)*
government *(p. 13)*

laissez-faire capitalism *(p. 25)*
liberty *(p. 25)*
limited government *(p. 25)*
majority rule, minority rights *(p. 26)*

oligarchy *(p. 13)*
pluralism *(p. 16)*
political culture *(p. 24)*
political efficacy *(p. 8)*

political equality *(p. 25)*
politics *(p. 15)*
popular sovereignty *(p. 26)*
power *(p. 15)*

representative democracy/
    republic *(p. 15)*
totalitarian government *(p. 14)*

For Further Reading

Dahl, Robert. *Democracy and Its Critics.* New Haven, CT: Yale University Press, 1989.

Dalton, Russell. *The Good Citizen: How a Younger Generation Is Reshaping American Politics* Rev. ed. Washington, DC: Congressional Quarterly Press, 2008.

Delli Carpini, Michael X., and Scott Keeter. *What Americans Know about Politics and Why It Matters.* New Haven, CT: Yale University Press, 1996.

Fischer, Claude S., and Michael Hout. *A Century of Difference: How America Changed in the Last One Hundred Years.* New York: Russell Sage Foundation, 2006.

Hibbing, John R., and Elizabeth Theiss-Morse. *Stealth Democracy: Americans' Belief about How Government Should Work.* New York: Cambridge University Press, 2002.

Huntington, Samuel. *Who Are We: The Challenges to America's National Identity.* New York: Simon & Schuster, 2004.

Jamieson, Kathleen Hall. *Everything You Think You Know about Politics . . . and Why You're Wrong.* New York: Basic Books, 2000.

Lasswell, Harold. *Politics: Who Gets What, When, How.* New York: Meridian Books, 1958.

Page, Benjamin I., and Lawrence R. Jacobs. *Class War? What Americans Really Think about Economic Inequality.* Chicago: University of Chicago Press, 2009.

Tocqueville, Alexis de. *Democracy in America.* Translated by Phillips Bradley. New York: Knopf, Vintage Books, 1945; orig. published 1835.

Zakaria, Fareed. *The Future of Freedom.* New York: Norton, 2003.

Recommended Web Sites

American Democracy Project
www.aascu.org/programs/adp/
This is an effort by the Association of State Colleges and Universities to increase political engagement among college students. See what opportunities are available for you to become politically active.

Americans for Informed Democracy
www.aidemocracy.org
A nonpartisan organization that promotes democracy and seeks to build a new generation of globally conscious leaders. Find out how you can be politically active and coordinate a town hall meeting on campus, attend a leadership retreat, or publish your opinions on democracy.

DiversityInc
http://diversityinc.com
This site is dedicated to the promotion of American diversity and education. Here you can read about the issues that directly affect American minorities.

For Democracy
www.fordemocracy.com
Most Americans know little about our government. Log on to this independent site to find a plethora of information on the history of American democracy and related current events.

Future of Freedom Foundation
www.fff.org
This organization promotes individual liberty, free markets, private property, and limited government. Find out how some people are trying to protect freedom in the United States.

Institute for Learning Technologies
www.ilt.columbia.edu/publications/digitext.html#
Columbia University's Institute for Learning Technologies provides general information on early political thinkers such as Aristotle, Hobbes, Locke, and Rousseau. Take a moment to read some of the writings on topics such as popular sovereignty, democracy, and limited government.

Mobilize.org
http://mobilize.org
This all-partisan network is dedicated to educating, empowering, and energizing young people. Find out how politics affects America's youth and what they are doing about it by being engaged and active.

U.S. Census Bureau
www.census.gov
The Web site for the Bureau of the Census offers a statistical look at our country's population and economy. Check out some of the statistics to get a better idea of American diversity.

When the framers of the Constitution met in 1787, they set out to establish a political system that would protect liberty and place limits on government. They also believed a powerful government required a broad popular base. However, they debated how best to protect liberty and how to balance democracy with other concerns.

The Founding and the Constitution

WHAT GOVERNMENT DOES AND WHY IT MATTERS The framers of the U.S. Constitution knew why government mattered. In the Constitution's preamble, the framers tell us that the purposes of government are to promote justice, to maintain peace at home, to defend the nation from foreign foes, to provide for the welfare of the citizenry, and, above all, to secure the "blessings of liberty" for Americans. The remainder of the Constitution spells out a plan for achieving these objectives. The plan includes provisions for the exercise of legislative, executive, and judicial powers and a recipe for the division of powers among the federal government's branches and between the national and state governments. The framers' conception of why government matters and how it is to achieve its goals has been America's political blueprint for more than two centuries.

The story of America's Founding and the Constitution is generally presented as something both inevitable

focusquestions

- What events led to the Declaration of Independence and the Articles of Confederation?

- How did the Constitution attempt to improve America's governance?

- What are the major institutions and rules established by the Constitution?

- Why was the Constitution controversial at the time of the Founding?

- How has the Constitution changed over the past 200 years?

and glorious: it was inevitable that the American colonies would break away from Great Britain to establish their own country; and it was glorious in that the country established the best of all possible forms of government under a new constitution, which was easily adopted and quickly embraced, even by its critics. In reality, though, America's successful breakaway from Britain was by no means assured, and the Constitution was in fact highly controversial. Moreover, its ratification and durability were often in doubt. George Washington, the man chosen to preside over the Constitutional Convention of 1787, thought the document produced that hot summer in Philadelphia would probably last no more than twenty years, at which time leaders would have to convene again to come up with something new.

That Washington's expectation proved wrong is, indeed, a testament to the enduring strength of the Constitution. America's longstanding values of liberty, equality, and democracy were all major themes of the founding period and are all elements of the U.S. Constitution. However, the Constitution was a product of political bargaining and compromise, formed in very much the same way political decisions are made today. This fact is often overlooked because of what the historian Michael Kammen has called the "cult of the Constitution"—a tendency of Americans, going back more than a century, to venerate, sometimes to the point of near worship, the Founders and the document they created.[1] As this chapter will show, the Constitution reflects high principle as well as political self-interest. It also defines the relationship between American citizens and their government.

chaptercontents

● What events led
to the Declaration
of Independence
and the Articles of
Confederation?

● The First Founding: Interests and Conflicts

Competing ideals and principles often reflect competing interests, and so it was in Revolutionary America. The American Revolution and the American Constitution were outgrowths and expressions of a struggle among economic and political forces within the colonies. Five sectors of society had interests that were important in colonial politics: (1) the New England merchants; (2) the southern planters; (3) the "royalists"—holders of royal lands, offices, and patents (licenses to engage in a profession or business activity); (4) shopkeepers, artisans, and laborers; and (5) small farmers. Throughout the eighteenth century, these groups were in conflict over issues of taxation, trade, and commerce. For the most part, however, the southern planters, the New England merchants, and the royal office and patent holders—groups that together made up the colonial elite—were able to maintain a political alliance that held in check the more radical forces representing shopkeepers, laborers, and small farmers. After 1760, however, by seriously threatening the interests of New England merchants and southern planters, British tax and trade policies split the colonial elite, permitting radical forces to expand their political influence, and set in motion a chain of events that culminated in the American Revolution.[2]

British Taxes and Colonial Interests

Beginning in the 1760s, the debts and other financial problems confronting the British government forced it to search for new revenue sources. This search rather quickly led to the Crown's North American colonies, which, on the whole, paid remarkably little in taxes to their parent country. The British government reasoned that a sizable fraction of its debt was, in fact, attributable to the expenses it had incurred in defense of the colonies during the French and Indian War, which ended in 1763, driving France from North America. The British also considered the cost of the continuing protection that British forces were giving the colonists from Indian attacks and that the British navy was providing for colonial shipping. Thus, during the 1760s, Britain sought to impose new, though relatively modest, taxes on the colonists.

Like most governments of the period, the British regime had limited ways in which to collect revenues. The income tax, which in the twentieth century became the single most important source of governmental revenues, had not yet been developed. For the most part, in the mid-eighteenth century, governments relied on tariffs, duties, and other taxes on commerce, and it was to such taxes, including the Stamp Act, that the British turned during the 1760s.

The Stamp Act and other taxes on commerce, such as the Sugar Act of 1764, which taxed sugar, molasses, and other commodities, most heavily affected the two groups in colonial society whose commercial interests and activities were most extensive—the New England merchants and the southern planters. Under the famous slogan "no taxation without representation," the merchants and planters together sought to organize opposition to these new taxes. In the course of the struggle against British tax measures, the planters and merchants broke with their royalist allies and turned to their former adversaries—the shopkeepers, small farmers, laborers, and artisans—for help. With the assistance of these groups, the merchants and planters organized demonstrations and a boycott of British goods that ultimately forced the Crown to rescind most of its new taxes.

This picture of a segmented snake, printed in Benjamin Franklin's newspaper, urged the colonies to unite during the French and Indian War, 1756–63. Again during the Revolutionary War, cooperation among the states was crucial to the independence movement.

The British helped radicalize colonists through bad policy decisions in the years before the Revolution. For example, Britain gave the ailing East India Company a monopoly on the tea trade in the American colonies. Colonists feared the monopoly would hurt colonial merchants' business and protested by throwing East India Company tea into Boston Harbor in 1773.

From the perspective of the merchants and planters, however, the British government's decision to eliminate most of the hated taxes brought a victorious conclusion to their struggle with the mother country. They were anxious to end the unrest they had helped to arouse, and they supported the British government's efforts to restore order. Indeed, most respectable Bostonians supported the actions of the British soldiers involved in the Boston Massacre. In their subsequent trial, the soldiers were defended by John Adams, a pillar of Boston society and a future president of the United States. Adams asserted that the soldiers' actions were entirely justified, provoked by "a motley rabble of saucy boys, Negroes and mulattos, Irish teagues and outlandish Jack tars." All but two of the soldiers were acquitted.[3]

Despite the efforts of the British government and the better-to-do strata of colonial society, it proved difficult to bring an end to the political strife. The more radical forces representing shopkeepers, artisans, laborers, and small farmers, who had been mobilized and energized by the struggle over taxes, continued to agitate for political and social change within the colonies. These radicals, led by individuals such as Samuel Adams, a cousin of John Adams, asserted that British power supported an unjust political and social structure within the colonies, and began to advocate an end to British rule.[4]

Political Strife and the Radicalizing of the Colonists

The political strife within the colonies was the background for the events of 1773–74. In 1773, the British government granted the politically powerful East India Company a monopoly on the export of tea from Britain, eliminating a lucrative form of trade for colonial merchants. To add to the injury, the East India Company sought to sell the tea directly in the colonies instead of working through the colonial merchants. Tea was an extremely important commodity during the 1770s, and these British actions posed a serious threat to the New England merchants. Together with

for critical **analysis**

Conflicts over taxes did not end with the American Revolution. Why is tax policy almost always controversial?

their southern allies, the merchants once again called on their radical adversaries for support. The most dramatic result was the Boston Tea Party of 1773, led by Samuel Adams.

This event was of decisive importance in American history. The merchants had hoped to force the British government to rescind the Tea Act, but they did not support any demands beyond this one. They did not seek independence from Britain. Samuel Adams and the other radicals, however, hoped to provoke the British government to take actions that would alienate its colonial supporters and pave the way for a rebellion. This was precisely the purpose of the Boston Tea Party, and it succeeded. By dumping the East India Company's tea into Boston Harbor, Adams and his followers goaded the British into enacting a number of harsh reprisals. Within five months after the incident in Boston, the House of Commons passed a series of acts that closed the port of Boston to commerce, changed the provincial government of Massachusetts, provided for the removal of accused persons to Britain for trial, and most important, restricted movement to the West—further alienating the southern planters, who depended on access to new western lands. These acts of retaliation confirmed the worst criticisms of Britain and helped radicalize Americans. Radicals such as Samuel Adams and Christopher Gadsden of South Carolina had been agitating for more-violent measures to deal with Britain. But ultimately they needed Britain's political repression to create widespread support for independence.

Thus, the Boston Tea Party set in motion a cycle of provocation and retaliation that in 1774 resulted in the convening of the First Continental Congress—an assembly of delegates from all parts of the country—that called for a total boycott of British goods and, under the prodding of the radicals, began to consider the possibility of independence from British rule. The eventual result was the Declaration of Independence.

The Declaration of Independence

In 1776, the Second Continental Congress appointed a committee consisting of Thomas Jefferson of Virginia, Benjamin Franklin of Pennsylvania, Roger Sherman of Connecticut, John Adams of Massachusetts, and Robert Livingston of New York to draft a statement of American independence from British rule. The Declaration of Independence, written by Jefferson and adopted by the Second Continental Congress, was an extraordinary document in both philosophical and political terms. In philosophic terms, the Declaration was remarkable for its assertion that certain rights, called "unalienable rights"—including life, liberty, and the pursuit of happiness—could not be abridged by governments. In the world of 1776, a world in which some kings still claimed to rule by divine right, this was a dramatic statement. In political terms, the Declaration was remarkable because, despite the differences of interest that divided the colonists along economic, regional, and philosophical lines, it identified and focused on problems, grievances, aspirations, and principles that might unify the various colonial groups. The Declaration was an attempt to identify and articulate a history and set of principles that might help to forge national unity.[5]

Britain eventually sent troops to subdue the American colonists. Grant Wood's Midnight Ride of Paul Revere (1931) depicts Revere alerting colonists to the British army's arrival. The subsequent battle between colonial and British forces at Concord and Lexington began the Revolutionary War.

THE DECLARATION OF INDEPENDENCE.
JULY 4TH 1776.

The year after fighting began between American colonists and the British army, the Continental Congress voted for independence on July 2, 1776, and approved the Declaration of Independence two days later, on July 4.

The Articles of Confederation

Having declared their independence, the colonies needed to establish a governmental structure. In November of 1777, the Continental Congress adopted the **Articles of Confederation**—the United States' first written constitution. Although it was not ratified by all the states until 1781, it was the country's operative constitution for almost twelve years, until March 1789.

However, almost from the moment of adoption, moves were afoot to reform and strengthen the Articles. The first goal of the Articles had been to limit the powers of the central government. The relationship between the national government and the states was called a **confederation**; as provided under Article II, "each state retains its sovereignty, freedom, and independence." It was not unlike the contemporary relationship between the United Nations and its member states. The central government was given no president or any other presiding officer. The entire national government was vested in a Congress, with execution of its few laws to be left to the individual states. And the Articles gave Congress very little power to exercise. Its members were not much more than delegates or messengers from the state legislatures: their salaries were paid out of the state treasuries; they were subject to immediate recall by state authorities; and each state, regardless of its size, had only one vote. All thirteen states had to agree to any amendments to the Articles.

Under the Articles of Confederation, Congress was given the power to declare war and make peace, to make treaties and alliances, to coin or borrow money, and to regulate trade with the Native Americans. It could also appoint the senior officers of the United States Army, but the national government had no army for those officers to command because the nation's armed forces were composed of the state militias. Moreover, the central government could not prevent one state from discriminating against other states in the competition for foreign commerce. These extreme limits on the power of the national government made the Articles of Confederation hopelessly impractical.[6]

Articles of Confederation
America's first written constitution; served as the basis for America's national government until 1789

confederation a system of government in which states retain sovereign authority except for the powers expressly delegated to the national government

● The Second Founding:
From Compromise to Constitution

The Declaration of Independence and the Articles of Confederation were not sufficient to hold the new nation together as an independent and effective nation-state. A series of developments following the armistice with the British in 1783 highlighted the shortcomings of the Articles of Confederation.

International Standing and Balance of Power

There was a special concern for the country's international position. Competition among the states for foreign commerce allowed the European powers to play the states off against each other, which created confusion on both sides of the Atlantic. At one point during the winter of 1786–87, John Adams of Massachusetts, a leader in the independence struggle, was sent to negotiate a new treaty with the British, one that would cover disputes left over from the war. The British government responded that since the United States under the Articles of Confederation was unable to enforce existing treaties, it would negotiate with each of the thirteen states separately.

At the same time, the United States faced a threat from Spain, which still held vast territories in North and South America. Well-to-do Americans—in particular the New England merchants and southern planters—were especially troubled by the influence that "radical" forces exercised in the Continental Congress and in the governments of several of the states. The colonists' victory in the Revolutionary War had not only ended British rule but also significantly changed the balance of political power within the new states. As a result of the Revolution, one key segment of the colonial elite—the royal land, office, and patent holders—was stripped of its economic and political privileges. In fact, many of these individuals, along with tens of thousands of other colonists who considered themselves loyal British subjects, left for Canada after the British surrender. And although the pre-Revolutionary elite was weakened, the pre-Revolutionary radicals were now better organized than ever before and were the controlling forces in such states as Pennsylvania and Rhode Island, where they pursued economic and political policies that struck terror in the hearts of the pre-Revolutionary political establishment. In Rhode Island, for example, between 1783 and 1785, a legislature dominated by representatives of small farmers, artisans, and shopkeepers had instituted economic policies, including drastic currency inflation, that frightened business and property owners throughout the country. Of course, the central government under the Articles of Confederation was powerless to intervene.

The Annapolis Convention

The continuation of international weakness and domestic economic turmoil led many Americans to consider whether their newly adopted form of government might not already require revision. In the fall of 1786, many state leaders accepted an invitation from the Virginia legislature for a conference of representatives of all the states. Delegates from five states actually attended. This conference, held in Annapolis, Maryland, was the first step toward the second founding. The one positive thing that came out of the Annapolis Convention was a carefully worded resolution calling on the Congress to send commissioners to Philadelphia at a later

In the winter of 1787, Daniel Shays led a makeshift army against the federal arsenal at Springfield to protest heavy taxes levied by the Massachusetts legislature. The rebellion proved the Articles of Confederation too weak to protect the fledgling nation.

time "to devise such further provisions as shall appear to them necessary to render the Constitution of the Federal Government adequate to the exigencies of the Union."[7] This resolution was drafted by Alexander Hamilton, a thirty-four-year-old New York lawyer who had played a significant role in the Revolution as George Washington's secretary and who would play a still more significant role in framing the Constitution and forming the new government in the 1790s. But the resolution did not necessarily imply any desire to do more than improve and reform the Articles of Confederation.

Shays's Rebellion

It is quite possible that the Constitutional Convention of 1787 in Philadelphia would never have taken place at all except for a single event that occurred during the winter following the Annapolis Convention: Shays's Rebellion.

Daniel Shays, a former army captain, led a mob of farmers in a rebellion against the government of Massachusetts. The purpose of the rebellion was to prevent foreclosures on their debt-ridden land by keeping the county courts of western Massachusetts from sitting until after the next election. The state militia dispersed the mob, but for several days Shays and his followers terrified the state government by attempting to capture the federal arsenal at Springfield, provoking an appeal to the Congress to help restore order. Within a few days, the state government regained control and captured fourteen of the rebels. (All were eventually pardoned.) In 1787, a newly elected Massachusetts legislature granted some of the farmers' demands.

Although the incident ended peacefully, its effects lingered and spread. Washington summed it up: "I am mortified beyond expression that in the moment of our acknowledged independence we should by our conduct verify the predictions of our transatlantic foe, and render ourselves ridiculous and contemptible in the eyes of all Europe."[8]

The Congress under the Confederation had been unable to act decisively in a time of crisis. This provided critics of the Articles of Confederation with precisely the evidence they needed to push Hamilton's Annapolis resolution through the Congress. Thus, the states were asked to send representatives to Philadelphia to discuss constitutional revision. Delegates were eventually sent by every state except Rhode Island.

The Constitutional Convention

Delegates selected by the state governments convened in Philadelphia in May 1787, with political strife, international embarrassment, national weakness, and local rebellion fixed in their minds. Seventy-four delegates were chosen, fifty-five attended, and thirty-nine eventually signed the Constitution. Recognizing that these issues were symptoms of fundamental flaws in the Articles of Confederation, the delegates soon abandoned the plan to revise the Articles and committed themselves to a second founding—a second, and ultimately successful, attempt to create a legitimate and effective national system of government. This effort occupied the convention for the next five months.

A Marriage of Interest and Principle For years, scholars have disagreed about the motives of the Founders in Philadelphia. Among the most controversial views of the framers' motives is the "economic interpretation" put forward by the historian Charles Beard and his disciples.[9] According to Beard's account, America's Founders were a collection of securities speculators and property owners whose only aim was personal enrichment. From this perspective, the Constitution's lofty principles were little more than sophisticated masks behind which the most venal interests sought to enrich themselves.

Contrary to Beard's approach is the view that the framers of the Constitution *were* concerned with philosophical and ethical principles. Indeed, the framers sought to devise a system of government consistent with the dominant philosophical and moral principles of the day. But in fact, these two views belong together; the Founders' interests were reinforced by their principles. The convention that drafted the American Constitution was chiefly organized by the New England merchants and southern planters. Although the delegates representing these groups did not all hope to profit personally from an increase in the value of their securities, as Beard would have it, they did hope to benefit in the broadest political and economic sense by breaking the power of their radical foes and establishing a system of government more compatible with their long-term economic and political interests. Thus, the framers sought to create a new government capable of promoting commerce and protecting property from radical state legislatures. At the same time, they hoped to fashion a government less susceptible than the existing state and national regimes to populist forces hostile to the interests of the commercial and propertied classes.

The Great Compromise The proponents of a new government fired their opening shot on May 29, 1787, when Edmund Randolph of Virginia offered a resolution that proposed corrections and enlargements in the Articles of Confederation. The proposal, which showed the strong influence of James Madison, was not a simple motion. It provided for virtually every aspect of a new government. (There is no verbatim record of the debates, but Madison was present during virtually all of the deliberations and kept full notes on them.)[10]

The portion of Randolph's motion that became most controversial was called the **Virginia Plan.** This plan provided for a system of representation in the national legislature based on the population of each state or the proportion of each state's

Virginia Plan a framework for the Constitution, introduced by Edmund Randolph, which called for representation in the national legislature based on the population of each state

Opponents of the Articles called for a new Constitutional Convention to explore a stronger form of national government. George Washington, a hero of the Revolution, presided over the convention.

revenue contribution to the national government, or both. (Randolph also proposed a second branch of the legislature, but it was to be elected by the members of the first branch.) Since the states varied enormously in size and wealth, the Virginia Plan was thought to be heavily biased in favor of the large states.

While the convention was debating the Virginia Plan, more delegates were arriving in Philadelphia and were beginning to mount opposition to it. Their resolution was introduced by William Paterson of New Jersey and known as the **New Jersey Plan**. The main proponents of the New Jersey Plan were delegates from the less populous states, which included Delaware, New Jersey, Connecticut, and New York, who asserted that the more populous states, such as Virginia, Pennsylvania, North Carolina, Massachusetts, and Georgia, would dominate the new government if representation were to be determined by population. The smaller states argued that each state should be equally represented in the new regime regardless of that state's population.

The issue of representation threatened to wreck the entire constitutional enterprise. Delegates conferred, factions maneuvered, and tempers flared. James Wilson of Pennsylvania told the small-state delegates that if they wanted to disrupt the union they should go ahead. The separation could, he said, "never happen on better grounds." Small-state delegates were equally blunt. Gunning Bedford of Delaware declared that the small states might look elsewhere for friends if they were forced. "The large states," he said, "dare not dissolve the confederation. If they do the small ones will find some foreign ally of more honor and good faith, who will take them by the hand and do them justice." These sentiments were widely shared. The union, as Oliver Ellsworth of Connecticut put it, was "on the verge of dissolution, scarcely held together by the strength of a hair."

The outcome of this debate was the Connecticut Compromise, also known as the **Great Compromise**. Under the terms of this compromise, in the first branch of Congress—the House of Representatives—the representatives would be apportioned

New Jersey Plan a framework for the Constitution, introduced by William Paterson, which called for equal state representation in the national legislature regardless of population

Great Compromise the agreement reached at the Constitutional Convention of 1787 that gave each state an equal number of senators regardless of its population, but linked representation in the House of Representatives to population

The Looking Glass for 1787 *showcases Connecticut's debate about the newly drafted Constitution. In the cartoon, Federalists stand for trade and commerce. Antifederalists say "Tax Luxary"* [sic] *and "Success to Shays"— showing the cartoonist's Federalist leaning.*

Who Benefits from the Great Compromise?

The Great Compromise attempted to balance power between large and small states in the new Congress. The charts show the difference in representation for states in the House and Senate in the first Congress (1789–1791). In the Senate, each state has equal representation, which in the first Congress meant each had 1/13 of all seats. In the House, the number of seats apportioned to each state is based on population; thus, the larger states have more representation.

Representation in the First Congress

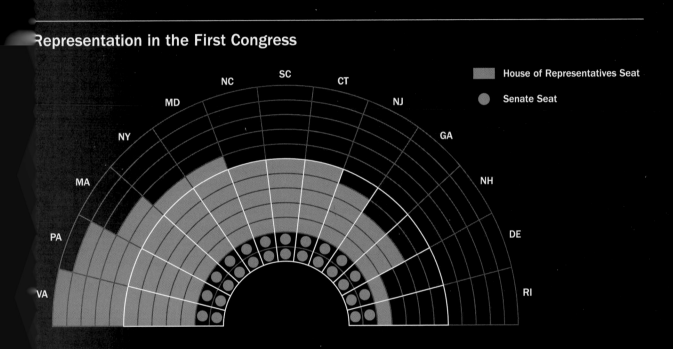

House of Representatives Seat

Senate Seat

State Populations, 1790*

1.	Virginia	747,610
2.	Pennsylvania	433,373
3.	Massachusetts	378,787
4.	New York	340,120
5.	Maryland	319,728
6.	North Carolina	393,751
7.	South Carolina	249,073
8.	Connecticut	237,946
9.	New Jersey	184,139
10.	Georgia	82,548
11.	New Hampshire	141,885
12.	Delaware	59,096
13.	Rhode Island	68,825

The framers calculated the number of representatives per state in 1787 using population estimates. The first census was not taken until 1790. Total state population includes slave population. Slaves were counted as 3/5 of a person for purposes of apportioning seats in the House.

SOURCE: U.S. Census Bureau, www.census.gov (accessed 7/27/10).

for critical analysis

1. At the Constitutional Convention, large states supported a plan—the Virginia Plan—to make the whole Congress look like the House. Small states supported a plan—the New Jersey Plan—to make the whole Congress look like the Senate. How would each have benefitted from their favored plans?

2. What are the advantages of equal representation by states? What are the drawbacks? In your opinion, do the advantages outweigh the disadvantages?

according to the number of inhabitants in each state. This, of course, was what delegates from the large states had sought. But in the second branch—the Senate—each state would have an equal vote regardless of its size; this provision addressed the concerns of the small states. This compromise was not immediately satisfactory to all the delegates. Indeed, two of the most vocal members of the small-state faction, John Lansing and Robert Yates of New York, were so incensed by the concession that their colleagues had made to the large-state forces that they stormed out of the convention. In the end, however, both sets of forces preferred compromise to the breakup of the Union, and the plan was accepted.

The Question of Slavery: The Three-fifths Compromise The story so far is too neat, too easy, and too anticlimactic. If it were left here, it would only contribute to American mythology. After all, the notion of a **bicameral** (two-chambered) legislature was very much in the air in 1787. Some of the states had had bicameral legislatures for years. The Philadelphia delegates might well have gone straight to the adoption of two chambers based on two different principles of representation even without the dramatic interplay of conflict and compromise. But a far more fundamental issue had to be confronted before the Great Compromise could take place: the issue of slavery.

Many of the conflicts that emerged during the Constitutional Convention were reflections of the fundamental differences between the slave and the nonslave states—differences that pitted the southern planters and New England merchants against one another. This was the first premonition of a conflict that would almost destroy the Republic in later years. In the midst of debate over large versus small states, Madison observed,

> The great danger to our general government is the great southern and northern interests of the continent, being opposed to each other. Look to the votes in Congress, and most of them stand divided by the geography of the country, not according to the size of the states.[11]

More than 90 percent of the country's slaves resided in five states—Georgia, Maryland, North Carolina, South Carolina, and Virginia—where they accounted for 30 percent of the total population. In some places, slaves outnumbered nonslaves by as much as ten to one. If the Constitution were to embody any principle of national supremacy, some basic decisions would have to be made about the place of slavery in the general scheme. Madison hit on this point on several occasions as different aspects of the Constitution were being discussed. For example, he observed,

> It seemed now to be pretty well understood that the real difference of interests lay, not between the large and small but between the northern and southern states. The institution of slavery and its consequences formed the line of discrimination. There were five states on the South, eight on the northern side of this line. Should a proportional representation take place it was true, the northern side would still outnumber the other: but not in the same degree, at this time; and every day would tend towards an equilibrium.[12]

Northerners and southerners eventually reached agreement through the **Three-fifths Compromise**. The seats in the House of Representatives would be apportioned according to a "population" in which five slaves would count as three free persons. The slaves would not be allowed to vote, of course, but the number of representatives would be apportioned accordingly.

bicameral having a legislative assembly composed of two chambers or houses; distinguished from unicameral

Three-fifths Compromise the agreement reached at the Constitutional Convention of 1787 that stipulated that for purposes of the apportionment of congressional seats, every slave would be counted as three-fifths of a person

The issue of slavery was the most difficult one faced by the framers, and it nearly destroyed the Union. Although some delegates believed slavery to be morally wrong, an evil and oppressive institution that made a mockery of the ideals and values espoused in the Constitution, morality was not the issue that caused the framers to support or oppose the Three-fifths Compromise. Whatever they thought of the institution of slavery, most delegates from the northern states opposed counting slaves in the distribution of congressional seats. Wilson of Pennsylvania, for example, argued that if slaves were citizens they should be treated and counted like other citizens. If, on the other hand, they were property, then why should not other forms of property be counted toward the apportionment of representatives? But southern delegates made it clear that if the northerners refused to give in, they would never agree to the new government. William R. Davie of North Carolina heatedly said that it was time "to speak out." He asserted that the people of North Carolina would never enter the Union if slaves were not counted as part of the basis for representation. Without such agreement, he asserted ominously,

Despite the Founders' emphasis on liberty, the new Constitution allowed slavery, counting each slave as three-fifths of a person in apportioning seats in the House of Representatives. In this 1792 painting, Liberty Displaying the Arts and Sciences, *the books, instruments, and classical columns at the left contrast with the kneeling slaves at the right—illustrating the divide between America's rhetoric of liberty and equality and the realities of slavery.*

"the business was at an end." Even southerners such as Edmund Randolph of Virginia, who conceded that slavery was immoral, insisted on including slaves in the allocation of congressional seats. This conflict between the southern and northern delegates was so divisive that many came to question the possibility of creating and maintaining a union of the two. Pierce Butler of South Carolina declared that the North and South were as different as Russia and Turkey. Eventually, the North and South compromised on the issue of slavery and representation. Indeed, northerners even agreed to permit a continuation of the odious slave trade to keep the South in the Union. But in due course, Butler proved to be correct, and a bloody war was fought when the disparate interests of the North and the South could no longer be reconciled.

● The Constitution

The political significance of the Great Compromise and the Three-fifths Compromise was to reinforce the unity of the mercantile and planter forces that sought to create a new government. The Great Compromise reassured those who feared that a new governmental framework would reduce the importance of their own local or regional influence. The Three-fifths Compromise temporarily defused the rivalry between the merchants and planters. Their unity secured, members of the alliance supporting the establishment of a new government moved to fashion a constitutional framework consistent with their economic and political interests.

In particular, the framers sought a new government that, first, would be strong enough to promote commerce and protect property from radical state legislatures such as Rhode Island's. This became the constitutional basis for national control over commerce and finance, as well as for the establishment of national judicial supremacy and the effort to construct a strong presidency. Second, the framers sought to prevent what they saw as the threat posed by the "excessive democracy" of the state and national governments under the Articles of Confederation. This led to such constitutional principles as bicameralism (division of the Congress into two chambers), **checks and balances**, staggered terms in office, and indirect election (selection of the president by an **electoral college** rather than directly by voters). Third, the framers, lacking the power to force the states or the public at large to accept the new form of government, sought to identify principles that would help to secure support. This became the basis of the constitutional provision for direct popular election of representatives and, subsequently, for the addition of the **Bill of Rights** to the Constitution. Finally, the framers wanted to be certain that the government they created did not pose even more of a threat to its citizens' liberties and property rights than did the radical state legislatures they feared and despised. To prevent the new government from abusing its power, the framers incorporated principles such as the **separation of powers** and **federalism** into the Constitution. Let us assess the major provisions of the Constitution's seven articles (listed in Box 2.1) to see how each relates to these objectives.

The Legislative Branch

In Article I, Sections 1–7, the Constitution provided for a Congress consisting of two chambers—a House of Representatives and a Senate. Members of the House of Representatives were given two-year terms in office and were to be elected

checks and balances mechanisms through which each branch of government is able to participate in and influence the activities of the other branches. Major examples include the presidential veto power over congressional legislation, the power of the Senate to approve presidential appointments, and judicial review of congressional enactments.

electoral college the presidential electors from each state who meet after the popular election to cast ballots for president and vice president

Bill of Rights the first ten amendments to the U.S. Constitution, ratified in 1791; they ensure certain rights and liberties to the people

separation of powers the division of governmental power among several institutions that must cooperate in decision making

federalism a system of government in which power is divided, by a constitution, between a central government and regional governments

directly by the people. Members of the Senate were to be appointed by the state legislatures (this was changed in 1913 by the Seventeenth Amendment, which instituted direct election of senators) for six-year terms. These terms were staggered so that the appointments of one-third of the senators would expire every two years. The Constitution assigned somewhat different tasks to the House and Senate. Though the approval of each body was required for the enactment of a law, the Senate alone was given the power to ratify treaties and approve presidential appointments. The House, on the other hand, was given the sole power to originate revenue bills.

The character of the legislative branch was directly related to the framers' major goals. The House of Representatives was designed to be directly responsible to the people in order to encourage popular consent for the new Constitution and to help enhance the power of the new government. At the same time, to guard against "excessive democracy," the power of the House of Representatives was checked by the Senate, whose members were to be appointed by the states for long terms rather than be elected directly by the people. The purpose of this provision, according to Alexander Hamilton, was to avoid "an unqualified complaisance to every sudden

BOX 2.1

The Seven Articles of the Constitution

1. The Legislative Branch
   House: two-year terms, elected directly by the people.
   Senate: six-year terms (staggered so that only one-third of the Senate changes in any given election), appointed by state legislature (changed in 1913 to direct election).
   Expressed powers of the national government: collecting taxes, borrowing money, regulating commerce, declaring war, and maintaining an army and a navy; all other power belongs to the states, unless deemed otherwise by the elastic (necessary and proper) clause.
   Exclusive powers of the national government: states are expressly forbidden to issue their own paper money, tax imports and exports, regulate trade outside their own borders, and impair the obligation of contracts; these powers are the exclusive domain of the national government.

2. The Executive Branch
   Presidency: four-year terms (limited in 1951 to a maximum of two terms), elected indirectly by the electoral college.
   Powers: can recognize other countries, negotiate treaties, grant reprieves and pardons, convene Congress in special sessions, and veto congressional enactment.

3. The Judicial Branch
   Supreme Court: lifetime terms, appointed by the president with the approval of the Senate.
   Powers: include resolving conflicts between federal and state laws, determining whether power belongs to the national government or the states, and settling controversies between citizens of different states.

4. National Unity and Power
   Reciprocity among states: establishes that each state must give "full faith and credit" to official acts of other states, and guarantees citizens of any state the "privileges and immunities" of every other state.

5. Amending the Constitution
   Procedure: requires approval by two-thirds of Congress and adoption by three-fourths of the states.

6. National Supremacy
   The Constitution and national law are the supreme law of the land and cannot be overruled by state law.

7. Ratification
   The Constitution became effective when approved by nine states.

breeze of passion, or to every transient impulse which the people may receive."[13] Staggered terms of service in the Senate, moreover, were intended to make that body even more resistant to popular pressure. Since only one-third of the senators would be selected at any given time, the composition of the institution would be protected from changes in popular preferences transmitted by the state legislatures. This would prevent what James Madison called "mutability in the public councils arising from a rapid succession of new members."[14] Thus, the structure of the legislative branch was designed to contribute to governmental power, to promote popular consent for the new government, and at the same time to place limits on the popular political currents that many of the framers saw as a radical threat to the economic and social order.

The issues of power and consent were important throughout the Constitution. Section 8 of Article I specifically listed the powers of Congress, which include the authority to collect taxes, to borrow money, to regulate commerce, to declare war, and to maintain an army and navy. By granting Congress these powers, the framers indicated very clearly that they intended the new government to be far more influential than its predecessor. At the same time, by defining the new government's most important powers as belonging to Congress, the framers sought to promote popular acceptance of this critical change by reassuring citizens that their views would be fully represented whenever the government exercised its new powers.

As a further guarantee to the people that the new government would pose no threat to them, the Constitution implied that any powers not listed were not granted at all. This is the doctrine of **expressed powers**. The Constitution grants only those powers specifically expressed in its text. But the framers intended to create an active and powerful government, and so they included the **elastic clause**, sometimes known as the necessary and proper clause, which signified that the enumerated powers were meant to be a source of strength to the national government, not a limitation on it. The national government could exercise each power with the utmost vigor, but it could seize no new powers without a constitutional amendment. In the absence of such an amendment, any power not enumerated was conceived to be "reserved" to the states (or the people).

expressed powers specific powers granted by the Constitution to Congress (Article I, Section 8) and to the president (Article II)

elastic clause Article I, Section 8, of the Constitution (also known as the necessary and proper clause), which enumerates the powers of Congress and provides Congress with the authority to make all laws "necessary and proper" to carry them out

Although there was much acrimonious debate and necessary compromise as the new Constitution was written, this print suggests that farmers, artisans, and "gentlemen" alike supported it after its ratification.

The Executive Branch

The Constitution provided for the establishment of the presidency in Article II. As Alexander Hamilton commented, the presidential article aimed toward "energy in the Executive." It did so in an effort to overcome the natural tendency toward stalemate that was built into the bicameral legislature as well as into the separation of powers among the three branches. The Constitution afforded the president a measure of independence from the people and from the other branches of government—particularly the Congress.

In line with the framers' goal of increased power to the national government, the president was granted the unconditional power to accept ambassadors from other countries; this amounted to the power to "recognize" other countries. The president was also given the power to negotiate treaties, although their acceptance required the approval of the Senate by a two-thirds vote. The president was given the unconditional right to grant reprieves and pardons, except in cases of impeachment. And the president was provided with the power to appoint major departmental personnel, to convene Congress in special session, and to veto congressional enactments. (The veto power is formidable, but it is not absolute, since Congress can override it by a two-thirds vote.)

The framers hoped to create a presidency that would make the federal government rather than the states the agency capable of timely and decisive action to deal with public issues and problems. This was the meaning of the "energy" that Hamilton hoped to impart to the executive branch.[15] At the same time, however, the framers sought to help the president withstand excessively democratic pressures by creating a system of indirect rather than direct election through a separate electoral college.

The Judicial Branch

In establishing the judicial branch in Article III, the Constitution reflected the framers' preoccupations with nationalizing governmental power and checking radical democratic impulses while guarding against potential interference with liberty and property from the new national government itself.

Under the provisions of Article III, the framers created a court that was to be literally a supreme court of the United States, and not merely the highest court of the national government. The most important expression of this intention was granting the Supreme Court the power to resolve any conflicts that might emerge between federal and state laws. In particular, the Supreme Court was given the right to determine whether a power was exclusive to the national government, concurrent with the states, or exclusive to the states. In addition, the Supreme Court was assigned jurisdiction over controversies between citizens of different states. The long-term significance of this provision was that as the country developed a national economy, it came to rely increasingly on the federal judiciary, rather than on the state courts, for the resolution of disputes.

Judges were given lifetime appointments to protect them from popular politics and from interference by the other branches. This, however, did not mean that the judiciary would remain totally impartial to political considerations or to the other branches, for the president was to appoint the judges, and the Senate to approve the appointments. Congress would also have the power to create inferior (lower) courts, to change the jurisdiction of the federal courts, to add or subtract federal judges, and even to change the size of the Supreme Court.

No explicit mention is made in the Constitution of **judicial review**—the power of the courts to render the final decision when there is a conflict of interpretation of the Constitution or of laws between the courts and Congress, the courts and the executive branch, or the courts and the states. The Supreme Court eventually assumed the power of judicial review. Its assumption of this power, as we shall see in Chapter 15, was based not on the Constitution itself but on the politics of later decades and the membership of the Court.

National Unity and Power

Various provisions in the Constitution addressed the framers' concern with national unity and power, including Article IV's provisions for comity (reciprocity) among states and among citizens of all states. Each state was prohibited from

for critical analysis
The framers sought to create an "energetic" presidency, but some observers believe that the presidency has become too powerful. Has the presidency become too powerful?

judicial review the power of the courts to review and, if necessary, declare actions of the legislative and executive branches invalid or unconstitutional. The Supreme Court asserted this power in *Marbury v. Madison*.

discriminating against the citizens of other states in favor of its own citizens. The Supreme Court was charged with deciding in each case whether a state had discriminated against goods or people from another state. The Constitution restricted the power of the states in favor of ensuring enough power to the national government to give the country a free-flowing national economy.

The framers' concern with national supremacy was also expressed in Article VI, in the **supremacy clause**, which provided that national laws and treaties "shall be the supreme Law of the Land." This meant that all laws made under the "Authority of the United States" would be superior to all laws adopted by any state or any other subdivision, and the states would be expected to respect all treaties made under that authority. The supremacy clause also bound the officials of all governments—state and local as well as federal—to take an oath of office to support the national Constitution. This meant that every action taken by the United States Congress would have to be applied within each state as though the action were in fact state law.

supremacy clause Article VI of the Constitution, which states that laws passed by the national government and all treaties are the supreme law of the land and superior to all laws adopted by any state or any subdivision

Amending the Constitution

The Constitution established procedures for its own revision in Article V. Its provisions are so difficult that Americans have availed themselves of the amending process only seventeen times since 1791, when the first ten amendments were adopted. Many other amendments have been proposed in Congress, but fewer than forty of them have even come close to fulfilling the Constitution's requirement of a two-thirds vote in Congress, and only a fraction have gotten anywhere near adoption by three-fourths of the states. Article V also provides that the Constitution can be amended by a constitutional convention. Occasionally, proponents of particular measures, such as a balanced-budget amendment, have called for a constitutional convention to consider their proposals. Whatever the purpose for which it were called, however, such a convention would presumably have the authority to revise America's entire system of government.

Ratifying the Constitution

The rules for the ratification of the Constitution were set forth in Article VII. Nine of the thirteen states would have to ratify, or agree on, the terms in order for the Constitution to be formally adopted.

Constitutional Limits on the National Government's Power

Although the framers sought to create a powerful national government, they also wanted to guard against possible misuse of that power. To that end, the framers incorporated two key principles into the Constitution—the separation of powers and federalism. A third set of limitations, in the form of the Bill of Rights, was added to the Constitution to help secure its ratification when opponents of the document charged that it paid insufficient attention to citizens' rights.

The Separation of Powers No principle of politics was more widely shared at the time of the 1787 founding than the principle that power must be used to balance power. The French political theorist Baron de la Brède et de Montesquieu (1689–1755) believed that this balance was an indispensable defense against tyranny. His

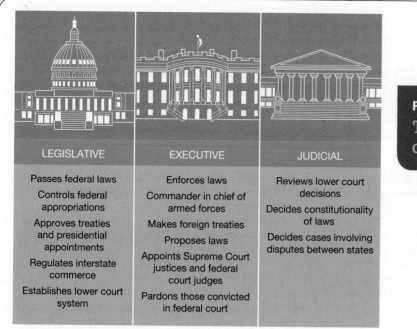

FIGURE 2.1
The Separation of Powers

LEGISLATIVE	EXECUTIVE	JUDICIAL
Passes federal laws	Enforces laws	Reviews lower court decisions
Controls federal appropriations	Commander in chief of armed forces	Decides constitutionality of laws
Approves treaties and presidential appointments	Makes foreign treaties	Decides cases involving disputes between states
Regulates interstate commerce	Proposes laws	
Establishes lower court system	Appoints Supreme Court justices and federal court judges	
	Pardons those convicted in federal court	

writings, especially his major work, *The Spirit of the Laws*, "were taken as political gospel" at the Philadelphia Convention.[16] Although the principle of the separation of powers was not explicitly stated in the Constitution, the entire structure of the national government was built precisely on Article I, the legislature; Article II, the executive; and Article III, the judiciary (see Figure 2.1).

However, separation of powers is nothing but mere words on parchment without a method to maintain the separation. The method became known by the popular label "checks and balances" (see Figure 2.2). Each branch is given not only its own powers but also some power over the other two branches. Among the most familiar checks and balances are the president's veto as a power over Congress and Congress's power over the president through its control of appointments to high executive posts and to the judiciary. Congress also has power over the president with its control of appropriations and (by the Senate) the right of approval of treaties. The judiciary was assumed to have the power of judicial review over the other two branches.

Another important feature of the separation of powers is the principle of giving each of the branches a distinctly different constituency. Theorists such as Montesquieu called this a "mixed regime," with the president chosen indirectly by electors, the House by popular vote, the Senate (originally) by state legislature, and the judiciary by presidential appointment. By these means, the occupants of each branch would tend to develop very different outlooks on how to govern, different definitions of the public interest, and different alliances with private interests.

Federalism Compared with the confederation principle of the Articles of Confederation, federalism was a step toward greater centralization of power. The delegates agreed that they needed to place more power at the national level, without completely undermining the power of the state governments. Thus, they devised a

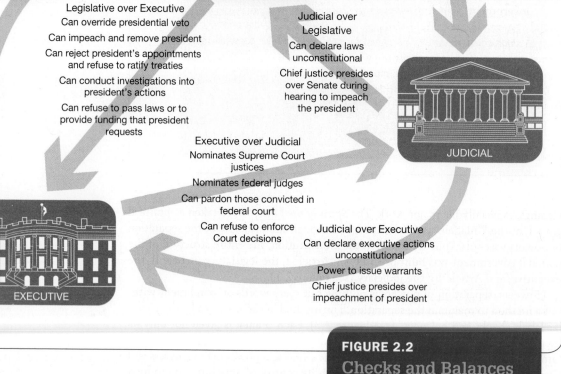

Executive over Legislative
Can veto acts of Congress
Can call Congress into a special session
Carries out, and thereby interprets, laws passed by Congress
Vice president casts tie-breaking vote in the Senate

LEGISLATIVE

Legislative over Judicial
Can change size of federal court system and the number of Supreme Court justices
Can propose constitutional amendments
Can reject Supreme Court nominees
Can impeach and remove federal judges

Legislative over Executive
Can override presidential veto
Can impeach and remove president
Can reject president's appointments and refuse to ratify treaties
Can conduct investigations into president's actions
Can refuse to pass laws or to provide funding that president requests

Judicial over Legislative
Can declare laws unconstitutional
Chief justice presides over Senate during hearing to impeach the president

JUDICIAL

Executive over Judicial
Nominates Supreme Court justices
Nominates federal judges
Can pardon those convicted in federal court
Can refuse to enforce Court decisions

Judicial over Executive
Can declare executive actions unconstitutional
Power to issue warrants
Chief justice presides over impeachment of president

EXECUTIVE

FIGURE 2.2
Checks and Balances

system of two sovereigns—the states and the nation—with the hope that competition between the two would be an effective limitation on the power of both.

The Bill of Rights Late in the Philadelphia Convention, a motion was made to include a list of citizens' rights in the Constitution. After a brief debate in which hardly a word was said in its favor and only one speech was made against it, the motion was almost unanimously turned down. Most delegates sincerely believed that since the federal government was already limited to its expressed powers, further protection of citizens was not needed. The delegates argued that the states should adopt bills of rights because their greater powers needed greater limitations. But almost immediately after the Constitution was ratified, a movement arose to adopt a national bill of rights. This is why the Bill of Rights, adopted in 1791, comprises the first ten amendments to the Constitution rather than being part of the body of it. We will have a good deal more to say about the Bill of Rights in Chapter 4.

● The Fight for Ratification

The first hurdle faced by the Constitution was ratification by state conventions of delegates elected by the people of each state. This struggle for ratification was carried out in thirteen separate campaigns. Each involved different people, moved at a different pace, and was influenced by local as well as national considerations. Two sides faced off throughout the states, however, calling themselves **Federalists** and **Antifederalists** (see Table 2.1). The Federalists (who more accurately should have called themselves "Nationalists," but who took their name to appear to follow in the revolutionary tradition) supported the Constitution and preferred a strong national government. The Antifederalists opposed the Constitution and preferred a federal system of government that was decentralized; they took their name by default, in reaction to their better-organized opponents. The Federalists were united in their support of the Constitution, whereas the Antifederalists were divided over what they believed the alternative to the Constitution should be.

During the struggle over ratification of the Constitution, Americans argued about great political issues and principles. How much power should the national government be given? What safeguards were most likely to prevent the abuse of power? What institutional arrangements could best ensure adequate representation for all Americans? Was tyranny of the many to be feared more than tyranny of the few?

Federalists those who favored a strong national government and supported the Constitution proposed at the American Constitutional Convention of 1787

Antifederalists those who favored strong state governments and a weak national government and who were opponents of the Constitution proposed at the American Constitutional Convention of 1787

Federalists versus Antifederalists

During the ratification struggle, thousands of essays, speeches, pamphlets, and letters were presented in support of and in opposition to the proposed Constitution. The best-known pieces supporting ratification of the Constitution were the eighty-five essays written, under the name of "Publius," by Alexander Hamilton, James Madison, and John Jay between the fall of 1787 and the spring of 1788. These *Federalist Papers*, as they are collectively known today, defended the principles of the Constitution and sought to dispel fears of a national authority. The Antifederalists published essays of their own, arguing that the new Constitution betrayed the Revolution and was a step toward monarchy. Among the best of the Antifederalist works were the essays, usually attributed to the New York State Supreme Court justice Robert Yates, that were written under the name of "Brutus" and published in the *New York Journal* at the same time the *Federalist Papers* appeared. The Antifederalist view was also ably presented in the pamphlets and letters written by a former delegate to the Continental Congress and future U.S. senator, Richard Henry Lee of Virginia, using the pen name "The Federal Farmer." These essays highlight the major differences of opinion between Federalists and Antifederalists. Federalists appealed to basic principles of government in support of their nationalist vision. Antifederalists cited equally fundamental precepts to support their vision of a looser confederacy of small republics.

Federalist Papers a series of essays written by Alexander Hamilton, James Madison, and John Jay supporting the ratification of the Constitution

Representation One major area of contention between the two sides was the question of representation. The Antifederalists asserted that representatives must be "a true picture of the people, . . . [possessing] the knowledge of their circumstances and their wants."[17] This could be achieved, argued the Antifederalists, only in small, relatively homogeneous republics such as the existing states. In their view, the size and extent of the entire nation precluded the construction of a truly

TABLE 2.1

Federalists versus Antifederalists

	FEDERALISTS	ANTIFEDERALISTS
Who were they?	Property owners, creditors, merchants	Small farmers, frontiersmen, debtors, shopkeepers, some state government officials
What did they believe?	Believed that elites were most fit to govern; feared "excessive democracy"	Believed that government should be closer to the people; feared concentration of power in hands of the elites
What system of government did they favor?	Favored strong national government; believed in "filtration" so that only elites would obtain governmental power	Favored retention of power by state governments and protection of individual rights
Who were their leaders?	Alexander Hamilton, James Madison, George Washington	Patrick Henry, George Mason, Elbridge Gerry, George Clinton

representative form of government. As Brutus put it, "Is it practicable for a country so large and so numerous . . . to elect a representation that will speak their sentiments? . . . It certainly is not."[18]

Federalists, for their part, saw no reason that representatives should be precisely like those they represented. In the Federalist view, one of the great advantages of representative government over direct democracy was precisely the possibility that the people would choose as their representatives individuals possessing ability, experience, and talent superior to their own. In Madison's words, rather than serving as a mirror or reflection of society, representatives must be "[those] who possess [the] most wisdom to discern, and [the] most virtue to pursue, the common good of the society."[19]

Although the terms of discussion have changed, this debate over representation continues today. Some argue that representatives must be very close in life experience, race, and ethnic background to their constituents to truly understand the needs and interests of those constituents. This argument is made by contemporary proponents of giving the states more control over social programs. This argument is also made by proponents of "minority districts"—legislative districts whose boundaries are drawn so as to guarantee that minorities will be able to elect their own representative to Congress. Opponents of this practice, which we will explore further in Chapter 10, have argued in court that it is discriminatory and unnecessary; blacks, they say, can be represented by whites and vice versa. Who is correct? It would appear that this question can never be answered to everyone's complete satisfaction.

Tyranny of the Majority A second important issue dividing Federalists and Antifederalists was the threat of **tyranny**—unjust rule by the group in power. Both opponents and defenders of the Constitution frequently affirmed their fear of tyrannical rule. Each side, however, had a different view of the most likely source of tyranny and, hence, of the way in which to forestall the threat.

tyranny oppressive government that employs cruel and unjust use of power and authority

● Why was the
Constitution
controversial at
the time of the
Founding?

From the Antifederalist perspective, the great danger was the tendency of all governments—including republican governments—to become gradually more and more "aristocratic" in character, wherein the small number of individuals in positions of authority would use their stations to gain more and more power over the general citizenry. In essence, the few would use their power to tyrannize the many. For this reason, Antifederalists were sharply critical of those features of the Constitution that divorced governmental institutions from direct responsibility to the people—institutions such as the Senate, the executive, and the federal judiciary. The latter, appointed for life, presented a particular threat: "I wonder if the world ever saw . . . a court of justice invested with such immense powers, and yet placed in a situation so little responsible," protested Brutus.[20]

The Federalists, too, recognized the threat of tyranny, but they believed that the danger particularly associated with republican governments was not aristocracy but majority tyranny. The Federalists were concerned that a popular majority, "united and actuated by some common impulse of passion, or of interest, adverse to the rights of other citizens," would endeavor to "trample on the rules of justice."[21] From the Federalist perspective, it was precisely those features of the Constitution that the Antifederalists attacked as potential sources of tyranny that actually offered the best hope of averting the threat of oppression. The size and extent of the nation, for instance, was for the Federalists a bulwark against tyranny because a majority would have difficulty uniting in a large and populous nation.

Governmental Power A third major difference between Federalists and Antifederalists was the issue of governmental power. Both opponents and proponents of the Constitution agreed on the principle of **limited government**. They differed, however, on the fundamentally important question of how to place limits on governmental action. Antifederalists favored limiting and enumerating the powers granted to the national government in relation both to the states and to the people at large. To them, the powers given the national government ought to be "confined to certain defined national objects.[22] Otherwise, the national government would "swallow up all the power of the state governments."[23] Antifederalists bitterly attacked the supremacy clause and the elastic clause of the Constitution as unlimited and dangerous grants of power to the national government.[24] Antifederalists also demanded that a bill of rights be added to the Constitution to place limits on the government's exercise of power over the citizenry.

Federalists favored the construction of a government with broad powers. They wanted a government that had the capacity to defend the nation against foreign foes, guard against domestic strife and insurrection, promote commerce, and expand the nation's economy. Antifederalists shared some of these goals but still feared governmental power. Hamilton pointed out, however, that these goals could not be achieved without allowing the government to exercise the necessary power. Federalists acknowledged that every power could be abused but argued that the way to prevent misuse of power was not by depriving the government of the powers needed to achieve national goals. Instead, they argued that the threat of abuse of power would be mitigated by the Constitution's internal checks and controls. As Madison put it, "the power surrendered by the people is first divided between two distinct governments, and then the portion allotted to each subdivided among distinct and separate departments. Hence, a double security arises to the rights of the people. The different governments will control each other, at the same time that each will be controlled by itself."[25] The Federalists' concern with avoiding unwarranted limits on governmental power led them to oppose a bill of

limited government a principle of constitutional government; a government whose powers are defined and limited by a constitution

rights, which they saw as nothing more than a set of unnecessary restrictions on the government.

The Federalists acknowledged that abuse of power remained a possibility but felt that the risk had to be taken because of the goals to be achieved. "The very idea of power included a possibility of doing harm," said the Federalist John Rutledge during the South Carolina ratification debates. "If the gentleman would show the power that could do no harm," Rutledge continued, "he would at once discover it to be a power that could do no good."[26] This aspect of the debate between the Federalists and the Antifederalists, perhaps more than any other, continues to reverberate through American politics. Should the nation limit the federal government's power to tax and spend? Should Congress limit the capacity of federal agencies to issue new regulations? Should the government endeavor to create new rights for minorities, the disabled, and others? What is the proper balance between promoting equality and protecting liberty? Though the details have changed, these are the same great questions that have been debated since the Founding.

Reflections on the Founding

The final product of the Constitutional Convention would have to be considered an extraordinary victory for the groups that had most forcefully called for the creation of a new system of government to replace the Articles of Confederation. Antifederalist criticisms forced the Constitution's proponents to accept the addition of a bill of rights designed to limit the powers of the national government. In general, however, it was the Federalist vision of America that triumphed. The Constitution adopted in 1789 created the framework for a powerful national government that for more than 200 years has defended the nation's interests, promoted its commerce, and maintained national unity. In one notable instance, the national government fought and won a bloody war to prevent the nation from breaking apart. And despite this powerful government, the system of internal checks and balances has functioned reasonably well, as the Federalists predicted, to prevent the national government from tyrannizing its citizens.

Of course, the groups whose interests were served by the Constitution in 1789, mainly the merchants and planters, are not the same groups that benefit from the Constitution's provisions today. Once incorporated into the law, political principles often take on lives of their own and have consequences that were never anticipated by their original champions. Indeed, many of the groups that benefit from constitutional provisions today did not even exist in 1789. Who would have thought that the principle of free speech would influence the transmission of data on the Internet? Who would have predicted that commercial interests that once sought a powerful government might come, two centuries later, to denounce governmental activism as "socialistic"? Perhaps one secret of the Constitution's longevity is that it did not confer permanent advantage on any one set of economic or social forces.

Although they were defeated in 1789, the Antifederalists present us with an important picture of a road not taken and of an America that might have been. Would the country have been worse off if it had been governed by a confederacy of small republics linked by a national administration with severely limited powers? Were the Antifederalists correct in predicting that a government given great power in the hope that it might do good would, through "insensible progress," inevitably turn to evil purposes? Two hundred years of government under the federal Constitution are not necessarily enough to answer these questions definitively. Time must tell.

Federalists versus Antifederalists: The Debate Gets Personal

Historians often cite the *Federalist Papers* and the letters by "Brutus" as the venues where the philosophies of Federalists and Antifederalists were debated. However, the issues surrounding the debate and rivalries that emerged were also prevalent in popular culture in the forms of cartoons, poems, and editorials. The feud between the Federalist Representative Roger Griswold of Connecticut and the Antifederalist Representative Matthew Lyon of Vermont in 1798 illustrates how popular culture has long been a means to communicate political information and opinions to the American public.

Lyon was an Irish immigrant who advocated direct democracy and, like many Antifederalists, was suspicious of the intentions of elected representatives. During informal discussions in the House of Representatives, Lyon spoke loudly about ill-intentioned Connecticut representatives who, he argued, were not interested in carrying out the wishes of their constituents, but rather in maintain-

ing their own power and pursuing their own selfish goals.[a]

The Connecticut Representative Roger Griswold, who was within earshot of Lyon's comments, responded by approaching Lyon and asking if he would march into Connecticut wearing his "wooden sword." Griswold's comments were an allusion to Lyon's dishonorable discharge from the military during the Revolutionary War.

Lyon's response was simple. He spat on Griswold. When Congress took a vote on whether to expel Lyon for this violation, the Federalists did not have the two-thirds majority necessary to do so. So Roger Griswold attempted to take matters into his own hands—literally. Armed with a new hickory walking stick, Griswold rose from his seat in the Congress, approached Lyon, and bludgeoned him approximately twenty times in the head.

The ongoing saga was the topic of many cartoons, editorials, and poems, including one detailed cartoon, "Congressional Pugilists" (another word for boxers). The cartoon shows Griswold holding a hickory

cane above his head and attempting to hit Lyon, who is grasping at a set of fireplace tongs in his own defense. Perhaps most interesting to note are the expressions of onlookers who are either pleased or outraged by the attack, illustrating the partisan environment in Congress at the time.

Some poems and cartoons criticized Congress and expressed alarm over the health of the nation and its developing government. Of particular concern was the young nation's reputation around the world. Others caricatured Griswold or Lyon, taking one side or the other.

The Griswold-Lyon affair illustrates that popular culture's prominent role in American politics is not a modern phenomenon. Although this feud dominated the headlines of traditional Federalist and Antifederalist publications, rumors of the scuffle spread quickly through more accessible avenues.

[a]Brian T. Neff, "Fracas in Congress: The Battle of Honor between Matthew Lyon and Roger Griswold," *Essays in History* 41 (1999).

for critical analysis

1. How might popular media facilitate quick dissemination of information?

2. Are cartoons and other political humor capable of communicating complex ideas? Or do they reduce politics to mere caricatures?

● The Citizen's Role and the Changing Constitution

The Constitution has endured for more than two centuries as the framework of government. But it has not endured without change. Without change, the Constitution might have become merely a sacred text, stored under glass.

Amendments: Many Are Called, Few Are Chosen

amendment a change added to a bill, law, or constitution

The need for change was recognized by the framers of the Constitution, and provisions for **amendment** were incorporated into Article V. Four methods of amendment are provided for in Article V:

1. Passage in House and Senate by two-thirds vote; then ratification by majority vote of the legislatures of three-fourths (thirty-eight) of the states.

2. Passage in House and Senate by two-thirds vote; then ratification by conventions called for the purpose in three-fourths of the states.

3. Passage in a national convention called by Congress in response to petitions by two-thirds of the states; ratification by majority vote of the legislatures of three-fourths of the states.

4. Passage in a national convention, as in (3); then ratification by conventions called for the purpose in three-fourths of the states.

Figure 2.3 illustrates each of these possible methods. Since no amendment has ever been proposed by national convention, however, methods (3) and (4) have never been employed. And method (2) has been employed only once (the Twenty-first Amendment, which repealed the Eighteenth, or Prohibition, Amendment). Thus, method (1) has been used for all the others.

The Constitution has proved to be extremely difficult to amend. In the history of efforts to amend the Constitution, the most appropriate characterization is "many

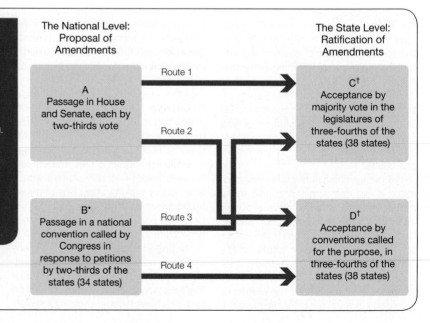

FIGURE 2.3

Four Ways the Constitution Can Be Amended

*This method of proposal has never been employed. Thus amendment routes 3 and 4 have never been attempted.

†For each amendment proposal, Congress has the power to choose the method of ratification, the time limit for consideration by the states, and other conditions of ratification. The movement to repeal Prohibition in the Twenty-first Amendment was the only occasion in which route 2 was used successfully.

The National Level: Proposal of Amendments

The State Level: Ratification of Amendments

A Passage in House and Senate, each by two-thirds vote

Route 1

Route 2

C† Acceptance by majority vote in the legislatures of three-fourths of the states (38 states)

B* Passage in a national convention called by Congress in response to petitions by two-thirds of the states (34 states)

Route 3

Route 4

D† Acceptance by conventions called for the purpose, in three-fourths of the states (38 states)

The American Constitution: A Model for the World?

The U.S. Constitution is often said to be both the world's oldest written constitution and a continuing model for the nations of the world. These assertions are *partly* accurate. Nearly two millennia before the delegates to America's Constitutional Convention met in Philadelphia, Greek city-states had produced written constitutions.[a] And closer to home, all the first American states possessed written constitutions. Nevertheless, it might be said that the U.S. Constitution is the world's oldest written document that formally organizes the governmental processes of an entire nation.

As to the second assertion, the U.S. Constitution has indeed frequently been a model for others, but other nations' constitution writers often consciously sought to avoid rather than imitate American-style institutions and practices. One important American idea that has been widely copied is that of having a written constitution. After America wrote its constitution in 1789, both Poland and France adopted written constitutions in 1791. The French became so enamored of constitution writing that they put forth four

different constitutions during the 1790s alone, as successive revolutionary governments seized power.[b] As revolutions swept Europe during the nineteenth and early twentieth centuries, every new government viewed a written constitution both as an important legitimating instrument and as a declaration that the new regime categorically rejected the despotic and arbitrary practices of its predecessor. Today, virtually all the world's democracies have written constitutions. Britain, Israel, and New Zealand remain important exceptions.[c] Ironically, possession of a written constitution has become such an important attribute of political legitimacy and symbol of freedom that even some despotic regimes have sham constitutions to provide the appearance, albeit not the substance, of popular government. For example, the former Soviet Union often boasted that it possessed the world's most democratic constitution.

Among the world's constitutional democracies, some have copied elements of the U.S. Constitution, but most have chosen patterns of government quite different from the American model. Judi-

cial review of statutes, an American political innovation, has been adopted by most democracies. In a number of instances, too, new constitutions have incorporated the principle of federalism to deal with the problem of ethnic or regional divisions. For example, with American encouragement, both Iraq and Afghanistan have made federalism an important principle in their new constitutional documents. However, it remains to be seen if these constitutions will survive after American troops leave those countries. Few democracies have copied the American system of separation of powers and checks and balances, with most opting, instead, for parliamentary government. Even the Japanese and German constitutions, written under the supervision of American occupation authorities following World War II, created parliamentary systems.

In addition to providing for parliamentary government, most of the world's constitutions have departed from the American model by providing extensive lists of rights. For example, the constitution of the Czech Republic includes a lengthy "Charter of Fundamental Rights and Freedoms."

Thus, although the U.S. Constitution inspired many other nations to develop a written constitution, the precise form that national constitutions take can diverge considerably from the American model.

[a]Kim Lane Scheppele, "Constitutions around the World," www.constitutioncenter.org (accessed 2/9/08).
[b]Scheppele, "Constitutions."
[c]Scheppele, "Constitutions."

for critical analysis

1. Is America's Constitution appropriate for every nation? Which elements might have universal validity? Which features might be relevant mainly to the United States?

2. The U.S. Constitution is a brief document, whereas many new constitutions are lengthy documents. What are the advantages and disadvantages of America's constitutional model?

for critical analysis

It is very difficult to amend the Constitution. Should it be made easier? Would our system of government be more democratic if our Constitution could be revised more easily?

are called, few are chosen." Since 1789, more than 11,000 amendments have been formally offered in Congress. Of these, Congress officially proposed only twenty-nine, and twenty-seven of these were eventually ratified by the states. Two of these—Prohibition and its repeal—cancel each other out, so that for all practical purposes, only twenty-five amendments have been added to the Constitution since 1791.

The Case of the Equal Rights Amendment

The Equal Rights Amendment (ERA) is a case study of a proposed amendment that almost succeeded. In fact, the ERA is one of the very few proposals that got the necessary two-thirds vote in Congress yet failed to obtain the ratification of the requisite thirty-eight states.

On October 12, 1971, the U.S. House of Representatives approved the Equal Rights Amendment by the required two-thirds majority; the Senate followed suit on March 22, 1972. The amendment was simple:

Sec. 1. Equality of rights under the law shall not be denied or abridged by the United States or by any State on account of sex.

Sec. 2. The Congress shall have the power to enforce, by appropriate legislation, the provisions of this article.

Sec. 3. This amendment shall take effect two years after the date of ratification.

The congressional resolution provided for the accustomed method of ratification through the state legislatures rather than by state conventions—route (1) rather than route (2) in Figure 2.3—and that it had to be completed within seven years, by March 22, 1979.

Since the amendment was the culmination of nearly a half-century of efforts, and since the women's movement had spread its struggle for several years prior to 1971, the amendment was ratified by twenty-eight state legislatures during the very first year. But opposition forces who saw the ERA as an expression of radical feminism quickly organized into the "Stop ERA" movement. By the end of 1974, five more states had ratified the amendment, but three states that had ratified it in 1973—Idaho, Nebraska, and Tennessee—had afterward voted to rescind their ratification. This posed an unprecedented problem: whether a state legislature had the right to rescind its approval. The Supreme Court refused to deal with this question, insisting that it was a political question to be settled by Congress. If the ERA had been ratified by the thirty-eight-state minimum, Congress would have had to decide whether to respect the rescissions or to count them as ratifications.

This point was rendered moot by events. By the end of 1978, thirty-five state legislatures had ratified the ERA—counting the three rescinding legislatures as ratifiers. But even counting them, the three additional state ratifications necessary to reach thirty-eight became increasingly difficult to get. In each of the remaining fifteen states, the amendment had already been rejected at least once. The only hope of the ERA forces was that the 1978 elections would change the composition of some of those state legislatures. Pinning their hopes on that, the ERA forces turned back to Congress and succeeded in getting an extension of the ratification deadline to June 30, 1982. This was an especially significant victory, because it was the first time Congress had extended the time limit since it began placing time restrictions on ratification in 1917. But this victory in Washington failed to impress any of the fifteen holdout legislatures. June 30, 1982, came and went, and the ERA was, for the time being at least, laid to rest. It was beaten by the efforts of Stop

ERA and by the emergence of conservatism generally, which had culminated in Ronald Reagan's election as president.[27]

Which Were Chosen? An Analysis of the Twenty-seven

There is more to the amending difficulties than the politics of campaigning and voting. It would appear that only a limited number of changes can actually be made through the Constitution. Most efforts to amend the Constitution have failed because they were simply attempts to use the Constitution as an alternative to legislation for dealing directly with a public problem.

The twenty-five successful amendments, on the other hand, are concerned with the structure or composition of government (see Table 2.2). This is consistent with the dictionary, which defines *constitution* as the makeup or composition of something. And it is consistent with the concept of a constitution as "higher law," because the whole point and purpose of a higher law is to establish a framework within which government and the process of making ordinary law can take place. Even those who would have preferred more changes in the Constitution have to agree that there is great wisdom in this principle. A constitution ought to enable legislation and public policies to take place, but it should not determine what that legislation or those public policies ought to be.

For those whose hopes for change center on the Constitution, it must be emphasized that the amendment route to social change is, and always will be, extremely limited. Through a constitution it is possible to establish a working structure of government, and through a constitution it is possible to establish basic rights of citizens by placing limitations on the powers of that government. Once these things have been accomplished, the real problem is how to extend rights to those people who do not already enjoy them. Of course, the Constitution cannot enforce itself. But it can and does have a real influence on everyday life because a right or an obligation set forth in the Constitution can become a cause of action in the hands of an otherwise powerless person.

Private property is an excellent example. Property is one of the most fundamental and well-established rights in the United States; but it is well established not because it is recognized in so many words in the Constitution but because legislatures and courts have made it a crime for anyone, including the government, to trespass or to take away property without compensation.

A constitution is good if it produces the cause of action that leads to good legislation, good case law, and appropriate police behavior. A constitution cannot eliminate power. But its principles can be a citizen's dependable defense against the abuse of power.

Opponents of gay marriage have proposed amending the Constitution to define marriage as a union between one man and one woman. Several states have passed amendments to their state constitutions banning gay marriage. Should marriage become a federal matter and be addressed through constitutional amendment?

lments to the Constitution

AMENDMENT	PURPOSE	YEAR PROPOSED	YEAR ADOPTED
I	*Limits on Congress:* Congress is not to make any law establishing a religion or abridging speech, press, assembly, or petition freedoms.		
II, III, IV	*Limits on Executive:* The executive branch is not to infringe on the right of people to keep arms (II), is not arbitrarily to take houses for a militia (III), and is not to engage in the search or seizure of evidence without a court warrant swearing to belief in the probable existence of a crime (IV).		
V, VI, VII, VIII	*Limits on Courts:** The courts are not to hold trials for serious offenses without provision for a grand jury (V), a petit (trial) jury (VII), a speedy trial (VI), presentation of charges (VI), confrontation of hostile witnesses (VI), immunity from testimony against oneself (V), and immunity from more than one trial for the same offense (V). Neither bail nor punishment can be excessive (VIII), and no property can be taken without just compensation (V).		
IX, X	*Limits on National Government:* All rights not enumerated are reserved to the states or the people.		
XI	Limited jurisdiction of federal courts over suits involving the states.	1794	1798
XII	Provided separate ballot for vice president in the electoral college.	1803	1804
XIII	Eliminated slavery and eliminated the right of states to allow property in persons.	1865[†]	1865
XIV	(Part 1) Provided a national definition of citizenship.[†]	1866	1868
XIV	(Part 2) Applied due process of Bill of Rights to the states.	1866	1868
XV	Extended voting rights to all races.	1869	1870
XVI	Established national power to tax incomes.	1909	1913
XVII[§]	Provided direct election of senators.	1911	1913
XIX	Extended voting rights to women.	1919	1920
XX	Eliminated "lame duck" session of Congress.	1932	1933
XXII	Limited presidential term.	1947	1951
XXIII	Extended voting rights to residents of the District of Columbia.	1960	1961
XXIV	Extended voting rights to all classes by abolition of poll taxes.	1962	1964
XXV	Provided presidential succession in case of disability.	1965	1967
XXVI	Extended voting rights to citizens aged 18 and over.	1971	1971**
XXVII	Limited Congress's power to raise its own salary.	1789	1992

*These amendments also impose limits on the law-enforcement powers of federal (and especially) state and local executive branches.

[†]The Thirteenth Amendment was proposed January 31, 1865, and adopted less than a year later, on December 18, 1865.

[†]In defining *citizenship*, the Fourteenth Amendment actually provided the constitutional basis for expanding the electorate to include all races, women, and residents of the District of Columbia. Only the "eighteen-year-olds' amendment" should have been necessary, since it changed the definition of citizenship. The fact that additional amendments were required following the Fourteenth suggests that voting is not considered an inherent right of U.S. citizenship. Instead, it is viewed as a privilege.

[§]The Eighteenth Amendment, ratified in 1919, outlawed the sale and transportation of liquor. It was repealed by the Twenty-first Amendment ratified in 1933.

**The Twenty-sixth Amendment holds the record for speed of adoption. It was proposed on March 23, 1971, and adopted on July 5, 1971.

The Supreme Court and Constitutional Amendment

Although the process of constitutional amendment outlined in Article V has seldom been used successfully, another form of constitutional revision is constantly at work in the United States. This is, of course, judicial interpretation of the Constitution. As the Supreme Court reviews cases, it interprets the meaning of the Constitution and its amendments. In some instances, the Court may give concrete definition to abstract constitutional principles. For example, the Constitution's Fifth Amendment asserts in general terms that individuals accused of crimes are entitled to procedural rights. The Supreme Court, in a series of decisions, established principles giving effect to those rights. Every viewer of television crime programs knows that, when arrested, individuals must receive *Miranda* warnings informing them of their right to refuse to speak and their right to counsel. These warnings are the result of a 1966 Supreme Court decision interpreting the meaning and implications of the Fifth Amendment.

In some instances, the Supreme Court does more than interpret or flesh out constitutional provisions. It seems to modify or augment the text itself. For example, in decisions in 1965 and 1973 on birth control and abortion, the Court said that Americans were constitutionally entitled to a right of privacy. No such right is mentioned anywhere in the Constitution. Similarly, the Court has held that the First Amendment prohibits many forms of government support for religion and many forms of religious exercise in public institutions, such as schools. By doing this, the Court was saying that the framers of the First Amendment simply meant that the government was prohibited from declaring one religion to be the nation's official faith. They did not intend to prohibit nondenominational school prayer.

Of course, much of the Supreme Court's power is itself based on constitutional interpretation rather than the text of the document. The Supreme Court claims the power of judicial review—the power to render the final decision when there is a conflict of interpretations of the Constitution or federal law among the courts, Congress, the executive branch, or the states. Nowhere does the Constitution mention this power. In a number of early cases, the Supreme Court asserted that the Constitution gave it the power of judicial review, and it was able to rewrite the Constitution to enhance its own power.

Some commentators denounce constitutional amendment by the judiciary and demand that judges limit themselves to "strict construction" of the Constitution, adhering closely to the words of the document's text. Critics of this perspective, on the other hand, assert that the Constitution is a living document subject to change as conditions warrant. Proponents of the idea of the *living Constitution* argue that the judiciary is the institution best qualified to adjust the Constitution's principles to new problems and times. Advocates of strict construction and champions of the living Constitution disagree about the desirability of constitutional amendment by the courts, but both acknowledge its reality.

Thinking Critically about Liberty, Equality, and Democracy

The Constitution's framers placed individual liberty ahead of all other political values. Their concern for liberty led many of the framers to distrust both democracy and equality. They feared that democracy could degenerate into a majority

Amending the Constitution

On March 23, 1971, Congress passed a joint resolution in support of the Twenty-sixth Amendment, which lowered the legal voting age from twenty-one to eighteen. Less than four months later, the amendment was ratified by the states, achieving this status faster than any other amendment in U.S. history. Key to the success of the Twenty-sixth Amendment, which effectively enfranchised 11 million new voters aged eighteen to twenty, was a groundswell of activism by America's youth. Angry about the U.S. war in Vietnam, young Americans pushed for ratification with the slogan "Old enough to fight, old enough to vote." Members of Congress and representatives in the state legislatures heard their outcry. By the time the 1972 elections rolled around, young people finally had a constitutionally protected right to participate.

Although only one other amendment has been ratified since the Twenty-sixth, countless others have been introduced by members of Congress or promoted by interested members of the public. All of them have the potential to affect the lives of Americans of all ages. Some of the better-known proposals include these:

—The Federal Marriage Amendment, which would define marriage as a union between a man and a woman and expressly prohibit gay marriage.

—The Every Vote Counts Amendment, which would replace the Electoral College with the direct election of the president and vice president.

—The Religious Equality Amendment, which would permit prayer in public school ceremonies and class meetings and protect the teaching of creationism in public schools.

—The English Language Amendment, which would make English the official language of the United States.

—The Flag Desecration Amendment, which would prohibit the desecration (including burning) of the American flag.

If you get involved in these debates, either by pushing for passage of an amendment or working to defeat a proposal, you can have an impact on the actual content of our Constitution. There are several ways to get involved:

● To see exactly what amendments have been proposed in Congress, you can search the Library of Congress archives (at www.thomas.gov.) using the phrase "proposing an amendment to the Constitution" (since most resolutions begin this way).

● When you see the sponsor of the bill, you can contact him or her directly to voice your support or opposition via telephone, letter, or e-mail. An alphabetical list of all members of the House is available at www.house.gov. You can contact senators at www.senate.gov.

● Find an organization that is working on your side of this issue with a quick Internet search of the amendment, or by searching for news articles about the amendment on Lexis/Nexis, a service that is available through most college and university library systems. Once you identify an organization, you can decide if you want to contribute money to the group, perhaps sign an online petition, or participate in one of their rallies or meetings.

● Each of the fifty states is governed by a constitution, most of which are much easier to amend than the U.S. Constitution. For example, while the Federal Marriage Amendment has not passed in Congress, at least a dozen states have amended their constitutions to ban same-sex marriage. Getting involved at the state level can have a true impact. A good resource on state-level policy is the Pew Research Center's www.stateline.org.

tyranny in which the populace, perhaps led by a rabble-rousing demagogue, would trample on liberty. As to equality, the framers were products of their time and place; our contemporary ideas of racial and gender equality would have been foreign to them. The framers were concerned primarily with another manifestation of equality: they feared that those without property or position might be driven by what some called a "leveling spirit" to infringe on liberty in the name of greater economic or social equality. Indeed, the framers believed that this leveling spirit was most likely to produce demagoguery and majority tyranny. As a result, the basic structure of the Constitution—separated powers, internal checks and balances, and federalism—was designed to safeguard liberty, and the Bill of Rights created further safeguards for liberty. At the same time, however, many of the Constitution's other key provisions, such as indirect election of senators and the president, as well as the appointment of judges for life, were designed to limit democracy and, hence, the threat of majority tyranny.

By championing liberty, however, the framers virtually guaranteed that democracy and even a measure of equality would sooner or later evolve in the United States. For liberty promotes the growth of political activity and the expansion of political participation. In James Madison's famous phrase, "Liberty is to faction as air is to fire."[28] Where they have liberty, more and more people, groups, and

The Eighteenth Amendment was passed in 1919 and prohibited the manufacture, transportation, and sale of alcoholic beverages. Repealed in 1933 by the Twenty-first Amendment, the Prohibition Amendment can be seen as an attempt to legislate through the amendment process.

interests will almost inevitably engage in politics and gradually overcome whatever restrictions might have been placed on participation. This is precisely what happened in the early years of the American Republic. During the Jeffersonian period, political parties formed. During the Jacksonian period, many state suffrage restrictions were removed and popular participation greatly expanded. Over time, liberty is conducive to democracy.

Liberty does not guarantee that everyone will be equal. It does, however, reduce the threat of inequality in one very important way. Historically, the greatest inequalities of wealth, power, and privilege have arisen where governments have used their power to allocate status and opportunity among individuals or groups. From the aristocracies of the early modern period to twentieth-century despotisms, the most extreme cases of inequality are associated with the most tyrannical regimes.

The other side of the coin, however, is that the absence of government intervention in economic affairs—in the name of liberty—may mean that there is no antidote to the inevitable inequalities of wealth produced by the marketplace. Economic inequalities, in turn, may lead to inequalities in political power as wealthy groups and individuals use their superior resources to elect politicians friendly to them and their aims and to influence the legislative process. Thus, liberty is a complex matter. In the absence of liberty, inequality is virtually certain. The existence of liberty, however, poses its own threat to political equality. Can we fully reconcile liberty and equality? Doing so remains a constant challenge in a democratic society.

Another limitation of liberty as a political principle is that the idea of limits on government action can also inhibit effective government. Take one of the basic tasks of government, the protection of citizens' lives and property. A government limited by concerns over the rights of those accused of crimes may be limited in its ability to maintain public order. Recently, the U.S. government has asserted that protecting the nation against terrorists requires law enforcement measures that seem at odds with legal and constitutional formalities. The conflict between liberty and governmental effectiveness is another tension at the heart of the American constitutional system.

Liberty is sometimes confused with the absence of government. The framers of the Constitution, though, saw liberty as a purpose or goal of government, not a characteristic of the absence of government. The government they created was designed to "secure the Blessings of Liberty" by maintaining order, keeping the peace, and intervening where necessary to allow citizens to conduct their affairs in safety and freedom. Every generation of Americans ponders and reconsiders the work of the framers.

for critical analysis

What are our Constitution's greatest strengths? What are its most pronounced weaknesses? If you were a framer, what would you change in the Constitution? Why?

studyguide

Practice Quiz

 Find a diagnostic Web Quiz with 34 additional questions on the StudySpace Web site: www.wwnorton.com/we-the-people

The First Founding: Interests and Conflicts

1. In their fight against British taxes such as the Stamp Act and the Sugar Act of 1764, New England merchants allied with which of the following groups? *(p. 39)*
   a) artisans
   b) southern planters
   c) laborers
   d) all of the above

2. How did the British attempt to raise revenue in the North American colonies? *(p. 39)*
   a) income tax
   b) taxes on commerce
   c) expropriation and government sale of land
   d) government asset sales

3. The first governing document in the United States was *(p. 42)*
   a) the Declaration of Independence.
   b) the Articles of Confederation and Perpetual Union.
   c) the Constitution.
   d) none of the above.

4. Where was the execution of laws conducted under the Articles of Confederation? *(p. 42)*
   a) the presidency
   b) the Congress
   c) the states
   d) the expanding federal bureaucracy

The Second Founding: From Compromise to Constitution

5. Which of the following was *not* a reason that the Articles of Confederation seemed too weak? *(p. 43)*
   a) the lack of a single voice in international affairs
   b) the power of radical forces in the Congress
   c) the impending "tyranny of the states"
   d) the power of radical forces in several states

6. Which event led directly to the Constitutional Convention by providing evidence that the government created under the Articles of Confederation was unable to act decisively in times of national crisis? *(p. 44)*
   a) the Boston Tea Party
   b) the Boston Massacre
   c) Shays's Rebellion
   d) the Annapolis Convention

7. The draft constitution that was introduced at the start of the Constitutional Convention was authored by *(p. 45)*
   a) Edmund Randolph
   b) Thomas Jefferson
   c) James Madison
   d) George Clinton

8. Which state's proposal embodied a principle of representing states in the Congress according to their size and wealth? *(p. 45)*
   a) Connecticut
   b) Maryland
   c) New Jersey
   d) Virginia

9. The agreement reached at the Constitutional Convention that determined that every slave would be counted as a fraction of a person for the purposes of taxation and representation in the House of Representatives was called the: *(p. 48)*
   a) Connecticut Compromise
   b) Three-fifths Compromise
   c) Great Compromise
   d) Virginia Plan

The Constitution

10. What mechanism was instituted in the Congress to guard against "excessive democracy"? *(p. 50)*
    a) bicameralism
    b) staggered Senate terms
    c) appointment of senators for long terms
    d) all of the above

11. Which of the following best describes the Supreme Court as understood by the Founders? *(p. 53)*
    a) the highest court of the national government
    b) arbiter of disputes within the Congress
    c) a figurehead commission of elders
    d) a supreme court of the nation and its states

12. Theorists such as Montesquieu referred to the principle of giving each branch of government a distinctly different constituency as: *(p. 55)*
    a) mixed regime.
    b) confederation.
    c) limited government.
    d) federalism.

The Fight for Ratification

13. Which of the following were the Antifederalists most concerned with? *(p. 59)*
    a) interstate commerce
    b) the protection of property
    c) the distinction between principles and interests
    d) the potential for tyranny in the central government

The Citizen's Role and the Changing Constitution

14. Which of the following best describes the process of amending the Constitution? *(pp. 62–64)*
    a) It is difficult and has rarely been used successfully to address specific public problems.
    b) It is difficult and has frequently been used successfully to address specific public problems.
    c) It is easy and has rarely been used successfully to address specific public problems.
    d) It is easy and has frequently been used successfully to address specific public problems.

Thinking Critically about Liberty, Equality, and Democracy

15. Which political value was most important for the framers of the Constitution? *(p. 67)*
    a) majority rule
    b) individual liberty
    c) political equality
    d) popular sovereignty

Chapter Outline

Find a detailed Chapter Outline on the StudySpace Web site: www.wwnorton.com/we-the-people

Key Terms

Find Flashcards to help you study these terms on the StudySpace Web site: www.wwnorton.com/we-the-people

amendment *(p. 62)*
Antifederalists *(p. 57)*
Articles of Confederation *(p. 42)*
bicameral *(p. 48)*
Bill of Rights *(p. 50)*
checks and balances *(p. 50)*
confederation *(p. 42)*
elastic clause *(p. 52)*

electoral college *(p. 50)*
expressed powers *(p. 52)*
federalism *(p. 50)*
Federalist Papers (p. 57)
Federalists *(p. 57)*
Great Compromise *(p. 46)*
judicial review *(p. 53)*
limited government *(p. 59)*

New Jersey Plan *(p. 46)*
separation of powers *(p. 50)*
supremacy clause *(p. 54)*
Three-fifths Compromise *(p. 48)*
tyranny *(p. 58)*
Virginia Plan *(p. 45)*

For Further Reading

Amar, Akhil Reed. *America's Constitution: A Biography*. New York: Random House, 2006.

Beard, Charles. *An Economic Interpretation of the Constitution of the United States*. New York: Macmillan, 1913.

Breyer, Stephen G. *Active Liberty: Interpreting Our Democratic Constitution*. New York: Knopf, 2005.

Dahl, Robert A. *How Democratic Is the American Constitution?* 2nd ed. New Haven, CT: Yale University Press, 2002.

Ellis, Joseph. *American Creation: Triumphs and Tragedies at the Founding of the Republic*. New York: Knopf, 2007.

Hamilton, Alexander, James Madison, and John Jay. *The Federalist Papers. Edited by Isaac Kramnick*. New York: Viking, 1987.

Holton, Woody. *Unruly Americans and the Origins of the Constitution*. New York: Hill and Wang, 2007.

Jensen, Merrill. *The Articles of Confederation*. Madison: University of Wisconsin Press, 1963.

Keller, Morton. *America's Three Regimes*. New York: Oxford University Press, 2009.

Lewis, Anthony. *Freedom for the Thought That We Hate: A Biography of the First Amendment*. New York: Basic Books, 2008.

Main, Jackson Turner. *The Social Structure of Revolutionary America*. Princeton, NJ: Princeton University Press, 1965.

Rossiter, Clinton. *1787: Grand Convention*. New York: Macmillan, 1966.

Storing, Herbert, ed. *The Complete Anti-Federalist*. 7 vols. Chicago: University of Chicago Press, 1981.

Winik, Jay. *The Great Upheaval: America and the Birth of the Modern World, 1788–1800*. New York: HarperCollins, 2007.

Recommended Web Sites

The American Civil Liberties Union
www.aclu.org
The ACLU is committed to protecting, for all individuals, the freedoms found in the Bill of Rights. This sometimes controversial organization constantly monitors the government for violations of liberty and encourages its members to take political action.

Archiving Early America
www.earlyamerica.com
Revolutionary Americans were motivated by a variety of competing ideals, principles, and interests. Visit this Web site to learn more about the early colonists and the founding of our government.

Constitution Finder
http://confinder.richmond.edu
Is the American Constitution a model for the world? Explore the constitutions of many different nations and see what elements of the U.S. Constitution can be found in the governing documents of other countries.

Find Law
http://findlaw.com/casecode/state.html
The Find Law Web site provides all fifty states' constitutions. Click on your state and try to identify such constitutional principles as bicameralism, staggered terms of office, checks and balances, and separation of powers.

The National Archives
www.archives.gov
This government site provides information about and actual digital images of such founding documents as the Declaration of Independence, the U.S. Constitution, and the Bill of Rights.

The National Constitution Center
www.constitutioncenter.org
The National Constitution Center in Philadelphia maintains a Web site that provides in-depth instructional analysis of the U.S. Constitution. Check out the Interactive Constitution function and follow the document from its Preamble through the Twenty-seventh Amendment.

Oyez
www.oyez.org
This Web site for U.S. Supreme Court Media has an excellent search engine for finding information on Supreme Court cases. See how the Court has interpreted the Constitution over time.

The PBS Liberty! Series
www.pbs.org/ktca/liberty
The PBS *Liberty!* series on the American Revolution offers an in-depth look at the Revolutionary War and includes information on historical events such as the Constitutional Convention.

The Supreme Court of the United States
www.supremecourtus.gov
The Web site for the U.S. Supreme Court provides information on recent decisions. Take a moment to read some oral arguments, briefs, or opinions.

In a federal system, state and local governments establish many of the rules that affect people's everyday lives. For example, in 2008, California passed a law that made it illegal to send text messages while driving. Other states have passed their own laws related to using cell phones and e-mail while behind the wheel.

DON'T TEXT
WHILE DRIVING
JAN 1ST

Ct Your Tax Dollars
AT WORK

HIGHWAY IMPROVEMENT
YEAR OF COMPLETION : 2009
STATE HIGHWAY FUNDS

A. Tarantino & Sons
POULTRY & SEAFOOD
415-822-3366
San Francisco
Family Owned and Operated Since 1917

Federalism

WHAT GOVERNMENT DOES AND WHY IT MATTERS In the fall of 2009, the federal Department of Transportation held a two-day summit on the dangers of texting and using cell phones while behind the wheel. Scientists presented evidence that texting or sending e-mail while driving is as dangerous as driving under the influence of alcohol; witnesses related dramatic and tragic stories about loved ones killed by distracted drivers; and drivers who themselves had caused fatal auto accidents while texting talked about how their lives had been forever changed. Yet it is the states, not the federal government, that are responsible for the laws that govern driving. And at the time of the national summit, states had adopted a wide variety of laws related to driving and texting. Eighteen states banned texting while driving, but the penalties varied widely. In Utah, the state with the most severe laws, a texting driver who caused a fatal accident faced the same penalties as a drunken driver; a driver simply caught texting could receive up to three months in jail and up to $750 in fines. In California, where texting and driving was also outlawed, the fine could be as low as $20.[1]

Although the states have formal responsibility for laws relating to health and safety, the federal government does have the power to influence state laws. The federal government can affect what states do by withholding

focusquestions

● What does the Constitution say about the powers of the national government and of the states?

● How did the federal government become much stronger over time?

● What major developments do we see in the federal framework since the 1930s?

● How do debates over federalism reflect Americans' views on liberty, equality, and democracy?

federal funds or by offering incentives for state action. In 1984, it pressured state governments to change their laws governing the age at which a person could legally drink alcohol, raising this to twenty-one years of age. The incentive was linking federal highway funding to the state's drinking age. The states quickly complied. In 2009, members of Congress introduced similar legislation that would require states to enact tough laws prohibiting drivers from texting while driving or risk losing federal highway funds. A competing bill offered states extra transportation funds as an incentive to enact texting bans.[2] The new concerns over the dangers of distracted driving engaged one of the oldest questions in American government: What is the responsibility of the federal government and what is the responsibility of the states? When should there be uniformity across the states and when is it better to let states adopt a diverse set of laws? Which approach serves the common good?

The United States is a federal system, in which the national government shares power with lower levels of government. Throughout American history, lawmakers, politicians, and citizens have wrestled with questions about how responsibilities should be allocated across the different levels of government. Some responsibilities, such as international relations, clearly lie with the federal government. Others, such as divorce laws, are controlled by state governments. In fact, most of the rules and regulations that Americans face in their daily lives are set by state and local governments. However, many government responsibilities are shared in American federalism and require cooperation among local, state, and federal governments. The debate about "who should do what" remains one of the most important discussions in American politics.

chaptercontents

Federalism in the Constitution

The Constitution has had its most fundamental influence on American life through **federalism**. Federalism can be defined as the division of powers and functions between the national government and the state governments. Governments can organize power in a variety of ways. One of the most important distinctions is between unitary and federal governments. In a **unitary system**, the central government makes the important decisions, and lower levels of government have little independent power. In such systems, lower levels of government primarily implement decisions made by the central government. In France, for example, the central government was once so involved in the smallest details of local activity that the minister of education boasted that by looking at his watch he could tell what all French schoolchildren were learning at that time because the central government set the school curriculum. In a **federal system**, by contrast, the central government shares power or functions with lower levels of government, such as regions or states. Nations with diverse ethnic or language groupings, such as Switzerland and Canada, are most likely to have federal arrangements. In federal systems, lower levels of government often have significant independent power to set policy in some areas, such as education and social programs, and to impose taxes. Yet the specific ways in which power is shared vary greatly: no two federal systems are exactly the same.

The United States was the first nation to adopt federalism as its governing framework. With federalism, the framers sought to limit the national government by creating a second layer of state governments. American federalism recognized two sovereigns in the original Constitution and reinforced the principle in the Bill of Rights by granting a few "expressed powers" to the national government and reserving all the rest to the states.

federalism a system of government in which power is divided, by a constitution, between a central government and regional governments

unitary system a centralized government system in which lower levels of government have little power independent of the national government

federal system a system of government in which the national government shares power with lower levels of government, such as states

The Powers of the National Government

As we saw in Chapter 2, the **expressed powers** granted to the national government are found in Article I, Section 8, of the Constitution. These seventeen powers include the power to collect taxes, to coin money, to declare war, and to regulate commerce (which, as we will see, became a very important power for the national government). Article I, Section 8, also contains another important source of power for the national government: the **implied powers** that enable Congress "to make all Laws which shall be necessary and proper for carrying into Execution the foregoing Powers." Not until several decades after the Founding did the Supreme Court allow Congress to exercise the power granted in this **necessary and proper clause**, but, as we shall see later in this chapter, this doctrine allowed the national government to expand considerably the scope of its authority, although the process was a slow one. In addition to these expressed and implied powers, the Constitution affirmed the power of the national government in the supremacy clause (Article VI), which made all national laws and treaties "the supreme Law of the Land."

expressed powers specific powers granted by the Constitution to Congress (Article I, Section 8), and to the president (Article II)

implied powers powers derived from the necessary and proper clause of Article I, Section 8, of the Constitution. Such powers are not specifically expressed, but are implied through the expansive interpretation of delegated powers

necessary and proper clause Article I, Section 8, of the Constitution, it provides Congress with the authority to make all laws "necessary and proper" to carry out its expressed powers

The Powers of State Government

One way in which the framers sought to preserve a strong role for the states was through the Tenth Amendment to the Constitution. The Tenth Amendment states that the powers that the Constitution does not delegate to the national government or prohibit to the states are "reserved to the States respectively, or to the people." The Antifederalists, who feared that a strong central government would encroach on individual liberty, repeatedly pressed for such an amendment as a way of limiting national power. Federalists agreed to the amendment because they did not think it would do much harm, given the powers of the Constitution already granted to the national government. The Tenth Amendment is also called the reserved powers amendment because it aims to **reserve powers** to the states.

The most fundamental power that the states retain is that of coercion—the power to develop and enforce criminal codes, to administer health and safety rules, to regulate the family via marriage and divorce laws. The states have the power to regulate individuals' livelihoods; if you're a doctor or a lawyer or a plumber or a barber, you must be licensed by the state. Even more fundamental, the states have the power to define private property—private property exists because state laws against trespass define who is and is not entitled to use a piece of property. If you own a car, your ownership isn't worth much unless the state is willing to enforce your right to possession by making it a crime for anyone else to drive your car without your consent. These are fundamental matters, and the powers of the states regarding these domestic issues are much greater than the powers of the national government, even today.

A state's authority to regulate these fundamental matters is commonly referred to as the **police power** of the state and encompasses the state's power to regulate the health, safety, welfare, and morals of its citizens. Policing is what states do—they coerce you in the name of the community in order to maintain public order. And this was exactly the type of power that the Founders intended the states to exercise.

In some areas, the states share **concurrent powers** with the national government, whereby they retain and share some power to regulate commerce and to affect the currency—for example, by being able to charter banks, grant or deny corporate charters, grant or deny licenses to engage in a business or practice a trade, and regulate the quality of products or the conditions of labor. This issue of concurrent versus exclusive power has come up from time to time in our history, but wherever there is a direct conflict of laws between the federal and the state levels, the issue will most likely be resolved in favor of national supremacy.

State Obligations to Each Other

The Constitution also creates obligations among the states. These obligations, spelled out in Article IV, were intended to promote national unity. By requiring the states to recognize actions and decisions taken in other states as legal and proper, the framers aimed to make the states less like independent countries and more like components of a single nation.

Article IV, Section I, calls for "Full Faith and Credit" among states, meaning that each state is normally expected to honor the "public Acts, Records, and judicial Proceedings" that take place in any other state. So, for example, if a couple is married in Texas—marriage being regulated by state law—in most cases Missouri must also recognize that marriage, even though the couple was not married under Missouri state law.

This **full faith and credit clause** has recently become embroiled in the controversy over gay and lesbian marriage. Since 2004, when Massachusetts became the first state to make same-sex marriage legal, six additional states have passed laws that allowed gays and lesbians to marry. California's law, however, was short-lived: in

reserved powers powers, derived from the Tenth Amendment to the Constitution, that are not specifically delegated to the national government or denied to the states

police power power reserved to the state government to regulate the health, safety, and morals of its citizens

concurrent powers authority possessed by *both* state and national governments, such as the power to levy taxes

full faith and credit clause provision from Article IV, Section 1, of the Constitution, requiring that the states normally honor the public acts and judicial decisions that take place in another state

● What does the
Constitution say
about the powers
of the national
government and
of the states?

November 2008, voters overturned the law only five months after it was enacted. Initially, Massachusetts did not allow same-sex couples from other states to marry in Massachusetts, but in 2008, the state dropped this provision. Now same-sex couples from all over the country can marry in Massachusetts.

The question concerning the full faith and credit clause is whether these marriages will be recognized by states that do not themselves allow same-sex marriage. If a practice is against their "strong public policy," states are not obligated to recognize it—even if it has been sanctioned by other states. A look at the history of interracial marriage offers some perspective on how much leeway states have to recognize marriages performed in other states. In 1952, thirty states prohibited interracial marriage. In 1967, when the Supreme Court struck down such laws as unconstitutional, sixteen states still had these statutes on the books. Many of the states that prohibited interracial marriage also refused to recognize such marriages performed in other states. But many states that outlawed interracial marriage did recognize out-of-state marriages, depending on the circumstances.[3] In the case of gay marriage, only New York, Rhode Island, and the District of Columbia have enacted laws that recognize out-of-state marriages of same-sex partners. In California, the governor signed a law in 2009 granting recognition of gay and lesbian marriages that were performed out-of-state during the five-month period that these marriages were legal in California.[4]

Most states, however, do not recognize same-sex marriages performed in other states. And to underscore their opposition to same-sex marriage, a large majority of states have enacted provisions against gay marriage. By 2009, forty-one states had passed "defense of marriage acts" that define marriage as a union between one man and one woman only. Most of these states also outlaw recognition of gay marriages in other states. Anxious to show its disapproval of gay marriage, Congress passed the Defense of Marriage Act in 1996, which declared that states will *not* have to recognize a same-sex marriage, even if it is legal in one state. The act also said that the federal government will not recognize gay marriage—even if it is legal under state law—and that gay marriage partners will not be eligible for the federal benefits, such as Medicare and Social Security, normally available to spouses.[5]

Gay marriage is not the only issue in which the "full faith and credit" clause has come into play. It has also played a role in conflicts over gay adoption. In these cases, however, the courts have so far ruled that the full faith and credit clause requires states to accept the legal decisions of other states. Three states—Florida, Mississippi, and Utah—explicitly ban gay adoption and several other states sharply restrict it. An Oklahoma law banned state agencies from recognizing adoption orders to gay and lesbian couples approved in states that permit such adoption. Effectively, this meant that Oklahoma refused to issue birth certificates for children born in Oklahoma but legally adopted by same-sex couples from other states. In 2007 a federal appeals court struck down the Oklahoma law, ruling that the full faith and credit clause required Oklahoma to honor adoption orders approved by

Should same-sex marriages performed in one state be legally recognized in another state? State laws vary, and despite the Constitution's full faith and credit clause, these differences can lead to debate over controversial issues.

From the Entertainment World to State and Local Politics

Under the American version of federalism, state governments have considerable power, and states and regions have their own lively political cultures. For example, in states, cities, and towns across the country, popular entertainers occasionally enter political life, drawing on their fame to get elected and to maintain their appeal while in office. These candidates often reflect the popular culture most prominent in their regions. In the South, for example, country music stars who run for office may have the advantage of widespread name recognition. In California, Hollywood stars have played an important role in state politics for decades.

Perhaps the most famous country music star to hold high state office was Jimmie Davis, known for his song "You Are My Sunshine." Recorded in 1940, the song became an international hit and propelled Davis into superstardom. Although he had held only minor public offices prior to 1944, Davis was easily elected governor of Louisiana.

Film and television stars have used their fame to win office most frequently in California. When rumors began to circulate in 2003 that the action film star Arnold Schwarzenegger might run for governor of California, many found the idea far-fetched. Yet, Schwarzenegger very effectively used his fame to build excitement and energy around his candidacy. Schwarzenegger drew on his show-business skills throughout the campaign, attracting enormous crowds and regularly using his most famous one-liners, "Hasta la vista, baby" and "I'll be back." Although the glow of stardom faded after a few years in office, Schwarzenegger—now "the Governator"—was re-elected in 2006.

Other actors have also won office in California. The most famous actor-turned-politician was Ronald Reagan, who was elected governor in 1966 and went on to become president in 1980. At the local level, Clint Eastwood, of spaghetti westerns and *Dirty Harry* fame, and the singer Sonny Bono both served as mayors. Although Eastwood decided to leave politics after one term, Bono went on to make politics his career, serving two terms in the House of Representatives.

In Minnesota, the pro wrestler Jesse "The Body" Ventura shocked the political establishment when he won election as governor in 1998. Known for his bad-boy persona as a wrestler, Ventura launched his political career by winning election as mayor of a Minneapolis suburb. He ran for governor as a third-party candidate who promised a big departure from politics as usual.

In 2006, the country musician and comic Kinky Friedman ran for governor of Texas on a similar platform, bringing in Ventura to help him campaign. Although he stood little chance of winning, Friedman attracted considerable media attention and distinguished himself from the career politicians in the race with slogans like "How Hard Could It Be?" and "Why the Hell Not?"

Entertainers have the advantage of name recognition when they enter politics. In state and local elections, such recognition alone may be enough to offset charges of inexperience. However, once in office, popular entertainers who enter state and local politics have varied careers. While some leave office after one term, others go on to make a career in politics. Popular entertainers who start their careers in state and local politics may also find it hard to attain sufficient stature to enter the national political arena. Moreover, the broad (but shallow) appeal that allows celebrities to win office may make it difficult for them to govern effectively. Research shows that celebrities often lack the firm base of political support needed to govern.[a]

[a]Darrell M. West and John M. Orman, *Celebrity Politics* (Upper Saddle River, NJ: Prentice Hall, 2003).

for critical analysis

1. Why have more entertainers sought political office at the state and local level rather than the national level?

2. Have entertainers won office in your state or local governments? How did their careers in show business affect their ability to govern?

courts in other states.[6] For a further discussion of gay and lesbian marriage, see Chapter 5.

Article IV, Section 2, known as the "comity clause," also seeks to promote national unity. It provides that citizens enjoying the **privileges and immunities** of one state should be entitled to similar treatment in other states. What this has come to mean is that a state cannot discriminate against someone from another state or give special privileges to its own residents. For example, in the 1970s, when Alaska passed a law that gave residents preference over nonresidents in obtaining work on the state's oil and gas pipelines, the Supreme Court ruled the law illegal because it discriminated against citizens of other states.[7] This clause also regulates criminal justice among the states by requiring states to return fugitives to the states from which they have fled. Thus, in 1952, when an inmate escaped from an Alabama prison and sought to avoid being returned to Alabama on the grounds that he was being subjected to "cruel and unusual punishment" there, the Supreme Court ruled that he must be returned according to Article IV, Section 2.[8] This example highlights the difference between the obligations among states and those among different countries. In 1997, France refused to return an American fugitive because he might be subject to the death penalty, which does not exist in France.[9] The Constitution clearly forbids states from doing something similar.

States' relationships with each other are also governed by the interstate compact clause (Article I, Section 10), which states that "No State shall, without the Consent of Congress . . . enter into any Agreement or Compact with another State." The Court has interpreted the clause to mean that states may enter into agreements with each other, subject to congressional approval. Compacts are a way for two or more states to reach a legally binding agreement about how to solve a problem that crosses state lines. In the early years of the Republic, states turned to compacts primarily to settle border disputes. Today compacts are used for a wide range of issues but are especially important in regulating the distribution of river water, addressing environmental concerns, and operating transportation systems that cross state lines.[10]

privileges and immunities clause provision from Article IV, Section 2, of the Constitution, that a state cannot discriminate against someone from another state or give its own residents special privileges

home rule power delegated by the state to a local unit of government to manage its own affairs

Local Government and the Constitution

Local government occupies a peculiar but very important place in the American system. In fact, the status of American local government is probably unique in world experience. First, it must be pointed out that local government has no status in the U.S. Constitution. *State* legislatures created local governments, and *state* constitutions and laws permit local governments to take on some of the responsibilities of the state governments. Most states amended their own constitutions to give their larger cities **home rule**—a guarantee of noninterference in various areas of local affairs. But local governments enjoy no such recognition in the Constitution. Local governments have always been subject to ultimate control by the states. This imbalance of power means that state governments could legally dissolve local governments or force multiple local governments to consolidate into one large locality. Local governments have no protected standing at all in the federal Constitution.[11]

Local governments became administratively important in the early years of the Republic because the states possessed little administrative capability. They relied on local governments—cities and counties—to implement state laws. Local government was an alternative to a statewide bureaucracy (see Table 3.1).

TABLE 3.1	
89,527 Governments in the United States	
TYPE	NUMBER
National	1
State	50
County	3,033
Municipal	19,492
Townships	16,519
School districts	13,051
Other special districts	37,381

SOURCE: U.S. Census Bureau, www.census.gov (accessed 7/14/08).

The Changing Relationship between the Federal Government and the States

At the time of the Founding, the states far outstripped the federal government in their size and power to influence the lives of ordinary Americans. In the system of shared powers between the states and the federal government, the states were most active in economic and social regulation, while Washington took a much more hands-off approach. Even so, the federal government gradually expanded its powers in the wake of important Supreme Court decisions. However, it was not until the New Deal in the 1930s that the federal government gained vast new powers.

Restraining National Power with Dual Federalism

dual federalism the system of government that prevailed in the United States from 1789 to 1937, in which most fundamental governmental powers were shared between the federal and state governments

As we have noted, the Constitution created two layers of government: the national government and the state governments. The consequences of this **dual federalism** are fundamental to the American system of government in theory and in practice; they have meant that states have done most of the fundamental governing. For evidence, look at Table 3.2. It lists the major types of public policies by which Americans were governed for the first century and a half under the Constitution. We call it the "traditional system" because it prevailed for much of American history and because it closely approximates the intentions of the framers of the Constitution.

Under the traditional system, the national government was quite small compared with both the state governments and the governments of other Western nations. Not only was it smaller than most governments of that time, but it was also actually very narrowly specialized in the functions it performed. The national government built or sponsored the construction of roads, canals, and bridges (internal improvements). It provided cash subsidies to shippers and shipbuilders and distributed free or low-priced public land to encourage western settlement and business ventures. It placed relatively heavy taxes on imported goods (tariffs), not only to raise revenues but also to protect "infant industries" from competition from the more advanced European enterprises. It protected patents and provided for a common currency, also to encourage and facilitate enterprises and to expand markets.

What do these functions of the national government reveal? First, virtually all the functions were aimed at assisting commerce. It is quite appropriate to refer to the traditional American system as a "commercial republic." Second, virtually none of the national government's policies directly coerced citizens. The emphasis of governmental programs was on assistance, promotion, and encouragement—the allocation of land or capital where they were insufficiently available for economic development.

Meanwhile, state legislatures were actively involved in economic regulation during the nineteenth century. In the United States, then and now, private property exists only in state laws and state court decisions regarding property, trespass, and real estate. American capitalism took its form from state property and trespass laws, as well as from state laws and court decisions regarding contracts, markets, credit, banking, incorporation, and insurance. Laws concerning slavery were a subdivision of property law in states where slavery existed. The practice of important professions, such as law and medicine, was and is illegal, except as provided for by state law. Marriage, divorce, and the registration of births and adoptions of children have always been regulated by state law. To educate or not to educate a child has been a decision governed more by state laws than by parents, and not at all by national law. It is important to note also that virtually all criminal laws—regarding everything from trespass to murder—have been state laws. Most of the criminal laws adopted by Congress are concerned with the District of Columbia and other federal territories.

All this (and more, as shown in the middle column of Table 3.2) demonstrates that most of the fundamental governing in the United States was done by the states. The contrast between national and state policies, as shown by Table 3.2, demonstrates the difference in the power vested in each. The list of items in the middle column could actually have been made longer. Moreover, each item on the list is a category of law that fills many volumes of statutes and court decisions.

TABLE 3.2

The Federal System: Specialization of Governmental Functions in the Traditional System (1800–1933)

NATIONAL GOVERNMENT POLICIES (DOMESTIC)	STATE GOVERNMENT POLICIES	LOCAL GOVERNMENT POLICIES
Internal improvements	Property laws (including slavery)	Adaptation of state laws to local conditions
Subsidies	Estate and inheritance laws	Public works
Tariffs	Commerce laws	Contracts for public works
Public lands disposal	Banking and credit laws	Licensing of public accommodations
Patents	Corporate laws	Assessible improvements
Currency	Insurance laws	Basic public services
	Family laws	
	Morality laws	
	Public health laws	
	Education laws	
	General penal laws	
	Eminent domain laws	
	Construction codes	
	Land-use laws	
	Water and mineral laws	
	Criminal procedure laws	
	Electoral and political parties laws	
	Local government laws	
	Civil service laws	
	Occupations and professions laws	

In 1815, President James Madison called for a federally funded program of "internal improvements," which was one of the few policy roles for the national government during the first half of the nineteenth century. By improving transportation through the construction of roads and canals, the government fostered the growth of the market economy and boosted federal power.

This contrast between national and state governments is all the more impressive because it is basically what the framers of the Constitution intended. Since the 1930s, the national government has expanded into local and intrastate matters, far beyond what anyone could have foreseen in 1790, 1890, or even in the 1920s. But this significant expansion of the national government did not alter the basic framework. The national government has become much larger, but the states have continued to be central to the American system of government.

Herein lies probably the most important point of all: the fundamental impact of federalism on the way the United States is governed comes not from any particular provision of the Constitution but from the framework itself, which has determined the flow of government functions and, through that, the political development of the country. By allowing state governments to do most of the fundamental governing, the Constitution saved the national government from many policy decisions that might have proven too divisive for a large and very young country. There is no doubt that if the Constitution had provided for a unitary rather than a federal system, the war over slavery would have come in 1789 or 1809 rather than in 1861; and if it had come that early, the South might very well have seceded and established a separate, slaveholding nation.

In helping the national government remain small and aloof from the most divisive issues of the day, federalism contributed significantly to the political stability of the nation, even as the social, economic, and political systems of many of the states and regions of the country were undergoing tremendous, profound, and sometimes violent, change.[12] As we shall see, some important aspects of federalism have changed, but the federal framework has survived two centuries and a devastating civil war.

Federalism and the Slow Growth of the National Government's Power

Having created the national government, and recognizing the potential for abuse of power, the states sought through federalism to constrain the national government. The "traditional system" of a weak national government prevailed for over a century despite economic forces favoring its expansion and despite Supreme Court cases giving a pro-national interpretation to Article I, Section 8, of the Constitution.

That article delegates to Congress the power "to regulate commerce with foreign nations, and among the several States and with the Indian tribes." This **commerce clause** was consistently interpreted *in favor* of national power by the Supreme Court for most of the nineteenth century. The first and most important case favoring national power over the economy was *McCulloch v. Maryland*.[13] This case involved the question of whether Congress had the power to charter a national bank, since such an explicit grant of power was nowhere to be found in Article I, Section 8. Chief Justice John Marshall answered that the power could be "implied" from other powers that were expressly delegated to Congress, such as the "powers to lay and collect taxes; to borrow money; to regulate commerce; and to declare and conduct a war."

By allowing Congress to use the necessary and proper clause to interpret its delegated powers expansively, the Supreme Court created the potential for an unprecedented increase in national government power. Marshall also concluded that whenever a state law conflicted with a federal law (as in the case of *McCulloch v. Maryland*), the state law would be deemed invalid since the Constitution states that "the Laws of the United States . . . shall be the supreme Law of the Land." Both parts of this great case are pro-national, yet Congress did not immediately seek to expand the policies of the national government.

Another major case, *Gibbons v. Ogden*, in 1824, reinforced this nationalistic interpretation of the Constitution. The important but relatively narrow issue was whether the state of New York could grant a monopoly to Robert Fulton's steamboat company to operate an exclusive service between New York and New Jersey. Chief Justice Marshall argued that New York State did not have the power to grant this particular monopoly. In order to reach this decision, Marshall had to define what Article I, Section 8, meant by "commerce among the several states." He insisted that the definition was "comprehensive," extending to "every species of commercial intercourse." He did say that this comprehensiveness was limited "to that commerce which concerns more states than one," giving rise to what later came to be called "interstate commerce." *Gibbons* is important because it established the supremacy of the national government in all matters affecting interstate commerce.[14] But what would remain uncertain during several decades of constitutional discourse was the precise meaning of interstate commerce.

Backed by the implied powers decision in *McCulloch* and by the broad definition of "interstate commerce" in *Gibbons*, Article I, Section 8, was a source of power for the national government as long as Congress sought to facilitate commerce through subsidies, services, and land grants. But later in the nineteenth century, when the national government sought to use those powers to *regulate* the economy rather than merely to promote economic development, federalism and the concept of interstate commerce began to operate as restraints on, rather than sources of, national power. Any effort of the national government to regulate commerce in such areas as fraud, the production of impure goods, the use of child labor, or the existence of dangerous working conditions or long hours was declared unconstitutional by the Supreme Court as a violation of the concept of interstate commerce. Such legislation meant that the federal government was entering the factory and the workplace—local areas—and was attempting to regulate goods that had not passed into commerce. To enter these local workplaces was to exercise police power—the power reserved to the states for the protection of the health, safety, and morals of

commerce clause Article I, Section 8, of the Constitution, which delegates to Congress the power "to regulate commerce with foreign nations, and among the several States and with the Indian tribes." This clause was interpreted by the Supreme Court in favor of national power over the economy

their citizens. No one questioned the power of the national government to regulate businesses that intrinsically involved interstate commerce, such as railroads, gas pipelines, and waterway transportation. But well into the twentieth century, the Supreme Court used the concept of interstate commerce as a barrier against most efforts by Congress to regulate local conditions.

This aspect of federalism was alive and well during an epoch of tremendous economic development, the period between the Civil War and the 1930s. It gave the American economy a freedom from federal government control that closely approximated the ideal of free enterprise. The economy was never entirely free, of course; in fact, entrepreneurs themselves did not want complete freedom from government. They needed law and order. They needed a stable currency. They needed courts and police to enforce contracts and prevent trespass. They needed roads, canals, and railroads. But federalism, as interpreted by the Supreme Court for seventy years after the Civil War, made it possible for business to have its cake and eat it, too. Entrepreneurs enjoyed the benefits of national policies facilitating commerce and were protected by the courts from policies regulating commerce.[15]

In 1916, the national government passed the Keating-Owen Child Labor Act, which excluded from interstate commerce all goods manufactured by children under fourteen. The act was ruled unconstitutional by the Supreme Court, and the regulation of child labor remained in the hands of state governments until the 1930s.

All this changed after 1937, when the Supreme Court issued a series of decisions that laid the groundwork for a much stronger federal government. Most significant was the Court's dramatic expansion of the commerce clause. By throwing out the old distinction between interstate and intrastate commerce, the Court converted the commerce clause from a source of limitations to a source of power for the national government. The Court upheld acts of Congress protecting the rights of employees to organize and engage in collective bargaining, regulating the amount of farmland in cultivation, extending low-interest credit to small businesses and farmers, and restricting the activities of corporations dealing in the stock market. The Court also upheld many other laws that contributed to the construction of the "welfare state."[16] With these rulings, the Court decisively signaled that the era of dual federalism was over. In the future, Congress would have very broad powers to regulate activity in the states.

The Changing Role of the States

As we have seen, the Constitution contained the seeds of a very expansive national government—in the commerce clause. For much of the nineteenth century, federal power remained limited. The Tenth Amendment was used to bolster arguments in favor of **states' rights**, which in their extreme version claimed that the states did not have to submit to national laws when they believed the national government had exceeded its authority. These arguments in favor of states' rights were voiced less often after the Civil War. But the Supreme Court continued to use the Tenth Amendment to strike down laws that it thought exceeded national power, including the Civil Rights Act passed in 1875.

In the early twentieth century, however, the Tenth Amendment appeared to lose its force. Reformers began to press for national regulations to limit the power of large corporations and to preserve the health and welfare of citizens. The Supreme Court approved some of these laws but it struck down others, including a law combating child labor. The Court stated that the law violated the Tenth Amendment because only states should have the power to regulate conditions of employment. By the late 1930s, however, the Supreme Court had approved such an expansion of federal power that the Tenth Amendment appeared irrelevant. The desire to promote equal conditions across the country had elevated the federal government over the states. In fact, in 1941, Justice Harlan Fiske Stone declared that the Tenth Amendment was simply a "truism," that it had no real meaning.[17]

Yet the idea that some powers should be reserved to the states did not go away. One reason is that groups with substantive policy interests often support states' rights as a means for achieving their policy goals. For example, in the 1950s, southern opponents of the civil rights movement revived the idea of states' rights to support racial segregation. In 1956, ninety-six southern members of Congress issued a "Southern Manifesto" in which they declared that southern states were not constitutionally bound by Supreme Court decisions outlawing racial segregation. They believed that states' rights should override individual rights to liberty and formal equality. With the triumph of the civil rights movement, the slogan of "states' rights" became tarnished by its association with racial inequality.

The 1990s saw a revival of interest in the Tenth Amendment and important Supreme Court decisions limiting federal power. Much of the interest in the Tenth Amendment stemmed from conservatives who believed that a strong federal government encroaches on individual liberties. They believed such freedoms

states' rights the principle that the states should oppose the increasing authority of the national government. This principle was most popular in the period before the Civil War

States' rights have been embraced by many causes in the past fifty years. Governor George Wallace of Alabama, a vocal supporter of states' rights, defiantly turned back U.S. Attorney General Nicholas Katzenbach, who tried to enroll two black students at the University of Alabama at Tuscaloosa in 1963.

devolution a policy to remove a program from one level of government by delegating it or passing it down to a lower level of government, such as from the national government to the state and local governments

for critical analysis

How have Supreme Court decisions affected the balance of power between the federal government and the states? Has the Supreme Court favored the federal government or the states?

are better protected by returning more power to the states through the process of **devolution**. In 1996, Bob Dole, the Republican presidential candidate, carried a copy of the Tenth Amendment in his pocket as he campaigned, pulling it out to read at rallies.[18] The Supreme Court's ruling in *United States v. Lopez* in 1995 fueled further interest in the Tenth Amendment.[19] In that case, the Court, stating that Congress had exceeded its authority under the commerce clause, struck down a federal law that barred handguns near schools. This was the first time since the New Deal that the Court had limited congressional powers in this way. In 1997, the Court again relied on the Tenth Amendment to limit federal power in *Printz v. United States*.[20] The decision declared unconstitutional a provision of the Brady Handgun Violence Prevention Act that required state and local law enforcement officials to conduct background checks on handgun purchasers. The Court declared that this provision violated state sovereignty guaranteed in the Tenth Amendment because it required state and local officials to administer a federal regulatory program. The Court also limited the power of the federal government over the states in a 1996 ruling that prevented Native Americans from the Seminole tribe from suing the state of Florida in federal court. A 1988 law had given Indian tribes the right to sue a state in federal court if the state did not negotiate in good faith over issues related to gambling casinos on tribal land. The Supreme Court's ruling appeared to signal a much broader limitation on national power by raising new questions about whether individuals can sue a state if it fails to uphold federal law.[21]

In 2003, the Court surprised many observers by ruling against the state of Nevada's challenge to the application of the federal Family and Medical Leave Act to Nevada state employees. The act guarantees workers time off (without pay) for family care responsibilities. The Court's decision, which required Nevada state government to abide by the Family and Medical Leave Act, appeared to conflict with earlier decisions immunizing states against lawsuits on the basis of age and disability discrimination. Perhaps most surprising was the support of former Chief Justice William Rehnquist, a strong proponent of states' rights. In his opinion, Rehnquist

International Trade Agreements and the States

The Constitution reserves for the federal government the power to make foreign policy and to enter into treaties. Yet the expansion of the global economy over the past three decades has also increased the importance of the international arena for state and local governments. For states, the expansion of international trade offers new opportunities to promote economic development but also presents enormous frustrations. This is because international trade agreements may tie the hands of states and because states have little formal voice in the provisions of these agreements.

One of the most important such trade agreements is the North American Free Trade Act (NAFTA), a treaty signed by Canada, the United States, and Mexico in 1992 to open trade across the national borders of these three countries. It also created new trade rules that each national government is obligated to follow. Although American state governments were not involved in creating these trade rules, the new rules may significantly restrict their own policies. Other trade agreements, such as those negotiated through the World Trade Organization (WTO), also may limit what states can do. Other trade agreements that have recently aroused concern in the states are proposed rulings that would label many common state procurement policies as barriers to trade and therefore unenforceable. Procurement policies determine who can sell goods and provide services to the state. States often impose conditions on the companies with which they do business. For example, some states have policies requiring them to buy local or American-made products in an effort to reduce the offshoring of jobs. Other states impose requirements aimed at improving the environment, including provisions for buying goods with recycled content, or doing business with firms that use renewable energy sources. These conditions vary from state to state and are a product of the political process in different states. As Governor John Baldacci of Maine noted in a 2006 letter to the U.S. trade representative, "The state of Maine's procurement laws have been developed to protect the interests of Maine's citizens and businesses and to reflect the state's commitment to spend its citizens' tax dollars in a socially and environmentally responsible way."[a]

The states have challenged these proposed rulings as an infringement on state sovereignty. And some states have started to pass legislation to ensure that trade agreements are scrutinized by the state legislature. For example, in 2007, the Hawaii state legislature passed legislation—over the governor's veto—to ensure that only the state legislature can approve or reject the terms relating to procurement in international trade agreements. It became the third state to pass such legislation, joining Rhode Island and Maryland.

One of the major complaints that states have is that they have no voice in the process of formulating trade agreement provisions even when such agreements significantly limit their sovereignty and regulatory authority. Five state legislatures (California, Washington, Maine, North Carolina, and Minnesota) have created formal committees on international trade and federalism. These committees aim to give their state greater capacity to assess the impact of trade agreements, and to gain expert and constituency views about the trade and state economic development policies. These committees are also a point of contact between the state legislatures and the U.S. trade representative and the members of Congress on issues related to trade and economic development. The potential for trade agreements to restrict the traditional democratic decision-making powers of the states means that in the future, states will have to consider the international repercussions of their actions as a normal part of state lawmaking.

[a]www.citizens.org (accessed 9/25/07).

for critical analysis

1. How do international treaties such as NAFTA and international organizations such as the World Trade Organization affect the sovereign powers of the states?

2. What are states doing to ensure that their interests are considered when the federal government enters into international trade agreements?

Especially since the mid-1990s, Republican Party leaders have contended that the national government has grown too powerful at the expense of the states and argued that the Tenth Amendment should restrict the growth of national power.

argued that family care issues were so strongly gender related that the Family and Medical Leave Act was necessary to prevent unconstitutional discrimination against women. Such protection against unconstitutional discrimination justified overriding state immunity in Rehnquist's view. Some analysts viewed the decision, in which the Court showed that on fundamental matters of civil rights federal law would supersede state sovereignty, as potentially a key turning point in judicial rulings on federalism.

The expansion of the power of the national government has not left the states powerless. The state governments continue to make important laws. No better demonstration of the continuing influence of the federal framework can be offered than that the middle column of Table 3.2 is still a fairly accurate characterization of state government today. In each of these domains, however, states must now share power with the federal government.

Who Does What? Public Spending and the Federal Framework

Questions about how to divide responsibilities between the states and the national government first arose more than 200 years ago, when the framers wrote the Constitution to create a stronger union. But they did not solve the issue of who should do what. There is no "right" answer to that question; each generation of Americans has provided its own answer. In recent decades, Americans have grown distrustful of the federal government and have supported giving more responsibility to the states.[22] Even so, they still want the federal government to set standards, promote equality, and provide security.

Political debates about the division of responsibility often take sides: some people argue for a strong federal role to set national standards whereas others say the states should do more. These two goals are not necessarily at odds. The key is to find the right balance. During the first 150 years of American history, that balance favored state power. But the balance began to shift toward Washington in the 1930s. In this section, we will look at how the balance shifted, and then we will consider current efforts to reshape the relationship between the national government and the states.

The New Deal

The New Deal of the 1930s signaled the rise of a more active national government. The door to increased federal action opened when states proved unable to cope with the demands brought on by the Great Depression. Before the depression, states and localities took responsibility for addressing the needs of the poor, usually through private charity. But the extent of the need created by the depression quickly exhausted local and state capacities. By 1932, 25 percent of the workforce was unemployed. The jobless lost their homes and settled into camps all over the country, called "Hoovervilles," after President Herbert Hoover. Elected in 1928, the year before the depression hit, Hoover steadfastly maintained that the federal government could do little to alleviate the misery caused by the depression. It was a matter for state and local governments, he said.

Yet demands mounted for the federal government to take action. In Congress, some Democrats proposed that the federal government finance public works to aid the economy and put people back to work. Other members of Congress introduced legislation to provide federal grants to the states to assist them in their relief efforts. None of these measures passed while Hoover remained in the White House.

When Franklin Delano Roosevelt took office in 1933, he energetically threw the federal government into the business of fighting the depression. He proposed a variety of temporary measures to provide federal relief and work programs. Most of the programs he proposed were to be financed by the federal government but administered by the states. In addition to these temporary measures, Roosevelt presided over the creation of several important federal programs designed to provide future economic security for Americans.

Federal Grants

For the most part, the new national programs that the Roosevelt administration developed did not directly take power away from the states. Instead, Washington typically redirected states by offering them **grants-in-aid**, whereby Congress appropriates money to state and local governments on the condition that the money be spent for a particular purpose defined by Congress.

The principle of the grant-in-aid can be traced back to the nineteenth-century land grants that the national government made to the states for the improvement of agriculture and farm-related education. Since farms were not in "interstate commerce," it was unclear whether the Constitution permitted the national government to provide direct assistance to agriculture. Grants made to the states, but designated for farmers, presented a way of avoiding the question of constitutionality while pursuing what was recognized in Congress as a national goal.

grants-in-aid programs through which Congress provides money to state and local governments on the condition that the funds be employed for purposes defined by the federal government

During the Great Depression, the national government became more active in regulating the economy and supporting the poor. New Deal programs sought to aid those affected by the depression, such as residents of this Hooverville outside of Seattle, which was photographed in 1933.

Franklin Roosevelt's New Deal expanded the range of grants-in-aid into social programs, providing grants to the states for financial assistance to poor children. Congress added more grants after World War II, creating new programs to help states fund activities such as providing school lunches and building highways. Sometimes the national government required state or local governments to match the national contribution dollar for dollar, but in some programs, such as the development of the interstate highway system, the congressional grants provided 90 percent of the cost of the program.

These types of federal grants-in-aid are also called **categorical grants** because the national government determines the purposes, or categories, for which the money can be used. For the most part, the categorical grants created before the 1960s simply helped the states perform their traditional functions.[23] During the 1960s, however, the national role expanded and the number of categorical grants increased dramatically. For example, during the 89th Congress (1965–66) alone, the number of categorical grant-in-aid programs grew from 221 to 379.[24] The value of categorical grants also has risen dramatically, increasing in value from $2.3 billion in 1950 to an estimated $467 billion in 2008. The grants authorized during the 1960s announced national purposes much more strongly than did earlier grants. One of the most important—and expensive—was the federal Medicaid program, which provides states with grants to pay for medical care for the poor, the disabled, and many nursing home residents (see Figure 3.1).

categorical grants congressional grants given to states and localities on the condition that expenditures be limited to a problem or group specified by law

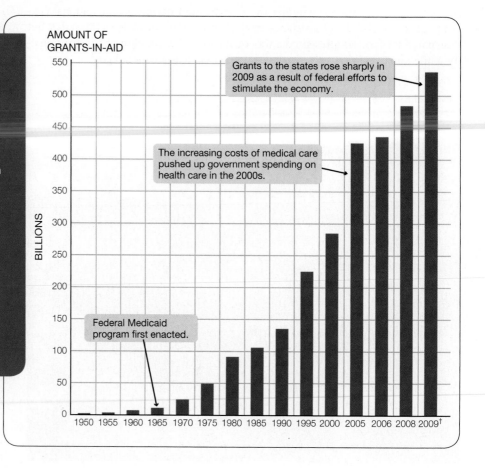

FIGURE 3.1

Historical Trend of Federal Grants-in-Aid,* 1950–2009

Spending on federal grants-in-aid to the states has grown dramatically since 1990. These increases reflect the growing public expectations about what government should do. What has been the most important cause of the steady increase in these grants?

*Excludes outlays for national defense, international affairs, and net interest.
†Estimate

SOURCE: Office of Management and Budget, www.gpoaccess.gov (accessed 6/18/10).

AMOUNT OF GRANTS-IN-AID

Grants to the states rose sharply in 2009 as a result of federal efforts to stimulate the economy.

The increasing costs of medical care pushed up government spending on health care in the 2000s.

Federal Medicaid program first enacted.

Many of the categorical grants enacted during the 1960s were **project grants**, which require state and local governments to submit proposals to federal agencies. In contrast to the older **formula grants**, which used a formula (composed of such elements as need and state and local capacities) to distribute funds, the new project grants made funding available on a competitive basis. Federal agencies would give grants to the proposals they judged to be the best. In this way, the national government acquired substantial control over which state and local governments got money, how much they got, and how they spent it.

Cooperative Federalism

The growth of categorical grants created a new kind of federalism. If the traditional system of two sovereigns performing highly different functions could be called dual federalism, historians of federalism suggest that the system since the New Deal could be called **cooperative federalism**. The political scientist Morton Grozdins characterized this as a move from "layer-cake federalism" to "marble-cake federalism,"[25] in which intergovernmental cooperation and sharing have blurred a once-clear distinguishing line, making it difficult to say where the national government ends and the state and local governments begin (see Figure 3.2). Figure 3.3 demonstrates the financial basis of the marble-cake idea.

For a while in the 1960s, however, it appeared as if the state governments would become increasingly irrelevant to American federalism. Many of the new federal grants bypassed the states and instead sent money directly to local governments and even to local nonprofit organizations. The theme heard repeatedly in Washington was that the states simply could not be trusted to carry out national purposes.[26]

One of the reasons that Washington distrusted the states was because of the way African American citizens were treated in the South. The southern states' forthright defense of segregation, justified on the grounds of states' rights, helped to tarnish the image of the states as the civil rights movement gained momentum. The national officials who planned the War on Poverty during the 1960s pointed to the racial exclusion practiced in the southern states as a reason for bypassing state governments. The political scientist James Sundquist described how the "Alabama syndrome" affected the War on Poverty: "In the drafting of the Economic Opportunity Act, an 'Alabama syndrome' developed. Any suggestion within the poverty task force that the states be given a role in the administration of the act

project grants grant programs in which state and local governments submit proposals to federal agencies and for which funding is provided on a competitive basis

formula grants grants-in-aid in which a formula is used to determine the amount of federal funds a state or local government will receive

cooperative federalism a type of federalism existing since the New Deal era in which grants-in-aid have been used strategically to encourage states and localities (without commanding them) to pursue nationally defined goals. Also known as "intergovernmental cooperation"

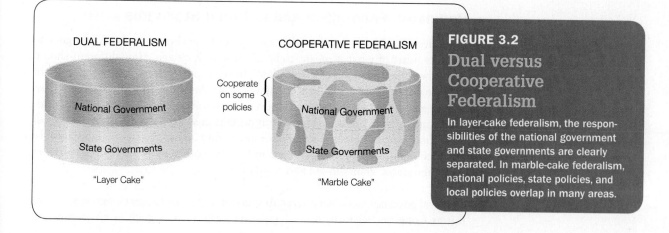

DUAL FEDERALISM

COOPERATIVE FEDERALISM

Cooperate on some policies

National Government

State Governments

"Layer Cake"

National Government

State Governments

"Marble Cake"

FIGURE 3.2

Dual versus Cooperative Federalism

In layer-cake federalism, the responsibilities of the national government and state governments are clearly separated. In marble-cake federalism, national policies, state policies, and local policies overlap in many areas.

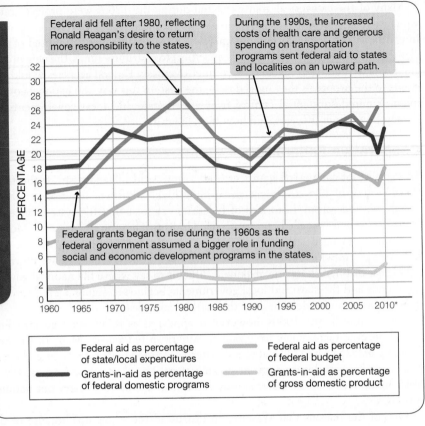

FIGURE 3.3

The Rise, Decline, and Recovery of Federal Aid

The level of federal aid has varied over the past several decades as program costs and politics have affected the role the national government plays in funding state and local services. The data in this figure show a rise, decline, and recovery of federal aid. What factors contributed to each of these trends?

*Estimate

SOURCE: Office of Management and Budget, www.gpoaccess.gov (accessed 3/26/08).

Federal aid fell after 1980, reflecting Ronald Reagan's desire to return more responsibility to the states.

During the 1990s, the increased costs of health care and generous spending on transportation programs sent federal aid to states and localities on an upward path.

Federal grants began to rise during the 1960s as the federal government assumed a bigger role in funding social and economic development programs in the states.

Federal aid as percentage of state/local expenditures

Federal aid as percentage of federal budget

Grants-in-aid as percentage of federal domestic programs

Grants-in-aid as percentage of gross domestic product

was met with the question, 'Do you want to give that kind of power to [the Alabama governor] George Wallace?'"[27]

Yet even though many national policies of the 1960s bypassed the states, other new programs, such as Medicaid—the health program for the poor—relied on state governments for their implementation. In addition, as the national government expanded existing programs run by the states, states had to take on more responsibility. These new responsibilities meant that the states were playing a very important role in the federal system.

Regulated Federalism and National Standards

The question of who decides what each level of government should do goes to the very heart of what it means to be an American citizen. How different should things be when one crosses a state line? In what policy areas is it acceptable for states to differ? In what areas should states be similar? How much inequality across the states is acceptable? Supreme Court decisions about the fundamental rights of American citizens provide the most important answers to these questions. Over time, the Court has pushed for greater uniformity across the states. In addition to legal decisions, the national government uses two other tools to create similarities across the states: grants-in-aid and regulations.

Grants-in-aid, as we have seen, are incentives: Congress gives money to state and local governments if they agree to spend it for the purposes Congress specifies. But as Congress began to enact legislation in new areas, such as environmental

> **What major developments do we see in the federal framework since the 1930s?**

In 2005, the Supreme Court ruled that the federal government had the right to prosecute individuals for using medical marijuana, even in states that had made such use legal. Despite the Court's ruling, some states have continued to permit the dispensing and use of medical marijuana.

policy, it also imposed additional regulations on states and localities. Some political scientists call this a move toward **regulated federalism**.[28] The national government began to set standards of conduct or required the states to set standards that met national guidelines. The effect of these national standards is that state and local policies in the areas of environmental protection, social services, and education are more uniform from coast to coast than are other nationally funded policies.

Some national standards require the federal government to take over areas of regulation formerly overseen by state or local governments. Such **preemption** occurs when state and local actions are found to be inconsistent with federal requirements. In some cases, federal laws and regulations are more stringent than state laws. For example, as federal regulations proliferated after the 1970s, Washington increasingly preempted state and local action in many different policy areas. These preemptions required the states to abide by tougher federal rules in policies as diverse as air and water pollution, occupational health and safety, and access for the handicapped. The regulated industries often oppose such laws because they increase the cost of doing business. After 1994, when Republicans controlled Congress, the federal government used its preemption power in business's favor, limiting the ability of states to tax and regulate industry. For example, the Internet Tax Freedom Act (ITFA), first enacted by Congress in 1998 and then renewed in 2001, 2004, and 2007, prohibits states and localities from taxing Internet access services. Congress is not the only federal body that can preempt the states; federal regulatory agencies can also issue rules that override state law. One controversial case involved a 2006 Food and Drug Administration drug-labeling rule preempting state laws that allow individuals to sue drug companies in state courts. Opponents—many of them trial lawyers—charged that such rules amount to "stealth preemption" that "will deprive consumers of their right to hold negligent corporations accountable for injuries caused by defective products."[29] Supporters claimed that the rules were a proper use of federal authority. Preemption by federal agency rules attracted the attention of the Democratic Congress in 2007, prompting the Senate Judiciary Committee to hold hearings to investigate whether federal agencies were

regulated federalism a form of federalism in which Congress imposes legislation on states and localities, requiring them to meet national standards

preemption the principle that allows the national government to override state or local actions in certain policy areas; in foreign policy, the willingness to strike first in order to prevent an enemy attack

"usurping congressional and state authority."[30] Although the Republicans came to power promising to grant more responsibility to the states, they ended up reducing state control in many areas by preemption.

State and local governments often contest federal preemptions. For example, in 2001, Attorney General John Ashcroft declared that Oregon's law permitting doctor-assisted suicide was illegal under federal drug regulations. Oregon took the Justice Department to federal court, which ruled in favor of the local law, stating that the federal government had overstepped its boundaries. In January 2006, the Supreme Court ruled in a 6-to-3 vote that the attorney general did not have the authority to outlaw the Oregon law. Individuals have also challenged federal preemption. In 2009, the Supreme Court ruled against a drug manufacturer and in favor of a woman whose arm had to be amputated after she was improperly injected with a drug designed to counter nausea.[31] Although the drug company knew that such complications could arise, it argued that it was not responsible for the amputation because federal regulations did not require it to warn against this danger in labeling the drug. The Court, however, found the company liable for the damage. In its decision, the Court made it clear that federal regulations could not preempt state consumer protections and that states had the power to adopt protections that are stricter than those of the federal government.

After only a few months in office, President Obama reversed the Bush administration's use of federal regulations to limit state laws. Under the new policy, federal regulations should preempt state laws only in extraordinary cases. The president directed agency leaders to review the regulations that had been put in place over the past ten years and consider amending them if they interfered with the "legitimate prerogatives of the states."[32]

The growth of national standards has created some new problems and has raised questions about how far federal standardization should go. One problem that emerged in the 1980s was the increase in **unfunded mandates**—regulations or new conditions for receiving grants that impose costs on state and local governments for which they are not reimbursed by the national government. The growth of unfunded mandates was the product of a Democratic Congress, which wanted to achieve liberal social objectives, and a Republican president, who opposed increased social spending. Between 1983 and 1991, Congress mandated standards in many policy areas, including social services and environmental regulations, without providing additional funds to meet those standards. Altogether, Congress enacted twenty-seven laws that imposed new regulations or required states to expand existing programs.[33] For example, in the late 1980s, Congress ordered the states to extend the coverage provided by Medicaid, the medical insurance program for the poor. The aim was to make the program serve more people, particularly poor children, and to expand services. But Congress did not supply additional funding to help states meet these new requirements; the states had to shoulder the increased financial burden themselves.

States and localities quickly began to protest the cost of unfunded mandates. Although it is very hard to determine the exact cost of federal regulations, the Congressional Budget Office estimated that between 1983 and 1990, new federal regulations cost states and localities between $8.9 and $12.7 billion.[34] States complained that mandates took up so much of their budgets that they were not able to set their own priorities.

These burdens became part of a rallying cry to reduce the power of the federal government—a cry that took center stage when a Republican Congress was elected in 1994. One of the first measures the new Congress passed was an act to limit the

unfunded mandates regulations or conditions for receiving grants that impose costs on state and local governments for which they are not reimbursed by the federal government

cost of unfunded mandates, the Unfunded Mandate Reform Act (UMRA). Under this law, Congress must estimate the cost of any proposal it believes will cost more than $50 million.

Despite considerable talk about unfunded mandates, the federal government has not acted to help states pay for existing mandates, many of which have grown very costly over the years. New national problems inevitably raise the question of "who pays?" Since 2001, the costs of homeland security have fallen heavily on the states. In 2003, states, faced with their worst fiscal crises in sixty years, complained that the federal assistance provided for homeland security was far too little. At its annual meetings that year, the National Governors' Association declared homeland security an unfunded mandate with which the federal government should help more. The relationship between national security needs and state and local capabilities remains an unsettled area.

More recently, concern about unfunded mandates has arisen around health care reform. As Congress sought to enact major new health care legislation, one strategy it considered was a major expansion of Medicaid, the program that serves low-income people. But because Medicaid is partly funded by the states, any major increase in Medicaid recipients could pose a significant fiscal burden on the states. Already strapped for cash by the recession, governors pressed Congress to provide additional resources to fund the increased expenses resulting from new federal regulations.[35]

New Federalism and State Control

In 1970, the mayor of Oakland, California, told Congress that his city had twenty-two separate employment and training programs but that few poor residents were being trained for jobs that were available in the local labor market.[36] National programs had proliferated as Congress enacted many small grants, but little effort was made to coordinate or adapt programs to local needs. Today many governors argue for more control over such national grant programs. They complain that national grants do not allow for enough local flexibility and instead take a "one size fits all" approach.[37] These criticisms point to a fundamental problem in American federalism: how to get the best results for the money spent. Do some divisions of responsibility between states and the federal government work better than others? Since the 1970s, as states have become more capable of administering large-scale programs, the idea of devolution—transferring responsibility for policy from the federal government to the states and localities—has become popular.

Proponents of more state authority have looked to **block grants** as a way of reducing federal control. Block grants are federal grants that allow the states considerable leeway in spending federal money. President Nixon led the first push for block grants in the early 1970s, as part of his **New Federalism**.

The debate over health care legislation raised concern about unfunded mandates, as state governments worried that Congress would require them to pay some of the costs of universal health care. Although the final legislation did not place the burden on states, several states threatened not to comply with a national health plan.

● What major developments do we see in the federal framework since the 1930s?

for critical analysis

Should states be required to implement unfunded mandates? Are Americans better off or worse off as a result of devolution?

block grants federal grants-in-aid that allow states considerable discretion in how the funds are spent

New Federalism attempts by Presidents Nixon and Reagan to return power to the states through block grants

INSURANCE PROFITS are BAD FOR MY HEALTH

www.HealthCareForAmericaNow.org

Nixon's block grants consolidated programs in the areas of job training, community development, and social services into three large block grants. These grants imposed some conditions on states and localities as to how the money should be spent, but not the narrow regulations contained in the categorical grants. In addition, Congress provided an important new form of federal assistance to state and local governments called **general revenue sharing**. Revenue sharing provided money to local governments and counties with no strings attached; localities could spend the money as they wished. In enacting revenue sharing, Washington acknowledged both the critical role that state and local governments play in implementing national priorities and their need for increased funding and enhanced flexibility in order to carry out that role (see Figure 3.4). Reagan's version of New Federalism also looked to block grants. Like Nixon, Reagan wanted to reduce the national government's control and return power to the states. In all, Congress created twelve new block grants between 1981 and 1990.[38]

Another way of letting the states do more is by having the national government do less. When Nixon implemented block grants he increased federal spending. But Reagan's block grants cut federal funding by 12 percent. His view was that the states could spend their own funds to make up the difference, if they chose to do so. Revenue sharing was also eliminated during the Reagan administration, leaving localities to fend for themselves. The Republican Congress elected in 1994 took this strategy even further, supporting block grants as well as substantial cuts in federal programs. Their biggest success was the 1996 welfare reform law, which delegated to states important new responsibilities. Most of the other major proposed block grants or spending reductions failed to pass Congress or were vetoed by President Clinton. The Republican congressional leadership had found that it was much easier to promise a "devolution revolution" than to deliver on that promise.[39]

Neither block grants nor reduced federal funding have proven to be magic solutions to the problems of federalism. For one thing, there is always a trade-off between accountability—that is, whether the states are using funds for the

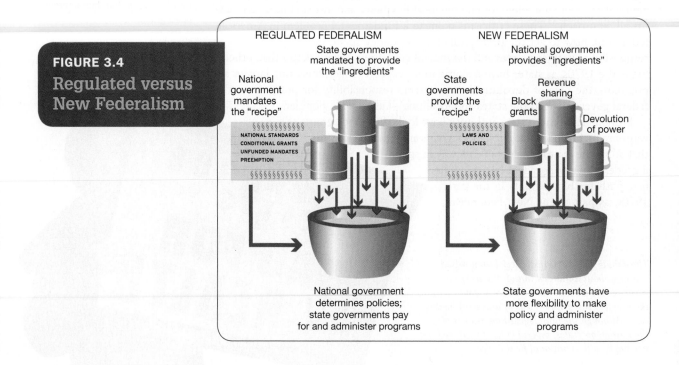

FIGURE 3.4
Regulated versus New Federalism

REGULATED FEDERALISM

State governments mandated to provide the "ingredients"

National government mandates the "recipe"

§§§§§§§§§§§
NATIONAL STANDARDS
CONDITIONAL GRANTS
UNFUNDED MANDATES
PREEMPTION
§§§§§§§§§§§

National government determines policies; state governments pay for and administer programs

NEW FEDERALISM

National government provides "ingredients"

State governments provide the "recipe"

Revenue sharing

Block grants

Devolution of power

§§§§§§§§§§§
LAWS AND
POLICIES

§§§§§§§§§§§

State governments have more flexibility to make policy and administer programs

purposes intended—and flexibility. Accountability and proper use of funds continue to be troublesome issues. Even after block grants were created, Congress reimposed regulations in order to increase the states' accountability. If the objective is to have accountable and efficient government, it is not clear that state bureaucracies are any more efficient or more capable than national agencies. In Mississippi, for example, the state Department of Human Services spent money from the child care block grant for office furniture and designer salt and pepper shakers that cost $37.50 a pair. As one Mississippi state legislator said, "I've seen too many years of good ol' boy politics to know they shouldn't [transfer money to the states] without stricter controls and requirements."[40]

Most discussion of New Federalism has focused on increased state control over government spending programs. On balance, we have seen, states did gain more power over spending policies during the 1980s and 1990s. But at times the federal government has moved to limit state discretion over spending in cases where it thinks states are too generous. For example, in 2007, President Bush issued regulations that prevented states from providing benefits under the State Child Health Insurance Program (SCHIP) to children in families well above the poverty line. New federal rulings also barred states from providing chemotherapy to illegal immigrants, who are guaranteed emergency medical treatment under Medicaid, the federal and state health program for the poor.[41] These new rules have embroiled states and the federal government in sharp conflicts over state discretion in spending decisions, once the hallmark of New Federalism. As Figure 3.5 indicates, federalism has changed dramatically over the course of American history. Finding the right balance among states and the federal government is an evolving challenge for American democracy.

Devolution: For Whose Benefit?

Since the expansion of the national government in the 1930s, questions about "who does what" have frequently provoked conflict in American politics. Why does such an apparently simple choice set off such highly charged political debate? One reason is that many decisions about federal versus state responsibility have implications for who benefits from government action.

Let's consider the benefits of federal control versus devolution in the realm of **redistributive programs**. These are programs designed primarily for the benefit of the poor. Many political scientists and economists maintain that states and localities should not be in charge of redistributive programs. They argue that since states and local governments have to compete with each other, they do not have the incentive to spend their money on the needy people in their areas. Instead, they want to keep taxes low and spend money on things that promote economic development.[42] In this situation, states might engage in a "race to the bottom": if one state cuts assistance to the poor, neighboring states will institute similar or deeper cuts

redistributive programs economic policies designed to control the economy through taxing and spending, with the goal of benefiting the poor

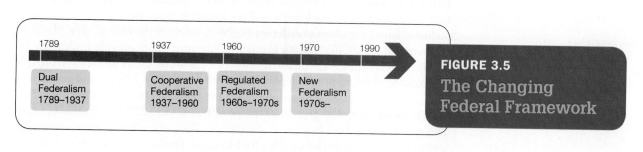

FIGURE 3.5
The Changing Federal Framework

1789   1937   1960   1970   1990

Dual Federalism 1789–1937   Cooperative Federalism 1937–1960   Regulated Federalism 1960s–1970s   New Federalism 1970s–

The debate over national versus state control of speed limits arose in 1973, when gas prices skyrocketed and supplies became scarce. Drivers nationwide were forced to wait in long lines at gas stations. The federal government responded to the gas crisis by instituting a national 55-mile-per-hour speed limit.

both to reduce expenditures and to discourage poorer people from moving into their states. As one New York legislator put it, "The concern we have is that unless we make our welfare system and our tax and regulatory system competitive with the states around us, we will have too many disincentives for business to move here. Welfare is a big part of that."[43]

In 1996, when Congress enacted a major welfare reform law, it followed a different logic. By changing welfare from a combined federal-state program into a block grant to the states, Congress gave the states more responsibility for programs that serve the poor. Most of those who initially supported the law opposed the current welfare system and hoped to reduce welfare spending. They defended their decision to devolve significant responsibility to the states by arguing that states could act as "laboratories of democracy" by experimenting with many different approaches to find those that best met the needs of their citizens.[44] As states altered their welfare programs in the wake of the new law, they did indeed design diverse approaches. For example, Minnesota adopted an incentive-based approach that offers extra assistance to families that take low-wage jobs. Other states have more "sticks" than "carrots" in their welfare programs. For example, six states impose very strict time limits on receiving welfare, allowing recipients less than the five-year limit in the federal legislation. After the passage of the law, welfare rolls declined dramatically. On average they declined by more than half from their peak in 1994; in twelve states the decline was 70 percent or higher. Politicians have cited these statistics to claim that the poor have benefited from greater state control of welfare, yet analysts caution that the reality is more complex. Most studies have found that the majority of those leaving welfare remain in poverty.

States have long adopted different eligibility rules for the federal-state Medicaid program and State Child Health Insurance Programs, which provide health care for low-income families. Although federal law set a floor requiring all states to provide Medicaid to children in families with incomes below 100–133 percent of the federal poverty level, twenty-four states made benefits available to children in families with incomes up to 250 percent of the poverty line ($51,625 for a family of four). The new health reform legislation, enacted in 2010, still allows states considerable leeway in determining who qualifies for Medicaid. The law raises the federal floor to include families with incomes lower than 138 percent of the poverty line but allows states to provide coverage to those with incomes above the new federal minimum.

In some decisions about federalism, local concerns are overridden in the name of the national interest. The question of speed limits provides an example. Speed limits had traditionally been a state and local responsibility. But in 1973, at the height of the oil shortage, Congress passed legislation to withhold federal highway funds from states that did not adopt a maximum speed limit of 55 miles per hour (mph). The lower speed limit, it was argued, would reduce energy consumption by cars. Although Congress had not formally taken over the authority to set speed limits, the power of its purse was so important that every state adopted the new speed limit. The national interest in energy conservation had outweighed local preferences for higher speed limits. As the crisis faded, concern about energy conservation diminished. The national speed limit lost much of its support, even though it was found to have reduced the number of traffic deaths. In 1995, Congress repealed the penalties for higher speed limits, and states once again became free to set their own speed limits. Many states with large rural areas raised their maximum to 75 mph; Montana initially set unlimited speeds in the rural areas during daylight hours. Research indicates that numbers of highway deaths have indeed risen in the states that increased the limits.[45]

Because the division of responsibility in the federal system has important implications for who benefits, few conflicts over state versus national control will ever be settled once and for all. As new evidence becomes available about the costs and benefits of different arrangements, it provides fuel for ongoing debates about what are properly the states' responsibilities and what the federal government should do. Likewise, changes in the political control of the national government usually provoke a rethinking of responsibilities as new leaders seek to alter federal arrangements for the benefit of the groups they represent.

Federalism since 2000

During the past ten years, many of the most controversial issues in American politics—including the appropriate size of public social spending, the rights and benefits of immigrants (legal as well as undocumented), what government should do about global warming, and questions about whether and how government should regulate business and moral behavior—have been fought out through the federal system. Politicians of all stripes regularly turn to the federal government to override decisions made by states. Likewise, when the federal government proves unable or unwilling to act, advocates and politicians try to achieve their goals in states and localities. In many cases, it is up to the courts to decide which level of government should have the final say.

Although conservatives proclaim their preference for a small federal government and their support for more state autonomy, in fact, they often expand the federal government and limit state autonomy. During the presidency of George W. Bush the growth of government, the activist free-spending Republican Congress, and a series of Supreme Court rulings supporting federal power over the states made it clear that conservatives do

In 1995, Congress removed its speed limit restrictions and gave the states the right to determine their own road speeds. As a result, speed limits went up on many highways.

not always support small government, nor do they always favor returning power to the states. Once in power, many conservatives not only discovered that they needed a strong federal government to respond to public demands but also found that they could use federal power to advance conservative policy goals.

For President Bush, the importance of a strong federal government dawned with force after the terrorist attacks in 2001. Aware that the American public was looking to Washington for protection, Bush worked with Congress to pass the USA PATRIOT Act, which greatly increased the surveillance powers of the federal government. A year later, he created the enormous new federal Department of Homeland Security.

President Bush also expanded federal control and enhanced spending in policy areas far removed from concerns about security. The 2001 No Child Left Behind Act introduced unprecedented federal intervention in public education, traditionally a state and local responsibility. New, detailed federal testing requirements and provisions stipulating how states should treat failing schools were major expansions of federal authority in education. When a number of states threatened to defy some of the new federal requirements, Bush's Department of Education relaxed its tough stance and became more flexible in enforcing the act. But the administration did not back down entirely, leading to several legal challenges to different aspects of the law.

At times, federal officials who oppose what states are doing have directly overridden state decisions or deliberately reduced the scope for state action. In 2005, the case of Terri Schiavo, a brain-damaged woman who had been in a coma for fifteen years, attracted widespread attention. After more than a decade of court rulings, the Florida state court decreed in 2005 that Schiavo's feeding tube should be removed in accordance with her husband's wishes. Unwilling to let the state court's decision stand, congressional leaders unleashed a major campaign to circumvent it. The fanfare surrounding the case—with Senate Majority Leader (and medical doctor) Bill Frist pronouncing Schiavo conscious after watching her on videotape—led to widespread charges that Congress had greatly overstepped its role. Conservatives themselves were split on the issue, with one Republican charging, "My party is demonstrating that they are for states' rights unless they don't like what the states are doing."[46]

In the Supreme Court, too, many decisions began to support a stronger federal role over the states. This was surprising to many observers because in the 1990s, it had appeared that the Rehnquist Court was embarked on a "federalism revolution" designed to return more power to the states. Instead, in several key decisions, the Court reaffirmed the power of the federal government. Decisions to uphold the federal Family and Medical Leave Act and the Americans with Disabilities Act asserted federal authority against state claims of immunity from the acts. In one important 2005 case, the Court upheld the right of Congress to ban medical marijuana, even though eleven states had legalized its use. Overturning a lower court ruling that said Congress did not have authority to regulate marijuana when it had been grown for noncommercial purposes in a single state, the Supreme Court ruled that the federal government did have the power to regulate use of all marijuana under the commerce clause.

Perhaps the most closely watched federalism case in 2006 was the challenge to Oregon's "right to die" law, which allows doctors to prescribe lethal doses of medicine for terminally ill patients who request it. Challengers claimed the law was illegal because Congress has the right to outlaw such use of drugs under the Controlled Substances Act, which regulates prescription drugs. In a 6-to-3 decision, the Court ruled in Oregon's favor. Despite this victory for states, the narrow focus of

for critical analysis

The role of the national government has changed significantly from the Founding era to the present. Do you think the framers of the Constitution would be pleased with the current balance of power between the national government and the state governments?

Who Benefits from Federal Spending?

Residents of every state pay taxes to the federal government, and every state receives money from the federal government. However, in any given year, some states receive more in federal spending than residents pay in federal taxes, while in other states, residents pay more to the federal government than their state gets back. These ratios vary from year to year. This map shows how much federal spending each state received for each dollar paid in federal taxes in 2005.

- Over $1.50
- $1.01 – 1.50
- $1.00
- $0.80 – 1.00
- Under $0.80

Federal Spending per Dollar of Federal Taxes

#	Amount	State	#	Amount	State	#	Amount	State
1.	$2.03	New Mexico	18.	$1.30	Maryland	35.	$0.94	Texas
2.	$2.02	Mississippi	19.	$1.27	Tennessee	36.	$0.93	Oregon
3.	$1.84	Alaska	20.	$1.21	Idaho	37.	$0.92	Michigan
4.	$1.78	Louisiana	21.	$1.19	Arizona	38.	$0.88	Washington
5.	$1.76	West Virginia	22.	$1.12	Kansas	39.	$0.86	Wisconsin
6.	$1.68	North Dakota	23.	$1.11	Wyoming	40.	$0.82	Massachusetts
7.	$1.66	Alabama	24.	$1.10	Iowa	41.	$0.81	Colorado
8.	$1.53	South Dakota	25.	$1.10	Nebraska	42.	$0.79	New York
9.	$1.51	Kentucky	26.	$1.08	Vermont	43.	$0.78	California
10.	$1.51	Virginia	27.	$1.08	North Carolina	44.	$0.77	Delaware
11.	$1.47	Montana	28.	$1.07	Pennsylvania	45.	$0.75	Illinois
12.	$1.44	Hawaii	29.	$1.07	Utah	46.	$0.72	Minnesota
13.	$1.41	Maine	30.	$1.05	Indiana	47.	$0.71	New Hampshire
14.	$1.41	Arkansas	31.	$1.05	Ohio	48.	$0.69	Connecticut
15.	$1.36	Oklahoma	32.	$1.01	Georgia	49.	$0.65	Nevada
16.	$1.35	South Carolina	33.	$1.00	Rhode Island	50.	$0.61	New Jersey
17.	$1.32	Missouri	34.	$0.97	Florida	n/a	$5.55	Distr. of Columbia

for critical analysis

1. Which states received the most federal dollars relative to taxes paid in 2005? Which states received the least? Did your state receive more in federal spending than residents paid in federal taxes?

2. Conservative Republicans generally prefer less federal spending. Is this preference at odds with the fact that many states with a majority of Republican voters receive more federal money per tax dollar than average?

SOURCE: The Tax Foundation, "Federal Spending Received Per Dollar of Taxes Paid by State, 2005," taxfoundation.org (accessed 5/11/10).

the ruling and the dissenting opinion by the new Chief Justice, John G. Roberts, Jr., indicated that the power of the federal government over the states would continue to be a contentious legal issue.

In other policy areas, states and localities have forged their own policies because the federal government has not acted. One of the most controversial of these issues is immigration legislation. In the first half of 2009, for example, state legislatures introduced more than 1,400 bills related to immigration.[47] Many state and local laws that govern immigration are not controversial but some of them raise critical questions about what is the federal role and what are the responsibilities of state and local governments. In April 2010, Arizona enacted an extremely controversial immigration measure that required immigrants to carry identity documents and required police to ask about immigration status when they stop drivers they suspect of being illegal immigrants. The federal Department of Justice quickly launched a review of the law and appeared poised to sue Arizona to prevent its implementation.

The presence of an estimated 12 million unauthorized immigrants in communities across the country is an especially volatile issue that affects many aspects of state lawmaking. In 2007, the federal Department of Homeland Security enlisted state and local officials in the effort to enforce federal immigration law. Under the program, state and local law enforcement agencies can be deputized to arrest suspected unauthorized immigrants and to check the immigration status of those apprehended on unrelated offenses. Yet the aggressive use of these powers in some localities has led to calls for ending the program. In 2009, the Justice Department stripped Joe Arpaio, sheriff of Maricopa County (Phoenix), Arizona, of the authority to make immigration sweeps. Arpaio had gained national attention for his harsh treatment of those rounded up in immigration raids, which included housing the immigrants in tent cities in the Arizona desert and putting female inmates in chain gangs. The federal government did not eliminate the program, however. Instead, it vowed to exercise greater oversight over local actions.[48]

In its first year, the Obama administration signaled a much stronger role for the federal government on some dimensions but more flexibility for state action in other matters. The stronger federal role was most evident in the measures to jump-start the failing economy. In February 2009, Congress enacted the American Recovery and Reinvestment Act (ARRA), a $787 billion measure that, in addition to tax cuts, offered states substantial one-time funds for a variety of purposes, including education, road building, unemployment insurance, and health care. Many governors, strapped for cash, welcomed the new funds. Others, however, worried that the federal government was using ARRA to dictate state spending priorities. Some of these governors sought to use the funds for purposes not allowed in the legislation or refused parts of the funds that they believed would tie their hands in the future. For example, Governor Mark Sanford of South Carolina, a Republican, asked the federal government for a waiver that would permit his state to use approximately $700 million of its estimated $2.8 billion ARRA allocation to pay down the state's debt. When the waiver was denied, Sanford vowed to reject the federal funds; however, the state legislature overrode his decision.[49] Several states objected to the unemployment funds, which required states to expand eligibility for unemployment insurance to many part-time and temporary workers. A handful of Republican governors, including Haley Barbour of Mississippi, Bobby Jindal of Louisiana, Bob Riley of Alabama, Mark Sanford of South

for critical analysis

Why did the Department of Homeland Security's program that enlists state and local agencies in enforcing federal immigration law become controversial? How has the Obama administration altered the program?

In 2009, the federal government approved billions of dollars to help states recover from the economic crisis. However, some state governors—including Haley Barbour of Mississippi (left) and Bobby Jindal of Louisiana (right)—refused to accept federal funds that came with requirements they considered objectionable.

Take Action at the State Level

College campuses across the country are largely alcohol-free zones, as the majority of their student populations are under twenty-one and thus ineligible to purchase alcoholic drinks. This national standard is a relatively new phenomenon. The legal drinking age had traditionally been a state-level issue, with Congress unable to legislate directly on age requirements. However, in 1984, Congress threatened to withhold national transportation funds from any state that refused to pass a law prohibiting the sale of alcohol to those under twenty-one. Because most states relied heavily on these federal funds, every state except Louisiana quickly raised its legal drinking age (Louisiana signed on in 1995).

The debate over the legal drinking age illustrates the essence of federalism—determining which policy areas should be the domain of the federal government and which issues should be reserved to the states. Many of the key issues currently facing us as a nation have been caught in this struggle between federal and state power.

The No Child Left Behind (NCLB) Act, for example, requires states to test all children in grades 3 through 8 on math and reading and imposes penalties on schools that fail to improve over time. Proponents of these national mandates argue that they are necessary to ensure that all children in the country, regardless of their home state, are provided quality education. Yet others, including many local and state officials, complain that the federal government requirements are too narrow or do not address the needs of their states.

State policy on stem-cell research is similarly charged. Under the Bush administration, the federal government imposed limits on federally funded embryonic-stem-cell research. Some state governments responded to these limitations by attempting to set even stricter guidelines in their own states (often banning it outright). Others took the opposite position, passing legislation that specifically guarantees the right to conduct such research or appropriating state funds to support stem-cell studies.

These examples illustrate the ways in which federal and state policies can overlap, sometimes creating a web of legislation and other times resulting in a national standard. Untangling this web can be tricky, but fortunately resources are available that can help you learn more about an issue, contact groups involved in the debate, and lend your own voice to the discussion.

- To begin, you can educate yourself about how your state addresses a host of issues ranging from health to the environment to civil rights by visiting the Pew Research Center's Web site www.stateline.org/live/. This Web site provides an in-depth look at key issues facing the states, presents comparisons among various state policies, and sometimes offers links to advocacy groups on different sides of the debate.

- After learning more about the issue from a state perspective, you can read comments from other readers, post your own comment, or share the entire article with friends.

- If one of these issues captures your interest or passion or anger, you might have a better chance of affecting policy at the state level (where there is generally greater access to legislators and fewer competing activists) than on the national level.

- In the abortion debate, for example, you might choose to write a letter or e-mail to your state representative or senator advocating either an expansion or restriction of abortion rights in your state.

- You might even want to circulate a petition to get an initiative on the ballot that will set state law on the issue. The Initiative and Referendum Institute at the University of Southern California (www.iandrinstitute.org) has information on this process.

Whatever your choice—to educate yourself, to express your opinion, or to join with others in action—the states provide fifty different arenas for effecting political change.

Carolina, and Rick Perry of Texas refused to accept the funds on the grounds that expanded eligibility would place a burden on employers in the future. A majority of states, however, changed their laws in response to the federal requirements.[50]

In other ways, the Obama White House signaled that it would allow the states more leeway for action than under the Bush administration. This was particularly true in the domains of social policy and the environment when states sought to enact laws more stringent than those of the federal government. In the memo reversing the Bush policy of preemption, the White House noted, "Throughout our history, State and local governments have frequently protected health, safety, and the environment more aggressively than has the national Government."[51] Its new policy aimed to keep the federal government from infringing on these more aggressive state actions.

● Thinking Critically about the Federal System

It is often argued that liberals prefer a strong federal government because they value equality more than liberty. Conservatives are said to prefer granting more power to states and localities because they care most about liberty. Although this greatly oversimplifies liberal and conservative views about government, such arguments underscore the reality that ideas about federalism are linked to different views about the purposes of government. For what ends should government powers be used? What happens when widely shared national values conflict in practice? The connections between federalism and our fundamental national values have made federalism a focus of political contention throughout our nation's history.

The Constitution limited the power of the federal government in order to promote liberty. This decision reflected the framers' suspicions of centralized power, based on their experience with the British Crown. The American suspicion of centralized power lives on today in widespread dislike of "big government," which generally evokes a picture of a bloated federal government. But over the course of our history we have come to realize that the federal government is also an important guarantor of liberty. As we'll see in Chapter 4, it took enhanced federal power to ensure that local and state governments adhered to the fundamental constitutional freedoms in the Bill of Rights.

One of the most important continuing arguments for a strong federal government is its role in ensuring equality. A key puzzle of federalism is deciding when differences across states represent the proper democratic decisions of the states and when such differences represent inequalities that should not be tolerated. Sometimes a decision to eliminate differences is made on the grounds of equality and individual rights, as in the Civil Rights Act of 1964, which outlawed legal segregation. At other times, a stronger federal role is justified on the grounds of national interest, as in the case of the oil shortage and the institution of a 55-mph speed limit in the 1970s. Advocates of a more limited federal role often point to the value of democracy. Public actions can more easily be tailored to fit distinctive local or state desires if states and localities have more power to make policy. Viewed this way, variation across states can be an expression of democratic will.

A decade ago, many Americans had grown disillusioned with the federal government and supported efforts to give the states more responsibilities. A 1997 poll, for example, found that Americans tended to have the most confidence in governments that were closest to them. Thirty-eight percent expressed "a great deal" of confidence in local government, 32 percent in state government, and 22 percent

for critical **analysis**

What would be the advantages and disadvantages of a unitary system in which the federal government had all the power? What would be the advantages and disadvantages of a fully decentralized system in which states had all the power?

in the federal government. Nearly two-thirds of those polled believed that shifting some responsibility to states and localities would help achieve excellence in government. After the terrorist attacks of 2001, however, support for the federal government soared. With issues of security topping the list of citizens' concerns, the federal government, which had seemed less important with the waning of the Cold War, suddenly reemerged as the central actor in American politics. As one observer put it, "Federalism was a luxury of peaceful times."[52] Yet polls show that trust in the federal government gradually dropped over the decade. In 2002, 64 percent of Americans expressed a positive view of the federal government; by 2008, only 37 percent did. In 2009, favorable views of the federal government climbed to 42 percent, a noticeable increase but still well below the highs obtained right after the terrorist attacks. Public views about state governments are generally more positive and more stable. However, the recession of 2008–2009 took a toll: those expressing a favorable view of states dropped from 62 percent in 2002 to 50 percent in 2009. Local governments remain most popular, with positive ratings of 67 percent in 2002 and 60 percent in 2009.[53]

American federalism remains a work in progress. As public problems shift and as local, state, and federal governments change, questions about the relationship between American values and federalism naturally emerge. The different views that people bring to this discussion suggest that concerns about federalism will remain a central issue in American democracy.

● How do debates over federalism reflect Americans' views on liberty, equality, and democracy?

studyguide

Practice Quiz

Find a diagnostic Web Quiz with 41 additional questions on the StudySpace Web site: www.wwnorton.com/we-the-people

The Federal Framework

1. Which term describes the sharing of powers between the national government and the state governments? *(p. 77)*
   a) separation of powers
   b) federalism
   c) checks and balances
   d) shared powers

2. Which amendment to the Constitution stated that the powers not delegated to the national government or prohibited to the states were "reserved to the states"? *(pp. 77–78)*
   a) First Amendment
   b) Fifth Amendment
   c) Tenth Amendment
   d) Twenty-sixth Amendment

3. A state government's authority to regulate the health, safety, and morals of its citizens is frequently referred to as *(p. 78)*
   a) the reserved power.
   b) the police power.
   c) the concurrent power.
   d) the implied power.

4. Which constitutional clause has been central in debates over gay and lesbian marriage because it requires that states normally honor the public acts and judicial decisions of other states? *(p. 78)*
   a) full faith and credit clause
   b) privileges and immunities clause
   c) necessary and proper clause
   d) interstate commerce clause

5. Many states have amended their constitutions to guarantee that large cities will have the authority to manage local affairs without interference from state government. This power is called *(p. 81)*
   a) home rule.
   b) preemption.
   c) states' rights.
   d) new federalism.

6. The system of federalism that allowed states to do most of the fundamental governing from 1789 to 1937 was *(p. 82)*
   a) home rule.
   b) regulated federalism.
   c) dual federalism.
   d) cooperative federalism.

7. In which case did the Supreme Court create the potential for increased national power by ruling that Congress could use the necessary and proper clause to interpret its delegated powers broadly? *(p. 85)*
   a) *United States v. Lopez*
   b) *Printz v. United States*
   c) *McCulloch v. Maryland*
   d) *Gibbons v. Ogden*

8. In 1937, the Supreme Court laid the groundwork for a stronger federal government by *(pp. 85–88)*
   a) issuing a number of decisions that dramatically narrowed the definition of the commerce clause.
   b) issuing a number of decisions that dramatically expanded the definition of the commerce clause.
   c) issuing a number of decisions that struck down the supremacy clause.
   d) issuing a number of decisions that struck down the privileges and immunities clause.

9. The process of returning more of the responsibilities of governing from the national level to the state level is known as *(p. 88)*
   a) dual federalism.
   b) devolution.
   c) preemption.
   d) home rule.

Who Does What? The Changing Federal Framework

10. One of the most powerful tools by which the federal government has attempted to get the states to act in ways that are desired by the federal government is by *(p. 91)*
    a) providing grants-in-aid.
    b) requiring licensing.
    c) granting home rule.
    d) defending states' rights.

11. The form of regulated federalism that allows the federal government to take over areas of regulation formerly overseen by states or local governments is called *(p. 95)*
    a) categorical grants.
    b) formula grants.

c) project grants.
d) preemption.

12. When state and local governments must conform to costly regulations or conditions in order to receive grants but do not receive reimbursements for their expenditures from the federal government it is called: *(p. 96)*
    a) a reciprocal grant.
    b) an unfunded mandate.
    c) general revenue sharing.
    d) a counterfunded mandate.

13. To what does the term *New Federalism* refer? *(p. 97)*
    a) the national government's regulation of state action through grants-in-aid
    b) the type of federalism relying on categorical grants
    c) efforts to return more policy-making discretion to the states through the use of block grants
    d) the recent emergence of local governments as important political actors

14. A recent notable example of the process of giving the states more responsibility for administering government programs is *(p. 99)*
    a) campaign finance reform.
    b) prison reform.
    c) trade reform.
    d) welfare reform.

Thinking Critically About Liberty versus Equality in the Federal System

15. Which of the following is not an argument in support of a strong federal government? *(pp. 106–7)*
    a) A strong federal government is sometimes needed to ensure equality.
    b) A strong federal government is sometimes needed to guarantee liberty.
    c) A strong federal government is sometimes needed to protect national interests.
    d) These are all arguments in support of a strong federal government.

Chapter Outline

 Find a detailed Chapter Outline on the StudySpace Web site: www.wwnorton.com/we-the-people

Key Terms

 Find Flashcards to help you study these terms on the StudySpace Web site: www.wwnorton.com/we-the-people

general revenue sharing *(p. 98)*
grants-in-aid *(p. 91)*
home rule *(p. 81)*
implied powers *(p. 77)*
necessary and proper
  clause *(p. 77)*

New Federalism *(p. 97)*
police power *(p. 78)*
preemption *(p. 95)*
privileges and immunities
  clause *(p. 81)*
project grants *(p. 93)*

redistributive programs *(p. 99)*
regulated federalism *(p. 95)*
reserved powers *(p. 78)*
states' rights *(p. 87)*
unfunded mandates *(p. 96)*
unitary system *(p. 77)*

For Further Reading

Bensel, Richard. *Sectionalism and American Political Development: 1880–1980*. Madison: University of Wisconsin Press, 1984.

Bowman, Ann O'M., and Richard Kearny. *The Resurgence of the States*. Englewood Cliffs, NJ: Prentice-Hall, 1986.

Derthick, Martha. *Keeping the Compound Republic: Essays on American Federalism*. Washington, DC: Brookings Institution Press, 2001.

Donahue, John D. *Disunited States*. New York: Basic Books, 1997.

Elazar, Daniel. *American Federalism: A View from the States*. 3rd ed. New York: Harper & Row, 1984.

Feiock, Richard C., and John T. Scholz, *Self-Organizing Federalism: Collaborative Mechanisms to Mitigate Institutional Collective Action Dilemmas*. New York: Cambridge University Press, 2009.

Gerston, Larry N. *American Federalism: A Concise Introduction*. Armonk, NY: M. E. Sharpe, 2007.

Grodzins, Morton. *The American System*. Chicago: Rand McNally, 1974.

Johnson, Kimberly S. *Governing the American State: Congress and the New Federalism, 1877–1929*. Princeton, NJ: Princeton University Press, 2007.

Kettl, Donald. *The Regulation of American Federalism*. Baltimore: Johns Hopkins University Press, 1987.

Van Horn, Carl E. *The State of the States*. 4th ed. Washington DC: Congressional Quarterly Press, 2005.

Recommended Web Sites

Constitution Finder
http://confinder.richmond.edu
  Governments can organize power in either unitary or federal systems. Examine the constitutions of different countries throughout the world and try to identify how those governments organize power.

Council of State Governments
www.csg.org
  This organization provides information on a variety of state-federal policy areas. See what current issues concerning federalism are of prime importance to the state governments on this site.

Federalism Project
www.federalismproject.org
  The Federalism Project of the American Enterprise Institute advocates competitive federalism and the empowering of states through devolution.

Governing.com
www.governing.com
  See what state-federal issues are important to your local government officials on the Web site for *Governing* magazine.

National Conference of State Legislatures
www.ncsl.org
National Governors Association
www.nga.org

These are two of the largest organizations dedicated to representing state and local government interests at the federal level.

Oyez: U.S. Supreme Court Media
www.oyez.org
  Read here about one of the most important U.S. Supreme Court decisions regarding the division of federal and state power in the case of *McCulloch v. Maryland*.

Urban Institute
www.newfederalism.urban.org
  New Federalism gives state governments more flexibility to make public policy and administer programs. The Urban Institute's "Assessing the New Federalism" policy center takes a statistical look at the success and failure of recent government programs.

U.S. Census Bureau
www.census.gov
  The Census Bureau maintains one of the largest collections of data about social and economic conditions of the nation's fifty states.

World Federalist Movement
www.wfm.org
  This international organization is dedicated to the division of power and authority among all local, state, and international governmental agencies. Generally, it promotes federalism and constitutional democracy throughout the world.

Freedom of speech is one of the liberties protected by the First Amendment. Even speech that is hostile or offensive—such as the views expressed by these Ku Klux Klan members—cannot be prohibited so long as they do not incite illegal action.

Civil Liberties

WHAT GOVERNMENT DOES AND WHY IT MATTERS Today in the United States, we often take for granted the liberties contained within the Bill of Rights. Few citizens of other countries can make such a claim. In fact, few people in recorded history have enjoyed such protections, including American citizens before the 1960s. For more than 170 years after its ratification by the states in 1791 the Bill of Rights meant little to most Americans. As we shall see in this chapter, guaranteeing the liberties articulated in the Bill of Rights to all Americans required a long struggle. As recently as the early 1960s, criminal suspects in state cases did not have to be informed of their rights, some states required daily Bible readings and prayers in their public schools, and some communities regularly censored reading material that they deemed to be obscene.

Thomas Jefferson said that a bill of rights "is what people are entitled to against every government on earth." Note the emphasis—people *against* government. Civil liberties are *protections from* improper government action. Some of these restraints are substantive liberties, which put limits on *what* the government shall and shall not have power to do—such as establishing a religion, quartering troops in private homes without consent, or seizing private property

focusquestions

- How were civil liberties "nationalized"?
- How does the First Amendment protect freedom of religion?
- How does the First Amendment protect free speech?
- Does the Second Amendment mean people have a right to own guns?
- What rights do people have if they are accused of a crime?
- Do people have a "right to privacy"?

without just compensation. Other restraints are procedural liberties, which deal with *how* the government is supposed to act. Civil liberties require a delicate balance between governmental power and governmental restraint. The government must be kept in check, with severe limits on its powers; yet, at the same time, the government must be given enough power to defend liberty and its benefits from those who seek to deprive others of them. This chapter will explore how this balance is struck. We will see how the Supreme Court, an undemocratic institution, is especially important in establishing the balance. Civil liberties also reflect how well the democratic principle of majority rule with minority rights works. The rights enumerated in the Bill of Rights and enforced through the courts can provide an important check on the power of the majority.

chapter contents

● A Brief History of the Bill of Rights

When the first Congress under the newly ratified Constitution met in late April of 1789, the most important item of business was the consideration of a proposal to add a bill of rights to the Constitution. Such a proposal had been turned down with little debate in the waning days of the Philadelphia Constitutional Convention in 1787, not because the delegates were against rights but because, as the Federalists, led by Alexander Hamilton, later argued, it was "not only unnecessary in the proposed Constitution but would even be dangerous."[1] First, according to Hamilton, a bill of rights would be irrelevant to a national government that was given only delegated powers in the first place. To put restraints on "powers which are not granted" could provide a pretext for governments to claim more powers than were in fact granted: "For why declare that things shall not be done which there is no power to do?"[2] Second, the Constitution was to Hamilton and the Federalists a bill of rights in itself, or contained provisions that amounted to a bill of rights without requiring additional amendments (see Table 4.1). For example, Article I, Section 9, included the right of **habeas corpus**, which prohibits the government from depriving a person of liberty without an open trial before a judge.

Despite the power of Hamilton's arguments, when the Constitution was submitted to the states for ratification, Antifederalists, most of whom had not been delegates in Philadelphia, picked up on the argument of Thomas Jefferson (who also had not been a delegate) that the omission of a bill of rights was a major imperfection of the new Constitution. The Federalists conceded that in order to gain ratification they would have to make an "unwritten but unequivocal pledge" to add a bill of rights that would include a confirmation (in what became the Tenth Amendment) of the understanding that all powers not expressly delegated to the national government or explicitly prohibited to the states were reserved to the states.[3]

"After much discussion and manipulation . . . at the delicate prompting of Washington and under the masterful prodding of Madison," the House of Representatives adopted seventeen amendments; of these, the Senate adopted twelve. Ten of the amendments were ratified by the necessary three-fourths of the states on December 15, 1791; from the start these ten were called the **Bill of Rights** (see Box 4.1).[4] The protections against improper government action contained in the Constitution and the Bill of Rights represent important **civil liberties**.

Nationalizing the Bill of Rights

The First Amendment provides that "Congress shall make no law . . ." But this is the only amendment in the Bill of Rights that addresses itself exclusively to the national government. For example, the Second Amendment provides that "the right of the

habeas corpus a court order demanding that an individual in custody be brought into court and shown the cause for detention

Bill of Rights the first ten amendments to the U.S. Constitution, ratified in 1791; they ensure certain rights and liberties to the people

civil liberties areas of personal freedom with which governments are constrained from interfering

Although the Bill of Rights has specified certain rights and liberties since it was ratified in 1791, the interpretation and protection of those rights and liberties has evolved over time. Many feared that the government's actions in the fight against terrorism following September 11, 2001, represented a turn away from protecting civil liberties.

TABLE 4.1

Rights in the Original Constitution (Not in the Bill of Rights)

CLAUSE	RIGHT ESTABLISHED
Article I, Sec. 9	guarantee of *habeas corpus*
Article I, Sec. 9	prohibition of **bills of attainder**
Article I, Sec. 9	prohibition of ***ex post facto* laws**
Article I, Sec. 9	prohibition against acceptance of titles of nobility, etc., from any foreign state
Article III	guarantee of trial by jury in state where crime was committed
Article III	treason defined and limited to the life of the person convicted, not to the person's heirs

bill of attainder a law that declares a person guilty of a crime without a trial

***ex post facto* law** a law that declares an action to be illegal after it has been committed

people to keep and bear Arms, shall not be infringed." And the Fifth Amendment says, among other things, that "no person shall . . . be twice put in jeopardy of life or limb" for the same crime. Since the First Amendment is the only part of the Bill of Rights that is explicit in its intention to put limits on Congress and therefore on the national government, a fundamental question inevitably arises: Do the remaining provisions of the Bill of Rights put limits only on the national government, or do they limit the state governments as well?

The Supreme Court first answered this question in 1833 by ruling that the Bill of Rights limited only the national government and not the state governments.[5] But in 1868, when the Fourteenth Amendment was added to the Constitution, the question arose once again. The Fourteenth Amendment reads as if it were meant to impose the Bill of Rights on the states:

> No *State* shall make or enforce any law which shall abridge the privileges or immunities of citizens of the United States; nor shall any *State* deprive any person of life, liberty, or property, without due process of law; nor deny to any person within its jurisdiction the equal protection of the laws [emphasis added].

This language sounds like an effort to extend the Bill of Rights in its entirety to all citizens, wherever they might reside.[6] Yet this was not the Supreme Court's interpretation of the amendment for nearly a hundred years. Within five years of ratification of the Fourteenth Amendment, the Court was making decisions as though the amendment had never been adopted.[7]

The only change in civil liberties during the first fifty-odd years following the adoption of the Fourteenth Amendment came in 1897, when the Supreme Court held that the due-process clause of the Fourteenth Amendment did in fact prohibit states from taking property for a public use without just compensation.[8] However, the Supreme Court had selectively "incorporated" into the Fourteenth Amendment only the property protection provision of the Fifth Amendment and no other clause of the Fifth or any other amendment of the Bill of Rights. In other words,

BOX 4.1

The Bill of Rights

Amendment I: Limits on Congress
Congress cannot make any law establishing a religion or abridging freedoms of religious exercise, speech, assembly, or petition.

Amendments II, III, IV: Limits on the Executive
The executive branch cannot infringe on the right of the people to keep arms (II), cannot arbitrarily take houses for militia (III), and cannot search for or seize evidence without a court warrant swearing to the probable existence of a crime (IV).

Amendments V, VI, VII, VIII: Limits on the Judiciary
The courts cannot hold trials for serious offenses without provision for a grand jury (V), a trial jury (VII), a speedy trial (VI), presentation of charges and confrontation by the accused of hostile witnesses (VI), and immunity from testimony against oneself and immunity from trial more than once for the same offense (V). Furthermore, neither bail nor punishment can be excessive (VIII), and no property can be taken without "just compensation" (V).

Amendments IX, X: Limits on the National Government
Any rights not enumerated are reserved to the state or the people (X), and the enumeration of certain rights in the Constitution should not be interpreted to mean that those are the only rights the people have (IX).

although according to the Fifth Amendment "due process" applied to the taking of life and liberty as well as property, only property was incorporated into the Fourteenth Amendment as a limitation on state power.

No further expansion of civil liberties via the Fourteenth Amendment occurred until 1925, when the Supreme Court held that freedom of speech is "among the fundamental personal rights and 'liberties' protected by the due process clause of the Fourteenth Amendment from impairment by the states."[9] In 1931, the Court added freedom of the press to that short list protected by the Bill of Rights from state action; in 1939, it added freedom of assembly.[10]

But that was as far as the Court was willing to go. As late as 1937, the Supreme Court was still unwilling to nationalize civil liberties beyond the First Amendment. The Constitution, as interpreted by the Supreme Court in *Palko v. Connecticut*, left standing the framework in which the states had the power to determine their own law on a number of fundamental issues. *Palko* established the principle of **selective incorporation,** by which the provisions of the Bill of Rights were to be considered one by one and selectively applied as limits on the states through the Fourteenth Amendment.[11] In order to make clear that "selective incorporation" should be narrowly interpreted, Justice Benjamin Cardozo, writing for an 8-to-1 majority, asserted that although many rights have value and importance, not all are of the same value and importance:

> [Not all rights are of] the very essence of a scheme of ordered liberty. To abolish them is not to violate a "principle of justice so rooted in the traditions and conscience of our people as to be ranked as fundamental." . . . What is true of jury trials and indictments is true also . . . of the immunity from compulsory self-incrimination

selective incorporation the process by which different protections in the Bill of Rights were incorporated into the Fourteenth Amendment, thus guaranteeing citizens protection from state as well as national governments [as in *Palko*]. . . . This too might be lost, and justice still be done. . . . If the Fourteenth Amendment has absorbed them [for example, freedom of thought and speech], the process of absorption has had its source in the belief that neither liberty nor justice would exist if they were sacrificed.

Palko left states with most of the powers they had possessed even before the adoption of the Fourteenth Amendment, including the power to pass laws segregating the races—a power, in fact, that the thirteen former Confederate states chose to continue to exercise on into the 1960s, despite *Brown v. Board of Education* in

TABLE 4.2

Incorporation of the Bill of Rights into the Fourteenth Amendment

SELECTED PROVISIONS AND AMENDMENTS	INCORPORATED	KEY CASE
Eminent domain (V)	1897	Chicago, Burlington, and Quincy R.R. v. Chicago
Freedom of speech (I)	1925	Gitlow v. New York
Freedom of press (I)	1931	Near v. Minnesota
Free exercise of religion (I)	1934	Hamilton v. Regents of the University of California
Freedom of assembly (I) and freedom to petition the government for redress of grievances (I)	1937	DeJonge v. Oregon
Freedom of assembly (I)	1939	Hague v. CIO
Non-establishment of state religion (I)	1947	Everson v. Board of Education
Freedom from unnecessary search and seizure (IV)	1949	Wolf v. Colorado
Freedom from warrantless search and seizure (IV) ("exclusionary rule")	1961	Mapp v. Ohio
Freedom from cruel and unusual punishment (VIII)	1962	Robinson v. California
Right to counsel in any criminal trial (VI)	1963	Gideon v. Wainwright
Right against self-incrimination and forced confessions (V)	1964	Mallory v. Hogan Escobedo v. Illinois
Right to counsel and remain silent (V)	1966	Miranda v. Arizona
Right against double jeopardy (V)	1969	Benton v. Maryland
Right to bear arms (II)	2010	McDonald v. Chicago

1954. The constitutional framework also left states with the power to engage in searches and seizures without a warrant, to indict accused persons without a grand jury, to deprive accused persons of trial by jury, to deprive persons of their right not to have to testify against themselves, to deprive accused persons of their right to confront adverse witnesses, and to prosecute accused persons more than once for the same crime.[12] Few states chose to use these kinds of powers, but some states did, and the power to do so was available for any state whose legislative majority or courts so chose.

So, until 1961, only the First Amendment and one clause of the Fifth Amendment had been clearly incorporated into the Fourteenth Amendment as binding on the states as well as on the national government.[13] After that, one by one, most of the important provisions of the Bill of Rights were incorporated into the Fourteenth Amendment and applied to the states. Table 4.2 shows the progress of this revolution in the interpretation of the Constitution.

The final provision of the Bill of Rights to be incorporated by the Supreme Court was the Second Amendment, which protects the right to bear arms. In the 2010 case of *McDonald v. Chicago* (08-1521), the Court held that the right of an individual "to keep and bear arms" is incorporated by the due process clause of the Fourteenth Amendment and applies to the states.[14]

The best way to examine the Bill of Rights today is the simplest way—to take the major provisions one at a time. Some of these provisions are settled areas of law, and others are not. The Court can reinterpret any one of them at any time.

The First Amendment and Freedom of Religion

Congress shall make no law respecting an establishment of religion, or prohibiting the free exercise thereof; or abridging the freedom of speech, or of the press; or the right of the people peaceably to assemble, and to petition the Government for a redress of grievances.

The Bill of Rights begins by guaranteeing freedom, and the First Amendment provides for that freedom in two distinct clauses: "Congress shall make no law [1] respecting an establishment of religion, or [2] prohibiting the free exercise thereof." The first clause is called the "establishment clause," and the second is called the "free exercise clause."

Separation between Church and State

The **establishment clause** and the idea of "no law" regarding the establishment of religion could be interpreted in several possible ways. One interpretation, which probably reflects the views of many of the First Amendment's authors, is that the government is prohibited from establishing an official church. Official state churches, such as the Church of England, were common in the eighteenth century and were viewed by many Americans as inconsistent with a republican form of

establishment clause the First Amendment clause that says that "Congress shall make no law respecting an establishment of religion." This law means that a "wall of separation" exists between church and state

The First Amendment affects everyday life in a multitude of ways. Because of its ban on state-sanctioned religion, the Supreme Court ruled in 2000 that student-initiated public prayer at school is illegal. Pregame prayer at public schools violates the establishment clause of the First Amendment.

Lemon test a rule articulated in *Lemon v. Kurtzman* that government action toward religion is permissible if it is secular in purpose, neither promotes nor inhibits the practice of religion, and does not lead to "excessive entanglement" with religion

government. Indeed, many American colonists had fled Europe to escape persecution for having rejected state-sponsored churches. A second possible interpretation is the view that the government may not take sides among competing religions but is not prohibited from providing assistance to religious institutions or ideas as long as it shows no favoritism. The United States accommodates religious beliefs in a variety of ways, from the reference to God on U.S. currency to the prayer that begins every session of Congress. These forms of religious establishment have never been struck down by the courts.

The third view regarding religious establishment, which for many years dominated Supreme Court decision making in this realm, is the idea of a "wall of separation" between church and state that cannot be breached by the government. The concept of a wall of separation was Jefferson's formulation and has figured in many Supreme Court cases arising under the establishment clause. For two centuries, Jefferson's words have had a powerful impact on our understanding of the proper relationship between church and state in America.

Despite the seeming absoluteness of the phrase "wall of separation," there is ample room to disagree on how high the wall is or of what materials it is composed. For example, the Court has been consistently strict in cases of school prayer, striking down such practices as Bible reading,[15] nondenominational prayer,[16] a moment of silence for meditation, and pregame prayer at public sporting events.[17] In each of these cases, the Court reasoned that school-sponsored observations, even of an apparently nondenominational character, are highly suggestive of school sponsorship and therefore violate the prohibition against establishment of religion. On the other hand, the Court has been quite permissive (and some would say inconsistent) about the public display of religious symbols, such as city-sponsored Nativity scenes in commercial or municipal areas.[18] And although the Court has consistently disapproved of government financial support for religious schools, even when the purpose has been purely educational and secular, the Court has permitted certain direct aid to students of such schools in the form of busing, for example. In 1971, after thirty years of cases involving religious schools, the Court attempted to specify some criteria to guide its decisions and those of lower courts, indicating, for example, in a decision invalidating state payments for the teaching of secular subjects in parochial schools, circumstances under which the Court might allow certain financial assistance. The case was *Lemon v. Kurtzman;* in its decision, the Supreme Court established three criteria to guide future cases, in what came to be called the ***Lemon* test**. The Court held that government aid to religious schools would be accepted as constitutional if (1) it had a secular purpose, (2) its effect was neither to advance nor to inhibit religion, and (3) it did not entangle government and religious institutions in each other's affairs.[19]

Although these restrictions make the *Lemon* test hard to pass, imaginative authorities are finding ways to do so, and the Supreme Court has demonstrated a willingness to let them. For example, in 1995, the Court narrowly ruled that a student religious group at the University of Virginia could not be denied student activities funds merely because it was a religious group espousing a particular viewpoint about a deity. The Court called the denial "viewpoint discrimination" that violated the free speech rights of the group.[20]

In 2004, the question of whether the phrase "under God" in the Pledge of Allegiance violates the "establishment clause" was brought before the Court. Written in 1892, the pledge had been used in schools without any religious references. But in 1954, in the midst of the Cold War, Congress voted to change the Pledge, in response to the "godless Communism" of the Soviet Union. The conversion was made by adding two key words, so that the revised version read: "I pledge allegiance to the flag of the United States of America and to the Republic for which it stands, one nation *under God*, indivisible, with liberty and justice for all."

Ever since the change was made, there has been a consistent murmuring of discontent from those who object to an officially sanctioned profession of belief in a deity as a violation of the religious freedom clause of the First Amendment. When saying the pledge, those who object to the phrase have often simply stayed silent during the two key words and then resumed for the rest of the pledge. In 2003, Michael A. Newdow, the atheist father of a kindergarten student in a California elementary school, forced the issue to the surface when he brought suit against the local school district. Newdow argued that the reference to God turned the daily recitation of the pledge into a religious exercise. A federal court ruled that although students were not required to recite the pledge at all, having to stand and listen to "under God" still violated the First Amendment's "establishment clause."

In 2005, the Supreme Court ruled that this display of the Ten Commandments at the Texas State Capitol in Austin did not violate the separation of church and state. However, the Court found that displays of the Ten Commandments inside two courthouses in Kentucky were unconstitutional.

The case was appealed to the Supreme Court and on June 14, 2004—exactly fifty years to the day after the adoption of "under God" in the pledge—the Court ruled that Newdow lacked a sufficient personal stake in the case to bring the complaint. This inconclusive decision by the Supreme Court left "under God" in the pledge while keeping the issue alive for possible resolution in a future case.

In 2005 the Supreme Court ruled, also inconclusively, on government-sponsored displays of religious symbols. Two 2005 cases involved displays of the Ten Commandments. In *Van Orden v. Perry*, the Court decided by a 5-to-4 margin that a display of the Ten Commandments at the Texas state capital did not violate the Constitution.[21] However, in *McCreary v. ACLU*, decided at the same time and also by a 5-to-4 margin, the Court determined that a display of the Ten Commandments inside two Kentucky courthouses was unconstitutional.[22] Justice Stephen Breyer, the swing vote in the two cases, said that the display in *Van Orden* had a secular purpose, whereas the displays in *McCreary* had a purely religious purpose. The key difference between the two cases is that the Texas display had been exhibited in a large park for forty years with other monuments related to the development of American law without any objections raised until this case, whereas the Kentucky display was erected much more recently and initially by itself, suggesting to some justices that its posting had a religious purpose. But most observers saw little difference between the two cases. Even Breyer was hard-pressed to explain his shifting votes except to say that *Van Orden* was a "borderline" case. Obviously, the issue of government-sponsored displays of religious symbols has not been settled.

Free Exercise of Religion

The **free exercise clause** protects the right to believe and to practice whatever religion one chooses; it also protects the right to be a nonbeliever. The precedent-setting case involving free exercise is *West Virginia State Board of Education v. Barnette* (1943), which involved the children of a family of Jehovah's Witnesses who refused to salute and pledge allegiance to the American flag on the grounds that their religious faith did not permit it. Three years earlier, the Court had upheld such a requirement and had permitted schools to expel students for refusing to salute the flag. But the entry of the United States into a war to defend democracy coupled with the ugly treatment to which the Jehovah's Witnesses' children had been subjected induced the Court to reverse itself and to endorse the free exercise of religion even when it may be offensive to the beliefs of the majority.[23]

Although the Supreme Court has been fairly consistent and strict in protecting the free exercise of religious belief, it has taken pains to distinguish between religious beliefs and *actions* based on those beliefs. In one case, for example, two Native Americans had been fired from their jobs for smoking peyote, an illegal drug. They claimed that they had been fired from their jobs illegally because smoking peyote was a religious sacrament protected by the free exercise clause. The Court disagreed with their claim in an important 1990 decision,[24] but Congress supported the claim and it went on to engage in an unusual controversy with the Court, involving the separation of powers as well as the proper application of the separation of church and state. Congress literally reversed the Court's 1990 decision with the enactment of the Religious Freedom Restoration Act of 1993 (RFRA), forbidding any federal agency or state government to restrict a person's free exercise of religion unless the federal agency or state government demonstrates that

for critical analysis

Despite the establishment clause, the United States still uses the motto "In God We Trust" and calls itself "one nation, under God." This Indiana license plate was introduced in 2007. Do you think this license plate is a violation of the separation of church and state?

its action "furthers a compelling government interest" and "is the least restrictive means of furthering that compelling governmental interest." One of the first applications of the RFRA was to a case brought by St. Peter's Catholic Church against the city of Boerne, Texas, which had denied permission to the church to enlarge its building because the building had been declared a historic landmark. The case went to federal court on the argument that the city had violated the church's religious freedom as guaranteed by Congress in RFRA. The Supreme Court declared RFRA unconstitutional, but on grounds rarely utilized, if not unique to this case: Congress had violated the separation of powers principle, infringing on the powers of the judiciary by going so far beyond its law-making powers that it ended up actually expanding the scope of religious rights rather than just enforcing them. The Court thereby implied that questions requiring a balancing of religious claims against public policy claims were reserved strictly to the judiciary.[25]

The First Amendment and Freedom of Speech and the Press

> Congress shall make no law . . . abridging the freedom of speech, or of the press . . .

Freedom of speech and of the press have a special place in American political thought. To begin with, democracy depends on the ability of individuals to talk to each other and to disseminate information and ideas. It would be difficult to conceive how democratic politics could function without free and open debate. Such debate, moreover, is seen as an essential mechanism for determining the quality or validity of competing ideas. As Justice Oliver Wendell Holmes said, "the best test of truth is the power of the thought to get itself accepted in the competition of the market. . . . That at any rate is the theory of our Constitution."[26] What is sometimes called the "marketplace of ideas" receives a good deal of protection from the courts. In 1938 the Supreme Court held that any legislation that attempts to restrict speech "is to be subjected to a more exacting judicial scrutiny . . . than are most other types of legislation."[27] This higher standard of judicial review came to be called strict scrutiny.

The doctrine of strict scrutiny places a heavy burden of proof on the government if it seeks to regulate or restrict speech. Americans are assumed to have the right to speak and to broadcast their ideas unless some compelling reason can be identified to stop them. But strict scrutiny does not mean that speech can never be regulated. Over the past 200 years, the courts have scrutinized many different forms of speech and constructed different principles and guidelines for each. According to the courts, although virtually all speech is protected by the Constitution, some forms of speech are entitled to a greater degree of protection than others. Let us examine what the federal courts have said about some of the major forms of speech.

Political Speech Political speech was the activity of greatest concern to the framers of the Constitution, even though some found it the most difficult form of speech to tolerate. Within seven years of the ratification of the Bill of Rights in 1791, Congress adopted the infamous Alien and Sedition Acts, which, among other things, made it a crime to say or publish anything that might tend to defame or bring into disrepute the government of the United States.

The first modern free speech case arose immediately after World War I. It involved persons who had been convicted under the federal Espionage Act of 1917 for opposing U.S. involvement in the war. The Supreme Court upheld the Espionage Act and refused to protect the speech rights of the defendants on the grounds that their activities—appeals to draftees to resist the draft—constituted a **"clear and present danger"** to security.[28] This is the first and most famous "test" for when government intervention or censorship can be permitted.

It was only after the 1920s that real progress toward a genuinely effective First Amendment was made. Since then, political speech has been consistently protected by the courts even when it has been deemed "insulting" or "outrageous." Here is the way the Supreme Court put it in one of its most important statements on the subject:

> The constitutional guarantees of free speech and free press do not permit a State to forbid or proscribe advocacy of the use of force or of law violation *except where such advocacy is directed to inciting or producing imminent lawless action and is likely to incite or produce such action* [emphasis added].[29]

In other words, as long as speech falls short of actually inciting action, it cannot be prohibited, even if it is hostile to or subversive of the government and its policies. This statement was made in the case of a Ku Klux Klan leader, Charles Brandenburg, who had been arrested and convicted of advocating "revengent" action against the president, Congress, and the Supreme Court, among others, if they continued "to suppress the white, Caucasian race." Although Brandenburg was not carrying a weapon, some of the members of his audience were. Nevertheless, the Supreme Court reversed the state courts and freed Brandenburg while also declaring Ohio's Criminal Syndicalism Act unconstitutional because it punished persons who "advocate, or teach the duty, necessity, or propriety [of violence] as a means of accomplishing industrial or political reform"; or who publish materials or "voluntarily assemble . . . to teach or advocate the doctrines of criminal syndicalism." The Supreme Court argued that the statute did not distinguish "mere advocacy" from "incitement to imminent lawless action." It would be difficult to go much further in protecting freedom of speech.

Another area of recent expansion of political speech—the participation of wealthy persons and corporations in political campaigns—was opened up in 1976, with the Supreme Court's decision in *Buckley v. Valeo*. Campaign finance reform laws of the early 1970s, arising out of the Watergate scandal, sought to put severe limits on campaign spending. In the *Buckley* case, a number of important provisions were declared unconstitutional on the basis of a new principle that spending money by or on behalf of candidates is a form of speech protected by the First Amendment. (For more details, see Chapter 10.)

The issue came up again in 2003, with passage of a new and still more severe campaign finance law, the Bipartisan Campaign Reform Act (BCRA). In *McConnell v. FEC* (Federal Election Commission), the 5-to-4 majority seriously reduced the area of speech protected by the *Buckley v. Valeo* decision by holding that Congress was well within its power to put limits on the amounts individuals could spend, and to put severe limits on the amounts of "soft money" that corporations and their PACs could spend. The Court argued that "the selling of access . . . has given rise to the appearance of undue influence [that justifies] regulations impinging on First Amendment rights . . . in order to curb corruption or the appearance of corruption."[30] In the *McConnell* case, the Court also upheld BCRA's limitations on "issue advertising." The Act prohibited political advocacy groups from running ads that mentioned a candidate within thirty days of a primary election and sixty days of a general election. This ban was justified on the argument that wealthy special interests could affect election outcomes with last-minute ad campaigns. However, in its 2007 decision in the case of *Federal Election Commission v. Wisconsin Right to Life*, the Court reversed itself, declaring that such ads were protected speech and could not be prohibited so long as they focused mainly on issues and were not simply appeals to vote for or against a specific candidate.[31]

In 2008, in the case of *Davis v. Federal Election Commission*, the Supreme Court struck down another element of BCRA, the so-called millionaire's amendment, which had increased contribution limits for opponents of self-funded, wealthy candidates.[32] Even more recently, in the 2010 case of *Citizens United v. Federal Election Commission*, the Supreme Court declared that the First Amendment prohibited BCRA's ban on corporate funding of independent political broadcasts aimed at electing or defeating particular candidates.[33] The case arose in 2008 when Citizens United, a conservative nonprofit organization, sought to show its film, *Hillary: The Movie*, a documentary aimed at attacking Clinton's presidential bid during the 2008 Democratic primaries. In its 5–4 decision, the Supreme Court ruled that the Constitution prohibits the government from regulating political speech and that therefore the government could not ban this type of political spending by corporations. The Court's decision in this case has been controversial. Republicans, seeing themselves as the main beneficiaries of corporate ads, hailed the decision as a victory for free speech. Democrats denounced the decision, with President Obama calling it, "a major victory for big oil, Wall Street banks, health insurance companies, and the other powerful interests that marshal their power every day in Washington to drown out the voices of everday Americans."[34] Congressional Democrats said they would consider ways to rewrite the law to circumvent the Court's decision.

Symbolic Speech, Speech Plus, and the Rights of Assembly and Petition The First Amendment treats the freedoms of assembly and petition as equal to the freedoms of religion and political speech. Freedom of assembly and freedom of petition are closely associated with speech but go beyond it to speech associated with action. Since at least 1931, the Supreme Court has sought to protect actions that are designed to send a political message. (Usually the purpose of a symbolic act is not only to send a direct message but also to draw a crowd—to do something spectacular in order to attract spectators to the action and thus strengthen the message.) Therefore the Court held unconstitutional a California statute making it a felony to display a red flag "as a sign, symbol or emblem of opposition to organized government."[35] Although today there are limits on how far one can go with actions that symbolically convey a message, the protection of such action is very broad. Thus, although the Court upheld a federal statute making it a crime to burn draft cards to protest the Vietnam War on the grounds that the government had a compelling interest in preserving draft cards as

The Supreme Court has interpreted the freedom of speech as extending to symbolic acts of political protest, such as flag burning. On several occasions—most recently in 2006—a resolution for a constitutional amendment to ban flag burning has passed in the House of Representatives but has never found enough support in the Senate.

part of the conduct of the war itself, it considered the wearing of black armbands to school a protected form of assembly for symbolic action.

Another example is the burning of the American flag as a symbol of protest. In 1984, at a political rally held during the Republican National Convention in Dallas, Texas, a political protester burned an American flag in violation of a Texas statute that prohibited desecration of a venerated object. In a 5-to-4 decision, the Supreme Court declared the Texas law unconstitutional on the grounds that flag burning was expressive conduct protected by the First Amendment.[36] Congress reacted immediately with a proposal for a constitutional amendment reversing the Court's Texas decision, and when the amendment failed to receive the necessary two-thirds majority in the Senate, Congress passed the Flag Protection Act of 1989. Protesters promptly violated this act, and their prosecution moved quickly into the federal district court, which declared the new law unconstitutional. The Supreme Court, in another 5-to-4 decision, affirmed the lower court decision.[37] A renewed effort began in Congress to propose a constitutional amendment that would reverse the Supreme Court and place this form of expressive conduct outside the realm of protected speech or assembly. Since 1995, the House of Representatives has four times passed a resolution for a constitutional amendment to ban flag burning, but each time the Senate has failed to go along.[38] In a 2003 decision the Supreme Court struck down a Virginia cross-burning statute. In that case, the Court ruled that states could make cross burning a crime as long as the statute requires prosecutors to prove that the act of setting fire to the cross was intended to intimidate. Former Justice Sandra Day O'Connor wrote for the majority that the First Amendment permits the government to forbid cross burning as a "particularly virulent form of intimidation" but not when the act was "a form of symbolic expression."[39] This decision will almost inevitably become a more generalized First Amendment protection of any conduct, including flag burning, that can be shown to be a form of symbolic expression.

Closer to the original intent of the assembly and petition clause is the category of **"speech plus"**—following speech with physical activity such as picketing, distributing leaflets, and other forms of peaceful demonstration or assembly. Such assemblies are consistently protected by courts under the First Amendment; state and local laws regulating such activities are closely scrutinized and frequently overturned. But the same assembly on private property is quite another matter and can in many circumstances be regulated. For example, the directors of a shopping center can lawfully prohibit an assembly protesting a war or supporting a ban on abortion. Assemblies in public areas can also be restricted under some circumstances, especially when the assembly or demonstration jeopardizes the health, safety, or rights of others. This condition was the basis of the Supreme Court's decision to uphold a lower court order that restricted the access abortion protesters had to the entrances of abortion clinics.[40]

An unusual "speech plus" case decided in 2006 was *Rumsfeld v. FAIR.*[41] A number of law schools had banned military recruiters from their campuses to protest the military's antigay policies. The government responded by threatening to cut off federal funding to schools that joined the ban. The schools argued, in turn, that the government was violating their constitutional right to voice opposition to its policies. The Supreme Court ruled that the government could require schools to host recruiters as a condition for funding. Recruitment, said the Court, was not a form of expression protected by the Constitution; schools remained completely free to voice their opposition to the military's policies even as they hosted the recruiters.

"speech plus" speech accompanied by conduct such as sit-ins, picketing, and demonstrations; protection of this form of speech under the First Amendment is conditional, and restrictions imposed by state or local authorities are acceptable if properly balanced by considerations of public order

Freedom of the Press

For all practical purposes, freedom of speech implies and includes freedom of the press. With the exception of the broadcast media, which are subject to federal regulation, the press is protected under the doctrine against **prior restraint**. Beginning with the landmark 1931 case of *Near v. Minnesota*, the U.S. Supreme Court has held that, except under the most extraordinary circumstances, the First Amendment of the Constitution prohibits government agencies from seeking to prevent newspapers or magazines from publishing whatever they wish.[42] Indeed, in the case of *New York Times v. U.S.*, the so-called *Pentagon Papers* case, the Supreme Court ruled that the government could not even block publication of secret Defense Department documents furnished to the *New York Times* by an opponent of the Vietnam War who had obtained the documents illegally.[43] In a 1990 case, however, the Supreme Court upheld a lower court order restraining Cable News Network (CNN) from broadcasting tapes of conversations between the former Panamanian dictator Manuel Noriega and his lawyer, supposedly recorded by the U.S. government. By a vote of 7 to 2, the Court held that CNN could be restrained from broadcasting the tapes until the trial court in the Noriega case had listened to the tapes and had decided whether their broadcast would violate Noriega's right to a fair trial.

Another press freedom issue that the courts have often been asked to decide is the question of whether journalists can be compelled to reveal their sources of information. Journalists assert that if they cannot assure sources of confidentiality, the flow of information will be reduced and press freedom effectively curtailed. Government agencies, however, aver that names of news sources may be relevant to criminal or even national-security investigations. More than thirty states have "shield laws," which to varying degrees, protect journalistic sources. There is, however, no federal shield law. The Supreme Court has held that the press has no constitutional right to withhold information in court.[44] In 2005, a *New York Times* reporter, Judith Miller, was jailed for contempt of court for refusing to tell a federal grand jury the name of a confidential source in a case involving the leaked identity

prior restraint an effort by a governmental agency to block the publication of material it deems libelous or harmful in some other way; censorship. In the United States, the courts forbid prior restraint except under the most extraordinary circumstances

Journalists often claim that the right to protect the names of their sources is essential to a free press. In 2005, a New York Times reporter, Judith Miller, went to jail rather than reveal the name of a confidential source in court.

of the CIA analyst Valerie Plame. Plame's husband, Joseph Wilson, had been critical of the Bush administration's Iraq policies.

Libel and Slander Some speech is not protected at all. If a written statement is made in "reckless disregard of the truth" and is considered damaging to the victim because it is "malicious, scandalous, and defamatory," it can be punished as **libel**. If an oral statement of such nature is made, it can be punished as **slander**.

Today, most libel suits involve freedom of the press, and the realm of free press is enormous. Historically, newspapers were subject to the law of libel, which provided that newspapers that printed false and malicious stories could be compelled to pay damages to those they defamed. In recent years, however, American courts have greatly narrowed the meaning of libel and made it extremely difficult, particularly for politicians or other public figures, to win a libel case against a newspaper. In the important 1964 case of *New York Times v. Sullivan*, the Court held that to be deemed libelous, a story about a public official not only had to be untrue, but also had to result from "actual malice" or "reckless disregard" for the truth.[45] In other words, the newspaper had to print false and malicious material *deliberately*. In practice, it is nearly impossible to prove that a paper deliberately printed maliciously false information, and it is especially difficult for a politician or other public figure to win a libel case. Essentially, the print media have been able to publish anything they want about a public figure.

However, in at least one case, the Court has opened up the possibility for public officials to file libel suits against the press. In 1985, the Court held that the press was immune to libel only when the printed material was "a matter of public concern." In other words, in future cases a newspaper would have to show that the public official was engaged in activities that were indeed *public*. This new principle has made the press more vulnerable to libel suits, but it still leaves an enormous realm of freedom for the press. For example, the Reverend Jerry Falwell, the leader of the Moral Majority, lost his libel suit against *Hustler* magazine even though the magazine had published a cartoon of Falwell showing him having drunken intercourse with his mother in an outhouse. A unanimous Supreme Court rejected a jury verdict in favor of damages for "emotional distress" on the grounds that parodies, no matter how outrageous, are protected because "outrageousness" is too subjective a test and thus would interfere with the free flow of ideas protected by the First Amendment.[46]

With the emergence of the Internet as an important communications medium, the courts have had to decide how traditional libel law applies to Internet content. In 1995, the New York courts held that an online bulletin board could be held responsible for the libelous content of material posted by a third party. To protect Internet service providers, Congress subsequently enacted legislation absolving service providers of responsibility for third-party posts. The federal courts have generally upheld this law and declared that providers are immune to suits regarding the content of material posted by others.[47]

Obscenity and Pornography If libel and slander cases can be difficult because of the problem of determining the truth of statements and whether those statements are malicious and damaging, cases involving pornography and obscenity can be even stickier. It is easy to say that pornography and obscenity fall outside the realm of protected speech, but it is impossible to draw a clear line defining exactly where protection ends and unprotected speech begins. Not until 1957 did the Supreme Court confront this problem, and it did so with a definition of obscenity that may

libel a written statement made in "reckless disregard of the truth" that is considered damaging to a victim because it is "malicious, scandalous, and defamatory"

slander an oral statement, made in "reckless disregard of the truth," which is considered damaging to the victim because it is "malicious, scandalous, and defamatory"

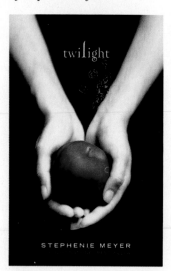

One of the more visible issues of free speech has been the banning of certain books in public schools. For example, in 2009, one of the most frequently banned books was Twilight, *a vampire saga by Stephenie Meyer.*

have caused more confusion than it cleared up. In writing the Court's opinion, Justice William Brennan defined obscenity as speech or writing that appeals to the "prurient interest"—that is, books, magazines, films, and other material whose purpose is to excite lust as this appears "to the average person, applying contemporary community standards." Even so, Brennan added, the work should be judged obscene only when it is "utterly without redeeming social importance."[48] Instead of clarifying the Court's view, Brennan's definition actually caused more confusion. In 1964, Justice Potter Stewart confessed that, although he found pornography impossible to define, "I know it when I see it."[49]

All attempts by the courts to define pornography and obscenity have proved impractical because each instance required courts to screen thousands of pages of print material and feet of film alleged to be pornographic. The vague and impractical standards that had been developed meant ultimately that almost nothing could be banned on the grounds that it was pornographic and obscene. An effort was made to strengthen the restrictions in 1973, when the Supreme Court expressed its willingness to define pornography as a work that (1) as a whole, is deemed prurient by the "average person" according to "community standards"; (2) depicts sexual conduct "in a patently offensive way"; and (3) lacks "serious literary, artistic, political, or scientific value." This definition meant that pornography would be determined by local rather than national standards. Thus, a local bookseller might be prosecuted for selling a volume that was a best-seller nationally but that was deemed pornographic locally.[50] This new definition of standards did not help much either, and not long after 1973 the Court began again to review all such community antipornography laws, reversing most of them.

In recent years, the battle against obscene speech has been against "cyberporn"— pornography on the Internet. Opponents of this form of expression argue that it should be banned because of the easy access children have to the Internet. The first major effort to regulate the content of the Internet occurred on February 1, 1996, when the 104th Congress passed major telecommunications legislation. Attached to the Telecommunications Act was an amendment, called the Communications Decency Act (CDA), that was designed to regulate the online transmission of obscene material. The constitutionality of the CDA was immediately challenged in court by a coalition of interests led by the American Civil Liberties Union (ACLU). In the 1997 case of *Reno v. ACLU*, the Supreme Court struck down the CDA, ruling that it suppressed speech that "adults have a constitutional right to receive" and that governments may not limit the adult population to messages that are fit for children. Supreme Court Justice John Paul Stevens described the Internet as the "town crier" of the modern age and said that the Internet was entitled to the greatest degree of First Amendment protection possible.[51] Congress again tried limiting children's access to Internet pornography with the 2001 Children's Internet Protection Act, which required public libraries to install antipornography filters on all library computers with Internet access. Though the act made cooperation a condition for receiving federal subsidies, it did permit librarians to unblock a site at the request of an adult patron. The law was challenged, and in 2003 the Court upheld it, asserting that its provisions did not violate library patrons' First Amendment rights.[52] In 2003, Congress enacted the PROTECT Act that outlawed efforts to sell child pornography via the Internet. The Supreme Court upheld this act in the 2008 case of *U.S. v. Williams* in which the majority said that criminalizing efforts to purvey child pornography did not violate free speech guarantees.[53]

In 2000, the Supreme Court also extended the highest degree of First Amendment protection to cable (not broadcast) television. In *U.S. v. Playboy Entertainment*

Group, the Court struck down a portion of the Telecommunications Act of 1996 that required cable TV companies to limit the broadcast of sexually explicit programming to late night hours. In its decision, the Court noted that the law already provided parents with the means to restrict access to sexually explicit cable channels through various blocking devices. Moreover, such programming could come into the home only if parents decided to purchase such channels in the first place.

Fighting Words and Hate Speech Speech can also lose its protected position when it moves toward the sphere of action. "Expressive speech," for example, is protected until it moves from the symbolic realm to the realm of actual conduct—to direct incitement of damaging conduct with the use of so-called **fighting words**. In 1942, the Supreme Court upheld the arrest and conviction of a man who had violated a state law forbidding the use of offensive language in public. He had called the arresting officer a "goddamned racketeer" and "a damn Fascist." When his case reached the Supreme Court, the arrest was upheld on the grounds that the First Amendment provides no protection for such offensive language because such words "are no essential part of any exposition of ideas."[54] This case was reaffirmed in a much more famous and more important case decided at the height of the Cold War, when the Supreme Court held that

> there is no substantial public interest in permitting certain kinds of utterances: the lewd and obscene, the profane, the libelous, and the insulting or "fighting" words— those which by their very utterance inflict injury or tend to incite an immediate breach of the peace.[55]

Since that time, however, the Supreme Court has reversed almost every conviction based on arguments that the speaker had used "fighting words." But again, it does not mean this is an absolutely settled area. In recent years, the increased activism of minority and women's groups has prompted a movement against words that might be construed as offensive to members of a particular group. But how should we determine what words are "fighting words" and therefore fall outside the protections of the freedom of speech?

One category of conditionally protected speech is the speech of high school students in public schools. In 1986, the Supreme Court backed away from a broad protection of student free speech rights by upholding the punishment of a high school student for making a sexually suggestive speech. The Court opinion held that such speech interfered with the school's goal of teaching students the limits of socially acceptable behavior.[56] Two years later the Supreme Court took another conservative step by restricting students' speech and press rights even further, defining them as part of the educational process and not to be treated with the same standard as adult speech in a regular public forum.[57] A later case involving high school students is the 2007 case of *Morse v. Frederick*.[58] This case dealt with the policies of Juneau-Douglas High School in Juneau, Alaska. In 2002, the Olympic torch relay passed Juneau on its way to Salt Lake City for the opening of the Winter Olympics. As the torch passed Juneau-Douglas High, a senior, Joseph Frederick, unfurled a banner that read, "Bong Hits 4 Jesus." The school's principal promptly suspended Frederick, who then brought suit for reinstatement, alleging that his free-speech rights had been violated. Like most of America's public schools, Juneau High prohibits assemblies or expressions on school grounds that advocate illegal drug use. Schools say that some federal aid is contingent on this policy. Civil libertarians, of course, see such policies as restricting students' right to free speech.

fighting words speech that directly incites damaging conduct

for critical analysis

Should hate speech be protected? Is it contradictory that many who strongly support free thought and expression draw the line on protecting "thought we hate"?

The Supreme Court has ruled that high school students' speech can be restricted. In a 2007 case involving a student who displayed the banner, at left, the Court found that the school principal had not violated the student's right to free speech by suspending him.

Speaking for the Court's majority, Chief Justice Roberts said that the First Amendment did not require schools to permit students to advocate illegal drug use.

In addition, scores of universities have attempted to develop speech codes to suppress utterances deemed to be racial or ethnic slurs. Similar developments have taken place in large corporations, both public and private, in which many successful complaints and lawsuits have been brought, alleging that the words of employers or their supervisors create a "hostile or abusive working environment." The Supreme Court has held that "sexual harassment" that creates a "hostile working environment" includes "unwelcome sexual advances, requests for sexual favors, and other *verbal* or physical conduct of a sexual nature"[59] [emphasis added]. A fundamental free speech issue is involved in these regulations of hostile speech.

Many jurisdictions have drafted ordinances banning hate speech forms of expression designed to assert hatred toward one or another group, be they African Americans, Jews, Muslims, or others. Such ordinances seldom pass constitutional muster. The leading Supreme Court case in this realm is the 1992 decision in *R.A.V. v. City of St. Paul.*[60] Here, a white teenager was arrested for burning a cross on the lawn of a black family in violation of a municipal ordinance that banned cross burning. The Court ruled that such an ordinance must be *content neutral,* that is, not prohibiting actions directed at some groups but not others. The statute in question prohibited only cross burning—typically an expression of hatred of African Americans. Since a statute banning all forms of hateful expression would be deemed overly broad, the *R.A.V.* standard suggests that virtually all hate speech is constitutionally protected.

Commercial Speech Commercial speech, such as newspaper or television advertisements, does not have full First Amendment protection because it cannot be considered political speech. Initially considered to be entirely outside the protection of the First Amendment, commercial speech made gains during the twentieth century. However, some commercial speech is still unprotected and therefore regulated. For example, the regulation of false and misleading advertising by the Federal Trade Commission is an old and well-established power of the federal government. The Supreme Court long ago approved the constitutionality of laws prohibiting the electronic media from carrying cigarette advertising.[61] The Court has upheld a state university ban on Tupperware parties in college dormitories.[62] It has upheld city ordinances prohibiting the posting of all commercial signs on public property (as long as the ban is total, so that there is no hint of censorship).[63] And the Supreme Court, in a heated 5-to-4 decision written by Chief Justice William Rehnquist, upheld Puerto Rico's statute restricting gambling advertising aimed at residents of Puerto Rico.[64]

However, the gains far outweigh the losses in the effort to expand the protection commercial speech enjoys under the First Amendment. "In part, this reflects the growing appreciation that commercial speech is part of the free flow of information necessary for informed choice and democratic participation."[65] For example, the Court in 1975 struck down a state statute making it a misdemeanor to sell or circulate newspapers encouraging abortions; the Court ruled that the statute infringed on constitutionally protected speech and on the right of the reader to make informed choices.[66] On a similar basis, the Court reversed its own earlier decisions upholding laws that prohibited dentists and other professionals from advertising their services. For the Court, medical service advertising was a matter of health that could be advanced by the free flow of information.[67] In 1996, the Supreme Court struck down Rhode Island laws and regulations banning the advertisement of liquor prices as a violation of the First Amendment.[68] And in a 2001 case, the Supreme Court ruled that a Massachusetts ban on all cigarette advertising violated the First Amendment right of the tobacco industry to advertise its products to adult consumers.[69] These instances of commercial speech are significant in themselves, but they are all the more significant because they indicate the breadth and depth of the freedom existing today to direct appeals to a large public, not only to sell goods and services but also to mobilize people for political purposes.

The Second Amendment and the Right to Bear Arms

A well regulated Militia, being necessary to the security of a free State, the right of the people to keep and bear Arms, shall not be infringed.

The point and purpose of the Second Amendment is the provision for militias; they were to be the backing of the government for the maintenance of local public order. "Militia" was understood at the time of the Founding to be a military or police resource for state governments, and militias were specifically distinguished from armies and troops, which came within the sole constitutional jurisdiction of Congress.

Thus, the right of the people "to keep and bear Arms" is based on and associated with participation in state militias. The reference to citizens keeping arms underscored the fact that in the 1700s, state governments could not be relied on to provide firearms to militia members, so citizens eligible to serve in militias (white

The Second Amendment arouses as much controversy as the First. It is constitutionally guaranteed, although an estimated 80 percent of Americans support some form of gun control.

males between the ages of eighteen and forty-five) were expected to keep their own firearms at the ready. In the late nineteenth century, some citizens sought to form their own *private* militias, but the Supreme Court cut that short with a ruling that militias are a military or police resource of state governments.[70] In 2008, the U.S. Supreme Court declared that the Second Amendment also protected an individual's right to possess a firearm for private use.[71] In the *Heller* case, the Court struck down a District of Columbia law that was designed to make it nearly impossible for private individuals to legally purchase firearms. The District of Columbia is an entity of the federal government, and the Court did not indicate that its ruling applied to state firearms laws. However, in the 2010 case of *McDonald v. Chicago*, the Court struck down a Chicago firearms ordinance and applied the Second Amendment to the states as well,[72] making this the first new incorporation decision by the Court in forty years.

Rights of the Criminally Accused

Except for the First Amendment, most of the battle to apply the Bill of Rights to the states was fought over the various protections granted to individuals who are accused of a crime, who are suspects in the commission of a crime, or who are brought before the court as a witness to a crime. The Fourth, Fifth, Sixth, and Eighth Amendments, taken together, are the essence of the **due process of law**, even though this fundamental concept does not appear until the very last words of the Fifth Amendment. In the next sections we will look at specific cases that illuminate the dynamics of this important constitutional issue. The procedural safeguards that we will discuss may seem remote to most law-abiding citizens, but

due process of law the right of every citizen against arbitrary action by national or state governments

they help define the limits of government action against the personal liberty of every citizen. Many Americans believe that "legal technicalities" are responsible for setting many actual criminals free. In many cases, that is absolutely true. In fact, setting defendants free is the very purpose of the requirements that constitute due process. One of America's traditional and most strongly held juridical values is that "it is far worse to convict an innocent man than to let a guilty man go free."[73] In civil suits, verdicts rest on "the preponderance of the evidence"; in criminal cases, guilt has to be proven "beyond a reasonable doubt"—a far higher standard. The provisions for due process in the Bill of Rights were added in order to improve the probability that the standard of "reasonable doubt" will be respected.

A loophole in gun purchase laws allowed a student at Virginia Tech with a history of mental illness to purchase the handguns that he used to kill thirty-two fellow students and wound many others. Following the tragedy, both the state of Virginia and the national government strengthened the requirements for background checks on gun buyers.

The Fourth Amendment and Searches and Seizures

The right of the people to be secure in their persons, houses, papers, and effects, against unreasonable searches and seizures, shall not be violated, and no Warrants shall issue, but upon probable cause, supported by Oath or affirmation, and particularly describing the place to be searched, and the persons or things to be seized.

The purpose of the Fourth Amendment is to guarantee the security of citizens against unreasonable (i.e., improper) searches and seizures. In 1990, the Supreme Court summarized its understanding of the Fourth Amendment brilliantly and succinctly: "A search compromises the individual interest in privacy; a seizure deprives the individual of dominion over his or her person or property."[74] But how are we to define what is reasonable and what is unreasonable?

The 1961 case of *Mapp v. Ohio* illustrates the beauty and the agony of one of the most important of the procedures that have grown out of the Fourth Amendment—the **exclusionary rule**, which prohibits evidence obtained during an illegal search from being introduced in a trial. Acting on a tip that Dollree (Dolly) Mapp was harboring a suspect in a bombing incident, several policemen forcibly entered Ms. Mapp's house, claiming they had a warrant to look for the bombing suspect. The police did not find the bombing suspect but did find some materials connected to a local numbers racket (an illegal gambling operation) and a quantity of "obscene materials," in violation of an Ohio law banning possession of such materials. Although the warrant was never produced, the evidence that had been seized was admitted by a court, and Ms. Mapp was charged and convicted of illegal possession of obscene materials.

By the time Ms. Mapp's appeal reached the Supreme Court, the issue of obscene materials had faded into obscurity, and the question before the Court was whether any evidence produced under the circumstances of the search of her home was admissible. The Court's opinion affirmed the exclusionary rule: under the Fourth Amendment (applied to the states through the Fourteenth Amendment), "all evidence obtained by searches and seizures in violation of the Constitution . . . is inadmissible."[75] This means that even people who are clearly guilty of the crime of which they are accused must not be convicted if the only evidence for their conviction was obtained illegally. This idea was expressed by Supreme Court

exclusionary rule the ability of courts to exclude evidence obtained in violation of the Fourth Amendment

Justice Benjamin Cardozo nearly a century ago when he wrote that "the criminal is to go free because the constable has blundered."

The exclusionary rule is the most severe restraint ever imposed by the Constitution and the courts on the behavior of the police. The exclusionary rule is a dramatic restriction because it rules out precisely the evidence that produces a conviction; it frees those people who are *known* to have committed the crime of which they have been accused. Because it works so dramatically in favor of persons known to have committed a crime, the Court has since softened the application of the rule. In recent years, the federal courts have relied on a discretionary use of the exclusionary rule, whereby they make a judgment as to the "nature and quality of the intrusion." It is thus difficult to know ahead of time whether a defendant will or will not be protected from an illegal search under the Fourth Amendment.[76]

In a number of instances, such as in the course of an arrest, the authorities can conduct searches without obtaining warrants. In other instances, the authorities may obtain warrants in anticipation of some subsequent need. In 2006, in the case of *U.S. v. Grubbs*, the Supreme Court ruled that the police could conduct searches using such "anticipatory warrants."[77] These warrants are issued when the police know that incriminating material is not yet present but have reason to believe that it will eventually arrive at a particular premises. The warrant is held until the police are ready to conduct their search.

Another recent issue involving the Fourth Amendment is the controversy over mandatory drug testing. Such tests are most widely applied to public employees, and in an important case the Supreme Court has upheld the U.S. Customs Service's drug-testing program for its employees.[78] The same year the Court approved drug and alcohol tests for railroad workers if they were involved in serious accidents.[79] After Court approvals of those two cases in 1989, more than forty federal agencies initiated mandatory employee drug tests. These growing practices gave rise to public appeals against the general practice of "suspicionless testing" of employees, in violation of the Fourth Amendment. A 1995 case, in which the Court upheld a public school district's policy requiring all students participating in interscholastic sports to submit to random drug tests, surely contributed to the efforts of federal, state, and local agencies to initiate random and suspicionless drug and alcohol testing.[80] The most recent cases suggest, however, that the Court is beginning to consider limits on the war against drugs. In a decisive 8-to-1 decision in 2007, the Court applied the Fourth Amendment as a shield against "state action that diminishes personal privacy" when the officials in question are not performing high-risk or safety-sensitive tasks.[81]

More recently, the Court found it unconstitutional for police to use trained dogs in roadblocks set up to look for drugs in cars. Unlike drunk-driving roadblocks, where public safety is directly involved, narcotics roadblocks "cannot escape the Fourth Amendment's requirement that searches be based on suspicion of individual wrongdoing."[82] In 2007, the Court extended protection against unlawful searches to passengers in cars that have been stopped by the police. Passengers, said the Court, have the same right as drivers to challenge the validity of a search.[83] The Court also ruled that a public hospital cannot constitutionally test maternity patients for illegal drug use without their consent,[84] and that the police may not use thermal imaging devices to detect suspicious patterns of heat emerging from private homes without obtaining the usual search warrant.[85] In 2009, the Court ruled against an Arizona school district that conducted a strip search of a thirteen-year-old student suspected of hiding ibuprofen in her underwear.[86]

In the case of Dollree Mapp v. Ohio, *the Supreme Court interpreted the Fourth Amendment to mean that if incriminating material is found through illegal search and seizure, it cannot be used as evidence in court.*

The Fifth Amendment

No person shall be held to answer for a capital, or otherwise infamous crime, unless on a presentment or indictment of a Grand Jury, except in cases arising in the land or naval forces, or in the Militia, when in actual service in time of War or public danger; nor shall any person be subject for the same offence to be twice put in jeopardy of life or limb; nor shall be compelled in any criminal case to be a witness against himself, nor be deprived of life, liberty, or property, without due process of law; nor shall private property be taken for public use, without just compensation.

grand jury jury that determines whether sufficient evidence is available to justify a trial; grand juries do not rule on the accused's guilt or innocence

Grand Juries The first clause of the Fifth Amendment, the right to a **grand jury** to determine whether a trial is warranted, is considered "the oldest institution known to the Constitution."[87] Grand juries play an important role in federal criminal cases. However, the provision for a grand jury is the one important civil liberties provision of the Bill of Rights that was not incorporated into the Fourteenth Amendment to apply to state criminal prosecutions. Thus, some states operate without grand juries. In such states, the prosecuting attorney simply files a "bill of information" affirming that there is sufficient evidence available to justify a trial. If the accused person is to be held in custody, the prosecutor must take the available information before a judge to determine that the evidence shows probable cause.

double jeopardy the Fifth Amendment right providing that a person cannot be tried twice for the same crime

Double Jeopardy "Nor shall any person be subject for the same offence to be twice put in jeopardy of life or limb" is the constitutional protection from **double jeopardy**, or being tried more than once for the same crime. The protection from double jeopardy was at the heart of the *Palko* case in 1937, which, as we saw earlier in this chapter, also established the principle of selective incorporation of the Bill of Rights. In that case, the state of Connecticut had indicted Frank Palko for first-degree murder, but a lower court had found him guilty of only second-degree murder and sentenced him to life in prison. Unhappy with the verdict, the state of Connecticut appealed the conviction to its highest court, won the appeal, got a new trial, and then succeeded in getting Palko convicted of first-degree murder. Palko appealed to the Supreme Court on what seemed an open-and-shut case of double jeopardy. Yet, although the majority of the Court agreed that this could indeed be considered a case of double jeopardy, they decided that double jeopardy was *not* one of the provisions of the Bill of Rights incorporated into the Fourteenth Amendment as a restriction on the powers of the states. It took more than thirty years for the Court to nationalize the constitutional protection against double jeopardy. Palko was eventually executed for the crime, because he lived in the state of Connecticut rather than in a state whose constitution included a guarantee against double jeopardy.

The modern interpretation of the Fifth Amendment was shaped by the 1966 case Miranda v. Arizona. *Ernesto Miranda confessed to kidnapping and rape. Since he was never told that he was not required to answer police questions, his case was appealed on the grounds that his right against self-incrimination had been violated.*

Self-Incrimination Perhaps the most significant liberty found in the Fifth Amendment, and the one most familiar to many Americans who watch television crime shows, is the guarantee that no citizen "shall be compelled in any criminal case to be a witness against himself." The most famous case concerning self-incrimination is one of such importance that Chief Justice Earl Warren assessed its results as going "to the very root of our concepts of American criminal jurisprudence."[88] Twenty-three-year-old Ernesto Miranda was sentenced to between twenty and

very concept of sovereignty. The Fifth Amendment neither invents eminent domain nor takes it away; its purpose is to put limits on that inherent power through procedures that require a showing of a public purpose and the provision of fair payment for the taking of someone's property. This provision is now universally observed in all U.S. principalities, but it has not always been meticulously observed.

The first modern case confronting the issue of public use involved a "mom and pop" grocery store in a run-down neighborhood on the southwest side of the District of Columbia. In carrying out a vast urban redevelopment program, the city government of Washington, D.C., took the property as one of a large number of privately owned lots to be cleared for new housing and business construction. The owner of the grocery store, and his successors after his death, took the government to court on the grounds that it was an unconstitutional use of eminent domain to take property from one private owner and eventually to turn that property back, in altered form, to another private owner. The store owners lost their case. The Supreme Court's argument was a curious but very important one: the "public interest" can mean virtually anything a legislature says it means. In other words, since the overall slum clearance and redevelopment project was in the public interest, according to the legislature, the eventual transfers of property that were going to take place were justified.[90] This principle was reaffirmed in the 2005 case of *Kelo v. City of New London*, where the Court held that the city could seize land from one private owner and transfer it to another as part of a redevelopment plan.[91]

The Sixth Amendment and the Right to Counsel

In all criminal prosecutions, the accused shall enjoy the right to a speedy and public trial, by an impartial jury of the State and district wherein the crime shall have been committed, which district shall have been previously ascertained by law, and to be informed of the nature and cause of the accusation; to be confronted with the witnesses against him; to have compulsory process for obtaining witnesses in his favor, and to have the Assistance of Counsel for his defence.

Like the exclusionary rule of the Fourth Amendment and the self-incrimination clause of the Fifth Amendment, the "right to counsel" provision of the Sixth Amendment is notable for freeing defendants who seem to the public to be patently guilty as charged. Other provisions of the Sixth Amendment, such as the right to a speedy trial and the right to confront witnesses before an impartial jury, are less controversial in nature.

Gideon v. Wainwright is the perfect case study because it involved a disreputable person who seemed patently guilty of the crime of which he was convicted. In and out of jails for most of his fifty-one years, Clarence Earl Gideon received a five-year sentence for breaking and entering a poolroom in Panama City, Florida. While serving time in jail, Gideon became a fairly well qualified "jailhouse lawyer," made his own appeal on a handwritten petition, and eventually won the landmark ruling on the right to counsel in all felony cases.[92]

The right to counsel has been expanded rather than contracted during the past few decades, when the courts have become more conservative. For example, although at first the right to counsel was met by judges assigning lawyers from the community as a formal public obligation, most states and cities now have created an office of public defender; these state-employed professional defense lawyers typically provide poor defendants with much better legal representation. And, although these defendants cannot choose their private defense attorney, they do

The Rights of the Accused from Arrest to Trial

No improper searches and seizures (Fourth Amendment)

No arrest without probable cause (Fourth Amendment)

Right to remain silent (Fifth Amendment)

No self-incrimination during arrest or trial (Fifth Amendment)

Right to be informed of charges (Sixth Amendment)

Right to counsel (Sixth Amendment)

No excessive bail (Eighth Amendment)

Right to grand jury (Fifth Amendment)

Right to open trial before a judge (Article I, Section 9)

Right to speedy and public trial before an impartial jury (Sixth Amendment)

Evidence obtained by illegal search not admissible during trial (Fourth Amendment)

Right to confront witnesses (Sixth Amendment)

No double jeopardy (Fifth Amendment)

No cruel and unusual punishment (Eighth Amendment)

have the right to appeal a conviction on the grounds that the counsel provided by the state was deficient. For example, in 2003 the Supreme Court overturned the death sentence of a Maryland death-row inmate, holding that the defense lawyer had failed to fully inform the jury of the defendant's history of "horrendous childhood abuse."[93] Moreover, the right to counsel extends beyond serious crimes to any trial, with or without jury, that holds the possibility of imprisonment.[94] In the 2006 case of *U.S. v. Gonzalez-Lopez*, the Court held that a defendant had been deprived of his Sixth Amendment rights because the trial court had refused to allow him to make use of the particular counsel of his own choosing.[95]

The Eighth Amendment and Cruel and Unusual Punishment

The Eighth Amendment prohibits "excessive bail," "excessive fines," and "cruel and unusual punishment." Virtually all the debate over Eighth Amendment issues focuses on the last clause of the amendment: the protection from "cruel and unusual punishment." One of the greatest challenges in interpreting this provision consistently is that what is considered "cruel and unusual" varies from culture to culture and from generation to generation.

In 1972, the Supreme Court overturned several state death penalty laws, not because they were cruel and unusual but because they were being applied in a capricious manner—that is, blacks were much more likely than whites to be sentenced to death, and the poor more likely than the rich, and men more likely than women.[96] Very soon after that decision, a majority of states revised their capital-punishment provisions to meet the Court's standards.[97] Since 1976, the Court has consistently upheld state laws providing for capital punishment, although the Court also continues to review numerous death-penalty appeals each year.

Between 1976 and 2009, states executed 1,161 people. Most of those executions occurred in southern states, with Texas leading the way at 430. As of 2009, thirty-six states had adopted some form of capital punishment, a move approved of by about three-quarters of all Americans.

Although virtually all criminal conduct is regulated by the states, Congress has also jumped on the bandwagon, imposing capital punishment for more than fifty federal crimes. Despite the seeming popularity of the death penalty, the debate has become, if anything, more intense. In 1997, for example, the American Bar Association passed a resolution calling for a halt to the death penalty until concerns about its fairness—that is, whether its application violates the principle of equality—and about ensuring due process are addressed.

Many death-penalty supporters praise its deterrent effects on other would-be criminals. Although studies of capital crimes usually fail to demonstrate any direct deterrent effect, the punishment's failure to act as a deterrent may be due to the lengthy delays—typically years and even decades—between convictions and executions. A system that eliminates undue delays might enhance deterrence. And deterring even one murder or other heinous crime, proponents argue, is ample justification for such laws. Beyond that

Thirty-seven states currently have the death penalty for the most serious crimes. Although a majority of Americans support the death penalty, it has always been controversial and is sometimes seen as a violation of the Eighth Amendment.

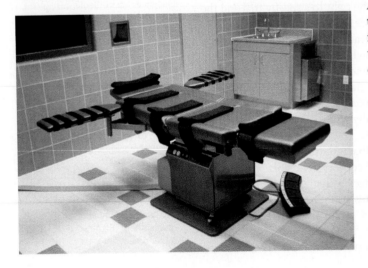

The Death Penalty

The United States is the only Western democracy that continues to make use of capital punishment as a form of criminal sanction. Thirty-seven of the fifty states provide for the death penalty, as do the federal government and the military. Since 1976, the states have executed more than one thousand convicted criminals. In 2007 alone, forty-two individuals were put to death by state authorities. Though this is a small number compared with, say, China, which may have executed as many as 8,000 persons for a variety of crimes in 2006, it was enough executions to rank the United States sixth, just behind Sudan, in its use of execution as a form of punishment.

Though a majority of Americans support capital punishment, America's continuing use of the death penalty has put the United States at odds with its European allies and with Canada and Mexico, which have all abolished capital punishment. One area of conflict concerns the extradition of criminals. If an individual charged with or convicted of a crime flees to another country, the fugitive's home country may ask that he or she be returned home to face trial or punishment. The United States has extradition treaties with many nations. In recent years, however, a number of European nations have resisted extraditing fugitives to the United States if there has been a possibility that they might face a death sentence on their return.

One of the most important of these cases involved Jens Soering. Soering was arrested in the United Kingdom in 1986 on a U.S. extradition warrant charging that he and his girlfriend had murdered her parents in Virginia. The European Court of Human Rights ruled that Soering's extradition to the United States would violate the European Convention on Human Rights, which prohibited torture or other degrading forms of punishment, because, if convicted in Virginia, he could be sentenced to death. To obtain Soering's extradition, the United States had to assure Britain that he would not be prosecuted for capital murder. Subsequently, Soering was returned, tried, and sentenced to ninety-nine years in prison. Since the Soering case, European authorities have generally made extradition to the United States conditional on American assurances that the individual sought by American authorities would not face capital charges if he or she were returned.

A second realm in which America's continuing use of capital punishment has created conflict with other nations stems from the 1963 Vienna Convention on Consular Relations. This treaty, signed by the United States and 162 other nations, requires the authorities to notify foreign nationals in their custody of their right to contact their own consulates for assistance before they are brought to trial. Police and courts in the United States often fail to comply with this obligation. As a result, a number of foreigners have been convicted of capital crimes and sentenced to death without having been allowed to contact their consulates for help. In 2001, the International Court of Justice ruled that the United States violated its treaty obligations with Germany by executing a German citizen, Walter LaGrand, without notifying him of his treaty rights. In recent years, the Mexican government has challenged the convictions and death sentences of several Mexican nationals in the United States on the grounds that they were not allowed to contact the Mexican consulate in a timely manner. In 2003, Mexico won a judgment against the United States in the International Court of Justice, but the U.S. Supreme Court ruled that Texas courts were not bound by this decision. Generally, U.S. courts have not been particularly hospitable to Vienna Convention claims.

SOURCE: William A. Schabas, "Indirect Abolition: Capital Punishment's Role in Extradition Law and Practice," *Loyola Los Angeles International and Comparative Law Review* 25 (2003): 581–604.

for critical analysis

1. America's continued use of capital punishment has complicated its relations with its neighbors and allies. Should the United States adjust its laws to accommodate the wishes of other nations?

2. What might explain why the United States continues to use capital punishment, whereas other Western nations have abandoned the practice?

argument, the death penalty is seen as a proper expression of retribution, echoed in the biblical phrase "an eye for an eye." People who commit vicious crimes deserve to forfeit their lives in exchange for the suffering they have inflicted.

Death-penalty opponents are quick to point out that the death penalty has not been proved to deter crime, either in the United States or abroad. In fact, America is the only Western nation that still executes criminals. If the government is to serve as an example of proper behavior, say foes, it has no business sanctioning killing when incarceration will similarly protect society. Furthermore, according to death-penalty foes, execution is expensive—more expensive than life imprisonment—precisely because the government must make every effort to ensure that it is not executing an innocent person. Curtailing legal appeals would make the possibility of a mistake too great. And although most Americans do support the death penalty, people also support life without the possibility of parole as an alternative. Race also intrudes in death-penalty cases: people of color (who are more likely to face economic deprivation) are disproportionately more likely to be sentenced to death, whereas whites charged with identical crimes are less likely to be given the ultimate punishment.

The proper use of the death penalty has long troubled the Supreme Court, which has struggled to establish principles to govern executions. In recent years, the Court has issued a number of death penalty opinions, declaring that death was too harsh a penalty for a child rapist[98] and invalidating a death sentence for black defendant when the prosecutor had improperly excluded African Americans from the jury.[99] In a decision that received worldwide attention, the Court ruled that the International Court of Justice had no authority to order a Texas court to reopen a death penalty case involving a foreign national.[100] The Court also upheld Kentucky's policy of execution by lethal injection despite arguments that this form of execution was likely to cause considerable pain.[101]

● The Right to Privacy

right to privacy the right to be left alone, which has been interpreted by the Supreme Court to entail free access to birth control and abortions

A **right to privacy** was not granted in the Bill of Rights, but a clause in the Fourth Amendment provides for "the right of the people to be secure in their persons, houses, papers, and effects, against unreasonable searches and seizures." In a 1928 case, Justice Louis Brandeis argued in a dissent that the Fourth Amendment should be extended to a more general principle of "privacy in the home."[102] Another step in this direction was taken when several Jehovah's Witnesses directed their children not to salute the flag or say the Pledge of Allegiance in school because the first of the Ten Commandments prohibits the worship of "graven images." They lost their case in 1940, but the Supreme Court reversed itself in 1943, holding that the 1940 case was "wrongly decided." The Court recognized "a right to be left alone" as part of the free-speech clause of the First Amendment.[103] Another small step was taken in 1958, when the Supreme Court recognized "privacy in one's association" in its decision that the state of Alabama could not use the membership list of the National Association for the Advancement of Colored People (NAACP) in state investigations.[104]

Birth Control The sphere of privacy was formally recognized in 1965, when the Court ruled that a Connecticut statute forbidding the use of contraceptives violated the right of marital privacy. Estelle Griswold, the executive director of the

Planned Parenthood League of Connecticut, was arrested by the state of Connecticut for providing information, instruction, and medical advice about contraception to married couples. She and her associates were found guilty as accessories to the crime and fined $100 each. The Supreme Court reversed the lower court decisions and declared the Connecticut law unconstitutional because it violated "a right of privacy older than the Bill of Rights—older than our political parties, older than our school system."[105] Justice William O. Douglas, author of the majority decision in the *Griswold* case, argued that this right of privacy is also grounded in the Constitution, because it fits into a "zone of privacy" created by a combination of the Third, Fourth, and Fifth Amendments. A concurring opinion, written by Justice Arthur Goldberg, attempted to strengthen Douglas's argument by adding that "the concept of liberty . . . embraces the right of marital privacy though that right is not mentioned explicitly in the Constitution [and] is supported by numerous decisions of this Court . . . and *by the language and history of the Ninth Amendment"* (emphasis added).[106]

Abortion The right to privacy was confirmed and extended in 1973 in one of the most important Supreme Court decisions in American history: *Roe v. Wade*. This decision established a woman's right to seek an abortion and prohibited states from making abortion a criminal act.[107] The Burger Court's decision in *Roe* took a revolutionary step toward establishing the right to privacy. It is important to emphasize that the preference for privacy rights and for their extension to include the rights of women to control their own bodies was not something the Supreme Court invented in a vacuum. Most states did not regulate abortions in any fashion until the 1840s, at which time only six of the twenty-six existing states had any regulations governing abortion. In addition, many states had begun to ease their abortion restrictions well before the 1973 *Roe* decision, although in recent years a number of states have reinstated some restrictions on abortion.

By extending the umbrella of privacy, this sweeping ruling dramatically changed abortion practices in America. In addition, it galvanized and nationalized the abortion debate. Groups opposed to abortion, such as the National Right to Life Committee, organized to fight the new liberal standard, while abortion rights groups sought to maintain that protection. In recent years, the legal standard shifted against abortion rights supporters in two key Supreme Court cases.

In *Webster v. Reproductive Health Services* (1989), the Court narrowly upheld (by a 5-to-4 majority) the constitutionality of restrictions on the use of public medical facilities for abortion.[108] And in the 1992 case of *Planned Parenthood v. Casey*, another 5-to-4 majority of the Court upheld *Roe* but narrowed its scope, refusing to invalidate a Pennsylvania law that significantly limits freedom of choice. The Court's decision defined the right to an abortion as a "limited or qualified" right subject to regulation by the states as long as the regulation does not constitute an "undue burden."[109] In the 2000 case of *Stenberg v. Carhart*, the Court, by a vote of 5-to-4, struck down Nebraska's ban on partial-birth abortions because the law had the "effect of placing a substantial obstacle in the path of a woman seeking an abortion."[110] However, in the 2006 case of *Ayotte v. Planned Parenthood*, the Court held that a law requiring parental notification before a minor could obtain an abortion was not an undue burden.[111] And, in *Gonzales v. Carhart*, the Court effectively reversed its earlier *Carhart* decision by upholding the federal partial-birth abortion ban, which was virtually identical to the Nebraska law it had struck down in 2000.[112]

forcriticalanalysis

Read the Third, Fourth, Fifth, and Ninth Amendments in the Appendix at the end of this book. In your opinion, do American citizens have a right to privacy?

Facebook and the Right to Privacy

While the Bill of Rights does not grant citizens a formal right to privacy, over the years the Supreme Court has weighed in on the extent to which the Fourth Amendment speaks to a citizen's right to be left alone. The explosion in digital media like the Internet has increased the salience of this "right to privacy" debate.

With over 350 million users, the popular social networking site Facebook.com has become a cultural and technological phenomenon. It has also become a "right to privacy" minefield. With individual pages on which users upload "status updates," photos, videos, and links, the site offers users a place to share information about themselves and update friends and acquaintances about their latest news and thoughts. These activities are tracked in users' "Newsfeeds" where individuals can observe the activities of other users in their social networks.

In September 2006, when Facebook first introduced the Newsfeed to its users, the outcry was immediate. Users overwhelmingly reacted with anger to the "broadcasting" of their personal information to others on the site. Facebook's founder, Mark Zuckerberg, replied that the Newsfeed would remain a feature of the site, though with the addition of privacy controls.

However, there is ongoing concern about what kind of access users want other individuals to have to their personal information. Stories abound about users whose status updates either got them fired from their jobs or caught in various lies or indiscretions. While new privacy settings launched in December 2009 allowed users to make privacy selections on a per-post basis, details like users' names, pictures, gender, and friend networks became categorized as "publicly available information" (PAI), meaning anyone online could view these details.

Of greatest concern to privacy advocates like the Electronic Frontier Foundation (EFF) and the American Civil Liberties Union (ACLU) is the accessing of personal data by outside entities through the use of Facebook Applications or "Apps." Facebook Apps such as quizzes or games like Mafia Wars and Farmville all grant software developers access to user information, which companies can then consolidate and sell. Interestingly, these outside entities not only get access to the personal data of the actual users taking the quizzes or playing the games but those users' "friends'" data.

But why would details about who your friends are or what you had for dinner matter? Zuckerberg says that in most users' minds, it doesn't. In January 2010, Zuckerberg argued, "People have really gotten comfortable not only sharing more information and different kinds, but more openly and with more people." He went on to describe privacy as a "social norm" that has been "evolving over time."

The concern, according to groups like the EFF and the ACLU, is that sophisticated use of Facebook data allows outside groups to identify with great accuracy such personal details as a user's sexual orientation and political or religious beliefs. The possibility of such sensitive information becoming a commodity that can be bought and sold is dangerous, they argue, as it introduces the possibility of discrimination. Until these complex privacy issues surrounding Facebook are resolved, perhaps users should simply be aware that much Facebook user data is not technically private. Without a formal "right to privacy" in the Bill of Rights, the protected status of personal information—from the government and outside entities—is certain to be a source of debate for years to come.

[a]Morphy, E. (2006). *Facebook Scrambles to Appease Outraged Users.* TechNewsWorld. 11 September. www.technewsworld.com (accessed 8/12/07).
[b]*Privacy, Security, and Social Networking APIs* (2008). Dr. Dobb's Journal. 4 February. www.ddj.com (accessed 2/4/08).
[c]Bankston, K. (2009). *Facebook's New Privacy Changes: The Good, the Bad, and the Ugly.* Electronic Frontier Foundation. 9 December. www.eff.org (accessed 7/1/10).
[d]Ozer, N. (2009). *Facebook Privacy in Transition—But Where is it Heading?* American Civil Liberties Union of Northern California. 9 December. www.aclunc.org (accessed 7/1/10).

for critical analysis

1. Why are Web sites like Facebook raising new questions about the right to privacy?

2. Should the Constitution be amended to include an explicit right to privacy? What other ways could the government protect privacy?

Homosexuality In the last two decades, the right to be left alone began to include the privacy rights of homosexuals. One morning in Atlanta, Georgia, in the mid-1980s, Michael Hardwick was arrested by a police officer who discovered him in bed with another man. The officer had come to serve a warrant for Hardwick's arrest for failure to appear in court to answer charges of drinking in public. One of Hardwick's unknowing housemates invited the officer to look in Hardwick's room, where he found Hardwick and another man engaging in "consensual sexual behavior." He was then arrested under Georgia's laws against heterosexual and homosexual sodomy. Hardwick filed a lawsuit against the state, challenging the constitutionality of the Georgia law. Hardwick won his case in the federal court of appeals. The state of Georgia, in an unusual move, appealed the court's decision to the Supreme Court. The majority of the Court reversed the lower court decision, holding against Mr. Hardwick, on the grounds that "the federal Constitution confers [no] fundamental right upon homosexuals to engage in sodomy," and that therefore there was no basis to invalidate "the laws of the many states that still make such conduct illegal and have done so for a very long time."[113]

Seventeen years later and to almost everyone's surprise, the Court overturned *Bowers v. Hardwick* with a dramatic pronouncement that gays are "entitled to respect for their private lives"[114] as a matter of constitutional due process. With *Lawrence v. Texas* (2003), the state legislatures no longer had the authority to make private sexual behavior a crime.[115] Drawing from the tradition of negative liberty, the Court maintained: "In our tradition the State is not omnipresent in the home. And there are other spheres of our lives and existence outside the home, where the State should not be a dominant presence." Explicitly encompassing lesbians and gay men within the umbrella of privacy, the Court concluded that the "petitioners are entitled to respect for their private lives. The State cannot demean their existence or control their destiny by making their private sexual conduct a crime." This decision added substance to the "right of privacy."[116]

The Right to Die Another area ripe for litigation and public discourse is the so-called right to die. A number of highly publicized physician-assisted suicides in the 1990s focused attention on whether people have a right to choose their own death and to receive assistance in carrying it out. Can this become part of the privacy right? Or is it a new substantive right? The Supreme Court has not definitively answered this question. However, the Court refused to intervene in the well-publicized case of Terri Schiavo, a woman who, as described in Chapter 3, suffered irreversible brain damage and was kept alive in a vegetative state via a feeding tube for fifteen years. During this period, Schiavo's husband, who wanted to withdraw life support, battled her parents, who wanted support continued indefinitely. The case was heard multiple times in the Florida state courts and the federal courts. In 2005, Schiavo's husband finally prevailed, and she was removed from life support and

The case of Terri Schiavo brought out strong reactions on both sides of the debate over the "right to die." Schiavo's husband ultimately won the right to remove the feeding tubes that had kept her alive in a vegetative state for many years.

subsequently died. In the 2006 case of *Gonzales v. Oregon*, however, the Supreme Court did intervene to uphold an assisted-suicide law. The law allowed doctors to use drugs to facilitate the deaths of terminally ill patients who requested such assistance.[117] Thus, although the Court has not ruled definitively on the right-to-die question, it does not seem hostile to the idea.

● Thinking Critically about the Future of Civil Liberties

In the months after the September 11 terrorists attacks against the United States, President George W. Bush issued a series of executive orders to combat the threat of terrorism. The president authorized the indefinite detention of individuals whom he designated enemy combatants at the Guantánamo Bay military prison in Cuba, the creation of special military tribunals to try enemy combatants, and the initiation of a massive warrantless surveillance program by the National Security Agency to monitor communications into and out of the United States in search of indications of terrorist activity. The president averred that these policies were necessary to protect the nation, but each of the president's orders was denounced by civil libertarians as an intrusion on constitutional rights and was challenged in the courts.

In the 2004 case of *Hamdi v. Rumsfeld*, the Supreme Court ruled that those declared enemy combatants could challenge their detention before a judge, but the Court affirmed the president's power to declare even U.S. citizens to be enemy combatants.[118] In 2006, in the case of *Hamdan v. Rumsfeld*, the Court invalidated the military tribunals established by presidential order because their procedures were not in accord with current law. The Court, however, accepted the principle that the president could order the creation of such tribunals as long as their procedures had some statutory basis. Congress provided that basis in the 2006 Military Commissions Act, which mainly reaffirmed the procedures that had been devised by the president.[119] The act also seemed partially to reverse the *Hamdi* decision by declaring that prisoners at Guantánamo could not present habeas corpus petitions to the federal courts challenging their detention. The legality of that portion of the act is currently being debated in the federal courts.

As for the NSA surveillance program, in 2007 the Sixth Circuit Court of Appeals upheld the validity of the program, but the American Civil Liberties Union has appealed the decision to the supreme Court. Under new rules established by President Bush, the NSA requests warrants from the Foreign Intelligence Surveillance (FISA) Court, a secretive panel established to hear top-secret cases. The president, however, reserved the right to order warrantless searches if he deemed them to be necessary. As these war on terror cases illustrate, battles over civil liberties are not abstract, historical matters. They are part or our lives today.

When President Obama took office in 2009, many civil libertarians were confident that the new administration would move quickly to curb what many saw as the civil liberties abuses of the Bush years, primarily associated with the "war on terror." After Obama's first year in office, however, civil libertarians gave the president a mixed review. Anthony Romero, director of the American Civil Liberties Union (ACLU), declared that the Obama administration had "made some significant strides toward restoring civil liberties and the rule of law."[120] Nevertheless, the ACLU took the Obama administration to task for continuing a number of Bush's policies.

Free Speech on Campus

In September 1964, administrators from the University of California at Berkeley prohibited student civil rights activists from distributing information and collecting donations on campus, even though other less controversial groups were allowed to do so. Students reacted strongly and passionately to the administration's actions. Hundreds participated in a series of protests and sit-ins over the course of several months. Their collective action, known as the Free Speech Movement, ultimately resulted in the restoration of their civil liberties.

Free-speech issues continue to be debated on college campuses today. For example, student groups opposed to affirmative action have recently staged satirical bake sales, where the purchase price for baked goods is adjusted based on the buyer's race and ethnicity. Basically, Caucasians and Asians are asked to pay more and African Americans and Latinos are charged less. College administrators—acting with the support of other student groups—have shut down these bake sales, arguing that they violate university discrimination policies. These universities have asserted that their obligation to protect individuals from discrimination is greater than the need to protect free speech.

If you are interested in this debate—or concerned about the protection of civil liberties in general—there are many ways to get involved. As a first step, you might want to explore the free-speech provisions on your campus. Will the school tolerate *all* speech, or just speech that does not violate certain community standards? Who has the power to make these decisions? Where do you stand? To find out more, you could

- Find out what rights are guaranteed to you in the student handbook. Most colleges and universities provide online access to their handbooks.

- E-mail or call the editor of the campus newspaper and find out if it has ever been censored by the administration or if the staff has freedom-of-press issues.

Once you learn what rights you have, you can move on to informing and motivating your fellow students about any issue or issues of concern to you. Here are some of the kinds of activities and events you can organize on your own or with a group of students who share your concern:

- Host prominent speakers who will talk about your issue and address questions from the audience. Talk to some professors who might be interested in this issue. They may have suggestions for speakers, and their department might help you by contacting the speaker, providing money or making arrangements. If they can't help you, chances are they can connect you with an on-campus organization that can.

- Plan or participate in debates with students or campus groups that have different views on your issue. Contact leaders of the groups to invite them to a public debate. For example, if your campus has had an affirmative action bake sale, you could contact leaders of the sale and their key opponents about coming together for a discussion.

- Invite professors and students to participate in a roundtable discussion about a civil-liberties issue. National Constitution Day (September 17) is a good day to plan such a discussion. Many political science departments have money set aside to host activities on this day. The chair of the department can provide you with information about their plans.

- Set up tables in high-traffic locations at lunchtime to disseminate information or to gather signatures for a petition relevant to your issue.

- Make contact with national political groups that share your position. They may be able to provide you with materials for dissemination and other resources.

The dilemma of balancing liberty and security has continued during the Obama administration. The introduction of full-body scanners at some airports was criticized as an intrusion on individual rights but also has been defended as a necessary step to prevent terrorist attacks.

Thus, while Obama issued executive orders closing the Guantanamo Bay prison, which housed a number of terrorist suspects, the prison actually remained open holding detainees without charge or trial while the administration considered what to do with them. Similarly, Obama ordered an end to the harsh interrogation of terrorist suspects countenanced by the Bush administration. Obama had little interest in investigating charges of prisoner abuse by the military and intelligence agencies. The ACLU criticized Obama for not bringing an end to government spying on Americans, monitoring of political activists, and the continued use of secret detentions and removals of terrorist suspects to overseas facilities.

Most Democrats believe that America's reputation in the world has been hurt by the image of prisoners held without proper legal process and are eager to find ways to restore America's reputation as a bastion of liberty. At the same time, however, the administration does not wish to see dangerous foes of the United States do harm to Americans. The dilemma of liberty versus security is rarely easy to resolve.

studyguide

Practice Quiz

 Find a diagnostic Web Quiz with 33 additional questions on the StudySpace Web site: www.wwnorton.com/we-the-people

A Brief History of the Bill of Rights

1. From 1789 until the 1960s, the Bill of Rights put limits on *(pp. 113–16)*
a) the national government only.
b) the state government only.
c) both the national and state governments.
d) neither the national nor the state government.

2. The amendment that provided the basis for the modern understanding of the government's obligation to protect civil rights was the *(p. 114)*
a) First Amendment.
b) Ninth Amendment.
c) Fourteenth Amendment.
d) Twenty-second Amendment.

3. Which of the following rights were not included in the original Constitution? *(pp. 114–15)*
a) prohibition of bills of attainder
b) prohibition of *ex post facto* laws
c) guarantee of *habeas corpus*
d) none—They were all included in the original Constitution.

4. Which of the following provided that all of the protections contained in the Bill of Rights applied to the states as well as the national government? *(pp. 115–17)*
a) the Fourteenth Amendment
b) *Palko v. Connecticut*
c) *Gitlow v. New York*
d) none of the above

5. The process by which some of the liberties in the Bill of Rights were applied to the states (or nationalized) is known as *(p. 115)*
a) selective incorporation.
b) judicial activism.
c) civil liberties.
d) establishment.

6. Which of the following provisions of the Bill of Rights was incorporated in 2010? *(p. 117)*
a) the right to bear arms
b) the right to counsel in any criminal trial
c) the right against self-incrimination
d) freedom from unnecessary searches and seizures

The First Amendment and Freedom of Religion

7. Which of the following protections are *not* contained in the First Amendment? *(pp. 117–30)*
a) the establishment clause
b) the free exercise clause
c) freedom of the press
d) All of the above are First Amendment protections.

8. The so-called *Lemon* test, derived from the Supreme Court's ruling in *Lemon v. Kurtzman,* concerns the issue of *(p. 118)*
a) school desegregation.
b) aid to religious schools.
c) prayer in school.
d) obscenity.

The First Amendment and Freedom of Speech and the Press

9. Under which conditions can the government regulate speech? *(pp. 121–22)*
a) when the speech presents a clear and present danger to society
b) when the speech incites damaging conduct
c) when the speech is made in reckless disregard of the truth and is considered damaging to the victim because it is malicious, scandalous, and defamatory
d) all of the above

10. Which of the following describes a written statement made in "reckless disregard of the truth" that is considered damaging to a victim because it is "malicious, scandalous, and defamatory"? *(p. 126)*
a) slander
b) libel
c) fighting words
d) expressive speech

Rights of the Criminally Accused

11. The Fourth, Fifth, Sixth, and Eighth Amendments, taken together, define *(p. 131)*
a) due process of law.
b) free speech.
c) the right to bear arms.
d) civil rights of minorities.

12. In *Mapp v. Ohio,* the Supreme Court ruled that *(p. 132)*
    a) evidence obtained from an illegal search could not be introduced in a trial.
    b) a person cannot be tried twice for the same crime.
    c) persons under arrest must be informed prior to police interrogation of their rights to remain silent and to have the benefits of legal counsel.
    d) government has the right to take private property for public use if just compensation is provided.

13. Which famous case deals with Sixth Amendment issues? *(p. 137)*
    a) *Miranda v. Arizona*
    b) *Mapp v. Ohio*
    c) *Gideon v. Wainwright*
    d) *Terry v. Ohio*

The Right to Privacy

14. In what case was a right to privacy first found in the Constitution? *(p. 140)*
    a) *Griswold v. Connecticut*
    b) *Roe v. Wade*
    c) *Baker v. Carr*
    d) *Planned Parenthood v. Casey*

15. In which case did the Supreme Court rule that state governments no longer had the authority to make private sexual behavior a crime? *(p. 143)*
    a) *Webster v. Reproductive Health Services*
    b) *Gonzales v. Oregon*
    c) *Lawrence v. Texas*
    d) *Bowers v. Hardwick*

Chapter Outline

Ⓢ **Find a detailed Chapter Outline on the StudySpace Web site: www.wwnorton.com/we-the-people**

Key Terms

Ⓢ **Find Flashcards to help you study these terms on the StudySpace Web site: www.wwnorton.com/we-the-people**

bill of attainder *(p. 114)*
Bill of Rights *(p. 113)*
civil liberties *(p. 113)*
"clear and present danger" test *(p. 122)*
double jeopardy *(p. 134)*
due process of law *(p. 131)*
eminent domain *(p. 136)*

establishment clause *(p. 117)*
ex post facto law *(p. 114)*
exclusionary rule *(p. 132)*
fighting words *(p. 128)*
free exercise clause *(p. 120)*
grand jury *(p. 134)*
habeas corpus *(p. 113)*
Lemon test *(p. 118)*

libel *(p. 126)*
Miranda rule *(p. 136)*
prior restraint *(p. 125)*
right to privacy *(p. 140)*
selective incorporation *(p. 115)*
slander *(p. 126)*
"speech plus" *(p. 124)*

For Further Reading

Barendt, Eric. *Freedom of Speech.* 2nd ed. New York: Oxford University Press, 2007.

Brandon, Mark. *The Constitution in Wartime.* Durham, NC: Duke University Press, 2005.

Cash, Arthur. *John Wilkes: The Scandalous Father of Civil Liberties.* New Haven, CT: Yale University Press, 2007.

Cook, Byrne. *Reporting the War: Freedom of the Press from the American Revolution to the War on Terror.* New York: Palgrave Macmillan, 2007.

Domino, John. *Civil Rights and Liberties in the 21st Century.* 3rd ed. New York: Longman, 2009.

Dworkin, Ronald. *Justice in Robes.* Cambridge, MA: Belknap Press, 2006.

Fisher, Louis. *Military Tribunals and Presidential Power.* Lawrence: University Press of Kansas, 2005.

Friendly, Fred W. *Minnesota Rag: The Dramatic Story of the Landmark Supreme Court Case that Gave New Meaning to Freedom of the Press.* New York: Vintage, 1982.

Glendon, Mary Ann. *Rights Talk: The Impoverishment of Political Discourse.* New York: Free Press, 1991.

Hentoff, Nat. *The First Freedom: The Tumultuous History of Free Speech in America.* New York: Basic Books, 1994.

Lewis, Anthony. *Gideon's Trumpet.* New York: Random House, 1964.

Sundby, Scott. *A Life and Death Decision: A Jury Weighs the Death Penalty.* New York: Palgrave Macmillan, 2007.

Recommended Web Sites

The American Civil Liberties Union (ACLU)
www.aclu.org

The ACLU is committed in protecting for all individuals the freedoms found in the Bill of Rights. This sometimes controversial organization constantly monitors the government for violations of liberty and encourages its members to take political action.

Electronic Privacy Information Center
http://epic.org/privacy

For an extensive list of privacy issues, go to the Web page for the Electronic Privacy Information Center. Here you will find civil liberties concerns as they relate to all forms of information technology, including the Internet.

The Free Expression Network
www.freeexpression.org

The Free Expression Network is an organization "dedicated to preserving the right to free expression." On its Web site you can find links to important First Amendment issues and organizations.

Freedom Forum
www.freedomforum.org

Freedom of speech and freedom of the press are considered critical in any democracy; however, only some kinds of speech are fully protected against restrictions. Freedom Forum is a nonpartisan agency that investigates and analyzes such First Amendment restrictions.

National Abortion and Reproductive Rights Action League
www.naral.org
National Right to Life Committee
www.HRIC.org

The National Abortion and Reproductive Rights Action League and the National Right to Life Committee are two of the nation's largest interest groups weighing in on the abortion issue. See what these opposing groups have to say about privacy rights.

Religious Freedom Page
http://religiousfreedom.lib.virginia.edu

The establishment clause of the U.S. Constitution has been interpreted to mean a "wall of separation" between government and religion. On the Religious Freedom Page you can find information on a variety of issues pertaining to religious freedom in the United States and around the world.

U.S. Supreme Court Media
www.oyez.org

This Web site for U.S. Supreme Court media has a great search engine for finding information on cases affecting civil liberties, such as *Lemon v. Kurtzman*, *Miranda v. Arizona*, *Mapp v. Ohio*, and *New York Times v. Sullivan*, to name a few.

The civil rights movement of the 1950s and 1960s relied on various nontraditional political tactics. These students protested segregation by sitting at a whites-only lunch counter. The black civil rights movement inspired a new wave of movements for equality for many groups in American society.

Civil Rights

WHAT GOVERNMENT DOES AND WHY IT MATTERS In 1960, four black students from North Carolina A&T State University made history: the four freshmen sat down at Woolworth's whites-only lunch counter in Greensboro, North Carolina, challenging the policies of segregation that kept blacks and whites in separate public and private accommodations across the South. Day after day the students sat at the counter, ignoring the taunts of onlookers, determined to break the system of segregation. Their actions and those of many other students, clergy members, and ordinary citizens finally did abolish such practices as separate white and black park benches, water fountains, and waiting rooms; the end of segregation meant opening access to public and private institutions on equal terms to all. But the victories of the civil rights movement did not come cheaply: many marchers, freedom riders, and sit-in participants were beaten; some were murdered.

Today, the Greensboro lunch counter is a part of history, on display at the Smithsonian Institution in Washington, D.C. Many goals of the civil rights movement that aroused such controversy in 1960 are now widely accepted as part of the American commitment to equal rights. But the question of what is meant by "equal rights" is hardly settled. Although most Americans reject the idea that government should create equal outcomes for its citizens, they do widely endorse government action to prohibit public and private discrimination, and they support the idea of equality of opportunity. However, even

focusquestions

- **What legal developments and political movements expanded civil rights?**
- **How have different groups won protection of their rights?**
- **Why do Americans disagree about affirmative action?**

this concept is elusive. When past denial of rights creates unequal starting points for some groups, should government take additional steps to ensure equal opportunity? What kinds of groups should be specially protected against discrimination? Should the disabled receive special protection? Should gays and lesbians? Finally, what kinds of steps are acceptable to remedy discrimination, and who should bear the costs? These questions are at the heart of contemporary debates over civil rights.

The answers that Americans give to these questions have shifted dramatically over the course of our nation's history. But ideas about civil rights did not change easily; advocates who challenged barriers to civil rights often struggled against strong resistance. The election of Barack Obama as the nation's first black president is a testament to the successes of those struggles but does not by itself alter persistent social and economic differences across racial lines. The black civil rights movement inspired a new wave of movements for equality, as groups including women, gays and lesbians, Native Americans, Latinos, and the disabled launched campaigns for equal rights.

This chapter will show how inequalities between races and genders were tolerated and even enforced by law during much of our country's history. Although the United States was founded on the ideals of liberty, equality, and democracy, its history of civil rights reveals a gap between these principles and actual practice. This history also reveals how the struggle to attain those ideals has helped narrow this gap. Closer to the present day, the struggle for political and social equality also shows how liberty and equality are not mutually supportive. In fact, these principles are often in conflict with one another. This chapter's concluding discussion of affirmative action illustrates this conflict.

chaptercontents

The Struggle for Civil Rights

● What legal developments and political movements expanded civil rights?

In the United States, the history of slavery and legalized racial **discrimination** against African Americans coexists uneasily with a strong tradition of individual liberty. Indeed, for much of our history Americans have struggled to reconcile such exclusionary racial practices with our notions of individual rights. With the adoption of the Fourteenth Amendment in 1868, **civil rights** became part of the Constitution, guaranteed to each citizen through "**equal protection** of the laws." This equal protection clause launched a century of political movements and legal efforts to press for racial equality.

For African Americans, the central fact of political life has been a denial of full citizenship rights for most of American history. By accepting the institution of slavery, the Founders embraced a system fundamentally at odds with the "Blessings of Liberty" promised in the Constitution. Their decision set the stage for two centuries of African American struggles to achieve full citizenship. For women as well, electoral politics was a decidedly masculine world. Until 1920, not only were women barred from voting in national politics, but electoral politics was closely tied to such male social institutions as lodges, bars, and clubs. Yet the exclusion of women from this political world did not prevent them from engaging in public life. Instead, women carved out a "separate sphere" for their public activities. Emphasizing female stewardship of the moral realm, women became important voices in social reform well before they won the right to vote.[1] For example, prior to the Civil War, women played leading roles in the abolitionist movement.

discrimination use of any unreasonable and unjust criterion of exclusion

civil rights obligation imposed on government to take positive action to protect citizens from any illegal action of government agencies as well as of other private citizens

equal protection clause provision of the Fourteenth Amendment guaranteeing citizens "the equal protection of the laws." This clause has been the basis for the civil rights of African Americans, women, and other groups

African American men won the right to vote after the Civil War, and many former slaves began registering and voting in state elections as early as 1867. This political influence soon evaporated in the face of Jim Crow laws and the end of Reconstruction.

Slavery and the Abolitionist Movement

No issue in the nation's history so deeply divided Americans as that of the abolition of slavery. The importation and subjugation of Africans kidnapped from their native lands was a practice virtually as old as the country itself: the first slaves brought to what became the United States arrived in 1619, a year before the Plymouth colony was established in Massachusetts. White southerners built their agricultural economy (especially cotton production) on a large slave labor force. By 1840, nearly half of the populations of Alabama and Louisiana consisted of black slaves. Even so, only about a quarter of southern white families owned slaves.

The subjugation of blacks through slavery was so much a part of southern culture that efforts to restrict or abolish slavery were met with fierce resistance. Despite the manifest cruelties of the slave system, southerners referred to the system by the quaint term *peculiar institution*. The label meant little to slavery's opponents, however, and an abolitionist movement grew and spread among northerners in the 1830s (although abolitionist sentiment could be traced back to the pre-Revolutionary era). The movement was most closely identified with the writing of William Lloyd Garrison. Slavery had been all but eliminated in the North by this time, but few northerners favored outright abolition. In fact, most whites held attitudes toward blacks that would be considered racist today.

The abolitionist movement spread primarily through local organizations in the North. Antislavery groups coalesced in New York, Ohio, New Hampshire, Pennsylvania, New Jersey, and Michigan. In addition to forming antislavery societies, the movement spawned two political parties: the Liberty Party, a staunchly antislavery party, and the Free Soil Party, a larger but more moderate party that sought primarily to restrict the spread of slavery into new western territories. In 1857, the infamous case of *Dred Scott v. Sandford* "roused passions as never before"[2] by splitting the country deeply with its holding that Scott had no due process rights because as a slave he was his master's permanent property regardless of his master's having taken him to a free state or territory.[3]

Some opponents of slavery took matters into their own hands, aiding in the escape of runaway slaves along the Underground Railroad. Even today, private homes and churches scattered throughout the Northeast that were used to hide blacks on their trips to Canada attest to the involvement of local citizenry. In the South, a similar, if contrary, fervor prompted mobs to break into post offices in order to seize and destroy antislavery literature.

The emotional power of the slavery issue was such that it precipitated the nation's bloodiest conflict, the Civil War. From the ashes of the Civil War came the Thirteenth, Fourteenth, and Fifteenth Amendments, which would redefine civil rights from that time on.

The Link to the Women's Rights Movement

The quiet upstate New York town of Seneca Falls played host to what would later come to be known as the starting point of the modern women's movement. Convened in July 1848 and organized by the activists Elizabeth Cady Stanton (who lived in Seneca Falls) and Lucretia Mott, the Seneca Falls Convention drew three hundred delegates to discuss and formulate plans to advance the political and social rights of women.

The centerpiece of the convention was its Declaration of Sentiments and Resolutions. Patterned after the Declaration of Independence, the Seneca Falls document declared, "We hold these truths to be self-evident: that all men and women are created equal," and "The history of mankind is a history of repeated injuries

Although a few women could vote in the early American republic, such as these New Jersey women who satisfied state property qualifications, laws were soon enacted to block women from the ballot box. At the beginning of the nineteenth century, no American woman could legally vote.

and usurpations on the part of man toward woman, having in direct object the establishment of an absolute tyranny over her." The most controversial provision of the declaration, nearly rejected as too radical, was the call for the right to vote for women. Although most of the delegates were women, about forty men participated, including the renowned abolitionist Frederick Douglass.

The link to the antislavery movement was not new. Stanton and Mott had attended the World Anti-slavery Convention in London in 1840 but had been denied delegate seats because of their sex. This rebuke helped precipitate the 1848 convention. The movements for women's rights and the abolition of slavery were also closely linked with the temperance movement (because alcohol abuse was closely linked to male abuses of women). The convergence of the antislavery, temperance, and suffrage movements was reflected in the views and actions of other women's movement leaders, such as Susan B. Anthony.

The convention and its participants were subjected to widespread ridicule, but similar conventions were organized in other states, and in the same year, New York State passed the Married Women's Property Act in order to restore the right of a married woman to own property.

The Civil War Amendments to the Constitution

The hopes of African Americans for achieving full citizenship rights initially seemed fulfilled when three constitutional amendments were adopted after the Civil War: the **Thirteenth Amendment** abolished slavery; the **Fourteenth Amendment** guaranteed equal protection under the law; and the **Fifteenth Amendment** guaranteed voting rights for blacks. Protected by the presence of federal troops, African American men were able to exercise their political rights immediately after the war. During Reconstruction, blacks were elected to many political offices: two black senators were elected from Mississippi and a total of fourteen African

Thirteenth Amendment one of three Civil War amendments; abolished slavery

Fourteenth Amendment one of three Civil War amendments; guaranteed equal protection and due process

Fifteenth Amendment one of three Civil War amendments; guaranteed voting rights for African American men

Americans were elected to the House of Representatives between 1869 and 1877. African Americans also held many state-level political offices. As voters and public officials, black citizens found a home in the Republican Party, which had secured the ratification of the three constitutional amendments guaranteeing black rights. After the war, the Republican Party continued to reach out to black voters as a means to build party strength in the South.[4]

This political equality was short-lived, however. The national government withdrew its troops from the South and turned its back on African Americans in 1877. In the Compromise of 1877, southern Democrats agreed to allow the Republican candidate, Rutherford B. Hayes, to become president after a disputed election. In exchange, northern Republicans dropped their support for the civil liberties and political participation of African Americans. After that, southern states erected a Jim Crow system of social, political, and economic inequality that made a mockery of the promises in the Constitution. The first **Jim Crow laws** were adopted in the 1870s in each southern state to criminalize intermarriage of the races and to segregate trains and depots. These were promptly followed by laws segregating all public accommodations, and within ten years all southern states had adopted laws segregating the schools.

Around the same time, some women pressed for the right to vote at the national level immediately after the Civil War, when male ex-slaves won the franchise. Politicians in both parties rejected women's suffrage as disruptive and unrealistic. Women also started to press for the vote at the state level in 1867 when a referendum to give women the vote in Kansas failed. Frustration with the general failure to win reforms in other states accelerated suffrage activism. In 1872, Susan B. Anthony and several other women were arrested in Rochester, New York, for illegally registering and voting in that year's national election. (The men who allowed the women to register and vote were also indicted; Anthony paid their expenses and eventually won presidential pardons for them.) At her trial, Judge Ward Hunt ordered the jury to find her guilty without deliberation. Yet Anthony was allowed to address the court, saying, "Your denial of my citizen's right to vote is the denial of my right of consent as one of the governed, the denial of my right

Jim Crow laws laws enacted by southern states following Reconstruction that discriminated against African Americans

The 1896 Supreme Court case of Plessy v. Ferguson *upheld legal segregation and created the "separate but equal" rule, which fostered national segregation. Overt discrimination in public accommodations was common.*

of representation as one of the taxed, the denial of my right to a trial of my peers as an offender against the law."[5] Hunt assessed Anthony a fine of $100 but did not sentence her to jail. Anthony refused to pay the fine.

Civil Rights and the Supreme Court: "Separate but Equal"

Resistance to equality for African Americans in the South led Congress to adopt the Civil Rights Act of 1875, which attempted to protect blacks from discrimination by proprietors of hotels, theaters, and other public accommodations. But the Court declared the Civil Rights Act of 1875 unconstitutional on the grounds that the act sought to protect blacks against discrimination by *private* businesses, whereas the Fourteenth Amendment, according to the Court's interpretation, was intended to protect individuals from discrimination only against actions by *public* officials of state and local governments.

In 1896, the Court went still further, in the infamous case of *Plessy v. Ferguson*, by upholding a Louisiana statute that *required* segregation of the races on trolleys and other public carriers (and by implication in all public facilities, including schools). Homer Plessy, a man defined as "one-eighth black," had violated a Louisiana law that provided for "equal but separate accommodations" on trains and a $25 fine for any white passenger who sat in a car reserved for blacks or any black passenger who sat in a car reserved for whites. The Supreme Court held that the Fourteenth Amendment's "equal protection of the laws" was not violated by racial distinction as long as the facilities were equal, thus establishing the **"separate but equal" rule** that prevailed through the mid-twentieth century. People generally pretended that segregated accommodations were equal as long as some accommodation for blacks existed. The Court said that although "the object of the [Fourteenth] Amendment was undoubtedly to enforce the absolute equality of the two races before the law, . . . it could not have intended to abolish distinctions based on color, or to enforce social, as distinguished from political, equality, or a commingling of the two races upon terms unsatisfactory to either."[6] What the Court was saying in effect was that the use of race as a criterion of exclusion in public matters was not unreasonable.

Organizing for Equality

The National Association for the Advancement of Colored People (NAACP)
The creation of a "Jim Crow" system in the southern states and the lack of a legal basis for "equal protection under the laws" prompted the beginning of a long process in which African Americans built organizations and devised strategies for asserting their constitutional rights.

One such strategy sought to win political rights through political pressure and litigation. This approach was championed by the NAACP, established by a group of black and white reformers in 1909. Among the NAACP's founders was W. E. B. Du Bois, one of the most influential and creative thinkers on racial issues of the twentieth century. Because the northern black vote was so small in the early decades of the twentieth century, the organization relied primarily on the courts to press for black political rights. After the 1920s, the NAACP built a strong membership base, with some strength in the South, which would be critical when the civil rights movement gained momentum in the 1950s.

The great migration of blacks to the North beginning around World War I enlivened a protest strategy. Although protest organizations had existed in the nineteenth century, the continuing migration of blacks to the North made protest

"separate but equal" rule doctrine that public accommodations could be segregated by race but still be equal

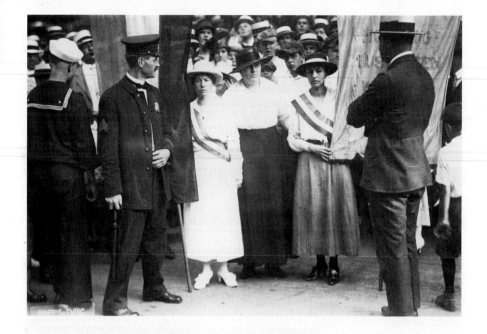

People had been agitating for women's right to vote since the 1830s, especially during the Civil War era. Here, early-twentieth-century suffragists protest in front of the White House. Women gained the constitutional right to vote in 1920.

an increasingly useful tool. The black labor leader A. Philip Randolph forced the federal government to address racial discrimination in hiring practices during World War II by threatening a massive march on Washington. The federal government also grew more attentive to blacks as their voting strength increased as a result of the northward migration. By the 1940s, the black vote had swung away from Republicans, but the Democratic hold on black votes was by no means absolute.

Women's Organizations and the Right to Suffrage Suffragists used the occasion of the Constitution's centennial in 1887 to protest the continued denial of their rights. For these women, the centennial represented "a century of injustice." The unveiling of the Statue of Liberty, depicting liberty as a woman, in New York Harbor in 1886 prompted women's rights advocates to call it "the greatest hypocrisy of the nineteenth century," in that "not one single woman throughout the length and breadth of the Land is as yet in possession of political Liberty."[7]

The climactic movement toward suffrage was formally launched in 1878 with the introduction of a proposed constitutional amendment in Congress. Parallel efforts were made in the states. Many states granted women the right to vote before the national government did; western states with less entrenched political systems opened politics to women earliest. When Wyoming became a state in 1890, it was the first state to grant full suffrage to women. Colorado, Utah, and Idaho all followed suit in the next several years. Suffrage organizations grew— the National American Woman Suffrage Association (NAWSA), formed in 1890, claimed two million members by 1917—and staged mass meetings, parades, petitions, and protests. NAWSA organized state-by-state efforts to win the right for women to vote. A more militant group, the National Woman's Party, staged pickets and got arrested in front of the White House to protest President Wilson's opposition to a constitutional amendment granting women this right. Finally in 1920, the Nineteenth Amendment was ratified, guaranteeing women the right to vote.

Litigating for Equality after World War II

The shame of discrimination against black military personnel during World War II, plus revelations of Nazi racial atrocities, moved President Harry S. Truman finally to bring the problem to the White House and national attention, with the appointment in 1946 of the President's Commission on Civil Rights. In 1948, the commission submitted its report, *To Secure These Rights*, which laid bare the extent of the problem of racial discrimination and its consequences. The report also revealed the success of experiments with racial integration in the armed forces during World War II to demonstrate to southern society that it had nothing to fear. But the committee recognized that the national government had no clear constitutional authority to pass and implement civil rights legislation. The committee proposed tying civil rights legislation to the commerce power, although it was clear that discrimination was not itself part of the flow of interstate commerce.[8] The committee even suggested using the treaty power as a source of constitutional authority for civil rights legislation.[9]

As for the Supreme Court, it had begun to change its position on racial discrimination before World War II by being stricter about the criterion of equal facilities in the "separate but equal" rule. In 1938, for example, the Court rejected Missouri's policy of paying the tuition of qualified blacks to out-of-state law schools rather than admitting them to the University of Missouri Law School.[10]

After the war, modest progress resumed. In 1950, the Court rejected Texas's claim that its new "law school for Negroes" afforded education equal to that of the all-white University of Texas Law School. Without confronting the "separate but equal" principle itself, the Court's decision anticipated its future civil rights rulings by opening the question of whether *any* segregated facilities could be truly equal.[11]

But in ordering the admission of blacks to all-white state law schools, the Supreme Court did not directly confront the "separate but equal" rule because the Court needed only to recognize the absence of any *equal* law school for blacks. The same was true in 1944, when the Supreme Court struck down the southern practice of "white primaries," which legally excluded blacks from participation in the nominating process. Here the Court simply recognized that primaries could no longer be regarded as the private affairs of the parties but were an integral aspect of the electoral process. This made parties "an agency of the State," and therefore any practice of discrimination against blacks was "state action within the meaning of the Fifteenth Amendment."[12] The most important pre-1954 decision was probably *Shelley v. Kraemer*, in which the Court ruled against the widespread practice of "restrictive covenants," whereby the seller of a home added a clause to the sales contract requiring the buyer to agree not to sell the home later to any non-Caucasian, non-Christian, and so on. The Court ruled that although private persons could sign such restrictive covenants, they could not be judicially enforced, since the Fourteenth Amendment prohibits any organ of the state, including the courts, from denying equal protection of its laws.[13]

Although none of those pre-1954 cases confronted "separate but equal" and the principle of racial discrimination as such, they were extremely significant to black leaders in the 1940s and gave them encouragement to believe that at last they had an opportunity and enough legal precedent to change the constitutional framework itself. Much of this legal work was done by the Legal Defense and Educational Fund of the NAACP. Until the late 1940s, lawyers working for the Legal Defense Fund had concentrated on winning small victories within that framework. Then, in 1948, the Legal Defense Fund upgraded its approach by simultaneously filing suits

The NAACP was formed in 1909 to promote the political rights of blacks. In the decades following the 1920s, the NAACP expanded its membership significantly and played an important role in the civil rights movement of the 1950s and 1960s.

Brown v. Board of Education
the 1954 Supreme Court decision that struck down the "separate but equal" doctrine as fundamentally unequal. This case eliminated state power to use race as a criterion of discrimination in law and provided the national government with the power to intervene by exercising strict regulatory policies against discriminatory actions

in different federal districts and through each level of schooling from unequal provision of kindergarten for blacks to unequal sports and science facilities in all-black high schools. After nearly two years of these mostly successful equalization suits, the lawyers decided the time was ripe to confront the "separate but equal" rule head-on, but they felt they needed some heavier artillery to lead the attack. Their choice was the African American lawyer Thurgood Marshall, who had been fighting, and often winning, equalization suits since the early 1930s. Marshall was pessimistic about the readiness of the Supreme Court for a full confrontation with segregation itself and the constitutional principle sustaining it. But the unwillingness of Congress after the 1948 election to consider fair employment legislation seems to have convinced Marshall that the courts were the only hope.

The Supreme Court must have come to the same conclusion because during the four years following 1948 there emerged a clear impression that the Court was willing to take more civil rights cases on appeal. Yet this was no guarantee that the Court would reverse *on principle* the separate but equal precedent of *Plessy v. Ferguson.* All through 1951 and 1952, as cases were winding slowly through the lower court litigation maze, intense discussions and disagreements arose among NAACP lawyers as to whether a full-scale assault on *Plessy* was good strategy or whether it might not be better to continue with specific cases alleging unequal treatment and demanding relief with a Court-imposed policy of equalization.[14] But for some lawyers such as Marshall, these kinds of victories could amount to a defeat. For example, under the leadership of Governor James F. Byrnes, a former Supreme Court justice, South Carolina had undertaken a strategy of equalization of school services on a large scale to satisfy the *Plessy* rule and to head off or render moot litigation against the principle of separate but equal.

In the fall of 1952, the Court had on its docket cases from Kansas, South Carolina, Virginia, Delaware, and the District of Columbia challenging the constitutionality of school segregation. Of these, the case filed in Kansas became the chosen one. It seemed to be ahead of the pack in its district court, and it had the special advantage of being located in a state outside the Deep South.[15]

Oliver Brown, the father of three girls, lived "across the tracks" in a low-income, racially mixed Topeka neighborhood. Every school-day morning, Linda Brown took the school bus to the Monroe School for black children about a mile away. In September 1950, Oliver Brown took Linda to the all-white Sumner School, which was closer to home, to enter her into the third grade in defiance of state law and local segregation rules. When they were refused, Brown took his case to the NAACP, and soon thereafter ***Brown v. Board of Education*** was born. In mid-1953, the Court announced that the several cases on their way up would be re-argued within a set of questions having to do with the intent of the Fourteenth Amendment. Almost exactly a year later, the Court responded to those questions in one of the most important decisions in its history.

In deciding the *Brown* case, the Court, to the surprise of many, basically rejected as inconclusive all the learned arguments about the intent and the history of the Fourteenth Amendment and committed itself to considering only the consequences of segregation:

Does segregation of children in public schools solely on the basis of race, even though the physical facilities and other "tangible" factors may be equal, deprive the children of the minority group of equal educational opportunities? We believe that it does. . . . We conclude that in the field of public education the doctrine of "separate but equal" has no place. Separate educational facilities are inherently unequal.[16]

The *Brown* decision altered the constitutional framework in two fundamental respects. First, after *Brown*, the states no longer had the power to use race as a criterion of discrimination in law. Second, the national government from then on had the power (and eventually the obligation) to intervene with strict regulatory policies against the discriminatory actions of state or local governments, school boards, employers, and many others in the private sector.

Civil Rights after *Brown v. Board of Education*

Brown v. Board of Education withdrew all constitutional authority to use race as a criterion of exclusion, and it signaled more clearly the Court's determination to use the **strict scrutiny** test in cases related to racial discrimination. This meant that the burden of proof would fall on the government—not on the challengers—to show that the law in question *was* constitutional.[17] Although the use of strict scrutiny in cases relating to racial discrimination would give an advantage to those attacking racial discrimination, the historic decision in *Brown v. Board of Education* was merely a small opening move. First, most states refused to cooperate until sued, and many ingenious schemes were employed to delay obedience (such as paying the tuition for white students to attend newly created "private" academies). Second, even as southern school boards began to cooperate by eliminating their legally enforced (*de jure*) school segregation, extensive actual (*de facto*) school segregation remained in the North as well as in the South, as a consequence of racially segregated housing that could not be reached by the 1954–55 *Brown* principles. Third, discrimination in employment, public accommodations, juries, voting, and other areas of social and economic activity were not directly touched by *Brown*.

School Desegregation, Phase One Although the District of Columbia and some of the school districts in the border states began to respond almost immediately to court-ordered desegregation, the states of the Deep South responded with a carefully planned delaying tactic commonly called "massive resistance" by the more demagogic southern leaders and "nullification" and "interposition" by the centrists. Either way, southern politicians stood shoulder to shoulder to declare that the Supreme Court's decisions and orders were without effect. The legislatures in these states enacted statutes ordering school districts to maintain segregated schools and state superintendents to terminate state funding wherever there was racial mixing in the classroom. Some southern states violated their own long traditions of local school autonomy by centralizing public school authority under the governor or the state board of education and gave themselves the power to close the schools and to provide alternative private schooling wherever local school boards might be tending to obey the Supreme Court.

Most of these plans of "massive resistance" were tested in the federal courts and were struck down as unconstitutional.[18] But southern resistance was not confined to legislation. For example, in Arkansas in 1957, Governor Orval Faubus mobilized the Arkansas National Guard to intercede against enforcement of a federal court order to integrate Little Rock Central High School, and President Eisenhower was forced to deploy U.S. troops and literally place the city under martial law. The

strict scrutiny test used by the Supreme Court in racial discrimination cases and other cases involving civil liberties and civil rights, which places the burden of proof on the government rather than on the challengers to show that the law in question is constitutional

de jure literally, "by law"; legally enforced practices, such as school segregation in the South before the 1960s

de facto literally, "by fact"; practices that occur even when there is no legal enforcement, such as school segregation in much of the United States today

for critical analysis

Describe the changes in American society between the *Plessy v. Ferguson* and the *Brown v. Board of Education* decisions. How might changes in society have interacted with the changes in civil rights policy in America since the *Brown* case?

Supreme Court considered the Little Rock confrontation so historically important that the opinion it rendered in that case was not only agreed to unanimously but was, unprecedentedly, signed personally by every one of the justices.[19] The end of massive resistance, however, became simply the beginning of still another southern strategy. "Pupil placement" laws authorized school districts to place each pupil in a school according to a whole variety of academic, personal, and psychological considerations, never mentioning race at all. This put the burden of transferring to an all-white school on the nonwhite children and their parents, making it almost impossible for a single court order to cover a whole district, let alone a whole state. This delayed desegregation a while longer.[20]

Social Protest and Congressional Action Ten years after *Brown*, fewer than 1 percent of black school-age children in the Deep South were attending schools with whites.[21] A decade of frustration made it fairly obvious to all observers that adjudication alone would not succeed. The goal of "equal protection" required positive, or affirmative, action by Congress and by administrative agencies. And given massive southern resistance and a generally negative national public opinion toward racial integration, progress would not be made through courts, Congress, or federal agencies without intense, well-organized support. Figure 5.1 shows the increase in civil rights demonstrations for voting rights and public accommodations during the fourteen years following *Brown*. Organized civil rights demonstrations began to mount slowly but surely after *Brown v. Board of Education*. By the 1960s, the many organizations that made up the civil rights movement had accumulated experience and built networks capable of launching large-scale direct-action campaigns against southern segregationists. The Southern Christian Leadership Conference, the Student Nonviolent Coordinating Committee, and many other organizations had built a movement that stretched across the South. The movement used the

"Massive resistance" among white southerners attempted to block the desegregation attempts of the national government. For example, at Little Rock Central High School in 1957, an angry mob of white students prevented black students from entering the school.

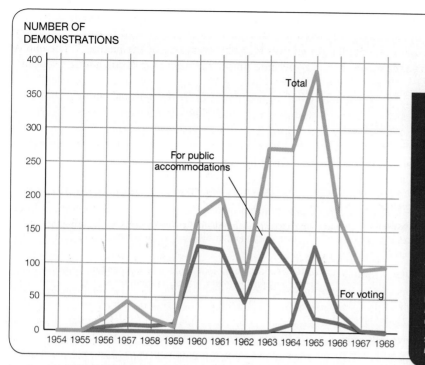

NUMBER OF DEMONSTRATIONS

400

350

300

250

200

150

100

50

0

1954 1955 1956 1957 1958 1959 1960 1961 1962 1963 1964 1965 1966 1967 1968

Total

For public accommodations

For voting

FIGURE 5.1

Peaceful Civil Rights Demonstrations, 1954–68

Peaceful demonstrations were an important part of the civil rights movement. Why did the number of demonstrations grow after 1955? Why do you think the focus shifted from public accommodations to voting rights after 1964?

NOTE: The data are drawn from a search of the *New York Times* index for all references to civil rights demonstrations.

SOURCE: Jonathan D. Casper, *The Politics of Civil Liberties* (New York: Harper & Row, 1972), 90.

media to attract nationwide attention and support. In the massive March on Washington in 1963, the Reverend Martin Luther King, Jr., staked out the movement's moral claims in his famous "I Have a Dream" speech. The image of protesters being beaten, attacked by police dogs, and set upon with fire hoses did much to win broad sympathy for the cause of black civil rights and to discredit state and local governments in the South. In this way, the movement created intense pressure for a reluctant federal government to take more assertive steps to defend black civil rights.

The first modern effort to legislate in the field of civil rights was made in 1957, but the law contained only a federal guarantee of voting rights, without any powers of enforcement, although it did create the Civil Rights Commission to study abuses. Much more important legislation for civil rights followed, especially the Civil Rights Act of 1964. It is important to observe here the mutual dependence of the courts and legislatures: the legislatures need constitutional authority to act, and the courts need legislative assistance to implement court orders and focus political support. Consequently, even as the U.S. Congress finally moved into the field of school desegregation (and other areas of "equal protection"), the courts continued to exercise their powers, not only by placing court orders against recalcitrant school districts but also by extending and reinterpreting aspects of the "equal protection" clause to support legislative and administrative actions (see Table 5.1).

The Civil Rights Acts

The right to equal protection of the laws could be established and, to a certain extent, implemented by the courts. But after a decade of very frustrating efforts, the courts and Congress ultimately came to the conclusion that the federal courts alone were not adequate to the task of changing the social rules, and that legislation and administrative action would be needed.

Three civil rights acts were passed during the first decade after the 1954 Supreme Court decision in *Brown v. Board of Education*. But these acts were of

TABLE 5.1

Cause and Effect in the Civil Rights Movement

Political action and government action spurred each other to produce dramatic changes in American civil rights policies.

JUDICIAL AND LEGAL ACTION	POLITICAL ACTION
1954 *Brown v. Board of Education*	
	1955 Montgomery, Alabama, bus boycott
1956 Federal courts order school integration, especially one ordering Autherine Lucy admitted to University of Alabama, with Governor Wallace officially protesting	
1957 Civil Rights Act creating Civil Rights Commission; President Eisenhower sends paratroops to Little Rock, Arkansas, to enforce integration of Central High School	**1957** Southern Christian Leadership Conference (SCLC) formed, with Martin Luther King, Jr., as president
1960 First substantive Civil Rights Act, primarily voting rights	**1960** Student Nonviolent Coordinating Committee formed to organize protests, sit-ins, freedom rides
1961 Interstate Commerce Commission orders desegregation on all buses and trains, and in terminals	
1961 JFK favors executive action over civil rights legislation	
1963 JFK shifts, supports strong civil rights law; assassination; LBJ asserts strong support for civil rights	**1963** Nonviolent demonstrations in Birmingham, Alabama, lead to King's arrest and his "Letter from Birmingham Jail"
	1963 March on Washington
1964 Congress passes historic Civil Rights Act covering voting, employment, public accommodations, education	
1965 Voting Rights Act	**1965** King announces drive to register 3 million blacks in the South
1966 War on Poverty in full swing	**Late 1960s** Movement dissipates: part toward litigation, part toward community action programs, part toward war protest, part toward more militant "Black Power" actions

only marginal importance. The first two, in 1957 and 1960, established that the Fourteenth Amendment to the Constitution, adopted almost a century earlier, could no longer be disregarded, particularly with regard to voting. The third, the Equal Pay Act of 1963, was more important, but it was concerned with women, did not touch the question of racial discrimination, and had no enforcement mechanisms.

By far the most important piece of legislation passed by Congress concerning equal opportunity was the Civil Rights Act of 1964. It not only put some teeth in the voting rights provisions of the 1957 and 1960 acts but also went far beyond voting to attack discrimination in public accommodations, segregation in the schools, and, at long last, the discriminatory conduct of employers in hiring, promoting, and laying off their employees. Discrimination against women was also included, extending the important 1963 provisions. The 1964 act seemed bold at the time, but it was enacted ten years after the Supreme Court had declared racial discrimination "inherently unequal" under the Fifth and Fourteenth Amendments. And it was enacted long after blacks had demonstrated that discrimination was no longer acceptable. The choice in 1964 was not between congressional action or inaction but between legal action and expanded violence.

Public Accommodations After the passage of the 1964 Civil Rights Act, public accommodations quickly removed some of the most blatant forms of racial discrimination. Signs defining "colored" and "white" restrooms, water fountains, waiting rooms, and seating arrangements were removed and a host of other practices that relegated black people to separate and inferior arrangements were ended. In addition, the federal government filed more than 400 antidiscrimination suits in federal courts against hotels, restaurants, taverns, gas stations, and other "public accommodations."

Many aspects of legalized racial segregation—such as separate Bibles in the courtroom—seem like ancient history today. But the issue of racial discrimination in public settings is by no means over. In 1993, six African American Secret Service agents filed charges against the Denny's restaurant chain for failing to serve them; white Secret Service agents at a nearby table had received prompt service. Similar charges citing discriminatory service at Denny's restaurants surfaced across the country. Faced with evidence of a pattern of systematic discrimination and numerous lawsuits, Denny's paid $45 million in damages to plaintiffs in Maryland and California in what is said to be the largest settlement ever in a public accommodations case.[22] The Denny's case shows how effective the Civil Rights Act of 1964 can be in challenging racial discrimination. In addition to the settlement, the chain vowed to expand employment and management opportunities for minorities in Denny's restaurants. Other forms of racial discrimination in public accommodations are harder to challenge, however. For example, there is considerable evidence that taxicabs often refuse to pick up black passengers.[23] Such practices may be common, but they are difficult to prove and remedy through the law.

School Desegregation, Phase Two The 1964 Civil Rights Act also declared discrimination by private employers and state governments (school boards, etc.) illegal, then went further to provide for administrative agencies to help the courts implement these laws. Title IV of the act, for example, authorized the executive branch, through the Justice Department, to implement federal court orders to desegregate schools, and to do so without having to wait for individual parents to bring complaints. Title VI of the act vastly strengthened the role of the executive branch and the credibility of court orders by providing that federal grants-in-aid to state and local governments for education must be withheld from any school system practicing racial segregation. Title VI became the most effective weapon for desegregating schools outside the South because the situation in northern communities was more subtle and difficult to reach. In the South, the problem was segregation by law coupled with overt resistance to the national government's efforts to change the situation. In contrast, outside the South, segregated facilities were the outcome of hundreds of thousands of housing choices made by individuals and families. Once racial residential patterns emerged, racial homogeneity, property values, and neighborhood schools and churches were defended by Realtors, neighborhood organizations, and the like. Thus, in order to eliminate discrimination nationwide, the 1964 Civil Rights Act (1) gave the president through the Office for Civil Rights of the Justice Department the power to withhold federal education grants,[24] and (2) gave the attorney general of the United States the power to initiate suits (rather than having to await complaints) wherever there was a "pattern or practice" of discrimination.[25]

In the decade following the 1964 Civil Rights Act, the Justice Department brought legal action against more than 500 school districts. During the same period, administrative agencies filed actions against 600 school districts, threatening to suspend federal aid to education unless real desegregation steps were taken.

Busing One step taken toward desegregation was busing children from poor urban school districts to wealthier suburban ones. In 1971, the Supreme Court held that state-imposed desegregation could be brought about by busing children across school districts, even where relatively long distances were involved:

> If school authorities fail in their affirmative obligations, judicial authority may be invoked. Once a right and a violation have been shown, the scope of a district court's equitable powers to remedy past wrongs is broad. . . . Bus transportation [is] a normal and accepted tool of educational policy.[26]

But the decision went beyond that, adding that under certain limited circumstances even racial quotas could be used as the "starting point in shaping a remedy to correct past constitutional violations," and that pairing or grouping of schools and reorganizing school attendance zones would also be acceptable.

Three years later, however, this principle was severely restricted when the Supreme Court determined that only cities found guilty of deliberate and de jure racial segregation would have to desegregate their schools.[27] This ruling had the effect of exempting most northern states and cities from busing because school

The 1964 Civil Rights Act made desegregation a legal requirement. The policy of busing from black neighborhoods to white schools bitterly divided the black and white communities in Boston. In 1976, a protestor waved an American flag threateningly at an innocent black bystander—a lawyer on his way to his office—as another white man sought to help him get out of the way.

segregation in northern cities is generally de facto segregation that results from segregated housing and from thousands of acts of private discrimination against blacks and other minorities.

Boston provides the best illustration of the agonizing problem of making further progress in civil rights in the schools under the constitutional framework established by these decisions. Boston school authorities were found guilty of deliberately building school facilities and drawing school districts "to increase racial segregation." After vain efforts by Boston school authorities to draw up an acceptable plan to remedy the segregation, federal judge W. Arthur Garrity ordered an elaborate desegregation plan of his own, involving busing between the all-black neighborhood of Roxbury and the nearby white, working-class community of South Boston. Opponents of this plan were organized and eventually took the case to the Supreme Court, where *certiorari* (the Court's device for accepting appeals; see Chapter 15) was denied; this had the effect of approving Judge Garrity's order. The city's schools were so segregated and uncooperative that even the conservative administration of President Richard Nixon had already initiated a punitive cutoff of funds. But many liberals also criticized Judge Garrity's plan as being badly conceived because it involved two neighboring communities with a history of tension and mutual resentment. The plan worked well at the elementary school level but proved so explosive at the high school level that it generated a continuing crisis for the city of Boston and for the whole nation over court-ordered, federally directed desegregation in the North.[28]

Additional progress in the desegregation of schools is likely to be extremely slow unless the Supreme Court decides to permit federal action against de facto segregation and against the varieties of private schools and academies that have sprung up for the purpose of avoiding integration. The prospects for further school integration diminished with a Supreme Court decision handed down on January 15, 1991. The opinion, written for the Court by Chief Justice William Rehnquist, held that lower federal courts could end supervision of local school boards if those boards could show compliance "in good faith" with court orders to desegregate and could show that "vestiges of past discrimination" had been eliminated "to the extent practicable."[29] It is not necessarily easy for a school board to prove that the new standard has been met, but this was the first time since *Brown* and the 1964 Civil Rights Act that the Court had opened the door at all to retreat.

That door of retreat was opened further by a 1995 decision in which the Court ruled that the remedies being applied in Kansas City, Missouri, were improper.[30] In accordance with a lower court ruling, the state was pouring additional funding into salaries and remedial programs for Kansas City schools, which had a history of segregation. The aim of the spending was to improve student performance and to attract white students from the suburbs into the city schools. The Supreme Court declared the interdistrict goal improper and reiterated its earlier ruling that states can free themselves of court orders by showing a good-faith effort. This decision indicated the Court's new willingness to end desegregation plans even when predominantly minority schools continue to lag significantly behind white suburban schools. In 2007, the Court's ruling in *Parents Involved in Community Schools v. Seattle School District No. 1* limited still further the measures that can be used to promote school integration. The case involved school-assignment plans voluntarily initiated by the cities of Seattle and Louisville. By making race one factor in assigning students to schools, the cities hoped to achieve greater racial balance across the public schools. The court ruled that these plans—even though the cities voluntarily adopted them—were unconstitutional because they discriminated against white students on the basis of race. Many observers described the decision as the end of the *Brown* era because it eliminated one of the few public strategies

forcritical **analysis**

Many people believe that despite the significance of the *Brown v. Board of Education* decision, it has failed to fulfill its promise. What did *Brown* really accomplish? Can courts bring about social change?

left to promote racial integration. Others argued that Justice Anthony Kennedy's concurring opinion, which recognized the harm of racial isolation, may provide the basis for new efforts to promote integration in the future.[31]

Outlawing Discrimination in Employment Despite the agonizingly slow progress of school desegregation, some progress was made in other areas of civil rights during the 1960s and 1970s. Voting rights were established and fairly quickly began to revolutionize southern politics. Service on juries was no longer denied to minorities. But progress in the right to participate in politics and government dramatized the relative lack of progress in the economic domain, and it was in this area that battles over civil rights were increasingly fought.

The federal courts and the Justice Department entered this area through Title VII of the Civil Rights Act of 1964, which outlawed job discrimination by all private and public employers, including governmental agencies (such as fire and police departments) that employed more than fifteen workers. We have already seen (in Chapter 3) that the Supreme Court gave "interstate commerce" such a broad definition that Congress had the constitutional authority to cover discrimination by virtually any local employers.[32] Title VII makes it unlawful to discriminate in employment on the basis of color, religion, sex, or national origin, as well as race.

Title VII delegated some of the powers to enforce fair-employment practices to the Justice Department's Civil Rights Division and others to a new agency created in the 1964 act, the Equal Employment Opportunity Commission (EEOC). By executive order, these agencies had the power of the national government to revoke public contracts for goods and services and to refuse to engage in contracts for goods and services with any private company that could not guarantee that its rules for hiring, promotion, and firing were nondiscriminatory. Executive orders in 1965, 1967, and 1969 by Presidents Johnson and Nixon extended and reaffirmed nondiscrimination practices in employment and promotion in the federal government service. And in 1972, President Nixon and a Democratic Congress cooperated to strengthen the EEOC by giving it authority to initiate suits rather than waiting for grievances.

But one problem with Title VII was that the complaining party had to show that deliberate discrimination was the cause of the failure to get a job or a training opportunity. Rarely does an employer explicitly admit discrimination on the basis of race, sex, or any other illegal reason. Recognizing the rarity of such an admission, the courts have allowed aggrieved parties (the plaintiffs) to make their case if they can show that an employer's hiring practices had the *effect* of exclusion. A leading case in 1971 involved a "class action" by several black employees in North Carolina attempting to show with statistical evidence that blacks had been relegated to only one department in the Duke Power Company, which involved the least desirable, manual-labor jobs, and that they had been kept out of contention for the better jobs because the employer had added attainment of a high school education and the passing of specially prepared aptitude tests as qualifications for higher jobs. The Supreme Court held that although the statistical evidence did not prove intentional discrimination, and although the requirements were race-neutral in appearance, their effects were sufficient to shift the burden of justification to the employer to show that the requirements were a "business necessity" that bore "a demonstrable relationship to successful performance."[33] The ruling in this case was subsequently applied to other hiring, promotion, and training programs.[34]

Voting Rights Although 1964 was the *most* important year for civil rights legislation, it was not the only important year. In 1965, Congress significantly strengthened legislation protecting voting rights by barring literacy and other tests as a condition for voting in six southern states,[35] by setting criminal penalties for interference with efforts to vote, and by providing for the replacement of local registrars with federally appointed registrars in counties designated by the attorney general as significantly resistant to registering eligible blacks to vote. The right to vote was further strengthened with ratification in 1964 of the Twenty-fourth Amendment, which abolished the poll tax, and in 1975 with legislation permanently outlawing literacy tests in all fifty states and mandating bilingual ballots or oral assistance for Spanish-speakers, Chinese, Japanese, Koreans, Native Americans, and Eskimos.

In the long run, the laws extending and protecting voting rights could prove to be the most effective of all the great civil rights legislation because the progress in black political participation produced by these acts has altered the shape of American politics. In 1965, in the seven states of the Old Confederacy covered by the Voting Rights Act (VRA), 29.3 percent of the eligible black residents were registered to vote, compared with 73.4 percent of the white residents (see Table 5.2). Mississippi was the extreme case, with 6.7 percent black and 69.9 percent white registration. In 1967, a mere two years after implementation of the voting rights laws, 52.1 percent of the eligible blacks in the seven states were registered, comparing

TABLE 5.2

Registration by Race and State in Southern States Covered by the Voting Rights Act (VRA)

The VRA had a direct impact on the rate of black voter registration in the southern states, as measured by the gap between white and black voters in each state. Further insights can be gained by examining changes in white registration rates before and after passage of the VRA as well as by comparing the gaps between white and black registration. Why do you think registration rates for whites increased significantly in some states and dropped in others? What impact could the increase in black registration have had on public policy?

	BEFORE THE ACT*			AFTER THE ACT* 1971–72		
	WHITE	BLACK	GAP[†]	WHITE	BLACK	GAP
Alabama	69.2%	19.3%	49.9%	80.7%	57.1%	23.6%
Georgia	62.6	27.4	35.2	70.6	67.8	2.8
Louisiana	80.5	31.6	48.9	80.0	59.1	20.9
Mississippi	69.9	6.7	63.2	71.6	62.2	9.4
North Carolina	96.8	46.8	50.0	62.2	46.3	15.9
South Carolina	75.7	37.3	38.4	51.2	48.0	3.2
Virginia	61.1	38.3	22.8	61.2	54.0	7.2
TOTAL	73.4	29.3	44.1	67.8	56.6	11.2

*Available registration data as of March 1965 and 1971—72.
[†]The gap is the percentage-point difference between white and black registration rates.

SOURCE: U.S. Commission on Civil Rights, *Political Participation* (1968), Appendix VII: Voter Education Project, Attachment to Press Release, October 3, 1972.

white primary

favorably with 79.5 percent of the eligible whites, a gap of 27.4 points. By 1972, the gap between black and white registration in the seven states was only 11.2 points, and in Mississippi the gap had been reduced to 9.4 points. At one time, white leaders in Mississippi attempted to dilute the influence of this growing black vote by **gerrymandering** districts to ensure that no blacks would be elected to Congress. But the black voters changed Mississippi before Mississippi could change them. In 1988, 11 percent of all elected officials in Mississippi were black. This was up one full percentage point from 1987 and closely approximates the size of the national black electorate, which at the time was just over 11 percent of the American voting-age population. Mississippi's blacks had made significant gains (as they had in other Deep South states) as elected state and local representatives, and Mississippi was one of only eight states in the country in which a black judge presided over the highest state court. (Four of the eight were Deep South states.)[36]

> **gerrymandering** apportionment of voters in districts in such a way as to give unfair advantage to one racial or ethnic group or political party

Several provisions of the 1965 Act had been scheduled to expire in 2007. However, in 2006, responding to charges that black voters still faced discrimination at the polls, Congress renewed the Act for another twenty-five years. Pressure for renewal of the Act had been intense since the disputed 2000 presidential election. The U.S. Commission on Civil Rights conducted hearings on the election in Florida, at which black voters testified about being turned away from the polls, about being wrongly purged from the voting rolls, and about the unreliable voting technology in their neighborhoods. On the basis of this testimony and after an analysis of the vote, the Commission charged that there had been extensive racial discrimination.[37]

Housing The Civil Rights Act of 1964 did not address housing, but in 1968, Congress passed another civil rights act specifically to outlaw housing discrimination. Called the Fair Housing Act, the law prohibited discrimination in the sale or rental of most housing—eventually covering nearly all the nation's housing. Housing was among the most controversial of discrimination issues because of deeply entrenched patterns of residential segregation across the United States. Such segregation was not simply a product of individual choice. Local housing authorities deliberately segregated public housing, and federal guidelines had sanctioned discrimination in Federal Housing Administration mortgage lending, effectively preventing blacks from joining the exodus to the suburbs in the 1950s and 1960s. Nonetheless, Congress had been reluctant to tackle housing discrimination, fearing the tremendous controversy it could arouse. But just as the housing legislation was being considered in April 1968, the civil rights leader Martin Luther King, Jr., was assassinated; this tragedy brought the measure unexpected support in Congress.

Although it pronounced sweeping goals, the Fair Housing Act had little effect on housing segregation because its enforcement mechanisms were so weak. Individuals believing they had been discriminated against had to file suit themselves. The burden was on the individual to prove that housing discrimination had occurred, even though such discrimination is often subtle

The mortgage crisis that led to foreclosures on many homes hit minority communities especially hard. Civil rights organizations argued that some lenders discriminated against African American and Hispanic home buyers, making it harder for them to get a fair deal on a mortgage.

and difficult to document. Although local fair-housing groups emerged to assist individuals in their court claims, the procedures for proving discrimination proved a formidable barrier to effective change. These procedures were not altered until 1988, when Congress passed the Fair Housing Amendments Act. This new law put more teeth in the enforcement procedures and allowed the Department of Housing and Urban Development (HUD) to initiate legal action in cases of discrimination. With vigorous use, these provisions may prove more successful than past efforts at combating housing discrimination.[38]

Other avenues for challenging residential segregation also had mixed success. HUD tried briefly in the early 1970s to create racially "open communities" by withholding federal funds to suburbs that refused to accept subsidized housing. Confronted with charges of "forced integration" and bitter local protests, however, the administration quickly backed down. Efforts to prohibit discrimination in lending have been somewhat more promising. Several laws passed in the 1970s required banks to report information about their mortgage lending patterns, making it more difficult for them to engage in **redlining**, the practice of refusing to lend to entire neighborhoods. The 1977 Community Reinvestment Act required banks to lend in neighborhoods in which they do business. Through vigorous use of this act, many neighborhood organizations have reached agreements with banks that, as a result, have significantly increased investment in some poor neighborhoods. Even so, racial discrimination in home-mortgage lending remains a significant issue. In 2007, the issue of predatory lending—offering loans well above market rates, often with complex provisions that borrowers do not understand—attracted nationwide attention as the number of home foreclosures skyrocketed. Several lawsuits charged that these loans were particularly targeted at minority borrowers.[39] In 2009, civil rights organizations, several states, including California, Massachusetts, New York, and Illinois, and some cities, including Baltimore, filed charges against banks and other lenders claiming they had illegally discriminated against African American and Latino home buyers. Minority home buyers, the suits charged, had been offered subprime mortgage products—with higher interest rates—in contrast to whites with similar income levels, who were offered lower-interest-rate loans.[40]

redlining a practice in which banks refuse to make loans to people living in certain geographic locations

● The Universalization of Civil Rights

Even before equal employment laws began to have a positive effect on the economic situation of blacks, something far more dramatic began happening—the universalization of civil rights. The right not to be discriminated against was being successfully claimed by the other groups listed in Title VII of the 1964 Civil Rights Act—those defined by sex, religion, or national origin—and eventually by still other groups defined by age or sexual preference. This universalization of civil rights has become the new frontier of the civil rights struggle.

Once gender discrimination began to be seen as an important civil rights issue, other groups rose to demand recognition and active protection of their civil rights. Under Title VII, any group or individual can try, and in fact is encouraged to try, to convert goals and grievances into questions of rights and of the deprivation of those rights. A plaintiff must establish only that his or her membership in a group is an unreasonable basis for discrimination—that is, that it cannot be proven to be a "job-related" or otherwise clearly reasonable and relevant decision. In America today, the list of individuals and groups claiming illegal discrimination is lengthy.

for critical analysis

If airport security personnel were permitted to detain and inspect people who appear to be from the Middle East, would it be "ethnic profiling," in violation of civil rights laws? Or would it be a reasonable exception to civil rights under the equal protection clause?

Women and Gender Discrimination

Title VII provided a valuable tool for the growing women's movement in the 1960s
and 1970s. In fact, in many ways the law fostered the growth of the women's movement. The first major campaign of the National Organization for Women (NOW)
involved picketing the Equal Employment Opportunity Commission for its refusal
to ban sex-segregated employment advertisements. NOW also sued the *New York
Times* for continuing to publish such ads after the passage of Title VII. Another
organization, the Women's Equity Action League (WEAL), pursued legal action
on a wide range of sex-discrimination issues, filing lawsuits against law schools and
medical schools for discriminatory admission policies, for example.

Building on these victories and the growth of the women's movement, feminist
activists sought an "Equal Rights Amendment" (ERA) to the Constitution. The proposed amendment was short: its substantive passage stated that "equality of rights
under the law shall not be denied or abridged by the United States or by any State on
account of sex." The amendment's supporters believed that such a sweeping guarantee of equal rights was a necessary tool for ending all discrimination against women
and for making gender roles more equal. Opponents charged that it would be socially disruptive and would introduce changes—such as coed restrooms—that most
Americans did not want. The amendment easily passed Congress in 1972 and won
quick approval in many state legislatures, but it fell three states short of the thirty-
eight needed to ratify the amendment by the 1982 deadline for its ratification.[41]

Despite the failure of the ERA, gender discrimination expanded dramatically as
an area of civil rights law. In the 1970s, the conservative Burger Court (under Chief
Justice Warren Burger) helped to establish gender discrimination as a major and
highly visible civil rights issue. Although the Burger Court refused to treat gender
discrimination as the equivalent of racial discrimination,[42] it did make it easier for
plaintiffs to file and win suits on the basis of gender discrimination by applying an
"intermediate" level of review to these cases.[43] This **intermediate scrutiny** is midway between traditional rules of evidence, which put the burden of proof on the
plaintiff, and the doctrine of strict scrutiny, which requires the defendant to show
not only that a particular classification is reasonable but also that there is a need or
compelling interest for it. Intermediate scrutiny shifts the burden of proof partially
onto the defendant, rather than leaving it entirely on the plaintiff.

intermediate scrutiny test
used by the Supreme Court in
gender discrimination cases,
which places the burden of proof
partially on the government and
partially on the challengers to
show that the law in question is
unconstitutional

Have Women Achieved Equal Rights?

Title VII of the 1964 Civil Rights Act prohibits gender discrimination, and the Supreme Court has consistently upheld the principle that women should have the same rights as men. Since 1960, the United States has made great strides toward gender equality in some areas, but as the data show, still has a long way to go in other areas.

Education

% of college students

1960 — 39% Women

1970 — 39% Women

1980 — 42% Women

1990 — 45% Women

2000 — 48% Women

2008 — 51% Women

Politics

% of members of Congress and state legislatures

1960 — Congress 4% Women

1970 — Congress 2% Women

1980 — State Legislatures 11% Congress 2% Women

1990 — State Legislatures 17% Congress 6% Women

2000 — State Legislatures 23% Congress 13% Women

2008 — State Legislatures 25% Congress 17% Women

Income

Women's weekly earnings as a percentage of men's, by occupation

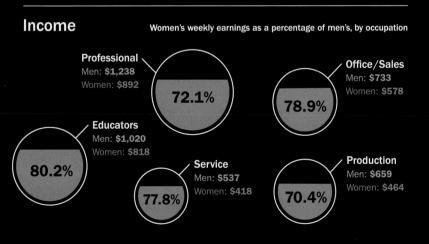

Professional
Men: **$1,238**
Women: **$892**
72.1%

Office/Sales
Men: **$733**
Women: **$578**
78.9%

Educators
Men: **$1,020**
Women: **$818**
80.2%

Service
Men: **$537**
Women: **$418**
77.8%

Production
Men: **$659**
Women: **$464**
70.4%

for critical analysis

1. How much do each of these factors—education, political office holders, and income— say about gender equality in the United States?

2. While most Americans support the principle of equal opportunity for all groups, there is disagreement over how much the government should do to ensure equal outcomes. Discuss the difference between equal opportunity and equal outcomes in the context of women's rights.

SOURCES: U.S. Census Bureau, census.gov; Center for American Women and Politics, cawp.rutgers.edu; Bureau of Labor Statistics, Women in the Labor Force: A Databook (2009 Edition), Table 18, (accessed 6/24/10).

One major step was taken in 1992, when the Court decided in *Franklin v. Gwinnett County Public Schools* that violations of Title IX of the 1972 Education Act could be remedied with monetary damages.[44] Title IX forbade gender discrimination in education, but it initially sparked little litigation because of its weak enforcement provisions. The Court's 1992 ruling that monetary damages could be awarded for gender discrimination opened the door for more legal action in the area of education. The greatest impact has been in the areas of sexual harassment—the subject of the *Franklin* case—and in equal treatment of women's athletic programs. The potential for monetary damages has made universities and public schools take the problem of sexual harassment more seriously. Colleges and universities have also started to pay more attention to women's athletic programs. In the two years after the *Franklin* case, complaints to the Education Department's Office for Civil Rights about unequal treatment of women's athletic programs nearly tripled. In several high-profile legal cases, some prominent universities were ordered to create more women's sports programs; many other colleges and universities have begun to add more women's programs in order to avoid potential litigation.[45] In 1997, the Supreme Court refused to hear a petition by Brown University challenging a lower court ruling that the university establish strict sex equity in its athletic programs. The Court's decision meant that in colleges and universities across the country, varsity athletic positions for men and women must reflect their overall enrollment numbers.[46]

In 1996, the Supreme Court made another important decision about gender and education by putting an end to all-male schools supported by public funds. It ruled that the Virginia Military Institute's (VMI) policy of not admitting women was unconstitutional.[47] Along with the Citadel, another all-male military college in South Carolina, VMI had never admitted women in its 157-year history. VMI argued that the unique educational experience it offered—including intense physical training and the harsh treatment of freshmen—would be destroyed if women students were admitted. The Court, however, ruled that the male-only policy denied "substantial equality" to women. Two days after the Court's ruling, the Citadel announced that it would accept women. VMI considered becoming a private institution in order to remain all-male, but in September 1996, the school board finally voted to admit

Kim Messer, pictured here with a group of male cadets, was one of the first women admitted to the Citadel, a military college in South Carolina. The Supreme Court ruled in 1996 that state-sponsored schools must be open to both men and women.

women. The legal decisions may have removed formal barriers to entry, but the experience of the new female cadets at these schools was not easy. The first female cadet at the Citadel, Shannon Faulkner, won admission in 1995 under a federal court order but quit after four days. Although four women were admitted to the Citadel after the Supreme Court decision, two of the four quit several months later. They charged harassment from male students, including attempts to set the female cadets on fire.[48]

Courts began to find sexual harassment a form of sex discrimination during the late 1970s. Although sexual harassment law applies to education, most of the law of sexual harassment has been developed by courts through interpretation of Title VII of the Civil Rights Act of 1964. In 1986, the Supreme Court recognized two forms of sexual harassment. One type is "quid pro quo" harassment, which involves an explicit or strongly implied threat that submission is a condition of continued employment. The second is harassment that creates offensive or intimidating employment conditions that amount to a "hostile environment."[49]

Employers and many employees have worried that hostile-environment sexual harassment is too ambiguous. When can an employee bring charges? When is the employer liable? In 1986, the Court said that sexual harassment may be legally actionable even if the employee did not suffer tangible economic or job-related losses in relation to it. In 1993, the Court said that sexual harassment may be legally actionable even if the employee did not suffer tangible psychological costs as a result of it.[50] In two 1998 cases, the Court further strengthened the law when it said that whether or not sexual harassment results in economic harm to the employee, an employer is liable for the harassment if it was committed by someone with authority over the employee—by a supervisor, for example. But the Court also said that an employer may defend itself by showing that it had a sexual harassment prevention and grievance policy in effect.[51]

The fight against gender discrimination as an important part of the civil rights struggle has coincided with the rise of women's politics as a discrete movement in American politics. As with the struggle for racial equality, the relationship between changes in government policies and political action suggests that changes in government policies to a great degree produce political action. Today, the existence of a powerful women's movement derives in large measure from the enactment of Title VII of the Civil Rights Act of 1964 and from the Burger Court's vital steps in applying that law to protect women. The recognition of women's civil rights has become an issue that in many ways transcends the usual distinctions of American political discourse. In the heavily partisan debate over the federal crime bill enacted in 1994, for instance, the section of the bill that enjoyed the widest support was the Violence against Women Act, whose most important feature was that it defined gender-biased violent crimes as a matter of civil rights and created a civil rights remedy for women who have been the victims of such crimes. The Supreme Court's 2000 decision ruling the act unconstitutional signaled a defeat for women's rights. Another setback occurred in 2007, when the Court ruled against a claim of pay discrimination at work. The case, *Ledbetter v. Goodyear Tire and Rubber Co.*, involved a woman supervisor named Lily Ledbetter who learned late in her career that she was being paid up to 40 percent less than male supervisors, including those with less seniority. Ledbetter filed a grievance with the Equal Employment Opportunity Commission charging sex discrimination. The Supreme Court denied her claim, ruling that according to the law, workers must file their grievance 180 days after the discrimination occurs. Many observers found the ruling unfair because workers often do not know about pay differentials until well after the initial decision to discriminate has been made. Justice Ruth Bader Ginsburg, the only female member of the Court, marked her disagreement by reading her dissent aloud, a rare occurrence. In January 2009, the Lily Ledbetter Fair Pay Act became the first bill that President Obama signed into law. The new law gave workers expanded rights to sue in cases, such as Ledbetter's, when an employee learns of discriminatory treatment well after it has started.

Latinos

The labels "Latino" and "Hispanic" encompass a wide range of groups with diverse national origins, distinctive cultural identities, and particular experiences. As a result, the civil rights issues have varied considerably by group and by place. For example, the early political experiences of Mexican Americans were shaped by race and by region. For the earliest Mexican Americans in the Southwest, the United States came to them, rather than the other way around. In 1848, under the Treaty of Guadalupe Hidalgo, Mexico ceded to the United States territory that now comprises Arizona, California, New Mexico, and parts of Colorado, Nevada, and Utah, as well as extending the Texas border to the Rio Grande. Although the treaty guaranteed full civil rights to the residents of these territories, Mexican Americans in fact experienced ongoing discrimination, which they sought to remedy through the courts. In 1898 the courts reconfirmed Mexican Americans' formal political rights, including the right to vote. In many places, however, and especially in Texas, Mexican Americans were segregated and prevented from voting through such means as the white primary and the poll tax.[52] There were regional differences too. In contrast to the northeastern and midwestern cities to which most European ethnics immigrated, the Southwest did not have a tradition of ethnic mobilization associated with machine politics. Particularly after the political reforms enacted in the first decade of the twentieth century, city politics in the Southwest was dominated by a small group of Anglo elites. In the countryside, when Mexican Americans participated in politics, it was often as part of a political organization dominated by a white landowner, or *patrón*.

The earliest Mexican American independent political organizations included the League of United Latin American Citizens (LULAC), founded in 1929, and the GI Forum, created in 1948. Both groups worked to stem discrimination against Mexican Americans. Discrimination against Mexicans in the Southwest was widespread. Texas established separate schools for Mexicans, and the practice of segregated education was also widespread in southern California. Mexicans also experienced severe discrimination in the housing markets, often banned by restrictive covenants from buying or renting houses in many neighborhoods. LULAC pursued a legal strategy like the NAACP's to eliminate the segregation of Mexican American students. One of its earliest victories came in 1931, when it successfully challenged a Texas school district's decision to establish separate schools for Anglos and Mexicans.[53] LULAC also litigated the 1947 *Mendez v. Westminster* case, which overturned school segregation in Orange County, California. This case was an important precursor to *Brown v. Board of Education*, and many of the same actors were involved. For example, Thurgood Marshall of the NAACP, the lead attorney on *Brown* (and later a Supreme

The 1947 Mendez v. Westminster *case challenged segregation of Mexican American students in California and was an important precursor to later school segregation cases. In 2007, a U.S. postal stamp was issued to commemorate the* Mendez *case.*

Court justice), filed a brief supporting desegregation in the *Mendez* case. Moreover, Earl Warren, the California governor who signed the legislation outlawing school segregation there after the *Mendez* decision, served as chief justice when the Supreme Court ruled on *Brown* seven years later. In 2007, the *Mendez* case received national recognition as an important landmark in civil rights with a U.S. postal stamp bearing the words "toward equality in our schools."[54] By the late 1950s, the first Mexican American was elected to Congress, and four others followed in the 1960s. In the late 1960s a new kind of Mexican American political movement was born. Inspired by the black civil rights movement, Mexican American students launched boycotts of high school classes in East Los Angeles, Denver, and San Antonio. Students in colleges and universities across California joined in as well. Among their demands were bilingual education, an end to discrimination, and more cultural recognition. In Crystal City, Texas, which had been dominated by Anglo politicians despite a population that was overwhelmingly Mexican American, the newly formed La Raza Unida Party took over the city government.[55]

Since that time, Latino political strategy has developed along two tracks. One is a traditional ethnic-group path of voter registration and voting along ethnic lines. The second is a legal strategy using the various civil rights laws designed to ensure fair access to the political system. The Mexican American Legal Defense and Education Fund (MALDEF), founded in 1968, has played a key role in designing and pursuing the latter strategy.

Immigrants and Civil Rights Since the 1960s, rights for Latinos have been intertwined with immigrant rights. Latino organizations opposed the Immigration Reform and Control Act of 1986 because it imposed sanctions on employers who hire undocumented workers. Such sanctions, they feared, would lead employers to discriminate against Latinos. These suspicions were confirmed in a 1990 report by the General Accounting Office that found employer sanctions had created a "widespread pattern of discrimination" against Latinos and others who appear foreign.[56] Organizations such as MALDEF monitor and challenge such discrimination. These groups have turned their attention to the rights of legal and illegal immigrants, as anti-immigrant sentiment has grown in recent years.

The Supreme Court has ruled that unauthorized immigrants are eligible for education and emergency medical care but can be denied other social benefits; for much of American history legal immigrants were treated much the same as citizens. But growing immigration—including an estimated 300,000 unauthorized immigrants per year—and mounting economic insecurity have undermined these practices. Groups of voters across the country now strongly support drawing a sharper line between immigrants and citizens. The movement to deny benefits to noncitizens gathered steam in California, which experienced sharp economic distress in the early 1990s and has the highest levels of immigration of any state. In 1994, Californians voted in favor of Proposition 187, denying unauthorized immigrants all services except emergency medical care. Supporters of the measure hoped to discourage unauthorized immigration and to pressure those already in the country to leave. Opponents contended that denying basic services to unauthorized

Some states and cities have tried to address illegal immigration by enacting stricter laws than those under consideration by Congress. This worker protested one such law with a sign reading "I am a day laborer, not a criminal."

immigrants risked creating a subclass of residents in the United States whose lack of education and poor health would threaten all Americans. In 1994 and 1997, a federal court declared most of Proposition 187 unconstitutional, affirming previous rulings that unauthorized immigrants should be granted public education. A booming economy helped to reduce public concern about unauthorized immigration, but these worries soon emerged again.

Questions about the rights of unauthorized immigrants became especially contentious in 2007. That year, Congress considered a complex compromise bill—running some 761 pages long—that attempted to accomplish three goals: increase border security to reduce the entrance of undocumented immigrants; provide unauthorized immigrants who had been in the country for at least five years with a pathway to legal citizenship; and ensure employers an adequate supply of temporary immigrant workers through a guest worker program. The compromise failed in the face of opposition from the Right, which disliked the provisions for creating a path to legal citizenship, and from the Left, which opposed the proposed guest worker program.

In the aftermath of the failed legislation, unauthorized immigrants have continued to be a hot-button political issue with important repercussions for civil rights. Antagonism against unauthorized immigration has spilled over into violence against Latinos. One issue for civil rights groups is to ensure that, when warranted, such violence is classified as a hate crime by the federal Justice Department. Such crimes carry significantly heavier penalties than would otherwise be the case. The National Council of La Raza and the Mexican American Legal Defense and Education Fund (MALDEF) have pressed the Justice Department to classify the murders of a Mexican man in Shenandoah, Pennsylvania, as a hate crime. Although the teenage perpetrators beat the man to death and shouted ethnic slurs, in 2009 a local jury imposed a very light sentence on the defendants. MALDEF collected 50,000 signatures, which it brought to the Justice Department, urging that the murder be declared a hate crime.[57] Another ongoing issue is a federal program that works with local and state law enforcement agencies to enforce federal immigration laws. Initiated by the Department of Homeland Security in the final years of the Bush administration, the program has drawn sharp criticism from civil rights groups for engaging in racial profiling and violating civil rights. In some areas, local officials have initiated immigrant "sweeps," rounding up Latinos, many of whom were legal immigrants or even American citizens. A broad coalition of civil rights organizations have opposed the program, and the congressional Hispanic Caucus called on the new president to end it. Even so, the Obama administration announced that it would expand the program, although it vowed to exercise greater federal oversight to ensure against civil rights violations. It also sought to redirect the program to focus on major drug offenders, violent criminals, and those already in prison.[58] At the same time, the administration revoked the authority of Maricopa County (Phoenix) Sheriff Joe Arpaio to act as an agent of the federal government. Arpaio attracted national attention and three federal investigations for his flamboyant immigrant sweeps and his harsh treatment of those he has detained. Arizona drew national attention in April 2010 when it enacted a new law requiring immigrants to carry identity documents with them at all times and giving the police greater powers to stop anyone they suspect of being an unauthorized immigrant. Opponents, including President Obama, charged that the law would lead to racial profiling of Latinos and to violation of their civil rights. The law sparked a political backlash, with some cities, including Los Angeles, announcing that they would boycott Arizona, and the federal Justice Department poised to launch a

for critical analysis

In 2010, Arizona passed a law requiring immigrants to carry immigration documents at all times and authorizing the police to detain anyone suspected of being illegally in the country. Critics charged that this law invited discrimination against Hispanics. Why are immigration and the rights of immigrants so controversial?

legal challenge against the law. Yet, public opinion polls showed that nearly 60 percent of those polled supported the tough measure. In the absence of new federal legislation that addresses the large numbers of undocumented immigrants in the country, the conflicting policies and lawsuits are likely to continue.

Asian Americans

Like the term "Latino," the label "Asian American" encompasses a wide range of people from very different national backgrounds who came to the United States at different moments in history. As a consequence, they have had very diverse experiences.

The early Asian experience in the United States was shaped by a series of naturalization laws dating back to 1790, the first of which declared that only white aliens were eligible for citizenship. Chinese immigrants began arriving in California in the 1850s, drawn by the boom of the gold rush, but they were immediately met with hostility. The virulent antagonism toward Chinese immigrants in California led Congress in 1870 to declare Chinese immigrants ineligible for citizenship. In 1882, the first Chinese Exclusion Act suspended the entry of Chinese laborers.

At the time of the Exclusion Act, the Chinese community was composed predominantly of single male laborers, with few women and children. The few Chinese children in San Francisco were initially denied entry to the public schools; only after parents of American-born Chinese children pressed legal action were the children allowed to attend public school. Even then, however, they were segregated into a separate Chinese school. American-born Chinese children could not be denied citizenship, however; this right was confirmed by the Supreme Court in 1898, when it ruled in *United States v. Wong Kim Ark* that anyone born in the United States was entitled to full citizenship.[59] Still, new Chinese immigrants were barred from the United States until 1943, after China had become a key wartime ally and Congress repealed the Chinese Exclusion Act and permitted Chinese residents to become citizens.

The earliest Japanese immigrants, who came to California in the 1880s at the height of the anti-Chinese movement, faced similar discrimination. Like Chinese immigrants, Japanese immigrants were ineligible to become citizens because of their race. During the first part of the twentieth century, California and several other western states enacted laws that denied Japanese immigrants the right to own property. The denial of basic civil rights to Japanese Americans culminated in the decision to remove forcibly Americans of Japanese descent as well as Japanese noncitizen residents from their homes and confine them in internment camps during World War II. Despite a vigorous legal challenge, the Supreme Court ruled that the internment was constitutional on the grounds of military necessity.[60] Not until the Civil Liberties Act of 1988 did the federal government formally acknowledge this denial of civil rights as a "grave injustice" that had been "motivated largely by racial prejudice, wartime hysteria, and a failure of political leadership."[61] Along with a formal apology from the president, Congress issued each surviving internee a $20,000 check.

Asian immigration increased rapidly after the 1965 Immigration Act, which lifted discriminatory quotas. In spite of this and other developments, limited English proficiency barred many new Asian American and Latino immigrants from full participation in American life. Two developments in the 1970s, however, established rights for language minorities. In 1974, the Supreme Court ruled in *Lau v. Nichols*, a suit filed on behalf of Chinese students in San Francisco, that school districts have to provide education for students whose English is limited.[62] It did not mandate bilingual education, but it established a duty to provide instruction that the students could understand. As we saw earlier, the 1970 amendments to the Voting Rights Act permanently outlawed literacy tests in all fifty states and mandated bilingual ballots or oral assistance for those who speak Spanish, Chinese, Japanese, Korean, Native American languages, or Eskimo languages.

Native Americans

The political status of Native Americans was left unclear in the Constitution. But by the early 1800s, the courts had defined each of the Indian tribes as a nation. As members of Indian nations, Native Americans were declared noncitizens of the United States. The political status of Native Americans changed in 1924, when congressional legislation granted citizenship to all persons born in the United States. A variety of changes in federal policy toward Native Americans during the 1930s paved the way for a later resurgence of their political power. Most important was the federal decision to encourage Native Americans on reservations to establish local self-government.[63]

The Native American political movement gathered force in the 1960s, as Native Americans began to use protest, litigation, and assertion of tribal rights to improve

Asian immigrants faced discrimination throughout much of American history. During World War II, Americans of Japanese descent were forced from their homes and confined in internment camps. At the time, the Supreme Court supported this denial of civil rights as a necessary security measure.

Human Rights and International Politics

When Barack Obama entered office, many observers expected the United States to place a stronger emphasis on human rights in its international engagement. In some respects, the new administration has fulfilled their hopes, but in other ways, it has pursued international policies that some view as hostile to the goal of promoting human rights around the world.

In March 2009, the new administration signaled that it would engage international concerns about human rights when it sought and won a seat on the United Nations Human Rights Council. The Bush administration had refused to join the council on the grounds that the UN was biased and that the United States could better protect international human rights by remaining on the outside.

However, when it comes to foreign policy, the Obama administration has made it clear that advancing human rights is not its sole goal. Instead, the administration has balanced support for human rights with the recognition that the United States often has to work with countries that may violate those rights.

For example, concerned with offending the Chinese president before their November 2009 meeting, Obama delayed a meeting with the Dalai Lama who has led a long resistance to Chinese rule in Tibet. This was in sharp contrast to the approach taken by President George W. Bush, who presented the Dalai Lama with the Congressional Gold Medal. Obama's decision was seen as part of a broader effort by the administration to cultivate Chinese support, a strategy that has been called "strategic reassurance." On her visit to China soon after becoming secretary of state, Hillary Clinton suggested that concern for human rights should not "interfere with the global economic crisis, the global climate-change crisis, and the security crisis"—a reference to the U.S. desire for North Korean nuclear disarmament—all of which required the Chinese to work with the United States.[a]

The Obama administration's stance toward Burma provides another example of its effort to balance human rights advocacy with foreign policy realism. Burma (also known as Myanmar) is ruled by a military junta that seized power almost five decades ago and has blocked democratic elections ever since. The United States has long imposed sanctions on Burma for its failure to hold elections and for its continued imprisonment of opposition leaders, most notably Nobel Peace Prize winner Aung San Suu Kyi. However the Obama administration has concluded that sanctions alone haven't worked. Therefore in late September of 2009, the administration announced that it would start talks with the country's military junta for the first time. At the same time, it declared that it would increase humanitarian assistance to the country.

Striking the right balance between human rights and achieving America's other international interests is not simple. As the Obama administration seeks to advance America's interests in the world, it will have to determine how best to reconcile these interests with its support for international human rights.

[a] John Pomfret. "Obama's Meeting with the Dalai Lama Is Delayed," *Washington Post*, October 5, 2009, www.washingtonpost.com (accessed 10/24/09).

for critical analysis

1. How has the Obama administration sought to balance support for human rights and America's international interests?

2. Are symbolic meetings, such as that with the Dalai Lama, important for advancing international human rights? Will better relations with Chinese leaders lead to stronger human rights in the long run or will they compromise America's ability to serve as a leader in this field?

their situation. In 1968, Dennis Banks, Herb Powless, and Clyde Bellecourt co-founded the American Indian Movement (AIM), the most prominent Native American rights organization. AIM won national attention in 1969 when 200 of its members, representing twenty different tribes, took over the famous prison island of Alcatraz in San Francisco Bay, claiming it for Native Americans. The federal government responded to the rise in Indian activism with the Indian Self-Determination and Education Assistance Act, which began to give Indians more control over their own land.[64]

As a language minority, Native Americans were also affected by the 1975 amendments to the Voting Rights Act and the *Lau* decision. The *Lau* decision established the right of Native Americans to be taught in their own languages. This marked quite a change from the boarding schools once run by the Bureau of Indian Affairs, at which members of Indian tribes had been forbidden to speak their own languages. In addition to these language-related issues, Native Americans have sought to expand their rights on the basis of their sovereign status. Since the 1920s and 1930s, Native American tribes have sued the federal government for illegally seizing land, seeking monetary reparations and land as damages. Both types of damages have been awarded in such suits, but only in small amounts. Native American tribes have been more successful in winning federal recognition of their sovereignty. Sovereign status has, in turn, allowed them to exercise greater self-determination. Most significant in economic terms was a 1987 Supreme Court decision that freed Native American tribes from most state regulations prohibiting gambling. The establishment of casino gambling on Native American lands has brought a substantial flow of new income into desperately poor reservations.

Disabled Americans

The concept of rights for the disabled began to emerge in the 1970s as the civil rights model spread to other groups. The seed was planted in a little-noticed provision of the 1973 Rehabilitation Act, which outlawed discrimination against individuals on the basis of disabilities. As in many other cases, the law itself helped give rise to the movement demanding rights for the handicapped.[65] Modeling itself on the NAACP's Legal Defense Fund, the disability movement founded a Disability Rights Education and Defense Fund to press its legal claims. The movement achieved its greatest success with the passage of the Americans with Disabilities Act (ADA) of 1990, which guarantees equal employment rights and access to public businesses for the disabled. Claims of discrimination in violation of this act are considered by the Equal Employment Opportunity Commission. The impact of the law has been far-reaching, as businesses and public facilities have installed ramps, elevators, and other devices to meet the act's requirements.[66] In 1998, the Supreme Court interpreted the ADA to apply to people with HIV. Until then, ADA was interpreted as covering people with AIDS but not people with HIV. The case arose when a dentist was asked to fill a cavity for a woman with HIV; he refused unless the procedure was done in a hospital setting. The woman sued, and her complaint was that HIV had already disabled her because it was discouraging her from having children. (The act prohibits discrimination in employment, housing, and health care.) Despite widespread concerns that the ADA was being expanded too broadly and the costs were becoming too burdensome, corporate America did not seem to be disturbed by the Court's ruling. Stephen Bokat, general counsel of the U.S. Chamber of Commerce, said businesses in general had already been accommodating people with HIV as well as with AIDS and that the case presented no serious problem.[67]

The Aged

Age discrimination in employment is illegal. The 1967 federal Age Discrimination in Employment Act (ADEA) makes age discrimination illegal when practiced by employers with at least twenty employees. Many states have added to the federal provisions with their own age discrimination laws, and some such state laws are stronger than the federal provisions. The major lobbyist for seniors, the AARP, formerly the American Association of Retired Persons (see Chapter 11), with its claim to over 30 million members, has been active in keeping these laws on the books and making sure that they are vigorously implemented. Rights for older workers received a setback in a 2009 Supreme Court decision in the case of *Gross v. FBL Financial Services*.[68] The Court ruled that a fifty-four-year-old employee who had challenged his dismissal on the grounds of age discrimination would have to show that his demotion was a direct result of discrimination. This was a major change in the law: in the past, the burden of proof was on employers to demonstrate that they had valid reasons other than age for demoting or terminating one of their employees.

Gays and Lesbians

In less than thirty years, the gay and lesbian movement has become one of the largest civil rights movements in contemporary America. Beginning with street protests in the 1960s, the movement has grown into a well-financed and sophisticated lobby. The Human Rights Campaign is the primary national political action committee (PAC) focused on gay rights; it provides campaign financing and volunteers to work for candidates endorsed by the group. The movement has also formed legal-rights organizations, including the Lambda Legal Defense and Education Fund.

Gay and lesbian rights drew national attention in 1993, when President Bill Clinton confronted the question of whether gays should be allowed to serve in the military. As a candidate, Clinton had said he favored lifting the ban on homosexuals in the military. The issue set off a huge controversy in the first months of Clinton's presidency. After nearly a year of deliberation, the administration enunciated a compromise: its "Don't ask, don't tell" policy. This policy allows gays and lesbians to serve in the military as long as they do not openly proclaim their sexual orientation or engage in homosexual activity. The administration maintained that the ruling would protect gays and lesbians against witchhunting investigations, but many gay and lesbian advocates expressed disappointment, charging the president with reneging on his campaign promise. In March 2010, the Pentagon instituted interim rules that make it more difficult for gays and lesbians whose sexual orientation is disclosed by a third party to be discharged, but only Congress can repeal the 1993 law.

But until 1996, there was no Supreme Court ruling or national legislation explicitly protecting gays and lesbians from discrimination. The first gay-rights case that the Court decided, *Bowers v. Hardwick*, ruled against a right to privacy that would protect consensual homosexual activity.[69] After the *Bowers* decision, the

In 2008, California voters passed Proposition 8, which restricted marriage to couples consisting of a man and woman. Opponents of the proposition argued that same-sex couples should be treated equally under the law and allowed the right to marry.

gay and lesbian rights movement sought suitable legal cases to test the constitutionality of discrimination against gays and lesbians, much as the black civil rights movement had done in the late 1940s and 1950s. As one advocate put it, "lesbians and gay men are looking for their *Brown v. Board of Education*."[70] Test cases stemmed from local ordinances restricting gay rights (including the right to marry), job discrimination, and family law issues such as adoption and parental rights. In 1996, the Supreme Court, in *Romer v. Evans*, explicitly extended fundamental civil rights protections to gays and lesbians, by declaring unconstitutional a 1992 amendment to the Colorado state constitution that prohibited local governments from passing ordinances to protect gay rights.[71] The decision's forceful language highlighted the connection between gay rights and civil rights as it declared discrimination against gay people unconstitutional.

In *Lawrence v. Texas* (2003), the Court overturned *Bowers* and struck down a Texas statute criminalizing certain intimate sexual conduct between consenting partners of the same sex.[72] A victory for lesbians and gays every bit as significant as *Roe v. Wade* was for women, *Lawrence v. Texas* extends at least one aspect of civil liberties to sexual minorities: the right to privacy. However, this decision by itself does not undo the various exclusions that deprive lesbians and gays of full civil rights, including the right to marry, which became a hot-button issue in 2004 and remains one today.

In San Francisco hundreds of gays and lesbians lined up to obtain marriage licenses after the mayor directed the county clerk to issue licenses to same-sex couples in defiance of California law. A significant victory came in 2004, when the Supreme Judicial Court of Massachusetts ruled that under that state's constitution, gay men and lesbians were entitled to marry. After that, six other states passed laws that allowed gays and lesbians to marry. In California, however, voters repealed the law five months later; in 2009 voters in Maine rolled back the law permitting gay marriage as well. In 2009, gay rights advocates won a significant victory of a different kind in national politics. New legislation extended the definition of hate crimes to include crimes against gays and transgendered people. Such legislation had been sought since the 1998 murder of Matthew Shepard, a Wyoming college student who was brutally slain because of his sexual orientation. The new law allows for tougher penalities when a crime is designated a hate crime.

● Affirmative Action

Not only has the politics of rights spread to increasing numbers of groups in American society since the 1960s, it has also expanded its goal. The relatively narrow goal of equalizing opportunity by eliminating discriminatory barriers evolved into the far broader goal of **affirmative action**—compensatory action to overcome the consequences of past discrimination. Affirmative action policies take race or some other status into account in order to provide greater opportunities to groups that have previously been at a disadvantage due to discrimination.

President Lyndon Johnson put the case emotionally in 1965: "You do not take a person who, for years, has been hobbled by chains . . . and then say you are free to compete with all the others, and still just believe that you have been completely fair."[73] Johnson attempted to inaugurate affirmative action by executive orders directing agency heads and personnel officers to pursue vigorously a policy of minority employment in the federal civil service and in companies doing business with the national government. But affirmative action did not become a prominent goal of the national government until the 1970s.

affirmative action government policies or programs that seek to redress past injustices against specified groups by making special efforts to provide members of these groups with access to educational and employment opportunities

Television and Public Opinion Regarding Minority Groups

Americans' support for the rights of minority groups often hinges on the way they perceive those groups, and some researchers believe that television plays a significant role in shaping people's perceptions of minority groups.

Depictions of African Americans in popular culture have a long and complicated history, from the mocking portrayals in early radio and television programs like *Amos 'n' Andy* to contemporary programs like *Everybody Hates Chris.* In the late 1980s, the sitcom *The Cosby Show* provoked concern that portrayals of upper-middle class African Americans could create a false perception of African American affluence. In 1989, the chair of Harvard's department of African American Studies, Henry Louis Gates Jr., argued that there was a fundamental disconnect between the socioeconomic status of African Americans in programs such as *Cosby* and the actual status o f most African Americans at the time. *The Cosby Show* starred Bill Cosby as a successful doctor married to a lawyer. The problem, according to critics such as Gates, was that, "As the dominant representation of blacks on TV, it suggests that blacks are solely responsible for their social conditions, with no acknowledgement of the severely constricted life opportunities that most black people face."[a] In fact, according to one study   of white viewers, exposure   to the affluent *Cosby* family led some to believe that affirmative action was unnecessary.

A different concern about television portrayals of African Americans is that the mass media may contribute to perceptions of black men as criminals. Some research has shown that news coverage of crime tends to portray African American suspects as more threatening than white suspects. Studies confirm that negative stereotypical portrayals of African Americans on television foster negative attitudes toward African Americans among white audience members. Similarly, recent research suggests that the television and film portrayal of Hispanics as drug lords may contribute to enduring public views that Latinos are prone to violent behavior.

Public opinion about gays and lesbians may also be linked to recent trends in media. Traditionally, gays and lesbians in America have been one of the most marginalized minority groups. Yet, the political scientist Alan Yang has presented data showing that Americans are becoming more accepting of gays and lesbians and same-sex marriage. During this same time period, portrayals of gays and lesbians on television have become more diverse and more frequent. One example of a popular program featuring gay characters was the comedy *Will and Grace,* which debuted on NBC in 1998. While the show received criticism from some who said it reinforced gay stereotypes (the flamboyant character Jack in particular), other research suggests that the program had positive effects on the status of gays in society. As reality television shows have gained, gays and lesbians have also been well represented on such shows as *Top Chef, Project Runway,* and *Queer Eye for the Straight Guy.*

But how might these portrayals of minorities on television translate into public opinion and eventually policy concerning rights? According to one theory, viewing programs including minority characters is associated with lower levels of prejudice. Another view is that television portrayals of minority groups are influenced by public opinion, not the other way around.

[a]H. L. Gates, "TV's Black World Turns—But Stays Unreal," *New York Times,* November 12, 1989, sec. 2, p. 1.

for critical analysis

1. Do you think that the way minority groups are portrayed on television is likely to have a major effect on support for those groups' rights?

2. Even if public opinion toward gays and lesbians shifts dramatically over the next several years, will that necessarily translate into more rights for gays? What are some factors that might foster a gap between public opinion toward gays and public policy toward gay rights?

Affirmative action also took the form of efforts by the agencies in the Department of Health, Education, and Welfare to shift their focus from "desegregation" to "integration."[74] Federal agencies—sometimes with court orders and sometimes without them—required school districts to present plans for busing children across district lines, for pairing schools, for closing certain schools, and for redistributing faculties as well as students, under pain of loss of grants-in-aid from the federal government. The guidelines issued for such plans constituted preferential treatment to compensate for past discrimination, and without this legislatively assisted approach to integration orders, there would certainly not have been the dramatic increase in black children attending integrated classes. The yellow school bus became a symbol of hope for many and a signal of defeat for others.

Affirmative action was also initiated in the area of employment opportunity. The Equal Employment Opportunity Commission often has required plans whereby employers must attempt to increase the number of their minority employees, and the Office of Federal Contract Compliance Programs in the Department of Labor has used the threat of contract revocation for the same purpose. Increases in the number of minorities did not require formal quotas.

The Supreme Court and the Burden of Proof

Efforts by the executive, legislative, and judicial branches to shape the meaning of affirmative action today tend to center on a key issue: What is the appropriate level of review in affirmative action cases—that is, on whom should the burden of proof be placed, the plaintiff or the defendant? Affirmative action was first addressed formally by the Supreme Court in the case of Allan Bakke (see Table 5.3). Bakke, a white male, brought suit against the University of California at Davis Medical School on the grounds that in denying him admission the school had discriminated against him on the basis of his race (that year the school had reserved 16 of 100 available slots for minority applicants). He argued that his grades and test scores had ranked him well above many students who had been accepted at the school and that the only possible explanation for his rejection was that those others accepted were black or Latino, whereas he was white. In 1978, Bakke won his case before the Supreme Court and was admitted to the medical school, but the Court stopped short of declaring affirmative action unconstitutional. The Court rejected the procedures at the University of California because its medical school had used both a quota *and* a separate admissions system for minorities. The Court accepted the argument that achieving "a diverse student body" was a "compelling public purpose," but found that the method of a rigid quota of student slots assigned on the basis of race was incompatible with the equal protection clause. Thus, the Court permitted universities (and presumably other schools, training programs, and hiring authorities) to continue to take minority status into consideration, but limited severely the use of quotas to situations in which (1) previous discrimination had been shown, and (2) it was used more as a guideline for social diversity than as a mathematically defined ratio.[75]

For nearly a decade after *Bakke*, the Supreme Court was tentative and permissive about efforts by universities, corporations, and governments to experiment with affirmative action programs.[76] But in 1989, with the case of *Wards Cove Packing Co. v. Atonio*, the Court backed away further from affirmative action by easing the way for employers to prefer white males, holding that the burden of proof of unlawful discrimination should be shifted from the defendant (the employer) to the plaintiff (the person claiming to be the victim of discrimination).[77] Congress

TABLE 5.3

Supreme Court Rulings on Affirmative Action

CASE	COURT RULING
Regents of the University of California v. Bakke, 438 U.S. 265 (1978)	Affirmative action upheld, but quotas and separate admission for minorities rejected; burden of proof on defendant
Wards Cove v. Atonio, 490 U.S. 642 (1989)	All affirmative action programs put in doubt: burden of proof shifted from defendant to plaintiff (victim), then burden of proof shifted back to employers (defendants)
St. Mary's Honor Center v. Hicks, 113 S.Ct. 2742 (1993)	Required victim to prove discrimination was intentional
Adarand Constructors v. Peña, 515 U.S. 200 (1995)	All race-conscious policies must survive "strict scrutiny," with burden of proof on government to show the program serves "compelling interest" to redress past discrimination
Hopwood v. Texas, 78 F3d 932 (5th Cir., 1996)	Race can *never* be used as a factor in admission, even to promote diversity (Supreme Court refusal to review limited application to the Fifth Circuit—Texas, Louisiana, Mississippi)
Gratz v. Bollinger, 123 S.Ct. 2411 (2003)	Rejection of a "mechanical" point system favoring minority applicants to University of Michigan as tantamount to a quota; *Bakke* reaffirmed
Grutter v. Bollinger, 123 S.Ct. 2325 (2003)	Upheld race-conscious admission to Michigan Law School, passing strict scrutiny with diversity as a "compelling" state interest, as long as admission was "highly individualized" and not "mechanical" as in *Gratz*

reacted with the Civil Rights Act of 1991, which shifted the burden of proof in employment discrimination cases back to employers.

In 1995, the Supreme Court's ruling in *Adarand Constructors v. Peña* further weakened affirmative action. This decision stated that race-based policies, such as preferences given by the government to minority contractors, must survive strict scrutiny, placing the burden on the government to show that such affirmative action programs serve a compelling government interest and are narrowly tailored to address identifiable past discrimination.[78] President Clinton responded to the *Adarand* decision by ordering a review of all government affirmative action policies and practices and adopted an informal policy of trying to "mend, not end" affirmative action.

This betwixt and between status of affirmative action was how things stood in 2003, when the Supreme Court took two cases against the University of Michigan that were virtually certain to clarify, if not put closure on, affirmative action. The first suit, *Gratz v. Bollinger* (the university president), was against the University of Michigan's undergraduate admissions policy and practices, alleging that by using a point-based ranking system that automatically awarded 20 points (out of 150) to African American, Latino, and Native American applicants, the university discriminated unconstitutionally against white students of otherwise equal or superior academic qualifications. The Supreme Court agreed, 6-to-3, arguing that something tantamount to a quota was involved because undergraduate admissions lacked the necessary "individualized consideration," employing instead a "mechanical one," based too much on the favorable minority points.[79] The Court's ruling in *Gratz v. Bollinger* was not surprising, given *Bakke*'s (1978) holding against quotas and given recent decisions calling for strict scrutiny of all racial classifications, even those that are intended to remedy past discrimination or promote future equality.

The second case, *Grutter v. Bollinger*, broke new ground. Grutter sued the law school on the grounds that it had discriminated in a race-conscious way against white applicants with equal or superior grades and law boards. A precarious majority of 5-to-4 aligned the majority of the Supreme Court with Justice Powell's lone plurality opinion in *Bakke* for the first time. In *Bakke*, Powell argued that (1) diversity in education is a compelling state interest and (2) race could be constitutionally considered as a plus factor in admissions decisions. In *Grutter*, the Court reiterated Powell's holding and, applying strict scrutiny to the law school's policy, found that the law school's admissions process is narrowly tailored to the school's compelling state interest in diversity because it gives a "highly individualized, holistic review of each applicant's file" in which race counts but is not used in a "mechanical" way.[80] The Court's ruling that racial categories can be deployed to serve a compelling state interest puts affirmative action on stronger ground. Even so, a 2006 state referendum (see below) outlawing affirmative action led the University of Michigan to abandon its affirmative action program in 2007.

Referenda on Affirmative Action

The courts have not been the only center of action: during the 1990s, challenges to affirmative action also emerged in state and local politics. One of the most significant state actions was the passage of the California Civil Rights Initiative, also known as Proposition 209, in 1996. Proposition 209 outlawed affirmative action programs in the state and local governments of California, thus prohibiting state and local governments from using race or gender preferences in their decisions about hiring, contracting, or university admissions. The political battle over Proposition 209 was heated, and supporters and defenders took to the streets as well as the airwaves to make their cases. When the referendum was held, the measure passed with 54 percent of the vote, including 27 percent of the black vote, 30 percent of the Latino vote, and 45 percent of the Asian American vote.[81] In 1997, the Supreme Court refused to hear a challenge to the new law. California's Proposition 209 was framed as a civil rights initiative: "the state shall not discriminate against, or grant preferential treatment to, any individual or group on the basis of race, sex, color, ethnicity, or national origin." Different wording can produce quite different outcomes, as a 1997 vote on affirmative action in Houston revealed. There, the ballot initiative asked voters whether they wanted to ban affirmative action in city contracting and hiring, not whether they wanted to end preferential treatment. Fifty-five percent of Houston voters decided in favor of affirmative action.[82] In 2006, 58 percent of Michigan voters voted to support a measure outlawing affirmative action in public education, contracting, and employment. Modeled after California's Proposition 209—and championed by the California anti-affirmative activist Ward Connerly—Michigan's Proposition 2 amended the state constitution to prohibit affirmative action. Although University of Michigan officials initially declared that they would continue to use affirmative action criteria in the admissions process until all legal appeals were exhausted, in early 2007 the university announced that it would stop using affirmative action procedures in admissions. Buoyed by their success in Michigan, affirmative action opponents planned to place similar initiatives on the ballot in other states. However, they succeeded in gaining sufficient signatures to bring the measure before voters only in Colorado and Nebraska. In Colorado the initiative failed to obtain voter approval in 2008, while the voters approved the measure in Nebraska.

Thinking Critically about the Affirmative Action Debate

The election of Barack Obama as the nation's first black president fueled discussions about whether America's racial problems had been solved. Polls taken just before Obama's inauguration revealed a sharp upturn in positive views about progress toward racial equality. In January 2009, 49 percent of those polled responded positively when asked whether the vision of Dr. Martin Luther King, Jr.'s "I Have a Dream" speech had been achieved. This response was some 15 percent higher than in March 2008. The swing toward a positive assessment was particularly striking among African Americans, 69 percent of whom said that King's vision had been realized; only 34 percent of African Americans had responded positively to the same question ten months earlier.[83] Yet the euphoria about racial equality did not last for long. A Gallup poll in October 2009 revealed that broad attitudes about America's racial divisions remained remarkably stable. When asked whether they were hopeful that a solution to problems between blacks and whites would be worked out, 56 percent responded positively. This response was nearly identical to that in 1963, when 55 percent indicated that they were hopeful. After Obama's election the proportion of those believing that racism against blacks was widespread dropped somewhat. Even so, in October 2009, nearly three-quarters of blacks and close to half of all whites continued to view racism against blacks as a widespread problem.[84]

Such beliefs indicate that the election of a black president will not make the debate about affirmative action disappear. Conflicts over affirmative action will persist because Americans hold fundamentally different views about whether and how the government should recognize racial distinctions. At the risk of gross oversimplification, we can divide the sides by two labels: liberals and conservatives.[85] The conservatives' argument against affirmative action can be reduced to two major points. The first is that rights in the American tradition are *individual* rights, and affirmative action violates this concept by concerning itself with "group rights," an idea said to be alien to the American tradition. The second point has to do with quotas. Conservatives would argue that the Constitution is "color blind" and that any discrimination,

The election of Barack Obama as the country's first black president raised questions about whether America's racial problems had been solved, and whether policies like affirmative action were still needed. Does the election of an African American as president mean we are closer to achieving racial equality?

even if it is called positive or benign discrimination, ultimately violates the equal protection clause.

The liberal side agrees that rights ultimately come down to individuals but argues that since the essence of discrimination is the use of unreasonable and unjust criteria of exclusion to deprive *an entire group* of access to something valuable the society has to offer, then the phenomenon of discrimination itself has to be attacked on a group basis. Although many agree that there has been progress toward racial equality (see Table 5.4), liberals argue that race still matters. Liberals can also use Supreme Court history to support their side because the first definitive interpretation of the Fourteenth Amendment by the Court in 1873 stated that

> the existence of laws in the state where the newly emancipated Negroes resided, which discriminated with gross injustice and hardship against them *as a class*, was the evil to be remedied by this clause [emphasis added].[86]

Liberals also have a response to the other conservative argument concerning quotas. The liberal response is that the Supreme Court has already accepted ratios—a form of quota—that are admitted as evidence to prove a "pattern or practice of discrimination" sufficient to reverse the burden of proof—to obligate the employer to show that there was *not* an intent to discriminate. Liberals can also argue that benign quotas often have been used by Americans both to compensate for some bad action in the past or to provide some desired distribution of social characteristics—sometimes called diversity. For example, a long and respected policy in the United States is that of "veterans' preference," on the basis of which the government automatically gives extra consideration in hiring to persons who have served the country in the armed forces. The justification is that ex-servicepeople deserve compensation for having made sacrifices for the good of the country. And the goal of social diversity has justified "positive discrimination," especially in higher education, the very institution where conservatives have most adamantly argued against positive quotas for blacks and women. For example, all of the Ivy League schools and many other private colleges and universities regularly

TABLE 5.4

Americans' Opinions on Racial Equality

Black and white Americans disagree somewhat on issues of affirmative action and progress toward racial equality. Do you think African Americans have achieved racial equality, will soon achieve racial equality, will not achieve racial equality in your lifetime, or will never achieve racial equality?

	ALL ACHIEVED %	WILL SOON ACHIEVE %	WON'T ACHIEVE IN LIFETIME %	WILL NEVER ACHIEVE %	UNSURE %
All	37	31	19	8	4
Blacks	11	38	32	17	3
Whites	40	31	19	7	4

SOURCE: ABC News/Washington Poll, January 12–15, 2010. www.pollingreport.com (accessed 7/2/10).

Civil Rights on Campus

Imagine, for a moment, **your** campus as it might have been in 1950. The student body would be largely white because higher education for nonwhites was almost unthinkable unless they attended a handful of largely segregated minority institutions. The diverse faculty that you see today would be mostly absent. For example, women were discouraged from teaching and researching the subjects that they do today. If they did teach, women were often relegated to teaching home economics–related courses. The list of differences that would characterize your campus then versus now goes beyond these examples. But the point is simple—civil rights activism since 1950 has brought about significant social change.

Today there are many groups dedicated to advancing the cause of civil rights. For example, gay and lesbian groups argue that their civil rights are discriminated against on the basis of their sexuality. They believe, among other things, that their inability to marry in most states prevents them from enjoying many of the benefits

that married heterosexual couples enjoy, such as tax deductions and the right to have a same-sex partner recognized by hospitals as a legal decision maker if the other partner is incapacitated.

Other groups advocating greater civil rights include undocumented immigrants and their supporters, who argue that despite their status as illegal citizens, they should still be afforded civil rights and legal protections because of the labor and financial contributions they make to society. For example, many immigrants pay Social Security taxes but never receive Social Security benefits. These and other groups have joined traditional civil rights organizations that continue to advocate for greater civil rights protections.

However, there is not always agreement that the civil rights of certain groups are being violated. For example, to many, the civil rights of women are not compromised by excluding them from certain combat positions in the military. For others this policy seems a clear civil rights violation.

Campuses often bring together diverse groups of people with different ideas regarding how society should function. The following ideas present ways that you can engage your fellow students on the issue of civil rights at your college or university.

- Identify whether your college or university practices affirmative action in recruiting and admissions. For example, are certain racial and ethnic groups recruited more heavily, and do they receive different considerations during the admissions process? What about the consideration that's given to students whose parents are alumni of the same college?

- Weigh in on what you think about your institution's affirmative action policies by writing a letter to the editor of your school newspaper, then see what kind of responses your letter generates. If your campus has a radio station, try using that as a vehicle for expressing your opinion about affirmative action at your college.

- Find out what kind of groups on campus organize students with similar backgrounds. For example, the National Council of La Raza often has campus chapters for Latino students; the LGBT (lesbian, gay, bisexual, and transgendered) community may have a student organization on your campus. If you find one that you can identify with, consider joining and exploring the activism that group is engaged in to advocate for civil rights on campus.

- Help organize a debate about civil rights on campus, perhaps through an organization such as those mentioned earlier. You can invite student panelists as well as representatives of interest groups on both sides of the issue that you'll be debating. The American Civil Liberties Union is one such group to contact for people who take a more liberal approach to civil rights issues. The American Conservative Union may be useful for putting you in touch with those who hold a conservative interpretation of civil rights.

and consistently reserve admissions places for some students whose qualifications in a strict academic sense are below those of others who are not admitted. These schools not only recruit students from minority groups, they also set aside places for the children of loyal alumni and of their own faculty, even when, in a pure competition solely and exclusively based on test scores and high school records, many of those same children would not have been admitted. These practices are not conclusive justification in themselves, but they certainly underscore the liberal argument that affirmative or compensatory action for minorities who have been unjustly treated in the past is not alien to American experience.

If we think of the debate about affirmative action in terms of American political values, it is clear that conservatives emphasize liberty, whereas liberals stress equality. Conservatives believe that using government actively to promote equality for minorities and women infringes on the rights of white men. Lawsuits challenging affirmative action often cite this "reverse discrimination" as a justification. Liberals, on the other hand, traditionally have defended affirmative action as the best way to achieve equality. In recent years, however, the debate over affirmative action has become more complex and has created divisions among liberals. These divisions stem from growing doubts among some liberals about whether affirmative action can be defended as the best way to achieve equality and about the tensions between affirmative action and democratic values. One recent study of public opinion found that many self-identified liberals were angry about affirmative action.[87] These liberals felt that in the name of equality, affirmative action actually violates norms of fairness and equality of opportunity by giving special advantages to some. Moreover, it is argued, affirmative action is broadly unpopular and is therefore questionable in terms of democratic values. Because our nation has a history of slavery and legalized racial discrimination, and because discrimination continues to exist (although it has declined over time), the question of racial justice, more than any other issue, highlights the difficulty of reconciling our values in practice (see Table 5.4).

studyguide

Practice Quiz

Find a diagnostic Web Quiz with 31 additional questions on the StudySpace Web site: www.wwnorton.com/we-the-people

The Struggle for Civil Rights

1. When did civil rights become part of the Constitution? (p. 153)
   a) in 1789 at the Founding
   b) with the adoption of the Fourteenth Amendment in 1868
   c) with the adoption of the Nineteenth Amendment in 1920
   d) in the 1954 *Brown v. Board of Education* case

2. Which of the following could be described as a Jim Crow law? (p. 156)
   a) a law criminalizing interracial marriage
   b) a law requiring blacks and whites to attend different schools
   c) a law segregating all public accommodations, such as hotels, restaurants, and theaters
   d) all of the above

3. Which civil rights case established the "separate but equal" rule? *(p. 157)*
   a) *Plessy v. Ferguson*
   b) *Brown v. Board of Education*
   c) *Regents of the University of California v. Bakke*
   d) *Adarand Constructors v. Peña*

4. The judicial test that places the burden of proof on government to show that a race-based policy serves a compelling government interest and is narrowly tailored to address identifiable past discrimination is called *(p. 161)*
   a) strict scrutiny.
   b) intermediate scrutiny.
   c) *de facto* segregation.
   d) *de jure* segregation.

5. Which of the following organizations established a Legal Defense Fund to challenge segregation? *(pp. 159–61)*
   a) the Association of American Trial Lawyers
   b) the National Association for the Advancement of Colored People
   c) the Student Nonviolent Coordinating Committee
   d) the Southern Christian Leadership Council

6. "Massive resistance" refers to efforts by southern states during the late 1950s and early 1960s to *(p. 161)*
   a) build public housing for poor blacks.
   b) defy federal mandates to desegregate public schools.
   c) give women the right to have an abortion.
   d) bus black students to white schools.

7. Which of the following made discrimination by private employers and state governments illegal? *(p. 164)*
   a) the Fourteenth Amendment
   b) *Brown v. Board of Education*
   c) the 1964 Civil Rights Act
   d) *Regents of the University of California v. Bakke*

8. The Voting Rights Act of 1965 significantly extended and protected voting rights by doing which of the following? *(p. 169)*
   a) barring literacy tests as a condition for voting in six southern states
   b) setting criminal penalties for interference with voting efforts
   c) providing for the replacement of local registrars with federally appointed registrars in counties designated as resistant to registering blacks to vote
   d) all of the above

The Universalization of Civil Rights

9. In what way does the struggle for gender equality most resemble the struggle for racial equality? *(p. 171)*
   a) There has been very little political action in realizing the goal.
   b) Changes in government policies to a great degree produced political action.
   c) The Supreme Court has not ruled on the issue.
   d) No legislation has passed adopting the aims of the movement.

10. Which of the following is *not* an example of an area in which women have made progress since the 1970s in guaranteeing certain civil rights? *(p. 175)*
    a) sexual harassment
    b) integration into all-male publicly supported universities
    c) more equal funding for college women's varsity athletic programs
    d) the passage of the Equal Rights Amendment

11. The Supreme Court's decision in *Mendez v. Westminster* was significant because it *(p. 176)*
    a) served as a precursor for *Brown v. Board of Education* by ruling that the segregation of Anglos and Mexican Americans into separate schools was unconstitutional.
    b) determined that anyone born in the United States was entitled to full citizenship.
    c) held that public accommodations could be segregated by race but still be equal.
    d) eliminated state power to use race as a criterion for discrimination in law.

12. Which of the following civil rights measures dealt with access to public businesses and accommodations? *(p. 182)*
    a) the 1990 Americans with Disabilities Act
    b) the 1964 Civil Rights Act
    c) neither a nor b
    d) both a and b

13. Which of the following cases represents the *Brown v. Board of Education* case for lesbians and gay men? *(p. 184)*
    a) *Bowers v. Hardwick*
    b) *Lau v. Nichols*
    c) *Romer v. Evans*
    d) There has not been a Supreme Court ruling explicitly protecting gays and lesbians from discrimination.

Affirmative Action

14. In what case did the Supreme Court find that rigid quotas are incompatible with the equal protection clause of the Fourteenth Amendment? *(p. 186)*
    a) *Regents of the University of California v. Bakke*
    b) *Brown v. Board of Education*
    c) *United States v. Nixon*
    d) *Immigration and Naturalization Service v. Chadha*

15. The Supreme Court's decision in *Grutter v. Bollinger* was significant because *(p. 188)*
    a) it stated that race can never be used as a factor in university admissions.
    b) it stated that diversity is a compelling state interest and that university admissions that take racial categorized into account are constitutional as long as they are highly individualized.
    c) it outlawed quotas and separate university admission standards for members of minority groups.
    d) it rejected mechanical point systems that favor minority applicants in university admissions.

Chapter Outline

Find a detailed Chapter Outline on the StudySpace Web site: www.wwnorton.com/we-the-people

Key Terms

Find Flashcards to help you study these terms on the StudySpace Web site www.wwnorton.com/we-the-people

affirmative action *(p. 184)*
Brown v. Board of Education (p. 160)
civil rights *(p. 153)*
de facto (p. 161)
de jure (p. 161)
discrimination *(p. 153)*

equal protection clause *(p. 153)*
Fifteenth Amendment *(p. 155)*
Fourteenth Amendment *(p. 155)*
gerrymandering *(p. 170)*
intermediate scrutiny *(p. 172)*

Jim Crow laws *(p. 156)*
redlining *(p. 171)*
"separate but equal" rule *(p. 157)*
strict scrutiny *(p. 161)*
Thirteenth Amendment *(p. 155)*

For Further Reading

Chen, Anthony S. *The Fifth Freedom: Jobs, Politics, and Civil Rights in the United States, 1941–1972.* Princeton, NJ: Princeton University Press, 2009.

Garrow, David J. *Bearing the Cross: Martin Luther King and the Southern Christian Leadership Conference: A Personal Portrait.* New York: Morrow, 1986.

Greenberg, Jack. *Crusaders in the Courts: How a Dedicated Band of Lawyers Fought for the Civil Rights Revolution.* New York: Basic Books, 1994.

Katznelson, Ira. *When Affirmative Action Was White: The Untold Story of Racial Inequality in Twentieth-Century America.* New York: Norton, 2006.

Klinkner, Philip A., with Rogers M. Smith. *The Unsteady March: The Rise and Decline of Racial Equality in America.* Chicago: University of Chicago Press, 1999.

McClain, Paula D., and Joseph Stewart, Jr. *"Can We All Get Along?" Racial Minorities in American Politics.* 4th ed. Boulder, CO: Westview Press, 2005.

Mink, Gwendolyn. *Hostile Environment: The Political Betrayal of Sexually Harassed Women.* Ithaca, NY: Cornell University Press, 2000.

Nava, Michael. *Created Equal: Why Gay Rights Matter to America.* New York: St. Martin's, 1994.

Rosales, Francisco. *Chicano! The History of the Mexican American Civil Rights Movement.* Houston: Arte Público Press, 1997.

Rosenberg, Gerald N. *The Hollow Hope: Can Courts Bring About Social Change?* Chicago: University of Chicago Press, 1991.

Russell, Nancy. *Freedom Is Not Enough: The Opening of the American Workplace.* Cambridge, MA: Harvard University Press, 2006.

Valelly, Richard. *The Voting Rights Act.* Washington, DC: Congressional Quality Press, 2005.

Recommended Web Sites

ADA Home Page
www.ada.gov
The Americans with Disabilities Act (ADA), enacted in 1990, guarantees equal employment rights and access to public businesses for the physically disabled. The U.S. Department of Justice maintains this Web site, which offers general information on ADA standards, changes in regulation, and policy enforcement.

Dr. Martin Luther King, Jr., Research and Education Institute
http://mlk-kpp01.stanford.edu
Dr. Martin Luther King, Jr., was a key leader in the fight for civil rights and desegregation. At this Web site you can find Dr. King's important speeches and papers, as well as other information about social injustice.

Equal Employment Opportunity Commission (EEOC)
www.eeoc.gov

This Web site provides information on the federal agency and current employment laws. At this site you can even find out how someone might file a harassment or discrimination charge against an employer.

Equality Now
www.equalitynow.org

This is an organization dedicated to ending gender discrimination around the world. Read about how this group is fighting for the rights of women in Africa or campaigning against female genital mutilation and sex trafficking.

Federal Bureau of Investigation
www.fbi.gov/hq/cid/civilrights/hate.htm

Civil rights violations fall under the jurisdiction of the Federal Bureau of Investigation. Find out what steps the FBI is taking to combat the problem of hate crimes and view some comprehensive statistical data.

Human Rights Campaign (HRC)
www.hrc.org
Gay and Lesbian Alliance against Defamation (GLAAD)
www.glaad.org

These two prominent interest groups are dedicated to equal rights for gays and lesbians and ending gender discrimination.

League of United Latin American Citizens (LULAC)
www.lulac.org

LULAC has worked to stem discrimination against Mexican Americans since World War II and is now the largest and oldest Hispanic organization in the United States. See what this group is doing to guarantee racial equality based on the Fourteenth Amendment's equal protection clause.

Mexican American Legal Defense and Education Fund (MALDEF)
www.maldef.org

MALDEF is the leading nonprofit Latino litigation, advocacy, and educational outreach institution in the United States. At this site, you will learn about litigation and other activities that MALDEF has initiated related to the rights of Latinos and of immigrants more generally.

NAACP
www.naacp.org

The NAACP is one of the oldest and largest civil rights organizations that is dedicated to equal rights and putting an end to racial discrimination. This group was particularly influential in the landmark case *Brown v. Board of Education*, which led to the desegregation of public schools.

National Organization for Women
www.now.org
Feminist Majority Foundation
www.feminist.org

These leading women's rights groups continue to fight for gender equality and equal rights.

U.S. Commission on Civil Rights
www.usccr.gov

The U.S. Commission on Civil Rights was created by Congress in the late 1950s and continues to investigate complaints of discrimination in American society.

U.S. Supreme Court Media
www.oyez.org

This Web site has a good search engine for finding information on such landmark civil rights cases as *Plessy v. Ferguson, Brown v. Board of Education, Lawrence v. Texas,* and *United States v. Wong Kim Ark*, to name only a few.

How closely should the government follow public opinion? In 2010, public opinion was sharply divided over health care reform. Some Americans opposed any further government intervention in the health care industry.

6

Public Opinion

WHAT GOVERNMENT DOES AND WHY IT MATTERS In a democracy, we expect the government to pay attention to public opinion. If the government's programs and policies do not seem consistent with popular preferences, we often begin to question the legitimacy of the government's actions. In 2007 and 2008, many Americans questioned why American forces remained in Iraq even though most Americans had concluded that it was time to bring the troops home. Americans also wonder why, on issues ranging from gun control through health care, the government never seems to be able to do what the public wants. Policy makers reply that the people often speak with many voices that are hard to reconcile and interpret. Sometimes, say public officials, their job is to do what's right even if it is unpopular. President George W. Bush, for example, once pointed to the fact that President Abraham Lincoln became quite unpopular as the Civil War dragged on. If Lincoln had allowed himself to be guided by public opinion, the United States might not exist today.

Another concern when we consider how closely government should

focusquestions

- What are political values and how are they formed?

- How do people form opinions about specific issues?

- How can we accurately measure public opinion?

- Does the American government follow public opinion?

follow public opinion is the fact that many Americans have very little knowledge about government. For example, in one widely reported survey, 71 percent of Americans could not name their own member of Congress and 81 percent could not identify both of their own state's senators.[1]

Americans like to believe that public opinion is an important force in political life. The economist Joseph Schumpeter, however, once observed that public opinion was the "product," not the "motive power" of the political process. By this comment he meant that public opinion was seldom, if ever, a driving force in politics. Instead, according to Schumpeter, politics was driven by the contending politicians, parties, and social forces that worked to win control of the government and to shape national policy. Such groups might seek to mold public opinion as part of their effort to bring about the policy and personnel changes they desired. So, for example, groups seeking changes in banking policy, farm policy, or military policy frequently mount public relations campaigns to secure public support for their goals. The appearance of popular support, in turn, might help these groups build a stronger case in Congress or even in the White House. In this model of the political process, public opinion plays, at best, an intermediate role. It does not control policy. Instead, groups that hope to change policy find it useful—sometimes even essential—to change public opinion along the way.

Of course, Schumpeter may have been too cynical, and he lacked modern tools with which to study public opinion. Often, members of the public have well-established opinions that cannot easily be molded by elites. As President Lincoln might have told Schumpeter, you can't fool all the people all the time.

Thus, when it comes to public opinion, the question of what the government does and why it matters is complicated. We certainly want the government to pay attention to public opinion. But, in some instances, when the government seems to be following public opinion it is actually responding to powerful forces that were able to shape opinion as they worked to control policy.

chaptercontents

● Understanding Public Opinion

The term **public opinion** is used to denote the values and attitudes that people have about issues, events, and personalities. Although the terms are sometimes used interchangeably, it is useful to distinguish between values and beliefs on the one hand, and attitudes or opinions on the other. **Values (or beliefs)** are a person's basic orientations to politics. Values underlie deep-rooted goals, aspirations, and ideals that shape an individual's perceptions of political issues and events. Liberty, equality, and democracy are basic political values that most Americans hold. Another useful term for understanding public opinion is *ideology*. **Political ideology** refers to a complex set of beliefs and values that, as a whole, form a general philosophy about government. As we shall see, liberalism and conservatism are important ideologies in America today.

For example, many Americans believe that governmental solutions to problems are inherently inferior to solutions offered by the private sector. This general belief, in turn, may lead individuals to have negative views of specific government programs even before they know much about them. An **attitude (or opinion)** is a specific view about a particular issue, personality, or event. An individual may have an opinion about Barack Obama or an attitude toward American policy in Iraq. The attitude or opinion may have emerged from a broad belief about Democrats or military intervention, but an attitude itself is very specific. Some attitudes may be short-lived.

When we think of opinion, we often think in terms of differences of opinion. The media are fond of reporting and analyzing political differences between blacks and whites, men and women, the young and old, and so on. Certainly, Americans differ on many issues, and often these differences do seem to be associated with race, religion, gender, age, or other social characteristics. Today, Americans seem divided on domestic issues such as health care and on issues of foreign policy such as what to do in Iraq and Afghanistan.

public opinion citizens' attitudes about political issues, leaders, institutions, and events

values (or beliefs) basic principles that shape a person's opinions about political issues and events

political ideology a cohesive set of beliefs that forms a general philosophy about the role of government

attitude (or opinion) a specific preference on a particular issue

Even among Americans who supported health care reform in 2010, opinion was divided over the various plans that had been proposed.

Political Values

As we review these differences, however, it is important to remember that Americans also agree on a number of matters. Indeed, most Americans share a common set of values, including a belief in the principles—if not always the actual practice—of liberty, equality, and democracy. Equality of opportunity has always been an important theme in American society. Americans believe that all individuals should be allowed to seek personal and material success. Moreover, Americans generally believe that such success should be linked to personal effort and ability, rather than to family connections or other forms of special privilege. Similarly, Americans have always voiced strong support for the principle of individual liberty. They typically support the notion that governmental interference with individuals' lives and property should be kept to the minimum consistent with the general welfare (although in recent years Americans have grown accustomed to greater levels of governmental intervention than would have been deemed appropriate by the founders of liberal theory). And most Americans also believe in democracy. They presume that every person should have the opportunity to take part in the nation's governmental and policy-making processes and to have some say in determining how they are governed.[2] Figure 6.1 offers some indication of this American consensus on fundamental values: 89 percent believe that gays should have equal employment rights (2008), 56 percent are worried about government monitoring of personal information (2007), and 69 percent agree that any group should be free to assemble (2007).

Obviously, the principles that Americans espouse have not always been put into practice. For two hundred years, Americans were able to believe in the principles of equality of opportunity and individual liberty while denying them in practice to generations of African Americans. Yet it is important to note that the strength of the principles ultimately helped to overcome practices that deviated from those principles. Proponents of slavery and, later, of segregation, were defeated in the arena of public opinion because their practices differed so sharply from the fundamental principles accepted by most Americans. Ironically, in contemporary politics, Americans' fundamental commitment to equality of opportunity has led to divisions over racial policy. In particular, both proponents and opponents of affirmative

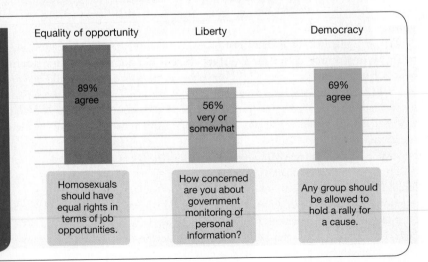

FIGURE 6.1
American's Support for Fundamental Values

Americans support equality of opportunity, liberty, and democracy in principle, but do they always support these values in practice? What limits, if any, do you think Americans favor when it comes to equality, liberty, and democracy?

SOURCES: Gallup Poll, 2008; Opinion Dynamics, 2007; and New England Survey Research Associates, 2007.

Equality of opportunity — 89% agree — Homosexuals should have equal rights in terms of job opportunities.

Liberty — 56% very or somewhat — How concerned are you about government monitoring of personal information?

Democracy — 69% agree — Any group should be allowed to hold a rally for a cause.

action programs cite their belief in equality of opportunity as the justification for their position. Proponents see these programs as necessary to ensure equality of opportunity, whereas opponents believe that affirmative action is a form of preferential treatment that violates basic American values.[3]

Forms of Disagreement

Agreement on fundamentals by no means implies that Americans do not differ with each other on a wide variety of issues. American political life is characterized by vigorous debate on economic policy, foreign policy, and social policy issues; race relations; environmental affairs; and a host of other matters.

As we will see later in this chapter, differences of political opinion are often associated with such variables as income, education, and occupation. Similarly, factors such as race, gender, ethnicity, age, religion, and region—which not only influence individuals' interests but also shape their experiences and upbringing—have enormous influence on their beliefs and opinions. For example, individuals whose incomes differ substantially have different views on the desirability of a number of important economic and social programs. In general, the poor—who are the chief beneficiaries of these programs—support them more strongly than do those who are wealthier and pay more of the taxes that fund the programs. Similarly, blacks and whites have different views on questions of civil rights and civil liberties—presumably reflecting differences of interest and historical experience. In recent years, many observers have begun to take note of a number of differences between the views expressed by men and those supported by women, especially on foreign-policy questions, where women appear to be much more concerned with the dangers of war. Let us see how such differences develop.

How Political Values Are Formed

People's attitudes about political issues and personalities tend to be shaped by their underlying political beliefs and values. For example, an individual who has basically negative feelings about government intervention into America's economy and society would probably be predisposed to oppose the development of new health care and social programs. Similarly, someone who distrusts the military would likely be suspicious of any call for the use of American troops. The processes through which these underlying political beliefs and values are formed are collectively called **political socialization.**

The process of political socialization is important. Probably no nation, and certainly no democracy, could survive if its citizens did not share some fundamental beliefs. If Americans had few common values or perspectives, it would be very difficult for them to reach agreement on particular issues. In contemporary America, some elements of the socialization process tend to produce differences in outlook, whereas others promote similarities. Four of the most important **agencies of socialization** that foster differences in political perspectives are the family, membership in social groups, education, and prevailing political conditions.

No list of agencies of socialization can fully explain the development of a given individual's basic political beliefs. In addition to the factors that are important for everyone, forces that are unique to each individual play a role in shaping political orientations. For one person, the character of an early encounter with a member of another racial group can have a lasting impact on that individual's view of the world. For another, a highly salient political event, such as the Vietnam War, can

political socialization the induction of individuals into the political culture; learning the underlying beliefs and values on which the political system is based

agencies of socialization social institutions, including families and schools, that help to shape individuals' basic political beliefs and values

leave an indelible mark on that person's political consciousness. For a third person, some deep-seated personality characteristic, such as paranoia, for example, may strongly influence the formation of political beliefs. Nevertheless, knowing that we cannot fully explain the development of any given individual's political outlook, let us look at some of the most important agencies of socialization that do affect one's beliefs.

Influences on Our Political Values

The Family Most people acquire their initial orientation to politics from their families. As might be expected, differences in family background tend to produce divergent political outlooks. Although relatively few parents spend much time teaching their children about politics, political conversations occur in many households and children tend to absorb the political views of parents and other caregivers, perhaps without realizing it. Studies have suggested, for example, that party preferences are initially acquired at home. Children raised in households in which the primary caregivers are Democrats tend to become Democrats themselves, whereas children raised in homes where their caregivers are Republicans tend to favor the GOP (Grand Old Party, a traditional nickname for the Republican Party).[4] Similarly, children reared in politically liberal households are more likely than not to develop a liberal outlook, whereas children raised in politically conservative settings are likely to see the world through conservative lenses. Obviously, not all children absorb their parents' political views. Two of the late conservative Republican president Ronald Reagan's three children, for instance, rejected their parents' conservative values and became active on behalf of Democratic candidates. Moreover, even those children whose views are initially shaped by parental values may change their minds as they mature and experience political life for themselves. Nevertheless, the family is an important initial source of political orientation for everyone.

Social Groups Another important source of divergent political orientations and values are the social groups to which individuals belong. Social groups include those to which individuals belong involuntarily—national, religious, gender, and racial groups, for example—as well as those to which people belong voluntarily, such as political parties, labor unions, and educational and occupational groups. Some social groups have both voluntary and involuntary attributes. For example, individuals are born with a particular social-class background, but as a result of their own actions people may move up—or down—the social scale.

Membership in social groups can affect political values in a variety of ways. Membership in a particular group can give individuals important experiences and perspectives that shape their view of political and social life. In American society, for example, the experiences of blacks and whites can differ significantly. Blacks are a minority and have been victims of persecution and discrimination throughout American history. Blacks and whites also have different educational and occupational opportunities, often live in separate communities, and may attend separate schools. Such differences tend to produce distinctive political outlooks. For example, in 2009, 92 percent of black respondents but only 56 percent of white respondents approved of the way President Obama had been handling race relations since he became president.[5] In a similar vein, blacks and whites responded differently to the case of the white Cambridge, Massachusetts, police officer James Crowley who arrested an African American Harvard professor, Henry Louis Gates, Jr., for

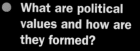

Members of various social groups may see political issues in different ways. After a racially-charged incident in 2009 involving Harvard professor Henry Louis Gates Jr. (second from left) and police officer James Crowely (second from right), President Obama tried to address the tensions surrounding the incident by bringing the two men together for a "beer summit" at the White House.

disorderly conduct when the officer answered a report that a man was breaking into a residence. It turned out later that Gates had locked himself out of his own house and was attempting to gain access but was angry and uncooperative when questioned by the police. Asked to indicate with which of these individuals they sympathized, white respondents to a 2009 poll sympathized with the police officer by a 45 to 29 percent margin. Blacks, on the other hand, sympathized with the professor by a margin of 61 percent to 19 percent.[6]

As this example suggests, blacks and whites differ considerably in their perceptions of the extent of racism in America (see figure 6.2). In a 2009 survey, 49 percent of white respondents thought racism was not rare in the United States while 47 percent thought it was fairly or very common. Among African Americans, on the other hand, 86 percent thought racism was common while 12 percent said it was rare.[7] Interestingly, Hispanic Americans, who have also been victims of racism in the United States, are less likely than African Americans to see America as currently a racist society. In response to a 2008 CBS News/*New York Times* survey, 52 percent of Hispanic Americans and 55 percent of white Americans said race relations in the United States were generally good. Only 29 percent of black Americans agreed.[8]

Men and women have important differences of opinion as well. Reflecting differences in social roles, political experience, and occupational patterns, women tend to be less militaristic than men on issues of war and peace, more likely than men to favor measures to protect the environment, and more supportive than men of government social and health care programs (see Table 6.1). Perhaps because of these differences on issues, women are more likely than men to vote for Democratic candidates. This tendency of men's and women's opinions to differ is called the **gender gap**.

Political party membership can be another factor affecting political orientations.[9] Partisans tend to rely on party leaders and spokespersons for cues on the appropriate positions to take on major political issues. In recent years, congressional redistricting

gender gap a distinctive pattern of voting behavior reflecting the differences in views between women and men

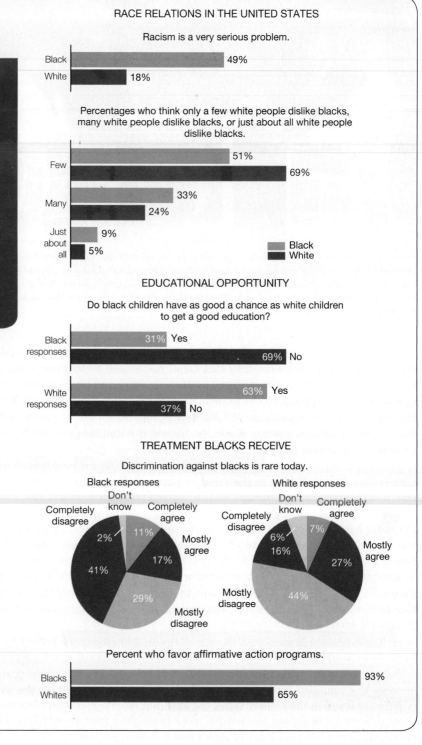

RACE RELATIONS IN THE UNITED STATES

Racism is a very serious problem.

- Black 49%
- White 18%

Percentages who think only a few white people dislike blacks, many white people dislike blacks, or just about all white people dislike blacks.

- Few: 51% (Black), 69% (White)
- Many: 33% (Black), 24% (White)
- Just about all: 9% (Black), 5% (White)

Black / White

EDUCATIONAL OPPORTUNITY

Do black children have as good a chance as white children to get a good education?

- Black responses: 31% Yes, 69% No
- White responses: 63% Yes, 37% No

TREATMENT BLACKS RECEIVE

Discrimination against blacks is rare today.

Black responses
- Don't know 2%
- Completely agree 11%
- Mostly agree 17%
- Mostly disagree 29%
- Completely disagree 41%

White responses
- Don't know 7%
- Completely agree 6%
- Mostly agree 27%
- Mostly disagree 44%
- Completely disagree 16%

Percent who favor affirmative action programs.

- Blacks 93%
- Whites 65%

TABLE 6.1

Disagreements among Men and Women on National Security Issues

For the most part, fewer women than men favor the use of military force as an instrument of foreign policy. Is this pattern reflected consistently in the data? What might explain gender differences in this realm?

GOVERNMENT ACTION	PERCENTAGE APPROVING OF ACTION	
	MEN	WOMEN
Agree that torture of terror suspects is acceptable	50	31
Favor withdrawing troops from Iraq within a year	43	55
Agree NSA surveillance program is needed	60	50
Oppose sending more troops to Iraq	52	69
Favor cutting off funding for Iraq war	48	57
Believe U.S. should send more troops to Afghanistan (2009)	49	36

SOURCES: ABC, 2009; *Ms.*, 2006; UPI/Zogby, 2007, *USA Today*, 2007; *Washington* Post/ABC, 2007; CBS, 2009.

and partisan realignment in the South have reduced the number of conservative Democrats and all but eliminated liberal Republicans from the Congress and from positions of prominence in the party. As a result, the leadership of the Republican Party has become increasingly conservative, whereas that of the Democratic Party has become more and more liberal. These changes in the positions of party leaders have been reflected in the views of party adherents and sympathizers in the general public. According to recent studies, differences between Democratic and Republican partisans on a variety of political and policy questions are greater today than during any other period for which data are available. On issues of national security, for example, Republicans have become very "hawkish," whereas Democrats have become quite "dovish." In October 2003, for instance, 85 percent of Republicans compared with 39 percent of the Democrats surveyed thought America's war against Iraq had been a good idea.[10] By March 2006, only 34 percent of Democrats surveyed by the Pew Research Center thought the war would succeed, but 74 percent of Republicans remained optimistic. By 2007, 60 percent of all Republicans still supported the war. Gaps on domestic social and economic issues were nearly as broad.

Religion may also affect individuals' attitudes. Religions provide a historical experience and philosophical perspective that lead their members to see the world in different ways. In the United States, for example, members of America's Christian majority are not likely to be offended by the display of Christian symbols in schools and other government buildings. Jews and members of other minority religious groups, on the other hand, often view such displays through their own historical lens as an effort to undermine their religions. Similarly, many commonplace elements of American secular culture, such as clothing styles, may be deeply offensive to an individual raised in a conservative Muslim tradition.

forcritical analysis

In 2008, religious conservatives were often called "values voters." What values did these voters support? Did their opponents lack values?

Membership in a social group can affect individuals' political orientations in another way: through the efforts of groups themselves to influence their members. Labor unions, for example, often seek to inform their members through meetings, rallies, and literature. These activities are designed to shape union members' understanding of politics and to make them more amenable to supporting the political positions favored by union leaders. Similarly, organization can sharpen the impact of membership in an involuntary group. Women's groups, black groups, religious groups, and the like usually endeavor to structure their members' political views through intensive educational programs. The importance of such group efforts can be seen in the impact of group membership on political opinion. Women who belong to women's organizations, for example, are likely to differ more from men in their political views than women without such group affiliation.[11] Other analysts have found that African Americans who belong to black organizations are likely to differ more from whites in their political orientations than blacks who lack such affiliations.[12]

In many cases, no particular efforts are required by groups to affect their members' beliefs and opinions. Often, individuals will consciously or unconsciously adapt their views to those of the groups with which they identify. For example, an African American who is dubious about affirmative action is likely to come under considerable peer pressure and internal pressure to modify his or her views. In this

Religion may affect attitudes about political and social issues. In 2008, these Christian teenagers demanded more restrictions on popular culture content that they considered harmful to young people.

and other cases, dissenters are likely gradually to shift their own views to conform to those of the group. The political psychologist Elisabeth Noelle-Neumann has called this process the "spiral of silence."[13]

A third way that membership in social groups can affect political beliefs is through what might be called objective political interests. On many economic issues, for example, the interests of the rich and the poor differ significantly. Inevitably, these differences of interest will produce differences of political outlook. James Madison and other framers of the Constitution thought that the inherent gulf between the rich and the poor would always be the most important source of conflict in political life. Certainly today, struggles over tax policy, welfare policy, health care policy, and so forth are fueled by differences of interest between wealthier and poorer Americans. In a similar vein, objective differences of interest between senior citizens and younger Americans can lead to very different views on such diverse issues as health care policy, Social Security, and criminal justice. To take another example, in recent decades major differences of opinion and political orientation have developed between American civilians and members of the armed services. Military officers, in particular, are far more conservative in their domestic and foreign policy views than the public at large and are heavily Republican in their political leanings.[14] It is interesting to note that support for the Republicans among military officers climbed sharply during the 1980s and 1990s, decades in which the GOP championed large military budgets. Could this be another case of objective interests swaying ideology?

It is worth pointing out again that, like the other agencies of socialization, group membership can never fully explain a given individual's political views. One's unique personality and life experiences may produce political views very different from those of the group to which one might nominally belong. This is why some African Americans are conservative Republicans, or why an occasional wealthy businessperson is also a socialist. Group membership is conducive to particular outlooks, but it is not determinative.

Differences in Education A third important source of differences in political perspectives comes from a person's education. In some respects, of course, schooling is a great equalizer. Governments use public education to try to teach all children a common set of civic values. It is mainly in school that Americans acquire their basic belief in liberty, equality, and democracy. In history classes, students are taught that the Founders fought for the principle of liberty. Through participation in class elections and student government, students are taught the virtues of democracy. In the course of studying such topics as the Constitution, the Civil War, and the civil rights movement, students are taught the importance of equality. These lessons are repeated in every grade in a variety of contexts. It is no wonder they are such an important element in Americans' beliefs.

At the same time, however, differences in educational attainment are strongly associated with differences in political outlook. In particular, those who attend college are often exposed to philosophies and modes of thought that will forever distinguish them from their friends and neighbors who do not pursue college diplomas. Table 6.2 outlines some general differences of opinion that are found between college graduates and other Americans.

In recent years, conservatives have charged that liberal college professors indoctrinate their students with liberal ideas. College does seem to have some "liberalizing" effect on students, but, more significantly, college seems to convince students of the importance of political participation and of their own capacity

TABLE 6.2

Education and Public Opinion

The figures show the percentage of respondents in each category who agree with the statement. Are college graduates generally more or less liberal than other Americans? Which data support your claim? Can you think of economic or political explanations for these findings?

ISSUES	EDUCATION			
	GRADE SCHOOL	HIGH SCHOOL	SOME COLLEGE	COLLEGE GRAD.
1. Women and men should have equal roles.	38%	75%	83%	86%
2. Abortion should never be allowed.	21	10	7	4
3. The government should adopt national health insurance.	35	47	42	49
4. The United States should not concern itself with other nations' problems.	45	26	20	8
5. Government should see to fair treatment in jobs for African Americans.	49	28	30	45
6. Government should provide fewer services to reduce government spending.	8	17	19	27

SOURCE: The American National Election Studies, 2004 data, provided by the Inter-University Consortium for Political and Social Research, University of Michigan.

for having an impact on politics and policy. Thus, one of the major differences between college graduates and other Americans can be seen in levels of political participation. College graduates vote, write "letters to the editor," join campaigns, take part in protests, and, generally, make their voices heard. Does this mean that college graduates are turned into dangerous radicals by liberal professors? Quite the contrary: college seems to convince individuals that it is important to involve themselves in the nation's politics.

Political Conditions A fourth set of factors that shape political orientations and values are the conditions under which individuals and groups are recruited into and involved in political life. Although political beliefs are influenced by family background and group membership, the precise content and character of these views is, to a large extent, determined by political circumstances. For example, in the nineteenth century, millions of southern Italian peasants left their homes. Some migrated to cities in northern Italy; others came to cities in the United States. Many of those who moved to northern Italy were recruited by socialist and communist parties and became mainstays of the forces of the Italian Left. At the same time, their cousins and neighbors who migrated to American cities were recruited by urban patronage machines and became mainstays of political conservatism. In both instances, group membership influenced political beliefs. Yet the character of those beliefs varied enormously with the political circumstances in which a given group found itself.

Similarly, the views held by members of a particular group can shift drastically over time, as political circumstances change. For example, American white southerners were staunch members of the Democratic Party from the Civil War through

Is There a Culture War in America?

Around recent elections, Ameri-cans listening to the news heard a lot about a "culture war" in America being waged between "blue states" (states won by Democratic presidential candidates) and "red states" (states won by Republican presidential candidates)—indicating to some that there were two Americas, the Republican one and the Democratic one. According to this view, Americans are deeply divided along lines drawn by their opinions on religion, morality, and certain political values.

The question of whether a true culture war exists in America is the subject of an ongoing battle among political scientists and other scholars, but the "two Americas" said to result from the culture war present clearly identifiable stereotypes in American popular culture. One often-cited example is the "NASCAR dad." Journalist Bill Schneider described the stereotype of the NASCAR fan as "male, southern, rural, blue collar and Republican."[a]

Stereotypes of liberal Americans also exist in popular culture. A political advertisement paid for by the conservative group Club for Growth that aired during the 2004 presidential primaries played on caricatures of liberals. In the ad, an older man (an actor) states, "I think Howard Dean should take his tax-hiking, government-expanding, latte-drinking, sushi-eating, Volvo-driving, *New York Times*–reading . . . ," and a woman completes the thought, "body-piercing, Hollywood-loving, left-wing freak show back to Vermont where it belongs."

One of the less predictable places that these two Americas intersect is in animated television programming. The writer Brian C. Anderson, for example, claims that Comedy Central's controversial program *South Park* is a clear attack on liberal elitism, hyperenvironmentalism, and political correctness, through the program's characteristically shocking plotlines and language. The *New York Times* columnist Matt Bai suggests that the Fox series *King of the Hill*, on the other hand, is a more realistic and nuanced depiction of middle-American values. In *King of the Hill*, Hank Hill and his wife, Peggy, live in a suburban American town, and Hank—a NASCAR fan and gun owner—"finds himself struggling to adapt to new phenomena: art galleries and yoga stu-dios, latte-sipping parents who ask their kids to call them by their first names and encourage them to drink responsibly."[b]

In 2008, Republicans chose Sarah Palin, a self-styled "hockey mom" to be their vice-presidential candidate partly on the assumption that Palin would appeal to the "Joe Six-Packs" in the electorate, the blue-collar families uneasy with the liberalism of the Democrats. Much was made of the fact that Palin liked to hunt and knew how to field dress a moose. Her husband Todd's blue-collar origins were also emphasized by Republican campaigners.

Latte-drinking, yoga-practicing liberals and moose-hunting, NASCAR-watching conservatives are extreme oversimplifications of a diverse and nuanced American population, yet these stereotypes persist in popular culture and sometimes in political discourse.

[a]"George Bush Prepares to Campaign for Reelection," *Insight*, CNN Transcript, December 3, 2003, http://transcripts.cnn.com/TRANSCRIPTS/0312/03/i_ins.00.html (accessed 3/31/08).
[b]M. Bai, "'King of the Hill' Democrats?" *New York Times*, June 26, 2005.

for critical analysis

1. Some commentators have pointed out that much of America is "purple" rather than "red" or "blue." To what extent do you believe that the red state/blue state stereotypes apply to your state?

2. What are some of the core political values that a majority of Americans agree on? What factors may account for differences in political values among Americans?

the 1960s. As members of this political group, they became key supporters of liberal New Deal and post–New Deal social programs that greatly expanded the size and power of the American national government. Since the 1960s, however, southern whites have shifted in large numbers to the Republican Party. Now they provide a major base of support for efforts to scale back social programs and to reduce sharply the size and power of the national government. The South's move from the Democratic to the Republican camp took place because of white southern opposition to the Democratic Party's racial policies and because of determined Republican efforts to win white southern support. It was not a change in the character of white southerners but a change in the political circumstances in which they found themselves that induced this major shift in political allegiances and outlooks in the South.

The moral of this story is that a group's views cannot be inferred simply from the character of the group. College students are not inherently radical or inherently conservative. Jews are not inherently liberal. Southerners are not inherently conservative. Men are not inherently supportive of the military. Any group's political outlooks and orientations are shaped by the political circumstances in which that group finds itself, and those outlooks can change as circumstances change. Quite probably, the generation of American students now coming of political age will have a very different view of the use of American military power from that of their parents—members of a generation that reached political consciousness during the 1960s, when opposition to the Vietnam War and military conscription was an important political phenomenon.

From Political Values to Ideology

As we have seen, people's beliefs about government can vary widely. But for some individuals, this set of beliefs can fit together into a coherent philosophy about government. This set of underlying orientations, ideas, and beliefs through which we come to understand and interpret politics is called a political ideology. Ideologies take many different forms. Some people may view politics primarily in religious terms. During the course of European political history, for example, Protestantism and Catholicism were often political ideologies as much as they were religious creeds. Each set of beliefs not only included elements of religious practice but also involved ideas about secular authority and political action. Other people may see politics through racial lenses. Nazism was a political ideology that placed race at the center of political life and sought to interpret politics in terms of racial categories.

In America today, a variety of ideologies compete for attention and support. Libertarians, for example, argue that government is a wasteful and dangerous institution that should be limited to as few activities as possible. Socialists, on the other hand, argue that more government control is necessary to promote justice and reduce economic and political inequality. Environmentalists view global warming and other threats to the world's environment as the most important issues facing humanity today. Although many subscribe to these and other ideas, most Americans describe themselves as either liberals or conservatives. Liberalism and conservatism are political ideologies that include beliefs about the role of the government, ideas about public policies, and notions about which groups in society should properly exercise power (see Boxes 6.1 and 6.2). These ideologies can be seen as the end results of the process of political socialization that was discussed in the preceding section.

Classically, a liberal was an individual who favored individual initiative and was suspicious of the motives of governments and of its ability to manage economic and social affairs. Liberals saw government as the foe of freedom. The proponents of a larger and more active government called themselves "progressives." In the early twentieth century, though, many liberals and progressives coalesced around the doctrine of "social liberalism," which represented a recognition that government action might be needed to preserve individual liberty. Today's liberals are social liberals rather than classical liberals.

Thus, today, the term **liberal** has come to imply support for political and social reform; extensive government intervention in the economy; the expansion of federal social services; and more vigorous efforts on behalf of the poor, minorities, and women, as well as greater concern for consumers and the environment. In social and cultural areas, liberals generally support abortion rights, are concerned with the rights of persons accused of crime, and oppose state involvement with religious institutions and religious expression. In international affairs, liberal positions are usually seen as including support for arms control, opposition to the development and testing of nuclear weapons, support for aid to poor nations, opposition to the use of American troops to influence the domestic affairs of developing nations, and support for international organizations such as the United Nations. Of course, liberalism is not monolithic. For example, among individuals who view themselves as liberal, many support American military intervention when it is tied to a humanitarian purpose, as in the case of America's military action in Kosovo in 1998–99. Most liberals supported the former president Bush's war on terrorism, even when some of the president's actions seemed to curtail civil liberties.

By contrast, the term **conservative** today is used to describe those who generally support the social and economic status quo and are suspicious of efforts to introduce new political formulae and economic arrangements. Conservatives believe strongly that a large and powerful government poses a threat to citizens' freedom. Ironically, today's conservatives espouse the views of classical liberalism. Premodern conservatives were the defenders of monarchy and aristocracy—doctrines that seem completely out of place today. Today, in the domestic arena, conservatives generally oppose the expansion of governmental activity, asserting that solutions to social and economic problems can be developed in the private sector. Conservatives particularly oppose efforts to impose government regulation on business, pointing out that such regulation is frequently economically inefficient and costly and can ultimately lower the entire nation's standard of living. As for social and cultural positions, many conservatives oppose abortion, support school prayer, are more concerned for the victims than for the perpetrators of crimes, oppose school busing, and support traditional family arrangements. In international affairs, conservatism has come to mean support for the maintenance of American military power. Like liberalism, conservatism is far from a monolithic ideology. Some conservatives support many government social programs. The Republican George W. Bush called himself a "compassionate conservative" to indicate that he favored programs that assist the poor and needy. Other conservatives dismissed Bush as a "big government" Republican and not a true conservative. Some of these individuals joined the 2009 "Tea Party" movement to protest President Obama's efforts to expand the role of the federal government. Some conservatives oppose efforts to outlaw abortion, arguing

liberal today this term refers to those who generally support social and political reform; extensive governmental intervention in the economy; the expansion of federal social services; more vigorous efforts on behalf of the poor, minorities, and women; and greater concern for consumers and the environment

conservative today this term refers to those who generally support the social and economic status quo and are suspicious of efforts to introduce new political formulae and economic arrangements. Conservatives believe that a large and powerful government poses a threat to citizens' freedom

During the 1960s and early 1970s, anti–Vietnam War protestors staged numerous demonstrations.

that government intrusion in this area is as misguided as government intervention in the economy. Such a position is sometimes called "libertarian." The political pundit Pat Buchanan has angered many fellow conservatives by opposing government action in the form of American military intervention in other regions. Many conservatives charge Buchanan with advocating a form of American "isolationism" that runs counter to contemporary conservative doctrine. The real political world is far too complex to be seen in terms of a simple struggle between liberals and conservatives.

To some extent, contemporary liberalism and conservatism can be seen as differences of emphasis with regard to the fundamental American political values of liberty and equality. For liberals, equality is the most important of the core values. Liberals encourage government action in such areas as college admissions and business practices to enhance race, class, and gender equality. For conservatives, on the other hand, liberty is the core value. Conservatives oppose many efforts of the government, however well intentioned, to intrude into private life and the marketplace. For example, in October 2008, many conservative Republican members of Congress voted against the Bush administration's emergency plan to end the nation's financial crisis because they opposed the partial government takeover of banks and other financial institutions that would result from the plan. Some conservatives believed that even the risk of a financial meltdown did not justify the expansion of government power in the marketplace. This simple formula for distinguishing liberalism and conservatism, however, is not always accurate, because political ideologies seldom lend themselves to neat or logical characterizations. Often political observers search for logical connections among the various positions identified with liberalism or with conservatism, and they are disappointed or puzzled when they are unable to find a set of coherent philosophical principles that define and unite the several elements of either of these sets of beliefs. On the liberal side, for example, what is the logical connection between opposition to U.S. government intervention in the affairs of foreign nations and calls for greater intervention in America's economy and society? On the conservative side, what is

for critical analysis

Describe the differences between liberal and conservative ideologies in American politics. Using one social or demographic group as an example, describe some factors that may have shaped the ideological orientation of that particular group.

BOX 6.1

Profile of a Liberal: Representative Nancy Pelosi

- Supports abortion rights.

- Opposes prayer in the public schools.

- Supports affirmative action.

- Favors expanded health coverage for all Americans.

- Wants to bring an end to the war in Iraq.

- Advocates increased funding for education.

- Supports further increases in the minimum wage.

the logical relationship between opposition to governmental regulation of business and support for a government ban on abortion? Indeed, the latter would seem to be just the sort of regulation of private conduct that conservatives claim to abhor.

Frequently, the relationships among the various elements of liberalism or of conservatism are political rather than logical. One underlying basis of liberal views is that all or most are criticisms of or attacks on the foreign and domestic policies and cultural values of the business and commercial strata that have been prominent in the United States for the past century. In some measure, the tenets of contemporary conservatism are this elite's defense of its positions against its enemies, who include organized labor, minority groups, and some intellectuals and professionals. Thus, liberals attack business and commercial elites by advocating more governmental regulation, including consumer protection and environmental regulation, opposing new military weapons programs, and supporting expensive social programs. Conservatives counterattack by asserting that governmental regulation of the economy is ruinous and that new military weapons are needed in a changing world, and they seek to stigmatize their opponents for showing no concern for the rights of "unborn" Americans.

Of course, it is important to note that many people who call themselves liberals or conservatives accept only part of the established liberal or conservative agendas. Some Republicans, for example, who are fiscal conservatives favoring low taxes and small government are, nevertheless, social liberals favoring gay rights and access to abortion. Similarly, some religious and social conservatives support expansion of the government's health and welfare services. There is nothing illogical about these positions. Since the relationships among the various tenets of liberal and conservative beliefs are often politically determined rather than dictated by logic, individuals often find themselves agreeing with part but not all of a particular political creed.

BOX 6.2

Profile of a Conservative: House Speaker John Boehner

- Wants to trim the size of the federal government.

- Wants to diminish government regulation of business.

- Favors prayer in the public schools.

- Opposes gay rights legislation.

- Favors making most abortions illegal.

- Supports harsher treatment of criminals.

- Opposes many affirmative action programs.

- Favors tax cuts.

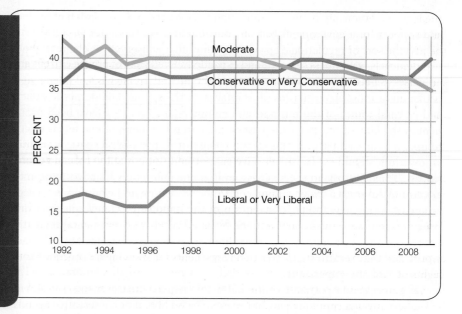

FIGURE 6.3

Americans' Shifting Ideology, 1972–2009

Over the past two decades, more Americans have identified themselves as "conservatives" than "liberals." During this same period, however, Americans have elected two Democratic presidents and have, several times, elected Democratic majorities in Congress. What might account for this apparent discrepancy between ideology and partisanship?

SOURCE: Gallup.com (accessed 8/5/10).

Americans' ideological preferences, moreover, are not carved in stone. They shift over time in response to political events, the appeals of political leaders, and life changes. During the 1980s and 1990s, the number of Americans describing themselves as conservatives seemed to be increasing, perhaps in response to Republican assertions that government was a problem rather than a solution. In recent years, Americans have looked to the government for solutions to such problems as international terrorism and economic crisis and, perhaps as a result, as Figure 6.3 indicates, more Americans have been describing themselves as liberals.

How We Form Political Opinions

An individual's opinions on particular issues, events, and personalities emerge as he or she evaluates these phenomena through the lenses of the beliefs and orientations that, taken together, form his or her political ideology. Thus, if a conservative is confronted with a plan to expand federal social programs, he or she is likely to express opposition to the endeavor without spending too much time pondering the specific plan. Similarly, if a liberal is asked to comment on the former conservative president George W. Bush, he or she is not likely to hesitate long before offering a negative view. Underlying beliefs and ideologies tend automatically to color people's perceptions and opinions about politics.

Opinions on particular issues, however, are seldom fully shaped by underlying ideologies. Few individuals possess ideologies so cohesive and intensely held that they will automatically shape all their opinions. Indeed, when we occasionally encounter individuals with rigid worldviews, who see everything through a particular political lens, we tend to dismiss them as "ideologues," or lacking common sense.

Although ideologies color our political perspectives, they seldom fully determine our views. This is true for a variety of reasons. First, as noted earlier, most individuals' ideologies contain internal contradictions. Take, for example, a conservative view of the issue of abortion. Should conservatives favor outlawing abortion as an appropriate

● How do people
form opinions about
specific issues?

means of preserving public morality, or should they oppose restrictions on abortion because these represent government intrusions into private life? Or take the issue of America's response to terrorism. Should conservatives support the government's eavesdropping, warrantless searches, and expanded surveillance of private citizens and businesses as needed to defend the nation, or should they be concerned about allowing the government so much power to intrude into private lives? In this instance, as in many others, ideology can point in different directions.

Second, individuals may have difficulty linking particular issues or personalities to their own underlying beliefs. Some issues defy ideological characterization. For example, should conservatives have supported or opposed the federal government's 2008-09 efforts to prevent the collapse of a number of major banking firms and two of America's major automakers? On the one hand, a conservative might oppose massive government intervention in the nation's economy. On the other hand, a conservative might favor actions designed to rescue American capitalism in a time of crisis. In a similar vein, should liberals have welcomed this display of the importance of government intervention in the face of market failure or should they have resented the expenditure of tax dollars to rescue greedy corporations? The federal government's response to the 2008–09 financial crisis was too complex to be viewed through simple ideological lenses. No wonder many conservatives were divided on the issue.

Finally, most people have at least some conflicting underlying attitudes. Most conservatives support *some* federal programs—defense, or tax deductions for businesses, for example—and wish to see them, and hence the government, expanded. Many liberals favor American military intervention in other nations for what they deem to be humanitarian purposes but generally oppose American military intervention in the affairs of other nations.

Thus, most individuals' attitudes on particular issues do not spring automatically from their ideological predispositions. It is true that most people have deeply rooted beliefs that help to shape their opinions on particular issues, but two other factors are also important: a person's knowledge of political issues, and outside influences on that person's views.

Political Knowledge

As we have seen, general political beliefs can guide the formation of opinions on specific issues, but an individual's beliefs and opinions are not always consistent with each other. Studies of political opinion have shown that most people don't hold specific and clearly defined opinions on every political issue. As a result, they are easily influenced by others. What best explains whether citizens are generally consistent in their political views or inconsistent and open to the influence of others? The key is knowledge and information about political issues. In general, knowledgeable citizens are better able to evaluate new information and to determine whether it is relevant to and consistent with their beliefs and opinions. As a result, better-informed individuals can recognize their political interests and act consistently on behalf of them.

One of the most obvious and important examples of this proposition is voting. Despite the predisposition of voters to support their own party's candidates (see Chapter 9 for a discussion of party identification), millions of voters are affected by the information they receive about candidates during a campaign. During the 2008 presidential campaign, for instance, voters weighed the arguments of Barack Obama against those of John McCain about who was more qualified to oversee the U.S. economy. Many Republican voters turned to Obama because they held the GOP responsible for the nation's financial crisis and found Obama's economic proposals more credible than those put forward by John McCain. Thus citizens can use information and judgment to overcome their predispositions. Without some political knowledge, citizens would have a difficult time making sense of the complex political world in which they live.

This point brings up two questions, however. First, how much political knowledge is necessary for one to act as an effective citizen? And second, how is political knowledge distributed throughout the population? In an important study of political knowledge in the United States, the political scientists Michael X. Delli Carpini and Scott Keeter found that the average American exhibits little knowledge of political institutions, processes, leaders, and policy debates.[15] Many Americans cannot even name their own congressional representative. Does this ignorance of key political facts matter?

Another important concern is the character of those who possess and act on the political information that they acquire. Political knowledge is not evenly distributed throughout the population. Those with higher education, income, and occupational status and who are members of social or political organizations are more likely to know about and be active in politics. An interest in politics reinforces an individual's sense of **political efficacy** and provides more incentive to acquire additional knowledge and information about politics. Those who don't think they can have an effect on government tend not to be interested in learning about or participating in politics. As a result, individuals with a disproportionate share of income and education also have a disproportionate share of knowledge and influence and are better able to get what they want from government.

Because becoming truly knowledgeable about politics requires a substantial investment of time and energy, many Americans seek to acquire political information and to make political decisions "on the cheap," making use of shortcuts that seem to relieve them of having to engage in a lengthy process of information gathering and evaluation. One "inexpensive" way to become informed is to take cues from trusted others—the local minister, the television commentator or newspaper editorialist, an interest-group leader, friends and relatives.[16] Along the same lines, a common shortcut for political evaluation and decision making is to assess new issues and events through the lenses of one's more general beliefs and orientations. Thus, if a conservative learns of a plan to expand federal social programs, he or she might express opposition to the endeavor without spending too much time pondering the specific proposal. Similarly, if a liberal is told that Republican leaders are backing a major overhaul of the Social Security system, he or she will probably not need to read thousands of pages of economic projections before expressing disapproval of the GOP's efforts.

Neither of these shortcuts, however, is entirely reliable. As we saw above, general ideological orientations can be poor guides to decision making in concrete instances. And taking cues from others may lead individuals to accept positions they would not support if they had more information. For example, few Americans read the details of the health care reform proposals debated in the House and Senate in 2009 but, instead, took their cues from politicians whose views they assumed were similar to their own. Yet many liberals who took their cues from President Obama might have preferred no bill at all to a bill without the "public option" that the president agreed to drop. And many conservatives who took their cues from House and Senate Republican leaders might have found much to like in the legislation these politicians castigated.

political efficacy the ability to influence government and politics

How Americans View the World and Vice Versa

When they are not being accused of seeking to conquer the world, Americans are often charged with failing to pay enough attention to international affairs. It is true that many Americans lack a basic knowledge of world history and geography and have considerable difficulty naming the leaders of other nations. Several surveys have indicated that some Americans think Canada is one of the 50 states.

Nevertheless, Americans do have strong opinions about which foreign nations are America's friends in the world and which are its foes. Topping the list of friends is Great Britain, seen by 74 percent of recent poll respondents as a "close ally." Curiously, 2 percent of those surveyed viewed Britain as an enemy. Perhaps they have not forgotten King George's mistreatment of the colonists in 1775. When it comes to China, now one of America's most important trading partners, only 9 percent of Americans believe China is a close ally, whereas 54 percent think China is not friendly or even is America's enemy. It is interesting to note also that France, traditionally an American ally, came to be viewed less favorably than Russia, America's Cold War adversary, in the wake of vocal French opposition to America's Middle East policy.

Just as Americans have opinions about the world, citizens of other nations have their own opinions about America. Americans sometimes complain that their efforts on behalf of other nations are not properly appreciated and feel envied and disliked by the rest of the world. Only Kenyan, Nigerian, and Filipino respondents to a recent survey had an overwhelmingly positive view of America. Even normally friendly Europeans seem to have developed a negative view of the United States.

During the American occupation of Iraq, antagonism toward American foreign policy has hardened even more in most Muslim countries. An overwhelming majority of those polled in the Middle East expressed strongly anti-American senti-

ment. The enduring popularity of Osama bin Laden in these countries also reinforces Muslim attitudes generally toward the United States. Worldwide, a majority of people believed that the United States' war on terror is actually an attempt to control the Middle East's oil or to dominate the world. The Bush administration's foreign policies earned few converts abroad and lost support at home as well.

for critical analysis

1. What are the factors shaping the ways Americans view other nations and how others view America?

2. Should Americans care about how they are seen around the world? Why or why not?

1778   1943

AMERICANS
will always fight for liberty

Governments frequently attempt to influence public opinion. This 1943 poster was intended to build support for World War II by associating it with the American Revolution.

Although understandable and, perhaps, inevitable, widespread inattentiveness to politics weakens American democracy in two ways. First, those who lack political information or resort to inadequate shortcuts to acquire and assess information cannot effectively defend their own political interests and can easily become victims or losers in political struggles. The presence, moreover, of large numbers of politically inattentive or ignorant individuals means that the political process can more easily be manipulated by the various institutions and forces that seek to shape public opinion.

Political Knowledge and Political Inequality If knowledge is power, lack of knowledge can be an enormous source of political weakness and contribute greatly to political inequality. When individuals are unaware of their interests or how to pursue them, it is virtually certain that political outcomes will not favor them. One example is in the realm of taxation. Over the past several decades, the United States has substantially reduced the rate of taxation paid by its wealthiest citizens. Most recently, tax cuts signed into law by George W. Bush provided a tax break mainly for the top 1 percent of the nation's wage earners; further tax cuts proposed by the president offered additional benefits to this privileged stratum. Surprisingly, however, polling data show that millions of middle-class and lower-middle-class Americans who did not stand to benefit from the president's tax cuts seemed to favor them, nonetheless. The explanation for this odd state of affairs appears to be lack of political knowledge. Millions of individuals who were unlikely to derive much advantage from President Bush's tax policy thought they would. The political scientist Larry Bartels has called this phenomenon "misplaced self-interest."[17] Upper-bracket taxpayers, who are usually served by an army of financial advisers, are unlikely to suffer from this problem.

The Influence of Political Leaders, Private Groups, and the Media

When individuals attempt to form opinions about particular political issues, events, and personalities, they seldom do so in isolation. Typically, they are confronted with—sometimes bombarded by—the efforts of a host of individuals and groups seeking to persuade them to adopt a particular point of view. Someone trying to decide what to think about Hillary Clinton, Barack Obama, or John McCain could hardly avoid an avalanche of opinions expressed through the media, in meetings, or in conversations with friends. The **marketplace of ideas** is the interplay of opinions and views that takes place as competing forces attempt to persuade as many people as possible to accept a particular position on a particular event. Given constant exposure to the ideas of others, it is virtually impossible for most individuals to resist some modification of their own beliefs. For example, as we saw earlier, African Americans and white Americans disagree on a number of matters. Yet as the political scientists Paul Sniderman and Edward Carmines have shown, considerable cross-racial agreement has evolved on fundamental issues of race and civil rights.[18] Three forces that play important roles in shaping opinions in the marketplace are the government, private groups, and the news media.[19]

marketplace of ideas the public forum in which beliefs and ideas are exchanged and compete

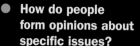
Government and the Shaping of Public Opinion All governments attempt, to a greater or lesser extent, to influence, manipulate, or manage their citizens' beliefs. But the extent to which public opinion is actually affected by governmental public-relations efforts is probably limited. The government—despite its size and power—is only one source of information and evaluation in the United States. Very often, governmental claims are disputed by the media, by interest groups, and at times by opposing forces within the government itself. Often, too, governmental efforts to manipulate public opinion backfire when the public is made aware of the government's tactics. Thus, in 1971, the United States government's efforts to build popular support for the Vietnam War were hurt when CBS News aired its documentary "The Selling of the Pentagon," which purported to reveal the extent and character of governmental efforts to sway popular sentiment. In this documentary, CBS demonstrated the techniques, including planted news stories and faked film footage, that the government had used to misrepresent its activities in Vietnam. These revelations, of course, undermined popular trust in all governmental claims.

A hallmark of the Clinton administration was the steady use of techniques like those used in election campaigns to bolster popular enthusiasm for White House initiatives. The president established a political "war room," similar to the one that operated in his campaign headquarters, where representatives from all departments met daily to discuss and coordinate the president's public-relations efforts. Many of the same consultants and pollsters who directed the successful Clinton campaign were also employed in the selling of the president's programs.[20]

After he assumed office in 2001, President George W. Bush asserted that political leaders should base their programs on their own conception of the public interest rather than the polls. This, however, did not mean that Bush ignored public opinion. Bush relied on the pollster Jan van Lohuizen to conduct a low-key operation, sufficiently removed from the limelight to allow the president to renounce polling while continuing to make use of survey data.[21] At the same time, the Bush White House developed an extensive public relations program, led by the former presidential aide Karen P. Hughes, to bolster popular support for the president's policies. Hughes, working with the conservative TV personality Mary Matalin, coordinated White House efforts to maintain popular support for the administration's war against terrorism. These efforts included presidential speeches, media appearances by administration officials, numerous press conferences, and thousands of press releases presenting the administration's views.[22] The White House also made a substantial effort to sway opinion in foreign countries, even sending officials to present the administration's views on television networks serving the Arab world.

Like its predecessors, the Obama administration has sought to shape public opinion in the United States and abroad. President Obama is an excellent speaker and the administration has relied upon the power of the president's oratory to build support for its initiatives in domestic and foreign policy. When Obama visited China, the Chinese government, fearing that he would use his media presence to captivate the nation, drastically limited Obama's live media exposure.

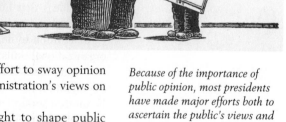

Because of the importance of public opinion, most presidents have made major efforts both to ascertain the public's views and to promote opinions favorable to themselves and their policies. Bill Clinton was often criticized for retaining a number of pollsters to chart shifts in public opinion on a daily basis.

Private Groups and the Shaping of Public Opinion We have already seen how the government tries to shape public opinion. But the ideas that become prominent in political life are also developed and spread by important economic and political groups searching for issues that will advance their causes. One example is the "right-to-life" issue, which has inflamed American politics over the past thirty years.

The notion of the right to life, whose proponents seek to outlaw abortion and overturn the Supreme Court's *Roe v. Wade* decision, was developed and heavily promoted by conservative politicians who saw the issue of abortion as a means of uniting Catholic and Protestant conservatives and linking both groups to the Republican Party. These politicians convinced Catholic and evangelical Protestant leaders that they shared similar views on the question of abortion, and they worked with religious leaders to focus public attention on the negative issues in the abortion debate. To advance their cause, leaders of the movement sponsored well-publicized Senate hearings, where testimony, photographs, and other exhibits were presented to illustrate the violent effects of abortion procedures. At the same time, publicists for the movement produced leaflets, articles, books, and films such as *The Silent Scream* to highlight the agony and pain ostensibly felt by the "unborn" when they were being aborted. All this underscored the movement's claim that abortion was nothing more or less than the murder of millions of innocent human beings. Finally, Catholic and evangelical Protestant religious leaders were organized to denounce abortion from their church pulpits and, increasingly, from their electronic pulpits on the Christian Broadcasting Network (CBN) and the various other television forums available for religious programming. Religious leaders also organized demonstrations, pickets, and disruptions at abortion clinics throughout the nation.[23] The abortion rights issue remains a potent one.

Typically, ideas are marketed most effectively by groups with access to financial resources, public or private institutional support, and sufficient skill or education to select, develop, and draft ideas that will attract interest and support. Thus, the development and promotion of conservative themes and ideas in recent years have been greatly facilitated by the millions of dollars that conservative corporations and business organizations such as the Chamber of Commerce and the Public Affairs Council spend each year on public information and what is now called in corporate circles "issues management." In addition, conservative business leaders have contributed millions of dollars to such conservative institutions as the Heritage Foundation, the Hoover Institution, and the American Enterprise Institute.[24] Many of the ideas that helped those on the Right influence political debate were first developed and articulated by scholars associated with institutions such as these.

In addition to financial assets, liberal intellectuals and professionals have ample organizational skills; access to the media; and practice in creating, communicating, and using ideas. During the past three decades, the chief vehicle through which liberal intellectuals and professionals have advanced their ideas has been the "public interest group," an institution that relies heavily on voluntary contributions of time, effort, and interest on the part of its members. Through groups such as Common Cause, the National Organization for Women, the Sierra Club, Friends of the Earth, and Physicians for Social Responsibility, intellectuals and professionals have been able to apply their organizational skills and educational resources to developing and promoting ideas.[25] Often, research conducted in universities and in liberal "think tanks" such as the Brookings Institution provides the ideas on which liberal politicians rely. For example, the welfare reform plan introduced by the Clinton administration in 1994 originated with the work of a former Harvard professor, David Ellwood. Ellwood's academic research led him to the conclusion that the nation's welfare system would be improved if services to the poor were expanded in scope but limited in duration. His idea was adopted by the 1992 Clinton campaign, which was searching for a position on welfare that would appeal to both liberal and conservative Democrats. The Ellwood plan seemed perfect: it promised liberals an immediate expansion of welfare benefits, yet it held out to conservatives the idea that welfare recipients would receive benefits only for a limited period of time. The Clinton welfare reform plan even borrowed phrases from Ellwood's book *Poor Support*.[26]

The journalist and author Joe Queenan has correctly observed that although political ideas can erupt spontaneously, they almost never do. Instead, he says,

issues are usually manufactured by tenured professors and obscure employees of think tanks. . . . It is inconceivable that the American people, all by themselves, could independently arrive at the conclusion that the depletion of the ozone layer poses a dire threat to our national well-being, or that an immediate, across-the-board cut in the capital-gains tax is the only thing that stands between us and the economic abyss. The American people do not have that kind of sophistication. They have to have help.[27]

The Media and Public Opinion The communications media are among the most powerful forces operating in the marketplace of ideas. As we shall see in Chapter 7, the mass media are not simply neutral messengers for ideas developed by others. Instead, the media have an enormous impact on popular attitudes and opinions. Over time, the ways in which the mass media report political events help to shape the underlying attitudes and beliefs from which opinions emerge. For example, for the past thirty years, the national news media have relentlessly investigated personal and official wrongdoing on the part of politicians and public officials. This continual media presentation of corruption in government and venality in politics has undoubtedly fostered the general attitude of cynicism and distrust that exists in the general public.

Opponents and proponents of a woman's right to choose often clash with one another. Large well-financed groups on both sides of the debate try to influence public opinion and government policy.

for critical analysis

Politicians, governments, and a host of groups endeavor to shape public perceptions of issues, events, and personalities. What are some of the ways these actors try to mold opinion? How can we distinguish between information and propaganda?

At the same time, the ways in which media coverage interprets or frames specific events can have a major impact on popular responses and opinions about these events.[29] Because media framing can be important, the Bush administration sought to persuade broadcasters to follow its lead in its coverage of terrorism and America's response to terrorism in the months following the September 11 attacks. Broadcasters, who found themselves targets of anthrax-contaminated letters apparently mailed by terrorists, needed little persuasion. For the most part, the media praised the president for his leadership and presented the administration's military campaign in Afghanistan and domestic antiterrorist efforts in a positive light. Even newspapers such as the *New York Times*, which had strongly opposed Bush in the 2000 election and questioned his fitness for the presidency, asserted that he had grown into the job. In the aftermath of the 2003 Iraq war, however, media coverage of the Bush administration became more critical. Formerly supportive media accused the president of failing both to anticipate the chaos and violence of postwar Iraq and to develop a strategy that would allow America to extricate itself from its involvement in Iraq. The president, for his part, accused the media of failing to present an accurate picture of his administration's successes in Iraq.

Measuring Public Opinion

As recently as fifty years ago, American political leaders gauged public opinion by people's applause and by the presence of crowds at meetings. This direct exposure to the people's views did not necessarily produce accurate knowledge of public opinion. It did, however, give political leaders confidence in their public support—and therefore confidence in their ability to govern by consent.

Abraham Lincoln and Stephen Douglas debated each other seven times during the summer and autumn of 1858, two years before they became presidential nominees. Their debates took place before audiences in parched cornfields and courthouse squares. A century later, the presidential debates, although seen by millions, take place before a few reporters, technicians, and audiences instructed not to applaud or make noise in television studios that might as well be on the moon. Only rarely can politicians experience the public's response directly. This distance between leaders and followers is one of the agonizing problems of modern democracy. The media send information to millions of people, but they are not yet as efficient at getting information back to leaders. Is government by consent possible where the scale of communication is so large and impersonal? In order to compensate for the decline in their ability to experience public opinion for themselves, leaders have turned to science, in particular to the science of opinion polling.

public-opinion polls scientific instruments for measuring public opinion

It is no secret that politicians and public officials make extensive use of **public-opinion polls** to help them decide whether to run for office, what policies to support, how to vote on important legislation, and what types of appeals to make in their campaigns. President Lyndon Johnson was famous for carrying the latest Gallup and Roper poll results in his pocket, and it is widely believed that he began to withdraw from politics because the polls reported losses in public support for him. All recent presidents and other major political figures have worked closely with polls and pollsters.

Who Supported Health Care Reform?

Public opinion on specific policies can be hard to measure. In the months leading up to the passage of the Health Care Act of 2010, polls on health care legislation frequently contradicted one another, with some showing a majority of Americans opposing health care legislation and others showing a majority in favor.

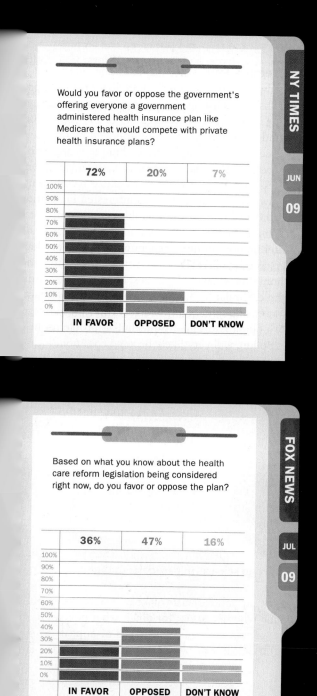

NY TIMES **JUN 09**

Would you favor or oppose the government's offering everyone a government administered health insurance plan like Medicare that would compete with private health insurance plans?

72%	20%	7%
IN FAVOR	OPPOSED	DON'T KNOW

FOX NEWS **JUL 09**

Based on what you know about the health care reform legislation being considered right now, do you favor or oppose the plan?

36%	47%	16%
IN FAVOR	OPPOSED	DON'T KNOW

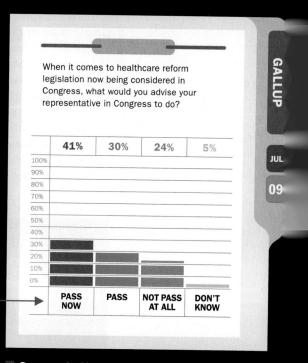

GALLUP **JUL 09**

When it comes to healthcare reform legislation now being considered in Congress, what would you advise your representative in Congress to do?

41%	30%	24%	5%
PASS NOW	PASS	NOT PASS AT ALL	DON'T KNOW

- Pass a new health care reform law by the end of this year
- Pass a new health care reform law but not necessarily this year
- Not pass a new health care reform law at all

for critical analysis

1. **What are some of the possible reasons for the differences in these polling results?**

2. **Given the difficulty of measuring public opinion on many issues, how much should lawmakers take public opinion into account?**

SOURCES: "In Poll, Wide Support for Government-Run Health," *New York Times*, June 20, 2009; Uncertainty on Health Care Reform," FoxNews.com, July 23, 2009; Most in U.S. Want Healthca · Reform, but Vary on Urgency," Gallup.com, July 24, 2009.

Constructing Public Opinion from Surveys

The population in which pollsters are interested is usually quite large. To conduct their polls they first choose a **sample** of the total population. The selection of this sample is important. Above all, it must be representative: the views of those in the sample must accurately and proportionately reflect the views of the whole. To a large extent, the validity of the poll's results depends on the sampling procedure used.

Sampling Techniques and Selection Bias The most common techniques for choosing such a sample are probability sampling and random digit dialing. In **probability sampling**, the pollster begins with a listing of the population to be surveyed. This listing is called the "sampling frame." After each member of the population is assigned a number, a table of random numbers or a computerized random selection process is used to select those to be surveyed. This technique is appropriate when the entire population can be identified. For example, all students registered at Texas colleges and universities can be identified from college records, and a sample of them can easily be drawn. When the pollster is interested in a national sample of Americans, however, this technique is not feasible, as no complete list of Americans exists.[30] National samples are usually drawn using a technique called **random digit dialing**. A computer random-number generator is used to produce a list of as many ten-digit numbers as the pollster deems necessary. Given that more than 95 percent of American households have telephones, this technique usually results in a random national sample. Similar techniques can be used to construct an Internet-based sample. Today, some polls contact respondents through the Internet. Still in its infancy, this form of polling is plagued by technical problems. In the years to come, though, Internet polling will very likely become common.[31]

sample a small group selected by researchers to represent the most important characteristics of an entire population

probability sampling a method used by pollsters to select a representative sample in which every individual in the population has an equal probability of being selected as a respondent

random digit dialing a polling method in which respondents are selected at random from a list of ten-digit telephone numbers, with every effort made to avoid bias in the construction of the sample

Though public opinion is important, it is not always easy to interpret, and polls often fail to predict accurately how Americans will vote. In 1948, election-night polls showed Thomas Dewey defeating Harry S. Truman for the presidency.

The importance of sampling was brought home early in the history of political polling. A 1936 *Literary Digest* poll predicted that the Republican presidential candidate Alf Landon would defeat the Democrat Franklin Delano Roosevelt in that year's presidential election. The actual election, of course, ended in a Roosevelt landslide. The main problem with the survey was what is called **selection bias** in drawing the sample. The pollsters had relied on telephone directories and automobile registration rosters to produce a sampling frame. During the Great Depression, only wealthier Americans owned telephones and automobiles. Thus, the millions of working-class Americans who constituted Roosevelt's principal base of support were excluded from the sample. A more recent instance of polling error caused by selection bias was the 1998 Minnesota gubernatorial election. A poll conducted by the *Minneapolis Star Tribune* just six weeks before the election showed Jesse Ventura running a distant third to the Democratic candidate, Hubert Humphrey III, who seemed to have the support of 49 percent of the electorate, and the Republican candidate, Norm Coleman, whose support stood at 29 percent. Only 10 percent of those polled said they were planning to vote for Ventura. On election day, Ventura won more votes than either Humphrey and Coleman. Analysis of exit-poll data showed why the preelection polls had been so wrong. In an effort to be more accurate, preelection pollsters' predictions often take account of the likelihood that respondents will actually vote. This is accomplished by polling only people who have voted in the past or by correcting for past frequency of voting. The *Star Tribune* poll was conducted only among individuals who had voted in the previous election. Ventura, however, brought to the polls not only individuals who had not voted in the last election but also many people who had never voted before in their lives. Twelve percent of Minnesota's voters in 1998 said they came to the polls only because Ventura was on the ballot. This surge in turnout was facilitated by the fact that Minnesota permits same-day voter registration. (See Chapter 10 for a discussion of the consequences of registration rules.) Thus, the pollsters were wrong because Ventura changed the composition of the electorate.[32]

In recent years, the issue of selection bias has been further complicated by the fact that growing numbers of individuals refuse to answer pollsters' questions or use such devices as answering machines and "Caller ID" to screen unwanted callers. If pollsters could be certain that those who responded to their surveys simply reflected the views of those who refused to respond, there would be no problem. Some studies, however, suggest that the views of respondents and nonrespondents can differ, especially along social-class lines. Middle- and upper-middle-class individuals are more likely to be willing to respond to surveys than their working-class counterparts.[33] Thus far, "nonresponse bias" has not undermined a major national survey, but the possibility of a future *Literary Digest* fiasco should not be ignored.

Sample Size The degree of reliability in polling is also a function of sample size. The same sample is needed to represent a small population as to represent a large population. The typical size of a sample ranges from 450 to 1,500 respondents. This number, however, reflects a trade-off between cost and degree of precision desired. The degree of accuracy that can be achieved with even a small sample can be seen from the polls' success in predicting election outcomes. The chance that the sample used does not accurately represent the population from which it is drawn is called the **sampling error** or *margin of error*. A typical survey of 1,500 respondents will have a sampling error of approximately 3 percent. When a preelection poll indicates 51 percent of voters surveyed favor the Republican candidate and

selection bias polling error that arises when the sample is not representative of the population being studied, which creates errors in overrepresenting or underrepresenting some opinions

sampling error polling error that arises based on the small size of the sample

TABLE 6.3

Two Pollsters and Their Records (1948–2008)

Since their poor showing in 1948, the major pollsters have been close to the mark in every national presidential election. In 2000, though, neither Gallup nor Harris accurately predicted the outcome. From what you have learned about polling, what were some of the possible sources of error in these two national polls?

	HARRIS	GALLUP	ACTUAL OUTCOME
2008			
McCain	44%	43%	46%
Obama	50	51	53
2004			
Bush	49%	49%	51%
Kerry	48	49	48
Nader	1	1	0
2000			
Bush	47%	48%	48%
Gore	47	46	49
Nader	5	4	3
1996			
Clinton	51%	52%	49%
Dole	39	41	41
Perot	9	7	8
1992			
Clinton	44%	44%	43%
Bush	38	37	38
Perot	17	14	19
1988			
Bush	51%	53%	54%
Dukakis	47	42	46
1984			
Reagan	56%	59%	59%
Mondale	44	41	41
1980			
Reagan	48%	47%	51%
Carter	43	44	41
Anderson		8	

(continued)

49 percent support the Democratic candidate, the outcome is too close to call because it is within the margin of error of the survey. A figure of 51 percent means that between 48 and 54 percent of voters in the population favor the Republicans, while a figure of 49 percent indicates that between 46 and 52 percent of all voters support the Democrats. Thus, in this example, a 52–48 percent Democratic victory would still be consistent with polls predicting a 51–49 percent Republican triumph.

Table 6.3 shows how accurate two of the major national polling organizations actually have been in predicting the outcomes of presidential elections. Pollsters have been mostly correct in their predictions.

	HARRIS	GALLUP	ACTUAL OUTCOME
1976			
Carter	48%	48%	51%
Ford	45	49	48
1972			
Nixon	59%	62%	61%
McGovern	35	38	38
1968			
Nixon	40%	43%	43%
Humphrey	43	42	43
Wallace	13	15	14
1964			
Johnson	62%	64%	61%
Goldwater	33	36	39
1960			
Kennedy	49%	51%	50%
Nixon	41	49	49
1956			
Eisenhower	NA	60%	58%
Stevenson		41	42
1952			
Eisenhower	47%	51%	55%
Stevenson	42	49	44
1948			
Truman	NA	44.5%	49.6%
Dewey		49.5	45.1

NOTE: All figures except those for 1948 are rounded. NA = Not asked.

SOURCES: Data from the Gallup Poll and the Harris Survey (New York: Chicago Tribune–New York News Syndicate, various press releases 1964–2004). Courtesy of the Gallup Organization and Louis Harris Associates.

Survey Design Even with reliable sample procedures, surveys may fail to reflect the true distribution of opinion within a target population. One frequent source of **measurement error** is the wording of survey questions. The precise words used in a question can have an enormous impact on the answers it elicits. The validity of survey results can also be adversely affected by poor question format, faulty ordering of questions, inappropriate vocabulary, ambiguity of questions, or questions with built-in biases. Often, seemingly minor differences in the wording of a question can convey vastly different meanings to respondents and thus produce quite different response patterns (see Box 6.3). For example, for many years the University of Chicago's National Opinion Research Center has asked respondents whether they think the federal government is spending too much, too little, or about the right amount of money on "assistance for the poor." Answering the question posed this way, about two-thirds of all respondents seem to believe that the government is spending too little. However, the same survey also asks whether the government spends too much, too little, or about the right amount for "welfare." When the word "welfare" is substituted for "assistance for the poor," about half of all respondents indicate that too much is being spent.[34]

> **measurement error** failure to identify the true distribution of opinion within a population because of errors such as ambiguous or poorly worded questions

BOX 6.3

It Depends on How You Ask

THE SITUATION
The public's desire for tax cuts can be hard to measure. In 2000, pollsters asked what should be done with the nation's budget surplus and got different results depending on the specifics of the question.

THE QUESTION
President Clinton has proposed setting aside approximately two-thirds of an expected budget surplus to fix the Social Security system. What do you think the leaders in Washington should do with the remainder of the surplus?

VARIATION 1
Should the money be used for a tax cut, or should it be used to fund new government programs?

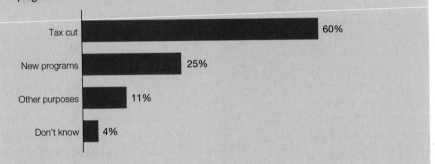

Tax cut	60%
New programs	25%
Other purposes	11%
Don't know	4%

VARIATION 2
Should the money be used for a tax cut, or should it be spent on programs for education, the environment, health care, crime fighting, and military defense?

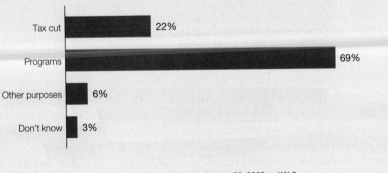

Tax cut	22%
Programs	69%
Other purposes	6%
Don't know	3%

SOURCE: Pew Research Center, reported in the *New York Times*, January 30, 2000, p. WK 3.

push polling a polling technique in which the questions are designed to shape the respondent's opinion

Push Polling In recent years, a new form of bias has been introduced into surveys by the use of a technique called **push polling**. This technique is not intended to yield accurate information. Instead, it involves asking a respondent a loaded question about a political candidate designed to elicit the response sought by the pollster and, simultaneously, to shape the respondent's perception of the candidate in question. One of the most notorious uses of push polling occurred in the 2000 South Carolina Republican presidential primary, in which George W. Bush defeated John McCain and went on to win the presidency. Callers working for Bush supporters asked Conservative white voters if they would be more or less likely to vote for

McCain if they knew that he had fathered an illegitimate black child. Because McCain often campaigned with a daughter whom he and his wife had adopted from Mother Teresa's orphanage in Bangladesh, many voters accepted the premise of the "poll." This push poll was often cited by McCain as one of the political smear tactics that had made him reluctant to expose his family to the stresses of the 2008 presidential race. More than one hundred consulting firms across the nation now specialize in push polling.[35] Calling push polling the "political equivalent of a drive-by shooting," Representative Joe Barton (R-Tex.) launched a congressional investigation into the practice.[36] Push polls may be one reason that Americans are becoming increasingly skeptical about the practice of polling and increasingly unwilling to answer pollsters' questions.[37]

Illusion of Saliency During the early days of a political campaign, when voters are asked which candidates they do, or do not, support, the answer they give often has little significance, because the choice is not yet important to them. Their preferences may change many times before the actual election. This is part of the explanation for the phenomenon of the postconvention "bounce" in the popularity of presidential candidates, which is usually observed after the Democratic and Republican national conventions. Respondents' preferences reflected the amount of attention a candidate had received during the conventions rather than strongly held views.

Salient interests are interests that stand out beyond others, that are of more than ordinary concern to respondents in a survey or to voters in the electorate. Politicians, social scientists, journalists, or pollsters who assume something is important to the public, when in fact it is not, create an **illusion of saliency**. The problem of saliency has become especially acute as a result of the proliferation of media polls that allow journalists to make news when none really exists. Polling diminishes journalists' dependence on news makers. A poll commissioned by a news agency can provide the basis for a good story even when candidates, politicians, and other news makers refuse to cooperate by engaging in newsworthy activities. Thus, on days when little or nothing is actually taking place in a political campaign, poll results, especially apparent changes in candidate popularity margins, can provide exciting news. Several times during the 2008 presidential campaign, for example, small changes in the relative standing of the Democratic and Republican candidates produced banner headlines around the country. Stories about what the candidates actually did or said often took second place to reporting the "horse race."

Interestingly, because rapid and dramatic shifts in candidate margins tend to take place when voters' preferences are least fully formed, horse-race news is most likely to make the headlines when it is actually least significant.[38] In other words, media interest in poll results is inversely related to the actual salience of voters' opinions and the significance of the polls' findings. However, by influencing perceptions, especially those of major contributors, media polls can influence political realities.

Bandwagon Effect The most noted, but least serious, of polling problems is the **bandwagon effect**, which occurs when polling results influence people to support the candidate marked as the probable victor. Some scholars argue that this bandwagon effect can be offset by an "underdog effect" in favor of the candidate who is trailing in the polls.[39] However, a candidate who demonstrates a lead in the polls usually finds it considerably easier to raise campaign funds than a candidate whose poll standing is poor. With these additional funds, poll leaders can often afford to pay for television time and other campaign activities that will cement their advantage.

salient interests attitudes and views that are especially important to the individual holding them

illusion of saliency the impression conveyed by polls that something is important to the public when actually it is not

bandwagon effect a shift in electoral support to the candidate whom public opinion polls report as the front-runner

● Thinking Critically about Public Opinion and Democracy

A major purpose of democratic government, with its participatory procedures and representative institutions, is to ensure that political leaders will heed public opinion. And, indeed, a good deal of evidence suggests that they do. There are many instances in which public policy and public opinion do not coincide, but most studies suggest that in general, the government's actions are consistent with citizens' preferences.[40] Of course, consistency does not mean that policy makers slavishly follow public opinion. In many instances, policy makers work assiduously to shape public opinion before following its dictates.[41]

In addition, areas of disagreement always arise between opinion and policy. For example, the majority of Americans favored stricter governmental control of handguns for years before Congress finally adopted the modest restrictions on firearms purchases embodied in the Brady bill and the Violent Crime Control Act, passed in 1993 and 1994, respectively. Similarly, most Americans—blacks as well as whites—oppose school busing to achieve racial balance, yet such busing continues to be used in many parts of the nation. Most Americans are far less concerned with the rights of the accused than the federal courts seem to be. Most Americans usually oppose U.S. military intervention in other nations' affairs, yet such interventions continue to take place in such regions as Iraq, and often win public approval after the fact. Of course, the overwhelming majority of Americans supported the Bush administration's decision to attack Afghanistan after September 11.

Several factors can contribute to a lack of consistency between opinion and governmental policy. First, the nominal majority on a particular issue may not be as intensely committed to its preference as the adherents of the minority viewpoint. An intensely committed minority may often be more willing to commit its time, energy, efforts, and resources to the affirmation of its opinions than an apathetic, even if large, majority. In the case of firearms, for example, although the proponents of gun control are by a wide margin the majority, most do not regard the issue as one of critical importance to themselves and are not willing to commit much effort to advancing their cause. The opponents of gun control, by contrast, are intensely committed, well organized, and well financed, and as a result are usually able to carry the day.

A second important reason that public policy and public opinion may not coincide has to do with the character and structure of the American system of government. The framers of the U.S. Constitution, as we saw in Chapter 2, sought to create a system of government that was based on popular consent but that did not invariably and automatically translate shifting popular sentiments into public policies. As a result, the American governmental process includes arrangements such as an appointed judiciary that can produce policy decisions that may run contrary to prevailing popular sentiment—at least for a time.

Perhaps the inconsistencies between opinion and policy could be resolved if we made broader use of a mechanism currently employed by a number of states—the initiative and referendum. This procedure allows propositions to be placed on the ballot and voted into law by the electorate, bypassing most of the normal machinery of representative government. Hundreds of initiatives were proposed in 2008 on abortion, gay marriage, taxes, and animal rights; and in 2009, voters in Maine approved the medical use of marijuana, one of dozens of initiatives on state ballots that year.

Become a Savvy Consumer of Polls

In a recent *Washington Post* poll, 69 percent of respondents under age thirty said they preferred a "bigger government with bigger services" over a smaller one with fewer services. This preference stands in stark contrast to the opinions of Americans ages thirty and up, a majority of whom favor smaller government.

More important, this gap in opinion is not an isolated phenomenon. Similar disparities exist between the attitudes of young and older Americans on a host of other issues. For example, when compared with older adults, today's youth are more supportive of plans to privatize Social Security, more likely to argue that economic growth needs to be balanced by environmental concerns, more tolerant of the rights of gays and lesbians, and the most supportive of affirmative action programs.

As you read this, you may wonder if the public-opinion differences between young people and older Americans are real, or if they've been manufactured by pollsters, politicians, or pundits trying to push their various agendas. This is a legitimate concern. Indeed, although accurate polls can yield important information about public opinion, it is not uncommon for polls to be manipulated and distorted by those who have a stake in the findings. In this case, you can trust the numbers; the data cited above come from scientific opinion polls, designed and fielded by reputable scholars or polling agencies.

But how do you know when to trust a poll? If you were buying a new computer or car or smartphone, you'd learn something about its properties (or its manufacturer) in order to evaluate its worth. You can easily become a savvy consumer of polls as well. For the most part, this involves asking a few key questions, such as the ones listed below.

- *Who's behind the poll?* This means asking not just who paid for the poll but who actually conducted the interviews and published the results. Most news outlets include this information in their coverage, but if you find a reference to a poll in a candidate's promotional material or an interest group's solicitation, you may need to contact the campaign or group for more information.

- *Who participated in the poll?* This includes determining how many people were interviewed, if they were chosen scientifically (rather than by self-selection, for example), and if the respondents were representative of a larger population. Bigger samples aren't necessarily better—it is more important that the sample was selected through a scientific (usually random) method and that the characteristics of the respondents generally match those of the group they are supposed to represent. For example, are there more women than men in the sample? Are respondents balanced in terms of region, religion, and ethnicity? Should they be?

- *Is there a margin of error (also called sampling error) associated with the poll?* If this information is included in the description of the survey results, it is a good sign that the sample was drawn scientifically.

- *Is the wording or the order of the questions suspicious?* Even a scientifically selected poll can be susceptible of other biases. For example, two questions about the same topic using similar, but not exactly the same, wording can elicit very different responses. Poll numbers can also be affected by the order in which questions were asked. Most polling organizations will include an exact copy of their questionnaire along with their analysis. Almost all online news outlets provide a link to the full set of questions.

- *Could this be considered a pseudopoll or a push poll?* Both of these types of polls are problematic, for different reasons. Pseudopolls, often found on Web sites, are not accurate measures of public opinion because respondents simply decide for themselves that they want to participate rather than being selected scientifically. As we saw in this chapter, push polls are not really polls at all but an attempt to spread negative rumors or innuendos about a candidate for office under the guise of a poll.

Initiatives such as these seem to provide the public with an opportunity to express its will. The major problem, however, is that government by initiative offers little opportunity for reflection and compromise. Voters are presented with a proposition, usually sponsored by a special-interest group, and are asked to take it or leave it. Perhaps the true will of the people, not to mention their best interest, might lie somewhere between the positions taken by various interest groups. Perhaps, for example, California voters might have wanted affirmative action programs to be modified but not scrapped altogether as Proposition 209 mandated. In a representative assembly, as opposed to a referendum campaign, a compromise position might have been achieved that was more satisfactory to all the residents of the state. This is one reason the framers of the U.S. Constitution strongly favored representative government rather than direct democracy.

When all is said and done, even without the initiative and the referendum, there can be little doubt that in general the actions of the American government do not remain out of line with popular sentiment for very long. We can take these as signs of a vital and thriving democracy.

In the years following the 2003 Iraq war, an increasing number of Americans opposed the presence of U.S. troops in Iraq. By 2006, less than 25% of Americans approved of the government's Iraq policy. What are some possible reasons that the government didn't bring their Iraq policy into line with public opinion right away?

studyguide

Practice Quiz

Find a diagnostic Web Quiz with 39 additional questions on the StudySpace Web site: www.wwnorton.com/we-the-people

Understanding Public Opinion

1. The term *public opinion* is used to describe *(p. 199)*
   a) the collected speeches and writings made by a president during his or her term in office.
   b) the analysis of events broadcast by news reporters during the evening news.
   c) the beliefs and attitudes that people have about issues.
   d) decisions of the Supreme Court.

2. Variables such as income, education, race, gender, and ethnicity *(p. 201)*
   a) often create differences of political opinion in America.
   b) have consistently been a challenge to America's core political values.
   c) have little impact on political opinions.
   d) help explain why public opinion polls are so unreliable.

3. Which of the following is an agency of socialization? *(p. 201)*
   a) the family
   b) social groups
   c) education
   d) all of the above

4. The process by which Americans learn political beliefs and values is called *(p. 201)*
   a) brainwashing.
   b) propaganda.
   c) indoctrination.
   d) political socialization.

5. When men and women respond differently to issues of public policy, they are demonstrating an example of *(p. 203)*
   a) liberalism.
   b) educational differences.
   c) the gender gap.
   d) party politics.

6. Members of a social group often have similar political beliefs because *(pp. 201–07)*
   a) groups frequently endeavor to structure their members' political views through educational programs, meetings, rallies, and other activities.

   b) individuals may consciously or unconsciously adapt their views to those of the groups with which they identify.
   c) they share objective political interests.
   d) all of the above

7. A politician who opposes abortions, government regulation of business, and gay rights legislation would be best described as a *(p. 211)*
   a) liberal.
   b) conservative.
   c) libertarian.
   d) socialist.

How We Form Political Opinions

8. The fact that the public is inattentive to politics and must frequently rely on informational shortcuts has which of the following effects on American democracy? *(pp. 216–18)*
   a) strengthens it by providing politicians with more freedom to act on a wider variety of issues
   b) strengthens it by increasing the number of people who participate in politics
   c) weakens it by making it easier for various institutions and political actors to manipulate the political process
   d) has no effect on it

9. Which of the follo[...] external influence[...] formed? *(pp. 218–[...])*
   a) the governmen[...]
   b) private interest groups
   c) the media
   d) the Constitution

Measuring Public Opinion

10. Which of the following is the term used in public-opinion polling to denote the small group representing the opinions of the whole population? *(p. 224)*
   a) control group
   b) sample
   c) micropopulation
   d) respondents

11. A poll that includes many poorly worded or ambiguous questions has a high degree of *(p. 227)*
    a) sampling error.
    b) measurement error.
    c) selection bias.
    d) validity error.

12. A push poll is a poll in which *(pp. 228–29)*
    a) the questions are designed to shape the respondent's opinion rather than measure the respondent's opinion.
    b) the questions are designed to measure the respondent's opinion rather than shape the respondent's opinion.
    c) the questions are designed in order to reduce measurement error.
    d) none of the above.

13. When politicians, pollsters, journalists, or social scientists assume something is important to the public when in fact it is not, they are creating *(p. 229)*
    a) an illusion of saliency.
    b) an illusion of responsibility.
    c) a gender gap.
    d) an elitist issue.

14. A familiar polling problem is the "bandwagon effect," which occurs when *(p. 229)*
    a) the same results are used over and over again.
    b) polling results influence people to support the candidate marked as the probable victor in a campaign.
    c) polling results influence people to support the candidate who is trailing in a campaign.
    d) background noise makes it difficult for a pollster and a respondent to communicate with each other.

Thinking Critically About Public Opinion and Democracy

15. Which of the following statements best characterizes the relationship between public opinion and public policy in the United States? *(pp. 230–32)*
    a) They always coincide because the American system of government requires that politicians slavishly follow majority public opinion.
    b) They always coincide because the American public shifts their preferences to support whatever actions government takes.
    c) They never coincide because the American system of government was not designed to account for public opinion.
    d) They generally coincide but sometimes do not because the American system of government includes many arrangements, such as an appointed judiciary, that can produce policy decisions that may run contrary to prevailing popular sentiment.

Chapter Outline

 Find a detailed Chapter Outline on the StudySpace Web site: www.wwnorton.com/we-the-people

Key Terms

Find Flashcards to help you study these terms on the StudySpace Web site: www.wwnorton.com/we-the-people

For Further Reading

Althaus, Scott. *Collective Preferences in Democratic Politics.* New York: Cambridge University Press, 2003.

Bartels, Larry. *Unequal Democracy.* Princeton, NJ: Princeton University Press, 2008.

Berinsky, Adam. *Silent Voices: Public Opinion and Political Participation in America.* Princeton, NJ: Princeton University Press, 2005.

Bishop, George. *The Illusion of Public Opinion.* New York: Rowman and Littlefield, 2004.

Clawson, Rosalee, and Zoe Oxley. *Public Opinion: Democratic Ideals and Democratic Practice.* Washington, DC: Congressional Quarterly Press, 2008.

Erikson, Robert, and Kent Tedin. *American Public Opinion.* 7th ed. New York: Longman, 2004.

Fiorina, Morris. *Culture War: The Myth of a Polarized America.* New York: Longman, 2005.

Gallup, George. *The Pulse of Democracy.* New York: Simon & Schuster, 1940.

Ginsberg, Benjamin. *The Captive Public: How Mass Opinion Promotes State Power.* New York: Basic Books, 1986.

Glynn, Carol, et al., ed. *Public Opinion.* Boulder, CO: Westview, 2004.

Jacobs, Lawrence R., and Robert Y. Shapiro. *Politicians Don't Pander: Political Manipulation and the Loss of Democratic Responsiveness.* Chicago: University of Chicago Press, 2000.

Lee, Taeku. *Mobilizing Public Opinion.* Chicago: University of Chicago Press, 2002.

Lippman, Walter. *Public Opinion.* New York: Harcourt, Brace, 1922.

Norrander, Barbara, and Clyde Wilcox. *Understanding Public Opinion.* Washington: Congressional Quarterly Press, 2009.

Zaller, John. *The Nature and Origins of Mass Opinion.* New York: Cambridge University Press, 1992.

Recommended Web Sites

American Association for Public Opinion Research
www.aapor.org
This Web site is one of the premier academic sites for public opinion data on a host of political and social topics.

eTalkinghead
http://directory.etalkinghead.com
Political blogs have become an increasingly popular way for Americans to express and discuss political opinions. This Web page provides a directory of political blogs by ideology and issue.

Gallup
www.gallup.com
The Gallup Organization has been involved in the scientific study of public opinion for over seventy years and is very highly regarded. This Web site contains public-opinion data archives, video archives, and international polls.

The Political Compass
www.politicalcompass.org
A political ideology is a cohesive set of beliefs that form a general philosophy about government; however, people are often unsure if they are liberal, moderate, or conservative. Go to the Web site for The Political Compass and take the test to see if it helps you identify your ideology.

Polling Report
http://pollingreport.com
This independent, nonpartisan resource tracks trends in American public opinion. On this site you will find countless political opinion polls by all of the major media outlets, all in one place.

Public Agenda
www.publicagenda.org
Measuring public opinion from surveys can be problematic. Often samples contain selection bias, or surveys have measurement error. Public Agenda is an organization that studies public opinion on major policy issues. Its Web site contains critiques of public opinion.

ThisNation.com
www.thisnation.com/socialization.html
The process through which underlying political beliefs and values are formed is called political socialization. This civic-minded Web page offers a brief discussion of political socialization with some related Web links.

The media play an essential role in American democracy. One function of the media is to communicate information about the government to the people. Here, former House Speaker Nancy Pelosi holds a press conference to announce the Democrats' plan for withdrawing troops from Iraq.

The Media

WHAT GOVERNMENT DOES AND WHY IT MATTERS One area in which our government's role is intended to be minimal is the realm of the news media. The Constitution's First Amendment guarantees freedom of the press, and most Americans believe that a free press is an essential condition for both liberty and democratic politics. Certainly, the press is usually ready to denounce any government action that smacks of censorship or news manipulation. Nevertheless, attempts to silence or discredit the opposition press have a long history in America dating back to the infamous Alien and Sedition Acts, which were enacted by the Federalists in an attempt to silence the Republican press. Presidents and other high-ranking government officials are not the only ones who seek to control the media. Evenly lowly bureaucrats sometimes view press freedom as a nuisance rather than an essential aspect of popular government. In 2009, for example, low-level U.S. Army officials barred a *Stars & Stripes* reporter, Heath Druzin, from continuing to cover a military unit in Iraq because they believed Druzin's stories did not reflect positively on the army's achievements. Though *Stars & Stripes* receives some government funding, it is not subject to Pentagon authority and is occasionally critical of military policies.[1]

Candidates for political office also complain frequently about the media. During the 2008 primary campaign, Hillary Clinton frequently asserted that the media were treating her opponent, and eventual Democratic nominee, Senator Barack Obama, with kid gloves while giving her candidacy generally negative treatment. Echoing Clinton's complaint, during a famous skit on *Saturday Night Live* (*SNL*), the Hillary Clinton character was subjected to a good deal of indignity by reporters,

focusquestions

- **What role do the news media play in politics?**
- **What factors determine what is "news"?**
- **How can the media influence politics?**

while the Obama character was fawned over. Of course, the *SNL* skit belied its own point by demonstrating that Clinton, too, could count upon some segments of the media for support.

In a similar vein, during the general election campaign in 2008, Republicans complained that the media, MSNBC in particular, were strongly anti-McCain and pro-Obama in their coverage. Democrats replied that MSNBC was very fair, while other media outlets, Fox in particular, evidenced constant anti-Obama and pro-McCain bias. Republican candidate John McCain normally had good relations with the press. During the course of the campaign, however, McCain began to attack the media regarding their alleged bias. Complaints from McCain and his advisers became especially sharp after the national media began to question his choice of Sarah Palin as the GOP's vice-presidential candidate. The media regarded Palin as unprepared and unqualified for the job and generally gave her negative coverage.

The media are vitally important in a democracy. Without the media's investigations and exposés, citizens would be forced to rely entirely on the information politicians and the government provide to them. This would hardly afford citizens a proper opportunity to evaluate issues and form reasoned opinions. Critical media play an essential role in a nation whose citizens hope to govern themselves.

Presumably, the only way that the media might avoid charges of bias by one side or the other would be to avoid presenting negative information about either side. But, of course, we rely upon the media to "vet" candidates by digging into their public claims and private records to help ensure that the individuals we elect to office are sufficiently trustworthy to hold positions of responsibility. Politicians who are the subjects of media revelations, of course, declare that their private lives are not the public's business and castigate the media for prying. However, when the media reveal that a politician has lied, cheated, stolen, or engaged in inappropriate sexual relationships, they are warning us that this individual may not be suited to hold high office. By looking closely at the actions of politicians, the media give us an opportunity to choose a better government.

chaptercontents

● The Media Industry and Government

The American news media are among the world's freest and most vast. Americans literally have thousands of available options to find political reporting. This wide variety of newspapers, newsmagazines, broadcast media, and Web sources regularly present information that is at odds with the government's claims, as well as editorial opinions sharply critical of high-ranking officials. The freedom to speak one's mind is one of the most cherished of American political values. Yet although thousands of media companies exist across the United States, surprisingly little variety appears in what is reported about national events and issues.

Types of Media

Americans get their news from three main sources: broadcast media (radio and television), print media (newspapers and magazines), and, increasingly, the Internet (see page 241). Each of these sources has distinctive characteristics.

Broadcast Media Television news reaches more Americans than any other single news source. Tens of millions of individuals watch national and local news programs every day. Television news, however, covers relatively few topics and provides little depth of coverage. It serves the extremely important function of alerting viewers to issues and events, but generally doesn't provide much more than a series of **sound bites**, brief quotes and short characterizations of the day's events. Because they are aware of the character of television news coverage, politicians and other news makers often seek to manipulate the news by providing the media with sound bites that will dominate news coverage for at least a few days. Thus, for example, in 2009, when pundits attacked President Obama for accepting the Nobel Peace Prize at the same time that he was sending more troops to Afghanistan, Obama disarmed his critics by declaring, "I do not view it as a recognition of my own accomplishments, but rather as an affirmation of American leadership on behalf of aspirations held by people in all nations." Or, responding to critics who said his health care proposals would interject the government between the doctor and the patient, Obama said, "If you like your doctor or your health care provider, you can keep them." One of the most famous presidential sound bites in recent history was George H. W. Bush's 1988 declaration, "Read my lips: no new taxes." Two years later he was, in effect, bitten by his own sound bite when he signed legislation that included new taxes. Twenty-four-hour news stations such as Cable News Network (CNN) offer more detail and commentary than the networks' half-hour evening news shows. Even CNN and the others, however, offer more headlines and sound bites than analysis, especially during their prime-time broadcasts.

Politicians generally consider local broadcast news a friendlier venue than the national news. National reporters are often inclined to criticize and question, whereas local reporters are more likely to accept the pronouncements of national leaders at face value. For this reason, presidents often introduce new proposals in a series of short visits to a number of cities—indeed, sometimes flying from airport stop to airport stop—in

sound bites short snippets of information aimed at dramatizing a story rather than explaining its substantive meaning

When President Obama announced his plan for increasing troop levels in Afghanistan in 2009, he knew that coverage of his speech in the news media would quickly reach tens of millions of Americans.

addition to or instead of making a national presentation. For example, in 2009, in a nationally televised speech, President Barack Obama announced his plan to reduce violence in Afghanistan, and then made a number of local speeches around the country promoting the same theme. National reporters questioned the president's plans, but local news coverage was overwhelmingly positive.

Radio news is also essentially a headline service, but without pictures. In the short time—usually five minutes per hour—they devote to news, radio stations announce the day's major events without providing much detail. In major cities, all-news stations provide a bit more coverage of major stories, but for the most part these stations fill the day with repetition rather than detail. All-news stations such as Washington, D.C.'s WTOP or New York's WCBS assume that most listeners are in their cars and that, as a result, the people in the audience change throughout the day as listeners reach their destinations. Thus, rather than use their time to flesh out a given set of stories, they repeat the same stories each hour to present them to new listeners. In the 1990s, radio talk shows became important sources of commentary and opinion. A number of conservative radio hosts such as Rush Limbaugh and Sean Hannity have huge audiences and have helped to mobilize support for conservative political causes and candidates.

Print Media Newspapers are critically important even though they are not the primary news source for most Americans. The print media are important for three reasons. First, as we shall see later in this chapter, the broadcast media rely on leading newspapers such as the *New York Times* and the *Washington Post* to set their news agenda. The broadcast media engage in very little actual reporting; they primarily cover stories that have been "broken," or initially reported, by the print media. For example, sensational charges that President Bill Clinton had an affair with a White House intern were reported first by the Drudge Report, a popular blog, and then picked up by the *Washington Post* and *Newsweek* before being trumpeted around the world by the broadcast media. It is only a slight exaggeration to observe that if an event is not covered in the *New York Times*, it is not likely to appear on the *CBS Evening News*. Second, the print media are important because they tend to provide more detailed and complete information, offering a better context for analysis. Third, the print media are important because they are the prime source of news for educated and influential individuals. The nation's economic, social, and political elites tend to rely on the detailed coverage provided by the print media to inform and influence their views about important public matters. The print media may have a smaller audience than their cousins in broadcasting, but they have an especially influential audience.

The Internet The Internet has been growing in importance as a news source. Every day, millions of Americans scan one of many news sites on the Internet for coverage of current events. Younger Americans are more likely to rely on the Internet than on almost any other news source (see page 241). One great advantage of the Internet is that it allows frequent updating. After the September 11 terrorist attacks, many Americans relied on the Internet for news about terrorism, bioterrorism, and the military campaign in Afghanistan.

In July 2007, candidates for the 2008 Democratic presidential nomination participated in a debate carried online on YouTube. This format allowed ordinary Americans from across the country to make comments and ask questions. One viewer played a guitar and sang a song that he had apparently composed about taxes. He then asked whether any of the famous politicians participating in the

Who Follows the News—and How?

In a democracy like the United States, people need political knowledge to understand current issues and their government's actions. However, just over half of all American adults report following the news regularly. With the rise of the Internet as a news source, Americans are increasingly likely to get political information online, with most getting news from multiple sources on a typical day.

News Sources Used on a Typical Day

Percentage of American adults who report regularly following the news

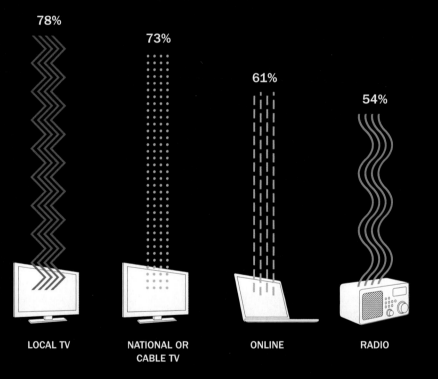

78%	73%	61%	54%	50%	17%
LOCAL TV	NATIONAL OR CABLE TV	ONLINE	RADIO	LOCAL NEWSPAPER	NATIONAL NEWSPAPER

Who Follows News "All or Most of the Time," by Age

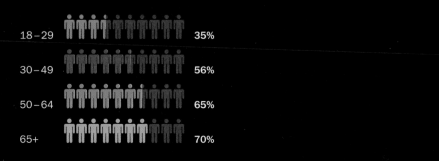

18–29	35%
30–49	56%
50–64	65%
65+	70%

SOURCE: Pew Internet and American Life Project, "Understanding the Participatory News Consumer," March 2010.

for critical analysis

1. How do younger Americans compare to older Americans in terms of following the news? What might explain the different rates of news consumption across age groups?

2. Radio and newspapers were once the dominant news sources. What are some of the likely consequences of the shift toward television and online news?

debate could help him deal with a recent speeding ticket. A lesbian couple asked whether any of the candidates would allow them to marry. Barack Obama was asked whether he was "authentically black" and replied that he proved he was black every time he tried to hail a cab in New York City.[2] As the 2008 campaign proceeded, candidates or their supporters placed a number of ads on YouTube that were seen by millions of viewers.[3] During the general election, John McCain developed a series of YouTube ads mocking Barack Obama and comparing him to empty-headed media celebrities like Paris Hilton. In August 2008, Hilton responded with her own YouTube videos comparing McCain to the wizened *Star Wars* character Yoda.

Political entrepreneurs have also used the Internet to organize online advocacy groups to raise money, make their positions known through e-mail and letter campaigns, and provide support for politicians who accepted their views. For example, Chris Hughes, one of the founders of the social networking site Facebook, helped the Obama presidential campaign establish a Facebook site that allowed Obama supporters to register as the senator's "friends." At the site's resource center, the senator's friends could download flyers, videos, and other campaign materials. In the site's "groups" section, the senator's friends could create or join online groups to share ideas and organize events and fund-raisers. The site's fund-raising section allowed the senator's friends to set personal fund-raising goals and to invite other registered friends to help them reach it. The Obama site attracted more than a million visitors during the campaign for the 2008 Democratic presidential nomination.[4]

In 2007, candidates for the Democratic and Republican presidential nominations participated in debates sponsored by YouTube and CNN. The questions for the candidates were submitted directly by voters, who posted videos of their questions.

In addition, a growing number of readers turn to informal sources of Internet news and commentary called *Web logs*, or "blogs." Blogs are published online and generally feature personal opinion and commentary on national and world events. Some "bloggers," as the authors of blogs are called, achieve fame, or at least notoriety, among online readers for their political and social views. In 2002 and 2003, the Howard Dean presidential campaign relied on hundreds of friendly bloggers to publicize the candidate's views and to help raise tens of millions of dollars in small contributions to finance what turned out to be his unsuccessful presidential bid.[5] Dean's tactics were a direct precursor to Barack Obama's 2008 campaign, which raised hundreds of millions of dollars in contributions via the Internet.

Inspired by Dean's example, two Democratic activists, Benjamin Rahn and Matt DeBergalis, created a Web site they called "ActBlue" to promote online Democratic fund-raising. ActBlue specializes in a practice called "bundling," which permits the campaign contributions of many individuals to be tied, or "bundled," together on behalf of a particular candidate. The practice is legal as long as no individual contribution exceeds the limits set by campaign-finance laws. As of October 2008, ActBlue had raised more than $50 million for Democratic candidates. Numerous, liberal Democratic candidates appealed for funds via YouTube videos that directed donors to ActBlue. For example, one campaigner posted a YouTube video in which he promised to subject himself to a variety of cyberspace humiliations if viewers met a series of donation targets. The video was watched more than 16,000 times on YouTube.[6] The ActBlue Web site lists the names of a number of Democratic candidates and allows users to decide to which ones they wish to donate. One analyst called it "one-stop shopping" for political donors.[7]

A number of blogs such as the Daily Kos and the Drudge Report have thousands of regular readers who often comment on and critique stories presented by the print and broadcast media. In recent years, bloggers have uncovered a number of major factual errors in media reports and forced the networks and newspapers to print and broadcast corrections. In addition, a number of bloggers have proven adept at recognizing faked or photoshopped photographs in news stories. Sharp-eyed bloggers noticed that major news outlets including the *New York Times, Los Angeles Times, Reuters, Associated Press*, and others had presented doctored photos in their reports from Iraq, Afghanistan, and the Israeli-Palestinian conflict.[8]

Although the Internet and the blogosphere are often seen as liberal and Democratic strongholds, conservatives have stepped up their efforts to make use of the new media. Over the past three years, conservative talk radio hosts and conservative bloggers have built an informal alliance to attack Democratic candidates and policies with which they disagree. In 2007, for example, conservative bloggers regularly posted material opposing the proposed immigration bill that would have given legal status to many illegal immigrants currently in the United States. Conservative talk-radio hosts relied on the bloggers to provide critical commentary that they could broadcast on their radio programs.[9] This alliance also played a role in numerous attacks launched against Barack Obama in 2008, including the charge that Obama was actually a Muslim, and not a Christian, as he says he is, and was not born in the United States, which is a requirement for being president.

The Power of the New Media Contemporary technology is opening new avenues for popular political participation. The Internet has become a powerful tool for political organization. Blogs and other Internet forums allow the rapid dissemination of information, ideas and opinions outside the control of the government or

The Internet, Blogs, and the Transformation of Political News

The American media are in the middle of a dramatic transformation. As rates of traditional news consumption drop, use of the Internet as a source of political information is on the rise. In fact, the delivery of political information via the Internet may be redefining contemporary journalism.

According to a 2008 study by the Pew Research Center, half of Americans under the age of fifty use the Internet as a source of political news. Although many of these users are turning to the Internet to read online versions of their favorite newspapers, a growing portion are turning to blogs. Political blogs often make use of articles, reports, statistics, and photos available on the Internet to research stories. These sites may provide personal commentary, links to various sources, and alternative versions of news stories that are reported in the mainstream media. They are updated frequently, usually with a series of relatively short entries.

In addition to growing readership, blogs have the potential to influence mainstream journalism and even political events. In 2004, for example, after a *60 Minutes* story claimed that George W. Bush received preferential treatment while serving in the Texas Air National Guard, conservative bloggers mounted a campaign against CBS and the news anchor Dan Rather for reporting a story that was based on forged documents. In the weeks that followed, CBS admitted that the documents had not been properly authenticated, and Dan Rather announced that he would resign. Bloggers saw Rather's downfall as a victory by the "new media" over the old media. In 2008, a blogger recorded comments made by Barack Obama about "bitter" blue-collar workers and posted them online. This event became a major story, as Obama's ability to reach out to small-town voters came into question.

As blogs have attracted the attention of voters, and policy makers, many politicians have begun blogs of their own. In the 2004 election, Howard Dean's popular Blog for America was the first Web log hosted by a presidential campaign. In 2008, the Obama and McCain campaign Web sites both had blogs. Moreover, the candidates increasingly cultivated relationships with bloggers, and an unprecedented number of bloggers were authorized to cover the 2008 party conventions. In 2009 and 2010, opponents and proponents of health care reform battled in the blogosphere.

Although blog readership and influence appear to be on the rise, many Americans remain skeptical about the accuracy of information found on blogs. In fact, the Pew Internet and American Life Project reports that although a record 46 percent of Americans had used the Internet for campaign news in spring 2008, 60 percent of Internet users believed that "the internet is full of misinformation and propaganda" that mislead voters. The full impact of blogs on news media and American politics remains to be seen.

SOURCE: Pew Internet & American Life Project, "The internet and the 2008 election," June 15, 2008, www .pewinternet.org (accessed 6/19/08).

---

for critical analysis

1. What are some possible drawbacks of receiving political information mainly from blogs? What advantages might blog readers have over traditional news consumers?

2. Thanks in large part to the Internet, Americans can now get news from more sources than ever. Do you think this will have an effect on participation in politics?

other institutions. To be sure, many of the ideas and opinions found in the various Web logs are unsupported by research or careful reasoning. Moreover, corporations and politicians have learned to create and use blogs for their own purposes. Blogs, nevertheless, sharply lower the technological and financial barriers that previously prevented all but a few individuals and interests from reaching mass audiences and potentially increase the ability of ordinary people to engage in effective political action. In 2008, bloggers were responsible for some of the most negative aspects of the presidential campaign. While the candidates themselves generally took the high road, focusing on issues and problems, Democratic and Republican bloggers often focused on negative stories and even scurrilous rumors. Thus, Republican bloggers circulated the unfounded claim that Barack Obama was a Muslim intent on subverting the U.S. government. Democratic bloggers circulated stories about John McCain's personal history and made much of an allegation that Sarah Palin's infant son was actually her daughter's baby. These blog-driven rumors became widespread and received attention in the mainstream media.

Magnifying the power of the Internet is the universal availability of digital cameras. Particularly since cell phones are now equipped with cameras, millions of Americans have the capacity to photograph or film events that they may witness. At the same time, Internet sites such as YouTube permit users to upload photos and video clips that are then viewed by hundreds of thousands of subscribers and are sometimes picked up by the mainstream media for even wider dissemination. In 2006, a YouTube video showing Senator George Allen making a racist comment to one of his opponent's campaign workers caused an uproar. Allen, who had been positioning himself for a possible 2008 presidential race, was defeated for reelection to the Senate from Virginia, when his victory had previously been seen as a sure thing. His presidential aspirations were dashed. With a bit of technology, citizens had ended the career of a once-powerful politician. This example illustrates the way in which technology can have a strong effect on popular politics.

Regulation of the Broadcast Media

In some countries, the government controls media content. In other countries, the government owns the broadcast media (e.g., the BBC in Britain) but it does not tell the media what to say. In the United States, the government neither owns nor controls the communications networks, but it does regulate the content and ownership of the broadcast media.

As we saw in Chapter 4, in the United States, the print media are essentially free from government interference. The broadcast media, on the other hand, are subject to federal regulation. American radio and television are regulated by the Federal Communications Commission (FCC), an independent agency established in 1934. Radio and TV stations must have FCC licenses that must be renewed every five years. Licensing provides a mechanism for allocating radio and TV frequencies to prevent broadcasts from interfering with and garbling each other. License renewals are almost always granted automatically by the FCC. Indeed, renewal requests are now filed by postcard.

Through regulations prohibiting obscenity, indecency, and profanity, the FCC has also sought to prohibit radio and television stations from airing explicit sexual and excretory references between 6 A.M. and 10 P.M. These are the hours when children are most likely to be in the audience. Generally speaking, FCC regulation applies only to the over-the-air broadcast media. It does not apply to cable television, the Internet, or satellite radio. As a result, explicit sexual content and graphic

for critical analysis

How do the media distort political reality? How do politicians use the media for their own purposes? What are the consequences for American democracy when the electorate is informed through such a filter? How might the quality of political information in America be improved?

Federal Communications Commission (FCC) regulations prohibit obscenity, indecency, and profanity in American television and radio broadcasts. The radio personality Howard Stern incurred millions of dollars in FCC fines before moving to satellite radio, which is not regulated by the FCC.

equal time rule the requirement that broadcasters provide candidates for the same political office equal opportunities to communicate their messages to the public

right of rebuttal a Federal Communications Commission regulation giving individuals the right to have the opportunity to respond to personal attacks made on a radio or television broadcast

fairness doctrine a Federal Communications Commission requirement for broadcasters who air programs on controversial issues to provide time for opposing views. The FCC ceased enforcing this doctrine in 1985

language that would fall afoul of the rules on broadcast television is regularly available on cable channels. This fact explains why "shock jock" Howard Stern, who regularly incurred fines and penalties on broadcast radio, moved his program to satellite radio. A number of bills have been introduced in recent congresses to extend the rules to cable TV and satellite radio, but none have succeeded so far.

For more than sixty years, the FCC also sought to regulate and promote competition in the broadcast industry, but in 1996 Congress passed the Telecommunications Act, a broad effort to do away with most regulations in effect since 1934. The act loosened restrictions on media ownership and allowed telephone companies, cable television providers, and broadcasters to compete with each other for telecommunication services. Following the passage of the act, several mergers between telephone and cable companies and among different segments of the entertainment media produced an even greater concentration of media ownership.

The Telecommunications Act of 1996 also included an attempt to regulate the content of material transmitted over the Internet. This law, known as the Communications Decency Act, made it illegal to make "indecent" sexual material on the Internet accessible to those under eighteen years old. The act was immediately denounced by civil libertarians and brought to court as an infringement of free speech. The case reached the Supreme Court in 1997, and the act was ruled an unconstitutional infringement of the First Amendment's right to freedom of speech (see Chapter 4).

Although the government's ability to regulate the content of the electronic media on the Internet has been questioned, the federal government has used its licensing power to impose several regulations that can affect the political content of radio and TV broadcasts. The first of these is the **equal time rule**, under which broadcasters must provide candidates for the same political office equal opportunities to communicate their messages to the public. If, for example, a television station sells commercial time to a state's Republican gubernatorial candidate, it may not refuse to sell time to the Democratic candidate for the same position. Under the terms of the Telecommunications Act, during the forty-five days before an election, broadcasters are required to make time available to candidates at the lowest rate charged for that time slot. However, the Bipartisan Campaign Reform Act of 2002 requires that to obtain the lowest rate, candidates must acknowledge their sponsorship of ads. This is why every political ad from a candidate ends with the words "I am _____ and I approve this message."

The second regulation affecting the content of broadcasts is the **right of rebuttal**, which requires that individuals be given the opportunity to respond to personal attacks. In the 1969 case of *Red Lion Broadcasting Company v. FCC*, for example, the U.S. Supreme Court upheld the FCC's determination that a radio station was required to provide a liberal author with an opportunity to respond to a conservative commentator's attack that the station had aired.[10]

For many years, a third important federal regulation was the **fairness doctrine**. Under this doctrine, broadcasters who aired programs on controversial issues were required to provide time for opposing views. In 1985, however, the FCC stopped enforcing the fairness doctrine on the grounds that there were so many radio and television stations—to say nothing of newspapers and newsmagazines—that in all likelihood many different viewpoints were already being presented without each station's being required to try to present all sides of an argument. Critics of this FCC decision charge that in many media markets the number of competing viewpoints is small. During the past several years, Democrats such as Nancy Pelosi, John Kerry, and Richard Durbin have sought to revive the fairness doctrine in response to what they see as the "unfairness" of conservative talk radio.

Organization and Ownership of the Media

The United States boasts nearly 2,000 television stations, approximately 1,400 daily newspapers, and more than 13,000 radio stations (20 percent of which are devoted to news, talk, or public affairs).[11]

Even though the number of TV and radio stations and daily newspapers reporting news in the United States is enormous, the number of sources of national news is actually quite small—several wire services, four broadcast networks, public radio and television, two elite newspapers, three newsmagazines, and a scattering of other sources such as the national correspondents of a few large local papers and the small independent radio networks. More than three-fourths of the daily newspapers in the United States are owned by a large media conglomerate such as the Hearst, McClatchy, or Gannett corporation; thus the diversity of coverage and editorial opinion in American newspapers is not so broad as it might seem. Much of the national news that is published by local newspapers is provided by one wire service, the Associated Press, while additional coverage is provided by services run by several major newspapers such as the *New York Times* and the *Chicago Tribune*. More than five hundred of the nation's television stations are affiliated with one of the four networks and carry that network's evening news reports. Dozens of others carry PBS (Public Broadcasting System) news. Several hundred local radio stations also carry network news or National Public Radio news broadcasts. At the same time, although there are only three truly national newspapers, the *Wall Street Journal*, the *Christian Science Monitor*, and *USA Today*, two other papers, the *New York Times* and the *Washington Post*, are read by political leaders and other influential Americans throughout the nation. National news is also carried to millions of Americans by two major newsmagazines—*Time* and *Newsweek*, though both are declining in readership. Beginning in the late 1980s, CNN became another major news source for Americans, especially after its spectacular coverage of the Persian Gulf war. However, the number of news sources has remained essentially the same. Even the availability of new electronic media on the Internet has failed to expand the number of news sources. Most national news available on the World Wide Web, for example, consists of electronic versions of the conventional print or broadcast media.

The trend toward the homogenization of national news has been hastened by dramatic changes in media ownership, which became possible in large part due to the relaxation of government regulations in the 1980s and 1990s. The enactment of the 1996 Telecommunications Act opened the way for further consolidation in the media industry, and a wave of mergers and consolidations has further reduced the field of independent media across the country. For example, the Australian press baron Rupert Murdoch owns the Fox network plus a host of radio, television, and newspaper properties around the world. In 2007, Murdoch won control of the *Wall Street Journal*, making him one of the wold's most powerful publishers. A small number of giant corporations now control a wide swath of media holdings, including television networks, movie studios, record companies, cable channels and local cable providers, book publishers, magazines, and newspapers. These developments have prompted questions about whether enough competition exists among

forcritical**analysis**

In recent years, a number of major media corporations have acquired numerous newspapers, television stations, and radio properties. Is media concentration a serious problem? Why or why not?

the media to produce a diverse set of views on political and corporate matters or whether the United States has become the prisoner of media monopolies.[12]

Media Ownership and Political Equality Increasing concentration of media ownership raises a number of major issues (see this chapter's Policy Debate). One of the most important relates to political equality. Access to the print and broadcast media is such an important political resource that for all intents and purposes, political forces that lack media access have only a very limited opportunity to influence the political process. As major newspapers, television stations, and radio networks fall into fewer and fewer hands, the risk increases that less popular or minority viewpoints and the politicians who express them will have difficulty finding a public forum in which to disseminate their ideas. Increasingly, such individuals turn to the Internet and its numerous blogs and other Web sites to express their views. The problem, however, is that ideas presented on the Internet tend to be read mainly by those who already agree with them. The Internet can be an important mechanism for linking communities of adherents, but it is less effective than radio, television, and the print media for reaching new audiences. Hence, growing concentration and consolidation in the print and broadcast industries are important policy problems.

Nationalization of the News

In general, the national news media cover more or less the same sets of events, present similar information, and emphasize similar issues and problems. Indeed, the national news services watch each other quite carefully. It is very likely that a major story carried by one service will quickly find its way into the pages or programming of the others. As a result, in the United States a rather centralized national news has developed, through which a relatively uniform picture of events, issues, and problems is presented to the entire nation.[13] The nationalization of the news began in the early 1900s, was accelerated by the development of radio networks in the 1920s and 1930s and by the creation of the television networks after the 1950s, and has been further strengthened by the recent trends toward concentrated media ownership. This nationalization of news content has very important consequences for the American political system.

Nationalization of the news has contributed greatly to the nationalization of politics and of political perspectives in the United States. Prior to the development of the national media and the nationalization of news coverage, news traveled very slowly. Every region and city saw national issues and problems primarily through a local lens. Concerns and perspectives varied greatly from region to region, city to city, and village to village. Today, in large measure as a result of the nationalization of the media, residents of all parts of the country share similar pictures of the day's events.[14] They may not agree on everything, but most see the world in similar ways.

The exception to this pattern can be found with those Americans whose chief source of news is something other than the "mainstream" national media. Some radio stations and print media are aimed exclusively at specific racial, ethnic, or religious groups. These individuals are likely to develop and retain a perception of the news that is quite different from that of "mainstream" America. For example, some conservative talk radio listeners are still interested in discussions asserting that President Obama is not a U.S. citizen and, hence, not eligible to serve as president of the United States.

Web blogs are a form of news enclave for the like-minded. Generally speaking, individuals seek out blogs with which they are likely to agree. The blogs function to reinforce people's preexisting ideas and to provide them with information to bolster their established beliefs. Thus, liberals might turn to Daily Kos, conservatives to PoliPundit, those with an interest in military issues to Military.com, and so forth. It is unusual for individuals to venture into what they regard as unfriendly parts of the blogosphere.

● News Coverage

Because of the important role the media can play in national politics, understanding the factors that affect media coverage is vitally important. What accounts for the media's agenda of issues and topics? What explains the character of coverage? Why does a politician receive good or bad press? What factors determine the interpretation, or "spin," that a particular story will receive? Although a host of minor factors play a role, three major factors are important: (1) the journalists, or producers, of the news; (2) the sources or topics of the news; and (3) the audience for the news.

Journalists

Media content and news coverage are inevitably affected by the views, ideals, and interests of those who seek out, write, and produce news and other stories. At one time, newspaper publishers exercised a great deal of influence over their papers' news content. Publishers such as William Randolph Hearst and Joseph Pulitzer became political powers through their manipulation of news coverage. Hearst, for example, almost single-handedly pushed the United States into war with Spain in 1898 through his newspapers' relentless coverage of the alleged brutality employed by Spain in its efforts to suppress a rebellion in Cuba, at that time a Spanish

Prior to the Iraq war, the Bush administration invited more than one hundred news correspondents and photographers to accompany American forces into battle. These "embedded" journalists developed considerable rapport with the soldiers and provided generally sympathetic war coverage.

colony. The sinking of the American battleship *Maine* in Havana Harbor under mysterious circumstances gave Hearst the ammunition he needed to force a reluctant President McKinley to lead the nation into war.

More important than publishers, for the most part, are the reporters. Those who cover the news for the national media generally have a good deal of discretion or freedom to interpret stories and, as a result, have an opportunity to interject their views and ideals into news stories. For example, the personal friendship and respect that some reporters felt for Franklin Roosevelt or John Kennedy helped to generate more favorable news coverage for these presidents. Likewise, the dislike and distrust many reporters felt for Richard Nixon was also communicated to the public. In the case of Ronald Reagan, the disdain that many journalists felt for the president was communicated in stories suggesting that he was often asleep or inattentive when important decisions were made.

Conservatives have long charged that the liberal biases of reporters and journalists result in distorted news coverage. A 2004 survey conducted by the Pew Research Center found that 34 percent of national news reporters identified themselves as liberal, whereas only 7 percent said they were conservative.[15] In a similar vein, a 2005 study by the University of Connecticut found that 52 percent of the journalists surveyed voted Democratic, 19 percent voted Republican, and 21 percent refused to say.[16]

The linkage between journalists and liberal ideas is by no means absolute. Most reporters, to be sure, attempt to maintain some measure of balance or objectivity whatever their personal political views. In addition, a number of important newspaper owners and publishers have decidedly conservative views and have built a set of conservative media entities to oppose what they perceive as the liberal media. This complex includes two newspapers, the *Wall Street Journal* and the *Washington Times*, several magazines such as the *American Spectator,* and a host of conservative radio and television talk programs. Also important is the media baron Rupert Murdoch, creator of Fox Network News and the financial force behind the *Weekly Standard.* Murdoch sees Fox as a conservative alternative to the more liberal networks and has staffed Fox with rather conservative broadcast personalities. To some extent, ideological diversity and polarization have also been encouraged by the proliferation of news sources. When there were few news sources, each appealed to the same broad national audience and, accordingly, maintained a middle-of-the-road stance. Now that there are many news sources, some seek to position themselves within a discrete ideological or partisan niche.

Probably more important than ideological bias is a selection bias in favor of news that the media view as having a great deal of audience appeal because of its dramatic or entertainment value. In practice, this bias often results in news coverage that focuses on crimes and scandals, especially those involving prominent individuals, despite the fact that the public obviously looks to the media for information about important political debates. For example, even though most journalists may be Democrats, this partisan predisposition did not prevent an enormous media frenzy in January 1998 when reports surfaced that President Clinton (a Democrat) might have had an affair with a White House intern, Monica Lewinsky. Once a hint of blood appeared in the water, partisanship and ideology were swept away by the piranhalike instincts journalists often manifest.

In addition to professional reporters, today's news is increasingly being covered by "citizen journalists" wielding digital cameras who post information and photos to blogs, YouTube, and other sites. The largest and most prominent group of citizen journalists calls itself OffTheBus.net, an online journalism project that has grown to a force of 7,500 volunteers who attend events, solicit interviews, and take pictures. One OffTheBus correspondent, Mayhill Fowler, broke two major stories in

2008, one involving a comment by Barack Obama about "bitter small-town voters," and the other, a story about former president Bill Clinton's criticism of a *Vanity Fair* writer.[17]

Subjects of the News

News coverage is also influenced by the individuals or groups who are subjects of the news or whose interests and activities are actual or potential news topics. The president, in particular, has the power to set the news agenda through speeches and actions. All politicians, for that matter, seek to shape or manipulate their media images by cultivating good relations with reporters as well as through news leaks and staged news events.

A *leak* is the disclosure of confidential information to the news media. Leaks may emanate from a variety of sources, including "whistle-blowers," lower-level officials who hope to publicize what they view as their bosses' improper activities. In 1971, for example, a minor Defense Department staffer named Daniel Ellsberg sought to discredit official justifications for America's involvement in Vietnam by leaking top-secret documents to the press. The "Pentagon Papers" were published by the *New York Times* and the *Washington Post* after the U.S. Supreme Court ruled that the government could not block their release.[18] Similarly, in 2005 President George W. Bush was infuriated when he learned that a still-unidentified source, presumed to be a whistle-blower, leaked information concerning the president's secret orders authorizing the National Security Agency to conduct clandestine surveillance of suspected terrorists without obtaining a warrant. Bush ordered the Justice Department to launch a probe of the leak. In 2006, another unidentified source leaked part of a secret intelligence summary that seemed to contradict the administration's claims of progress in the war in Iraq. In 2009, a leak to the journalist Bob Woodward infuriated the Pentagon by revealing General Stanley McChrystal's secret report to the president on the failures of American military efforts in Afghanistan.

Most leaks, though, originate not with low-level whistle-blowers but rather with senior government officials and prominent politicians and political activists. These

In 2009, shortly after President Obama announced a "surge" of 30,000 additional troops in Afghanistan, defense secretary Robert Gates visited Afghanistan and made the administration's case for the surge in a series of interviews.

Politicians sometimes deliberately leak confidential information to the press, in the hope of influencing news coverage. In 2007, Vice President Cheney's chief of staff, Lewis "Scooter" Libby, was convicted of obstructing an investigation into the Bush administration's illegal leak of a covert CIA official's identity.

individuals cultivate long-term relationships with journalists to whom they regularly leak confidential information, knowing that it is likely to be published on a priority basis in a form acceptable to them. Their confidence is based on the fact that journalists are likely to regard high-level sources of confidential information as valuable assets whose favor must be retained. For example, Lewis "Scooter" Libby, Vice President Cheney's chief of staff, was apparently such a valuable source of leaks to so many prominent journalists that his name was seldom even mentioned in the newspapers, despite his prominence in Washington and his importance as a decision maker.[19] Further, the more recipients of leaked information strive to keep their sources secret, the more difficulty other journalists will have in checking its validity.

Through such tacit alliances with journalists, prominent figures can manipulate news coverage and secure the publication of stories that serve their purposes. One recent case that revealed the complexities of this culture of leaks was the 2005 Valerie Plame affair. Plame was an undercover CIA analyst who happened to be married to Joseph Wilson, a prominent career diplomat. Wilson had angered the Bush White House by making a number of statements that were critical of the president's policies in Iraq. In an apparent effort to discredit Wilson, one or more administration officials informed prominent journalists that Plame had improperly used her position to help Wilson. In so doing, these officials may have violated a federal statute prohibiting disclosure of the identities of covert intelligence operatives. The subsequent investigation revealed that the story had been leaked to several journalists, including the *Washington Post*'s Bob Woodward, who did not use it; and the *New York Times*'s Judith Miller, who did. Miller initially refused to name her source and spent several weeks in jail for contempt of court after refusing to testify before a federal grand jury looking into the leak. After Miller finally testified, Scooter Libby was charged with having been the source of the leak, though it later emerged that the leak actually came from a former State Department official, Richard Armitage. The leak in the Plame case came to light only because it was illegal. Thousands of other leaks each year are quietly and seamlessly incorporated into the news.

Also seamlessly incorporated into daily news reports each year are thousands of press releases. The press release, sometimes called a news release, is a story written by an advocate or publicist and distributed to the media in the hope that journalists will publish it with little or no revision and under their own bylines. The inventor of the press release was a famous New York public relations consultant named Ivy Lee. In 1906, a train operated by one of Lee's clients, the Pennsylvania Railroad, was involved in a serious wreck. Lee quickly wrote a story about the accident that presented the railroad in a favorable light and distributed the account to reporters. Many papers published Lee's slanted story as their own objective account of events and the railroad's reputation for quality and safety remained intact. Consistent with Lee's example, today's press release presents facts and perspectives that serve an advocate's interests but is written in a way that mimics the factual news style of the paper, periodical, or television news program to which it has been sent. It is quite difficult for the audience to distinguish a well-designed press release from an actual news story. Newspapers, of course, realize that they are allowing themselves to be used, but they have a strong financial incentive to publish press releases that, in effect, allow them to fill their pages at little cost.

The capacity of news subjects to influence the news is hardly unlimited. Media consultants and issues managers may shape the news for a time, but it is generally not difficult for the media to penetrate the smoke screens thrown up by news sources if they have a reason to do so. Thus, for example, despite the administration's media management, media accounts of continuing U.S. casualties in Afghanistan, coupled with stories about the corruption and incompetence of the Afghan government, forced the Obama administration to declare in 2009 that America's commitment to Afghanistan was not open-ended and to indicate that there would be a timetable for the removal of American forces from that country.

Occasionally, a politician proves incredibly adept at surviving repeated media attacks. Bill Clinton, for example, was able to survive repeated revelations of sexual improprieties, financial irregularities, lying to the public, and illegal campaign fundraising activities. Clinton and his advisers crafted what the *Washington Post* called a "toolkit" for dealing with potentially damaging media revelations. This toolkit included techniques such as chiding the press, browbeating reporters, referring inquiries quickly to lawyers who would not comment, and acting quickly to change the agenda. These techniques helped Clinton maintain a favorable public image despite the Monica Lewinsky scandal and even the humiliation of a formal impeachment and trial.

The Power of Consumers

The print and broadcast media are businesses that, in general, seek to show a profit. This means that, like any other business, they must cater to the preferences of consumers. This has very important consequences for the content and character of the news media.

Catering to the Audience In general, and especially in the political realm, the print and broadcast media and the publishing industry are not only responsive to the interests of consumers generally but are particularly responsive to the interests and views of the better-educated and more affluent segments of their audience. The preferences of these audience segments have a profound effect on the content and orientation of the press, of radio and television programming, and of books, especially in the areas of news and public affairs.[20]

Although affluent consumers do watch television programs and read periodicals whose contents are designed simply to amuse or entertain, the one area that most directly appeals to the upscale audience is that of news and public affairs. The affluent—who are also typically well-educated—are the core audience of news-magazines, journals of opinion, books dealing with public affairs, such newspapers as the *New York Times* and the *Washington Post*, and broadcast news and weekend and evening public-affairs programs. Although other segments of the public also read newspapers and watch television news, their level of interest in world events, national political issues, and the like is closely related to their level of education. As a result, upscale Americans are overrepresented in the news and public-affairs audience. The concentration of these strata in the audience makes news, politics, and public affairs potentially very attractive topics to advertisers, publishers, radio broadcasters, and television executives. As a result, topics in which the upper-middle class is interested, such as the stock market, scientific and literary affairs, and international politics, receive extensive coverage.

At the same time, however, entire categories of events, issues, and phenomena of interest to lower-middle- and working-class Americans receive scant attention from the national print and broadcast media. For example, trade-union news and events are discussed only in the context of major strikes or revelations of corruption. No network or national periodical routinely covers labor organizations. Religious

During the 1960s, civil rights protesters learned a variety of techniques designed to elicit sympathetic media coverage. Television images of police brutality in Alabama led directly to the enactment of the 1965 Civil Rights Act.

and church affairs receive little coverage. The activities of veterans', fraternal, ethnic, and patriotic organizations are also generally ignored.

The Media and Conflict Although the media respond most to the upscale audience, groups that cannot afford the services of media consultants and issues managers can publicize their views and interests through protest. Frequently, the media are accused of encouraging conflict and even violence because the audience mostly watches news for the entertainment value that conflict can provide. Clearly, conflict can be an important vehicle for attracting the attention and interest of the media, and thus gives an opportunity for media attention to groups otherwise lacking the financial or organizational resources to broadcast their views. But although conflict and protest can succeed in drawing media attention, these methods ultimately do not allow groups from the bottom of the social ladder to compete effectively in the media.

The chief problem with protest as a media technique is that, in general, the media on which the protesters depend have considerable discretion in reporting and interpreting the events they cover. For example, should the media focus on the conflict itself, rather than the issues or concerns that created the conflict? The answer to this question is typically determined by the media, not by the protesters. This means that media interpretation of protest activities is more a reflection of the views of the groups and forces to which the media are responsive—as we have seen, usually segments of the upper-middle class—than it is a function of the wishes of the protesters themselves. It is worth noting that civil rights protesters received their most favorable media coverage during the 1960s, when a segment of the white upper-middle class saw blacks as potential political allies in the Democratic Party.

Typically, upper-middle-class protesters—including many student demonstrators—have little difficulty securing favorable publicity for themselves and their causes. Upper-middle-class protesters are often more skilled than their lower-class counterparts in the techniques of media manipulation. That is, they typically are better educated about how to package messages for media consumption. For example, it is important to know at what time of day a protest should occur if it is to be carried on the evening news. Similarly, the setting, definition of the issues, character of the rhetoric used, and so on all help to determine whether a protest will receive favorable media coverage. Moreover, upper-middle-class protesters can often produce their own media coverage through "underground" newspapers, college newspapers, student radio and television stations, and the Internet. The same resources and skills that generally allow upper-middle-class people to publicize their ideas are usually not left behind when segments of this class choose to engage in disruptive forms of political action. This helps to explain why relatively small groups of antitax activists who call themselves the Tea Party movement were able to play a major role in the 2010 Republican primaries and general election. Tea Party was, of course, a label designed to refer to America's original antitax rebels.

● Media Power in American Politics

The content and character of news and public affairs programming—what the media choose to present and how they present it—can have far-reaching political consequences. Media disclosures can greatly enhance—or fatally damage—the careers of public officials. Media coverage can rally support for—or intensify opposition to—national policies. The media can shape and modify, if not fully form, public perceptions of events, issues, and institutions.

Shaping Events

In recent American political history, the media have played a central role in at least three major events. First, the media were a critically important factor in the civil rights movement of the 1950s and 1960s. Television images showing peaceful civil rights marchers attacked by club-swinging police helped to generate sympathy among northern whites for the civil rights struggle and greatly increased the pressure on Congress to bring an end to segregation.[21] Second, the media were instrumental in compelling the Nixon administration to negotiate an end to American involvement in the Vietnam War. Beginning in 1967, the national media, reacting in part to a shift in elite opinion, portrayed the war as misguided and unwinnable and, as a result, helped to turn popular sentiment against continued American involvement.[22]

Finally, the media were central actors in the Watergate affair, which ultimately forced President Richard Nixon, the landslide victor in the 1972 presidential election, to resign from office in disgrace. The relentless series of investigations launched by the *Washington Post*, the *New York Times*, and the television networks led to the disclosures of the various abuses of which Nixon was guilty and ultimately forced him to choose between resignation and almost certain impeachment.

The Sources of Media Power

agenda setting the power of the media to bring public attention to particular issues and problems

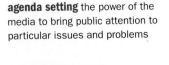

Agenda Setting The power of the media stems from several sources. The first is **agenda setting**, which means that the media help to set the agenda for political discussion. Groups and forces that wish to bring their ideas before the public in order to generate support for policy proposals or political candidacies must somehow secure media coverage. If the media are persuaded that an idea is newsworthy, then they may declare it an "issue" that must be confronted or a "problem" to be solved, thus clearing the first hurdle in the policy-making process. On the other hand, if an idea lacks or loses media appeal, its chance of resulting in new programs or policies is diminished.

For example, in the fall of 2001, President Bush had little difficulty convincing the media that terrorism and his administration's campaign to combat terrorist attacks merited a dominant place on the agenda. In 2002 and 2003, American military campaigns in Afghanistan and Iraq easily dominated the news. Some stories have such overwhelming significance that political leaders' main concern is not whether the story will receive attention but whether they will figure prominently and positively in media accounts. This was certainly true in 2005, when disastrous hurricanes struck the Gulf Coast. There was no question that these storms and the damage they caused would be on the national agenda. The question was how blame and credit would be apportioned. Local, state, and national leaders, including the president, sought to escape blame for the region's lack of preparedness and to take credit for emergency and relief efforts. Eventually, the Bush administration and the Federal Emergency Management Agency (FEMA) were blamed for the disaster. In 2008–09 the global financial crisis and the severe economic recession that ensued dominated the news agenda.

In April 2004, 60 Minutes II's broadcast of the story of American soldiers' abuse of Iraqi inmates at Abu Ghraib prison was seen around the world and led to accusations of brutality and torture. Initial efforts by the Bush administration to contain the Iraq prison scandal and limit the blame to a handful of soldiers and immediate senior officers failed.

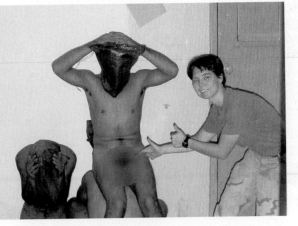

Even as the crisis eased, continuing media attention created enormous pressure for the government to "do something" and a sense among many Americans that not enough was being done by the Obama administration to cope with economic problems. A similar phenomenon could be seen in 2010 when the Obama administration seemed helpless to deal with a massive oil spill in the Gulf of Mexico.

In many instances, the media serve as conduits for agenda-setting efforts by competing groups and forces. Occasionally, however, journalists themselves play an important role in setting the agenda of political discussion. For example, whereas many of the scandals and investigations surrounding President Clinton were initiated by his political opponents, the Watergate scandal that destroyed Nixon's presidency was in some measure initiated and driven by the *Washington Post* and the national television networks.

Framing A second source of the media's power, known as **framing**, is their power to decide how the American people interpret political events and results. For example, in 2009 by always referring to the Obama administration's health care initiative as "reform," the media was tacitly framing the legislation in a positive way. Americans generally approve of the idea of "reform" and are likely to support ideas labeled as reforms. Had the media framed the initiative as "health care rationing," which some Republicans called it, the proposal would easily have been defeated.

Media frames were quite important during the 2008 election. From the perspective of the national media, one of the most important aspects of the 2008 election was that for the first time in American history an African American was making a serious bid for the presidency of the United States. The media appeared to regard this aspect of the campaign as more significant than Hillary Clinton's bid to become the first woman to serve as president. Partly because they regarded the fact that Obama was America's first significant black presidential candidate as supremely important,

framing the power of the media to influence how events and issues are interpreted

This famous photograph of the aftermath of a napalm attack was one of many media images that shaped the American public's views on the Vietnam War. Media accounts critical of the war helped to turn public opinion against it and hastened the withdrawal of American troops.

the media gave Obama much more attention and scrutiny than they afforded other candidates. This extra attention frequently allowed Obama to dominate the news and led his opponents constantly to charge that the media were biased in his favor. It may be true that many reporters and commentators supported Obama. Nevertheless, if he had been an inept candidate, the extra coverage he received would only have amplified his weakness. Obama, however, was able to take full advantage of the extra media attention he was given to generate popular enthusiasm for his campaign and raise tens of millions of dollars in small contributions via the Internet. By devoting enormous quantities of ink and air time to Obama, the media were not so much exhibiting bias as reflecting what they saw as the historic importance of the story. Extra media coverage, in turn, gave Obama an extra opportunity—which he seized—to display his intelligence and ability to the electorate.

In terms of media coverage, Sarah Palin's candidacy was almost the opposite of Obama's experience. One reason that John McCain chose Palin as his vice-presidential running mate was a calculation that the media would find Palin sufficiently new and interesting to divert their attention from Obama. Palin's acceptance speech at the Republican convention in which she described herself as a simple "hockey mom," and declared that the difference between a hockey mom and a pit bull was "lipstick," captured the media's interest and briefly gave the GOP a stage to rival Obama's. Palin, however, was not able to put her extra media exposure to good use. After two disastrous network interviews in which Palin appeared unable to answer the simplest questions, the media generally dismissed the Alaska governor as inept and uninformed, and resumed their focus on Obama.

Priming A third important media power is **priming**. This occurs when media coverage affects the way the public evaluates political leaders, issues, and events. For example, nearly unanimous media praise for President Bush's speeches to the nation in the wake of the September 11 terrorist attacks prepared, or *primed*, the public to view Bush's subsequent response to terrorism in an extremely positive light, even though some aspects of the administration's efforts, most notably those in the realm of bioterrorism, were quite problematic.

In the case of political candidates, the media have considerable influence over whether a particular individual will receive public attention, whether a particular individual will be taken seriously as a viable contender, and whether the public will evaluate a candidate's performance favorably. Thus, if the media find a candidate interesting, they may treat him or her as a serious contender even though the facts of the matter seem to suggest otherwise. In a similar vein, the media may declare that a candidate has "momentum," a mythical property that the media confer on candidates if they happen to exceed the media's expectations. Midway through the 2008 Democratic primaries, the media declared that Barack Obama had momentum, as his fund-raising and poll numbers exceeded early expectations. Nothing Hillary Clinton was able to do seemed to deprive Obama of the coveted momentum the media had granted him.

Typically, media coverage of election campaigns focuses on the "horse race" (that is, who is ahead and by how much) to the detriment of attention to issues and candidate records. In the year preceding the 2008 national elections, several candidates fought for the Democratic and Republican presidential nominations. From the outset, it appeared that Senator Hillary Clinton was nearly certain to become the Democratic nominee. Looking for a horse race, however, the national media gave enormous publicity to Senator Barack Obama. Newspapers and magazines ran hundreds of positive profiles of Obama, touting him as the first serious African

priming process of preparing the public to take a particular view of an event or political actor

What the Media Tell Americans about the World and the World about America

It is often said that we live in an age of "globalization," when events anywhere in the world affect everyone in the world. Nevertheless, the American news media are surprisingly parochial in their orientation. Few news organizations have foreign bureaus or foreign correspondents. Indeed, in the face of globalization, the number of foreign bureaus operated by major news organizations has actually decreased. One veteran CBS reporter, Tom Fenton, said that when he joined the network in 1970, "I was one of three correspondents in the Rome bureau. We had bureaus in Paris, Bonn, Warsaw, Cairo, and Nairobi. Now you can count the number of foreign correspondents on two hands and have three fingers left over."[a] Despite vital American interests in the Middle East, most reporters know very little about the history, culture, and languages of the region. U.S. correspondents sent to cover the Iraq war could not speak directly with Iraqis or understand Arabic news media.[b]

On a typical Sunday, most major American newspapers devote roughly 20 percent of their news coverage to international events. It is interesting to note that the bulk of the international news featured in these papers involved war, terrorism, and political violence. To the extent that Americans derive their understanding of the world from the newspapers, they might reasonably see much of it as a very dangerous place.

However, before we dismiss the American news media as parochial, we should compare U.S. coverage of international events with that presented on the same day by one of the world's oldest and most famous newspapers, *The Times* of London. *The Times* did, indeed, devote a considerably greater portion of its news coverage to international events than did the American newspapers. Slightly more than 44 percent of the stories in *The Times* focused on world affairs—twice the percentage found in the typical American paper.

The Times and other international newspapers devote enormous attention to the United States because America's economic and military power mean that American actions are likely to have important consequences throughout the world. In their news pages and editorial commentary, newspapers in Europe, Asia, Africa, Latin America, and the Middle East seek to dissect American policy to understand its intentions and significance for their own nations. Often, this coverage is less than flattering, even when American policy appears to be successful. Most European newspapers were sharply critical of the Bush administration's decision to go to war against Iraq without UN approval and, in 2009, the president of the European Union called the Obama administration's economic policies, "a road to Hell" that would cause global inflation. However, not all foreign news coverage of U.S. politics is critical.

[a]Michael Massing, "The Unseen War," *New York Review of Books*, May 29, 2003, p. 17.
[b]Massing, "Unseen War," p. 17.

for critical analysis

1. In 2004, American news coverage of the abuse of Iraqi prisoners by U.S. soldiers shocked the world. Should the American media present a more positive image of the United States to foreigners?

2. American newspapers offer more coverage of local events than of world affairs. What factors might explain the local focus of the American press?

American presidential contender. Hardly a negative word about Obama was uttered on the air or in print. Obama was even allowed to appear in a *Saturday Night Live* Halloween skit poking fun at Clinton, who was portrayed as a witch.[23] Months of positive coverage helped transform Obama into a serious presidential contender.

The media's power to influence people's evaluation of public figures is not absolute. Throughout the last decade, politicians implemented new techniques for communicating with the public and shaping their own images. For instance, Bill Clinton pioneered the use of town meetings and television entertainment programs as a means of communicating directly with voters in the 1992 election. During the 2000 presidential race between Bush and Gore, both candidates made use of town meetings, as well as talk shows and entertainment programs such as *The Oprah Winfrey Show, The Tonight Show with Jay Leno,* and *Saturday Night Live,* to reach mass audiences. During a town meeting, talk show, or entertainment program, politicians are free to craft their own images without interference from journalists.

In 2008, the McCain campaign quickly determined that Sarah Palin, the vice-presidential nominee, was not quite ready for prime-time media exposure. Palin had little experience outside her own state and was not conversant with most national political issues. Accordingly, GOP strategists sought to limit Palin's media exposure to situations in which she would not be subjected to the sort of intensive questioning that might reveal her limitations.

The Rise of Adversarial Journalism

The political power of the news media vis-à-vis the government has greatly increased in recent years through the growing prominence of "adversarial journalism"—a form of reporting in which the media adopt a hostile posture toward the government and public officials.

During the nineteenth century, American newspapers were completely subordinate to the political parties. Newspapers depended on official patronage—legal notice and party subsidies—for their financial survival and were controlled by party leaders. (A vestige of that era survived into the twentieth century in such newspaper names as the *Springfield Republican* and the *St. Louis Globe-Democrat*.) At the turn of the century, with the development of commercial advertising, newspapers became financially independent. This made possible the emergence of a formally nonpartisan press.

Presidents were the first national officials to see the opportunities in this development. By communicating directly to the electorate through newspapers and magazines, Theodore Roosevelt and Woodrow Wilson established political constituencies for themselves, independent of party organizations, and strengthened their own power relative to Congress. President Franklin Delano Roosevelt used the radio, most notably in his famous fireside chats, to reach out to voters throughout the nation and to make himself the center of American politics. FDR was also adept at developing close personal relationships with reporters that enabled him to obtain favorable news coverage despite the fact that in his day a majority of newspaper owners and publishers were staunch conservatives. Following Roosevelt's example, subsequent presidents have all sought to use the media to enhance their popularity and power. For example, through televised news conferences, President John F. Kennedy mobilized public support for his domestic and foreign-policy initiatives.

During the 1950s and early 1960s, a few members of Congress also made successful use of the media—especially television—to mobilize national support for their causes. Senator Estes Kefauver of Tennessee became a major contender for

for critical analysis

Before he left office in June 2007, the long-time British prime minister Tony Blair called the news media a "feral beast." Why are many politicians hostile to media? Do you share their views?

the presidency and won a place on the 1956 Democratic national ticket as a result of his dramatic televised hearings on organized crime. Senator Joseph McCarthy of Wisconsin made himself a powerful national figure through his well-publicized investigations of alleged communist infiltration of key American institutions. These senators, however, were more exceptional than typical. Through the mid-1960s, the executive branch continued to generate the bulk of news coverage, and the media became a cornerstone of presidential power.

The Vietnam War shattered this relationship between the press and the presidency. During the early stages of U.S. involvement, American officials in Vietnam who disapproved of the way the war was being conducted leaked information critical of administrative policy to reporters. Publication of this material infuriated the White House, which pressured publishers to block its release—on one occasion, President Kennedy went so far as to ask the *New York Times* to reassign its Saigon correspondent. However, the national print and broadcast media—the network news divisions, the national news weeklies, the *Washington Post*, and the *New York Times*—discovered an audience for critical coverage and investigative reporting among segments of the public skeptical of administration policy. As the Vietnam conflict dragged on, critical media coverage fanned antiwar sentiment. Moreover, growing opposition to the war among liberals encouraged some members of Congress, most notably Senator J. William Fulbright, chair of the Senate Foreign Relations Committee, to break with the president. In turn, these shifts in popular and congressional sentiment emboldened journalists and publishers to continue to present critical news reports. Through this process, journalists developed a commitment to adversarial journalism, while a constituency emerged that would rally to the defense of the media when it came under White House attack.

This pattern, established during the Vietnam War, endured through the 1970s and into the 1980s. Political forces opposed to presidential policies, many members of Congress, and the national news media began to find that their interests often overlapped. Opponents of the Nixon, Carter, Reagan, and Bush administrations

In an effort to avoid tough questions from interviewers on traditional news programs, politicians increasingly seek out opportunities to reach the public through entertainment or "soft news" programs. Bill Clinton played his saxophone on The Arsenio Hall Show *and discussed his choice of underwear with a teenage interviewer on MTV. George W. Bush also made good use of appearances on entertainment programs, appearing on* The Tonight Show with Jay Leno *and other programs.*

Adversarial journalism has become common in politics as reporters aggressively pursue stories that are critical of politicians and their actions. In 2008, intense media coverage of inflammatory remarks made by Barack Obama's preacher Jeremiah Wright presented a challenge for the Obama campaign.

welcomed news accounts critical of the conduct of executive agencies and officials in foreign affairs and in such domestic areas as race relations, the environment, and regulatory policy. In addition, many senators and representatives found it politically advantageous to champion causes favored by the antiwar, consumer, or environmental movements because, by conducting televised hearings on such issues, they were able to mobilize national constituencies, to become national figures, and in a number of instances to become serious contenders for their party's presidential nomination.

As for the national media, aggressive use of the techniques of investigation, publicity, and exposure allowed them to enhance their autonomy and carve out a prominent place for themselves in American government and politics. The power derived by the press from adversarial journalism is one of the reasons that the media seem to relish opportunities to attack political institutions and to publish damaging information about important public officials. Increasingly, media coverage has come to influence politicians' careers, the mobilization of political constituencies, and the fate of issues and causes.

Adversarial, or "attack," journalism has become commonplace in America, and some critics have suggested that the media have contributed to popular cynicism and the low levels of citizen participation that characterize contemporary American political processes. But before we begin to think about means of compelling the media to adopt a more positive view of politicians and political issues, we should consider the possibility that media criticism is one of the major mechanisms of political accountability in the American political process. Without aggressive media coverage, would we have known of Bill Clinton's misdeeds or, for that matter, those of Richard Nixon? Without aggressive media coverage, would important questions be raised about the conduct of American foreign and domestic policy? It is easy to criticize the media for their aggressive tactics, but would our democracy function effectively without the critical role of the press? Vigorous and critical media are needed as the "watchdogs" of American politics. Of course, in October 2001, the adversarial relationship between the government and the media was at least temporarily transformed into a much more supportive association as the media helped rally the American people for the fight against terrorism.

for critical analysis

In wartime, can media criticism of government action aid the nation's enemies? Should there be limits on media criticism of the government during time of war? Or does criticism actually enhance the nation's strength?

The adversarial relationship between the government and segments of the press, however, resumed in the wake of the 2003 Iraq war. Such newspapers as the *Washington Post* and the *New York Times* castigated President Bush for going to war without the support of some of America's major allies. When American forces failed to uncover evidence that Iraq possessed weapons of mass destruction—a major reason cited by the administration for launching the war—these newspapers intimated that the war had been based on intelligence failures, if not outright presidential deceptions. The president, as noted earlier, denounced the media for distorting his record. Thus, after a brief interlude of post–September 11 harmony, the customary hostilities between politicians and the press resumed.

● Thinking Critically about Media Power and Democracy

The free media are an institution absolutely essential to democratic government. Ordinary citizens depend on the media to investigate wrongdoing, to publicize and explain governmental actions, to evaluate programs and politicians, and to bring

Become an Informed and Vocal News Critic

Americans today are less trusting of what's being reported by major news outlets than they were in the not too distant past, and many of the traditional sources of news and information—newspapers and the nightly news on television—have seen sizable reductions in their audience. The number of Americans who tune into national news on TV is down by around half since the early 1970s.

Although dissatisfaction with the media is on the rise across all age groups, young people are among the most likely to have negative things to say about the news media. In fact, recent surveys have shown that around one in four young Americans get the majority of their news and information from comedy shows like *The Daily Show with Jon Stewart* and *The Colbert Report*, and similar numbers say a candidate endorsement by Jon Stewart could sway their votes on Election Day. The content of these shows, which satirize the sensational and melodramatic style of mainstream news

programming, resonates with media-savvy young Americans.

In an attempt to make mainstream news more attractive to young people, news editors have instituted changes in recent years. For example, CNN created its "Headline News" channel, which features fast-paced news and allows viewers to "dip in and dip out," thus catering to the tendency among younger Americans to consume news quickly and to channel surf. Many networks have added younger and more diverse anchors to their news desks. Hiring anchors who don't fit the mold of the "older white guy" is an attempt to connect with younger, more diverse viewers. Moreover, news organizations have expanded their reach by offering free access to companion Web sites. For example, at NBC only about a quarter of the TV news audience for its national news program is under thirty-four, but 54 percent of visitors to the network's MSNBC Web site fall into this age demographic.

Of course, changing the look of how news is delivered doesn't necessarily

address the complaints voiced by young Americans about the news media. But what these steps do suggest is that media industry leaders take audience reaction seriously and are willing to adapt rather than lose influence with a generation of potential readers, listeners, and viewers.

If you're interested in digging a little deeper into the mass media's news coveage, here are some things that you can do to become a more informed consumer of news and information:

- People often complain that the news media seem biased. Rather than adhering to norms of objectivity, the news is often reported from a liberal or conservative perspective. Instead of accepting this complaint at face value, try a little experiment yourself. Spend some time watching, reading, and listening to news from two sources, one that is considered "conservative" and the other "liberal" (for example, Fox News and NPR, or the editorial pages of the *Wall Street Journal* and *New York Times*). Do you agree with the characterization of these organizations as biased?

- Make your voice heard if you have concerns about news that's presented in a partisan fashion. Let the editors, hosts, writers, and owners of the broadcast or print media know that you expect more objectivity in the news that's being presented.

- Spend some time checking out "new" and "alternative" media. Many blogs provide readers with a portal to information across a variety of sources, often with commentary. A few to consider are the Huffington Post (www .huffingtonpost.com), the Drudge Report (www.drudgereport.com), the Daily Dish (andrewsullivan.theatlantic.com), and the Daily Kos: State of the Nation (www.dailykos.com).

During President Richard Nixon's second term in office, the Washington Post *reporters Carl Bernstein and Bob Woodward (above) played an important role in uncovering the Watergate conspiracy that eventually led to Nixon's resignation.*

to light matters that might otherwise be known to only a handful of governmental insiders. In short, without free and active media, popular government would be virtually impossible. Citizens would have few means through which to know or assess the government's actions—other than the claims or pronouncements of the government itself. Moreover, without active—indeed, aggressive—media, citizens would be hard-pressed to make informed choices among competing candidates at the polls. Of course, by continually emphasizing deceptions and wrongdoing by political figures, the media encourage the public to become cynical and distrustful, not only of the people in office but of the government and the political process themselves. A widespread sense that all politics is corrupt or deceptive can easily lead to a sense that nothing can be done. In this way, the media's adversarial posture may contribute to the low levels of political participation seen in America today.

Today's media are not only adversarial but also increasingly partisan. Debates about the liberalism and conservatism of the mass media point out that many readers and viewers perceive a growing bias in newspapers, radio, and television. Blogs and other Internet outlets, of course, are often unabashedly partisan. To some extent, increasing ideological and partisan stridency is an inevitable result of the expansion and proliferation of news sources. When the news was dominated by three networks and a handful of national papers, each sought to appeal to the entire national audience. This required a moderate and balanced tone so that consumers would not be offended and jump ship to a rival network or newspaper. Today, there are so many news sources that few can aim for a national audience. Instead, each targets a partisan or ideological niche and aims to develop a strong relationship with consumers in that audience segment by catering to their biases and predispositions. The end result may be to encourage greater division and disharmony among Americans.

At the same time, the declining power of party organizations (as we will see in Chapter 9) has made politicians ever more dependent on favorable media coverage. National political leaders and journalists have had symbiotic relationships, at least since FDR's presidency, but initially politicians were the senior partners. They benefited from media publicity, but they were not totally dependent on it as long as they could still rely on party organizations to mobilize votes. Journalists, on the other hand, depended on their relationships with politicians for access to information and would hesitate to report stories that might antagonize valuable sources for fear of being excluded from the flow of information in retaliation.

With the decline of party organizations, journalists have less fear that their access to information can be restricted in retaliation for negative coverage. Such freedom gives the media enormous power. The media can make or break reputations, help to launch or to destroy political careers, and build support for or rally opposition to programs and institutions.[24] Wherever there is so much power, at least the potential exists for its abuse or overly zealous use. All things considered, free media are so critically important to the maintenance of a democratic society that Americans must be prepared to take the risk that the media will occasionally abuse their power. The forms of governmental control that would prevent the media from misusing their power would also certainly destroy freedom. The ultimate beneficiaries of free and active media are the American people.

studyguide

Practice Quiz

 Find a diagnostic Web Quiz with 31 additional questions on the StudySpace Web site: www.wwnorton.com/we-the-people

The Media Industry and Government

1. Which of the following statements is *not true about old-fashioned newspapers? (p. 240)*
   a) They typically offer readers a better context for analysis by providing more detailed and complete information than other forms of media.
   b) They are the read on a daily basis by almost all Americans.
   c) They serve as the primary source of news for the nation's social and political elites.
   d) Broadcast media organizations rely heavily on newspapers to set their news agenda.

2. In general, FCC regulations apply only to *(p. 245)*
   a) cable television.
   b) Internet Web sites.
   c) over-the-air broadcast media.
   d) satellite radio.

3. The now defunct requirement that broadcasters provide time for opposing views when they air programs on controversial issues was called *(p. 246)*
   a) the equal time rule.
   b) the fairness doctrine.
   c) the right of rebuttal.
   d) the response rule.

4. The nationalization of the news has been influenced by which of the following trends in ownership of the media? *(p. 246)*
   a) the purchase of influential newspapers by foreign corporations
   b) the fragmentation of ownership of all media in the United States
   c) the wave of mergers and consolidations following the passage of the 1996 Telecommunications Act
   d) the purchase of the major news networks by the national government

5. Which of the following best describes national news in the United States? *(p. 248)*
   a) fragmented and localized
   b) nationalized and centralized
   c) centralized but still localized
   d) none of the above

6. Which of the following can be considered an example of a news enclave? *(p. 248)*
   a) Web blogs
   b) letters to the editor

c) readers of the *New York Times*
d) people who watch CNN

News Coverage

7. Which of the following have an impact on the nature of media coverage of politics? *(p. 249)*
   a) reporters
   b) political actors
   c) news consumers
   d) all of the above

8. The newspaper publisher William Randolph Hearst was responsible for encouraging U.S. involvement in which war? *(p. 249)*
   a) the Spanish-American War
   b) the Vietnam War
   c) the U.S. war with Mexico
   d) the Gulf War

9. Which of the following is *not* an explanation for why media coverage may be relatively uninfluenced by the predominantly liberal political preferences of journalists? *(p. 250)*
   a) Most reporters attempt to maintain some measure of balance and objectivity in their reporting.
   b) Journalists always cover all government officials—regardless of their partisanship—in a favorable light.
   c) Journalists have a stronger preference for stories that are dramatic and have a great deal of value than for stories that support their own political preferences.
   d) A number of important newspaper owners and publishers have decidedly conservative views that may influence coverage.

10. Which of the following is a strategy available to poor people to increase their coverage by the news media? *(p. 255)*
    a) protest
    b) media consultants
    c) television advertising
    d) newspaper advertising "time sharing"

Media Power in American Politics

11. The media's powers to determine what becomes a part of political discussion and to shape how

political events are interpreted are known as (pp. 256–57)
a) issue definition and protest power.
b) agenda setting and framing.
c) the illusion of saliency and the bandwagon effect.
d) the equal time rule and the right of rebuttal.

12. Media coverage of election campaigns typically focuses on which of the following? (p. 258)
a) the details of each candidate's domestic policy proposals
b) the details of each candidate's foreign policy proposals
c) the records of each of the candidates
d) the "horse race" (that is, who is ahead and by how much)

13. Which of the following has *not* been a consequence of the emergence of adversarial (or "attack") journalism? (pp. 260–62)
a) It has led the media to adopt a more positive view of politicians and political issues.
b) It has enhanced the media's autonomy from politicians and allowed them to carve out a prominent place for themselves in the political process.
c) It has increased the likelihood that the media will act as the much-needed "watchdog" of American politics.
d) It has led to accusations that the media is creating popular cynicism and depressing levels of political participation.

14. Which of the following best describes the media's role in the Watergate affair? (p. 262)
a) They played a central role in reporting on President Nixon's resignation once he left office but did little to reveal his abuses of power to the public while he was president.
b) They played a central role in President Nixon's decision to resign from the presidency by revealing his abuses of power to the public.
c) They played a central role in disproving claims that President Nixon had abused his power while in office.
d) They played almost no role in the Watergate affair because they refused to investigate claims that President Nixon had abused his power.

Thinking Critically about Media Power and Democracy

15. The declining power of party organizations has had which of the following effects on the power of the media in the United States? (p. 264)
a) made the media less powerful because politicians are no longer forced to follow the fairness doctrine
b) made the media more powerful because politicians must now rely on the media to mobilize votes
c) made the media more powerful because politicians can no longer raise money through campaign contributions
d) had no effect on the power of the media

Chapter Outline

Find a detailed Chapter Outline on the StudySpace Web site: www.wwnorton.com/we-the-people

Key Terms

Find Flashcards to help you study these terms on the StudySpace Web site: www.wwnorton.com/we-the-people

agenda setting (p. 256)
equal time rule (p. 246)
fairness doctrine (p. 246)

framing (p. 257)
priming (p. 258)

right of rebuttal (p. 246)
sound bites (p. 239)

For Further Reading

Armstrong, Jerome, and Markos Zuniga. *Crashing the Gate: Netroots, Grassroots, and the Rise of People-Powered Politics.* New York: Chelsea Green, 2006.

Campbell, Richard, Christopher Martin, and Bettina Fabos. *Media and Culture.* New York: St. Martin's Press, 2009.

Cook, Timothy. *Governing with the News: The News Media as a Political Institution.* Chicago: University of Chicago Press, 1997.

De Zengotita, Thomas. *Mediated: How the Media Shapes Our World and the Way We Live in It.* New York: Bloomsbury, 2006.

Fenton, Tom. *Bad News: The Decline of Reporting, the Business of News, and the Danger to Us All.* New York: HarperCollins, 2005.

Graber, Doris, ed. *Media Power in American Politics.* 5th ed. Washington, DC: Congressional Quarterly Press, 2006.

Hamilton, James T. *All the News That's Fit to Sell.* Princeton, NJ: Princeton University Press, 2004.

Jamieson, Kathleen, and Paul Waldman. *The Press Effect.* New York: Oxford University Press, 2004.

Jenkins, Henry. *Convergence Culture: Where Old and New Media Collide.* New York: New York University Press, 2008.

Kellner, Douglas. *Media Spectacle and the Crisis of Democracy.* Boulder, CO: Paradigm, 2005.

Rich, Frank. *The Greatest Story Ever Sold.* New York: Penguin, 2006.

Starr, Paul. *The Creation of the Media.* New York: Basic Books, 2004.

Weaver, David, et al. *The American Journalist in the 21st Century: U.S. News People at the Dawn of a New Millennium.* New York: Erlbaum, 2006.

Recommended Web Sites

Accuracy in Media
www.aim.org

This nonprofit, watchdog group attempts to ensure accuracy in media reporting by identifying botched or slanted stories and then "setting the record straight." Check out the media monitor, special reports, and press releases to see what current stories may be cause for concern.

Drudge Report
www.drudgereport.com

The Web site for the Drudge Report is a great source page for all the world's breaking news and most recent columns. Any consumer of the news will appreciate this handy guide to specific columnists and opinion pages of major publications.

Federal Communications Commission
www.fcc.gov

The FCC is an independent regulatory agency established by the U.S. government in 1934 to regulate the broadcast media. On the official FCC Web site you can read about the rules and regulations that affect the media, along with other current topics of interest.

FOX News.com
www.foxnews.com/politics

CNN Politics.com
www.cnn.com/POLITICS

The New York Times
www.nytimes.com/pages/politics/index.html

Political news sites provide a good variety of perspectives on the news from conservative to liberal.

Journalism.org
www.journalism.org

This nonprofit, nonpolitical site, sponsored by the Project for Excellence in Journalism, examines the overall performance of the press as providers of information. Their aim is to help both consumers and producers of the news understand what the press is delivering and hopefully make it better.

National Newspaper Association
www.nnawes.org

The NNA is one of the oldest and largest professional associations in the print media today. As ownership of major newspapers fall into fewer and fewer hands, the NNA is trying to protect, promote, and enhance America's community newspapers.

Newseum
www.newseum.org

Newseum is the Web page for an interactive museum of news journalism. On this site you can browse the front pages of over 500 daily national and international newspapers and explore the galleries and theaters of the news museum in Washington, D.C.

The Pew Research Center for the People and the Press
http://people-press.org

This independent survey research organization studies attitudes toward the press and numerous political issues.

For much of American history, formal barriers restricted the right to vote and created a pattern of unequal participation in politics. Today, most of those barriers have been eliminated, but voter turnout remains relatively low, especially among young voters. In 2008, these voters cast their ballots at a polling station in a fraternity house near the UCLA campus.

Political Participation and Voting

WHAT GOVERNMENT DOES AND WHY IT MATTERS In 2008, the Obama campaign sought to mobilize new voters, reaching out especially to young voters. As the first major-party African American candidate for president, Obama also spurred a huge mobilization among black voters. In the 2004 election, Republicans held the advantage in recruiting volunteers and in mobilizing the electorate. In 2008, by contrast, Democrats had a much more extensive operation for registering new voters, contacting potential supporters, and turning them out to vote. The pendulum swung again in 2010, when Tea Party activists energized Republican voters.

In many ways, the Obama campaign rewrote the rules for engaging supporters in electoral campaigns. The campaign paid special attention to young voters, seeking to replace cynicism and apathy with idealism and hope. Connecting through the Internet and other new technologies, volunteers found many opportunities to participate. The campaign opened

focusquestions

- What are the ways people participate in politics?

- How do different groups of Americans participate in politics?

- Why do some people participate in politics while others don't?

many offices across the country, making it easier for potential supporters to connect with campaign activities. In 2010, Republican activists made effective use of many of the same techniques.

The combination of excitement and mobilization in the 2008 elections spurred more than 71 percent of eligible voters to register, a modern record. Participation increased among many categories of voters. African Americans turned out at historically high levels, inspired by the first major-party black presidential candidate in American history. Young voters also increased their turnout, with 51 percent of eighteen- to twenty-nine-year-olds voting.[1] However, Democrats had trouble mobilizing African Americans and young voters for the 2010 midterm elections. Young voters, who made up 18 percent of the electorate in 2008, only made up slightly more than 10 percent in 2010.

Who votes and participates in other ways affects the issues that candidates and elected officials put at the top of their agenda. However, despite the recent increases, turnout among younger voters remains relatively low. Registering, learning about the issues, and distinguishing among the candidates are often not easy tasks for first-time voters. For many young people, the decision to stay away from politics has been reinforced by their perception that politics is "a dirty, distance spectator sport, whose players don't seem interested in their ideas or their issues."[2]

Recent polls show that young people share many of the same concerns as older voters, but their views on how to address issues are often distinct. For example, young adults prefer more lenient immigration policies than older voters. They also tend to be more positive about the role of government and express support for stronger environmental laws than older people do.[3] Yet young people's relatively lower rates of participation mean that a narrower set of policy options receives serious attention, while the approaches favored by a majority of younger people are neglected. When young people participate in greater numbers, the scope of public debate is broadened, and the possibilities of approaching old problems in new ways expand.

chaptercontents

Forms of Political Participation

Political participation refers to a wide range of activities, designed to influence government. Today, voting has come to be seen as the normal or typical form of citizen political activity. Yet ordinary people took part in politics long before the advent of the election or any other formal mechanism of popular involvement in political life. If there is any natural or spontaneous form of popular political participation, it is the riot rather than the election. The urban riot and the rural uprising were common in both Europe and America prior to the nineteenth century and not entirely uncommon even in the twentieth century. Urban riots played an important role in American politics in the 1960s and 1970s. Even as recently as 1999, riots during the Seattle, Washington, meeting of the World Trade Organization helped labor unions and other opponents of trade liberalization to slow the pace of change in the rules governing world trade.

political participation political activities, such as voting, contacting political officials, volunteering for a campaign, or participating in a protest, whose purpose is to influence government

Most Americans would not consider taking part in a riot. Yet for much of the twentieth century, fewer Americans exercised their right to vote. Only recently has participation begun to move up again. Participation in presidential elections dropped significantly after 1960, when 64 percent of eligible voters cast ballots. In 1996, participation reached a new low when only 52 percent of eligible voters went to the polls. In 2004, major efforts to get out the vote brought turnout to over 60 percent. This was the first significant increase in voting in recent years. The trend continued in 2008, when nearly 62 percent of the population eligible to vote did so. Turnout for midterm elections (that is, elections that fall between presidential elections) is typically lower; for local elections, even lower.[4]

Of course, voting and rioting are not the only forms of participation available to Americans. Citizens can contact political officials, sign petitions, attend public meetings, join organizations, give money to a politician or a political organization, volunteer in a campaign, write a letter to the editor or write an article about an issue, or participate in a protest or rally. Such activities differ from voting because they can communicate much more detailed information to public officials than voting can. Voters may support a candidate for many reasons, but their actual votes do not indicate specifically what they like and don't like, nor do they tell officials how intensely voters feel about issues. A vote can convey only a general sense of approval or disapproval. By writing a letter or engaging in other kinds of political participation, people can convey much more specific information, telling public officials exactly what issues they care most about and what their views on those issues are. For that reason these other political activities are often more satisfying than voting. And citizens who engage in these other activities are more likely to try to influence state and local politics

Protests and rallies are forms of political participation. At this rally, demonstrators gathered in support of immigrants' rights. They hoped to draw attention to their cause and to influence the government to adopt policies that would result in better conditions for immigrant workers.

rather than national politics; in voting, people find the national scene more interesting than state and local politics.[5]

Nonelectoral political activity takes many forms: some of the most prominent in recent years include lobbying, public relations, litigation, and protest. Although interest groups often dominate these forms of nonelectoral political activity because they pour large sums of money into it, ordinary citizens also seek to influence politics through diverse strategies. **Lobbying** is an effort by groups or individuals to take their case directly to elected or appointed officials. By voting, citizens seek to determine who will govern. By lobbying, citizens attempt to determine what those in power will do. As we will see in Chapter 11, many interest groups employ professional lobbyists to bring their views to lawmakers. At the same time, however, thousands of volunteers lobby Congress and the bureaucracy each year on behalf of citizen groups such as the Sierra Club and the Home School Legal Defense Fund.[6] The hundreds of thousands of citizens who call or write to members of Congress each year, seeking to influence their votes, are also engaged in lobbying.

Public relations is an effort to sway public opinion on behalf of an issue or cause. Most private citizens cannot afford to launch major advertising campaigns the way that deep-pocketed interest groups do, but they often find other public relations strategies. Letters to the editor can help attract wider attention to issue. Giving public presentations to community organizations is also a form of public relations. When Mothers Against Drunk Driving (MADD) started in the early 1980s, the two women who launched the organization had no money or political connections. Candy Lightner, whose daughter was killed by a drunk driver, sought to raise awareness of the problem by starting a newsletter and speaking to local community groups who began to invite her to their meetings.[7] Only after the awareness raising of these early public relations strategies did the organization begin to get politicians to listen to their concerns.

In some cases, efforts to influence public opinion can backfire. In September 2007, when General David Petraeus appeared before Congress to report on the progress of the war in Iraq, the progressive antiwar group MoveOn.org sought to challenge his positive account of the war with a public-relations strategy. MoveOn bought a full-page advertisement in the *New York Times* bearing the headline, "General Petraeus or General Betray Us?" Although MoveOn's membership approved of the ad, it provoked an outcry of opposition among critics who charged that MoveOn was undermining the Iraq war effort and unfairly smearing an upstanding military leader. Both houses of Congress passed resolutions condemning the advertisement.

Litigation is an attempt to use the courts to achieve a goal. In recent years, citizen groups and even individuals have used the federal courts more and more frequently to affect public policy. Using the so-called citizen-suit provisions of a number of federal statutes, citizen groups play an active role in shaping policy in such areas as air and water quality, preservation of endangered species, civil rights, and the rights of persons with disabilities. Use of the courts by citizen groups is encouraged by federal and state fee-shifting provisions that allow plaintiffs (those bringing a case in court) to recover legal fees from the government or the defendant, as well as by class-action rules that allow an individual to bring suit on behalf of large groups. We will learn more about this form of participation in Chapter 15.

Though most Americans reject violent **protest** or terrorism for political ends, peaceful protest is generally recognized as a legitimate and important form of

lobbying a strategy by which organized interests seek to influence the passage of legislation by exerting direct pressure on members of the legislature

public relations an attempt, usually through the use of paid consultants, to establish a favorable relationship with the public and influence its political opinions

litigation a lawsuit or legal proceeding; as a form of political participation, an attempt to seek relief in a court of law

protest participation that involves assembling crowds to confront a government or other official organization

political activity and is protected by the First Amendment. During the 1960s and 1970s, hundreds of thousands of Americans took part in peaceful protests that helped bring an end to legalized racial segregation. In recent years, peaceful marches and demonstrations have been employed by a host of groups ranging from opponents of the war in Iraq to antiabortion activists to conservative Tea Party activists. Protest is widely valued as a strategy that is available to all groups. The largest public protests in recent years were staged by immigrants and their supporters in 2006. The spark for the protest was opposition to a House bill that branded unauthorized immigrants and those who assisted them as felons. The protest, which took place in cities across the country, drew unexpectedly large crowds, estimated at 500,000 in Los Angeles, 300,000 in Chicago, and tens of thousands in many other cities. Galvanized by Spanish-language radio and the organizational power of the Catholic church, the large numbers turning out to march across the country stunned even the organizers. As one organizer put it, "People are joining in so spontaneously, it's almost like the immigrants have risen. I would call it a civil rights movement reborn in this country."[8] In 2009, conservative activists concerned about the growth of government and the prospect of health reform launched protests across the country. Tens of thousands of these protesters converged on Washington in September 2009 to attract national attention to their concern that Obama was taking the country in the wrong direction.[9]

Alternative forms of political action generally require more time, effort, or money than voting does. It is not surprising, then, that far fewer people engage in these forms of political participation than vote. In a 2008 survey of participation, for example, 76 percent of those questioned reported voting in the last election. (This figure is higher than the percentages reported in exit polls because people tend to overstate their voting habits in surveys.) In contrast, just 22 percent of respondents said they had attended a local community meeting in the previous year; 16 percent said they had contacted a public official. Only 10 percent of those surveyed reported giving money to a candidate's campaign during the election, while 9 percent said they had attended a rally or political meeting. Fewer than 5 percent of those questioned said they had actually spent time volunteering for a political campaign[10] (see Figure 8.1).

Whether voting is as effective or satisfying as these other forms of political action is an open question. It is clear, however, that for most Americans, voting remains the most accessible and most important form of political activity. Moreover, precisely because of the time, energy, and money often required to lobby, litigate, and even demonstrate, these forms of political action are often, albeit not always, dominated by better-educated and wealthier Americans. As we will see, voting participation in America is also somewhat biased in favor of those with greater wealth and, especially, higher levels of education. Nevertheless, the right to vote gives ordinary Americans a more equal chance to participate in politics than almost any other form of political activity. In the remainder of this chapter, therefore, we will turn to voting in America.

Beginning in 2009, the conservative Tea Party movement staged numerous protests to express their objections to the federal government's economic stimulus plan.

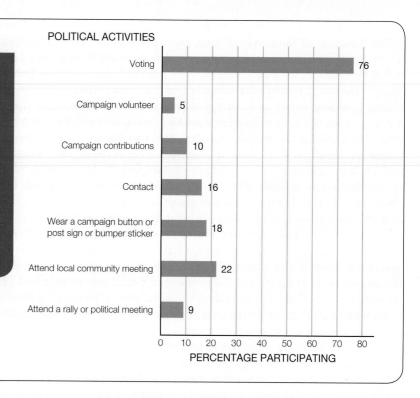

FIGURE 8.1

Political Participation

Political activities such as volunteering generally take more time and effort than voting. When asked about various forms of political participation, 76 percent of respondents said they voted in the most recent election. (This number is higher than the actual turnout because people tend to overstate their voting habits in surveys.)

SOURCE: The American National Election Studies (ANES).

POLITICAL ACTIVITIES

Voting — 76
Campaign volunteer — 5
Campaign contributions — 10
Contact — 16
Wear a campaign button or post sign or bumper sticker — 18
Attend local community meeting — 22
Attend a rally or political meeting — 9

PERCENTAGE PARTICIPATING

Voting

Despite the availability of many alternatives, in practice, citizen participation in American politics is generally limited to voting and a small number of other electoral activities (for example, campaigning). It is true that voter turnout in the United States is relatively low. But when, for one reason or another, Americans do seek to participate, their participation generally takes the form of voting.

The preeminent position of voting in the American political process is not surprising. The American legal and political environment is overwhelmingly weighted in favor of electoral participation. The availability of the right to vote, or **suffrage,** is, of course, a question of law. And civic education, also to a large extent mandated by law, encourages citizens to believe that electoral participation is the appropriate way to express opinions and grievances. As a result of closely contested recent elections and major efforts to increase turnout, electoral participation has increased in recent years, from a little over 54 percent in the 2000 presidential election to 60 percent in 2004 and nearly 62 percent in 2008.[11] However it is still true that the least well-off Americans are the least likely to vote, while the wealthiest Americans are the most likely to vote; in 2008, just 54 percent of those earning under $25,000 a year voted in the presidential election, compared with 79 percent of those earning more than $100,000 a year.[12]

Voting Rights In principle, states determine who is eligible to vote. During the nineteenth and early twentieth centuries, the right to vote was not distributed equally across the American population. Voter eligibility requirements often varied greatly from state to state. Some states openly abridged the right to vote on the

suffrage the right to vote; also called franchise

Some states have tried to make voting easier by offering early voting, voting by mail or same-day voter registration, in an effort to increase participation. In 2010, 32 states offered early voting.

basis of race; others did not. Some states imposed property restrictions on voting; others had no such restrictions. Most states mandated lengthy residency requirements, which meant that persons moving from one state to another sometimes lost their right to vote for as much as a year. In more recent years, however, constitutional amendments, federal statutes, and federal court decisions have limited states' discretion in the area of voting rights. Individual states may establish brief residency requirements, generally fifteen days, for record-keeping purposes. Beyond this, states have little or no power to regulate suffrage.

Today in the United States, all native-born or naturalized citizens over the age of eighteen, with the exception of those imprisoned for a felony, in most states and, in many states, people who have a felony conviction even if they are not in prison, have the right to vote. During the colonial and early national periods of American history, the right to vote was generally restricted to white males over the age of twenty-one. Many states also limited voting to those who owned property or paid more than a specified amount of annual tax. Property and tax requirements began to be rescinded during the 1820s, however, and had generally disappeared by the end of the Civil War.

By the time of the Civil War, blacks had won the right to vote in most northern states. In the South, black voting rights were established by the Fifteenth Amendment, ratified in 1870, which prohibited denial of the right to vote on the basis of race. Despite the Fifteenth Amendment, the voting rights of African Americans were effectively rescinded during the 1880s by the states of the former Confederacy. During this period, the southern states created what was called the "Jim Crow" system of racial segregation. As part of this system, a variety of devices, such as **poll taxes** and literacy tests, were used to prevent virtually all blacks from voting. During the 1950s and 1960s, through the civil rights movement led by Dr. Martin Luther King, Jr., and others, African Americans demanded the restoration of their voting rights. Their goal was accomplished through the enactment of the 1965

poll tax a state-imposed tax on voters as a prerequisite for registration. Poll taxes were rendered unconstitutional in national elections by the Twenty-fourth Amendment, and in state elections by the Supreme Court in 1966

for critical analysis

Describe the expansion of suffrage in the United States since the Founding. Why might the government have denied participation to so many for so long? What forces influenced the expansion of voting rights?

Voting Rights Act, which provided for the federal government to register voters in states that discriminated against minority citizens. The result was the reenfranchisement of southern blacks for the first time since the 1860s.

Women won the right to vote in 1920, with the adoption of the Nineteenth Amendment. This amendment resulted primarily from the activities of the women's suffrage movement, led by Elizabeth Cady Stanton, Susan B. Anthony, and Carrie Chapman Catt during the late nineteenth and early twentieth centuries. The "suffragists," as they were called, held rallies, demonstrations, and protest marches for more than half a century before achieving their goal. The cause of women's suffrage was ultimately advanced by World War I. President Woodrow Wilson and members of Congress became convinced that women would be more likely to support the war effort if they were granted the right to vote. For this same reason, women were given the right to vote in Great Britain and Canada during World War I.

The most recent expansion of the right to vote in the United States took place in 1971, during the Vietnam War, when the Twenty-sixth Amendment was ratified, lowering the voting age from twenty-one to eighteen. Unlike black suffrage and women's suffrage, which came about in part because of the demands of groups that had been deprived of the right to vote, the Twenty-sixth Amendment was not a response to the demands of young people to be given the right to vote. Instead, many policy makers hoped that the right to vote would channel the disruptive protest activities of students involved in the anti–Vietnam War movement into peaceful participation at the ballot box.

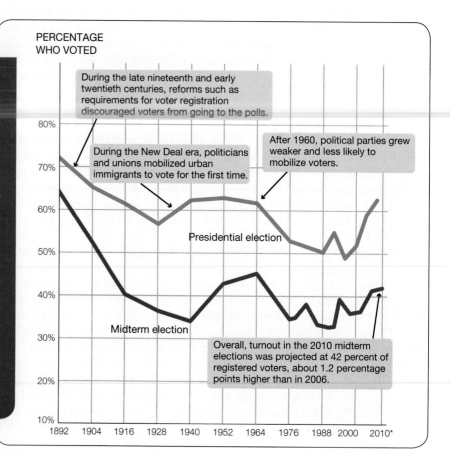

FIGURE 8.2
Voter Turnout in Presidential and Midterm Elections, 1892–2010

Since the 1890s, participation in elections has declined substantially. One pattern is consistent across time: more Americans tend to vote in presidential election years than in years when only congressional and local elections are held. What are some of the reasons that participation rose and fell during the last century?

SOURCES: Erik Austin and Jerome Clubb, *Political Facts of the United States since 1789* (New York: Columbia University Press, 1986), 378–79; and U.S. Census Bureau, www.census .gov (accessed 4/7/08); Matthew Daly, "Voter Turnout Increases from Last Midterm in 2006," *Washington Post*, November 3, 2010. *estimate

PERCENTAGE WHO VOTED

During the late nineteenth and early twentieth centuries, reforms such as requirements for voter registration discouraged voters from going to the polls.

During the New Deal era, politicians and unions mobilized urban immigrants to vote for the first time.

After 1960, political parties grew weaker and less likely to mobilize voters.

Presidential election

Midterm election

Overall, turnout in the 2010 midterm elections was projected at 42 percent of registered voters, about 1.2 percentage points higher than in 2006.

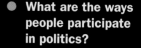

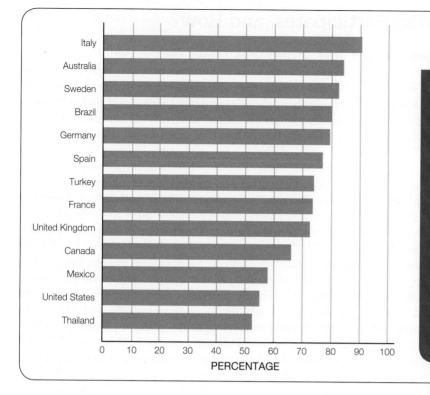

FIGURE 8.3
Voter Turnout around the World, 1945–2008

Although the United States is the oldest mass democracy, rates of voter turnout are substantially higher in other countries. In many of these countries, election days are holidays and voting is compulsory. Do you think that either of these reforms would increase voting in the United States?

NOTE: Average between 1945 and 2008.

SOURCE: International Institute of Democracy and Electoral Assistance. www.idea.int/vt/ (accessed 12/5/09); note that for some of the countries, the most recent election data are from 2007; for Brazil the average is calculated for the period after 1989, when democracy was restored.

Voting and Civic Education Laws cannot completely explain why most people vote rather than rioting or lobbying. If public attitudes were unfavorable to elections, it is doubtful that legal remedies alone would have much impact.

Positive public attitudes about voting do not come into being in a completely spontaneous manner. Americans are taught to equate citizenship with electoral participation. Civic training, designed to give students an appreciation for the American system of government, is a legally required part of the curriculum in every elementary and secondary school. Although it is not so often required by law, civic education usually manages to find its way into college curricula as well.

Voter Participation Although the United States has developed a system of civic education and a legal basis for nearly universal suffrage, America's rate of voter participation, or **turnout**, is low. About 62 percent of those eligible participate in national presidential elections. Barely one-third of eligible voters take part in midterm congressional elections, though in 2006 and 2010 turnout rose to more than 40 percent (see Figure 8.2). Turnout in state and local races that do not coincide with national contests is typically even lower. In most European countries and other Western democracies, by contrast, national voter turnout is usually between 70 and 90 percent[13] (see Figure 8.3).

Figure 8.4 shows the marked differences in voter turnout linked to ethnic group, education level, employment status, and age. This trend has created a political process whose class bias is so obvious and egregious that, if it continues, it raises serious questions about the health of American democracy. If it is only the voices of the more affluent that are heard during election time, the issues that concern lower-income Americans may not find a place at the top of the political agenda.

turnout the percentage of eligible individuals who actually vote

● Who Participates, and How?

Participation and New Technologies During the presidential campaign of 2008, Americans used the Internet in large numbers to watch campaign-related videos, read blogs, and send e-mails. They also signed up to receive text messages from campaigns informing them about new developments and urging them to participate in nearby campaign events. Many who received campaign messages forwarded them to their friends. For the first time in a national election cycle, over half of American adults used some kind of Internet channel to learn about the candidates or express their views.[14] Many analysts and political activists hoped that the widespread use of the Internet and other new technologies would promote greater participation and begin to alter the socioeconomic bias in participation. However, recent studies suggest that only among young people is there any indication that the use of new media may weaken the long-standing pattern of socioeconomic bias in participation.

Young Americans are particularly likely to participate in politics through the Internet or other new technologies. While all demographic groups used the Internet during the 2008 campaign, research shows that the numbers were especially marked for younger Americans. Nearly three-quarters of adults aged eighteen to twenty-four relied on the Internet to connect to the political process, compared to less than half of those aged fifty-five to sixty-four, and only 22 percent of Americans sixty-five or older. While all age groups used the Internet to forward political commentary to other people, adults under thirty were more than twice as likely as any other age group to post their own views on Internet sites. Younger Americans were especially likely to belong to a social networking site and more inclined to use their social networking site profiles for political communication. In fact, 65 percent of those eighteen to twenty-four used their social networking site for political communication, compared to only 36 percent for those aged forty-five or older.

Obama supporters were considerably more active than McCain supporters in their use of the Internet during the 2008 campaign. For example, among online political users, 26 percent of those who voted for Obama posted their views online via blogs, social networking sites, or some other site. Only 15 percent of those who voted for McCain reported posting their views online.[15] In 2010, both parties made extensive use of these technologies.

Despite the widespread use of the new technologies, the most recent research suggests that these new ways of participating have not yet significantly altered the socioeconomic bias in participation. A recent study found that when it comes to political activities that can be pursued offline and online, such as writing to a politician or donating money, the relationship between participation and socioeconomic status largely tracks the entrenched pattern in which the participation of lower-income, lower-education groups lags behind those with higher incomes and higher levels of education. For example, among those with incomes of less than $20,000 a year, 18 percent were active in offline political activities during 2008 and 8 percent active in online activities; for those earning $100,000 or more, 45 percent were active in offline and 35 in online activities.[16] However, when it comes to new forms of engagement made possible by the Internet, such as writing comments on a blog or posting political content on a social networking site, the socioeconomic gap narrows considerably.[17] If this trend continues, it suggests that growing use of Internet media for political activity may help reduce America's well-known gap in participation between the poor and the affluent.

ho Voted in 2008?

Voting rates vary substantially by age, race and ethnicity, education, and employment status. If Americans from some groups have more of a say in who gets elected, they effectively have more of a say in government and what policies get passed. In 2008, African Americans reported voting at higher rates than any other group. In virtually every election, older Americans are more likely to vote than younger Americans, and college graduates are more likely to vote than those with less education. Americans with jobs also turn out in higher numbers than the unemployed.

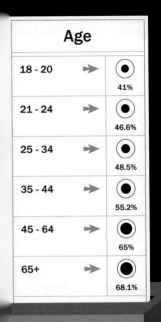

Age

18 - 20	41%
21 - 24	46.6%
25 - 34	48.5%
35 - 44	55.2%
45 - 64	65%
65+	68.1%

AGE

Race

White	66.1%
African American	64.7%
Hispanic	49.9%
Asian	47.6%

RACE

Education

8 years or less	23.4%
Some high school	42.8%
High school graduate	50.9%
Some college	65%
College graduate	73.3%

EDUCATION

Employment

Employed	60.1%
Unemployed	48.8%

MPLOYMENT

Key

Percentage of Population Reporting They Voted in 2008

Less →→→ More

for critical analysis

1. Which groups have the highest rates of voter turn Which groups have the lowest? How might this af whose interests are represented in governmer

2. Compare these statistics 2008 with Figure 8.4 sho voting patterns over time. How did turnout rates in 2008 compare with earlie elections? Among which groups did participation increase the most in 200:

J.S. Census Bureau.
reflect the percentage of voting-age U.S. citizens who reported voting in the 2008 presidential election.

African Americans

As we saw in Chapter 5, political and legal pressure and protest all played a part in the modern civil rights movement, which took off in the 1950s. The movement drew on an organizational base and network of communication rooted in black churches, the NAACP, and black colleges.

The nonviolent protest tactics adopted by local clergy members, including Rev. Martin Luther King, Jr., eventually spread across the South and brought national attention to the movement. The clergy organized into a group called the Southern Christian Leadership Conference (SCLC). Students also played a key role. The most important student organization was the Student Nonviolent Coordinating Committee (SNCC). In 1960, four black students sat down at the lunch counter of the Greensboro, North Carolina, Woolworth's department store, which like most southern establishments did not serve African Americans. Their sit-in was the first of many. Through a combination of protest, legal action, and political pressure, the civil rights movement compelled a reluctant federal government to enforce black civil and political rights.

The victories of the civil rights movement made blacks full citizens and stimulated a tremendous growth in the number of black public officials at all levels of government, as blacks exercised their newfound political rights. Yet despite these successes, racial segregation remains a fact of life in the United States, and new problems have emerged. Most troubling is the persistence of black urban poverty, now coupled with deep social and economic isolation.[18] These conditions raise new questions about African American political participation. One question concerns black political cohesion: Will blacks continue to vote as a bloc, given the sharp economic differences that now divide a large black middle class from an equally large group of deeply impoverished African Americans? A second question concerns the benefits of participation: How can political participation improve the lives of African Americans, especially of the poor?

Public opinion and voting evidence indicate that African Americans continue to vote as a bloc despite their economic differences.[19] Surveys of black voters show that blacks across the income spectrum believe that their fates are linked because of their race. This sense of shared experience and a common fate has united blacks at the polls and in politics.[20] Since the 1960s, blacks have overwhelmingly chosen Democratic candidates, and black candidates have sought election under the Democratic banner. Republican hostility to affirmative action and other programs of racial preference is likely to sharply check any large-scale black migration to the Republican Party. After Hurricane Katrina, President George W. Bush's popularity among blacks fell to new lows. The rap singer Kanye West caused a stir when he went off script at a fund-raising telethon for hurricane relief, declaring that the poor federal response to the hurricane showed that "George Bush doesn't care about black people." Despite the controversy that surrounded West's remarks, his sentiments were echoed weeks later in polls showing that only 2 percent of blacks approved of the job that President Bush was doing.

At the same time, however, the black community and its political leadership have been considerably frustrated about the benefits of loyalty to the Democratic Party. Some analysts argue that the structure of party competition makes it difficult for African Americans to win policy benefits through political participation. Because Republicans have not sought to win the black vote and Democrats take it for granted, neither party is willing to support bold measures to address the problems of poor African Americans. With Barack Obama running in 2008 as the first black major-party candidate for president, African American interest in the election

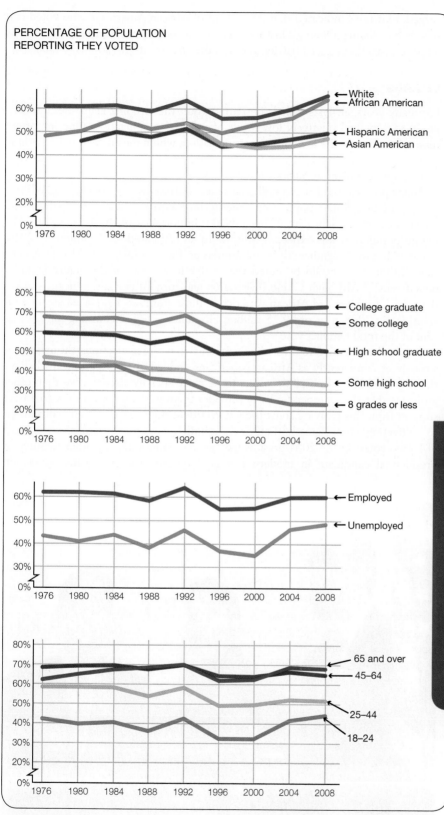

PERCENTAGE OF POPULATION
REPORTING THEY VOTED

← White
← African American

← Hispanic American
← Asian American

← College graduate

← Some college

← High school graduate

← Some high school

← 8 grades or less

← Employed

← Unemployed

→ 65 and over
← 45–64

→ 25–44

→ 18–24

FIGURE 8.4

The Percentage of Americans Who Voted, 1976–2008

Voting rates vary substantially by race and ethnicity, education, employment status, and age. Which groups have the highest rates of voter turnout? Among which groups has participation increased the most since 1992?

SOURCES: U.S. Census Bureau, "Reported Voting and Registration by Race, Hispanic Origin, Sex, and Age Groups: November 1964 to 2008"; "Reported Voting and Registration by Region, Educational Attainment, and Labor Force: November 1964 to 2008," www.census.gov (accessed 11/24/09).

surged. Exit polls indicated that 95 percent of African Americans who voted cast ballots for Obama. Obama's historic victory engendered widespread pride among all Americans that a racial barrier as old as the country itself had finally fallen.

Latinos

For many years, analysts called the Latino vote "the sleeping giant" because as a group Latinos had relatively low levels of political mobilization. One important reason for this was the low rate of naturalization, which meant that many Latinos, as noncitizens, were not eligible to vote. Among those who were eligible to vote, registration and turnout rates were relatively low.

Today political parties and politicians view Latinos as a political group of critical importance. Rapid population growth, increased political participation, and uncertain party attachment all magnify the importance of the Latino vote. The Latino population was expected to grow to an estimated 49.7 million by 2010, making Hispanics significantly more numerous, for example, than African Americans (although it should be noted that a significant part of this figure includes noncitizens).[21] Although Latino registration and turnout is still significantly lower than that of whites and African Americans, those numbers have been steadily increasing. By 2008, a record 9.75 million Hispanics voted, accounting for 7.4 percent of the total national vote.[22]

Latinos have tended to favor the Democrats in national elections, though not as strongly or consistently as African Americans. Indeed, many Republicans believe that the tendency of Hispanic voters to be more socially conservative than other groups within the Democratic Party provides them with an opportunity to attract support from this growing constituency. President Bush was especially committed to cultivating support in the Latino community, winning upward of 44 percent of Latino voters in the 2004 presidential election, more than any other Republican presidential candidate in modern history. However, the significant opposition

for critical analysis

How significant a factor was the Latino vote in the 2008 election? Why does the percent of eligible Latinos voting still lag behind that of other groups?

Latinos are a growing force in American politics but still turn out at lower rates than some other groups. In 2010, the Hispanic Republicans of Texas launched an effort to increase Latino representation in state and local politics.

among Republicans to immigration reform, along with the party's unfavorable position on an array of economic issues of concern to Hispanics, saw Latinos return to their more typical Democratic voting patterns in 2006 and 2008. Polls showed that Barack Obama won 67 percent of the Latino vote, compared to 31 percent for John McCain.

President Obama, much like his predecessor, has actively courted Hispanic voters. Nowhere was this more evident than in his nomination in May 2009 of Sonia Sotomayor to be the nation's first Latina Supreme Court Justice. The president also appointed two Latino lawmakers—Ken Salazar and Hilda Solis—to his cabinet and named a record number of Hispanics to positions within the administration. Obama's support for immigration reform and his domestic policy agenda have both attracted support from Latinos. Polling suggested, for example, that the Democratic effort to expand health insurance coverage was far more popular within the Hispanic community than the nation at large, possibly owing to the higher than average number of Latinos without insurance coverage (one survey found that 20 percent of registered Latino voters had lacked insurance coverage at some point in the preceding two years; the number among noncitizen Latinos is considered to be far higher).[23] Finally, the administration has aggressively reached out to Spanish-speaking media in an effort to connect to Latino voters: it held the first bilingual White House press briefing and partnered with Univision and Telemundo to broadcast White House events. Latino voters retained their strong allegiance to Democratic candidates in the 2010 midterm elections.[24]

Asian Americans

The diversity of national backgrounds among Asian Americans has impeded the development of group-based political power. No one national group dominates among the Asian American population. This diversity means that Asian Americans—or, to

Although Asian Americans come from diverse national backgrounds and hold diverse political opinions, efforts have been made recently to increase overall turnout among Asian American voters and increase their influence as a group. In 2008, the Center for Asian Americans United for Self-Empowerment (CAUSE) undertook a major effort to register Asian Pacific voters.

use the broader census-based category, Asian Pacific Islanders (commonly referred to as Asian Pacific Americans or APAs)—often have different political concerns stemming from their different national backgrounds and experiences in the United States. Historically, these groups have united most effectively around common issues of ethnic discrimination or anti-Asian violence in the United States. For example, discriminatory immigration policies or discrimination in access to federal mortgage policies provided a common focus in the past.

With an estimated population of 15 million in 2009, APAs are also a smaller group than whites, Hispanics, and African Americans. However, in particular states, such as California, where 33 percent of APAs live, the group has the potential to become an important political presence. Turnout rates among APAs have been generally lower than those of other groups, though they have been gradually increasing; in 2008, 47.6 percent of APAs turned out to vote, the second-highest percentage turnout since the Census began tracking APA electoral participation in 1990.[25] In terms of political orientation, APAs are a diverse group, but they have been moving, along with other minority groups, toward the Democratic Party in recent elections. Although a majority of Asian Americans voted Republican in the early 1990s, in the 2000s APAs have been voting increasingly Democratic, with 62 percent casting their ballot for Barack Obama in the 2008 presidential election, compared to just 35 percent for John McCain.[26]

In recent years there have been efforts to mobilize a more united Asian American political presence. For example, a group initially called Chinese Americans United for Self-Empowerment (CAUSE) changed its name to the Center for Asian Americans United for Self-Empowerment to reflect a panethnic identity. In 2004, CAUSE produced a thirty-second video titled "The Least Likely," which was shown on MTV. The video's title referred to the fact that Asian Pacific youth are the least likely to vote compared with other young voters. In the video, prominent Asian American actors urged Asian Pacific youth to vote. CAUSE launched a major effort to register Asian voters for the 2008 election. Since 2000, another group, called the 80–20 Initiative, has sought to mobilize Asian Americans to vote as a bloc in order to increase their political power. Since 2000, the 80–20 Initiative has endorsed Democratic candidates for president.

Women versus Men

gender gap a distinctive pattern of voting behavior reflecting the differences in views between women and men

The ongoing significance of gender issues in American politics is best exemplified by the emergence of a **gender gap**—a distinctive pattern of male and female voting decisions—in electoral politics. Although proponents of women's suffrage had expected women to make a distinctive impact on politics as soon as they won the vote, not until the 1980s did voting patterns reveal a clear difference between male and female votes. In 1980, men voted heavily for the Republican candidate, Ronald Reagan; women divided their votes between Reagan and the incumbent Democratic president, Jimmy Carter. Since that election, gender differences have emerged in congressional and state elections as well. Women tend to vote in higher numbers for Democratic candidates, whereas Republicans win more male votes. In the 2004 election, George W. Bush narrowed the gender gap substantially, winning 48 percent of the female vote.[27] By 2006 the gender gap had reappeared, with 55 percent of women voting Democratic and only 43 percent Republican.[28] As the general election got under way in 2008, observers expressed doubt about how women would vote, especially the disappointed supporters of Hillary Clinton. Republicans hoped that Governor Sarah Palin of Alaska as the vice-presidential

Women won the right to vote with the adoption of the Nineteenth Amendment in 1920, in part because many officials were convinced that women's suffrage would increase female support for American involvement in World War I. Women have generally been less likely than men to support military activities.

candidate would draw support from women. In the end, women voted strongly Democratic in 2008, with exit polls showing that 58 percent of women cast their ballots for the Obama-Biden ticket and 43 percent for the McCain-Palin ticket.

Behind these voting patterns are differing assessments of key policy issues. For one thing, more women than men take liberal positions on political issues; women are more likely than men to oppose military activities and support social spending. For example, 54 percent of women approved of the U.S. decision to send troops to Saudi Arabia in 1991, compared with 78 percent of men. The military campaign in Afghanistan was a rare exception to this pattern of gender differences: in 2001, 85 percent of women and 89 percent of men expressed support for the war in Afghanistan.[29] The gender gap returned with the war in Iraq. During the war, in 2003, 79 percent of men supported the war, compared with 65 percent of women. This split continued during the debate about when to withdraw from Iraq. In 2007, 51 percent of men stated that they were in favor of keeping troops in Iraq until civil order was restored, whereas only 35 percent of women supported keeping troops there with such an indefinite time horizon.[30] On social programs, women tend to want stronger action from government: 37 percent of men express satisfaction with the Social Security and Medicare systems, whereas only 33 percent of women do; 45 percent of men were content with the quality of public education, whereas only 39 percent of women were. Men were also more likely to be satisfied that they could get ahead through hard work, with 73 percent satisfied, but only 65 percent of women agreed.[31] It is important to note that these differences do not mean that all women vote more liberally than all men. In fact, the voting differences between women who are homemakers and women who are in the workforce are almost as large as the differences between men and women. The sharpest differences are found between married men and single women, with single women tending to take the most liberal positions.[32]

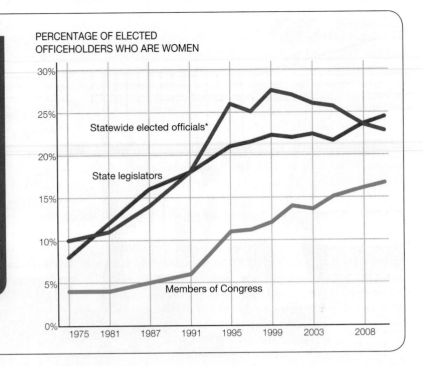

FIGURE 8.5

Increase in Number of Women in Elective Office, 1975–2010

The number of women holding elected office has always been larger in state offices than in Congress. When did the percentage of women elected to office begin to rise more rapidly?

*Governors, attorneys general, etc.

SOURCES: Cynthia Costello, Shari Miles, and Anne J. Stone, eds., *The American Woman, 2001–2002* (New York: Norton, 2002), 328; and Center for American Women and Politics, www.cawp.rutgers .edu (accessed 7/5/10).

PERCENTAGE OF ELECTED
OFFICEHOLDERS WHO ARE WOMEN

Statewide elected officials*

State legislators

Members of Congress

Another key development in gender politics in recent years is the growing number of women in political office (see Figure 8.5). Journalists dubbed 1992 the "Year of the Woman" because so many women were elected to Congress: women doubled their numbers in the House and tripled them in the Senate. By 2009, women held 17.2 percent of the seats in the House of Representatives, including that held by the first female Speaker of the House, Nancy Pelosi. That number appeared poised to drop to around 16 percent in 2011, the first decline in 30 years. A total of seventeen women served in the 100-person Senate in 2009, which represented an all-time high for an institution that had only had thirty-eight female senators in its entire history.[33] Organizations supporting female candidates have worked to encourage more women to run for office and have supported them financially. In addition to the bipartisan National Women's Political Caucus (NWPC), the Women's Campaign Fund and EMILY's List provide prochoice Democratic women with early campaign financing, which is critical to establishing electoral momentum. (The acronym of the latter group stands for Early Money Is Like Yeast.) Recent research has shown that the key to increasing the numbers of women in political office is to encourage more women to run for election. Women are disadvantaged as candidates not because they are women but because male candidates are more likely to have the advantage of incumbency.[34] Although women in public office by no means take uniform positions on policy issues, surveys show that, on the whole, female legislators are more supportive of women's rights, health care spending, and children's and family issues.[35] Recent surveys have shown that the public judges public officials differently on the basis of gender. While women are seen as better at dealing with issues such as education and health care and are viewed as more skilled in working out compromises, the public views male officials as far more capable in dealing with national security and defense, and crime and public safety.[36]

Women candidates gained special prominence in the 2008 elections, with Senator Hillary Clinton's spirited campaign for the Democratic presidential nomination and the selection of Alaska's governor Sarah Palin to run as vice president on the Republican ticket. Although neither succeeded in winning office, their campaigns marked important milestones in the road to power for women politicians. Clinton's near-miss for the Democratic presidential nomination, in particular, is likely to make it easier for women to be considered credible presidential candidates in the future.

Religious Identity and Politics

Religious identity plays an important role in American life. For some people, religious groups provide an organizational infrastructure for participating in politics around issues of special group concern. Black churches, for example, were instrumental in the civil rights movement, and black religious leaders continue to play important roles in national and local politics. Jews have also been active as a group in politics, but less through religious bodies than through a variety of social-action agencies. Such agencies include the American Jewish Congress, the American Jewish Committee, and the Anti-Defamation League.

For most of American history, religious values have been woven deeply into the fabric of public life. Public school students began the day with prayers or Bible reading; city halls displayed crèches during the Christmas season. Practices that were religiously proscribed—most notably abortion—were also forbidden under law. But over the past thirty-five years, a variety of court decisions greatly reduced this kind of religious influence on public life. In 1962, the Supreme Court ruled in *Engel v. Vitale* that prayer in public schools was unconstitutional—that government should not be in the business of sponsoring official prayers. Bible reading was prohibited the following year. By 1973, with *Roe v. Wade*, the Court had made abortion legal.[37]

These decisions drew the condemnation of many Catholic and Protestant leaders. They also helped to spawn a countermovement of religious activists seeking to roll back these decisions and to find a renewed role for religion in public life. The mobilization of religious organizations and other groups that aim to reintroduce their view of morality into public life has been one of the most significant political developments of the past two and a half decades. Some of the most divisive conflicts in politics today, such as those over abortion and gay marriage, hinge on differences over religious and moral issues. These divisions have become so significant and so broad that they now constitute a major clash of cultures with repercussions throughout the political system and across many different areas of policy.

One of the most significant elements of this new politics has been the mobilization of white evangelical Protestants into a cohesive and politically shrewd organization aligned with the Republican Party. The Moral Majority, the first broad political organization of evangelical Christians, became a notable political force in the 1980 election, when it aligned with the Republican Party, eventually backing Ronald Reagan for president. Over the next few years, evangelicals strengthened their movement by registering voters and mobilizing them with sophisticated, state-of-the-art political techniques. Their success was evident in the 1984 election, when 80 percent of evangelical Christian voters cast their ballots for Reagan. The 1988 election was a turning point in the political development of the Christian right. The televangelist Pat Robertson ran for president, and, although his candidacy was unsuccessful, his effort laid the groundwork for future political strength. Robertson's supporters gained control of some state Republican parties and won positions of power in others. With this new organizational base and sharply honed political skills, Robertson formed a new organization, the Christian Coalition. This organization became one of the most important groups in American politics during the 1990s because of its ability to reach and mobilize a large grassroots base.

President George W. Bush was closely aligned with religious conservatives. Many analysts viewed the former president's faith-based initiative, which sought to funnel government assistance to religious groups engaged in charitable work, as a way to reward conservative Christian groups for supporting his election. In fact, conservative religious groups spoke out against the initiative at first because they feared that government control would accompany federal dollars.[38]

The religious right played an important role in mobilizing voters to support George W. Bush in the 2004 election. In 2008, the religious right was less excited about the candidacy of John McCain, who had clashed with these groups during the 2000 Republican primaries. The nomination of the more socially conservative Sarah Palin as vice-presidential candidate greatly increased the enthusiasm of the religious right for the Republican ticket. Although Barack Obama sought to win this group over, exit polls showed that Democrats made only marginal gains among white evangelical Christians, who voted overwhelmingly Republican.

Age and Participation

One of the most significant patterns in political participation is the generational divide. Older people have much higher rates of participation than young people. This division is especially apparent in the different voting rates of the two groups. In the 2008 presidential elections, youth turnout was at its highest level in decades, with 51 percent of those aged eighteen to twenty-nine voting. However, this figure is still far lower than the number of older (sixty-five and over) voters who turned out: an estimated 70 percent of those voters cast ballots in 2008.[39] Moreover, in midterm elections, youth turnout has historically been extremely low. Therefore, while both groups make up a similar proportion of the population, the political voice of the elderly is typically much stronger because of their consistently higher voting rates. When the Twenty-sixth Amendment to the Constitution granted eighteen- to twenty-year-olds the right to vote in 1971, many believed this group would be a significant new voice in politics. Instead, voting participation of the young declined quite dramatically. During recent elections, a major effort to mobilize young voters reversed this downward trend.

One reason younger people vote less is that political campaigns have rarely targeted young voters. A study of political advertising in the 2000 elections found that 64 percent of campaign television advertising was directed at people over fifty. Only 14.2 percent of advertising was aimed at eighteen- to thirty-four-year-olds.[40] This creates a vicious cycle: the less political campaigns appeal to younger voters, the less likely they are to participate, and the less they participate, the less likely they will be targeted by political campaigns.

Another reason that political campaigns target older voters is that the elderly are better organized to participate than young people. The most important organization representing the elderly is AARP, which has a membership of 40 million. Although only a small fraction of the members are active in the organization, AARP's ability to mobilize many thousands of individuals to weigh in on policy proposals has made the organization one of the most powerful in Washington. Young people have no comparable organization. The United States Student Association has represented college students since the 1950s, but its numbers are much smaller and it does not have the same organizational capacity to mobilize its members as AARP. Other organizations, such as Third Millennium, have emerged to represent the voice of young people in politics. But like most advocacy organizations, these groups do not have a membership base and have little capacity to mobilize.

Since the early 1990s, several campaigns have been designed to increase the participation of young voters. Rock the Vote, which began in 1990, uses musicians and actors to urge young people to vote. It has spawned other initiatives aimed at young voters, including Rap the Vote and Rock the Vote a lo Latino. Active mobilization by such groups helped the youth vote increase in every election since 2000. Aware of the potential importance of young voters, political campaigns in the 2008 election appealed to the youth vote by turning to new technologies. Candidates posted videos on YouTube and created MySpace and Facebook pages in order to be visible in media frequented by young people. Independent mobilization efforts also sought to register and mobilize young people to vote. Older organizations joined forces with new ones to devise the best strategies for reaching young people. For example, an organization called Young Voter Strategies, which launched a major registration and get-out-the-vote drive for the 2006 midterm elections, merged with Rock the Vote in 2007 in order to mobilize young voters in 2008.[41]

The Obama campaign made young voters central to its electoral strategy. The campaign sought to increase participation of young voters through a major voter registration campaign. Although predictions of a massive youth turnout did not prove true, 22.3 million or 51 percent of eighteen- to twenty-nine-year-olds turned

At this 2008 Rock the Vote concert, musicians such as Pharrell Williams, from the band N*E*R*D, performed to support efforts to get young people to vote. Particularly since 2000, campaigns like Rock the Vote have contributed to increases in the youth vote.

out to vote, which represented a slight increase from 2004 and a big increase from the 2000 election, in which just 40 percent of young voters cast ballots.[42] Exit polls showed that 66 percent of these younger voters cast their ballots for Barack Obama.[43] Obama retained strong support among young voters in 2010, but their turnout was substantially lower.

Although young people have historically been less likely to engage in politics than older generations, they have a strong interest in community service. One recent survey found that 19 percent of young people are involved in community service projects, with numbers higher among those with college experience.[44] Another survey found that 57 percent of young people felt that they could have a role in solving the problems in their community. Yet that same survey revealed cynicism about politics, with 61 percent of young people responding that "politics is a way for the powerful to keep themselves powerful."[45]

● Explaining Political Participation

Political participation is skewed toward those with more education and more money. To understand these current patterns we must go back to a basic question: Why do people participate in politics? Simple as it seems, there are different ways to answer this question.

Socioeconomic Status

socioeconomic status status in society based on level of education, income, and occupational prestige

The first explanation for political participation points to the characteristics of individuals. One of the most important and consistent results of surveys about participation is that Americans with higher levels of education, more income, and higher-level occupations—what social scientists call higher **socioeconomic status**—participate much more in politics than do those with less education and less income. Education level alone is the strongest predictor of most kinds of participation, but income becomes important—not surprisingly—when it comes to making contributions. In addition to education and income, other individual characteristics also affect participation. For example, African Americans and Latinos are less likely to participate than are whites, although when differences in education and income are taken into account, both groups participate at the same levels or higher levels than do whites. Finally, young people are far less likely to participate in politics than are older people. The proportion of young people that vote has declined in almost every single election since 1972. The jump in the participation of young voters in the 2004 and 2006 elections was a significant exception to this downward trend.[46] As we have seen, the 2008 elections continued the trend of increased participation among young people. Even with these substantial gains over the past four years, younger people continue to vote at lower rates than older people. Exit polls conducted during the 2008 elections also indicated that more affluent voters continued to vote in greater numbers than those with lower incomes.[47]

Although they give us a picture of who participates and who does not, explanations based on individual characteristics leave many questions open. One of the biggest questions is why the relationship between education and participation—so strong in surveys—does not seem to hold true over time. As Americans have become more educated, with more people finishing high school and attending college, we would expect to see more people participating in politics. Yet participation has declined, not increased.[48] During the nineteenth century, participation in

Digital Media and the New Political Engagement

The Internet has paved the way for new forms of political activism, and the nature and definition of political participation has begun to evolve. From Youtube mash-ups to Facebook groups, citizens now have ways of participating that extend far beyond signing a petition or attending a rally.

For example, in March 2007, an online video entitled "Vote Different" became an instant viral sensation. The video was a parody mash-up of an Apple computer advertisement from 1984. In the video released in 2007, the screen projects a giant black and white image of Hillary Clinton's face, reciting a monotonous campaign speech. An athlete swinging a sledgehammer dons the Obama campaign's logo on her white tank top. After shattering the giant television screen, the spot closes with the printed text: "On January 14th, the Democratic Primary will Begin. And you'll see why 2008 won't be like '1984.'"

The creator of "Vote Different," Phil de Vellis, had no direct connection to the Obama campaign. He had made the video spot on his own, using standard editing software on his home computer, uploaded it to the Internet, and forwarded the link to a handful of political blogs. As de Vellis himself stated in a brief essay in the *Huffington Post*, "This ad was not the first citizen ad, and it will not be the last. The game has changed."

Following "Vote Different," numerous citizen-generated political mash-ups and parodies became viral hits, grabbing the attention of bloggers and mainstream journalists alike. The scantily clad "Obama Girl" sang that she had "A Crush on Obama." Artist will.i.am produced a song and video entitled "Yes We Can" that set Obama's New Hampshire primary concession speech to music. Thousands of political mash-ups made their way through cyberspace, adding to the political conversation, and potentially empowering citizens in the process. According to a 2009 report by the Pew Internet and American Life Project, these kinds of creative online political activities saw huge increases in 2008.

While the act of creating a political video or mash-up clearly requires time and political engagement, what about Twitter and Facebook? Just how participatory or political are behaviors like "tweeting" about politics or joining a political group on Facebook? While clicking to become a fan of McCain or Obama might not necessarily indicate a deeply engaged from of political activity, it is important to consider the broader potential of these social networking technologies. Facebook has the potential to connect citizens and activists to one another to help spread information in an inexpensive way. Twitter has the ability to mobilize large groups of people in collective action, by spreading breaking news and identifying key locations and events in real time. And, these digital technologies permit such interconnectivity and communication without having to rely upon corporate or state-controlled mass communication systems.

The Internet presents a potential shift in how information flows between elites and the masses—or, alternatively, between government and the people. Instead of "top-down" forms of communication designed by political parties or political campaigns, such as political ads, press events, or even mass mailings, the Internet facilitates communication between citizens and from citizens back to political candidates and parties. In this way, citizens in the online world transform from passive recipients of political information to active producers, gatherers, and disseminators of political information.

for critical analysis

1. How has the Internet made it easier for individual citizens to communicate political messages to a broad range of people? How is this form of participation different from the forms that were available to citizens in the past?

2. What do these new forms of political communication mean for candidates, politicians, and parties who may no longer have close control over political messages?

presidential elections was 20 percent higher than current levels. Moreover, politics was a much more vibrant and encompassing social activity: large numbers of people joined in parades, public meetings, and electioneering.[49] This puzzle suggests that we need to look beyond the characteristics of individuals to the larger social and political setting to understand changes in patterns of participation over time.

Civic Engagement

civic engagement a sense of concern among members of the political community about public, social, and political life, expressed through participation in social and political organizations

The social setting can affect political participation in a variety of ways. One recent study argued that participation depends on three elements: resources (including time, money, and know-how), **civic engagement** (are you concerned about public issues, and do you feel that you can make a difference?), and recruitment (are you asked to participate, especially by someone you know?).[50] Whether people have resources, feel engaged, and are recruited depends very much on their social setting—what their parents are like, whom they know, what associations they belong to. For example, in the United States, churches are one important social institution in helping to foster political participation. Through their church activities people learn the civic skills that prepare them to participate in the political world more broadly. It is often through church activities that people learn to run meetings, write newsletters, or give speeches and presentations. Churches are also an important setting for meeting people and creating networks for recruitment, since people are more likely to participate if asked by a friend or an acquaintance.

As this model suggests, if fewer people belong to social organizations, they may be less likely to participate in politics. The United States has often been called a nation of joiners because of our readiness to form local associations to address common problems. As early as the 1830s, the French political thinker and historian Alexis de Tocqueville singled out this tendency to form associations as a most distinctive American trait.[51] There is evidence, however, that Americans no longer join organizations as much as they did in the past. This declining membership raises concerns that the civic engagement that ordinary Americans once exhibited is deteriorating. These concerns are magnified by declining levels of social trust, which further contribute to the tendency to pull back from public engagement.[52] There are many possible reasons for the decline in organizational membership and social trust, and consequently in civic engagement. Television, for example, keeps people in their houses and away from meetings or other, more civic, engagements.[53] Crime can also reduce civic engagement by reducing social trust, making people suspicious and unwilling to take part in neighborhood activities.

Another way to explain the decline in civic engagement is to look at how the experiences of different generations might make them more or less oriented toward civic engagement. The generation that came of age during the Great Depression and World War II has been called the "long civic generation" because this group tends to participate in politics and associational life much more than previous or later generations. During the 1930s, people looked to government to help them with economic hardships, and in the 1940s, the same generation fought World War II, a popular war in which the entire country pulled together.[54] Later generations have not experienced such popular common causes to bring them together in the public sphere: their wars have been less popular and their great social causes more divisive. In addition, political life has seemed much less inspiring, filled with accusations of wrongdoing and constant investigations into possible scandal. Such a generational perspective makes sense because people form habits and beliefs in their early years that are very important in how they participate later in life. A generational perspective also helps explain why participation did not decline during

● Why do some
people participate
in politics while
others don't?

the twentieth century, but instead started out low in the early 1900s, rose from the 1930s through the 1960s, and then began to fall once again.

However, arguments about declining public trust and generational effects may not give enough attention to the political setting in which participation takes place. The organization of politics itself plays a key role in channeling participation in particular directions and in encouraging or discouraging people from participating. Participation depends on whether there are formal obstacles in the political system, what people think political engagement has to offer them, and, most important, whether political parties and politicians try to mobilize people into politics.

Formal Obstacles

Formal obstacles can greatly decrease participation. As we saw earlier in the chapter, in the South prior to the 1960s, the widespread use of the poll tax and other measures such as the white primary essentially deprived black Americans (and many poor whites) of the right to vote during the first part of the twentieth century. This system of legal segregation meant that black Americans in the South had few avenues for participating in politics. With the removal of these legal barriers in the 1960s, black political participation shot up, with rates of turnout approaching those of southern whites as early as 1968.[55]

Another important political factor reducing voter turnout in the United States is our nation's peculiar registration rules. In every American state but North Dakota, individuals who are eligible to vote must register with the state election board before they are actually allowed to vote. Registration requirements were introduced at the end of the nineteenth century in response to the demands of the Progressive movement. Progressives hoped to make voting more difficult both to reduce multiple voting and other forms of corruption, and to discourage immigrant and working-class voters from going to the polls. In some states, registration requirements reduced voter turnout by as much as 50 percent. Once voters are

Registration requirements make it harder to vote because voters have to plan ahead and register, rather than just showing up at the polls on election day. Some groups try to increase voting rates by getting more people registered in advance of elections.

registered, they participate at very high levels—80 to 90 percent of those registered have voted in recent elections.

Registration requirements particularly depress the participation of those with little education and low incomes because registration requires a greater degree of political involvement and interest than does the act of voting itself. To vote, a person need be concerned only with the particular election campaign at hand. Requiring individuals to register before the next election forces them to make a decision to participate on the basis of an abstract interest in the electoral process rather than a simple concern with a specific campaign. Such an abstract interest in electoral politics is largely a product of education. Those with relatively little education may become interested in political events once the issues of a particular campaign become salient, but by that time it may be too late to register. Young people tend to assign a low priority to registration even if they are well educated. Moreover, because young people tend to move more often than older people, registration requirements place a greater burden on them. As a result, personal registration requirements not only diminish the size of the electorate but also tend to create an electorate that is, on average, better educated, higher in income and social status, and composed of fewer young people, African Americans, and other minorities than the citizenry as a whole (see Figure 8.6). In Europe, there is typically no registration burden on the individual voter; voter registration is handled automatically by the government. This is one reason that voter turnout rates in Europe are higher than those in the United States.

As might be expected, in states that do not require registration (North Dakota) or that allow registration on the day of the election (Minnesota, Idaho, Maine, Montana, New Hampshire, Wisconsin, Iowa, and Wyoming), voter turnout is not only higher than average, but younger and less affluent voters turn out in larger percentages.[56] Minnesota's same-day rule played an important role in the surprise 1998 gubernatorial victory of the colorful former professional wrestler Jesse Ventura. Ventura won the votes of many young men who had not been registered until they came to the polls on Election Day. Without same-day registration, Ventura's electoral chances would have been considerably smaller.

Over the years, voter registration restrictions have been modified somewhat to make registration easier. But the removal of formal obstacles is not enough to ensure that people participate, as the example of the National Voter Registration Act passed in 1993 shows. Popularly known as the Motor Voter Act, the law aimed to increase participation by making it easier to register to vote. The cumbersome process of registering (and staying registered after moving) has often been singled out as a barrier to participation. The new law aimed to remove this obstacle by allowing people to register when they apply for a driver's license and at other public facilities. Although voter registration increased, turnout did not. An estimated 3.4 million people registered to vote as a result of the Motor Voter Act, but turnout in the 1996 election—the first presidential election held after the law went into effect—actually declined by 6 percent from that in 1992.[57] The very limited success of the Motor Voter Act suggests that people need motivation to participate, not simply the removal of barriers.

One formal obstacle to participation that has grown more important in recent years is the restriction on the voting rights of people who have committed a felony. Forty-eight states and the District of Columbia prohibit prison inmates who are serving a felony sentence from voting.[58] In thirty-six states, felons on probation or parole are not permitted to vote. There are also numerous restrictions on the voting rights of felons who have served their sentences. In eleven states, a felony record can result in a lifetime ban on voting. With the sharp rise in incarceration rates

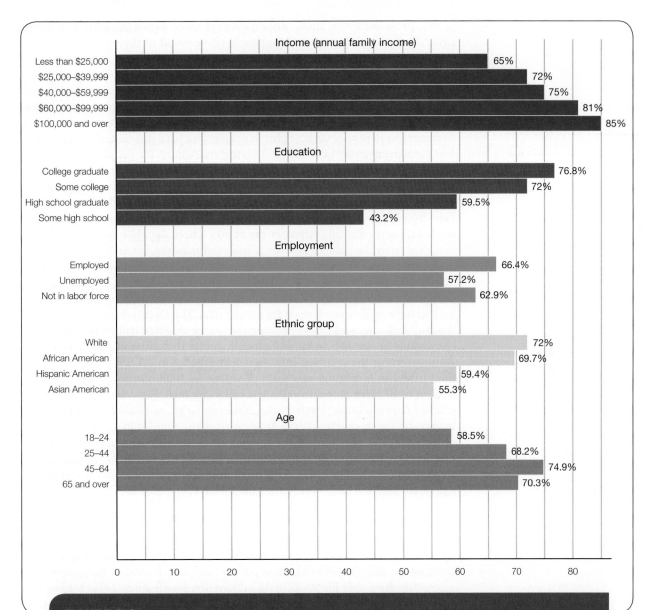

FIGURE 8.6

Voter Registration Rates by Social Group, 2008

Some political analysts argue that registration requirements depress turnout. The percentage of the population that is registered to vote varies according to education level, employment status, race and ethnicity, and age. Are people with a lower income more or less likely to register to vote? Are less educated people more or less likely to register? Would the rates of participation among these groups change if registration requirements were altered?

Sources: U.S. Census Bureau, "Reported Voting and Registration by Race, Hispanic Origin, Sex, and Age Groups: November 1964 to 2008"; "Reported Voting and Registration by Region, Educational Attainment, and Labor Force: November 1964 to 2008," www.census.gov (accessed 11/24/09); U.S. Census Bureau, "Reported Voting and Registration by Region, Educational Attainment, and Labor Force: November 1964 to 2008," www.census.gov (accessed 11/24/09); Douglass R. Hess and Jody Herman, "Representational Bias in the 2008 Electorate," November 2009, www.projectvote.org (accessed 11/21/09).

in the 1980s and 1990s, these restrictions have had a significant impact on voting rights. By one estimate, 5.3 million people (2.4 percent of the voting-age population) have lost their voting rights as a result of these restrictions. These restrictions disproportionately affect minorities because 60 percent of the prison population is black or Latino. One in eight black men cannot vote because of a criminal record. In the states that deny the vote to all ex-felons, nearly one in three black men has lost the right to vote.[59] Concern over the impact of these voting restrictions has led to campaigns to restore voting rights to people who have committed a felony. Since 1997, nineteen states have reduced voting restrictions for people with a felony record. As a consequence of these reforms, an estimated 760,000 persons regained the right to vote.[60] Such reforms may have an important impact on politics: one study showed that if all people with felony records had been allowed to vote, Al Gore would have won the 2000 election.[61] The impact of felon disenfranchisement has been especially strong in the South, where Republican candidates have benefited from the reduction in the numbers of minority voters.

Another type of formal obstacle has received less attention. In the United States, elections are held on Tuesdays, regular working days. By contrast, in most European counties, elections are held on Sundays or holidays. In some countries, such as India, polls remain open for several days. The United States has addressed this problem somewhat by expanding the use of absentee ballots and instituting early voting or voting by mail. In Colorado, a state that promotes absentee voting, 78.6 percent of the vote was cast via absentee ballot in 2008.[62] Oregon has gone the furthest in instituting new ways of voting: in 1998, Oregon voters approved a measure allowing voters to cast their ballots by mail. Early and absentee voting reached unprecedented levels in the 2008 campaign, as Democrats in particular made early voting central to their campaign strategy. One estimate put the number of early votes at one-third of the total in 2008, with Obama outperforming his Election Day totals in critical states that permitted early voting.[63] Although studies are divided on whether early voting promotes higher turnout, there is widespread agreement that the early vote helped the Obama campaign in 2008.[64]

Political Mobilization

The political setting can play an important role in motivating people to vote. When elections are closely contested, more people tend to vote. And in political settings where they think their input will make a difference, people are more likely to participate. One study of black political participation, for example, found that blacks were more likely to vote, participate in campaigns, and contact public officials in cities run by a black mayor. Their greater attention to city politics and their belief that city government is more responsive to their concerns helps to spark participation.[65]

But the most significant factor affecting participation is whether people are mobilized by parties, candidates, interest groups, and social movements. A recent comprehensive study of the decline in participation in the United States found that fully half of the drop-off could be accounted for by reduced **mobilization** efforts.[66] People are much more likely to participate when someone—preferably someone they know—asks them to get involved.

A series of experiments conducted by the political scientists Donald Green and Alan Gerber demonstrates the importance of personal contact for mobilizing voters. Evaluating the results of several get-out-the-vote drives, Gerber and Green showed that face-to-face interaction with a canvasser greatly increased the chances that the person contacted would go to the polls. They estimated that personal contact

mobilization the process by which large numbers of people are organized for a political activity

During the nineteenth century, America's political parties worked hard to mobilize voters, using everything from barbecues to bribes to get out the vote. On the day of a presidential election, hundreds of thousands of party workers handed out leaflets, knocked on doors, and even provided free transportation to those unable to get to the polls on their own.

boosted turnout by 9.8 percent. The impact of direct mail was much smaller, causing only a 0.6 percent increase in voting.[67] Impersonal calls from a phone bank had no effect on voter turnout. Green and Gerber also evaluated the impact of mobilization on young voters, studying a series of get-out-the-vote campaigns conducted near college campuses during the 2000 election. In these campaigns, phone contacts that were chattier and more informal than standard phone-bank messages increased turnout by an estimated 5 percent. Face-to-face contact again proved even more powerful, increasing turnout by 8.5 percent.[68] Recent research has shown that text messaging also has a positive impact on youth turnout. In 2008 one study showed that sending text messages to young voters on the day of a presidential primary election increased turnout by 4.6 percent; messages specifically sent on the day before the election increased turnout by 2.1 percent.[69]

In previous decades, political parties, organizations, and social movements relied on personal contact to mobilize voters. As we will see in Chapter 9, during the nineteenth century, American political party machines employed hundreds of thousands of workers to organize and mobilize voters as well as to bring them to the polls. The result was an extremely high rate of turnout, typically more than 90 percent of eligible voters.[70] But political party machines began to decline in strength in the beginning of the twentieth century and by now have, for the most part, disappeared. Without party workers to encourage them to go to the polls and even to bring them there if necessary, many eligible voters will not participate.

By the late twentieth century, political parties had become essentially fund-raising and advertising organizations rather than mobilizers of people. The experience of a Connecticut woman during the 1996 election was typical. Hoping to participate in the campaign, she sent a check to the Democratic Party and asked how she could volunteer. She subsequently received many more requests to donate money but she was never informed of any other way to become involved.[71] Interest groups

for critical analysis

Why is voter turnout so low in the United States? What are the consequences of low levels of voter turnout?

In recent elections, political parties have used a combination of old and new technologies to mobilize voters. In 2010, candidates and party activists used the Internet as a way to reach out to potential voters, and they also knocked on doors and held rallies (like this one for Florida gubernatorial candidate Rick Scott) to try to motivate likely supporters.

also reduced their efforts at direct mobilization. Although the number of interest groups grew dramatically, the connection that most interest-group members had to these groups often extended no further than their checkbook. Rather than being a means for contact by a friend or an acquaintance to take part in a political activity, belonging to an organization was likely to bring requests through the mail for donations. And rather than providing a venue for meeting new people and widening your circle of engagement, organizational membership was more likely to land your name on yet another mailing list, generating still more requests for funds. In the past, social movements, such as the labor movement in the 1930s and the civil rights movement of the 1960s, played an important role in mobilizing people into politics.

The competitiveness of national elections since 2000 has motivated both parties to build strong organizations to reach voters and turn them out on election day. The trend started in the 2002 midterm elections when Georgia Republicans built strong support through traditional door-to-door political mobilization. For the last three days before the election, they organized a "72-hour task force" of volunteers who made sure their voters went to the polls. The spectacular success of the strategy—an unexpected Republican sweep in Georgia—meant that both parties sought to deploy such strategies in future elections.

In the 2004 elections, Republicans were more successful in their organizational efforts than Democrats. Republicans built an organization with more than 1.4 million volunteers who were trained to make calls, go door-to-door to register voters, write letters to the editor in support of former president Bush, post blogs on the Web, and phone in to local radio talk shows. During the 2008 campaign, the Democrats built a more extensive organization to contact and turn out voters than did Republicans. Barack Obama's campaign made mobilization a centerpiece of its strategy from the start. Inspired by the Republican strategies of 2004 and by Obama's own experience as a community organizer, the campaign sought to build

● Why do some
people participate
in politics while
others don't?

an organized base of volunteers to go door-to-door seeking support for their candidate. Many of Obama's crucial primary victories relied on direct voter mobilization, including his initial win in Iowa and his later success in states that used the caucus system to select presidential candidates.

These victories in the primaries led the Obama campaign to build a nationwide organization of paid staff and volunteers for the general election. The expansion of the electorate through mobilization became a central pillar of the Obama strategy. The campaign opened more than 700 offices in the battleground states, where paid staff coordinated the work of tens of thousands of volunteers. The Internet played a significant role in the mobilization strategy: text messages, e-mails, and the campaign Web site made it easy for volunteers to connect with mobilization efforts, either by signing up to join a neighborhood team or by securing a list of voters to be contacted by phone. The campaign paid special attention to registering and turning out new voters—especially young voters.

The McCain campaign put less emphasis on building an organization of paid staff and volunteers. McCain's reputation as a maverick in the Republican Party meant that many of the party's core voters—who accounted for the bulk of volunteers in past elections—were not initially enthusiastic about his candidacy. The selection of Governor Sarah Palin of Alaska as the vice-presidential nominee sent a burst of energy though the party faithful, sparking a wave of volunteering. The McCain campaign fielded significant ground operations to mobilize voters in battleground states. Even so, the McCain campaign's capacity to mobilize voters remained far weaker and less extensive than that of the Democrats. Obama's significant fund-raising advantage allowed him to create a much larger field operation than McCain could support.

Analyses of the 2008 election suggested that the organization and mobilization on the part of the Democrats helped Barack Obama win the White House. By mobilizing support in places where Democrats had not seriously contended in the past, the Obama campaign expanded the electoral map. Some of the new states won by Democrats, including North Carolina, substantially increased their turnout rates. The marriage of technology, money, and field organization that the Obama campaign assembled for the 2008 campaign is sure to be imitated in future elections.

forcritical analysis

Why do efforts at direct mobilization seem to be more successful than television advertising in promoting voter turnout? How is the Internet becoming an important tool for increasing political participation?

● Thinking Critically about Political Participation and Liberty, Equality, and Democracy

Over the course of our history, as we have seen, the American political community has expanded to make our politics more closely match our fundamental values of liberty, equality, and democracy. But for much of the twentieth century, our political institutions failed to mobilize an active citizenry. The demobilized citizenry gave rise to an uneven pattern of political participation at odds with American notions of equality and democracy. Since 2000, a series of highly competitive national elections has spurred political campaigns to pay much more attention to drawing voters into the political process. At same time, new technologies—the Internet, texting, and social networking sites—have provided citizens with novel ways to learn about and engage with politics. These new media have also supplied political

Become a Voter (and More)

The 2008 elections marked a new high in youth involvement in political campaigns. From January 2008, when 65,000 young adults braved frigid temperatures to attend the Iowa caucuses, to the moment the polls closed on the night of November 4, young people participated in a broad range of campaign activities. Some young people became fully engaged, working as volunteers, knocking on doors to support their candidate and help get out the vote. For others, greater involvement meant checking candidate Web sites, signing up to receive texts, or simply paying more attention to the presidential campaign that they had in past years.

All of this activity translated into an increased presence for young people in the 2008 electorate. The 2008 election was the first time in many years in which the voting rate of young people (under thirty) increased, while that of the rest of the electorate did not grow.[a] Despite this upsurge in youth participation and voting, young people have a long way to go before they catch up to the participation rates of older voters.

If you are a citizen and eighteen years old, you are eligible to vote in all federal, state, and local elections. In most states, however, you must register to vote approx-imately thirty days before Election Day. In general, registration is fairly simple, but it does require a bit of time and effort.

- *Register.* The easiest method is to use several online resources to get you started. Various organizations such as the League of Women Voters (www.lwv.org), Rock the Vote (www.rockthevote.org), or the National Association of Secretaries of State (www.canivote.org) allow you to see the voter registration guidelines particular to your state. Most states require individuals to print out and complete a voter registration form that you must then mail to your local registrar's office, although some states ask that you complete a request for an official voter registration form that they mail to you.

- *Request an absentee ballot.* If you go to college away from home, you can choose to register to vote at school or at your "home" address. If you choose to register at your home address, you will most likely have to vote absentee, which will require an additional request for an absentee ballot. The League of Women Voters and the National Association of Secretaries of State Web sites cited above can help you find the right paperwork for your state.

- *Know where and when to vote.* Once you're registered to vote, you'll want to make sure you know where to go, when the polls are open, and what kind of identification is required of you. The League of Women Voters Web site can answer all of these questions for you.

- *Sign up to be an election judge.* Local election officials are often desperate for young poll workers to help monitor and manage polling places on Election Day. (The average age of a poll worker is seventy-two!) With a little bit of training, you can participate in this process—and get paid for your work. There is no national program, but the National Association of Secretaries of State Web site has a link that will connect you to your local offices.

- *Learn about the candidates and issues.* Deciding whom to vote for can be a difficult choice, especially when it comes to less publicized state and local races, initiatives and referendums, and the retention of judges. In some local races (such as school board elections), the candidates are not affiliated with political parties, which may make the decision even harder. However, with a little time on the Internet, you can learn a lot about the candidates and the ballot questions. Some election offices will send out sample ballots that will allow you to see ahead of time what you will be asked to vote on, including the names of various candidates. Other organizations (such as those listed in the first point above) provide information about candidates' stands on various issues. Or, armed with the candidates' names, you can check out their own Web sites. Often, local newspapers will publish a list of endorsements just prior to the election.

[a]Douglas R. Hess and Jody Herman, "Representational Bias in the 2008 Electorate," November 2009, www.projectvote.org (accessed 12/5/09).

leaders and candidates with additional avenues for reaching out to citizens. The gains in promoting participation in recent years raise three pressing questions. First, how far have these changes gone to rebalancing the skewed pattern of participation? Second, what will it take for the uptick in political engagement to gain further momentum? And finally, what is at stake for American values in the efforts to sustain the increased political engagement of the recent past?

Over the past decade, participation in elections has indeed grown. Moreover, the excitement generated by the 2008 campaign drew younger people and people of color into politics in new ways. As we have seen, participation among voters under thirty grew while that of the rest of the electorate remained stable. And, at 65 percent, African American turnout was nearly equal to that of whites for the first time in modern electoral history. Young African Americans and Latinos in particular increased their participation. These are hopeful signs for the future, since habits of participation learned early in life tend to set a pattern for lifelong political engagement. Despite these positive indications, there is still a long way to go before the imbalance participation is righted. Even with the intense mobilization that surrounded the 2008 campaign, older people voted in far greater numbers than younger people, and many more high-income voters came to the polls than did lower-income voters. Postelection analyses showed that only 54 percent of those with incomes under $25,000 a year voted in 2008, compared with 79 percent of those earning over $100,000 a year.[72]

These results indicate that the socioeconomic bias in American politics remains an important concern. What would it take to build on the increased political engagement among citizens of all backgrounds? One of the most important factors in sustaining engagement is the sense that voters, not well-off interests and individuals, can help shape what government actually does. During Obama's first year as president, many Americans felt frustrated that Wall Street appeared to benefit from the administration's efforts to shore up the economy while most Americans continued to suffer from the deep economic recession. For decades, reformers have sought to amplify the voice of ordinary Americans by limiting the role of money in politics. But the Supreme Court greatly limited the scope for reform in an important decision in 1976, when it ruled that individual contributions to candidates were a form of free speech and that it would be a curtailment of liberty to forbid such spending so long as it was not formally connected with a political campaign.[73] Many reformers remain dissatisfied with the Court's decision because they believe that allowing money to play such an important role in politics undermines political equality. Critics also do not think that restricting direct spending on candidates is a significant infringement of liberty. The Bipartisan Campaign Finance Reform Act (upheld by the Supreme Court in 2003) limited donations to parties. But because interest groups quickly created new organizations to attract funds, the law did little to reduce the importance of money in campaigns. The Supreme Court's 2010 ruling in *Citizens United v. Federal Election Commission* promised to increase the role of money in campaigns. Defending campaign spending as free speech, the court ruled that corporations and labor unions could directly spend unlimited amounts of money in favor of candidates as long as they did not coordinate with the campaign organization. The decision ensured that the role of money in politics is likely to grow larger, not smaller, in the future. (See Chapter 10 for a discussion of this reform.)

Public institutions can play an important role in helping people understand our values in practice and find acceptable balances among them. Yet there are indications that our institutions are increasingly less able to perform this role. Some

for critical analysis

As voter turnout has declined since its peak in the late 1800s, inequality in political participation has become more severe. Why are upper-income Americans more likely to be voters than lower-income Americans?

people argue that the behavior of American elites—the upper-middle class and the corporate community—has been the driving factor in the weakening of American democracy. Many American elites no longer participate in broad public institutions; instead, they send their children to private schools, obtain their medical care from generous private insurance plans, and hire private police to ensure their security. This "secession of the rich" has had damaging consequences for American democracy because these groups no longer have a stake in what happens in the public sector. Their main interest is in keeping taxes low and protecting themselves from public problems.[74] Yet clearly individuals have the right to participate as they wish and to purchase the services they think they need. But what happens when these individual choices undermine our ability to bring people together to hammer out their differences about what our values should mean in practice?

American political culture has supplied a core set of values that has helped knit together a culturally diverse nation. But the scope and meaning of these values has shifted over the course of history. In the past, these values were applied selectively, and some people were excluded from the definition of the American political community. Today, a more inclusive definition has evolved. Nonetheless, new questions about the role of our institutions in promoting political engagement and broad-based participation have emerged. We now face serious questions about what our values mean in a political system that seems irrelevant to many people and in which higher-income citizens have a disproportionately strong voice. The answers given to these questions today will shape the meaning of the American dream for future generations.

studyguide

Practice Quiz

Forms of Political Participation

1. What is the most common form of political participation? *(p. 271)*
   a) lobbying
   b) contributing money to a campaign
   c) protesting
   d) voting

2. Which of the following is not a form of political participation? *(p. 272)*
   a) volunteering in a campaign
   b) attending an abortion-rights rally
   c) contributing to the Democratic Party
   d) watching the news on television

3. Which of the following best describes the electorate in the United States before the 1820s? *(p. 275)*
   a) landowning white males over the age of twenty-one
   b) all white males
   c) all literate males
   d) "universal suffrage"

4. Women won the right to vote in _____ with the adoption of the _____ Amendment. *(p. 276)*
   a) 1791; Fifth
   b) 1868; Fourteenth
   c) 1920; Nineteenth
   d) 1971; Twenty-sixth

5. Civic education takes place during *(p. 277)*
   a) elementary school.
   b) high school.
   c) election campaigns.
   d) all of the above

6. Since 1892, voter turnout in presidential election years has *(p. 277)*
   a) been consistently higher than in years when only congressional and local elections are held.
   b) been consistently lower than in years when only congressional and local elections are held.
   c) been the same as in years when only congressional and local elections are held.
   d) consistently increased.

Who Participates, and How?

7. Which of the following is *not* an indicator of the ongoing significance of gender issues in American politics? *(pp. 284–86)*
   a) the emergence of a gender gap
   b) the decrease in the number of women holding public office
   c) the increase in the number of women holding public office
   d) the continued importance of political issues of special concern to women

8. Which of the following statements most accurately characterizes the rates of political participation among different age groups? *(p. 288)*
   a) Older people have much lower rates of participation than young people.
   b) Older people have much higher rates of participation than young people.
   c) Both older people and younger people participate in politics at extremely low rates.
   d) Both older people and younger people participate in politics at extremely high rates.

Explaining Political Participation

9. Americans who do vote are more likely to be _____ than the population as a whole. *(p. 290)*
   a) wealthy
   b) white
   c) better educated
   d) all of the above

10. A sense of concern among members of a political community about public, social, and political life, expressed through participation in social and political organizations, is referred to as *(p. 292)*
   a) political efficacy.
   b) political trust.
   c) civic engagement.
   d) political mobilization.

11. Which of the following are examples of obstacles to political participation for African Americans? *(p. 293)*
   a) mobilization and levels of civic engagement
   b) the Civil Rights Acts of 1957 and 1964
   c) poll taxes and white primaries
   d) churches and community centers

12. Which of the following factors is not currently an obstacle to voting in the United States? *(pp. 294–96)*
   a) registration requirements
   b) that elections occur on Tuesdays
   c) the restriction of voting rights for people who have committed a felony
   d) literacy tests

13. After passage of the Motor Voter Act in 1993, participation in the 1996 elections *(p. 294)*
   a) increased dramatically.
   b) increased somewhat.
   c) declined somewhat.
   d) was not affected, since few people registered to vote as a result of the act.

14. Of all the factors explaining political participation, which is the most important? *(p. 299)*
   a) the mobilization of people by political institutions
   b) socioeconomic status
   c) civic engagement
   d) level of education

Thinking Critically about Political Participation and Liberty, Equality, and Democracy

15. The "secession of the rich" refers to *(p. 302)*
   a) the growing tendency of many wealthy Americans not to vote in elections.
   b) the growing tendency of many wealthy Americans to move out of the country.
   c) the growing tendency of many wealthy Americans to refuse to pay taxes.
   d) the growing tendency of many wealthy Americans not to participate in broad public institutions such as public education.

Chapter Outline

 Find a detailed Chapter Outline on the StudySpace Web site: www.wwnorton.com/we-the-people

Key Terms

Find Flashcards to help you study these terms on the StudySpace Web site: www.wwnorton.com/we-the-people

civic engagement *(p. 292)*

gender gap *(p. 284)*

litigation *(p. 272)*

lobbying *(p. 272)*

mobilization *(p. 296)*

political participation *(p. 271)*

poll tax *(p. 275)*

protest *(p. 272)*

public relations *(p. 272)*

socioeconomic status *(p. 290)*

suffrage *(p. 274)*

turnout *(p. 277)*

For Further Reading

Crenson, Matthew A., and Benjamin Ginsberg. *Downsizing Democracy: How America Sidelined Its Citizens and Privatized Its Public.* Baltimore: Johns Hopkins University Press, 2004.

Dalton, Russell J. *The Good Citizen: How a Younger Generation Is Reshaping American Politics.* Washington, DC: Congressional Quarterly Press, 2007.

Green, Donald P., and Alan S. Gerber. *Get Out the Vote! How to Increase Voter Turnout.* Washington, DC: Brookings Institution Press, 2004.

Hahn, Hahrie. 2009. *Moved to Action: Motivation, Participation, and Inequality in American Politics.* Stanford, CA: Stanford University Press.

Manza, Jeff, and Christopher Uggen. *Locked Out: Felon Disenfranchisement and American Democracy.* New York: Oxford University Press, 2006.

Patterson, Thomas E. *The Vanishing Voter: Public Involvement in an Age of Uncertainty.* New York: Vintage, 2003.

Putnam, Robert D. *Bowling Alone: The Collapse and Revival of American Community.* New York: Simon & Schuster, 2000.

Rosenstone, Steven J., and John Mark Hansen. *Mobilization, Participation and Democracy in America.* New York: Macmillan, 1993.

Schudson, Michael. *The Good Citizen: A History of American Civic Life.* New York: Free Press, 1998.

Verba, Sidney, Kay Lehman Schlozman, and Henry Brady. *Voice and Equality: Civic Voluntarism in American Politics.* Cambridge, MA: Harvard University Press, 1995.

Zukin, Cliff, Scott Keeter, Molly Andolina, Krista Jenkins, and Michael X. Delli Carpini. *A New Engagement? Political Participation, Civic Life and the Changing American Citizen.* New York: Oxford University Press, 2006.

Recommended Web Sites

CQ MoneyLine

http://moneyline.cq.com/pml/home.do

Campaign contributions are a form of political participation that is both necessary and controversial. This Web site uses data from the Federal Election Commission (FEC) to publish the names of those who give elected officials campaign money and those who may be receiving preferential treatment.

Declare Yourself

http://declareyourself.com

Statistics on political participation show that older people are much more likely to vote than are young people. Declare Yourself is a national nonpartisan, nonprofit campaign dedicated to closing the intergenerational divide by energizing and empowering a new movement of young voters.

League of Women Voters
www.lwv.org

Established in 1920 as part of the women's suffrage movement, the League of Women Voters encourages informed and active participation in government.

Project Vote
www.projectvote.org

Since 1982, Project Vote has worked to increase the participation of low-income, minority, youth, and other marginalized and under-represented voters. The organization sponsors voter registration drives, get-out-the-vote programs, and monitors election laws across the states. As a community organizer, Barack Obama worked for Project Vote, registering voters in Chicago.

Project Vote Smart
www.votesmart.org

This nonpartisan site is dedicated to providing citizens with information on political candidates and elected officials. Here you can easily view candidates' biographical information, positions on issues, and voting records, so that you can make an informed choice on Election Day.

U.S. Census Bureau: Voting and Registration
www.census.gov/population/www/socdemo/voting.html

The U.S. Census Bureau collects statistics on voting and registration by various demographic and socioeconomic characteristics. See if you can find differences in voter turnout by race, age, sex, or socioeconomic status.

Following the 2010 elections, the Republican Party reclaimed some of the power it had lost in the 2008 elections. A new Republican majority took control of the House of Representatives, led by Representative John Boehner.

Political Parties

WHAT GOVERNMENT DOES AND WHY IT MATTERS In the United States, political parties force the government to concern itself with the needs of its citizens. Strong parties and energetic party competition make it more likely that the political system will support basic American values.

Liberty requires coherent and well-organized opposition to those in power. Political equality is enhanced when parties organize the collective political energies of those who, as individuals, might lack the resources and knowledge to compete with elites and interest groups. Democracy is promoted when parties mobilize large numbers of individuals to participate in the political arena.

Over the past 200 years, Americans' conception of political parties has changed considerably. In the early years of the Republic, parties were seen as threats to the social order. In his 1796 "Farewell Address," President George Washington warned his countrymen to shun partisan politics. Nonetheless, the party-building activities of the

focusquestions

- Why do political parties exist?
- How has the American party system changed over time?
- How are the major political parties organized?
- What groups tend to support the Republicans and Democrats?
- What is the role of parties in elections?
- How do parties influence the policies passed by government?

Jeffersonians, Jacksonians, and their successors made American politics more egalitarian and democratic. Today, political parties are a core feature of the American political system. They provide guideposts for citizens and politicians alike by helping to organize the political world and simplify complex policy debates. In Congress, parties are key in setting the terms of policy conflict; they also exercise significant influence over the votes of individual members of Congress on many important issues. Parties also play central roles in mobilizing citizens to vote and, through their competition, help to ensure that the public voice is heard in policy making.

The importance of parties in organizing congressional debate and mobilizing citizens was evident in the 2009 debate over health care. Democratic party leaders in the House of Representatives and in the Senate worked to build support among their members for a bill, forging compromises and applying pressure, where necessary. Although the bill passed the House with 84 percent support from Democrats and won all 60 Democratic votes in the Senate, crafting a compromise between the two houses of Congress presented a major challenge. With one less Democratic vote after a special election in Massachusetts, Democratic leaders had to work hard to win support of enough Democrats in the House and Senate to send a final bill to the President. The role of parties was also evident in the nearly unanimous opposition of the Republican Party to the health bills. Republican opposition stemmed from both policy and political concerns. Most Republicans preferred policy approaches that require less government regulation of the market and less public spending. As the opposition party, however, Republicans were also aware that a major policy win would likely strengthen Democrats. Republican Party leaders mobilized staunch opposition to the Democratic health reform proposals both the House and the Senate. In the end, only one Republican in the House voted for health reform. Unified Republican opposition led Senate Democratic leaders to use the reconciliation process, a procedure that requires only a majority vote to pass legislation, in order to enact their health care reform.

chapter contents

What Are Political Parties?

Political parties, like interest groups, are organizations that seek influence over government. Ordinarily, they can be distinguished from interest groups on the basis of their orientation. A party seeks to control the government by electing its members to office and thereby controlling the government's personnel. As we will see in Chapter 11, interest groups usually accept government and its personnel as givens and try to influence government policies through them.

In the United States today, the relationship between parties and government is more complex than this basic definition suggests. Political parties have been the chief points of contact between government, on the one side, and groups and forces in society, on the other. Through organized political parties, social forces can gain some control over governmental policies and personnel. Simultaneously, the government often seeks to organize and influence important groups in society through political parties. All political parties have this dual character: they are instruments through which citizens and government attempt to influence one another.

As long as political parties have existed, they have been criticized for introducing selfish, "partisan" concerns into public debate and national policy. Yet political

political parties organized groups that attempt to influence the government by electing their members to important government offices

The Democratic Party of the United States is the world's oldest political party. It can trace its history back to Thomas Jefferson's Jeffersonian Republicans and, later, to Andrew Jackson's Jacksonian Democrats. The Jacksonians expanded voter participation and ushered in the political era of the common person, as shown in this image of Jackson's inauguration celebration.

parties are extremely important to the proper functioning of a democracy. As we will see, parties expand popular political participation, promote more effective choice, and smooth the flow of public business in the Congress. Our problem in America today is not that political life is too partisan but that our parties are not strong enough to function effectively. This is one reason that America has such low levels of popular political involvement. Unfortunately, some reforms currently being implemented, such as restrictions on so-called soft money, might further erode party strength in America.

● The Two-Party System in America

two-party system a political system in which only two parties have a realistic opportunity to compete effectively for control

Although George Washington and many other leaders of his time considered partisan politics unhealthy, the **two-party system** emerged early in the history of the new Republic. Beginning with the Federalists and the Jeffersonian Republicans in the late 1780s, two major parties have dominated national politics, although which particular two parties they were has changed with the times and issues. This two-party system has culminated in today's Democrats and Republicans (see Figure 9.1).

Historically, parties form in one of two ways. The first, which could be called "internal mobilization," occurs when political conflicts break out and government officials and competing factions seek to mobilize popular support. This is precisely what happened during the early years of the American Republic. Competition in the Congress between northeastern merchants and southern agricultural factions led first the southerners and then the northeasterners to attempt to organize their supporters. The result was the foundation of America's first national parties—the Jeffersonians, whose primary base was in the South, and the Federalists, whose strength was greatest in the New England states.

The second way that parties may form, which could be called "external mobilization," takes place when a group of politicians outside government organizes popular support to win governmental power. For example, during the 1850s, a group of state politicians who opposed slavery, especially the expansion of slavery in America's territorial possessions, built what became the Republican Party by constructing party organizations and mobilizing popular support in the Northeast and West.

America's two major parties now, of course, are the Democrats and the Republicans. Both trace their roots back over 150 years to the nineteenth century and have evolved over time. Since they were formed, the two major parties have undergone significant shifts in their positions and goals, and their membership. These changes within the parties have been prompted by issues and events as well as by demographic and social developments. Parties also change as they compete with one another to win support among voters and interest groups for political office, different policies, and enduring power. Because of this, it is important to understand parties in relation to one another.

Party Systems

Historians often refer to the set of parties that are important at any given time as a nation's "party system." The most obvious feature of a party system is the number of major parties competing for power. The United States has usually had a two-party

Third Parties*
and
Independents

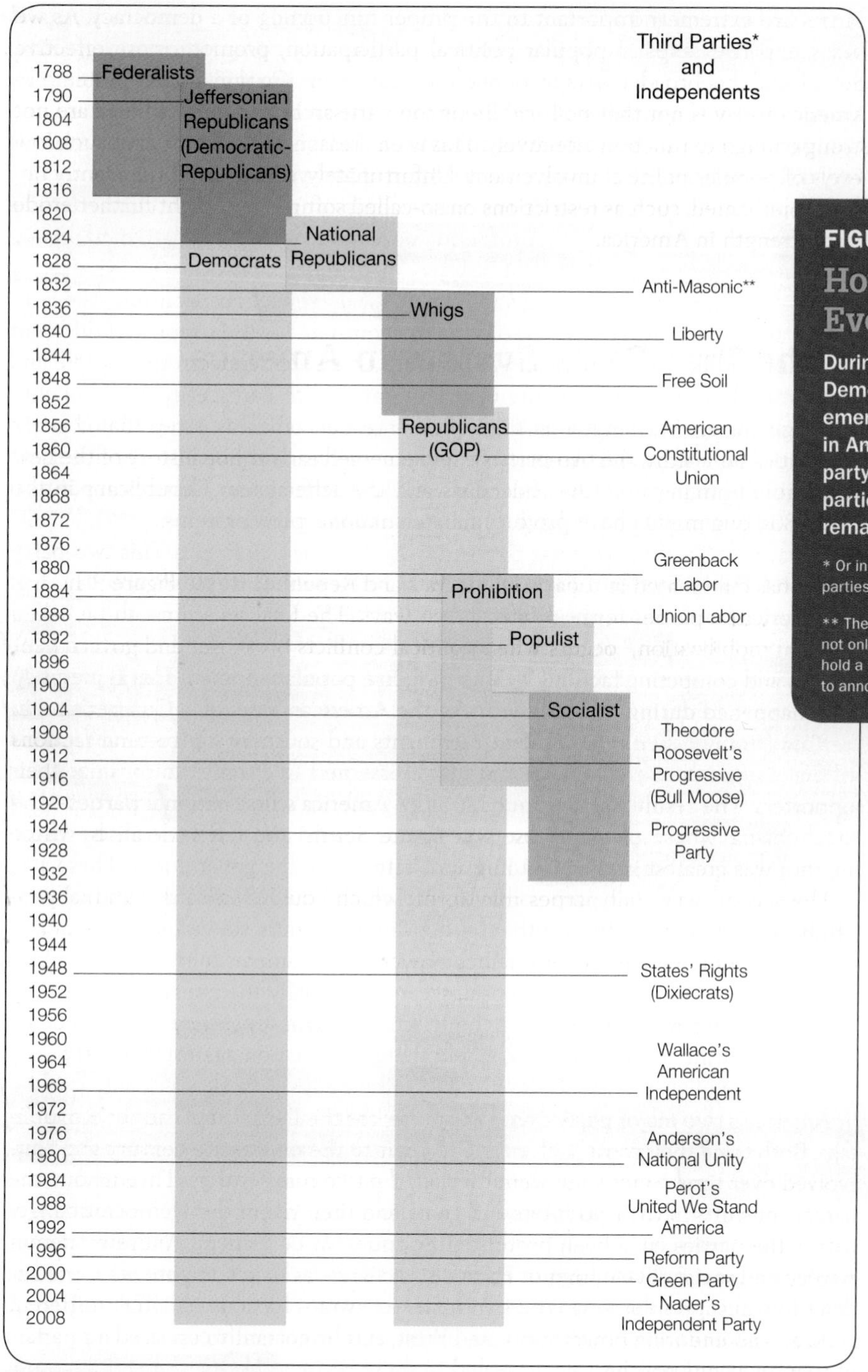

FIGURE 9.1

How the Party System Evolved

During the nineteenth century, the Democrats and the Republicans emerged as the two dominant parties in American politics. As the American party system evolved, many third parties emerged, but few of them remained in existence for very long.

* Or in some cases, fourth parties; most of these parties lasted through only one term.

** The Anti-Masonics had the distinction of being not only the first third party but also the first party to hold a national nominating convention and the first to announce a party platform.

system, meaning that only two parties have a serious chance to win national elections. Of course, we have not always had the same two parties, and, as we shall see below, minor parties often put forward candidates.

The term *party system*, however, refers to more than just the number of parties competing for power. It also includes the organization of the parties, the balance of power between and within party coalitions, the parties' social and institutional bases, and the issues and policies around which party competition is organized. Seen from this broader perspective, the character of a nation's party system can change even if the number of parties remains the same and even when the same two parties seem to be competing for power. Today's American party system is very different from the country's party system of fifty years ago, but the Democrats and Republicans continue to be the major competing forces. The character of a nation's party system can have profound consequences for the relative influences of social forces, the importance of political institutions, and even the types of issues and policies that reach the nation's political agenda. For example, the contemporary American political parties mainly compete for the support of different groups of middle-class Americans. As a result, issues that concern the middle and upper-middle classes, such as the environment, health care, retirement benefits, and taxation, are very much on the political agenda, whereas issues that concern working-class and poorer Americans, such as welfare and housing, receive short shrift from both parties.[1] Over the course of American history, changes in political forces and alignments have produced six distinctive party systems.

The First Party System: Federalists and Jeffersonian Republicans The first party system emerged in the 1790s and pitted the Federalists against the Jeffersonian Republicans. The Federalists spoke mainly for New England merchants and supported a program of protective tariffs to encourage manufacturing, assumption of the states' Revolutionary War debts, the creation of a national bank, and resumption of commercial ties with Britain. The Jeffersonians, led by southern agricultural interests, opposed these policies and instead favored free trade, the promotion of agricultural over commercial interests, and friendship with France. The Federalists sought, unsuccessfully, to use the force of law against the Jeffersonians by enacting the Alien and Sedition Acts to outlaw criticism of the government. These acts, however, proved virtually impossible to enforce, and the Jeffersonians gradually expanded their base from the South into the Middle Atlantic states. In the election of 1800, Jefferson defeated the incumbent Federalist president, John Adams, and led his party to power. Over the following years, the Federalists gradually weakened. The party disappeared altogether after the pro-British sympathies of some Federalist leaders during the War of 1812 led to charges of treason against the party.

From the collapse of the Federalists until the 1830s, America had only one political party, the Jeffersonian Republicans, who gradually came to be known as the Democrats. This period of one-party politics is sometimes known as the Era of Good Feelings to indicate the absence of party competition. Throughout this period, however, there was intense factional conflict within the Democratic Party, particularly between the supporters and opponents of General Andrew Jackson, America's great military hero of the War of 1812. Jackson's opponents united to deny him the presidency in 1824, but Jackson won elections in 1828 and 1832. Jackson's support was in the South and West, and he generally espoused a program of free trade and policies that appealed to those regions. During the 1830s, groups opposing Jackson united to form a new political force—the Whig Party—thus giving rise to the second American party system.

The Second Party System: Democrats and Whigs During the 1830s and 1840s, the Democrats and the Whigs built party organizations throughout the nation; they both sought to enlarge their bases of support by expanding the right to vote. They increased the number of eligible voters through the elimination of property restrictions and other barriers to voting—at least voting by white males. This was not the last time that party competition would pave the way for expansion of the electorate. Support for the new Whig Party was stronger in the Northeast than in the South and West and stronger among merchants than among small farmers. Hence, in some measure, the Whigs were the successors of the Federalists. Yet conflict between the two parties revolved more around personalities than policies. The Whigs were a diverse group united more by opposition to the Democrats than by agreement on programs. In 1840, the Whigs won their first presidential election under the leadership of General William Henry Harrison, a military hero known as "Old Tippecanoe." The Whig campaign carefully avoided issues—since the party could agree on almost none—and emphasized the personal qualities and heroism of the candidate. The Whigs also invested heavily in campaign rallies and entertainment to win the hearts, if not exactly the minds, of the voters. The 1840 campaign came to be called the "hard cider" campaign because of the practice of using food and especially drink to win votes.

During the late 1840s and early 1850s, conflicts over slavery produced sharp divisions within both the Whig and the Democratic parties despite the efforts of party leaders to develop compromises. By 1856, the Whig Party had all but disintegrated under the strain, and many Whig politicians and voters, along with antislavery Democrats, joined the new Republican Party, which pledged to ban slavery from the western territories. In 1860, the Republicans nominated Abraham Lincoln for the presidency. Lincoln's victory strengthened southern calls for secession from the Union and, soon thereafter, for all-out civil war.

THE REPUBLICANS IN NOMINATING CONVENTION IN THEIR WIGWAM AT, CHICAGO, MAY, 1860.

The Republican Party was formed during the 1850s as a coalition of antislavery and other forces. The party's nomination of Abraham Lincoln for the presidency at the 1860 convention sparked the secession of the South and of the Civil War.

The Civil War and Post–Civil War Party System: Republicans and Democrats

During the course of the war, President Lincoln depended heavily on Republican governors and state legislatures to raise troops, provide funding, and maintain popular support for a long and bloody military conflict. The secession of the South had stripped the Democratic Party of many of its leaders and supporters, but the Democrats remained politically competitive throughout the war and nearly won the 1864 presidential election because of war weariness on the part of the northern public. With the defeat of the Confederacy in 1865, some congressional Republicans sought to convert the South into a Republican bastion through a program of Reconstruction that enfranchised newly freed slaves. This Reconstruction program collapsed in the 1870s as a result of disagreement within the Republican Party in Congress and violent resistance to Reconstruction by southern whites. With the end of Reconstruction, the former Confederate states regained full membership in the Union and full control of their internal affairs. Throughout the South, African Americans were deprived of political rights, including the right to vote, despite post–Civil War constitutional guarantees to the contrary. The post–Civil War South was solidly Democratic in its political affiliation, and with a firm southern base, the national Democratic Party was able to confront the Republicans on a more or less equal basis. From the end of the Civil War to the 1890s, the Republican Party remained the party of the North, with strong business and middle-class support, while the Democrats were the party of the South, with support also from working-class and immigrant groups.

The System of 1896: Republicans and Democrats During the 1890s, profound and rapid social and economic changes led to the emergence of a variety of protest parties, including the Populist Party, which won the support of hundreds of thousands of voters in the South and West. The Populists appealed mainly to small farmers but also attracted western mining interests and urban workers as well. In the 1892 presidential election, the Populist Party carried four states and elected governors in eight. In 1896, the Populist Party effectively merged with the Democrats, who nominated William Jennings Bryan, a Democratic senator with pronounced Populist sympathies, for the presidency. The Republicans nominated the conservative senator William McKinley. In the ensuing campaign, northern and midwestern businesses made an all-out effort to defeat what they saw as a radical threat from the Populist-Democratic alliance. When the dust settled, the Republicans had won a resounding victory. The GOP had carried the more heavily populated northern and midwestern states and confined the Democrats to their smaller bases of support in the South and far West. For the next thirty-six years, the Republicans were the nation's majority party, carrying seven of nine presidential elections and controlling both houses of Congress in fifteen of eighteen contests. The Republican Party of this era was very much the party of American business, advocating low taxes, high tariffs on imports, and a minimum of government regulation. The Democrats were far too weak to offer much opposition. Southern Democrats, moreover, were too concerned with maintaining the region's autonomy on issues of race to challenge the Republicans on other fronts.

The New Deal Party System: Reversal of Fortune Soon after the Republican presidential candidate Herbert Hoover won the 1928 presidential election, the nation's economy collapsed. The Great Depression, which produced unprecedented economic hardship, stemmed from a variety of causes, but from the perspective of millions of Americans the Republican Party did not do enough to promote economic recovery. In 1932, Americans elected Franklin Delano Roosevelt (FDR) and a

During the 1960s, disagreements over civil rights divided the Democratic Party, as white southern Democrats objected to the civil rights policies passed by the Kennedy and Johnson administrations. Their movement away from the Democratic Party set the stage for Republican Richard Nixon's victory in the presidential election of 1968.

solidly Democratic Congress. FDR developed a program for economic recovery that he dubbed the "New Deal." Under the auspices of the New Deal, the size and reach of America's national government increased substantially. The federal government took responsibility for economic management and social welfare to an extent that was unprecedented in American history. Roosevelt designed many of his programs specifically to expand the political base of the Democratic Party. He rebuilt the party around a nucleus of unionized workers, upper-middle-class intellectuals and professionals, southern farmers, Jews, Catholics, and African Americans that revitalized the Democrats. This so-called New Deal coalition made the Democrats the nation's majority party for the next thirty-six years. Republicans groped for a response to the New Deal and often wound up supporting popular New Deal programs such as Social Security in what was sometimes derided as "me too" Republicanism.

The New Deal coalition was severely strained during the 1960s by conflicts over civil rights and the Vietnam War. The struggle over civil rights initially divided northern Democrats who supported the civil rights cause from white southern Democrats who defended the system of racial segregation. Subsequently, as the civil rights movement launched a northern campaign aimed at securing access to jobs and education and an end to racial discrimination in such realms as housing, northern Democrats also split, often along income lines. The struggle over the Vietnam War further divided the Democrats, with upper-income liberal Democrats strongly opposing the Johnson administration's decision to send U.S. forces to fight in Southeast Asia. These schisms within the Democratic Party provided an opportunity for the GOP, which returned to power in 1968 under the leadership of Richard Nixon.

The Contemporary American Party System In the 1960s, conservative Republicans argued that "me-tooism" was a recipe for continual failure and sought to reposition the GOP as a genuine alternative to the Democrats. In 1964, for example, the Republican presidential candidate Barry Goldwater, author of a book titled *The Conscience of a Conservative*, argued in favor of substantially reduced levels of taxation and spending, less government regulation of the economy, and the elimination of many federal social programs. Though Goldwater was defeated by Lyndon Johnson, the ideas he espoused continued to be major themes for the Republican Party. It took Richard Nixon's "southern strategy" to give the GOP the votes it needed to end Democratic dominance of the political process. Nixon appealed strongly to disaffected white southerners, and with the help of the independent candidate and former Alabama governor George Wallace, he sparked the shift of voters that eventually gave the once-hated "party of Lincoln" a strong position in all the states of the former Confederacy. During the 1980s, under the leadership of Ronald Reagan, Republicans added two additional important groups to their coalition. The first were religious conservatives who were offended by Democratic support for abortion and gay rights as well as alleged Democratic disdain for traditional cultural and religious values. The second were working-class whites who were drawn to Reagan's tough approach to foreign policy as well as his positions against affirmative action.

While Republicans built a political base around economic and social conservatives and white southerners, the Democratic Party maintained its support among a majority of unionized workers and upper-middle-class intellectuals and professionals. Democrats also appealed strongly to racial minorities. The 1965 Voting Rights Act had greatly increased black voter participation in the South and helped the Democratic Party retain some House and Senate seats in southern states. And whereas the GOP appealed to social conservatives, the Democrats appealed strongly to Americans concerned with abortion rights, gay rights, feminism, environmentalism, and other progressive social causes.

The Republican Party, widened its appeal in the second half of the twentieth century. Groups previously associated with the Democratic Party—particularly white blue-collar workers and white southern Democrats—have been increasingly attracted to Republican presidential candidates (for example, Dwight D. Eisenhower, Richard Nixon, Ronald Reagan, George H. W. Bush, and George W. Bush). Yet Republicans generally did not do as well at the state and local levels until the 1990s. In 1994, however, the Republican Party finally won a majority in both houses of Congress, in large part because of the party's growing strength in the South.

During the 1990s, conservative religious groups, which had been attracted to the Republican camp by its opposition to abortion and support for school prayer, made a concerted effort to expand their influence within the party. This effort led to conflict between these members of the "religious right" and more traditional "country-club" Republicans, whose major concerns were economic matters such as taxes and federal regulation of business. The coalition between these two wings won control of both houses of Congress in 1994 and was able to retain control of both houses in 1996, despite President Clinton's reelection in that year. In 2000, George W. Bush sought to unite the party's centrist and right wings behind a program of tax cuts, education reform, military strength, and family values. However, by 2006, the public's disapproval of the Bush administration and the war in Iraq led to major losses for Republicans in both houses of Congress. Campaigning during the worst financial crisis since the 1930s and burdened with a president whose approval ratings had sunk to historic lows, Republicans fared poorly in the 2008 elections. With the party in disarray, contending factions sought to redefine a strategy that would allow Republicans to regain the influence they had enjoyed in the early days of George W. Bush's presidency.

In 2008, Democrats sought to reach beyond their base by appealing to moderate voters in states that had once been Republican strongholds. After the 2008 elections, Democrats controlled the Congress as well as the presidency for the first time since 1995. Obama's post-partisan rhetoric of "one America" signaled the party's efforts to move beyond the social cleavages that had dominated politics since the 1960s. However, the continuation of sharp partisan differences in Congress signaled that intense party conflict would continue to characterize American politics.

Electoral Alignments and Realignments

The points of transition between party systems in American history are sometimes called periods of **electoral realignment**. During these periods, the electoral coalitions that support the parties and the balance of power between the parties are redefined. Figure 9.2 charts the sequence of party systems and realignments in American history. Party loyalties in contemporary America continue to be in a state of flux, as party identification among some voters has grown stronger, but the percentage of voters who declare no party loyalty remains at an all-time high.[2]

Although scholars dispute the timing of realignments, there is some agreement that five have occurred since the Founding. The first took place around 1800, when the Jeffersonian Republicans defeated the Federalists and became the dominant force in American politics. The second realignment took place in about 1828, when the Jacksonian Democrats seized control of the White House and the Congress. The third period of realignment centered on 1860. During this period, the newly founded Republican Party led by Abraham Lincoln won power, in the process destroying the Whig Party, which had been one of the nation's two major parties since the 1830s. During the fourth realignment, centered on the election of 1896, the Republicans reasserted their dominance of the national government, a dominance that had been weakening since the 1880s. The fifth realignment took place during the period 1932–36, when the Democrats, led by Franklin Delano Roosevelt, took control of the White House and Congress and, despite sporadic interruptions, maintained control of both through the 1960s. After that time, American party politics was characterized primarily by **divided government**, wherein the presidency is controlled by one party while the other party controls one or both houses of Congress.

In historical terms realignments occur when new issues, combined with economic or political crises, mobilize new voters and persuade large numbers of voters to reexamine their traditional partisan loyalties and permanently shift their support from one party to another. For example, during the 1850s, diverse regional, income, and business groups supported one of the two major parties, the Democrats or the Whigs, on the basis of their positions on various economic issues, such as internal improvements, the tariff, monetary policy, and banking. This economic alignment was shattered during the 1850s. The newly formed Republican Party campaigned on the basis of opposition to slavery and, in particular, opposition to the expansion of slavery into the territories. The issues of slavery and sectionalism produced divisions within both the Democratic and the Whig parties, ultimately leading to the dissolution of the latter, and these issues compelled voters to reexamine their partisan allegiances. Many northern voters who had supported the Whigs or the Democrats on the basis of their economic stands shifted their support to the

electoral realignment the point in history when a new party supplants the ruling party, becoming in turn the dominant political force. In the United States, this has tended to occur roughly every thirty years

divided government the condition in American government wherein the presidency is controlled by one party while the opposing party controls one or both houses of Congress

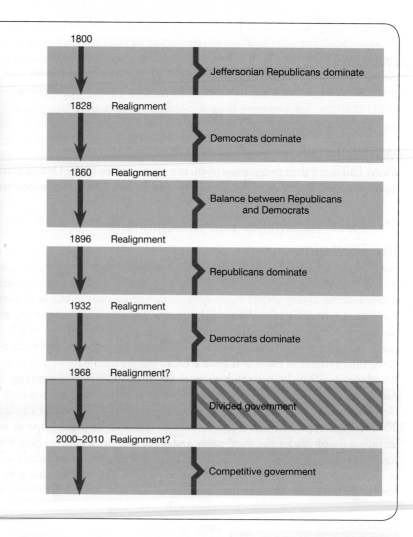

1800
Jeffersonian Republicans dominate

1828   Realignment
Democrats dominate

1860   Realignment
Balance between Republicans and Democrats

1896   Realignment
Republicans dominate

1932   Realignment
Democrats dominate

1968   Realignment?
Divided government

2000–2010 Realignment?
Competitive government

Republicans as slavery replaced tariffs and economic concerns as the central item on the nation's political agenda. Many southern Whigs shifted their support to the Democrats. The new sectional alignment of forces that emerged was solidified by the trauma of the Civil War and persisted almost to the turn of the century.

In 1896, this sectional alignment was at least partially supplanted by an alignment of political forces based on economic and cultural factors. During the economic crises of the 1880s and 1890s, the Democrats forged a coalition consisting of economically hard-pressed midwestern and southern farmers, as well as small-town and rural economic interests. These groups tended to be native-stock, fundamentalist Protestants. The Republicans, on the other hand, put together a coalition comprising most of the business community, industrial workers, and city dwellers. In the election of 1896, the Republican candidate, William McKinley, emphasizing business, industry, and urban interests, defeated the Democrat, William Jennings Bryan, who spoke for sectional interests, farmers, and fundamentalism. Republican dominance lasted until 1932.

Such periods of electoral realignment in American politics have had extremely important institutional and policy results. Realignments occur when new issue concerns, coupled with economic or political crises, weaken the established political elite and permit new groups of politicians to create coalitions of forces capable of capturing and holding the reins of governmental power. The construction of new governing coalitions during these realigning periods has effected major changes in American governmental institutions and policies. Each period of realignment was a turning point in American politics. The choices made by the national electorate during these periods have helped shape the course of American political history for the following generation.[3]

American Third Parties

Although the United States is said to have a two-party system, the country has always had more than two parties. Typically, **third parties** in the United States have represented social and economic interests that for one or another reason were not given voice by the two major parties.[4] Such parties have had a good deal of influence on ideas and elections in the United States. The Populists, a party centered in the rural areas of the West and Midwest, and the Progressives, spokesmen for the urban middle classes in the late nineteenth and early twentieth centuries, are the most important examples in the past 100 years. More recently, Ross Perot, who ran in 1992 as an independent and in 1996 as the Reform Party's nominee, impressed voters with his folksy style; he garnered almost 19 percent of the votes cast in the 1992 presidential election. Table 9.1 lists the top candidates in the presidential election of 2008, including the top third-party and independent candidates who ran. In addition to the candidates listed in Table 9.1, the Green Party, the Socialist Party, the Prohibition Party, and several other parties nominated candidates for the presidency in 2008. In order to have even any realistic chance of winning, a candidate needs to appear on the ballot in at least enough states to reach a total of 270 electoral votes. However, most of the third-party and independent candidates in 2008 did not appear on the ballot in enough states to have any hope of winning. Including Ralph Nader, the third-party and independent candidates gained no electoral votes for president, and most of them disappeared immediately after the presidential election. Third-party and independent candidacies also arise at the state and local levels. In New York, the Liberal and Conservative parties have been

> How has the American party system changed over time?

third parties parties that organize to compete against the two major American political parties

TABLE 9.1

Parties and Candidates in 2008

In the 2008 presidential election, in addition to the Democratic and Republican nominees, several candidates appeared on the ballot in one or more states.

CANDIDATE	PARTY	VOTE TOTAL*	PERCENTAGE OF VOTE*
Barack Obama	Democratic	64,629,649	53%
John McCain	Republican	56,887,996	46%
Ralph Nader	Independent	667,045	0.5%
Robert L. Barr, Jr.	Libertarian	493,987	0.4%
Charles O. Baldwin	Independent	177,690	0.1%
Alan Keyes	Independent	35,299	0%

*With 99 percent of votes tallied.

SOURCE: http://elections.foxnews.com/tracker.html (accessed 11/6/08).

on the ballot for decades. In 1998, Minnesota elected a third-party governor, the former professional wrestler Jesse Ventura. In 2002, the Green Party candidate for governor in Massachusetts, Jill Stein, may have affected the race between Mitt Romney and his Democratic rival by drawing votes away from the Democrats in a close race. And in 2006, the entertainer Kinky Friedman mounted a somewhat credible campaign, as an independent candidate for the governorship of Texas.

Although the Republican Party was only the third American political party to make itself permanent (by replacing the Whigs), other third parties have enjoyed an influence far beyond their electoral size. This was because large parts of their programs were adopted by one or both of the major parties, which sought to appeal to the voters mobilized by the new party, and so to expand their own electoral strength. The Democratic Party, for example, became a great deal more liberal when it adopted most of the Progressive program early in the twentieth century. Many socialists felt that President Roosevelt's New Deal had adopted most of their party's program, including old-age pensions, unemployment compensation, an agricultural marketing program, and laws guaranteeing workers the right to organize into unions.

This kind of influence explains the short lives of third parties. Their causes are usually eliminated when the major parties absorb their programs and draw their supporters into the mainstream. There are, of course, additional reasons for the short duration of most third parties. One is the usual limitation of their electoral support to one or two regions. Populist support, for example, was primarily midwestern. The 1948 Progressive Party, with Henry Wallace as its candidate, drew nearly half its votes from the state of New York. The American Independent Party polled nearly 10 million popular votes and forty-five electoral votes for George Wallace in 1968—the most electoral votes polled by a third-party candidate since Theodore Roosevelt. But all of Wallace's electoral votes and the majority of his popular vote came from the states of the Deep South.

Americans usually assume that only the candidates nominated by one of the two major parties have any chance of winning an election. Thus, a vote cast for a third-party or independent candidate is often seen as a vote wasted. Voters who would prefer a third-party candidate may feel compelled to vote for the major-party candidate whom they regard as the "lesser of two evils" to avoid wasting their votes in a futile gesture. Third-party candidates must struggle—usually without success—to overcome the perception that they cannot win. Thus, in 1996, many voters who favored Ross Perot gave their votes to Bob Dole or Bill Clinton on the presumption that Perot was not really electable.

Under federal election law, any minor party receiving more than 5 percent of the national presidential vote is entitled to federal funds, though considerably less than the major parties receive. The Reform Party qualified by winning 8.2 percent in 1996. Ralph Nader, the Green Party candidate in 2000, hoped to win the 5 percent of the vote that would entitle the Green Party to federal funds. Though Nader may have drawn enough liberal votes in New Hampshire and Florida to give those states—and the national election—to the GOP, hopes of achieving the 5 percent threshold were dashed. Nader, nevertheless, resumed his presidential campaign in 2004 and 2008, although he had little impact in either race. The other third-party and independent candidates who ran in 2008 fell even farther from the 5 percent mark. The Libertarian candidate, Bob Barr, running on a platform of smaller government and more individual freedom, received less than half a percentage point of the vote and just under half a million votes. The Independent candidates Charles Baldwin and Alan Keyes each received fewer than 200,000 votes in 2008.

In 2000, Ralph Nader ran as the candidate of the Green Party and won 3 percent of the vote, mainly at the expense of the Democratic candidate, Al Gore. Many observers believed that Gore would have won the 2000 election had Nader dropped out. In 2004 and 2008, Nader ran again as an independent candidate, receiving less than 1 percent of the vote.

Third parties are active not only in presidential races. During the 2002 off-year elections, third-party candidates ran for state office and for congressional seats in many states. Libertarian Party gubernatorial candidates received at least 2 percent of the vote in fifteen states, including a whopping 11 percent of the vote in Wisconsin. Green Party candidates also were active throughout the nation. Whereas the Green Party generally draws votes that might have been cast for Democrats, the Libertarians tend to be supported by individuals who might otherwise have voted for the GOP's candidate. Thus, the Libertarians' strong showing in Wisconsin helped to bring about a Democratic victory in that state in 2002. The Tea Party movement had a considerable impact on the Republican Party primaries in 2010, when Tea Party activists defeated several incumbents and candidates endorsed by Republican Party leaders. Some high profile Tea Party candidates, including Rand Paul (R. KY) then went on to win office in the 2010 midterm elections, but on the whole the Tea Party succeeded in electing only about 32 percent of their candidates. Although it took the name "Tea Party" and sponsored a national convention, the Tea Party movement is not a formal party. It is an organized challenge to incumbents by the most conservative wing of the Republican Party.[5]

As many scholars have pointed out, third-party prospects are also hampered by America's **single-member-district** plurality election system. In many other nations, several individuals can be elected to represent each legislative district. This is called a system of **multiple-member districts**. In this type of system, the candidates of weaker parties have a better chance of winning at least some seats, and voters, less concerned about wasting ballots, are usually more willing to support minor-party candidates.

Reinforcing the effects of the single-member district, the **plurality system** of voting (see Chapter 10) generally has the effect of setting what could be called a high threshold for victory. To win a plurality race, candidates usually must secure many more votes than they would need under most European systems of **proportional representation**. For example, to win an American plurality election in a single-member district where there are only two candidates, a politician must win more than 50 percent of the votes cast. To win a seat from a European multiple-member district under proportional rules, a candidate may need to win only 15 or 20 percent of the votes cast. This high American threshold discourages minor parties and encourages the various political factions that might otherwise form minor parties to minimize their differences and remain within the major-party coalitions.[6]

However, it is not strictly accurate to assert (as some scholars have) that America's single-member plurality election system is the major cause of its historical two-party pattern. All that can be said is that American election law depresses the number of parties likely to survive over long periods of time in the United States. There is nothing magical about two. Indeed, the single-member plurality system of election can also discourage second parties. After all, if one party consistently receives a large plurality of the vote, people may eventually come to see their vote *even for the second party* as a wasted effort. This happened to the Republican Party in the Deep South before World War II.

Party Organization

In the United States, **party organizations** exist at virtually every level of government (see Figure 9.3). These organizations are usually committees made up of a number of active party members. State law and party rules prescribe how such committees are constituted. Usually, committee members are elected at local party

single-member district an electorate that is allowed to select only one representative from each district; the normal method of representation in the United States

multiple-member district an electorate that selects all candidates at large from the whole district; each voter is given the number of votes equivalent to the number of seats to be filled

plurality system a type of electoral system in which, to win a seat in the parliament or other representative body, a candidate need only receive the most votes in the election, not necessarily a majority of votes cast

proportional representation a multiple-member district system that allows each political party representation in proportion to its percentage of the total vote

party organization the formal structure of a political party, including its leadership, election committees, active members, and paid staff

FIGURE 9.3
How American Parties Are Organized

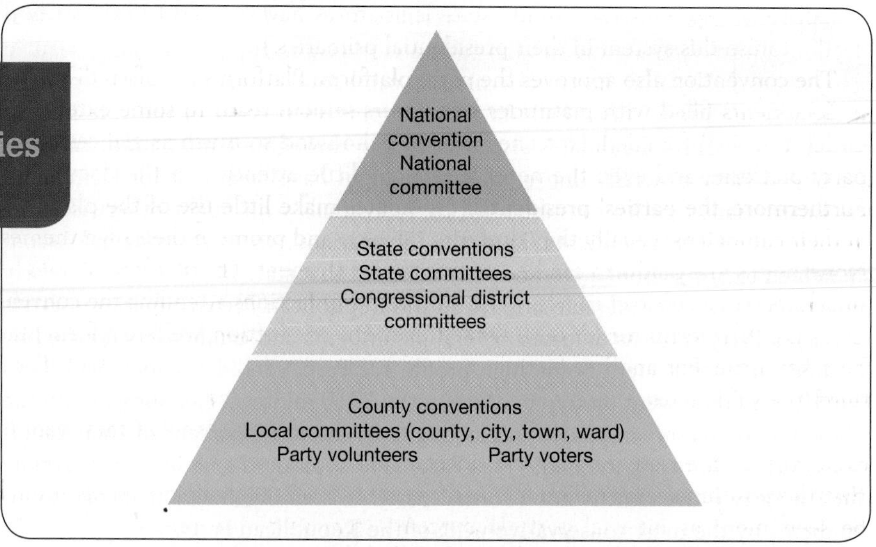

National
convention
National
committee

State conventions
State committees
Congressional district
committees

County conventions
Local committees (county, city, town, ward)
Party volunteers   Party voters

caucus (political) a normally closed meeting of a political or legislative group to select candidates, plan strategy, or make decisions regarding legislative matters

national convention a national party political institution that nominates the party's presidential and vice presidential candidates, establishes party rules, and writes and ratifies the party's platform

meetings—called **caucuses**—or as part of the regular primary election. The best-known examples of these committees are at the national level—the Democratic National Committee and the Republican National Committee.

National Convention

At the national level, the party's most important institution is the **national convention**. The convention, held every four years, is attended by delegates from each of the states; as a group, they nominate the party's presidential and vice-presidential candidates, draft the party's campaign platform for the presidential race, and approve changes in the rules and regulations governing party procedures. Before World War II, presidential nominations occupied most of the time, energy, and effort expended at the national convention. The nomination process required days of negotiation and compromise among state party leaders and often required many ballots before a nominee was selected. In recent years, however, presidential candidates have essentially nominated themselves by capturing enough delegate support in primary elections to win the official nomination on the first ballot. The actual convention has played little or no role in selecting the candidates.

The convention's other two tasks, determining the party's rules and its platform, remain important. Party rules can determine the relative influence of competing factions within the party and can also increase or decrease the party's chances for electoral success. In 1972, for example, the Democratic National Convention adopted a new set of rules favored by the party's liberal wing. Under these rules, state delegations to the Democratic convention were required to include women and members of minority groups in rough proportion to those groups' representation among the party's membership in that state. Liberals correctly calculated that women and African Americans would generally support liberal ideas and candidates. The rules also called for the use of proportional representation—a voting system liberals thought would give them an advantage by allowing the election of more women and minority delegates. (Although Republican rules do not require proportional representation, some state legislatures have moved to compel both parties to use this system in their presidential primaries.)

The convention also approves the party **platform.** Platforms are often dismissed as documents filled with platitudes that voters seldom read. To some extent this criticism is well founded. Not one voter in a thousand so much as glances at the party platform, and even the news media pay little attention to the documents. Furthermore, the parties' presidential candidates make little use of the platforms in their campaigns; usually they prefer to develop and promote their own themes. Nonetheless, the platform can be an important document. The platform should be understood as a contract in which the various party factions attending the convention state their terms for supporting the ticket. For one faction, welfare reform may be a key issue. For another faction, tax reduction may be more important. For a third, the critical issue might be deficit reduction. When one of these "planks" is included in the platform, its promoters are asserting that this is what they want in exchange for their support for the ticket, while other party factions are agreeing that the position seems reasonable and appropriate. Thus, party platforms should be seen more as internal party documents than as public pledges. The 2008 Democratic platform, for example, included a plank aimed at cities, promising to "strengthen the federal commitment to cities." Urban areas have long formed the backbone of Democratic political strength. A party plank pledging aid to cities and metropolitan areas rewards a key constituency whose enthusiastic support is crucial to a Democratic victory. Because party platforms are written more for the delegates than for ordinary voters, they tend to be less centrist than the presidential candidates themselves. A presidential candidate hoping to win over "swing" voters in addition to the party faithful has to stake out more moderate positions. Thus, the 2008 Republican platform presented more extreme views on issues like environmental regulation and the rights of same-sex couples than those of John McCain.

> **platform** a party document, written at a national convention, that contains party philosophy, principles, and positions on issues

Delegates from each state attend the party's national convention. In 2008, Democratic Party delegates from Wisconsin supported Barack Obama after he won the Wisconsin primary.

National Committee

Between conventions, each national political party is technically headed by its national committee. For the Democrats and Republicans, these are called the Democratic National Committee (DNC) and the Republican National Committee (RNC), respectively. These national committees raise campaign funds, head off factional disputes within the party, and endeavor to enhance the party's media image. The actual work of each national committee is overseen by its chairperson. Michael Steele, who became the chair of the RNC in 2009, is the former lieutenant governor of Maryland and the first African American to chair the RNC. The Democratic National Committee is chaired by Tim Kaine, a former governor of Virginia, whose bipartisan appeal fit with the new aspirations of the party to expand its base. Other committee members are generally major party contributors or fund-raisers and serve in a largely ceremonial capacity. Prior to the enactment of campaign finance reforms in 2002, during every election cycle the DNC and RNC each raised tens of millions of dollars of so-called soft money that could be used to support party candidates throughout the nation. The 2002 Bipartisan Campaign Reform Act (BCRA), sometimes known as the McCain-Feingold Act, outlawed this practice. To circumvent BCRA, however, each party has established a set of "shadow parties." These are groups nominally organized to promote and publicize political issues and, as such, can claim tax-exempt status under Section 527 of the Internal Revenue Code, which defines and provides tax-exempt status for nonprofit political advocacy groups. Such groups are sometimes called **527 committees** because of this provision of the tax code.

Under the law, 527 committees can raise and spend unlimited amounts of money as long as their activities are not coordinated with those of the formal party organizations. Although some 527 committees are actually independent, many are directed by former Republican and Democratic party officials and run shadow campaigns on behalf of the parties.[7] In the 2008 election cycle, more soft money was funneled through nonprofit organizations formed specifically to support particular candidates. This change was the result of a 2007 Supreme Court decision that overturned parts of the BCRA, allowing corporations, including nonprofits, to run issue advertisements in the days leading up to the primaries and general elections.[8] Soft money played a less prominent role in the 2008 election in part because the presidential candidates and their parties created such successful fund-raising operations. But a diverse array of outside groups, including the U.S. Chamber of Commerce, the National Rifle Association, and Defenders of Wildlife Action Fund, continued to raise and spend large sums of money on competitive congressional races. The Supreme Court's decision in the 2010 *Citizens United v. FEC* case changed the terms for campaigning in 2010. Some analysts predicted that by allowing corporations to engage in unlimited independent spending on political advertisements for candidates, the ruling could make parties and 527s less significant in future campaigns.

Whichever party controls the White House, the party's national committee chair is appointed by the president. Typically, this means that that party's national committee becomes little more than an

527 committees nonprofit independent groups that receive and disburse funds to influence the nomination, election, or defeat of candidates. Named after Section 527 of the Internal Revenue Code, which defines and grants tax-exempt status to nonprofit advocacy groups

New parties are formed in the United States every year, but few last more than one or two electoral cycles. Why do new parties tend to be so short-lived? Would our political system function better with more than two major parties?

adjunct to the White House staff. For a first-term president, the committee devotes the bulk of its energy to the reelection campaign. The national committee chair of the party not in control of the White House is selected by the committee itself and usually takes a broader view of the party's needs, raising money and performing other activities on behalf of the party's members in Congress and in the state legislatures.

Congressional Campaign Committees

Each party also forms House and Senate campaign committees to raise funds for House and Senate election campaigns. Their efforts may or may not be coordinated with the activities of the national committees. Within the party that controls the White House, the national committee and the congressional campaign committees are often rivals, since both groups are seeking donations from the same people but for different candidates: the national committee seeks funds for the presidential race, while the congressional campaign committees approach the same contributors for support for the congressional contests. In recent years, the Republican Party has attempted to coordinate the fund-raising activities of all its committees. Republicans have sought to give the GOP's national institutions the capacity to invest funds in those close congressional, state, and local races where they can do the most good. The Democrats soon followed suit. Their aggressive stance and party unity allowed them to win back Congress in 2006.

State and Local Party Organizations

Each of the two major parties has a central committee in each state. The parties traditionally also have county committees and, in some instances, state senate district committees, judicial district committees, and in the case of larger cities, citywide party committees and local assembly district "ward" committees as well. Congressional districts also may have party committees.

Some cities also have precinct committees. Precincts are not districts from which any representative is elected but instead are legally defined subdivisions of wards that are used to register voters and set up ballot boxes or voting machines. A precinct is typically composed of 300 to 600 voters. Well-organized political parties—especially the famous old machines of New York, Chicago, and Boston—provided for "precinct captains" and a fairly tight group of party members around them. Precinct captains were usually members of long standing in neighborhood party clubhouses, which were important social centers as well as places for distributing favors to constituents.[9]

During the nineteenth and early twentieth centuries, many cities, counties, and occasionally even a few states had such well-organized parties that they were called **machines** and their leaders were called "bosses." Some of the great reform movements in American history were motivated by the excessive powers and abuses of these machines and their bosses. But few, if any, machines are left today. Traditional party machines depended heavily on **patronage**, their power to control government jobs. With thousands of jobs to dispense, party bosses were able to recruit armies of political workers who, in turn, mobilized millions of voters. Today, because of civil-service reform, party leaders no longer control many positions. Nevertheless, state and local party organizations are very active in recruiting candidates and conducting voter registration drives. In addition, under current federal law, state and local party organizations can spend unlimited amounts of money on "party-building" activities such as voter registration and get-out-the-vote drives (though in some states such practices are limited by state law). As a result, for many years the

machines strong party organizations in late-nineteenth- and early-twentieth-century American cities. These machines were led by "bosses" who controlled party nominations and patronage

patronage the resources available to higher officials, usually opportunities to make partisan appointments to offices and to confer grants, licenses, or special favors to supporters

national party organizations, which had enormous fund-raising abilities but were restricted by law in how much they could spend on candidates, transferred millions of dollars to the state and local organizations. The state and local parties, in turn, spent these funds, sometimes called "**soft money**," to promote national, as well as state and local, political activities. In this process, local organizations became linked financially to the national parties and American political parties became somewhat more integrated and nationalized than ever before. At the same time, the state and local party organizations came to control large financial resources and play important roles in elections despite the collapse of the old patronage machines.[10]

The Bipartisan Campaign Reform Act (McCain-Feingold) of 2002 prohibits soft-money contributions to national, state, and local political parties for federal election activity. Critics of the act argue that it weakens political parties and strengthens interest groups, which remain free to spend as much as they wish as long as their expenditures are not formally coordinated with a candidate's own campaign. In the 2008 election cycle, soft-money groups played an important though relatively low-profile role. For example, the National Rifle Association planned to spend $40 million on advertisements and efforts to turn gun owners out to vote. The Planned Parenthood Action Fund sponsored advertisements describing the candidates' positions on reproductive issues and aimed to contact and turn out sympathetic women voters in battleground states.

● Parties and the Electorate

Party organizations are more than just organizations; they are made up of millions of rank-and-file members. Individual voters tend to develop **party identification** with one of the political parties. Although it is a psychological tie, party identification also has a rational component. Voters generally form attachments to parties that reflect their views and interests. Once those attachments are formed, however, they are likely to persist and even to be handed down to children, unless some very strong factors convince individuals that their party is no longer an appropriate object of their affections. In some sense, party identification is similar to brand loyalty in the marketplace: consumers choose a brand of automobile for its appearance or mechanical characteristics and stick with it out of loyalty, habit, and unwillingness to reexamine their choices constantly, but they may eventually change if the old brand no longer serves their interests.

Although the percentage of independents is high, most Americans continue to identify with either the Republican Party or the Democratic Party (see Figure 9.4). Party identification gives citizens a stake in election outcomes that goes beyond the particular race at hand. This is why strong party identifiers are more likely than other Americans to go to the polls and, of course, are more likely than others to support the party with which they identify. **Party activists** are drawn from the ranks of the strong identifiers. Activists are those who not only vote but also contribute their time, energy, and effort to party affairs. No party could succeed without the thousands of volunteers who undertake the mundane tasks needed to keep the organization going. Many party activists devote their time to politics because they have strong beliefs on particular policy issues. Across a range of issues, the views of party activists tend to be more extreme than the views of the party's rank-and-file voters. The views of Democratic activists are more liberal than those of Democratic voters, whereas the views of Republican activists are more conservative than those of Republican voters. One study that compared the views of party

soft money money contributed directly to political parties and other organizations for political activities that is not regulated by federal campaign spending laws; in 2002 federal law prohibited unregulated donations to national party committees

party identification an individual voter's psychological ties to one party or another

party activists partisans who contribute time, energy, and effort to support their party and its candidates

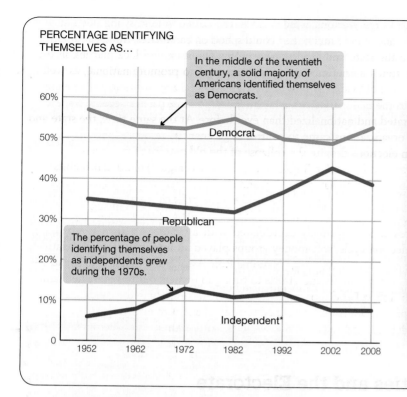

PERCENTAGE IDENTIFYING THEMSELVES AS...

In the middle of the twentieth century, a solid majority of Americans identified themselves as Democrats.

Democrat

Republican

The percentage of people identifying themselves as independents grew during the 1970s.

Independent*

1952 1962 1972 1982 1992 2002 2008

FIGURE 9.4

Americans' Party Identification, 1952–2008

Over time, the Democrats lost strength as more Americans identify themselves as Republicans and independents. Why do you think the percentage of people identifying themselves as independents grew during the 1970s?

SOURCES: 1952 to 2004: American National Election Studies; 2006–2008: Gallup.com (accessed 7/15/10). *Independents who said they leaned toward one party are counted with that party.

activists and rank-and-file voters across a range of issues found that since the 1990s, the views of Republican party activists have diverged most sharply from those of the average voter.[11]

Group Affiliations

The Democratic and Republican parties are currently America's only truly national parties. They are the only political organizations that draw support from most regions of the country and from Americans of every racial, economic, religious, and ethnic group. The two parties do not draw equal support from members of every social stratum, however. In the United States today, a variety of group characteristics are associated with party identification. These include race and ethnicity, gender, religion, class, ideology, region, and age.

Race and Ethnicity Since the 1930s and Franklin Delano Roosevelt's New Deal, African Americans have been overwhelmingly Democratic in their party identification. More than 90 percent of African Americans describe themselves as Democrats and support Democratic candidates in national, state, and local elections. In 2008, 95 percent of African Americans supported the Democratic candidate, Senator Barack Obama. Latino voters do not form a monolithic bloc, by contrast. Cuban Americans have generally leaned Republican in their party affiliations, whereas Mexican Americans favored the Democrats by a small margin. Other Latino voters, including those from Puerto Rico, have tended to be overwhelmingly Democratic. This mix of partisan preferences shifted strongly toward the Democrats in 2008, when the exit polls showed that 67 percent of Latinos supported Senator Obama, and 31 percent of Latinos voted for Senator McCain. The Latino vote is particularly important because it can help alter the electoral map. In 2008, the Latino vote in swing states such as Florida, Colorado, New Mexico, and Nevada helped bring the Democrats to victory. Asian Americans have been divided in past elections, but in 2008, 62 percent of Asian Americans voted for Barack Obama, and 35 percent voted for John McCain.

Gender Women are somewhat more likely to support Democrats, and men are somewhat more likely to support Republicans, in surveys of party affiliation. This difference is known as the **gender gap**. The gender gap has varied between 6 and 11 percent since 1992. For example, in 1992, 47 percent of women voted for Bill Clinton compared to 41 percent of men. The gap grew to 11 percent in 1996, when 54 percent of women supported Clinton and only 43 percent of men did. George W. Bush's first election, in 2000, had a sizable gender gap of 53 percent support among men and 43 percent among women. In 2004, the gender gap decreased slightly, with 55 percent of men voting for Bush compared with 48 percent of women. In 2008, the gap remained on the small side, with 56 percent of women and 49 percent of men supporting Barack Obama for president. Obama's near-majority support among men was the highest for a Democratic candidate in many years.

gender gap a distinctive pattern of voting behavior reflecting the differences in views between women and men

A large majority of evangelical Christians identify with the Republican party. In 2008, John McCain sought the support of Reverend Jerry Falwell and other Christian leaders, attempting to reassure them that the Republicans would continue to support policies they favored.

Religion Jews are among the Democratic Party's most loyal constituent groups and have been since the New Deal. Nearly 90 percent of all Jewish Americans describe themselves as Democrats. Catholics were also once a strongly pro-Democratic group but have been shifting toward the Republican Party since the 1970s, when the GOP began to focus on abortion and other social issues deemed to be important to Catholics. Protestants are more likely to identify with the Republicans than with the Democrats. Protestant fundamentalists, in particular, have been drawn to the GOP's conservative stands on social issues, such as school prayer and abortion. The importance of religious conservatives to the Republican Party became quite evident in 2001. After his victory in the November 2000 presidential election, George W. Bush announced that his administration would seek to award federal grants and contracts to religious groups. By using so-called faith-based groups as federal contractors, Bush was seeking to reward religious conservatives for their past loyalty to the GOP and to ensure that these groups would have a continuing stake in Republican success. Religious conservatives, particularly white born-again Christians, overwhelmingly supported President Bush in 2004, accounting for one-third of his votes. Almost 80 percent of white born-again Christians voted for President Bush; only 21 percent supported Kerry. Yet the 2004 election results also revealed that religiosity—as measured by frequency of attendance at religious services—had a larger impact on voting than denominational affiliation. Voters who attended religious services weekly were more likely to vote for Bush, regardless of their religion, than were voters who were less observant. In 2008 it appeared that the white evangelical vote might be somewhat more open to voting Democratic, and Barack Obama sought to appeal to this group.[12] However, exit polls showed that white evangelicals continued to vote overwhelmingly Republican, giving McCain 76 percent of their votes.

Class The patterns of class voting that emerged from the New Deal of the 1930s were simple: upper-income Americans were considerably more likely to affiliate with the Republicans, whereas lower-income Americans were far more likely to identify with the Democrats. This divide is reflected in the differences between the two parties on economic issues. In general, the Republicans support cutting taxes and social spending—positions that reflect the interests of the wealthy. The Democrats, however, favor increasing social spending, even if this requires increasing taxes—a position consistent with the interests of less-affluent Americans. These broad trends remain true today, but beginning in the 1970s, many white working class voters, concerned about "law and order" and racial liberalism, started voting Republican. Often called "Reagan Democrats" because so many voted for Reagan in the 1980s, some of these voters have remained in the Republican Party. Analysts disagree about the trend of class voting because there is no widely accepted definition of class. When the electorate is divided into thirds on the basis of income, the relationship between lower-income voters and Democratic allegiance remains strong. When class is measured by education, however, white workers without a college degree have voted heavily for Republicans in recent elections.[13]

Ideology Ideology and party identification are very closely linked. Most individuals who describe themselves as conservatives identify with the Republican Party, whereas most who call themselves liberals support the Democrats. This division has increased in recent years as the two parties have taken very different positions on social and economic issues. Before the 1970s, when party differences were more blurred, it was not uncommon to find Democratic conservatives and Republican liberals. Both of these species are rare today. Yet important differences remain among conservatives and among liberals. Economic conservatives care most about reducing government regulation and taxes. Social conservatives are concerned about social issues such as abortion and gay marriage. The Republican Party includes both groups, but at times the interests of these two kinds of conservatives conflict. Likewise, many Democrats who are economic liberals, in favor of generous social spending, are conservative when it comes to matters such as gun control.

When the leading candidates in the 2008 presidential election emerged as Hillary Clinton, a woman; Barack Obama, an African American; and John McCain, who would be the oldest American president if elected, observers questioned how the traditional affiliations of racial, gender, and age groups would play out.

Region After the 2000 election, red and blue maps appeared showing the regional distribution of the vote. Democrats, represented as "Blue America," were clustered on the coasts and the upper Midwest. Republicans, represented as "Red America," were concentrated in the Mountain West, the Southwest, and the South.

The explanations for these regional variations are complex. Between the Civil War and the 1960s, the "Solid South" was a Democratic bastion. Today the South is solidly Republican. Southern Republicanism has come about because conservative white southerners identify the Democratic Party with the civil rights movement and with liberal positions on abortion, school prayer, and other social issues. Republican strength in the South is also related to the weakness of organized labor in these regions, as well as to the dependence of the two regions on military programs supported by the Republicans. Democratic strength in the Northeast and Midwest is a function of the continuing influence of organized labor in the large cities of this region, as well as of the region's large population of minority and elderly voters, who benefit from Democratic social programs. The coastal West, especially California, shifted toward the Democrats in the 1990s, in part because of the growing importance of the Latino vote.

Age Age is another factor associated with partisanship. In 2008, the shift toward the Democratic party affected all age groups, but it was particularly strong among young voters. Polls showed that, while older voters preferred Democrats by 11–12 percent, those born after 1977 favored Democrats by 24 percent. There is nothing about a particular numerical age that leads to a particular party loyalty. Instead, individuals from the same age cohort are likely to have experienced a similar set of events during the period when their party loyalties were formed. Thus, Americans between the ages of fifty and sixty-four came of political age during the Cold War, Vietnam, and civil rights eras. Apparently among voters whose initial perceptions of politics were shaped during this period, more responded favorably to the role played by the Democrats than to the actions of the Republicans. Young people who came of age during the Bush presidency had the strongest Democratic Party identification of any age group.

Figure 9.5 indicates the relationship between party identification and a number of social criteria. Race, religion, and income seem to have the greatest influence on Americans' party affiliations. None of these social characteristics are inevitably linked to partisan identification, however. There are black Republicans, southern white Democrats, Jewish Republicans, and even an occasional conservative Democrat. The general party identifications just discussed are broad tendencies that both reflect and reinforce the issue and policy positions the two parties take in the national and local political arenas.

● Parties and Elections

Parties play an important role in the electoral process. They provide the candidates for office, get out the vote, and facilitate mass electoral choice.

Recruiting Candidates

One of the most important but least noticed party activities is the recruitment of candidates for local, state, and national office. Each election year, candidates must be found for thousands of state and local offices as well as congressional seats. Where

Who Identifies with Which Party?

Gender	Men		42%	11%	47%
	Women		34%	11%	55%
Age	18-29		33%	10%	58%
	30-49		39%	10%	50%
	50-64		38%	11%	51%
	65 and over		40%	11%	49%
Race	White		44%	10%	46%
	Black		7%	8%	86%
	Hispanic		27%	11%	62%
	All others		15%	12%	73%
Income	Under $20K		24%	12%	63%
	$20K–$29,999		32%	10%	58%
	$30K–$49,999		36%	9%	54%
	$50K–$74,999		51%	8%	41%
	$75K and over		48%	8%	45%
Region	East		34%	11%	55%
	Midwest		38%	12%	50%
	South		41%	10%	49%
	West		37%	10%	53%
Education	< High school		27%	13%	60%
	High school grad.		38%	11%	52%
	College grad.		43%	10%	47%
	Postgraduate		38%	9%	53%

Party identification varies by income, race, and gender. For example, as these statistics from 2008 show, Americans with higher incomes are significantly more likely to support the Republican Party. Women and African Americans are more likely than white men to identify with the Democratic Party.

Republican Party

Democratic Party

Independent

for critical analysis

1. How do younger Americans differ from older Americans in their party identification? How—and how much—do regions of the country differ?

2. Do you think of yourself as a Democrat, Republican, or independent? Are other Americans of your gender, age, race, region, and income level likely to share your party preference?

SOURCE: Harold W. Stanley and Richard G. Niemi, *Vital Statistics on American Politics, 2009-2010* (Washington, DC: Congressional Quarterly Press, 2009), pp. 108-9.

they do not have an incumbent running for reelection, party leaders attempt to identify strong candidates and to interest them in entering the campaign.

An ideal candidate will have an unblemished record and the capacity to raise enough money to mount a serious campaign. Party leaders are usually not willing to provide financial backing to candidates who are unable to raise substantial funds on their own. For a House seat this can mean several hundred thousand dollars; for a Senate seat a serious candidate must be able to raise several million dollars. Often, party leaders have difficulty finding attractive candidates and persuading them to run. Candidate recruitment is problematic in an era when political campaigns often involve mudslinging, and candidates must assume that their personal lives will be intensely scrutinized in the press.[14]

Nominations

Article I, Section 4, of the Constitution makes only a few provisions for elections. It delegates to the states the power to set the "times, places, and manner" of holding elections, even for U.S. senators and representatives. It does, however, reserve to Congress the power to make such laws if it chooses to do so. The Constitution has been amended from time to time to expand the right to participate in elections. Congress has also occasionally passed laws about elections, congressional districting, and campaign practices. But the Constitution and the laws are almost completely silent on nominations, setting only citizenship and age requirements for candidates. The president must be at least thirty-five years of age, a native-born citizen, and a resident of the United States for fourteen years. A senator must be at least thirty, a U.S. citizen for at least nine years, and a resident of the state he or she represents. A member of the House must be at least twenty-five, a U.S. citizen for seven years, and a resident of the state he or she represents.

nomination the process by which political parties select their candidates for election to public office

Nomination is the process by which a party selects a single candidate to run for each elective office. The nominating process can precede the election by many months, as it does when the many candidates for the presidency are eliminated from consideration through a grueling series of debates and state primaries until there is only one survivor in each party—the party's nominee.

When more than one person aspires to an office, the choice can divide friends and associates. In comparison to such an internal dispute, the electoral campaign against the opposition is almost fun, because there the fight is against the declared adversaries.

Getting Out the Vote

The actual election period begins immediately after the nominations. Throughout American history, this has been a time of glory for the political parties, whose popular base of support is fully displayed. All the paraphernalia of party committees and all the committee members are activated into local party workforces.

The first step in the electoral process involves voter registration. This aspect of the process takes place all year round. There was a time when party workers were responsible for virtually all of this kind of electoral activity, but they have been supplemented (and in many states virtually displaced) by civic groups such as the League of Women Voters, unions, and chambers of commerce.

Those who have registered have to decide on Election Day if they will actually go to the polling place, stand in line, and vote for the various candidates and referenda on the ballot. If they are voting by mail in one of the states that allows this, they have to request the ballot, fill it out, and return it. Political parties, candidates, and campaigning can make a big difference in convincing voters to vote. In recent years, each of the two major parties has developed extensive data files on hundreds of millions of potential voters. The GOP has called its archive "Voter Vault," while the Democratic file was originally called "Demzilla" and later "VoteBuilder," created by a private software company called Voter Activation Network. In the mid-2000s, the Democratic National Committee began to use this state-of-the-art Web-based system for collecting and sharing voter information in a bid to compete with the technologically sophisticated Republicans. In the 2008 election, the DNC made the voter file available to state parties, and this technology became one of the keys to the successful mobilization and get-out-the-vote activities of Democrats in 2008. These elaborate data files allow the two parties to bring their search for votes, contributions, and campaign help down to named individuals. Voter mobilization, once an art, has now become a science.

Facilitating Voter Choice

On any general-election ballot, there are likely to be only two or three candidacies where the nature of the office and the characteristics and positions of the candidates are well known to voters. But what about the choices for judges, the state comptroller, the state attorney general, and many other elective positions? And what about referenda? This method of making policy choices is being used more and more as a means of direct democracy. A referendum may ask: Should there be a new bond issue for financing the local schools? Should there be an amendment to the state constitution to increase the number of county judges? In 1996, Californians approved Proposition 209, a referendum that called for an end

Party affiliations help voters decide whom and what to vote for when they are unfamiliar with all of the candidates and issues. Parties provide information directly through voter guides and materials campaign, such as yard signs.

to most statewide affirmative action programs, including those employed for college admission. Another famous proposition, on the 1978 California ballot, was a referendum to reduce local property taxes. It started a taxpayer revolt that spread to many other states. By the time the revolt had spread, most voters knew where they stood on the issue. But the typical referendum question is one on which few voters have clear and knowledgeable positions. Parties and campaigns help by providing information when voters must choose among obscure candidates and vote on unclear referenda.

● Parties and Government

When the dust of the campaign has settled, does it matter which party has won? It does. Especially when the parties are sharply divided ideologically, as they have been in recent years, the party that controls government can make significant changes by moving policy in new directions.

Parties and Policy

One of the most familiar complaints about American politics is that the two major parties try to be all things to all people and are therefore indistinguishable from each other. Data and experience give some support to this observation. Parties in the United States are not programmatic or ideological, as they have sometimes been in Britain or other parts of Europe. But this does not mean there are no differences between them. Since the 1980s, important differences have emerged between the positions of Democratic and Republican party leaders on a number of key issues, and these differences are still apparent today. For example, the national leadership of the Republican Party supports maintaining high levels of military spending, cuts in social programs, tax relief for middle- and upper-income voters, tax incentives for businesses, and the "social agenda" backed by members of conservative religious denominations. The national Democratic leadership, on the other hand, supports expanded social welfare spending, cuts in military spending, increased regulation of business, and a variety of consumer and environmental programs.

These differences reflect differences in philosophy and differences in the core constituencies to which the parties seek to appeal. The Democratic Party at the national level seeks to unite organized labor, the poor, members of racial minorities, and liberal upper-middle-class professionals. The Republicans, by contrast, appeal to business, upper-middle- and upper-class groups in the private sector, white working-class voters, and social conservatives. Often, party leaders will seek to develop issues they hope will add new groups to their party's constituent base. During the 1980s, for example, under the leadership of Ronald Reagan, the Republicans devised a series of "social issues," including support for school prayer, opposition to abortion, and opposition to affirmative action, designed to cultivate the support of white southerners. This effort was extremely successful in increasing Republican strength in the once solidly Democratic South. In the 1990s, under the leadership of Bill Clinton, who called himself a "new Democrat," the Democratic Party sought to develop new social programs designed to solidify the party's base among working-class and poor voters, and new, somewhat more conservative economic programs aimed at attracting the votes of middle- and upper-middle-class voters. In 2000, George W. Bush labeled himself a "compassionate conservative"

Partisanship in the Media

Although partisan media figures like Rush Limbaugh and Michael Moore have no formal relationships with the Republican or Democratic parties, they often play a significant role in mobilizing party supporters. Strongly partisan media serve a useful function for the political parties, because while they speak to the party's base, party leaders can maintain a distance from polarizing figures such as Limbaugh and Moore and focus on appealing to people toward the middle of the political spectrum.

The conservative political talk radio host Rush Limbaugh began his career in 1988, soon after the Federal Communications Commission rescinded the Fairness Doctrine, allowing radio stations to air opinion commentary without giving equal attention to the opposing point of view. Limbaugh earned notoriety for his unapologetic criticism of liberal fiscal and social policies, and his colorful insults. Throughout the 1990s, *The Rush Limbaugh Show* grew in popularity and soon attracted the largest number of talk radio listeners in the country.

In 1996, the comedian and political satirist Al Franken wrote a book titled *Rush Limbaugh Is a Big Fat Idiot and Other Observations,* in which he criticized Limbaugh and Republican political leaders. In 2003, Franken published another sa-

tirical book, *Lies and the Lying Liars Who Tell Them: A Fair and Balanced Look at the Right,* that caused a legal battle with Fox News. In 2004, Franken became one of the founders of the Air America Radio Network, airing news and satire from a progressive liberal perspective. He is now a U.S. senator from Minnesota.

In 2004, the filmmaker Michael Moore released his controversial documentary *Fahrenheit 9/11,* which criticized the Bush administration's response to the terrorist attacks of September 11. By the end of the film's first day in theaters, *Fahrenheit 9/11* was the top-grossing documentary in the nation's history. However, many accused the filmmaker of creating an unfair and inaccurate portrayal of the administration's policies, and some theater owners refused to show the documentary.[a]

The question often asked about strongly partisan programs, books, and films is, "Do these messages persuade the public?" Because their audiences tend to favor the creator's point of view in the first place, the persuasive power of overtly partisan media is limited. A study by the National Annenberg Election Survey found that the audiences of Rush Limbaugh's talk radio show and Michael Moore's documentary were about equivalent in size and about as far

apart as they could be in terms of public opinion regarding George W. Bush, the Iraq war, and whether or not the country was moving "in the right direction." As the survey's director Kathleen Jamieson explained, "One-sided partisan communication tends to attract an audience of believers and reinforces their beliefs rather than change their minds."[b]

The legal scholar Cass Sunstein argues that the rise of such fragmented media may have negative consequences for the health of the democracy.

As digital media expand Americans' content options, it will become easier for citizens to see and hear only the topics and points of view that they favor. Partisan media is not a negative in and of itself. If people listen to Rush Limbaugh in the morning and watch Rachel Maddow in the evening, they might obtain the conservative and liberal perspectives, which could thwart the polarization effect. But how many liberals are listening to Limbaugh? How many conservatives are watching Maddow?

[a]"Less Moore, *Fahrenheit 9/11* in Iowa," *Chicago Sun-Times,* July 5, 2004.
[b]National Annenberg Election Survey, "*Fahrenheit 9/11* Viewers and Limbaugh Listeners about Equal in Size Even Though They Perceive Two Different Nations, Annenberg Data Show," press release, August 3, 2004, www.annenbergpublicpolicycenter.org

for critical analysis

1. If tuning in to partisan media that favors our preexisting opinions is bad for society, what is the answer? Should writers and producers be required to include opposing points of view?

2. Party leaders tend to distance themselves from highly partisan media figures, even as they rely on them to help maintain the support of their base. Why?

to signal the Republican base that he was a conservative while seeking to reassure moderate and independent voters that he was not an opponent of federal social programs.

As these examples suggest, parties do not always support policies just because their constituents already favor those policies. Instead, party leaders can play the role of **policy entrepreneurs**, seeking ideas and programs that will expand their party's base of support while eroding that of the opposition. It is one of the essential characteristics of party politics in America that a party's programs and policies often lead, rather than follow, public opinion. Like their counterparts in the business world, party leaders seek to identify and develop "products" (programs and policies) that will appeal to the public. The public, of course, has the ultimate voice. With its votes it decides whether or not to "buy" new policy offerings.

Thus, for example, in 2010 many Republican congressional candidates vowed to repeal the major health care reform act signed by President Obama earlier in the year.

Parties in Congress

The ultimate test of the party system is its relationship to and influence on the institutions of government. Congress, in particular, depends more on the party system than is generally recognized. For one thing, the speakership of the House is essentially a party office. All the members of the House take part in the election of the Speaker. But the actual selection is made by the **majority party**, that is, the party that holds a majority of seats in the House. (The other party is known as the **minority party**.) When the majority-party caucus presents a nominee to the entire House, its choice is then invariably ratified in a straight vote along party lines.

The committee system of both houses of Congress is also a product of the two-party system. Although the whole membership adopts the rules that organize committees and the rules that define the jurisdiction of each like ordinary legislation, parties shape all other features of the committees. For example, each party is assigned a quota of members for each committee, depending on the percentage of total seats held by the party. On the rare occasions when an independent or third-party candidate is elected, the leaders of the two parties must agree against whose quota this member's committee assignments will count. Presumably the member will not be able to serve on any committee until the question of quota is settled.

As we shall see in Chapter 12, the assignment of individual members to committees is a party decision. Each party has a "committee on committees" to make such decisions. Granting permission to transfer to another committee is also a party decision. Moreover, advancement up the committee ladder toward the chair is a party decision. Since the late nineteenth century, most advancements have been automatic—based on the length of continual service on the committee. This seniority system has existed only because of the support of the two parties, however, and either party can depart from it by a simple vote. During the 1970s, both parties reinstituted the practice of reviewing each chair—voting anew every two years on whether the same person would continue to hold each committee's chair. In their 1994 campaign document, the "Contract with America," House Republican candidates pledged to limit committee and subcommittee chairs to three two-year terms if the GOP won control of Congress. For years, Republicans had argued that entrenched Democratic committee chairs had become powerful, arrogant, and indifferent to the popular will. When Republicans took control of Congress in 1994, they reaffirmed their pledge to limit the terms of committee and subcommittee chairs. As they approached the 2000 congressional elections, however, some GOP leaders came to regret the commitment they had made six years earlier. However, in 2001, Republicans lived up to their 1995 pledge to limit House committee chairs to three terms. Incumbent chairmen were forced to step down but were generally replaced by the most senior Republican member of each committee.

The continuing importance of parties in Congress became especially evident in the months after the Republicans won control of Congress in 1994. The Republican leadership was able to maintain nearly unanimous support among party members on vote after vote as it sought to implement the GOP's legislative agenda. Democrats were rarely able to match the strong party discipline of Republicans in Congress. After 2006, however, when Democrats won back the Congress, they showed considerably more party discipline than they had in past decades. After Obama's election, Republican members of Congress also showed remarkable party discipline in rejecting the President's major initiatives ranging from the economic stimulus to the major health care act.

President and Party

As we saw earlier, the party that wins the White House is always led, in title anyway, by the president. The president normally depends on fellow party members in Congress to support his legislative initiatives. At the same time, members of the party in Congress hope that the president's programs and personal prestige will help them raise campaign funds and secure reelection. Strong presidents with broad popular support can depend on party ties to enact their legislation in Congress. These presidents also dominate the party apparatus so that it promotes their legislative agenda. Yet there has been a trade-off in using the party machinery to support the president's legislative agenda and building it to support the party in congressional elections. The political scientist Daniel Galvin argues that since the Eisenhower presidency, Republicans have paid much more attention to party building than Democrats.[15] Given their minority status in the electorate for much of the past fifty years, Republican presidents sought to enhance the party's capabilities to mobilize voters and win elections. George W. Bush's adviser Karl Rove hoped to build a strong party apparatus that would ensure a permanent Republican majority. Democratic presidents put much less energy into building the party apparatus, focusing instead on their legislative agenda and their own reelection. It was only after the 2004 election defeat that Democrats began to pour their energies into building a stronger party. Under the chairmanship of Howard Dean, a previous presidential candidate and a former Vermont governor, the Democratic National Committee invested heavily in new technology and in creating party mobilizing capabilities in states across the country, not just the traditionally "blue" states that reliably voted Democratic.

The Obama campaign benefited from this period of intense capacity building and used this party machinery as a springboard for its own mobilizing organization, Obama for America. With detailed information about Democratic Party activists, Obama for America's database became an important political resource for the mobilizing capacities of the Democratic Party. After Obama took office, the organization was renamed Organizing for America (OFA) and became an independent project of the Democratic National Committee. During Obama's first year in office, the president used Organizing for America to mobilize grassroots support for his legislative agenda. As we saw in the introduction, OFA took a very active part in lobbying members of Congress to support health care reform. Organizing for America provides training for volunteers to learn how to become organizers and it has established offices in nearly every state.

Political Parties and the World

Few Americans are aware of the international involvements of our two major political parties. Since the mid-1980s each political party has been associated with a formal foreign policy institute. The International Republican Institute (IRI) was founded in 1983, and the National Democratic Institute for International Affairs (NDI) was established in 1985. Each party's institute is led by a cadre of the party's former officials and elected officeholders.

Both the IRI and the NDI work to encourage citizen participation and democracy throughout the world, particularly in regions that lack a historical and institutional base for democratic politics. Both party institutes work with local politicians, civic leaders, and community activists to encourage understanding of democratic political techniques and respect for democratic values.

Although the programs of the party institutes have many similarities, they diverge in ways that reflect the differences between the two American political parties. NDI programs pay special attention to women and young people—groups cultivated by the Democratic Party in

the United States—and to trade unions, another bulwark of the U.S. Democratic Party. Thus, for example, an NDI program in Senegal was designed to increase the involvement of women in local government and in the leadership of the nation's political parties.

The IRI, for its part, has emphasized cultivating relationships with government officials and business leaders, and whereas the NDI's approach is decidedly grassroots in character, the IRI, like the Republican Party, emphasizes political technology. For example, in Macedonia, the IRI has taught public officials the elements of media relations, public-opinion polling, and "message development." Differences are also evident

in which countries each institute emphasizes. For example, the IRI pays special attention to the issue of democracy in Cuba, reflecting the significance of the Cuban American vote to the Republican Party.

Although promoting democracy sounds uncontroversial, intervention into the affairs of other countries can lead to results that are anything but democratic. The case of the IRI's activities in Haiti provide an example. A 2006 investigative article in the *New York Times* charged that the IRI deliberately worked to destabilize democracy in Haiti in 2003–04.[a] At the time, Haiti was in a political crisis, with two opposing sides seeking to reach a political reconciliation. According to interviews and public records, the IRI's representative in Haiti provided one-sided support to the opponents of the elected president, Bertrand Aristide. Aristide was a controversial leader who was seen as a voice for Haiti's poor. Although the U.S. ambassador to Haiti at the time protested the involvement of the IRI, the group continued to operate with little accountability. Aristide's opponents launched a coup in 2004, sending the country into chaos for years to come.

Despite criticism, the IRI has grown and in 2008 employed 400 people working on democracy projects in seventy countries.[b]

[a]Walt Bogdanich and Jenny Nordberg, "Mixed U. S. Signals Helped Tilt Haiti toward Chaos," *New York Times*, January 29, 2006, p. 1.
[b]Mike McIntire, "Democracy Group Gives Donors Access to McCain," *New York Times*, July 28, 2008, p. A1.

for critical analysis

1. What are the similarities and differences between the NDI and the IRI? Do these parallel the similarities and differences between the Democratic and Republican parties?

2. How can Americans ensure that the activities of groups such as the IRI and NDI are accountable to the taxpayers who fund them?

Thinking Critically about the Role of Parties in a Democracy

Americans often express frustration with party conflict. Many voters were attracted to Barack Obama's appeal as a "postpartisan" candidate who would bring the country together. Some expressed disappointment when party conflict continued to characterize policy debates after the election. Yet healthy political parties are extremely important for maintaining political equality, democracy, and liberty in America. First, strong parties are generally an essential ingredient for effective electoral competition by groups lacking substantial economic or institutional resources. Party building has typically been the strategy pursued by groups that must organize the collective energies of large numbers of individuals to counter their opponents' superior material means or institutional standing. Historically, disciplined and coherent party organizations were generally developed first by groups representing the political aspirations of the working classes. Parties, the French political scientist Maurice Duverger notes, "are always more developed on the Left than on the Right because they are always more necessary on the Left than on the Right."[16] In the United States, the first mass party was built by the Jeffersonians as a counterweight to the superior social, institutional, and economic resources that the incumbent Federalists could deploy. In a subsequent period of American history, a similar set of circumstances impelled the efforts of the Jacksonians to construct a coherent mass party organization. Only by organizing the power of numbers could the Jacksonian coalition hope to compete successfully against the superior resources that its adversaries could mobilize.

In the United States, the political success of party organizations forced their opponents to copy them in order to meet the challenge. It was, as Duverger points out, "contagion from the Left" that led politicians of the Center and Right to attempt to build strong party organizations.[17] These efforts were sometimes successful. In the United States during the 1830s, the Whig Party, which was led by northeastern business interests, carefully copied the effective organizational techniques the Jacksonians had devised. The Whigs won control of the national government in 1840. But even when groups nearer the top of the social scale responded in kind to organizational efforts by their inferiors, the net effect nonetheless was to give lower-class groups an opportunity to compete on a more equal footing. In the absence of coherent mass organization, middle- and upper-class factions almost inevitably have a substantial competitive edge over their lower-class rivals. When both sides organize, the net effect is erosion of the relative advantage of the well-off.

Second, political parties are bulwarks of liberty. The Constitution certainly provides for freedom of speech, freedom of assembly, and freedom of the press. Maintaining these liberties, though, requires more than parchment guarantees. Of course, as long as freedom is not seriously threatened, abstract guarantees suffice to protect it. If, however, those in power actually threaten citizens' liberties, the preservation of freedom may come to depend on the presence of a coherent and well-organized opposition. As we saw earlier in this chapter, in the first years of the Republic, it was not the Constitution or the courts that preserved free speech in the face of Federalist efforts to silence the government's critics; it was the vigorous action of the Jeffersonian-Republican opposition that saved liberty. To this day, the presence of an opposition party is a fundamentally important check on attempts by those in power to skirt the law and infringe on citizens' liberties. For example, twenty-five years ago, although it was the news media that revealed President Richard Nixon's abuses of power, the concerted efforts of Nixon's Democratic opponents in Congress were required finally to drive the president from office. More recently, the Democratic Party played this role in challenging George W. Bush's program to authorize domestic wiretaps without a warrant.

Third, parties promote voter turnout. Party competition has long been known to be a key factor in stimulating voting. As the political scientists Stanley Kelley, Richard Ayres, and William Bowen note, competition gives citizens an incentive to vote and politicians an incentive to get them to vote.[18] The origins of the American national electorate can be traced to the competitive organizing activities of the Jeffersonian Republicans and the Federalists. According to the historian David Fischer,

The Federalists, although initially reluctant, soon learned the techniques of mobilizing voters: "mass meetings, barbecues, stump-speaking, festivals of many kinds, processions and parades, runners and riders, door-to-door canvassing, the distribution of tickets and ballots, . . . free transportation to the polls, outright bribery and corruption of other kinds."[20]

The result of this competition for votes was described by the historian Henry Jones Ford in his classic *Rise and Growth of American Politics*.[21] Ford examined the popular clamor against John Adams and Federalist policies in the 1790s that made government a "weak, shakey affair" and appeared to contemporary observers to mark the beginnings of a popular insurrection against the government.[22] Attempts by the Federalists initially to suppress mass discontent, Ford observed, might have "caused an explosion of force which would have blown up the government."[23] What intervened to prevent rebellion was Jefferson's "great unconscious achievement," the creation of an opposition party that served to "open constitutional channels of political agitation."[24] The creation of the Jeffersonian Republican Party diverted opposition to the administration into electoral channels. Party competition gave citizens a sense that their votes were valuable and that it was thus not necessary to take to the streets to have an impact upon political affairs. Whether or not Ford was correct in crediting party competition with an ability to curb civil unrest, it is clear that competition between the parties promoted voting.

Finally, political parties make democratic government possible. We often do not appreciate that democratic government is a contradiction in terms. Government implies policies, programs, and decisive action. Democracy, on the other hand, implies an opportunity for all citizens to participate fully in the governmental process. The contradiction is that full participation by everyone is often inconsistent with getting anything done. At what point should participation stop and governance begin? How can we make certain that popular participation will result in a government capable of making decisions and developing needed policies? The problem of democratic government is especially acute in the United States because of the system of separated powers bequeathed to us by the Constitution's framers. This system means that it is very difficult to link popular participation and effective decision making. Often, after the citizens have spoken and the dust has settled, no single set of political forces has been able to win control of enough of the scattered levers of power to actually do anything. Instead of government, we have a continual political struggle.

Strong political parties are a partial antidote to the inherent contradiction between participation and government. Strong parties can both encourage popular

for critical **analysis**

What are the principal issues dividing the two major parties today? What are the chief areas of agreement between the two parties? Do the parties agree or disagree on questions of liberty and democracy?

Become a Party Activist

When Evan Blewett arrived as a student at DePaul University in September 2006, one of the first groups he joined was the DePaul Democrats. He quickly became actively involved—first serving as membership director, then as treasurer, and finally filling the job of political director. As a member of the DePaul Democrats, Evan has had countless opportunities to work in local, state, and federal elections. Officials in the Democratic Party and local Democratic candidates have turned to Evan and his fellow campus Democrats to help staff their campaigns. One candidate paid students $50 a day to help in her run for office, eventually paying more than $15,000 to DePaul students.

The DePaul Democrats have used their connections to Democratic Party officials to bring speakers to campus, including numerous local politicians, many members of Congress serving in the House and Senate, and even Barack Obama when he was a presidential candidate.

And Evan has used these experiences to build his own political credentials. Indeed, using a network built through these experiences, Evan became a volunteer for Obama's campaign, coordinating the student invitations to the candidate's Chicago kickoff speech, traveling to key primary races, and finally landing a full-time paid position in Obama's headquarters for summer 2008.

Whether you want a lifetime of politics or simply want some exposure to the inside activities of a political party, an important first step may be to decide which political party best represents your own values. Most Americans who identify with a particular party choose the Democratic Party or the Republican Party, although others opt for minor parties such as the Green Party, the Natural Law Party, or the Peace and Freedom Party.

- If you're unsure which party best represents your views, you can take several online "tests" (such as the one at www.politicalcompass.org/test) to see how your views line up with the policies espoused by the different political parties.

- Once you've found out which party best represents your views, see if your campus has a student organization that is affiliated with this party. Most schools have campus chapters of the Democratic and Republican parties, and some even have organizations associated with minor parties. These campus chapters are likely to be in contact with groups on nearby campuses, as well as the local and state offices of the parties themselves.

- If your campus does not currently have a College Republicans or College Democrats group, you can contact the national party committees for guidance on how to build your own chapter and helpful hints on reaching out to expand your membership. Visit www.crnc.org for the College Republican National Committee or www.collegedems.com for the College Democrats of America.

- As a member of one of these student organizations, you can have party-affiliated speakers come to campus to speak to your group, or to a larger campuswide event. The national organization will even contact the speaker and arrange the details for you.

- You can also apply for an internship in local, state, or national party offices. Often you can do this directly through the party's Web site (which often has a link to an application), and many schools or political science departments also have internship coordinators who can help you find a position. You may even be able to receive academic credit for your involvement.

At election time, party workers try to increase turnout among potential voters who are likely to support their candidates. By promoting political participation, parties contribute to a healthy democracy.

involvement and convert participation into effective government. After the 1960s, many analysts began to express concern that American parties had become too weak to play their role in organizing political conflict, promoting participation, developing coherent policy programs, and enacting them into government. One prominent scholar even proclaimed in 1969 that we had seen "the end of American party politics."[25] Among the trends that these scholars noted was a decline of partisan attachment within the electorate, the growth in the numbers of voters identifying as independents, and a rise in so-called split-ticket voting. This trend, sometimes termed *dealignment*, first emerged in the late 1960s; it was seen as a product of growing social diversity and educational attainment, trends that made voters less reliant on parties to guide their political decision making. The growth of the mass media, particularly television, also seemed to reduce the role of parties in elections, as television tends to focus on the personality of individual candidates rather than the "institution" of the party. This period also saw a massive increase in the number and influence of interest groups that, in many ways, seemed to be doing the job that traditional party organizations once fulfilled, such as mobilizing voters and raising money.

Parties also seemed to be becoming increasingly detached from their own candidates and officeholders. The introduction of primaries and open caucuses, first for congressional candidates and later, in 1972, for presidential nominations, excluded the party elites that had previously selected candidates. In the view of many, there was now very little the party could do to influence candidate campaigns. Unsurprisingly, once in office, it seemed that political parties had little influence over their members. This lack of influence was further compounded by the dominance of something known as the "seniority system." Under this system, members of Congress gained powerful committee positions based not on loyalty to the party but on the longevity of their service. The result, at least until the mid-1970s, was historically low levels of "party unity" in Congress on key votes.

More recently, parties appear to have grown stronger. There is solid evidence that there is ideological polarization along party lines in Congress, with growing levels of party unity in roll-call voting. Since the mid-1970s, the power of the party leadership within Congress has also grown significantly, with party leaders now more able to remove "wayward" committee chairmen and members. In elections, parties have become more active again and are taking on a new, important role in recruiting candidates, coordinating campaigns, mobilizing voters, and raising money.[26] While many ordinary voters have not polarized as much as have members of Congress, a large number of the most active voters have developed stronger partisan attachments.[27]

There is an old saying that politics is the art of compromise, but politics is more than that—it is also the challenge of making choices. Parties help to crystallize a world of possible government actions into a set of distinct choices. In so doing, they make it easier for ordinary citizens to understand politics, evaluate candidates, and make their own choices.

● How do parties influence the policies passed by government

studyguide

Practice Quiz

Ⓢ **Find a diagnostic Web Quiz with 36 additional questions on the StudySpace Web site: www.wwnorton.com/we-the-people**

What Are Political Parties?

1. A political party is different from an interest group in that a political party (p. 309)
   a) seeks to control the entire government by electing its members to office and thereby controlling the government's personnel.
   b) seeks to control only limited, very specific functions of government.
   c) is entirely nonprofit.
   d) has a much smaller membership.

Two-Party System in America

2. External mobilization occurs when (p. 310)
   a) a politician seeks to pursue a moderate course that places him or her midway between the positions of conservative Republicans and liberal Democrats.
   b) the presidency is controlled by one party while the opposing party controls one or both houses of Congress.
   c) a group of politicians outside government organizes popular support to win governmental power.
   d) political conflicts within government break out and competing factions seek to mobilize popular support.

3. Which party was founded as a political expression of the antislavery movement? (p. 313)
   a) American Independent
   b) Prohibition
   c) Republican
   d) Democratic

4. The periodic episodes in American history in which an "old" dominant political party is replaced by a "new" dominant political party are called (p. 317)
   a) constitutional revolutions.
   b) party turnovers.
   c) presidential elections.
   d) electoral realignments.

5. Historically, when do realignments occur? (p. 317)
   a) typically, every twenty years
   b) whenever a minority party takes over Congress
   c) when large numbers of voters permanently shift their support from one party to another
   d) in odd-numbered years

6. A proportional-representation electoral system is (p. 321)
   a) a multiple-member district system that gives each political party representation in proportion to its percentage of the total vote.
   b) a single-member district system that gives each political party representation in proportion to its percentage of the total vote.
   c) a multiple-member district system where the candidate with the most votes wins the election.
   d) a single-member district system where the candidate with the most votes wins the election.

Party Organization

7. On what level are U.S. political parties organized? (pp. 321–26)
   a) national
   b) state

c) county
d) all of the above

8. Which of the following is *not* determined at a party's national convention? *(p. 322)*
    a) the party's candidates for president and vice president
    b) the party's campaign platform for the presidential race
    c) the congressional committees party representatives will be assigned to
    d) the rules and regulations governing party procedures.

9. An independent, nonprofit group that receives and disburses funds to influence election campaigns is called *(p. 324)*
    a) a 527 committee.
    b) a political machine.
    c) a party organization.
    d) a third party.

10. Through which mechanism did party leaders in the late nineteenth and early twentieth centuries maintain their control? *(p. 325)*
    a) civil service reform
    b) soft money contributions
    c) machine politics
    d) electoral reform

Parties and the Electorate

11. Which of the following best describes the changes in Americans' party identification since 1952? *(p. 327)*
    a) The number of Democrats has declined and been surpassed by the number of Republicans.
    b) The number of Democrats has declined but remains larger than the number of Republicans.
    c) The number of Democrats and Republicans has always been roughly the same.
    d) The number of independents has always been larger than the number of Republicans and Democrats combined.

Parties and Elections

12. Parties today are most important in the electoral process in *(p. 330)*
    a) recruiting and nominating candidates for office.
    b) financing all of the campaign's spending.
    c) providing millions of volunteers to mobilize voters.
    d) creating a responsible party government.

Parties and Government

13. Which of the following features of the committee system are determined by the whole membership of each house of Congress rather than by decisions within each party? *(p. 336)*
    a) the assignments of individual members to particular committees.
    b) the rules defining the jurisdiction of each committee.
    c) the ability of individual members to transfer from one committee to another.
    d) the use of the seniority system for determining committee chairs.

14. Which of the following statements best describes party-building activities from the 1960s to 2004 *(p. 337)*
    a) Both political parties ignored party-building activities.
    b) Democrats and Republicans have paid equally high levels of attention to party.
    c) Democrats have paid more attention to party building than Republicans.
    d) Republicans have paid more attention to party building than Democrats.

Thinking Critically about the Role of Parties in a Democracy

15. Which of the following was *not* seen as an important cause of dealignment? *(p. 342)*
    a) the growth of the mass media
    b) the massive increase in the number and influence of interest groups
    c) the increase in educational attainment
    d) the greater reliance of political parties on soft money

Chapter Outline

Find a detailed Chapter Outline on the StudySpace Web site: www.wwnorton.com/we-the-people

Key Terms

Find Flashcards to help you study these terms on the StudySpace Web site: www.wwnorton.com/we-the-people

caucus (political) *(p. 322)*
divided government *(p. 317)*
electoral realignment *(p. 317)*

527 committees *(p. 324)*
gender gap *(p. 328)*
machines *(p. 325)*

majority party *(p. 336)*
minority party *(p. 336)*
multiple-member district *(p. 321)*

For Further Reading

Aldrich, John H. *Why Parties? The Origin and Transformation of Political Parties in America.* Chicago: University of Chicago Press, 1995.

Galvin, Daniel J. *Presidential Party Building: Dwight D. Eisenhower to George W. Bush.* Princeton, NJ: Princeton University Press, 2009.

Gerring, John. *Party Ideologies in America.* New York: Cambridge University Press, 1998.

Green, Donald, Bradley Palmquist, and Eric Schickler. *Partisan Hearts and Minds: Political Parties and the Social Identities of Voters.* New Haven, CT: Yale University Press, 2002.

Green, John C., and Paul S. Herrnson, eds. *Responsible Partisanship? The Evolution of American Political Parties since 1950.* Lawrence: University Press of Kansas, 2002.

Karol, David. *Party Position Change in American Politics: Coalition Management.* New York: Cambridge University Press, 2009.

Maisel, L. Sandy. *Political Parties and Elections: A Very Short Introduction.* New York: Oxford University Press, 2007.

McCarty, Nolan, Keith Poole, and Howard Rosenthal. *Polarized America: The Dance of Ideology and Unequal Riches.* Cambridge, MA: MIT Press, 2006.

Milkis, Sidney M. *Political Parties and Constitutional Government: Remaking American Democracy.* Baltimore: Johns Hopkins University Press, 1999.

Shefter, Martin. *Political Parties and the State: The American Historical Experience.* Princeton, NJ: Princeton University Press, 1994.

Recommended Web Sites

D.C.'s Political Report
www.dcpoliticalreport.com/Disclaimer.htm
This is a great resource page for political parties, with a special focus on American third parties. Here you can find almost every organization that identifies itself as a political party, including such obscure groups as the American Beer Drinker's Party or the Scorched Earth Party.

Democratic Party
www.dnc.org
Republican Party
www.GOP.com, www.rnc.org
These are the official Web sites for the Democrats and Republicans. Compare the platforms of the two main U.S. parties and see if there's "not a dime's worth of difference" between the two of them.

Green Party
www.gp.org
Libertarian Party
www.lp.org
Reform Party National Committee
http://reformparty.org
The Green Party, Libertarian Party, and Reform Party are three of the largest and most successful third parties in recent years. Find out what these parties are trying to accomplish and why their candidates run when they have little or no chance of winning.

National Annenberg Election Survey
http://annenbergpublicpolicycenter.org
Individual voters tend to develop psychological ties to one party or another. The National Annenberg Election Survey (NAES) uses survey data to track party identification by state every two years. Find out if your state has more Democratic or Republican identifiers.

Politics1.com
www.politics1.com/parties.htm
Politics1 is a nonpartisan site that provides an extensive list of political parties in the United States. Here you will find numerous party links as well as an abundance of historical information on America's third parties and biographies of leading politicians.

PoliTxts: Party Platforms since 1840
http://janda.org/politxts/PartyPlatforms/listing.html
Party platforms contain the party philosophy, principles, and positions on issues and are customarily approved at a national convention. Compare and contrast major party platforms for every presidential election year since 1840 on this page, compiled by Kenneth Janda.

The Tea Party movement played a notable role in the 2010 elections. For example, with the support of Tea Party groups, Rand Paul of Kentucky won the Republican primary and then the general election for senator.

Campaigns and Elections

WHAT GOVERNMENT DOES AND WHY IT MATTERS In November 2008, Americans chose Senator Barack Obama, a Democrat, to be their forty-fourth president. Obama defeated the Republican candidate, Senator John McCain, by a margin of more than 7 million votes out of some 120 million votes cast, posting 53 percent of the popular vote to McCain's 46 percent. A half century after the enactment of the 1965 Voting Rights Act enfranchised millions of black voters, Obama became America's first nonwhite president. Americans also elected an overwhelmingly Democratic Congress in 2008.

By 2010, however, many voters had become disenchanted with the performance of the administration and the Democratic Congress. Many liberal Democrats thought the president had not done enough to end America's military involvement in the Middle East or to advance a progressive social agenda. Republican conservatives, on the other hand, blamed the president and Congress for the failure of

focusquestions

- What are the basic rules of American elections?
- How are campaigns typically conducted?
- What are the major features of presidential elections?
- What factors influence voters' decisions?
- What factors shaped the outcomes of the 2008 and 2010 elections?
- How do candidates raise the money they need to run?

the economy to fully recover from the 2008–09 recession and were concerned with the long-term costs and consequences of Democratic social and economic programs. As a result, the Democrats suffered heavy losses in the 2010 midterm elections and the president saw his agenda threatened by a newly assertive GOP.

In the aftermath of these elections, most pundits focused on explaining voters' choices and their implications for the nation's politics and policies. These are important topics, but it is also worthwhile to think a bit about the overall significance of elections.

In democracies, elections promote leadership accountability because the threat of defeat at the polls exerts pressure on those in power to conduct themselves in a responsible manner and to take account of popular interests and wishes when they make their decisions. It is because of this need to anticipate the dissatisfaction of their constituents that elected officials constantly monitor public-opinion polls as they decide what positions to take on policy issues.

Although elections allow citizens a chance to participate in politics, they also allow the government a chance to exert a good deal of control over when, where, how, and which of its citizens will participate. Electoral processes are governed by a variety of rules and procedures that allow those in power a significant opportunity to regulate the character—and perhaps also the consequences—of mass political participation.

chapter contents

Elections in America

In the United States, elections are held at regular intervals. National presidential elections take place every four years, on the first Tuesday in November; congressional elections are held every two years on the same Tuesday. (Congressional elections that do not coincide with a presidential election are sometimes called **midterm elections**.) Elections for state and local office also often coincide with national elections. Some states and municipalities, however, prefer to schedule their local elections in years that do not coincide with national contests to ensure that local results will not be affected by national trends.

In the American federal system, the responsibility for organizing elections rests largely with state and local governments. State laws specify how elections are to be administered, determine the boundaries of electoral districts, and specify candidate and voter qualifications. Elections are administered by state, county, and municipal election boards that are responsible for establishing and staffing polling places and verifying the eligibility of individuals who come to vote.

Types of Elections

Three types of elections are held in the United States: primary elections, general elections, and runoff elections. Americans occasionally also participate in a fourth voting process, the referendum, but the referendum is not actually an election.

Primary elections are held to select each party's candidates for the general election. In the case of local and statewide offices, the winners of primary elections face one another as their parties' nominees in the general election. At the presidential level, however, primary elections are indirect; they are used to select state delegates to the national nominating conventions, at which the major party presidential candidates are chosen. America is one of the only nations in the world to hold primary elections. In most countries, nominations are controlled by party officials, as they once were in the United States. The primary system was introduced at the turn of the century by Progressive reformers who hoped to weaken the power of party leaders by taking candidate nominations out of their hands.

Under the laws of some states, only registered members of a political party may vote in a primary election to select that party's candidates. This is called a **closed primary**. Other states allow all registered voters to decide on the day of the primary in which party's primary they will participate. This is called an **open primary**.

The primary is followed by the general election—the decisive electoral contest. The winner of the general election is elected to office for a specified term. In some states, however, mainly in the Southeast, if no candidate wins an absolute majority in the primary, a runoff election is held before the general election. This situation is most likely to arise if there are more than two candidates, none of whom receives a majority of the votes cast. A runoff election is held between the two candidates who received the largest number of votes.

Twenty-four states also provide for referendum voting, as we saw in Chapter 1. The **referendum** process allows citizens to vote directly on proposed laws or other governmental actions. In recent years, voters in several states have voted to set limits on tax rates, to block state and local spending proposals, and to prohibit social services for illegal immigrants. Although it involves voting, a referendum is not an election. The election is an institution of representative government. Through an election, voters choose officials to act for them. The referendum, by contrast, is

midterm elections congressional elections that do not coincide with a presidential election; also called off-year elections

primary elections elections held to select a party's candidate for the general election

closed primary a primary election in which voters can participate in the nomination of candidates, but only of the party in which they are enrolled for a period of time prior to primary day

open primary a primary election in which the voter can wait until the day of the primary to choose which party to enroll in to select candidates for the general election

referendum the practice of referring a measure proposed or passed by a legislature to the vote of the electorate for approval or rejection

In 2010, voters in Missouri decided several referenda, including a proposition to block government-mandated health insurance.

an institution of direct democracy; it allows voters to govern directly without intervention by government officials. The validity of referenda results, however, is subject to judicial action. If a court finds that a referendum outcome violates the state or national constitution, it can overturn the result. This happened in the case of a 1995 California referendum curtailing social services to illegal aliens.[1] In 2010, more than 180 measures appeared on state ballots—most relating to taxes, budgets, and governmental administration. For example, Washington voters were asked to decide whether future state tax increases should require a two-thirds legislative majority.

Eighteen states also have legal provisions for **recall** elections. The recall is an electoral device that allows voters to remove governors and other state officials from office prior to the expiration of their terms. Generally speaking, a recall effort begins with a petition campaign. For example, in California, if 12 percent of those who voted in the last general election sign petitions demanding a special recall election, one must be scheduled by the state board of elections. In 2003, California voters blamed Governor Gray Davis for the state's $38 billion budget deficit, allowing his opponents to secure enough signatures to force a vote. In October 2003, Davis became only the second governor in American history to be recalled by his state's electorate. Under California law, voters are also asked to choose a replacement for the official whom they dismiss. Californians in 2003 elected Arnold Schwarzenegger to be their governor. In 2008, a number of politicians faced recall elections. For example, Michigan voters were given an opportunity to recall House Speaker Andy Dillon, who made enemies when he backed a state income tax increase. And, in an ironic twist, the California prison guards union launched an (unsuccessful) effort to recall Governor Arnold Schwarzenegger. Federal officials, such as the president and members of Congress, are not subject to recall.

recall procedure to allow voters an opportunity to remove state officials from office before their terms expire

The Criteria for Winning

In some countries, to win a seat in the parliament or other governing body, a candidate must receive an absolute majority (50 percent plus 1) of all the votes cast in the relevant district. This type of electoral system is called a **majority system** and, in the United States, is used in primary elections by some southern states. Majority systems usually include a provision for a runoff election between the two top candidates, because if the initial race draws several candidates, there is little chance that any one will receive a majority.

In other nations, candidates for office need not win an absolute majority of the votes cast to win an election. Instead, victory is awarded to the candidate who receives the most votes, regardless of the actual percentage this represents. A candidate receiving 50 percent, 30 percent, or 20 percent of the vote can win if no other candidate received more votes. This type of electoral system is called a **plurality system** and is used in virtually all general elections in the United States.

Most European nations employ a third type of electoral system, called **proportional representation**. Under proportional rules, competing political parties are awarded legislative seats in rough proportion to the percentage of the popular votes cast that each party won. A party that wins 30 percent of the vote will receive roughly 30 percent of the seats in the parliament or other representative

majority system a type of electoral system in which, to win a seat in the parliament or other representative body, a candidate must receive a majority of all the votes cast in the relevant district

plurality system a type of electoral system in which, to win a seat in the parliament or other representative body, a candidate need only receive the most votes in the election, not necessarily a majority of votes cast

proportional representation a multiple-member district system that allows each political party representation in proportion to its percentage of the total vote

body. In the United States, proportional representation is used by many states in presidential primary elections.

In general, proportional representation works to the advantage of smaller or weaker groups in society, whereas plurality and majority rules tend to help larger and more powerful forces. Proportional representation benefits smaller or weaker groups because it usually allows a party to win legislative seats with fewer votes than would be required under a majority or plurality system. In Europe, for example, a party that wins 10 percent of the national vote might win 10 percent of the parliamentary seats. In the United States, by contrast, a party that wins 10 percent of the vote would probably win no seats in Congress. Because they give small parties little chance of success, plurality and majority systems tend to reduce the number of competitive political parties. Proportional representation, on the other hand, tends to increase the number of parties. In part because of its use of plurality elections, the United States has usually had only two significant political parties, whereas with proportional representation, many European countries have developed multiparty systems.

Electoral Districts

The boundaries for congressional and state legislative districts in the United States are redrawn by the states usually every ten years in response to population changes determined by the census. This redrawing of district boundaries is called **redistricting**. The character of district boundaries is influenced by several factors. Some of the most important influences have been federal court decisions. In the 1963 case of *Gray v. Sanders*, and in the 1964 cases of *Wesberry v. Sanders* and *Reynolds v. Sims*, the Supreme Court held that legislative districts within a state must include roughly equal populations, so as to accord with the principle of "one person, one vote."[2] During the 1980s, the Supreme Court also declared that legislative districts should, insofar as possible, be contiguous, compact, and consistent with existing political subdivisions.[3]

Despite judicial intervention, state legislators routinely seek to influence electoral outcomes by manipulating the organization of electoral districts. This strategy is called **gerrymandering**, named for a nineteenth-century Massachusetts governor, Elbridge Gerry, who was alleged to have designed a district in the shape of a salamander to promote his party's interests. The principle of gerrymandering is simple: different distributions of voters among districts can produce different electoral results. For example, by dispersing the members of a particular group across two or more districts, state legislators can dilute their voting power and prevent

redistricting the process of redrawing election districts and redistributing legislative representatives. This happens every ten years to reflect shifts in population or in response to legal challenges in existing districts

gerrymandering apportionment of voters in districts in such a way as to give unfair advantage to one racial or ethnic group or political party

The drawing of electoral districts is always a matter of controversy, with opponents accusing one another of "gerrymandering"—drawing district boundaries in such a way as to serve a particular group's interests. The original gerrymander was a districting plan attributed to the Massachusetts governor Elbridge Gerry (1744–1814) that had the shape of a salamander.

In a number of recent cases, black, white, and Hispanic voters have claimed to be the victims of racial gerrymanders. For instance, in 1995 the Supreme Court held that one Georgia district, which was 64 percent African American, was unfairly based on race. Meanwhile, no challenge was made to Texas's 6th District, which was predominantly white. In 2006, the Supreme Court rejected part of a Texas redistricting plan on the grounds that it suppressed minority votes, though the Court upheld most of the plan.

benign gerrymandering attempts to draw district boundaries so as to create districts made up primarily of disadvantaged or underrepresented minorities

majority-minority district a gerrymandered voting district that improves the chances of minority candidates by making selected minority groups the majority within the district

them from electing a representative in any district. Alternatively, by concentrating the members of a group or the adherents of the opposing party in as few districts as possible, state legislators can try to ensure that their opponents will elect as few representatives as possible. In recent years, the federal government has supported what is sometimes called **benign gerrymandering** through the creation of congressional districts made up primarily of minority group members. This practice was intended to increase the number of African Americans elected to public office. The Supreme Court has viewed this effort as constitutionally dubious, however. Beginning with the 1993 case of *Shaw v. Reno*, the Court has generally rejected efforts to create such **majority-minority districts**.[4] The Court has asserted that districting based exclusively on racial criteria is unlawful.

The Ballot

Before the 1890s, voters cast ballots according to political parties. Each party printed its own ballots, listed only its own candidates for each office, and employed party workers to distribute its ballots at the polls. Because only one party's candidates appeared on any ballot, it was very difficult for a voter to cast anything other than a straight party vote.

The advent of a new, neutral ballot brought a significant change to electoral procedure. The new ballot was prepared and administered by the state rather than the parties. Each ballot was identical and included the names of all candidates for office. This ballot reform made it possible for voters to make their choices on the basis of the individual rather than the collective merits of a party's candidates. Because all candidates for the same office now appeared on the same ballot, voters were no longer forced to choose a straight party ticket. This gave rise to the phenomenon of split-ticket voting in American elections.

If a voter supports candidates from more than one party in the same election, he or she is said to be casting a split-ticket vote. Voters who support only one party's candidates are casting a straight-ticket vote. Straight-ticket voting occurs most often when a voter casts a ballot for a party's presidential candidate and then "automatically" votes for the rest of that party's candidates. The result of this voting pattern is known as the **coattail effect**.

Prior to the reform of the ballot, it was not uncommon for an entire incumbent administration to be swept from office and replaced by an entirely new set of officials. In the absence of a real possibility of split-ticket voting, the electorate could express any desire for change only as a vote against all candidates of the party in power. Because of this, the possibility always existed, particularly at the state and local levels, that an insurgent slate committed to policy change could be swept into power. The party ballot thus increased the potential impact of elections on the government's composition. Although this potential may not always have been realized, the party ballot at least increased the chance that electoral decisions could lead to policy changes. By contrast, because it permitted choice on the basis of candidates' individual appeals, ticket splitting led to increasingly divided partisan control of government.

The actual ballots used by voters vary from county to county across the United States. Some counties employ paper ballots; others use mechanical voting machines or computerized systems. Not surprisingly, the controversy surrounding Florida's presidential vote in 2000 led to a closer look at the different balloting systems, and it became apparent that some of them produced unreliable results. When many counties moved to introduce computerized voting systems, critics warned that they might be vulnerable to unauthorized use or "hacking." During the 2008 Ohio primaries a software error was discovered that potentially affected electronic voting machines used in thirty-four states. The machine's manufacturer moved to correct the error before the November national elections, and the 2008 and 2010 elections produced few complaints about electronic voting.

> **coattail effect** the result of voters casting their ballot for president or governor and "automatically" voting for the remainder of the party's ticket

The Electoral College

In the early history of popular voting, nations often made use of indirect elections. In these elections, voters would choose the members of an intermediate body. These members would, in turn, select public officials. The assumption underlying such processes was that ordinary citizens were not really qualified to choose their leaders and could not be trusted to do so directly. The last vestige of this procedure in America is the **electoral college**, the group of electors who formally select the president and vice president of the United States.

When Americans go to the polls on Election Day, they are technically not voting directly for presidential candidates. Instead, voters within each state are choosing among slates of electors selected by each state's party and pledged, if elected, to support that party's presidential candidate. In each state (except Maine and Nebraska), the slate that wins casts all the state's electoral votes for its party's candidate.[5] Each state is entitled to a number of electoral votes equal to the number of the state's senators and representatives combined, for a total of 538 electoral votes for the fifty states and the District of Columbia. Occasionally, an elector will break his or her pledge and vote for the other party's candidate. For example, in 1976, when the Republicans carried the state of Washington, one Republican elector from that state refused to vote for Gerald Ford, the Republican presidential nominee. Many states have now enacted statutes formally binding electors to

> **electoral college** the presidential electors from each state who meet after the popular election to cast ballots for president and vice president

their pledges, but some constitutional authorities doubt whether such statutes are enforceable.

In each state, the electors whose slate has won proceed to the state's capital on the Monday following the second Wednesday in December and formally cast their ballots. The ballots are sent to Washington and tallied by the Congress in January; then the name of the winner is formally announced. If no candidate were to receive a majority of all electoral votes, the names of the top three candidates would be submitted to the House, where each state would be able to cast one vote. Whether a state's vote would be decided by a majority, plurality, or some other fraction of the state's delegates would be determined under rules established by the House.

In 1800 and 1824, the electoral college failed to produce a majority for any candidate. In the election of 1800, Thomas Jefferson, the Jeffersonian Republican Party's presidential candidate, and Aaron Burr, that party's vice-presidential candidate, received an equal number of votes in the electoral college, throwing the election into the House of Representatives. (The Constitution at that time made no distinction between presidential and vice-presidential candidates, specifying only that the individual receiving a majority of electoral votes would be named president.) Some members of the Federalist Party in Congress suggested that they should seize the opportunity to damage the Republican cause by supporting Burr and denying Jefferson the presidency. The Federalist leader Alexander Hamilton put a stop to this mischievous notion, however, and made certain that his party supported Jefferson. Hamilton's actions enraged Burr and helped lead to the infamous duel between the two men, in which Burr killed Hamilton. The Twelfth Amendment, ratified in 1804, was designed to prevent a repetition of such an inconclusive election by providing for separate electoral college votes for president and vice president.

In the 1824 election, four candidates—John Quincy Adams, Andrew Jackson, Henry Clay, and William H. Crawford—divided the electoral vote; no one of them received a majority. The House of Representatives eventually chose Adams over the others, even though Jackson had won more electoral and popular votes. After 1824, the two major political parties had begun to dominate presidential politics to such an extent that by December of each election year, only two candidates remained for the electors to choose between, thus ensuring that one would receive

Some of the devices that have been used to record votes in the United States are notably prone to errors that can affect election results. For example, in 2000 in Florida's Palm Beach County, some voters were confused by the "butterfly ballot," which made it difficult to match candidates and votes. In the 2008 elections, many of the nation's voters cast their ballots on electronic touch-screen machines. Critics of touch-screen voting systems, however, question the machines for their accuracy and security against fraud.

a majority. This freed the parties and the candidates from having to plan their campaigns to culminate in Congress, and Congress very quickly ceased to dominate the presidential selection process.

On all but three occasions since 1824, the electoral vote has simply ratified the nationwide popular vote. Since electoral votes are won on a state-by-state basis, it is mathematically possible for a candidate who receives a nationwide popular plurality to fail to carry states whose electoral votes would add up to a majority. Thus, in 1876, Rutherford B. Hayes was the winner in the electoral college despite receiving fewer popular votes than his rival, Samuel Tilden. In 1888, Grover Cleveland received more popular votes than Benjamin Harrison, but received fewer electoral votes. And in 2000, Al Gore outpolled his opponent, George W. Bush, by more than 500,000 votes, but narrowly lost the electoral college by a mere four electoral votes.

● Election Campaigns

A **campaign** is an effort by political candidates and their supporters to win the backing of donors, political activists, and voters in their quest for political office. Campaigns precede every primary and general election. Because of the complexity of the campaign process, and because of the amount of money that candidates must raise, presidential campaigns usually begin almost two years before the November presidential elections. The campaign for any office consists of a number of steps. Candidates must first organize an exploratory committee consisting of supporters who will help them raise funds and bring their names to the attention of the media and potential donors. This step is relatively easy for a candidate currently in the office. The current officeholder is called an **incumbent**. Incumbents usually are already well-known and have little difficulty attracting supporters and contributors, unless of course they have been subject to damaging publicity while in office.

campaign an effort by political candidates and their supporters to win the backing of donors, political activists, and voters in their quest for political office

incumbent a candidate running for reelection to a position that he or she already holds

Advisers

The next step in a typical campaign involves recruiting advisers and creating a formal campaign organization (see Figure 10.1). Most candidates, especially for national or statewide office, will need a campaign manager, a media consultant, a pollster, a financial adviser, and a press spokesperson, as well as a staff director to coordinate the activities of volunteer and paid workers. For a local campaign, candidates generally need hundreds of workers. State-level campaigns call for thousands of workers, and presidential campaigns require tens of thousands of workers nationwide.

Professional campaign workers, including the managers, consultants, and pollsters required in a modern campaign, prefer to work for candidates who seem to have a reasonable chance of winning. Candidates seen as having little chance of winning often have difficulty hiring the most experienced professional consultants. Professional political consultants have taken the place of the old-time party bosses who once controlled political campaigns. Most consultants who direct campaigns specialize in politics, although some are drawn from the ranks of corporate advertising and may work with commercial clients in addition to politicians. Campaign consultants conduct public opinion polls, produce television commercials, organize direct-mail campaigns, and develop the issues and advertising messages the candidate will use to mobilize support. George W. Bush's former chief political strategist, Karl Rove, not only played a key role in two presidential campaigns but is also widely credited

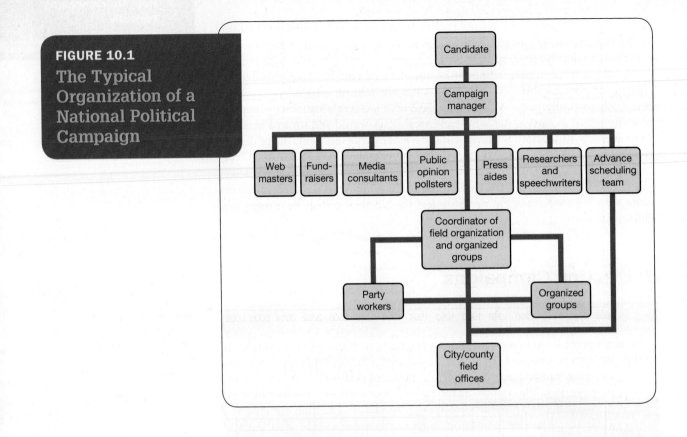

The Typical Organization of a National Political Campaign

with crafting the strategy that brought about a Republican victory in the 2002 national congressional races.

Together with their advisers, candidates must begin serious fund-raising efforts at an early stage in the campaign. To have a reasonable chance of winning a seat in the House of Representatives, a candidate may need to raise more than $500,000. To win a Senate seat, a candidate may need ten times that much. Candidates generally begin raising funds long before they face an election. Once in office, members of Congress find it much easier to raise campaign funds and are thus able to outspend their challengers (see Figure 10.2).[6] Members of the majority party in the House and Senate are particularly attractive to donors who want access to those in power.[7] Presidential candidates in particular must raise huge amounts of money. In 2008, Barack Obama set new fund-raising records. His early fund-raising produced more than $200 million, one-third in contributions of less than $200. Ultimately, Obama raised nearly $750 million, an unprecedented figure.

Polling

Another important element of a campaign is public-opinion polling. To be competitive, a candidate must collect voting and poll data to assess the electorate's needs, hopes, fears, and past behavior. Polls are conducted throughout most political campaigns. Surveys of voter opinion provide the basic information that candidates and their staffs use to craft campaign strategies—that is, to select issues, to assess their own strengths and weaknesses as well as those of the opposition, to check voter

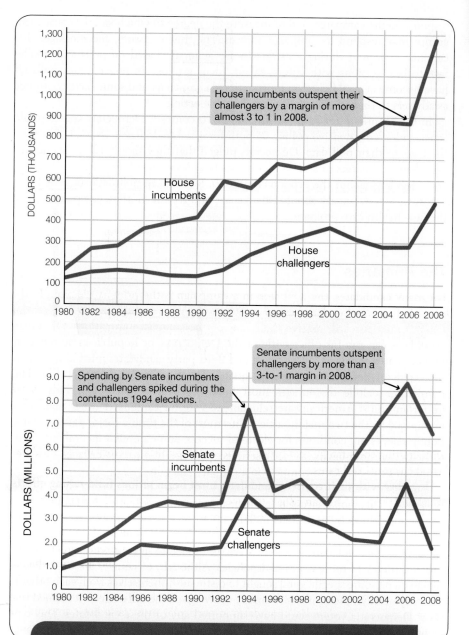

FIGURE 10.2

Average House and Senate Campaign Expenditures, 1980–2008 (Net Dollars)

The average amount spent by House and Senate incumbents to secure reelection has risen sharply in recent years, whereas spending by challengers has remained more stable. What would you expect to see as a consequence of this trend? Is legislation needed to level the playing field?

SOURCES: Norman J. Ornstein, Thomas E. Mann, and Michael J. Malbin. eds., *Vital Statistics on Congress, 2001–2002* (Washington, DC: American Enterprise Institute, 2002), 87, 93; and Campaign Finance Institute, www.cfinst.org (accessed 1/17/09).

response to the campaign, and to measure the degree to which various constituent groups may respond to campaign appeals. The themes, issues, and messages that candidates present during a campaign are generally based on polls and smaller face-to-face sessions with voters, called "focus groups." In recent years, pollsters have become central figures in most national campaigns, and some have continued as advisers to their clients after they win the election.

In the months prior to the 2008 and 2010 contests, Democrats and Republicans conducted extensive polling on both foreign and domestic issues. In 2008, on the basis of their poll data, Democrats judged that they should campaign against President Bush's record and emphasize such issues as health care reform and voters' misgivings about the economy. In 2010, Republican poll data suggested that voters were now uneasy about "Obamacare" and led the GOP to campaign against the new health care program.

The Primaries

For many candidates, the next step in a campaign is the primary election. In the case of all offices but the presidency, state and local primary elections determine which candidates will receive the major parties' official nominations. Of course, candidates can run for office without the Democratic or Republican nomination. In most states, however, independent and third-party candidates must obtain many thousands of petition signatures to qualify for the general election ballot. This requirement alone discourages most independent and third-party bids. More important, most Americans are reluctant to vote for candidates other than those nominated by the two major parties. Thus most of the time, a major party nomination is a necessary condition for electoral success. Some popular incumbents coast to victory without having to face a serious challenge. In most major races, however, candidates can expect to compete in a primary election.

There are essentially two types of primary contests: the personality clash and the ideological, or factional, struggle. In the first category are primaries that simply reflect competing efforts by ambitious individuals to secure election to office. In 2008, for example, the major Democratic presidential hopefuls, Hillary Rodham Clinton, Barack Obama, and John Edwards, were all moderate liberals who agreed on the broad outlines of most issues and policies. Although, of course, these candidates disagreed on some specifics and sought to distinguish themselves from each other in a variety of ways, the similarities greatly outweighed the differences. It seemed that most Democratic voters could have supported any of these candidates. This type of primary contest can be very healthy for a political party because it can enhance interest in the campaign and can produce a nominee with the ability to win the general election.

The second type of primary—the ideological struggle—can have different consequences. Ideological struggles usually occur when one wing or faction of a party decides that it is not willing to compromise its principles for the sake of the party's electoral success. Early in the 2008 race, religious conservatives backed a presidential bid by the former Arkansas governor Mike Huckabee, an evangelical minister. Huckabee's campaign brought the issue of religion and politics to the forefront, dividing the economic conservatives from the religious conservatives in the GOP coalition. When John McCain won the GOP nomination, religious conservatives threatened to sit out the general election. However, when McCain designated Sarah

Palin as his running mate, religious conservatives were pleased. Palin had strong religious ties and was a stalwart foe of abortion. In the wake of the Palin nomination, religious conservatives stopped denouncing McCain and rushed to embrace the Republican ticket.

Presidential Elections

Although they also involve primary elections, the major party presidential nominations follow a pattern that is quite different from the nominating process employed for other political offices. In some years, particularly when an incumbent president is running for reelection, one party's nomination may not be contested. If, however, the Democratic or Republican presidential nomination is contested, candidates typically compete in primaries or presidential nominating caucuses in all fifty states, attempting to capture national convention delegates. Most states hold primary elections to choose the delegates for national conventions. A few states hold a **caucus**, a nominating process that begins with precinct-level meetings throughout the state. Some caucuses, called **open caucuses**, are open to anyone wishing to attend. Other states use **closed caucuses**, open only to registered party members. Citizens attending the caucuses typically elect delegates to statewide conventions at which delegates to the national party conventions are chosen.

caucus (political) a normally closed meeting of a political or legislative group to select candidates, plan strategy, or make decisions regarding legislative matters

The primaries and caucuses begin in January of a presidential election year and end in June (see Figure 10.3). The early ones are most important because they can help front-running candidates secure media attention and financial support. Gradually, the primary and caucus process has become "front loaded," with states vying with each other to increase their political influence by holding their nominating processes first. Traditionally, the New Hampshire primary and the Iowa caucuses are considered the most important of the early events, and candidates spend months courting voter support in these two states. A candidate who performs well in Iowa and New Hampshire will usually be able to secure support and better media coverage for subsequent races. A candidate who fares badly in these two states may be written off as a loser. As they sought their parties' 2008 presidential nominations, the leading Democratic and Republican candidates campaigned intensely in Iowa and New Hampshire. The Democrats Hillary Clinton, Barack Obama, and John Edwards spent long hours in the two states, greeting voters, seeking endorsements and launching media blitzes. On the GOP side, John McCain, Rudy Giuliani, and Mike Huckabee fought tooth and nail for the support of Republican voters.

open caucus a presidential nominating caucus open to anyone who wishes to attend

closed caucus a presidential nominating caucus open only to registered party members

As noted in Chapter 9, the Democratic Party requires that state presidential primaries allocate delegates on the basis of proportional representation; Democratic candidates win delegates in rough proportion to their percentage of the primary vote. The Republican Party does not require proportional representation, but most states have now written proportional representation requirements into their election laws. A few states use the **winner-take-all system**, by which the candidate with the most votes wins all the party's delegates in that state.

When the primaries and caucuses are concluded, it is usually clear which candidates have won their parties' nominations. For example, in 2008, John McCain had effectively wrapped up the Republican nomination by the first week in March. Barack Obama and Hillary Clinton, though, fought for the Democratic nomination until the beginning of June.

winner-take-all system a system in which all of a state's presidential nominating delegates are awarded to the candidate who wins the most votes, while runners-up receive no delegates

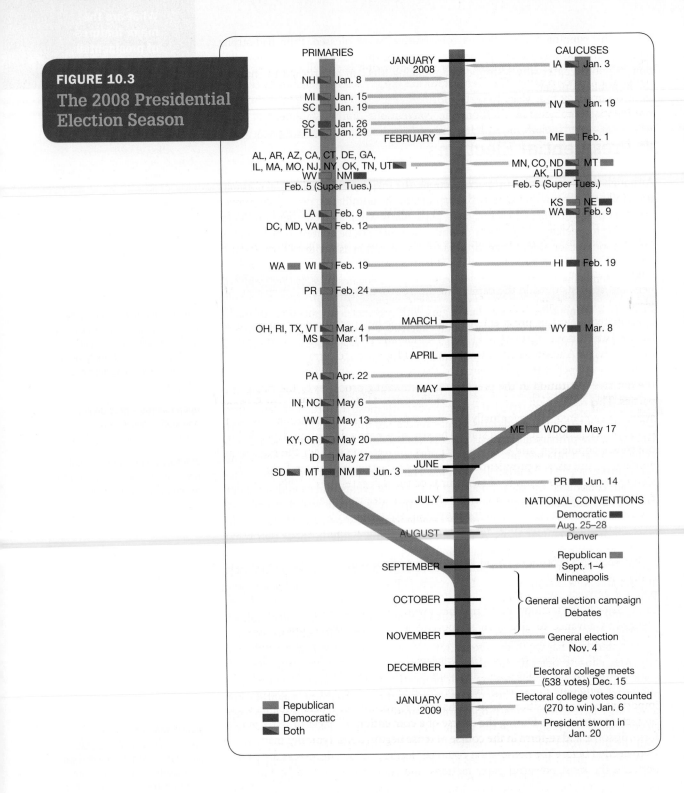

FIGURE 10.3
The 2008 Presidential
Election Season

PRIMARIES

CAUCUSES

JANUARY 2008

IA — Jan. 3

NH — Jan. 8

MI — Jan. 15
SC — Jan. 19

NV — Jan. 19

SC — Jan. 26
FL — Jan. 29

FEBRUARY

ME — Feb. 1

AL, AR, AZ, CA, CT, DE, GA,
IL, MA, MO, NJ, NY, OK, TN, UT
WV — NM
Feb. 5 (Super Tues.)

MN, CO, ND — MT
AK, ID
Feb. 5 (Super Tues.)

KS — NE
WA — Feb. 9

LA — Feb. 9

DC, MD, VA — Feb. 12

WA — WI — Feb. 19

HI — Feb. 19

PR — Feb. 24

MARCH

WY — Mar. 8

OH, RI, TX, VT — Mar. 4
MS — Mar. 11

APRIL

PA — Apr. 22

MAY

IN, NC — May 6

WV — May 13

KY, OR — May 20

ME — WDC — May 17

ID — May 27

JUNE

SD — MT — NM — Jun. 3

PR — Jun. 14

JULY

NATIONAL CONVENTIONS
Democratic —
Aug. 25–28
Denver

AUGUST

SEPTEMBER

Republican —
Sept. 1–4
Minneapolis

OCTOBER

General election campaign
Debates

NOVEMBER

General election
Nov. 4

DECEMBER

Electoral college meets
(538 votes) Dec. 15

JANUARY
2009

Electoral college votes counted
(270 to win) Jan. 6

President sworn in
Jan. 20

Republican
Democratic
Both

The Convention

The one major step that remains before a nomination is actually awarded is the national party convention. The Democratic and Republican national party conventions occur every four years to certify formally each party's presidential and vice-presidential nominees. In addition, the conventions draft a statement of party principles, called a **platform**, and determine the rules that will govern party activities for the next four years.

platform a party document, written at a national convention, that contains party philosophy, principles, and positions on issues

The History of Political Conventions For more than fifty years after America's founding, presidential nominations were controlled by each party's congressional caucus—all the party's members in the House and the Senate. Critics referred to this process as the "King Caucus" and charged that it did not take proper account of the views of party members throughout the nation. In 1824, the King Caucus method came under severe attack when the Democratic Party caucus failed to nominate Andrew Jackson, the candidate with the greatest support among both party members and activists outside the capital. In the 1830s, the party convention was devised as a way of allowing party leaders and activists throughout the nation to participate in selecting presidential candidates. The first party convention was held by the Anti-Masonic Party in 1831. The Democratic Party held its first convention in 1832, when Andrew Jackson was nominated for a second term.

As it developed during the course of the next century, the convention became the decisive institution in the presidential nominating processes of the two major parties. The convention was a genuine deliberative body in which party factions argued, negotiated, and eventually reached a decision. The convention was composed of delegations from each state. The size of a state's delegation depended on the state's population, and each delegate was allowed one vote for the purpose of nominating the party's presidential and vice-presidential candidates. Before 1936, victory required the support of two-thirds of the delegates. Until 1968, state delegations voted according to the unit rule, which meant that all the members of the state delegation would vote for the candidate favored by the majority of the state's delegates. This practice was designed to maximize a state's influence in the nominating process. The unit rule was abolished in 1968.

Between the 1830s and World War II, national convention delegates were generally selected by a state's party leaders. Usually the delegates were public officials, political activists, and party notables from all regions of the state, representing most major party factions. Some delegates would arrive at the convention having pledged in advance to give their support to a particular presidential candidate. Most delegates were uncommitted, however. This fact, coupled with the unit rule, allowed state party leaders (i.e., the delegates) to negotiate with each other and with presidential candidates for their support. State party leaders might agree to support a candidate in exchange for a promise to name them or their followers to important national positions, or in exchange for promises of federal programs and projects for their state. During the course of a convention, alliances of states would form, dissolve, and re-form in the course of tense negotiations. Typically, many votes were needed before the nomination could be decided. Often, deadlocks developed between the most powerful party factions, and state leaders would be forced to find a compromise, or "dark-horse," candidate. Among the more famous dark-horse nominees were James Polk in 1844 and Warren Harding in 1920. Although he was virtually unknown, Polk won the Democratic nomination when it became clear that none of the more established candidates could win. Similarly, Harding,

In the past, each party's nominees for president and vice president were chosen and announced at the national convention. Today, presidential and vice-presidential candidates are chosen in a series of primary elections and local caucuses, though they deliver acceptance speeches at the conventions.

another political unknown, won his nomination after the major candidates had fought one another to a standstill.

In its day, the convention was seen as a democratic reform. In later years, however, new generations of reformers came to view the convention as a symbol of rule by party leaders. The convention also strengthened the independence and power of the presidency by taking the nominating process out of the hands of Congress.

Contemporary Party Conventions Whereas the traditional party convention was a deliberative assembly, the contemporary convention acts more to ratify than to determine the party's presidential and vice-presidential nominations. Today, as we saw earlier in this chapter, the nomination is actually determined in a series of primary elections and local party caucuses held in virtually all fifty states during several months prior to the convention. These primaries and caucuses determine how each state's convention delegates will vote. Candidates now arrive at the convention knowing who has enough delegate support in hand to assure a victory in the first round of balloting. State party leaders no longer serve as power brokers, and the party's presidential and vice-presidential choices are made relatively quickly.

Even though the party convention no longer controls presidential nominations, it still has a number of important tasks. The first of these is the adoption of party rules concerning such matters as convention delegate selection and future presidential primary elections. In 1972, for example, the Democratic convention accepted rules requiring convention delegates to be broadly representative of the party's membership in terms of race and gender. After those rules were passed, the convention refused to seat several state delegations that were deemed not to meet this standard.

Another important task for the convention is the drafting of a party platform—a statement of principles and pledges around which the delegates can unite. Although the two major parties' platforms tend to contain many similar principles and platitudes, differences between the two platforms can be significant. In recent years, for example, the Republican platform has advocated tax cuts and taken strong positions on such social issues as affirmative action and abortion. The Democratic platforms, on the other hand, have focused on the importance of maintaining welfare and regulatory programs. A close reading of the party platforms can reveal some of the ideological differences between the parties.

Convention Delegates Today, convention **delegates** are generally political activists with strong positions on social and political issues. Generally, Republican delegates tend to be more conservative than Republican voters as a whole, whereas Democratic delegates tend to be more liberal than the majority of Democratic voters. In states such as Michigan and Iowa, local party caucuses choose many of the delegates who will actually attend the national convention. In most of the remaining states, primary elections determine how a state's delegation will vote, but the actual delegates are selected by state party officials. Delegate votes won in primary elections are apportioned to candidates on the basis of proportional representation. Thus, a candidate who received 30 percent of the vote in the California Democratic primary would receive roughly 30 percent of the state's delegate votes at the party's national convention.

delegates political activists selected to vote at a party's national convention

As was mentioned earlier, the Democratic Party requires that a state's convention delegation be representative of that state's Democratic electorate in terms of race, gender, and age. Republican delegates, by contrast, are more likely to be male and white. The Democrats also reserve slots for elected Democratic Party officials, called **superdelegates**. All the Democratic governors and about 80 percent of the party's members of Congress now attend the national convention as delegates.

superdelegate a convention delegate position, in Democratic conventions, reserved for party officials

Convention Procedure Each party convention lasts several days. The convention usually begins with the selection of party committees, including the credentials, rules, and platform committees, and the election of a temporary convention chairperson. This individual normally delivers a keynote address highlighting the party's appeals and concerns. After all the delegates have been seated by the credentials committee, a permanent chair is elected. This person presides over the presidential and vice-presidential nominations, the adoption of a party platform, and any votes on rules that are proposed by the rules committee.

Although the actual presidential nomination is effectively decided before the convention, the names of a number of candidates are generally put in nomination and speeches made on their behalf at the convention. To be nominated is considered an honor, and ambitious politicians are eager for the media attention, however brief, that such a nomination brings.

The nominating speeches, as well as speeches by party notables, are carefully scrutinized by the mass media, which report and analyze the major events of the convention. During the 1950s and 1960s, the television networks provided "gavel-to-gavel" coverage of the Democratic and Republican national conventions. Today, however, the major television networks carry convention highlights only. Because the parties are eager to receive as much media coverage as possible, they schedule convention events in order to reach large television audiences. The parties typically try to present the actual presidential nomination and the nominee's acceptance speech during prime viewing time, normally between 8:00 and 11:00 P.M. on a weeknight.

After the nominating speeches are concluded, the voting begins. The names of the states are called alphabetically and the state delegation's vote is reported by its chairperson. During this process, noisy and colorful demonstrations are staged in support of the nominees. When the nomination is formally decided, a lengthy demonstration ensues, with bands and colorful balloons celebrating the conclusion of the process. The party's vice-presidential candidate is usually nominated the next day. This individual is almost always selected by the presidential nominee, and the choice is merely ratified by the convention. In 2008, Barack Obama chose Senator Joseph Biden of Delaware, who brought extensive foreign policy experience to the ticket. John McCain chose Governor Sarah Palin of Alaska, partly in the hope that her very conservative stance on social issues would appeal to the religious right.

Once the nominations have been settled and most other party business has been resolved, the presidential and vice-presidential nominees deliver acceptance speeches. These speeches are opportunities for the nominees to begin their formal campaigns on a positive note, and they are usually meticulously crafted to make as positive an impression on the electorate as possible.

The General Election Campaign and High-Tech Politics

For those candidates lucky enough to survive the nominating process, the last hurdle is the general election. There are essentially two types of general election in the United States today. The first type is the organizationally driven, labor-intensive election. In general, local elections and many congressional races fall into this category. Candidates campaign in such elections by recruiting large numbers of volunteer workers to hand out leaflets and organize rallies. The candidates make appearances at receptions, community group meetings, and local events, and even in shopping malls and on busy street corners. Generally, local and congressional campaigns depend less on issues and policy proposals and more on hard work designed to make the candidate more visible than his or her opponent. Statewide campaigns, some congressional races, and, of course, the national presidential election fall into the second category: the media-driven, capital-intensive electoral campaign.

In the nineteenth and early twentieth centuries, political campaigns were waged by the parties' enormous armies of patronage workers. Throughout the year, party workers cultivated the support of voters by assisting them with legal problems, helping them find jobs, and serving as liaisons with local, state, and federal agencies. On Election Day, throughout the nation hundreds of thousands of party workers marched from house to house reminding their supporters to vote, helping the aged and infirm to reach the polls, and calling in the favors they had accrued during the year. Campaigns resembled the maneuvers of huge infantries vying for victory. Historians have, in fact, referred to this traditional style of party campaigning as "militarist."

Contemporary political campaigns rely less on infantries and more on "air power." That is, rather than deploying huge armies of workers, contemporary campaigns

The Age of the Talk Show Campaign

Modern day political candidates are increasingly likely to seek out voters through non-news television programs such as talk shows, late-night comedy shows, or MTV. Candidates and campaign strategists have discovered that such entertainment venues provide candidates the chance to be seen by viewers who might not otherwise pay attention to the campaign. Less formal shows also allow candidates to show softer or more humorous sides of their personalities. As contemporary politics has become increasingly attentive to candidates' personalities and character, these venues have become a "must" for candidates.

During the 2008 presidential election, Democratic candidates Hillary Clinton and Barack Obama had separate appearances on *The Tonight Show with Jay Leno*, *The Late Show with David Letterman*, and *Saturday Night Live*. Obama danced on stage with *Ellen* and had a heart-to-heart on *Oprah*.

The former Arkansas governor and GOP candidate Mike Huckabee appeared on Leno and Letterman, and even jokingly offered Comedy Central's Stephen Colbert a slot as his VP running mate. The Republican presidential nominee Senator John McCain and his wife Cindy had a sit-down with the ladies of ABC's *The View*. Meanwhile, both McCain and his running mate, Governor Sarah Palin, made separate appearances on *Saturday Night Live* in the weeks running up to the general election.

The appearance of presidential candidates on entertainment television shows is something that would have seemed surprising and inappropriate to audiences prior to 1968. It was in September of that year that Republican Richard Nixon was the first presidential candidate to appear on an entertainment program, delivering the catchphrase "Sock it to me," on the popular variety show *Laugh In*.

Yet, in the 1970s and 80s political candidates continued to campaign almost exclusively in the traditional television forums: political advertisements, presidential debates, and network news programs. The tide seemed to change in 1992 when Bill Clinton appeared on the popular late-night *Arsenio Hall Show* wearing sunglasses and playing the saxophone, and in a town hall style question and answer session on MTV. Also in 1992, independent presidential candidate Ross Perot announced his intention to run for president on the soft-news talk show *Larry King Live*.

Research generally indicates that these appearances can help candidates. When viewers see interviews with political candidates on late-night comedy programs, or see them poking fun at themselves on comedy shows, the audience is more likely to judge the candidate on personal qualities like how much a candidate "cares about people like me." This can be advantageous to candidates whose personalities are warm or inspiring.

And while it is generally found that talk show interviews are friendly and easygoing, not all entertainment appearances go smoothly. For example, during their appearance on *The View* in 2008, John McCain and his wife Cindy were challenged to defend McCain's approval of campaign ads that they claimed were misleading. Following the interview, Cindy McCain told reporters that the hosts of *The View* had "picked their bones clean." Clearly talk and comedy shows provide candidates with an additional way to reach voters—but whether the appearance will definitely help the candidate's image remains to be seen.

SOURCES: Baum, M. A. (2005). "Talking the Vote: Why Presidential Candidates Hit the Talk Show Circuit." *American Journal of Political Science, 49,* 213–234; Moy, P. and Xenos, M. A. & Hess, V. K. (2006). "Priming Effects of Late-Night Comedy." *International Journal of Public Opinion Research, 18,* 198–210; and Cindy McCain: "Tough interviewers 'picked our bones clean'" (2008) CNN.com. Sept 14.

for critical analysis

1. If you were a presidential candidate, would you choose to be interviewed on talk shows? Why or why not?

2. Do you think presidential candidate appearances on talk shows contribute to a more informed electorate? Are they good for democracy? Why or why not?

make use of a number of communications techniques to reach voters and bid for their support. Six techniques are especially important.

Polling Surveys of voter opinion provide the information that candidates and their staffs use to craft campaign strategies. Candidates employ polls to select issues, to assess their own strengths and weaknesses (as well as those of the opposition), to check voter response to the campaign, and to determine the degree to which various constituent groups are susceptible to campaign appeals. Virtually all contemporary campaigns for national and statewide office as well as many local campaigns make extensive use of opinion polling.

The Broadcast Media Extensive use of the broadcast media, television in particular, is the hallmark of the modern political campaign. Candidates endeavor to secure as much positive news and feature coverage as possible. This type of coverage is called *free media* because the cost of air time is borne by the media themselves. Candidates can secure free media coverage by participating in newsworthy events. Incumbents introduce legislation, sponsor hearings, undertake inspection tours of fires and floods, meet with delegations of foreign dignitaries, and so on, to capture the attention of the television cameras. Challengers announce new policy proposals, visit orphanages and senior centers, and demand that their opponents agree to a series of debates. Generally speaking, incumbents have the advantage in securing free media time.

In addition to pursuing free media coverage, candidates spend millions of dollars for *paid media* time, in the form of television and radio ads. Many of these ads consist of fifteen-, thirty-, or sixty-second **spot advertisements** that permit a candidate's message to be delivered to a target audience before uninterested or hostile viewers can tune it out. Examples of extremely effective spot ads include George H. W. Bush's 1988 "Willie Horton" ad, which implied that Bush's opponent, Michael Dukakis, coddled criminals, and Lyndon Johnson's 1964 "daisy girl" ad, which suggested that his opponent, Barry Goldwater, would lead the United States into nuclear war. A successful 2008 spot ad promoting Hillary Clinton's candidacy presented an image of Senator Clinton surrounded by children and cradling a baby. "She changed our way of thinking when she introduced universal health care to America," the narrator intones. The ad ended with the often-repeated Clinton line, "If you're ready for change, she's ready to lead."[8] The ad was designed to soften Clinton's image while declaring her leadership experience in a realm that most Americans believe should be a legislative priority. Television spot ads are used to establish candidate name recognition, to create a favorable image of the candidate and a negative image of the opponent, to link the candidate with desirable groups in the community, and to communicate the candidate's stands on selected issues.

In a typical campaign, candidates will begin with biographical ads to acquaint voters with appealing aspects of their backgrounds. As the campaign progresses, candidates air ads dealing with important issues. In 2008, the presidential candidates presented ads focusing on taxes, foreign policy, health care, and Social Security during the middle rounds of the campaign. In the closing weeks of a campaign, candidates often unleash "attack ads," questioning the opponent's character or judgment. During their October 15, 2008, presidential debate, Obama and McCain criticized one another for running negative campaigns. McCain, however, insisted that his most controversial attack ads, accusing Obama of associating with William Ayers, a 1960s radical who had become a community activist in Chicago, were completely fair and pointed to questions about Obama's character that merited consideration. In the same debate, McCain repeated questions about Obama's ties

spot advertisement a fifteen-, thirty-, or sixty-second television campaign commercial that permits a candidate's message to be delivered to a target audience

to ACORN, a liberal group accused of fraudulently registering large numbers of ineligible Democratic voters and other forms of election fraud.

In addition to ads sponsored by the candidates, numerous campaign ads are sponsored by the political parties and by political advocacy groups seeking to influence the outcome of the election. As discussed in Chapter 4, the 2003 Bipartisan Campaign Reform Act (BCRA) prohibited advocacy groups from running ads that mentioned a candidate's name within thirty days of a primary election and sixty days of a general election. The nominal purpose of the ban was to prevent well-heeled groups from conducting ad blitzes just before an election that might distort the results. When they voted for the ban, though, many members of Congress saw it as what is sometimes called "incumbent relief legislation," designed to make it even more difficult for opponents to defeat entrenched incumbents. In its 2007 decision in *Federal Election Commission v. Wisconsin Right to Life*, the Supreme Court struck down the ad ban as an unconstitutional restriction on speech. The

---

BOX 10.1

Electing the President: Steps in the Process

Formation of an Exploratory Committee. Formed 18–24 months before the election, this committee of supporters begins the process of fund-raising and bringing the candidate's name to the attention of the media and influential groups. At the end of several weeks of "exploration" the prospective candidate will announce whether or not he or she intends to seek office.

Fund-raising. A successful presidential candidate will need to raise several hundred million dollars and may begin even before forming an exploratory committee. Candidates must develop fund-raising strategies, recruit expert fund-raisers, and quickly build a substantial campaign chest to secure early media attention and to convince political professionals that they are serious contenders.

Campaigning. Candidates begin campaigning months before the primary elections and caucuses that start in January of the election year. Campaign strategies may include public appearances, meetings with local leaders and groups, and ad campaigns.

The Party Debates. Each major political party organizes a series of televised discussions among its prospective candidates. For many candidates, these debates represent an early opportunity to impress large television audiences.

The Primaries and Caucuses. In each state, the Democratic and Republican parties each hold a primary election or a caucus (rules vary from state to state) to select delegates to the party's national convention. The delegates are then awarded to candidates in rough proportion to the votes each candidate receives in the state's primary or caucus contest.

The Convention. The Democratic and Republican parties hold national conventions in August and September prior to the November general election, where their nomination for president is "officially" announced. The presidential nominee announces his or her vice-presidential running mate and both deliver acceptance speeches.

The General Election Campaign. Candidates campaign all across the nation—focusing on states considered key to their chances of victory—seeking votes and continuing to raise money. If a candidate accepts public funding, they are prohibited from raising private funds.

The Debates. In October, the presidential candidates engage in several televised debates along with one vice presidential debate. The debates can be decisive in winning over—or failing to win over—undecided voters.

The November Election. Voters in each state cast ballots. In most states, the presidential candidate who wins a majority of votes in the state wins all of that state's votes (as cast by its electors) in the electoral college. Disputes over vote counting are taken to the courts, and recounts may be ordered.

The Electoral College. The electors meet in December and their votes are counted in January. However, there is usually already a clear winner at the end of Election Day in November.

The Inauguration. The new president is officially inaugurated on January. 20.

1992 presidential campaign introduced two new media techniques that are still important today: the talk show interview and the "electronic town hall meeting." Candidates used interviews on television and radio talk shows to reach the large audiences drawn to this popular entertainment program format. The **town meeting** format allows candidates the opportunity to appear in an auditorium like setting and interact with ordinary citizens, thus underlining the candidates' concern with the views and needs of the voters. Moreover, both talk-show appearances and town meetings allow candidates to deliver their messages to millions of Americans without the input of journalists or commentators who might criticize or question the candidates' assertions.

town meeting a media format in which candidates meet with ordinary citizens. Allows candidates to deliver messages without the presence of journalists or commentators

Another use of the broadcast media in contemporary campaigns is the televised candidate debate. Televised presidential debates began with the famous 1960 Kennedy-Nixon clash. Today, both presidential and vice-presidential candidates hold debates, as do candidates for statewide and even local offices. Debates allow candidates to reach voters who have not fully made up their minds about the election. Moreover, debates can increase the visibility of lesser-known candidates. In 1960, John F. Kennedy's strong performance in the presidential debate was a major factor in bringing about his victory over the much better-known Richard Nixon.

Phone Banks Through the broadcast media, candidates communicate with voters en masse and impersonally. Phone banks, on the other hand, allow campaign workers to make personal contact with hundreds of thousands of voters. Personal contacts of this sort are thought to be extremely effective. Again, polling data identify the groups that will be targeted for phone calls. Computers select phone numbers from areas in which members of these groups are concentrated. Staffs of paid or volunteer callers, using computer-assisted dialing systems and prepared scripts, then place calls to deliver the candidate's message. The targeted groups are generally those identified by polls as either uncommitted or weakly committed, as well as strong supporters of the candidate who are contacted simply to encourage them to vote. In 2008, the campaigns also placed hundreds of thousands of automated "robo calls" urging voters to support their candidates.

Despite the growing use of high-tech campaign techniques, candidates still rely on volunteer campaign workers to help get their messages out. Volunteers often go door-to-door, canvassing to encourage supporters of their candidate to get out and vote on Election Day.

Direct Mail Direct mail is both a vehicle for communicating with voters and a mechanism for raising funds. The first step in a direct-mail campaign is the purchase or rental of a computerized mailing list of voters deemed to have some particular perspective or social characteristic. Often magazine subscription lists or lists of donors to various causes are employed. For example, a candidate interested in reaching conservative voters might rent subscription lists from the *National Review, Human Events*, or *Conservative Digest*; a candidate interested in appealing to liberals might rent subscription lists from the *New York Review of Books* or *The Nation*. Considerable fine-tuning is possible. After obtaining the appropriate mailing lists, candidates usually send pamphlets, letters, and brochures describing themselves and their views to voters believed to be sympathetic. Different types of mail appeals are made to different electoral subgroups. Often the letters sent to voters are personalized. The recipient is addressed by name in the text and the letter appears actually to

American Campaign Techniques Conquer the World

Since the 1950s, American election campaigns have been characterized by a reliance on technology in place of organization and personnel and by the rise of a new type of campaigner, the professional political consultant, in place of the old-time party boss. More and more, these campaign methods and even the consultants who wield them have spread to other parts of the world. American campaign consultants with their polls and phone banks and spot ads have directed campaigns in Europe, Latin America, and Asia. One American consultant recently said, "[We have] worked a lot in South America, Israel, [and the] Philippines and one of the things that I've discovered through that work is that the tools and techniques and strategies that we have developed here are applicable everywhere."[a]

This phenomenon, which is sometimes called the Americanization of politics, has important political implications. For the most part, the substitution of technology for organization in political campaigns works to the advantage of politicians

and political forces representing the upper ends of the social spectrum versus those representing the lower classes. Strong party organization was generally introduced by working-class parties as a way of maximizing their major political resource—the power of numbers. When politics is based mainly on organization and numbers, working-class parties can compete quite successfully. The growing use of technology in place of organization shifts the advantage to middle- and upper-class parties, which generally have better access to the financial resources needed to fuel the polls and television ads on which new-style campaigns depend.

In Britain and France, new techniques were introduced first by conservative

parties and then copied by their opponents. The development of the new technology in Europe and other parts of the world followed the American pattern.

This phenomenon is now becoming apparent in Africa. For example, in Kenya's 2008 presidential contest, President Mwai Kibaki made use of consultants, opinion polls, and media technology in his nation's presidential race. The linchpin of Kibaki's effort was the cell-phone campaign. Many Kenyan voters, especially in rural areas, lack Internet access or television service. Most, however, own cell phones. The president's ads, plastered on billboards throughout the nation, provided a cell-phone number and urged voters to call in their views. Voters were also likely to receive cell-phone calls and text messages from Kibaki supporters asking them to vote for the president. Not to be outdone, Kibaki's main rival, the populist Raila Odinga, hired Dick Morris, a former consultant to Bill Clinton, to offer advice to his campaign. Odinga used television ads designed by a media consultant and organized his own cell-phone campaign.[b]

Unfortunately, when Kibaki lost the election, he refused to cede power and a period of fighting ensued before a power-sharing agreement was reached. American consultants scurried for cover when the bullets flew.

[a]Paul Baines, Fritz Plasser, and Christian Scheucher, "Operationalising Political Marketing: A Comparison of US and Western European Consultants and Managers," Middlesex University Discussion Paper Series, No. 7, July 1999.
[b]Stephanie McCrummen, "Kenya Tests New Style of Politicking," *Washington Post*, December 22, 2007, p. A10.

for critical analysis

1. Which foreign political parties were first to adopt American-style campaign techniques? Why?
2. What are the political implications and consequences of the shift from old-fashioned campaign styles to American-style, technology-intensive politics?

have been signed by the candidate. Of course, these "personal" letters and even signatures are generated by a computer.

In addition to its use as a political advertising medium, direct mail has also become an important source of campaign funds. Computerized mailing lists permit campaign strategists to pinpoint individuals whose interests, background, and activities suggest that they may be potential donors to the campaign. Letters of solicitation are sent to these potential donors. Some of the money raised is then used to purchase additional mailing lists. Direct-mail solicitation can be enormously effective.

Professional Public Relations Modern campaigns and the complex technology they rely on are typically directed by professional public-relations consultants. Virtually all serious contenders for national and statewide office retain the services of professional campaign consultants. Increasingly, candidates for local office, too, have come to rely on professional campaign managers. Consultants offer candidates the expertise necessary to conduct accurate opinion polls, produce television commercials, organize direct-mail campaigns, and make use of sophisticated computer analyses.

The Internet The Internet has become a major weapon in modern political campaigns. Although "netwar" has been a factor in politics since the 1990s, the 2008 campaigns made Internet tactics more central to their political strategies than ever before. Beginning with the primaries, every campaign developed a Web strategy for fund-raising, generating interest in the candidate, mobilizing supporters, and getting out the vote. The Clinton primary campaign made extensive use of the Internet to mobilize potential supporters and to raise money. The Edwards campaign used the Web to contact liberal activists who might have seen him as

In the 2008 presidential race, the Obama campaign developed an innovative Web site with features based on social networking sites like Facebook. Obama supporters were able to create their own pages on the site for fund-raising and networking.

an alternative to Clinton and Obama. The Obama campaign, for its part, used the Internet to create events such as walkathons and fund-raisers all around the country. Both Obama and John McCain created social networking sites that allow supporters to post information about themselves and to chat with each other. These sites help build enthusiasm and are potent fund-raising tools. Obama's site was built by Thomas Gensemer and the company Blue State Digital. Obama's Web site played a major role in the Illinois senator's ability to raise money and build strong ties to supporters.[9]

Campaigns and Political Equality: From Labor-Intensive to Capital-Intensive Politics

The displacement of organizational methods by technology is, in essence, a shift from labor-intensive to capital-intensive competitive electoral practices. Campaign tasks that were once performed by masses of party workers with some cash now require fewer personnel but a great deal more money, for the new political style depends on polls, computers, and other electronic paraphernalia. Of course, even when workers and organization were the key electoral tools, money had considerable political significance. Nevertheless, during the nineteenth century, national political campaigns in the United States employed millions of people. Indeed, as many as 2.5 million individuals did political work during the 1880s.[10] The direct cost of campaigns, therefore, was relatively low. For example, in 1860, Abraham Lincoln spent only $100,000—which was approximately twice the amount spent by his chief opponent, Stephen A. Douglas.

Modern campaigns depend heavily on money. Each element of contemporary political technology is enormously expensive. A sixty-second spot announcement on prime-time network television costs hundreds of thousands of dollars each time it is aired. Opinion surveys can be quite expensive; polling costs in a statewide race can easily reach or exceed the six-figure mark. Campaign consultants can charge substantial fees. The inauguration of a serious national direct-mail campaign requires at least $1 million in "front-end cash" to pay for mailing lists, brochures, letters, envelopes, and postage.[11] Even debate preparation requires substantial staff work, research, and, of course, money. It is the expense of new technology that accounts for the enormous cost of recent American national elections.

Certainly "people power" is not irrelevant to modern political campaigns. Candidates continue to utilize the political services of tens of thousands of volunteer workers. Nevertheless, in the contemporary era, even the recruitment of campaign workers has become a matter of electronic technology. Employing a technique called "instant organization," paid telephone callers use phone banks to contact individuals in areas targeted by a computer (which they do when contacting potential voters, as we discussed before). Volunteer workers are recruited from among these individuals. A number of campaigns—Richard Nixon's 1968 presidential campaign was the first—have successfully used this technique.

The displacement of organizational methods by technology has the farthest-reaching implications for the balance of power among contending political groups. Labor-intensive organizational tactics allowed parties whose chief support came from groups nearer the bottom of the social scale to use the numerical superiority of their forces as a partial counterweight to the institutional and economic resources more readily available to the opposition. The capital-intensive technological format, by contrast, has given a major boost to the political fortunes of those forces whose sympathizers are better able to furnish the large sums now needed to

for critical **analysis**

In recent years, the Internet has become a prominent campaign tool. Does the Internet make electoral campaigns more democratic? Does it make them less democratic? Or are its effects neutral?

compete effectively.[12] Indeed, the new technology permits financial resources to be more effectively harnessed and exploited than was ever before possible.

Dominated by expensive technology, electoral politics has become a contest in which the wealthy and powerful have a decided advantage. Perhaps the use of the Internet is the only exception. Through the Internet, political candidates have been able to raise millions of dollars in small contributions from tens of thousands of donors. To maximize the power of online fund-raising, Internet "bundlers" such as ActBlue combine thousands of small contributions to make major donations to particular candidates. For example, in 2007 ActBlue raised over $4 million from 54,000 online donors for John Edwards's campaign for the Democratic presidential nomination.[13] Despite the potential of the Internet, online fund-raising produced only 5 to 10 percent of the more than $3 billion spent by or on behalf of candidates in the 2008 national elections. For the bulk of their funds, both political parties are compelled to rely heavily on the support of well-funded special interests—a situation that has become clear in the fund-raising scandals that have plagued both parties in recent years. We shall return to this topic later in this chapter.

How Voters Decide

Whatever the capacity of those with the money and power to influence the electoral process, it is the millions of individual decisions on Election Day that ultimately determine electoral outcomes. Sooner or later the choices of voters weigh more heavily than the schemes of campaign advisers or the leverage of interest groups.

Three factors influence voters' decisions at the polls: partisan loyalty, issues and policy concerns, and candidate characteristics.

Partisan Loyalty

Many studies have shown that most Americans identify more or less strongly with one or the other of the two major political parties. Partisan loyalty was considerably stronger during the 1940s and 1950s than it is today. But even now most voters feel a certain sense of identification or kinship with the Democratic or Republican party. This sense of identification is often handed down from parents to children and is reinforced by social and cultural ties. Partisan identification predisposes voters in favor of their party's candidates and against those of the opposing party (see Figure 10.4). At the level of the presidential contest, issues and candidate personalities may become very important, although even here many Americans supported John McCain or Barack Obama in the 2008 race only because of partisan loyalty. But partisanship is more likely to assert itself in the less-visible races, where issues and the candidates are not as well-known. State legislative races, for example, are often decided by voters' party ties. Once formed, voters' partisan loyalties seldom change. Voters tend to keep their party affiliations unless some crisis causes them to reexamine the bases of their loyalties and to conclude that they have not given their support to the appropriate party. During these relatively infrequent periods of electoral change, millions of voters can change their party ties. For example, at the beginning of the New Deal era, between 1932 and 1936, millions of former Republicans transferred their allegiance to Franklin Roosevelt and the Democrats.

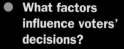
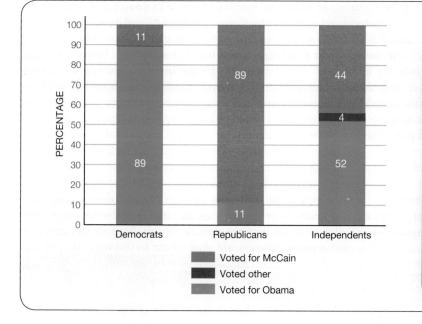

Issues

Issues and policy preferences are a second factor influencing voters' choices at the polls. Voters may cast their ballots for the candidate whose position on economic issues they believe to be closest to their own. Similarly, they may select the candidate who has what they believe to be the best record on foreign policy. Issues are more important in some races than others. If candidates actually "take issue" with each other, that is, articulate and publicize very different positions on important public questions, then voters are more likely to be able to identify and act on whatever policy preferences they may have.

The ability of voters to make choices on the basis of issue or policy preferences is diminished, however, if competing candidates do not differ substantially or do not focus their campaigns on policy matters. Very often, candidates deliberately take the safe course and emphasize topics that will not be offensive to any voters. Thus, candidates often trumpet their opposition to corruption, crime, and inflation. Presumably, few voters favor these things. Although it may be perfectly reasonable for candidates to take the safe course and remain as inoffensive as possible, this candidate strategy makes it extremely difficult for voters to make their issue or policy preferences the basis for their choices at the polls.

Voters' issue choices usually involve a mix of their judgments about the past behavior of competing parties and candidates and their hopes and fears about candidates' future behavior. Political scientists call choices that focus on future behavior **prospective voting**, whereas those based on past performance are called **retrospective voting**. To some extent, whether prospective or retrospective evaluation is more important in a particular election depends on the strategies of competing candidates. Candidates always endeavor to define the issues of an election in terms that will serve their interests. Incumbents running during a period of prosperity will seek to take credit for the economy's happy state and define the election as revolving around their record of success. This strategy encourages voters to make retrospective

prospective voting voting based on the imagined future performance of a candidate

retrospective voting voting based on the past performance of a candidate

judgments. By contrast, an insurgent running during a period of economic uncertainty will tell voters it is time for a change and ask them to make prospective judgments. Thus, Bill Clinton focused on change in 1992 and prosperity in 1996, and through well-crafted media campaigns was able to define voters' agenda of choices.

In 2008, no incumbent was running for the presidency. Democrats, however, sought to portray John McCain, the Republican candidate, as simply a continuation of the failed Bush administration and took every opportunity to link McCain to Bush's unpopular economic and foreign policies. McCain, for his part, portrayed himself as a "maverick" who had often disagreed with Bush and other Republicans. In the end, voters associated a Republican White House with their economic woes and took out their frustrations on the Republican candidate.

The Economy As we identify the strategies and tactics employed by opposing political candidates and parties, we should keep in mind that the best-laid plans of politicians often go awry. Election outcomes are affected by a variety of forces that candidates for office cannot fully control. Among the most important of these forces is the condition of the economy. If voters are satisfied with their economic prospects, they tend to support the party in power, while voter unease about the economy tends to favor the opposition. Thus, George H. W. Bush lost in 1992 during an economic downturn even though his victory in the Middle East had briefly given him a 90 percent favorable rating in the polls. And Bill Clinton won in 1996 during an economic boom even though voters had serious concerns about his moral fiber. As we shall see later in this chapter, the 2008 financial crisis gave Barack Obama and the Democrats a significant advantage. Over the past quarter-century, the "Consumer Confidence Index," calculated by the Conference Board, a business research group, has been a fairly accurate predictor of presidential outcomes. The index is based on surveys asking voters how optimistic they are about the future of the economy. It would appear that a generally rosy view, indicated by a score over 100, augurs well for the party in power. An index score under 100, suggesting that voters are pessimistic about the economy's trend, suggests that incumbents should worry about their own job prospects (see Figure 10.5). Just before the November, 2010 elections, the Consumer Confidence Index stood at 50.2, which turned out to be a good predictor of the heavy losses the Democrats would sustain at the polls.

Candidate Characteristics

Candidates' personal attributes always influence voters' decisions. Some analysts claim that voters prefer tall candidates to short ones, candidates with shorter names to candidates with longer names, and candidates with lighter hair to candidates with darker hair. Perhaps these rather frivolous criteria do play some role. But the more important candidate characteristics that affect voters' choices are race, ethnicity, religion, gender, geography, and social background. In general, voters prefer candidates who are closer to themselves in terms of these categories; voters presume that such candidates are likely to have views and perspectives close to their own. Moreover, they may be proud to see someone of their ethnic, religious, or geographic background in a position of leadership. This is why, for many years, politicians sought to "balance the ticket," making certain that their party's ticket included members of as many important groups as possible.

Just as candidates' personal characteristics may attract some voters, they may repel others. Many voters are prejudiced against candidates of certain ethnic, racial, or

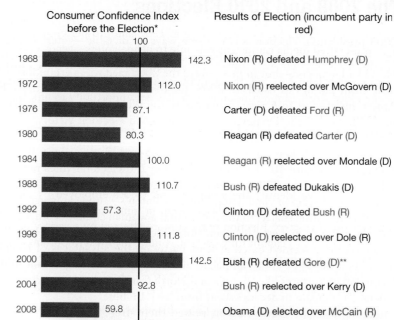

Consumer Confidence Index before the Election*

Results of Election (incumbent party in red)

Year	CCI	Result
1968	142.3	Nixon (R) defeated Humphrey (D)
1972	112.0	Nixon (R) reelected over McGovern (D)
1976	87.1	Carter (D) defeated Ford (R)
1980	80.3	Reagan (R) defeated Carter (D)
1984	100.0	Reagan (R) reelected over Mondale (D)
1988	110.7	Bush (R) defeated Dukakis (D)
1992	57.3	Clinton (D) defeated Bush (R)
1996	111.8	Clinton (D) reelected over Dole (R)
2000	142.5	Bush (R) defeated Gore (D)**
2004	92.8	Bush (R) reelected over Kerry (D)
2008	59.8	Obama (D) elected over McCain (R)

FIGURE 10.5
Consumer Confidence and Presidential Elections

Since 1968, the Consumer Confidence Index has been a reliable predictor of incumbents' political fortunes. Was the result of the 2008 election consistent with this trend? What issues other than the economy influenced the 2008 election?

*Survey was bimonthly prior to 1977 so figures for 1968, 1972, and 1976 are for October and they are for September from 1983 on.

**Gore won the popular vote but Bush was elected by the Electoral College.

SOURCE: Bloomberg Financial Markets.

religious groups. And for many years voters were reluctant to support the candidacies of women, although this appears to be changing. Indeed, the fact that in 2008 the Democratic candidate was a black man and the Republican vice-presidential candidate a woman indicates the ongoing collapse of previously rigid political barriers.

Voters also pay attention to candidates' personality characteristics, such as "decisiveness," "honesty," and "vigor." In recent years, integrity has become a key election issue. In 2008, Republicans frequently questioned Barack Obama's character, pointing to his association with the 1960s radical William Ayers, and with his outspoken black minister, Rev. Jeremiah Wright. Democrats, for their part, attacked Sarah Palin for alleged abuses of power in Alaska. However, voters seemed less concerned with these matters than with the ability of the candidates to deal with the nation's economic woes. In hard times, the electorate tends to become impatient with partisan mudslinging.

for critical analysis

Do American political campaigns help voters make decisions? Or do they produce more confusion than enlightenment?

● The 2008 and 2010 Elections

The 2008 presidential election was in some ways predictable—voters wanted a change from a very unpopular Republican administration and, perhaps predictably, elected a Democrat—but in many ways the 2008 race was a groundbreaking departure from politics as usual. In 2008, for the first time in the nation's history, Americans elected an African American to the White House. Senator Barack Obama of Illinois led the Democratic Party to a solid electoral victory, securing 53 percent of the popular vote versus the Republican candidate, Senator John McCain, who were 46 percent. Obama won a 365-to-173 majority in the Electoral College (see Figure 10.5), far more than the 270 electoral votes needed to claim the presidency. The 2008 presidential election was also notable because of the prominence of women candidates. Hillary Clinton's strong campaign for the Democratic nomination shattered the notion that a woman couldn't compete seriously for the nation's highest office, and John McCain's selection of Sarah Palin as his running mate seemed based at least partly on the advantages of having a woman on the ticket. The 2008 campaigns also brought about a significant shift in the electoral map, as states like Virginia and North Carolina that hadn't supported a Democratic candidate in decades went from "red" to "blue."

As noted above, the Democrats increased their strength in both houses of Congress in 2008, adding eight seats in the Senate, giving them a larger majority. Democrats also gained at least twenty-two seats in the House of Representatives to win a 256-to-178 majority in the lower chamber. Because of enormous interest in the presidential campaign, the increasing use of absentee and pre-Election Day voting, and well-financed voter registration drives conducted mainly by the Democrats, more than 120 million Americans cast ballots in 2008, a number comparable to the level of turnout reached in 2004. In the 2010 midterm elections, however, the GOP was able to recover much of the ground it had ceded to the Democrats in 2008. Riding a tidal wave of popular dissatisfaction with the Obama administration and Congress, Republicans regained control of the House of Representatives and increased their numbers in the Senate as well.

The 2008 Primaries

The 2008 Democratic and Republican primaries and caucuses to select the parties' candidates for the presidency began January 3 with the Iowa Democratic caucuses. The actual campaigns, of course, began early in 2007 as ambitious politicians assessed their chances and started the long process needed to raise the tens of millions of dollars required to launch a presidential candidacy. On the Republican side, the front-runner was John McCain. The Arizona senator had campaigned for the Republican nomination in 2000, only to be defeated by Bush in a primary contest remembered for the victor's smear tactics. McCain, the son and grandson of U.S. Navy admirals, was a Vietnam War hero whose body still bore the marks of having been severely tortured by the North Vietnamese after he was captured when his plane was shot down during a bombing mission. McCain had a distinguished career in the Senate and was the chief sponsor of several major pieces of legislation, including the McCain-Feingold campaign reform law. When the Republicans had last controlled the Senate, McCain had chaired the Foreign

*Hillary Clinton was seen as the
front-runner for the Democratic
nomination in the months leading up to the primaries. How
to address the ongoing war in
Iraq was an issue debated by
the Democratic candidates, and
Clinton was criticized by some
Democrats for initially supporting the war.*

Relations Committee and was regarded in Washington as one of the Senate's
foreign policy experts. Despite his national prominence, McCain was generally
not well-liked in Republican circles. The party's business wing was suspicious of
McCain because of his reformist bent and often found him annoyingly hypocritical for continually denouncing the role of big money in politics while frequently
approaching corporate donors and lobbyists to ask for their support. For its
part, the GOP's social-conservative base distrusted McCain, whom they saw as
uninterested—at best—in the various social issues they regarded as having paramount political importance. Traditional Republicans might have preferred Mitt
Romney, a successful businessperson and former governor of Massachusetts, but
the GOP's evangelical Protestant cadres did not like the idea of Romney, a Mormon,
as their party's candidate. Social conservatives supported former Arkansas governor and evangelical minister, Mike Huckabee, an articulate politician whose sense
of humor made him a successful guest on *Saturday Night Live.* Other Republicans,
Ron Paul, Rudy Giuliani, and Fred Thompson, excited little interest.

After losing the Iowa caucuses to Huckabee and struggling to raise money,
McCain regained his political and financial footing and was able to drive his
opponents from the race. McCain had effectively secured the Republican nomination by the beginning of March. Though Republicans appeared to have no serious
alternative to McCain, the Arizona senator's candidacy did not excite the party.
A large segment of the GOP's conservative base was uninspired by McCain, and
some saw him as a liberal in Republican clothing.

Clinton Versus Obama On the Democratic side, the clear front-runner for
the presidential nomination was the New York senator and former first lady Hillary
Rodham Clinton. Senator Clinton was famous, her husband was extraordinarily
popular among Democrats, and her contacts and position as a New York senator
meant that she would be able to count on tens of millions of dollars in campaign
contributions. Most pundits predicted an easy Clinton victory. Other Democratic
contenders included former North Carolina senator and 2004 vice-presidential candidate John Edwards, former New Mexico governor Bill Richardson, congressman

Dennis Kucinich, former Alaska senator Mike Gravel, and senators Joe Biden, Chris Dodd, and Barack Obama. Biden, Dodd, and Richardson, along with Gravel and Kucinich, generated relatively little interest and quickly dropped out. Edwards was popular among his fellow trial lawyers, who contributed enough money to his campaign to keep him in through the end of January, though with little chance of success. The surprise of the Democratic primary contest was, of course, Senator Barack Obama.

Obama was a first-term senator from Illinois, having arrived in Washington in 2004. He had won a measure of national celebrity by delivering a rousing key-note address at the 2004 Democratic national convention. Many Democrats' first opportunity to see Obama as a serious contender came in the Democratic debates. Prior to and during the primary contests, it has become conventional for each party's contenders to hold televised debates on various issues of national interest. Twenty-six debates between the Democratic hopefuls were scheduled, beginning in April 2007, with the last debate in April 2008. For the most part, the debaters acquitted themselves well, committing few gaffes. Media analysts generally thought Clinton had a somewhat stronger command of the issues, though some thought Edwards spoke more forcefully. However, the true winner of the primary-season debates was Obama. The Illinois senator was not necessarily more articulate, more knowledgeable, or more passionate about important issues than Clinton, Edwards, and the others, but observers were impressed that at debate after debate the virtually unknown senator stood toe-to-toe with his more seasoned and famous opponents and held his own. Obama's impressive performance electrified liberal Democrats, excited young voters, intrigued the media, and ignited the enthusiasm of black Democrats, even if most were initially dubious that Obama could succeed. This enthusiastic response to Obama's debate appearances swelled the ranks of Obama supporters, inspired donors to write checks, and gave Obama the means to compete against Clinton and Edwards.

Over the next six months, Clinton and Obama battled furiously in state after state. Edwards dropped out of the race, and Obama had established himself as a contender with the potential to defeat the once seemingly invincible Clinton. Obama was particularly popular with younger voters and with liberals who resented what they saw as Clinton's early equivocation on the Iraq war. Black politicians—many of whom considered Bill Clinton an important ally during his presidency—initially supported Hillary Clinton, assuming she would win. But as their constituents rallied to Obama, and it became clear that Obama's candidacy actually had a chance, the Illinois senator was able to garner overwhelming black support. Some pundits said it was ironic that the first woman to mount a serious presidential bid and the first black person to mount such a bid were pitted against one another. For the news media, however, in this battle of the firsts, Obama's candidacy was the more important first. Clinton was seen as an established figure on the political scene—a powerful senator from New York, former first lady, and wife of perhaps the most powerful figure in the Democratic Party. Clinton's status in some ways worked against her. To some commentators it appeared that Clinton had already been co-president for eight years and was no longer a first.

By late spring, it became clear that Obama would be the Democratic presidential nominee. The result was close. Under Democratic rules, 2,118 delegates were needed to win the nomination. In the various primaries and caucuses, Obama had won 1,763 delegates to Clinton's 1,640. This effectively left the decision to the party's 796 "superdelegates," party officials and notables chosen to attend the convention. At the outset, most superdelegates had backed Clinton. As the

In his bid for the presidency, John McCain strived to distance himself from George W. Bush, whose popularity had reached record lows before the 2008 election. However, Americans' reluctance to elect another Republican after the Bush administration's poor performance contributed to McCain's defeat.

race wore on, however, sentiment shifted toward Obama. Some saw Obama as the better candidate, while others worried that black Democrats—20 percent of the party's electoral strength—would stay home on Election Day if Obama was denied the nomination. With 438 superdelegates supporting Obama, he could count on 2,201 votes. Clinton briefly weighed taking her candidacy to the floor of the convention to be decided there, but ultimately, on June 3, withdrew and announced that she and her husband would staunchly support Obama in the general election.

The General Election

At the August 2008 Democratic national convention, speaker after speaker extolled Obama's virtues. Obama chose Senator Joseph Biden of Delaware as his vice-presidential running mate. Biden, chair of the Senate Foreign Relations Committee, was selected at least partly in response to questions about Obama's scant foreign policy experience. In addition, Biden had working- class roots in Pennsylvania. Democrats hoped that Biden would appeal to the so-called "Joe Six-pack" voters, blue-collar workers whom the Democrats needed in such battleground states as Ohio and Pennsylvania.

The Republican convention, which opened a few days after the Democratic convention ended, began without much fanfare. Hurricane Gustav, which was bearing down on the Gulf states, led the Republicans to cancel many of the first day's events, as they wanted to make clear that they were taking a possible natural disaster seriously. Rather than attending the convention, President Bush addressed the delegates via video. Moreover, although John McCain won the primary battle and was respected for his military service, he was not an especially beloved figure among rank-and-file Republicans. Nevertheless, McCain excited and energized Republicans when he chose Sarah Palin, the little-known governor of Alaska, as his vice-presidential running mate and "introduced" her to the GOP base at the convention. Palin, a religious conservative who opposed abortion, excited many Republicans who had been cool toward McCain.

Palin's vice-presidential acceptance speech, which might otherwise have been watched by a handful of diehard Republicans, attracted more than 50 million curious viewers when it was broadcast from the convention. Palin rose to the occasion and delivered a strong speech, filled with memorable quips and emphasizing issues of character and family values. "A star is born," declared the conservative commentator Pat Buchanan after the speech. Unfortunately for the GOP, Palin's star faded rapidly as the inexperienced governor proved unequal to the demands of a national campaign. In television interviews, including one with Katie Couric on CBS, Palin seemed to know little about current political issues and problems, and could do no more than repeat Republican talking points that she seemed to have committed to memory. Despite her reasonably good performance in the nationally televised vice-presidential debate, Palin was declared "clearly out of her league," even by staunchly Republican commentators who wondered aloud if Palin could seriously be entrusted with the presidency if anything happened to McCain.

Despite the brief surge of enthusiasm generated by the selection of Palin, the McCain ticket struggled throughout the campaign. From the beginning the deck seemed stacked against the Republicans. Despite his protestations of independence, the fact remained that McCain was a Republican and, hence, tied to the Bush administration. Obama and the Democrats, moreover, held an enormous fund-raising advantage over McCain and the Republicans. Knowing that he would have difficulty raising money from traditional GOP donors, McCain had decided to accept public funding for the general election. This would give his campaign some $84 million to spend on organizing, advertising, and voter registration but would prohibit him from raising additional funds from private sources. McCain hoped Republican Party fund-raising would add considerably to this figure. Obama, on the other hand, became the first major-party candidate since the law was enacted to forgo general election public funding. Obama was, instead, able to step up his Internet and conventional fund-raising, which eventually produced in the neighborhood of $700 million, an astonishing total that more than doubled the previous

Republican voters were initially enthusiastic about McCain's choice of Governor Sarah Palin of Alaska as his running mate. However, Palin stumbled in television interviews, including an interview with CBS's Katie Couric in which Palin's answers sometimes seemed incoherent (left). Palin's poor performance was the subject of widely viewed skits on Saturday Night Live (right), in which comedian Tina Fey impersonated Palin, in one case using Palin's own words from the interview with Katie Couric.

record set by the Republicans in 2004. His campaign's extraordinary fund-raising prowess gave Obama and the Democrats some $200 million more to spend than was available to McCain and the Republicans.

Lack of money was not McCain's only problem. Beginning in 2008, the nation experienced a serious financial crisis that began with a decline in home sales and a wave of mortgage foreclosures, and continued with billions of dollars of losses in mortgage-based securities. Toward the end of September, the stock market lost more than a third of its value, wiping out trillions of dollars in investments. Some of the nation's leading financial institutions, such as the venerable Lehman Brothers, failed and a host of others seemed poised to close their doors. Since all these events took place while the Republicans controlled the White House, the Democrats were quick to blame the Bush administration's economic policies for the crisis though, in truth, congressional Democrats had often protected such institutions as Fannie Mae and Freddie Mac that were at the root of the problem. Nevertheless, Republican presidential chances seemed to decline with the stock market as the GOP bore the brunt of the public's anger and concern.

The Debates Obama helped his cause enormously in the three televised presidential debates held in September and October. He responded with evident knowledge and intelligence to questions on matters of domestic and foreign policy. So, for that matter, did McCain. But McCain, the Washington veteran, was expected to have answers to policy questions. Obama was the newcomer who had been chided for his inexperience. Like Kennedy, Reagan, and Clinton before him, Obama bore the burden of reassuring voters that he measured up to the job of being president. In the debates, Obama spoke clearly and incisively on education, economic policy, health policy, and the wars in Iraq and Afghanistan. McCain, to be sure, had actual experience in all these areas while Obama only spoke well, but the same had been true of—and enough for—Kennedy, Reagan, and Clinton.

Even more important was Obama's manner. By contrast with the often twitchy McCain, Obama was smooth, calm, and reassuring. Many commentators observed that Obama appeared "presidential," and that this helped more and more Americans feel comfortable with his candidacy. Following the debates, Obama's approval ratings rose steadily and the McCain campaign faltered. Republicans were reduced to efforts to portray Obama as the friend of the 1960s radical William Ayers, with whom Obama had had a casual connection in the past. Obama easily parried these attacks by presenting his new friends, such establishment figures as the billionaire investor Warren Buffett, former secretary of state Colin Powell, and former Federal Reserve head Paul Volcker.

Obama's Victory Throughout October, Obama led consistently in the national polls, but by single-digit margins. Given the faltering economy, an unpopular president, and the Democrats' enormous financial advantage, the GOP should have been heading for a train wreck of epic proportions and yet, until late October when Obama's lead increased, McCain trailed only by three- to five-point margins in the polls. Some analysts of opinion data thought the problem was race. A white Democratic candidate, according to some mathematical models of public opinion, would have enjoyed a much stronger lead in the polls, perhaps an additional six or seven points. Some analysts worried whether Obama's lead was even as strong as it looked. These analysts pointed to the so-called Bradley effect, a phantom lead in the polls produced when white voters, reluctant to display overt signs of racism, lie to pollsters about their intentions. This is allegedly what

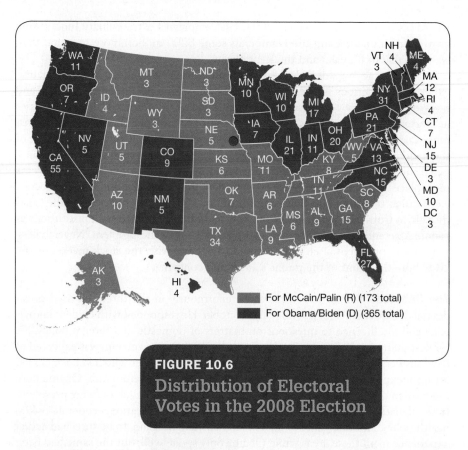

FIGURE 10.6

Distribution of Electoral Votes in the 2008 Election

happened in 1982 when Los Angeles, Mayor Tom Bradley lost the California gubernatorial race after leading his white opponent in the polls. While asserting that race would not be a factor in the 2008 election, Obama cautioned his supporters not to be overconfident.

In the end, racial antipathy did not determine the outcome of the 2008 presidential election. Some voters undoubtedly opposed Obama because of his race while others supported him on the same grounds. But, given America's long history of slavery, segregation, and racial antagonism, the most important fact of the election was that tens of millions of white voters—some reluctantly—had voted for a black man for the presidency of the United States. Remarkably, Obama ran better among white voters than the Democratic candidate, John Kerry, had in 2004. Obama polled 43 percent of the white vote, two points more than the percentage polled by Kerry. Obama also ran well among Latinos (66 percent), young people (66 percent), and among black voters, where he took 95 percent of the vote. Two Democratic constituencies, women and Jews, who had favored Hillary Clinton in the primaries gave their support to Obama in the general election. Obama won 56 percent of the vote among women and 78 percent among Jews. The most important issue cited by voters who cast ballots for Obama was the economy. More than 60 percent said that their chief policy reason for supporting Obama over McCain was a belief that Obama and the Democrats would be better able to restore the nation's economic health. Obama won by a total of 365 electoral votes to 173 for McCain (see Figure 10.6).

Who Supported Obama in 2008?

Barack Obama defeated John McCain in the 2008 presidential election, winning 53% of the popular vote to McCain's 46%. The map in Figure 10.6, to the left, shows who won each state; there, red seems to dominate. However, if we adjust the map to show each state in proportion to its population, blue states—those won by Obama—clearly dominate.

Election Results by State's Population

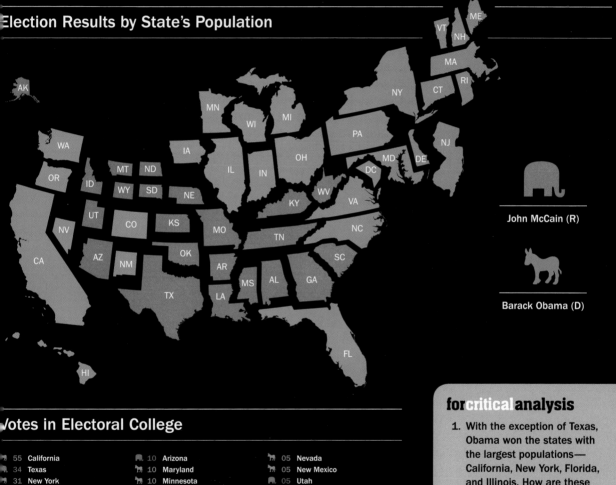

John McCain (R)

Barack Obama (D)

Votes in Electoral College

55	California	10	Arizona	05	Nevada			
34	Texas	10	Maryland	05	New Mexico			
31	New York	10	Minnesota	05	Utah			
27	Florida	10	Wisconsin	05	West Virginia			
21	Illinois	09	Alabama	04	Hawaii			
21	Pennsylvania	09	Colorado	04	Idaho			
20	Ohio	09	Louisiana	04	Maine			
17	Michigan	08	Kentucky	04	New Hampshire			
15	Georgia	08	South Carolina	04	Rhode Island			
15	New Jersey	07	Connecticut	03	Alaska			
15	North Carolina	07	Iowa	03	Delaware			
13	Virginia	07	Oklahoma	03	District Of Columbia			
12	Massachusetts	07	Oregon	03	Montana			
11	Indiana	06	Arkansas	03	North Dakota			
11	Missouri	06	Kansas	03	South Dakota			
11	Tennessee	06	Mississippi	03	Vermont			
11	Washington	05	Nebraska	03	Wyoming			

SOURCE: Mark Newman, "Maps of the 2008 US presidential election results," www.personal.umich.edu/~mejn/election/2008/ (accessed 7/8/10).

for critical analysis

1. With the exception of Texas, Obama won the states with the largest populations—California, New York, Florida, and Illinois. How are these states different from those that McCain won? What do these differences tell us about the political differences between more densely populated areas (urban areas) and those with lower populations (rural areas)?

2. What do you think causes the differences between urban and rural America? Do you think these differences will continue long into the future?

The 2010 Elections

In 2010, after nearly two years in office, President Obama and his Democratic allies in the 111th Congress could point to an impressive set of accomplishments. Prodded by the president, Congress had enacted a major overhaul of the nation's health care system—a feat that had eluded previous Democratic presidents Bill Clinton and Jimmy Carter. Under the terms of what came to be known in the press as "Obamacare," tens of millions of previously uninsured Americans would potentially be eligible to purchase low-cost or federally subsidized health insurance policies through state-based insurance exchanges. Insurance companies would be prohibited from denying coverage to individuals with preexisting conditions.

Obama and congressional Democrats also enacted a major new law aimed at protecting the nation's financial system from a future crisis like the one that nearly brought about a global financial catastrophe in 2008–09. Under the financial overhaul law, banks would be subject to tighter regulation and prohibited from engaging in some of the risky activities that contributed to the collapse of several major banking institutions and the larger economic crisis. Among other provisions, the law revamped the mortgage system to protect borrowers, discourage risky loans, and establish a new consumer protection agency to oversee consumer lending and the practices of credit card issuers.

During the same two years, Congress enacted and the president signed into law a massive financial bailout act, a law helping impoverished children obtain health insurance, a law making it easier for women to sue their employers for wage discrimination, a law reforming the Pentagon's weapons procurement policies, and a host of other laws aimed at strengthening the nation's economy, improving social services, and promoting equal rights.

Yet, despite the successes claimed by Obama and his allies, public opinion polls taken throughout the summer and fall of 2010 indicated that the Democrats were likely to lose a large number of congressional seats in the November 2010 midterm elections. It is usually the case that the president's party will lose some congressional seats in midterm elections. Members swept to victory on the president's coattails are more vulnerable as some voters drawn to the polls by the presidential campaign lose interest and fail to turn out for the midterm elections. Projections in 2010, however, seemed to suggest that the Democrats could expect a far greater midterm drubbing at the polls than usual. The nation's economy remained sluggish, with unusually high rates of unemployment. At the same time, many Democrats were unsatisfied with Obama's accomplishments and less interested in supporting their party in 2010. Many Republicans, on the other hand, were outraged by the Obama agenda and were determined to punish the Democrats in the 2010 elections. The news media referred to this phenomenon as the "enthusiasm gap."

A Crisis of Enthusiasm?

Democrats, particularly liberal Democrats, had pinned enormous hopes on the Obama administration and the large Democratic congressional majorities elected in 2008. Liberals saw an opportunity for an expansion of domestic social programs. They were confident that Obama—a frequent senatorial critic of Bush-era foreign policy—would bring a quick end to the wars in Iraq and Afghanistan and would present a less bellicose image to the world. Liberals were also certain that the administration and Congress would not only end the nation's economic crisis but also bring an end to the laissez-faire economic policies they believed had led to the crisis in the first place. Liberals hoped, too, that the administration would develop a new immigration policy that would present a more welcoming face to the millions of illegal immigrants living in the United States.

On each of these dimensions, however, liberal Democrats found reasons to be less than satisfied with the performance of President Obama and the congressional Democratic leadership. Obamacare represented a major expansion of federal social policy. Yet, many liberals had hoped for a program of national health insurance, perhaps along the lines of an expansion of Medicare to cover all Americans. Other liberals argued that the plan should at least offer a "public option" of national health insurance for some Americans. The enacted legislation, though, with its reliance on private insurers seemed, to some, a weak beginning and, to others, a sell-out to the health insurance industry.

In the realm of foreign policy, the administration did declare that America's combat role in Iraq had ended—despite the continuing presence of tens of thousands of American troops in that country—and at the same time stepped up combat operations in Afghanistan. The Obama administration's new package of economic regulations satisfied some liberal demands, though liberal and progressive groups denounced the law's many loopholes, such as exemptions granted to community banks and auto dealers, from oversight by the newly created Consumer Financial Products Agency. Finally, in the controversial area of immigration reform, the administration enraged liberals by delaying the introduction of new proposals while the opponents of immigration reform enacted restrictive legislation at the state level. All in all, liberal Democrats' initial enthusiasm for Obama had diminished sharply as they judged the president's performance to lag sharply behind his promises.[14]

A Cup of Tea?

The same Obama administration policies that produced a decline of political engagement among liberal Democrats produced outrage and a sharp increase in political involvement among conservative Republicans. Many conservatives were infuriated by the president's social and economic programs. While liberal Democrats thought health care reform had not gone far enough, conservatives saw Obamacare as a costly government takeover of a major industry and an unwarranted intrusion into the lives of all Americans. While liberals saw the administration's financial reform program as a law filled with loopholes, conservatives saw a policy that would strangle America's financial services industry. While liberals thought Obama had not done enough to end America's military involvement in the Middle East, conservatives saw a lack of commitment to America's military strength. And, while liberals were unhappy with the lack of progress on immigration reform, conservatives saw an administration unwilling to protect America's borders from a flood of illegals. Hence the policies that left liberals disenchanted and disengaged, drove new legions of outraged conservatives into the political arena.

The most visible manifestation of conservative anger was the Tea Party movement that arose in late 2008 and early 2009 in response to the Obama administration's economic stimulus plans and health care reform plan. The tea party concept caught on over the Internet and through conservative blogs. Soon Tea Party activists began holding meetings and demonstrations throughout the nation

Christine O'Donnell was one of several Tea Party-backed candidates who won primary elections by appealing to dissatisfied Republican voters, but whose lack of qualifications made if difficult to win the general election.

to protest the administration's policies. The Tea Party movement first made its political weight felt in the January 2010 special election to fill the seat vacated by the death of long-time U.S. Senator Ted Kennedy of Massachusetts. With the support of local Tea Party groups who recruited thousands of volunteers for his campaign, political newcomer Scott Brown, a vocal opponent of Obamacare, became the first Republican senator to be elected from Massachusetts since 1972. Subsequently, Tea Party activists campaigned vigorously in the 2010 Republican primaries, often supporting conservative insurgents against more established mainstream Republicans. For example, in New York, with the backing of local Tea Party groups, real-estate developer Carl Paladino defeated former Representative Rick Lazio in the Republican gubernatorial primary. In Kentucky, Tea Party groups supported Rand Paul, who won comfortably over the official Republican pick to run for senator. In Alaska, Tea Party favorite Joe Miller defeated U.S. Senator Lisa Murkowski in the Republican primary (though Murkowski went on to stage a strong comeback in the general election as an independent).

In several primaries, victorious Tea Party–backed candidates seemed to have significant political liabilities that threatened to undermine Republican chances in the general election. In primaries, where voter turnout tends to be low, relatively small groups of ideologically motivated activists can sometimes bring about the nomination of candidates who do not fare well in the general election, where the electorate is larger and ideologically more diverse. For example, in Delaware, the Tea Party movement's favored candidate Christine O'Donnell defeated Representative Mike Castle in the Republican U.S. senatorial primary. Castle was a veteran member of Congress and was favored to win the seat in November. O'Donnell, on the other hand, while enthusiastically supported by conservative Republican activists, seemed poorly suited for a general election campaign. Research by the Democratic opposition quickly revealed that O'Donnell had embellished her academic record, had failed to pay a portion of her college tuition until sued by the university, and had once claimed (on television) to have dabbled in witchcraft. Despite the enthusiasm of her supporters in the primaries, O'Donnell's liabilities made it easy for a little known, but apparently better qualified, Democrat to prevail in the general election.

Super PACs

Republicans also hoped to benefit from the effects of the Supreme Court's 2010 decision in the case of *Citizens United v. Federal Election Commission*, which opened the way for unlimited corporate funding of political broadcasts calling for the election or defeat of particular candidates.[15] Following what it saw as the logic of the Supreme Court's decision, the Federal Election Commission (FEC) ruled that individuals and organizations could form so-called "independent expenditure-only committees" that would be allowed to raise and spend unlimited amounts of money to advocate for or against candidates so long as their efforts were not coordinated with those of the candidates.

Quickly, dozens of new organizations were formed by pro-Democratic and pro-Republican activists (the media dubbed these new groups "super PACs") to accept unlimited contributions from corporations and directly campaign for or against candidates. Republicans took the lead in super-PAC fund-raising, forming such groups as American Crossroads, which was set up by former Republican White House advisers Karl Rove and Edward Gillespie.[16] In the late days before the November election, an alliance of pro-Republican super PACs launched a $50 million coordinated advertising campaign designed to help GOP House and Senate candidates. This campaign allowed a number of Republican challengers to offset the fund-raising advantage that would otherwise have been enjoyed by their incumbent Democratic foes.[17] Democrats were slower to take advantage of the new fund-raising environment, but in the closing days of the election, a coalition of Democratic super PACS led by public-employee unions raised millions of dollars to help Democratic candidates.

The Election

On November 2, 2010, America went to the polls and handed the GOP a solid victory. With several races still undecided in the days after the election, Republicans added at least sixty seats in the House of Representatives, taking control of that chamber. The GOP would now have the opportunity to elevate its own congressional leaders: John Boehner of Ohio would take Democrat Nancy Pelosi's place as Speaker, and Eric Cantor of Virginia was expected to assume the position of Majority Leader.

In Senate contests, the Republicans had a number of major successes but failed to add enough seats to win a majority in the upper chamber. The GOP added seats, giving it forty-six Senate seats, enough to sustain filibusters if necessary. Several long-time Democratic incumbents, including Blanche Lincoln of Arkansas and Russ Feingold of Wisconsin, were defeated. Republicans, for their part, elected several Tea Party favorites, including Rand Paul in Kentucky, Mario Rubio in Florida, and Mike Lee in Utah. One Democrat who won a hard-fought race against a Tea Party–backed challenger was Senate Majority Leader Harry Reid of Nevada, who

had been behind in the polls as recently as a week before the election. Reid defeated Sharron Angle who garnered nationwide publicity when she told Reid to "man up" during their televised debate.

Republicans also fared well in elections for state offices, gaining majorities in nineteen state legislative chambers and winning ten gubernatorial seats. These victories could prove quite important for the GOP as the state legislatures would soon begin the process of redrawing congressional district boundaries based on the 2010 census. In most states, the party that controls the state legislature has the power to draw district boundaries that help its own candidates and hurt the opposition.

Surveys showed Senate Majority Leader Harry Reid lagging among voters in the days before the November 2010 election, but when the votes were tallied, he held onto his seat. Despite losing several seats in the Senate to Republicans, Democrats held onto a majority.

A Referendum on Democratic Leadership

What accounted for the drubbing suffered by the Democrats in 2010? Consistent with the usual pattern seen in midterm elections, many of the voters who had been drawn to the polls by Obama in the 2008 presidential election stayed home in 2010. Young voters, for example, accounted for 18 percent of the electorate in 2008 but only 10 percent in 2010.[18] The GOP benefitted, moreover from the energy and efforts of the Tea Party movement and from newfound fund-raising advantages.

In addition to these factors, though, Democrats were defeated by the economy and the perception that their economic policies were not solving the nation's problems. In November 2010, 14.8 million Americans were unemployed—more than 4 million more than had been unemployed when President Obama took office. Not surprisingly, a majority of voters agreed that the economy was the most important issue facing the country, and an overwhelming 94 percent of those who voted for the Republicans said they were worried about the direction of the nation's economy.[19]

Many of those who supported Republican candidates saw the 2010 midterm elections as an opportunity to voice their disappointment with President Obama, the congressional Democratic leadership, and the government in general, particularly in the realm of economic policy. Among those who gave their votes to the GOP, 55 percent thought that the president's economic stimulus package had hurt the economy and 35 percent thought it had made no difference; among those who voted for the GOP, 88 percent thought the president's policies would hurt the country and 90 percent disapproved of the way Congress was doing its job; among those who voted for the GOP, 41 percent thought President Obama was most to blame for the nation's economic problems; and among those who voted for the GOP, 43 percent described themselves as angry about the way the federal government was working, with another 50 percent saying they were dissatisfied but not angry. The electorate's message seemed clear: It was time for a change.

But even if the electorate's message was clear, the election's results seemed unlikely to produce a clear response from the government. The 2010 election ushered in a period of divided government, with the Democrats controlling the Senate and the White House and the Republicans dominating the House of Representatives. The two parties pledged to work together for the nation's welfare, but past experience suggested this would prove difficult.

● Money and Politics

Modern national political campaigns are fueled by enormous amounts of money. In 2008, incumbent candidates in competitive races for the House of Representatives typically spent close to $2 million to hold on to their seats. In Senate races, the average winner spent more than $4 million. In recent years, some Senate contests have cost $25 million or more, as have some races for governorships. In fact, 2010 California Republican gubernatorial candidate, Meg Whitman, spent more than $160 million, including $140 million of her own money in an ultimately unsuccessful bid for office.

Sources of Campaign Funds

In 2008, according to the Center for Responsive Politics, roughly $3 billion was spent by candidates for federal offices. About 10 percent of this total came from political action committees (PACs), mainly in support of congressional races, and the remainder from individual donors. Several million individuals donated money to political campaigns in 2008, some in contributions of as little as five or ten dollars. One of the sources of Barack Obama's fund-raising advantage in the 2008 campaign was his ability to generate more than 2 million small- and medium-size contributions to his campaign.[20] Another $500 million in 2008 was raised and spent by individuals and advocacy groups—the so-called 527 and 501c(4) groups operating outside the structure of the Democratic and Republican campaigns. According to early estimates, as much as $4 billion was spent by candidates and their supporters during the 2010 midterm elections in the wake of federal court decisions which eliminated many of the previous limits on campaign spending.

Individual Donors Politicians spend a great deal of time asking people for money. Money is solicited via direct mail, through the Internet, over the phone, and in numerous face-to-face meetings. Under federal law, individual donors may

Fund-raising is a major part of political campaigns. Candidates and parties meet with individual donors and leaders of important groups in an effort to amass campaign funds. Here, Governor Mitch Daniels of Indiana speaks at a fund-raiser for the Republican Party.

donate as much as $2,300 per candidate per election, $5,000 per PAC per calendar year (to a maximum of $65,500), $28,500 per national party committee per calendar year, and $10,000 to state and local committees per calendar year (to a maximum of $42,700). Federal rules also impose an overall limit on individual contributors of $108,200 per election cycle. Individuals may also contribute freely to 527 committees and to 501c(4) groups. Additionally, they may attempt to enhance their influence by "bundling" their contributions with those of friends and associates.

political action committee (PAC)
a private group that raises and distributes funds for use in election campaigns

Political Action Committees Political action committees (PACs) are organizations established by corporations, labor unions, or interest groups to channel the contributions of their members into political campaigns. Under the terms of the 1971 Federal Elections Campaign Act, which governs campaign finance in the United States, PACs are permitted to make larger contributions to any given candidate than individuals are allowed to make (see Box 10.2). Moreover, allied or related PACs often coordinate their campaign contributions, greatly increasing the amount of money a candidate actually receives from the same interest group. More than 4,500 PACs are registered with the Federal Election Commission, which oversees campaign finance practices in the United States. Nearly two-thirds of all PACs represent corporations, trade associations, and other business and professional

BOX 10.2

Federal Campaign Finance Regulation

Campaign Contributions
No individual may contribute more than $2,300 to any one candidate in any single election. Individuals may contribute as much as $28,500 to a national party committee and up to $5,000 to a political action committee. Full disclosure is required for contributions over $100. Candidates may not accept cash contributions over $100.

Political Action Committees (PAC)
Any corporation, labor union, trade association, or organization may establish a PAC. PACs must contribute to the campaigns of at least five different candidates and may contribute as much as $5,000 per candidate in any given election.

Soft Money
The national parties are prohibited from raising campaign funds to be transferred to state party organizations.

Independent Spending
527 committees are tax-exempt groups that raise money for votes mobilization and issue advocacy. 501(c)(4) committees are tax-exempt groups that can spend up to half their revenue for political advocacy without being required to disclose their donors. Independent expenditure committees (super PACs) can raise and spend unlimited amounts of money for political ads.

Presidential Elections
Candidates in presidential primaries may receive federal matching funds if they raise at least $5,000 in each of twenty states. The money raised must come in contributions of $250 or less. The amount raised by candidates in this way is matched by the federal government. Candidates who accept public funding in the primaries must adhere to an overall spending limit, which was set at $42 million for 2008. In the general election, candidates may accept public funding, currently $84 million. Candidates who accept such funding may spend no money beyond their federal allotments, though political parties may work to support their candidacies. Minor-party candidates may get partial federal funding.

Federal Election Commission (FEC)
The six-member FEC supervises federal elections, collects and publicizes campaign finance records, and investigates violations of federal campaign finance law.

groups. Alliances of bankers, lawyers, doctors, and merchants all sponsor PACs. One example of a PAC is the National Beer Wholesalers' Association PAC, which for many years was known as "SixPAC." Labor unions also sponsor PACs, as do ideological, public interest, and nonprofit groups. The National Rifle Association sponsors a PAC, as does the Sierra Club. Many congressional and party leaders have established PACs, known as leadership PACs, to provide funding for their political allies.

The Candidates On the basis of the Supreme Court's 1976 decision in *Buckley v. Valeo*, the right of individuals to spend their *own* money to campaign for office is a constitutionally protected matter of free speech and is not subject to limitation. Thus, extremely wealthy candidates often contribute millions of dollars to their own campaigns. The New Jersey Democrat Jon Corzine, for example, spent approximately $60 million of his own funds in a successful U.S. Senate bid in 2000 and another $40 million when he ran for governor of New Jersey in 2005. The only exception to the *Buckley* rule concerns presidential candidates who accept federal funding for their general election campaigns. Such individuals are limited to $50,000 in personal spending.

Independent Spending—527, 501c(4), and Super PAC Committees Committees known as **527s** and **501c(4)s** are independent groups that are currently not covered by the campaign-spending restrictions imposed in 2002 by the Bipartisan Campaign Reform Act (BCRA). These groups, named for the sections of the tax code under which they are organized, can raise and spend unlimited amounts on political advocacy as long as their efforts are not coordinated with those of any candidate's campaign. A 527 is a group established specifically for the purpose of political advocacy, whereas a 501c(4) is a nonprofit group such as an environmental or other public interest group that also engages in advocacy. A 501c(4) may not spend more that half its revenues for political purposes. Unlike a 527, a 501c(4) is not required to disclose where it gets its funds or exactly what it does with them. As a result, it has become a common practice for wealthy and corporate donors to route campaign contributions far in excess of the legal limits through 501c(4)s. In 2008, 527s and 501c(4)s raised and spent hundreds of millions of dollars on campaign ads and other activities promoting issues. Because they are not subject to contribution or spending limits, 527s and 501c(4)s have been able to raise three times as much money as PACs. In the 2008 national elections the top 527s were mainly, but not exclusively, supportive of the Democrats. These included the Service Employees International Union, America Votes, EMILY's List, and Citizens United. Table 10.1 lists the top donors to 527 committees in 2008. A new form of independent group, the independent expenditure committee or "super PAC," came about as a result of an FEC ruling that the Supreme Court's decision in *Citizens United v. FEC* permitted individuals and organizations to form committees that could raise unlimited amounts of money to run advertising for and against candidates so long as their efforts were not coordinated with those of the candidates. Super PACs played an important role in the 2010 midterm elections.

Political Parties Before 2002, most campaign dollars took the form of soft money, or unregulated contributions to the national parties nominally to assist in party building or voter registration efforts rather than for particular campaigns. Federal campaign finance legislation crafted by Senators John McCain and Russell

527 committees nonprofit independent groups that receive and disburse funds to influence the nomination, election, or defeat of candidates. Named after Section 527 of the Internal Revenue Code, which defines and provides tax-exempt status for nonprofit advocacy groups

501c(4) committees nonprofit groups that also engage in issue advocacy. Under Section 501c(4) of the federal tax code such a group may spend up to half its revenue for political purposes

TABLE 10.1

Top Donors to 527 Committees, 2008

DONOR	TOTAL DONATIONS
Service Employees International Union	$30,999,124
American Federation of State, County, and Municipal Employees	$5,581,604
Soros Fund Management	$5,150,000
Shangri-La Entertainment	$4,850,000
Las Vegas Sands	$4,359,820
Fund for America	$4,020,000
Oak Spring Farms	$3,480,000
Friends of America Votes	$3,225,425
United Food and Commercial Workers	$3,179,000
United Brotherhood of Carpenters	$2,786,690
Pharmaceutical Product Development, Inc.	$2,740,790
International Union of Operating Engineers	$1,865,000
National Association of Realtors	$1,556,600
America Votes	$1,450,000
Democratic Governors Association	$1,265,000
Sheet Metal Workers	$1,225,000
Templeton Foundation	$1,086,200
Bonanza Oil	$1,050,000
Trust Asset Management	$1,000,000

SOURCE: Center for Responsive Politics, based on records released October 21, 2008.

Feingold and enacted in 2002 sought to ban soft money by prohibiting the national parties from soliciting and receiving contributions from corporations, unions, or individuals and prevented them from directing such funds to their affiliated state parties. However, it did not reduce the overall importance of money in politics, and political parties continue to play a major role in financing political campaigns. Under federal rules, a national political party committee may make unlimited "independent expenditures" advocating support for its own presidential candidate or advocating the defeat of the opposing party's candidate as long as these expenditures are not coordinated with the candidate's own campaign. A national party committee may also spend up to $19 million in coordination with its presidential candidate's campaign even if its candidate has accepted public funding. Thus, for example, even though John McCain accepted full public funding, the national Republican Party helped fund McCain's advertising up to the federal limit. State and local party organizations may spend unlimited funds for grassroots presidential campaign activities such as voter registration drives, phone banks, and campaign materials. In 2008, Republican Party efforts partly, but not fully, offset Barack Obama's enormous fund-raising advantage over John McCain.

Public Funding The Federal Elections Campaign Act also provides for public funding of presidential campaigns. As they seek a major-party presidential nomination, candidates become eligible for public funds by raising at least $5,000 in individual contributions of $250 or less in each of twenty states. Candidates who reach this threshold may apply for federal funds to match, on a dollar-for-dollar basis, all individual contributions of $250 or less they receive. Currently, candidates who accept matching funds may spend no more than $42 million, including matching funds, in their presidential primary campaigns. The funds are drawn from the Presidential Election Campaign Fund. Taxpayers can contribute $3 to this fund, at no additional cost to themselves, by checking a box on the first page of their federal income tax returns. Major-party presidential candidates receive a lump sum (currently nearly $85 million) during the summer prior to the general election. They must meet all their general expenses from this money. Third-party candidates are eligible for public funding only if they received at least 5 percent of the vote in the previous presidential race. This stipulation effectively blocks preelection funding for third-party or independent candidates, although a third party that wins more than 5 percent of the vote can receive public funding after the election. In 1980, John Anderson convinced banks to lend him money for an independent candidacy on the strength of poll data showing that he would receive more than 5 percent of the vote and thus would obtain public funds with which to repay the loans. Under current law, no candidate is required to accept public funding for either the nominating races or general presidential election. Candidates who do not accept public funding are not affected by any expenditure limits. In 2008, John McCain accepted public funding for the general election campaign, receiving $84 million, but Barack Obama declined, choosing to rely on his own fund-raising prowess. Obama was ultimately able to outspend McCain by a wide margin. As a result, many observers believe that the 2008 race may be the last time that a major-party candidate will forgo his or her own fund-raising in favor of public funding. Candidates who accept public funding may not engage in fund-raising for their own campaigns with one exception: publicly funded candidates may raise money to meet the costs of complying with federal campaign laws and other legal

During the 2004 presidential campaign, dozens of independent 527 committees spent hundreds of millions of dollars on television advertising. One of the most notorious of these ads was the "Swift Boat Veterans for Truth," which challenged John Kerry's military record and activism against the Vietnam War.

Influence Campaigns and Elections Before You Cast Your Vote

Although young Americans have been less likely to vote in elections then older Americans, young Americans have influenced the ways campaigns and elections are conducted.

For example, demonstrations that were driven largely by young protesters against the 1968 Democratic convention led directly to changes in the contemporary nomination system. Today, candidates for the party's presidential nomination must appeal directly to voters through primaries and caucuses. However, this was not the case in 1968 and before, when party nominees were handpicked by party elites. Unhappy with the chosen candidate in 1968—Hubert Humphrey—young protesters turned out on the streets of Chicago to demonstrate against his nomination. Chicago police responded with force to the peaceful protests. The Democratic Party, fearing similar uprisings in subsequent elections, reformed their nominating process to give the people more of a say through primaries and caucuses. The Republican Party quickly followed suit.

Fast-forward to more recent times. The 2008 campaign for president was unique because of the campaign activism that it inspired among high school and college-aged youth. For example, CNN and YouTube partnered to present two debates in the 2008 primary elections—one for Democratic and the other for Republican candidates. Recognizing that young people are a driving force behind YouTube, allowing individuals to submit their own questions to the candidates this way was intended to bring a more youthful perspective to the debates. Moreover, candidates are increasingly turning to Internet sites like Facebook and MySpace for connecting with young voters.

These are just a few of many examples that demonstrate how young people have influenced campaigns and elections. If you're interested in ensuring that voices such as yours continue to shape campaigns and elections in this country, here are a few suggestions for getting involved.

- Volunteer for a campaign. Whether the campaign is at the campus, local, or national level, candidates are always grateful for volunteers. One of the easiest ways to find out whom to contact about volunteering is by visiting Project Vote Smart's Web site (www.votesmart.org). By entering your zip code, you can find out who is running for specific offices in your area. Contact information for each candidate is provided in the event you choose to volunteer.

- Invite a candidate (or two or three) to your college in order to engage in either a discussion with interested students or a forum among a variety of candidates. The best way to go about this is to work with a campus organization, such as your student government association or the College Republicans or Democrats. In addition to congressional candidates, you can consider candidates running for statewide and local offices.

- Host a gathering to watch a debate. Debates are a key way for voters to gain information about where candidates stand on issues. However, most people who watch debates do so by themselves. You might consider checking out DebateWatch (www.debates.org). It provides information about hosting a gathering of people to watch a debate together and discuss what they hear from the candidates.

and accounting costs, up to a total of 5 percent of their campaign expenditures. Hence in 2008, John McCain raised more than $4 million for the "McCain-Palin Compliance Fund."

Implications for Democracy

The important role played by private funds in American politics affects the balance of power among contending social groups. Politicians need large amounts of money to campaign successfully for major offices. This fact inevitably ties their interests to the interests of the groups and forces that can provide this money. In a nation as large and diverse as the United States, to be sure, campaign contributors represent many different groups and often represent clashing interests. Business groups, labor groups, environmental groups, and pro-choice and right-to-life forces all contribute millions of dollars to political campaigns. One set of trade associations may contribute millions to win politicians' support for telecommunications reform, whereas another set may contribute just as much to block the same reform efforts. Insurance companies may contribute millions of dollars to Democrats to win their support for changes in the health care system, whereas physicians may contribute equal amounts to prevent the same changes from becoming law.

Interests that donate large amounts of money to campaigns expect and often receive favorable treatment from the beneficiaries of their largesse. For example, in 2000 a number of major interest groups with specific policy goals made substantial donations to the Bush presidential campaign. These interests included airlines, energy producers, banks, tobacco companies, and a number of others. After Bush's election, these interests pressed the new president to promote their legislative and regulatory agendas. For instance, MBNA America Bank was a major donor to the 2000 Bush campaign. The bank and its executives gave Bush $1.3 million. The bank's president helped raise millions more for Bush and personally gave an additional $100,000 to the president's inaugural committee after the election. All told, MBNA and other banking companies donated $26 million to the GOP in 2000. Within weeks of his election, President Bush signed legislation providing MBNA and the others with something they had sought for years—bankruptcy laws making it more difficult for consumers to escape credit card debts.

Similarly, a coalition of manufacturers led by the U.S. Chamber of Commerce and the National Association of Manufacturers also provided considerable support for Bush's 2000 campaign. This coalition sought, among other things, the repeal of federal rules promulgated in 2000 by the federal Occupational Safety and Health Administration (OSHA), which were designed to protect workers from repetitive motion injuries. Again, within weeks of his election, the president approved a resolution rejecting the rules. In 2010, a number of corporate interests and labor unions took advantage of the Supreme Court's lifting of restrictions on campaign spending to pour tens of millions of dollars into congressional races. Corporate America, for the most part, supported the GOP. Labor, particularly public-sector unions fearing job cuts under the Republicans, gave tens of millions of dollars to support Democrats.

Despite the diversity of contributors, not all interests play a role in financing political campaigns. Only those interests that have a good deal of money to spend can make their interests known in this way. The poor and the downtrodden also live in America and have an interest in the outcome of political campaigns. Who speaks for them? Who benefits from the American system of private funding of campaigns?

for critical **analysis**

Democratic elections are virtually an American invention, yet voter participation in the United States today is lower than voting rates in many other nations. What might be done to enhance the democratic character of American electoral politics?

Rules governing campaign finance have been the object of intense debate in recent years. Many Americans believe that government is "for sale to the highest bidder" and shudder when they watch political candidates raise millions of dollars from corporations, labor unions, lobby groups, and wealthy individuals.

● Thinking Critically about the Electoral Process

As we have seen throughout this book, Americans' most fundamental values often clash, leaving us perplexed as to the best way to proceed. In the realm of electoral politics, the question of campaign finance produces such a clash of values. On the one hand, most Americans are wary of the high cost of campaigns and the apparently sinister role of campaign contributions in the political process. Through their contributions, wealthy individuals and well-funded interest groups seek to influence election outcomes, the behavior of elected officials, and, through so-called issue advertising, even the tenor of the political debate.

The problem, however, is that we find ourselves with a case of competing political ends. Although reform of spending practices may appear to advance the goal of political equality, it might do so at the expense of liberty. Don't we want to encourage vigorous and lively political debate—even though it may be expensive? Should not any group of citizens be free to promote its political ideas at its own expense? These are questions worth pondering, and as we often see in political life, they are dilemmas with no quick and easy solution.

studyguide

Practice Quiz

 Find a diagnostic Web Quiz with 39 additional questions on the StudySpace Web site: www.wwnorton.com/we-the-people

Elections in America

1. A closed primary is a primary election in which *(p. 349)*
   a) one's vote is kept private.
   b) only registered members of the party may vote.
   c) only registered members of the party may run.
   d) voting is conducted by mail

2. Beginning with the 1993 case *Shaw v. Reno*, the Supreme Court has *(p. 352)*
   a) generally rejected efforts to create majority-minority districts and asserted that districting based exclusively on race is unlawful.
   b) generally supported efforts to create majority-minority districts and asserted that districting based exclusively on race is lawful.
   c) generally rejected efforts to create majority-minority districts but asserted that districting based exclusively on race is lawful.
   d) refused to rule on the question of whether districting based exclusively on race is lawful.

3. The neutral ballot made it possible for voters to *(p. 352)*
   a) vote the party line.
   b) vote for a split ticket.
   c) send clear mandates for policy change.
   d) both a and b

4. If a state has ten members in the U.S. House of Representatives, how many electoral votes does that state have? *(p. 353)*
   a) two
   b) ten
   c) twelve
   d) can't tell from this information

Election Campaigns

5. The average amount of money spent by House incumbents to secure reelection has: *(p. 357)*
   a) been surpassed by the average amount of money spent by challengers since 1980.
   b) remained the same as the average amount spent by challengers since 1980.
   c) increased at a greater rate than the average amount spent by challengers since 1980.
   d) decreased at a greater rate than the average amount spent by challengers since 1980.

Presidential Elections

6. A political party meeting to nominate a presidential candidate that is open only to registered party members is called *(p. 359)*
   a) an open caucus.
   b) a closed caucus.
   c) an open primary.
   d) a closed primary.

7. The unit rule was *(p. 361)*
   a) a system by which candidates won delegates in rough proportion to the percentage of the primary vote they received.
   b) a Democratic Party requirement that convention delegates be broadly representative of the party's membership in terms of race and gender.
   c) a guideline that said all members of a state's delegation should vote for the candidate favored by the majority of the state's delegates at party conventions.
   d) a federal policy that forced legislative districts within a state to include roughly equal populations.

8. What was the most fundamental change in national conventions in the twentieth century? *(p. 362)*
   a) They no longer nominate presidential candidates.
   b) Now party platforms are written at the convention.
   c) The participation of electoral officials in conventions has continued to decline.
   d) none of the above

9. A committee of supporters that is organized to fund-raise and draw attention to a potential presidential candidate is typically referred to as *(p. 363)*
   a) a superdelegate committee.
   b) an exploratory committee.
   c) a 527 committee.
   d) a political action committee.

10. Which of the following is *not* an important communication technique for contemporary political campaigns? *(pp. 364–68)*
    a) polling
    b) direct mail
    c) phone banks
    d) gerrymandering

How Voters Decide

11. Which of the following is *not* a factor that influences voters' decisions? *(pp. 372–75)*
    a) partisanship
    b) issues
    c) candidate characteristics
    d) the electoral system used to determine the winner

12. Partisan loyalty *(p. 372)*
    a) is often handed down from parents to children.
    b) changes frequently.
    c) has little impact on electoral choice.
    d) is mandated in states with closed primaries.

13. When a voter decides which candidate to vote for based on past performance, the voter is engaged in *(p. 373)*
    a) prospective voting.
    b) retrospective voting.
    c) candidate-centered voting.
    d) ticket splitting.

Money and Politics

14. In *Buckley v. Valeo,* the Supreme Court ruled that *(p. 391)*
    a) PAC donations to campaigns are constitutionally protected.
    b) the right of individuals to spend their own money to campaign is constitutionally protected.
    c) the political system is corrupt.
    d) the Federal Elections Campaign Act is unconstitutional.

15. In 2002, federal campaign finance legislation crafted by John McCain and Russell Feingold sought to *(pp. 391–92)*
    a) ban soft money by prohibiting national parties from soliciting and receiving contributions from corporations, unions, or individuals.
    b) increase the amount of soft money in elections by encouraging national parties to solicit and receive contributions from corporations, unions, and individuals.
    c) ban candidates from using their own personal resources in election campaigns.
    d) ban 527 committees from receiving and disbursing funds to influence elections.

Chapter Outline

 Find a detailed Chapter Outline on the StudySpace Web site: www.wwnorton.com/we-the-people

Key Terms

Find Flashcards to help you study these terms on the StudySpace Web site: www.wwnorton.com/we-the-people

benign gerrymandering *(p. 352)*
campaign *(p. 355)*
caucus (political) *(p. 359)*
closed caucus *(p. 359)*
closed primary *(p. 349)*
coattail effect *(p. 353)*
delegates *(p. 363)*
electoral college *(p. 353)*
501c(4) committees *(p. 391)*
527 committees *(p. 391)*
gerrymandering *(p. 351)*

incumbent *(p. 355)*
majority system *(p. 350)*
majority-minority district *(p. 352)*
midterm elections *(p. 349)*
open caucus *(p. 359)*
open primary *(p. 349)*
platform *(p. 361)*
plurality system *(p. 350)*
political action committee (PAC) *(p. 390)*
primary elections *(p. 349)*

proportional representation *(p. 350)*
prospective voting *(p. 373)*
recall *(p. 350)*
redistricting *(p. 351)*
referendum *(p. 349)*
retrospective voting *(p. 373)*
spot advertisement *(p. 366)*
superdelegate *(p. 363)*
town meeting *(p. 368)*
winner-take-all system *(p. 359)*

For Further Reading

Abramson, Paul, John Aldrich, and David Rohde. *Change and Continuity in the 2008 Elections.* Washington, DC: Congressional Quarterly Press, 2009.

Ackerman, Bruce, and Ian Avres. *Voting with Dollars.* New Haven, CT: Yale University Press, 2004.

Browning, Graeme. *Electronic Democracy.* New York: Cyberage, 2002.

Ginsberg, Benjamin, and Martin Shefter. *Politics by Other Means: Institutional Conflict and the Declining Significance of Elections in America.* New York: Norton, 1999.

Heilemann, John, and Mark Halperin. *Game Change: Obama and the Clintons, McCain and Palin, and the Race of a Lifetime.* New York: Harper, 2010.

Maass, Matthias. *The World Views of the 2008 U.S. Presidential Election.* New York: Palgrave, 2009.

Nelson, Michael, ed. *The Elections of 2008.* Washington, DC: Congressional Quarterly Press, 2009.

Polsby, Nelson, Aaron Wildavsky, and David Hopkins. *Presidential Elections.* 12th ed. New York: Rowman and Littlefield, 2007.

Raymond, Allen, and Ian Spiegelman. *How to Rig an Election.* New York: Simon & Schuster, 2008.

Schier, Steven. *You Call This an Election?* Washington, DC: Georgetown University Press, 2003.

Wayne, Stephen. *Is This Any Way to Run a Democratic Election?* 3rd ed. Washington, DC: Congressional Quarterly Press, 2007.

Recommended Web Sites

Center for Voting and Democracy
www.fairvote.org
The Center for Voting and Democracy is dedicated to open access to voting, equal representation, and a voice for all Americans. Read about some of their electoral reform proposals such as runoff elections, proportional representation, and alternatives to the electoral college.

The Color of Money
www.colorofmoney.org
Campaign funding affects the balance of power among contending social groups in America. Politicians are tied to groups that provide them with the large amounts of money needed to campaign for major office. This Web site examines federal campaign contributions with a focus on race and ethnicity to show how campaign money has the potential to skew government policy decisions.

ElectionMail.com
www.electionmail.com
Are you thinking about running for office? Whether you aspire to be student government president or president of the United States, here you can find links to affordable political printing, including political brochures, campaign literature, and campaign signs.

Federal Election Commission
www.fec.gov
The Federal Election Commission (FEC) is an independent government agency that was created in 1975 to administer and enforce the Federal Election Campaign Act (FECA). At the official FEC Web site you can read about the rules and regulations that govern the financing of federal elections and other topics of interest.

JibJab.com
www.jibjab.com
This Web site became famous for its political video clips during the 2004 presidential campaign. For a good laugh check out some of the political jokes or rummage through the video archives to find one of the original Bush or Kerry clips.

MultiEducator.com
www.multied.com/elections/
MultiEducator's History Central Web site features a major section on elections. Here you can find the history of every U.S. national election, including popular and electoral votes, turnout, and a map of the states carried by each competing candidate.

National Archives and Records Administration
www.archives.gov/federal-register/electoral-college/index.html
The U.S. National Archives and Records Administration's Electoral College page is a great resource on presidential elections. Find answers to frequently asked questions about our electoral system, read about how electors vote, or try predicting who will win the next presidential election with the electoral college calculator.

OpenSecrets.org
www.opensecrets.org
Campaign funds come from a variety of sources, including individual donors, political action committees (PACs), self-contributions, independent spending, parties, and public funding. At this site you can research funding for all federal officials, including your own members of Congress.

Project Vote Smart
www.votesmart.org
Project Vote Smart is a nonpartisan site dedicated to providing citizens with information on political candidates and elected officials. Here you can easily view a candidate's biographical information, position on issues, and voting record, so that you can make an informed choice on Election Day.

Voter Information Services
www.vis.org
Voter Information Services (VIS) is a nonpartisan, nonprofit organization dedicated to helping interested citizens learn about their elected members of Congress. Here you can obtain a Congressional Report Card for your members of Congress and find out where they stand on the issues.

Many organized groups, including business groups, try to influence the government. When Congress considered various forms of health care legislation in 2009 and 2010, the health insurance and pharmaceutical industries lobbied for laws that would benefit them. Here, Angela Braly, the CEO of the health insurance company WellPoint, testifies before Congress.

Groups and Interests

WHAT GOVERNMENT DOES AND WHY IT MATTERS In 2009 and early 2010, the major item on the congressional agenda was health care reform. President Obama had made health care his main legislative priority and congressional Democrats promised to craft legislation that would increase the availability and affordability of health care for all Americans. The health care industry is among America's largest and includes insurance companies, hospitals, physicians, pharmaceutical companies, medical device manufacturers, and a host of other people and institutions. Each of these interests was, of course, determined to make certain that it was not hurt by and, indeed, would benefit from the law that might eventually be enacted. To promote their interests, more than 300 industry groups deployed hundreds of lobbyists and spent nearly $1 billion on lobbying and campaign contributions in 2009. Many of the lobbyists employed by health care groups were former members of Congress and former congressional staffers with close ties to key lawmakers. Over 350 individuals who had previously worked in the

focusquestions

- Why are some interests represented by organized groups—but others are not?
- Why has the number of interest groups grown?
- How do interest groups try to influence the government?
- What are the arguments for and against regulating interest groups?

congressional leadership offices or for key members of committees involved in writing health legislation, along with thirteen former members of Congress, represented health care clients in 2008 and 2009.[1]

One important consequence of this lobbying effort was that the health insurance industry was able to secure language in the health care measure signed into law in 2010 that will require 40 million Americans to buy health insurance while blocking a "public option" or expansion of Medicare that might compete with the private insurance companies. Polls suggested that most Americans favored a publicly financed health care option or an expansion of Medicare, but, of course, most Americans do not employ lobbyists.

The case of health care reform exemplifies the power of interest groups in action. Tens of thousands of organized groups have formed in the United States, ranging from civic associations to huge nationwide groups such as the National Rifle Association (NRA), whose chief cause is opposition to restrictions on gun ownership, or Common Cause, a public-interest group that advocates a variety of liberal political reforms. Despite the array of interest groups in American politics, however, we can be sure that not all interests are represented equally nor that the results of this group competition are always consistent with the common good.

In this chapter we will examine the nature and consequences of interest-group politics in the United States.

chaptercontents

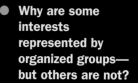

Why are some interests represented by organized groups— but others are not?

The Character of Interest Groups

The framers of the U.S. Constitution feared the power that could be wielded by organized interests. Yet they believed that interest groups thrived because of liberty— the freedom that all Americans enjoy to organize and to express their views. If the government were given the power to regulate or in any way to forbid efforts by organized interests to interfere in the political process, the government would in effect have the power to suppress liberty. The solution to this dilemma was presented by James Madison:

> Take in a greater variety of parties and interest [and] you make it less probable that a majority of the whole will have a common motive to invade the rights of other citizens. . . . [Hence the advantage] enjoyed by a large over a small republic.[2]

According to Madison, a good constitution encourages multitudes of interests so that no single interest, which he called a "faction," can ever tyrannize the others. The basic assumption is that competition among interests will produce balance, with all the interests regulating each other.[3] Today, this Madisonian principle of regulation is called **pluralism**. According to pluralist theory, all interests are and should be free to compete for influence in the United States. Moreover, according to pluralist doctrine, the outcome of this competition is compromise and moderation, since no group is likely to be able to achieve any of its goals without accommodating itself to some of the views of its many competitors.[4]

An **interest group** is an organized group of people that makes policy-related appeals to government. This definition of interest groups includes membership organizations as well as businesses, corporations, universities, and other institutions that do not accept members. Individuals form groups in order to increase the chance that their views will be heard and their interests treated favorably by the government. Interest groups are organized to influence governmental decisions.

Interest groups are sometimes referred to as "lobbies." Interest groups are also sometimes confused with political action committees, which are actually groups

pluralism the theory that all interests are and should be free to compete for influence in the government. The outcome of this competition is compromise and moderation

interest group individuals who organize to influence the government's programs and policies

As long as there is government, there will be interests trying to influence it. During the 1890s, for instance, business interests fought for protective tariffs from Congress and President McKinley. This 1897 cartoon satirizes their success in capturing Congress.

Public interest groups often advocate for interests that are not addressed by traditional lobbies. For example, in addition to many other activities, the Public Interest Research Group (PIRG) publishes an annual toy safety report to help protect consumers and to encourage policymakers to address problems in this area.

that focus on influencing elections rather than trying to influence the elected (see Chapter 10). One final distinction that we should make is that interest groups are also different from political parties: interest groups tend to concern themselves with the *policies* of government; parties tend to concern themselves with the *personnel* of government.

The number of interest groups in the United States is enormous, and millions of Americans are members of one or more groups, at least to the extent of paying dues or attending an occasional meeting. By representing the interests of such large numbers of people and encouraging political participation, organized groups can and do enhance American democracy. Organized groups educate their members about issues that affect them. Groups lobby members of Congress and the executive, engage in litigation, and generally represent their members' interests in the political arena. Groups mobilize their members for elections and grassroots lobbying efforts, thus encouraging participation. Interest groups also monitor government programs to make certain that their members are not adversely affected by these programs. In all these ways, organized interests can be said to promote democratic politics. But because not all interests are represented equally, interest-group politics works to the advantage of some and the disadvantage of others.

It is also important to remember that not all organized interests are successful. Struggles among interest groups have winners and losers, and even large groups well represented in Washington are sometimes defeated in political struggle. In recent years, for example, despite relentless lobbying, physicians' groups such as the American Medical Association (AMA) have been unable to persuade Congress to increase Medicare funding for physicians' services. One reason for this failure is that physicians are forced to compete for funding with insurers, drug companies, and hospitals. The doctors have simply been overmatched.

Common Types of Interest Groups

Business and Agricultural Groups Interest groups come in as many shapes and sizes as the interests they represent. When most people think about interest groups, they immediately think of groups with a direct economic interest in governmental actions. These groups are generally supported by groups of producers or manufacturers in a particular economic sector. Examples of this type of group include the National Petroleum Refiners Association and the American Farm Bureau Federation. At the same time that these types of broadly representative groups are active in Washington, specific companies, such as Exxon, IBM, and General Motors, may be active on certain issues that are of particular concern to them.

Labor Groups Labor organizations are equally active lobbyists. The AFL-CIO, the United Mine Workers, and the Teamsters are all groups that lobby on behalf of organized labor. In recent years, groups have arisen to further the interests of public employees, the most significant among these being the American Federation of State, County, and Municipal Employees (AFSCME).

Professional Associations Professional lobbies such as the American Bar Association and the American Medical Association have been particularly successful in furthering their members' interests in state and federal legislatures. Financial institutions, represented by organizations such as the American Bankers Association and the National Savings and Loan League, although often less visible than other lobbies, also play an important role in shaping legislative policy.

Public Interest Groups Recent years have witnessed the growth of a powerful "public interest" lobby, purporting to represent interests whose concerns are not addressed by traditional lobbies. These groups have been most visible in the consumer protection and environmental policy areas, although public interest groups cover a broad range of issues. The Natural Resources Defense Council, the Sierra Club, the Union of Concerned Scientists, and Common Cause are all examples of public interest groups.

Ideological Groups Closely related to and overlapping public interest groups are ideological groups, organized in support of a particular political or philosophical perspective. People for the American Way, for example, promotes liberal values, whereas the Christian Coalition focuses on conservative social goals, and the National Taxpayers Union campaigns to reduce the size of the federal government.

Public-Sector Groups The perceived need for representation on Capitol Hill has generated a public-sector lobby in the past several years, including the National League of Cities and the "research" lobby. The latter group comprises think tanks and universities that have an interest in obtaining government funds for research and support, and it includes such institutions as Harvard University, the Brookings Institution, and the American Enterprise Institute. Indeed, universities have expanded their lobbying efforts even as they have reduced faculty positions and course offerings.[5]

What Interests Are Not Represented?

It is difficult to categorize unrepresented interests precisely because they are not organized and are not able to present to us (or governments) their identity and their demands. The political scientist David Truman referred to these interests as "potential interest groups."[6] And he is undoubtedly correct that at any time, as long as there is freedom, any interest shared by a lot of people can develop through "voluntary association" into a genuine interest group that can demand, usually successfully, to get some representation. But the fact remains that many interests—very widely shared interests—do not get organized and recognized. Such "potential interests" might include grandparents, tall people, or undergraduates.

Organizational Components

Although interest groups are many and varied, most share certain key organizational components. These include leadership, money, an agency or office, and members.

First, every group must have a leadership and decision-making structure. For some groups, this structure is very simple. For others, it can be quite elaborate

● Why are some interests represented by organized groups— but others are not?

forcriticalanalysis

The 2007 energy bill increased subsidies for ethanol and other biofuels despite concerns that the costs of producing ethanol are greater than the savings generated by its use. What types of groups do you think are likely to be part of the "biofuels coalition" that lobbies for ethanol?

Do Foreign Interests Exert Influence in the United States?

Discussions of interest groups often focus on the efforts of competing domestic forces—business, labor, public interest groups, and so on—to influence the government. Often, however, foreign interests and foreign governments also lobby vigorously to influence U.S. policy. Much of this lobbying is undertaken by foreign firms hoping to do business in the United States or directly with the U.S. government on favorable terms. For example, every year Americans purchase billions of dollars of goods manufactured in China. In some instances, these Chinese products have failed to comply with American health and safety standards, leading to demands that the United States restrict Chinese imports. To protect their access to the U.S. market, Chinese firms, like those in many other countries, retain the services of international trade lobbyists. These lobbyists guide foreign firms through the intricacies of U.S. laws and customs and introduce foreign executives to American power brokers, movers, and shakers. Some see international trade lobbyists as corporate traitors, but American lobbyists and their counterparts in other countries play an important role in promoting world trade and diminishing international rivalries.

Questions of loyalty are also often raised by the activities of another form of foreign lobby in the United States—the ethnic lobby. Many Americans retain a sense of identification with their family's country of origin or with those who share their religion in another country. Individuals with such ethnic or religious ties to another country are often willing to lobby vigorously on its behalf. The best-known case is that of the pro-Israel lobby. Through such organizations as AIPAC, the American Israel Public Affairs Committee, some Jewish Americans have worked to secure American military,

financial, and economic support for Israel since that nation's founding. Largely because of the pro-Israel lobby's activities, Israel is the largest recipient of American foreign aid and is usually supported by the United States in its conflicts with the Arab nations of the Middle East. Interestingly, Jewish Americans are not the only pro-Israel lobbyists. Israel is also strongly supported by so-called Christian Zionists, evangelical Protestants who see Israel's existence as the fulfillment of biblical prophecy.

In addition to the pro-Israel lobby, a number of other ethnic lobbies are active in Washington. Americans from the Indian subcontinent have lobbied effectively for the improvement of U.S.–Indian relations. Some Irish Americans have lobbied against British rule in Northern Ireland. Recently, despite a good deal of lobbying by Armenian Americans, Congress failed to pass a resolution condemning the murder of hundreds of thousands of Armenians by Turkish forces between 1914 and 1917. Turkey, an important U.S. military ally, was able to defeat the resolution with a lobbying campaign of its own.

Often, lobbying by foreign firms and governments is accompanied by extensive public-relations campaigns. One foreign government that lobbies vigorously in the United States and also spends tens of millions of dollars each year on public relations is the Kingdom of Saudi Arabia. For example, a recent issue of *The New Republic*—a magazine read mainly by upper-middle-class professionals and

intellectuals in New York, Washington, and Boston—the Kingdom of Saudi Arabia sponsored a full-page ad promoting its efforts to combat terrorism.[a]

In point of fact, however, the Saudi government's long-standing practice has been to subsidize and support Islamic radicals as long as they do not make trouble within Saudi Arabia.[b] The Saudi ad campaign is designed to gloss over this rather embarrassing and politically inconvenient fact.

[a]*New Republic*, December 5, 2005, back cover.
[b]Craig Unger, *House of Bush, House of Saud* (New York: Scribners, 2004).

for critical analysis

1. Should foreign firms be allowed to lobby in the United States?
2. Is it un-American or disloyal for ethnic and religious groups to lobby on behalf of a foreign country with which they identify?

and involve hundreds of local chapters that are melded into a national apparatus. Interest-group leadership is, in some respects, analogous to business leadership. Many interest groups are initially organized by political entrepreneurs with a strong commitment to a particular set of goals. Such entrepreneurs see the formation of a group as a means both for achieving those goals and for enhancing their own influence in the political process. Just as is true in the business world, however, successful groups often become bureaucratized; the initial entrepreneurial leadership is replaced by a paid professional staff. In the 1960s, for example, Ralph Nader led a loosely organized band of consumer advocates ("Nader's Raiders") in a crusade for product safety that resulted in the enactment of a number of pieces of legislation and numerous regulations, such as the requirement that all new cars be equipped with seat belts. Today, Nader remains active in the consumer movement, and his ragtag band of raiders has been transformed into a well-organized and well-financed phalanx of interlocked groups led by professional staffs.

Second, every interest group must build a financial structure capable of sustaining an organization and funding the group's activities. Most interest groups rely on membership dues and voluntary contributions from sympathizers. Many also sell some ancillary services to members, such as insurance and vacation tours. Third, most groups establish an agency that actually carries out the group's tasks. This may be a research organization, a public relations office, or a lobbying office in Washington or a state capital.

Finally, almost all interest groups must attract and keep members. Somehow, groups must persuade individuals to invest the money, time, energy, or effort required to take part in the group's activities. Members play a larger role in some groups than in others. In **membership associations**, group members actually serve on committees and engage in projects. In the case of labor unions, members may march on picket lines; in the case of political or ideological groups, members may participate in demonstrations and protests. In another set of groups, **staff organizations**, a professional staff conducts most of the group's activities; members are called on only to pay dues and make other contributions. Among the well-known public interest groups, some, such as the National Organization for Women (NOW), are membership groups; others, such as Defenders of Wildlife and the Children's Defense Fund, are staff organizations.

The "Free Rider" Problem Whether they need individuals to volunteer or merely to write checks, both types of groups need to recruit and retain members. Yet many groups find this task difficult, even when it comes to recruiting members who agree strongly with the group's goals. Why? As the economist Mancur Olson explains, the benefits of a group's success are often broadly available and cannot be denied to nonmembers.[7] Such benefits can be called **collective goods**. This term is usually associated with certain government benefits, but it can also be applied to beneficial outcomes of interest-group activity. Following Olson's own example, suppose a number of private property owners live near a mosquito-infested swamp. Each owner wants this swamp cleared. But if one or a few of the owners were to clear the swamp alone, their actions would benefit all the other owners as well, without any effort on the part of those other owners. Each of the inactive owners would be a **free rider** on the efforts of the ones who cleared the swamp. Thus, there is a disincentive for any of the owners to undertake the job alone.

Since the number of concerned owners is small in this particular case, they might eventually be able to organize themselves to share the costs as well as enjoy

Although there have always been groups trying to influence the government, since the 1960s the number of organized interests in Washington, D.C., has increased substantially. For instance, the consumer activist Ralph Nader, shown here at a demonstration in support of mandatory airbags in cars, founded a network of consumer advocacy groups.

membership association an organized group in which members actually play a substantial role, sitting on committees and engaging in group projects

staff organization a type of membership group in which a professional staff conducts most of the group's activities

collective goods benefits, sought by groups, that are broadly available and cannot be denied to nonmembers

free riders those who enjoy the benefits of collective goods but did not participate in acquiring them

the benefits of clearing the swamp. But suppose the numbers of interested people are increased. Suppose the common concern is not the neighborhood swamp but polluted air or groundwater involving thousands of residents in a region, or in fact millions of residents in a whole nation. National defense is the most obvious collective good whose benefits are shared by every resident, regardless of the taxes they pay or the support they provide. As the number of involved persons increases, or as the size of the group increases, the free-rider phenomenon becomes more of a problem. Individuals do not have much incentive to become active members and supporters of a group that is already working more or less on their behalf. The group would no doubt be more influential if all concerned individuals were active members—if there were no free riders. But groups do not reduce their efforts just because free riders get the same benefits as dues-paying activists. In fact, groups may try even harder precisely because there are free riders, with the hope that the free riders will be encouraged to join in.

Why Join? Despite the free-rider problem, interest groups offer numerous incentives to join. Most important, they make various "selective benefits" available only to group members. These benefits can be information related, material, solidary, or purposive. Of course, groups sometimes offer combinations of benefits. Membership in a community association, for example, can offer its members a sense of belonging (solidary benefit), involvement in community decision making (purposive benefit), and reduced rates on homeowners' insurance (material benefit). Table 11.1 gives some examples of the range of benefits in each of these categories.

informational benefits special newsletters, periodicals, training programs, conferences, and other information provided to members of groups to entice others to join

  Informational benefits are the most widespread and important category of selective benefits offered to group members. Information is provided through conferences, training programs, and newsletters and other periodicals sent automatically to those who have paid membership dues.

material benefits special goods, services, or money provided to members of groups to entice others to join

  Material benefits include anything that can be measured monetarily, such as special services, goods, and even money. Groups can offer a broad range of material benefits to attract members. These benefits often include discount purchasing, shared advertising, and, perhaps most valuable of all, health and retirement insurance.

solidary benefits selective benefits of group membership that emphasize friendship, networking, and consciousness raising

  Another option identified on Table 11.1 is that of **solidary benefits**. The most notable of this class of benefits are the friendship and "networking" opportunities that membership provides. Another benefit that has become extremely important to many of the newer nonprofit and citizen groups is "consciousness raising." One example of this can be seen in the claims of many women's organizations that active participation conveys to each member of the organization an enhanced sense of her own value and a stronger ability to advance individual as well as collective rights. Members of associations based on ethnicity, race, or religion also derive solidary benefits from interacting with individuals they perceive as sharing their own histories, values, and perspectives.

purposive benefits selective benefits of group membership that emphasize the purpose and accomplishments of the group

  A fourth type of benefit involves the appeal of the purpose of an interest group. An example of these **purposive benefits** is businesses' joining trade associations to further their economic interests. Similarly, individuals join consumer, environmental, or other civic groups to pursue goals important to them. Many of the most successful interest groups of the past twenty years have been citizen groups or public interest groups, whose members are brought together largely around shared ideological goals, including government reform, election and campaign reform, civil rights, economic equality, "family values," or even opposition to government itself.

TABLE 11.1

Selective Benefits of Interest Group Membership

CATEGORY	BENEFITS
Informational benefits	Conferences
	Professional contacts
	Training programs
	Publications
	Coordination among organizations
	Research
	Legal help
	Professional codes
	Collective bargaining
Material benefits	Travel packages
	Insurance
	Discounts on consumer goods
Solidary benefits	Friendship
	Networking opportunities
Purposive benefits	Advocacy
	Representation before government
	Participation in public affairs

SOURCE: Adapted from Jack Walker, Jr., *Mobilizing Interest Groups in America: Patrons, Professions, and Social Movements* (Ann Arbor: University of Michigan Press, 1991), 86.

AARP and the Benefits of Membership One group that has been extremely successful in recruiting members and mobilizing them for political action is AARP (formerly called the American Association of Retired Persons). AARP was founded in 1958 as a result of the efforts of a retired California high school principal, Ethel Percy Andrus, to find affordable health insurance for herself and for the thousands of members of the National Retired Teachers Association (NRTA). In 1955 she found an insurer who was willing to give NRTA members a low group rate. In 1958, partly at the urging of the insurer (who found that insuring the elderly was quite profitable), Andrus founded AARP. For the insurer it provided an expanded market; for Andrus it was a way to serve the ever-growing elderly population, whose problems and needs were expanding along with their numbers and their life expectancy.

Today, AARP is a large and powerful organization with 38 million members and an annual income of $900 million. In addition, the organization receives $90 million in federal grants. Its national headquarters in Washington, D.C., staffed by nearly 3,000 full-time employees, is so large that it has its own zip code. Its monthly periodical, *AARP The Magazine*, has a circulation larger than the combined circulations of *Time, Newsweek,* and *U.S. News & World Report.*[8]

How did this large organization overcome the free-rider problem and recruit 38 million older people as members? First, no other organization on earth has ever provided more successfully the selective benefits necessary to overcome the free-rider problem. It helps that AARP began as an organization to provide affordable

During the 2003 national debate over Medicare reform and prescription drug pricing, it was the support of senior citizen groups for a new Medicare bill that ultimately allowed the bill to prevail in Congress.

for critical analysis

Could college students be organized as an interest group? What would such a group advocate? What might be some impediments to the creation of a National Organization of College Students?

health insurance for aging members rather than as an organization to influence public policy. But that fact only strengthens the argument that members need short-term individual benefits if they are to invest effort in a longer-term and less concrete set of benefits. As AARP evolved into a political interest group, its leadership also added more selective benefits for individual members. They provided guidance against consumer fraud, offered low-interest credit cards, evaluated and endorsed products that were deemed of best value to members, and provided auto insurance and a discounted mail-order pharmacy.

In a group as large as AARP, members are bound to disagree on particular subjects, often creating serious factional disputes. But the resources of AARP are so extensive that its leadership has been able to mobilize itself for each issue of importance to the group. One of its most successful methods of mobilization for political action is the "telephone tree," with which AARP leaders can quickly mobilize thousands of members for and against proposals that affect Social Security, Medicare, and other questions of security for the aging. A "telephone tree" in each state enables the state AARP chair to phone all of the AARP district directors, who then can phone the presidents of the dozens of local chapters, who can call their local officers and individual members. Within twenty-four hours, thousands of individual AARP members can be contacting local, state, and national officials to express their opposition to proposed legislation. It is no wonder that AARP is respected and feared throughout Washington. In 2009, AARP's endorsement of the health care bill proposed by the House leadership convinced many wavering members of Congress to support the bill rather than risk offending the powerful lobby group.

The Characteristics of Members

Membership in interest groups is not randomly distributed in the population. People with higher incomes, higher levels of education, and management or professional occupations are much more likely to become members of groups than are those who occupy the lower rungs on the socioeconomic ladder.[9] Well-educated, upper-income business and professional people are more likely to have the time and the money and to have acquired through the educational process the concerns and skills needed to play a role in a group or association. Moreover, for business and professional people, group membership may provide personal contacts and access to information that can help advance their careers. At the same time, of course, corporate entities—businesses and the like—usually have ample resources to form or participate in groups that seek to advance their causes.

The result is that interest-group politics in the United States tends to have a very pronounced upper-class bias. Certainly, many interest groups and political associations have a working-class or lower-class membership—labor organizations or welfare-rights organizations, for example—but the great majority of interest groups and their members are drawn from the middle and upper-middle classes. In general, the "interests" served by interest groups are the interests of society's "haves." Even when interest groups take opposing positions on issues and policies, the conflicting positions they espouse usually reflect divisions among upper-income strata rather than conflicts between the upper and lower classes.

In general, to obtain adequate political representation, forces from the bottom rungs of the socioeconomic ladder must be organized on the massive scale associated

● Why has the number
of interest groups
grown?

with political parties. Parties can organize and mobilize the collective energies of large numbers of people who, as individuals, may have very limited resources. Interest groups, on the other hand, generally organize smaller numbers of the better-to-do. Thus, the relative importance of political parties and interest groups in American politics has far-ranging implications for the distribution of political power in the United States. As we saw in Chapter 9, political parties have declined in influence in recent years. Interest groups, on the other hand, as we shall see in the next section, have become much more numerous, more active, and more influential in American politics.

● The Proliferation of Groups

Interest groups and concerns about them are not new phenomena. As long as there is government, as long as government makes policies that add value or impose costs, and as long as there is liberty to organize, interest groups will abound; and if government expands, so will interest groups. There was, for example, a spurt of growth in the national government during the 1880s and 1890s, arising largely from the first government efforts at economic intervention to fight large monopolies and to regulate some aspects of interstate commerce. In the latter decade, a parallel spurt of growth occurred in national interest groups, including the imposing National Association of Manufacturers (NAM) and numerous other trade associations. Many groups organized around specific agricultural commodities as well. This period also marked the beginning of the expansion of trade unions as interest groups. Later, in the 1930s, interest groups with headquarters and representation in Washington began to grow significantly, concurrent with that decade's historic and sustained expansion within the national government (see Chapter 3).

Over the past decades, there has been an even greater increase both in the number of interest groups seeking to play a role in the American political process and in the extent of their opportunity to influence that process. This explosion of interest-group activity has two basic origins: first, the expansion of the role of government during this period; and second, the coming of age of a new and dynamic set of political forces in the United States—forces that have relied heavily on "public interest" groups to advance their causes.

The Expansion of Government

Modern governments' extensive economic and social programs have powerful politicizing effects, often sparking the organization of new groups and interests. The activities of organized groups are usually viewed in terms of their effects on governmental action. But interest-group activity is often as much a consequence as an antecedent of governmental programs. Even when national policies begin as responses to the appeals of pressure groups, government involvement in any area can be a powerful stimulus for political organization and action by those whose interests are affected. For example, during the 1970s, expanded federal regulation of the automobile, oil, gas, education, and health care industries impelled each of these interests to increase substantially its efforts to influence the government's behavior. These efforts, in turn, spurred the organization of other groups to augment or counter the activities of the first.[10] Similarly, federal social programs have occasionally sparked political organization and action on the part of clientele groups seeking to influence the distribution of benefits and, in turn, the organization of groups opposed to the programs or their cost. For example, federal programs and court decisions in such areas as abortion and school prayer were the stimuli for political organization and action by fundamentalist religious groups. Thus, the expansion of government in recent decades has also stimulated increased group activity and organization.

The New Politics Movement and Public Interest Groups

The second factor accounting for the explosion of interest-group activity in recent years has been the emergence of a new set of forces in American politics that can collectively be called the "New Politics" movement.

The **New Politics movement** is made up of upper-middle-class professionals and intellectuals for whom the civil rights and antiwar movements were formative experiences, just as the Great Depression and World War II had been for their parents. The crusade against racial discrimination and the Vietnam War led these young men and women to see themselves as a political force in opposition to the public policies and politicians associated with the nation's postwar regime. In more recent years, the forces of New Politics have focused their attention on such issues as environmental protection, women's rights, and nuclear disarmament.

Members of the New Politics movement constructed or strengthened public interest groups such as Common Cause, the Sierra Club, the Environmental Defense Fund, Physicians for Social Responsibility, and the National Organization for Women. New Politics forces were able to influence the media, Congress, and even the judiciary and enjoyed a remarkable degree of success during the late 1960s and early 1970s in securing the enactment of policies they favored. New Politics activists played a major role in securing the enactment of environmental, consumer, and occupational health and safety legislation.

Among the factors contributing to the rise and success of New Politics forces was technology. In the 1970s and 1980s, computerized direct-mail campaigns allowed public interest groups to reach hundreds of thousands of potential sympathizers and contributors. Today, the Internet and e-mail serve the same function. Electronic communication allows relatively small groups to identify even more efficiently and mobilize their adherents throughout the nation. Individuals with perspectives that might be in the minority can become aware of each other and mobilize for national political action through the magic of electronic politics.

New Politics groups seek to distinguish themselves from other interest groups—business groups, in particular—by styling themselves as **public interest groups**, terminology that suggests they serve the general good rather than their own selfish interest. These groups' claims to represent *only* the public interest should be viewed with caution, however. It is not uncommon to find decidedly private interests seeking to hide behind the term "public interest." For example, the benign-sounding Partnership to Protect Consumer Credit is a coalition of credit-card companies fighting for less federal regulation of credit abuses, and Project Protect is a coalition of logging interests promoting increased timber cutting.[11] Citizens for a Better Medicare actually represents the pharmaceutical industry. A bill rejected by the Senate in 2006 would have required lobbying groups to disclose their actual identities but was attacked by the industry as a threat to free speech.

New Politics movement a political movement that began in the 1960s and 1970s, made up of professionals and intellectuals for whom the civil rights and antiwar movements were formative experiences. The New Politics movement strengthened public interest groups

public interest groups groups that claim they serve the general good rather than only their own particular interest

forcriticalanalysis

Interest groups often use aliases in their advertising. For example, Americans for Balanced Energy Choices is an alias for a coal-industry trade group. Should lobbying groups be required to disclose their actual identities?

● Strategies: The Quest for Political Power

Interest groups work to improve the probability that they and their policy interests will be heard and treated favorably by all branches and levels of the government. The quest for political influence or power takes many forms. Insider strategies include access to key decision makers and use of the courts. Outsider strategies include going public and using electoral politics. These strategies do not exhaust all the possibilities, but they paint a broad picture of ways that groups utilize their resources in the fierce competition for power (see Figure 11.1).

Many groups employ a mix of insider and outsider strategies. For example, environmental groups such as the Sierra Club lobby members of Congress and key congressional staff members, participate in bureaucratic rule making by offering comments and suggestions to agencies on new environmental rules, and bring lawsuits under various environmental acts like the Endangered Species Act, which authorizes groups and citizens to come to court if they believe the act is being violated. At the same time, the Sierra Club attempts to influence public opinion through media campaigns and to influence electoral politics by supporting candidates who they believe share their environmental views and opposing candidates they view as foes of environmentalism.

Direct Lobbying

Lobbying is an attempt by a group to influence the policy process through persuasion of government officials. Most Americans tend to believe that interest groups exert their influence through direct contact with members of Congress, but lobbying encompasses a broad range of activities that groups engage in with all sorts of government officials and the public as a whole.

The 1946 Federal Regulation of Lobbying Act defines a lobbyist as "any person who shall engage himself for pay or any consideration for the purpose of attempting to influence the passage or defeat of any legislation of the Congress of the United States." The 1995 Lobbying Disclosure Act requires all organizations employing lobbyists to register with Congress and to disclose whom they represent, whom they lobby, what they are looking for, and how much they are paid. More than 34,000 lobbyists are currently registered.[12]

Lobbying involves a great deal of activity on the part of someone speaking for an interest. Lobbyists badger and buttonhole legislators, administrators, and committee staff members with facts about pertinent issues and facts or claims about public support of certain issues or facts.[13] Lobbyists can serve a useful purpose in the legislative and administrative processes by providing this kind of information. In 1978, during debate on a bill to expand the requirement for lobbying disclosures, the Democratic senators Edward Kennedy of Massachusetts and Dick Clark of Iowa joined with the Republican senator Robert Stafford of Vermont to issue the following statement: "Government without lobbying could not function. The flow of information to Congress and to every federal agency is a vital part of our democratic system."[14]

Lobbying Congress Today, lobbyists attempt to influence the policy process in a variety of ways.[15] Traditionally, however, the term *lobbyist* referred mainly to individuals who sought to influence the passage of legislation in the Congress. The First

lobbying a strategy by which organized interests seek to influence the passage of legislation by exerting direct pressure on members of the legislature

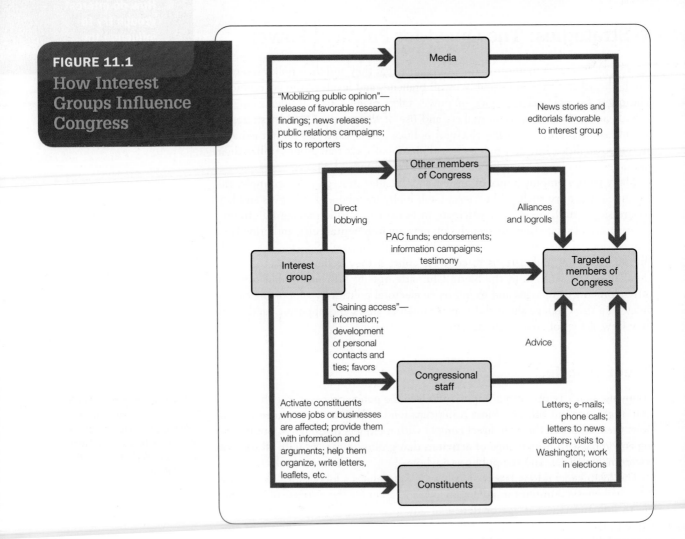

FIGURE 11.1
How Interest Groups Influence Congress

Media

"Mobilizing public opinion"—release of favorable research findings; news releases; public relations campaigns; tips to reporters

News stories and editorials favorable to interest group

Other members of Congress

Direct lobbying

Alliances and logrolls

Interest group

PAC funds; endorsements; information campaigns; testimony

Targeted members of Congress

"Gaining access"—information; development of personal contacts and ties; favors

Advice

Congressional staff

Activate constituents whose jobs or businesses are affected; provide them with information and arguments; help them organize, write letters, leaflets, etc.

Letters; e-mails; phone calls; letters to news editors; visits to Washington; work in elections

Constituents

Amendment to the Constitution provides for the right to "petition the Government for a redress of grievances." But as early as the 1870s, "lobbying" became the common term for petitioning. Petitioning cannot take place on the floor of the House or Senate. Therefore, petitioners must confront members of Congress in the lobbies of the legislative chamber; this activity gave rise to the term *lobbying*.

The influence of lobbyists, in many instances, is based on personal relationships and behind-the-scenes services they are able to perform for lawmakers. Many of Washington's top lobbyists have close ties to important members of Congress or were themselves important political figures, thus virtually guaranteeing that clients will have direct access to congressional leaders. According to the Capitol Hill newspaper, *The Hill*, examples include Jim Blanchard of DLA Piper, who was a governor of Michigan; Chuck Brain of Capitol Hill Strategies, who worked in the White House Legislative Affairs office under President Clinton; Al D'Amato of Park Strategies, who was a senator from New York; Mitchell Feuer of Rich Feuer Group, who was counsel to the Senate Banking Committee; and Broderick Johnson of Bryan Cave, who was a senior aide in the Clinton White House. The list goes on.[16] Some important lobbyists have more than a business relationship to lawmakers. Quite a few are married to prominent political figures. For example, Linda Daschle of LHD and Associates is the wife of former Senate Majority Leader Tom Daschle, and Hadassah Lieberman, wife of Senator Joseph Lieberman, was for many years a lobbyist for the pharmaceutical industry.

Corporate interests also endeavor to be strategic in their choice of lobbyists. Many of Washington's lobbyists also serve as campaign treasurers and major fundraisers for political candidates.[17] Lobbyists like Peter Hart, Tommy Boggs, Peter Knight, Ken Duberstein, and Vin Weber are influential, in part, because of their ability to raise money for politicians. Interest groups will often hire lobbyists whom they know to be key fund-raisers for the politicians they hope to influence. In so doing, they are not making a campaign contribution that would have to be reported to the Federal Election Commission but are nevertheless seeking to ensure that the lobbyist promoting their interests will be seen by the targeted politician as an important source of campaign money. For example, a coalition of television networks seeking to loosen rules governing their ownership of local TV stations hired Gregg Hartley as their lobbyist. Hartley, formerly a top aide to former House Majority Whip Roy Blunt, whose support the coalition sought, was one of Blunt's top fund-raisers. Companies hiring Hartley to lobby for them were almost certain of receiving a positive reception from Blunt. Many members of Congress list lobbyists as treasurers of their reelection committees.[18] Several members of the powerful House Appropriations Committee sponsor political action committees headed by lobbyists with business before the committee.[19]

Interest groups also have substantial influence in setting the legislative agenda and in helping to craft specific language in legislation. Today, sophisticated lobbyists win influence by providing information about policies to busy members of Congress. As one lobbyist noted, "You can't get access without knowledge. . . . I can go in to see [the former Energy and Commerce Committee chair] John Dingell, but if I have nothing to offer or nothing to say, he's not going to want to see me."[20] In recent years, interest groups have also begun to build broader coalitions and comprehensive campaigns around particular policy issues.[21] These coalitions do not rise from the grass roots but instead are put together by Washington lobbyists who launch comprehensive lobbying campaigns that combine stimulated grassroots activity with information and campaign funding for members of Congress. In recent years, the Republican leadership worked so closely with lobbyists that critics charged that the boundaries between lobbyists and legislators had been erased and that lobbyists had become "adjunct staff to the Republican leadership."[22]

Lobbyists also often testify on behalf of their clients at congressional committee and agency hearings. Lobbyists talk to reporters, place ads in newspapers, and organize letter-writing and e-mail campaigns. Lobbyists also play an important role in fund-raising, helping to direct clients' contributions to members of Congress and presidential candidates.

Concern about business having too much influence in Washington dates back to the early days of the country. Here, a mid-nineteenth-century cartoon lampoons the ease with which corporate executives could bribe politicians.

POLITICAL MARKET.

In 2008, the Senate Commerce and Labor Committee heard from lobbyists for the "payday loan" industry, which offers small loans at very high interest rates. Public advocacy groups complained that the payday lenders were taking advantage of consumers and should be regulated more closely by government. Lobbyists for the lenders argued that the industry provides a beneficial service to consumers and does not need stricter regulation.

What happens to interests that do not engage in extensive lobbying? They often find themselves "Microsofted." In 1998, the software giant was facing antitrust action from the Justice Department and had few friends in Congress. One member of the House, Representative Billy Tauzin (R-La.), told Microsoft's chairman, Bill Gates, that without an extensive investment in lobbying, the corporation would continue to be "demonized." Gates responded by quadrupling Microsoft's lobbying expenditures and hiring a group of lobbyists with strong ties to Congress. The result was congressional pressure on the Justice Department resulting in a settlement of the Microsoft suit on terms favorable to the company. Similarly, in 1999, members of Congress advised Wal-Mart that its efforts to win approval to operate savings and loans in its stores were doomed to failure if the retailer did not greatly increase its lobbying efforts. "They don't give money. They don't have congressio-nal representation—so nobody here cares about them," said one influential member. Like Microsoft, Wal-Mart learned its lesson, hired more lobbyists, and got what it wanted.[23] By 2005, Wal-Mart had become a seasoned political player, creating a "war room" in its Arkansas headquarters. Staffed by a phalanx of veteran political operatives from both parties, the war room is the nerve center of the giant retailer's lobbying and public relations efforts.[24] Today, Wal-Mart spends about $5 million a year on its lobbying efforts. Its rivals Costco and Target together barely spend $1 million.

Lobbying the President So many individuals and groups clamor for the president's time and attention that only the most skilled and best-connected members of the lobbying community can hope to influence presidential decisions. Typically, a president's key political advisers and fund-raisers will include individuals with ties to the lobbying industry who can help their friends gain access to the White House. For example, one of President George W. Bush's top fund-raisers was Tom Kuhn, a Washington lobbyist representing the electric power industry. Kuhn, also the president's personal friend and college classmate, was able to prevent the EPA from imposing new controls on electric power plant emissions of mercury, representing a savings of hundreds of millions of dollars for the industry. During the 2008 presidential campaign, Barack Obama said, "Lobbyists won't find a job in my White House." However, soon after his election, Obama appointed David Axelrod as his senior adviser. Before joining the Obama campaign and administration, Axelrod was a partner in ASK Public Strategies, a consulting group that worked for a number of firms. ASK helped the giant Illinois utility Commonwealth Edison seek a major rate hike. At least thirty other senior Obama administration officials have a lobbying background.[25] The lobbying industry is so much a part of Washington that it probably would have been impossible for the president to keep his campaign pledge.

Lobbying the Executive Branch Even when an interest group is very successful at getting its bill passed by Congress and signed by the president, the prospect of full and faithful implementation of that law is not guaranteed. Often, a group and its allies do not pack up and go home as soon as the president turns their lobbied-for new law over to the appropriate agency. On average, 40 percent of interest-group representatives regularly contact both legislative and executive branch organizations, whereas 13 percent contact only the legislature and 16 percent only the executive branch.[26]

In some respects, interest-group access to the executive branch is promoted by federal law. The Administrative Procedure Act, first enacted in 1946 and frequently amended in subsequent years, requires most federal agencies to provide notice and an opportunity for comment before implementing proposed new rules and regulations. This "notice and comment rule-making" is designed to allow interests an opportunity to make their views known and to participate in the implementation of federal legislation that affects them. In 1990, Congress enacted the Negotiated Rulemaking Act to encourage administrative agencies to engage in direct and open negotiations with affected interests when developing new regulations. These two pieces of legislation—which have been strongly enforced by the federal courts—have played an important role in opening the bureaucratic process to interest-group influence. Today, few federal agencies would consider attempting to implement a new rule without consulting affected interests, who are sometimes known in Washington as "stakeholders."[27]

Interest groups may also try to influence the president's decisions. In 2009, President Obama met with business leaders to discuss how a new health care policy would affect their employees' health insurance plans.

Cultivating Access

In 2005, one prominent Washington lobbyist, Jack Abramoff, was indicted on numerous charges of fraud and violations of federal lobbying laws. During the investigation of his activities, it was revealed that Abramoff, along with his associate, Michael Scanlon, had collected tens of millions of dollars from several American Indian tribes that operated lucrative gambling casinos. Indian gambling is currently a $16 billion industry in the United States. What Abramoff provided in exchange was access to key members of Congress who helped his clients shut down rival casino operators. Abramoff was closely associated with several House members, including the former House majority leader Tom DeLay as well as senators John Cornyn, Conrad Burns, and David Vitter. Millions of tribal dollars apparently found their way into the campaign war chests of Abramoff's friends in Congress. Thus, through a well-connected lobbyist, money effectively purchased access and influence. Abramoff and several of his associates subsequently pled guilty to federal bribery and fraud charges. Abramoff was sentenced to more than five years in prison. In a similar vein, Representative Randy "Duke" Cunningham of California was found guilty of accepting $2.4 million in bribes from a defense contractor. Cunningham allegedly used his position on a defense appropriations subcommittee to funnel millions of dollars in contracts to the firm. In 2009, Representative William Jefferson of Louisiana was found guilty of accepting bribes. Jefferson acquired considerable notoriety when FBI agents found $90,000 hidden in the congressman's freezer.

For the most part, though, access to decision makers does not require bribes or other forms of illegal activity. In many areas, interest groups, government agencies, and congressional committees routinely work together for mutual benefit. The interest group provides campaign contributions for members of Congress and lobbies for larger budgets for the agency. The agency, in turn, provides government contracts for the interest group and constituency services for friendly members of Congress. The congressional committee or subcommittee supports the agency's budgetary requests and programs that the interest group favors. Figure 11.2 illustrates one of the most important access patterns in recent American political history: that of the defense industry. Each such pattern, or **iron triangle**, is almost literally a triangular shape, with one point in an executive-branch program, another point in a Senate or House legislative committee or subcommittee, and a third point in some highly stable and well-organized interest group. The points in the triangular relationship are mutually supporting; they count as access only if they last over a long period of time. For example, access to a legislative committee or subcommittee requires that at least one member of it support the interest group in question. This member also must have built up considerable seniority in Congress. An interest cannot feel comfortable about its access to Congress until it has one or more of its "own" people with ten or more years of continuous service on the relevant committee or subcommittee.

A number of important policy domains, such as the environmental and welfare arenas, are controlled not by highly structured and unified iron triangles

iron triangle the stable, cooperative relationship that often develops among a congressional committee, an administrative agency, and one or more supportive interest groups. Not all of these relationships are triangular, but the iron triangle is the most typical

Most interest groups use legal means to try to influence lawmakers. However, in 2009, Louisiana congressman William Jefferson was found guilty of accepting bribes, including $90,000 in cash that was discovered in his freezer.

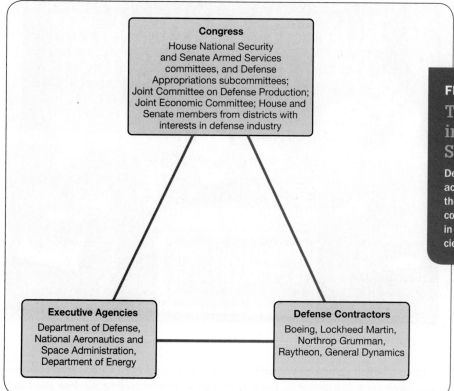

Congress

House National Security and Senate Armed Services committees, and Defense Appropriations subcommittees; Joint Committee on Defense Production; Joint Economic Committee; House and Senate members from districts with interests in defense industry

Executive Agencies

Department of Defense, National Aeronautics and Space Administration, Department of Energy

Defense Contractors

Boeing, Lockheed Martin, Northrop Grumman, Raytheon, General Dynamics

FIGURE 11.2

The Iron Triangle in the Defense Sector

Defense contractors are powerful actors in shaping defense policy; they act in concert with defense committees and subcommittees in Congress and executive agencies concerned with defense.

but by rival **issue networks**. These networks consist of like-minded politicians, consultants, public officials, political activists, and interest groups having some concern with the issue in question. Activists and interest groups recognized as being involved in the area, the "stakeholders," are customarily invited to testify before congressional committees or give their views to government agencies considering action in their domain.

To counter the growing influence of the lobbying industry, stricter guidelines regulating the actions of lobbyists have been adopted in the last decade. For example, as of 1993, businesses may no longer deduct lobbying costs as a business expense. Trade associations must report to members the proportion of their dues that goes to lobbying, and that proportion of the dues may not be reported as a business expense either. The most important attempt to limit the influence of lobbyists was the 1995 Lobbying Disclosure Act, which significantly broadened the definition of people and organizations that must register as lobbyists. This led, as we saw earlier, to more than 34,000 registrations.

In 1996, Congress passed legislation limiting the size of gifts to its own members: no gift could be more than $50, and no member could receive more than $100 from a single source. It also banned the practice of honoraria for giving speeches, which special interests had used to supplement congressional salaries. In 2007, congressional Democrats secured the enactment of a new package of ethics rules designed to fulfill their 2006 campaign promise to bring an end to lobbying abuses. The new rules prohibited lobbyists from paying for most meals, trips, parties, and gifts for members of Congress. Lobbyists were also required to disclose the amounts and

issue network a loose network of elected leaders, public officials, activists, and interest groups drawn together by a specific policy issue

After the Abramoff scandal, in which a prominent lobbyist pleaded guilty to conspiring to bribe members of Congress, both parties called for reform of the lobbying process. In 2007, Democrats in the House of Representatives passed new ethics rules designed to end lobbying abuses.

sources of small campaign contributions they collected from clients and "bundled" into large contributions. And interest groups were required to disclose the funds they used to rally voters to support or oppose legislative proposals. According to the *Washington Post*, however, within a few weeks lobbyists had learned how to circumvent many of the new rules, and lobbying firms were as busy as ever.[28]

Using the Courts (Litigation)

Interest groups sometimes turn to litigation when they lack access or when they are dissatisfied with government in general or with a specific government program and feel they have insufficient influence to change the situation. Interest groups can use the courts to affect public policy in at least three ways: (1) by bringing suit directly on behalf of the group itself, (2) by financing suits brought by individuals, or (3) by filing a companion brief as an amicus curiae (literally "friend of the court") to an existing court case (see Chapter 15 for a discussion of amicus curiae briefs).

Among the most significant modern illustrations of the use of the courts as a strategy for political influence are those that accompanied the "sexual revolution" of the 1960s and the emergence of the movement for women's rights.

The 1973 Supreme Court case of *Roe v. Wade*, which took away a state's power to ban abortions, sparked a controversy that brought conservatives to the fore on a national level.[29] These conservative groups made extensive use of the courts to whittle away at the scope of the privacy doctrine. They obtained rulings, for example, that prohibit the use of federal funds to pay for voluntary abortions. And in 1989, right-to-life groups were able to use a strategy of litigation that significantly undermined the *Roe v. Wade* decision, namely, in the case of *Webster v. Reproductive Health Services* (see Chapter 4), which restored the right of states to place restrictions on abortion.[30] The *Webster* case brought more than 300 interest groups on both sides of the abortion issue to the Supreme Court's door.

Another significant illustration of using the courts for political influence is found in the history of the NAACP. The most important of these court cases was, of course, *Brown v. Board of Education of Topeka, Kansas,* in which the U.S. Supreme Court held that legal segregation of the schools was unconstitutional.[31]

Business groups also frequently use the courts because of the number of government programs applied to them. Litigation involving large businesses is most mountainous in such areas as taxation, antitrust, interstate transportation, patents, and product quality and standardization. Often a business is brought to litigation against its will by virtue of initiatives taken against it by other businesses or by government agencies. But many individual businesses bring suit themselves to influence government policy. Major corporations and their trade associations pay tremendous amounts of money each year in fees to the most prestigious Washington law firms. Some of this money is expended in gaining access. A great proportion of it, however, is used to keep the best and most experienced lawyers prepared to represent the corporations in court or before administrative agencies when necessary.

New Politics forces made significant use of the courts during the 1970s and 1980s, and judicial decisions were instrumental in advancing their goals. Facilitated by changes in the rules governing access to the courts ("standing" is discussed in Chapter 15), the New Politics agenda was clearly visible in court decisions handed down in several key policy areas. In the environmental policy area, New Politics groups were able to force federal agencies to pay attention to environmental issues, even when the agency was not directly involved in activities related to environmental quality. For example, the Federal Trade Commission (FTC) became very responsive to the demands of New Politics activists during the 1970s and 1980s. The FTC stepped up its activities considerably, litigating a series of claims arising under regulations prohibiting deceptive advertising in cases ranging from false claims for over-the-counter drugs to inflated claims about the nutritional value of children's cereal.

Mobilizing Public Opinion

Going public is a strategy that attempts to mobilize the widest and most favorable climate of opinion. Many groups consider it imperative to maintain this climate at all times, even when they have no issue to fight about. An increased use of this kind of strategy is usually associated with modern advertising. As early as the 1930s, political analysts were distinguishing between the "old lobby" of direct group representation before Congress and the "new lobby" of public-relations professionals addressing the public at large to reach Congress.[32]

Institutional Advertising One of the best-known ways of going public is the use of **institutional advertising**. A casual scanning of important mass-circulation magazines and newspapers will provide numerous examples of expensive and well-designed ads by the major oil companies, automobile and steel companies, other large corporations, and trade associations. The ads show how much these organizations are doing for the country, for the protection of the environment, or for the defense of the American way of life. Their purpose is to create and maintain a strongly positive association between the organization and the community at large in the hope that they can draw on these favorable feelings as needed for specific political campaigns later on.

institutional advertising
advertising designed to create a positive image of an organization

Protests and Demonstrations Many groups resort to going public because they lack the resources, the contacts, or the experience to use other political strategies. The sponsorship of boycotts, sit-ins, mass rallies, and marches by Martin Luther King, Jr.'s, Southern Christian Leadership Conference (SCLC) and related organizations during the 1950s and 1960s is one of the most significant and successful cases of going public to create a more favorable climate of opinion by calling attention to abuses. The success of these events inspired similar efforts on the part of women. Organizations such as the National Organization for Women (NOW) used public strategies in their drive for legislation and in their efforts to gain ratification of the Equal Rights Amendment. In 2004 and 2005, antiwar groups demonstrated near President Bush's ranch in Crawford, Texas, to demand an end to the American military presence in Iraq. The protestors were led by Cindy Sheehan, whose son had been killed while serving in Iraq.

grassroots mobilization a lobbying campaign in which a group mobilizes its membership to contact government officials in support of the group's position

Grassroots Mobilization Another form of going public is **grassroots mobilization**. In such a campaign, a lobby group mobilizes its members and their families throughout the country to write to their elected representatives in support of the group's position.

Among the most effective users of the grassroots effort in contemporary American politics is the religious right. Networks of evangelical churches have the capacity to generate hundreds of thousands of letters and phone calls to Congress and the White House. For example, the religious right was outraged when President Clinton announced soon after taking office that he planned to end the military's ban on gay and lesbian soldiers. The Reverend Jerry Falwell, an evangelical leader, called on viewers of his television program to dial a telephone number that would add their names to a petition urging Clinton to retain the ban on gays in the military. Within a few hours, 24,000 people had called to support the petition.[33]

Grassroots campaigns have been so effective throughout the last few years that a number of Washington consulting firms have begun to specialize in this area. In

Many interest groups stage protests and demonstrations to draw attention to their cause and mobilize public opinion. This Sierra Club demonstration was intended to call attention to the problem of toxic pollution in Oregon's Willamette River.

2007, for example, a grassroots firm called Grassfire.org led the drive to kill the immigration reform bill supported by President Bush and a number of congressional Democrats that would have legalized the status of many illegal immigrants. Grassfire.org used the Internet and talk radio programs to generate a campaign that yielded 700,000 signatures on petitions opposing the bill. The petitions, along with tens of thousands of phone calls, letters, and e-mails generated by Grassfire and several other groups led to the bill's defeat in the U.S. Senate.[34]

Many members of Congress, are becoming quite skeptical of such methods, charging that these are not genuine grassroots campaigns but instead represent "Astroturf lobbying" (a play on the name of an artificial grass used on many sports fields). Such Astroturf campaigns, often using e-mail, have increased in frequency in recent years as members of Congress have grown more and more skeptical of Washington lobbyists and far more concerned about demonstrations of support for a particular issue by their constituents. Often, unfortunately, Astroturf campaigns are carefully scripted efforts on behalf of corporate interests using names designed to disguise their true goals to help them gather public support for their efforts. For example, the Save Our Species Alliance is an industry group seeking to weaken the Endangered Species Act, and Citizens for Asbestos Reform seeks to limit the ability of individuals harmed by asbestos from seeking redress in the courts. The Committee to Protect America's Health Care is a coalition of for-profit hospitals that runs ads calling for increased federal funding for those entities. Voices for Choices was the alias used by a coalition of telecommunications companies that unsuccessfully advertised on behalf of continued regulation of local phone services. Both Americans for Balanced Energy Choices and the Coalition for Affordable and Reliable Energy sponsor ads promoting the virtues of coal as an energy source. "Some of us invest lots of time and money into making the world cleaner," announces the pitchman for Americans for Balanced Energy Choices. "And one thing that's helping is electricity from coal." By the logic of these aliases, a coalition of strip-mining interests might call itself Citizens for a Cleaner Earth while perhaps a coalition of health insurers, companies notorious for raising premiums but refusing to pay subscribers' claims, might operate under the alias Citizens against Costly Medical Services. A Senate bill proposed in 2007 would have required lobby groups using such aliases to disclose their true identities. Many groups treated this proposal as a vicious attack on their freedom of speech. Wayne LaPierre, president of the National Rifle Association, suggested that this sort of disclosure requirement would have thwarted the activities of the Revolutionary-era pamphleteer Tom Paine and perhaps undermined the American Revolution. The proposal ultimately failed.

Using Electoral Politics

In addition to attempting to influence members of Congress and other government officials, interest groups also seek to use the electoral process to elect the right legislators in the first place and to ensure that those who are elected will owe them a debt of gratitude for their support. If we view matters in perspective, groups invest far more resources in lobbying than in electoral politics. Nevertheless, financial support and campaign activism can be important tools for organized interests.

Political Action Committees By far the most common electoral strategy interest groups employ is that of giving financial support to the parties or to particular candidates. But such support can easily cross the threshold into outright bribery. Therefore, Congress has occasionally made an effort to regulate this strategy. For example, the Federal Election Campaign Act of 1971 (amended in 1974) limits campaign contributions and requires that each candidate or campaign committee itemize the full name and address, occupation, and principal business of each person who contributes more than $100. These provisions have been effective up to a point, considering the rather large number of embarrassments, indictments, resignations, and criminal convictions in the aftermath of the Watergate scandal.

The Watergate scandal was triggered by the illegal entry of Republican workers into the office of the Democratic National Committee in the Watergate apartment and hotel complex. But an investigation quickly revealed numerous violations of campaign- finance laws, involving millions of dollars in unregistered cash from corporate executives to President Nixon's reelection committee. Many of these revelations were made by the famous Ervin Committee, named for its chair, Senator Sam J. Ervin (D-N.C.). The committee's official name and jurisdiction was the Senate Select Committee to Investigate the 1972 Presidential Campaign Activities.

political action committee (PAC) a private group that raises and distributes funds for use in election campaigns

Reaction to Watergate produced further legislation on campaign finance in 1974 and 1976, but the effect was to restrict individual rather than interest-group campaign activity. Today, individuals may contribute no more than $2,300 to any candidate for federal office in any primary or general election. A **political action committee (PAC)**, however, can contribute $5,000, provided it contributes to at least five different federal candidates each year. Beyond this, the laws permit corporations, unions, and other interest groups to form PACs and to pay the costs of soliciting funds from private citizens for the PACs. In other words, PACs are interest groups that choose to operate in the electoral arena in addition to whatever they do within the interest-group system. The option to form a PAC was made available by law only in the early 1970s. Until then, it was difficult—if not downright illegal—for corporations, including unions, to get directly involved in elections by supporting parties and candidates.

Electoral spending by interest groups has been increasing steadily despite the flurry of reform following Watergate. The dollar amounts for each year reveal the growth in electoral spending. The number of PACs has also increased significantly—from 480 in 1972 to more than 5,000 in 2008 (see Figure 11.3). Although the reform legislation of the early and mid-1970s attempted to reduce the influence that special interests have over elections, the effect has been almost the exact opposite. Opportunities for legally influencing campaigns are now widespread. The total extent of spending on national elections for 2008 was approximately $3 billion. PACs contributed about one-third of this amount. Another third was contributed in soft money raised by 527 and 501c(4) groups, which are not regulated by the Federal Election Commission.

Given the enormous costs of television commercials, polls, computers, and other elements of contemporary political technology, most politicians are eager to receive PAC contributions and are at least willing to give a friendly hearing to the needs and interests of contributors. Most politicians probably will not simply sell their services to the interests that fund their campaigns, but there is some evidence that interest groups' campaign contributions do influence the overall pattern of political behavior in Congress and in the state legislatures.

Indeed, PACs and campaign contributions provide organized interests with such a useful tool for gaining access to the political process that calls to abolish PACs have been quite frequent among political reformers. Concern about PACs grew through the 1980s and 1990s, creating a constant drumbeat for reform of federal election laws. Proposals were introduced in Congress on many occasions, perhaps the most celebrated being the McCain-Feingold bill, which became the Bipartisan Campaign Reform Act (BCRA) of 2002. When originally proposed in 1996, McCain-Feingold was aimed at reducing or eliminating PACs. But in a stunning

Celebrity Involvement with Groups and Interests

Interest groups sometimes rely on the involvement of celebrities—such as actors, musicians, and sports figures—to help attract media attention and gain access to politicians. But when Bono lobbies for debt relief for Africa or Angelina Jolie discusses the plight of refugees, do they actually help advance the causes that they represent? Is their involvement good for democracy and the political process?

Endorsing political candidates, making public statements for or against certain policies, and even becoming official representatives of certain groups have become common forms of political activism for entertainment-world celebrities. In their book *Celebrity Politics,* Darrell West and John Ormond argue that the American mass media pay attention to a celebrity's opinion on a political issue simply because it is the viewpoint of someone famous—not because of any special insight or expertise that person has. The perceived importance of what celebrities do and say is reinforced by the news-coverage style of "infotainment" shows like *Inside Edition* and *Extra.* West and Ormond argue that this trend encourages citizens to view politics

as show business and spectacle rather than something in which they ought to participate.

Others are more positive about the role of celebrities in politics. Hans Riemer of Rock the Vote believes that the involvement of celebrities like rock stars in political life engages young Americans. "If musicians are politically engaged, then young people are going to be politically engaged," says Riemer.[a] In fact, data from Harvard's Kennedy School of Government Vanishing Voter project suggests that the many celebrities involved in "get out the vote" campaigns have contributed to first-time voters going to the polls.

Celebrities certainly bring media attention to the groups they support, as in the cases of Richard Gere's work for a free Tibet, Michael J. Fox's support for stem cell research, and the late Charlton Heston's involvement with the National Rifle Association. Members of Congress often invite celebrities to speak before committees to increase the chances of their policy negotiations getting on the news. (This phenomenon is discussed further in Chapter 12's Politics and Popular Culture unit.)

Experiments by political scientists David Jackson and Thomas Darrow suggest that celebrity support can improve public opinion surrounding politicians or policies *if* those celebrities are well-liked. A problem for organizations represented by celebrities arises when those celebrities are not seen as likable or credible. "Sometimes [celebrity representation] works against a cause if the general public perceives the celebrity as flaky or out of the mainstream," admits Bob Oettinger, president of Celebrity Outreach Foundation, an orga-

nization that helps coordinate charities and celebrity spokespeople.[b] Moreover, some studies have suggested that many Americans do not like celebrity endorsements of specific policies.[c]

Celebrity involvement with specific interests seems likely to increase in the future, thanks in part to organizations like Oettinger's that match up celebrities with political groups. The dynamic is straightforward: celebrities want to enhance their reputations by being associated with good causes, and interest groups want media attention. But, as illustrated by the ongoing debates over the effectiveness of celebrities in politics, it is unclear whether this trend is ultimately good for the causes celebrities represent or for American democracy.

[a]P. Brownfeld, "Musicians Try to Tune Fans In to Causes, Candidates," December 16, 2003, Foxnews.com (accessed 4/28/08).
[b]"Celebrities Use Status to Stump for Causes," January 9, 2002, Foxnews.com (accessed 4/28/08).
[c]R. Leiby, "Reliable Source," *The Washington Post*, October 26, 2004.

for critical analysis

1. Do you think "celebrity politics" discourages citizen participation by promoting a "sit down and watch" approach to political life? Or do you believe celebrities can foster participation among people who might not otherwise pay attention to the causes they represent?

2. What are some of the other ways that interest groups can attract media attention and gain access to policy makers?

425

about-face, when campaign finance reform was adopted in 2002, it did not restrict PACs in any significant way. Rather, it eliminated unrestricted "soft money" donations to the national political parties (see Chapter 10). One consequence of this reform, as we saw in Chapters 9 and 10, was the creation of a host of new organizations known as 527 committees. These are often directed by former party officials but are nominally unaffiliated with the two parties. This change has had the effect of strengthening interest groups and weakening parties.

Activist groups carefully keep their campaign spending separate from party and candidate organizations to avoid the restrictions of federal campaign finance laws. As long as a group's campaign expenditures are not coordinated with those of a candidate's own campaign, the group is free to spend as much money as it wishes. Such expenditures are viewed as "issue advocacy" and are protected by the First Amendment. This view was reaffirmed by the Federal Election Commission, which ruled in May 2004 that spending by 527 committees was not limited by BCRA.

One powerful but little-known campaign finance tactic is the formation of strategic alliances between corporate interest groups and ideological or not-for-profit groups. A corporate interest may find it useful to hide its campaign contributions by laundering them through a not-for-profit. For example, in the late 1990s, a variety of gambling interests opposed a bill that would have prohibited Internet gambling. Members of Congress were reluctant to accept money directly from what might have seemed to be unsavory sources. At the direction of the former Washington super-lobbyist Jack Abramoff, the affected gambling interests made contributions to religious groups led by Ralph Reed, the former executive director of the Christian Coalition, and Rev. Louis P. Sheldon, founder of the Traditional Values Coalition, as well as tax reform groups headed by Grover Norquist. In turn, these groups lobbied against the Internet gambling ban, providing laundered campaign funds for prominent members of Congress. This tactic, called "money swapping," is fairly common. The Clinton administration allegedly engaged in extensive money

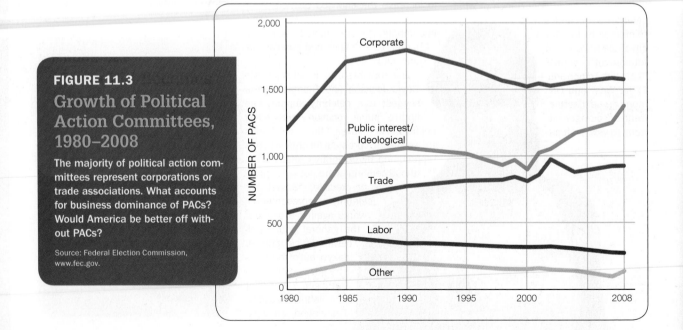

FIGURE 11.3
Growth of Political Action Committees, 1980–2008

The majority of political action committees represent corporations or trade associations. What accounts for business dominance of PACs? Would America be better off without PACs?

Source: Federal Election Commission, www.fec.gov.

Who Is Represented by PACs?

PACs representing business interests have been the dominant category since the FEC started tracking PACs in 1974. The number of "nonconnected" or ideological PACs has also grown in recent years. These groups are not connected to a specific corporation, labor organization, or membership association, and work to elect candidates who support their ideals or agenda. However, in terms of contributions to candidates, spending by ideological groups is dwarfed by the combined contributions of PACs from various business sectors.

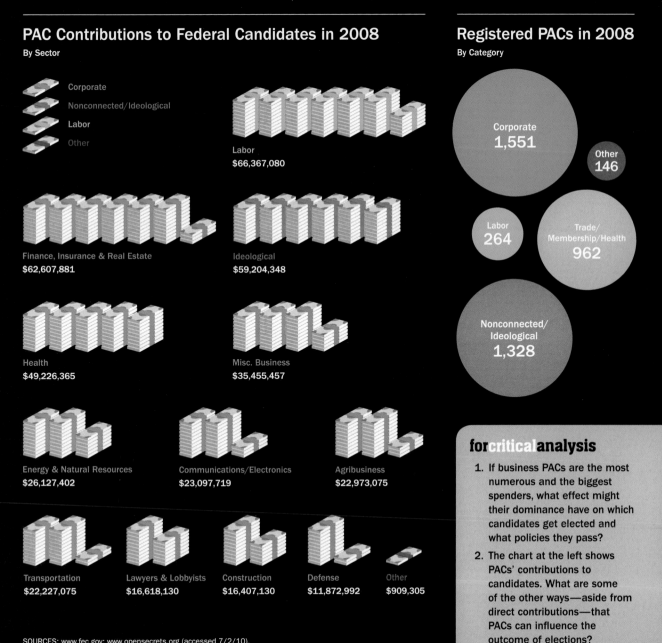

PAC Contributions to Federal Candidates in 2008
By Sector

Corporate
Nonconnected/Ideological
Labor
Other

Labor
$66,367,080

Finance, Insurance & Real Estate
$62,607,881

Ideological
$59,204,348

Health
$49,226,365

Misc. Business
$35,455,457

Energy & Natural Resources
$26,127,402

Communications/Electronics
$23,097,719

Agribusiness
$22,973,075

Transportation
$22,227,075

Lawyers & Lobbyists
$16,618,130

Construction
$16,407,130

Defense
$11,872,992

Other
$909,305

Registered PACs in 2008
By Category

Corporate
1,551

Other
146

Labor
264

Trade/Membership/Health
962

Nonconnected/Ideological
1,328

for critical analysis

1. If business PACs are the most numerous and the biggest spenders, what effect might their dominance have on which candidates get elected and what policies they pass?

2. The chart at the left shows PACs' contributions to candidates. What are some of the other ways—aside from direct contributions—that PACs can influence the outcome of elections?

SOURCES: www.fec.gov; www.opensecrets.org (accessed 7/2/10).

swapping with such organizations as the International Brotherhood of Teamsters. In one case, a foreign national hoping to influence the administration was advised that a direct contribution would be illegal. Instead, Democratic fund-raisers advised this individual to make a contribution to Teamster president Ron Carey's reelection campaign. The Teamsters, in turn, made a legal contribution to the Clinton campaign. Such money swapping is illegal but almost impossible to prove.

Campaign Activism Financial support is not the only way that organized groups seek influence through electoral politics. Sometimes activism can be even more important than campaign contributions. Campaign activism on the part of conservative groups played a very important role in bringing about the Republican capture of both houses of Congress in the 1994 congressional elections. For example, Christian Coalition activists played a role in many races, including those in which Republican candidates were not overly identified with the religious right. One postelection study suggested that more than 60 percent of the more than 600 candidates supported by the Christian right were successful in state, local, and congressional races in 1994.[35] The efforts of conservative Republican activists to bring voters to the polls is one major reason that turnout among Republicans exceeded Democratic turnout in a midterm election for the first time since 1970. This increased turnout was especially marked in the South, where the Christian Coalition was most active. In many congressional districts, Christian Coalition efforts on behalf of the Republicans were augmented by grassroots campaigns launched by the NRA and the National Federation of Independent Business (NFIB). The NRA had been outraged by Democratic support for gun-control legislation, and the NFIB had been energized by its campaign against employer mandates in the failed Clinton health care reform initiative. Both groups are well-organized at the local level and were able to mobilize their members across the country to participate in congressional races.

The Initiative Another political tactic that interest groups sometimes use is sponsorship of ballot initiatives at the state level. The initiative, a device adopted by a number of states around 1900, allows proposed laws to be placed on the general election ballot and submitted directly to the state's voters. This procedure bypasses the state legislature and the governor. The initiative was originally promoted by late-nineteenth-century Populists as a mechanism that would allow the people to govern directly. Populists saw the initiative as an antidote to interest group influence in the legislative process.

Many studies have suggested that, ironically, most initiative campaigns today are actually sponsored by interest groups seeking to circumvent legislative opposition to their goals. In recent years, for example, initiative campaigns have been sponsored by the insurance industry, trial lawyers' associations, and tobacco companies.[36] The success of business groups promoting anti-tax initiatives and conservative activists seeking to ban same-sex marriage led liberal activists to develop their own initiative campaigns to promote issues such as same-sex marriage, clean energy, and abortion rights. In 1998, liberal activists established the Ballot Initiative Strategy Center (BISC) to provide national coordination for these efforts. These efforts have led to successes such as the 2010 Oregon campaign for Propositions 66 and 67 that increased taxes for corporations and high-income wage earners. The role of interest groups in initiative campaigns should come as no surprise, since such campaigns can cost millions of dollars.

for critical analysis

Describe the different techniques of influence that organized interests employ. When is one technique preferable to another?

Take an Interest in Interest Groups

The words "interest group" often conjure up images of powerful lobbyists working on behalf of people far removed from yourself and your peers. For example, AARP, formerly the American Association of Retired Persons, represents more than 35 million people who are fifty years of age and older and is one of the most politically powerful groups in existence today. It's probably safe to say that the effectiveness of AARP in influencing Social Security and Medicare reform doesn't strike most college students as something that's likely to change their lives anytime soon.

However, groups formed by young Americans lobbied successfully for the College Cost Reduction and Access Act, a measure that was ultimately passed by Congress in 2007. Among other things, the act increases Pell Grants, reduces interest on certain college loans, and makes the rate of loan repayment partially dependent on how much one earns. In short, it attempts to address one of the most vexing problems faced by young Americans today—affording a college education—especially as college increasingly seems a necessity in life rather than a choice. Students and other

young people were at the forefront of activism around getting this bill passed.

Campus chapters of U.S. PIRG, a federation of state Public Interest Research Groups, were involved with mobilizing youth around this particular legislation. PIRG and the College Cost Reduction and Access Act is a terrific example of the power of interest groups in the United States and the ways in which youth are often involved in lobbying for solutions to social and political problems. As easy as it is to buy the conventional wisdom that interest groups are a political force used only by people older and wealthier than you, it's simply not the case.

The following ideas for getting involved will help you think through issues like interest-group representation and influence. You don't necessarily need to become an activist yourself to gain a better understanding of what interest groups actually do in our democracy.

- Identify the issues you care the most about in politics today and find out if there are any interest groups that advocate on behalf of those issues. You might consider joining one or two in order to show your support and to better

understand the ways in which interest groups cultivate members and represent their interests in state and national governments. An easy way to learn about relevant issues of the day is to visit the Web site for Campus Activism (www.campusactivism.org) and check out their list of issues and campaigns that are going on around the country to help address them.

- If you find a group for which you feel a close affinity, consider forming a campus chapter. There are a lot of groups that will gladly help students start campus chapters. Some that come to mind include the American Association for University Women (www.aauw.org) and Amnesty International (www.amnesty.org).

- Find out how those who represent you in Congress measure up according to interest groups. As you'll see when you visit the link to interest-group ratings on the Project Vote Smart Web site (www.votesmart.org), interest groups assess how consistently elected officials vote for legislation that's supportive of group interests. You may find a few surprising scores tied to those who represent you in Congress.

- Interest groups often get a bad rap in American politics, mainly because people think they have too much influence over elected officials who end up responding to them more than average voters. These concerns are especially heightened during an election year because people believe that candidates are "bought and sold" by way of campaign donations from interest groups. Look up the McCain-Feingold Act, which was intended to reduce the influence of interest groups' money in elections. If you are still concerned about the influence of interest groups and think further reform is needed, e-mail your member of Congress, using the contact information at www.house.gov or www.senate.gov.

Thinking Critically about Groups and Interests: The Dilemmas of Reform

We would like to think that policies are products of legislators' concepts of the public interest. Yet the truth of the matter is that few programs and policies ever reach the public agenda without the vigorous support of important national interest groups. In the realm of economic policy, social policy, international trade policy, and even such seemingly interest-free areas as criminal justice policy—where, in fact, private prison corporations lobby for longer sentences for lawbreakers—the activity of interest group is a central feature.

James Madison wrote that "liberty is to faction as air is to fire."[37] By this he meant that the organization and proliferation of interests were inevitable in a free society. To seek to place limits on the organization of interests, in Madison's view, would be to limit liberty itself. Madison believed that interests should be permitted to regulate themselves by competing with each other. As long as competition among different interests was free, open, and vigorous—that is, as long as pluralism thrived—there would be some balance of power among them and no one interest would be able to dominate the political or governmental process.

There is considerable competition among organized groups in the United States. For example, pro-choice and anti-abortion forces continue to be locked in a bitter struggle. Nevertheless, interest-group politics is not as free of bias as Madisonian theory might suggest. Although the weak and poor do occasionally become organized to assert their rights, interest-group politics is generally a form of political competition in which the wealthy and powerful are best able to engage. In the realm of group politics, liberty seems inconsistent with equality.

Moreover, although groups sometimes organize to promote broad public concerns, interest groups more often represent relatively narrow, selfish interests. Small, self-interested groups can be organized much more easily than large and more diffuse collectives. For one thing, the members of a relatively small group—say, bankers or hunting enthusiasts—are usually able to recognize their shared interests and the need to pursue them in the political arena. Members of large and more diffuse groups—say, consumers or potential victims of firearms—often find it difficult to recognize their shared interests or the need to engage in collective action to achieve them.[38]

To make matters still more complicated, group politics seems to go hand in hand with government. As we saw earlier, government programs often lead to a proliferation of interest groups as competing forces mobilize to support, oppose, or take advantage of the government's actions. Often, the government explicitly encourages the formation of interest groups. Agencies such as the Department of Veterans Affairs, the Social Security Administration, and the Department of Agriculture devote a great deal of energy to the organization and mobilization of groups of "stakeholders" to support the agencies and their efforts. One reason that the Social Security program has endured despite its fiscal shortcomings is that it is so strongly supported by a powerful group—AARP. Significantly, the Social Security Administration played an important early

forcritical**analysis**

How has the U.S. government sought to regulate interest-group activity in order to balance the competing values of liberty and equality? What else might government do to make group politics less biased?

Some citizens worry that well-funded narrow interests, such as business groups, are better able to organize and lobby the government, while ordinary citizens have less influence in politics.

role in the formation of AARP, precisely because agency executives realized that this group could become a useful ally.

The responsiveness of government agencies to interest groups is a challenge to democracy. Groups sometimes seem to have a greater impact than voters on the government's policies and programs. Yet, before we decide that we should do away with interest groups, we should think carefully: If there were no organized interests, would the government pay more attention to ordinary voters? Or would the government simply pay less attention to everyone? In his work *Democracy in America*, Alexis de Tocqueville argued that the proliferation of groups promoted democracy by encouraging governmental responsiveness. Does group politics foster democracy or impede democracy? It does both.

● **What are the arguments for and against regulating interest groups?**

studyguide

Practice Quiz

Ⓢ Find a diagnostic Web Quiz with 30 additional questions on the StudySpace Web site: www.wwnorton.com/we-the-people

The Character of Interest Groups

1. The theory that competition among organized interests will produce balance with all the interests regulating over another is *(p. 403)*
   a) pluralism.
   b) elite power politics.
   c) democracy.
   d) socialism.

2. Groups that have an interest in obtaining government funds for research, such as Harvard University, the Brookings Institution and the American Enterprise Institute, are referred to as *(p. 405)*
   a) public sector groups.
   b) public interest groups.
   c) professional associations.
   d) ideological groups.

3. To overcome the free-rider problem, groups *(pp. 407–08)*
   a) provide general benefits.
   b) litigate.
   c) go public.
   d) provide selective benefits.

4. Politically organized religious groups often make use of *(p. 408)*
   a) material benefits.
   b) solidary benefits.
   c) purposive benefits.
   d) none of the above.

5. Which of the following best describes the reputation of AARP in the Washington community? *(p. 409)*
   a) it is respected and feared.
   b) it is supported and well-liked by all political forces.
   c) it is believed to the ineffective.
   d) it wins the political battles it fights.

The Proliferation of Groups

6. Which of the following is an important reason for the enormous increase in the number of groups seeking to influence the American political system? *(p. 411)*
   a) the decrease in the size and activity of government during the last few decades.
   b) the increase in the size and activity of government during the last few decades.
   c) the increase in the number of people identifying themselves as an independent in recent decades.
   d) the increase in the amount of soft money in election campaigns in recent decades.

7. Which types of interest groups are most often associated with the New Politics movement? *(p. 412)*
   a) public-interest groups.
   b) professional associations.
   c) government groups.
   d) labor groups.

Strategies: The Quest for Political Power

8. Access politics, exemplified by defense contractions acting in concert with congressional committees and executive agencies, is an example of *(p. 418)*
   a) campaign activism.
   b) public interest politics.
   c) an iron triangle.
   d) the role of conservative interest groups.

9. A loose network of elected leaders, public officials, activists, and interest groups drawn together by a public policy issue is referred to as *(p. 419)*
   a) an issue network.
   b) an iron triangle.

c) a political action committee

d) pluralism

10. In which of the following ways do interest groups use the courts to affect public polity? *(p. 420)*
    a) filing *amicus* briefs.
    b) bringing lawsuits.
    c) financing those filing suit.
    d) all of the above.

11. Which of the following is *not* a way for an interest group to use a "going public" strategy? *(pp. 421–22)*
    a) institutional advertising
    b) grassroots mobilization
    c) protests and demonstrations
    d) lobbying the executive branch

12. According to this text, what is the limit a PAC can contribute to a candidate in a primary or general election campaign? *(p. 424)*
    a) $1,000
    b) $5,000
    c) $10,000
    d) $50,000

13. Which of the following is *not* an activity in which interest groups frequently engage? *(p. 426)*
    a) starting their own political party
    b) litigation
    c) lobbying
    d) contributing to compaigns

14. "Money swapping" occurs when *(p. 426)*
    a) a member of a congressional committee trades his or her vote for a cash payment from an interest group.
    b) an interest group combines its compaign spending with that of a political party or candidate organization.
    c) a lobbyist is paid to testify before a congressional committee.
    d) a corporate interest group attempts to hide its campaign contributions by laundering them through a not-for-profit group.

Thinking Critically about Groups and Interests: The Dilemmas of Reform

15. Which of the following statements is true about the kinds of groups that are likely to organize? *(p. 430)*
    a) small, self-interested groups can be organized more easily than large and diffuse groups.
    b) small, self-interested groups can be organized less easily than large and diffuse groups.
    c) small, self-interested groups are just as easy to organize as large and diffuse groups.
    d) small, self-interested groups are only easy to organize when large and diffuse groups have already organized.

Chapter Outline

 Find a detailed Chapter Outline on the StudySpace Web site: www.wwnorton.com/we-the-people

Key Terms

Find Flashcards to help you study these terms on the StudySpace Web site: www.wwnorton.com/we-the-people

collective goods *(p. 407)*
free riders *(p. 407)*
grassroots mobilization *(p. 422)*
informational benefits *(p. 408)*
institutional advertising *(p. 421)*
interest group *(p. 403)*

iron triangle *(p. 418)*
issue network *(p. 419)*
lobbying *(p. 413)*
material benefits *(p. 408)*
membership association *(p. 407)*
New Politics movement *(p. 412)*

pluralism *(p. 403)*
political action committee (PAC) *(p. 424)*
public interest groups *(p. 412)*
purposive benefits *(p. 408)*
solidary benefits *(p. 408)*
staff organization *(p. 407)*

For Further Reading

Ainsworth, Scott. *Analyzing Interest Groups*. New York: Norton, 2002.

Alexander, Robert, ed. *The Classic of Interest Group Behavior*. New York: Wadsworth, 2005.

Baumgartner, Frank, Jeffrey M. Berry, Beth L. Leech, David C. Kimball, and Marie Hojnacki. *Lobbying and Policy Change: Who Wins, Who Loses and Why*. Chicago: University of Chicago Press, 2009.

Berry, Jeffrey. *Interest Group Society.* 5th ed. New York: Longman, 2008.

Cigler, Allan J., and Burdett A. Loomis, eds. *Interest Group Politics.* 7th ed. Washington, DC: Congressional Quarterly Press, 2006.

Esterling, Kevin. *The Political Economy of Expertise.* Ann Arbor: University of Michigan Press, 2004.

Goldstein, Kenneth. *Interest Groups, Lobbying and Participation in America.* New York: Cambridge University Press, 2008.

Kaiser, Robert. *So Damn Much Money: The Triumph of Lobbying and the Corrosion of American Government.* New York: Vintage, 2010.

Kollman, Kenneth W. *Outside Lobbying: Public Opinion and Interest Group Strategies.* Princeton, NJ: Princeton University Press, 1998.

Lowi, Theodore J. *The End of Liberalism: The Second Republic of the United States.* 2nd ed. New York: Norton, 1979.

Moe, Terry M. *The Organization of Interests: Incentives and the Internal Dynamics of Political Interest Groups.* Chicago: University of Chicago Press, 1980.

Nownes, Anthony. *Total Lobbying: What Lobbyists Want and How They Try to Get It.* New York: Cambridge University Press, 2006.

Olson, Mancur, Jr. *The Logic of Collective Action: Public Goods and the Theory of Groups.* Cambridge, MA: Harvard University Press, 1965.

Rozell, Mark, Clyde Wilcox, and David Madland. *Interest Groups in American Campaigns.* Washington, DC: Congressional Quarterly Press, 2005.

Sheingate, Adam. *The Rise of the Agricultural Welfare State: Institutions and Interest Group Power in the United States, France, and Japan.* Princeton, NJ: Princeton University Press, 2003.

Strolovitch, Dara. *Affirmative Advocacy: Race, Class and Gender in Interest Group Politics.* Chicago: University of Chicago Press, 2007.

Truman, David B. *The Governmental Process: Political Interests and Public Opinion.* New York: Knopf, 1951.

Recommended Web Sites

AARP
www.aarp.org

AARP (formerly the American Association of Retired Persons) is one of the largest and most significant interest groups in the United States. Read about the history of this organization, its group benefits, and how it is affecting political issues and elections.

AFL-CIO Legislative Alert Center
www.aflcio.org/issues/legislativealert/

Created in 1955, the AFL-CIO represents over 10 million working men and women. See how this influential labor group is active and involved in political issues.

American Civil Liberties Union
www.aclu.org
American Conservative Union
www.conservative.org

The American Civil Liberties Union and the American Conservative Union are two of the nation's largest and most influential ideological interest groups. See what these opposing groups have to say about our government and current political issues.

American Israel Public Affairs Committee (AIPAC)
www.aipac.org

Due to globalization, interest groups cannot limit their activities to only one country. Decisions made in Washington, D.C., can affect countries around the world. The American Israel Public Affairs Committee (AIPAC) works with Republicans and Democrats to maintain a strong relationship between the United States and Israel.

MoveOn
www.moveon.org

This progressive interest group is dedicated to bringing ordinary citizens back into the political process and electing liberal members of government. See how this group uses electoral politics, via political action committees and campaign activism, to achieve its agenda.

National Rifle Association
www.nra.org
Coalition to Stop Gun Violence
www.csgv.org
Brady Campaign to Prevent Gun Violence
www.bradycampaign.org

Lobbying is an attempt by a group to influence the policy process by persuading government officials. These three groups employ a variety of lobbying techniques on the issue of gun control.

U.S. PIRG (United States Public Interest Research Group)
www.uspirg.org

This public interest group stands up for ordinary citizens. Its special emphasis is on consumer rights and the environment. U.S. PIRG mobilizes public opinion via institutional advertising, social movements, and grassroots efforts. PIRG chapters can be found in most states and at many colleges and universities.

World Wildlife Fund
www.wwf.org

The World Wildlife Fund is dedicated to protecting nature. They provide information to policy makers about conservation and advocate policies to help preserve the natural environment.

In addition to its lawmaking powers, Congress plays a critical role in American democracy as a representative institution. The members of Congress—100 senators and 435 representatives—represent the voices of the people across America. Yet some observers worry that Congress does not represent all voices equally.

IN GOD WE TRUST

Congress

WHAT GOVERNMENT DOES AND WHY IT MATTERS In 2009, Congress passed the Credit Card Accountability, Responsibility, and Disclosure (CARD) Act of 2009, a law restricting many credit card company practices that had resulted in higher payments for customers. Credit card companies could no longer routinely raise interest rates on existing balances. The law also prevented them from charging a fee to customers who exceeded their borrowing limit unless these customers had explicitly requested this service. One part of the law directly targeted consumers under the age of twenty-one. After the law went into effect, young consumers would find it harder to get a credit card because they were now required to get permission from their parents or show that they could make the payments themselves. This provision was intended to help young people avoid getting into debt that would be a burden to pay off. The law also banned practices familiar to most college students, such as the offer of free pizza or T-shirts in exchange for signing up for a new credit card account.[1]

The same year, Congress enacted the Student Aid and Fiscal Responsibility Act, a law designed to make more loans available to college students by having the federal government lend directly to students. The law would eliminate the role of the banks, which under the existing system received large subsidies from the government to offer loans. By eliminating these subsidies the new law would save an estimated $68 billion

focusquestions

- Do members of Congress do what their constituents want?

- How is Congress organized?

- What are the main steps in passing a law?

- How does Congress decide which laws to pass?

- What other powers does Congress have?

over ten years, nearly half of which would be used to provide more aid to students. The legislation would also block a planned increase in the interest rate on student loans, keeping the rate at 3.4 percent instead of the projected increase to 6.8 percent. Most student groups and associations representing colleges supported the bill, while banks and other lenders opposed it.[2] Opponents charged that the legislation would reduce jobs and reduce choice. They called it a "Washington takeover."

Congress has vast authority over most aspects of American life. Laws related to federal spending, taxing, and regulation all pass through Congress. While the debates over these laws are often hard to follow because they are complex and technical or heated and partisan, it is important for the American people to learn about that Congress is doing. As the examples above indicate, actions taken—or not taken—in Congress affect the everyday choices that people face and the opportunities they can expect in life. With so much information about Congress available on the Internet, it is not hard to get beyond the heated rhetoric and simplistic headlines and ask your own questions about a proposed law. How will it affect my life and the lives of people I care about? What is the impact on our country? Making laws is often compared to making sausage, because it is such a complex—and often ugly—process. Even so, it is vital for citizens to monitor what Congress does because the laws it passes are so central to our lives.

chaptercontents

Congress: Representing the American People

Congress is the most important representative institution in American government. Each member's primary responsibility is to the district, to his or her **constituency**, not to the congressional leadership, a party, or even Congress itself. Yet the task of representation is not a simple one. Views about what constitutes fair and effective representation differ, and constituents may have very different expectations of their representatives. Members of Congress must consider these diverse views and expectations as they represent their districts.

constituency the residents in the area from which an official is elected

House and Senate: Differences in Representation

The framers of the Constitution provided for a **bicameral** legislature—that is, a legislative body consisting of two chambers. As we saw in Chapter 2, the framers intended each of these chambers, the House of Representatives and the Senate, to serve a different constituency. Members of the Senate, appointed by state legislatures for six-year terms, were to represent the elite members of society. Today, members of the House and Senate are elected directly by the people. The 435 members of the House are elected from districts apportioned according to population; the 100 members of the Senate are elected by state, with two senators from each. Senators continue to have much longer terms in office and usually represent much larger and more diverse constituencies than do their counterparts in the House (see Table 12.1).

bicameral having a legislative assembly composed of two chambers or houses; opposite of unicameral

The House and Senate play different roles in the legislative process. In essence, the Senate is the more deliberative of the two bodies—the forum in which any and all ideas that senators raise can receive a thorough public airing. The House is the more centralized and organized of the two bodies—better equipped to play a routine role in the governmental process. In part, this difference stems from the different rules governing the two bodies. These rules give House leaders more control over the legislative process and allow House members to specialize in certain legislative areas. The rules of the much smaller Senate give its leadership relatively little power and discourage specialization.

TABLE 12.1

Differences between the House and the Senate

	HOUSE	SENATE
Minimum age of member	25 years	30 years
U.S. citizenship	At least 7 years	At least 9 years
Length of term	2 years	6 years
Number representing each state	1–53 per state (depends on population)	2 per state
Constituency	Local	Local and national

For its first 128 years, Congress was a decidedly masculine world. In 1917, three years before the ratification of the Nineteenth Amendment, Jeanette Rankin (R-Mont.) (pictured back row, far right) became the first woman to serve in Congress.

Both formal and informal factors contribute to differences between the two chambers of Congress. Differences in the length of terms and requirements for holding office, specified by the Constitution, generate differences in how members of each body develop their constituencies and exercise their powers of office. The result is that members of the House most effectively and frequently serve as the agents of well-organized local interests with specific legislative agendas—for instance, used-car dealers seeking relief from regulation, labor unions seeking more favorable legislation, or farmers looking for higher subsidies. The small size and relative homogeneity of their constituencies and the frequency with which they must seek re-election make House members more attuned to the legislative needs of local interest groups.

Senators, on the other hand, serve larger and more heterogeneous constituencies. As a result, they are somewhat better able than members of the House to act as the agents for groups and interests organized on a statewide or national basis. Moreover, with longer terms in office, senators have more time to consider "new ideas" or to bring together new coalitions of interests rather than simply serving existing ones.

Sociological versus Agency Representation

We have become so accustomed to the idea of representative government that we tend to forget what a peculiar concept representation really is. A representative claims to act or speak for some other person or group. But how can one person be trusted to speak for another? How do we know that those who call themselves our representatives are actually speaking on our behalf, rather than simply pursuing their own interests?

sociological representation a type of representation in which representatives have the same racial, gender, ethnic, religious, or educational backgrounds as their constituents. It is based on the principle that if two individuals are similar in background, character, interests, and perspectives, then one could correctly represent the other's views

agency representation the type of representation in which a representative is held accountable to a constituency if he or she fails to represent that constituency properly. This is incentive for good representation when the personal back grounds, views and interests of the representative differ from those of his or her constituency

There are two circumstances under which one person reasonably might be trusted to speak for another. The first of these occurs if the two individuals are so similar in background, character, interests, and perspectives that anything said by one would very likely reflect the views of the other as well. This principle is at the heart of what is sometimes called **sociological representation**—the sort of representation that takes place when representatives have the same racial, gender, ethnic, religious, or educational backgrounds as their constituents. The assumption is that sociological similarity helps to promote good representation; thus, the composition of a properly constituted representative assembly should mirror the composition of society.

The second circumstance under which one person might be trusted to speak for another occurs if the two are formally bound together so that the representative is in some way accountable to those he or she is supposed to represent. If representatives can somehow be punished for failing to speak properly for their constituents, then we know they have an incentive to provide good representation even if their own personal backgrounds, views, and interests differ from they backgrounds of those they represent. This principle is called **agency representation**—the sort of representation that takes place when constituents have the power to hire and fire their representatives.

Both sociological and agency representation play a role in the relationship between members of Congress and their constituencies.

The Social Composition of the U.S. Congress The extent to which the U.S. Congress is representative of the American people in a sociological sense can be seen by examining social characteristics of the House and Senate today. For example, the religious affiliations of members of both the House and Senate are overwhelmingly Protestant—the distribution is very close to the proportion in the population at large—although the Protestant category comprises more than fifteen denominations. Catholics are the second largest category of religious affiliation, and Jews a much smaller third category.[3] Religious affiliations directly affect congressional debate on a limited range of issues where different moral views are at stake, such as abortion.

African Americans, women, Hispanic Americans, and Asian Americans have increased their congressional representation in the past two decades (see Figure 12.1), but the representation of minorities in Congress is still not comparable to their proportions in the general population. In 2010, seventy-eight women served in the House (up from only twenty-nine in 1990). After the Democrats won a majority in the House in November 2006, Nancy Pelosi (D-Calif.) became the first female Speaker of the House and held that position through 2010. In 2010, seventeen women served in the Senate. Since many important contemporary national issues cut along racial and gender lines, pressure for reform in the representative process is likely to continue until these groups are fully represented.

The occupational backgrounds of members of Congress have always been a matter of interest because so many issues split along economic lines that are relevant to occupations and industries. The legal profession is the dominant career of most members of Congress prior to their election. Public service or politics is also a significant background, with many members coming from positions in state and local government. In addition, many members of Congress also have important ties to business and industry.[4] Although Congress has become much more diverse in recent years, in 2010 it was still 72 percent male and 84 percent white. Moreover, members of Congress are much more highly educated than most Americans. More than nine in ten members hold university degrees, and close to half of them have law degrees.[5] This is not a portrait of the U.S. population. Congress is not a sociological microcosm of American society.

Can Congress still legislate fairly or take account of a diversity of views and interests if it is not a sociologically representative assembly? The task is certainly much more difficult. Yet there is reason to believe it can. Representatives, as we shall see shortly, can serve as the agents of their constituents, even if they do not precisely mirror their sociological attributes. Yet sociological representation is a matter of some importance, even if it is not an absolute prerequisite for fair legislation by members of the House and Senate. At the least, the social composition of a representative assembly is important for symbolic purposes—to demonstrate to groups in the population that the government takes them seriously. If Congress is not representative symbolically, then its own authority—and indeed that of the entire government—would be reduced.[6]

Representatives as Agents A good deal of evidence indicates that whether or not members of Congress share their constituents' sociological characteristics, they

● Do members of Congress do what their constituents want?

for critical analysis

Why is sociological representation important? If congressional representatives have racial, religious, or educational backgrounds similar to those of their constituents, are they better representatives? Why or why not?

The increase in the number of African Americans in Congress in the last forty years is shown by the membership of the Congressional Black Caucus, which had forty-two members in 2010. Caucus members are shown here at a press conference about the government's response to Hurricane Katrina, which was especially devastating to the African American community in the Gulf states.

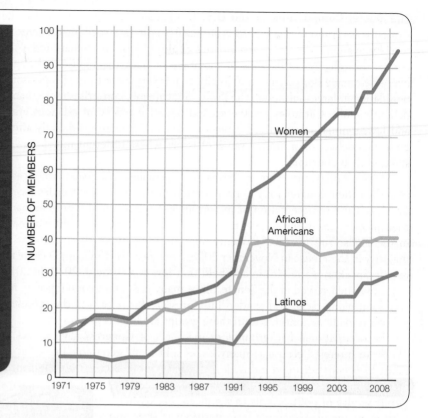

do work very hard to speak for their constituents' views and serve their constituents' interests in the governmental process. The idea of representative as agent is similar to the relationship of lawyer and client. True, the relationship between the member of Congress and as many as 660,000 "clients" in the district, or the senator and millions of "clients" in the state, is very different from that of the lawyer and client. But the criteria of performance are comparable. One expects at the very least that each representative will constantly seek to discover the interests of the constituency and will speak for those interests in Congress and in other centers of government.[7]

There is constant communication between constituents and congressional offices, and communication has grown dramatically with the Internet. The volume of e-mail from constituents and advocacy groups has grown so large so quickly that congressional offices have struggled to find effective ways to respond in a timely manner.[8] At the same time, members of Congress have found new ways to communicate with constituents. They have created Web sites describing their achievements, established a presence on social networking sites, and issued e-newsletters that alert constituents to timely issues. Many have also set up blogs and use Twitter accounts to establish a more informal style of communication with constituents.

The seriousness with which members of the House attempt to behave as representatives can be seen in the amount of time they spend on behalf of their constituents. One way to measure of the amount of time members of Congress devote to constituency service (called "case work") is to look at the percentage

Who Are the Members of Congress?

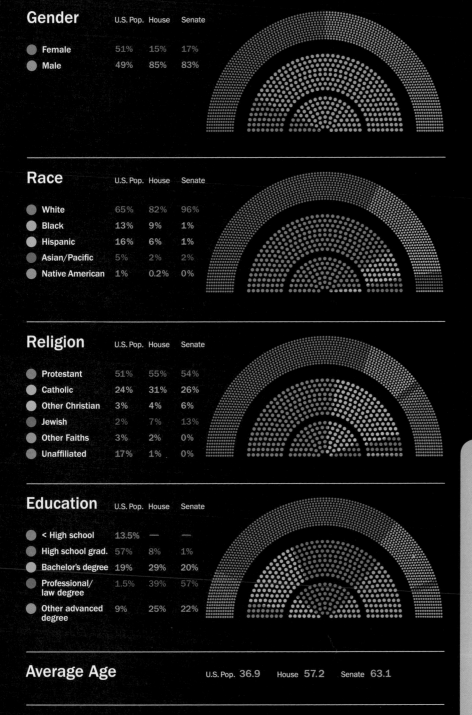

Gender

	U.S. Pop.	House	Senate
Female	51%	15%	17%
Male	49%	85%	83%

Race

	U.S. Pop.	House	Senate
White	65%	82%	96%
Black	13%	9%	1%
Hispanic	16%	6%	1%
Asian/Pacific	5%	2%	2%
Native American	1%	0.2%	0%

Religion

	U.S. Pop.	House	Senate
Protestant	51%	55%	54%
Catholic	24%	31%	26%
Other Christian	3%	4%	6%
Jewish	2%	7%	13%
Other Faiths	3%	2%	0%
Unaffiliated	17%	1%	0%

Education

	U.S. Pop.	House	Senate
< High school	13.5%	—	—
High school grad.	57%	8%	1%
Bachelor's degree	19%	29%	20%
Professional/ law degree	1.5%	39%	57%
Other advanced degree	9%	25%	22%

Average Age

U.S. Pop. 36.9	House 57.2	Senate 63.1

Key

U.S. Population

Senate

House of Representatives

Although the number of women, African Americans, and Latinos in Congress has increased in recent decades, Congress is still much less diverse than the American population. Members of Congress are predominantly male, white, Protestant Christian, and most commonly come from a professional and educational background as lawyers. These data compare the 111th Congress, which took office in 2009, with the U.S. population as a whole.

forcritical analysis

1. Does it matter if the backgrounds of members of Congress reflect the population as a whole? Can members still represent their constituents effectively if they do not come from similar backgrounds?

2. Visit www.house.gov and www.senate.gov to identify your representatives in Congress and visit their Web pages. How similar are their backgrounds to yours? How closely do their policy positions, as expressed on their web pages, match your own?

SOURCES: Mildred L. Amer, "Membership of the 111th Congress: A Profile," CRS Report R40086, February 4, 2010. U.S. Census Bureau, www.census.gov (accessed 3/5/10).

of personal House and Senate staff (personal staff being non–committee member staff) assigned to district and state offices. In 1972, 22.5 percent of House members' personal staff were located in district offices; by 2005 the number had grown to 50.7 percent.[9] For the Senate, the staff in state offices grew from 12.5 percent in 1972 to 39 percent in 2005. The service that these offices provide is not merely a matter of writing and mailing letters. It includes talking to constituents, providing them with minor services, presenting special bills for them, and attempting to influence decisions by regulatory commissions on their behalf.

Although no members of Congress are above constituency pressures (and they would not want to be), on many issues constituents do not have very strong views, and representatives are free to act as they think best. Foreign policy issues often fall into this category, although that is less true since the Iraq war aroused strong feelings. But in many districts there are two or three issues on which constituents have such pronounced opinions that representatives feel they have little freedom of choice. For example, representatives from districts that grow wheat, cotton, or tobacco probably will not want to exercise a great deal of independence on relevant agricultural legislation. In oil-rich states such as Oklahoma and Texas, senators and members of the House are likely to be leading advocates of oil interests. For one thing, representatives are probably fearful of voting against their district interests; for another, the districts are unlikely to have elected representatives who would *want* to vote against them.

The influence of constituencies is so pervasive that both parties have strongly embraced the informal rule that nothing should be done to endanger the re-election chances of any member. Party leaders obey this rule fairly consistently by not asking any member to vote in a way that might conflict with a district interest.

The Electoral Connection

The sociological composition of Congress and the activities of representatives once they are in office are very much influenced by electoral considerations. Three factors related to the U.S. electoral system affect who gets elected and what they do once in office. The first set of issues concerns who decides to run for office and which candidates have an edge over others. The second issue is that of incumbency advantage. Finally, the way congressional district lines are drawn can greatly affect the outcome of an election. Let us examine more closely the impact that these considerations have on representation.

Who Runs for Congress Voters' choices are restricted from the start by who decides to run for office. In the past, decisions about who would run for a particular elected office were made by local party officials. A person who had a record of service to the party, or who was owed a favor, or whose "turn" had come up might be nominated by party leaders for an office. Today, few party organizations have the power to slate candidates in that way. Instead, parties try to ensure that well-qualified candidates run for Congress. During the 1990s, the Republican Party developed "farm teams" of local officials who were groomed to run for Congress. Their success led Democrats to attempt a similar strategy. Even so, the decision to run for Congress is a personal choice. One of the most important factors determining who runs for office is a candidate's individual ambition.[10] A potential candidate may also assess whether he or she can attract enough money to mount a credible campaign. The ability to raise money depends on connections with other politicians, interest groups, and national party organizations. In the past, the difficulty of raising campaign funds posed a disadvantage to female candidates. Since the 1980s, however, a number of powerful political action committees (PACs) have emerged to recruit women and fund their campaigns. The largest of them, EMILY's List, has become one of the most powerful fund-raisers of all PACs. Recent research shows that money is no longer the barrier it once was to women running for office.[11] Even so, women candidates tend to face more competition in their primary elections.

Features distinctive to each congressional district also affect the field of candidates. Among them are the range of other political opportunities that may lure potential candidates away. In addition, the way the congressional district overlaps with state legislative boundaries may affect a candidate's decision to run. A state-level representative or senator who is considering running for the U.S. Congress is more likely to assess her prospects favorably if her state district coincides with the congressional district (because the voters will already know her). And for any candidate, decisions about running must be made early, because once money has been committed to already declared candidates, it is harder for new candidates to break into a race. Thus, the outcome of a November election is partially determined many months earlier, when decisions to run are finalized.

Incumbency Incumbency plays a very important role in the American electoral system and in the kind of representation citizens get in Washington. Once in office, members of Congress possess an array of tools that they can use to stack the deck in favor of their re-election. The most important of these is constituency service: taking care of the problems and requests of individual voters. Through such services and through regular newsletter mailings, the incumbent seeks to establish a "personal" relationship with his or her constituents. The success of this strategy is evident in the high rates of re-election for congressional incumbents: as high as 98 percent for House members and 90 percent for members of the Senate in recent years (see Figure 12.2). It is also evident in what is called "sophomore surge"—the tendency for candidates to win a higher percentage of the vote when seeking future terms in office. Based on early estimates of the 2010 elections, approximately 86 percent of incumbents were re-elected in the House and roughly 90 percent in the Senate.

Incumbency can help a candidate by scaring off potential challengers. In many races, potential candidates may decide not to run because they fear that the incumbent simply has too much money or is too well liked or too well known. Potential challengers may also decide that a district's partisan leanings are too unfavorable. It often takes exceptional circumstances to persuade strong candidates to run against well-established incumbents. The efforts of incumbents to raise funds to ward off potential challengers start early. A Connecticut Democrat, Joe Courtney, who earned the nickname "Landslide Joe" with his ninety-one-vote margin of victory in 2006, began fund-raising for the 2008 election even before he was sworn in for his first term. In addition, the Democratic Congressional Campaign Committee placed him on its Frontline team, a group of the twenty-nine most vulnerable Democrats. The Democratic leadership took special efforts to raise the profile of these members of Congress. For example, Courtney and others in the Frontline team received

● Do members of Congress do what their constituents want?

incumbency holding a political office for which one is running

In 2010, Senator Arlen Specter (pictured below) lost the Pennsylvania Democratic primary to a challenger, ending Specter's thirty-year career in the Senate. It is typically difficult for challengers to defeat incumbents who have held office for a long time, but as a former Republican who joined the Democrats only the year before, Specter was vulnerable to rising anti-incumbent sentiment.

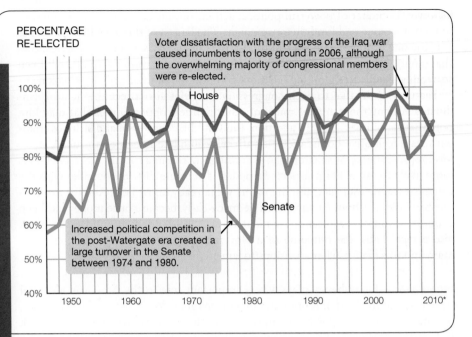

FIGURE 12.2

The Power of Incumbency

Members of Congress who run for re-election have a very good chance of winning. Senators have at times found it difficult to use the power of incumbency to protect their seats, as the sharp decline in Senate incumbency rates between 1974 and 1980 indicates. Has the incumbency advantage generally been greater in the House or in the Senate?

SOURCES: Norman J. Ornstein et al., eds., *Vital Statistics on Congress, 1999–2000* (Washington, DC: AEI Press, 2000), 57–58; and authors' update.
*estimate

PERCENTAGE RE-ELECTED

Voter dissatisfaction with the progress of the Iraq war caused incumbents to lose ground in 2006, although the overwhelming majority of congressional members were re-elected.

House

Senate

Increased political competition in the post-Watergate era created a large turnover in the Senate between 1974 and 1980.

high-profile speaking assignments on the floor of Congress and were appointed to key congressional committees. In 2008, Courtney won his seat by a comfortable margin, and he was easily re-elected in 2010.[12]

The advantage of incumbency thus tends to preserve the status quo in Congress. This fact has implications for the social composition of Congress. For example, incumbency advantage makes it harder for women to increase their numbers in Congress because most incumbents are men. Women who run for open seats (for which there are no incumbents) are just as likely to win as male candidates.[13] Supporters of **term limits** argue that such limits are the only way to get new faces into Congress. They believe that incumbency advantage and the tendency of many legislators to view politics as a career mean that very little turnover will occur in Congress unless limits are imposed on the number of terms a legislator can serve.

Yet the percentage of incumbents who are returned to Congress after each election also depends on how many members decide to run again. Because each year some members decide to retire, turnover in Congress is greater than the reelection rates of incumbents suggest. On average, 10 percent of the House and Senate decide to retire each election. In some years, the number of retirements is higher, as in 1992, when 20 percent of House members decided to retire; thus, the 90 percent of incumbents who were reelected that year were a subset of all the eligible incumbents (80 percent). The precarious economy and the backlash against the party in power made 2008 and 2010 difficult election years for some incumbents. In 2008, many vulnerable Republican incumbents decided to retire rather than face a strong challenger. And again in 2010, a number of Republican and Democratic

term limits legally prescribed limits on the number of terms an elected official can serve

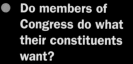
incumbents declined to run for re-election. Democrats felt particularly vulnerable since their party controlled the presidency and both houses of Congress in a year when economic woes contributed to strong anti-incumbent sentiment. Some of the Democrats who dropped out represented marginal districts, which had often voted Republican in the past. Others, such as Senator Christopher Dodd of Connecticut, a five-term Democrat, recognized that public opinion had turned against them and decided not to continue in a race that looked like an uphill battle.[14] Even with these retirements during primaries, a large number of Democratic incumbents lost their seats in 2010.

Apportionment and Redistricting The final factor that affects who wins a seat in Congress is the way congressional districts are drawn. Every ten years, state legislatures must redraw congressional districts to reflect population changes. Because the number of congressional seats has been fixed at 435 since 1929, redistricting is a zero-sum process; in order for one state to gain a seat, another must lose one. The process of allocating congressional seats among the fifty states is called **apportionment**. States with population growth gain additional seats; states with population declines or less population growth lose seats. Over the past several decades, the shift of the American population to the South and the West has greatly increased the size of the congressional delegations from these regions (see Figures 12.3 and 12.4). Census estimates projected that this trend would continue after the 2010 census. Texas was likely to emerge as the biggest winner, with a gain of three additional seats; Arizona, Florida, Georgia, Nevada, South Carolina, Utah, and Washington were all in line to add one extra seat.[15]

apportionment the process, occurring after every decennial census, that allocates congressional seats among the fifty states

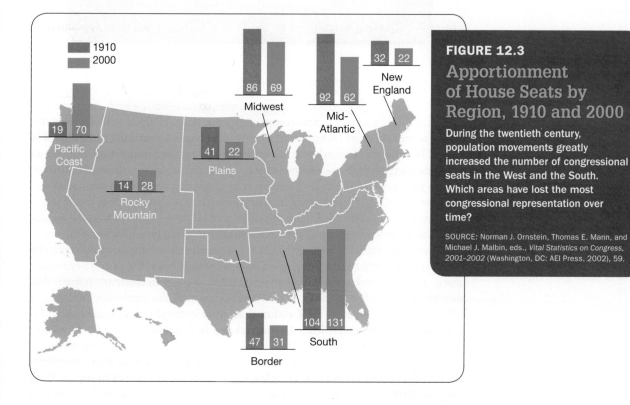

FIGURE 12.3

Apportionment of House Seats by Region, 1910 and 2000

During the twentieth century, population movements greatly increased the number of congressional seats in the West and the South. Which areas have lost the most congressional representation over time?

SOURCE: Norman J. Ornstein, Thomas E. Mann, and Michael J. Malbin, eds., *Vital Statistics on Congress, 2001–2002* (Washington, DC: AEI Press, 2002), 59.

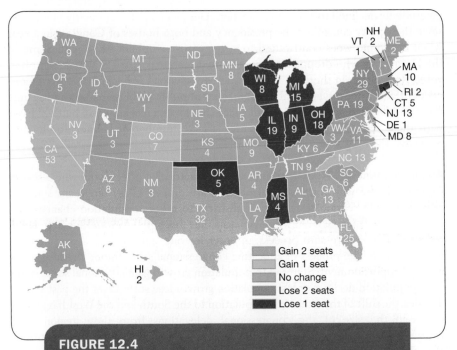

FIGURE 12.4

Results of Congressional Reapportionment, 2000

States in the West and parts of the South were the big winners in the reapportionment of House seats following the 2000 census. The old manufacturing states in the Midwest and Mid-Atlantic regions were the biggest losers. Which states have the greatest number of House seats?

redistricting the process of redrawing election districts and redistributing legislative representatives. This happen every ten years to reflect shifts in population or in response to legal challenges to existing districts

gerrymandering apportionment of voters in districts in such a way as to give unfair advantage to one racial or ethnic group or political party

Not surprisingly, **redistricting** is a highly political process: districts are shaped to create an advantage for the majority party in the state legislature, which controls the redistricting process. In this complex process, those charged with drawing districts use sophisticated computer technologies to come up with the most favorable district boundaries. Redistricting can create open seats and may pit incumbents of the same party against one another, ensuring that one of them will lose. Redistricting can also give an advantage to one party by clustering voters with some ideological or sociological characteristics in a single district, or by separating those voters into two or more districts. The manipulation of electoral districts to serve the interests of a particular group is known as **gerrymandering** (see Chapter 10).

In the redistricting following the 2000 census, the close balance of power in the House—with party control hinging on only six seats—made the process especially charged. Both Republicans and Democrats went to court to challenge remaps that they viewed as unfair. In 2003, Texas Republicans took the unprecedented step of redrawing the lines set in 2001 rather than waiting for the next census. After an unusual episode in which Texas Democrats fled to Oklahoma and New Mexico to prevent passage of the plan, the state legislature eventually approved the new map. Redistricting attracts close political attention because the way districts are drawn always benefits one party over the other. Republicans are expected to benefit from the post-2010 redistricting, in part as a result of the population gains in states that have tended to vote Republican in the past. But they will also benefit because Republicans control the state legislatures in the majority of the states in line to gain additional seats, and they may be able to redraw the districts in ways that maximize the Republicans' advantage.[16]

As we saw in Chapter 10, since the passage of the 1982 amendments to the Voting Rights Act of 1965, race has become a major—and controversial—consideration in drawing voting districts. These amendments, which encouraged the creation of districts in which members of racial minorities have decisive majorities, have greatly increased the number of minority representatives in Congress. After the 1991–92 redistricting, the number of predominantly minority districts doubled, rising from twenty-six to fifty-two. Among the most fervent supporters of the new minority districts were white Republicans, who used the opportunity to create more districts dominated by white Republican voters. These developments raise thorny questions about representation. Some analysts argue that the system may grant minorities greater sociological representation but has made it more difficult for minorities to win substantive policy goals. Others dispute this argument, noting that the strong surge of Republican voters was a more significant factor in Republican congressional victories than any Democratic losses due to racial redistricting.[17]

In 1995, the Supreme Court limited racial redistricting in *Miller v. Johnson*, in which the Court stated that race could not be the predominant factor in creating electoral districts.[18] Yet concerns about redistricting and representation have not disappeared. The distinction between race being the "predominant" factor and its being one factor among many is very hazy. Because the drawing of district boundaries affects incumbents as well as the field of candidates who decide to run for office, it continues to be a key battleground on which political parties fight about the meaning of representation.

Direct Patronage

As agents of their constituents, members of Congress often have an opportunity to provide direct benefits, or **patronage**, for their district. The most important of these opportunities for direct patronage is in legislation that has been described half-jokingly as the **pork barrel**. This type of legislation specifies a project to be funded within a particular district. Many observers of Congress argue that pork-barrel bills are the only ones that some members are serious about moving toward actual passage, because they are seen as so important to members' re-election bids.

A common form of pork barreling is the "earmark," the practice through which members of Congress insert into bills language that provides special benefits for their own constituents. When the Democrats took over Congress in 2007, they vowed to limit the use of earmarks, which had grown from 1,439 per year in 1995 to 15,268 in 2006. More troubling, earmarks were connected to congressional scandals. For example, the Republican House member Randy "Duke" Cunningham (R-Calif.) was sent to jail in 2005 for accepting bribes by companies hoping to receive earmarks in return.[19] The House passed a new rule requiring that those representatives supporting each earmark identify themselves and guarantee that they had no personal financial stake in the requested project. A new ethics law applied similar provisions to the Senate as well. The new requirements appear to have had some impact: the 2007 military bill, for example, cut in half the value of earmarks contained in the military bill passed in 2006. But in the midst of the sharp economic downturn in 2009, Congress passed a bill designed to stimulate

● **Do members of Congress do what their constituents want?**

for critical analysis

How does redistricting alter the balance of power in Congress? Why do political parties care so much about the redistricting process?

patronage the resources available to higher officials, usually opportunities to make partisan appointments to offices and to confer grants, licenses, or special favors to supporters

pork barrel (or pork) appropriations made by legislative bodies for local projects that are often not needed but that are created so that local representatives can win re-election in their home districts

the economy, which contained more than 8,000 earmarks. In many cases, Republicans and some Democrats who voted against the bill later were happy to take credit from their constituents for the earmarks they had placed in it. In his 2010 State of the Union address, President Obama called for Congress to publish a list of all earmark requests on a single Web site. Reformers hope that such transparency will cause members of Congress to think twice before they request an earmark.[20]

Highway bills are a favorite vehicle for congressional pork-barrel spending. A 2005 highway bill was full of such items, containing more than 6,000 projects earmarked for specific congressional districts. Among them were such projects as $3.5 million for horse trails in Virginia and $5 million for a parking garage in downtown Bozeman, Montana. These measures often have little to do with transportation needs, instead serving as evidence that congressional members can bring federal dollars back home. Perhaps the most extravagant item in the 2005 bill—and the one least needed for transportation—was a bridge in Alaska designed to connect a barely populated island to the town of Ketchikan, population just under 8,000. At a cost that could soar to $2 billion, the bridge would replace an existing five-minute ferry ride. The Alaska representative Don Young (R) proudly claimed credit for such pork-barrel projects. At the suggestion that Alaska's senior senator, Ted Stevens (R), chairman of the Senate Appropriations committee, might be the reason Alaska got these projects, Young pretended to be offended, saying, "If he's the chief porker, I'm upset."[21] After Hurricane Katrina, growing concern about the rising budget deficit made "the bridge to nowhere" a symbol of wasteful congressional spending. Sensitive to this criticism, Congress removed the earmarks for the bridge from the final legislation. Even so, it allowed Alaska to keep the funds for other unspecified transportation projects. In 2007, the state quietly dropped the project.

A limited amount of other direct patronage also exists (see Figure 12.5). One important form of constituency service is intervention with federal administrative agencies on behalf of constituents. Members of the House and Senate and their staff members spend a great deal of time on the telephone and in administrative offices seeking to secure favorable treatment for constituents and supporters. Among the kinds of services that members of Congress offer to constituents is assistance for senior citizens who are having Social Security or Medicare benefit eligibility problems. They may also assist constituents in finding federal grants for which they may be eligible to apply. As Representative Pete Stark (D-Calif.) said on his Web site, "We cannot make the decision for a federal agency on such matters, but we can make sure that you get a fair shake."[22] A small but related form of patronage is getting an appointment to one of the military academies for the child of a constituent. Traditionally, these appointments are allocated one to a district.

A different form of patronage is the **private bill**—a proposal to grant some kind of relief, special privilege, or exemption to the person named in the bill. The private bill is a type of legislation, but it is distinguished from a public bill, which is supposed to deal with general rules and categories of behavior, people, and institutions. As many as 75 percent of all private bills introduced (and one-third of the ones that pass) are concerned with providing relief for foreign nationals who do not have resident status in the United States but who the sponsoring member of Congress believes are deserving of citizenship. For example, in 2007 Gene Green (D-Tex.) sponsored a private bill to obtain legal status for an undocumented couple in danger of being deported whose son had died as a marine in Iraq.[23]

Private legislation is a congressional privilege that is often abused, but it is impossible to imagine members of Congress giving it up completely. It is one of the

private bill a proposal in Congress to provide a specific person with some kind of relief, such as a special exemption from immigration quotas

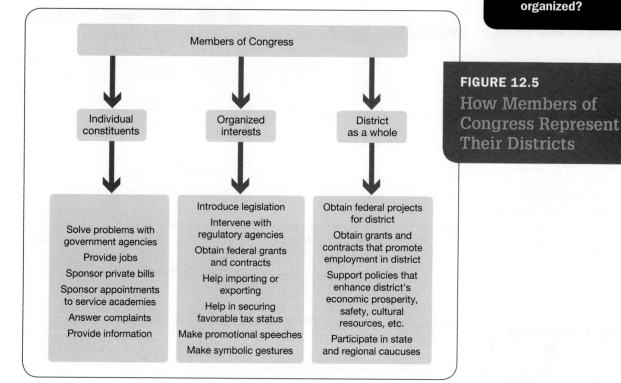

FIGURE 12.5
How Members of Congress Represent Their Districts

Members of Congress

Individual constituents	Organized interests	District as a whole
Solve problems with government agencies Provide jobs Sponsor private bills Sponsor appointments to service academies Answer complaints Provide information	Introduce legislation Intervene with regulatory agencies Obtain federal grants and contracts Help importing or exporting Help in securing favorable tax status Make promotional speeches Make symbolic gestures	Obtain federal projects for district Obtain grants and contracts that promote employment in district Support policies that enhance district's economic prosperity, safety, cultural resources, etc. Participate in state and regional caucuses

easiest, cheapest, and most effective forms of patronage available to each member. It can be defended as an indispensable part of the process by which members of Congress seek to fulfill their role as representatives. And obviously they like the privilege because it helps them win re-election.

● The Organization of Congress

The United States Congress is not only a representative assembly. It is also a legislative body. For Americans, representation and legislation go hand in hand, but many parliamentary bodies in other countries are representative without the power to make laws. It is no small achievement that the U.S. Congress both represents and governs.

To exercise its power to make laws, Congress must first bring about something close to an organizational miracle. The building blocks of congressional organization include the political parties, the committee system, congressional staff, the caucuses, and the parliamentary rules of the House and Senate. Each of these factors plays a key role in the organization of Congress and in the process through which Congress formulates and enacts laws.

Party Leadership in the House

Every two years, at the beginning of a new Congress, the members of each party gather to elect their House leaders. House Republicans call this the **conference**. House Democrats call theirs the **caucus**. The elected leader of the majority party

conference a gathering of House Republicans every two years to elect their House leaders. Democrats call their gathering the caucus

caucus (political) a normally closed meeting of a political or legislative group to select candidates, plan strategy, or make decisions regarding legislative matters

Speaker of the House the chief presiding officer of the House of Representatives. The Speaker is the most important party and House leader, and can influence the legislative agenda, the fate of individual pieces of legislation, and members' positions within the House

majority leader the elected leader of the majority party in the House of Representatives or in the Senate. In the House, the majority leader is subordinate in the party hierarchy to the Speaker of the House

minority leader the elected leader of the minority party in the House or Senate

whip a party member in the House or Senate responsible for coordinating the party's legislative strategy, building support for key issues, and counting votes

is later proposed to the whole House and is automatically elected to the position of **Speaker of the House**, with voting along straight party lines. The House majority conference or caucus then also elects a **majority leader**. The minority party goes through the same process and selects the **minority leader**. Each party also elects a **whip** to line up party members on important votes and to relay voting information to the leaders.

Next in order of importance for each party after the Speaker and majority or minority leader is what Democrats call the Steering and Policy Committee (Republicans have a separate steering committee and a separate policy committee), whose tasks are to assign new legislators to committees and to deal with the requests of incumbent members for transfers from one committee to another. Currently, the Speaker serves as chair of the Democratic Steering and Policy Committee, while the minority leader chairs the Republican Steering Committee. At one time, party leaders strictly controlled committee assignments, using them to enforce party discipline. Today, in principle, representatives receive the assignments they want. But several individuals often seek assignments to the most important committees, which gives the leadership an opportunity to cement alliances when it resolves conflicting requests.

Generally, representatives seek assignments that will allow them to influence decisions of special importance to their districts. Representatives from farm districts, for example, may request seats on the Agriculture Committee.[24] Seats on powerful committees such as Ways and Means, which is responsible for tax legislation, and Appropriations are especially popular.

Party Leadership in the Senate

Within the Senate, the president pro tempore exercises primarily ceremonial leadership. Usually, the majority party designates a member with the greatest seniority to serve in this capacity. Real power is in the hands of the majority leader and minority leader, each elected by party conference. Together they control the Senate's calendar, or agenda for legislation.

In 2006, Nancy Pelosi (D-CA) became the first woman Speaker of the House of Representatives. Minority Leader John Boehner (R-OH), who handed her the gavel that year, took over as Speaker in 2011 after Republicans won a majority in the House in the 2010 elections.

Each party also elects a Policy Committee, which advises the leadership on legislative priorities. The structure of majority party leadership in the House and the Senate is shown in Figures 12.6 and 12.7.

Legislative Agendas

Along with these tasks of organization, congressional party leaders may also seek to establish a legislative agenda. Since the New Deal, presidents have taken the lead in creating legislative agendas. (This trend is discussed in Chapter 13.) When congressional leaders have been faced with a White House controlled by the opposing party, they have attempted to devise their own agendas. Democratic leaders of Congress sought to create a common Democratic perspective in 1981 when Ronald Reagan became president. The Republican Congress elected in 1994 expanded on this idea, calling its agenda the "Contract with America." From 2000 to 2006, with both houses of Congress in the hands of Republicans, congressional leaders worked closely with the Republican White House. In 2007, when Democrats took over Congress, House Speaker Nancy Pelosi sought to promote party unity with a plan to pass six key pieces of legislation in the first hundred hours of Democratic congressional control. Although the House succeeded in passing the six measures, most of them died in the Senate. The pattern of the Democratic House passing legislation that then became bottled up in the Senate continued into 2009–2010. Because a Senate minority of forty-one can block legislation by using the filibuster, the Democratic leadership found it difficult to enact legislation with a cohesive Republican minority. It meant that the Democratic leadership had to keep every Senate Democrat (and two independents who voted with the Democrats) on board—and add one or two Republican votes after they lost two members—to enact legislation. As the Republicans prepared to take over the House in 2010, they stressed reducing the deficit, extending the Bush-era tax cuts for all, including the very wealthy, and rolling back key provisions in the comprehensive health care legislation enacted in 2010.

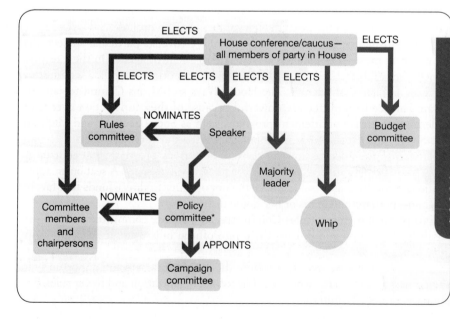

FIGURE 12.6

Majority Party Structure in the House of Representatives

*Includes Speaker, majority leader, chief and deputy whips, caucus chair, chairs of five major committees, members elected by regional caucuses, members elected by recently elected representatives, and at-large members appointed by the Speaker.

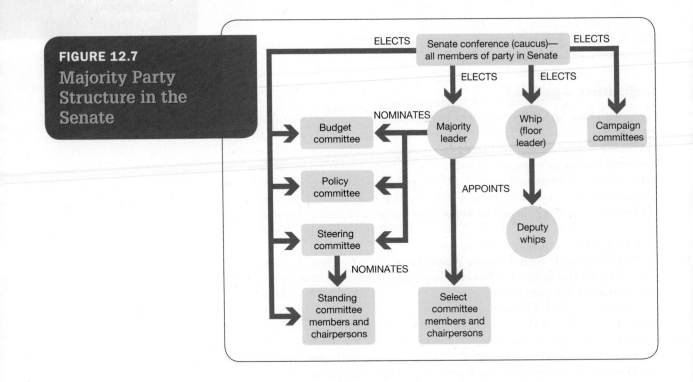

FIGURE 12.7
Majority Party Structure in the Senate

The Committee System

The committee system is central to the operation of Congress. At each stage of the legislative process, Congress relies on committees and subcommittees to do the hard work of sorting through alternatives and writing legislation. There are several different kinds of congressional committees: standing committees, select committees, joint committees, and conference committees.

Standing Committees The most important arenas of congressional policy making are **standing committees**. These committees continue in existence from one session of Congress to the next; they have the power to propose and write legislation. The jurisdiction of each standing committee covers a particular subject matter, which in most cases parallels a major department or agency in the executive branch (see Table 12.2). Among the most important standing committees are those in charge of finances. The House Ways and Means Committee and the Senate Finance Committee are powerful because of their jurisdiction over taxes, trade, and expensive entitlement programs such as Social Security and Medicare. The Senate and House Appropriations committees also play important ongoing roles because they decide how much funding various programs will actually receive; they also determine exactly how the money will be spent. A seat on an appropriations committee allows a member the opportunity to direct funds to a favored program—perhaps one in his or her home district.

Except for the House Rules Committee, all standing committees receive proposals for legislation and process them into official bills. The House Rules Committee decides the order in which bills come up for a vote on the House floor and determines the specific rules that govern the length of debate and opportunity for amendments. The Senate, which has less formal organization and fewer rules, does not have a rules committee.

standing committee a permanent committee with the power to propose and write legislation that covers a particular subject, such as finance or agriculture

TABLE 12.2

Permanent Committees of Congress

HOUSE COMMITTEES

Agriculture	Judiciary
Appropriations	Natural Resources
Armed Services	Oversight and Government Reform
Budget	Rules
Education and Labor	Science and Technology
Energy and Commerce	Small Business
Financial Services	Standards of Official Conduct
Foreign Affairs	Transportation and Infrastructure
Homeland Security	Veterans' Affairs
House Administration	Ways and Means

SENATE COMMITTEES

Agriculture, Nutrition, and Forestry	Foreign Relations
Appropriations	Health, Education, Labor, and Pensions
Armed Services	Homeland Security and Governmental Affairs
Banking, Housing, and Urban Affairs	Judiciary
Budget	Rules and Administration
Commerce, Science, and Transportation	Select Intelligence
Energy and Natural Resources	Small Business and Entrepreneurship
Environment and Public Works	Veterans' Affairs
Finance	

Select Committees Select committees are usually not permanent and usually do not have the power to present legislation to the full Congress. (The House and Senate Select Intelligence committees are permanent, however, and do have the power to report legislation.) These committees hold hearings and serve as focal points for the issues they are charged with considering. Congressional leaders form select committees when they want to take up issues that fall outside the jurisdictions of existing committees, to highlight an issue, or to investigate a particular problem. Examples of select committees investigating political scandals include the Senate Watergate Committee of 1973, the committees set up in 1987 to investigate the Iran-Contra affair, and the Whitewater Committee of 1995–96. Select committees set up to highlight ongoing issues have included the House Select Committee on Hunger, established in 1984, and the House Select Committee on Energy Independence and Global Warming, created in 2007. A few select committees have remained in existence for many years, such as the select committees on aging; hunger; children, youth, and families; and narcotics abuse and control. In 1995, however, congressional Republicans abolished most of these select committees, both to streamline operations and to remove a forum used primarily by Democratic representatives and their allies. In 2003, an

select committee a (usually) temporary legislative committee set up to highlight or investigate a particular issue or address an issue not within the jurisdiction of existing committees

important select committee, the House Select Homeland Security Committee, was created to oversee the new Department of Homeland Security. Unlike most select committees, this one had the ability to present legislation. Initially the committee had only temporary status. It was made a regular permanent committee in 2005.

joint committee a legislative committee formed of members of both the House and Senate

Joint Committees **Joint committees** involve members from both the Senate and the House. There are four such committees: economic, taxation, library, and printing. These joint committees are permanent, but they do not have the power to present legislation. The Joint Economic Committee and the Joint Taxation Committee have often played important roles in collecting information and holding hearings on economic and financial issues.

conference committee a joint committee created to work out a compromise on House and Senate versions of a piece of legislation

Conference Committees Finally, **conference committees** are temporary committees whose members are appointed by the Speaker of the House and the presiding officer of the Senate. These committees are charged with reaching a compromise on legislation once it has been passed by the House and the Senate. Conference committees play an extremely important role in determining what laws are actually passed, because they must reconcile any differences in the legislation passed by the House and Senate.

In 2003, conference committees became controversial when Democrats prevented several of them from convening. The Democrats took this action to protest their near exclusion from conference committees on major energy, health care, and transportation laws. When control of Congress is divided between two parties, each is guaranteed significant representation in conference committees. When a single party controls both houses, the majority party is not obligated to offer such representation to the minority party. Democrats complained that Republicans took this power to the extreme by excluding Democrats and adding new provisions to legislation at the conference-committee stage. When the Democrats returned to power in 2007, they also largely bypassed the conference committees. When their early efforts to reach compromises in the conference were derailed by partisan differences, the Democrats began making closed-door agreements between top leaders in the House and the Senate. Although the process facilitated compromises across the two chambers, it meant that important changes to bills were made in private, without the transparency that would have been part of the conference-committee process.[25]

seniority ranking given to an individual on the basis of length of continuous service on a committee in Congress

Politics and the Organization of Committees Within each committee, hierarchy has usually been based on seniority. **Seniority** is determined by years of continuous service on a particular committee, not years of service in the House or Senate. In general, each committee is chaired by the most senior member of the majority party. But the principle of seniority is not absolute. Both Democrats and Republicans have violated it on occasion. When the Republicans took over the House in 1995, they violated the principle of seniority in the selection of key committee chairs. Newt Gingrich, House Speaker at the time, defended the new practice with an allusion to football, saying, "You've got to carry the moral responsibility of fielding the team that can win or you cheat the whole conference."[26] Since then, Republicans continued to depart from the principle of seniority in selecting committee chairs, often choosing on the basis of loyalty or fund-raising abilities rather than seniority. In 2007, Democrats returned to the seniority principle for choosing committee chairs. However, they altered traditional practices in other ways by offering freshman Democrats choice committee assignments in order to increase their chances of re-election.[27]

Over the years, Congress has reformed its organizational structure and operating procedures. Most changes have been made to improve efficiency, but some reforms have also been a response to political considerations. In the 1970s, for example, a series of reforms substantially altered the organization of power in Congress. Among the most important changes put into place at that time were an increase in the number of subcommittees and greater autonomy for subcommittee chairs. Subcommittees are responsible for considering a specific subset of issues under a committee's jurisdiction. One of the driving impulses behind these reforms was an effort to reduce the power of committee chairs. In the past, committee chairs exercised considerable power; they determined hearing schedules, selected subcommittee members, and appointed committee staff. Some chairs used their power to block consideration of bills they opposed. By enhancing subcommittee power and allowing more members to chair subcommittees and appoint subcommittee staff, the reforms undercut the power of committee chairs.

Yet the reforms of the 1970s created new problems for Congress. As a consequence of the reforms, power became more fragmented, making it harder to reach agreement on legislation. The Republican leadership of the 104th Congress (1995–97) sought to reverse the fragmentation of congressional power and concentrate more authority in the party leadership. To this end they reduced the number of subcommittees and limited the time committee chairs could serve to three terms. They made good on this promise in 2001, when they replaced thirteen committee chairs. As a consequence of these changes, committees no longer have the central role they once held in policy making. When the Democrats took control of Congress in 2007, they decided to retain some of the Republican reforms, including the term limits on committee chairs. Even so, the Democratic leadership's deference to the long experience and expertise of some of the Democratic committee chairs gave committees more clout than during the Republican Congresses of previous years. But sharp partisan divisions among members of Congress have made it difficult for committees to deliberate and bring bipartisan expertise to bear on policy making as in the past. With committees less able to engage in effective decision making and often unable to act, it has become more common in recent years for party-driven legislation to go directly to the floor, bypassing committees.[28]

The Staff System: Staffers and Agencies

The congressional institution second in importance only to the committee system is the staff system. Every member of Congress employs many staff members whose tasks include handling constituency requests and, to a large extent, dealing with legislative details and the activities of administrative agencies. Staffers often bear the primary responsibility for formulating and drafting proposals, organizing hearings, dealing with administrative agencies, and negotiating with lobbyists. Indeed, legislators typically deal with each other through staff, rather than through direct personal contact. Representatives and senators together employ 11,500 staffers in their Washington and home offices. Staffers even develop policy ideas, draft legislation, and, in some instances, have a good deal of influence over the legislative process.

In addition to the personal staffs of individual senators and representatives, Congress also employs roughly 2,000 committee staffers. These individuals make up the permanent staff that stays attached to every House and Senate committee regardless of turnover in Congress and that is responsible for organizing and

Members of Congress rely heavily on their personal staffs and on committee staffs, who often play an important role in the legislative process. Here, Senator Orrin Hatch (right) talks with two aides during a Judiciary Committee meeting.

staff agency a legislative support agency responsible for policy analysis

caucus (congressional) an association of members of Congress based on party, interest, or social group, such as gender or race

administering the committee's work, including doing research, scheduling, organizing hearings, and drafting legislation. Committee staffers can play key roles in the legislative process. One example of the importance that members of Congress attach to committee staffers was the conflict over hiring a new staff director for the House Ethics Committee (officially known as the Committee on Standards of Official Conduct) in 2005. The Ethics Committee has the power to investigate members for unethical practices and can issue reprimands or censures when it finds members in violation of House rules. The staff director is critical in determining how energetically and effectively the committee investigates alleged ethics violations. With allegations of ethics violations swirling around the congressional leadership and criminal investigations into the congressional lobbyist Jack Abramoff under way, the Ethics Committee was in a pivotal position. But for the first half of 2005, the committee was at a standstill as Republicans and Democrats fought over who would have the job of staff director. Although the House rules call for the committee staff director to be nonpartisan, the committee chair, Doc Hastings (R-Wash.), initially sought to appoint a partisan Republican to the job. After nearly half a year of wrangling, Hastings agreed to appoint a staff director acceptable to both parties.

Not only does Congress employ personal and committee staff, it has also established **staff agencies** designed to provide the legislative branch with resources and expertise independent of the executive branch. These agencies enhance Congress's capacity to oversee administrative agencies and to evaluate presidential programs and proposals. They include the Congressional Research Service, which performs research for legislators who wish to know the facts and competing arguments relevant to policy proposals or other legislative business; the Government Accountability Office, through which Congress can investigate the financial and administrative affairs of any government agency or program; and the Congressional Budget Office, which assesses the economic implications and likely costs of proposed federal programs, such as health care reform proposals. A fourth agency, the Office of Technology Assessment, which provided Congress with analyses of scientific or technical issues, was abolished in 1995.

Informal Organization: The Caucuses

In addition to the official organization of Congress, an unofficial organizational structure also exists—the caucuses. **Caucuses** are groups of senators or representatives who share certain opinions, interests, or social characteristics. A large number of caucuses are composed of legislators representing particular economic or policy interests, such as the Travel and Tourism Caucus, the Steel Caucus, the Mushroom Caucus, and Concerned Senators for the Arts. Legislators who share common backgrounds or social characteristics have organized caucuses such as the Congressional Black Caucus, the Congressional Caucus for Women's Issues, and the Hispanic Caucus. All these caucuses seek to advance the interests of the groups they represent by promoting legislation, encouraging Congress to hold hearings, and pressing administrative agencies for favorable treatment. In recent years, some caucuses have evolved into powerful lobbying organizations, well funded by interest groups. For example, the Sportsmen's Caucus receives funds from a nonprofit foundation that itself benefits from donations from the National Rifle Association, sports equipment manufacturers, and firearms manufacturers.

● What are the main
steps in passing a
law?

● Rules of Lawmaking: How a Bill Becomes a Law

The institutional structure of Congress is a key factor in shaping the legislative process. A second and equally important set of factors is the rules of congressional procedure. These rules govern everything from the introduction of a **bill** through its submission to the president for signing (see Figure 12.8). Not only do these regulations influence the fate of every bill, they also help to determine the distribution of power in the Congress.

bill a proposed law that has been sponsored by a member of Congress and submitted to the clerk of the House or Senate

Committee Deliberation

The first step in getting a law passed is drafting legislation. Members of Congress, the White House, and federal agencies all take roles in developing and drafting initial legislation. These bills are then officially submitted by a senator or representative to the clerk of the House or Senate and referred to the appropriate committee for deliberation. During the course of its deliberations, the committee typically refers the bill to one of its subcommittees, which may hold hearings, listen to expert testimony, and amend the proposed legislation before referring it to the full committee for consideration. The full committee may then accept the recommendation of the subcommittee or hold its own hearings and prepare its own amendments.

The next steps in the process are the **committee markup** sessions, in which committees rewrite bills to reflect changes discussed during the hearings. In the partisan fighting that has characterized Congress in recent years, the minority party has charged that its members are often not given enough time to study proposed legislation before markup. Conflict over this issue drew the Capitol police to the House in 2003 and almost resulted in a fistfight among representatives when Democrats protested their treatment by the House Ways and Means Committee. Charging that they had been given a complex pension bill only ten hours before markup, House Democrats walked out. The ensuing commotion, with Republicans calling the police and a Democratic congressman threatening a Republican, presented a sorry spectacle for the evening news. Although Democrats lost a resolution to censure the committee for its actions, the committee chair, Bill Thomas (R-Calif.), later broke down in tears as he apologized on the House floor.

committee markup session in which a congressional committee rewrites legislation to incorporate changes discussed during hearings on the bill

Frequently, the committee and subcommittee do little or nothing with a bill that has been submitted to them. Many bills are simply allowed to "die in committee" with little or no serious consideration given to them. Often, members of Congress introduce legislation that they neither expect nor desire to see enacted into law but present merely to please a constituency group. These bills die a quick and painless death. Other pieces of legislation have ardent supporters and die in committee only after a long battle. But in either case, most bills are never reported out of the committees to which they are assigned. In a typical congressional session, 95 percent of the roughly 8,000 bills introduced die in committee.

The relative handful of bills that are presented out of committee must, in the House, pass one last hurdle within the committee system—the Rules Committee. This committee determines the rules that will govern action on the bill on the House floor. In

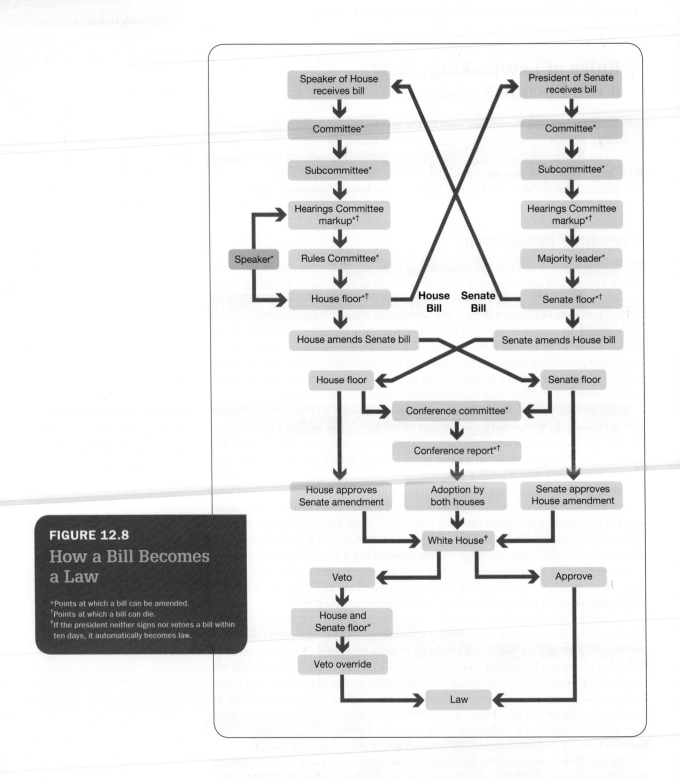

FIGURE 12.8

How a Bill Becomes a Law

*Points at which a bill can be amended.
†Points at which a bill can die.
‡If the president neither signs nor vetoes a bill within
ten days, it automatically becomes law.

particular, the Rules Committee allots the time for debate and decides to what extent amendments to the bill can be proposed from the floor. A bill's supporters generally prefer a **closed rule**, which puts severe limits on floor debate and amendments. Opponents of a bill usually prefer an **open rule**, which permits potentially damaging floor debate and makes it easier to add amendments that may cripple the bill or weaken its chances for passage. Thus, the outcome of the Rules Committee's deliberations can be extremely important, and the committee's hearings can be an occasion for sharp conflict. In recent years, the Rules committee has become less powerful because the House leadership exercises so much influence over its decisions.

One of the most important changes in the way Congress operates is the reduced importance of committees. Since 1995, committees have lost considerable influence as power has shifted upward to the legislative leadership. This means that committees typically do not deliberate for very long or call witnesses. In some cases, the leadership has bypassed committees altogether, bringing legislation directly to the floor. Nonetheless, committees continue to play an important role in the legislative process, especially on issues that are not sharply partisan.[29]

Debate

The next step in getting a law passed is debate on the floor of the House and Senate. Party control of the agenda is reinforced by the rule giving the Speaker of the House and the president of the Senate the power of recognition during debate on a bill. Usually the chair knows the purpose for which a member intends to speak well in advance of the occasion. Spontaneous efforts to gain recognition are often foiled. For example, the Speaker may ask, "For what purpose does the member rise?" before deciding whether to grant recognition.

In the House, virtually all the time allotted by the Rules Committee for debate on a given bill is controlled by the bill's sponsor and by its leading opponent. In almost every case, these two people are the committee chair and the ranking minority member of the committee that processed the bill—or those they designate. These two participants are, by rule and tradition, granted the power to allocate most of the debate time in small amounts to members who are seeking to speak for or against the measure. Preference in the allocation of time goes to the members of the committee whose jurisdiction covers the bill.

In the Senate, the leadership has much less control over floor debate. Indeed, the Senate is unique among the world's legislative bodies for its commitment to unlimited debate. Once given the floor, a senator may speak as long as he or she wishes. On a number of memorable occasions, senators have used this right to prevent action on legislation that they oppose. Through this tactic, called the **filibuster**, small minorities or even one individual in the Senate can force the majority to give in. During the 1950s and 1960s, for example, opponents of civil rights legislation often sought to block its passage by staging a filibuster. Filibusters can be ended by a Senate vote to cut off debate, called **cloture**. From 1917 to 1975, it took two-thirds of the Senate or sixty-seven votes to end a filibuster. In 1975, the Senate changed the rules to three-fifths of the Senate or sixty votes needed for cloture. The threat of a filibuster ensures that, in crafting legislation and proposing judicial appointments, the majority takes into account the viewpoint of the political minority. For much of American history, senators only rarely used the filibuster. In the last twenty years, however, the filibuster has become so common that observers routinely note that it takes sixty votes to get anything passed in the Senate. The 110th Congress (2007–08) holds the record, with 134 cloture votes; midway

● **What are the main steps in passing a law?**

closed rule a provision by the House Rules Committee limiting or prohibiting the introduction of amendments during debate

open rule a provision by the House Rules Committee that permits floor debate and the addition of new amendments to a bill

filibuster a tactic used by members of the Senate to prevent action on legislation they oppose by continuously holding the floor and speaking until the majority backs down. Once given the floor, senators have unlimited time to speak, and it requires a vote of three-fifths of the Senate to end a filibuster

cloture a rule allowing a majority of two-thirds or three-fifths of the members of a legislative body to set a time limit on debate over a given bill

through, the 111th Congress (2009–10) appeared poised to hold a comparable number of cloture votes. Frustrated at the difficulty of moving his agenda through the Senate, President Obama noted in his 2010 State of the Union Address, "You had to cast more votes to break filibusters last year than in the entire 1950s and '60s combined."[30] Yet the filibuster is a tool that both parties have used; with a sixty-seven-vote majority required to eliminate it, the filibuster is likely to remain a feature of American politics for the foreseeable future.

Although it is the best known, the filibuster is not the only technique used to block Senate debate. Under Senate rules, members have virtually unlimited ability to propose amendments to a pending bill. Each amendment must be voted on before the bill can come to a final vote. The introduction of new amendments can be stopped only by unanimous consent. This, in effect, can permit a determined minority to filibuster by amendment, indefinitely delaying the passage of a bill. Senators can also place "holds," or stalling devices, on bills to delay debate. Senators place holds on bills when they fear that openly opposing them will be unpopular. Because holds are kept secret, the senators placing the holds do not have to take public responsibility for their actions. There have been several efforts to eliminate holds. In 1997, opponents of this practice introduced an amendment that would have required publicizing the identity of the senator putting a bill on hold. But when the Senate voted on the measure, the proposal to end the practice of anonymous holds had "mysteriously disappeared."[31] Although no one took credit for killing the measure, it was evident that the majority of senators wanted to maintain the practice. In 2007, reformers succeeded in passing the Honest Leadership and Open Government Act. Although the new law did not eliminate holds, it contained provisions requiring Senators who impose a hold to identify themselves in the *Congressional Record* after six days and state the reasons for the hold.[32] Even with this provision, senators have continued to impose holds on legislation and especially on presidential appointees. Senator Richard Shelby (R-Ala.) aroused the ire of the White House in 2010 for placing a "blanket hold" on more than seventy presidential nominees. Unusual in its sweeping nature, Shelby's hold aimed to force the White House to support several defense-related contracts that would benefit the state of Alabama.[33]

After the 2010 Gulf oil spill, the Senate Environment and Public Works Committee held hearings on the disaster. Executives from BP America, Transocean Limited, and Halliburton were called to testify on their companies' roles in the spill.

Once a bill is debated on the floor of the House and the Senate, the leaders schedule it for a vote on the floor of each chamber. By this time, congressional leaders know what the vote will be; leaders do not bring legislation to the floor unless they are fairly certain it is going to pass. As a consequence, it is unusual for the leadership to lose a bill on the floor. On rare occasions, the last moments of the floor vote can be very dramatic, as each party's leadership puts its whip organization into action to make sure that wavering members vote with the party. In September 2008, the House of Representatives surprisingly rejected a $700 billion bank rescue plan, which dramatically, led the Dow Jones Industrial Index to decline nearly 7 percent in a single day—one of the biggest drops in recent history. As the *New York Times* reported, lawmakers were "almost speechless" on hearing that the bill did not pass; not only did the White House and the congressional leadership of both parties expect the bill to prevail, albeit narrowly, but so did the most ardent opponents of the bill. As the end of the voting period for members drew close, it was clear that the bill was going down to defeat, with 205 for the bill and 228 against. Since members of the House can change their votes until the voting period ends, the Speaker decided to extend the time to forty minutes in order to corral votes from members. As much as both Democratic and Republican leaders tried, they could not get enough members to switch their votes. A few days later, the House passed a revised version of the bill by 263 to 171 votes.[34]

Conference Committee: Reconciling House and Senate Versions of Legislation

Once a bill is out of committee and through both houses of Congress, it must be considered by a conference committee. Getting a bill out of committee and through one of the houses of Congress is no guarantee that the bill will be enacted into law. Frequently, bills that began with similar provisions in both chambers emerge with little resemblance to each other. Alternatively, a bill may be passed by one chamber but undergo substantial revision in the other chamber. In such cases, a conference committee composed of the senior members of the committees or subcommittees that initiated the bills may be required to iron out differences between the two pieces of legislation. Sometimes members or leaders will let objectionable provisions pass on the floor, knowing that they will get the chance to change what they want in conference. Usually, conference committees meet behind closed doors. Agreement requires a majority of each of the two delegations. Legislation that emerges successfully from a conference committee is more often a compromise than a clear victory of one set of forces over another.

When a bill comes out of conference, it faces one more hurdle. Before a bill can be sent to the president for signing, the House-Senate conference committee's version of the bill must be approved on the floor of each chamber. Usually such approval is given quickly. Occasionally, however, a bill's opponents use this round of approval as one last opportunity to defeat a piece of legislation.

Presidential Action

The final step in passing a law is presidential approval. Once adopted by the House and Senate, a bill goes to the president, who may choose to sign the bill into law or **veto** it. The veto is the president's constitutional power to reject a piece of legislation. To veto a bill, the president returns it unsigned within ten days to the house of Congress in which it originated. If Congress adjourns during the ten-day period, and the president has taken no action, the bill is also considered to be vetoed. This

veto the president's constitutional power to turn down acts of Congress. A presidential veto may be overridden by a two-thirds vote of each house of Congress

latter method is known as the **pocket veto**. The possibility of a presidential veto affects how willing members of Congress are to push for different pieces of legislation at different times. If they think a proposal is likely to be vetoed they might shelve it until a later time.

A presidential veto may be overridden by a two-thirds vote in both the House and Senate. A veto override says much about the support that a president can expect from Congress, and it can deliver a stinging blow to the executive branch. Presidents will often back down from a veto threat if they believe that Congress will override the veto.

How Congress Decides

What determines the kinds of legislation that Congress ultimately produces? According to the simplest theories of representation, members of Congress would respond to the views of their constituents. In fact, the process of creating a legislative agenda, drawing up a list of possible measures, and deciding among them is a very complex process, in which a variety of influences from inside and outside government play important roles. External influences include a legislator's constituency and various interest groups. Influences from inside government include party leadership, congressional colleagues, and the president. Let us examine each of these influences individually and then consider how they interact to produce congressional policy decisions.

Constituency

Because members of Congress, for the most part, want to be reelected, we would expect the views of their constituents to be a primary influence on the decisions that legislators make. Yet constituency influence is not so straightforward. In fact, most constituents do not even know what policies their representatives support. The number of citizens who do pay attention to such matters—the attentive public—is usually very small. Nonetheless, members of Congress spend a lot of time worrying about what their constituents think, because they realize that the choices they make may be scrutinized in a future election and used as ammunition by an opposing candidate. Because of this possibility, members of Congress try to anticipate their constituents' policy views.[35] Legislators are more likely to act in accordance with those views if they think that voters will take them into account during elections. In October 1998, for example, thirty-one House Democrats broke party ranks and voted in favor of an impeachment inquiry against President Clinton because they believed a "no" vote could cost them re-election that November. The White House successfully pressed to schedule the vote authorizing the use of force in Iraq right before the 2002 elections in order to pressure members to vote for it. In this way, constituents may affect congressional policy choices even when there is little direct evidence of their influence.

Members of Congress often spend a great deal of time in their electoral districts meeting with constituents. Representative Elijah E. Cummings of Maryland is shown here greeting constituents at an event in Baltimore.

Interest Groups

Interest groups are another important external influence on the policies that Congress produces. When members of Congress are making voting decisions, those interest groups that have some connection to constituents in particular members' districts are most likely to be influential. For this reason, interest groups with the ability to mobilize followers in many congressional districts may be especially influential in Congress. In recent years, Washington-based interest groups with little grassroots strength have recognized the importance of locally generated activity. They have, accordingly, sought to simulate grassroots pressure, using a strategy that has been nicknamed "Astroturf lobbying" (see Chapter 11). Such campaigns encourage constituents to sign form letters, postcards or emails, which are then sent to congressional representatives. Campaigns set up toll-free telephone numbers for a system in which simply reporting your name and address to the listening computer will generate a letter to your congressional representative. One Senate office estimated that such organized campaigns to demonstrate "grassroots" support account for two-thirds of the mail the office received. As such campaigns increase, however, they become less influential, because members of Congress are aware of how rare constituent interest actually is.[36]

Many interest groups now also use legislative "scorecards" that rate how members of Congress vote on issues of importance to that group. A high or low rating by an important interest group may provide a potent weapon in the next election. Interest groups can increase their influence over a particular piece of legislation by signaling their intention to include it in their scoring. Among the most influential groups that use scorecards, often posting them on their Web sites for members to see, are the National Federation of Independent Business, the AFL-CIO, National Right to Life, the League of Conservation Voters, and the National Rifle Association.

Interest groups also have substantial influence in setting the legislative agenda and in helping to craft specific language in legislation. Today, sophisticated lobbyists win influence by providing information about policies to busy members of Congress. In the 2009–2010 health reform effort, the biotechnology firm Genentech ghostwrote statements that more than a dozen members of Congress placed into the Congressional Record. Genentech's role came to light when it became evident that members had used the exact same language in their entries.[37] In recent years, interest groups have also begun to build broader coalitions and comprehensive campaigns around particular policy issues. These coalitions do not rise from the grass roots but instead are put together by Washington lobbyists who launch comprehensive lobbying campaigns that combine simulated grassroots activity with information and campaign funding for members of Congress.

Close financial ties between members of Congress and interest-group lobbyists often raise eyebrows because they suggest that interest groups get special treatment in exchange for political donations. Concerns about the influence of lobbyists in Congress mounted in the early 2000s when Republicans launched the K Street Project, named after the street in Washington where many high-powered lobbyists have offices. The K Street Project placed former Republican staffers in key lobbying positions and ensured a large flow of corporate cash into Republican coffers. Congressional relationships to lobbyists came under close scrutiny when the lobbyist Jack Abramoff—a self-proclaimed big supporter of the K Street Project—pled guilty in early 2006 to charges of conspiracy, mail fraud, and tax evasion in connection with his lobbying activities.

Celebrities, Capitol Hill, and the 2009 Health Care Debate

Celebrity involvement in politics on Capitol Hill has become standard practice in today's political environment, with stars from sports, music, Hollywood, and beyond vying for the spotlight on behalf of the causes they support.

For Brad Pitt, it's the redevelopment of Hurricane Katrina–ravaged New Orleans. For U2's front man Bono? Debt relief in Africa. Nicole Kidman? Violence against women overseas. Kelly Clarkson? Illegal downloading of music. Ben Affleck? The scientific promise of mapping the human genome. Mira Sorvino? The crisis in Darfur. And the list goes on.

According to research by Professor Harry Strine, over 400 celebrities have appeared as witnesses in congressional committee hearings since 1969. Because celebrities attract significant media attention, members of Congress capitalize on these appearances as opportunities to seem hip, amicable, and sympathetic to constituents back at home and to other members of Congress.

Meanwhile celebrities, although often unable to speak to the precise historical, scientific, or economic details of a policy proposal, do put a recognizable face on a cause and draw national attention to what might otherwise be considered a dull political debate.

Interestingly, unlike the treatment of non-celebrity witnesses at congressional hearings, celebrity witnesses are generally given the "star" treatment, according to Strine. When members of Congress interact with celebrity witnesses, their treatment tends to be appreciative, good-natured, and even coddling—with significant deference and respect. Celebrity witnesses are interrupted less frequently than non-celebrity witnesses and are shown far more solidarity and acceptance by members of Congress. The role of celebrity witnesses appears to be a strategic one aimed at fostering media coverage and fueling favorable discourse about a given topic.

Celebrities also get involved in congressional debate without ever showing up on Capitol Hill. During the recent health care debate, several stars participated in the conversation through indirect means including advocacy ads, online spots, and satirical parodies.

For example, Zach Braff and Donald Faison, actors who play fictional doctors on the comedy series *Scrubs*, starred in a humorous political ad from *Rock the Vote*. The ad highlighted the high rate of uninsured young people and advocated their involvement in the debate process. The humor Web site "Funny or Die" aired sketches and ad parodies including one starring *Saturday Night Live* funnyman Will Ferrell, *Madmen* star Jon Hamm, and *House* star Olivia Wilde. The spot, produced by the progressive advocacy group MoveOn and viewed by almost 3 million Americans, satirized the need to "protect health insurance executives" while advocating for the inclusion of a public health insurance option in the health care reform package.

Celebrity advocacy might not necessarily change the public's mind on an issue, but it can certainly draw media coverage to otherwise un-newsworthy congressional debates. This added attention helps set the national agenda regarding what issues take top billing on the public's radar. And, although some stars have experienced a backlash from the public as a result of unpopular stands—like Sean Penn and Janeane Garofalo for their criticism of the Iraq War in 2003, most stars see the risk as worthwhile. As the publicist Ken Sunshine puts it: "I represent successful artists who have been outspoken on a variety of issues, and they keep getting more successful. It is outrageous to play it safe in a world where nothing is very safe."

SOURCES: Johnson, T. "How Celeb Activists Handle Health Care Reform." *Variety.* October 31, 2009; Marlantes, L., Bradley, T., and Burns, Q. "Another Day, Another Star on Capital Hill," ABCnews.com (accessed 9/20/06). Strine IV, Harry C. "Your Testimony Was Splendid: The Treatment of Celebrities and Non-celebrities in Congressional Hearings," paper presented at the annual meeting of the Southern Political Science Association, January 5, 2006.

for critical analysis

1. Do you think celebrities should have the chance to address congressional committees even if they are not experts on the policies being discussed?

2. How can increased media attention—such as the buzz generated by celebrity appearances—affect policy decisions made by congressional committees?

Concern over such corruption led Congress to enact new ethics legislation in 2007. The new law set new restrictions on the gifts lobbyists can bestow on law-makers and limited privately funded travel. The law also prohibited members of Congress from lobbying for two years after they retire and required lawmakers to identify the earmarks they insert in legislation. It also aimed to shine light on the practice of "bundling," whereby lobbyists assemble money from a number of clients to make a single political donation. Now, lobbyists are required to disclose the names of the individual contributors to these political donations. Although the new law provides additional transparency, allowing the public to learn more about the relationship between lobbyists and members of Congress, it is widely viewed as lacking sufficient authority to go after those who are suspected of ethics violations.[38]

Party Discipline

In both the House and Senate, party leaders have a good deal of influence over the behavior of their party members. This influence, sometimes called "party discipline," was once so powerful that it dominated the lawmaking process. At the turn of the last century, party leaders could often command the allegiance of more than 90 percent of their members. A vote on which 50 percent or more of the members of one party take one position while at least 50 percent of the members of the other party take the opposing position is called a **party unity vote**. At the beginning of the twentieth century, nearly half of all **roll-call votes** in the House of Representatives were party votes. For much of the twentieth century, the number of party votes declined as bipartisan legislation became more common. The 1990s witnessed a return to strong party discipline as partisan polarization drew sharper lines between Democrats and Republicans, and congressional party leaders aggressively used their powers to promote party discipline. In 2005 party discipline was close to its all-time high.

Typically, party unity is greater in the House than in the Senate. House rules grant greater procedural control of business to the majority party leaders, which gives them more influence over House members. In the Senate, however, the leadership has few sanctions over its members. The former Senate minority leader Tom Daschle once observed that a Senate leader seeking to influence other senators has as incentives "a bushel full of carrots and a few twigs."[39]

Though it has not reached nineteenth-century levels, party unity has been on the rise in recent years because the divisions between the parties have deepened on many high-profile issues such as abortion, health care, and financial reform. (see Figure 12.9). Party unity scores rise when congressional leaders try to put a partisan stamp on legislation. For example, in 1995, then Speaker Newt Gingrich sought to enact a Republican Contract with America that few Democrats supported. The result was more party unity in the House than in any year since 1954. Republicans, especially in the House, exhibited very high party unity scores after they came to power in 1995. Since then, the polarization of political parties has shown up in very high party unity scores. In 2009, House Democrats voted with the majority 91 percent of the time, close to their all-time high of 92 percent in 2007 and 2008. In 2009, Senate Democrats set a record for party unity by voting with their caucus 91 percent of the time. Republicans were also very united, although at slightly lower levels. In 2009, House Republicans voted with their party 87 percent of the time; Senate Republicans voted with their party 85 percent of the time.

party unity vote a roll-call vote in the House or Senate in which at least 50 percent of the members of one party take a particular position and are opposed by at least 50 percent of the members of the other party

roll-call vote a vote in which each legislator's yes or no vote is recorded as the clerk calls the names of the members alphabetically

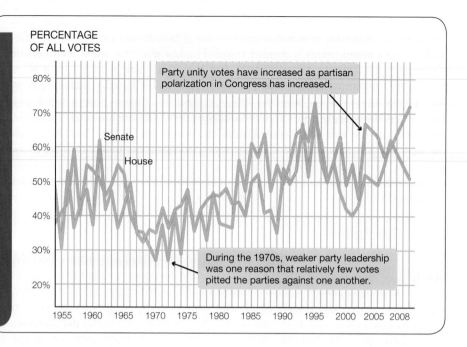

FIGURE 12.9

Party Unity Votes by Chamber

Party unity votes are roll-call votes in which a majority of one party lines up against a majority of the other party. Party unity votes increase when the parties are polarized and when the party leadership can enforce discipline. Why did the percentage of party unity votes decline in the 1970s? Why has it risen in recent years?

SOURCE: Richard, Rubin "Party Unity: An Ever Thicker Dividing Line," *CQ Weekly Online* (January 11, 2010), 122–31, library.cqpress.com (accessed 2/5/10).

To some extent, party unity is based on ideology and background. Republican members of the House are more likely than Democrats to have been elected by rural or suburban districts. Democrats are likely to be more liberal on economic and social questions than their Republican colleagues in both houses. These differences certainly help to explain roll-call divisions between the two parties. Ideology and background, however, are only part of the explanation of party unity. The other part has to do with party organization and leadership. Among the resources that party leaders have at their disposal are (1) leadership PACs, (2) committee assignments, (3) access to the floor, (4) the whip system, (5) logrolling, and (6) the presidency. Party leaders regularly use these resources, which are often effective in securing the support of party members.

Leadership Pacs Leaders have increased their influence over members in recent years with aggressive use of leadership political action committees. Leadership PACs are organizations that members of Congress use to raise funds that they then distribute to other members of their party running for election. Republican congressional leaders pioneered the aggressive use of leadership PACs to win their congressional majority in 1995, and the practice has spread widely since that time. The former House majority leader Tom DeLay was especially aggressive in raising funds, creating several important PACs, including Americans for a Republican Majority (ARMPAC), Retain Our Majority Program (ROMP), and the Republican Majority Issues Committee. In recent years, Democrats have also formed well-funded leadership PACs. For aspiring presidential candidates, leadership PACs can provide an initial infrastructure for the campaign and can help fund precampaign travel. This is how Hillary Clinton used her leadership PAC, HILLPAC, before she formally announced her candidacy in 2007. Money from leadership PACs can be directed to the most vulnerable candidates or to candidates who are having trouble raising money. The PACs enhance the power of the party and create a bond between the leaders and the members who receive their help.[40]

Committee Assignments Leaders can create debts among members by helping them get favorable committee assignments. These assignments are made early in the congressional careers of most members and cannot be taken from them if they later balk at party discipline. Nevertheless, if the leadership goes out of its way to get the right assignment for a member, this effort is likely to create a bond of obligation that can be called on without any other payments or favors. This is one reason the Republican leadership gave freshmen favorable assignments when the Republicans took over Congress in 1995. When she assumed the position of Speaker in 2007, Nancy Pelosi sought to spread power more widely by limiting the number of committees that any one member could chair. She also gave freshmen representatives access to key committees that would raise their political stature.[41] By offering attractive committee assignments to members in competitive races, especially to new members, she sought to boost her party's chances in the next elections.

Access to the Floor The most important everyday resource available to the parties is control over access to the floor. With thousands of bills awaiting passage and most members clamoring for access in order to influence a bill or to publicize themselves, floor time is precious. In the Senate, the leadership allows ranking committee members to influence the allocation of floor time—who will speak for how long; in the House, the Speaker, as head of the majority party (in consultation with the minority leader), allocates large blocks of floor time. Thus, floor time is allocated in both houses of Congress by the majority and minority leaders. More important, the Speaker of the House and the majority leader in the Senate possess the power of recognition. Although this power may not appear to be substantial, it is a formidable authority and can be used to stymie a piece of legislation completely or to frustrate a member's attempts to speak on a particular issue. Because the power is significant, members of Congress usually attempt to stay on good terms with the Speaker and the majority leader to ensure that they will continue to be recognized.

House Speaker Nancy Pelosi was particularly generous in offering freshmen Democrats and other especially vulnerable Democrats an opportunity to speak on the floor. As the House considered the six signature pieces of legislation in their first hundred hours, Pelosi ensured that twenty-nine of the most vulnerable Democrats—designated as the Frontline team—received prime-time speaking assignments.[42]

The Whip System Some influence accrues to party leaders through the whip system, which is primarily a communications network. Between twelve and twenty assistant and regional whips are selected to operate at the direction of the majority or minority leader and the whip. They take polls of all the members in order to learn their intentions on specific bills. This enables the leaders to know if they have enough support to allow a vote as well as whether the vote is so close that they need to put pressure on a few undecided members. Leaders also use the whip system to convey their wishes and plans to the members, but only in very close votes do they actually exert pressure on a member. In those instances, the Speaker or a lieutenant will go to a few party members who have indicated they will switch if their vote is essential. The

As Speaker of the House, Nancy Pelosi ensured that freshman Democrats—such as Steve Driehaus of Ohio, pictured here—had opportunities to speak on the floor. Despite this increased visibility, many Democratic freshmen, including Driehaus, lost their bids for re-election in 2010.

Although party discipline in Congress has declined in the past century, recent years have seen a new increase in party unity. In 2008, House and Senate Republicans appeared together to show that they were united in their support of a proposal for property tax cuts.

logrolling a legislative practice whereby agreements are made between legislators in voting for or against a bill; vote trading

whip system helps the leaders limit pressuring members to a few times per session.

The whip system helps maintain party unity in both houses of Congress, but it is particularly critical in the House of Representatives because of the large number of legislators whose positions and votes must be accounted for. The majority and minority whips and their assistants must be adept at inducing compromise among legislators who hold widely differing viewpoints. The whips' personal styles and their perception of their function significantly affect the development of legislative coalitions and influence the compromises that emerge. As Republican House whip from 1995 to 2002, Tom DeLay established a reputation as an effective vote counter and a tough leader, earning the nickname the Hammer. DeLay also expanded the reach of the whip, building alliances with Republicans outside of Congress, particularly those in ideological and business-oriented groups. Under DeLay's leadership these lobbyists effectively worked as part of the whip operation. As whip, DeLay also began a campaign to pressure trade associations to hire Republicans as their lobbyists, which was continued by his successor, Roy Blunt (R-Mo.). These relationships opened the congressional Republican leadership to accusations of corruption and led to DeLay's downfall as majority leader in 2006. Under the Democrats the whip system returned to its former status as an instrument of the Speaker. Speaker Pelosi used the whip system to promote diversity and strengthen party loyalty.

Logrolling An agreement between two or more members of Congress who have nothing in common except the need for support is called **logrolling**. The agreement states, in effect, "You support me on bill X and I'll support you on another bill of your choice." Since party leaders are the center of the communications networks in the two chambers, they can help members create large logrolling coalitions. Hundreds of logrolling deals are made each year, and although there are no official record-keeping books, it would be a poor party leader whose whips did not know who owed what to whom. In some instances, logrolling produces strange alliances. A most unlikely alliance emerged in Congress in October 1991, which one commentator dubbed "the corn for porn plot."[43] The alliance joined Senate supporters of the National Endowment for the Arts (NEA) with senators seeking limits on the cost of grazing rights on federal lands. The NEA, which provides federal funding to the arts, had been under fire from the conservative senator Jesse Helms (R-N.C.) for funding some controversial artists whose work Helms believed to be indecent. In an effort to prevent federal support for such works, Helms attached a provision to the NEA's funding that would have prohibited the agency from awarding grants to any work that in a "patently offensive way" depicted "sexual or excretory activities or organs." Supporters of the NEA condemned such restrictions as a violation of free speech and pointed out that many famous works of art could not have been funded under such restrictions. When it appeared that the amendment would pass, NEA supporters offered western senators a deal. In exchange for voting down the Helms amendment, they would eliminate a planned hike in grazing fees. Republican senators from sixteen western states switched their votes and defeated the Helms amendment. Although Helms called his defeat the product of "back-room deals and parliamentary flimflam," his amendment was simply the victim of the time-honored congressional practice of logrolling.[44]

The Presidency Of all the influences that maintain the clarity of party lines in Congress, the influence of the presidency is probably the most important. Indeed, the office is a touchstone of party discipline in Congress. Since the late 1940s, under President Harry Truman, presidents each year have identified a number of bills that they want to be considered part of their administration's program. By the mid-1950s, both parties in Congress began to look to the president for these proposals, which became the most significant part of Congress's agenda. The president's support is a criterion for party loyalty, and party leaders are able to use it to rally some members.

Weighing Diverse Influences

Clearly, many different factors affect congressional decisions. But at various points in the decision-making process, some factors are likely to be more influential than others. For example, interest groups may be more effective at the committee stage, when their expertise is especially valued and they are less obviously visible. Because committees play a key role in deciding what legislation actually reaches the floor of the House or Senate, interest groups can often put a halt to bills they dislike, or they can ensure that the options that do reach the floor are those that the groups' members support.

Once legislation reaches the floor and members of Congress are deciding among alternatives, constituent opinion will become more important. Legislators are also influenced very much by other legislators: many of their assessments about the substance and politics of legislation come from fellow members of Congress.

The influence of the external and internal forces described in the preceding section also varies according to the kind of issue being considered. On policies of great importance to powerful interest groups—farm subsidies, for example—those groups are likely to have considerable influence. On other issues, members of Congress may be less attentive to narrow interest groups and more willing to consider what they see as the general interest.

Finally, the mix of influences varies according to the historical moment. The close balance in Congress between Republicans and Democrats during the past fifteen years has made party leaders especially important in decision making.

● Beyond Legislation: Other Congressional Powers

In addition to the power to make the law, Congress has at its disposal an array of other instruments through which to influence the process of government. The Constitution gives the Senate the power to approve treaties and appointments. And Congress has a number of other powers through which it can share with the other branches the capacity to administer the laws.

What Is Congress's Role in Foreign Policy?

During World War II, national security dominated the congressional agenda. With the massive mobilization of American troops and economic production geared to support the war effort, domestic policy commanded only modest attention in Congress. Congress focused on supporting the president as the nation faced total mobilization for war. During other periods, Congress has been much less supportive of the president's foreign policy. For example, in the late 1960s, as widespread doubts about the wisdom of the Vietnam War began to grow, Congress convened hearings that questioned administration assumptions and priorities.

Americans disagree about Congress's proper role in foreign policy. Such disagreements become especially salient in times of war. Should Congress primarily support the president as commander in chief of the armed forces? Or should Congress play the role of watchdog, delving into the details of foreign policy to ensure that the president's policies best serve the public interest?

Intensive congressional scrutiny of the president's foreign policy is counterproductive, say those who believe Congress should unite behind the president.

In order to manage the nation's defense effectively, the national government must speak with one voice. Congressional objections to the president's priorities only strengthen the nation's enemies by weakening our resolve to take the measures needed to ensure our defense. Congress is more likely than the president to adopt a short-term, politicized perspective. Congress is also more likely to put domestic concerns ahead of foreign-policy priorities. These tensions grew more pronounced after public disenchantment with the war in Iraq gave control of Congress to the Democrats in the 2006 midterm election. House and Senate leaders pressed the president to announce a new strategy for reducing American forces in Iraq. The president insisted, however, that U.S. troops needed to stay in Iraq to end sectarian violence. In the

end, presidents are better equipped than Congress to know what needs to be done to conduct a successful foreign policy. They have a large national security apparatus with extensive expertise, and they are able to keep the big picture in mind.

Critics disagree, arguing that Congress has a vital role to play in foreign policy. The absence of ongoing congressional scrutiny can lead to poor policy, detached from democratic accountability. The continuing violence in Iraq and the lack of progress toward political stability provided only one example where congressional leaders claimed the Bush administration had lost touch with the electorate. From this viewpoint, democratic checks and balances must extend to foreign policy. If the executive branch refuses to adjust its foreign policies in response to public opinion, then Congress may have to exercise its power of the purse by cutting off funds. Ultimately, Congress must closely monitor the executive to ensure that the arguments and evidence for U.S. foreign policy are sound.

Former president Bush's handling of the war in Iraq and the threat of terrorism brought tensions between Congress and the White House to a level not seen since the Vietnam War. President Obama, however, found he was not immune to these tensions. Although Obama succeeded in winning congressional approval for additional troops in Afghanistan, many members of Congress did not support his request. The president's reputation rests far more heavily on success or failure in foreign policy than do the reputations of members of Congress. Meanwhile, Congress is more responsive to popular pressures that also have a place in foreign policy.

for critical analysis

1. Why is the president better equipped than Congress to conduct foreign policy, especially in matters such as the war against terrorism?

2. Why is congressional oversight essential to good foreign policy? How does the experience of the war in Iraq point to the importance of strong congressional involvement in foreign policy?

Oversight

Oversight, as applied to Congress, refers to the effort to oversee or to supervise how the executive branch carries out legislation. Oversight is carried out by committees or subcommittees of the Senate or the House, which conduct hearings and investigations in order to analyze and evaluate bureaucratic agencies and the effectiveness of their programs. Their purpose may be to locate inefficiencies or abuses of power, to explore the relationship between what an agency does and what a law intended, or to change or abolish a program. Most programs and agencies are subject to some oversight every year during the course of hearings on **appropriations**, that is, the funding of agencies and government programs.

Committees or subcommittees have the power to subpoena witnesses, take oaths, cross-examine, compel testimony, and bring criminal charges for contempt (refusing to cooperate) and perjury (lying under oath). Hearings and investigations are similar in many ways, but they differ on one fundamental point. A hearing is usually held on a specific bill, and the questions asked are usually intended to build a record with regard to that bill. In an investigation, the committee or subcommittee does not begin with a particular bill, but examines a broad area or problem and then concludes its investigation with one or more proposed bills.

In recent years, congressional oversight power has increasingly been used as a tool of partisan politics. The Republican Congress aggressively investigated President Clinton, racking up 140 hours of sworn testimony on whether the president had used the White House Christmas card list for partisan purposes. By contrast, the Republican-controlled Congress failed to scrutinize seriously the actions of the Bush administration during Bush's first six years in office. The investigation into the abuse of prisoners in Iraq's Abu Ghraib prison, for example, entailed only twelve hours of sworn testimony. Moreover, the few oversight hearings that the Republican Congress held mainly sought to support the leadership's policy goals—during a hearing on Arctic oil drilling, for example, much testimony was devoted to the benefits of such drilling. Congress also convened oversight hearings on issues

oversight the effort by Congress, through hearings, investigations, and other techniques, to exercise control over the activities of executive agencies

appropriations the amounts of money approved by Congress in statutes (bills) that each unit or agency of government can spend

In 2006, the Senate Judiciary Committee responded to concerns about President Bush's authorization of secret domestic surveillance by holding hearings on the program. Former attorney general Alberto Gonzales was called to testify and explain the administration's actions.

that had nothing to do with the executive branch, such as the high-profile hearings on steroid use in Major League Baseball in 2005 and 2008.[45]

When the Democrats took control of Congress in 2007, the congressional oversight role increased dramatically. To highlight the importance of oversight, Democrats renamed the House Government Reform Committee to be the House Oversight and Government Reform Committee and added four new subcommittees dedicated to oversight. They also hired over 200 new investigative staffers.[46] Armed with these resources, Congress stepped up the number of oversight hearings: during its first six months in power, the Democratic Congress held 942 oversight hearings, compared with 579 for the same period when Republicans controlled Congress in 2005.[47] Congress has been especially vigilant in using its oversight powers to investigate different dimensions of the financial crisis. Under the legislation passed in 2008, Congress appointed an oversight panel that would help it monitor the Treasury Department's implementation of the $700 billion Troubled Asset Relief Program (TARP, otherwise known as the bank bailout). That panel, headed by Harvard law professor Elizabeth Warren, submitted monthly reports to Congress throughout 2009 and held multiple public meetings across the country. Congress also enacted a law that created the Financial Crisis Inquiry Commission, a ten-member commission charged with holding hearings to establish the causes of the 2008 financial collapse.[48]

Advice and Consent: Special Senate Powers

The Constitution has given the Senate a special power, one that is not based on lawmaking. The president has the power to make treaties and to appoint top executive officers, ambassadors, and federal judges—but only "with the Advice and Consent of the Senate" (Article II, Section 2). For treaties, two-thirds of those present must concur; for appointments, a simple majority is required.

The power to approve or reject presidential requests also involves the power to set conditions. The Senate only occasionally exercises its power to reject treaties and appointments. Despite the recent debate surrounding judicial nominees, only a handful of judicial nominees have been rejected by the Senate during the past century, whereas hundreds have been approved.

Most presidents make every effort to take potential Senate opposition into account in treaty negotiations and will frequently resort to **executive agreements** with foreign powers instead of treaties. The Supreme Court has held that such agreements are equivalent to treaties, but they do not need Senate approval.[49] In the past, presidents sometimes concluded secret agreements without informing Congress of the agreements' contents, or even their existence. For example, American involvement in the Vietnam War grew in part out of a series of secret arrangements made between American presidents and the South Vietnamese during the 1950s and 1960s. Congress did not even learn of the existence of these agreements until 1969. In 1972, Congress passed the Case Act, which requires that the president inform Congress of any executive agreement within sixty days of its having been reached. This provides Congress with the opportunity to cancel agreements that it opposes. In addition, Congress can limit the president's ability to conduct foreign policy through executive agreement by refusing to appropriate the funds needed to implement an agreement. In this way, for example, Congress can modify or even cancel executive agreements to provide American economic or military assistance to foreign governments.

executive agreement an agreement, made between the president and another country, that has the force of a treaty but does not require the Senate's "advice and consent"

Impeachment

The Constitution also grants Congress the power of **impeachment** over the president, vice president, and other executive officials. Impeachment means to charge a government official (president or otherwise) with "Treason, Bribery, or other high Crimes and Misdemeanors" and bring them before Congress to determine their guilt. Impeachment is thus like a criminal indictment in which the House of Representatives acts like a grand jury, voting (by simple majority) on whether the accused ought to be impeached. If a majority of the House votes to impeach, the impeachment trial moves to the Senate, which acts like a trial jury by voting whether to convict and forcibly remove the person from office (this vote requires a two-thirds majority of the Senate).

Controversy over Congress's impeachment power has arisen over the grounds for impeachment, especially the meaning of "high Crimes and Misdemeanors." A strict reading of the Constitution suggests that the only impeachable offense is an actual crime. But a more commonly agreed-on definition is that "an impeachable offense is whatever the majority of the House of Representatives considers it to be at a given moment in history."[50] In other words, impeachment, especially impeachment of a president, is a political decision.

The political nature of impeachment was very clear in the two instances of impeachment that have occurred in American history. In the first, in 1867, President Andrew Johnson, a southern Democrat who had battled a congressional Republican majority over Reconstruction, was impeached by the House but saved from conviction by one vote in the Senate. In 1998, the House impeached President Bill Clinton on two counts, for lying under oath and obstructing justice, in the investigation into his sexual affair with the White House intern Monica Lewinsky. The vote was highly partisan, with only five Democrats voting for impeachment on each charge. In the Senate, where a two-thirds majority was needed to convict the president, only forty-five senators voted to convict on the first count of lying and fifty voted to convict on the second charge of obstructing justice. As in the House, the vote for impeachment was highly partisan, with all Democrats and only five Republicans supporting the president's ultimate acquittal.

The impeachment power is a considerable one; its very existence in the hands of Congress is a highly effective safeguard against the executive tyranny so greatly feared by the framers of the Constitution.

...My goal in this deposition was to be truthful...

Senate Volume III, Part 1, pp. 535-532

The Senate possesses the power to impeach federal officials. In American history, sixteen federal officials have been impeached, including two presidents, Andrew Johnson and Bill Clinton. During Clinton's trial in the House, Bill McCollum (R-Fla.), argued that lying under oath was sufficient grounds for removing Clinton from office.

impeachment the formal charge by the House of Representatives that a government official has committed "Treason, Bribery, or other high Crimes and Misdemeanors"

● Thinking Critically about Congress and Democracy

Much of this chapter has described the major institutional components of Congress and has shown how they work as Congress makes policy. But what do these institutional features mean for how Congress represents the American public? Does the organization of Congress promote the equal representation of all Americans? Or

Get Your Representatives in Congress Working for You

Most students in college today are receiving some sort of federal financial assistance in the form of Pell grants or subsidized loans. With college tuition rising faster than inflation, many students (and their families) view such assistance as absolutely essential to their ability to stay in school. Members of Congress are well aware of these concerns, thanks in part to the letters, e-mails, and personal visits from many young people who have contacted their representatives and senators and urged them to continue (or extend) such help. As the Get Involved box in Chapter 11 described, in 2007, Congress responded by passing the College Cost Reduction and Access Act, which overhauls the federal student aid program and raises the level of grants.

Voicing your opinion on issues that matter to you may seem difficult, but it is actually relatively easy. Members of Congress have strong incentives to listen to their constituents, and there are several ways that you can let them know how they can represent you better.

- *Know who is representing you in the House and Senate.* To locate your senators, simply go to the official U.S. Senate Web site (www.senate.gov) and use the drop-down menu to enter your state. You can find out who your representative is by visiting the U.S. House of Representatives Web site (www.house .gov) and entering your zip code.

- *Follow current policymaking.* Both the House and Senate Web sites have links to allow you to check what leg-islation is currently on the floor or in committee. You can also use the Library of Congress's Web site (www .thomas.loc.gov) to search for bills currently in Congress or to "browse" by sponsor to see what legislation has been introduced by your senators and representative this session. Contacting your member of Congress about an issue may be especially effective if a proposal related to that issue is currently under consideration.

- *Contact Congress directly.* You can phone Congress by calling the U.S. Capitol Switchboard at (202) 224-3121 and ask to be connected to your senators or your representative. You can send them e-mails through links on their home Web sites. Or you can send them a letter to their Washington, D.C., office (the address will be found on their Web site). You don't have to be an expert on the topic—you can simply ask them to "vote no" or "please support," or you can write a more detailed request. The Web site www.congress .org has tips on how to address your letters and e-mails, as well as guidance on what to write.

- *See your representative or senator in person.* Members of Congress spend a lot of time in their home districts and states, holding town hall meetings and listening to the concerns of their constituents. You can find out their schedules by e-mailing or calling their office, and then simply show up at a local event.

- *Apply for an internship.* Most members of Congress have internships that run either for a school term or for the summer. Your university's internship coordinator (and sometimes even the political science department) has probably worked with local congressional offices in the past and can help facilitate your application.

are there institutional features of Congress that allow some interests more access and influence than others?

As we noted at the beginning of this chapter, Congress instituted a number of reforms in the 1970s to make itself more accessible and to distribute power more widely within the institution. These reforms sought to respond to public views that Congress had become a stodgy institution ruled by a powerful elite that made decisions in private. We have seen that these reforms increased the number of subcommittees, prohibited most secret hearings, and increased the staff support for Congress. These reforms spread power more evenly throughout the institution and opened new avenues for the public to contact and influence Congress.

But the opening of Congress ultimately did not benefit the broad American public, as reformers had envisioned. In fact the congressional reforms enacted during the 1970s actually made Congress less effective and, ironically, more permeable to special interests. Open committee meetings made it possible for sophisticated interest groups to monitor and influence every aspect of developing legislation. The unanticipated, negative consequences of these reforms highlighted the trade-off between representation and effectiveness in Congress.[51] Efforts to improve representation by opening Congress up made it difficult for Congress to be effective.

For the Founders, Congress was the national institution that best embodied the ideals of representative democracy. Throughout our history, Congress has symbolized the American commitment to democratic values. Members of Congress, working to represent their constituents, bring these democratic values to life. A member of Congress can interpret his or her job as representative in two different ways: as a delegate or as a trustee. As a **delegate**, a member of Congress acts on the express preferences of his constituents; as a **trustee**, the member is more loosely tied to constituents and makes the decisions she thinks best. The delegate role appears to be the more democratic because it forces representatives to heed the desires of their constituents. But this requires the representative to be in constant touch with constituents; it also requires constituents to follow each policy issue very closely. The problem with this form of representation is that most people do not follow every issue so carefully; instead they focus only on extremely important issues or issues of particular interest to them. Many people are too busy to get the information necessary to make informed judgments even on issues they care about. Thus, adhering to the delegate form of representation takes the risk that the voices of only a few active and informed constituents get heard. Although it seems more democratic at first glance, the delegate form of representation may actually open Congress up even more to the influence of the voices of special interests.

Congressional members act as trustees, on the other hand, they may not pay sufficient attention to the wishes of their constituents. In this scenario, the only way the public can exercise influence is by voting every two years for representatives or every six years for senators. Yet most members of Congress take this electoral check very seriously. They try to anticipate the wishes of their constituents even when they don't know exactly what those interests are, because they know that unpopular decisions can be used against them in the coming election. What the public dislikes most about Congress stems from suspicions that Congress acts as neither a trustee nor a delegate of the broad public interest, but instead is swayed by narrow special interests with lots of money.[52] Ideally, representative democracy grants all citizens equal opportunity to select their leaders and to communicate

● **What other powers does Congress have?**

for critical **analysis**

Two of Congress's chief responsibilities are representation and lawmaking. How do these responsibilities support and reinforce one another? How might they also conflict with one another?

delegate a representative who votes according to the preferences of his or her constituency

trustee a representative who votes based on what he or she thinks is best for his or her constituency

for critical **analysis**

Why is it so hard to make the voice of the public heard over the special interests in Congress? What reforms can enhance the public's influence in congressional deliberations?

their preferences to these elected representatives. Yet, in reality, some citizens have more wealth, are more politically savvy, or belong to more effective organizations. Despite past efforts to reform Congress, these advantages provide special access to some interests even as they mute the voice of much of the American public. The dilemma that congressional reformers confront is how to devise safeguards that reduce the voices of special interests while allowing Congress to remain open to public influence.

studyguide

Practice Quiz

Find a diagnostic Web Quiz with 37 additional questions on the StudySpace Web site: www.wwnorton.com/we-the-people

Congress: Representing the American People

1. Because they have larger and more heterogeneous constituencies, senators *(p. 438)*
   a) are more attuned to the needs of localized interest groups.
   b) care more about re-election than House members.
   c) can better represent the national interest.
   d) face less competition in elections than House members.

2. What type of representation is described when constituents have the power to hire and fire their representative? *(p. 438)*
   a) agency representation
   b) sociological representation
   c) democratic representation
   d) trustee representation

3. Sociological representation is important in understanding the U.S. congress because *(p. 439)*
   a) members often vote on the basis of their religion.
   b) Congress is a microcosm of American society.
   c) the symbolic composition of Congress is important for the authority of the government.
   d) there is a distinct "congressional sociology."

4. Some have argued that the creation of minority congressional districts has *(p. 447)*
   a) lessened the sociological representation of minorities in Congress.
   b) made it more difficult for minorities to win substantive policy goals.

   c) been a result of the media's impact on state legislative politics.
   d) lessened the problem of "pork-barrel" politics.

5. One way members of Congress can work as agents of their constituents is by *(p. 447)*
   a) providing direct patronage.
   b) taking part in a party vote.
   c) joining a caucus.
   d) supporting term limits.

The Organization of Congress

6. Which of the following types of committees does not include members of both the House and the Senate? *(p. 454)*
   a) standing committee
   b) joint committee
   c) conference committee
   d) No committees include both House members and senators.

7. A series of reforms instituted by Congress in the 1970s, including an increase in the number of subcommittees and greater autonomy for subcommittee chairs, was intended to *(p. 455)*
   a) reduce the power of committee chairs.
   b) increase the power of committee chairs.
   c) secure re-election for all committee chairs.
   d) guarantee the electoral defeat of all committee chairs.

Rules of Lawmaking: How a Bill Becomes a Law

8. The difference between a closed rule and an open rule in the House is *(p. 459)*
   a) a closed rule puts severe limits on floor debate and amendments, whereas an open rule permits floor debate and makes amendments easier.
   b) an open rule puts severe limits on floor debate and amendments, whereas a closed rule permits floor debate and makes amendments easier.
   c) a closed rule allows journalists and members of the public to listen to debates about a bill, whereas an open rule prevents journalists and members of the public from listening to debates about the bill.
   d) an open rule allows journalists and members of the public to listen to debates about a bill, whereas a closed rule prevents journalists and members of the public from listening to debates about the bill.

9. Which of the following is not a technique that can be used to block debate about a bill in the Senate? *(pp. 459–60)*
   a) filibuster
   b) the introduction of new amendments
   c) cloture
   d) placing holds on bills

How Congress Decides

10. Which of the following is *not* an important influence on how members of Congress vote on legislation? *(p. 462)*
    a) the media
    b) constituency
    c) interest groups
    d) party leaders

11. Which of the following is *not* a resource that party leaders in Congress use to create party discipline? *(pp. 465–67)*
    a) committee assignments
    b) access to the floor
    c) the whip system
    d) roll-call votes

12. An agreement between members of Congress to trade support for each other's bills is known as *(p. 468)*
    a) oversight.
    b) filibuster.
    c) logrolling.
    d) patronage.

Beyond Legislation: Other Congressional Powers

13. When Congress conducts an investigation to explore the relationship between what a law intended and what an executive agency has done, it is engaged in *(p. 471)*
    a) oversight.
    b) advice and consent.
    c) executive agreement.
    d) direct patronage.

14. Which of the following statements about impeachment is *not* true? *(p. 473)*
    a) The president is the only official who can be impeached by Congress.
    b) The House of Representatives decides by simple majority vote whether the accused ought to be impeached.
    c) The Senate decides whether to convict and remove the person from office.
    d) There have only been two instances of impeachment in American history.

Thinking Critically about Congress and Democracy

15. What is the difference between a member of Congress acting as a delegate and a member of Congress acting as a trustee? *(p. 475)*
    a) A member of Congress acting as a delegate votes based on what he or she believes is best for the district they represent, whereas a member of Congress acting as a trustee votes according to the preferences of his or her constituency.
    b) A member of Congress acting as a delegate votes according to the preferences of his or her constituency, whereas a member of Congress acting as a trustee votes based on what he or she believes is best for the district they represent.
    c) A member of Congress acting as a delegate votes based on what the president tells him or her to do, whereas a member of Congress acting as a trustee votes according to what party leaders tell him or her to do.
    d) A member of Congress acting as a delegate votes based on what party leaders tell him or her to do, whereas a member of Congress acting as a trustee votes according to what the president tells him or her to do.

Chapter Outline

Find a detailed Chapter Outline on the StudySpace
Web site: www.wwnorton.com/we-the-people

Key Terms

Find Flashcards to help you study these terms on the
StudySpace Web site: www.wwnorton.com/we-the-people

agency representation *(p. 438)*
apportionment *(p. 445)*
appropriations *(p. 471)*
bicameral *(p. 437)*
bill *(p. 457)*
caucus (congressional) *(p. 456)*
caucus (political) *(p. 449)*
closed rule *(p. 459)*
cloture *(p. 459)*
committee markup *(p. 457)*
conference *(p. 449)*
conference committee *(p. 454)*
constituency *(p. 437)*
delegate *(p. 475)*

executive agreement *(p. 472)*
filibuster *(p. 459)*
gerrymandering *(p. 446)*
impeachment *(p. 473)*
incumbency *(p. 443)*
joint committee *(p. 454)*
logrolling *(p. 468)*
majority leader *(p. 450)*
minority leader *(p. 450)*
open rule *(p. 459)*
oversight *(p. 471)*
party unity vote *(p. 465)*
patronage *(p. 447)*
pocket veto *(p. 462)*

pork barrel (or pork) *(p. 447)*
private bill *(p. 448)*
redistricting *(p. 446)*
roll-call vote *(p. 465)*
select committee *(p. 453)*
seniority *(p. 454)*
sociological representation *(p. 438)*
Speaker of the House *(p. 450)*
staff agency *(p. 456)*
standing committee *(p. 452)*
term limits *(p. 444)*
trustee *(p. 475)*
veto *(p. 461)*
whip *(p. 450)*

For Further Reading

Adler, E. Scott. *Why Congressional Reforms Fail.* Chicago: University of Chicago Press, 2002.

Dodd, Lawrence C. and Bruce I. Oppenheimer, eds. *Congress Reconsidered.* 9th ed. Washington, DC: Congressional Quarterly Press, 2008.

Dodson, Debra L. *The Impact of Women in Congress.* New York: Oxford University Press, 2006.

Fenno, Richard F. *Homestyle: House Members in Their Districts.* Boston: Little, Brown, 1978.

Fiorina, Morris. *Congress: Keystone of the Washington Establishment.* 2nd ed. New Haven, CT: Yale University Press, 1989.

Fowler, Linda, and Robert McClure. *Political Ambition: Who Decides to Run for Congress?* New Haven, CT: Yale University Press, 1989.

Hamilton, Lee. *How Congress Works.* Bloomington: Indiana University Press, 2004.

Koger, Gregory. *Filibustering: A Political History of Obstruction in the House and Senate.* Chicago: University of Chicago Press, 2010.

Mann, Thomas E., and Norman J. Ornstein. *The Broken Branch: How Congress Is Failing America and How to Get It Back on Track.* New York: Oxford University Press, 2006.

Mayhew, David R. *Congress: The Electoral Connection.* New Haven, CT: Yale University Press, 1974.

Palmer, Barbara, and Denise Simon. *Breaking the Political Glass Ceiling: Women and Congressional Elections.* 2nd ed. New York: Routledge, 2008.

Redman, Eric. *The Dance of Legislation.* Seattle: University of Washington Press, 2001.

Recommended Web Sites

Cook Political Report
www.cookpolitical.com

The Cook Political Report, by Charlie Cook, is a nonpartisan analysis of electoral politics. Check out current House and Senate races for an in-depth analysis of past elections and previews of future congressional elections.

Library of Congress: Thomas
http://thomas.loc.gov

The Library of Congress's "Thomas" Web site is a superb place to find information about the U.S. Congress. Roll-call votes, current legislation, the full text of the *Congressional Record*, and committee reports are just a few of the archives you will find.

National Committee for an Effective Congress
www.ourcampaigns.com

Congressional redistricting is the process of redrawing House districts every ten years to account for shifts in population. For information about redistricting in your state, log on to the Redistricting Resource Center, provided by the National Committee for an Effective Congress.

Roll Call
www.rollcall.com

Roll Call, the newspaper of Capitol Hill, provides daily coverage on the members, legislation, and events taking place in and around the U.S. legislature.

The Sunlight Foundation and Taxpayers for Common Sense
http://earmarkwatch.org

Earmarks are language that members of Congress put into legislation that dedicates funds for specific uses, many whose broad benefits can be questioned. The Sunlight Foundation and Taxpayers for Common Sense are two watchdog groups that have joined forces to publish a database of congressional earmarks. Earmarks can be searched by state, congressional sponsor, recipient, and description of the project.

U.S. House of Representatives
www.house.gov
U.S. Senate
www.senate.gov

These are the official Web sites for the U.S. House of Representatives and the U.S. Senate. Here you can find information on your members of Congress, key congressional leaders, bills currently under consideration, and legislative committees.

Shortly after taking office in 2009, President Barack Obama signed the American Recovery and Reinvestment Act bill, which provided $787 billion to help stimulate the economy. As a new president, Obama inherited numerous challenges—like the economic recession—as well as vast powers.

13

The Presidency

WHAT GOVERNMENT DOES AND WHY IT MATTERS When the Obama administration took office in 2008, it inherited a host of problems and powers from its predecessor. Among the most important of these problems were the ongoing wars in Iraq and Afghanistan, continuing fears of terrorism, and the economic woes afflicting America and the world. During the 2008 campaigns, all the candidates had pledged to find new solutions to the global challenges facing America. And with the election over, Americans hoped for the best. Yet, in his first years in office, President Obama found the nation's problems to be difficult to solve. Despite a massive economic stimulus package, levels of unemployment remained high and the health of the nation's financial and housing markets remained in doubt. The war in Afghanistan ground on with the administration searching for a strategy that might bring an end to the conflict. And, as Americans were reminded by an attempt to smuggle powerful bombs onto two airplanes in October, 2010, the threat of terrorism had not been ended. And, of course, Obama encountered new problems such as the

focusquestions

- What powers does the Constitution give the president?

- What institutional resources do presidents have to help them exercise their powers?

- How have modern presidents become even more powerful?

- What are the implications of presidential government for democracy?

massive Gulf of Mexico oil spill in 2010 that threatened to become one of history's worst environmental disasters.

The new president also inherited a presidency vastly more powerful than the institution imagined by the framers of the U.S. Constitution. Ironically, the same wars that presented such an enormous challenge to the new administration also had the potential to enhance its power.

Presidential power generally seems to increase during times of war. For example, President Abraham Lincoln's 1862 declaration of martial law and Congress's 1863 legislation giving the president the power to make arrests and imprisonments through military tribunals amounted to a "constitutional dictatorship" that lasted through the Civil War and Lincoln's re-election in 1864. During World War II, Franklin Delano Roosevelt, like Lincoln, did not bother to wait for Congress but took executive action first and expected Congress to follow. One dissenter on the Supreme Court called the president's assumption of emergency powers "a loaded weapon ready for the hand of any authority that can bring forward a plausible claim of an urgent need."

The "loaded weapon" was seized again in September 2001, when Congress defined the World Trade Center and Pentagon attacks as an act of war and adopted a joint resolution authorizing the president to use "all necessary and appropriate force" against those responsible for the attacks. On the basis of this authorization, President Bush ordered the invasion of Afghanistan and began the reorganization of the nation's "homeland security." President Obama rescinded some Bush-era policies but disappointed many civil libertarians as he continued Bush's policy of vigorously asserting national security needs and government secrecy claims to block lawsuits and press access to information regarding the treatment of terror suspects.[1]

In this chapter, we examine the foundations of the American presidency and assess the origins and character of presidential power in the twenty-first century. National emergencies are one source of presidential power, but presidents are also empowered by democratic political processes and, increasingly, by their ability to control and expand institutional resources of the office.

chaptercontents

The Constitutional Basis of the Presidency

● What powers does the Constitution give the president?

The presidency was established by Article II of the Constitution, which begins by asserting, "The executive power shall be vested in a President of the United States of America." It goes on to describe the manner in which the president is to be chosen and defines the basic powers of the presidency. By vesting the executive power in a single president, the framers were emphatically rejecting proposals for various forms of collective leadership. Some delegates to the Constitutional Convention had argued in favor of a multiheaded executive or an "executive council" in order to avoid undue concentration of power in the hands of one individual. Most of the framers, however, were anxious to provide for "energy" in the executive. They hoped to have a president capable of taking quick and aggressive action. These framers thought a unitary executive would be more energetic than some form of collective leadership. They believed that a powerful executive would help to protect the nation's interests vis-à-vis other nations and promote the federal government's interests relative to the states.

The presidential selection process defined by Article II resulted from a struggle between those delegates who wanted the president to be selected by, and thus be responsible to, Congress and those delegates who preferred that the president be elected directly by the people. Direct popular election would create a more independent and more powerful presidency. With the adoption of a scheme of indirect election through an electoral college in which the electors would be selected by the state legislatures (and close elections would be resolved in the House of Representatives), the framers hoped to achieve a "republican" solution: a strong president responsible to state and national legislators rather than directly to the electorate. This indirect method of electing the president probably did dampen the power of most presidents in the nineteenth century.

The framers of the Constitution wanted an "energetic" presidency, capable of quick, decisive action. However, when George Washington was sworn in as the first president in 1789, the presidency was a less powerful office than it is today.

The presidency was strengthened somewhat in the 1830s with the introduction of the national convention system of nominating presidential candidates. Until then, presidential candidates had been nominated by their party's congressional delegates. This was the **caucus** system of nominating candidates, derisively called "King Caucus" because any candidate for president was beholden to the party's leaders in Congress to get the party's nomination and the support of the party's congressional delegation in the presidential election. The national nominating convention arose outside Congress to provide some representation for a party's voters who lived in districts where they weren't numerous enough to elect a member of Congress. The political party in each state made its own provisions for selecting delegates to attend the presidential nominating convention, and in virtually all states the selection was dominated by the party leaders. Only in recent decades have state laws intervened to regularize the selection process and to provide (in all but a few instances) for open election of delegates. The convention system quickly became the most popular method of nominating candidates for all elective offices and remained so until well into the twentieth century, when it succumbed to the criticism that it was a nondemocratic method dominated by a few leaders in a "smoke-filled room." But during the nineteenth century, it was seen as a victory for democracy against the congressional elite. And the national convention gave the presidency a base of power independent of Congress.

This additional independence did not immediately transform the presidency into the office familiar to us today, but the national convention did begin to open the presidency to larger social forces and newly organized interests in society. In other words, it gave the presidency a mass popular base that would eventually support and demand increased presidential power. Improvements in the telephone, the telegraph, and other forms of mass communication allowed individuals to share their complaints and allowed national leaders—especially presidents and presidential candidates—to reach out directly to people to ally themselves with, and even sometimes to create, popular groups and forces. Eventually, though more slowly, the presidential selection process began to be further democratized, with the adoption of primary elections through which millions of ordinary citizens were given an opportunity to take part in the presidential nominating process by popular selection of convention delegates.

But despite political and social conditions favoring the enhancement of the presidency, the development of presidential government as we know it today did not mature until the middle of the twentieth century. For a long period, even as the national government began to grow, Congress was careful to keep tight reins on the president's power. The real turning point in the history of American national government came during the administration of Franklin Delano Roosevelt. Since FDR and his "New Deal" of the 1930s, every president has been strong whether he was committed to the strong presidency or not.

● The Constitutional Powers of the Presidency

Whereas Section 1 of Article II explains how the president is to be chosen, Sections 2 and 3 outline the powers and duties of the president. These two sections identify two sources of presidential power. Some presidential powers are specifically established by the language of the Constitution. For example, the president is authorized to make treaties, grant pardons, and nominate judges and other public officials. These specifically defined powers are called the **expressed powers** of the office and cannot be revoked by Congress or any other agency without an amendment to the Constitution. Other expressed powers include the power to receive ambassadors and the command of the military forces of the United States.

In addition to the president's expressed powers, Article II declares that the president, "shall take Care that the Laws be faithfully executed." Since the laws are enacted by Congress, this language implies that Congress is to delegate to the president the power to implement or execute its will. Powers given to the president by Congress are called **delegated powers**. In principle, Congress delegates to the president only the power to identify or develop the means through which to carry out its decisions. So, for example, if Congress determines that air quality should be improved, it might delegate to a bureaucratic agency in the executive branch the power to identify the best means of bringing about such an improvement as well as the power actually to implement the cleanup process. In practice, of course, decisions about how to clean the air are likely to have an enormous impact on businesses, organizations, and individuals throughout the nation. As it delegates power to the executive, Congress substantially enhances the importance of the presidency and the executive branch. In most cases, Congress delegates power to bureaucratic agencies in the executive branch rather than to the president. As we shall see,

expressed powers specific powers granted by the Constitution to Congress (Article I, Section 8), and to the president (Article II)

delegated powers constitutional powers that are assigned to one governmental agency but that are exercised by another agency with the express permission of the first

The term imperial presidency *was popularized in 1973 by a book of that name written during the Vietnam era. President Lyndon B. Johnson, pictured here greeting American troops in Vietnam, believed that his presidential powers allowed, through the Gulf of Tonkin Resolution, any of the nation's resources to be used to fight the war in Vietnam.*

however, contemporary presidents have found ways to capture a good deal of this delegated power for themselves.

Presidents have claimed a third source of power beyond expressed and delegated powers. These are powers not specified in the Constitution or the law but said to stem from "the rights, duties and obligations of the presidency."[2] They are referred to as the **inherent powers** of the presidency and are most often asserted by presidents in times of war or national emergency. For example, after the fall of Fort Sumter and the outbreak of the Civil War, President Abraham Lincoln issued a series of executive orders for which he had no clear legal basis. Without even calling Congress into session, Lincoln combined the state militias into a ninety-day national volunteer force, called for 40,000 new volunteers, enlarged the regular army and navy, diverted $2 million in unspent appropriations to military needs, instituted censorship of the U.S. mails, ordered a blockade of southern ports, suspended the writ of habeas corpus in the border states, and ordered the arrest by military police of individuals whom he deemed to be guilty of engaging in or even contemplating treasonous actions.[3] Lincoln asserted that these extraordinary measures were justified by the president's inherent power to protect the nation.[4] Subsequent presidents, including Franklin Delano Roosevelt and George W. Bush, have had similar views.

Expressed Powers

The president's expressed powers, as defined by Sections 2 and 3 of Article II, fall into several categories:

1. *Military.* Article II, Section 2, provides for the power as "Commander in Chief of the Army and Navy of the United States, and of the Militia of the several States, when called in to the actual Service of the United States."

2. *Judicial.* Article II, Section 2, also provides the power to "grant Reprieves and Pardons for Offences against the United States, except in Cases of Impeachment."

3. *Diplomatic.* Article II, Section 2, also provides the power "by and with the Advice and Consent of the Senate to make Treaties." Article II, Section 3, provides the power to "receive Ambassadors and other public Ministers."

4. *Executive.* Article II, Section 3, authorizes the president to see to it that all the laws are faithfully executed; Section 2 gives the chief executive power to appoint, remove, and supervise all executive officers and to appoint all federal judges.

5. *Legislative.* Article I, Section 7 and Article II, Section 3 give the president the power to participate authoritatively in the legislative process.

Military The president's military powers are among the most important exercised by the chief executive. The position of **commander in chief** makes the president the highest military authority in the United States, with control of the entire defense establishment. The president is also head of the nation's intelligence network, which includes not only the Central Intelligence Agency (CIA) but also the National Security Council (NSC), the National Security Agency (NSA), the Federal Bureau of Investigation (FBI), and a host of less well known but very powerful international and domestic security agencies.

---

inherent powers powers claimed by a president that are not expressed in the Constitution, but are inferred from it

commander in chief the role of the president as commander of the national military and the state national guard units (when called into service)

The President versus the World: How Presidents Seized Control of the War Power

The 1973 War Powers Resolution provided that presidents could not deploy military forces for more than sixty days without securing congressional authorization. Many in Congress saw this time limit as a restraint on presidential action, though it gave the president more discretion than the framers of the Constitution had provided. President Gerald Ford had carefully followed the letter of the law when organizing a military effort to rescue American sailors held by North Korea. But this was the first and last time that the War Powers Act was fully observed. Between 1982 and 1986, President Reagan presented Congress with a set of military *faits accomplis* that undermined the War Powers Act and, in effect, asserted a doctrine of sole presidential authority in the security realm.

In October 1983, while American forces were still in Lebanon, President Reagan ordered an invasion of the Caribbean island of Grenada after a coup had led to the installation of a pro-Cuban government on the island. Congress threatened to invoke the War Powers Act, but Reagan withdrew American troops before the Senate acted. In 1986, Reagan ordered the bombing of Libya in response to a terrorist attack in Berlin that the administration blamed on Libyan agents. In both cases, Reagan acted without consulting Congress and claimed that his authority had come directly from the Constitution.

Reagan's successor, George H. W. Bush, ordered an invasion of Panama designed to oust the Panamanian strongman General Manuel Noriega. Congress made no official response to the invasion. In 1990–91, the Bush administration sent a huge American military force into the Persian Gulf in response to Iraq's invasion and occupation of Kuwait. Both houses of Congress voted to authorize military action against Iraq, but Bush made it clear that he did not feel bound by any congressional declaration. Indeed, the president later pointed out that he had specifically avoided asking Capitol Hill for "authorization" since such a request might improperly imply that Congress "had the final say in . . . an executive decision."[a]

In 1994, President Clinton planned an invasion of Haiti under the cover of a UN Security Council resolution. Congress expressed strong opposition to Clinton's plans, but he pressed forward nonetheless, claiming that he did not need congressional approval. In a similar vein, between 1994 and 1998, the administration undertook a variety of military actions in the former Yugoslavia without formal congressional authorization.

In 2001, President George W. Bush ordered an attack that soon toppled Afghanistan's Taliban regime. In 2003, Bush sent American forces to oust Saddam Hussein's government in Iraq. Bush had congressional support for his actions but, like his predecessors, asserted that he did not need Congress's permission to undertake military action. It is no longer clear what war powers, if any, remain in the hands of Congress.

[a]George H. W. Bush and Brent Scowcroft, *A World Transformed* (New York: Knopf, 1998), 441.

for critical analysis

1. Article I of the Constitution gives Congress the power to declare war. Why have modern presidents consistently refrained from asking Congress for such a declaration?

2. The late Edward Corwin said that the Constitution invited the president and Congress to struggle over war powers. What advantages have allowed presidents gradually to prevail in this struggle over the past century?

War and Inherent Presidential Power The Constitution gives Congress the power to declare war. Presidents, however, have gone a long way toward capturing this power for themselves. Congress has not declared war since December 1941, but since then, American military forces have engaged in numerous campaigns throughout the world under the orders of the president. When North Korean forces invaded South Korea in June 1950, Congress was actually prepared to declare war, but President Harry S. Truman decided not to ask for congressional action. Instead, Truman asserted that the president and not Congress could decide when and where to deploy America's military might. Truman dispatched American forces to Korea without a congressional declaration, and in the face of the emergency, Congress felt it had to acquiesce. Congress passed a resolution approving the president's actions, and this became the pattern for future congressional-executive relations in the military realm. The wars in Vietnam, Bosnia, Afghanistan, and Iraq, as well as a host of lesser conflicts, were all fought without declarations of war.

In 1973, Congress responded to presidential unilateralism by passing the **War Powers Resolution** over President Nixon's veto. This resolution reasserted the principle of congressional war power, required the president to inform Congress of any planned military campaign, and stipulated that forces must be withdrawn within sixty days in the absence of a specific congressional authorization for their continued deployment. Presidents, however, have generally ignored the War Powers Resolution, claiming inherent executive power to defend the nation. Thus, President George W. Bush responded to the 2001 attacks by Islamic terrorists by organizing a major military campaign to overthrow the Taliban regime in Afghanistan, which had sheltered the terrorists. In 2003, Bush ordered a major American campaign against Iraq, which he accused of posing a threat to the United States. U.S. forces overthrew the government of the Iraqi dictator, Saddam Hussein, and occupied the country. In both instances, Congress passed resolutions approving the president's actions, but the president was careful to assert that he did not need congressional authorization. The War Powers Resolution was barely mentioned on Capitol Hill and was ignored by the White House.

War Powers Resolution
a resolution of Congress that the president can send troops into action abroad only by authorization of Congress, or if American troops are already under attack or serious threat

In 2010, President Obama visited American troops in Afghanistan. A few months earlier, Obama ordered a "surge" of 30,000 reinforcements to be sent to Afghanistan. Although the strategy was controversial, even among Obama's own party, Congress approved funding for the increase in troops.

● What powers does
the Constitution
give the president?

Military Sources of Domestic Power The president's military powers extend into the domestic sphere. Article IV, Section 4, provides that the "United States shall [protect] every State . . . against Invasion . . . and . . . domestic Violence." Congress has made this an explicit presidential power through statutes directing the president as commander in chief to discharge these obligations.[5] The Constitution restrains the president's use of domestic force by providing that a state legislature (or governor when the legislature is not in session) must request federal troops before the president can send them into the state to provide public order. Yet this proviso is not absolute. First, presidents are not obligated to deploy national troops merely because the state legislature or governor makes such a request. And more important, the president may deploy troops in a state or city without a specific request from the state legislature or governor if the president considers it necessary to maintain an essential national service during an emergency, to enforce a federal judicial order, or to protect federally guaranteed civil rights.

One historic example of the unilateral use of presidential emergency power to protect the states against domestic disorder, even when the states don't request it, was the decision by President Dwight D. Eisenhower in 1957 to send troops into Little Rock, Arkansas, literally against the wishes of the state of Arkansas, to enforce court orders to integrate Little Rock's Central High School. The governor of Arkansas, Orval Faubus, had posted the Arkansas National Guard at the entrance to Central High School to prevent the court-ordered admission of nine black students. After an effort to negotiate with Governor Faubus failed, President Eisenhower reluctantly sent a thousand paratroopers to Little Rock; they stood watch while the black students took their places in the all-white classrooms. This case makes quite clear that the president does not have to wait for a request by a state legislature or governor before acting as a domestic commander in chief.[6]

However, in most instances of domestic disorder—whether from human or from natural causes—presidents tend to exercise unilateral power by declaring a "state of emergency," thereby making available federal grants, insurance, and direct assistance. In 1992, in the aftermath of the devastating riots in Los Angeles and the hurricanes in Florida, American troops were very much in evidence, sent in by the president, but more in the role of Good Samaritans than of military police. In 2005, President Bush declared a state of emergency to allow the Federal Emergency Management Agency (FEMA) to coordinate the government's response to Hurricane Katrina, an immense storm that devastated the city of New Orleans. Bush sent federal troops to bolster local efforts.

Military emergencies have typically also led to expansion of the domestic powers of the executive branch. This was true during the First and Second World Wars and has been true in the wake of the "war on terrorism" as well. Within a month of the September 11 attacks, the White House had drafted and Congress had enacted the USA PATRIOT Act, expanding the power of government agencies to engage in domestic surveillance activities, including electronic surveillance, and restricting judicial review of such efforts. The act also gave the attorney general greater authority to detain and deport aliens suspected of having terrorist affiliations. The following year, Congress created the Department of Homeland Security, combining offices from twenty-two federal agencies into one huge new cabinet department that would be responsible for protecting the nation from attack and responding to natural disasters. The new agency includes the Coast Guard, Transportation Safety Administration, Federal Emergency Management Administration, Immigration and Naturalization Service, and offices from the departments of Agriculture, Energy, Transportation, Justice, Health and Human Services, Commerce, and the General

The Roles of the President

Chief of State (acting on behalf of all Americans)

Commander in Chief (in charge of military)

Chief Jurist (judicial responsibilities)

Chief Diplomat (managing our relations with other nations)

Chief Executive (as "boss" of executive branch)

Chief Legislator (legislative powers)

Chief Politician (party leadership)

As head of state, the president is America's chief representative in dealings with other countries. At the first official state dinner, President Obama and Michelle Obama welcomed India's prime minister, Manmohan Singh, and his wife, Gursharan Kaur, to the White House.

Services Administration. The actual reorganization plan was drafted by the White House, but Congress weighed in to make certain that the new agency's workers had civil service and union protections.

Judicial The presidential power to grant reprieves, pardons, and amnesties involves power over all individuals who may be a threat to the security of the United States. Presidents may use this power on behalf of a particular individual, as did Gerald Ford when he pardoned Richard Nixon in 1974 "for all offenses against the United States which he . . . has committed or may have committed." Or they may use it on a large scale, as did President Andrew Johnson in 1868, when he gave full amnesty to all southerners who had participated in the "Late Rebellion," and President Carter in 1977, when he declared an amnesty for all the draft evaders of the Vietnam War. President Clinton issued a number of controversial individual pardons during his last weeks in office. President Bush, on the other hand, seldom issued pardons.[7] This power of life and death over others helped elevate the president to the level of earlier conquerors and kings by establishing him or her as the person before whom supplicants might come to make their pleas for mercy.

Diplomatic The president is America's "head of state"—its chief representative in dealings with other nations. As head of state the president has the power to make treaties for the United States (with the advice and consent of the Senate). When President Washington received Edmond Genêt ("Citizen Genêt") as the formal emissary of the revolutionary government of France in 1793 and had his cabinet officers and Congress back his decision, he established a greatly expanded interpretation of the power to "receive Ambassadors and other public Ministers," extending it to the power to "recognize" other countries. That power gives the president the almost unconditional authority to review the claims of any new ruling groups to determine whether they indeed control the territory and population of their country, so that they can commit it to treaties and other agreements.

In recent years, presidents have expanded the practice of using executive agreements instead of treaties to establish relations with other countries.[8] An **executive agreement** is exactly like a treaty because it is a contract between two countries, but an executive agreement does not require a two-thirds vote of approval by the Senate. There are actually two types of executive agreements. One is the executive-congressional agreement. For this type of agreement, the president will submit the proposed arrangement to Congress for a simple majority vote in both houses, usually easier for presidents to win than the two-thirds approval of the Senate that is required. The other type of executive agreement is the sole executive agreement, which is simply an understanding between the president and a foreign state and is not submitted to Congress for its approval. In the past, sole executive agreements were used to flesh out commitments already made in treaties or to arrange for matters well below the level of policy. Since the 1930s, however, presidents have entered into sole executive agreements on important issues when they were uncertain about their prospects for securing congressional approval of an agreement. For example, the General Agreement on Tariffs and Trade (GATT), one of the cornerstones of U.S. international economic policy in the post–World War II era, was based on an executive agreement. The courts have held that executive agreements have the force of law, as though they were formal treaties.

During the 1960s, Congress discovered that several presidents had entered into agreements with foreign governments and not informed Congress. This discovery led to the enactment of the 1972 Case-Zablocki Act, requiring the president to provide Congress each year with a complete list of all executive agreements signed during the course of that year. Presidents have not fully complied with this law. If they wish to keep an agreement secret, they call it by another name, such as "national security memorandum," and claim that it is not covered by the Case act.

Executive Power The most important basis of the president's power as chief executive is to be found in Article II, Section 3, which stipulates that the president must see that all the laws are faithfully executed, and Section 2, which provides that the president will appoint, remove, and supervise all executive officers, and appoint all federal judges (with Senate approval). The power to appoint the principal executive officers and to require each of them to report to the president on subjects relating to the duties of their departments makes the president the true chief executive officer (CEO) of the nation. In this manner, the Constitution focuses executive power and legal responsibility on the president. The famous sign on President Truman's desk, "The buck stops here," was not merely an assertion of Truman's personal sense of responsibility but was in fact his recognition of the legal and constitutional responsibility of the president. The president is subject to some limitations, because the appointment of all such officers, including ambassadors, ministers, and federal judges, is subject to a majority approval by the Senate. But these appointments are at the discretion of the president, and the loyalty and the responsibility of each appointee are presumed to be directed toward the president.

executive agreement an agreement, made between the president and another country, that has the force of a treaty but does not require the Senate's "advice and consent"

The Supreme Court's decision in U.S. v. Nixon is often seen as a blow to presidential power because Nixon was required to turn over secret tapes related to the Watergate scandal, despite his claim of executive privilege.

executive privilege the claim that confidential communications between a president and close advisers should not be revealed without the consent of the president

Another component of the president's power as chief executive is **executive privilege**. Executive privilege is the claim that confidential communications between a president and close advisers should not be revealed without the consent of the president. Presidents have made this claim ever since George Washington refused a request from the House of Representatives to deliver documents concerning negotiations of an important treaty. Washington refused (successfully) on the grounds that, first, the House was not constitutionally part of the treaty-making process and that, second, that diplomatic negotiations required secrecy.

Although many presidents have claimed executive privilege, the concept was not tested in the courts until the 1971 "Watergate" affair. President Richard Nixon refused congressional demands that he turn over secret White House tapes that congressional investigators thought would establish Nixon's complicity in illegal activities. In *United States v. Nixon* (418 U.S. 683, 1974), the Supreme Court ordered Nixon to turn over the tapes. The president complied with the order and was forced to resign from office. The *U.S. v. Nixon* case is often seen as a blow to presidential power but, in actuality, the Court's ruling recognized for the first time the validity of a claim of executive privilege, though holding that it did not apply in this particular instance. Subsequent presidents have cited *U.S. v. Nixon* in support of their claims of executive privilege. For example, the Bush administration successfully invoked executive privilege when it refused congressional demands for records of Vice President Dick Cheney's 2001 energy task force meetings.

The President's Legislative Power The president plays a role not only in the administration of government but also in the legislative process. Two constitutional provisions are the primary sources of the president's power in the legislative arena. The first of these is the portion of Article II, Section 3, providing that the president "shall from time to time give to the Congress Information of the State of the Union, and recommend to their Consideration such Measures as he shall judge necessary and expedient." The second of the president's legislative powers is the veto power assigned by Article I, Section 7.[9]

Delivering a "State of the Union" address does not at first appear to be of any great import. It is a mere obligation of the president to make recommendations for Congress's consideration. But as political and social conditions began to favor an increasingly prominent role for presidents, each president, especially since Franklin Delano Roosevelt, began to rely on this provision to become the primary initiator of proposals for legislative action in Congress and the principal source for public awareness of national issues, as well as the most important single individual participant in legislative decisions. Few today doubt that the president and the executive branch together are the primary source for many important congressional actions.[10]

veto the president's constitutional power to turn down acts of Congress. A presidential veto may be overridden by a two-thirds vote of each house of Congress

pocket veto a presidential veto that is automatically triggered if the president does not act on a given piece of legislation passed during the final ten days of a legislative session

The **veto** is the president's constitutional power to turn down acts of Congress (see Figure 13.1). It makes the president the most important single legislative leader.[11] No bill vetoed by the president can become law unless both the House and Senate override the veto by a two-thirds vote. In the case of a **pocket veto**, Congress does not have the option of overriding the veto, but must reintroduce the bill in the next session. A pocket veto can occur when the president is presented with a bill during the last ten days of a legislative session. Usually, if a president does not sign a bill within ten days, it automatically becomes law. But this is true only while Congress is in session. If a president chooses not to sign a bill presented within the last ten days of a legislative session, then Congress is out of session when the ten-day limit expires, and instead of becoming law, the bill is vetoed. Use of the veto varies according to the political situation that each president confronts. George W. Bush did not find it necessary to use his veto until 2007, when the Democrats

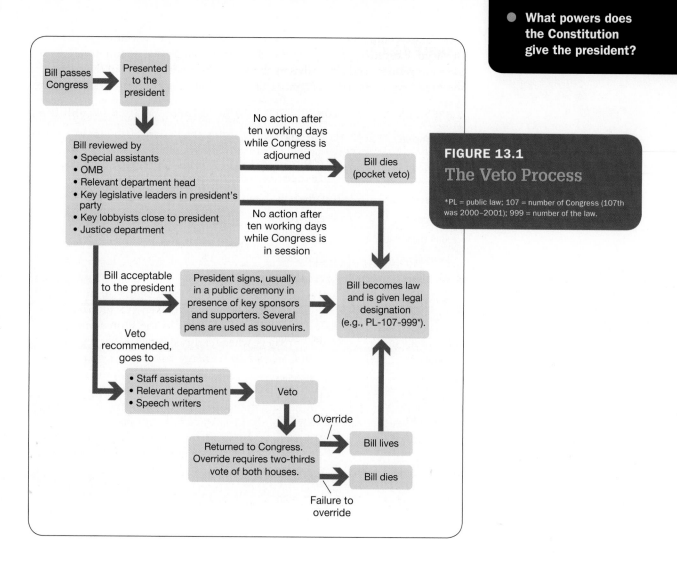

FIGURE 13.1
The Veto Process

*PL = public law; 107 = number of Congress (107th was 2000–2001); 999 = number of the law.

controlled both houses of Congress. During his last two years in office Bush vetoed eleven bills, including legislation designed to prohibit the use of harsh interrogation tactics, saying it "would take away one of the most valuable tools in the war on terror."[12] President Obama, who during his first two years in office enjoyed solid Democratic majorities in both houses of Congress, used his veto power only once during his first year, and that was to send back to Congress a stopgap spending bill enacted in December 2009 in case a winter storm prevented Congress from approving a defense bill. The actual bill was approved and the stopgap was no longer needed. As shown by Table 13.1, presidential vetoes are seldom overridden. Since the time of George Washington, presidents have used their veto power 2,560 times and on only 109 occasions has Congress overridden them.

Although this power is not explicitly stated, the Constitution also provides the president with the power of **legislative initiative**. The framers of the Constitution clearly saw legislative initiative as one of the keys to executive power. Initiative implies the ability to formulate proposals for important policies, and the president, as an individual with a great deal of staff assistance, is able to initiate decisive action more frequently than Congress, with its large assemblies that have to deliberate and debate before taking action. With some important exceptions, Congress banks

legislative initiative the president's inherent power to bring a legislative agenda before Congress

TABLE 13.1

Presidential Vetoes (1789–2008)

PRESIDENT	CONGRESSES	TOTAL VETOES	VETOES OVERRIDDEN
Washington	1st–4th	2	.....
Adams	5th–6th	.....	.....
Jefferson	7th–10th	.....	.....
Madison	11th–14th	7	.....
Monroe	15th–18th	1	.....
John Quincy Adams	19th–20th	.....	.....
Jackson	21st–24th	12	.....
Van Buren	25th–26th	1	.....
Harrison	27th	.....	.....
Tyler	27th–28th	10	1
Polk	29th–30th	3	.....
Taylor	31st	.....	.....
Fillmore	31st–32nd	.....	.....
Pierce	33rd–34th	9	5
Buchanan	35th–36th	7	.....
Lincoln	37th–39th	7	.....
Johnson	39th–40th	29	15
Grant	41st–44th	93	4
Hayes	45th–46th	13	1
Garfield	47th	.....	.....
Arthur	47th–48th	12	1
Cleveland	49th–50th	414	2
Harrison	51st–52nd	44	1
Cleveland	53rd–54th	170	5
McKinley	55th–57th	42	.....
Theodore Roosevelt	57th–60th	82	1
Taft	61st–62nd	39	1
Wilson	63rd–66th	44	6
Harding	67th	6	.....
Coolidge	68th–70th	50	4
Hoover	71st–72nd	37	3
Franklin D. Roosevelt	73rd–79th	635	9
Truman	79th–82nd	250	12
Eisenhower	83rd–86th	181	2
Kennedy	87th–88th	21	.....

(Continued on next page)

PRESIDENT	CONGRESSES	TOTAL VETOES	VETOES OVERRIDDEN
Johnson	88th–90st	30	.....
Nixon	91st–93rd	43	7
Ford	93rd–94th	66	12
Carter	95th–96th	31	2
Reagan	97th–100th	78	9
George H. W. Bush	101st–102nd	44	1
Clinton	103rd–106th	37	2
George W. Bush	107th–110th	10	3
Total	....	**2560**	**109**

on the president to set the agenda of public policy. And quite clearly, initiative confers power; there is power in being able to set the terms of discourse in the making of public policy.

For example, during the weeks immediately following September 11, George W. Bush took many presidential initiatives to Congress, and each was given almost unanimous support—from commitments to pursue al Qaeda and to the removal of the Taliban, the reconstitution of the Afghanistan regime, all the way to almost unlimited approval for mobilization of both military force and power over the regulation of American civil liberties. In a similar vein, President Obama moved quickly after his election to deal with the nation's financial emergency and to overhaul America's health care system. Congress quickly enacted the $787 billion financial stimulus package proposed by the president. On the matter of health care, however, conflicts broke out between congressional advocates of a variety of competing approaches and the House and Senate passed different bills, which would have to be reconciled in a conference and passed again by both House. However, before the reconciliation process could begin, a surprise victory by Scott Brown, a Republican, in the special election of January 2010 for the seat of Senator Ted Keanedy, who had died the previous August, in Massachusetts deprived Democrats of their previous filibuster-proof majority in the Senate. The president and congressional leaders rethought their strategy and in March 2010, the House passed the Senate version of the bill, eliminating the need for reconciliation.

The president's initiative does not end with policy making involving Congress and the making of laws in the ordinary sense of the term. The president has still another legislative role (in all but name) within the executive branch. This is designated as the power to issue **executive orders**. The executive order is first and foremost simply a normal tool of management, a power that virtually any CEO has to make "company policy"—rules-setting procedures, etiquette, chains of command, functional responsibilities, and so on. But evolving out of this normal management practice is a recognized presidential power to promulgate rules that have the effect and the formal status of legislation. Most presidential executive orders provide for the reorganization of structures and procedures or otherwise direct the affairs of the executive branch—either to be applied across the board to all agencies or applied in some important respect to a single agency or department. One of the most important examples is Executive Order No. 8248, September 8,

executive order a rule or regulation issued by the president that has the effect and formal status of legislation

1939, establishing the divisions of the Executive Office of the President. Another one of equal importance is President Nixon's executive order establishing the Environmental Protection Agency in 1970–71, which included establishment of the Environmental Impact Statement.

This legislative or policy leadership role of the presidency is an institutionalized feature of the office that exists independent of the occupant of the office. That is to say, anyone duly elected president would possess these powers regardless of his or her individual energy or leadership characteristics.[13]

Delegated Powers

Many of the powers exercised by the president and the executive branch are not found in the Constitution but are the products of congressional statutes and resolutions. Over the past century, Congress has voluntarily delegated a great deal of its own legislative authority to the executive branch. To some extent, this delegation of power has been an almost inescapable consequence of the expansion of government activity in the United States since the New Deal. Given the vast range of the federal government's responsibilities, Congress cannot execute and administer all the programs it creates and the laws it enacts. Inevitably, Congress must turn to the hundreds of departments and agencies in the executive branch or, when necessary, create new agencies to implement its goals. Thus, for example, in 2002, when Congress sought to protect America from terrorist attacks, it established a Department of Homeland Security and gave it broad powers in the realms of law enforcement, public health, and immigration. Similarly, in 1970, when Congress enacted legislation designed to improve the nation's air and water quality, it assigned the task of implementing its goals to a new Environmental Protection Agency (EPA) created by an executive order issued by President Nixon. Congress gave the EPA substantial power to set and enforce air- and water-quality standards.

As they implement congressional legislation, federal agencies collectively develop thousands of rules and regulations and issue thousands of orders and findings every year. Agencies interpret Congress's intent, promulgate rules aimed at implementing that intent, and issue orders to individuals, firms, and organizations throughout the nation designed to impel them to conform to the law. When it establishes an agency, Congress sometimes grants it only limited discretionary authority, providing very specific guidelines and standards that must be followed by the administrators charged with the program's implementation. Take the Internal Revenue Service (IRS), for example. Most Americans view the IRS as a powerful agency whose dictates can have an immediate and sometimes unpleasant impact on their lives. Yet congressional tax legislation is very specific and detailed and leaves little to the discretion of IRS administrators.[14] The agency certainly develops numerous rules and procedures to enhance tax collection. It is Congress, however, that establishes the structure of tax liabilities, tax exemptions, and tax deductions that determine each taxpayer's burdens and responsibilities.

In most instances, however, congressional legislation is not very detailed. Often, Congress defines a broad goal or objective and delegates enormous discretionary power to administrators to determine how that goal is to be achieved. For example, the 1970 act creating the Occupational Safety and Health Administration (OSHA) states, as Congress's purpose, "to assure so far as is possible every working man and woman in the nation safe and healthful working conditions." The act, however, neither defines such conditions nor suggests how they might be achieved.[15] The result is that agency administrators have enormous discretionary power to draft rules and regulations that have the effect of law. Indeed, the courts treat these administrative rules like congressional statutes. For all intents and purposes, when Congress creates an agency such as OSHA or the Department of Homeland Security, giving it a broad mandate to achieve some desirable outcome, it transfers its own legislative power to the executive branch.

During the nineteenth and early twentieth centuries, Congress typically wrote laws that provided fairly clear principles and standards to guide executive implementation. For example, the 1923 tariff act empowered the president to increase or decrease duties on certain manufactured goods in order to reduce the difference in costs between domestically produced products and those manufactured abroad. The act authorized the president to make the final determination, but his discretionary authority was quite constrained. The statute listed the criteria the president was to consider, fixed the permissible range of tariff changes, and outlined the procedures to be used to calculate the cost differences between foreign and domestic goods. When an importer challenged a particular executive decision as an abuse of delegated power, the Supreme Court had no difficulty finding that the president was merely acting in accordance with Congress's directives.[16]

At least since the New Deal, however, Congress has tended to give executive agencies broad mandates and to draft legislation that offers few clear standards or guidelines for implementation by the executive. For example, the 1933 National Industrial Recovery Act gave the president the authority to set rules to bring about *fair competition* in key sectors of the economy without ever defining what the term meant or how it was to be achieved.[17] Similarly, the 1938 Agricultural Adjustment Act, which led to a system of commodity price supports and agricultural production restrictions, authorized the secretary of agriculture to make agricultural marketing "orderly" without offering any guidance regarding the commodities to be affected, how markets were to be organized, or how prices should be determined. All these decisions were left to the discretion of the secretary and his agents.[18] This pattern of broad delegation became typical in the ensuing decades. The 1972 Consumer Product Safety Act, for example, authorizes the Consumer Product Safety Commission to reduce unreasonable risk of injury from household products but offers no suggestions to guide the commission's determination of what constitutes reasonable and unreasonable risks or how these are to be reduced.[19]

This shift from the nineteenth-century pattern of relatively well-defined congressional guidelines for administrators to the more contemporary pattern of broad delegations of congressional power to the executive branch is, to be sure, partially a consequence of the great scope and complexity of the tasks that America's contemporary government has undertaken. During much of the nineteenth century, the federal government had relatively few domestic responsibilities and Congress could pay close attention to details. Today, the operation of an enormous executive establishment and literally thousands of programs under varied and changing circumstances requires that administrators be allowed some considerable measure of discretion to carry out their jobs. Nevertheless, the end result is to shift power from Congress to the executive branch.

The Presidency as an Institution

The framers of the Constitution, as we saw, created a unitary executive because they thought this would make the presidency a more energetic institution. Nevertheless, since the ratification of the Constitution, the president has been joined by thousands of officials and staffers who work for, assist, or advise the chief executive

forcriticalanalysis

Presidents have expressed, delegated, and inherent sources of power. Which of the three do you think most accounts for the powers of the presidency?

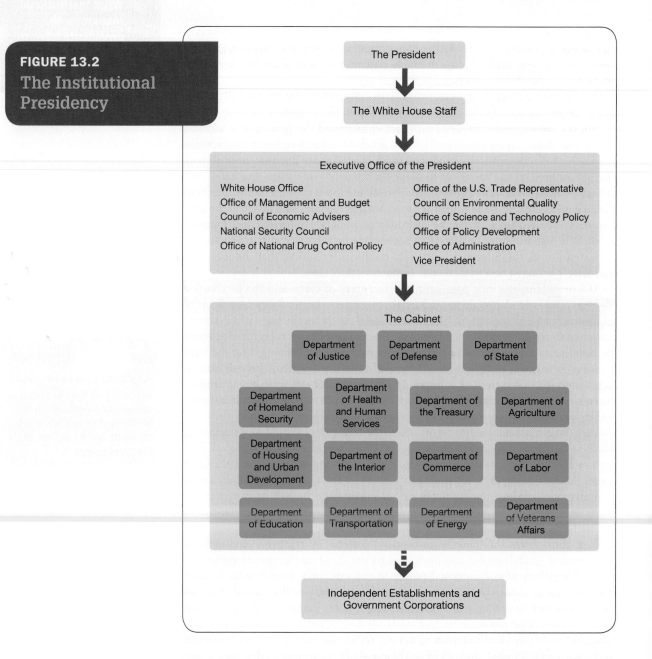

FIGURE 13.2
The Institutional Presidency

The President

The White House Staff

Executive Office of the President

White House Office
Office of Management and Budget
Council of Economic Advisers
National Security Council
Office of National Drug Control Policy

Office of the U.S. Trade Representative
Council on Environmental Quality
Office of Science and Technology Policy
Office of Policy Development
Office of Administration
Vice President

The Cabinet

Department of Justice | Department of Defense | Department of State

Department of Homeland Security | Department of Health and Human Services | Department of the Treasury | Department of Agriculture

Department of Housing and Urban Development | Department of the Interior | Department of Commerce | Department of Labor

Department of Education | Department of Transportation | Department of Energy | Department of Veterans Affairs

Independent Establishments and Government Corporations

(see Figure 13.2). Collectively, these individuals could be said to make up the institutional presidency and to give the president a capacity for action that no single individual, however energetic, could duplicate. The first component of the institutional presidency is the president's Cabinet.

The Cabinet

In the American system of government, the **Cabinet** is the traditional but informal designation for the heads of all the major federal government departments. The Cabinet has no constitutional status. Unlike in Great Britain and many other

Cabinet the secretaries, or chief administrators, of the major departments of the federal government. Cabinet secretaries are appointed by the president with the consent of the Senate

parliamentary countries, where the cabinet *is* the government, the American Cabinet is not a collective body. It meets but makes no decisions as a group. Each appointment must be approved by the Senate, but Cabinet members are not responsible to the Senate or to Congress at large. Cabinet appointments help build party and popular support, but the Cabinet is not a party organ. The Cabinet is made up of directors but is not a true board of directors.

Since Cabinet appointees generally have not shared political careers with the president or with each other, and since they may meet literally for the first time after their selection, the formation of an effective governing group out of this motley collection of appointments is unlikely. Although President Clinton's insistence on a Cabinet diverse enough to resemble American society could be considered an act of political wisdom, it virtually guaranteed that few of his appointees had ever spent much time working together or even knew the policy positions or beliefs of the other appointees.[20]

Some presidents have relied more heavily on an "inner Cabinet," the **National Security Council (NSC)**. The NSC, established by law in 1947, is composed of the president, the vice president, the secretary of state, and the secretary of defense, and other officials invited by the president. It has its own staff of foreign-policy specialists run by the special assistant to the president for national security affairs. For these highest appointments, presidents often turn to people from outside Washington, usually longtime associates. President Obama (at least in his early months in office) relied heavily on his chief of staff, Rahm Emanuel, who resigned in 2010 and was replaced by Pete Rouse; his former chief campaign strategist and now senior advisor, David Axelrod; the deputy chief of staff, Jim Messina; and the press secretary, Robert Gibbs.

Presidents have obviously been uneven and unpredictable in their reliance on the NSC and other subcabinet bodies because executive management is inherently a personal matter. Despite all the personal variations, however, one generalization can be made: presidents have increasingly preferred the White House staff to the Cabinet as their means of managing the gigantic executive branch.

The White House Staff

The **White House staff** is composed mainly of analysts and advisers.[21] Although many of the top White House staff members are given the title "special assistant" for a particular task or sector, the types of judgments they are expected to make and the kinds of advice they are supposed to give are a good deal broader and more generally political than those coming from the Executive Office of the President or from the Cabinet departments. The members of the White House staff also tend to be more closely associated with the president than other presidentially appointed officials.

From an informal group of fewer than a dozen people (popularly called the **Kitchen Cabinet**), and no more than four dozen at its height during Roosevelt presidency in 1937, the White House staff has grown substantially.[22] Richard Nixon employed 550 people in 1972. President Carter, who found so many of the requirements of presidential power distasteful, and who publicly vowed to keep his staff small and decentralized, built an even larger and more centralized staff. President Clinton reduced the White House staff by 20 percent, but a large White House staff is still essential.

National Security Council (NSC) a presidential foreign-policy advisory council composed of the president; the vice president; the secretary of state; the secretary of defense and other officials invited by the president

White House staff analysts and advisers to the president, often given the title "special assistant"

Kitchen Cabinet an informal group of advisers to whom the president turns for counsel and guidance. Members of the official Cabinet may or may not also be members of the Kitchen Cabinet

The Executive Office of the President

Executive Office of the President (EOP) the permanent agencies that perform defined management tasks for the president. Created in 1939, the EOP includes the Office of Management and Budget, the Council of Economic Advisers, the National Security Council, and other agencies

Created in 1939, the **Executive Office of the President (EOP)** is a major part of what is often called the "institutional presidency"—the permanent agencies that perform defined management tasks for the president. The most important and the largest EOP agency is the Office of Management and Budget (OMB). Its roles in preparing the national budget, designing the president's program, reporting on agency activities, and overseeing regulatory proposals make OMB personnel part of virtually every conceivable presidential responsibility. The status and power of the OMB have grown in importance with each successive president. At one time the process of budgeting was a "bottom-up" procedure, with expenditure and program requests passing from the lowest bureaus through the departments to "clearance" in OMB and thence to Congress, where each agency could be called in to reveal what its "original request" had been before OMB revised it. Now the budgeting process is "top-down": OMB sets the terms of discourse for agencies as well as for Congress. The director of OMB is now one of the most powerful officials in Washington.

The staff of the Council of Economic Advisers (CEA) constantly analyzes the economy and economic trends and attempts to give the president the ability to anticipate events rather than waiting and reacting to events. The Council on Environmental Quality was designed to do for environmental issues what the CEA does for economic issues. The National Security Council (NSC) is composed of designated Cabinet officials who meet regularly with the president to give advice on the large national security picture. The staff of the NSC assimilates and analyzes data from all intelligence-gathering agencies (CIA, etc.). Other EOP agencies perform more specialized tasks.

Somewhere between 1,500 and 2,000 highly specialized people work for EOP agencies.[23] The importance of each agency in the EOP varies according to the personal orientation of each president. For example, the NSC staff was of immense importance under President Nixon, especially because it served essentially as the personal staff of the presidential assistant Henry Kissinger. But it was of less importance to President George H. W. Bush, who looked outside the EOP altogether for military policy matters, turning much more to the Joint Chiefs of Staff and its chair at the time, General Colin Powell. Powell later served as Secretary of State under President George W. Bush.

The Vice Presidency

The vice presidency is a constitutional anomaly even though the office was created along with the presidency by the Constitution. The vice president exists for two purposes only: to succeed the president in case of death, resignation, or incapacitation and to preside over the Senate, casting a tie-breaking vote when necessary.[24]

The main value of the vice presidency as a political resource for the president is electoral. Traditionally, a presidential candidate's most important guideline in choosing a running mate is that he or she bring the support of at least one state (preferably a large one) not otherwise likely to support the ticket. Another guideline holds that the vice-presidential nominee should provide some regional balance and, wherever possible, some balance among various ideological or ethnic subsections of the party. It is very doubtful that John Kennedy would have won in 1960 without his vice-presidential candidate, Lyndon Johnson, and the contribution Johnson made to winning in Texas. Barack Obama chose Senator Joseph Biden of Delaware to be his running mate for a number of reasons. To begin with, Biden is Catholic and has blue-collar origins. Obama believed correctly that Biden would appeal to these important groups in such must-win states as Pennsylvania and Ohio. Perhaps even more important, Biden possesses enormous foreign policy experience and chaired the Senate Foreign Relations Committee. The Republicans had often pointed to Obama's lack of experience in the international realm as indicating that he was not ready to be president. Democrats hoped that Biden's presence on the ticket would put the "experience" issue to rest. Indeed, after John McCain designated Sarah Palin to be his vice-presidential running mate, Republicans found it difficult to claim that their ticket was more experienced than that of the Democrats.

As the institutional presidency has grown in size and complexity, most presidents of the past twenty-five years have sought to use their vice presidents as a management resource after the election. President Clinton for example, relied greatly on his vice president, Al Gore. Gore's most important task was to oversee the National Performance Review (NPR), an ambitious program to "reinvent" the way the federal government conducts its affairs. The presidency of George W. Bush resulted in unprecedented power and responsibility for his vice president, Dick Cheney, who helped shape the war on terror. In the Obama White House, Vice President Biden is said to be regarded as the "skeptic-in-chief."[25] Biden's role is to question and criticize policy recommendations made to the president until, of course, the president makes a decision and the vice president falls loyally into step.

The vice president is also important because, in the event of the death or incapacity of the president, he or she will succeed to the nation's highest office. During the course of American history, six vice presidents have had to replace presidents who died in office. One vice president—Gerald Ford—found himself at the head of the nation when President Richard Nixon was forced to resign as a result of the Watergate scandal. During the 2004 vice-presidential debates, Dick Cheney reminded Americans of the importance of the succession when he sought to distinguish himself from the Democratic vice-presidential nominee, John Edwards, by averring that he, unlike the less-experienced Edwards, had been chosen for his ability to serve as president if that became necessary.

Vice President Joseph Biden had thirty-five years' experience in the Senate before Barack Obama picked him as his running mate. In particular, Biden's foreign policy experience was seen as an important strength in the campaign and the Obama administration.

Until the ratification of the Twenty-fifth Amendment in 1965, the succession of the vice president to the presidency was a tradition, launched by John Tyler when he assumed the presidency after William Henry Harrison's death, rather than a constitutional or statutory requirement. The Twenty-fifth Amendment codified this tradition by providing that the vice president would assume the presidency in the event of the chief executive's death or incapacity and setting forth the procedures that would be followed. In the event that both the president and vice president are killed, the Presidential Succession Act of 1947 establishes an order of succession, beginning with the Speaker of the House and continuing with the president of the Senate and the Cabinet secretaries. This piece of legislation was adopted during the Cold War and prompted by fear of a nuclear attack. It has, however, taken on new importance in an age of global terrorism.

The First Spouse

The president serves as both chief executive and chief of state—the equivalent of Great Britain's prime minister and king rolled into one, simultaneously leading the government and serving as a symbol of the nation at official ceremonies and functions. Traditionally, most first ladies limited their activities to the ceremonial portion of the presidency. They greeted foreign dignitaries, visited other countries, and attended important national ceremonies.

Because they are generally associated exclusively with the head-of-state aspect of America's presidency, presidential spouses are usually not subject to the same sort of media scrutiny or partisan attack as that aimed at the president. However, some first spouses have had more influence over policy. Franklin Roosevelt's wife, Eleanor, was widely popular, but also widely criticized, for her active role in many elements of her husband's presidency. Hillary Clinton played a major political and policy role in Bill Clinton's presidency. During the 1992 campaign, Bill Clinton often implied that she would be active in the administration by joking that voters would get "two for the price of one." After the election, Hillary took a leading role in many policy areas, most notably heading the administration's health care reform effort. She also became the first first lady to seek public office on her own when she won a seat in the U.S. Senate in 2000 and then ran for president in 2008. Later, President Obama named Clinton secretary of state. Barack Obama's wife, Michelle, is a lawyer and served for a number of years as a senior administrator at the University of Chicago's Pritzker School of Medicine. Given her legal and policy background, Michelle Obama seemed likely to become a visible and activist first lady on the Hillary Clinton model, but in the first two years of the Obama presidency she played a mainly behind-the-scenes role.

The President and Policy

The president's powers and institutional resources, taken together, give the chief executive a substantial voice in the nation's policy-making processes. Strictly speaking, presidents cannot introduce legislation. Only members of Congress can formally propose new programs and policies. Nevertheless, a great many of the major bills acted on by the Congress are crafted by the president and his aides and then introduced by friendly legislators. Congress has come to expect the president to propose the government's budget, and the nation has come to expect presidential initiatives to deal with major problems. Some of these initiatives have come in the form of huge packages of programs—Franklin Roosevelt's "New Deal" and Lyndon Johnson's "Great Society." Sometimes presidents craft a single program they hope will have a significant impact on the nation and on their political fortunes. For example, Bill Clinton developed a major health care reform initiative whose political defeat marked a significant setback for his presidency. George W. Bush made the "war on terrorism" the centerpiece of his administration. To fight this war, Bush brought about the creation of a new Cabinet department—the Department of Homeland Security—and the enactment of such pieces of legislation as the USA PATRIOT Act to give the executive branch more power to deal with the terrorist threat. Going beyond terrorism, Bush also presided over a huge expansion of the Medicare program to provide prescription drug benefits for senior citizens. All this was achieved by a president who was said to lack a popular **mandate** in the wake of the controversial 2000 election. Bush

mandate a claim by a victorious candidate that the electorate has given him or her special authority to carry out promises made during the campaign

During the 2008 presidential campaign, Michelle Obama campaigned for her husband, speaking at rallies and appearing on talk shows. As first lady, she has worked on numerous issues, including childhood obesity.

THE WHITE HOUSE
WASHINGTON

Satire and Perceptions of the American Presidency

Because citizens rarely have direct experience with the president, the bulk of the information we use to evaluate the president comes to us through the mass media—in the forms of news reporting, presidential speeches, and press conferences, and also in the form of humorous and satirical portrayals of the president. Contemporary forms of political humor include political parodies and impersonations like Tina Fey's 2008 impersonation of Republican vice-presidential candidate Sarah Palin on *Saturday Night Live*, the nightly monologue jokes of the mainstream late-night political comedians like Jay Leno or David Letterman, and the more ironic and satirical news parody programs like *The Daily Show* or *The Colbert Report*.

Political humor aimed at government leaders has been a part of democratic societies since the Greek and Roman empires. Political humor and satire provide a nonviolent way of communicating concerns, exposing hypocrisy, and bringing to light a leader's flaws. Political scientist David Paletz has argued that instances of political humor can be placed on a spectrum ranging from "supportive" to "subversive." More supportive presidential political humor might poke fun at the president's physical appearance, habits, or general approach to governing, but would exhibit basic support for the administration and the institutions of goverment. More subversive presidential

political humor seeks to aggressively critique the individuals in power, their policies and practices, and the functions of our key institutions.

An example of subversive political humor would be segments on *The Daily Show* that aired after the U.S.'s engagement in the Iraq War in 2003. In one segment, Jon Stewart strongly criticized the Bush administration's Iraq War policies and juxtaposed clips of the president to highlight inconsistent or hypocritical policy decisions. Supportive political humor is more common on the mainstream late-night comedy shows, whose writers need to be careful not to alienate members of their bipartisan audience. While Leno and Letterman do include jokes critical of policy decisions, they are more likely to make lighthearted jokes about minor personal characteristics: Bush's misuse of vocabulary words, Kerry's protruding chin, Obama's big ears, or Palin's folksy accent.

Nonetheless, research shows that their monologues have an impact on the audience through repeated exposure—likely because the shows use the same targets and themes across programs and over time. Findings suggest that viewers of the network late-night comedy shows have more negative perceptions of the candidates on their most caricatured traits and issue positions. For example, late-night comedy viewers found Gore less inspiring than non-viewers in 2000, consistent with Gore's caricature as stiff and boring. In 2004, late-night jokes about Kerry as a flip-flopper and Bush's mishandling of the Iraq War (two dominant

themes in late-night monologues) caused participants to be more likely to cite those topics when asked about the two candidates—suggesting that late-night jokes can bring topics, traits, and policies to the forefront something that could impact presidential approval ratings.

With the election of Barack Obama in 2008, journalists and comedians began to tackle a difficult question: What will political humor look like under an Obama presidency?

A defining moment of political humor aimed at Obama aired on *Saturday Night Live* in October 2009. The actor Fred Amisen, impersonating the president while sitting in the Oval Office, spoke directly into the camera to allay Republican fears about a liberal agenda under his presidency. "When you look at my record," Armisen stated, "it's very clear what I've done so far. And that is. . . . nothing." As articulated in a CNN headline the following week, the sketch marked "the end of the honeymoon" for Obama and political humor writers.

SOURCES: Leopold, T., "SNL Obama Sketch Marks End of Honeymoon," CNN.com (accessed 10/7/09). Paletz, David L., "Political Humor and Authority: From Support to Subversion." *International Political Science Review, 11* (1990): 483–493. Young, D. G., "A Flip-Flopper and a Dumb Guy Walk into a Bar: Political Humor and Priming in the 2004 Campaign," *HUMOR: The International Journal of Humor Research, 19* (2010): 1–26.

for critical analysis

1. If people know that humor is not meant to be taken seriously, how could jokes shape public opinion of the president?

2. How can the public's feelings about the president affect the president's conduct and influence?

may have lacked a mandate, but the expressed and delegated powers of the office gave him the resources through which to prevail.

At one time, historians and journalists liked to debate the question of strong versus weak presidents. Some presidents, such as Lincoln and FDR, were called "strong" for their leadership and their ability to guide the nation's political agenda. Others, such as Buchanan and Coolidge, were seen as "weak" for failing to develop significant legislative programs and seeming to observe rather than shape political events. Today, the strong-versus-weak categorization has become moot. *Every president is strong.* This strength is not so much a function of personal charisma or political savvy as it is a reflection of the increasing power of the institution of the presidency. Let us see how this came about.

The Contemporary Bases of Presidential Power

During the nineteenth century, Congress was America's dominant institution of government, and members of Congress sometimes treated the president with disdain. Today, however, no one would assert that the presidency is an unimportant institution. Presidents seek to dominate the policy-making process and claim the power to lead the nation in time of war. The expansion of presidential power over the course of the past century has not come about by accident but as the result of an ongoing effort by successive presidents to enlarge the powers of the office.

Generally, presidents can expand their power in three ways: party, popular mobilization, and administration. In the first instance, presidents may construct or strengthen national partisan institutions with which to exert influence in the legislative process and through which to implement their programs. Alternatively, or in addition to the first tactic, presidents may use popular appeals to create a mass base of support that will allow them to subordinate their political foes. This tactic is called "going public."[26] Third, presidents may seek to bolster their control of established executive agencies or to create new administrative institutions and procedures that will reduce their dependence on Congress and give them a more independent governing and policy-making capability. Presidents' use of executive orders to achieve their policy goals in lieu of seeking to persuade Congress to enact legislation is, perhaps, the most obvious example.

Party as a Source of Power

All presidents have relied on the members and leaders of their own party to implement their legislative agendas. President George W. Bush, for example, worked closely with congressional GOP leaders on such matters as energy policy and Medicare reform. But the president does not control his own party; party members have considerable autonomy. Moreover, in America's system of separated powers, the president's party may be in the minority in Congress and unable to do much for the chief executive's programs (see Figure 13.3). Consequently, although their party is valuable to chief executives, it has not been a fully reliable presidential tool. As a result, contemporary presidents are more likely to use two other methods—popular mobilization and executive administration—to achieve their political goals.

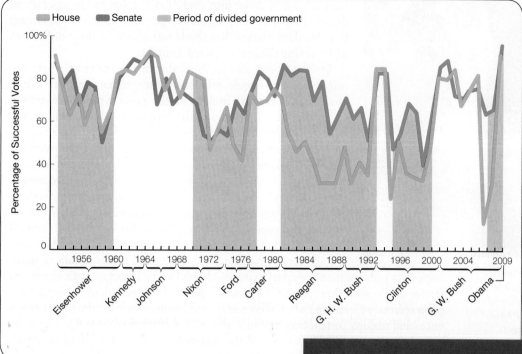

FIGURE 13.3

Presidential Success on Congressional Votes* (1953–2009)

Presidents have more success in Congress when their party is in the majority. Can you identify the periods when presidents had majority support in Congress and when they did not?

*Percentages based on votes on which presidents took a position.
SOURCE: *Congressional Quarterly*
CREDIT: *Nelson HSU/NPR*

Going Public

Popular mobilization as a technique of presidential power has its historical roots in the presidencies of Theodore Roosevelt and Woodrow Wilson and has, subsequently, become a weapon in the political arsenals of most presidents since the mid-twentieth century. In the nineteenth century, it was considered inappropriate for presidents to engage in personal campaigning on their own behalf or in support of programs and policies. When Andrew Johnson broke this unwritten rule and made a series of speeches vehemently seeking public support for his Reconstruction program, even some of Johnson's supporters were shocked at what they saw as his lack of decorum and dignity. The president's opponents cited his "inflammatory" speeches in one of the articles of impeachment drafted by the Congress.[27]

The first presidents to make systematic use of appeals to the public were Theodore Roosevelt and Woodrow Wilson, but the president who used public appeals most effectively was Franklin Delano Roosevelt. FDR was "firmly persuaded of the need to form a direct link between the executive office and the public."[28] Roosevelt developed a number of tactics aimed at forging such a link. He often embarked on speaking trips around the nation to promote his programs. On one such tour, he told a crowd, "I regain strength just by meeting the American people."[29] In addition, FDR made limited but important use of the new electronic medium the radio to reach millions of Americans. In his famous "fireside chats," the president, or at

President Franklin Delano Roosevelt's direct appeals to the American people allowed FDR to "reach over the heads" of congressional opponents and force them to follow his lead because their constituents demanded it.

least his voice, came into every living room in the country to discuss programs and policies and generally to assure Americans that Franklin Delano Roosevelt was aware of their difficulties and working diligently toward solutions.

Roosevelt was also an innovator in the realm of what now might be called press relations. When he entered the White House, FDR faced a mainly hostile press typically controlled by conservative members of the business establishment. As the president wrote, "All the fat-cat newspapers—85 percent of the whole—have been utterly opposed to everything the Administration is seeking."[30] Roosevelt hoped to be able to use the press to mold public opinion, but to do so he needed to circumvent the editors and publishers who were generally unsympathetic to his goals. To this end, the president worked to cultivate the reporters who covered the White House. Roosevelt made himself available for biweekly press conferences where he offered candid answers to reporters' questions and made certain to make important policy announcements that would provide the reporters with significant stories to file with their papers.[31] Roosevelt was the first president to designate a press secretary (Stephen Early), who was charged with organizing the press conferences and making certain that reporters observed the informal rules distinguishing presidential comments that were off the record from those that could be attributed directly to the president.

Every president since FDR has sought to craft a public-relations strategy that would emphasize the incumbent's strengths and maximize his popular appeal. For John F. Kennedy, handsome and quick-witted, the televised press conference was an excellent public-relations vehicle. Johnson and Nixon lacked Kennedy's charisma, but both were effective television speakers, usually reading from a prepared text. Bill Clinton made extensive use of televised town meetings—carefully staged events in which the president would not be asked the sorts of pointed questions preferred by reporters and which gave the president an opportunity to appear to consult with rank-and-file citizens about his goals and policies.

One Clinton innovation was to make the White House Communications Office an important institution within the Executive Office of the President (EOP). In a practice continued by George W. Bush, the Communications Office became responsible not only for responding to reporters' queries but also for developing and implementing a coordinated communications strategy—promoting the president's policy goals, developing responses to unflattering news stories, and making certain that a favorable image of the president would, insofar as possible, dominate the news. Barack Obama often relies on his own effective speaking abilities rather than material crafted by the Communications Office.

The Limits of Going Public Some presidents have been able to make effective use of popular appeals to overcome congressional opposition. Popular support, though, has not been a firm foundation for presidential power. The public is notoriously fickle. President George W. Bush maintained an approval rating of over 70 percent for more than a year following the September 11 terrorist attacks. By the end of 2005, however, President Bush's approval rating had dropped to 39 percent as a result of the growing unpopularity of the Iraq war, the administration's inept handling of hurricane relief, and several White House scandals, including the conviction of Vice President Cheney's chief of staff on charges of lying

Who Thinks the President Is Doing a Good Job?

In presidential approval polls, respondents are asked "Do you approve of the way the president is handling his job?" These graphs show the percentage of positive responses. As we can see, presidents generally experience broad shifts in popular approval. Perhaps not surprisingly, members of the president's own party are more likely to think the president is doing a good job, as in the case of Obama's handling of key issues.

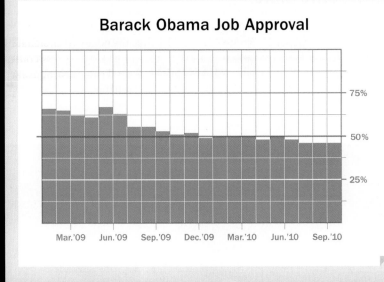

Barack Obama Job Approval

Obama's Handling of Issues

Percentage approving, by party identification

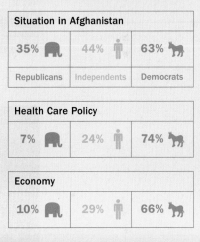

Situation in Afghanistan		
35%	44%	63%
Republicans	Independents	Democrats

Health Care Policy		
7%	24%	74%

Economy		
10%	29%	66%

Approval Ratings of Past Presidents

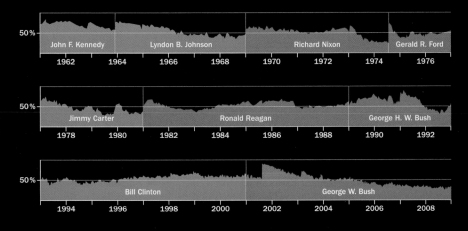

for critical analysis

1. What factors help to explain changes in presidential approval ratings? Can you identify some specific events that were associated with sharp upswings or drops in presidential approval?

2. Does popular approval really affect presidential power? How can popular feelings about the president affect the president's conduct and influence?

SOURCES: (Part 1) Gallup.com, "Obama Approval on Economy Down, on Foreign Affairs Up," February 8, 2010; (Part 2) Gallup.com, "Presidential Approval Ratings—Gallup Historical Statistics and Trends," (accessed 5/11/10).

to a federal grand jury. After America's triumph in the 1990 Persian Gulf War, President George H. W. Bush scored a remarkable 90 percent approval rating in the polls. Two years later, however, after the 1991 budget crisis, Bush's support plummeted and the president was defeated in his bid for re-election. During his first two years in office, Ronald Reagan's approval score ranged from a high of 59 percent in 1981 to a low of 37 percent in early 1983.[32] As Reagan's poll standing fell, his ability to overawe Democratic opponents and retain the support of wavering Republicans diminished sharply. Such declines in popular approval during a president's term in office are nearly inevitable and follow a predictable pattern (see Who Are Americans).[33] Presidents generate popular support by promising to undertake important programs that will contribute directly to the well-being of large numbers of Americans. Almost inevitably, presidential performance falls short of promises and popular expectations, leading to a sharp decline in public support and the ensuing collapse of presidential influence.[34]

The Administrative State

Contemporary presidents have increased the administrative capabilities of their office in three ways. First, they have enhanced the reach and power of the Executive Office of the President (EOP). Second, they have sought to increase White House control over the federal bureaucracy. Third, they have expanded the role of executive orders and other instruments of direct presidential governance. Taken together,

President Bill Clinton was a master of the televised town meeting, in which the president gives the appearance of consulting average citizens on important policy issues. Clinton's technique illustrated how campaign-style events could become tools to shape and sell national policy.

these three components of what might be called the White House "administrative strategy" have given presidents a capacity to achieve their programmatic and policy goals even when they are unable to secure congressional approval. Indeed, some recent presidents have been able to accomplish quite a bit without much congressional, partisan, or even public support.

The Executive Office of The President The Executive Office of the President has grown from six administrative assistants in 1939 to today's 400 employees working directly for the president in the White House office along with some 1,400 individuals staffing the several (currently eight) divisions of the Executive Office.[35] The creation and growth of the White House staff gives the president an enormously enhanced capacity to gather information, plan programs and strategies, communicate with constituencies, and exercise supervision over the executive branch. The staff multiplies the president's eyes, ears, and arms, becoming a critical instrument of presidential power.[36]

In particular, the Office of Management and Budget (OMB) serves as a potential instrument of presidential control over federal spending and hence a mechanism through which the White House has greatly expanded its power. The OMB has the capacity to analyze and approve all legislative proposals, not only budgetary requests, emanating from all federal agencies before being submitted to Congress. This procedure, now a matter of routine, greatly enhances the president's control over the entire executive branch. All legislation emanating from the White House as well as all executive orders also go through the OMB.[37] Thus, through one White House agency, the president has the means to exert major influence over the flow of money as well as the shape and content of national legislation.

Regulatory Review A second tactic that presidents have used to increase their power and reach is the process of regulatory review, through which presidents have sought to seize control of rule making by the agencies of the executive branch (see also Chapter 14). Whenever Congress enacts a statute, its actual implementation requires the promulgation of hundreds of rules by the agency charged with administering the law and giving effect to the will of Congress. Some congressional statutes are quite detailed and leave agencies with relatively little discretion. Typically, however, Congress enacts a relatively broad statement of legislative intent and delegates to the appropriate administrative agency the power to fill in many important details.[38] In other words, Congress typically says to an administrative agency, "Here is the problem: deal with it."[39]

The discretion Congress delegates to administrative agencies has provided recent presidents with an important avenue for expanding their own power. For example, President Clinton believed the president had full authority to order agencies of the executive branch to adopt such rules as the president thought appropriate.

During the course of his presidency, Clinton issued 107 directives to administrators ordering them to propose specific rules and regulations. In some instances, the language of the rule to be proposed was drafted by the White House staff; in other cases, the president asserted a priority but left it to the agency to draft the precise language of the proposal. Republicans, of course, denounced Clinton's actions as a usurpation of power.[40] However, after he took office, President George W. Bush made no move to surrender the powers Clinton had claimed—quite the contrary. Bush continued the Clinton-era practice of issuing presidential directives to agencies to spur them to issue new rules and regulations. In January 2009, President

Obama affirmed the importance of regulatory review but said his administration would take a close look at the review process to make certain that guidance to the federal agencies would be fair and would involve public participation.[41]

Governing by Decree: Executive Orders A fourth mechanism through which contemporary presidents have sought to enhance their power to govern unilaterally is through the use of executive orders and other forms of presidential decrees, including executive agreements, national security findings and directives, proclamations, reorganization plans, the signing of statements, and a host of others.[42] Executive orders have a long history in the United States and have been the vehicles for a number of important government policies, including the purchase of Louisiana, the annexation of Texas, the emancipation of the slaves, the internment of the Japanese, the desegregation of the military, the initiation of affirmative action, and the creation of important federal agencies, among them the EPA, the FDA, and the Peace Corps.[43]

Although wars and national emergencies produce the highest volume of executive orders, such presidential actions also occur frequently in peacetime (see Figure 13.4). In the realm of foreign policy, unilateral presidential actions in the form of executive agreements have virtually replaced treaties as the nation's chief foreign-policy instruments.[44] Presidential decrees, however, are often used for purely domestic purposes.

Presidents may not use executive orders to issue whatever commands they please. The use of such decrees is bound by law. If a president issues an executive order, proclamation, directive, or the like, in principle he does so pursuant to

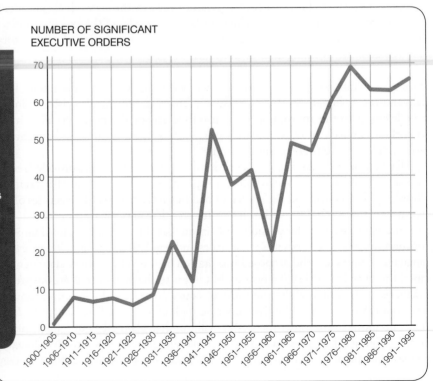

FIGURE 13.4

Significant Executive Orders, 1900–1995

Over the past century, presidents have made increasingly frequent use of executive orders to accomplish their policy goals. What factors explain this development? How has Congress responded to increased presidential assertiveness? What might explain the large number of executive orders issued during the 1940s?

SOURCE: William Howell, "The President's Powers of Unilateral Action: The Strategic Advantages of Acting Alone" (Ph.D. diss., Stanford University, 1999).

NUMBER OF SIGNIFICANT EXECUTIVE ORDERS

the powers granted to him by the Constitution or delegated to him by Congress, usually through a statute. When presidents issue such orders, they generally state the constitutional or statutory basis for their actions. For example, when President Truman ordered the desegregation of the armed services, he did so pursuant to his constitutional powers as commander in chief. In a similar vein, when President Johnson issued Executive Order No. 11246, he asserted that the order was designed to implement the 1964 Civil Rights Act, which prohibited employment discrimination. Where an executive order has no statutory or constitutional basis, the courts have held it to be void. The most important case on this point is *Youngstown Co. v. Sawyer,* the so-called steel seizure case of 1952.[45] Here, the Supreme Court ruled that President Truman's seizure of the nation's steel mills during the Korean War had no statutory or constitutional basis and was thus invalid.

A number of court decisions, though, have established broad boundaries that leave considerable room for presidential action. For example, the courts have held that Congress might approve presidential action after the fact or, in effect, ratify presidential action through "acquiescence," by not objecting for long periods of time or by continuing to provide funding for programs established by executive orders. In addition, the courts have indicated that some areas, most notably the realm of military policy, are presidential in character and have allowed presidents wide latitude to make policy by executive decree. Thus, within the very broad limits established by the courts, presidential orders can be and have been important policy tools.

President Clinton issued numerous orders designed to promote a coherent set of policy goals: protecting the environment, strengthening federal regulatory power, shifting America's foreign policy from a unilateral to a multilateral focus, expanding affirmative action programs, and helping organized labor in its struggles with employers.[46] President George W. Bush also did not hesitate to use executive orders—issuing more than 250 between his inauguration and the end of 2007. During his first months in office, Bush issued orders prohibiting the use of federal funds to support international family-planning groups that provided abortion-counseling services and placing limits on the use of embryonic stem cells in federally funded research projects. Throughout his administration, Bush made very aggressive use of executive orders in response to the threat of terrorism. In November 2001, for example, Bush issued a directive authorizing the creation of military tribunals to try noncitizens accused of involvement in acts of terrorism against the United States. In May 2007, Bush issued controversial national security directives that gave the president sole responsibility for determining when and how constitutional government could be reestablished in the event of a catastrophic attack on the United States.

During his first year in office, President Obama also issued a number of executive orders, many of which were designed to rescind Bush-era orders. Thus, Obama ordered the closing of the Guantánamo prison and ordered an end to what were deemed unlawful methods of interrogation of terror suspects. In February 2010, with many elements of his legislative agenda stalled in Congress, Obama indicated that he planned to make increased use of executive orders to advance energy, environmental, fiscal, and other domestic priorities.[47]

Signing Statements To negate congressional actions to which they objected, recent presidents have made frequent and calculated use of presidential **signing statements** when signing bills into law.[48] The signing statement is an announcement made by the president at the time of signing a congressional enactment into

signing statements announcements made by the president when signing bills into law, often presenting the president's interpretation of the law.

law, sometimes presenting the president's interpretation of the law as well as usually innocuous remarks predicting the many benefits the new law will bring to the nation. Occasionally, presidents have used signing statements to point to sections of the law they deemed improper or even unconstitutional, and to instruct executive branch agencies how they were to execute the law.[49] President Harry Truman, for example, accompanied his approval of the 1946 Hobbs Anti-Racketeering Act with a message offering his interpretation of ambiguous sections of the statute and indicating how the federal government would implement the new law.[50]

Presidents have made signing statements throughout American history, though many were not recorded and did not become part of the official legislative record. Ronald Reagan's attorney general, Edwin Meese, is generally credited with transforming the signing statement into a routine tool of presidential direct action.[51] Meese believed that carefully crafted signing statements would provide a basis for action by executive agencies and, perhaps even more important, would become part of the history and context of a piece of legislation if and when judicial interpretation became necessary. Indeed, to make certain that signing statements became part of the legislative history, Meese reached an agreement with the West Publishing Company to include them in its authoritative texts.[52]

With the way paved, Reagan, followed by George H. W. Bush, Clinton, and George W. Bush, proceeded to use detailed and artfully designed signing statements—prepared by the Department of Justice—to attempt to reinterpret congressional enactments. For example, when signing the Safe Drinking Water Amendments of 1986, President Reagan issued a statement that interpreted sections of the Act to allow discretionary enforcement when the Congress seemed to call for mandatory enforcement.[53] Reagan hoped the courts would accept his version of the statute when examining subsequent enforcement decisions. In other cases, Reagan used his signing statements to attempt to nullify portions of statutes. George W. Bush issued over 1,200 signing statements and used them to rewrite the law on numerous occasions. As a candidate, President Obama criticized Bush for excessive use of signing statements. Obama does not issue such statements but has declared that the reserves the right to ignore sections of bills he considers unconstitutional if objections have been lodged previously by the executive branch—in effect, a secret signing statement.[54]

The Advantages of The Administrative Strategy Through the course of American history, party leadership and popular appeals have played important roles in presidential efforts to overcome political opposition. Both party and appeals to the people continue to be instruments of presidential power. Reagan's tax cuts and Clinton's budget victories were achieved with strong partisan support. George W. Bush, lacking the oratorical skills of Reagan or Roosevelt, nevertheless made good use of sophisticated communications strategies to promote his agenda. Yet, as we saw, in the modern era parties have waned in institutional strength, and the effects of popular appeals have often proven evanescent. The limitations of the alternatives have increasingly impelled presidents to try to expand the administrative capabilities of the office and their own capacity for unilateral action as means of achieving their policy goals. And in recent decades, the expansion of the Executive Office, the development of regulatory review, the use of executive orders, the signing of statements, and the like have given presidents a substantial capacity to achieve significant policy results despite congressional opposition to their legislative agendas.

In principle, perhaps, Congress could respond more vigorously to unilateral policy making by the president than it has. Certainly a Congress willing to impeach a president should have the mettle to overturn his administrative directives. But the president has significant advantages in such struggles with Congress. In battles over presidential directives and orders, Congress is on the defensive, reacting to presidential initiatives. The framers of the Constitution saw "energy," or the ability to take the initiative, as a key feature of executive power.[55] When the president takes action by issuing an order or an administrative directive, Congress must initiate the cumbersome and time-consuming lawmaking process, overcome internal divisions, and enact legislation that the president may ultimately veto. Moreover, as the political scientist Terry Moe has argued, in such battles Congress faces a significant collective-action problem insofar as members are likely to be more sensitive to the substance of a president's actions and its effects on their constituents than to the more general implications of presidential power for the long-term vitality of their institution.[56]

Thinking Critically about Presidential Power and Democracy

The framers of the Constitution created a system of government in which the Congress and the executive branch were to share power. At least since the New Deal, however, the powers of Congress have waned, whereas those of the presidency have expanded dramatically. An instance of congressional retreat in the face of presidential assertiveness occurred in October 2002, when both houses of Congress, pressed by President George W. Bush, voted overwhelmingly to authorize the White House to use military force against Iraq. The resolution adopted by Congress allowed the president complete discretion to determine whether, when, and how to attack Iraq. The president had rejected language that might have implied even the slightest limitations on his prerogatives. Indeed, Bush's legal advisers had pointedly declared that the president did not actually need specific congressional authorization to attack Iraq if he deemed such action to be in America's interest. "We don't want to be in the legal position of asking Congress to authorize the use of force when the president already has that full authority," said one senior administration official. Few members of Congress even bothered to object to this apparent rewriting of the U.S. Constitution.

There is no doubt that Congress continues to be able to harass presidents and even, on occasion, to hand the White House a sharp rebuff. In the larger view, however, presidents' occasional defeats—however dramatic—have to be seen as

Obama campaigned on a platform of "change," and while he did overturn numerous Bush-era policies, he gave up few of the institutional powers that Bush and earlier presidents had claimed.

Work in the White House

Johanna Atienza was a twenty-year-old junior majoring in political science at a West Coast university when she learned from other students that her school had a Washington, D.C., internship program—and that it included the possibility of working in the White House. She was immediately interested: "What better way is there to learn about politics than from the inside?" She also felt that a semester in the nation's capital would help her to understand whether the people who worked in the federal government really cared about the average citizen.

Johanna spent considerable time and effort on the application and then waited for the response. When she received the letter informing her of her acceptance, she was thrilled. In early January, she moved to Washington, D.C., and was assigned to work with the people who scheduled travel for the president and the first lady. Over the next three months, Johanna met and worked with some of the top officials in the White House. She also had the opportunity to meet the president and first lady. Although it was exciting to wander around the maze of offices in the White House, Johanna reports, she was often so busy that she had little time to realize

that she was indeed wandering through White House corridors.

What did Johanna learn from her three-month participation in the day-to-day life of White House politics that she was unlikely to learn in a classroom? First, she was struck by the incredible complexity of the presidency and Washington politics. Procedures were detailed and time-consuming. Things moved remarkably slowly, if at all. Second, however, she gained tremendous respect for the people who work in the White House. They were dedicated people who worked long hours, often for little money. Even the older aides worked long hours and devoted themselves to public service.

- If this type of hands-on experience appeals to you, you can apply for the White House internship online at www.whitehouse.gov/government/wh-intern.html. Although each presidential administration varies the exact requirements, in general, students will have to complete an application form that includes several essay questions and is accompanied by two or three letters of recommendation. Once selected, interns must agree to a background check and a random drug test.

- Find out if your college offers course credit for internships in government. Although the internship is unpaid, students can usually arrange to earn course credits for their time and, if they work with their home institution, they can use student loans to help cover the cost of room and board.

If a semester in Washington, D.C., does not fit into your schedule, there are a lot of other ways to learn about the administration's policies and practices.

- Use the White House Web site to learn more about the president's policies. The WH Web page, www.whitehouse.gov, has links to at least a dozen top policy areas, where you can read what the president sees as the problem—and his proposed solution. This is only one side of the story, of course, but it is a good launching pad for further investigation.

- Ask questions through the White House Web site. There are also links that will allow you to ask a question about the historical background for various presidential traditions or submit a more policy-based query about the current administration's stance on a particular issue. If you're unsure what to ask, you can always read through the archive of others' questions—and the answers provided by the president's staff.

- Listen to the president. The president records a weekly radio address that is broadcast on radio stations across the country. You can listen to the most recent recording, or search the archives to hear what the president has to say—in his own words and in his own voice. While some addresses may seem only loosely connected to top issues of the day, others, particularly on key dates or anniversaries, will address more important issues. Both should give you a sense of the range of topics facing our nation's top administrator.

temporary setbacks in a gradual and decisive shift toward increased presidential power in the twenty-first century. Louis Fisher, America's leading authority on the separation of powers, recently observed that in what are arguably the two most important policy arenas, national defense and the federal budget, the powers of Congress have shown a "precipitous decline" for at least the past fifty years. The last occasion on which Congress exercised its constitutional power to declare war was December 8, 1941, and yet, since that time, American forces have been committed to numerous battles on every continent by order of the president. The much-hailed 1973 War Powers Resolution, far from limiting presidential power, actually allowed the president considerably more discretionary authority than he was granted by the Constitution. The War Powers Act gave the president the authority to deploy forces abroad without congressional authority for sixty days. The Constitution, though, seems to require congressional authorization before troops can be deployed for even one day. And presidents have ignored even these stipulations.

As to spending powers, the framers of the Constitution conceived the "power of the purse" to be Congress's most fundamental prerogative. For more than a century this power was jealously guarded by powerful congressional leaders such as the Taft-era House Speaker "Uncle" Joe Cannon, who saw congressional control of the budget as a fundamental safeguard against "Prussian-style" militarism and autocracy. Since the New Deal, however, successive Congresses have yielded to steadily increasing presidential influence over the budget process. In 1939, Congress allowed Franklin Delano Roosevelt to take a giant step toward presidential control of the nation's purse strings when it permitted him to bring the Bureau of the Budget (BoB) into the newly created Executive Office of the President. Roosevelt and his successors used the BoB (now called the OMB) effectively to seize the nation's legislative and budgetary agenda. In 1974, Congress attempted to respond to Richard Nixon's efforts to further enhance presidential control of spending when it enacted the Budget and Impoundment Control Act. This piece of legislation centralized Congress's own budgetary process and seemed to reinforce congressional power. Yet, less than ten years later, Congress watched as President Ronald Reagan essentially seized control the congressional budget process. Subsequently, as Fisher observes, lacking confidence in its own ability to maintain budgetary discipline, Congress has surrendered more and more power to the president.

Representative assemblies such as the United States Congress derive their influence from the support of groups and forces in civil society that believe these institutions serve their interests. Britain's Parliament ultimately overcame the Crown because it gradually won the confidence and support of the most important forces in civil society. A chief executive, such as the president of the United States, on the other hand, fundamentally derives power from the command of bureaucracies, armies, and the general machinery of the state. Presidents can certainly benefit from popular support. If we imagine, however, a fully demobilized polity in which neither institution could count on much support from forces in civil society, the president would still command the institutions of the state, whereas Congress would be without significant resources. In a fully mobilized polity, on the other hand, Congress might have a chance to counterbalance the president's institutional powers with the support of significant social forces.

A powerful presidency, a weak Congress, and a partially demobilized electorate are a dangerous mix. Presidents have increasingly asserted the right to govern unilaterally and now appear able to overcome most institutional and political constraints. Presidential power, to be sure, can be a force for good. To cite one example from the not-so-distant past, it was President Lyndon Johnson, more than Congress

for critical analysis

The presidency and Congress are both democratic institutions. Which is the more democratic? Why?

or the judiciary, who faced up to the task of smashing America's apartheid system. Yet, as the framers knew, unchecked power is always dangerous. Americans of the founding generation feared that unchecked presidential power would lead to *monocracy*—a republican form of monarchy without a king. Have we not taken more than one step in that direction? Inevitably, we will pay a price for our undemocratic politics.

studyguide

Practice Quiz

Find a dignostic Web Quiz with 34 additional questions on the StudySpace Web site: www.wwnorton.com/we-the-people

The Constitutional Basis for the Presidency

1. Which article of the Constitution establishes the presidency? *(p. 483)*
   a) Article I
   b) Article II
   c) Article III
   d) none of the above

2. Which of the following is *not* an expressed power of the president? *(pp. 484–85)*
   a) granting pardons
   b) declaring war
   c) nominating judges
   d) making treaties

The Constitutional Powers of the Presidency

3. Which of the following war powers does the Constitution *not* assign to the president? *(p. 486)*
   a) command of the army and navy of the United States
   b) the power to declare war
   c) command of the state militias
   d) The Constitution assigns all of the powers above to the president.

4. The War Powers Resolution of 1973 was an act passed by Congress that *(p. 488)*
   a) outlawed presidential use of executive agreements.
   b) created the National Security Council.
   c) granted the president the authority to declare war.
   d) stipulated military forces must be withdrawn within sixty days in the absence of a specific congressional authorization for their continued deployment.

5. Which of the following does not require the advice and consent of the Senate? *(p. 491)*
   a) an executive agreement
   b) a treaty
   c) Supreme Court nominations
   d) All of the above require the advice and consent of the Senate.

6. What did the Supreme Court rule in *U.S. v. Nixon*? *(p. 492)*
   a) Nixon had to turn his secret White House tapes over to congressional investigators because presidents do not have the power of executive privilege.
   b) Nixon did not have to turn his secret White House tapes over to congressional investigators because, in general, presidents have the power of executive privilege.
   c) Nixon had to turn his secret White House tapes over to congressional investigators but, in general, presidents have the power of executive privilege.
   d) Nixon did not have to turn his secret White House tapes over to congressional investigators but, in general, presidents do not have the power of executive privilege.

7. What are the requirements for overriding a presidential veto? *(p. 492)*
   a) fifty percent plus one vote in both houses of Congress
   b) two-thirds vote in both houses of Congress
   c) three-fourths vote in both houses of Congress
   d) a presidential veto cannot be overridden by Congress

8. When the president issues a rule or regulation that reorganizes or otherwise directs the affairs of the executive branch, such as the directives that established the Executive Office of the President and

the Environmental Protection Agency, it is called (p. 495)
a) an executive order.
b) an executive mandate.
c) administrative oversight.
d) legislative initiative.

The Presidency as an Institution

9. Which of the following statements about vice presidents is *not* true? (p. 500)
a) The vice president succeeds the president in case of death, resignation, or incapacitation.
b) The vice president casts the tie-breaking vote in the Senate when necessary.
c) Twelve vice presidents have had to replace presidents who died in office during American history.
d) Presidential candidates typically select a vice presidential candidate who is likely to bring the support a state that would not otherwise support the ticket.

10. The Office of Management and Budget is part of (p. 500)
a) the Executive Office of the President.
b) the White House staff.
c) the Kitchen Cabinet.
d) both a and b.

11. How many people work for agencies within the Executive Office of the President? (p. 500)
a) 25 to 50
b) 700 to 1,000
c) 1,500 to 2,000
d) 4,500 to 5,000

The Contemporary Bases of Presidential Power

12. What are the three ways that presidents can expand their power? (p. 504)
a) weakening national partisan institutions, avoiding popular appeals, and loosening their control of executive agencies
b) strengthening national partisan institutions, using popular appeals, and bolstering their control of executive agencies
c) weakening national partisan institutions, using popular appeals, and loosening their control of executive agencies

d) strengthening national partisan institutions, avoiding popular appeals, and bolstering their control of executive agencies

13. The Supreme Court case *Youngstown Co. v. Sawyer* was significant because (p. 511)
a) it showed that the courts would never invalidate an executive order.
b) it showed that the courts would invalidate executive orders that have no statutory or constitutional basis.
c) it asserted that pocket vetoes were unconstitutional.
d) it struck down the Budget and Impoundment Control Act.

14. When the president makes an announcement about his interpretation of a congressional enactment that he is signing into law, it is called (p. 511)
a) a signing statement.
b) an executive order.
c) legislative initiative.
d) executive privilege.

Thinking Critically about Presidential Power and Democracy

15. Which of the following best describes presidential and congressional power since the New Deal? (pp. 513–515)
a) The power of the president over the federal budget has increased but Congress has become more powerful than the president on national security issues.
b) The power of the president over national security issues has increased but Congress has become more powerful than the president on budgetary issues.
c) The power of the president over the federal budget and national defense has grown while the power of Congress over these areas has declined.
d) The power of the president over the federal budget and national defense has declined while the power of Congress over these areas has grown.

Chapter Outline

Ⓢ **Find a detailed Chapter Outline on the StudySpace Web site: www.wwnorton.com/we-the-people**

Key Terms

 Find Flashcards to help you study these terms on the StudySpace Web site: www.wwnorton.com/we-the-people

Cabinet *(p. 498)*
caucus (political) *(p. 484)*
commander in chief *(p. 486)*
delegated powers *(p. 485)*
executive agreement *(p. 491)*
Executive Office of the President (EOP) *(p. 500)*

executive order *(p. 495)*
executive privilege *(p. 492)*
expressed powers *(p. 485)*
inherent powers *(p. 486)*
Kitchen Cabinet *(p. 499)*
legislative initiative *(p. 493)*
mandate *(p. 502)*

National Security Council (NSC) *(p. 499)*
pocket veto *(p. 492)*
signing statements *(p. 511)*
veto *(p. 492)*
War Powers Resolution *(p. 488)*
White House staff *(p. 499)*

For Further Reading

Aberbach, Joel, and Mark Peterson, eds. *The Executive Branch.* New York: Oxford University Press, 2005.

Barber, James David. *The Presidential Character.* Englewood Cliffs, NJ: Prentice-Hall, 1992.

Crenson, Matthew, and Benjamin Ginsberg. *Presidential Power: Unchecked and Unbalanced.* New York: Norton, 2007.

Draper, Robert. *Dead Certain: The Presidency of George Bush.* New York: Free Press, 2007.

Edwards, George. *Why the Electoral College Is Bad for America.* New Haven, CT: Yale University Press, 2004.

Edwards, George, and Stephen Wayne. *Presidential Leadership: Politics and Policy Making.* New York: Wadsworth, 2009.

Hayes, Stephen F. *Cheney: The Untold Story of America's Most Powerful and Controversial Vice President.* New York: HarperCollins, 2007.

Lowi, Theodore J. *The Personal President: Power Invested, Promise Unfulfilled.* Ithaca, NY: Cornell University Press, 1985.

Milkis, Sidney M. *The President and the Parties: The Transformation of the American Party System since the New Deal.* New York: Oxford University Press, 1993.

Neustadt, Richard E. *Presidential Power: The Politics of Leadership from Roosevelt to Reagan.* Rev. ed. New York: Free Press, 1990.

Pfiffner, James. *Understanding the Presidency.* 6th ed. New York: Longman, 2010.

Pika, Joseph, and John A. Maltese. *Politics of the Presidency.* Washington, DC: Congressional Quarterly Press, 2009.

Skowronek, Stephen. *The Politics Presidents Make: Leadership from John Adams to Bill Clinton.* Cambridge, MA: The Belknap Press of Harvard University Press, 1997.

Yoo, John. *The Powers of War and Peace.* Chicago: University of Chicago Press, 2005.

Recommended Web Sites

Almanac of Policy Issues: War Powers Resolution
www.policyalmanac.org/world/archive/war_powers_resolution.shtml

The War Powers Resolution was passed in 1973 to define and limit the president's power during times of war. Read the full text of the resolution on this Web site.

Dave Leip's Atlas of U.S. Presidential Elections
www.uselectionatlas.org

For information on upcoming and past presidential elections, refer to this Web site. Experiment with the electoral college calculator to see how your state could affect the electoral outcome.

The American Presidency Project
www.americanpresidency.org

Directed by Gerhard Peters and John T. Woolley at UC Santa Barbara, this site contains over 88,000 documents related to the study of the presidency, including party platforms, candidates' remarks, statements of administration policy, documents released by the Office of the Press Secretary, and election debates. This site is also an excellent resource for data related to the study of the presidency.

The National Archives: Executive Branch
www.archives.gov/executive/

Research official executive branch documents at the Executive Branch Web site, provided by the U.S. National Archives and Records Administration.

Vicepresidents.com
www.vicepresidents.com

This Web site is dedicated to providing lots of interesting facts and archives about vice presidents, along with some lively humor.

The White House
www.whitehouse.gov

This is the official Web site of the White House. Here you can read about current presidential news, the president's Cabinet, executive orders, and presidential appointments.

White House Historical Association
www.whitehousehistory.org

The White House Historical Association is dedicated to the understanding, appreciation, and preservation of the White House. At its Web site you can find historical facts and take a detailed online tour of the numerous rooms and the property.

The White House: Past First Ladies
www.whitehouse.gov/history/firstladies/

The first lady is an important resource for the president in his role as head of state. Read about the current and past first ladies on this Web site.

The Coast Guard—an agency within the federal bureaucracy—led the efforts to contain and clean up the Deepwater Horizon oil spill in 2010. These efforts included relocating endangered wildlife that was threatened by the spill. Here, pelicans rescued from the oil slick are loaded onto Coast Guard planes for release in a safer wildlife reserve.

Bureaucracy in a Democracy

WHAT GOVERNMENT DOES AND WHY IT MATTERS Americans depend on government bureaucracies to accomplish the most spectacular achievements as well as the most mundane. Yet they often do not realize that public bureaucracies are essential for providing the services that they use every day and that they rely on in emergencies. On a typical day, a college student might check the weather forecast, drive on an interstate highway, mail the rent check, drink from a public water fountain, check the calories on the side of a yogurt container, attend a class, log on to the Internet, and meet a relative at the airport. Each of these activities is possible because of the work of a government bureaucracy: the U.S. Weather Service, the U.S. Department of Transportation, the U.S. Postal Service, the Environmental Protection Agency, the Food and Drug Administration, the student loan programs of the U.S. Department of Education, the Advanced Research Projects Agency (which developed the Internet in the 1960s), and the Federal Aviation Administration. Without the ongoing work of these agencies,

focusquestions

- What is the bureaucracy and why is it necessary?
- What are some of the major goals we expect federal agencies to promote?
- How have politicians tried to make the bureaucracy more efficient?
- Can the bureaucracy be controlled?

many of these common activities would be impossible, unreliable, or more expensive. Even though bureaucracies provide essential services that all Americans rely on, they are often disparaged by politicians and the general public alike. Criticized as "big government," many federal bureaucracies come into public view only when they are charged with fraud, waste, and abuse.

In emergencies, the national perspective on bureaucracy and, indeed, on "big government" shifts. After the September 11 terrorist attacks, all eyes turned to Washington. The federal government responded by strengthening and reorganizing the bureaucracy to undertake a whole new set of responsibilities designed to keep America safe. In the biggest government reorganization in over half a century, Congress created the Department of Homeland Security in 2002. The massive new department merged twenty-two existing agencies into a single department employing nearly 170,000 workers.

As we shall see in this chapter, Americans have a love/hate relationship with the federal bureaucracy. This ambivalence prompts politicians at times to promise that they will slash the federal bureaucracy or move government responsibilities to the private sector. Yet, they rarely follow through on such promises. Because Americans rely on government in so many aspects of their lives, significant reductions in the federal bureaucracy would create disruptions that no one wishes to experience.

chaptercontents

Bureaucracy and Bureaucrats

Bureaucracy is nothing more nor less than a form of organization, a complex structure of offices, tasks, and rules. To gain some objectivity, and to appreciate the universality of bureaucracy, let us take the word and break it into its two main parts—*bureau* and *cracy*. *Bureau*, a French word, can mean either "office" or "desk." *Cracy* is from the Greek word for "rule" or "form of rule." Taken together, *bureau* and *cracy* produce an interesting definition: Bureaucracy is a form of rule by offices and desks. Each member of an organization has an office, meaning a place as well as a set of responsibilities. That is, each "office" comprises a set of tasks that are specialized to the needs of the organization, and the person holding that office (or position) performs those specialized tasks. Specialization and repetition are essential to the efficiency of any organization. Therefore, when an organization is inefficient, it is often because it is not bureaucratized enough! But bureaucracies do not only perform specialized tasks that require routine action. As we shall see, they also undertake politically controversial tasks that require them to exercise a great deal of discretion and professional judgment. In many areas of policy, Congress writes laws that are very broad, and it is up to the bureaucracy to define what the policy will mean in practice. The decisions that bureaucrats make—often based on professional judgments—can themselves become politically contentious.

Both routine and exceptional tasks require the organization, specialization, and expertise found in bureaucracies. To provide services, government bureaucracies employ specialists such as meteorologists, doctors, and scientists. To do their jobs effectively, these specialists require resources and tools (ranging from paper to blood samples); they have to coordinate their work with others (for example, the traffic engineers must communicate with construction engineers); and there must be effective outreach to the public (for example, private doctors must be made aware of health warnings). Bureaucracy offers a way to coordinate the many different parts that must work together for the government to provide good services.

bureaucracy the complex structure of offices, tasks, rules, and principles of organization that are employed by all large-scale institutions to coordinate the work of their personnel

The Size of the Federal Service

For decades, politicians from both parties have asserted that the federal government is too big. Ronald Reagan led the way in 1981 with his statement that government was the problem, not the solution. Fifteen years later President Bill Clinton abandoned the traditional Democratic defense of government, declaring that "the era of big government is over." President George W. Bush voiced similar sentiments when he accepted his party's nomination for president in 2000, proclaiming "Big government is not the answer!" President Obama struck a different tone. Addressing Congress on the topic of health care reform, he noted that while Americans had a "healthy skepticism about government," they also believed that "hard work and responsibility should be rewarded by some measure of security and fair play" and recognized "that sometimes government has to step in to help deliver that promise."[2] Despite fears of bureaucratic growth getting out of hand, however, the federal service has hardly grown at all during the past thirty-five years; it reached its peak postwar level in 1968 with 3 million civilian employees plus an additional 3.6 million military personnel (a figure swollen by Vietnam). The number of civilian federal employees has since fallen to approximately 2.7 million in 2008; the number of military personnel totals only 1.4 million.[3]

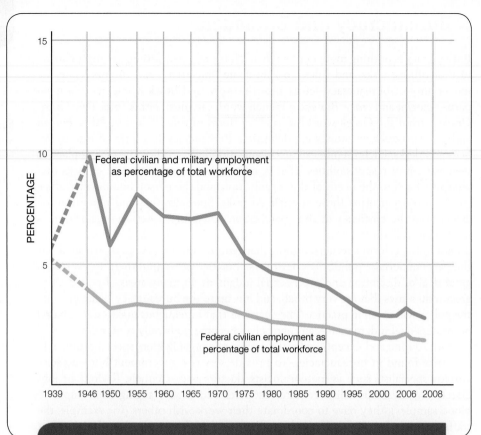

FIGURE 14.1

Employees in the Federal Service and in the National Workforce, 1946–2008

Since 1950, the ratio of federal employment to the total workforce has gradually declined. The lower line in this figure shows that the federal service has tended to grow at a rate that keeps pace with the economy and society. The upper line shows that variations in federal employment since 1946 have been in the military and are directly related to war and the Cold War. When did military employment begin its sharp decline?

SOURCES: "Federal Civilian Employment and Annual Payroll by Branch: 1970–2008," Table 484, and "Department of Defense Personnel: 1960–2008," Table 498—both tables are from the U.S. Census Bureau's *Statistical Abstract of the United States 2010*.

The growth of the federal service over the past fifty years is even less imposing when placed in the context of the total workforce and when compared with the size of state and local public employment. Figure 14.1 indicates that since 1950, the ratio of federal employment to the total workforce has been steady, and in fact has *declined* slightly in the past thirty years. In 1950, there were 4.3 million state and local civil service employees (about 6.5 percent of the country's workforce). In 2007, there were just over 19 million (nearly 14 percent of the workforce).[4] Federal employment, in contrast, exceeded 5 percent of the workforce only during World War II (not shown), and almost all of that temporary growth was military.

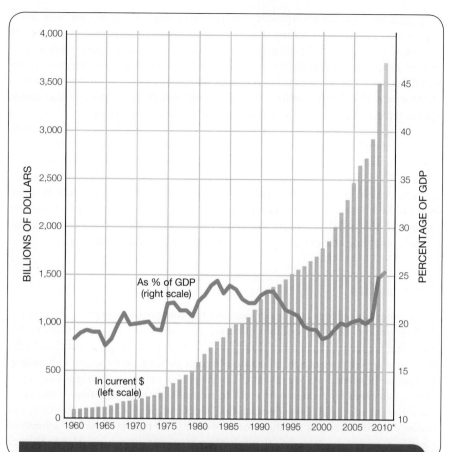

FIGURE 14.2

Annual Federal Outlays, 1960–2010

As the bars on this figure indicate, when measured in dollars, federal government spending, which supports the federal bureaucracy, shows dramatic increases over time. But as the trend line shows, federal spending as a percentage of gross domestic product has experienced significant ups and downs over time.

*Data for 2010 is estimated.

SOURCE: Office of Management and Budget, "Table 1.3: Summary of Receipts, Outlays, and Surpluses or Deficits in Current Dollars, Constant (FY 2005) Dollars, and as Percentages of GDP: 1940–2015," www.whitehouse.gov (accessed 2/15/10).

Another useful comparison is to be found in Figure 14.2. Although the dollar increase in federal spending shown by the bars looks impressive, the trend line indicating the relation of federal spending to the Gross Domestic Product (GDP) remained close to what it had been in 1960. This changed in 2009 when the recession pushed spending up dramatically, as the federal government sought to stimulate the economy, and spending rose on other recession-related programs, such as unemployment insurance. In 2009, the budget also reflected the costs of the wars in Iraq and Afghanistan which had not been included in the budgets of the Bush administrations.

In sum, the national government is indeed "very large," but it has not been growing any faster than the economy or society. The same is roughly true of the growth pattern of state and local public personnel. Bureaucracy keeps pace with society, despite people's seeming dislike of it, because the control towers, the prisons, the Social Security system, and other essential elements cannot be operated without bureaucracy. The United States certainly could not hope to protect the nation against terrorism without a large military and civilian bureaucracy.

Although the federal executive branch is large and complex, everything about it is commonplace. Bureaucracies are commonplace because they touch so many aspects of daily life. Government bureaucracies implement the decisions made through the political process. Bureaucracies are full of routine because that ensures the regular delivery of services and also ensures that each agency fulfills its mandate. Public bureaucracies are powerful because legislatures and chief executives, and indeed the people, delegate vast power to them to make sure a particular job is done—enabling citizens to be freer to pursue their private ends.

Bureaucrats

"Government by offices and desks" conveys to most people a picture of hundreds of office workers shuffling millions of pieces of paper. There is a lot of truth in that image, but we have to look more closely at what papers are being shuffled and why. More than seventy years ago, an astute observer defined bureaucracy as "continuous routine business."[5] As we saw at the beginning of this chapter, almost any organization succeeds by reducing its work to routines, with each routine being given to a different specialist. But specialization separates people from each other; one worker's output becomes another worker's input. The timing of such relationships is essential, and timing requires these workers to stay in communication with each other. In fact, bureaucracy was the first information network.

What Do Bureaucrats Do? Congress is responsible for making the laws but, in most cases, legislation only sets the broad parameters for government action. Bureaucracies are responsible for filling in the blanks by determining how the laws should be implemented. This requires bureaucracies to draw up much more detailed rules that guide the process of **implementation**. Bureaucracies also play a key role in enforcing the laws. Congress needs the bureaucracy to engage in rule making and implementation for several reasons. One is that bureaucracies employ people who have much more specialized expertise in specific policy areas than do members of Congress. Decisions about how to achieve many policy goals— from managing the national parks to regulating air quality to ensuring a sound economy—rest of the judgment of specialized experts. A second reason that Congress needs bureaucracy is that because updating legislation can take many years, bureaucratic flexibility can ensure that laws are administered in ways that take new conditions into account. Finally, members of Congress often prefer to delegate politically difficult decision making to bureaucrats.

One of the most important things that bureaucracies do is issue rules. The rules drawn up by government agencies provide more detailed and specific indications of what the policy actually will mean. For example, the Clean Air Act empowers the Environmental Protection Agency (EPA) to assess whether current or projected levels of air pollutants pose a threat to public health, to determine whether motor vehicle emissions are contributing to such pollution, and to create rules

implementation the efforts of departments and agencies to translate laws into specific bureaucratic rules and actions designed to regulate these emissions. Under the Bush Administration, the EPA claimed it did not have the authority to regulate a specific group of pollutants commonly referred to as "greenhouse gases" (for example, carbon dioxide). In 2007, the Supreme Court ruled that the EPA did have that authority and had to provide a justification for not regulating such emissions.[6] In the first year of the Obama administration, the agency ruled that greenhouse gases posed a threat to public health and that the emissions from new motor vehicles contributed to greenhouse gas pollution.[7] The agency then imposed new gas emission standards for automobiles, which would raise the average per vehicle fuel economy for new vehicles to 35.5 miles per gallon mile starting in 2016.[8] Not only will this finding by the EPA have a significant effect on the automobile industry, it could lead to far-reaching regulations in the future governing all greenhouse-gas generating industries.

The rule-making process is thus a highly political one. Once a new law is passed, the agency studies the legislation and proposes a set of rules to guide implementation. These proposed rules are then open to comment by anyone who wishes to weigh in. Representatives for the regulated industries and advocates of all sorts commonly submit comments. But anyone who wishes to can go to the Web site www.regulations.gov to read proposed rules, enter their own comments, and view the comments of others. Once rules are approved, they are published in the *Federal Register* and have the force of law.

In additional to rule making, bureaucracies play an essential role in enforcing the laws, in which they exercise considerable power over private actors. For example, in 2009, the Consumer Product Safety Commission fined Mattel $2.3 million for selling toys that contained lead, and another company, Mega Brands America, $1.1 million for failure to properly report a child fatality caused by one of its building sets.[9] In 2010, to comply with federal regulations, the auto manufacturer Toyota was forced to recall several car models after identifying problems with their gas pedals and accelerators. The National Highway Traffic Safety Commission launched an investigation of Toyota and found that Toyota knew of the defect but installed the accelerators in cars anyway. The National Highway Traffic Safety Commission charged the company an initial fine of $16.4 million for failing to notify regulators of these problems. It also left open the possibility of further fines pending investigations of other defects in the cars.[10]

Government bureaucrats do essentially the same things that bureaucrats in large private organizations do, and neither type deserves the disrespect after implied in the term *bureaucrat*. But because of the authoritative, coercive nature of government, far more constraints are imposed on public bureaucrats than on private bureaucrats, even when their jobs are the same. During the 1970s and 1980s, the length of time required to develop an administrative rule from a proposal to actual publication in the *Federal Register* (when it takes on full legal status) grew from an average of fifteen months to an average of thirty-five to forty months. Inefficiency? No. Most of the increased time is attributable to new procedures requiring more public notice, more public hearings, more hearings held

The rules established by regulatory agencies have the force of law. In 2010, the car company Toyota was forced by federal regulators to recall six million vehicles in the U.S. owing to safety defects with some models.

out in the field rather than in Washington, more cost-benefit analysis, and stronger legal obligations to prepare "environmental impact statements" demonstrating that the proposed rule or agency action will not have an unacceptably large negative impact on the human or physical environment.[11] Thus, a great deal of what is popularly paraded as the lower efficiency of public agencies can be attributed to the political, judicial, legal, and public-opinion restraints and extraordinarily high expectations imposed on public bureaucrats.

We will have more to say at the end of this chapter about bureaucratic accountability and the potential role of citizens in it. Suffice it to say here that if a private company such as Microsoft were required to open up all its decision processes and management practices to full view by the media, their competitors, and all interested citizens, Microsoft—despite its profit motive and the pressure of competition—would likely appear far less efficient, perhaps no more efficient than public bureaucracies.

A good case study of the important role agencies can play is the story of how ordinary federal bureaucrats created the Internet. Yes, it's true: what became the Internet was developed largely by the U.S. Department of Defense, and defense considerations still shape the basic structure of the Internet. In 1957, immediately following the profound American embarrassment over the Soviet Union's launching of Sputnik, Congress authorized the establishment of the Advanced Research Projects Agency (ARPA) to develop, among other things, a means of maintaining communications in the event the existing telecommunications network (the telephone system) was disabled by a strategic attack. Since the telephone network was highly centralized and therefore could have been completely disabled by a single attack, ARPA developed a decentralized, highly redundant network. Redundancy in this case improved the probability of functioning after an attack. The full design, called by the acronym of ARPANET, took almost a decade to create. By 1971, around twenty universities were connected to the ARPANET. The forerunner to the Internet was born.[12]

The Merit System: How to Become a Bureaucrat Although they face more inconveniences than their counterparts in the private sector, public bureaucrats are rewarded in part with greater job security than employees of most private organizations. More than a century ago, the federal government attempted to imitate business by passing the Civil Service Act of 1883, which was followed by almost universal adoption of equivalent laws in state and local governments. These laws required that appointees to public office be qualified for the job to which they are appointed. This policy came to be called the **merit system**; its ideal was not merely to put an end to political appointments under the "spoils system" but also to require adequate preparation for every job by holding competitive examinations through which the very best candidates were to be hired. At the higher levels of government agencies, including such posts as cabinet secretaries and assistant secretaries, many jobs are filled with political appointees and are not part of the merit system.

As a further safeguard against political interference (and to compensate for the lower-than-average pay given to public employees), merit system employees—genuine civil servants—were given legal protection against being fired without a show of cause. Reasonable people may disagree about the value of such job security and how far it should extend in the civil service, but the justifiable objective of this job protection—cleansing bureaucracy of political interference while upgrading performance—cannot be disputed.

merit system a product of civil service reform, in which appointees to positions in public bureaucracies must objectively be deemed qualified for those positions

Who Are "Bureaucrats"?

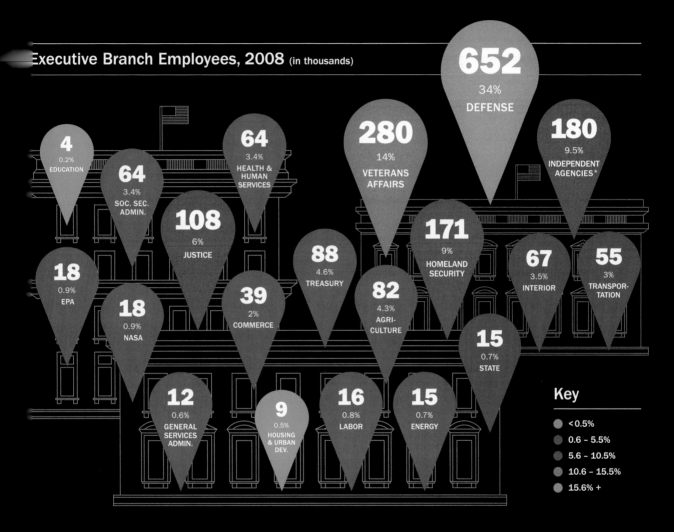

Executive Branch Employees, 2008 (in thousands)

4 — 0.2% EDUCATION

64 — 3.4% SOC. SEC. ADMIN.

64 — 3.4% HEALTH & HUMAN SERVICES

652 — 34% DEFENSE

280 — 14% VETERANS AFFAIRS

180 — 9.5% INDEPENDENT AGENCIES*

108 — 6% JUSTICE

88 — 4.6% TREASURY

171 — 9% HOMELAND SECURITY

67 — 3.5% INTERIOR

55 — 3% TRANSPORTATION

18 — 0.9% EPA

18 — 0.9% NASA

39 — 2% COMMERCE

82 — 4.3% AGRICULTURE

15 — 0.7% STATE

12 — 0.6% GENERAL SERVICES ADMIN.

9 — 0.5% HOUSING & URBAN DEV.

16 — 0.8% LABOR

15 — 0.7% ENERGY

Key

- ● < 0.5%
- ● 0.6 – 5.5%
- ● 5.6 – 10.5%
- ● 10.6 – 15.5%
- ● 15.6% +

Location

320 — 17% WASHINGTON D.C. AREA

1,589 — 83% – OTHER

Independent agencies include NASA, the EPA, and the Social Security Administration (shown here), as well as other agencies.

SOURCE: Bureau of Labor Statistics

Contrary to popular notions of "paper pushers," the people who work in the federal bureaucracy perform a range of tasks essential to the functioning of American society. Nearly two million executive branch employees are involved in protecting the nation's security, managing the economy, and promoting public welfare through various means including environmental protection and health and safety regulations. Most federal employees work outside the Washington, D.C. area.

for critical analysis

1. Which category of departments and agencies—security, economic, or public welfare—employs the most people? Why?

2. With two million people working for the executive branch, mostly outside of the Washington, D.C. area, how can Congress and the president be sure that they are serving the public's interests?

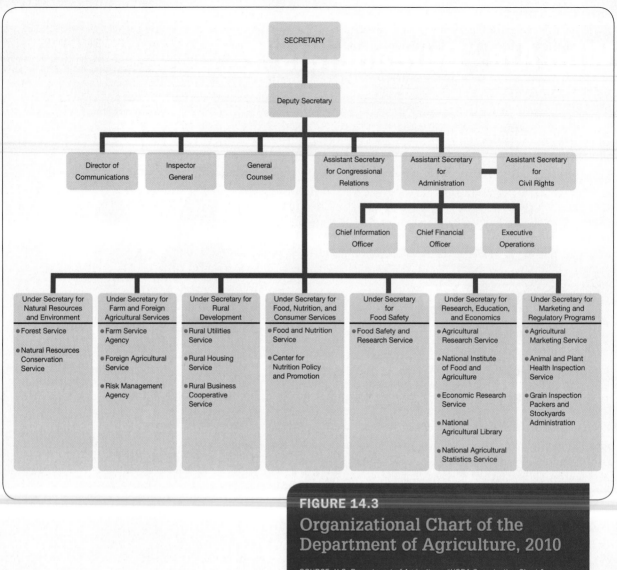

FIGURE 14.3

Organizational Chart of the Department of Agriculture, 2010

SOURCE: U.S. Department of Agriculture. "USDA Organization Chart." www
.usda.gov (accessed 2/15/10).

● The Organization of the Executive Branch

department the largest subunit of the executive branch. The secretaries of the fifteen departments form the Cabinet

Cabinet departments, agencies, and bureaus are the operating parts of the bureaucratic whole. Figure 14.3 is an organizational chart of one of the largest and most important of the fifteen **departments**, the Department of Agriculture. At the top is the head of the department, who in the United States is called the "secretary" of the department.[13] Below the secretary and the deputy secretary is a second tier of "under secretaries" who have management responsibilities for one or more operating agencies, shown in the smaller print directly below each undersecretary's title. Those operating agencies are the third tier of the department, yet they are the highest level of responsibility for the actual programs around which the entire department is organized. This third tier is generally called the "bureau level." Each

● What are some of
the major goals
we expect federal
agencies to
promote?

bureau-level agency usually operates under a statute, enacted by Congress, that set up the agency and gave it its authority and jurisdiction. The names of these bureau-level agencies are often quite well known to the public—the Forest Service and the Food Safety and Inspection Service, for example. These are the so-called line agencies, those that deal directly with the public. Sometimes these agencies are officially called "bureaus," such as the Federal Bureau of Investigation (FBI), which is a part of the third tier of the Department of Justice. But "bureau" is also the conventional term for this level of administrative agency, even though many agencies or their supporters have preferred over the years to adopt a more palatable designation, such as "service" or "administration." Each bureau is, of course, even further subdivided into divisions, offices, or units—all are parts of the bureaucratic hierarchy.

Not all government agencies are part of Cabinet departments. Some **independent agencies** are set up by Congress outside the departmental structure altogether, even though the president appoints and directs the heads of these agencies. Independent agencies usually have broad powers to provide public services that are either too expensive or too important to be left to private initiatives. Some examples of independent agencies are the National Aeronautics and Space Administration (NASA), the Central Intelligence Agency (CIA), and the Environmental Protection Agency (EPA). **Government corporations** are a third type of government agency but are more like private businesses performing and charging for a market service, such as delivering the mail (the United States Postal Service) or transporting railroad passengers (Amtrak).

independent agency an agency that is not part of a Cabinet department

government corporation a government agency that performs a service normally provided by the private sector

Yet a fourth type of agency is the independent regulatory commission, given broad discretion to make rules. The first regulatory agencies established by Congress, beginning with the Interstate Commerce Commission in 1887, were set up as independent regulatory commissions because Congress recognized that regulatory agencies are "minilegislatures," whose rules are exactly the same as legislation but require the kind of expertise and full-time attention that is beyond the capacity of Congress. Until the 1960s, most of the regulatory agencies that were set up by Congress, such as the Federal Trade Commission (1914) and the Federal Communications Commission (1934), were independent regulatory commissions. But beginning in the late 1960s and the early 1970s, all new regulatory programs, with two or three exceptions (such as the Federal Election Commission), were placed within existing departments and made directly responsible to the president. Since the 1970s, no major new regulatory programs have been established, independent or otherwise.

The different agencies of the executive branch can be classified into three main groups by the services that they provide to the American public. The first category of agencies provide services and products that seek to promote the public welfare. The second group of agencies work to promote national security. The third group provides services that help to maintain a strong economy. Let us look more closely at what each set of agencies offers to the American public.

● Promoting the Public Welfare

One of the most important activities of the federal bureaucracy is to promote the public welfare. Americans often think of government welfare as a single program that goes only to the very poor; but a number of federal agencies provide services, build infrastructure, and enact regulations designed to enhance the well-being of the vast majority of citizens. Departments that have important responsibilities for promoting the public welfare in this sense include the Department of Housing and Urban Development, the Department of Health and Human Services, the Department of Veterans Affairs, the Department of the Interior, the Department of Education, and the Department of Labor. Ensuring the public welfare is also the main activity of agencies in other departments, such as the Department of Agriculture's Food and Nutrition Service, which administers the federal school lunch program and food stamps. In addition, a variety of independent regulatory agencies enforce regulations that aim to safeguard the public health and welfare.

How Do Federal Bureaucracies Promote the Public Welfare? Federal bureaucracies promote the public welfare with a diverse set of services, products, and regulations. The Department of Health and Human Services (HHS), for example, administers the program that comes closest to the popular understanding of welfare—Temporary Assistance to Needy Families (TANF). Yet this program is one of the smallest activities of the department. HHS also oversees the National Institutes of Health (NIH), which is responsible for cutting-edge biomedical research. In addition, HHS is responsible for the two major health programs of the federal government: Medicaid, which provides health care for low-income families and for many elderly and disabled people, and Medicare, which is the health insurance available to all elderly people in the United States.

A different notion of the public welfare but one highly valued by most Americans is provided by the National Park Service, which is under the Department of the Interior. First created in 1916, the National Park Service is responsible for the care and upkeep of national parks. Since the nineteenth century, Americans have seen protection of the natural environment as an important public goal and have looked to federal agencies to implement laws and administer programs that preserve natural areas and keep them open to the public.

The United States has no "Department of Regulation" but has many **regulatory agencies**. Some of these are bureaus within departments, such as the Food and Drug Administration (FDA) within the Department of Health and Human Services and the Occupational Safety and Health Administration (OSHA) in the Department of Labor. As we saw earlier, other regulatory agencies are independent regulatory commissions, such as the Consumer Product Safety Commission, Federal Communications Commission (FCC) and the EPA. But whether departmental or independent, an agency or commission is regulatory if Congress delegates to it relatively broad powers over a sector of the economy or a type of commercial activity and authorizes it to make rules restricting the conduct of people and businesses within that jurisdiction. Rules made by regulatory agencies have the force and effect of law.

Through their activities, these agencies seek to promote the welfare of all Americans, often working behind the scenes. The FDA, for example, works to protect public health by setting standards for food processing and inspecting plants to ensure that those standards are met. The EPA sets standards to limit polluting emissions from automobiles, among other functions. EPA regulations required automobile manufacturers to change the way they designed cars. The result has been cleaner air in many metropolitan areas.

Bureaucracies, Clienteles, and the Public Some of the public agencies that provide services that enhance well-being are tied to a specific group or segment of American society that is often thought of as the main clientele of that agency.

regulatory agencies
departments, bureaus, or independent agencies whose primary mission is to impose limits, restrictions, or other obligations on the conduct of individuals or companies in the private sector

For example, the Department of Agriculture was established in 1862 to promote the interests of farmers. Likewise, the Department of Veterans Affairs has strong links to veterans' organizations, such as the American Legion and the Veterans of Foreign Wars. The Department of Education relies on teachers' organizations for support. Figure 14.4 is a representation of this type of politics. This configuration is known as an **iron triangle**, a pattern of stable relationships among an agency in the executive branch, a congressional committee or subcommittee, and one or more organized groups of agency clientele. (Iron triangles were discussed in detail in Chapter 11.)

These relationships with particular clienteles are often important in preserving agencies from political attack. During his 1980 campaign, Ronald Reagan promised to dismantle the Department of Education as part of his commitment to get government "off people's backs." After his election, President Reagan even appointed a secretary of the department who was publicly committed to eliminating it. Yet, by the end of his administration, the Department of Education was still standing and barely touched. In 1995, the Republican Congress vowed to eliminate the Department of Education, along with two other departments, but it, too, failed. The educational constituency of the department (its clientele) mobilized to save it each time.

Such clientele groups generally have more influence over federal agencies than do people who are not part of the clientele group. But the ability of clientele groups to get their way is not automatic, as agencies have to balance limited resources, competing interests, and political pressures. For example, the Department of Veterans Affairs long resisted the efforts of Vietnam veterans to be compensated for exposure to Agent Orange, a chemical defoliant used extensively during the Vietnam War. Veterans charged that exposure to Agent Orange had left them with a variety of diseases ranging from cancer to severe birth defects in their children. Only after decades of lobbying, lawsuits, and federally sponsored studies did the Department of Veterans Affairs provide assistance to affected veterans.

Moreover, federal agencies increasingly seek public support outside their direct clients for their activities. In some cases, key clientele groups will work to build

iron triangle the stable, cooperative relationship that often develops among a congressional committee, an administrative agency, and one or more supportive interest groups. Not all of these relationships are triangular, but the iron triangle is the most typical

The federal bureaucracy plays an important role in promoting public welfare. The EPA creates and enforces regulations related to the environment—for instance, preventing the pollution of groundwater. At left, an EPA manager examines a plastic liner that catches acid runoff from an abandoned copper mine in Nevada. The Centers for Disease Control and Prevention (at right), part of the Department of Health and Human Services, protects the health and safety of people through its work to reduce and eliminate infectious diseases, such as swine flu.

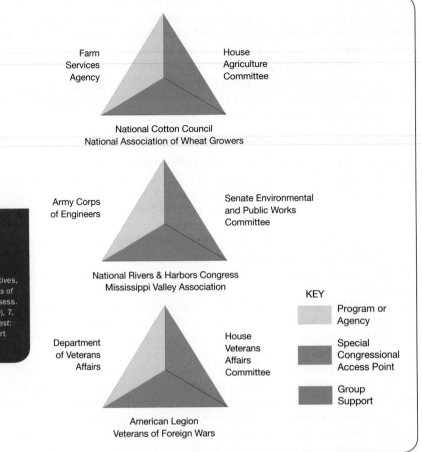

FIGURE 14.4

Iron Triangles

SOURCES: Adapted from U.S. House of Representatives, *Report of the Subcommittee for Special Investigations of the Committee on Armed Services,* 86th Cong., 1st sess. (Washington, DC: Government Printing Office, 1960), 7. Reprinted from Theodore J. Lowi, *Incomplete Conquest: Governing America,* 2nd ed. (New York: Holt, Rinehart and Winston, 1981), 139.

Farm Services Agency

House Agriculture Committee

National Cotton Council
National Association of Wheat Growers

Army Corps of Engineers

Senate Environmental and Public Works Committee

National Rivers & Harbors Congress
Mississippi Valley Association

KEY

Program or Agency

Special Congressional Access Point

Group Support

Department of Veterans Affairs

House Veterans Affairs Committee

American Legion
Veterans of Foreign Wars

---

for critical analysis

What is the impact of iron triangles on inequality in the United States? Do the ties among agencies, congressional committees, and organized groups promote inequality?

more widespread support for agency activities. For example, the AFL-CIO, which represents organized labor, built a broad coalition of student organizations, church groups, consumer groups, and civil rights activists opposed to sweatshops in the United States. These groups helped to support the Department of Labor's campaign to uncover and eliminate such manufacturing practices in the United States. Agency failure to consider public opinion can result in embarrassment, which bureaucrats prefer to avoid. The color-coded system that the Department of Homeland Security devised to warn about terrorism failed to command public respect. As soon as the system made its appearance, it came in for ridicule by late night comedians, who joked about the color-coding. The public gradually began to ignore the alerts, especially as suspicions mounted that the system was being politically manipulated. Eventually, the federal government stopped issuing new alerts.

Attentiveness to the public often means making the public aware of services and improving the way services are delivered. The Social Security Administration is an independent agency that administers old-age and disability insurance, the federal government's most important and expensive welfare program. Old-age insurance, or Social Security, is supported by AARP, an interest group representing people over fifty, generally considered to be the most powerful interest group operating in the United States today. But worried that younger workers are losing confidence in Social Security, the agency has recently begun to issue annual statements to each worker, outlining the benefits that they can count on from Social Security when they retire and indicating what benefits are available if they become disabled before retirement.

● What are some of the major goals we expect federal agencies to promote?

Providing National Security

One of the remarkable features of American federalism is that the most vital agencies for providing security for the American people are located in state and local governments—namely the police. But some agencies vital to maintaining national security are located in the national government, and they can be grouped into two categories: (1) agencies for control of conduct defined as a threat to internal national security and (2) agencies for defending American security from external threats. The departments of greatest influence in these two areas are Homeland Security, Justice, Defense, and State.

Agencies for Internal Security The task of maintaining domestic security changed dramatically after the terrorist attacks of September 11, 2001. The creation of the Department of Homeland Security in late 2002 signaled the high priority that domestic security would now have. The orientation of domestic agencies shifted as well, as agencies geared up to prevent terrorism, a task that differed greatly from their former charge of investigating crime. Along with this shift in responsibility, these agencies have acquired broad new powers—many of them controversial—including the power to detain terrorist suspects and to engage in extensive domestic intelligence-gathering about possible terrorists.

Before September 11, most of the effort put into maintaining national security took the form of legal work related to prosecuting federal crimes. The largest and most important unit of the Justice Department is the Criminal Division. Lawyers in the Criminal Division represent the United States government when it is the plaintiff enforcing the federal criminal laws, except for those cases (about 25 percent) specifically assigned to other divisions or agencies. Criminal litigation is handled by U.S. attorneys, who are appointed by the president. There is one U.S. attorney in each of the ninety-four federal judicial districts; he or she supervises the work of a number of assistant U.S. attorneys.

The Civil Division of the Justice Department deals with litigation in which the United States is the defendant being sued for injury and damages allegedly inflicted by a government official or agency. The missions of the other divisions of the Justice Department—Antitrust, Civil Rights, Environment and Natural Resources, and Tax—are described by their names.

When terrorism prevention took center stage, the Justice Department reoriented its activities accordingly. It was aided in its new mission by the USA PATRIOT Act, enacted soon after September 11. The act gave the Justice Department broad new powers, allowing the attorney general to detain any foreigner suspected of posing a threat to internal security. The Patriot Act also expanded the government's ability to use wiretaps and to issue search warrants without notifying suspects immediately. It required public libraries to keep lists of the public's book and Internet usage for federal inspection. Although initially popular with most Americans, these measures created concern about civil liberties. Despite these concerns, Congress renewed the act with only modest revisions in 2006.

Crime, Violence, and National Security on Television

Government agencies that are charged with providing national security, such as the Justice Department and the Department of Homeland Security, affect the lives of Americans every day. But the extent to which Americans accept the authority of these security agencies has varied over time. Violent real-world events may increase Americans' level of fear and result in increased support for security measures. After September 11, many Americans were willing to grant security agencies greater powers. Interestingly, mass media—particularly television—may also play a role in this process.

In the 1970s, George Gerbner and his colleagues at the Annenberg School of Communication began a line of research regarding the effects of violent television content on fear of crime, and the acceptance of authority and security presence. Because the television world is rife with crime and violence, Gerbner contends that viewers of television will see the world as a dangerous place. Gerbner warns that this causes citizens to favor martial policies of law and order, including a greater security presence and tougher punishment for criminals.[a]

Indeed, recent studies have confirmed that viewing television can increase citizens' fear of violence, crime, and terrorism. While exploring the effects of television viewing on fear and anxiety after the September 11 attacks, at least two studies found that the more television content people watched after the attacks, the greater their self-reported fear and anxiety. Yet both studies found that people who read the newspaper had lower levels of support for expanded police authority and restrictions on privacy in the interest of national security.

Entertainment programming may also affect viewers' attitudes about security and governmental authority. Another study analyzed the effects of exposure to crime dramas such as NYPD Blue on viewers' perceptions of crime as an important problem, and the extent to which viewers judged public officials on their performance on crime-related issues. The authors argued that crime dramas frequently "activate" the concept of crime in the minds of the viewers, causing viewers to think more about it when making political judgments.

Consider programs like the popular drama 24 starring Kiefer Sutherland as Jack Bauer. Each episode is laden with back-to-back violent encounters with thugs, spies, and terrorists, with a major criminal or terrorist threat always imminent. To what extent do these images increase citizens' acceptance of the authority of police and security agencies?

[a]G. Gerbner, L. Gross, M. Morgan, and N. Signorielli, "The 'Mainstreaming' of America: Violence Profile No. 11," *Journal of Communication* 30 (1980), 10–29.

for critical analysis

1. If television content increases viewers' fear and subsequent support for security agencies, is that good or bad for the functioning of American democracy? What if the television content makes the world seem more dangerous than it actually is?

2. After September 11, Americans were generally more willing to accept increased powers of security agencies. Why have critics argued that some of the measures these agencies have taken in the fight against terrorism are at odds with democracy?

What are some of the major goals we expect federal agencies to promote?

Since 2001, the Justice Department has played a central role in setting the balance between national security and civil liberties. In 2007, high-profile congressional hearings revealed extensive conflicts between the Justice Department and the White House over the use of warrantless wiretapping in the United States. These included a dramatic hospital scene in 2005 in which White House officials sought—unsuccessfully—to persuade the gravely ill former attorney general, John Ashcroft, to approve the continuation of the wiretapping program over the wishes of Justice Department officials. The hearings also exposed the fact that in 2005 the former attorney general, Alberto Gonzales, secretly approved the use of severe methods of interrogation—many classified as torture under the Geneva Convention—even after Congress had passed a law forbidding torture.[14]

Since its creation in 2002, the Department of Homeland Security has joined the Justice Department as the major bureaucracy charged with domestic security. The new department took over some of the security-oriented agencies previously controlled by other departments (see Table 14.1). For example, the Immigration and Naturalization Service (INS) was moved from Justice to Homeland Security. Once inside the new department, the INS was abolished. Immigration services were consolidated into U.S. Citizenship and Immigration Services. The enforcement functions of the old INS were combined with the U.S. Customs Services (formerly part of the Treasury Department) to create a new Bureau of Immigration and Customs Enforcement, known as ICE, in the Department of Homeland Security. ICE has extensive investigative capacities, with field offices around the United States and bureaus in over thirty countries. Other agencies that were transferred to the Department of Homeland Security include the Coast Guard, the Secret Service, and the Federal Emergency Management Agency.

Growing pains were evident in the department's first years as different bureaucratic cultures, now part of a single operation, sought to work together. The new department also quickly became embroiled in turf battles with the FBI (which remained in the Justice Department) as the two departments attempted to sort out their respective responsibilities for homeland security. The department's most public failure was its terrible performance during Hurricane Katrina. Not only did the agency fail to move quickly to assist stranded residents of New Orleans, it mismanaged contracts and grants associated with the recovery efforts. The heavy reliance of the Department of Homeland Security on private contractors has contributed to its failings. Without the staff to supervise the contractors adequately, the department became known for massive cost overruns and poor performance. Concerns about conflicts of interest between contractors and the agency have mounted. Alarm bells went off in 2007 when the Coast Guard, the largest agency under Homeland Security, renewed a $24 billion contract for fleet modernization only eleven days after department officials testified about major flaws in the program.[15]

Agencies for External National Security Two departments occupy center stage in maintaining external national security: the departments of State and Defense.

The State Department's primary mission is diplomacy. As the United States geared up to invade Afghanistan in 2001 and Iraq in 2003, Secretary of State Colin Powell took the lead in building the case for American action. Although diplomacy is the primary task of the State Department, diplomatic missions are only one of its organizational dimensions. As of 2010, the State Department comprised twenty-eight bureau-level units, each under the direction of an assistant secretary.[16]

for critical analysis

Why was the Department of Homeland Security created? What problems has the new agency faced?

These bureaus support the responsibilities of the elite of foreign affairs, the foreign service officers (FSOs), who staff U.S. embassies around the world and who hold almost all of the most powerful positions in the department below the rank of ambassador.[17] The ambassadorial positions, especially the plum positions in the major capitals of the world, are filled by presidential appointees, many of whom get their posts by having been important donors to the victorious political campaign.

Despite the importance of the State Department in foreign affairs, fewer than 20 percent of all U.S. government employees working abroad are directly under its authority. By far the largest number of career government professionals working abroad are under the authority of the Defense Department.

TABLE 14.1

The Shape of a Domestic Security Department

DEPARTMENT OF HOMELAND SECURITY	AGENCIES AND DEPARTMENTS THAT WERE MOVED TO THE DEPARTMENT OF HOMELAND SECURITY	DEPARTMENT OR AGENCY THEY WERE PREVIOUSLY UNDER	FROM THE 2010 BUDGET REQUEST	
			BUDGET REQUEST, IN MILLIONS	ESTIMATED NUMBER OF EMPLOYEES
Border and Transportation Security	U.S. Customs and Border Protection	Treasury Department	$11,437	58,105
	Immigration and Customs Enforcement	Justice Department	$5,763	20,134
	U.S. Citizenship and Immigration Services	Justice Department	$2,868	10,700
	National Protection and Program Directorate (includes domestic preparedness)	General Services Administration	$1,959	2,584
	Transportation Security Administration	Transportation Department	$7,794	51,949
	Federal Law Enforcement Training Center	Treasury Department	$288	1,103
Emergency Preparedness and Response	Federal Emergency Management Agency	Independent agency	$10,479	6,717
Domestic Nuclear Detection Office	(new)		$366	130
Science and Technology	(multiple programs)	Department of Energy	$968	404
Secret Service	Secret Service, including presidential protection units	Treasury Department	$1,710	7,055
Coast Guard	Coast Guard	Transportation Department	$9,956	49,954
Total DHS			$55,115	211,807

SOURCE: U.S. Department of Homeland Security, "Budget-in-Brief, Fiscal Year 2010," www.dhs.gov (accessed 2/16/10).

The creation of the Department of Defense by legislation between 1947 and 1949 was an effort to unify the two historic military departments, the War Department and the Navy Department, and to integrate them with a new department, the Air Force. Real unification, however, did not occur. The Defense Department simply added more pluralism to an already pluralistic national security establishment. That establishment became more complex in 1952, with the creation of the National Security Agency, charged with electronic surveillance and intelligence gathering.

The American military, following worldwide military tradition, is organized according to a "chain of command"—a tight hierarchy of clear responsibility and rank, made clearer by uniforms, special insignia, and detailed organizational charts and rules of order and etiquette. At the top of the military chain of command are chiefs of staff (called chief of naval operations in the navy, and commandant in the marines). These chiefs of staff also constitute the membership of the Joint Chiefs of Staff—the center of military policy and management.

In 2002, for the first time in our nation's history, the Defense Department created a regional commander in chief charged with homeland defense and command of military operations inside the nation's borders. The U.S. Northern Command is charged with providing emergency backup to state and local governments, which are the first responders to any security disaster. The creation of a regional command within the United States was an unprecedented move, breaching a long-standing line between domestic law enforcement and foreign military operations.

As the creation of a military capacity within the United States suggests, addressing the threat of terrorism calls for greater coordination of internal and external security. In 2004, the National Commission on Terrorist Attacks upon the United States (the 9/11 Commission) issued a widely read report that called for a major reorganization of bureaucratic responsibilities for internal and external security.[18] The report revealed that different departments of the American government had information that, if handled properly, might have prevented the attacks of September 11, 2001. To correct this, the commission made major recommendations designed to promote unity of effort across the bureaucracy.

The 9/11 Commission's work prompted a major reorganization of the fragmented intelligence community. In 2005, a new office, the Office of the Director of National Intelligence, took over responsibility for coordinating the efforts of the sixteen different agencies that gather intelligence. The DNI reports directly to the president each morning.

National Security and Democracy Of all the agencies in the federal bureaucracy, those charged with providing national security most often come into tension with the norms and expectations of American democracy. Two issues in particular arise as these agencies work to ensure the national security: (1) the trade-offs between respecting the personal rights of individuals versus protecting the general public and (2) the need for secrecy in matters of national security versus the public's right to know what the government is doing. Standards of what is an acceptable trade-off in each area vary depending on whether the country is at war or peace. The nature of the threat facing national security also affects judgments about the appropriate trade-offs. Needless to say, Americans often disagree about such threats and therefore take different views about what activities the government should be able to pursue to defend our national security. At the outset of the war on terrorism, the nation was unusually united in its support for a wide range of government security measures that would have been highly controversial in any other circumstance.

After September 11, the federal government assumed a new role in airport security. With the passage of the Secure Aviation and Transportation Act, the federal government became involved with screening passengers and baggage.

When national security is at stake, federal agencies have taken actions that are normally considered incompatible with individual rights. For example, in World War II, thousands of American citizens of Japanese descent were interned for national security reasons. Although the Supreme Court declared this action justified, the federal government has since acknowledged that it constituted unjustified discrimination and has offered reparations to those who were interned. In the 1960s, the FBI director J. Edgar Hoover authorized extensive wiretaps to eavesdrop on telephone calls of the civil rights leader Martin Luther King, Jr.; most people today would regard this an illegal invasion of his personal privacy. With the advent of the war on terrorism, the government gained unprecedented powers to detain foreign suspects, carry out wiretaps and searches, conduct secret military tribunals, and build an integrated law enforcement and intelligence system. Congress hastily enacted many of these sweeping provisions of the USA PATRIOT Act several weeks after the terrorist attacks, with little debate. Since then, extensive doubts about the broad powers of the Patriot Act have emerged. As denunciations of the act spread from civil libertarians on the left to libertarians on the right and to groups such as librarians and city governments, who objected to its surveillance provisions, Congress began to consider measures that would restrict federal power in order to protect individual liberties. When Congress debated renewing the Patriot Act in 2005–06, these concerns about individual liberties threatened to block renewal. The act that was finally approved in 2006 protected most libraries from having to turn over information to the government. Nonetheless, many in Congress felt the safeguards to individual liberties did not go far enough.

Protecting national security often requires the government to conduct its activities in secret. Yet, as Americans have come to expect a more open government in the past three decades, many critics believe that federal agencies charged with national security keep too many secrets from the American public. As one critic put it, "the United States government must rest, in the words of the Declaration of Independence, on 'the consent of the governed.' And there can be no meaningful consent where those who are governed do not know to what they are consenting."[19]

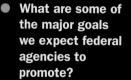

● What are some of
the major goals
we expect federal
agencies to
promote?

The effort to make information related to national security more available to the public began in 1966 with the passage of the Freedom of Information Act (FOIA). Strengthened in 1974 after Watergate, the act allows any person to request classified information from any federal agency. It is estimated that the federal government spends $339 million a year responding to 506, 471 requests for information.[20] The information obtained through the Freedom of Information Act often reveals unflattering or unsuccessful aspects of national security activities. One private organization, the National Security Archive, makes extensive use of the Freedom of

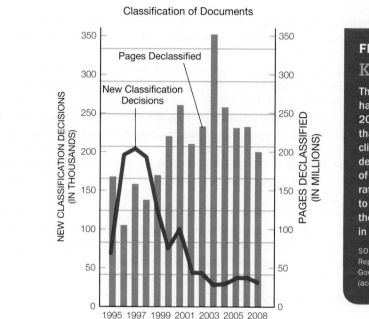

Classification of Documents

Pages Declassified

New Classification Decisions

FIGURE 14.5

Keeping Secrets

The number of classified documents has increased substantially since 2001, whereas the pages of material that have been declassified has declined sharply. Meanwhile, requests to declassify material under the Freedom of Information Act have increased at a rate that agencies have found difficult to manage. During what years was there a move toward more openness in government?

SOURCE: OpenTheGovernment.org, "Secrecy Report Card 09: Indicators of Secrecy in the Federal Government," p. 18, www.openthegovernment.org (accessed 2/17/10).

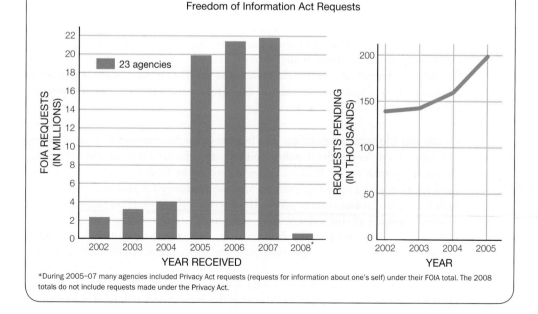

Freedom of Information Act Requests

*During 2005–07 many agencies included Privacy Act requests (requests for information about one's self) under their FOIA total. The 2008 totals do not include requests made under the Privacy Act.

Information Act to obtain information about the activities of national security agencies. The National Security Archive has published many of these documents on its Web site and maintains an archive in Washington, D.C., that is open to the public.

The tension between secrecy and democracy has sharpened dramatically with the threat of terrorism. The Freedom of Information Act has been curtailed, and the range of information deemed sensitive has greatly expanded. President Bush defended the new secrecy, declaring, "We're an open society, but we're at war. Foreign terrorists and agents must never again be allowed to use our freedoms against us." Although most Americans agreed that enhanced secrecy was needed to ensure domestic security, concerns about excessive secrecy mounted. Some analysts worried that secrecy would prevent Congress from carrying out its basic oversight responsibilities. They also claimed that much of the secrecy had nothing to do with national security. As a candidate President Obama promised to reduce government secrecy and in many respects he has moved in that direction. The day after his election, the president launched a process that would culminate in an Open Government Directive. He also instructed federal agencies that they should administer the FOIA law liberally: when in doubt, err on the side of openness. And in the most substantive change, at the end of his first year in office, Obama issued an executive order designed to promote more rapid declassification of secret documents. However, the new administration also continued some of the secrecy practices initiated in the Bush years. Most notably, the administration invoked the state secrets privilege to prevent lawsuits related to warrantless wiretapping and torture from going to trial.[21]

There are no easy answers to the questions about how the needs for national security should be reconciled with the values of a democratic society. It is clear, however, that in an era when national security is foremost in the public's mind, conflicts between democracy and secrecy are sure to increase.

Maintaining a Strong Economy

In our capitalist economic system, the government does not directly run the economy. Yet many federal government activities are critical to maintaining a strong economy. Foremost among these are the agencies responsible for fiscal and monetary policy. Other agencies, such as the Internal Revenue Service (IRS), transform private resources into use for public purposes. Tax policy may also strengthen the economy through decisions about whom to tax, how much, and when. Finally, the federal government, through such agencies as the Department of Transportation, the Commerce Department, and the Energy Department may directly provide services or goods that bolster the economy.

Fiscal and Monetary Agencies The best term for government activity affecting or relating to money is **fiscal policy**. "Fiscal" can refer to anything and everything having to do with public finance. However, we in the United States often reserve *fiscal* for taxing and spending policies and use *monetary* for policies having to do with banks, credit, and currency. Yet a third term, *welfare*, deserves to be treated as an equal member of this redistributive category.[22]

The administration of fiscal policy occurs primarily in the Treasury Department. In addition to collecting income, corporate, and other taxes, the Treasury also manages the enormous national debt—$13.1 trillion in 2010.[23] The debt is a fiscal instrument in the hands of the federal government that can be used—through manipulation of interest rates and through the buying and selling of government

fiscal policy the government's use of taxing, monetary, and spending powers to manipulate the economy

bonds—to slow down or to speed up the activity of the entire national economy, as well as to defend the value of the dollar in international trade. The Treasury Department is also responsible for printing U.S. currency, but currency is only a tiny proportion of the entire money economy. Most of the trillions of dollars used in the transactions of the private and public sectors of the U.S. economy exist in computerized accounts, not in actual currency.

Another important fiscal agency (although for technical reasons it is called an agency of monetary policy) is the **Federal Reserve System**, which is headed by the Federal Reserve Board. The Federal Reserve System (called simply the Fed) has authority over the interest rates and lending activities of the nation's most important banks. Congress established the Fed in 1913 as a clearinghouse responsible for adjusting the supply of money and credit to the needs of commerce and industry in different regions of the country. The Fed is also responsible for ensuring that banks do not overextend themselves, a policy that guards against a chain of bank failures during a sudden economic scare, such as occurred in 1929 and again in 2008. The Federal Reserve Board directs the operations of the twelve district Federal Reserve Banks, which are essentially "bankers' banks," serving the monetary needs of the hundreds of member banks in the national banking system.[24] The Treasury and the Federal Reserve took center stage when a string of bank failures threatened economic catastrophe in 2008. These agencies designed a $700 billion bailout package and persuaded Congress that a rapid response was needed to avert a worldwide depression. Although the Treasury and the Federal Reserve sprang into action when economic calamity loomed, critics charged that the crisis could have been prevented if these agencies had exercised more regulatory oversight over the financial sector during the previous decade. In 2010, the Congress and the president neared agreement on creating a new "Risk Council" to be headed by the treasury secretary, with the Federal Reserve chairman as his deputy. This new body would identify systemwide risks to the financial sector. The change would reduce the Federal Reserve's authority, removing its important oversight powers over banks.[25]

Revenue Agencies   One of the first actions Congress took under President George Washington was to create the Department of the Treasury, and probably its oldest function is the collection of taxes on imports, called tariffs. Now part of the United States Customs Service, federal customs agents are located at every U.S. seaport and international airport to oversee the collection of tariffs. But far and away the most important of the **revenue agencies** is the Internal Revenue Service. The Customs Service and the IRS are two of at least twelve bureaus within the Treasury Department.

The IRS is the government agency that Americans love to hate. As one expert put it, "probably no organization in the country, public or private, creates as much clientele *dis*favor as the Internal Revenue Service. The very nature of its work brings it into an adversary relationship with vast numbers of Americans every year."[26] Taxpayers complain about the IRS's needless complexity, its lack of sensitivity and responsiveness to individual taxpayers, and its overall lack of efficiency. Such complaints led Congress to pass the IRS Restructuring and Reform Act of 1998, which instituted a number of new protections for taxpayers. The law aimed to make IRS agents more "customer friendly" and limit the agency's ability to collect money owed

Federal Reserve System a system of twelve Federal Reserve Banks that facilitates exchanges of cash, checks, and credit; regulates member banks; and uses monetary policies to fight inflation and deflation

revenue agencies agencies responsible for collecting taxes. Examples include the Internal Revenue Service for income taxes, the U.S. Customs Service for tariffs and other taxes on imported goods, and the Bureau of Alcohol, Tobacco, Firearms and Explosives for collection of taxes on the sales of those particular products

The Treasury Department helps maintain the economy in various ways. Here, Treasury Secretary Timothy Geithner (right) meets with economic experts to discuss oversight of the Troubled Assets Relief Program, which was designed to address the financial crisis that began in 2008.

through liens on individual income or wages. It also mandated the firing of IRS employees who harass taxpayers or violate their rights. By 2005, however, concern was shifting toward the problem of tax dodgers. When a 2005 report indicated that the gap between true income and income reported to the IRS was at an all-time high, the IRS vowed to step up enforcement activities, focusing especially on foreign tax shelters favored by the wealthy. The Obama administration has put an emphasis on shutting down overseas tax "havens." Aided by a 13 percent increase in funding for enforcement, the IRS has become more aggressive about pursuing wealthy individuals suspected of avoiding U.S. tax by sheltering their income abroad. After the U.S. government reached deals with the Swiss and Maltese governments to turn over details of U.S. citizens with holdings in Swiss and Maltese banks, more than 14,000 U.S. taxpayers came forward as part of an amnesty program, with some accounts amounting to as much as $100 million.[27]

The politics of the IRS is most interesting because although thousands upon thousands of individual corporations and wealthy individuals have a strong and active interest in American tax policy, key taxation decisions are set by agreements among the president, the Treasury Department, and the leading members of the two tax committees in Congress, the House Ways and Means Committee and the Senate Finance Committee. External influence is not spread throughout the fifty states but is much more centralized in the majority political party, a few key figures in Congress, and a handful of professional lobbyists. Suspicions of unfair exemptions and favoritism are widespread, and they do exist, but these exemptions come largely from Congress, *not* from the IRS itself.

Economic Development Agencies Federal agencies also conduct programs designed to strengthen particular segments of the economy or to provide specific services aimed at strengthening the entire economy. Created in 1889, the Department of Agriculture is the fourth oldest Cabinet department. Its initial mission, to strengthen American agriculture through research and to assist farmers by providing information about effective farming practices, reflected the enormous importance of agriculture in the American economy. Through its Agricultural Extension

In recent years, there have been several attempts to "reinvent" government. In 1993, President Bill Clinton and Vice President Al Gore established the National Performance Review to reinvent government. Gore promoted this on David Letterman's show, where he railed against the government's procurement requirements, which even specified the number of pieces into which a government ashtray may shatter.

Service, the Department of Agriculture established an important presence in rural areas throughout the country. It also built strong support for its activities among the nation's farmers and at the many land-grant colleges, where agricultural research has been conducted for over one hundred years.

At first glance, the Department of Transportation, which oversees the nation's highway and air traffic systems, may seem to have little to do with economic development. But effective transportation is the backbone of a strong economy. The interstate highway system, for example, is widely acknowledged as a key factor in promoting economic growth in the decades after World War II. The departments of Commerce and Energy also oversee programs designed to ensure a strong economy. The Small Business Administration in the Department of Commerce provides loans and technical assistance to small businesses across the country.

In recent decades dissatisfaction with government has led to calls to keep government out of the economy. Yet if the federal government were to disappear, chances are high that the economy would fall into chaos. Agreement is widespread that the federal government should set the basic rules for economic activity and intervene—through such measures as setting interest rates—to keep the economy strong. Some analysts argue that the government's role should go beyond rule setting to include more active measures such as investment in infrastructure. These advocates of government action point to the economic benefits of government investments in the interstate highway system and the government research in the 1960s that led to the creation of the Internet.

Can the Bureaucracy Be Reformed?

When citizens complain that government is too bureaucratic, what they often mean is that government bureaucracies seem inefficient and waste money. The epitome of such bureaucratic inefficiency in the late 1980s was the Department of Defense, which was revealed to have spent $640 apiece for toilet seats and $435 apiece for hammers.[28] Many citizens also had personal experience with the federal government: a mountain of forms to fill out, lengthy waits, and unsympathetic service. Why can't government do better? many citizens asked. The application of new technologies and innovative management strategies in the private sector during the 1980s made government agencies look even more lumbering and inefficient by comparison. People were coming to expect faster service and more customer-friendly interactions in the private sector. But how can public-sector bureaucracies become more effective?

The government has sought to find various ways to make the federal bureaucracy more efficient. The key strategies used to promote bureaucratic reform include reinventing government, termination, devolution, and privatization. In general, Democratic administrations have aimed to make the existing bureaucracy work more effectively whereas Republican administrations have sought to reduce the bureaucracy, especially by contracting out government work to private companies.

Reinventing the Bureaucracy

In 1993, President Clinton launched the National Performance Review (NPR)—a part of his promise to "reinvent government"—to make the federal bureaucracy more efficient, accountable, and effective. Vice President Al Gore took charge of

The latest case of reinventing government is the largest and most complex yet, the creation of the Department of Homeland Security. Reorganizing the bureaucracy on this level has been a complicated procedure, as the organizational chart being held by Representative Jane Harman (D-Calif.) attests.

the new effort. The National Performance Review sought to prod federal agencies into adopting flexible, goal-driven practices. Clinton promised that the result would be a government that would "work better and cost less." Virtually all observers agreed that the NPR made substantial progress. Its original goal was to save more than $100 billion over five years, in large part by cutting the federal workforce by 12 percent (more than 270,000 jobs) by the end of 1999. Actually, by 2000, $136 billion in savings were already assured through legislative or administrative action, and the federal workforce had been cut by 426,200.[29] The streamlining of government business procedures did help make government work more effectively but it did not institute the more sweeping approach to reform preferred by some political leaders. These leaders have instead pursued efforts to terminate, devolve, or contract out government functions.

Termination

The only *certain* way to reduce the size of the bureaucracy is to eliminate programs. Variations in the levels of federal personnel and expenditures (as were shown in Figures 14.1 and 14.2) demonstrate the futility of trying to make permanent cuts in existing agencies. Furthermore, most agencies have a supportive constituency that will fight to reinstate any cuts that are made. Termination is the only way to ensure an agency's reduction; this is a rare occurrence, even in the Reagan administration and the first Bush administration, both of which proclaimed a strong commitment to the reduction of the national government. In fact, not a single national government agency or program was terminated during the twelve years of Reagan and George H. W. Bush. In the 1990s, Republicans did succeed in eliminating two small agencies.

The overall lack of success in terminating bureaucracy is a reflection of Americans' love/hate relationship with the national government. As antagonistic as Americans may be toward bureaucracy in general, they benefit from the services being rendered and protections being offered by particular bureaucratic agencies; that is, they fiercely defend their favorite agencies while perceiving no inconsistency between that defense and their antagonistic attitude toward the bureaucracy in general. A good case in point is the agonizing problem of closing military bases in the wake of the end of the Cold War with the former Soviet Union, when the United States no longer needed so many bases. Since every base was in some congressional member's district, it proved impossible for Congress to decide to close any of them. Consequently, between 1988 and 1990, Congress established a Defense Base Closure and Realignment Commission to decide on base closings, taking the matter out of Congress's hands altogether.[30] And even so, the process was slow and agonizing.

Elected leaders have come to rely on a more incremental approach to downsizing the bureaucracy. Much has been done by budgetary means, reducing the budgets of all agencies across the board by small percentages, and cutting some less-supported agencies by larger amounts. Yet these changes are still incremental, leaving the existence of agencies unaddressed.

An additional approach has been taken to thwart the highly unpopular regulatory agencies, which are so small (relatively) that cutting their budgets contributes virtually nothing to reducing the deficit. This approach is called **deregulation**, simply defined as a reduction in the number of rules promulgated by regulatory

deregulation a policy of reducing or eliminating regulatory restraints on the conduct of individuals or private institutions

agencies. President Reagan used this strategy successfully and was very proud of it. Presidents George H. W. Bush, Clinton, and George W. Bush have proudly followed Reagan's lead.

Devolution

The next best approach to genuine reduction of the size of the bureaucracy is **devolution**—downsizing the federal bureaucracy by delegating the implementation of programs to state and local governments. Devolution often alters the pattern of who benefits most from government programs. Opponents of devolution in social policy, for example, charge that it reduces the ability of the government to remedy inequality. They argue that state governments, which cannot run deficits as does the federal government and which have more limited taxing capabilities, will inevitably cut spending on programs that serve low-income residents. They point to the State Child Health Insurance Program, which was created in 1997 to extend health insurance to low-income children. When the economy was booming, states added children to the rolls and some even extended benefits to their parents. By 2002, however, as states faced significant budget crises many cut back on the state Children's Health Insurance Program. Although the federal government was initially able to compensate for state funding problems, states have found it difficult to keep pace with the rising number of children without health insurance. Moreover, because state revenues can fluctuate widely from year to year, states are often forced to cut back on expensive health coverage programs. By 2010, many states faced their worst budget crises since the Great Depression. Even though the federal government provided substantial assistance to states through a massive stimulus program, many states faced difficulties in funding health benefits for children.

Often the central aim of devolution is to provide more efficient and flexible government services. Yet by its very nature, devolution entails variation across the states. In some states, government services may improve as a consequence of devolution. In other states, services may deteriorate as the states use devolution as an opportunity to cut spending and reduce services. This has been the pattern in the implementation of the welfare reform passed in 1996, the most significant devolution of federal government social programs in many decades. Some states, such as Wisconsin, have used the flexibility of the reform to design innovative programs that respond to clients' needs; other states, such as Idaho, have virtually dismantled their welfare programs. Because the legislation placed a five-year lifetime limit on receiving welfare, the states will take on an even greater role in the future as current clients lose their eligibility for federal benefits. Welfare reform has been praised by many for reducing welfare rolls and responding to the public desire that welfare be a temporary program. At the same time, it has placed more low-income women and their children at risk for being left with no form of assistance at all, depending on the state in which they live.

This is the dilemma that devolution poses. Up to a point, variation can be considered one of the virtues of federalism. But dangers are inherent in large variations in the provisions of services and benefits in a democracy.

Privatization

Most of what is called "privatization" is the provision of government goods and services by private contractors under direct government supervision. Except for top-secret strategic materials, virtually all military hardware, from boats to bullets,

devolution a policy to remove a program from one level of government by delegating it or passing it down to a lower level of government, such as from the national government to the state and local governments

for critical analysis

Dissatisfied citizens have supported a range of bureaucratic reforms, including termination of agencies, devolution of responsibility to lower levels of government, and privatization. Are such reforms likely to make the bureaucracy more responsive to public wishes?

Creating the Capabilities for Nation Building

As the world's strongest democracy, the United States has consistently regarded its international role as one that should not only project the country's military power but also embody American values. The federal government's goals in promoting democracy abroad—previously focused on containing communism—have steadily grown to include all the different tasks that fall under the problem of nation building.

During the Cold War, the United States tried to contain the Soviet Union's efforts to establish communist ideology in the satellite regimes of Eastern Europe and the developing world. In the war on terrorism, by contrast, the United States confronted terrorist groups that wanted control in societies divided by fierce religious and ethnic conflicts. Instead of the tightly controlled governments of the Soviet satellite countries, these countries had only the most fragile political institutions. They were called fragile or failed states.

As the conflicts in Afghanistan and Iraq made clear, such conditions called for the

creation of new capabilities. Increasingly doubtful that the use of military force alone could create stable democracies in either country, Congress and the Executive Branch began to ask what skills were needed in order to strengthen political institutions and national cohesion in these countries. In August 2004, Congress authorized the State Department to create the Office of the Coordinator for Reconstruction and Stabilization (S/CRS).

The core mission of the S/CRS is to lead civilian capacity for stabilizing and reconstructing postconflict societies. In concrete terms, this mission involves many specialized tasks that have to be pursued in careful sequence. As military units establish day-to-day security, the

new office is responsible for mobilizing experts in areas including municipal administration; reconstruction of water supply, electricity, and telecommunications; humanitarian relief; housing; education; banking; agriculture; and the innumerable other specialties required for stabilizing war-torn countries. Other professionals were simultaneously charged with responsibility for strengthening political institutions and, where necessary, planting the seeds of entirely new institutions such as political parties, legislative assemblies, courts, and local governments. The role of the S/CRS is to mobilize civilian resources to respond rapidly when a crisis occurs.

Despite its overarching goals, the new office commands modest personnel and financial resources. Its core staff is relatively small because it is primarily charged with planning and coordinating other agencies. Equally important, under this new arrangement, the State Department office is expected to develop a civilian reserve corps of several hundred individuals drawn from federal agencies and nongovernmental organizations who can apply their expertise quickly to postconflict trouble spots.

The S/CRS has made considerable progress under the Obama administration. The organization is recruiting the active and standby component of its civilian corps of approximately 4,250 individuals.[31] The office has also issued the first ever set of strategic guidelines for all U.S. government agencies involved in civilian reconstruction and stabilization efforts in order to help coordinate their peacekeeping and peace-building activities.

for critical analysis

1. Why does the United States need so many different kinds of expertise to promote political stability in fragile and failed states?

2. What are the pros and cons of assigning responsibility for postconflict stabilization to the State Department instead of the Department of Defense?

is produced on a privatized basis by private contractors. Research services worth billions of dollars are bought under contract by governments; these private contractors are universities as well as ordinary industrial corporations and private "think tanks." **Privatization** simply means that a formerly public activity is picked up under contract by a private company or companies. But such programs are still very much government programs; they are paid for by government and supervised by government. Privatization downsizes the government only in that the workers providing the service are no longer counted as part of the government bureaucracy.

President George W. Bush made privatization a central component of his effort to reform the federal bureaucracy. The president introduced new procedures that would subject more than 800,000 federal jobs—nearly half the federal civilian workforce—to competitive outsourcing. If it were determined that a company could do the job more efficiently, the work would be contacted out. Under Bush, government outsourcing grew dramatically as the government sought to staff the new Department of Homeland Security and pursue wars in Afghanistan and Iraq without increasing the numbers of federal employees. One estimate of the growth of contracting showed that at the end of the Cold War in 1990, there were three and a half contractors and grantees for every civil servant; by 2005 the buildup connected with national security had altered the ratio to five and a half contractors and grantees for every civil servant.[32] From 2001 to 2008, spending on outside contractors more than doubled, reaching $500 billion per year.[33]

The central aim of privatization is to reduce the cost of government. Depending on how it is conducted, competitive outsourcing may not lead to extensive privatization; instead, competition may improve government performance by forcing federal agencies to reexamine how they can do their work more efficiently. When private contractors can perform a task as well as government can but for less money, taxpayers win. But private firms may not be more efficient or less costly than government. This is especially likely when there is little competition among private firms and when public bureaucracies are not granted a fair chance to bid in the contracting competition. When private firms have a monopoly on service provision, they may be less efficient than government and more expensive. In fact, there is no good evidence that privatization saves the government money. And problems of accountability arise with private contractors just as they do with government workers.

Concerns about adequate government oversight and accountability have escalated in recent years as the scale of contracting has dramatically increased. Payments for federal contracts grew from $209 billion in 2000 to $528 billion in 2008. In 2005, only 34 percent of existing contracts were subject to competition, whereas 45 percent were open to competition in 2000 (Figure 14.6).[34] Although military contracts account for much of the growth, contracting is common throughout the federal bureaucracy. In fact, contracting is now so widespread that it has been called a "virtual fourth branch of government."[35]

Much of the public attention to contracting has focused on the use of private contractors in Iraq and Afghanistan Congressional hearings revealed massive cost overruns by KBR (formerly a subsidiary of Halliburton, the firm that former vice president Dick Cheney headed), which held $9 billion in no-bid contracts to provide services ranging from supplying fuel for the military to cafeteria meals in Iraq. Army auditors have challenged $1.9 billion of KBR's bills as improper, citing violations ranging from unserved meals to inflated gas prices.[36]

Private security firms pose even more serious oversight issues. The Department of Defense has made heavy use of private security firms to provide services in

privatization removing all or part of a program from the public sector to the private sector

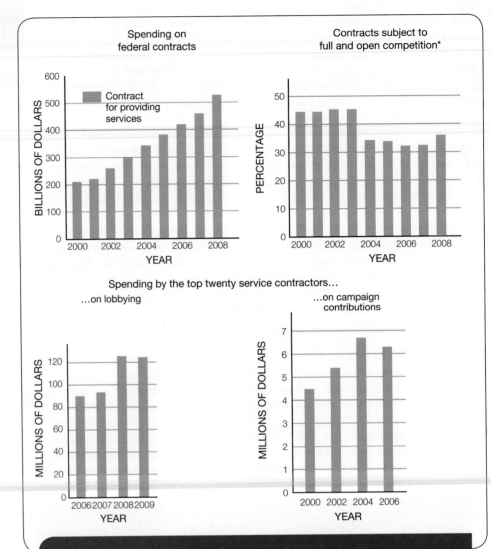

Spending on federal contracts

Contracts subject to full and open competition*

Spending by the top twenty service contractors...

...on lobbying

...on campaign contributions

FIGURE 14.6

Outsourcing the Government

As spending on federal contracts has grown, the number of contracts subject to open competition has declined substantially. At the same time, the rise in spending by private contractors on lobbying and campaign contributions raises questions about improper political influence on government contracting decisions.

*Includes both new contracts and payments against existing contracts.

SOURCES: Fedspending.org. "Summary of Federal Spending: Financial Assistance and Procurement," www .fedspending.org (accessed 2/18/10); Fedspending.org. "Federal Contract Awards by Extent of Competition," www.fedspending.org (accessed 2/18/10); Government Executive. "Top 200 Federal Contractors," August 15, 2009, www.govexec.com (accessed 2/18/10); Center for Responsive Politics. "Lobbying Database," www .opensecrets.org (accessed 2/18/10); Government Executive. "Top 200 Federal Contractors," August 15, 2009, www.govexec.com (accessed 2/18/10); Center for Responsive Politics. "Heavy Hitters," www.opensecrets.org (accessed 2/18/10).

Iraq and Afghanistan that were previously provided by the military directly. As of June 2009, there were 18,000 armed private security contractors in Iraq and Afghanistan compared with approximately 180,000 troops, with trends in Defense Department contracting indicating that the number of contractors is likely to increase.[37] High profile congressional hearings into the role of Blackwater, a private security firm, in civilian killings in Iraq illustrated the difficulties of relying on private contractors to conduct a war. With a billion dollars of government contracts, Blackwater played an essential role in providing security in Iraq. But many argue that its effectiveness came at a high cost. Because they are not bound by the same rules of conduct as the military, private security forces have been accused of being more likely than the regular military to kill civilians who posed little threat. Similarly, because the private military is not subject to the military code of justice, illegal behavior is difficult to sanction. The private military is also costlier. Noting that "sergeants in the military generally cost the Government between $50,000 to $70,000 per year" and that "a comparable position at Blackwater costs the Federal Government over $400,000, six times as much," congressional critics have questioned whether the private military is cost effective.[38] Disparities in pay are not only demoralizing to the troops, they also lure trained troops away from the military to the private contractors. Even more troubling is the possibility that private contractors undermined the mission in Iraq by creating hostility among the Iraqi people as reports of unprovoked civilian killings came to light.[39]

Although federal regulations forbid the outsourcing of "inherently governmental work," no clear line separates governmental and nongovernmental work. In most aspects of government activity, contract employees work side by side with government employees in what has been called a "blended workforce."[40] For example, many agencies that rely on technical expertise, such as the National Oceanographic and Atmospheric Administration, routinely rely on contractors. The rule against using contractors for inherently governmental work seems to have little impact. For example, in 2006 the General Services Administration hired a private firm, CACI International, to help it examine cases of fraud by other private contractors. Not only did the contract workers cost double their public counterparts, they were engaged in oversight of other private contractors, a clear conflict of interest.[41]

As alarm over the activities of contractors has grown, there have been several efforts to increase accountability. In 2002, the federal government created a centralized system to record how well contractors have performed. The aim of the database is to provide a resource for agencies as they make new contracts. However, research by the General Accountability Office showed that after seven years, the database was poorly documented and not often used in agency decision making.[42] As part of the 2009 National Defense Authorization Act, Congress called for the creation of an additional database that will record contractors who have legal or contract violations.[43] In 2008 Congress also responded to the concerns about contractors by creating a "Commission on Wartime Contracting." The commission, modeled on the 1941 Truman Commission set up to investigate wartime profiteering in World War II, has a two-year charge to investigate contracting abuse and waste in Afghanistan and Iraq. In contrast to the Truman Commission, however, the new commission does not have the power to subpoena witnesses.

Some members of Congress have sought to press for more far-reaching regulations on contractors. For example, Senator Chuck Schumer (D-N.Y.) and Chris Van Hollen (D-Md.) proposed new legislation in 2010 that would prohibit government contractors from making political contributions.[44] Members of Congress also proposed outlawing contractors from performing sensitive functions in war

One strategy to carry out the tasks of government is privatization. The United States' military operations have increasingly been privatized, with private contractors providing security services in Iraq and Afghanistan.

settings, including interrogations, security, and intelligence functions. Proposals for such major reforms, however, are difficult to enact given the strength and political connections of many federal contractors.

The Obama administration has sought to address the concerns about contracting in several ways. In July 2009, the White House Office of Management and Budget (OMB) took steps to reduce the government's reliance on outside contractors. Departments and agencies were told to cut contract spending by 7 percent over the next two years.[45] The White House, moreover, indicated a reduction in the estimated 160,000 contractors employed by the government in 2008, with more work being completed by government employees.

● Managing the Bureaucracy

By their very nature, bureaucracies pose challenges to democratic governance. Bureaucracies provide the expertise needed to implement the public will, but they can also become entrenched organizations that serve their own interests. The task is neither to retreat from bureaucracy nor to attack it, but to take advantage of its strengths while making it more accountable to the demands of democratic politics and representative government. This task will be the focus of the remainder of this chapter.

Over two hundred years, millions of employees, and trillions of dollars after the Founding, we must return to James Madison's observation, "You must first enable the government to control the governed; and in the next place oblige it to control itself."[46] Today the problem is the same, only now the process has a name: administrative accountability. Accountability implies that some higher authority will guide and judge the actions of the bureaucracy. The highest authority in a democracy is *demos*—the people—and the guidance for bureaucratic action is the popular will. But that ideal of accountability must be translated into practical terms by the president and Congress.

The President as Chief Executive

In 1937, President Franklin Roosevelt's Committee on Administrative Management gave official sanction to an idea that had been growing increasingly urgent: "The president needs help." The national government had grown rapidly during the preceding twenty-five years, but the structures and procedures necessary to manage the burgeoning executive branch had not yet been established. The response to the call for "help" for the president initially took the form of three management policies: (1) All communications and decisions that related to executive policy decisions must pass through the White House. (2) In order to cope with such a flow, the White House must have adequate staffs of specialists in research, analysis, legislative and legal writing, and public affairs. (3) The White House must have additional staff to follow through on presidential decisions—to ensure that those decisions are made, communicated to Congress, and carried out by the appropriate agency.

Making the Managerial Presidency Establishing a management capacity for the presidency began in earnest with FDR, but it did not stop there.[47] The story of the modern presidency can be told largely as a series of responses to the plea for managerial help. Indeed, each expansion of the national government into new policies and programs in the twentieth century was accompanied by a parallel expansion of the president's management authority. This pattern began even before FDR's presidency, with the policy innovations of President Woodrow Wilson between 1913 and 1920. Congress responded to Wilson's policies with the 1921 Budget and Accounting Act, which turned over the prime legislative power of budgeting to the White House. Each successive president has continued this pattern, creating what we now know as the "managerial presidency."

Presidents John Kennedy and Lyndon Johnson were committed both to government expansion and to management expansion, in the spirit of their party's hero, FDR. President Nixon also strengthened and enlarged the managerial presidency, but for somewhat different reasons. He sought the strongest possible managerial hand because he had to assume that the overwhelming majority of federal employees had sympathies with the Democratic Party, which had controlled the White House and had sponsored governmental growth for twenty-eight of the previous thirty-six years.[48]

President Jimmy Carter was probably more preoccupied with administrative reform and reorganization than any other president in the twentieth century. His reorganization of the civil service will long be recognized as one of the most significant contributions of his presidency. The Civil Service Reform Act of 1978 was the first major revamping of the federal civil service since its creation in 1883. The 1978 act abolished the century-old Civil Service Commission (CSC) and replaced it with three agencies, each designed to handle one of the CSC's functions on the theory that the competing demands of these functions had given the CSC an "identity crisis." The Merit Systems Protection Board (MSPB) was created to defend competitive merit recruitment and promotion from political encroachment. A separate Federal Labor Relations Authority (FLRA) was set up to administer collective bargaining and individual personnel grievances. The third new agency, the Office of Personnel Management (OPM), was created to manage recruiting, testing, training, and the retirement system. The Senior Executive Service was also created at this time to recognize and foster "public management" as a profession and to facilitate the movement of top, "supergrade" career officials across agencies and departments.[49]

Carter also tried to impose a stringent budgetary process on all executive agencies. Called "zero-based budgeting," it was a method of budgeting from the bottom up, whereby each agency was required to rejustify its entire mission rather than merely its next year's increase. Zero-based budgeting did not succeed, but the effort was not lost on President Reagan. Although Reagan gave the impression of being a laid-back president, he actually centralized management to an unprecedented degree. From Carter's "bottom-up" approach, Reagan went to a "top-down" approach, whereby the initial budgetary decisions would be made in the White House and the agencies would be required to fit within those decisions. This process converted the OMB into an agency of policy determination and presidential management.[50] President George H. W. Bush took Reagan's centralization strategy even further in using the White House staff instead of cabinet secretaries for managing the executive branch.[51]

President Clinton was often criticized for the way he managed his administration. His easygoing approach to administration led critics to liken his management style to college "bull sessions" complete with pizza and "all-nighters." Yet, as we have seen, Clinton also inaugurated one of the most systematic efforts "to change the way government does business" in his National Performance Review. Heavily influenced by the theories of management consultants who prized decentralization, customer responsiveness, and employee initiative, Clinton sought to infuse these new practices into government.[52]

George W. Bush was the first president with a degree in business. His management strategy followed a standard business school dictum: select skilled subordinates and delegate responsibility to them. Bush followed this model closely

Following the government's slow and inadequate response to Hurricane Katrina in 2005, some questioned President Bush's management of executive agencies. When Hurricane Rita threatened the Gulf states a month later, Bush worked closely with FEMA to make sure that the error was not repeated.

in his appointment of highly experienced officials to cabinet positions and in his selection of Dick Cheney for vice president. But critics contended that the Bush administration's distrust of the bureaucracy led it to exercise inappropriate political control. Political appointees occupied high agency positions that allowed them to suppress the work of agency experts when they threatened to undercut the administration's political goals.

Since taking office, the Obama administration has sought to reinvigorate federal agencies, reflecting the Democrats' greater support for strong government institutions. Obama's approach to the managerial presidency features a deep belief in the importance of scientific expertise in government service. The president's appointments to head key regulatory agencies, including the EPA, OSHA, and the FDA, reflected this conviction. Some of the new agency leaders were well-known academic experts; others had won recognition for their achievements in state or local administrative settings.

Decades of reform have increased the managerial capacity of the presidency, but such reforms themselves do not ensure democratic accountability—presidents must put their managerial powers to use. Although Ronald Reagan was an enormously popular president, he was faulted for his disengaged management style. During his administration, the National Security Council staff was not prevented from running its own policies toward Iran and Nicaragua for at least two years (1985–86) after Congress had explicitly restricted activities toward Nicaragua and the president had forbidden negotiations with Iran. The Tower Commission, appointed to investigate the Iran-Contra affair, concluded that although there was nothing fundamentally wrong with the institutions involved in foreign-policy making, there had been a "flawed process," "a failure of responsibility," and a thinness of the president's personal engagement in the issues. The Tower Commission found that "at no time did [President Reagan] insist upon accountability and performance review."[53] In 2008, Congress held hearings to investigate the financial crisis. Members grilled banking and insurance executives as well former chairman of the Federal Reserve, Alan Greenspan. Greenspan, once hailed as a financial wizard, memorably admitted that inadequate regulation of lending practices played a role in causing the crisis.

Presidents may also use their managerial capacities to limit democratic accountability if they believe it is a hindrance to effective government. Even in the unusual circumstances of the war on terrorism, critics question whether the Bush administration had been too quick to assert **executive privilege** and shield its actions from public scrutiny. In such circumstances, the separation of powers among the branches of government may be the best way to ensure democratic accountability.

executive privilege the claim that confidential communications between a president and close advisers should not be revealed without the consent of the president

● Congressional Oversight

Congress is constitutionally essential to responsible bureaucracy because ultimately the key to bureaucratic responsibility is legislation. When a law is passed and its intent is clear, the accountability for implementation of that law is also clear. Then the president knows what to "faithfully execute," and the responsible agency understands what is expected of it. But when Congress enacts vague legislation, agencies must resort to their own interpretations. The president and the federal courts often step in to tell agencies what the legislation intended. And so do the most intensely interested groups. Yet when everybody, from president to courts to interest groups, gets involved in the actual interpretation of legislative intent, to whom and to what is the agency accountable?

Congress's answer is **oversight**. The more power Congress has delegated to the executive, the more it has sought to reinvolve itself in directing the interpretation of laws through committee and subcommittee oversight of each agency. The standing committee system in Congress is well suited to oversight, inasmuch as most of the congressional committees and subcommittees have jurisdictions roughly parallel to one or more departments and agencies, and members of Congress who sit on these committees can develop expertise equal to that of the bureaucrats. The exception is the Department of Homeland Security, whose activities are now overseen by more than twenty committees. One of the central recommendations of the 9/11 Commission—as yet unimplemented—was to create a single committee with oversight of the DHS. Appropriations committees, as well as authorization committees, have oversight powers—as do their respective subcommittees. In addition to these, the Committee on Oversight and Government Reform in the House and the Homeland Security and Governmental Affairs Committee in the Senate have oversight powers not limited by departmental jurisdiction.

The best indication of Congress's oversight efforts is the use of public hearings, before which bureaucrats and other witnesses are summoned to discuss and defend agency budgets and past decisions. In 2007, for example, Congress held high-profile hearings on topics as diverse as the use of military contractors in Iraq, potentially improper dismissals of U.S. attorneys, and the failures of the Consumer Products Safety Commission to keep lead out of children's toys.

The data drawn from systematic studies of congressional committee and subcommittee hearings and meetings show quite dramatically that Congress has tried through oversight to keep pace with the expansion of the executive branch. The annual number of oversight hearings grew over time as the bureaucracy expanded. Oversight hearings in both the Senate and the House increased dramatically in the 1970s in the aftermath of Watergate. In recent years, oversight has become a topic of substantial political concern. After the Republicans took over Congress in 1995, they concentrated their oversight power on investigating scandal. When George W. Bush became president in 2001, congressional oversight virtually disappeared. In the words of the congressional scholars Thomas Mann and Norman Ornstein, Republican members of Congress saw "themselves as field lieutenants in the president's army far more than they [did] as members of a separate and independent branch of government."[54] In their view, Congress's failure to exercise its oversight role led to poor government performance and bureaucracies that were not accountable to the American people. After winning back Congress in 2006, the Democrats revived the oversight role. Congress has held oversight hearings on a wide range of topics. Hearings have examined many different aspects of the Iraq and Afghanistan wars, including the use of government contractors. Congress has also been very active in overseeing programs related to the recession, including the Troubled Asset Relief Program (TARP), which was instituted to help bail out the banks in 2008. When trouble with Toyota vehicles surfaced in 2010, Congress exercised its oversight powers to determine whether the company knew of the problems and withheld information from the National Highway Transportation Safety Agency.

Congress holds hearings to determine whether federal agencies are successfully performing their jobs. In 2009, Attorney General Eric Holder testified at a congressional hearing on oversight of the Justice Department. Members of Congress were concerned about a recent Justice Department decision to try the suspects in the 9/11 terrorist attacks in New York.

Navigate the Bureaucracy

To some, the idea of "getting involved" in something as complex as the federal, state, or even local bureaucracy can seem daunting. As you probably know by now, the bureaucracy has grown considerably in size in the last thirty-five or so years and now touches aspects of daily life ranging from protecting citizens from terrorist attacks, to protecting the environment, to making sure the food you eat is safe. These are all important issues that citizens should easily be able to get involved with, but given the size of bureaucracies these days, where do you jump in?

It's not that hard, actually, to make a difference in how bureaucracies respond to social and political problems. Often it's as simple as volunteering your efforts in order to bring greater attention to a problem so that a relevant bureaucratic agency does something to fix the problem.

For example, you may see news stories about people working together locally in order to help the homeless. College students are often part of volunteer efforts to count the homeless in order to provide government agencies with a good idea of how widespread the homeless problem is in a given area. This information is then used to help lobby health and human service agencies to provide increased and better housing and resources for those on the streets.

College students have also fought, with some success, bureaucracies on their own campuses over issues like peer-to-peer file sharing and music downloads on the campus network. Recognizing that this is a practice that's here to stay and students expect schools to not restrict access, colleges and universities across the country have begun offering free or cheap access to legal sites such as Napster, Rhapsody, and Ruckus.

So, even though the old adage "you can't fight city hall" is the conventional wisdom, there is room for people such as you to have an impact on the bureaucracy at all levels. Here are a few suggestions for getting involved in ways that range from limited to more concentrated activism.

- Start with something fairly simple. Ask yourself what political or social issue interests you and find out what bureaucratic agency is responsible for oversight and administering programs for that issue. Just trying to find out who to turn to with questions about your issue could be a lesson in and of itself. For example, you may be concerned with the treatment of veterans returning from active service in places like Iraq and Afghanistan. The Department of Veterans Affairs (www.va.gov) would be a good place to start for information on what the government is doing to help those returning with physical and psychological injuries.

- If you're interested in more active involvement in the bureaucracy, you should consider interning with a government agency in Washington, D.C. For example, you could spend a summer or even an entire semester earning academic credit while interning at bureaucratic agencies ranging from the Food and Drug Administration, to the Department of Housing and Urban Development, to the Department of Defense. This is probably the best way to get hands-on experience with the bureaucracy. One way to intern while earning academic credit is through attending the Washington Center (www.twc.edu).

- Finally, you could think about being an "ombudsperson" to help people deal with the bureaucracy. Grandparents and other elderly relatives often need help navigating the Social Security system, new immigrants are often in the dark about what to do in order to become legal citizens, and many high school students need help filling out forms for financial aid. Try visiting VolunteerMatch (www.volunteermatch.org), a Web site that puts people together with individuals and groups who are in need of unpaid assistance. You might even be able to use your affiliation with a campus organization, such as a fraternity or sorority, to encourage others to become volunteer ombudspersons, especially if charitable work is one of the organization's goals.

Individual members of Congress can also carry out oversight. Such inquiries addressed to bureaucrats are considered standard congressional "case work" and can turn up significant questions of public responsibility even when the motivation is only to meet the demand of an individual constituent. Oversight also takes place through communications between congressional staff and agency staff. In addition, Congress has created for itself three large agencies whose obligations are to engage in constant research on problems taking place in or confronted by the executive branch. These are the Government Accountability Office (GAO), the Congressional Research Service (CRS), and the Congressional Budget Office (CBO). Each of these agencies is designed to give Congress information independent of the information it can get directly from the executive branch through hearings and other communications.[55] Another source of information for oversight is directly from citizens through the Freedom of Information Act, which, as we have seen, gives ordinary citizens the right to gain access to agency files and agency data to determine whether derogatory information exists in the file about the citizens themselves and to learn about what the agency is doing in general. Nevertheless, the information citizens gain through FOIA can be effective only through the institutionalized channels of congressional committees and, on a few occasions, through public-interest litigation in the federal courts.

● Thinking Critically about Responsible Bureaucracy in a Democracy

The increasing use of federal contractors raises new questions about democratic accountability. When government work is contracted out, federal monitoring is essential to ensure that funds are spent in accordance with the public will and to confirm that the costs are fair. Yet government contracting is now so extensive that such monitoring has become extremely difficult. Even with monitoring, accountability may be hard to achieve. Many of the mechanisms of democratic accountability do not apply to private firms that contract to perform public work. For example, private corporations can resist FOIA requests, and they are not constrained by the same ethics rules as public employees. Moreover, because private firms do not have to disclose information about their operations in the same way that public bureaucracies do, Congress has much more limited oversight. The move to contracting out clearly presents major challenges to democratic accountability in the future.

One of the most troubling aspects of contracting is that private contractors donate millions of dollars each year to political campaigns and lobbying. As Figure 14.6 shows, the top twenty service contractors have substantially increased their spending on lobbying and political campaigns since 2000. These expenditures raise troubling questions about how assertive members of Congress are likely to be in scrutinizing the business practices of important political donors or in moving business from the private to the public sector.

As the president and Congress seek to translate the ideal of democratic accountability into practice, they struggle to find the proper balance between administrative discretion and the public's right to know. An administration whose every move is subject to intense public scrutiny may be hamstrung in its efforts to carry out the public interest. On the other hand, a bureaucracy that is shielded from the public eye may wind up pursuing its own interests rather than those of the public. The last century has seen a simultaneous movement toward strengthening the managerial capacity of the presidency and ensuring that bureaucratic decision making is more transparent. The purpose of these reforms has been to create an effective, responsive bureaucracy. But reforms alone cannot guarantee democratic accountability. Presidential and congressional vigilance in defense of the public interest is essential.

studyguide

Practice Quiz

Find a diagnostic Web Quiz with 39 additional questions on the StudySpace Web site: www.wwnorton.com/we-the-people

Bureaucracy and Bureaucrats

1. Which of the following best describes the growth of the federal service in the past thirty-five years? *(p. 523)*
   a) rampant, exponential growth
   b) little growth at all
   c) decrease in the total number of federal employees
   d) vast, compared to the growth of the economy and the society

2. What task must bureaucrats perform if Congress charges them with enforcing a law through explicit directions? *(p. 526)*
   a) implementation
   b) interpretation
   c) lawmaking
   d) quasi-judicial decision making

3. Which of the following was *not* a component of the Civil Service Act of 1883? *(p. 528)*
   a) the merit system
   b) a job security system
   c) a spoils system
   d) All of the above were associated with the Civil Service Act of 1883.

The Organization of the Executive Branch

4. Which of the following are *not* part of the executive branch? *(pp. 530–31)*
   a) Cabinet departments
   b) government corporations
   c) independent regulatory commissions
   d) All of the above are parts of the executive branch.

5. Which of the following is an example of a government corporation? *(p. 531)*
   a) National Aeronautics and Space Administration (NASA)
   b) United States Postal Service
   c) National Science Foundation
   d) Federal Express

Promoting the Public Welfare

6. Which of the following is *not* an example of a clientele agency? *(p. 533)*
   a) Department of Justice
   b) Department of Commerce
   c) Department of Agriculture
   d) Department of Housing and Urban Development

7. Which of the following was *not* a part of the USA PATRIOT Act? *(p. 535)*
   a) a provision allowing the attorney general to detain any foreigner suspected of posing a threat to internal security
   b) a provision expanding the government's ability to use wiretaps
   c) a provision creating the Department of Homeland Security
   d) a provision requiring public libraries to keep lists of the public's book and Internet usage for federal inspection

Can the Bureaucracy Be Reformed?

8. Which president instituted the bureaucratic reform of the National Performance Review? *(p. 545)*
   a) Richard Nixon
   b) Lyndon Johnson

c) Jimmy Carter
d) Bill Clinton

9. Deregulation refers to *(p. 546)*
    a) removing all or part of a program from the public sector to the private sector.
    b) a policy of reducing or eliminating regulatory restraints on the conduct of individuals or private institutions.
    c) a policy to remove a program from one level of government by passing it down to a lower level of government.
    d) reducing the overall number of regulatory agencies in the federal bureaucracy.

10. Which of the following is a way in which the bureaucracy might be reduced? *(p. 547)*
    a) devolution
    b) termination
    c) privatization
    d) all of the above

11. Which of the following best describes the changes in government contracting since 2000? *(p. 549)*
    a) Spending on government contracts has decreased while the number of government contracts subject to open competition has increased.
    b) Spending on government contracts has decreased while the number of government contracts subject to competition has decreased.
    c) Spending on government contracts has increased while the number of government contracts subject to open competition has decreased.
    d) Spending on government contracts has increased while the number of government contracts subject to open competition has increased.

Managing the Bureaucracy

12. Which of the following is a power sometimes invoked by presidents to shield their administration's actions from public scrutiny? *(p. 555)*
    a) executive privilege
    b) executive protection

c) congressional oversight
d) administrative adjudication

Congressional Oversight

13. The concept of oversight refers to the effort made by *(p. 556)*
    a) Congress to make executive agencies accountable for their actions.
    b) the president to make Congress accountable for its actions.
    c) the courts to make executive agencies responsible for their actions.
    d) the states to make the executive branch accountable for its actions.

14. Which of the following is *not* an agency created by Congress to engage in constant research on problems taking place in or confronted by the executive branch? *(p. 558)*
    a) Government Accountability Office
    b) Congressional Research Service
    c) Congressional Oversight Organization
    d) Congressional Budget Office

Thinking Critically about Responsible Bureaucracy in a Democracy

15. Which of the following is *not* an issue of democratic accountability raised by the growth in government contracting? *(p. 558)*
    a) Members of Congress may be reluctant to scrutinize the business practices of the private contractors who donate millions of dollars every year to political campaigns.
    b) Private contractors can resist Freedom of Information Act requests.
    c) Private contractors are always less efficient in using public funds than government agencies.
    d) Congressional oversight is limited because private contractors do not have to disclose information about their operations in the same way that public bureaucracies do.

Chapter Outline

Find a detailed Chapter Outline on the StudySpace Web site: www.wwnorton.com/we-the-people

Key Terms

Find Flashcards to help you study these teams on the StudySpace Web site: www.wwnorton.com/we-the-people

bureaucracy *(p. 523)*
department *(p. 530)*

deregulation *(p. 546)*
devolution *(p. 547)*

executive privilege *(p. 555)*
Federal Reserve System *(p. 543)*

fiscal policy *(p. 542)*
government corporation *(p. 531)*
implementation *(p. 526)*
independent agency *(p. 531)*

iron triangle *(p. 533)*
merit system *(p. 528)*
oversight *(p. 556)*

privatization *(p. 549)*
regulatory agencies *(p. 532)*
revenue agencies *(p. 543)*

For Further Reading

Aberbach, Joel D., and Mark A. Peterson, eds. *Institutions of American Democracy: The Executive Branch* (Institutions of American Democracy Series). New York: Oxford University Press, 2006.

Arnold, Peri E. *Making the Managerial Presidency: Comprehensive Organization Planning.* Princeton, NJ: Princeton University Press, 1986.

Kettl, Donald F., and James W. Fesler. *The Politics of the Administrative Process.* 4th ed. Washington, DC: Congressional Quarterly Press, 2008.

Light, Paul C. *A Government III Executed: The Decline of the Federal Service and How to Reverse It.* Cambridge, MA: Harvard University Press, 2008.

Verkuil, Paul. *Outsourcing Sovereignty: Why Privatization of Government Functions Threatens Democracy and What We Can Do about It.* New York: Cambridge University Press, 2007.

Weiner, Tom. *Legacy of Ashes: The History of the CIA.* New York: Doubleday, 2007.

Wildavsky, Aaron. *The New Politics of the Budget Process.* 2nd ed. New York: HarperCollins, 1992.

Wilson, James Q. *Bureaucracy: What Government Agencies Do and Why They Do It.* New York: Basic Books, 1989.

Wood, Dan B. *Bureaucratic Dynamics: The Role of Bureaucracy in a Democracy.* Boulder, CO: Westview, 1994.

Recommended Web Sites

Central Intelligence Agency
www.cia.gov
The Central Intelligence Agency (CIA) is one of several bureaucracies responsible for providing national security. A major problem facing this clandestine agency is how to provide security and meet the public's right to know what the government is doing. At the official Web site for the CIA, see what questions are often asked.

Department of Homeland Security
www.dhs.gov
The Department of Homeland Security was created after 9/11 to promote bureaucratic communication and domestic security. See what the department is doing to protect America from foreign threats.

Federal Emergency Management Agency
www.fema.org
In the aftermath of Hurricane Katrina, the Federal Emergency Management Agency (FEMA) became infamous for its role in the disaster relief efforts. View the disaster history of your state and see what FEMA is currently doing to prevent disasters and assist Americans in need.

Official U.S. Executive Branch Web Sites
www.loc.gov
This resource page at the Library of Congress Web site provides links to every federal department, independent agency, and regulatory commission in the federal bureaucracy.

Reason Foundation
reason.org/areas/topic/privatization
The Reason Foundation is dedicated to promoting libertarian principles and limited government. Their Web site includes studies and opinion pieses on a range of policy issues, including many related to the size and effectiveness of the federal bureaucracy.

Project on Government Oversight
www.pogo.org
The Project on Government Oversight is an independent, nonprofit organization that seeks to make government more accountable by investigating corruption and misconduct. Originally set up to focus on the military, this organization now examines all types of government bureaucracies.

U.S. Agency for International Development
www.usaid.gov
In 1961 Congress created the U.S. Agency for International Development (USAID) to provide economic and social development assistance to foreign countries. Often criticized for promoting American values and foreign policy objectives, USAID is currently involved in numerous global issues.

In 2010, Barack Obama nominated former Solicitor General Elena Kagan to the Supreme Court, bringing the number of women justices to three. Kagan's nomination was approved by the Senate, and she was sworn in by Chief Justice John Roberts (right) in August 2010.

The Federal Courts

WHAT GOVERNMENT DOES AND WHY IT MATTERS Many Americans may think of the Supreme Court as a distant and mysterious institution whose decisions affect giant corporations, wealthy individuals, and powerful politicians. They may see no direct relationship between the black-robed justices and the everyday lives of ordinary people. Occasionally, however, the Supreme Court is asked to hear questions that touch students' lives in a very direct way. One recent example, from 2007, is the case of *Morse v. Frederick*.[1] This case dealt with the policies of Juneau-Douglas High School in Juneau, Alaska. In 2002, the Olympic torch relay passed through Juneau on its way to Salt Lake City for the opening of the Winter Olympics. As the torch passed Juneau-Douglas High, a senior, Joseph Frederick, unfurled a banner that read, "Bong Hits 4 Jesus." The school's principal promptly suspended Frederick, who then brought suit for reinstatement, alleging that his right to freedom of speech had been violated.[2]

Like most of America's public schools, Juneau-Douglas High prohibits assemblies or expressions on school grounds that advocate illegal drug use. Schools say that some federal aid is contingent on this policy.

focusquestions

- What are the general types of cases and types of courts in our legal system?
- What are the different levels of federal courts?
- How does the Supreme Court exercise the power of judicial review?

Civil libertarians see such policies as restricting students' right to free speech—a right that has been recognized by the Supreme Court since a 1969 case when it said an Iowa public school could not prohibit students from wearing antiwar armbands. Unfortunately for Joseph Frederick, today's Supreme Court has a more conservative cast than it did in 1969. Speaking for the Court's majority, Chief Justice John G. Roberts said that the First Amendment did not require schools to permit students to advocate illegal drug use. This decision affected not only Joseph Frederick, but also millions of other students whose views might be seen as inappropriate by school administrators. Far from being a remote institution, the Supreme Court turns out to have reached into every public school in America.

Every year, nearly 25 million cases are tried in American courts, and one American in every nine is directly involved in litigation. Cases can arise from disputes between citizens, from efforts by government agencies to punish wrongdoing, or from citizens' efforts to prove that their rights have been infringed on as a result of government action—or inaction. Many critics of the U.S. legal system assert that Americans have become too litigious (ready to use the courts for all purposes). But the heavy use that Americans make of the courts is also an indication of the extent of conflict in American society. And given the existence of social conflict, it is far better that Americans seek to settle their differences through the courts rather than by fighting.

The framers of the American Constitution called the Supreme Court the "least dangerous branch" of American government. Today, it is not unusual to hear the Court described as an all-powerful "imperial judiciary." Before we can understand this transformation and its consequences, we must look in some detail at America's judicial process.

chaptercontents

The Legal System

Originally, a "court" was the place where a sovereign ruled—where the king or queen and governed. Settling disputes between citizens was part of governing. In modern democracies, courts and judges have taken over the power to settle controversies by hearing the facts on both sides and deciding which side possesses the greater merit. But since judges are not kings, they must have a basis for their authority. That basis in the United States is the Constitution and the law. Courts decide cases by hearing the facts on both sides of a dispute and applying the relevant law or principle to the facts. This can be a sensitive matter because courts have been given the authority to settle disputes not only between citizens but also between citizens and the government itself, where the courts are obliged to maintain the same neutrality and impartiality as they do in disputes involving two citizens. This is the essence of the "rule of law"—that "the state" and its officials must be judged by the same laws as the citizenry.

Cases and the Law

Court cases in the United States proceed under two broad categories of law: criminal law and civil law, each with myriad subdivisions.

Cases of **criminal law** are those in which the government charges an individual with violating a statute that has been enacted to protect public health, safety, morals, or welfare. In criminal cases, the government is always the **plaintiff** (the party that brings charges) and alleges that a criminal violation has been committed by a named **defendant**. Most criminal cases arise in state and municipal courts and involve matters ranging from traffic offenses to robbery and murder. Although the great bulk of criminal law is still a state matter, a large and growing body of federal criminal law deals with matters ranging from tax evasion and mail fraud to the sale of narcotics and acts of terrorism. Defendants found guilty of criminal violations may be fined or sent to prison.

criminal law the branch of law that regulates the conduct of individuals, defines crimes, and specifies punishment for criminal acts

plaintiff the individual or organization that brings a complaint in court

defendant the one against whom a complaint is brought in a criminal or civil case

The courts have the authority to settle disputes not only between individuals and other private entities but also between individuals and the government. In recent "enemy combatant" cases, the Supreme Court has ruled on the rights of prisoners being held in the U.S. base in Guantánamo, Cuba. In 2008, demonstrators dressed as Guantánamo detainees protested outside the Court.

civil law the branch of law that deals with disputes that do not involve criminal penalties

Cases of **civil law** involve disputes among individuals, groups, corporations, and other private entities, or between such litigants and the government in which no criminal violation is charged. Unlike criminal cases, the losers in civil cases cannot be fined or sent to prison, although they may be required to pay monetary damages for their actions. In a civil case, the one who brings a complaint is the plaintiff and the one against whom the complaint is brought is the defendant. The two most common types of civil cases involve contracts and torts. In a typical contract case, an individual or corporation charges that it has suffered because of another's violation of a specific agreement between the two. For example, the Smith Manufacturing Corporation may charge that Jones Distributors failed to honor an agreement to deliver raw materials at a specified time, causing Smith to lose business. Smith asks the court to order Jones to compensate it for the damage allegedly suffered. In a typical tort case, one individual charges that he or she has been injured by another's negligence or malfeasance. Medical malpractice suits are one example of tort cases. Another important area of civil law is administrative law, which involves disputes over the jurisdiction, procedures, or authority of administrative agencies. A plaintiff may assert, for example, that an agency did not follow proper procedures when issuing new rules and regulations. A court will then examine the agency's conduct in light of the Administrative Procedure Act, the legislation that governs agency rule making.

precedent a prior case whose principles are used by judges as the basis for their decision in a present case

In deciding cases, courts apply statutes (laws) and legal **precedents** (prior decisions). State and federal statutes, for example, often govern the conditions under which contracts are and are not legally binding. Jones Distributors might argue that it was not obliged to fulfill its contract with the Smith Corporation because actions by Smith, such as the failure to make promised payments, constituted fraud under state law. Attorneys for a physician being sued for malpractice, on the other hand, may search for prior instances in which courts ruled that actions similar to those of their client did not constitute negligence. Such precedents are applied under the doctrine of **stare decisis**, a Latin phrase meaning "let the decision stand."

stare decisis literally, "let the decision stand." The doctrine that a previous decision by a court applies as a precedent in similar cases until that decision is overruled

If a case involves the actions of the federal government or a state government, a court may also be asked to examine whether the government's conduct was consistent with the Constitution. In a criminal case, for example, defendants might assert that their constitutional rights were violated when the police searched their property. Similarly, in a civil case involving federal or state restrictions on land development, plaintiffs might assert that government actions violated the Fifth Amendment's prohibition against taking private property without just compensation. Thus, both civil and criminal cases may raise questions of constitutional law.

Types of Courts

trial court the first court to hear a criminal or civil case

court of appeals a court that hears appeals of trial court decisions

supreme court the highest court in a particular state or in the United States. This court primarily serves an appellate function

In the United States, systems of courts have been established both by the federal government and by the governments of the individual states. Both systems have several levels, as shown in Figure 15.1. More than 99 percent of all court cases in the United States are heard in state courts. The overwhelming majority of criminal cases, for example, involve violations of state laws prohibiting such actions as murder, robbery, fraud, theft, and assault. If such a case is brought to trial, it will be heard in a state **trial court**, in front of a judge and sometimes a jury, who will determine whether the defendant violated state law. If the defendant is convicted, he or she may appeal the conviction to a higher court, such as a state **court of appeals**, and from there to a court of last resort, usually called the state's **supreme court**.

Similarly, in civil cases, most litigation is brought in the courts established by the state in which the activity in question took place. For example, a patient bringing

● What are the general types of cases and types of courts in our legal system?

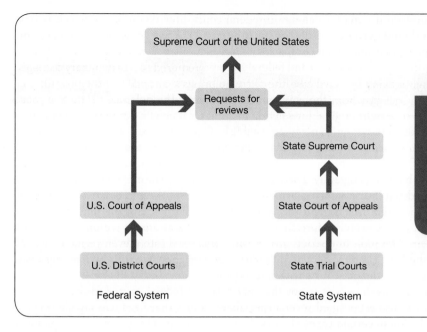

FIGURE 15.1

The U.S. Court System

The state and federal court systems parallel each other until they reach the U.S. Supreme Court. The Supreme Court hears appeals from both systems.

suit against a physician for malpractice would file the suit in the appropriate court in the state where the alleged malpractice occurred. The judge hearing the case would apply state law and state precedent to the matter at hand. There is some variation in court structure among the fifty states. Several states lack an intermediate appellate level. In these states, the court of last resort is the only appellate court. Two states, Oklahoma and Texas, have established two state courts of last resort, one for civil appeals and the other for criminal appeals. It should be noted that in both criminal and civil matters, most cases are settled before trial through negotiated agreements between the parties. In criminal cases these agreements are called **plea bargains**.

Although each state has its own set of laws, these laws have much in common from state to state. Murder and robbery, obviously, are illegal in all states, although the range of possible punishments for those crimes varies from state to state. Some states, for example, provide for capital punishment (the death penalty) for murder and other serious offenses; other states do not. However, some acts that are criminal offenses in one state may be legal in another state. Prostitution, for example, is legal in some Nevada counties, although it is outlawed in all other states. Considerable similarity among the states is also found in the realm of civil law. In the case of contract law, most states have adopted the Uniform Commercial Code in order to reduce interstate differences. In areas such as family law, however, which covers such matters as divorce and child custody arrangements, state laws vary greatly.

Cases are heard in the federal courts if they involve federal laws, treaties with other nations, or the U.S. Constitution; these areas are the official **jurisdiction** of the federal courts. In addition, any case in which the U.S. government is a party is heard in the federal courts. If, for example, an individual is charged with violating a federal criminal statute, such as evading the payment of income taxes, charges would be brought before a federal judge by a federal prosecutor. Civil cases involving the citizens of more than one state and in which more than $75,000 is at stake may be heard in either the federal or the state courts, usually depending on the preference of the plaintiff.

plea bargain a negotiated agreement in a criminal case in which a defendant agrees to plead guilty in return for the state's agreement to reduce the severity of the criminal charge or prison sentence the defendant is facing

jurisdiction the sphere of a court's power and authority

But even if a matter belongs in federal court, how do we know which federal court should exercise jurisdiction over the case? The answer to this seemingly simple question is somewhat complex. The jurisdiction of each federal court is derived from the U.S. Constitution and federal statutes. Article III of the Constitution gives the Supreme Court appellate jurisdiction in all federal cases and original jurisdiction in cases involving foreign ambassadors and issues in which a state is a party. Article III assigns original jurisdiction in all other federal cases to the lower courts that Congress was authorized to establish. Over the years, as Congress enacted statutes creating the federal judicial system, it specified the jurisdiction of each type of court it established. For the most part, Congress has assigned jurisdictions on the basis of geography. The nation is currently, by statute, divided into ninety-four judicial districts, including one court for each of three U.S. territories: Guam, the U.S. Virgin Islands, and the Northern Marianas. Each of the ninety-four U.S. district courts exercises jurisdiction over federal cases arising within its territorial domain. The judicial districts are, in turn, organized into eleven regional circuits and the D.C. circuit. Each circuit court exercises appellate jurisdiction over cases heard by the district courts within its region.

Geography, however, is not the only basis for federal court jurisdiction. Congress has also established several specialized courts that have nationwide original jurisdiction in certain types of cases. These include the U.S. Court of International Trade, created to deal with trade and customs issues, and the U.S. Court of Federal Claims, which handles damage suits against the United States. Congress has, in addition, established a court with nationwide appellate jurisdiction. This is the U.S. Court of Appeals for the Federal Circuit, which hears appeals involving patent law and those arising from the decisions of the trade and claims courts. Other federal courts assigned specialized jurisdictions by Congress include the U.S. Court of Veterans Appeals, which exercises exclusive jurisdiction over cases involving veterans' claims, and the U.S. Court of Military Appeals, which deals with questions of law arising from trials by court-martial.

With the exception of the claims court and the Court of Appeals for the Federal Circuit, these specialized courts were created by Congress on the basis of the powers the legislature exercises under Article I, rather than Article III, of the Constitution. Article III is designed to protect judges from political pressure by granting them life tenure and prohibiting reduction of their salaries while they serve. The judges of Article I courts, by contrast, are appointed by the president for fixed terms of fifteen years and are not protected by the Constitution from salary reduction. As a result, these "legislative courts" are generally viewed as less independent than the courts established under Article III of the Constitution. The three territorial courts were also established under Article I, and their judges are appointed for ten-year terms.

The appellate jurisdiction of the federal courts also extends to cases originating in the state courts. In both civil and criminal cases, a decision of the highest state court can be appealed to the U.S. Supreme Court by raising a federal issue. Appellants might assert, for example, that they were denied the right to counsel or otherwise deprived of the **due process of law** guaranteed by the federal Constitution, or they might assert that important issues of federal law were at stake in the case. The U.S. Supreme Court is not obligated to accept such appeals and will do so only if it believes that the matter has considerable national significance. We will return to this topic later in the chapter. In addition, in criminal cases, defendants who have been convicted in a state court may request a **writ of *habeas corpus*** from a

due process of law the right of every citizen against arbitrary action by national or state governments

writ of *habeas corpus* a court order that the individual in custody be brought into court and shown the cause for detention. *Habeas corpus* is guaranteed by the Constitution and can be suspended only in cases of rebellion or invasion

What are the
different levels of
federal courts?

federal district court. Sometimes known as the "Great Writ," *habeas corpus* is a court order to the authorities to release a prisoner deemed to be held in violation of his or her legal rights. In 1867, its distrust of southern courts led Congress to authorize federal district judges to issue such writs to prisoners whom they believed had been deprived of constitutional rights in state court. Generally speaking, state defendants seeking a federal writ of *habeas corpus* must show that they have exhausted all available state remedies and must raise issues not previously raised in their state appeals. Federal courts of appeals and, ultimately, the U.S. Supreme Court have appellate jurisdiction for federal district court *habeas* decisions.

Although the federal courts hear only a small fraction of all the civil and criminal cases decided each year in the United States, their decisions are extremely important. It is in the federal courts that the Constitution and federal laws that govern all Americans are interpreted and their meaning and significance established. Moreover, it is in the federal courts that the powers and limitations of the increasingly powerful national government are tested. Finally, through their power to review the decisions of the state courts, it is ultimately the federal courts that dominate the American judicial system.

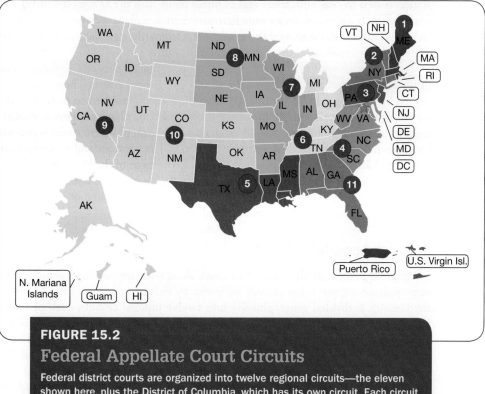

FIGURE 15.2

Federal Appellate Court Circuits

Federal district courts are organized into twelve regional circuits—the eleven shown here, plus the District of Columbia, which has its own circuit. Each circuit court hears appeals from lower federal courts within the circuit. A 13th federal circuit court—the U.S. Court of Appeals for the Federal Circuit—hears appeals from a number of specialized courts such as the U.S. Court of Federal Claims.

SOURCE: www.uscourts.gov/court_locator.aspx. (accessed 7/27/10).

Federal Jurisdiction

In 2008, federal district courts (the lowest federal level) received 349,969 cases. Though large, this number is approximately 1 percent of the number of cases heard by state courts. The federal courts of appeal listened to 61,104 cases in 2008 and about fifteen percent of the verdicts were appealed to the U.S. Supreme Court. Most of the cases filed with the Supreme Court are dismissed without a ruling on their merits. The Court has broad latitude to decide what cases it will hear and generally listens to only those cases it deems to raise the most important issues. Only eighty-three cases were given full-dress Supreme Court review in 2008–09.[3]

● Federal Trial Courts

original jurisdiction the authority to initially consider a case. Distinguished from appellate jurisdiction, which is the authority to hear appeals from a lower court's decision

Most of the cases of original federal jurisdiction are handled by the federal district courts. Courts of **original jurisdiction** are the courts that are responsible for discovering the facts in a controversy and creating the record on which a judgment is based. Although the Constitution gives the Supreme Court original jurisdiction in several types of cases, such as those affecting ambassadors and those in which a state is one of the parties, most original jurisdiction goes to the lowest courts—the trial courts. (In courts that have appellate jurisdiction, judges receive cases after the factual record is established by the trial court. Ordinarily, new facts cannot be presented before appellate courts.)

There are eighty-nine district courts in the fifty states, plus one in the District of Columbia and one in Puerto Rico, and three territorial courts. These courts are staffed by 679 federal district judges. District judges are assigned to district courts according to the workload; the busiest of these courts may have as many as twenty-eight judges. Only one judge is assigned to each case, except where statutes provide for three-judge courts to deal with special issues. The routines and procedures of the federal district courts are essentially the same as those of the lower state courts, except that federal procedural requirements tend to be stricter. States, for example, do not have to provide a grand jury, a twelve-member trial jury, or a unanimous jury verdict. Federal courts must provide all these things.

Federal Appellate Courts

Roughly 20 percent of all lower-court cases, along with appeals from some federal agency decisions, are subsequently reviewed by federal appeals courts. As noted, the country is divided geographically into twelve judicial circuits, each of which has a U.S. Court of Appeals. Every state, the District of Columbia, and each of the territories is assigned to the circuit in the continental United States that is closest to it. A thirteenth appellate court, the U.S. Court of Appeals for the Federal Circuit, has a subject matter, rather than a geographical, jurisdiction.

Except for cases selected for review by the Supreme Court, decisions made by the appeals courts are final. Because of this finality, certain safeguards have been built into the system. The most important is the provision of more than one judge for every appeals case. Each court of appeals has from six to twenty-eight permanent judgeships, depending on the workload of the circuit. Although normally three judges hear appealed cases, in some instances a larger number of judges sit together *en banc*.

Another safeguard is provided by the assignment of a Supreme Court justice as the circuit justice for each of the twelve circuits. The circuit justice deals with requests for special action by the Supreme Court. The most frequent and best-known action of circuit justices is that of reviewing requests for stays of execution when the full Court is unable to do so—primarily during the summer, when the Court is in recess.

The Supreme Court

The Supreme Court is America's highest court. Article III of the Constitution vests "the judicial power of the United States" in the Supreme Court, and this court is supreme in fact as well as form. The Supreme Court is the only federal court established by the Constitution. The lower federal courts are created by statute and can be restructured or, presumably, even abolished by the Congress. The Supreme Court is made up of the Chief Justice of the United States and eight Associate Justices. The **chief justice** presides over the Court's public sessions and conferences. In the Court's actual deliberations and decisions, however, the chief justice has no more authority than his colleagues. Each justice casts one vote. The chief justice, though, is always the first to speak and the last to vote when the justices deliberate. In addition, if the chief justice has voted with the majority, he decides which of the justices will write the formal opinion for the court. The character of the opinion can be an important means of influencing the evolution of the law beyond the mere affirmation or denial of the appeal on hand. To some extent, the influence of the chief justice is a function of his or her own leadership ability. Some chief justices, such as the late Earl Warren, have been able to lead the court in a new direction. In other instances, forceful associate justices, such as the late Felix Frankfurter, are the dominant figures on the Court.

The Constitution does not specify the number of justices who should sit on the Supreme Court; Congress has the authority to change the Court's size. In the early nineteenth century, there were six Supreme Court justices; later there were seven. Congress set the number of justices at nine in 1869, and the Court has remained that size ever since. In 1937, President Franklin D. Roosevelt, infuriated by several

chief justice justice on the Supreme Court who presides over the Court's public sessions and whose official title is Chief Justice of the United States

President George W. Bush nominated John Roberts (left photo, center) first as a Supreme Court justice, and then as chief justice after the death of former Chief Justice William Rehnquist. Although Roberts's nomination was approved fairly easily in the Senate, President Bush's next nominee, Samuel Alito (right) was subjected to harsher questioning before being confirmed. Democratic senators were worried that Alito, who was replacing a more moderate justice, would shift the overall balance of the Court toward the right.

Supreme Court decisions that struck down New Deal programs, asked Congress to enlarge the Court so that he could add a few sympathetic justices to the bench. Although Congress balked at Roosevelt's "court packing" plan, the Court gave in to FDR's pressure and began to take a more favorable view of his policy initiatives. The president, in turn, dropped his efforts to enlarge the Court.

How Judges Are Appointed

Federal judges are appointed by the president and confirmed by the Senate. They are generally selected from among the more prominent or politically active members of the legal profession. Many federal judges previously served as state court judges or state or local prosecutors. Before the president makes a formal nomination, however, the senators from the candidate's own state must indicate that they support the nominee. This is an informal but seldom violated practice called **senatorial courtesy**. If one or both senators from a prospective nominee's home state belong to the president's political party, the president will almost invariably consult them and secure their blessing for the nomination. Because the president's party in the Senate will rarely support a nominee opposed by a home-state senator from their ranks, this arrangement gives these senators virtual veto power over appointments to the federal bench in their own states. Senators also see nominations to the judiciary as a way to reward important allies and contributors in their states. If the state has no senator from the president's party, the governor or members of the state's House delegation may make suggestions. The practice of "courtesy" generally does not apply to Supreme Court appointments, only to district and circuit court nominations.

Federal appeals court nominations follow much the same pattern. Since appeals court judges preside over jurisdictions that include several states, however, senators do not have so strong a role in proposing potential candidates. Instead, potential appeals court candidates are generally suggested to the president by the Justice Department or by important members of the administration. The senators from the nominee's own state are still consulted before the president will formally act.

senatorial courtesy the practice whereby the president, before formally nominating a person for a federal judgeship, seeks the indication that senators from the candidate's own state support the nomination

TABLE 15.1

Supreme Court Justices, 2009 (in Order of Seniority)

NAME	YEAR OF BIRTH	PRIOR EXPERIENCE	APPOINTED BY	YEAR OF APPOINTMENT
Antonin Scalia	1936	Law professor, federal judge	Reagan	1986
Anthony Kennedy	1936	Federal judge	Reagan	1988
Clarence Thomas	1948	Federal judge	G. H. W. Bush	1991
Ruth Bader Ginsburg	1933	Federal judge	Clinton	1993
Stephen Breyer	1938	Federal judge	Clinton	1994
John Roberts, Jr. *Chief Justice*	1955	Federal judge	G. W. Bush	2005
Samuel Alito	1950	Federal judge	G. W. Bush	2006
Sonia Sotomayor	1954	Federal judge	Obama	2009
Elena Kagan	1960	Solicitor General	Obama	2010

Who Are Federal Judges?

One factor among many that presidents may take into account when selecting judicial nominees is diversity. The number of Supreme Court justices is relatively small, so it is easy to count the number of African Americans who have served as Supreme Court justices (2), female justices (4), and Hispanic justices (1). How diverse is the rest of the federal judiciary? The first section below shows the racial, ethnic, and gender composition of the lower federal courts.

Federal Judges in 2009, by Race and Gender

👤 = 10 Federal Judges

White Men 884

African American Men 79

Hispanic Men 53

White Women 193

African American Women 29

Hispanic Women 18

Appointments to Federal Courts, by Administration

● White Men
● White Women

● African American Men
● African American Women

● Hispanic Men
● Hispanic Women

KENNEDY/ JOHNSON — **NIXON/ FORD** — **CARTER** — **REAGAN** — **G.H.W. BUSH** — **CLINTON** — **G.W. BUSH**

KENNEDY/JOHNSON: 93%, 1%, 4%, <1%, 1%

NIXON/FORD: 95%, <1%, 3%, 1%

CARTER: 66%, 12%, 12%, 3%, 6%, <1%

REAGAN: 86%, 7%, 1%, <1%, 5%, <1%

G.H.W. BUSH: 72%, 16%, 7%, 1%, 4%

CLINTON: 52%, 23%, 12%, 4%, 2%

G.W. BUSH: 67%, 16%, 5%, 2%, 6%, 4%

for critical analysis

1. Would you describe the federal judiciary as diverse? Does racial, ethnic, and gender diversity of federal judges matter? Why or why not?

2. What similarities and differences do you notice among the judicial appointments of the presidents shown? What might account for the differences in terms of the diversity of their appointees?

SOURCE: Wheeler, Russell, "The Changing Face of the Federal Judiciary." Washington, DC: Brookings Institution; August 2009. Data in first section above are from August 2009.

There are no formal qualifications for service as a federal judge. In general, presidents endeavor to appoint judges who possess legal experience and good character and whose partisan and ideological views are similar to the president's own. Once the president has formally nominated an individual, the nominee must be considered by the Senate Judiciary Committee and confirmed by a majority vote in the full Senate. In recent years, a good deal of partisan conflict has surrounded judicial appointments. Senate Democrats have sought to prevent Republican presidents from appointing conservative judges while Senate Republicans have worked to prevent Democratic presidents from appointing liberal judges. During the early months of the Obama administration, Republicans were able to slow the judicial appointment process through various procedural maneuvers so that only three of the president's twenty-three nominations for federal judgeships were confirmed by the Senate.[4] Some of Obama's allies urged the president to take a more aggressive stance or risk allowing Republicans to block what had been considered a key Democratic priority.

If political factors play an important role in the selection of district and appellate court judges, they are decisive when it comes to Supreme Court appointments. Because the high court has so much influence over American law and politics, virtually all presidents have made an effort to select justices who share their own political philosophies.

It is important to note that five of the nine current justices as of 2010 were appointed by Republican presidents. This conservative majority, consisting of Chief Justice Roberts and Justices Alito, Kennedy, Scalia, and Thomas, has propelled the Court in a more conservative direction in a variety of areas. In 2009 and 2010, for example, in a series of 5–4 decisions, the Court overturned limits on corporate campaign spending, ruled that the Federal Communications Commission was justified in penalizing the use of expletives on the airwaves, and blocked a suit against former Attorney General John Ashcroft by a terrorist suspect alleging that the suspect had been mistreated in prison. Three members of the conservative bloc—Justices Alito, Thomas, and Roberts—are relatively young individuals who will likely serve on the Court for years, if not decades, to come. Through such judicial appointments, presidents continue to exercise influence long after they have passed from the political scene.

In recent decades, Supreme Court nominations have come to involve intense partisan struggle. Typically, after the president has named a nominee, interest groups opposed to the nomination have mobilized opposition in the media, the

In 2009, President Obama's first nominee to the Supreme Court, Sonia Sotomayor, was sworn in. Although a large Democratic majority in the Senate all but guaranteed Sotomayor would be confirmed, Republican senators grilled her for weeks on her approach to the law.

public, and the Senate. When President George H. W. Bush proposed the conservative judge Clarence Thomas for the Court, for example, liberal groups launched a campaign to discredit Thomas. After extensive research into his background, opponents of the nomination were able to produce evidence suggesting that Thomas had sexually harassed a former subordinate, Anita Hill. Thomas denied the charge. After contentious Senate Judiciary Committee hearings, highlighted by testimony from both Thomas and Hill, Thomas narrowly won confirmation.

Likewise, conservative interest groups carefully scrutinized Bill Clinton's somewhat more liberal nominees, hoping to find information about them that would sabotage their appointments. During his two opportunities to name Supreme Court justices, Clinton was compelled to drop several potential appointees because of information unearthed by political opponents.

In 2009, when President Obama nominated federal Judge Sonia Sotomayor to replace retiring Justice David Souter, conservatives denounced Sotomayor as a "reverse racist" because of her support for affirmative action. Many Republican senators, however, were reluctant to oppose a Hispanic nominee. For several years, the GOP has made efforts to attract America's rapidly growing Hispanic population. Republicans feared that opposing Sotomayor would undermine these efforts.[5] In 2010 Republicans severely criticized Obama's nomination of Elena Kagan, solicitor general and former Harvard law dean, to replace retiring Justice John Paul Stevens.

● How does the Supreme Court exercise the power of judicial review?

● The Power of the Supreme Court: Judicial Review

The phrase **judicial review** refers to the power of the judiciary to examine and, if necessary, invalidate actions undertaken by the legislative and executive branches if it finds them unconstitutional. The phrase is sometimes also used to describe the scrutiny that appellate courts give to the actions of trial courts, but, strictly speaking, this is an improper usage. A higher court's examination of a lower court's decisions might be called "appellate review," but it is not judicial review.

Judicial Review of Acts of Congress

Because the Constitution does not give the Supreme Court the power of judicial review over congressional enactments, the Court's exercise of it is something of a usurpation. It is not known whether the framers of the Constitution opposed judicial review, but "if they intended to provide for it in the Constitution, they did so in a most obscure fashion."[6] Disputes over the intentions of the framers were settled in 1803 in the case of *Marbury v. Madison*.[7] This case arose after Thomas Jefferson replaced John Adams in the White House. Jefferson's secretary of state, James Madison, refused to deliver an official commission to William Marbury, who had been appointed to a minor office by Adams just before he left the presidency. Marbury petitioned the Supreme Court to order Madison to deliver the commission. Jefferson and his followers did not believe that the Court had the power to undertake such an action and might have resisted the order. Chief Justice John Marshall was determined to assert the power of the judiciary but knew he must avoid a direct confrontation with the president. Accordingly, Marshall turned down Marbury's petition but gave as his reason the unconstitutionality of the legislation upon which Marbury had based his claim. Thus, Marshall asserted the power of judicial review but did so in a way that would not provoke a battle with Jefferson.

judicial review the power of the courts to review and, if necessary, declare actions of the legislative and executive branches invalid or unconstitutional. The Supreme Court asserted this power in *Marbury v. Madison*

In Marbury v. Madison *(1803), Chief Justice John Marshall established the Supreme Court's power to rule on the constitutionality of federal and state laws. This power makes the Court a lawmaking body.*

The Supreme Court's decision in this case established the power of judicial review. The Court said:

> It is emphatically the province and duty of the Judicial Department [the judicial branch] to say what the law is. Those who apply the rule to particular cases must, of necessity, expound and interpret that rule. If two laws conflict with each other, the Courts must decide on the operation of each. . . . So, if a law [e.g., a statute or treaty] be in opposition to the Constitution, if both the law and the Constitution apply to a particular case, so that the Court must either decide that case conformably to the law, disregarding the Constitution, or conformably to the Constitution, disregarding the law, the Court must determine which of these conflicting rules governs the case. This is of the very essence of judicial duty.

Although Congress and the president have often been at odds with the Court, its legal power to review acts of Congress has not been seriously questioned since 1803. One reason is that judicial power has been accepted as natural, if not intended. Another reason is that over more than two centuries, the Supreme Court has struck down only some 160 acts of Congress. When such acts do come up for review, the Court makes a self-conscious effort to give them an interpretation that will make them constitutional. In some instances, however, the Court reaches the conclusion that a congressional enactment directly violates the Constitution. For example, in 2007 and 2010, the high court struck down key portions of the Bipartisan Campaign Finance Reform Act, through which Congress had sought to regulate spending in political campaigns.[8] The Court found that provisions of the act limiting political advertising violated the First Amendment.

Judicial Review of State Actions

The power of the Supreme Court to review state legislation or other state action and to determine its constitutionality is neither granted by the Constitution nor inherent in the federal system. But the logic of the **supremacy clause** of Article VI of the Constitution, which declares the Constitution itself and laws made under its authority to be the supreme law of the land, is very strong. Furthermore, in the Judiciary Act of 1789, Congress conferred on the Supreme Court the power to reverse state constitutions and laws whenever they are clearly in conflict with the U.S. Constitution, federal laws, or treaties.[9] This power gives the Supreme Court appellate jurisdiction over all of the millions of cases that American courts handle each year.

The supremacy clause of the Constitution not only established the federal Constitution, statutes, and treaties as the "supreme Law of the Land," but also provided that "the Judges in every State shall be bound thereby, any Thing in the Constitution or Laws of the State to the Contrary notwithstanding." Under this authority, the Supreme Court has frequently overturned state constitutional provisions or statutes and state court decisions it deems to contravene rights or privileges guaranteed under the federal Constitution or federal statutes.

The civil rights arena abounds with examples of state laws that the Supreme Court has overturned because the statutes violated guarantees of due process and equal protection contained in the Fourteenth Amendment to the Constitution. For example, in the 1954 case of *Brown v. Board of Education*, the Court overturned statutes from Kansas, South Carolina, Virginia, and Delaware that either required or permitted segregated public schools on the basis that such statutes denied black

supremacy clause Article VI of the Constitution, which states that laws passed by the national government and all treaties are the supreme law of the land and superior to all laws adopted by any state or any subdivision

schoolchildren equal protection of the law. In 1967, in *Loving v. Virginia*, the Court invalidated a Virginia statute prohibiting interracial marriages.[10]

State statutes in other subject matter areas are equally subject to challenge. In *Griswold v. Connecticut*, the Court invalidated a Connecticut statute prohibiting the general distribution of contraceptives to married couples on the basis that the statute violated the couples' rights to marital privacy.[11] In *Brandenburg v. Ohio*, the Court overturned an Ohio statute forbidding any person to urge criminal acts as a means of inducing political reform. The statute had also prohibited anyone from joining any association that advocated such activities. The Court found that the statute punished "mere advocacy" and therefore violated the free speech provisions of the Constitution.[12]

Judicial Review of Federal Agency Actions

● How does the Supreme Court exercise the power of judicial review?

Although Congress makes the law, as we saw in Chapters 12 and 14, Congress can hardly administer the thousands of programs it has enacted and must delegate power to the president and to a huge bureaucracy to achieve its purposes. For example, if Congress wishes to improve air quality, it cannot possibly anticipate all the conditions and circumstances that may arise with respect to that general goal. Inevitably, Congress must delegate to the executive substantial discretionary power to make judgments about the best ways to bring about improved air quality in the face of changing circumstances. Thus, over the years, almost any congressional program will result in thousands and thousands of pages of administrative regulations developed by executive agencies nominally seeking to implement the will of the Congress.

Delegation of power to the executive poses a number of problems for Congress and the federal courts. If Congress delegates broad authority to the president, it risks seeing its goals subordinated to and subverted by those of the executive branch.[13] If Congress attempts to limit executive discretion by enacting precise rules and standards to govern the conduct of the president and the executive branch, it risks writing laws that do not conform to real-world conditions and that are too rigid to be adapted to changing circumstances.[14]

The issue of delegation of power has led to a number of court decisions over the past two centuries, generally revolving around the question of the scope of the delegation. Courts have also been called on to decide whether the rules and regulations adopted by federal agencies are consistent with Congress's express or implied intent.

As presidential power expanded during the New Deal era, one measure of increased congressional subordination to the executive was the enactment of laws that contained few, if any, principles limiting executive discretion. Congress enacted legislation, often at the president's behest, that gave the executive virtually unfettered authority to address a particular concern. For example, the Emergency Price Control Act of 1942 authorized the executive to set "fair and equitable" prices without offering any indication of what those terms might mean.[15] Although the Court initially challenged these delegations of power to the president during the New Deal, a confrontation with President Franklin Delano Roosevelt caused the Court to retreat from its position. Perhaps as a result, since then no congressional delegation of power to the president has been struck down as impermissibly broad. Particularly in recent years, the Supreme Court has found that so long as federal agencies developed rules and regulations "based upon a permissible construction" or "reasonable interpretation" of Congress's statute, the judiciary would accept the views of the executive branch. Generally, the courts give considerable

Protesters charged that the Supreme Court's decision in Bush v. Gore *unfairly handed the presidency to George W. Bush. However, in several cases related to presidential power in the war on terror, the Court ruled against the Bush administration's programs and procedures.*

deference to administrative agencies as long as those agencies have engaged in a formal rule-making process and can show that they have carried out the conditions prescribed by the various statutes governing agency rule making.

Judicial Review and Presidential Power

for critical analysis

During his 2005 confirmation hearings, senators asked Chief Justice Roberts why the Supreme Court was more willing to declare acts of Congress unconstitutional than it was to confront the president on the constitutionality of his actions. What reasons might you identify?

The federal courts are also called on to review the actions of the president. On many occasions, members of Congress and individuals and groups opposing the president's policies have challenged presidential orders and actions in the federal courts. In recent years, the federal bench has, more often than not, upheld assertions of presidential power in such realms as foreign policy, war and emergency powers, legislative power, and administrative authority. In June 2004, however, the Supreme Court ruled on three cases involving President George W. Bush's antiterrorism initiatives and claims of executive power and in two of the three cases appeared to place some limits on presidential authority.

One important case the Court decided was *Hamdi v. Rumsfeld*.[16] Yaser Esam Hamdi, apparently a Taliban soldier, was captured by American forces in Afghanistan and brought to the United States, where he was incarcerated at the Norfolk Naval Station. Hamdi was classified as an enemy combatant and denied civil rights,

How does the
Supreme Court
exercise the power
of judicial review?

including the right to counsel, despite the fact that he had been born in Louisiana and held American citizenship. In June 2004, the Supreme Court ruled that Hamdi was entitled to a lawyer and "a fair opportunity to rebut the government's factual assertions." However, the Supreme Court affirmed that the president possessed the authority to declare a U.S. citizen an enemy combatant and to order that such an individual be held in federal detention. Several of the justices intimated that once designated an enemy combatant, a U.S. citizen might be tried before a military tribunal and the normal presumption of innocence be suspended. One government legal adviser indicated that the effect of the Court's decision was minimal. "They are basically upholding the whole enemy combatant status and tweaking the evidence test," he said.[17] Thus the Supreme Court did assert that presidential actions were subject to judicial scrutiny and placed some constraints on the president's unfettered power. But at the same time, the Court affirmed the president's single most important claim—the unilateral power to declare individuals, including U.S. citizens, "enemy combatants" who could be detained by federal authorities under adverse legal circumstances.

Another important Supreme Court decision came in the 2006 case of *Hamdan v. Rumsfield* (126 S.Ct. 2749). Salim Hamdan was a Taliban fighter captured in Afghanistan and held at the Guantánamo Bay naval base. The Bush administration planned to try Hamdan before a military commission authorized by a 2002 presidential order. The Supreme Court ruled that the commissions created by the president planned to use procedures that violated federal law and U.S. treaty obligations. President Bush responded by demanding that Congress rewrite the law. Congress quickly obliged and enacted the Military Commissions Act, which gave the president statutory authority for his actions. In Section 7 of the Act, Congress declared that Guantánamo prisoners could not bring habeas corpus petitions to federal courts to seek their release. In the 2008 case of *Boumediene v. Bush* 06-1195 (2008), however, the Supreme Court struck down Section 7 and declared habeas corpus to be a fundamental right.

Judicial Review and Lawmaking

Much of the work of the courts involves the application of statutes to the particular case at hand. Over the centuries, judges have also developed a body of rules and principles of interpretation that are not grounded in specific statutes. This body of judge-made law is called common law.

The appellate courts, however, are in another realm. Their rulings can be considered laws, but they are laws governing the behavior only of the judiciary. The written opinion of an appellate court is about halfway between common law and statutory law. It is judge-made and draws heavily on the precedents of previous cases. But it tries to articulate the rule of law controlling the case in question and future cases like it. In this respect, it is like a statute. But it differs from a statute in that a statute addresses itself to the future conduct of citizens, whereas a written opinion addresses itself mainly to the willingness or ability of courts in the future to take cases and render favorable opinions. Decisions by appellate courts affect citizens by giving them a cause of action or by taking it away from them. That is, they open or close access to the courts.

A specific case illustrates the distinction. Before the Second World War, one of the most insidious forms of racial discrimination was the "restrictive covenant," a clause in a contract whereby the purchasers of a house agreed that if they later decided to sell it, they would sell only to a Caucasian. When a test case finally reached the Supreme Court in 1948, the Court ruled unanimously that citizens had a

Due process of law is an area in which federal courts have been critical in "making law" since the 1960s. In 2009, the Court heard the case of Savana Redding, who was strip searched by school officials who suspected she was hiding prescription pills. The Court ruled that the search was illegal.

right to discriminate with restrictive covenants in their sales contracts but that the courts could not enforce these contracts. Its argument was that enforcement would constitute violation of the Fourteenth Amendment provision that no state shall "deny to any person within its jurisdiction equal protection under the law."[18] The Court was thereby predicting what it would and would not do in future cases of this sort. Most states have now enacted statutes that forbid homeowners to place such covenants in sales contracts.

Many areas of civil law have been constructed in the same way—by judicial messages to other judges, some of which are codified eventually into legislative enactments. An example of great concern to employees and employers is that of liability for injuries sustained at work. Courts have sided with employees so often that it has become virtually useless for employers to fight injury cases. It has become "the law" that employers are liable for such injuries, without regard to negligence. But the law in this instance is simply a series of messages to lawyers that they should advise their corporate clients not to appeal injury decisions. In recent years, the Supreme Court has also been developing law in the realm of sexual harassment in the workplace. In a 2006 case, for example, the Supreme Court said that a victim of sexual harassment who was transferred from her job could sue her employer even though the company disciplined the perpetrator when the harassment was reported.[19]

The appellate courts cannot decide what types of behavior will henceforth be a crime. They cannot directly prevent the police from forcing confessions from suspects or intimidating witnesses. In other words, they cannot directly change the behavior of citizens or eliminate abuses of government power. What they can do, however, is make it easier for mistreated persons to gain redress.

In redressing wrongs, the appellate courts—and even the Supreme Court itself—often call for a radical change in legal principle. Changes in race relations, for example, would probably have taken a great deal longer if the Supreme Court had not rendered the 1954 decision *Brown v. Board of Education,* which redefined the rights of African Americans.

Similarly, the Supreme Court interpreted the doctrine of the separation of church and state so as to alter significantly the practice of religion in public institutions. For example, in a 1962 case, *Engel v. Vitale,* the Court declared that a once widely observed ritual—the recitation of a prayer by students in a public school—was unconstitutional under the establishment clause of the First Amendment. Almost all the dramatic changes in the treatment of criminals and of persons accused of crimes have been made by the appellate courts, especially the Supreme Court. The Supreme Court brought about a veritable revolution in the criminal process with three cases over less than five years: *Gideon v. Wainwright,* in 1963, established the obligation of state courts to provide legal counsel to defendants who could not afford their own attorneys. *Escobedo v. Illinois,* in 1964, gave suspects the right to remain silent and the right to have counsel present during questioning. But the *Escobedo* decision left confusions that allowed differing decisions to be made by lower courts. In *Miranda v. Arizona,* in 1966, the Supreme Court cleared up these confusions by setting forth what is known as the Miranda rule: arrested people have the right to remain silent, the right to be informed that anything they say can be held against them, and the right to counsel before and during police

● How does the
Supreme Court
exercise the power
of judicial review?

interrogation (see Chapter 4).[20] In 2000, the Supreme Court considered overruling *Miranda* in *Dickerson v. United States*, but it decided that the wide acceptance of Miranda rights in the legal culture is "adequate reason not to overrule" it.

One of the most significant changes brought about by the Supreme Court was the revolution in legislative representation unleashed by the 1962 case of *Baker v. Carr*.[21] In this landmark case, the Supreme Court held that it could no longer avoid reviewing complaints about the apportionment of seats in state legislatures. Following that decision, the federal courts went on to force reapportionment of all state, county, and local legislatures in the country.

The Supreme Court in Action

Given the millions of disputes that arise every year, the job of the Supreme Court would be impossible if it were not able to control the flow of cases and its own caseload. The Supreme Court has original jurisdiction in a limited variety of cases defined by the Constitution. The original jurisdiction includes (1) cases between the United States and one of the fifty states, (2) cases between two or more states, (3) cases involving foreign ambassadors or other ministers, and (4) cases brought by one state against citizens of another state or against a foreign country. The most important of these cases are disputes between states over land, water, or old debts. Generally, the Supreme Court deals with these cases by appointing a "special master," usually a retired judge, to actually hear the case and present a report. The Supreme Court then allows the states involved in the dispute to present arguments for or against the master's opinion.[22] The fact that a matter falls within the Supreme Court's jurisdiction does not mean that the Court will necessarily hear the case.

Rules of Access Over the years, the courts have developed specific rules that govern which cases within their jurisdiction they will and will not hear. In order to be heard by the courts, cases must meet certain criteria that are initially applied by the trial court but may be reconsidered by appellate courts. These rules of access can be broken down into three major categories: case or controversy, standing, and mootness.

Article III of the Constitution and Supreme Court decisions define judicial power as extending only to "cases and controversies." This means that the case before a court must be an actual controversy, not a hypothetical one, with two truly adversarial parties. The courts have interpreted this language to mean that they do not have the power to render advisory opinions to legislatures or agencies about the constitutionality of proposed laws or regulations. Furthermore, even after a law is enacted, the courts will generally refuse to consider its constitutionality until it is actually applied.

Parties to a case must also have **standing**—that is, they must show that they have a substantial stake in the outcome of the case. The traditional requirement for standing has been to show injury to oneself; that injury can be personal, economic, or even aesthetic. In order for a group or class of people to have standing (as in class-action suits), each member must show specific injury. This means that a general interest in the environment, for instance, does not provide a group with sufficient basis for standing.

The Supreme Court also uses a third criterion in determining whether it will hear a case: that of **mootness**. In theory, this requirement disqualifies cases that are brought too late—after the relevant facts have changed or the problem has been resolved by other means. The criterion of mootness, however, is subject to the

standing the right of an individual or organization to initiate a court case, on the basis of their having a substantial stake in the outcome

mootness a criterion used by courts to screen cases that no longer require resolution

The justices' preferences and priorities influence which cases are heard by the Supreme Court. Recently, the Court's conservative justices have been interested in cases involving challenges to affirmative action. In 2009, the Court found that officials in New Haven, Connecticut, including Mayor John DeStefano (pictured here), had discriminated against white firefighters in their efforts to protect the rights of minority firefighters.

discretion of the courts, which have begun to relax the rules of mootness, particularly in cases where a situation that has been resolved is likely to come up again. In the abortion case *Roe v. Wade*, for example, the Supreme Court rejected the lower court's argument that because the pregnancy had already come to term, the case was moot. The Court agreed to hear the case because no pregnancy was likely to outlast the lengthy appeals process.

Putting aside the formal criteria, the Supreme Court is most likely to accept cases that involve conflicting decisions by the federal circuit courts, cases that present important questions of civil rights or civil liberties, and cases in which the federal government is the appellant. Ultimately, however, the question of which cases to accept can come down to the preferences and priorities of the justices. If a group of justices believes that the Court should intervene in a particular area of policy or politics, they are likely to look for a case or cases that will serve as vehicles for judicial intervention. For many years, the Court was not interested in considering challenges to affirmative action or other programs designed to provide particular benefits to minorities. In recent years, however, several of the Court's more conservative justices have been eager to push back the limits of affirmative action and racial preference, and have therefore accepted a number of cases that would allow them to do so. In the 2009 case of *Ricci v. DeStefano*, for example, the Court ruled that officials in New Haven, Connecticut, had discriminated against white firefighters when they threw out the results of a test in which whites had outscored minority candidates for promotion. The Court said employers must have a "strong basis in evidence" that a test is defective, rather than simply relying on disparate outcomes.[23] The case is also notable because it was an appeal from a decision by Judge Sonia Sotomayor who, a few months later, joined the Supreme Court.

writ of certiorari a decision of at least four of the nine Supreme Court justices to review a decision of a lower court; from the Latin "to make more certain"

Writs Most cases reach the Supreme Court through a **writ of *certiorari*** (Figure 15.3). *Certiorari* is an order to a lower court to deliver the records of a particular case to be reviewed for legal errors. The term *certiorari* is sometimes shortened to *cert*, and cases deemed to merit certiorari are referred to as "certworthy." An

● How does the
Supreme Court
exercise the power
of judicial review?

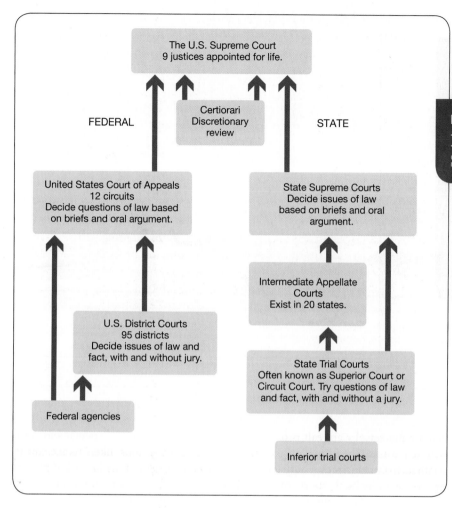

FIGURE 15.3
How Cases Reach the Supreme Court

The U.S. Supreme Court
9 justices appointed for life.

FEDERAL

Certiorari
Discretionary
review

STATE

United States Court of Appeals
12 circuits
Decide questions of law based
on briefs and oral argument.

State Supreme Courts
Decide issues of law
based on briefs and oral
argument.

Intermediate Appellate
Courts
Exist in 20 states.

U.S. District Courts
95 districts
Decide issues of law and
fact, with and without jury.

State Trial Courts
Often known as Superior Court or
Circuit Court. Try questions of law
and fact, with and without a jury.

Federal agencies

Inferior trial courts

individual who loses in a lower federal court or state court and wants the Supreme Court to review the decision has ninety days to file a petition for a writ of *certiorari* with the clerk of the U.S. Supreme Court. There are two types of petitions, paid petitions and petitions *in forma pauperis* (in the form of a pauper). The former requires payment of filing fees, submission of a certain number of copies, and compliance with a variety of other rules. For *in forma pauperis* petitions, usually filed by prison inmates, the Court waives the fees and most other requirements. Petitions for thousands of cases are filed with the Court every year (Figure 15.4).

Since 1972, most of the justices have participated in a "*certiorari* pool" in which their law clerks work together to evaluate the petitions. Each petition is reviewed by one clerk who writes a memo for all the justices participating in the pool summarizing the facts and issues and making a recommendation. Clerks for the other justices add their comments to the memo. After the justices have reviewed the memos, any one of them may place any case on the discuss list, which is circulated by the chief justice. If a case is not placed on the discuss list, it is automatically denied *certiorari*. Cases placed on the discuss list are considered and voted on during the justices' closed-door conference.

For *certiorari* to be granted, four justices must be convinced that the case satisfies Rule 10 of the Rules of the U.S. Supreme Court. Rule 10 states that *certiorari*

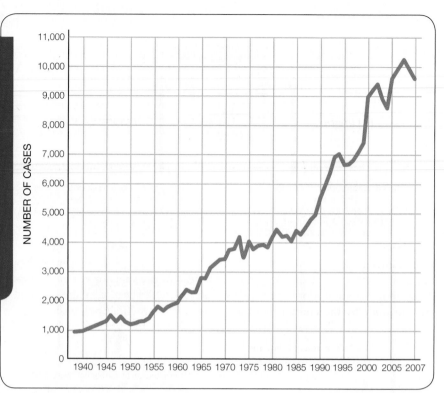

FIGURE 15.4

Cases Filed in the U.S. Supreme Court, 1938–2007 Terms*

*Number of cases filed in term starting in year indicated.

SOURCES: Years 1938–69, 1970–83, 1984–99: reprinted with permission from *The United States Law Week* (Washington, DC: Bureau of National Affairs), vol. 56, 3102; vol. 59, 3064; vol. 61, 3098; vol. 63, 3134; vol. 65, 3100; vol. 67, 3167; vol. 69, 3134 (copyright © Bureau of National Affairs Inc.); and 2000–05 U.S. Bureau of the Census. *Statistical Abstract of the United States*; 2006–07: Office of the Clerk, Supreme Court of the United States.

is not a matter of right but is to be granted only when there are special and compelling reasons. These include conflicting decisions by two or more circuit courts, conflicts between circuit courts and state courts of last resort, conflicting decisions by two or more state courts of last resort, decisions by circuit courts on matters of federal law that should be settled by the Supreme Court, and a circuit court decision on an important question that conflicts with Supreme Court decisions. It should be clear from this list that the Court will usually take action under only the most compelling circumstances—when there are conflicts among the lower courts about what the law should be, when an important legal question has been raised in the lower courts but not definitively answered, or when a lower court deviates from the principles and precedents established by the high court. The support of four justices is needed for *certiorari*, and few cases are able to satisfy this requirement. In recent sessions, although thousands of petitions were filed, the Court has granted *certiorari* to hardly more than eighty petitioners each year—about 1 percent of those seeking a Supreme Court review.

A handful of cases reach the Supreme court through avenues other than *certiorari*. One of these is the writ of certification. This writ can be used when a U.S. court of appeals asks the Supreme Court for instructions on a point of law that has never been decided. A second alternative avenue is the writ of appeal, which is used to appeal the decision of a three-judge district court.

Controlling the Flow of Cases

In addition to the judges, other actors play important roles in shaping the flow of cases through the federal courts: the solicitor general and federal law clerks.

The Solicitor General If any single person has greater influence than individual judges over the federal courts, it is the **solicitor general** of the United States. The solicitor general is the third-ranking official in the Justice Department (below the attorney general and the deputy attorney general) but is the top government lawyer in virtually all cases before the Supreme Court in which the government is a party. The solicitor general has the greatest control over the flow of cases; his or her actions are not reviewed by any higher authority in the executive branch. More than half the Supreme Court's total workload consists of cases under the direct charge of the solicitor general.

The solicitor general exercises especially strong influence by screening cases before any agency of the federal government can appeal them to the Supreme Court; indeed, the justices rely on the solicitor general to "screen out undeserving litigation and furnish them with an agenda to government cases that deserve serious consideration."[24] Typically, more requests for appeals are rejected than are accepted by the solicitor general. Agency heads may lobby the president or otherwise try to circumvent the solicitor general, and a few of the independent agencies have a statutory right to make direct appeals, but without the solicitor general's support, these requests are seldom reviewed by the Court. At best, they are doomed to *per curiam* ("by the court") rejection—rejection through a brief, unsigned opinion by the whole Court. Congress has given only a few agencies, including the Federal Communications Commission, the Federal Maritime Commission, and in some cases the Department of Agriculture (even though it is not an independent agency), the right to appeal directly to the Supreme Court without going through the solicitor general.

The solicitor general can enter a case even when the federal government is not a direct litigant by writing an *amicus curiae* ("friend of the court") brief. A friend of the court is not a direct party to a case but has a vital interest in its outcome. Thus, when the government has such an interest, the solicitor general can file an *amicus* brief, or a federal court can invite such a brief because it wants an opinion in writing. Other interested parties may file briefs as well.

In addition to exercising substantial control over the flow of cases, the solicitor general can shape the arguments used before the federal courts. Indeed, the Supreme Court tends to give special attention to the way the solicitor general characterizes the issues. The solicitor general is the person who appears most frequently before the Court and, theoretically at least, is the most disinterested. The credibility of the solicitor general is not hurt when several times each year he or she comes to the Court to withdraw a case with the admission that the government has made an error.

The solicitor general's sway over the flow of cases does not, however, entirely overshadow the influence of the other agencies and divisions in the Department of Justice. The solicitor general is counsel for the major divisions in the department, including the Antitrust, Tax, Civil Rights, and Criminal divisions. Their activities generate a great part of the solicitor general's agenda. This is particularly true of the Criminal Division, whose cases are appealed every day. These cases are generated by initiatives taken by the United States attorneys and the district judges before whom they practice.

Law Clerks Every federal judge employs law clerks to research legal issues and assist with the preparation of opinions. Each Supreme Court justice is assigned four clerks. The clerks are almost always honors graduates of the nation's most prestigious law schools. A clerkship with a Supreme Court justice is a great honor

solicitor general the top government lawyer in all cases before the Supreme Court where the government is a party

per curiam a brief, unsigned decision by an appellate court, usually rejecting a petition to review the decision of a lower court

amicus curiae literally, "friend of the court"; individuals or groups who are not parties to a lawsuit but who seek to assist the Supreme Court in reaching a decision by presenting additional briefs

and generally indicates that the fortunate individual is likely to reach the very top of the legal profession. The work of the Supreme Court clerks is a closely guarded secret, but it is likely that some justices rely heavily on their clerks for advice in writing opinions and in deciding whether the Court should hear an individual case. In a recent book, a former law clerk to the late justice Harry Blackmun charged that Supreme Court justices yielded "excessive power to immature, ideologically driven clerks, who in turn use that power to manipulate their bosses."[25]

Lobbying for Access: Interests and the Court

At the same time that the Court exercises discretion over which cases it will review, groups and forces in society often seek to persuade the justices to listen to their problems. Interest groups use several different strategies to get the Court's attention. Lawyers representing these groups try to choose the proper client and the proper case, so that the issues in question are most dramatically and appropriately portrayed. They also have to pick the right district or jurisdiction in which to bring the case. Sometimes they even have to wait for an appropriate political climate.

Group litigants have to plan carefully when to use and when to avoid publicity. They must also attempt to develop a proper record at the trial court level, one that includes some constitutional arguments and even, when possible, errors on the part of the trial court. One of the most effective strategies that litigants use in getting cases accepted for review by the appellate courts is to bring the same type of suit in more than one circuit (that is, to develop a "pattern of cases"), in the hope that inconsistent treatment by two different courts will improve the chance of a Supreme Court review.

Congress will sometimes provide interest groups with legislation designed to facilitate their use of litigation. One important recent example is the 1990 Americans with Disabilities Act (ADA), enacted after intense lobbying by public interest and advocacy groups. The ADA, in conjunction with the 1991 Civil Rights Act, opened the way for disabled individuals to make effective use of the courts to press their interests.

The two most notable users of the pattern-of-cases strategy in recent years have been the National Association for the Advancement of Colored People (NAACP) and the American Civil Liberties Union (ACLU). For many years, the NAACP (and its Defense Fund—now a separate group) has worked through local chapters and with many individuals to encourage litigation on issues of racial discrimination and segregation. Sometimes it distributes petitions to be signed by parents and filed with local school boards and courts, deliberately sowing the seeds of future litigation. The NAACP and the ACLU often encourage private parties to bring suit and then join the suit as *amici curiae*.

More recently, conservative advocacy groups have also used this strategy. For example, the Washington, D.C.–based Center for Individual Rights, has launched an active campaign of litigation to challenge affirmative action programs in college admissions and employment. In the case of *Hopwood v. Texas*, the center won a major victory against affirmative action, with the Fifth Circuit Court invalidating the University of Texas law school's program of preferential minority admissions.[26] In two very important subsequent cases, the center challenged the University of Michigan's minority admissions programs, which gave preferential treatment to minority applicants to the college of arts and sciences and to the law school. In 2003, the U.S. Supreme Court upheld the law school's program with certain

MGM v. Grokster: Digital Media and the Federal Courts

As digital technology evolves, America's federal courts find themselves bombarded by questions of intellectual property and copyright law. Some of the most recent high-profile cases involving the fate of digital technologies in the federal courts have involved P2P (peer-to-peer) networks such as Napster or Grokster, which are best known for facilitating the sharing of audio and video files between users.

Napster, the first well-known P2P file-sharing service, became popular soon after it was launched in 1999. Napster's creator, Shawn Fanning, was a student at Northeastern University when he began writing the program that would allow quick and convenient sharing of MP3 music files. Artists such as Metallica and Madonna criticized Napster, and music industry executives, fearing that Napster's distribution network was encouraging illegal exchanges of music and costing the industry millions, filed a lawsuit in 1999. In the spring of 2001, with over 25 million users, Napster was forced by the Ninth Circuit Court of Appeals to cease operations.

But with the shutdown of Napster, P2P technologies only became larger, less centralized, and more difficult to regulate. One example of the next generation of P2P networks was Grokster, a P2P file-sharing service without a centralized search engine. In 2003, Grokster was challenged by large media companies including AOL, Sony, Viacom, and Disney over the legality of their service. The U.S. District Court ruled in favor of Grokster, arguing that the company had no say over how its users chose to actually employ the technology. Judge Stephen Wilson pointed out that the service Grokster provided was similar to that of a VCR, in that it could be used for many *legal* purposes. "Grokster and Streamcast are not significantly different from companies that sell home video recorders or copy machines, both of which can be and are used to infringe copyrights," said Judge Wilson.[a]

After industry executives appealed the decision, the Ninth Circuit Court of Appeals—the same one that had shut down Napster three years earlier—heard the Grokster case. But unlike the Napster case in 2004, this time the court ruled in favor of the P2P network, citing the precedent of the 1984 Betamax case, which deemed VCR manufacturers not responsible for how individuals used their product. The court found that Grokster's file-sharing service was legal because it was decentralized, hence the company was not liable for the copyright infringements made by its users.[b] Frustrated by the ruling, the movie and music companies appealed to the Supreme Court. In response to the court's ruling, the Recording Industry Association of America began filing lawsuits against individual P2P users (many of them teenagers) for copyright infringement.

In 2005, the Supreme Court judged in favor of the music and movie industries, arguing that the legality of Grokster was not so much a function of the details of the technology but rather that Grokster's business model was predicated on the notion that users would share copyrighted material.

[a]R. Naraine, "Judge Rules in Favor of File-Swapping Sites," Internet News.com, April 25, 2003, www.internetnews.com (accessed 3/12/08).
[b]R. Smolla, "You Say Napster, I Say Grokster: What Do You Do When Technology Outpaces the Law?" Slate.com, December 13, 2004, www.slate.com (accessed 3/12/08).

for critical analysis

1. When the Supreme Court issued its decision on the *MGM v. Grokster* case, it did so based not on the technology behind the P2P service but on the company's business model. Why is this an important distinction? How might this decision contribute to setting a precedent in a way that a decision based on the technology itself might not have?

2. Should the courts be more accommodating of innovative technologies? Or should they do more to protect artists and "traditional" businesses?

RIAA Keep your Hands Off My iPod

changes. But the justices struck down the affirmative action rules that the under-graduate college applied.[27] In so doing, the Court forced colleges throughout the nation to place new restrictions on their affimative action efforts. The center has also sued the University of Washington over minority admissions, Alabama State University (a historically black school) over preferential treatment for whites, and a school district in Minnesota over preferential treatment for minorities in magnet school admissions.[28] Through this pattern of suits in federal and state courts, the center has sought to challenge and undermine the legal underpinnings of affirma-tive action.

In many states, it is considered unethical and illegal for attorneys to engage in "fomenting and soliciting legal business in which they are not parties and have no pecuniary right or liability." The NAACP was sued by the state of Virginia in the late 1950s in an attempt to restrict or eliminate its efforts to influence the pat-tern of cases. The Supreme Court reviewed the case in 1963, recognized that the strategy was being utilized, and held that the NAACP strategy was protected by the First and Fourteenth Amendments, just as other forms of speech and petition are protected.[29]

Thus, many pathbreaking cases are eventually granted *certiorari* because contin-ued refusal to review one or more of them would amount to a rule of law just as much as if the courts had handed down a written opinion. In this sense, the flow of cases, especially the pattern of significant cases, influences the behavior of the appellate judiciary.

The Supreme Court's Procedures

The Preparation The Supreme Court's decision to accept a case is the beginning of what can be a lengthy and complex process (see Figure 15.5). First, the attor-neys on both sides must prepare **briefs**—written documents in which the attorneys explain why the Court should rule in favor of their client. Briefs are filled with re-ferrals to precedents specifically chosen to show that other courts have frequently ruled in the same way the attorneys are asking the Supreme Court. The attorneys for both sides muster the most compelling precedents they can in support of their arguments.

As the attorneys prepare their briefs, they often ask sympathetic interest groups for their help. These groups are asked to file *amicus curiae* briefs that support the claims of one or the other litigant. In a case involving separation of church and state, for example, liberal groups such as the ACLU and Citizens for the Ameri-can Way are likely to be asked to file *amicus* briefs in support of strict separation, whereas conservative religious groups are likely to file *amicus* briefs advocating increased public support for religious ideas. Often, dozens of briefs will be filed on each side of a major case. *Amicus* filings are one of the primary methods used by interest groups to lobby the Court. By filing these briefs, groups indicate to the Court where they stand and signal to the justices that they believe the case to be an important one.

Oral Argument The next stage of a case is **oral argument**, in which attorneys for both sides appear before the Court to present their positions and answer the justices' questions. Each attorney has only a half hour to present his or her case, and this time includes interruptions for questions. Certain members of the Court, such as Justice Antonin Scalia, are known to interrupt attorneys dozens of times. Others, such as Justice Clarence Thomas, seldom ask questions. For an attorney, the opportunity to argue a case before the Supreme Court is a singular honor and

brief a written document in which attorneys explain, using case precedents, why the court should find in favor of their client

oral argument the stage in Supreme Court procedure in which attorneys for both sides appear before the Court to present their positions and answer questions posed by justices

a mark of professional distinction. It can also be a harrowing experience, when justices interrupt a carefully prepared presentation. Nevertheless, oral argument can be very important to the outcome of a case. It allows justices to understand better the heart of the case and to raise questions that might not have been addressed in the opposing sides' briefs. It is not uncommon for justices to go beyond the strictly legal issues and ask opposing counsel to discuss the implications of the case for the Court and the nation at large.

The Conference Following oral argument, the Court discusses the case in its Wednesday or Friday conference. The chief justice presides over the conference and speaks first; the other justices follow in order of seniority. The Court's conference is secret, and no outsiders are permitted to attend. The justices discuss the case and eventually reach a decision on the basis of a majority vote. If the Court is divided, a number of votes may be taken before a final decision is reached. As the case is discussed, justices may try to influence or change each other's opinions. At times, this may result in compromise decisions.

Opinion Writing After a decision has been reached, one of the members of the majority is assigned to write the **opinion**. This assignment is made by the chief justice, or by the most senior justice in the majority if the chief justice is on the losing side. The assignment of the opinion can make a significant difference to the interpretation of a decision. Every opinion of the Supreme Court sets a major precedent for future cases throughout the judicial system. Lawyers and judges in the lower courts will examine the opinion carefully to ascertain the Supreme Court's meaning. Differences in wording and emphasis can have important implications for future litigation. Thus, in assigning an opinion, the justices must give serious thought to the impression the case will make on lawyers and on the public, as well

opinion the written explanation of the Supreme Court's decision in a particular case

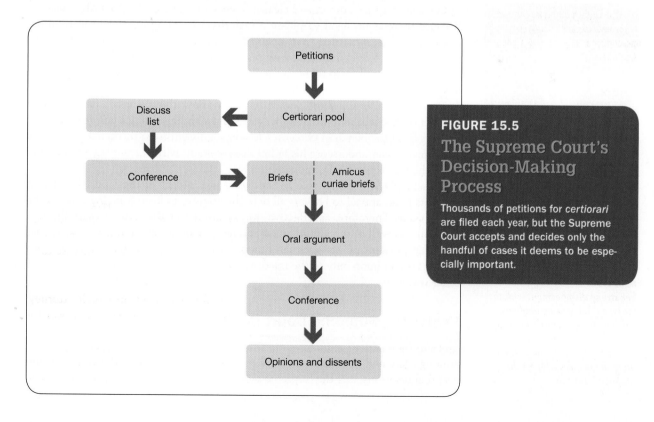

FIGURE 15.5
The Supreme Court's Decision-Making Process

Thousands of petitions for *certiorari* are filed each year, but the Supreme Court accepts and decides only the handful of cases it deems to be especially important.

as to the probability that one justice's opinion will be more widely accepted than another's.

One of the more dramatic instances of this tactical consideration occurred in 1944, when Chief Justice Harlan F. Stone chose Justice Felix Frankfurter to write the opinion in the "white primary" case *Smith v. Allwright*. The chief justice believed that this sensitive case, which overturned the southern practice of prohibiting black participation in nominating primaries, required the efforts of the most brilliant and scholarly jurist on the Court. But the day after Stone made the assignment, Justice Robert H. Jackson wrote a letter to Stone urging a change of assignment. In his letter, Jackson argued that Frankfurter, a foreign-born Jew from New England, would not win the South with his opinion, regardless of its brilliance. Stone accepted the advice and substituted Justice Stanley Reed, an American-born Protestant from Kentucky and a southern Democrat in good standing.[30]

Once the majority opinion is drafted, it is circulated to the other justices. Some members of the majority may agree with both the outcome and the rationale, but wish to emphasize or highlight a particular point. For that purpose, they draft a concurring opinion, called a *regular concurrence*. In other instances, one or more justices may agree with the majority but disagree with the rationale presented in the majority opinion. These justices may draft *special concurrences*, explaining their disagreements with the majority.

Dissent Justices who disagree with the majority decision of the Court may choose to publicize the character of their disagreement in the form of a **dissenting opinion**. The dissenting opinion is generally assigned by the senior justice among the dissenters. Dissents can be used to express irritation with an outcome or to signal to defeated political forces in the nation that their position is supported by at least some members of the Court. Ironically, the most dependable way an individual justice can exercise a direct and clear influence on the Court is to write a dissent. Because there is no need to please a majority, dissenting opinions can be more eloquent and less guarded than majority opinions. The current Supreme Court often produces 5-to-4 decisions, with dissenters writing long and detailed opinions that, they hope, will help them to convince a swing justice to join their side on the next round of cases dealing with a similar topic. During the Court's 2006–07 term, Justice Ruth Bader Ginsburg was so unhappy about the majority's decisions in a number of cases that she violated her own long-standing practice and read forceful dissents from the bench in two cases. Reading a dissent from the bench is one way that a justice can underscore his or her disagreement with current legal trends and point the way toward other possibilities.

Dissent plays a special role in the work and impact of the Court because it amounts to an appeal to lawyers all over the country to keep bringing cases of the sort at issue. Therefore, an effective dissent influences the flow of cases through the Court as well as the arguments that lawyers will use in later cases. Even more important, dissent points out that although the Court speaks with a single opinion, it is the opinion only of the majority—and one day the majority might go the other way.

Explaining Supreme Court Decisions

The Supreme Court explains its decisions in terms of law and precedent. But although law and precedent do have an effect on the Court's deliberations and eventual decisions, it is the Supreme Court that decides what laws actually mean

dissenting opinion a decision written by a justice in the minority in a particular case in which the justice wishes to express his or her reasoning in the case

On several recent occasions, Justice Ruth Bader Ginsburg read her dissenting opinions aloud from the bench, to emphasize her strong disagreement with the majority. Dissenting opinions can encourage lawyers to bring similar cases in the future by letting the public know that not all of the justices support the majority decision.

and what importance precedent will actually have. Throughout its history, the Court has shaped and reshaped the law. In the late nineteenth and early twentieth centuries, for example, the Supreme Court held that the Constitution, law, and precedent permitted racial segregation in the United States. Beginning in the late 1950s, however, the Court found that the Constitution prohibited segregation on the basis of race and indicated that the use of racial categories in legislation was always suspect. By the 1970s and 1980s, the Court once again held that the Constitution permitted the use of racial categories—when such categories were needed to help members of minority groups achieve full participation in American society. Since the 1990s, the Court has retreated from this position, too, indicating that governmental efforts to provide extra help to racial minorities could represent an unconstitutional infringement on the rights of the majority.

Activism and Restraint One element of judicial philosophy is the issue of activism versus restraint. Over the years, some justices have believed that courts should interpret the Constitution according to the stated intentions of its framers and defer to the views of Congress when interpreting federal statutes. Justice Felix Frankfurter, for example, advocated judicial deference to legislative bodies and avoidance of the "political thicket" in which the Court would entangle itself by deciding questions that were essentially political rather than legal in character. Advocates of **judicial restraint** are sometimes called "strict constructionists," because they look strictly to the words of the Constitution in interpreting its meaning.

The alternative to restraint is **judicial activism**. Activist judges such as Chief Justice Earl Warren believed that the Court should go beyond the words of the Constitution or a statute to consider the broader societal implications of its decisions. Activist judges sometimes strike out in new directions, promulgating new interpretations or inventing new legal and constitutional concepts when they believe these to be socially desirable. For example, Justice Harry Blackmun's opinion in *Roe v. Wade* was based on a constitutional right to privacy that is not found in the words of the Constitution but was, rather, from the Court's prior decision in *Griswold v. Connecticut*.[31] Blackmun and the other members of the majority in the *Roe* case argued that the right to privacy was implied by other constitutional provisions. In this instance of judicial activism, the Court knew the result it wanted to achieve and was not afraid to make the law conform to the desired outcome.

Activism and restraint are sometimes confused with liberalism and conservatism. For example, conservative politicians often castigate "liberal activist" judges and call for the appointment of conservative jurists who will refrain from reinterpreting the law. To be sure, some liberal jurists are activists and some conservatives have been advocates of restraint, but the relationships are by no means synonymous. Indeed, the Rehnquist court, dominated by conservatives, was among the most activist courts in American history, striking out in new directions in such areas as federalism and election law. The Roberts court is continuing along the same route. As the examples of these conservative courts illustrate, a judge may be philosophically conservative and believe in strict construction of the Constitution but also be jurisprudentially activist and believe that the courts must play an active an energetic role in policy making, if necessary striking down acts of Congress to ensure that the intent of the framers is fulfilled.

Political Ideology The second component of judicial philosophy is political ideology. The liberal or conservative attitudes of justices play an important role in their decisions.[32] Indeed, the philosophy of activism versus restraint is sometimes

judicial restraint judicial philosophy whose adherents refuse to go beyond the clear words of the Constitution in interpreting its meaning

judicial activism judicial philosophy that posits that the Court should go beyond the words of the Constitution or a statute to consider the broader societal implications of its decisions

for critical analysis

In its 2008 decision in the case of *District of Columbia v. Heller*, the Supreme Court struck down a District of Columbia law that prohibited most private citizens from keeping handguns in their homes. How does the *Heller* decision affect gun laws outside the District of Columbia?

a smokescreen for political ideology. In the past, liberal judges have often been activists, willing to use the law to achieve social and political change, whereas conservatives have been associated with judicial restraint. Interestingly, however, in recent years some conservative justices who have long called for restraint have actually become activists in seeking to undo some of the work of liberal jurists over the past three decades.

From the 1950s to the 1980s, the Supreme Court took an activist role in such areas as civil rights, civil liberties, abortion, voting rights, and police procedures. For example, the Supreme Court was more responsible than any other governmental institution for breaking down America's system of racial segregation. The Supreme Court virtually prohibited states from interfering with the right of a woman to seek an abortion and sharply curtailed state restrictions on voting rights. And it was the Supreme Court that placed restrictions on the behavior of local police and prosecutors in criminal cases. Since that time, however, the conservative justices appointed by presidents Ronald Reagan, George H. W. Bush, and George W. Bush have become the dominant bloc on the Court and, as we saw earlier, have moved the Court to the right on a number of issues, including affirmative action and abortion.

The political struggles of recent years amply illustrate the importance of judicial ideology. Is abortion a fundamental right or a criminal activity? How much separation must there be between church and state? Does application of the Voting Rights Act to increase minority representation constitute a violation of the rights of whites? The answers to these and many other questions cannot be found in the words of the Constitution. They must be located, instead, in the hearts and minds of the judges who interpret that text.

● Judicial Power and Politics

One of the most important institutional changes to occur in the United States during the past half-century has been the striking transformation of the role and power of the federal courts, and of the Supreme Court in particular. Understanding how this transformation came about is the key to understanding the contemporary role of the courts in America.

Traditional Limitations on the Federal Courts

For much of American history, the power of the federal courts was subject to a number of limitations.[33] To begin with, unlike other governmental institutions, courts cannot exercise power on their own initiative. Judges must wait until a case is brought to them before they can make authoritative decisions. Traditionally, moreover, courts were constrained by judicial rules of standing that limited access to the bench. Claimants who simply disagreed with governmental action or inaction could not obtain access. Access to the courts was limited to individuals who could show that they were particularly affected by the government's behavior in some area. This limitation on access to the courts diminished the judiciary's capacity to forge links with important political and social forces.

Second, courts were traditionally limited in the character of the relief they could provide. In general, courts acted only to offer relief or assistance to individuals and

The Supreme Court and International Law

For most of its history the American judiciary has been a particularly domestic institution. But in this epoch of globalization, the Court has had to give up what Justice Ruth Bader Ginsburg in 2003 called "our 'island' or 'lone ranger' mentality." Ginsburg went on to note that increasingly the justices were considering the perspectives of comparative and international law.

Along one path of change, numerous cases involving such things as interpreting the terms of an international treaty have arisen over "cross-border transactions" in which international law is not only relevant but could be the governing law. Such cases have given rise to the adoption of the United Nations Convention on Contracts for the International Sale of Goods (CISG), which the United States ratified in 1986. By the mid-1990s, U.S. courts had to deal with an increasing number of such cases, and the lower judges as well as the Supreme Court justices and their law clerks had a difficult time with these because they required research on international law and decisions by foreign courts. And our various courts continually disagree over the weight to put on the rulings of foreign tribunals: Are these foreign decisions to be taken as precedents in our courts? Or do U.S. courts apply U.S. law to such transnational cases?

A second path of change is the extent to which our courts should be influenced by international opinion and the decisions by foreign legislators and courts in their domestic disputes. One of the most striking was the 2003 decision that a Texas statute making it a crime for two persons of the same sex to engage in consensual sexual conduct violated the due process clause (*Lawrence v. Texas,* 123 S.Ct. 2472). More controversial than the ruling itself was part of its argument—that other nations, including Great Britain, had repealed such laws ten years earlier. Another decision of equal import was the 2002 decision in which the majority opinion noted that "within the world community the imposition of the death penalty for crimes committed by mentally retarded offenders is overwhelmingly disapproved." Chief Justice Rehnquist and Justice Scalia vigorously dissented on this point: "The viewpoints of other countries simply are not relevant . . . [and foreign] notions of justice are not always those of our people" (*Atkins v. Virginia,* 536 U.S. 304). More recently, in 2005, the International Task Force on Euthanasia and Assisted Suicide (ITFEA) filed an *amicus* brief in the case of *Gonzales v. Oregon.* This case involved Oregon's assisted-suicide law, which allows individuals to end their own lives under certain circumstances.

Another international influence is the UN Treaty to establish an International Criminal Court (ICC), to be given jurisdiction over the conduct of military personnel in any international campaign. Since its creation in 1998, 130 countries have signed the treaty. Although President Clinton signed for the United States, he continued to bargain over terms, and the U.S. Senate has never had to confront a vote on ratification. However, Clinton's signature committed the United States to avoid acting in any way that would undermine the treaty. Consequently, fears persist that U.S. military personnel could be subject to prosecution if one of the ratifying states comes forward with an allegation that a "war crime" has been committed. The Bush administration was generally hostile to the ICC, asserting that it was an agency lacking accountability and that its actions infringed on American sovereignty. The Obama administration, on the other hand, has indicated a desire to cooperate with the ICC and has suggested that it might be time to renegotiate and revise the treaty establishing the court to deal with American concerns and potentially secure U.S. ratification.

for critical analysis

1. Who should have jurisdiction if American soldiers at Abu Ghraib Prison in Baghdad are charged by the new Iraqi government with war crimes for mistreating Iraqi prisoners? Iraqi courts? American courts? the ICC?

2. Who should have jurisdiction if an American soldier is arrested by Iraqi police and charged with molesting an Iraqi woman?

not to broad social classes, again inhibiting the formation of alliances between the courts and important social forces.

Third, courts lacked enforcement powers of their own and were compelled to rely on executive or state agencies to ensure compliance with their edicts. If the executive or state agencies were unwilling to assist the courts, judicial enactments could go unheeded, as when President Andrew Jackson declined to enforce Chief Justice John Marshall's 1832 order to the state of Georgia to release two missionaries it had arrested on Cherokee lands. Marshall asserted that the state had no right to enter the Cherokee lands without their assent.[34] Jackson is reputed to have said, "John Marshall has made his decision, now let him enforce it." Congress and the president have ignored Supreme Court rulings in recent years as well. For example, in 1983 the Supreme Court declared that a practice known as the one-house legislative veto was unconstitutional. This practice entailed the enactment of legislation that could later be rescinded by either house of Congress if it was dissatisfied with the results. In the case of *Immigration and Naturalization Service v. Chadha*, the Court ruled that this amounted to the usurpation of executive power by the legislature.[35] Congress and the president, however, find the legislative veto procedure convenient and continue to use it by other names, despite the Court's ruling.

Fourth, federal judges are, of course, appointed by the president (with the consent of the Senate). As a result, the president and Congress can shape the composition of the federal courts and ultimately, perhaps, the character of judicial decisions. Finally, Congress has the power to change both the size and jurisdiction of the Supreme Court and other federal courts. In many areas, federal courts obtain their jurisdiction not from the Constitution but from congressional statutes. On a number of occasions, Congress has threatened to take matters out of the Court's hands when it was unhappy with the Court's policies.[36] For example, in 1996 Congress enacted several pieces of legislation designed to curb the jurisdiction of the federal courts. One of these laws was the Prison Litigation Reform Act, which limits the ability of federal judges to issue "consent decrees" under which the judges could take control of state prison systems. Another jurisdictional curb was included in the Immigration Reform Act, which prohibited the federal courts from hearing class-action suits against Immigration and Naturalization Service deportation orders. As to the size of the Court, on one memorable occasion, presidential and congressional threats to expand the size of the Supreme Court—Franklin Delano Roosevelt's "court packing" plan—encouraged the justices to drop their opposition to New Deal programs.

As a result of these limitations on judicial power, through much of their history the chief function of the federal courts was to provide judicial support for executive agencies and to legitimize acts of Congress by declaring them to be consistent with constitutional principles. Only on rare occasions have the federal courts dared to challenge Congress or the executive branch.[37]

Two Judicial Revolutions

Since the Second World War, however, the role of the federal judiciary has been strengthened and expanded. There have been two judicial revolutions in the United States since then. The first and more visible of these was the substantive revolution in judicial policy. As we saw earlier in this chapter and in Chapters 4 and 5, in policy

In 2005, the Supreme Court decided two cases involving displays of the Ten Commandments on government property. Christian activists paid close attention to the wording of the decisions, which allowed such displays in some circumstances.

areas, including school desegregation, legislative apportionment, and criminal procedure, as well as obscenity, abortion, and voting rights, the Supreme Court was at the forefront of a series of sweeping changes in the role of the U.S. government, and ultimately, in the character of American society.[38]

But at the same time that the courts were introducing important policy innovations, they were also bringing about a second, less visible revolution. During the 1960s and 1970s, the Supreme Court and other federal courts instituted a series of changes in judicial procedures that fundamentally expanded the power of the courts in the United States. First, the federal courts liberalized the concept of standing to permit almost any group that seeks to challenge the actions of an administrative agency to bring its case before the federal bench. In 1971, for example, the Supreme Court ruled that public interest groups could use the National Environmental Policy Act to challenge the actions of federal agencies by claiming that the agencies' activities might have adverse environmental consequences.[39]

Congress helped to make it even easier for groups dissatisfied with government policies to bring their cases to the courts by adopting Section 1983 of the U.S. Code, which permits the practice of "fee shifting"—that is, allowing citizens who successfully bring a suit against a public official for violating their constitutional rights to collect their attorneys' fees and costs from the government. Thus, Section 1983 encourages individuals and groups to bring their problems to the courts rather than to Congress or the executive branch. These changes have given the courts a far greater role in the administrative process than ever before. Many federal judges are concerned that federal legislation in areas such as health care reform would create new rights and entitlements that would give rise to a deluge of court cases. "Any time you create a new right, you create a host of disputes and claims," warned Barbara Rothstein, chief judge of the federal district court in Seattle, Washington.[40]

Become an Advocate for Justice

Do you think you can't affect the outcome of justice? Think again. Thousands of socially conscious youth convened in Jena, Louisiana, in 2007 to protest the sentences of the so-called "Jena 6." After black students at a local high school sat beneath a campus tree, which was historically claimed by white students, nooses were found dangling from the same tree. The heightened racial tensions were only exacerbated when the justice system appeared to treat white students lightly while coming down hard on black students who behaved similarly. In order to protest the perceived injustice of the criminal justice system to black defendants, more than 10,000 demonstrators, including a large number of young people, descended on the city of Jena for marches

and vigils. Their presence helped to overturn the original sentences of the "Jena 6."

If protesting what you believe to be an injustice in the court system isn't for you, there are plenty of other things that you can do to take a more active role in understanding and helping to shape the outcome of court cases in this country.

- Help wrongfully convicted inmates. The Innocence Project identifies and assists prison inmates who may be vindicated through the use of DNA testing and has helped to exonerate more than 200 inmates who were serving lengthy sentences or even facing the death penalty in prisons around the country. You don't have to be an attorney or someone skilled in the science of DNA testing in order to help to ensure that innocent people aren't sitting in prisons or even on death row. By visiting www .innocenceproject.org, you can find out about things that you can do to help, including spreading the word about the plight of wrongfully incarcerated individuals by hosting a screening of their recommended list of movies and television programs.

- Draw attention to the courts' role in key issues. Recent decisions by state Supreme Courts to declare legislation that defines marriage as a union between a man and woman unconstitutional have drawn considerable criticism from those opposed to what some call "legislating from the bench." By this, some accuse justices of using the courts to

become policy makers rather than arbiters of justice. Gay marriage isn't the only issue that critics have used to argue against this practice. Others include abortion, because the right to privacy isn't mentioned in the Constitution, and medical marijuana.

Talk to friends and family about what role the courts should play in settling policy disputes. If you feel comfortable enough, consider writing a letter to a newspaper editor about whether the courts should take a more active role in settling a certain issue or about an area in which they have intervened too much.

- Along similar lines, you can explore various perspectives on the courts' role in society. There are a variety of membership groups who are organized around a very clear idea of how the courts should interface with civil society. Some of them even have campus chapters nationwide in order to bring together like-minded young people around the principles of either judicial activism or judicial restraint. If exploring this dimension of the courts sounds interesting, you can check out the Web sites for the Federalist Society for Law and Public Policy Studies (www.fed-soc.org) and the People for the American Way (www.pfaw.org). You might even consider joining a campus chapter or starting one if it doesn't already exist, or even attending events that are sponsored by these groups nationwide.

- Listen to Supreme Court media files. The Web site for Oyez (www.oyez.org) has links to Supreme Court oral arguments and opinion announcements. Listening to how things unfold once a case makes its way to the Supreme Court can help to demystify what is often perceived as the most remote branch of government.

● How does the
Supreme Court
exercise the power
of judicial review?

Second, the federal courts broadened the scope of relief to permit themselves to act on behalf of broad categories or classes of persons in "class action" cases, rather than just on behalf of individuals.[41] A **class-action suit** is a procedural device that permits large numbers of persons with common interests to join together under a representative party to bring or defend a lawsuit. One example of a class-action suit is the case of *In re Agent Orange Product Liability Litigation*, in which a federal judge in New York certified Vietnam War veterans as a class with standing to sue a manufacturer of herbicides for damages allegedly incurred from exposure to the defendant's product while in Vietnam.[42] The class potentially numbered in the tens of thousands.

Third, the federal courts began to employ so-called structural remedies, in effect retaining jurisdiction of cases until the court's mandate had actually been implemented to its satisfaction.[43] The best known of these instances was federal judge W. Arthur Garrity's effort to operate the Boston school system from his bench in order to ensure its desegregation. Between 1974 and 1985, Judge Garrity issued fourteen decisions relating to different aspects of the Boston school desegregation plan that had been developed under his authority and put into effect under his supervision.[44] In 1985, as a result of a suit brought by the NAACP five years earlier, federal judge Leonard B. Sand imposed fines that would have forced the city of Yonkers, New York, into bankruptcy if it had refused to accept his plan to build public housing in white neighborhoods. Twenty-two years and $1.6 million in fines later, in 2007, the city finally gave in to the judge's ruling.

Through these three judicial mechanisms, the federal courts paved the way for an unprecedented expansion of national judicial power. In essence, liberalization of the rules of standing and expansion of the scope of judicial relief drew the federal courts into linkages with important social interests and classes, while the introduction of structural remedies enhanced the courts' ability to serve these constituencies. Thus, during the 1960s and 1970s, the power of the federal courts expanded in the same way the power of the executive expanded during the 1930s—through links with constituencies, such as civil rights, consumer, environmental, and feminist groups, that staunchly defended the Supreme Court in its battles with Congress, the executive, and other interest groups.

class-action suit a legal action by which a group or class of individuals with common interests can file a suit on behalf of everyone who shares that interest

for critical **analysis**

In what ways are courts, judges, and justices shielded from politics and political pressure? In what ways are they vulnerable to political pressure? Are the courts an appropriate place for politics?

● Thinking Critically about the Judiciary, Liberty, and Democracy

In the original conception of the framers, the judiciary was to be the institution that would protect individual liberty from the government. As we saw in Chapter 2, the framers believed that in a democracy the great danger was what they termed "tyranny of the majority"—the possibility that a popular majority, "united or actuated by some common impulse or passion," would "trample on the rules of justice."[45] The framers hoped that the courts would protect liberty from the potential excesses of democracy. And for most of American history, this was precisely the role the federal courts played. The courts' most important decisions were those that protected the freedoms—to speak, worship, publish, vote, and attend school—of groups and individuals whose political views, religious beliefs, or racial or ethnic backgrounds made them unpopular.

Today, Americans of all political persuasions seem to view the courts as useful instruments through which to pursue their goals rather than protectors of individual rights. Liberals and conservatives alike hope to use the courts as instruments of social policy. One side wants to ban abortion and the other to promote school integration. One side hopes to help business maintain its profitability, whereas the other wants to enhance the power of workers in the workplace. These may all be noble goals, but they present a basic dilemma for students of American government. If the courts are simply one more set of policy-making institutions, then who is left to protect the liberty of individuals?

studyguide

Practice Quiz

Find a diagnostic Web Quiz with 33 additional questions on the StudySpace Web site: www.wwnorton.com/we-the-people

The Legal System

1. What is the name for the body of law that involves disputes between private parties? *(p. 566)*
   a) civil law
   b) privacy law
   c) household law
   d) common law

2. By what term is the practice of the courts to uphold precedent known? *(p. 566)*
   a) *certiorari*
   b) *stare decisis*
   c) rule of four
   d) senatorial courtesy

3. Where do most trials in America take place? *(p. 566)*
   a) state and local courts
   b) appellate courts
   c) federal courts
   d) the Supreme Court

4. The term "writ of *habeas corpus*" refers to *(pp. 568–69)*
   a) a court order that an individual in custody be brought into court and shown the cause for his or her detention.
   b) a criterion used by courts to screen cases that no longer require resolution.

c) a decision of at least four of the nine Supreme Court justices to review a decision of a lower court.
   d) a short, unsigned decision by an appellate court, usually rejecting a petition to review the decision of a lower court.

Federal Jurisdiction

5. Under what authority is the number of Supreme Court justices decided? *(p. 571)*
   a) the president
   b) the chief justice
   c) Congress
   d) the Constitution

The Power of the Supreme Court: Judicial Review

6. The Supreme Court's decision in *Marbury v. Madison* was important because *(pp. 575–76)*
   a) it invalidated state laws prohibiting interracial marriage.
   b) it ruled that the recitation of prayers in public schools are unconstitutional under the establishment clause of the First Amendment.

c) it established that arrested people have the right to remain silent, the right to be informed that anything they say can be held against them, and the right to counsel before and during police interrogation.

d) it established the power of judicial review.

7. Which of the following cases involved the "right to privacy"? (p. 577)
   a) Griswold v. Connecticut
   b) Brown v. Board of Education
   c) Schneckloth v. Bustamante
   d) Marbury v. Madison

8. Which of the following Supreme Court cases did not involve the rights of criminal suspects? (p. 581)
   a) Miranda v. Arizona
   b) Escobedo v. Illinois
   c) Baker v. Carr
   d) Dickerson v. United States

9. Which of the following is not included in the original jurisdiction of the Supreme Court? (p. 581)
   a) cases between the United States and one of the fifty states
   b) cases involving challenges to the constitutionality of state laws
   c) cases between two or more states
   d) cases involving foreign ambassadors or other ministers

10. Which of the following does not influence the flow of cases heard by the Supreme Court? (pp. 584–85)
    a) the Supreme Court itself
    b) the solicitor general
    c) the attorney general
    d) law clerks

11. Which government official is responsible for arguing the federal government's position in cases before the Supreme Court? (p. 585)
    a) the vice president
    b) the attorney general
    c) the U.S. district attorney
    d) the solicitor general

12. Which of the following is a brief submitted to the Supreme Court by someone other than one of the parties in the case? (p. 585)
    a) amicus curiae
    b) habeas corpus

c) solicitor general
d) ex post brief

13. Justices who favored going beyond the words of the Constitution to consider the broader societal implications of the Supreme Court's decisions would be considered an advocate of which judicial philosophy? (p. 591)
    a) judicial restraint
    b) judicial activism
    c) judicial constitutionalism
    d) stare decisis

Judicial Power and Politics

14. Which of the following would not be accurately characterized as a traditional limitation on the power of the federal courts? (pp. 592–94)
    a) Courts lack enforcement powers of their own and are compelled to rely on executive or state agencies to ensure compliance with their rulings.
    b) Congress has the power to change both the size and jurisdiction of the federal courts.
    c) Courts can act to offer relief or assistance to broad social classes but not to specific individuals.
    d) Courts cannot exercise power on their own initiative and must wait for cases to be brought to them.

15. How have changes in judicial policy areas and judicial procedure affected the power of the federal judiciary since World War II? (pp. 594–95)
    a) Strong involvement in sweeping policy change has expanded the court's power, but changes in procedure have sought to limit judicial power.
    b) Changes in procedure have expanded the court's power, but the courts have played only minor roles in policy change.
    c) Both policy and procedure changes have expanded judicial power.
    d) Both policy and procedure changes have lessened judicial power.

Chapter Outline

Find a detailed Chapter Outline on the StudySpace Web site: www.wwnorton.com/we-the-people

Key Terms

Find Flashcards to help you study these terms on the StudySpace Web site: www.wwnorton.com/we-the-people

amicus curiae (p. 585)
brief (p. 588)
chief justice (p. 571)
civil law (p. 566)
class-action suit (p. 597)
court of appeals (p. 566)
criminal law (p. 565)
defendant (p. 565)
dissenting opinion (p. 590)
due process of law (p. 568)
judicial activism (p. 591)

judicial restraint (p. 591)
judicial review (p. 575)
jurisdiction (p. 567)
mootness (p. 581)
opinion (p. 589)
oral argument (p. 588)
original jurisdiction (p. 570)
per curiam (p. 585)
plaintiff (p. 565)
plea bargain (p. 567)
precedent (p. 566)

senatorial courtesy (p. 572)
solicitor general (p. 585)
standing (p. 581)
stare decisis (p. 566)
supremacy clause (p. 576)
supreme court (p. 566)
trial court (p. 566)
writ of certiorari (p. 582)
writ of habeas corpus (p. 568)

For Further Reading

Baum, Lawrence. *The Supreme Court.* Washington, DC: Congressional Quarterly Press, 2006.

Cross, Frank. *Decision Making in the U.S. Courts of Appeals.* Stanford, CA: Stanford University Press, 2007.

Epstein, Lee. *Constitutional Law for a Changing America.* Washington, DC: Congressional Quarterly Press, 2007.

Ginsburg, Ruth Bader. *Supreme Court Decisions and Women's Rights.* Washington DC: Congressional Quarterly Press, 2000.

Greenberg, Jan Crawford. *Supreme Conflict: The Inside Story of the United States Supreme Court.* New York: Penguin, 2008.

Hall, Kermit L., James W. Ely, Jr., and Joel B. Grossman. *The Oxford Companion to the Supreme Court of the United States.* 2nd ed. New York: Oxford University Press, 2005.

Irons, Peter. *A People's History of the Supreme Court.* New York: Penguin, 2006.

McClosky, Robert, and Sanford Levinson. *The American Supreme Court.* Chicago: University of Chicago Press, 2004.

O'Brien, David M. *Storm Center: The Supreme Court in American Politics.* 7th ed. New York: Norton, 2005.

Powe, Lucas. *The Supreme Court and the American Elite.* Cambridge, MA: Harvard University Press, 2009.

Raskin, Jamin B. *We the Students: Supreme Court Decisions for and about Students.* Washington, DC: Congressional Quarterly Press, 2003.

Rehnquist, William H. *The Supreme Court.* New York: Vintage, 2002.

Rosen, Jeffrey. *The Supreme Court: The Personalities and Rivalries That Defined America.* New York: Henry Holt, 2007.

Rosenberg, Gerald. *The Hollow Hope: Can Courts Bring about Social Change?* Chicago: University of Chicago Press, 1991.

Rossum, Ralph. *Antonin Scalia's Jurisprudence.* Lawrence: University Press of Kansas, 2006.

Sunstein, Cass. *Are Judges Political?* Washington, DC: Brookings Institution Press, 2006.

Toobin, Jeffrey. *The Nine: Inside the Secret World of the Supreme Court.* New York. Anchor Books 2008.

Whittington, Keith. *Political Foundations of Judicial Supremacy: The President, the Supreme Court, and Constitutional Leadership in U.S. History.* Princeton, NJ: Princeton University Press, 2008.

Recommended Web Sites

Concourts
www.concourts.net
The U.S. Supreme Court has the responsibility for examining and interpreting the Constitution. The Concourts Web site assumes a comparative perspective and looks at systems of constitutional review in over 150 countries.

FindLaw
www.findlaw.com
FindLaw's Web site provides answers to most legal questions and helps individuals find legal counsel.

Justice Talking
www.justicetalking.org
Justice Talking is a public radio program that examines current legal issues and important court cases.

Legal Information Institute
www.law.cornell.edu
The Legal Information Institute at Cornell University is a wonderful Web site for conducting legal research.

Office of the Solicitor General
www.usdoj.gov/osg
The solicitor general conducts litigation on behalf of the U.S. Supreme Court and has a tremendous amount of control over the cases that it hears. See what cases are currently being considered by this powerful official of the Justice Department.

U.S. Courts
www.uscourts.gov
The U.S. court system consists of trial, appellate, and supreme courts. The U.S. Courts Web site provides a look at the different types of courts in the federal judiciary.

U.S. Supreme Court
www.supremecourtus.gov
The Web site for the U.S. Supreme Court provides information on recent decisions. Take a moment to read some oral arguments, briefs, or court opinions.

U.S. Supreme Court Media
www.oyez.com
The Web site for U.S. Supreme Court Media has a great search engine for finding information on such landmark cases as *Marbury v. Madison, Miranda v. Arizona,* and *Roe v. Wade.*

Americans count on the government to ensure a prosperous economy. Here, Treasury Secretary Timothy Geithner gives an update on the Troubled Asset Relief Plan (TARP), a major component of the government's response to the recession that began in December 2007.

FINANCIAL STABILIT

and RECOVERY

16

Government and the Economy

WHAT GOVERNMENT DOES AND WHY IT MATTERS Since the 1930s, Americans have counted on the federal government to ensure a prosperous economy. Political leaders have a wide variety of tools they can use to improve economic performance. Among the most widely used are spending, tax cuts, and interest rate changes, all of which aim to stimulate economic activity or reduce inflation, and regulations that influence competition among firms. Political leaders' choice of economic tools depends on their perceptions about what the most pressing economic problem is, beliefs about which tools are most likely to be effective, and considerations about who is likely to benefit from the policy and who is likely to be hurt. Although economic policy is a highly technical field, the choice of policy tools is fundamentally a political decision.

In 2008, with the financial sector seemingly on the brink of collapse, the federal government launched a series of major interventions designed to prop up failing banks and insurance companies. It was not just financial institutions that faced collapse. As the economic instability spread, Washington bailed out other distressed

focusquestions

- **What are the major goals of economic policy?**
- **What are the tools of economic policy that the government can use?**
- **How do environmental policies intersect with the economy?**
- **Why is economic policy often controversial?**

industries, ending up as a major stakeholder in both the financial sector and the auto industry. The federal government also passed a sweeping package in 2009 to help stimulate the economy, save jobs, and make longer-term investments to help build future prosperity. As the economic crisis began to ebb, however, Congress struggled to implement enduring reforms to the financial regulatory system. Worries about the nation's ballooning debt mounted, and conflicts erupted over whether government had now gotten too big.

These developments raised fundamental questions about the role of the government in the economy. On one side of the spectrum are those who believe that the government should have a minimal role in the economy. Government's main purpose should be to set and enforce rules that ensure economic stability. This perspective is sometimes called the night watchman state.[1] At the other end of the spectrum are those who want to see the state actively engaged in shaping economic outcomes. Not only should the government promote economic growth in this perspective, it should step in to protect individuals from economic harm. The government's role in the economy should be active to shape the kind of society we want.

American economic policy has historically reflected the belief that individual liberty is the key to a thriving economy. In this view, the government's role is to set the basic rules that govern economic transactions and then stand back and let individuals engage in the market. However, periodically, Americans have demanded restrictions on market freedoms to protect the public. An array of laws governing competition and protecting consumers and the environment is the consequence of these democratic demands. Although American economic policy has not traditionally sought to reduce inequality, the growth in inequality over the past three decades has spurred new interest in understanding the impact of government policy on economic inequality.

chaptercontents

● The Goals of Economic Policy

The job of this chapter and the following chapter is to step beyond the politics and the institutions to look at the goals of government—the public policies. **Public policy** can be defined simply as an officially expressed purpose or goal backed by a sanction (a reward or a punishment). Public policy can be embodied in a law, a rule, a regulation, or an order. This chapter will focus on policies aimed at the economy.

At the most basic level, government makes it possible for the economy to function efficiently by setting the rules for economic exchange and punishing those who violate those rules. Among the most important rules for the economy are those that define property rights, contracts, and standards for goods. This kind of government rule making allows markets to expand by making it easier for people who do not know each other to engage in economic transactions. They no longer have to rely only on personal trust to do business. Likewise, government helps markets expand by creating money and standing behind its value. Money allows diverse goods to be traded and greatly simplifies economic transactions. The importance of government to basic market transactions is evident in periods when government authority is very weak. Governments that are on the losing side of wars, for example, are often so weak that they cannot enforce the basic rules needed for markets to function. In these settings, markets often break down, money loses its value, and economies contract as the basic conditions for doing business disappear.

Government involvement in the economy now extends far beyond these basic market-creating functions. As we shall see in this section, government has become involved in many aspects of the economy in order to promote the public well-being. Of course, there is often vigorous disagreement about the extent to which government should intervene in the economy to promote the public welfare. In addition, beliefs about which forms of government intervention in the economy are

public policy a law, rule, statute, or edict that expresses the government's goals and provides for rewards and punishments to promote their attainment

Americans often disagree about how much the government should be involved in the economy, and about the best ways to achieve economic goals. Many expressed concern that the government's 2008 and 2009 economic rescue measures helped big businesses but did not do enough to help ordinary individuals.

most necessary and most effective have changed over time. Although the policies have changed, government intervention in the economy has sought to achieve four fundamental goals. The first goal is to promote economic stability, the second is to stimulate economic growth, the third is to promote business development, and the fourth is to protect employees and consumers.

Promoting Stable Markets

public good a good or service that is provided by the government because it either is not supplied by the market or is not supplied in sufficient quantities

One way that the government promotes economic stability is by regulating competition and preventing monopolies. Monopolistic "trusts" became a particular concern in the late 1800s, and in 1904 President Teddy Roosevelt was depicted taking a swing at the railroad trust, the oil trust, and others that he believed were stifling competition.

One of the central reasons for government involvement in the economy is to protect the welfare and property of individuals and businesses.

Maintenance of law and order is one of the most important ways that government can protect welfare and property. The federal government has also enacted laws designed to protect individuals and businesses in economic transactions. Federal racketeering laws, for example, aim to end criminal efforts to control businesses through such illegal means as extortion and kickbacks.

Another way in which the government promotes economic stability is by regulating competition. Beginning in the nineteenth century, as many sectors of the national economy flourished, certain companies began to exert monopolistic control over those sectors. Decreased competition threatened the efficiency of the market and the equitable distribution of its benefits. As a result, the national government stepped in to "level the playing field."

Another major reason that Congress began to adopt national business regulatory policies was that the regulated companies themselves felt burdened by the inconsistencies among the states. These companies often preferred a single, national regulatory authority, no matter how burdensome, because it would ensure consistency throughout the United States; the companies could thereby treat the nation as a single market.[2]

The government also promotes economic stability by providing **public goods**. This term refers to facilities the state provides because no single participant can afford to provide those facilities. The provision of public goods may entail supplying the physical marketplace itself—such as the commons in New England towns or the provision of an interstate highway system to stimulate the trucking industry. The provision of public goods is essential to market operation, and the manner in which the government provides those goods will affect the market's character.

In the United States, public goods related to transportation have been particularly important in promoting economic development. From the first canal systems that spread commerce into the interior of the country to the contemporary public role in supporting and regulating air transportation, government has created the conditions for reliable and efficient business activity. In some cases, government will supply a public good to stimulate the economy and then allow private companies to take over. The federal government brought electricity to rural areas in the 1930s to promote economic development, but over time the provision of electricity has been taken over by private companies. Government often supplies public goods that are too big or too risky for private actors to tackle. Major dams and hydroelectric projects are an example. By bringing water and energy to new areas, such public projects transformed the American West. More recently, government-supplied public goods have enhanced public security through such measures as the

NO MOLLY-CODDLING HERE

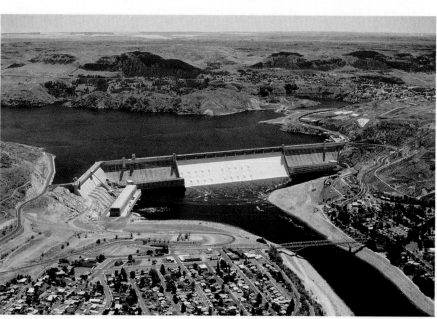

The government also provides public goods that support and stimulate the economy. The Grand Coulee Dam—a government facility in the state of Washington—was built to provide irrigation and electricity that were vital to economic development in the West.

federal takeover of airport security, the creation of a pharmaceutical stockpile to protect against bioterrorism, and the support for research to develop vaccines to counter bioterrorism agents. The 2009 American Recovery and Reinvestment Act offered funding for several future-oriented infrastructure investments including high-speed rail, high-speed internet access for rural areas, and funding to promote the development of "green" energy.

Promoting Economic Prosperity

In addition to setting the basic conditions that allow markets to function, governments may actively intervene in the economy to promote economic growth. Although the idea that government should stimulate economic growth can be traced back to Alexander Hamilton's views about promoting industry, it was not until the twentieth century that the federal government assumed such a role.

Measuring Economic Growth Since the 1930s, the federal government has carefully tracked national economic growth. Economic growth is measured in several different ways. The two most important measures are the Gross National Product (GNP), which is the market value of the goods and services produced in the economy, and the **Gross Domestic Product (GDP)**, the same measure but excluding income from foreign investments. In the late 1990s, the American economy grew at a rate of over 4 percent a year, a rate considered high by modern standards (see Figure 16.1). Growth was slower during the 2000s, averaging 1.9 percent annually. This was largely the result of two recessions: one in the early 2000s and the recession that began in 2008. In the middle part of the decade (2003–07), the economy grew at a strong 2.8 percent annually.[3]

Gross Domestic Product (GDP) the total value of goods and services produced within a country

The engine of American economic growth has shifted over the centuries. In the 1800s, our nation's rich endowment of natural resources was especially important in propelling growth. Manufacturing industries became the driving force of economic growth during the late nineteenth century as mass production made

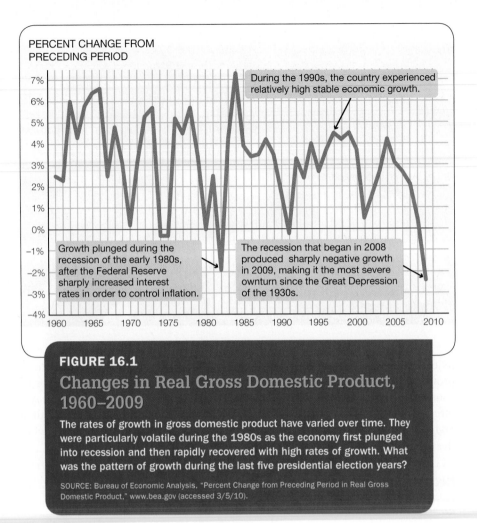

PERCENT CHANGE FROM
PRECEDING PERIOD

During the 1990s, the country experienced relatively high stable economic growth.

Growth plunged during the recession of the early 1980s, after the Federal Reserve sharply increased interest rates in order to control inflation.

The recession that began in 2008 produced sharply negative growth in 2009, making it the most severe ownturn since the Great Depression of the 1930s.

FIGURE 16.1

Changes in Real Gross Domestic Product, 1960–2009

The rates of growth in gross domestic product have varied over time. They were particularly volatile during the 1980s as the economy first plunged into recession and then rapidly recovered with high rates of growth. What was the pattern of growth during the last five presidential election years?

SOURCE: Bureau of Economic Analysis, "Percent Change from Preceding Period in Real Gross Domestic Product," www.bea.gov (accessed 3/5/10).

it possible to manufacture goods at a pace that was once unimaginable. In more recent times, the high-technology boom fostered unanticipated and vigorous economic growth that made the United States the envy of the world. Despite these very different economic engines, the basic prerequisites of growth are similar in each case: strong investment, technological innovation, and a productive workforce. Throughout the nation's history, the federal government has adopted policies to promote each of these conditions needed to sustain economic growth.

The most fundamental way that government affects investment is by promoting business, investor, and consumer confidence. When businesses fear political instability, unpredictable government action, or widespread disregard of the law, they are unlikely to invest. When consumers are insecure about the future, they are unlikely to spend. In 2008, the federal government enacted a $700 billion rescue plan to restore investor confidence after several large banks failed. Although the plan—known as the Troubled Assets Relief Program or the TARP—helped to stabilize the financial system, many Americans believed that it unfairly bailed out banks that had been behaving irresponsibly. The TARP became one of the most unpopular pieces of legislation related to the financial crisis in 2008. The Tea Party movement made the TARP one of its central targets. In the 2010 primaries, Tea Partiers castigated

Republican members of Congress who had supported the TARP and succeeded in replacing several of them with Tea Party–approved candidates.

The federal government also promotes investment through its regulation of financial markets. The most important federal agency in this regard is the Securities and Exchange Commission (SEC), created after the stock market crash of 1929. The SEC requires companies to disclose information about the stocks and bonds they are selling, inform buyers of the investment risks, and protect investors against fraud. In this way, the SEC helps to maintain investor confidence and a strong supply of capital for American business. The SEC came in for harsh criticism during the financial crisis in 2008. Analysts pointed to weak SEC oversight and regulation as an important factor in driving the financial sector to the brink of collapse. Major financial reforms enacted in 2010 substantially beefed up the SEC's enforcement capabilities and requires the agency to take the lead in implementing many of the key regulations.[4]

Public investment is another important source of growth in the American economy. In the 1930s and again in the late 1970s, the federal government promoted public investment as a means to spark economic growth. Some kinds of public investment promote growth as a byproduct of other more central objectives. One of the most important of these is military spending. Many analysts credited the rise in military spending associated with the war in Iraq with helping to spur economic growth in 2003.

The second important condition for economic growth is innovation. The federal government has sought to support innovation in a variety of ways. One of the most important is through the National Science Foundation. Created in 1950, the National Science Foundation supports basic research across a range of scientific fields. The aim is to advance fundamental knowledge that may be useful in many different applications.[5] Federal government sponsorship of health research began in the late 1800s. Today, the National Institutes of Health (NIH) conducts basic and applied research in biomedicine. The Human Genome Project—the effort to map the basic genetic structure of human life—was initiated by government researchers and only later taken up by private corporations. Recently, the NIH has taken the lead in basic research to counter bioterrorism. Its efforts to understand the biology of various infectious agents and to develop vaccines are expected to produce important new knowledge about the human immune system. Research sponsored by the military has long been an important source of innovation for the American economy. Such key twentieth-century innovations as radar and nuclear power stemmed from military research. And as we saw in Chapter 14, military research also created the technology for the twenty-first century with ARPANET, the precursor of the Internet.

A third fundamental condition for economic growth is a sufficient and productive workforce. Federal immigration policy has played a key role in ensuring an adequate supply of labor throughout American history. Immigration laws routinely give special priority to workers who have skills that are in demand among American employers. Immigrants with nursing degrees, for example, have long received special priority.

Today, a productive workforce is a highly educated workforce. Education, as we will see in Chapter 17, is primarily the responsibility of state and local governments. The federal government, however, supports the development of a productive workforce with a variety of programs to support higher education, such as educational grants, tax breaks, and loans. The federal government also sponsors a limited array of job-training programs that focus primarily on low-skilled workers. Some analysts argue that the federal government must do much more to support the development of a highly skilled workforce if the United States is to sustain economic growth in the future.

Full Employment Before the 1930s, neither the federal nor the state governments sought to promote full employment. Unemployment was widely viewed as an unfortunate occurrence that government could do little to alter. The New Deal response to the prolonged and massive unemployment of the Great Depression changed that view. The federal government put millions of people back to work on public projects sponsored by such programs as the Works Progress Administration (WPA). The bridges, walkways, and buildings they constructed can still be seen across the United States today. The federal government viewed these programs as temporary measures, however. As the buildup for World War II boosted the economy and unemployment melted away, the employment programs were dismantled.

The New Deal and government wartime spending, however, showed that government could help ensure full employment. Public expectations changed as well: Americans looked to the federal government to reduce unemployment after the war. Moreover, economic theory now supported their expectations. Keynes's theories that government could boost employment by stimulating demand had become very influential.

Federal policy placed the most emphasis on achieving full employment during the 1960s. Keynesian economists in the Council of Economic Advisers convinced President Kennedy to enact the first tax cut designed to stimulate the economy and promote full employment.[6] The policy was widely seen as a success, and unemployment declined to a low of 3.4 percent in 1968.

Favorable economic conditions in the 1990s reduced unemployment to record lows once again. Many analysts contended that the economy had changed so much that the old trade-offs between inflation and unemployment had ceased to exist.

Millions of Americans lost their jobs as the country slipped deeper into recession in 2008 and 2009. Government offices responsible for unemployment benefits, such as the one pictured here, were overwhelmed with new requests for help.

When the economy fell into recession in 2008, it became apparent that the American economy needed help. The economic crisis in the latter part of the decade led to the loss of an estimated 8 million jobs. The Obama administration and Congress responded by passing a sweeping stimulus package called the American Recovery and Reinvestment Act in 2009 to help encourage economic growth, save existing jobs, and make longer-term investments that would encourage job creation, such as investments in weatherization projects and clean technology construction. The nonpartisan Congressional Budget Office estimated that ARRA increased the number of full-time jobs between 2 to 4.8 million.[7] Yet, because unemployment remained high, ARRA did not get much public support for helping the economy and it attracted considerable criticism for contributing to the budget deficit. When President Obama proposed additional measures to stimulate the economy, he was unable to win sufficient support in Congress. When Congress considered a second stimulus bill focused on job creation, it succeeded in enacting a relatively small job creation package worth $15 billion, most of which consisted of tax credits for businesses that hire new employees.[8]

Low Inflation During the 1970s and early 1980s, **inflation**, a consistent increase in the general level of prices, was one of America's most vexing problems. There was much disagreement over what to do about it. The first effort, beginning in 1971, was the adoption of strict controls over wages, prices, dividends, and rents—that is, authorizing an agency in the executive branch to place limits on what wage people could be paid for their work, what rent their real estate could bring, and what interest they could get on their money. After two years of effort, these particular policies were fairly well discredited. Since oil prices had become so clearly a major source of inflation in the late 1970s, President Carter experimented with the licensing of imports of oil from the Middle East, with tariffs and excise taxes on unusually large oil profits made by producers, and with sales taxes on gasoline at the pump to discourage all casual consumption of gasoline. President Carter also attempted to reduce consumer spending in general by raising income taxes, especially Social Security taxes on employees.

inflation a consistent increase in the general level of prices

In the 1970s, the government tried to rein in high inflation that made many everyday goods too expensive for ordinary Americans. Unable to afford food at retail prices, these New York residents lined up to buy wholesale food from a warehouse.

The continuing high rate of inflation paved the way for an entirely different approach by President Reagan in the early 1980s. In place of oil import licensing and selective tax increases, President Reagan proposed and got a general tax cut. The Reagan theory was that if tax cuts were deep enough and were guaranteed to endure, they would increase the "supply" of money, would change people's psychology from pessimism to optimism, and would thereby encourage individuals and corporations to invest enough and produce enough to get the country out of inflation. At the same time, President Reagan supported the continuation of the high Social Security taxes enacted during the Carter administration, which probably went further than any other method to fight inflation by discouraging consumption. Inflation is caused by too many dollars chasing too few goods, bidding up prices. Any tax will take dollars out of consumption, but since the Social Security tax hits middle- and lower-middle-income people the heaviest, and since these middle-income people are the heaviest consumers, such a tax reduces consumer dollars. Another policy supported by the Reagan administration was restraining the amount of credit in the economy by pushing up interest rates.

Inflation was finally reduced from its historic highs of nearly 20 percent down toward 2 and 3 percent each year. Noting that the 1970s were America's only "peacetime inflation," the economist Bradford DeLong contends that it wasn't until inflation had risen to dizzying heights late in the decade that the Federal Reserve truly had a mandate to reduce inflation.[9] Once it had full political support for reducing inflation in 1979, the Federal Reserve raised interest rates sharply and brought inflation rates down at the same time that it provoked a sharp recession.

Promoting Business Development

During the nineteenth century, the national government was a promoter of markets. National roads and canals were built to tie states and regions together. National tariff policies promoted domestic markets by restricting imported goods; a tax on an import raised its price and weakened its ability to compete with similar domestic products. The national government also heavily subsidized the railroad system. Until the 1840s, railroads were thought to be of limited commercial value. But between 1850 and 1872, Congress granted over 100 million acres of public-domain land to railroad interests, and state and local governments pitched in an estimated $280 million in cash and credit. Before the end of the century, 35,000 miles of track existed—almost half the world's total at the time.

Railroads were not the only clients of federal support for the private markets. Many sectors of agriculture began receiving federal subsidies during the nineteenth century. Agriculture remains highly subsidized. In 2001, an environmental group caused a stir by putting the exact amounts of subsidies received by individual farmers on a widely publicized Web site. In 2005, 40 percent of farms in the United States received subsidies; by 2006 the total subsidy was estimated at more than $20 billion. One of the many criticisms of the farm subsidy program is that it disproportionately supports large-scale farmers rather than small family farmers. The list of farm subsidy recipients includes many large corporations.

The national government also promotes business development indirectly through **categorical grants** (see Chapter 3), whereby the national government offers grants to states on condition that the state (or local) government undertake a particular activity. Thus, in order to use motor transportation to improve national markets, a 900,000-mile national highway system was built during the 1930s, based

categorical grants congressional grants given to states and localities on the condition that expenditures be limited to a problem or group specified by the law on a formula whereby the national government would pay 50 percent of the cost if the state would provide the other 50 percent. Over twenty years, beginning in the late 1950s, the federal government constructed an additional 45,000 miles of interstate highways. In this program, the national government agreed to pay 90 percent of the construction costs on the condition that each state provide 10 percent of the costs of any portion of a highway built within its boundaries.[10] The tremendous growth of highways was a major boon to the automobile and trucking industries.

The federal government supports specific business sectors with direct subsidies, loans, and tax breaks. In 1953, the Small Business Administration (SBA) was created to offer loans, loan guarantees, and disaster assistance to small businesses. Recognizing that such businesses often find it harder to obtain financing and to recover from unexpected events such as fires, the federal government has provided assistance where the market would not. Today, the SBA provides more than $45 billion in such assistance to small businesses.

Among the many contemporary examples of policies promoting private industry, Sematech may be the most instructive. Sematech is a nonprofit research and development (R&D) consortium of major U.S. computer microchip manufacturers, set up in 1987 to work with government and academic institutions to reestablish U.S. leadership in semiconductor manufacturing. (The United States appeared to be in danger of losing out to the Japanese in this area during the 1980s.) The results of its research were distributed among the fourteen consortium members.[11] For nine years, industry and government together spent $1.7 billion to make the American microchip industry the leader in the world. The government contributed about half of the total expenditures. In 1997, federal funding was phased out. Industry leaders, convinced they no longer needed federal support, themselves initiated the break with government. At a critical moment, the federal government had stepped in to save the chip industry; it stepped out once that goal had been achieved.

Since September 11, 2001, the federal government has taken on a major role in promoting technological innovation related to national security. Even before the September 11 terrorist attacks, the CIA had set up its own venture-capital firm,

Since the early nineteenth century, the government has been an important promoter of business development in the United States. Beginning around 1850, federal, state, and local governments gave railroad companies the land on which to lay tracks and financial aid to construct the railroads. Railroads also received additional land from the government that they could sell at low prices to attract settlers to build along their lines.

In-Q-Tel (the "Q" stands for a character in the James Bond movies), to invest in high-tech start-ups whose work could enhance intelligence efforts. With defense and homeland security at the top of the national agenda, military spending increased by 20 percent during the first two years of the George W. Bush administration. A new emphasis on technological innovation accompanied the increase in spending. As a way to promote its access to the latest technology, the Department of Defense runs a $1 billion program that funds the early stages of research and development for innovative small firms.[12]

Protecting Employees and Consumers

Stable relations between business and labor are important elements of a productive economy. During the latter half of the nineteenth century, strikes over low wages or working conditions became a standard feature of American economic life. In fact, the United States has one of the most violent histories of labor relations in the world. Yet for most of American history, the federal government did little to regulate relations between business and labor. Local governments and courts often weighed in on the side of business by prohibiting strikes and arresting strikers.

As the economic depression enveloped the United States in the 1930s, massive strikes for union recognition and plummeting wages prompted the federal government to take action. Congress passed the 1935 National Labor Relations Act, which set up a new framework for industrial relations. The new law created a permanent agency, the National Labor Relations Board (NLRB), charged with overseeing union elections and collective bargaining between labor and industry. The federal government weighed in further on the side of organized labor in 1938, when it passed the Fair Labor Standards Act, which created the minimum wage.

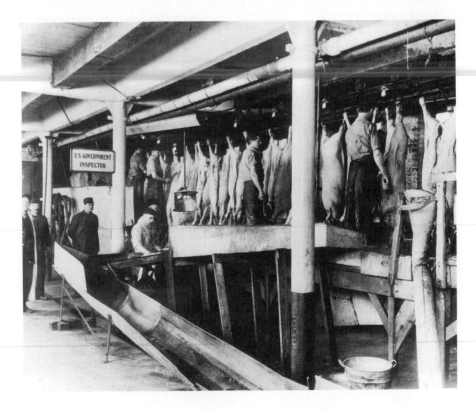

Protecting consumers has been a central goal of economic policy since the early twentieth century. In 1906, Congress passed the New Meat Inspection Act, which required that all meat intended for interstate commerce meet federal health standards. This photo shows a Chicago slaughterhouse immediately following the passage of the act.

Because it is not indexed to inflation, the value of the minimum wage declines if it is not raised periodically. Since 1938, conflicts over increasing the minimum wage have been a regular feature of American politics.

During the 1950s and 1960s, the federal government played an active role in industrial relations. The Department of Labor and occasionally even the president directly intervened in labor-management disputes to ensure peaceful industrial relations. Although Democrats were generally seen as more supportive of labor, both parties sought to achieve a balance between business and labor that would promote a strong, stable economy.

President Reagan made a decisive break with this tradition of compromise in 1981 when he fired striking air traffic controllers and hired permanent replacements to take their jobs. Politicians are now much less likely to intervene in labor relations.

Economic policies also protect consumers. The idea that the federal government should protect consumers emerged in the first decade of the 1900s. Upton Sinclair's graphic exposé about the unsanitary practices of the meatpacking industry, *The Jungle*, published in 1906, galvanized public concern about unsanitary food processing. These concerns prompted the U.S. Department of Agriculture to inspect packing plants and the meat they produced, stamping approved meats with the now familiar "USDA" certification. Similar concern about food and drug safety led to the creation of the Food and Drug Administration in 1927.

The movement for consumer protection took off again in the 1960s. The consumer advocate Ralph Nader's 1965 book *Unsafe at Any Speed* helped spark new demands for federal action. Nader's book showed that design flaws in the Corvair, a popular car model, had caused deaths that could have been prevented. Nader's book not only led to the demise of the Corvair, it galvanized calls for more federal action to protect consumers. The first response was the 1966 National Traffic and Motor Vehicle Safety Act, which gave the Department of Transportation responsibility for ensuring vehicle safety. Federal responsibility for consumer safety expanded in 1972 when Congress created the Consumer Product Safety Commission. The Commission, which is an independent agency, informs consumers about hazards associated with products and works with industry to set product standards. In cases where safety concerns are severe, it will see that such products are recalled. Through the Consumer Product Safety Commission, the Department of Transportation, and the Food and Drug Administration (which regulates food, drugs, and cosmetics), the federal government continues to play an active role in protecting the public from unsafe products.

In 2007, the Consumer Product Safety Commission became the target of vigorous criticism for failing to protect consumers from hazardous products. Recalls of popular children's toys, reports of injuries to children from magnetic toys, dogs and cats dying from tainted pet food, and reported dangers from imported toothpaste all raised questions about the agency's effectiveness. Congressional hearings probed the capacity of the agency to monitor consumer safety, given that its staff had declined from more than 800 in 1980 to 420 in 2007. At the same time that the staff declined, the growth of consumer products manufactured in China made the agency's job tougher. In 2008, 43 percent of imported consumer goods had been manufactured in China or Hong Kong; 85 percent of all product recalls came from imported products, and the vast bulk of those were manufactured in China, where rapid economic expansion and fewer consumer protections contributed to the problem.[13] Concern about the Consumer Product Safety Commission's ability to protect Americans led to a significant reform in 2008, which provided new resources to the agency and established new requirements governing toy safety.

for critical analysis

What does the American government do to ensure that the products that Americans buy are safe? What challenges does it face in making certain that products are safe?

Four Schools of Economic Thought

Not surprisingly, there are deep differences of opinion about whether, how much, and in what ways government should be involved in the economy. Ideas about the appropriate role for government have shifted in response to unanticipated or tenacious economic problems such as recession or inflation. As politicians, interest groups, and the public debate which goals are most important and appropriate for economic policy to achieve, their views are informed by underlying theories. Different theories about how the economy works present quite distinct roles for government.

The idea that government should have only a minimal role in the economy is often called **laissez-faire capitalism**. Proponents of laissez-faire (literally, "let to do") argue that the economy will flourish if the government leaves it alone. The argument for laissez-faire was first elaborated in the late 1700s by the great Scottish economist Adam Smith. Smith believed that most government involvement in the economy—such as the government-authorized monopolies that dominated trade in his day—depressed economic growth. Instead, he argued that competition among free enterprises would unleash economic energy, fostering growth and innovation. In his view, the self-seeking behavior of individuals, when subject to the discipline of market competition, would create products that consumers want at the best possible price. Smith praised "the invisible hand" of the market, by which he meant that millions of individual economic transactions together create a greater good—far better than the government could create. Smith believed that the government role should be restricted to national defense, establishing law and order (including the protection of private property), and providing basic public goods (such as roads) that facilitate commerce.

In the 1930s, the ideas of the British economist John Maynard Keynes laid the foundation for a revolution in thinking about the role of the government in the economy during periodic downturns. **Keynesians** argue that by pumping money into the economy, government can stimulate demand and create a cycle of increased production and jobs that will pull the economy out of recession. Governments can do this in several ways. For one, they can increase public spending through such measures as public works or public employment. Alternatively, governments can stimulate demand through temporary tax cuts. Tax cuts will allow workers to keep more of their earnings; their increased spending power will boost consumption and increase demand.[14]

After World War II, Keynesian ideas guided economic policy making across the industrialized world. By the 1960s, Keynesians believed they could ensure ongoing prosperity by "fine-tuning" the economy: policy makers could stimulate demand with spending or tax cuts when recession loomed and then cut back on spending or increase taxes when inflation threatened. President Richard Nixon, a Republican, reflected the strong consensus behind Keynesian ideas when he remarked, "I am now a Keynesian."

Yet, by the time Keynesian ideas became the accepted wisdom, new economic conditions threatened their effectiveness. Many observers argued that increased international trade made Keynesian remedies less useful. Confidence that the government can fine-tune the economy had diminished, and Keynesians lost the great influence they once had in economic policy.

In contrast to Keynesians, **monetarists** believe that the role of the government in managing the economy should be limited to regulating the supply of money. More active government management of the economy, monetarists argue, either has little effect or actually makes the economy worse. Monetarists do not believe that

laissez-faire capitalism an economic system in which the means of production and distribution are privately owned and operated for profit with minimal or no government interference

Keynesians followers of the economic theories of John Maynard Keynes, who argued that the government can stimulate the economy by increasing public spending or by cutting taxes

monetarists followers of economic theories that contend that the role of the government in the economy should be limited to regulating the supply of money

The economist John Maynard Keynes influenced economic policy with the idea that governments could remedy economic downturns by increasing public spending or cutting taxes.

government can act quickly enough to fine-tune the economy. Instead, they maintain that government should promote economic stability by regulating the money supply. The most prominent monetarist in the United States, the late economist Milton Friedman, recommended that the federal government let the growth in the money supply match the rate of economic growth. In this way, inflation could be kept low even as economic growth continued. This strict version of monetarism envisions a hands-off approach for the government; the theory calls for little exercise of discretion on the part of government officials. Instead, they must follow a simple rule about how much to increase the supply of money.

In the late 1970s, when high levels of inflation plagued the American economy, monetarists became especially influential in economic policy making. However, today it is impractical to implement a strict version of monetarism. Instead, economic policy makers have sought to manipulate interest rates to ensure a healthy and stable economy.

Proponents of **supply-side economics** believe that reducing the role of government in the economy will promote investment and spur economic growth. Reducing tax rates is the centerpiece of the supply-side economic strategy. Supply-siders maintain that lower tax rates create incentives for more productive and efficient use of resources. When individuals know they can keep more of their earnings, they are more likely to be productive workers and creative investors. The ideas behind supply-side economics emerged in the 1970s, when Keynesian solutions appeared to have little impact on the high rates of inflation and a sluggish economy.

Key thinkers associated with developing the ideas behind supply-side economics include the economists Robert Mundell, who won the Nobel Prize, and Arthur B. Laffer. Laffer became known for the "Laffer curve," which posited that there was an optimal rate of taxation. If taxes went above the optimal rate, tax revenues would shrink because economic activity would decline. In this perspective, decreasing taxes could yield more tax revenue by spurring economic activity. This view marked a shift for conservatives by placing more emphasis on tax cuts and less on budget deficits. Supply-side ideas were very influential in the administrations of the Republican presidents Ronald Reagan and George W. Bush, both of whom pointed to supply-side ideas as a sound reason for enacting significant tax cuts.

Monetarists such as the late economist Milton Friedman call for limiting government involvement in the economy.

supply-side economics posits that reducing the marginal rate of taxation will create a productive economy by promoting levels of work and investment that would otherwise be discouraged by higher taxes

● The Tools of Economic Policy

The U.S. economy is no accident; it is the result of specific policies that have expanded American markets and sustained massive economic growth. The Constitution provides that Congress shall have the power

> To lay and collect Taxes, . . . to pay the Debts and provide for the common Defence and general Welfare; . . . To borrow Money; . . . To coin Money [and] regulate the Value thereof. . . .

These clauses of Article I, Section 8, are the constitutional sources of the fiscal and monetary policies of the national government. The Constitution says nothing, however, about *how* these powers can be used, although the way they are used shapes the economy. As it works to meet the multiple goals of economic policy outlined above, the federal government relies on a broad set of tools that has evolved over time. Let us now turn to the actual tools designed to accomplish the goals of economic policy.

Monetary Policies

Monetary policies manipulate the growth of the entire economy by controlling the availability of money to banks. With a very few exceptions, banks in the United States are privately owned and locally operated. Until well into the twentieth century, banks were regulated, if at all, by state legislatures. Each bank was granted a charter, giving it permission to make loans, hold deposits, and make investments within that state. Although more than 25,000 banks continue to be chartered by the state, they are less important than they used to be in the overall financial picture, as the most important banks now are members of the federal banking system.

But banks did not become the core of American capitalism without intense political controversy. The Federalist majority in Congress, led by Alexander Hamilton, did in fact establish a Bank of the United States in 1791, but it was vigorously opposed by agrarian interests, led by Thomas Jefferson, who feared that the interests of urban, industrial capitalism would dominate such a bank. The Bank of the United States was terminated during the administration of Andrew Jackson, but the fear of a central, public bank lingered eight decades later, when Congress in 1913 established an institution—the **Federal Reserve System**—to integrate private banks into a single national system. The Federal Reserve System did not become a central bank in the European tradition but rather is composed of twelve Federal Reserve banks, each located in a major commercial city. The Federal Reserve banks are not ordinary banks; they are banker's banks that make loans to other banks, clear checks, and supply the economy with currency and coins. They also play a regulatory role over the member banks. Every national bank must be a member of the Federal Reserve System and must follow national banking rules. State banks and savings and loan associations may also join if they accept national rules. At the top of the system is the Federal Reserve Board—"the Fed"— comprising seven members appointed by the president (with Senate confirmation) for fourteen-year terms. The chairman of the Fed is selected by the president from among the seven members of the board for a four-year term. In all other concerns, however, the Fed is an independent agency (see Chapter 14) inasmuch as its members cannot be removed during their terms except "for cause," and the president's executive power does not extend to them or their policies. Nonetheless, observers charged the longtime Federal Reserve chairman, Alan Greenspan, with being attentive to politics, for example, in his endorsement of President George W. Bush's tax cuts. In his 2005 confirmation hearings to head the Fed, the economist Ben Bernanke promised Congress that he would be "strictly independent of all political influences."[15]

The major advantage that a bank gains from being in the Federal Reserve System is that it can borrow from the system. This enables banks to expand their loan operations continually, as long as there is demand for loans in the economy. On the other hand, it is this very access of member banks to the Federal Reserve System that gives the Fed its power: the ability to expand and contract the *amount of credit* available in the United States.

The Fed can affect the total amount of credit through the interest (called the discount rate) it charges on the loans it extends to member banks. If the Fed significantly decreases the discount rate, it can give a boost to a sagging economy. During 2001, the Fed cut interest rates eleven times to combat the combined effects of recession and the terrorist attacks. In the steep recession that began in 2008, the Fed acted aggressively. By December 2008, it had cut rates nine times from a high in September 2007 of 4.75 percent to a historically low zero percentage rate. Moreover, the Federal Reserve kept interest rates at that same level well into 2010 in an attempt to encourage lending again and thus economic growth.[16] If the Fed raises the discount rate, it can put a brake on the economy because the higher discount rate also increases the general interest rates charged by leading private banks to their customers. Although the Federal Reserve is responsible for ensuring high employment as well as price stability, it has been particularly important in fighting inflation. During the late 1970s and early 1980s, with inflation at record high levels, Federal Reserve Chairman Paul Volcker aggressively raised interest rates in order to dampen inflation. Although his actions provoked a sharp recession, they raised the stature of the Fed, demonstrating its ability to manage the economy. Because the Fed is so closely associated with inflation fighting, Senate Democrats pressed Ben Bernanke, President Bush's nominee to head the Fed, to indicate that he would view maximum employment as a goal of equal importance to that of fighting inflation.

A second power of the Fed is control over the **reserve requirement**—the amount of cash and negotiable securities every bank must hold readily available to cover withdrawals and checks written by its depositors. When the Fed decides to increase the reserve requirement, it can decrease significantly the amount of money banks have to lend; conversely, if the Fed lowers the reserve requirement, banks can be more liberal in extending more loans.[17]

A third power of the Fed is called **open-market operations**, whereby the Fed buys and sells government securities to increase or decrease the supply of money in the economy. When the Fed buys government securities in the open market, it increases the amount of money available to consumers to spend or invest; when it sells securities, it is reducing the money supply.

Finally, a fourth power is derived from one of the important services the Federal Reserve System renders, which is the opportunity for member banks to borrow

reserve requirement the amount of liquid assets and ready cash that banks are required to hold to meet depositors' demands for their money

open-market operations method by which the Open Market Committee of the Federal Reserve System buys and sells government securities, etc., to help finance government operations and to reduce or increase the total amount of money circulating in the economy

Ben Bernanke, appointed by President Bush to chair the Federal Reserve Board in 2005 and whose reappointment by President Obama was confirmed by the Senate in 2010, promised Congress that he would not be influenced by politics. The Fed seeks to regulate the U.S. economy by manipulating the supply of money and credit.

from each other. One of the original reasons for creating a Federal Reserve System was to balance regions of the country that might be vigorously expanding with other areas that might be fairly dormant: the national system would enable the banks in a growing region, facing great demand for credit, to borrow money from banks in regions of the country where the demand for credit is much lower. This exchange is called the "federal funds market," and the interest rate charged by one bank to another, the **federal funds rate**, can be manipulated just like the discount rate, to expand or contract credit.[18]

federal funds rate the interest rate on loans between banks that the Federal Reserve Board influences by affecting the supply of money available

The federal government also provides insurance to foster credit and encourage private capital investment. The Federal Deposit Insurance Corporation (FDIC) insures bank deposits up to $250,000. Another important promoter of investment is the federal insurance of home mortgages through the Department of Housing and Urban Development (HUD). By guaranteeing mortgages, the government can reduce the risks that banks run in making such loans, thus allowing banks to lower their interest rates and make such loans more affordable to middle- and lower-income families. Such programs have enabled millions of families who could not have otherwise afforded it to finance the purchase of a home.

This system began to unravel in the first decade of the 2000s with the growth of the subprime market for lending. This market made home loans available to people who could not otherwise afford to buy a home. At the same time, however, it created new instabilities in the market by offering risky loans that would become more costly due to adjustable interest rates. The slowing housing market in 2007 set off a wave of foreclosures as many homeowners discovered that they could not pay back their loans. After the recession hit in 2008, many more Americans lost their homes to foreclosures: by late 2010, an estimated 2.5 million homes had been lost. Estimates showed that an additional 3.3 million homes could be foreclosed over the next four years.[19]

The foreclosure crisis in turn sent shock waves through the financial system, as investment banks found themselves holding worthless loans. One casualty of the home loan meltdown was the Wall Street investment bank Bear Stearns, which faced bankruptcy early in March 2008. Seeking to limit the harm to the broader economy that such a bankruptcy would cause, Fed chairman Bernanke arranged for Bear Stearns to be bought—at bargain-basement prices—by JP Morgan Chase, another investment bank. In making this move, Bernanke was exercising powers of the Federal Reserve Act that had not been used since the 1930s.[20] After the firm Lehman Brothers collapsed in 2008 and several other investment banks and insurance companies moved closer to insolvency, the Federal Reserve also provided billions of dollars to banks so that they could continue to lend money for student loans, auto loans, and residential mortgages. In all, the Fed gave nearly $1.5 trillion ($1,500 billion) in emergency loans to financial institutions (almost all of that money has been or is expected to be paid back).[21] Although many were impressed by the swift action undertaken by the Fed, critics charged that its supervision of the banking system prior to the crisis had been too lax. This led to an unusually contentious set of Senate confirmation hearings for Chairman Bernanke, whom President Obama had renominated in 2009.

Fiscal Policies

fiscal policy the government's use of taxing, monetary, and spending powers to manipulate the economy

Fiscal policy includes the government's taxing and spending powers. Personal and corporate income taxes, which raise most of the U.S. government's revenues, are the most prominent examples. Although the direct purpose of an income tax is to raise revenue, each tax has a different impact on the economy, and government can attempt to plan for that impact.

Taxation During the nineteenth century, the federal government received most of its revenue from a single tax, the **tariff**. It also relied on excise taxes, which are taxes levied on specific products, such as tobacco and alcohol. As federal activities expanded in the 1900s, the federal government added new sources of tax revenue. The most important was the income tax, proposed by Congress in 1909, ratified by the states, and added to the Constitution in 1913 as the Sixteenth Amendment. The income tax is levied on individuals as well as corporations. With the creation of the Social Security system in 1935, social insurance taxes became an additional source of federal revenue.

Before World War II, individual income taxes accounted for only 14 percent of federal revenues.[22] The need to raise revenue for World War II made the income tax much more important. Congress expanded the base of the income tax so that most Americans paid income taxes after World War II. Table 16.1 shows several notable shifts that have occurred in taxes since 1960. Social insurance taxes now comprise a much greater share of federal revenues, rising from 15.9 percent of revenues in 1960 to an estimated 40.4 percent in 2010. Receipts from corporate income taxes have declined over the same time period, dropping from 23.2 percent of receipts in 1960 to 7.2 in 2010. The share of the federal individual income tax has remained fairly stable; it was 44 percent in 1960 and estimated at 43.2 percent in 2010.

One of the most important features of the American income tax is that it is a "progressive" or a "graduated" tax, with the heaviest burden carried by those most able to pay. A tax is called **progressive** if the rate of taxation goes up with each higher income bracket. A tax is called **regressive** if people in lower income brackets pay a higher proportion of their income toward the tax than people in higher income brackets. For example, a sales tax is deemed regressive because everybody pays at the same rate, so that people who make less money end up paying a greater share of their income in sales taxes than do people who make more money (assuming, as is generally the case, that as total income goes up the amount spent on sales-taxable purchases increases at a lower rate). The Social Security tax is another example of a regressive tax. In 2010, Social Security law applied a tax of 6.2 percent on the first $106,800 of income for the retirement program and an additional 1.45 percent on all income (without limit) for Medicare benefits, for a total of 7.65 percent in Social Security taxes. This means that a person earning an income of $106,800 pays $8,170 in Social Security taxes, a rate of 7.65 percent. But someone earning twice that income, $213,600, pays a total of $11,267 in Social Security taxes, a rate of 5.3 percent. As one's income continues to rise, the amount of Social Security taxes also rises (until the cap is reached), but the rate, or the percentage of one's income that goes to taxes, declines.

Although the primary purpose of the graduated income tax is, of course, to raise revenue, an important second objective is to collect revenue in such a way as to reduce the disparities of wealth between the lowest and the highest income brackets. We call this a policy of **redistribution**. Another policy objective of the income tax is the encouragement of the capitalist economy by rewarding investment. The tax laws allow individuals or companies to deduct from their taxable income any money they can justify as an investment or a "business expense"; this gives an incentive to individuals and companies to spend money to expand their production, their advertising, or their staff, and reduces the income taxes

tariff a tax on imported goods

progressive taxation taxation that hits upper income brackets more heavily

regressive taxation taxation that hits lower income brackets more heavily

redistribution a policy whose objective is to tax or spend in such a way as to reduce the disparities of wealth between the lowest and the highest income brackets

TABLE 16.1

Federal Revenues by Type of Tax as Percentage of Total Receipts, 1960–2010

The federal government collects revenue from a variety of different taxes. Most important is the individal income tax. Since 1960, revenues from the corporation income tax have fallen significantly. At the same time, taxes for social insurance and retirement programs have grown substantially. Does the federal government draw more of its revenue from progressive taxes or from regressive taxes?

YEAR	INDIVIDUAL INCOME TAXES	CORPORATION INCOME TAXES	SOCIAL INSURANCE AND RETIREMENT RECEIPTS	EXCISE TAXES	OTHER
1960	44.0	23.2	15.9	12.6	4.2
1970	46.9	17.0	23.0	8.1	4.9
1980	47.2	12.5	30.5	4.7	5.1
1990	45.2	9.1	36.8	3.4	5.4
2000	49.6	10.2	32.2	3.4	4.5
2001	49.9	7.6	34.9	3.3	4.3
2002	46.3	8.0	37.8	3.6	4.3
2003	44.5	7.4	40.0	3.8	4.3
2004	43.0	10.1	39.0	3.7	4.2
2005	43.1	12.9	36.9	3.4	3.8
2006	43.4	14.7	34.8	3.1	4.0
2007	45.3	14.4	33.9	2.5	3.9
2008	45.4	12.1	35.7	2.7	4.2
2009	43.5	6.6	42.3	3.0	4.7
2010 (est.)	43.2	7.2	40.4	3.4	5.7

SOURCE: Office of Management and Budget, "Percentage Composition of Receipts by Source: 1934–2015," *The Budget for Fiscal Year 2011, Historical Tables*, www.whitehouse.gov (accessed 3/7/10).

loophole incentive to individuals and businesses to reduce their tax liabilities by investing their money in areas that the government designates

businesses have to pay. These kinds of deductions are called incentives or "equity" by those who support them; others call them "**loopholes**." The tax laws of the 1980s actually closed a number of important loopholes in U.S. tax laws. But others still exist—on home mortgages and on business expenses, for example—and others will likely return, because there is a strong consensus among members of Congress, both Democrats and Republicans, that businesses often need such incentives. The differences between the two parties focus largely on which incentives are justifiable.[23]

The tax reform laws of 1981 and 1986 significantly reduced the progressiveness of the federal income tax. Drastic rate reductions were instituted in 1986. Before George W. Bush's 2001 reform, there were five tax brackets, ranging from a

15 percent tax on those in the lowest income bracket to 39.6 percent on those in the highest income bracket. Prior to the 1980s, the highest tax brackets sometimes were taxed at a rate of 90 percent on the last $1 million of taxable income earned in a given year. Meanwhile, Social Security taxes—the most regressive taxes of all—remain high and are likely to be increased.[24]

Taxes became a controversial issue during the George W. Bush administration. After passing major cuts in income tax rates in 2001, President Bush proposed and Congress passed a sweeping new round of cuts in 2003. Bush's plan was intended to promote investment by reducing taxes on most stock dividends, to spur business activity by offering tax breaks to small businesses, and to stimulate the economy by reducing the tax rates for all taxpayers. In 2006, Congress extended the rate reductions on dividends and capital gains, a move that estimates showed would cost the treasury $70 billion over five years. The argument for the tax cuts was largely a supply-side argument: the cuts would make for a prosperous economy. The president and his supporters pointed to the expanding economy and lower taxes for all as the fruit of the tax cuts. Opponents charged that it made no sense to cut taxes since the benefits of the tax cuts primarily go to the wealthy. They argue that not only do the rich already benefit from unequal patterns of growth that have sent their income skyrocketing, but tax cuts that disproportionately benefit the wealthy do not stimulate the economy, as supply-side theory predicts. Critics also charge that the tax cuts have caused the federal budget, which was in surplus when Bush took office, to fall into deficit.[25]

President Obama and the Democratic leadership proposed extending the tax cuts for everyone with annual incomes under $250,000; those making more would have their income taxes revert back to the rates in the 1990s. Republicans and some Democrats preferred to extend the tax cuts for everyone. With the 2010 mid-term elections approaching. Congress failed to reach an agreement on the Bush tax cuts. If Congress does not act by 2011, the rates will increase for all taxpayers.

Spending and Budgeting The federal government's power to spend is one of the most important tools of economic policy. Decisions about how much to spend affect the overall health of the economy. They also affect every aspect of American life from the distribution of income to the availability of different modes of transportation to the level of education in society. Not surprisingly, the fight for control over spending is one of the most contentious in Washington, as interest groups and politicians strive to determine the priorities and appropriate levels of spending. Decisions about spending are made as part of the annual budget process. During the 1990s, when the federal budget deficit first became a major political issue and when parties were deeply split on spending, the budget process became the focal point of the entire policy-making process. Even though the **budget deficit** disappeared in the late 1990s, the budget continued to dominate the attention of policy makers (Figure 16.2). With the rapid swing from budget surpluses in 2000 to record deficits by 2003, deficits once again emerged as a political issue. This time, however, Republican leaders, who had made deficits the focal point of politics in the mid-1990s, largely dismissed their importance. As House Majority Leader Tom DeLay put it, "The Soviet Union had a balanced budget. Well, you can raise taxes until you balance it, but the economy will go into the toilet."[26] Nonetheless, with deficits identified as causing future reductions in Social Security and other programs, deficits are likely to remain on the political agenda.

- **What are the tools of economic policy that the government can use?**

for critical analysis

What are the multiple goals of tax policy in America? How else might some of these goals be achieved? In what ways is the tax system in the United States progressive? In what ways is it regressive?

budget deficit amount by which government spending exceeds government revenue in a fiscal year

U.S. Budget Deficits and Surpluses, 1960–2010*

The federal deficit grew substantially during the 1980s under President Reagan. During the 1990s, the budget deficit declined significantly but then grew dramatically after 2001. When was the last time that the federal budget showed a surplus? Why did the budget deficit grow so much after 2001?

*Estimate

SOURCE: Office of Management and Budget, "Summary of Receipts, Outlays, and Surpluses or Deficits (–) as Percentages of GDP: 1930–2015," *The Budget for Fiscal Year 2011, Historical Tables,* www.whitehouse.gov (accessed 3/7/10).

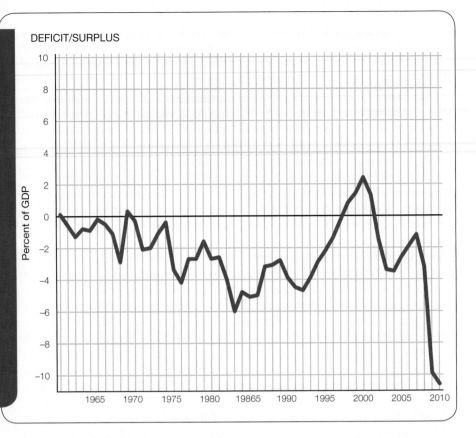

The president and Congress have each created institutions to assert control over the budget process. The Office of Management and Budget (OMB) in the Executive Office of the President is responsible for preparing the president's budget. This budget contains the president's spending priorities and the estimated costs of the president's policy proposals. It is viewed as the starting point for the annual debate over the budget. When different parties control the presidency and Congress, the president's budget may have little influence on the budget that is ultimately adopted. Members of the president's own party also may have different priorities. In 2009, President Obama made clear that he wanted to strip $1.75 billion in funding for new F-22 fighter jets from the defense budget, arguing that funding for the Cold War–era jets was wasteful. The Democratic-controlled Senate committee responsible for defense appropriations resisted that pressure and included the funding in the budget. In the end, the president won the battle and the measure was removed from the final bill.[27]

Congress has its own budget institutions. Congress created the Congressional Budget Office (CBO) in 1974 so that it could have reliable information about the costs and economic impact of the policies it considers. At the same time, Congress established a budget process designed to establish spending priorities and to consider individual expenditures in light of the entire budget. A key element of the process is the annual budget resolution, which designates broad targets for spending. By estimating the costs of policy proposals, Congress hoped to control spending and to reduce deficits. When the congressional budget process proved unable to hold down deficits in the 1980s, Congress established stricter measures to control spending, including "spending caps" that limit spending on some types of programs.

A very large and growing proportion of the annual federal budget is **mandatory spending**, expenditures that are, in the words of the OMB, "relatively uncontrollable." Interest payments on the national debt, for example, are determined by the actual size of the national debt. Legislation has mandated payment rates for such programs as retirement under Social Security, retirement for federal employees, unemployment assistance, Medicare, and farm price supports (see Figures 16.3 and 16.4). These payments increase with the cost of living; they increase as the average age of the population goes up; they increase as national and world agricultural surpluses go up. In 1970, 38.5 percent of the total federal budget was made up of these **uncontrollables**; in 1975, 52.5 percent fell into that category; and by 2010, around 59.5 percent was in the uncontrollable category. This means that the national government now can do very little **discretionary spending** that will allow it to counteract fluctuations in the business cycle.

Government spending as a fiscal policy works fairly well when deliberate deficit spending is used to stop a recession and to speed up the recovery period, but it does not work very well in fighting inflation, because elected politicians are politically unable to make the drastic expenditure cuts necessary to balance the budget, much less to produce a budgetary surplus.

mandatory spending federal spending that is made up of "uncontrollables," budget items that cannot be controlled through the regular budget process

uncontrollable a budgetary item that is beyond the control of budgetary committees and can be controlled only by substantive legislative action in Congress. Some uncontrollables, such as interest on the debt, are beyond the power of Congress, because the terms of payments are set in contracts

discretionary spending federal spending on programs that are controlled through the regular budget process

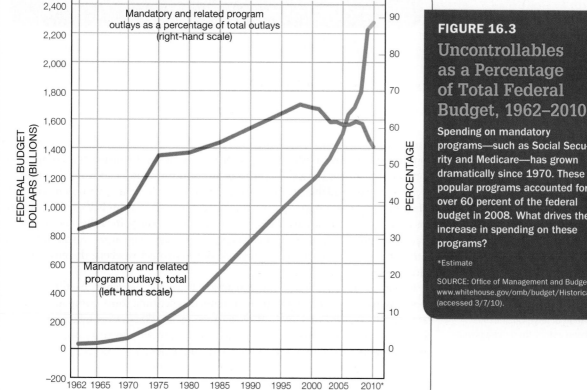

FIGURE 16.3

Uncontrollables as a Percentage of Total Federal Budget, 1962–2010

Spending on mandatory programs—such as Social Security and Medicare—has grown dramatically since 1970. These popular programs accounted for over 60 percent of the federal budget in 2008. What drives the increase in spending on these programs?

*Estimate

SOURCE: Office of Management and Budget, www.whitehouse.gov/omb/budget/Historicals (accessed 3/7/10).

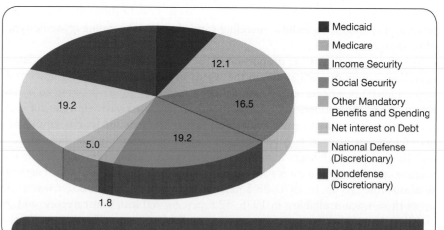

FIGURE 16.4
Budget Outlays of the Federal Government by Function, 2010*

The biggest items in the federal budget are mandatory programs, including Social Security and Medicare. These programs are supported by contributory taxes and enjoy broad support. It is easier to cut discretionary spending, because appropriations must be approved each year. With rising budget deficits and congressional unwillingness to raise taxes, discretionary spending—including defense, but especially domestic programs—are the easiest programs to cut.

*Estimate

SOURCE: Office of Management and Budget, www.whitehouse.gov (accessed 3/7/10).

Regulation and Antitrust Policy

Americans have long been suspicious of concentrations of economic power. Federal economic regulation aims to protect the public against potential abuses by concentrated economic power in two ways. First, the federal government can establish conditions that govern the operation of big businesses to ensure fair competition. For example, it can require business to make information about its activities and account books available to the public. Second, the federal government can force a large business to break up into smaller companies if it finds that the company has established a **monopoly**. This is called **antitrust policy**. In addition to economic regulation, the federal government engages in social regulation. Social regulation establishes conditions on businesses in order to protect workers, the environment, and consumers.

Federal regulatory policy was a reaction to public demands. As the American economy prospered throughout the nineteenth century, some companies grew so large that they were recognized as possessing "market power." This meant that they were powerful enough to eliminate competitors and to impose conditions on consumers rather than catering to consumer demand. The growth of billion-dollar corporations led to collusion among companies to control prices, much to the dismay of smaller businesses and ordinary consumers. Small businesses, laborers, farmers, and consumers all began to clamor for protective regulation. Although the states had been regulating businesses in one way or another all along, interest

monopoly the existence of a single firm in a market that controls all the goods and services of that market; absence of competition

antitrust policy government regulation of large businesses that have established monopolies

groups turned to Washington as economic problems appeared to be beyond the reach of the individual state governments. If markets were national, there would have to be national regulation.[28]

The first national regulatory policy was the Interstate Commerce Act of 1887, which created the first national independent regulatory commission, the Interstate Commerce Commission (ICC), designed to control the monopolistic practices of the railroads. Two years later, the Sherman Antitrust Act extended regulatory power to cover all monopolistic practices, including "trusts" or any other agreement between companies to eliminate competition. These were strengthened in 1914 with the enactment of the Federal Trade Act (creating the Federal Trade Commission, or FTC) and the Clayton Act. The only significant addition of economic regulatory policy beyond regulation of interstate trade, however, was the establishment in 1913 of the Federal Reserve System, which was given powers to regulate the banking industry along with its general monetary powers. At the same time, public demands to protect consumers led the federal government to enact a more limited number of social regulations. As we have seen, Upton Sinclair's best-seller about the meatpacking industry, *The Jungle*, led to the federal meat inspection program in 1906. Two decades later, the Food and Drug Administration was set up to test and regulate products viewed as essential to public health.

The modern epoch of comprehensive national regulation began in the 1930s. Most of the regulatory programs of the 1930s were established to regulate the conduct of companies within specifically designated sectors of American industry. For example, the jurisdiction of one agency was the securities industry; the jurisdiction of another was the radio (and eventually television) industry. Another was banking. Another was coal mining; still another was agriculture. At this time, Congress also set the basic framework of American labor regulation, including the rules for collective bargaining and the minimum wage.

When Congress turned once again to regulatory policies in the 1970s, it became still bolder, moving beyond the effort to regulate specific sectors of industry toward regulating some aspect of the entire economy. The scope or jurisdiction of such agencies as the Occupational Safety and Health Administration (OSHA), the Consumer Product Safety Commission (CPSC), and the Environmental Protection Agency (EPA) is as broad and as wide as the entire economy, indeed the entire society.

Despite occasional high-profile regulatory cases such as the one against Microsoft in the 1990s, the trend since the late 1970s has been against regulation. Businesses complained about the burden of the new regulations they confronted, and many economists began to argue that excessive regulation was hurting the economy. Congress and the president responded with a wave of **deregulation**. For example, President Reagan went about the task of changing the direction of regulation by way of "presidential oversight." Shortly after taking office, he gave the OMB authority to review all executive-branch proposals for new regulations. By this means, Reagan reduced the total number of regulations issued by federal agencies, dropping the number of pages in the *Federal Register* from 74,000 in 1980 to 49,600 in 1987.[29] By 2009 the *Federal Register* had grown to more than 69,000 pages. Nonetheless, the movement for deregulation became steadily more controversial during the presidency of George W. Bush. In the late 1980s and 1990s, many states had opened their electrical power markets to competition, resulting in lower prices. But in 2001, severe energy shortages in California caused power outages and skyrocketing prices. California officials charged that Enron and

deregulation a policy of reducing or eliminating regulatory restraints on the conduct of individuals or private institutions

other out-of-state suppliers had used their market power to drive up the price of energy and then used their political clout to dissuade federal regulators from intervening.

The financial crisis that began in 2008 put regulation on the agenda once again. As the economic emergency subsided, Congress began to consider long-term reform of the financial industry. A central question was how to create regulations that would prevent excessive risk-taking by investors, seen as the principal cause of the recession. The complex reform that Congress enacted in 2010 (the Dodd-Frank Wall Street Reform and Consumer Protection Act) included a range of new regulations on the financial industry. It created a Bureau of Consumer Financial Protection, placed under the auspices of the Federal Reserve but independent of it. The new agency has a broad mandate to regulate consumer financial products, such as mortgages and credit cards, to ensure that they are fair and competitive. The reform also created a new Financial Stability Oversight Council, headed by the Treasury Secretary. The new council is responsible for identifying risks to the economy before they spread.

Subsidies and Contracting

Subsidies and contracting are the carrots of economic policy. Their purpose is to encourage people to do something they might not otherwise do or to get people to do more of what they are already doing. Sometimes the purpose is merely to compensate people for something done in the past.

subsidy a government grant of cash or other valuable commodities, such as land, to an individual or an organization; used to promote activities desired by the government, to reward political support, or to buy off political opposition

Subsidies Subsidies are simply government grants of cash or other valuable commodities, such as land. Although subsidies are often denounced as "giveaways," they have played a fundamental role in the history of government in the United States. Subsidies were the dominant form of public policy of the national government and the state and local governments throughout the nineteenth century. They continue to be an important category of public policy at all levels of government. The first planning document ever written for the national government, Alexander Hamilton's Report on Manufactures, was based almost entirely on Hamilton's assumption that American industry could be encouraged by federal subsidies and that these were not only desirable but constitutional.

The thrust of Hamilton's plan was not lost on later policy makers. Subsidies in the form of land grants were given to farmers and to railroad companies to encourage western settlement. Substantial cash subsidies have traditionally been given to shipbuilders to help build the commercial fleet and to guarantee the use of their ships as military personnel carriers in time of war. Policies using the subsidy technique continued to be plentiful in the twentieth century, even after the 1990s when there was widespread public and official hostility toward subsidies. For example, in 2007, the annual value of corporate subsidies not including agriculture was estimated at more than $92 billion.[30]

Politicians have always favored subsidies because subsidies can be treated as "benefits" that can be spread widely in response to many demands that might otherwise produce profound political conflict. Subsidies can, in other words, be used to buy off the opposition.

Another secret to the popularity of subsidies is that those who receive the benefits do not perceive the controls inherent in them. In the first place, most of the resources available for subsidies come from taxation. (During the nineteenth century, there was a lot of public land to distribute, but that is no longer the case.)

Second, the effect of any subsidy has to be measured somewhat indirectly in terms of what people *would be doing* if the subsidy were not available. For example, many thousands of people settled in lands west of the Mississippi only because land subsidies were available. Similarly, hundreds of research laboratories exist in universities and corporations only because certain types of research subsidies from the government are available to fund them.

Contracting Like any corporation, a government agency must purchase goods and services by contract. The law requires open bidding for a substantial proportion of these contracts because government contracts are extremely valuable to businesses in the private sector and because the opportunities and incentives for abuse surrounding contracting are very great. But contracting is more than a method of buying goods and services. Contracting is also an important technique of policy because government agencies are often authorized to use their **contracting power** as a means of encouraging corporations to improve themselves, as a means of helping to build up whole sectors of the economy, and as a means of encouraging certain desirable goals or behavior, such as equal employment opportunity. For example, the infant airline industry of the 1930s was nurtured by the national government's lucrative contracts to carry airmail. A more recent example is the use of government contracting to encourage industries, universities, and other organizations to engage in research and development on a wide range of issues in basic and applied science.

> **contracting power** the power of government to set conditions on companies seeking to sell goods or services to government agencies

Military contracting has long been a major element in government spending. So tight was the connection between defense contractors and the federal government during the Cold War that as he was leaving office, President Eisenhower warned the nation to beware of the powerful "military-industrial complex." After the Cold War, as military spending and production declined, major defense contractors began to look for alternative business activities to supplement the reduced demand for weapons. For example, Lockheed Martin, the nation's largest defense contractor, began to bid on contracts related to welfare reform. Since the terrorist attacks of 2001, however, the military budget has been awash in new funds and military contractors are flooded with business. President Bush increased the Pentagon budget by more than 7 percent a year, requesting so many weapons systems that one observer called the budget a "weapons smorgasbord."[31] Military contractors geared up to produce not only weapons for foreign warfare but also surveillance systems to enhance domestic security.

for critical analysis

Think about a specific instance of government intervention in the American economy since the New Deal. What economic policy tool was used? What other tools might have been used? In your opinion, when is government action in the economy necessary?

● The Environment and the Economy

One of the most important reasons that the government intervenes in the economy is to protect the environment. Although federal interest in environmental conservation stretches back to the 1900s, federal regulation of industry grew more extensive with the rise of the modern environmental movement in the 1970s. Today, concern about global warming has put environmental issues front and center in debates about the economy. Not only must policy makers grapple with the costs of combating global warming but they must also assess the long-term impact of warming on the American economy and society. This is a fundamental challenge because the effects of global warming are likely to be very widely felt. At the same time, however, the specific consequences and the timing of their impact remain very uncertain.

In 1969, Cleveland's Cuyahoga River caught fire due to the industrial waste dumped into the water and became a symbol of the need for government regulation of polluting industries.

The wave of environmental policy enacted in the 1970s stemmed in large part from American prosperity in the 1960s. An affluent America with more time for leisure grew concerned about the quality of the environment and the need to preserve natural beauty. The consequences of economic growth that paid little attention to environmental impact were evident all over America. In 1969, Cleveland's Cuyahoga River, long a dumping ground for industrial waste, caught fire. Images of the burning river became especially vivid symbols of environmental neglect. The first "Earth Day" in 1970 celebrated this new set of concerns, which became a major feature of American politics in subsequent decades.[32]

A wave of new laws wrote environmental goals into policy. The 1969 National Environmental Policy Act (NEPA), the Clean Air Act Amendments of 1970, the 1972 Clean Water Act, and the 1974 Safe Drinking Water Act together established a new set of goals and procedures for protecting the environment. They are properly considered part of economic policy because they regulate the activities of virtually every aspect of the economy. NEPA, for example, requires federal agencies to prepare an environmental impact statement for every major development project that they propose. In this way, environmental impacts routinely become factored into considerations about whether a particular project is feasible or desirable.

Environmental disasters have often drawn attention to new environmental hazards and have prompted greater federal regulation. For example, during the mid-1970s the residents of the Love Canal neighborhood in Buffalo, New York, discovered that their neighborhood had been built on a toxic waste dump. Many of the chemicals in the soil were suspected carcinogens. At federal and state cost, residents were moved to new homes. Partly as a result of this highly publicized incident, Congress passed legislation to facilitate cleanup of hazardous waste sites. Yet government action and corporate liability are often bitterly contested issues in this area. As the book and film *A Civil Action*—about toxic waste in a Massachusetts community—demonstrated, identifying the sources of toxic pollution and linking such pollution to health hazards can be very difficult.[33]

Protecting the environment presents policy makers with difficult trade-offs. Compliance with environmental regulations can be very costly. Moreover, critics maintain that federal standards are sometimes too high. How clean should the air be? What is the difference between pure drinking water and safe drinking water? Who should bear the costs of providing environmental benefits? Not only do citizens, consumers, and businesses take different perspectives on these questions but the goals themselves often present a moving target. As new scientific evidence shows (or fails to find evidence for) new or suspected environmental hazards, conflicts over the proper government role emerge.

The Debate on Global Warming

Nowhere have these conflicts been more acute than in the debate over global warming. A large and growing body of scientific evidence suggests that greenhouse gas emissions from cars, power plants and other human-made sources are causing temperatures on Earth to rise.[34] The projected environmental consequences are dire: melting polar ice caps, extreme weather, droughts, fire, rising sea levels, and disease. All would have profound economic consequences. Yet these projections come with considerable uncertainty: how likely are most catastrophic scenarios? Should we prepare for the most damaging outcomes or only the most likely outcomes of global warming?[35] These questions are important because the costs of transforming the world's carbon-based technologies through lower energy use and newer green technologies are enormous. These questions are especially salient for the United States, which has the world's largest economy and is responsible for 25 percent of the world's greenhouse gas emissions but has only 10 percent of the world's population.[36] And because the United States relies so heavily on fossil fuels for its energy sources, the effort to reduce carbon emission requires a major shift in how we obtain and use energy.

As scientists have learned more about the effects of human activity on the climate, the issue of global warming has risen on the national agenda. The issue attracted broad attention in 2006 with the success of former vice president Al Gore's film *An Inconvenient Truth*. In 2007, the film won an Academy Award, and Gore, along with the UN's International Panel on Climate Change, received the Nobel Peace Prize for arousing public awareness about the dangers of global warming. American public opinion reflected the growing salience of global warming as a policy issue. For example, in 2007, 84 percent of Americans reported believing that human activity was at least a contributing factor in global warming.[37] However, the economic recession and political controversy over climate change seemed to shift public perceptions about the existence and importance of global warming. In 2010, only 57 percent of America reported believing that global climate change was happening at all, with just 50 percent of respondents "very" or "somewhat" worried about climate change. In another survey, respondents ranked climate change last in importance in a list of twenty-one top public policy issues.[38] In the same survey, just over half of the public said that they would support protecting the environment over stimulating the economy, while 36 percent chose the economy.[39] When asked whether or not the issue would affect their votes, just under half of the public said that global warming would be "extremely" or "very important" to their vote for president.[40] Some corporate leaders have also become increasingly concerned about global warming, sponsoring events to learn more about the problem

Former vice president Al Gore's 2006 film An Inconvenient Truth *attracted broad attention to the issue of global warming. The film won an Academy Award, and Gore was a corecipient of the Nobel Peace Prize for his efforts to raise public awareness.*

After the massive Deepwater Horizon oil spill in the Gulf of Mexico in 2010, the Obama administration faced stronger pressure to regulate off-shore drilling and its environmental impact. The oil spill was estimated to have leaked nearly five million barrels, making it the largest spill of its kind.

for critical analysis

What are some of the policies that can be used to address global warming? Which policies have the best chance of being enacted?

and joining coalitions to press for solutions. Moreover, many political leaders who have been skeptical about the reality and causes of global warming have come to accept that it poses a threat that must be addressed. At the end of his presidency, George W. Bush, who had been skeptical about climate change, sought to ward off critics by announcing "I take the issue seriously."[41] The Obama administration has made global warming an important focus of attention and encouraged federal agencies to move aggressively on this issue. In 2009, the Environmental Protection Agency began to set standards so that it could regulate greenhouse gas emissions under the Clean Air Act for the first time ever. The administration also proposed creating a new Climate Service that would centralize the collection and analysis of data on climate change across the world. The new attitude was epitomized by Commerce Secretary Gary Locke, who noted in his announcement of the planned Climate Service that "whether we like it or not, climate change represents a real threat."[42]

Environmental Policies

But how can the goal of a "greener America" be reached? Agreeing on policies to reduce greenhouse gas emissions remains extremely difficult. Policy makers charged with devising approaches to global warming have identified three basic policy approaches. The first is mitigation, or reduction of greenhouse gas emissions. The second is large-scale research and development to promote alternative technologies. The third consists of measures that allow us to adapt to a warmer climate. Each of these strategies entails potentially gargantuan costs in the form of higher energy prices, subsidies to industry, infrastructure projects, and relocation decisions. When specific policy proposals are discussed and these costs become apparent, the consensus for addressing global warming breaks down.

Mitigation: Reducing Emissions The mitigation approach, which seeks to reduce greenhouse gas emissions, has garnered the most attention from policy makers. Two policies that aim to achieve this goal are tougher standards for auto fuel mileage and higher taxes on gasoline. Both have been very controversial. Although the public strongly supports higher gas-mileage standards, auto companies resisted such standards for nearly thirty years after they were first put into place in the early 1970s. The 2007 energy bill's requirement that automobiles raise fuel efficiency rates by 40 percent—to 35 miles per gallon by 2020—was a breakthrough on this issue. Even so, when California and fifteen other states sought to require even tougher standards for fuel mileage, the Environmental Protection Agency rejected their request, citing the need for a single national standard. Proposals to increase gasoline taxes have so far been political nonstarters. Public opinion polls routinely show that a majority of Americans oppose a tax on gasoline as a way to reduce emissions, and few politicians want to sponsor such an unpopular policy.[43]

International agreements on climate change, such as the Kyoto Protocol, seek to reduce carbon emissions by establishing mandatory caps on the total amount of emissions developed countries can emit. Although the United States signed the protocol in 1997, congressional and presidential opposition prevented any effort to implement its provisions. Policy makers have since considered several ways to reduce carbon emissions. One of the most effective is a "carbon tax," which would tax the producers of energy. The higher costs would then be passed on to consumers. Yet only a handful of politicians have expressed interest in supporting carbon taxes, which could substantially raise the costs of all sorts of consumer products.

Proponents of reducing carbon emissions pinned their hopes on a "cap-and-trade" system as the most politically feasible strategy to achieve their goal. This approach sets a target for carbon emissions for each industry but allows companies to trade "carbon credits" with each other. This market-based system is attractive to political leaders because it achieves its goals by creating incentives for private actors and allows them flexibility as they seek to reduce emissions. More than twenty-three large firms, including leading auto makers, have joined environmentalists in a coalition called the U.S. Climate Action Partnership (USCAP) to press for a cap-and-trade system to reduce carbon emissions.[44] In 2009, the House of Representatives passed a landmark cap-and-trade bill aimed at reducing greenhouse gas emissions. However, opposition from some Democrats and most Republicans in the Senate made further movement toward final passage of cap-and-trade legislation unlikely. New signs of progress emerged, however, in early 2010, with three senators of both parties—Senators John Kerry (D-Mass.), Joseph Lieberman (I-Conn.), and Lindsey Graham (R-S.C.)—proposing legislation that would apply carbon controls to specific sectors of the economy rather than setting the overall national target envisioned by the cap-and-trade scheme. One of the central elements of the proposal was a requirement that power plants limit their emissions, with the cap becoming more stringent over the next decade. Another key provision was the imposition of a carbon tax on gasoline, with the money raised being used to fund alternative fuel vehicle technologies such as electric cars. Despite this progress, these proposals set fairly minimal emissions reduction standards on high-polluting industries.[45]

In the absence of congressional action, the Obama administration took steps to curb climate change, with the EPA announcing that it would set standards for greenhouse gas emissions for automobiles under the Clean Air Act, raising the fuel economy standards for new vehicles to 35.5 gallons beginning in 2012. Not only will this action by the EPA have a significant effect on the automobile industry,

The United States and Global Climate Change

Concerns about global warming began to surface more than two decades ago. The international scope of the question became apparent when more than 150 countries, including the United States, signed the United Nations Framework Convention on Climate Change (UNFCCC) in 1992 at the so-called Earth Summit in Rio de Janeiro. By 1997, the signatory parties agreed on the Kyoto Protocol for reducing the level of heat trapping gases in the earth's atmosphere. To achieve this goal, the Kyoto Protocol set binding targets for greenhouse gas emissions to be met by each country by the year 2012 at levels 5.2 percent lower than their 1990 levels.

Since the Kyoto Protocol, the United States has been a hesitant participant in international climate negotiations. The United States signed the protocol during the Clinton presidency, but disagreement quickly erupted over the economic costs that industry would incur if forced to lower greenhouse emissions. As a result, President Clinton never submitted

the protocol to the Senate for ratification. On taking office in 2001, President Bush then announced he would not submit the Kyoto agreement to the Senate because it exempted China and other developing countries from binding limits while imposing excessive costs on the U.S. economy.

Even as the scientific basis for global warming gained wider acceptance, the politics of implementing binding limits produced a growing split between wealthy industrialized countries and the developing world. China and Brazil argued that the industrialized countries and especially the United States had contributed far more to global warming over

time than developing countries. The industrialized leaders, especially the United States, should therefore shoulder the burden of limiting worldwide emissions while giving poorer countries a chance to develop their economies.

In the ensuing debates, many other Kyoto signatories also came to see the United States as a laggard in international efforts to control global warming. With only 10 percent of the world's population, the United States emitted approximately 25 percent of greenhouse gases, more than any other single country.

It was hoped that the 2009 Copenhagen Summit would produce a new legally binding international agreement with specific emission reduction targets for both developed and developing nations. Ultimately, however, the agreement fell well short of this goal: the meeting ended with no legally binding agreement and no deadline set to reach one. Wealthy nations agreed to provide funds to developing nations to help them integrate clean technology, though the sum of $10 billion a year was considered too low to be effective. The agreement did mark the first time the developing world, including major polluters such as China, India, and Brazil, committed to reducing their carbon output. This is particularly important as these countries will produce nearly all the growth in emissions over the coming decades.[a]

[a] Juliet Eilperin and Anthony Faiola, "Climate Deal Falls Short of Key Goals," *Washington Post,* December 19, 2009, www.washingtonpost.com (accessed 3/8/10).

for critical analysis

1. Why did many countries that signed the Kyoto Protocol come to see the United States as a laggard in efforts to control global warming?

2. Why was it so important to U.S. negotiators that mandatory limits on greenhouse gas emissions be applied to China as well as to the developed countries?

it could lead to far-reaching regulations in the future that could extend to all greenhouse-gas generating industries. EPA Administrator Lisa Jackson also allowed the State of California to impose increased greenhouse gas standards on automobile manufacturers.

Promoting Alternative Technologies Many analysts and politicians, however, prefer a second strategy, which centers on increasing research and development to promote alternative technologies. President Obama came out strongly in favor of a comprehensive energy and climate change bill that would, among other things, provide funding and large tax incentives for the production and adoption of clean-energy technologies. He also warned that the United States was falling behind other countries, including China, in the production of clean-energy products, arguing that this industry would be a vital source of millions of new jobs over the next few decades.[46]

The 2009 Recovery Act made several significant allocations designed to support alternative energy technology investment and improve energy efficiency. The act included $11 billion for improvements to the national electricity grid, $5 billion for "weatherization" projects, and $4.5 billion to improve energy efficiency in federal buildings. It also allocated $6.3 billion for state and local renewable energy and efficiency products, and $2 billion for grants to manufacturers of batteries that store large amounts of electric energy.

Green technologies may prove to be a boon for the American economy. Because highly skilled labor is required to produce most green technologies, America has a competitive advantage over many other countries. To be more precise, the production of green technologies—unlike other kinds of goods—cannot be outsourced to developing countries.

In addition to enhancing environmental quality and promoting economic growth, a move toward green technologies could significantly improve American national security. Indeed, because most oil money goes to Saudi Arabia and Iran, some argue that adopting more fuel-efficient technologies would take money away from regimes that support terrorism against the United States. As the author and *New York Times* columnist Thomas Friedman put it, "Green is the new red, white and blue."[47]

Part of the attraction of green technologies is that they appear to entail fewer politically difficult costs. A closer look, however, reveals that this is not entirely true. For example, the search for cleaner technologies has renewed interest in nuclear power. But nuclear power has long suffered from NIMBY (Not In My Backyard) problems: few people want a nuclear power plant close by. The question of how to dispose of nuclear waste poses similar problems. Plans to deposit nuclear waste in Nevada's Yucca Mountain became the target of considerable controversy, not only by people close by but also by those concerned with the dangers of transporting nuclear waste to Nevada. Even less dangerous technologies, such as wind farms, attract opposition, as the effort to establish a large wind farm off Cape Cod demonstrated.

Development of green technologies will no doubt be an important component of America's efforts to combat climate change. However, opposition to some of the new technologies and the time required to develop these alternatives mean that they are not the magic bullet that many proponents wish they were.

Adaptation Policies A final approach to climate change is adaptation to a warmer climate. Adaptation would entail a diverse set of policies, including establishment of green corridors, pest and disease control, water conservation to deal with drought, and new infrastructure such as seawalls to cope with rising sea levels.[48] Even more controversial measures, such as moving people away from low-lying areas, would be part of an adaptation strategy.

Many aspects of a deliberate adaptation strategy would be difficult to implement in the market-oriented, decentralized context of the United States. Although some European countries, such as the low-lying Netherlands, are relocating people as part of their adaptation strategy, American politicians have little stomach for initiating such controversial measures. Moreover, the combination of conservation and new infrastructure requires considerable public resources and broad coordination across multiple public agencies. Both are hard to achieve in the context of American politics. For example, the environmentally sensitive Sacramento Delta is extremely vulnerable to rising sea levels. The delta, a swath of land that lies below sea level, is economically important because it supplies much of northern California, including California agribusiness, with water. Yet decisions about what happens in the delta involve more than 200 government agencies.[49]

When deliberate adaptation does not occur, de facto adaptation may. Although no single event such as Hurricane Katrina can be attributed to climate change, the consequences of Katrina are relevant to global-warming scenarios. As in New Orleans, the most vulnerable people with the fewest resources will suffer the worst consequences of adaptation as they lose their homes and livelihoods. As in New Orleans and in recent urban heat waves, many will die. Many scientists believe that deliberate adaptation has to be part of our approach to climate change because even if we take major steps to mitigate carbon emissions and pour resources into developing new technologies, global warming has already arrived.[50]

Global climate change poses a difficult economic challenge for the United States. It presents the opportunity for American industry to take the lead in developing green technologies, placing the nation's economic prosperity on a fundamentally new base. Yet it also calls for government to enforce the reduction of carbon emissions and adapt current practices to a changing world. Many industries have expressed support for action to address climate change, but such a major economic transformation creates winners and losers. Firms, such as the auto companies, whose profits are jeopardized and workers whose jobs are threatened by change have successfully blocked bold action in the past. The diffuse long-term harms that global warming poses are hard to pit against the specific concentrated costs that face industries today. Nonetheless, growing recognition that climate change is real and poses potentially catastrophic consequences ensures that economic policy and environmental policy will be ever more closely intertwined in the future.

● The Politics of Economic Policy Making

Addressing economic challenges and maintaining a healthy economy are extremely important to political leaders. As presidents from Herbert Hoover (who presided over the beginning of the Great Depression of the 1930s) to Jimmy Carter (who faced double-digit inflation) discovered, voters will punish politicians for poor economic performance. Yet even though all politicians want a healthy economy, they often differ in their views about how to attain it. Moreover, politicians disagree about what the priorities of economic policy should be. Democrats and Republicans alike want to promote economic growth, but Democrats are generally more concerned about equality and unemployment than are Republicans. Republicans stress the importance of economic freedom for maintaining a healthy economy, whereas Democrats are often more willing to support economic regulation to attain social objectives. Such differences along party lines are not hard and fast divisions, however. The politics of economic policy making are also greatly influenced by economic ideas.

The Changing Federal Role in the Economy

Until 1929, most Americans believed that government had little to do with actively managing the economy. The world was guided by the theory that the economy, if left to its own devices, would produce full employment and maximum production. This traditional view of the relationship between government and the economy crumbled in 1929 before the stark reality of the Great Depression of 1929–33. Some misfortune befell nearly everyone. Around 20 percent of the workforce became unemployed, and few of these individuals had any monetary resources or the old family farm to fall back on. Banks failed, wiping out the savings of millions who had been prudent enough or fortunate enough to have any. Thousands of businesses closed, throwing middle-class Americans onto the bread lines alongside unemployed laborers and dispossessed farmers. The Great Depression proved to Americans that imperfections in the economic system could exist.

Demands grew for the federal government to act. In Congress, some Democrats proposed that the federal government finance public works to aid the economy and put people back to work. Other members introduced legislation to provide federal grants to the states to assist their relief efforts.

When President Franklin Delano Roosevelt took office in 1933, he energetically threw the federal government into the business of fighting the Depression. He proposed a variety of temporary measures to provide federal relief and work programs. Most of the programs he proposed were to be financed by the federal government but administered by the states. In addition to these temporary measures, Roosevelt presided over the creation of several important federal programs designed to provide future economic security for Americans. Since that time, the government has been instrumental in ensuring that the economy will never again collapse as it did during the Depression.

The experience of the 1930s transformed public expectations about federal government involvement in the economy. Since that time, the public has held the government—and the president in particular—responsible for ensuring a healthy economy.

As we have seen, Keynesian ideas, which used spending and tax policy to promote growth and low unemployment, dominated economic policy during the 1960s and during the first half of the 1970s. The Council of Economic Advisers (CEA) played a central role in economic policy during that time because the president relied on its advice about whether to stimulate or depress the economy. As Keynesian prescriptions became less effective, however, the CEA began to lose its central role. Since the late 1970s, when President Carter began to emphasize monetary policy, the chairman of the Federal Reserve has occupied the pivotal position in economic policy making. The long run of economic prosperity in the 1990s made the former Fed chairman Alan Greenspan into something of a cult figure. Universally praised by Democrats and Republicans alike for his management of the economy, Greenspan served four four-year terms as head of the Federal Reserve. As the economy fell into recession in the early 2000s, critics complained that Greenspan had lost his touch and had helped create the conditions for recession.

Coca-Cola and the Middle East: Brands as American Icons

"That's as American as apple pie," or so the expression goes. But perhaps a more accurate simile for contemporary American culture would be, "that's as American as Coca-Cola," or McDonald's, or Starbucks, or Microsoft, or Marlboro. As the American government helps promote American goods and services abroad, increasing numbers of people from around the world experience American culture through its brands. However, the world has long been engaged in a love/hate relationship with the ubiquity of American brands and the popular culture that accompanies them. While in many cases, people abroad are simply worried about American brands competing with local businesses, consumers around the globe also use their wallets to respond to American foreign policy and international economic policy.

Although the United States remains a leader in exports, in August 2005, the *Financial Times* reported that "anti-Americanism is hurting companies whose products are considered to be distinctly 'American.'" At the start of the 2003 war in Iraq, sales of Coca-Cola dropped 10 percent in the Middle East and McDonald's sales fell 7.5 percent. According to the *San Francisco Chronicle*, a 2005 study revealed that substantial proportions of opinion leaders in Canada, the United Kingdom, France, and Germany reported that they were less likely to buy American goods as a result of American foreign policy.

In some cases, local entrepreneurs in Europe and the Middle East have begun to offer goods and services to replace American brands. Take Coca-Cola, for example. Since it was placed on the

Arab League's official boycott list in 1967 for doing business in Israel, Coca-Cola has had hurdles to overcome with its public relations in the Middle East. Once placed on the list, Coca-Cola was perceived by some in the Middle East as a supporter of the Israeli military and of the Jewish religion. So strong was this rumor, in fact, that The Coca-Cola Company has a section on its Web site entitled "Middle East Rumors" where the company states that it "is not affiliated with any specific religion or ethnic group . . . [and] does not support or oppose governments, political or religious causes." Nonetheless, to many people around the world, Coke represents America—American culture, interests, and policy. Entrepreneurs have responded by offering alternatives to American goods, such as Mecca Cola, which was launched by

Tawfik Mathlouthi. Mathlouthi explains that Mecca Cola "is not just a drink. It is an act of protest against Bush and Rumsfeld and their policies."[a] The company has pledged to give 10 percent of profits to Palestinian children's charities and an additional 10 percent to European Nongovernmental Organizations (NGOs). Mecca Cola has quickly grown in popularity in Belgium, France, and Germany and is currently being introduced in the Middle East.

Many U.S. companies that have felt the effects of foreign boycotts abroad are engaging in campaigns to bring consumers back. One argument against local consumers' boycotts of American goods is that the bulk of the impact will not be felt in America but in the local communities where the boycotts take place. American companies are trying to convey the message that the people who will be hurt are local farmers, suppliers, and employees of the local plants—not American executives or politicians. However, they have had limited success in finding a solution. The shape of this solution, whether economic, political, or merely a matter of good public relations, has yet to emerge.

[a] Jon Fasman, "Freedom Coke: The Arab World's Foolish Boycott of American Food," Slate.com, March 25, 2003, www.slate.com (accessed 3/22/08).

for critical analysis

1. Do you think that boycotts of American products abroad will be successful in influencing American foreign policy? Why or why not?

2. Do you choose to buy or not buy certain goods or services for political reasons? To what extent do you believe your personal purchasing choices affect the company behind the products?

Presidents who preside over periods of economic downturn are generally punished by the electorate. In 1992, economic recession and relatively high levels of unemployment greatly improved the challenger Bill Clinton's presidential prospects, even though he was not widely known when he started campaigning. Clinton's campaign took as a central theme the unofficial slogan, "It's the economy, stupid." The uncertain direction of the economy made it an issue in the 2004 presidential campaign. Anxious not to repeat his father's experience in 1992, President George W. Bush claimed in 2004 that his policies were creating new jobs and touted the benefits of his tax cuts for middle-income families. Democrats countered that Bush's policies benefited the wealthy but left most Americans economically worse off.

Politics and the Great Recession of 2008

As the near-collapse of the financial sector in 2008 reverberated throughout the American (and world) economy, thousands of Americans lost their homes, banks refused to lend, and unemployment rose. The federal government, first under George Bush and then under Barack Obama, initiated large-scale government interventions in hopes of staving off the downward economic spiral. These included emergency measures to bail out failing companies, short-term stimulus to get the economy moving again, and proposals for regulations that would prevent similar financial meltdowns in the future. Even as the federal government moved to prevent the economy from plunging into depression, however, support for these measures wavered as fear of rising deficits, exploding long-term debt, and, more abstractly, "big government" grew.

As we have seen, propping up the financial sector presented an economic challenge for federal officials. Having made a number of ad hoc loans to a variety of financial institutions in early to mid-2008, the Treasury and Federal Reserve realized that they needed a more comprehensive approach as the financial crisis escalated after the collapse of investment bank Lehman Brothers and the rescue of the insurance company American International Group (AIG). Congress ultimately approved a $700 billion emergency "bailout" of financial institutions in October 2008 (known as the Troubled Asset Relief Program or TARP), which the Treasury Department drew on to infuse major financial institutions with capital.

It was not just major banking institutions that faced ruin. Auto companies, too, teetered on the edge of bankruptcy. Wishing to avoid the loss of hundreds of thousands of jobs in the automobile industry, the outgoing Bush administration controversially made emergency bridging loans to General Motors (GM), GM's car financing business (called GMAC), and Chrysler, in December 2008, using funds from the financial rescue plan package approved by Congress two months earlier. In return, both companies agreed to restructure their operations to cut costs and become more competitive. However, only a few months later, the companies returned to the federal government to ask for further assistance; by June 2009, GM and Chrysler had received a total of $82 billion in government assistance.[51] The federal government also effectively subsidized the earnings of auto manufacturers by approving $3 billion in subsidies over the course of 2009 for people willing to trade in their old cars for more fuel-efficient vehicles, a program commonly known as "cash for clunkers."[52] As a condition of receiving these subsidies, the bailed-out companies had to comply with the decisions of a federal "pay czar" responsible for ensuring that the subsidized industries did not provide excessive executive compensation. Although the Treasury Department estimated that

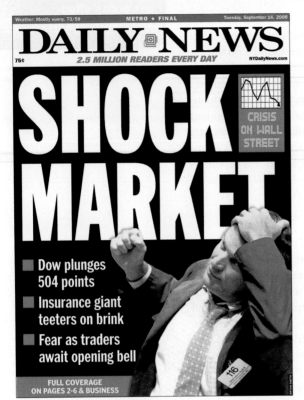

After the Lehmen Brothers investment bank collapsed and the giant insurance company AIG announced it was near collapse in September 2008, the stock market plummeted and Americans looked to the government to address the crisis. However, Democrats and Republicans disagreed about the best response.

taxpayers ultimately stood to lose $30 billion from the GM and Chrysler bailouts by 2010, the Treasury Department estimated the loss at $17 billion.[53]

By late 2010, the economy had stabilized sufficiently that many of the financial institutions that had received funds under TARP were able to pay the federal government back. The Congressional Budget Office estimated that TARP would end up costing the taxpayers $66 billion, far less than the initial $700 billion.[54] This did not include the hundreds of billions of dollars spent by the Federal Reserve in buying up mortgage-related debts held by banks.[55]

Congress also passed a sweeping package in 2009 to help stimulate the economy, save jobs (particularly in the public sector), and make longer-term investments that would help stimulate economic growth. The $789 billion American Recovery and Reinvestment Act (more commonly known as the "stimulus" bill of 2009) contained a number of measures to stimulate growth in the short term and prevent drastic cuts to public services. Among the most important measures in the act were reductions in individual and business taxes by $288 billion, which were designed to generate more spending and job hiring. The measure also spent $195.5 billion on aid, health insurance subsidies, and job training for low-income and unemployed workers, as well as $44.5 billion designed to limit teacher layoffs and cutbacks in local school districts. The rest of the investments not only aimed to create new jobs in the short term, they sought to be long-term investments in infrastructure and education that would help future growth.[56]

Although only some Republicans and Democrats had balked at supporting the financial bailout package in 2008, by early 2009 a sharp partisan rift had become evident. No Republicans in the House and only three in the Senate voted to support the 2009 stimulus package. Republicans denounced the House measure as overly tilted toward spending rather than tax cuts. But even when Senate Democrats added significant new tax cuts to the bill, most Republicans opposed it. While Democrats defended the measure as an infusion of funds needed to prevent a depression, Republicans denounced it as wasteful spending and made their opposition a defining stance toward the new Obama administration. Mounting unemployment complicated the political judgments about the stimulus; despite the injection of public funds into the economy, national unemployment rose to a seasonally adjusted rate of 9.6 in September 2010, with rates much higher in some states.[57] While those defending the stimulus measure argued that unemployment would have been still higher without it, the inability of the stimulus to bring unemployment rates down led opponents to brand it a failure.

Although economists largely agree that the bailouts and recovery spending prevented a depression and saved millions of jobs, there is significant controversy over the long-term effect of this historically high level of government spending. Opposition to the Recovery Act, for example, partly reflected a growing concern over the long-term sustainability of such large increases in government spending, particularly their effect on the growing national debt.[58] Over the past decade, large annual budget deficits have become common, requiring more borrowing by the government. As a consequence, the national debt has increased from 40 percent of annual

GDP in 2008 to 62 percent in 2010. The Office of Management and Budget estimates that the national debt will be equivalent to the entire GDP of the economy by 2012.[59] As the national debt has risen, so has the annual amount the government must pay to service the debt; by 2014, projections show that interest payments on the debt will amount to $514 billion, which is more than the annual spending on domestic programs.[60] Economists suggest that without broad tax increases and spending cuts, the deficit and debt will ultimately rise to unsustainable levels, leading foreign investors to demand higher interest rates or, perhaps, to stop lending money to the government altogether. Yet there is little political will to take these steps in either party, in large part because of deep public opposition to both tax increases and spending cuts. For example, one poll in early 2010 found that Americans oppose cutting government spending on health care and education by a two-to-one ratio, while 51 percent oppose lower military spending.[61]

Partisan divisions arose over what longer-term actions the federal government should take to prevent a similar economic collapse in the future. While a majority of Democrats favored strict regulations to limit the kinds of risky financial transactions that had caused the recession, most Republicans and some Democrats resisted stronger economic regulation. Efforts to craft a bipartisan legislation for financial regulation collapsed in early 2010 after months of negotiations. A central point of contention was how strong and independent the new consumer protection agency should be, with the Democrats deciding to press for a stronger measure.[62]

President Obama came to office vowing to pursue bipartisanship as he sought to revive the economy. Both tasks proved difficult to achieve. Rather than cementing a new consensus on the role of government in the economy, Obama's first two years in office were dogged by partisan rancor. Fueled by a combination of political maneuvering for partisan advantage and philosophical differences over the proper role of government and the economy, congressional Democrats and Republicans made partisan division the defining feature of politics.

Business and Labor in the Economy

The groups that influence decisions about economic policy are as wide-ranging as the objectives of policy. Consumer groups, environmentalists, businesses, and labor all attempt to shape economic policy. Of these groups, organized labor and business are the most consistent actors who weigh in across the spectrum of policies. In the past, organized labor was much more important in influencing economic policy than it is today. At the height of their strength in the 1950s, unions represented some 35 percent of the labor force. Today, labor unions, representing 12.3 percent of the labor force, are much less powerful in influencing economic policy. Democratic presidents continue to court labor because unions control resources and votes important to Democratic politicians, but labor's overall power has waned. On particular issues, organized labor can still exercise significant influence. For example, labor played a key role in Congress's decision to increase the minimum wage in 1996. Labor has recently sought to boost its political profile and has particularly sought to influence trade policy.

Business organizations are the most consistently powerful actors in economic policy. Business groups are most united around the goal of reducing government regulation. Organizations such as the U.S. Chamber of Commerce, which represents small business, and the Business Roundtable and the National Association of Manufacturers, which represent big business, actively worked to roll back government regulation in the 1970s and 1980s.

In addition to subsidies and tax breaks, business also relies on the federal government for protection against unfair foreign competition. For example, over the past several years, the film-production industry has lobbied Washington to help it compete with other countries where films can be made more cheaply than in the United States. This country loses an estimated $10 billion in annual revenues to these foreign competitors. Television shows and films with American locales are routinely filmed in Canada, where tax incentives and lower costs make production considerably cheaper. Industry representatives, fearing that Los Angeles could turn into a "rust belt" for film production, have sought legislation to secure wage credits.[63] The Screen Actors Guild went so far as to ask the federal government to investigate Canada for unfair trade practices.

● Thinking Critically about Economic Policy

Historically, Americans have been more concerned with ensuring economic liberty than with promoting economic equality. The widespread perception of openness and opportunity in American society has made Americans more tolerant than Europeans of economic inequality. American economic policy has rarely aimed to promote economic equality. Instead, economic policy has sought to ensure fairness in the marketplace and protect against the worst side effects of the free market. One of the central ways to ensure fair markets is to guard against the emergence of businesses so large that they can control markets. As we have seen, antitrust policy aims to break up such concentrations of power in the name of free and fair competition. The laws designed to strengthen labor in the 1930s likewise aimed to limit the power of big business by creating a countervailing power; they did not attempt directly to create equality. Consumer and environmental regulations are key economic policy protections against the worst side effects of the free market. Over time, as Americans have grown more concerned about the quality of life, policies in these areas have placed greater restrictions on the market. In a sense, economic prosperity and market success laid the foundation for such restrictions. As Americans felt more economically secure, they could afford to worry about how the economy affected the nonmaterial aspects of their lives, such as the environment. It is no accident that social regulation of the economy took off after the unprecedented prosperity of the 1960s.

The growth in economic inequality over the past three decades raises new questions about economic policy. Increased global competition, computerization, and the decline of unions and worker skills have all been identified as sources of the growth of inequality.[64] Taxes are another policy area that affects inequality. Depending on how they are designed, tax policies put relatively more money in the pockets of people with either lower or higher incomes. For example, tax cuts on investment income and reductions in the estate tax are more likely to increase the after-tax income of the wealthy because this group derives more of its income from investments and inheritances than do people with lower incomes.[65] Likewise, income-tax rates can be reduced for all groups, but depending on the proportion of tax cuts for each group, some income brackets may benefit more than others. One of the major criticisms of the tax cuts of 2001, 2003, and 2006 is that they increased the gap between rich and poor. They did so by allowing the rich to retain a greater proportion of their after-tax income than did middle- and lower-income taxpayers. The liberal Center for Budget and Policy Priorities analyzed the impact

The Income Gap

In recent decades, the difference or "gap" between the income going to the richest and poorest segments of the American population has been increasing. As the second graph shows, the after-tax income of the top 1 percent of earners has increased by over 250% since 1979, while those in the bottom fifth have only seen their income increase by 11 percent.

Pre-Tax Income, 1950–2008

In constant (2008) dollars

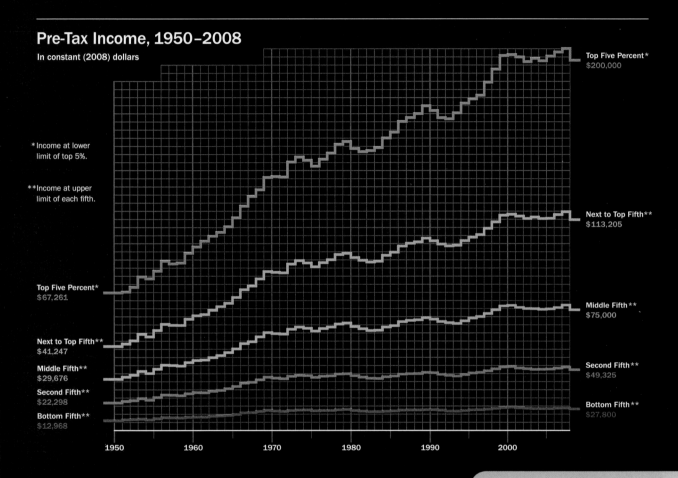

* Income at lower limit of top 5%.

** Income at upper limit of each fifth.

Top Five Percent*
$67,261

Next to Top Fifth**
$41,247

Middle Fifth**
$29,676

Second Fifth**
$22,298

Bottom Fifth**
$12,968

Top Five Percent*
$200,000

Next to Top Fifth**
$113,205

Middle Fifth**
$75,000

Second Fifth**
$49,325

Bottom Fifth**
$27,800

1950   1960   1970   1980   1990   2000

Change in Average After-Tax Income, 1979–2008

Top one percent +256%

Top Fifth +87%

Next to Top Fifth +32%

Middle Fifth +21%

Second Fifth +18%

Bottom Fifth +11%

for critical analysis

1. If average income has risen for all groups over the past thirty years, does it matter if some groups have their income increase more rapidly than others? Why or why not?

2. Democrats have often blamed Republican tax cuts for making the rich richer and the poor poorer. Should the government impose higher taxes on the rich to reduce income inequality? Why or why not?

SOURCES: Statistical Abstract of the United States, 2010, Table 678; Center on Budget and Policy Priorities, Income Gaps Hit Record Levels in 2006, New Data Show," April 17, 2009, www.cbpp.org (accessed 3/8/10).

of these tax cuts. As Figure 16.5 shows, the tax cuts allowed households in the bottom fifth of the income range to keep an additional 0.5 percent of their pretax income. For the middle-income group, after-tax income grew by 2.3 percent, while the top 20 percent gained 4.6 in after-tax income. The gains for the top 1 percent of households was much larger: an increase of 6.8 percent of after-tax income each year.[66] These differences matter because long-term trends in growth are widening the gap between rich and poor, as Figure 16.6 shows. Because after-tax incomes are *more unequal* as a consequence of the tax changes, liberals identify them as a regressive tax change.

Conservatives take a different view. They argue that even with these changes, the rich paid by far the greatest share of federal taxes. In fact, as the second half of Figure 16.5 shows, in 2005, the top fifth of households paid 68.7 percent of all taxes, whereas the bottom fifth paid less than 1 percent. Most crucial in judging the impact of the tax cuts, the rich paid a *larger share* of the total federal tax bill after the tax cuts than before. As Figure 16.5 shows, the share of the total tax bill fell for

FIGURE 16.5
Two Perspectives on Tax Cuts

Liberals and conservatives take different perspectives on the tax cuts introduced by President George W. Bush. Liberals charge that the cuts are regressive because they allow wealthy people to keep much more of their pretax income, as the top chart shows. Conservatives contend that the tax cuts benefited less-wealthy taxpayers because their share of the total tax burden declined while the tax burden of the richest taxpayers increased, as the bottom chart shows.

SOURCES: Center on Budget and Policy Priorities, www.cbpp.org; Congressional Budget Office, www.cbo.gov; and www.cbo.gov (accessed 3/22/08).

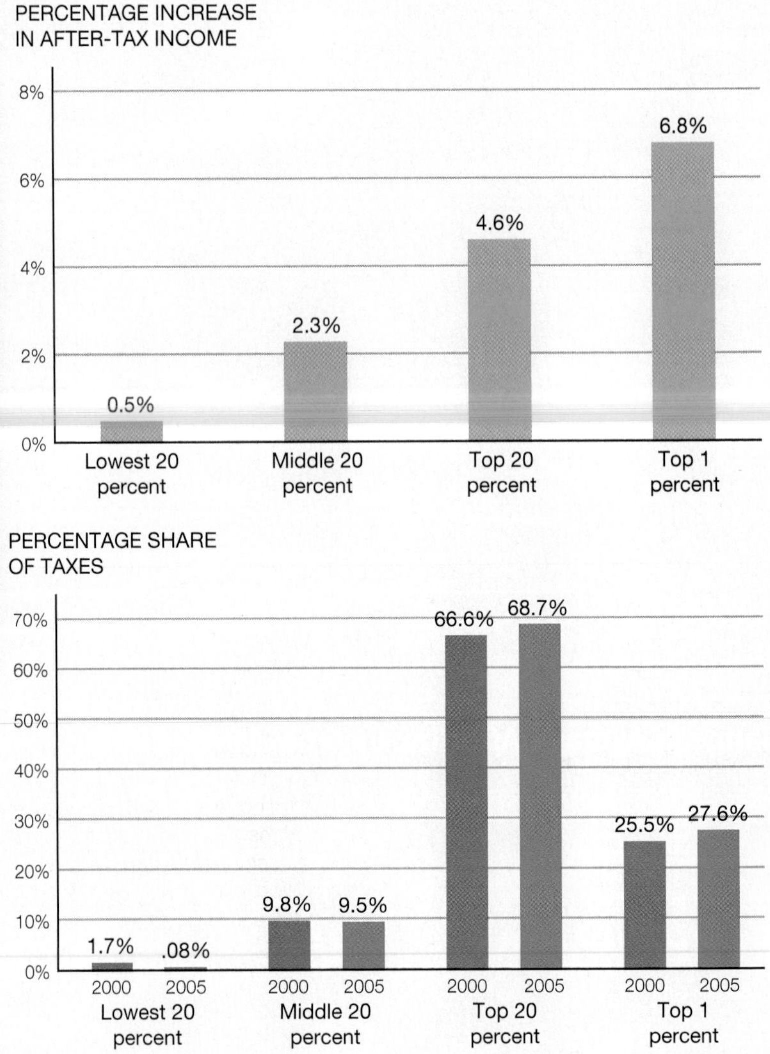

PERCENTAGE INCREASE IN AFTER-TAX INCOME

PERCENTAGE SHARE OF TAXES

Your Money and Politics

In the summer of 1998, a group of students formed the United Students Against Sweatshops. These young men and women were concerned about the working conditions of the laborers who made the apparel bearing their universities' logos. They argued that when schools and then students bought goods made in sweatshops, they were implicitly lending support to unjust labor practices. They wanted their universities to purchase products only from suppliers who agreed to a code of conduct that protected workers.

Many university administrations were reluctant to adopt anti-sweatshop policies, so students put on more pressure, sponsoring debates, holding street theater events, and in some instances even occupying the university president's office and staging hunger strikes. This persistence, amid constant negotiations, paid off, and by 2006, more than 150 universities had signed on to the Workers' Rights Commission, an independent organization that monitors the working conditions of apparel factories.

At the heart of these efforts was the belief that how students spend their money has an effect on other people throughout the world—and that they can use their money wisely, to reflect their values. Although the effort was aimed at workers in factories around the globe, the action was local—starting with their own campuses.

Individual citizens can have an impact on economic policies at any level and from any ideological direction.

- *Join an organization that promotes fiscal responsibility.* There are numerous organizations that are concerned about federal budgeting decisions. One of the most prominent is the Concord Coalition (www.concordcoalition.org), a bipartisan group that uses grassroots advocacy and public information campaigns to lobby for more efficient federal spending, which means taking steps to eliminate annual deficits and paying down the national debt.

- *Join an organization that promotes economic justice.* The Sargent Shriver National Center on Poverty Law (www.povertylaw.org), for example, provides information about the impact of economic policies on poor people in the United States. They advocate policies that will provide greater economic security (such as living wages and health care) for the poor.

- *Work to fight poverty.* There are a host of organizations that will connect you with opportunities to volunteer your time and effort with the less fortunate. The Corporation for National and Community Service (www.nationalservice.gov) is the federal government's clearinghouse for volunteer opportunities. You can also try www.dosomething.org or the U.S. Department of Education's Web site (www.ed.gov).

- *Work for economic justice on campus.* Find out if your university has signed on to the Workers' Rights Commission. If they haven't done so, and you feel they should, United Students Against Sweatshops (www.usas.org) can help you (or your school organization) to start a movement on campus. If your school is in compliance, you may want to follow the lead of students on other campuses and be an advocate for the rights (such as living wages) and benefits (such as health insurance) of service employees of the college or university.

- *Spend your money judiciously.* Every day, consumers make decisions about what companies to support (by buying their products) and what companies to oppose (by boycotting their goods or services) with every purchase they make. Some people will drink only fair-trade coffee, which is produced in a way that protects small farmers in coffee-producing countries. Others have boycotted Coca-Cola products to pressure the company to allow their workers in Colombia to unionize.

households in the lowest- and middle-income categories, but it increased for the top categories. Therefore, although the lowest group paid .09 percent *less* as a share of total taxes, the top 20 percent of earners paid 2.1 percent *more*.

What is fair? As long as the rich are still taxed at higher rates, should we worry that the tax cuts are making after-tax income distribution more unequal? After all, as the rich have gotten richer, they have paid an ever higher share of the total federal tax bill. The answer to this question depends on different views about the consequences of income inequality. Those who believe that the growth of income inequality harms the middle class by increasing prices or undermines democracy believe that tax policy should be designed to lessen these inequalities. Those who think that inequality is not a major problem believe that tax cuts give individuals incentives to be productive and thus promote economic growth. In this view, tax policies designed to reduce after-tax income inequalities would be harmful to the society and the economy.[67]

Are Americans concerned about inequality? Do they want economic policy to reduce inequality? A 2003 study by the Princeton political scientist Larry Bartels showed that the public is indeed aware of rising inequality and that a majority think it is a bad thing. Nonetheless, his research showed that people "fail to connect inequality and public policy." Part of the reason is that many people do not understand where they fit in the tax system. One survey showed that half of the respondents thought that "most families" have to pay the estate tax, when in fact only 2 percent of estates had to pay the tax. Americans' aversion to taxes can make it difficult to have a national debate about raising taxes on higher-income earners. This became evident in the waning days of the 2008 campaign. Questioned about his tax plan, Barack Obama defended his proposal to increase taxes for high earners and to allow many Bush-era tax cuts to expire, as scheduled, in 2010. Obama's casual remark that it made sense to "spread the wealth around" ignited a firestorm of criticism from his opponent John McCain, who had pledged not to raise taxes at all. The debate that ensued highlighted the difficulties in conducting a public debate about taxes and inequality.

If widespread concern about inequality is to drive changes in economic policy, the American public needs a better understanding of the relation between economic policy and inequality.

for critical analysis

How does economic policy affect inequality among Americans? Should economic policy makers take equality into account as they decide among different economic tools?

studyguide

Practice Quiz

Find a diagnostic Web Quiz with 37 additional questions on the StudySpace Web site: www.wwnorton.com/we-the-people

Goals of Economic Policy

1. Which of the following is *not* one of the reasons that government is involved in the economy? (pp. 606–07)
   a) to guarantee economic equality
   b) to protect property
   c) to regulate competition
   d) to provide public goods

2. The total value of goods and services produced within a country is referred to as (p. 607)
   a) the Gross National Product.
   b) the Gross Domestic Product.

c) the federal funds rate.
d) the Gini coefficient.

3. Inflation refers to *(p. 611)*
   a) a tax on imported goods.
   b) a consistent increase in the general level of prices.
   c) a consistent decrease in the general level of prices.
   d) an increase in the interest rate on loans between banks.

4. The argument for laissez-faire was first elaborated by *(p. 616)*
   a) James Madison.
   b) Adam Smith.
   c) Alan Greenspan.
   d) Milton Friedman.

5. Which of the following economic perspectives argues for an ongoing role for government in the economy? *(p. 616)*
   a) laissez-faire
   b) Keynesianism
   c) monetarism
   d) rational expectations

6. The theories of which economist were used to help justify the increase in government spending during the New Deal? *(p. 616)*
   a) John Maynard Keynes
   b) Milton Friedman
   c) Robert Lucas
   d) Alan Greenspan

The Tools of Economic Policy

7. Monetary policy seeks to influence the economy through *(p. 618)*
   a) taxing and spending.
   b) the availability of credit and money.
   c) foreign exchange of currency.
   d) administrative regulation.

8. Monetary policy is handled largely by *(p. 618)*
   a) Congress.
   b) the president.
   c) the Department of the Treasury.
   d) the Federal Reserve System.

9. A situation in which the government attempts to affect the economy through taxing and spending is an example of *(p. 620)*
   a) an expropriation policy.
   b) a monetary policy.
   c) a fiscal policy.
   d) eminent domain.

10. A tax that places a greater burden on those who are better able to afford it is called *(p. 621)*
    a) regressive.
    b) progressive.

c) a flat tax.
d) voodoo economics.

11. A policy whose objective is to tax or spend in such a way as to reduce the disparities of wealth between the highest and lowest income brackets is called *(p. 621)*
    a) antitrust policy.
    b) discretionary spending.
    c) deregulation.
    d) redistribution.

12. Which of the following statements best describes the U.S. budget deficit? *(p. 624)*
    a) The budget deficit grew substantially in the 1980s and declined substantially in the 1990s before rising sharply again in the 2000s.
    b) The budget deficit declined substantially in the 1980s and grew substantially in the late 1990s into the new 2000s.
    c) The budget deficit grew consistently between 1980 and the present.
    d) The budget deficit declined consistently between 1980 and the present.

13. Which of the following statements best describes spending in the federal budget? *(p. 625)*
    a) Mandatory and discretionary spending now make up approximately equal parts of the total budget.
    b) Mandatory spending has been outlawed and the total budget is now made up of discretionary spending.
    c) Mandatory spending is now a much larger percentage of the total budget than discretionary spending.
    d) Discretionary spending is now a much larger percentage of the total budget than mandatory spending.

The Environment and the Economy

14. A cap-and-trade system is an example of which kind of policy approach to global warming? *(p. 633)*
    a) mitigation
    b) promoting alternative technologies
    c) adaptation to a warmer climate
    d) Not In My Backyard (NIMBY)

The Politics of Economic Policy Making

15. Which groups currently have the most political influence in economic policy making? *(p. 641)*
    a) consumer groups
    b) labor unions
    c) business groups
    d) environmental groups

Chapter Outline

**Find a detailed Chapter Outline on the StudySpace
Web site: www.wwnorton.com/we-the-people**

Key Terms

**Find Flashcards to help you study these terms on the
StudySpace Web site: www.wwnorton.com/we-the-people**

antitrust policy *(p. 626)*
budget deficit *(p. 623)*
categorical grants *(p. 612)*
contracting power *(p. 629)*
deregulation *(p. 627)*
discretionary spending *(p. 625)*
federal funds rate *(p. 620)*
Federal Reserve System *(p. 618)*
fiscal policy *(p. 620)*
Gross Domestic Product (GDP) *(p. 607)*

inflation *(p. 611)*
Keynesians *(p. 616)*
laissez-faire capitalism *(p. 616)*
loophole *(p. 622)*
mandatory spending *(p. 625)*
monetarists *(p. 616)*
monetary policy *(p. 618)*
monopoly *(p. 626)*
open-market operations *(p. 619)*
progressive taxation *(p. 621)*

public good *(p. 606)*
public policy *(p. 605)*
redistribution *(p. 621)*
regressive taxation *(p. 621)*
reserve requirement *(p. 619)*
subsidy *(p. 628)*
supply-side economics *(p. 617)*
tariff *(p. 621)*
uncontrollable *(p. 625)*

For Further Reading

Auerbach, Alan J., David Card, and John M. Quigley, eds. *Public Policy and the Income Distribution.* New York: Russell Sage Foundation, 2006.

Bryner, Gary C. *Blue Skies, Green Politics: The Clean Air Act of 1990.* Rev. ed. Washington, DC: Congressional Quarterly Press, 1995.

Frank, Robert H. *Falling Behind: How Rising Inequality Harms the Middle Class.* Berkeley: University of California Press, 2007.

Friedman, Milton, and Walter Heller. *Monetary versus Fiscal Policy.* New York: Norton, 1969.

Greider, William. *Secrets of the Temple: How the Federal Reserve Runs the Country.* New York: Simon & Schuster, 1987.

Hacker, Jacob S., and Paul Pierson. *Winner-Take-All Politics: How Washington Made the Rich Richer—and Turned Its Back on the Middle Class* (New York: Simon & Schuster, 2010)

Harris, Richard A., and Sidney M. Milkis. *The Politics of Regulatory Change. 2nd ed.* New York: Oxford University Press, 1996.

Jacobs, Lawrence, and Theda Skocpol, eds. *Inequality and American Democracy: What We Know and What We Need to Learn.* New York: Russell Sage Foundation, 2005.

Page, Benjamin I., and Lawrence R. Jacobs. *Class War: What Americans Really Think about Economic Inequality.* Chicago: University of Chicago Press, 2009.

Schick, Allen. *The Federal Budget: Politics, Policy, Process.* 3rd ed. Washington, DC: Brookings Institution Press, 2007.

Stein, Robert M., and Kenneth N. Bickers. *Perpetuating the Pork Barrel: Policy Subsystems and American Democracy.* New York: Cambridge University Press, 1995.

Stiglitz, Joseph E. *Globalization and Its Discontents.* New York: Norton, 2003.

Weir, Margaret. *Politics and Jobs: The Boundaries of Employment Policy in the United States.* Princeton, NJ: Princeton University Press, 1992.

Recommended Web Sites

Board of Governors of the Federal Reserve System
www.federalreserve.gov

The Federal Reserve System consists of twelve banks that utilize monetary policy to fight inflation and deflation. Visit the "Fed's" official Web site to see how it is working to maintain a strong economy.

Citizens for Tax Justice
www.ctj.org

Review federal, state, and local tax laws at the Web site of Citizens for Tax Justice. This nonprofit organization is dedicated to educating ordinary citizens about tax laws and reducing the tax burden on low- and middle-income Americans.

National Bureau of Economic Research
www.nber.org

The National Bureau of Economic Research (NBER) is a nonprofit, nonpartisan organization dedicated to creating a better understanding of the economy. Take a minute to review some of their free research publications.

Tax Foundation
www.taxfoundation.org/research/topic/9.html

The Tax Foundation is a respected organization that has been providing Americans with information about tax policy for over fifty years. Click on your state to learn about current tax and spending policies.

Treasury Direct
www.treasurydirect.gov/govt/govt.htm

Treasury Direct, part of the U.S. Department of the Treasury, provides a statistical look at federal, state, and public debt.

U.S. Census Bureau: The 2010 Statistical Abstract
www.census.gov/compendia/statab/brief.html

The Annual Statistical Abstract, provided by the U.S. Census Bureau, makes available an abundance of statistics on education, welfare, housing, employment, and agriculture.

U.S. Department of Commerce
www.commerce.gov

The U.S. Department of Commerce promotes domestic and international commerce to foster economic progress. Review the initiatives and programs designed to encourage economic development.

Health care is an area of social policy that has been controversial. Although most Americans support universal access to health care, they disagree about the best way to ensure high-quality health care. As Congress considered various proposals in 2009 and 2010, the debate heated up.

Social Policy

WHAT GOVERNMENT DOES AND WHY IT MATTERS Social policies promote a range of public goals. The first is to protect against the risks and insecurities that most people face over the course of their lives. These include illness, disability, temporary unemployment, and the reduced earning capability that comes with old age. Most spending on social welfare in the United States goes to programs, such as Social Security and medical insurance for the elderly, that serve these purposes. These programs are widely regarded as successful and popular. Although large projected deficits in both programs have generated conflict about these policies, they are the least controversial areas of social spending.

Comprehensive health care reform is more controversial. Most Americans support universal access to health care, but when it comes to specific proposals, they often express doubts. Democrats experienced the public ambivalence about health care reform when they sought to enact major changes to the system in 2010. Although the Democratic Congress and the Obama administration succeeded in enacting landmark health care reform legislation, the reform remained an issue in the 2010 elections as Republicans appealed to voters' concerns about the new law's impact. Fear that reform will be too costly and will jeopardize current health care arrangements makes it difficult to devise a plan that has broad support. After its passage in March 2010, the Obama health care plan began to gain more support in public opinion. But as the 2010 elections approached, 40 percent of Americans still had an unfavorable view of the legislation while 49 percent favored it.[1]

focusquestions

- What do we mean by the "welfare state"?
- What are the goals of education, employment, health, and housing policies?
- Who benefits from social policies?

Two other goals of social policy have also been controversial: promoting equality of opportunity and assisting the poor. Although Americans admire the ideal of equal opportunity, there is no general agreement about what government should do to address inequalities of results: groups that have suffered from past inequality generally support much more extensive government action to promote equality of opportunity than do others. Yet most Americans support some government action, especially in the area of education.

The third goal of social policy—to alleviate poverty—has long generated controversy in the United States. Americans take pride in their strong work ethic and prize the value of self-sufficiency. As a result, the majority of Americans express suspicions that the able-bodied poor will not try hard enough to support themselves if they are offered too much assistance or if they receive the wrong kind of assistance. Yet Americans also recognize that poverty may be the product of past inequality of opportunity. Since the 1960s, a variety of educational programs and income-assistance policies have sought to end poverty and promote equal opportunity. Much progress has been made toward these goals. However, the disproportionate rates of poverty among minorities suggest that our policies have not solved the problem of unequal opportunity. Likewise, the high rates of child poverty challenge us to find new ways to assist the poor.

American social policy reflects the nation's views about which risks should be borne by the individual and which should be shared by society as a whole. As such, social policy reflects public wishes, as would be expected in a democracy. However, Americans often have quite different views about whether social policy should advance the value of equality. There is a broad consensus that equality of opportunity is not only desirable but also an essential part of American culture. There is much less agreement about which social policies are needed to promote equality of opportunity. Americans also have different views about how social policy affects liberty. Some argue that it entails no significant curtailment of liberty, whereas others believe that social policy reduces liberty by increasing the size of government and by raising taxes.

chaptercontents

● What do we mean
by the "welfare
state"?

● The Welfare State

For much of American history, local governments and private charities were in charge of caring for the poor. During the 1930s, when this largely private system of charity collapsed in the face of widespread economic destitution, the federal government created the beginnings of an American welfare state. The idea of the welfare state was new; it meant that the national government would oversee programs designed to promote economic security for all Americans—not just for the poor. The American system of social welfare comprises many different policies enacted over the years since the Great Depression. Because each program is governed by distinct rules, the kind and level of assistance available vary widely.

The History of the Social Welfare System

America has always had a welfare system, but until 1935, it was almost entirely private, composed of an extensive system of voluntary donations through churches and other religious groups, ethnic and fraternal societies, communities and neighborhoods, and philanthropically inclined wealthy individuals. Most often it was called "charity," and although it was private and voluntary, it was thought of as a public obligation.

There were great variations in the generosity of charity from town to town, but one thing seems to have been universal: the tradition of distinguishing between two classes of poverty—the "deserving poor" and the "undeserving poor." The deserving poor were the widows and orphans and others rendered dependent by some misfortune, such as the death or serious injury of the family's breadwinner in the course of honest labor. The undeserving poor were able-bodied persons unwilling to work, transients new to the community, and others of whom, for various reasons, the community did not approve. This private charity was a very subjective matter: the givers and their agents spent a great deal of time and resources examining the qualifications, both economic and moral, of the seekers of charity.

Before the Great Depression, much of the private charity was given in cash, called "outdoor relief." But because of fears that outdoor relief spawned poverty rather than relieving or preventing it, many communities set up settlement houses and other "indoor relief" institutions. Some of America's most dedicated and unselfish citizens worked in the settlement houses, and their efforts made a significant contribution to the development of the field of social work.

A still larger institution of indoor relief was the police station, where many of America's poor sought temporary shelter. But even in the severest weather, the homeless could not stay in police stations for many nights without being jailed as vagrants.[2] Indeed, the settlement houses and the police departments were not all that different in their approaches, since social workers in those days tended to consider "all social case work [to be] mental hygiene."[3] And even though not all social workers were budding psychiatrists, "it was true that they focused on counseling and other preventive techniques, obscuring and even ignoring larger structural problems."[4]

The severe limitations on financing faced by private charitable organizations and settlement houses slowly produced a movement

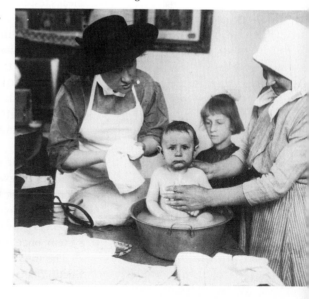

The creation of the modern welfare state in the 1930s shifted responsibility for alleviating poverty from private charities, such as settlement houses, to the government. Chicago's Hull House was one of the most famous settlement houses in the early twentieth century. There, social workers instructed the poor in methods of hygiene and child rearing.

In the early days of the Depression, much of the assistance for the destitute was provided by private groups, through projects such as New York City soup kitchens. Just a few years later, the government became responsible for providing food to needy families.

by many groups toward public assumption of some of these charitable or welfare functions. Workers' compensation laws were enacted in a few states, for example, but the effect of such laws was limited because they benefited only workers injured on the job, and of them, only those who worked for certain types of companies. A more important effort, one that led more directly to the modern welfare state, was public aid to mothers with dependent children. Beginning in Illinois in 1911, the movement for mothers' pensions spread to include forty states by 1926. Initially, such aid was viewed as simply an inexpensive alternative to providing "indoor relief" to mothers and their children. Moreover, applicants not only had to pass a rigorous means test but also had to prove that they were deserving, because the laws provided that assistance would be given only to individuals who were deemed "physically, mentally, and morally fit." In most states, a mother was deemed unfit if her children were illegitimate.[5]

In effect, these criteria proved to be racially discriminatory. Many African Americans in the South and ethnic immigrants in the North were denied benefits on the grounds of "moral unfitness." Furthermore, local governments were allowed to decide whether to establish such pension programs. In the South, many counties with large numbers of African American women refused to implement assistance programs.

Despite the spread of state government programs to assume some of the obligation to relieve the poor, the private sector remained dominant until the 1930s. Even as late as 1928, only 11.6 percent of all relief granted in fifteen of the largest cities came from public funds.[6] Nevertheless, the various state and local public experiences provided guidance and precedents for the national government's welfare system, once it was developed.

The traditional approach, dominated by the private sector with its severe distinction between deserving and undeserving poor, crumbled in 1929 before the stark reality of the Great Depression. During the depression, misfortune became so widespread and private wealth shrank so drastically that private charity was out of the question, and the distinction between deserving and undeserving became impossible to draw. Around 20 percent of the workforce immediately became unemployed; this figure grew as the depression stretched into years. Moreover, few of these individuals had any monetary resources or any family farm on which to fall back. Banks failed, wiping out the savings of millions who had been fortunate enough to have any savings at all. Thousands of businesses failed as well, throwing middle-class Americans onto the bread lines along with unemployed laborers, dispossessed farmers, and those who had never worked in any capacity whatever. The Great Depression proved to Americans that poverty could be a result of imperfections in the economic system as well as of individual irresponsibility. It also forced Americans to alter drastically their standards regarding who was deserving and who was not.

Once poverty and dependency were accepted as problems inherent in the economic system, a large-scale public-policy approach was not far away. By the time the Roosevelt administration took office in 1933, the question was not whether there was to be a public welfare system but how generous or restrictive that system would be.

Foundations of the Welfare State

If the welfare state were truly a state, its founding would be the Social Security Act of 1935. This act created two separate categories of welfare: contributory and noncontributory. The table on the Who Are Americans page lists the key programs in each of these categories, with the year of their enactment, the most recent figures on the number of Americans they benefit, and their cost to the federal government.

Contributory Programs The category of welfare programs that are financed by taxation can justifiably be called "forced savings"; these programs force working Americans to set aside a portion of their current earnings to provide income and benefits during their retirement years. These **contributory programs** are what most people have in mind when they refer to **Social Security** or social insurance. Under the original contributory program—old-age insurance—the employer and the employee were each required to pay equal amounts, which in 1937 were set at 1 percent of the first $3,000 of wages, to be deducted from the paycheck of each employee and matched by the same amount from the employer. This percentage has increased over the years; the contribution in 2010 was 7.65 percent subdivided as follows: 6.2 percent on the first $106,800 of income for Social Security benefits, plus 1.45 percent on all earnings for Medicare.[7]

Social Security may seem to be a rather conservative approach to welfare. In effect, the Social Security tax, as a forced saving, sends a message that people cannot be trusted to save voluntarily to take care of their own needs. But in another sense, it is quite radical. Social Security is not real insurance; workers' contributions do not accumulate in a personal account, as they would in an annuity. Consequently, contributors do not receive benefits in proportion to their own contributions, and this means that a redistribution of wealth is occurring. In brief, Social Security mildly redistributes wealth from higher- to lower-income people, and it quite significantly redistributes wealth from younger workers to older retirees.

contributory programs social programs financed in whole or in part by taxation or other mandatory contributions by their present or future recipients

Social Security a contributory welfare program into which working Americans contribute a percentage of their wages, and from which they receive cash benefits after retirement

After 1935, the federal government created new programs to help poor families. For example, the federally funded school lunch program provides nutritious meals for needy children.

Medicare a form of national health insurance for the elderly and the disabled

indexing periodic process of adjusting social benefits or wages to account for increases in the cost of living

cost-of-living adjustment (COLA) a change made to the level of benefits of a government program based on the rate of inflation

noncontributory programs social programs that provide assistance to people on the basis of demonstrated need rather than any contribution they have made

means testing a procedure by which potential beneficiaries of a public-assistance program establish their eligibility by demonstrating a genuine need for the assistance

Congress increased Social Security benefits every two or three years during the 1950s and 1960s. The biggest single expansion in contributory programs since 1935 was the establishment in 1965 of **Medicare**, which provides substantial medical services to elderly persons who are already eligible to receive old-age, survivors', and disability insurance under the original Social Security system. In 1972, Congress decided to end the grind of biennial legislation to increase benefits by establishing **indexing**, whereby benefits paid out under contributory programs would be modified annually by **cost-of-living adjustments (COLAs)** designed to increase benefits to keep up with the rate of inflation. But, of course, Social Security taxes (contributions) also increased after almost every benefit increase. This made Social Security, in the words of one observer, "a politically ideal program. It bridged partisan conflict by providing liberal benefits under conservative financial auspices."[8] In other words, conservatives could more readily yield to the demands of the well-organized and ever-growing constituency of elderly voters if benefit increases were automatic; liberals could cement conservative support by agreeing to finance the increased benefits through increases in the regressive Social Security tax rather than out of the general revenues coming from the more progressive income tax. (See Chapter 16 for a discussion of regressive and progressive taxes.)

Noncontributory Programs Programs to which beneficiaries do not have to contribute—**noncontributory programs**—are also known as "public assistance programs," or, derisively, as "welfare." Until 1996, the most important noncontributory program was Aid to Families with Dependent Children (AFDC)—originally called Aid to Dependent Children, or ADC—which was founded in 1935 by the original Social Security Act. In 1996, Congress abolished AFDC and replaced it with the Temporary Assistance to Needy Families (TANF) block grant. Eligibility for public assistance is determined by **means testing**, a procedure that requires applicants to show a financial need for assistance. Between 1935 and 1965, the government created programs to provide housing assistance, school lunches, and food stamps to other needy Americans.

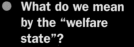
Like contributory programs, the noncontributory public assistance programs also made their most significant advances during the 1960s and 1970s. The largest single category of expansion was the establishment in 1965 of **Medicaid**, a program that provides extended medical services to all low-income persons who have already established eligibility through means testing under AFDC or TANF. Noncontributory programs underwent another major transformation during the 1970s in the level of benefits they provide. Besides being means tested, noncontributory programs are federal rather than national; grants-in-aid are provided by the national government to the states as incentives to establish the programs (see Chapter 3). Thus, from the beginning there were considerable disparities in benefits from state to state. The national government sought to rectify the disparities in levels of old-age benefits in 1974 by creating the Supplemental Security Income (SSI) program to augment benefits for the aged, the blind, and the disabled. SSI provides uniform minimum benefits across the entire nation and includes mandatory COLAs. States are allowed to be more generous if they wish, but no state is permitted to provide benefits below the minimum level set by the national government. As a result, twenty-five states increased their own SSI benefits to the mandated level.

The TANF program is also administered by the states and, as with the old-age benefits just discussed, benefit levels vary widely from state to state (see Figure 17.1). For example, in 2008, the states' monthly TANF benefits for a family of three varied from $170 in Mississippi to $923 in Alaska.[9] Even the most generous TANF payments are well below the federal poverty line. In 2010, the poverty level for a family of three included those earning less than $18,310 a year or $1,524 a month.[10]

The number of people receiving AFDC benefits expanded in the 1970s, in part because new welfare programs had been established during the mid-1960s: Medicaid (discussed earlier) and **food stamps**, which were formerly coupons that could be exchanged for food at most grocery stores and now come in the form of a debit

Medicaid a federally and state-financed, state-operated program providing medical services to low-income people

food stamps a debit card that can be used for food at most grocery stores; the largest in-kind benefits program

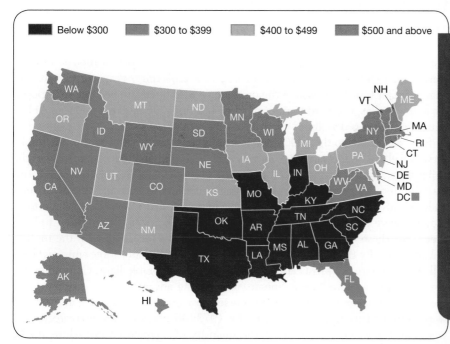

Below $300 $300 to $399 $400 to $499 $500 and above

FIGURE 17.1

Monthly Spending on TANF Benefits

Spending on TANF benefits varies widely across the country. In thirteen states, monthly benefits for a family of three are below $300; in fourteen states, they are above $500 a month. In which regions does spending on TANF benefits tend to be higher? In which regions is it generally lower?

SOURCE: Liz Schott and Zachary Levinson, *TANF Benefits Are Low and Have Not Kept Pace with Inflation* (Washington, DC: Center on Budget and Policy Priorities, November 24, 2008), www.cbpp.org (accessed 3/11/10).

in-kind benefits noncash goods and services provided to needy individuals and families by the federal government

card. These programs provide what are called **in-kind benefits**—noncash goods and services that would otherwise have to be paid for in cash by the beneficiary. Because AFDC recipients automatically received Medicaid and food stamps, these new programs created an incentive for poor Americans to establish their eligibility for AFDC.

Another, more complex reason for the growth of AFDC in the 1970s was that it became more difficult for the government to terminate people's AFDC benefits for lack of eligibility. In the 1970 case of *Goldberg v. Kelly*, the Supreme Court held that the financial benefits of AFDC could not be revoked without due process—that is, a hearing at which evidence is presented, and so on.[11] This ruling inaugurated the concept of **entitlement**, a class of government benefits with a status similar to that of property (which, according to the Fourteenth Amendment, cannot be taken from people "without due process of law"). *Goldberg v. Kelly* did not provide that the beneficiary had a "right" to government benefits; it provided that once a person's eligibility for AFDC was established, and as long as the program was still in effect, that person could not be denied benefits without due process. The decision left open the possibility that Congress could terminate the program and its benefits by passing a piece of legislation. If the welfare benefit were truly a property right, Congress would have no authority to deny it by a mere majority vote.

entitlement a legal obligation of the federal government to provide payments to individuals, or groups of individuals, according to eligibility criteria or benefit rules

Thus the establishment of in-kind benefit programs and the legal obstacles involved in terminating benefits contributed to the growth of the welfare state. But it is important to note that real federal spending on AFDC itself did not rise after the mid-1970s. Unlike Social Security, AFDC was not indexed to inflation; without cost-of-living adjustments, the value of AFDC benefits fell by more than one-third. Moreover, the largest noncontributory welfare program, Medicaid, actually devotes less than one-third of its expenditures to poor families; the rest goes to the disabled and the elderly in nursing homes.[12]

Welfare Reform

The unpopularity of welfare led to widespread calls for reform as early as the 1960s. Public-opinion polls consistently showed that Americans disliked welfare more than any other government program. Although a series of modest reforms were implemented starting in the late 1960s, it took thirty years for Congress to enact a major transformation in the program. Why did welfare become so unpopular, and why was it so hard to reform? How has the 1996 law that replaced AFDC with TANF changed welfare?

From the 1960s to the 1990s, opinion polls consistently showed that the public viewed welfare beneficiaries as "undeserving."[13] Underlying that judgment was the belief that welfare recipients did not want to work. The Progressive-era reformers who first designed AFDC wanted single mothers to stay at home with their children. Motivated by horror stories of children killed in accidents while their mothers were off working or of children tied up at home all day in order to keep them safe, these reformers believed that it was better for the child if the mother did not work. By the 1960s, as more women entered the labor force and as welfare rolls rose, welfare recipients appeared in a more unfavorable light. Common criticisms charged that welfare recipients were taking advantage of the system, that they were irresponsible people who refused to work. These negative assessments were amplified by racial stereotypes. By 1973, 46 percent of welfare recipients were African American. Although the majority of recipients were white, media

Who Benefits from Social Programs?

Almost all Americans benefit from public welfare programs at some point in their lives. The biggest public welfare programs are contributory programs like Social Security (retirement and old-age benefits) and Medicare. Programs that offer income maintenance benefits—including the TANF benefits that people sometimes refer to when they talk about "being on welfare"—are generally smaller and less expensive.

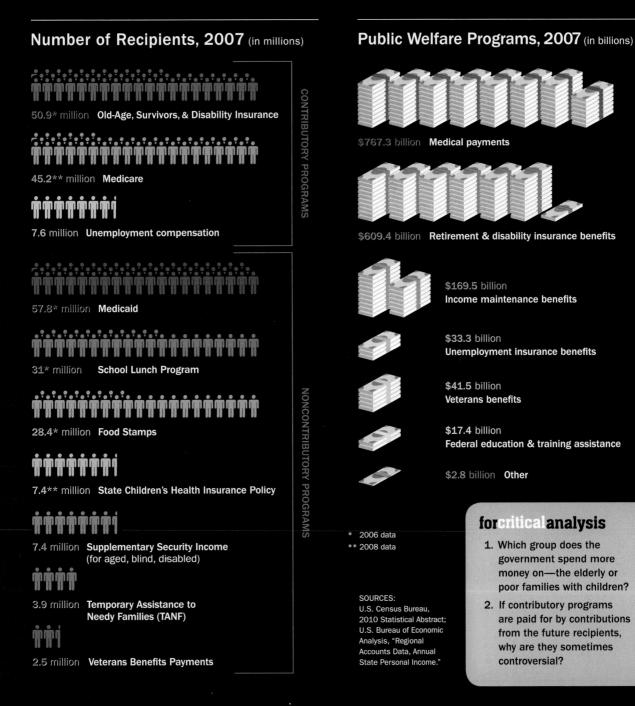

Number of Recipients, 2007 (in millions)

CONTRIBUTORY PROGRAMS

50.9* million   Old-Age, Survivors, & Disability Insurance

45.2** million   Medicare

7.6 million   Unemployment compensation

NONCONTRIBUTORY PROGRAMS

57.8* million   Medicaid

31* million   School Lunch Program

28.4* million   Food Stamps

7.4** million   State Children's Health Insurance Policy

7.4 million   Supplementary Security Income (for aged, blind, disabled)

3.9 million   Temporary Assistance to Needy Families (TANF)

2.5 million   Veterans Benefits Payments

Public Welfare Programs, 2007 (in billions)

$767.3 billion   Medical payments

$609.4 billion   Retirement & disability insurance benefits

$169.5 billion
Income maintenance benefits

$33.3 billion
Unemployment insurance benefits

$41.5 billion
Veterans benefits

$17.4 billion
Federal education & training assistance

$2.8 billion   Other

* 2006 data
** 2008 data

SOURCES:
U.S. Census Bureau,
2010 Statistical Abstract;
U.S. Bureau of Economic
Analysis, "Regional
Accounts Data, Annual
State Personal Income."

for critical analysis

1. Which group does the government spend more money on—the elderly or poor families with children?

2. If contributory programs are paid for by contributions from the future recipients, why are they sometimes controversial?

portrayals helped to create the widespread perception that the vast majority of welfare recipients were black. A careful study by Martin Gilens has shown how racial stereotypes of blacks as uncommitted to the work ethic reinforced public opposition to welfare.[14]

Despite public opposition, it proved difficult to reform welfare. Congress added modest work requirements in 1967 but little changed in the administration of welfare. A more significant reform in 1988 imposed stricter work requirements but also provided additional support services, such as child care and transportation assistance. This compromise legislation reflected a growing consensus that effective reform entailed a combination of sticks (work requirements) and carrots (extra services to make work possible). The 1988 reform also created a new system to identify the absent parent (usually the father) and enforce child-support payments.

These reforms were barely implemented when welfare rolls rose again with the recession of the early 1990s, reaching an all-time high in 1994. Sensing continuing public frustration with welfare, when Bill Clinton was a presidential candidate he vowed "to end welfare as we know it," an unusual promise for a Democrat. Once in office, Clinton found it difficult to design a plan that would provide an adequate safety net for recipients who were unable to find work. One possibility—to provide government jobs as a last resort—was rejected as too expensive. Clinton's major achievement in the welfare field was to increase the Earned Income Tax Credit. This credit allows working parents whose annual income falls below $43,352 (for a family of three or more) to file through their income tax return for an income supplement of up to $5,666, depending on their income and family size. It was a first step toward realizing Clinton's campaign promise to ensure that "if you work, you shouldn't be poor."

for critical analysis

Why was AFDC—commonly called "welfare"—such an unpopular program? How did welfare reform alter the way poor people are assisted? What direction should future reforms to the welfare law take?

Congressional Republicans proposed a much more dramatic reform of welfare, which Clinton, facing a campaign for reelection in 1996, signed. The Personal Responsibility and Work Opportunity Reconciliation Act (PRWORA) repealed AFDC. In place of the individual entitlement to assistance, the new law created block grants to the states and allowed states much more discretion in designing their cash-assistance programs to needy families. The new law also established time limits, restricting recipients to two years of assistance and creating a lifetime limit of five years. It imposed new work requirements on those receiving welfare, and it restricted most legal immigrants from receiving benefits. The aim of the new law was to reduce welfare caseloads, promote work, and reduce out-of-wedlock births. Notably, reducing poverty was not one of its stated objectives.

After this law was enacted, the number of families receiving assistance dropped by 60 percent nationwide (see Figure 17.2). The sharp decline in the number of recipients was widely hailed as a sign that the welfare reform was working. Indeed, former welfare recipients have been more successful at finding and keeping jobs than many critics of the law predicted. One important indicator of how welfare has changed is the proportion of funds it provides in cash assistance. Before the 1996 reform, assistance was provided largely in the form of a cash grant. By 2008, 70 percent of welfare funds were allocated for noncash assistance and 30 percent for cash assistance. This means that an increasing proportion of welfare funds is spent on such costs as assistance with transportation to work, temporary shelter, or one-time payments for emergencies so that people do not go on the welfare rolls. The orientation of assistance has shifted away from subsidizing people who are not in the labor force toward addressing temporary problems that low-income people face and providing assistance that facilitates work.[15] The law has been less successful in other respects: researchers have found no clear evidence that it has

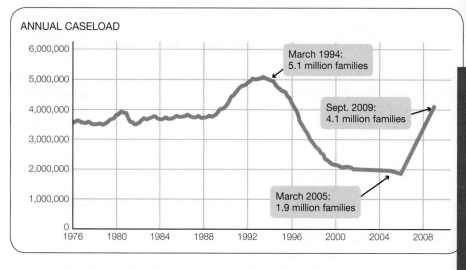

ANNUAL CASELOAD

March 1994:
5.1 million families

Sept. 2009:
4.1 million families

March 2005:
1.9 million families

FIGURE 17.2

Welfare
Caseload,
1982–2009

Welfare caseloads began to decline even before the 1996 reform. They have continued to plummet in the years since welfare reform. Welfare caseloads remained low even during the recession of the early 2000s. Does the decline in the welfare caseload show that the 1996 reform was successful?

SOURCE: U.S. Department of Health and Social Services, Administration for Children and Families, "TANF Total Number of Recipients, Fiscal Year 2009," www.acf.hhs.gov (accessed 3/12/10).

• What do we mean by the "welfare state"?

helped reduce out-of-wedlock births. And critics point out that most former welfare recipients are not paid enough to pull their families out of poverty. Moreover, many families eligible for food stamps and Medicaid stopped receiving these benefits when they left the welfare rolls. The law has helped reduce welfare caseloads, but it has done little to reduce poverty.[16]

Since 1996, two different perspectives on TANF reform have emerged. Democrats have proposed changes that would make the welfare law "an antipoverty weapon."[17] They hope to increase spending on child care, allow more education and training, and relax time limits for those working and receiving welfare benefits. Republicans, by contrast, have proposed stricter work requirements and advocated programs designed to promote marriage among welfare recipients.[18] In 2005 Congress renewed the TANF program and added new funding to promote marriage and fatherhood. As the economy soured in 2009 and 2010, welfare rolls began to move upward but at a very slow rate. The American Recovery and Reinvestment Act of 2009 included a TANF Emergency Fund that provided funds for states to create subsidized jobs for low-income parent and young adults. Despite these measures, many advocates for the poor worried that the state TANF programs were not assisting enough poor families.[19]

How Do We Pay for the Welfare State?

Since the 1930s, when the main elements of the welfare state were first created, spending on social policy has grown dramatically. Most striking has been the growth of entitlement programs, the largest of which are Social Security and Medicare. The costs of entitlement programs grew from 26 percent of the total federal budget in 1962 to 57 percent by 2010. Funds to pay for these social programs have come disproportionately from increases in payroll taxes. In 1970, social insurance taxes accounted for 23 percent of all federal revenues; in 2010 they had grown to 40.4 percent of all federal revenues.[20] During the same time period, corporate taxes fell from 17 percent to 7.2 percent of all federal revenues. Because the payroll tax is regressive, low- and middle-income families have carried the burden for funding increased social spending.

Although much public attention has centered on welfare and other social spending programs for the poor, such as food stamps, these programs account for only a small proportion of social spending. For example, even at its height, AFDC made up only 1 percent of the federal budget. In recent years, Congress has tightly controlled spending on most means-tested programs, and lawmakers and government officials currently express little concern that spending on such programs is out of control. The biggest spending increases have come in social insurance programs that provide broad-based benefits. Such expenditures are hard to control because these programs are entitlements, and the government has promised to cover all people who fit the category of beneficiary. So, for example, the burgeoning elderly population will require that spending on Social Security automatically increase in the future. Furthermore, because Social Security benefits are indexed to inflation, there is no easy way to reduce benefits. Spending on medical programs—Medicare and Medicaid—has also proved difficult to control, in part because of the growing numbers of people eligible for the programs but also because of rising health care costs. Health care expenditures have risen much more sharply than inflation in recent years (Figure 17.3).

Concern about social spending has centered on Social Security because the aging of the baby-boom generation will force spending up sharply in the coming decades. Indeed, under current law, the Social Security Trust Fund—the special government account from which Social Security payments are made—is projected to experience a shortfall beginning in 2037. Critics also contend that Americans are not getting their money's worth from Social Security and that workers would be better off if they could take at least part of the payroll tax that currently pays for Social Security and invest it in individual accounts. They highlight unfavorable rates of return in the current system, noting, for example, that a male worker born in 2000

for critical analysis

Is Social Security a policy "in crisis"? What changes are policy makers discussing to alter Social Security so that future generations can have a secure retirement?

FIGURE 17.3

Federal Social Spending, 1962–2015

Social Security and Medicare, the main entitlement programs that provide pensions and health insurance for people over sixty-five, have grown dramatically since 1962. The federal government spends far more on these two programs, which benefit all elderly people regardless of income, than it does on means-tested programs, which benefit the poor.

SOURCE: Office of Management and Budget, The President's Budget, Historical Tables, Table 8.1, Outlays by Budget Enforcement Act Category, 1962–2015; Table 16.1, Outlays for Health Programs:1962–2015, www .whitehouse.gov (accessed 3/12/10).

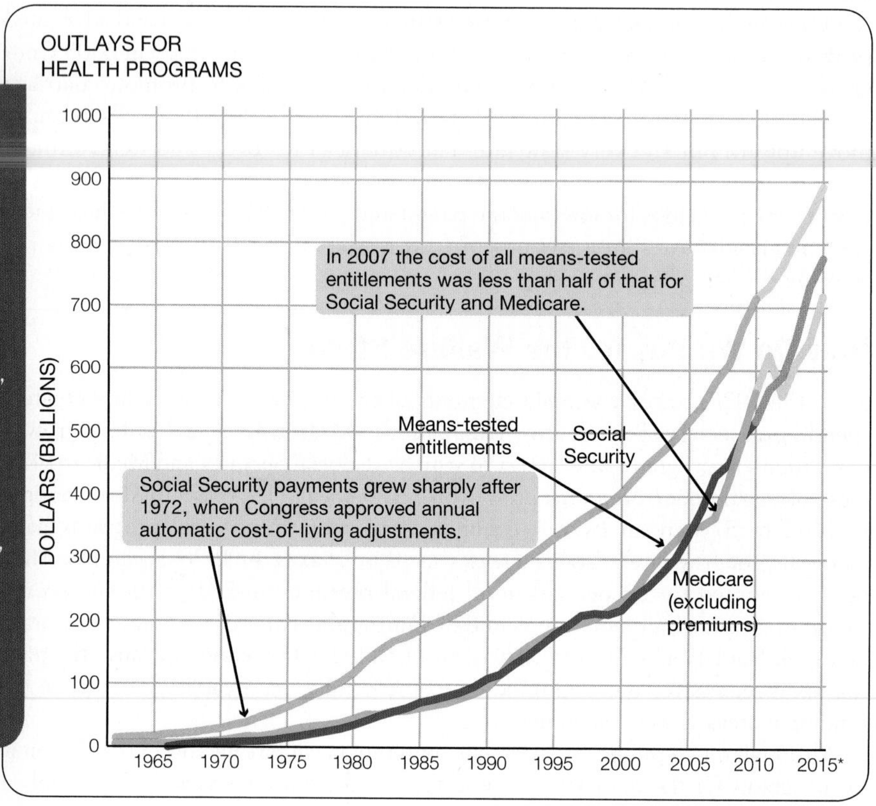

OUTLAYS FOR HEALTH PROGRAMS

In 2007 the cost of all means-tested entitlements was less than half of that for Social Security and Medicare.

Means-tested entitlements

Social Security

Social Security payments grew sharply after 1972, when Congress approved annual automatic cost-of-living adjustments.

Medicare (excluding premiums)

DOLLARS (BILLIONS)

who is single can expect to see a return of only 0.86 percent on his Social Security contributions. This is well below what an insured bank account would pay and far below stock market returns over the past decades.[21]

President George W. Bush came to office supporting Social Security reforms, including the creation of private retirement accounts. Soon after taking office, the president appointed a Social Security Commission, whose final report prominently featured individual accounts as a reform strategy. The commission recommended three reform plans, each of which offered workers the choice of contributing a portion (ranging from 2 to 4 percent) of the payroll tax to an individual account. The worker's traditional benefits would be reduced by the amount diverted to the individual account. According to the commission, individual plans would create a better system because they would allow workers to accumulate assets and build wealth, wealth that could be passed on to their children.[22]

Because Social Security is such a popular program, proposed changes that might weaken it are generally greeted with suspicion. Given the politically volatile character of debates about Social Security, the president backed off from proposing any changes in the program during his first term. Nonetheless, in 2004, immediately after his reelection, Bush announced that he would make Social Security reform a centerpiece of his next administration. Although the president did not put forth a precise plan, private accounts were at the heart of his approach to reform. During the first half of 2005, the president toured the country attempting to win support for his ideas. But he immediately faced huge opposition as unions and AARP mobilized to oppose him. AARP launched a national advertising campaign against private accounts with slogans designed to highlight the risks and radical nature of the president's proposal: "If we feel like gambling, we'll play the slots," and "If you have a problem with the sink, you don't tear down the entire house." Senate Democrats, displaying unusual unity, closed ranks against the president's ideas. By October 2005, the president had to admit that Social Security reform was dead.

Supporters of the current Social Security system contend that the system's financial troubles are exaggerated. They dispute arguments that deficits require cuts in Social Security. They point out that Social Security taxes were raised in 1983 and its trust funds officially placed "off budget" so that the program would be prepared to serve the aging baby-boom generation.[23] They argue that instead of saving that money, however, the federal government cut taxes on the wealthy and used Social Security taxes to finance the deficit. Advocates of the current system believe that many of Social Security's troubles could be solved by raising income taxes on the wealthy and eliminating the cap on payroll taxes. In 2010, only the first $106,800 income was subject to the payroll tax. If this cap were lifted, these critics argue, the resulting revenues would cut the expected shortfall in the Social Security Trust Fund in half.

Supporters of the current system are also deeply skeptical about the benefits of individual accounts. They charged that the president's commission presented a rosy scenario that overestimated likely gains through the stock market. When more realistic assumptions are adopted and the costs of the private accounts are considered, they argue, individual accounts do not provide higher benefits than the current system. Moreover, these critics note that individual accounts would do nothing to solve the budget crisis that Social Security will face.[24]

Finally, supporters of the present system emphasize that Social Security is not just a retirement account but a social insurance program that provides "income protection to workers and their families if the wage earner retires, becomes disabled or dies."[25] Because it provides this social insurance protection, supporters argue, Social Security's returns should not be compared with those of a private retirement account.

Recent reports have estimated that by 2037, the Social Security system will be unable to pay full benefits. President Bush advocated creating private retirement accounts as a way of reforming Social Security, but opponents of the plan successfully argued that it was too risky.

Opening Opportunity

equality of opportunity a widely shared American ideal that all people should have the freedom to use whatever talents and wealth they have to reach their fullest potential

The welfare state not only supplies a measure of economic security, it provides opportunity. The American belief in **equality of opportunity** makes such programs particularly important. Programs that provide opportunity keep people from falling into poverty, and they offer a hand up to those who are poor. At their best, opportunity policies allow all individuals to rise as high as their talents will take them. Four types of policies are most significant in opening opportunity: education policies, employment policies, health policies, and housing policies.

Education Policies

Those who understand American federalism from Chapter 3 already are aware that most of the education of the American people is provided by the public policies of state and local governments. What may be less obvious is that these education policies—especially the policy of universal compulsory public education—are the most important single force in the distribution and redistribution of opportunity in America.

For most of American history, the federal government has played only a minor role in education. In the early years of the nation, the federal government assisted schools through the Land Ordinance of 1785 and the Northwest Ordinance of 1787, both of which ensured that lands were set aside for public schools and their maintenance. In 1862 Congress established land-grant colleges with the Morrill Act. After World War II, the federal government stepped up its role in education policy with the enactment of the GI Bill of Rights of 1944, the National Defense Education Act (NDEA) of 1958, the Elementary and Secondary Education Act of 1965 (ESEA), and various youth and adult vocational training acts since 1958. Note, however, that since the GI Bill was aimed almost entirely at postsecondary schooling, the national government did not really enter the field of elementary education until after 1957.[26]

What finally brought the national government into elementary education was embarrassment that the Soviet Union had beaten the United States into space with the launching of Sputnik. The national policy under NDEA was aimed specifically at improving education in science and mathematics. General federal aid for education did not come until ESEA in 1965, which allocated funds to school districts with substantial numbers of children from families who were unemployed or earning less than $2,000 a year. By the early 1970s, federal expenditures for elementary and secondary education were running over $4 billion per year, and rose to a peak in 1980 at $4.8 billion.[27]

Ronald Reagan's administration signaled a new focus for federal education policy: the pursuit of higher standards. In 1983, the Department of Education issued *A Nation at Risk*, an influential report that identified low educational standards as the cause of America's declining international economic competitiveness. The report did not suggest any changes in federal policy, but it urged states to make excellence in education their primary goal. This theme was picked up again by President George H. W. Bush. Because Republicans have historically opposed a strong federal role in education, the initiatives of Reagan and Bush remained primarily advisory, but they were very influential in focusing educational reform on standards and testing, now widely practiced across the states.

The federal role was substantially increased by President George W. Bush's signature education act, the No Child Left Behind Act of 2001. This act created

for critical analysis

What factors led to the expansion of governmental power (both state and national) over social policy? What factors might lead to a decrease of governmental activity in social policy? How do you think social policy in the United States will change in the future?

stronger federal requirements for testing and school accountability. It requires that every child in grades 3 through 8 be tested yearly for proficiency in math and reading. For a school to be judged a success, it has to show positive test results for all subcategories of children—minority race and ethnicity, English learners, and disability—not just overall averages. Parents whose child is in a failing school have the right to transfer the child to a better school. Because of strong congressional opposition to creating a national test, the states were made responsible for setting standards and devising appropriate tests.

As we saw in Chapter 3, No Child Left Behind initially attracted broad bipartisan support, but it quickly generated considerable controversy. Many states branded it an unfunded mandate, noting that the law placed expensive new obligations on the schools to improve their performance but provided woefully inadequate resources. Teachers objected that "teaching to the test" undermined critical-thinking skills. In some states, up to half the schools failed to meet the new standards, presenting a costly remedial challenge. Under the federal law, they were required to improve student performance by providing such new services as supplemental tutoring, longer school days, and additional summer school.

Faced with these conflicts, the Obama administration sought a major overhaul of No Child Left Behind. Obama's proposal kept some of the features of the original law, including its emphasis on testing and standards. Yet the president's approach broadened the criteria for evaluating schools to include attendance and graduation rates. It also made academic progress, rather than test results, the main criterion for judging a school's academic success. Parts of the president's blueprint for reform immediately attracted controversy. One contentious issue was a proposal to change the criteria for allocating $14 billion in federal assistance to schools (called Title I funds) from a per-pupil formula to a system of competitive grants. The idea aroused intense opposition because it would greatly increase federal power over schools and alter long-standing patterns of funding. The provisions for holding teachers accountable for student achievement provoked antagonism. Teachers' unions charged that the president's plan made the teachers responsible for achievement but gave them no authority over education.[28] Although teachers' unions are a major Democratic backer, Democratic members of Congress appeared supportive of the president's proposals. Even so, controversies over the president's plan promised a vigorous legislative debate over the reform of No Child Left Behind.

The Obama administration has also been a strong supporter of charter schools. Charter schools are publicly funded schools that are free from the bureaucratic rules and regulations of the school district in which they are located. Charter schools are free to design specialized curricula and to use resources in ways they think most effective. Since the creation of the first charter schools in Minnesota in 1990, states across the country have passed legislation to allow them. Many states, however, proceeded slowly, establishing caps on the number of new charter schools that could be created each year. The Obama administration put its weight behind charter schools in one of its first pieces of legislation, the American Reinvestment

Education policy is the most important means of providing equal opportunity for all Americans. President George W. Bush's No Child Left Behind Act of 2001, an education reform bill passed by overwhelmingly bipartisan majorities in Congress, imposes stronger national requirements for school accountability and testing.

and Recovery Act, sometimes called the stimulus bill. The act included a new $4.3 billion program called Race to the Top, which offered competitive grants to state education systems. To be eligible for the grants, states had to agree to lift the caps on the number of charter schools that could be created each year. The administration proposed to continue the grant competition as a component of its No Child Left Behind reform.

Employment and Training Programs

Considering the importance that Americans attach to work and the high value they place on education, it is somewhat surprising that the United States does not have a strong system for employment and job training. Such programs have two goals. One is to prepare entry-level workers for new jobs or to retrain workers whose jobs have disappeared. A second goal is to provide public jobs during economic downturns when sufficient private employment is not available. Since the 1930s, the American employment and training systems have fared poorly in terms of expenditures, stability, and results.[29]

The first public employment programs were launched during the New Deal. These programs were created to use the power of the federal government to get people back to work again. An "alphabet soup" of federal programs sought to employ those who did not have jobs: the Civilian Conservation Corps (CCC) put young men to work on environmental projects in rural areas; and the Works Progress Administration (WPA) employed many different kinds of workers, from writers and artists to manual laborers. In the desperate circumstances of the Great Depression, these public employment programs enjoyed widespread support. But by the end of the 1930s, questions about corruption and inefficiency in employment programs reduced support for them.

Not until the 1960s did the federal government try again. This time, as part of the War on Poverty, government programs were designed to train and retrain workers, primarily the poor, rather than providing them with public employment. For the most part, the results of these programs were disappointing. It proved very difficult to design effective training policies in the federal system; lack of coordination and poor administration plagued the Great Society training programs. Concern about such administrative problems led Congress to combine funds for all the different training programs into a single block grant in 1973, via the Comprehensive Employment and Training Act (CETA). In doing this, Congress hoped that more local flexibility would create more effective programs.

CETA expanded greatly and, as unemployment rose sharply during the 1970s, became primarily a public-service employment program. The federal government provided funds to state and local governments to create jobs for the unemployed. At its peak, CETA had a budget of more than $10 billion and provided jobs for nearly 739,000 workers—12 percent of the nation's unemployed. But complaints soon arose that CETA was providing jobs primarily to people who were the most job ready and was doing little for the most disadvantaged. Congress abolished CETA in 1981, making it one of the only federal programs totally eliminated in the past thirty or so years.[30]

But job training remained a popular idea, and in 1982, Congress created a new program that supported local efforts: the Job Training Partnership Act (JTPA), which became the primary federal program. In addition to retraining adult workers, JTPA provided funding for summer jobs for youth. During the last years of the Clinton administration, the Workforce Investment Act sought to create a

for critical analysis

How did the WPA assist unemployed workers during the Depression of the 1930s? What does the government do to assist workers who lose their jobs today? Do you think that given increasing outsourcing of American jobs, the federal government should do more to help American workers?

● What are the
goals of education,
employment,
health, and housing
policies?

more flexible and accessible job-training system, allowing individual workers to select their own training programs. As part of its effort to stimulate the economy and to assist the unemployed, the Obama administration enacted a variety of new grant programs aimed at offering training for dislocated workers and young people as well as tax credits for employers who retain workers or hire new workers. President Obama also promoted the idea of "green jobs." The stimulus legislation provided funding for a number of training programs for jobs in the energy sector. In his first budget, the president proposed to provide seed funding for clean-energy technology.

As the American economy changes and many corporations transfer operations out of the country or downsize their workforces, the need for retraining has become more pressing. Such training is particularly important for the three-quarters of American workers who have not finished four years of college. Enhancing the ability of the federal government to assist American workers, who face increasing economic insecurity, is one of the most important challenges confronting policy makers today.

Health Policies

Until recent decades, no government in the United States—national, state, or local—concerned itself directly with individual health. But public responsibility was always accepted for *public* health. After New York City's newly created Board of Health was credited with holding down a cholera epidemic in 1867, most states followed with the creation of statewide public health agencies. Within a decade, the results were obvious. Between 1884 and 1894, for example, Massachusetts's rate of infant mortality dropped from 161.3 per 1,000 to 141.4 per 1,000.[31]

The U.S. Public Health Service (USPHS) has been in existence since 1798 but was a small part of public health policy until after World War II. Established in 1937 but little noticed for twenty years was the National Institutes of Health (NIH), an agency within the USPHS that was created to do biomedical research. Between 1950 and 2007, NIH expenditures by the national government increased from $160 million to $28 billion. NIH research on the link between smoking and disease led to one of the most visible public-health campaigns in American history. The Centers for Disease Control and Prevention (CDC), which monitors outbreaks of disease and implements prevention measures, coordinates such public-health campaigns. Subsequently, NIH's focus turned to cancer and acquired immunodeficiency syndrome (AIDS). As with smoking, this work on AIDS resulted in massive public-health education as well as new products and regulations.

Other recent commitments to the improvement of public health are the numerous laws aimed at cleaning up and defending the environment (including the creation in 1970 of the Environmental Protection Agency) and laws attempting to improve the health and safety of consumer products (regulated by the Consumer Product Safety Commission, created in 1972). Health policies aimed directly at the poor include Medicaid and nutritional programs, particularly food stamps and the school lunch program.

In 2010, federal grants to states for Medicaid totaled $251 billion, up from $41 billion in 1990. Federal programs for AIDS research, treatment, prevention, and income support had a budget of $226 billion in 2010, a major increase from the $2.9 billion spent in 1990.[32] President Clinton put greater emphasis on AIDS by appointing an "AIDS czar" to coordinate federal AIDS policy, and by giving this position Cabinet status. Bush continued the practice, appointing his own AIDS

The American Health Care System in Comparison

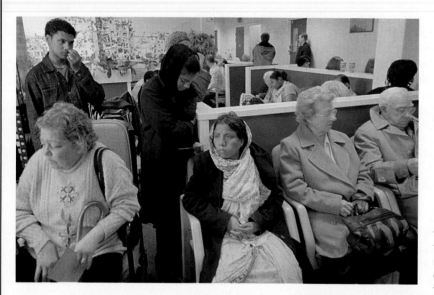

When compared with other advanced democracies, the United States is unique: it is the only one that does not provide universal access to health care. The American approach to health care is a patchwork of different programs. About 60 percent of Americans under the age of sixty-five receive health care from their employers who contract with private insurance companies to provide care. There is also a large federal role—accounting for half of all medical expenditures—composed of three different programs: Medicare, which provides health insurance for people over sixty-five; Medicaid, which covers low-income people, the disabled, and elderly people who need long-term care; and the State Children's Health Insurance Plan (SCHIP), a federal-state program for uninsured children.

The trouble with the American approach is twofold: it leaves some people without coverage, and it is expensive. Not all employers provide health insurance for their workers, and not all workers opt to purchase the health plans that employers offer. The number of unin-

sured in 2007 was 45.7 million, or around 16 percent of the population. Moreover, the American system is the world's most expensive. The costs of health care in the United States have made it increasingly difficult for individuals to pay for care, even with employer help. And employers complain that the costs of providing health care are making them uncompetitive in world markets.

The health systems in Europe and Canada rely on two different models to offer universal coverage at much lower cost than in the United States. The first model is the single-payer approach; the second is the compulsory insurance model.

In single-payer systems, the government plays the central role in collecting revenues to fund health care, and it pays for the care that is supplied. The fact that the government is the "single payer" allows it to bargain for the lowest prices from providers. The French system has been called the best in the world because of the broad coverage it provides at low costs, along with provisions that allow those who want to pay more for extra services to do so.[a]

The compulsory insurance model is used in Germany, the Netherlands, and Switzerland. In these countries, individuals make contributions to "sickness funds," which are public-private organizations that pay for and provide health care. Many of the funds are attached to work settings, similar to employer-provided health insurance in the United States. What is different in these systems is that the sickness funds are highly regulated by the government: funds are required to provide specific basic services and are not allowed to expel individuals if they lose their jobs.

The health care legislation passed by the U.S. Congress in 2010 is a step toward providing broader coverage, but it remains to be seen how well it addresses concerns about the American system.

[a]Victor G. Rodwin, "The Health Care System under French National Health Insurance: Lessons for Health Reform in the United States," *American Journal of Public Health* 93, no. 1 (2003), 31–37.

for critical analysis

1. What is a single-payer system of health care? How does it differ from that of the United States? What are some of the political obstacles to creating a single-payer system in the United States?

2. How do compulsory health insurance systems work? Do you think this system could work in the United States? Why or why not?

czar. However, the position has been a difficult balancing act among advocates, health care professionals, and the realities of government finances.

Health Care Reform

Until the passage of Patient Protection and Affordable Care Act in March 2010, the United States was the only advanced industrial nation without universal access to health care. Opposition from the American Medical Association, the main lobbying organization of doctors, prevented President Roosevelt from proposing national health insurance during the 1930s, when other elements of the welfare state became law. As a result, the United States developed a patchwork system: in early 2010, approximately 60 percent of the nonelderly population received health insurance through their employer, older Americans were covered through Medicare, and the poor and disabled were assisted with Medicaid. However, the growing costs of employer-provided insurance means that increasing numbers of workers cannot afford it. Many small employers cannot even afford to offer benefits because they are so expensive. And both Medicaid and Medicare face severe fiscal strain due to rising costs.

President Clinton's major attempt to reshape federal health policy, and the boldest policy initiative of his administration, was his effort to reform America's health care system. In September 1993, Clinton announced a plan with two key objectives: to limit the rising costs of the American health care system and to provide universal health insurance coverage for all Americans (more than 41 million Americans lacked health insurance). Clinton's plan at first garnered enormous public support and seemed likely to win congressional approval in some form. But the plan, which entailed a major expansion of federal administration of the health care system, gradually lost momentum as resistance to it took root among those who feared changes in a system that worked well for them. Although Clinton had pledged to make health care the centerpiece of his 1994 legislative agenda, no health care bill even came up for a full congressional vote that year. Following the failure of

Some recent public health initiatives have sought to promote healthier diets and combat obesity by requiring restaurants to provide calorie counts or by banning trans fat. As part of the 2010 health reform bill, the federal government stipulated that chain restaurants provide calorie counts for standard menu items, as at this Subway restaurant.

President Clinton's health care initiative, Congress passed a much smaller program expanding health insurance coverage for low-income children not already receiving Medicaid, called the State Children's Health Insurance Program.

Medicare Reform In 2003, Congress enacted a major reform of the Medicare program, which has provided health care to seniors since 1964. Most notably, Congress added a prescription-drug benefit to the package of health benefits for the elderly. The high cost of prescription drugs had been an issue of growing concern to millions of older Americans. Yet the bill proved very controversial. Critics charged that the bill included a sweetheart deal with drug companies, because the legislation contained a provision prohibiting the federal government from using its purchasing power to reduce drug prices. Many Democrats also objected to the legislation because it opened the door for private health plans to play a significant role in health care provision for the elderly. They feared that the entry of such plans would significantly weaken Medicare, which has been one of the most strongly supported federal social programs. Fiscal conservatives worried about the costs of the prescription-drug package. This concern escalated several months after the bill's passage when the administration issued new, much higher cost estimates for the prescription-drug benefit than the estimates presented when the bill was being debated. Adding fuel to the growing controversy over drug prices was the disclosure that the former Medicare administrator had prevented his chief actuary from releasing the higher cost estimates to Congress as it was considering the Medicare bill.

The conflict over Medicare reform highlights the problems surrounding health care more generally. A majority of Americans believe that government should ensure that all people receive adequate health care. Yet how to deliver such benefits and how to pay for them are extremely contentious issues. In the 2008 presidential campaign, once again, the old question captured political attention: why can't the richest country in the world provide access to health care for all its citizens?[33]

Health Care Legislation in 2010 After the 2008 election, the Obama administration and the Democratic Congress pressed forward with comprehensive health reform. Seeking to avoid the conflicts that broke out in Congress over the Clintons' fully formed and highly complex health reform proposal, Obama offered Congress broad principles for reform, not a detailed proposal. The administration aimed at covering most Americans who lacked health insurance with a reform strategy that built on the existing system. The plan that ultimately passed had three key features: the first was the creation of new state-based insurance exchanges where individuals could buy health insurance, along with insurance regulation that would prohibit insurers from denying benefits for a variety of reasons such as preexisting conditions; the second was a provision requiring uninsured individuals to purchase health insurance known as "the individual mandate"; and the third was a set of subsidies to help the uninsured and small businesses purchase insurance as well as an expansion of the public programs Medicaid and the SCHIP. One controversial provision considered was a "public option" that would allow individuals to purchase government-provided insurance from the insurance exchange. Aware that this idea had become a flashpoint for opponents, Democratic congressional leaders ultimately dropped it from consideration in their final negotiations.

Even so, opponents branded the reform proposals as "big government" and sometimes as "socialism," a charge that has been levied against health reform initiatives since the 1940s. Republicans closed ranks against the proposal, meaning that all the credit—or blame—for the act would fall on the Democrats.

Health Policy in Television and Film

For many Americans, issues surrounding health policy are complicated and may seem somewhat abstract until they affect friends, family, or themselves. While politicians and the news media can highlight important health policy issues, another less direct route of information and influence comes in the form of entertainment programming.

Primetime medical dramas like NBC's *ER* or Fox's *House* often illustrate how health policy affects individual citizens' lives, without abstractions or statistics. Programs like *ER* and *House* portray individual characters struggling with issues like malpractice, whether or not to resuscitate a loved one, or how they are going to afford their medical treatment. The

THIS MIGHT HURT A LITTLE.

MICHAEL MOORE
SiCKO

plots reveal the practical and emotional implications of these issues, and may make them more meaningful to the audience. Because of this potential influence on viewers, in some cases researchers have even worked with the writers and producers of medical dramas to make certain that the health information presented is accurate and helpful.

In addition, researchers are studying the content of medical dramas to determine how health policy debates are presented, who is engaged in the debates, and whether they are balanced. A report by the Kaiser Family Foundation from July 2002 concluded that the kinds of health policy debates presented in American medical dramas fell into two main categories: (1) resource issues like HMOs, Medicare, Medicaid, and disparities in insurance coverage, and (2) ethical issues such as patients' rights, end-of-life options, stem-cell research, and clinical drug trials. However, ethical issues, with their dramatic content, were far more likely to receive attention than were resource issues. Some issues such as the problems of long-term care or problems of the uninsured received little attention in these programs. Most policy debates presented in the programs were relevant to current legislative debates or other health policy discussions in the news. In general, the study found that medical shows present balanced portrayals of health policy debates, with both sides equally represented in the discussions.

The controversial filmmaker Michael Moore tackled health care in his 2007 film *Sicko*. Rather than attempting to balance both sides, Moore's message was very clear—the American system is deeply flawed and in desperate need of reform. *Sicko* relied on a series of vignettes to illustrate that the American health care system fails to serve not only those without health insurance but also

those who pay for it. Moore introduces, for example, a man who accidentally sawed off two fingers but can only afford to have one of the fingers sewn back on. Another story follows a 9/11 volunteer who is denied the treatment he needs for a lung condition he developed while digging through the rubble of the World Trade Center.

There is some evidence to suggest that *Sicko* may have had a significant impact on the debate about health care in America. A survey by the Kaiser Family Foundation found that although only 4 percent of the public had seen *Sicko,* 42 percent had heard or read about it. More important, of those who had seen, heard about, or read about *Sicko,* 43 percent said the movie made them more likely to think that the health care system in America needs reform and 27 percent said they were paying closer attention to the positions of presidential candidates on health care as a result of the film.[a]

[a]Survey by Henry J. Kaiser Family Foundation, Princeton Survey Research Associates International, August 2–8, 2007.

for critical analysis

1. What are some of the drawbacks of getting information about complex health policies from entertainment television and movies? What are some possible advantages?

2. Most Americans believe that the government should ensure that all citizens receive adequate health care. What are some of the obstacles to implementing universal health care? What are some possible solutions?

The Democrats did ultimately enact comprehensive health care reform in 2010 through a set of complex parliamentary maneuvers, but the politics of health care reform continued to loom large in the 2010 congressional elections. Republicans appealed to ongoing public uncertainty about the new legislation and promised to repeal it if they won control of Congress.

As noted in the chapter introduction, a sizeable minority of Americans opposed the act and a majority remained confused about exactly what the act would do. Seniors (those aged over 65) were among the strongest opponents of the law with 49 percent opposed to the law compared to 38 percent in favor.[34] Seniors were concerned that they would not see any new benefit from the law, since most already receive generous health coverage through the Medicare plan, with nearly half of seniors worried that they would have a harder time getting benefits under the new law. In fact, the law offers a mixture of new benefits to seniors along with higher premiums for higher income Medicare recipients. Tea Party activists also mobilized against the law. One poll showed that 68 percent of Tea Party activists viewed the law unfavorably.[35]

The new health reform law faced challenges in public opinion and from state governments. Twenty-one state attorney generals filed lawsuits against the legislation on the grounds that the provision requiring individuals to purchase health insurance expanded the Commerce Clause beyond its constitutional limits. The states also objected to provisions that required them to expand their Medicaid programs to cover more poor people. These suits began to wind their way through the federal court system and may well end up being decided by the Supreme Court.

Housing Policies

The United States has one of the highest rates of home ownership in the world, and the central thrust of federal housing policy has been to promote home ownership. The federal government has traditionally done much less to provide housing for low-income Americans who cannot afford to buy homes. Federal housing programs were first created during the Great Depression of the 1930s, when many Americans found themselves unable to afford housing.

Through public housing for low-income families, which originated in 1937 with the Wagner-Steagall National Housing Act, and subsidized private housing after 1950, the percentage of American families living in overcrowded conditions was reduced from 20 percent in 1940 to 9 percent in 1970. Federal policies made an even greater contribution to reducing "substandard" housing, defined by the U.S. Census Bureau as dilapidated houses without hot running water and without some other plumbing. In 1940, almost 50 percent of American households lived in substandard housing. By 1950, this had been reduced to 35 percent; by 1975, to 8 percent.[36] Despite these improvements in housing standards, federal housing policy until the 1970s was largely seen as a failure. Restricted to the poorest of the poor, marked by racial segregation and inadequate spending, public housing contributed to the problems of the poor by isolating them from shopping, jobs, and urban amenities. Dilapidated high-rise housing projects stood as a symbol of the failed American policy of "warehousing the poor." By the 1980s, the orientation of housing policy had changed: most federal housing policy for low-income Americans came in the form of housing vouchers (called Section 8 vouchers) that provided recipients with support to rent in the private market. Although this program did not promote the same kind of isolation of the poor, it was often useless in very active housing markets where the vouchers provided too little money to cover rental costs.

In 2008 and 2009, as a growing
number of Americans found they
could not afford the mortgages
on their homes, the government
authorized measures to help
people keep their homes. Critics
of the government's response said
that the measures did not do
enough to help homeowners and
were intended mainly to help big
financial companies.

The Clinton administration at first showed a strong ideological commitment
to encouraging housing policies and combating homelessness. But especially after
1994, the Clinton administration began to retreat. HUD Secretary Henry Cisneros
continually had to waive, virtually to the point of abandonment, a long-standing
one-for-one HUD rule that provided that for every public housing unit destroyed,
another would have to be built. The Bush administration placed less emphasis on
housing policy. It proposed transforming the federal voucher program into a block
grant to the states. The initiative, which never came to a vote in Congress, faced
opposition from housing proponents who feared that it would greatly reduce assistance to low-income renters.

Beginning in 2007 and 2008, a home loan foreclosure crisis presented the government with a different kind of housing problem. During the housing boom of the early
2000s, many homeowners received loans that they later could not afford to repay. As a
result, millions of homeowners were in danger of losing their homes as they defaulted
on their mortgage payments. Moreover, the magnitude of bad debt harmed banks and
threatened to destabilize the entire economy. The federal government responded with
a plan that would slow the rising interest rates that were the cause of the problem
for some homeowners. It also created several additional programs designed to help
homeowners facing foreclosure. However, these programs did not experience much
success. As a result, many people lost their homes, and the broader economy felt the
strain as the effects of the defaulted loans filtered through the economic system.

Who Gets What from Social Policy?

The two categories of social policy—contributory and noncontributory—generally
serve different groups of people. We can understand much about the development
of social policy by examining which constituencies benefit from different policies.

The strongest and most generous programs are those in which the beneficiaries
are widely perceived as deserving of assistance and also are politically powerful.

Because Americans prize work, constituencies that have "earned" their benefits in some way or those who cannot work because of a disability are usually seen as most deserving of government assistance. Politically powerful constituencies are those who vote as a group, lobby effectively, and mobilize to protect the programs from which they benefit.

When we study social policies from a group perspective, we can see that the elderly and the middle class receive the most benefits from the government's social policies and that children and the working poor receive the fewest. In addition, America's social policies do little to change the fact that minorities and women are more likely than white men to be poor.

The Elderly

The elderly are the beneficiaries of the two strongest and most generous social policies: old-age pensions (what we call Social Security) and Medicare (medical care for the elderly). As these programs have grown, they have provided most elderly Americans with economic security and have dramatically reduced the poverty rate among the elderly. In 1959, before very many people over the age of sixty-five received social insurance, the poverty rate for the elderly was 35 percent; by 2008, it had dropped to 9.7 percent.[37] Because of this progress, many people call Social Security the most effective antipoverty program in the United States.[38] This does not mean that the elderly are rich, however; in 2008, the median income of elderly households was $29,744, well below the national median income.[39] The aim of these programs is to provide security and prevent poverty rather than to assist people once they have become poor. And they have succeeded in preventing poverty among most of the aged.

One reason that Social Security and Medicare are politically strong is that the elderly are widely seen as a deserving population. They are not expected to work, because of their age. Moreover, both programs are contributory, and a work history is a requirement for receiving a Social Security pension. But these programs are

In 1995, the Republican-led Congress proposed cuts in Medicare spending, prompting vigorous protests from senior citizens. Fearing negative political repercussions in the 1996 elections, Congressional Republicans retreated from their efforts to overhaul the Medicare system. In 2003, the support of senior groups like AARP was critical to the passage of a new Medicare prescription drug plan.

also strong because they serve a constituency that has become quite powerful. The elderly are a very large group: in 2008, there were 38.9 million Americans over the age of sixty-five. Because Social Security and Medicare are not means tested, they are available to nearly all people over the age of sixty-five, whether they are poor or not. The size of this group is of great political importance because the elderly turn out to vote in higher numbers than the rest of the population.

In addition, the elderly have developed strong and sophisticated lobbying organizations that can influence policy making and mobilize elderly Americans to defend these programs against proposals to cut them. One important and influential organization that defends the interests of older people in Washington is AARP. The initials originally stood for the American Association of Retired Persons, but in 1999, the organization changed its name to its initials only. This is because 44 percent of AARP members work full or part time. AARP had over 40 million members in 2010, amounting to one-fifth of all voters. It also has a sophisticated lobbying organization in Washington, which employs twenty-eight lobbyists and a staff of 165 policy analysts.[40] (See Chapter 11 for more discussion of AARP's lobbying efforts.) Although AARP is the largest and the strongest organization of the elderly, other groups, such as the Alliance for Retired Americans, to which many retired union members belong, also lobby Congress on behalf of the elderly.

When Congress considers changes in programs that affect the elderly, these lobbying groups pay close attention. They mobilize their supporters and work with legislators to block changes they believe will hurt the elderly.[41] As we saw in Chapters 11 and 16, the power of this lobby was apparent in 2003, and in 2005, during the effort to reform Social Security. AARP had long opposed any reform that allowed private health care firms to provide Medicare benefits. But in 2003, it changed its position and supported the president's bill, which combined prescription drug benefits and an opening for private firms. AARP's vocal support—including its television advertisements in favor of the bill—was widely credited with making the legislative victory possible. In 2005, AARP switched sides and opposed the president's proposals to reform Social Security. AARP opposition was a key factor in the proposal's failure to attract political support. In 2009 and 2010, AARP came out in support of health reform, although it avoided endorsing any specific bill. Although thousands of members left the organization in protest, their actions had little impact given the size of the organization.

The Middle Class

Americans don't usually think of the middle class as benefiting from social policies, but government action promotes the social welfare of the middle class in a variety of ways. First, medical care and pensions for the elderly help the middle class by relieving them of the burden of caring for elderly relatives. Before these programs existed, old people were more likely to live with and depend financially on their adult children. Many middle-class families whose parents and grandparents are in nursing homes rely on Medicaid to pay nursing-home bills.

In addition, the middle class benefits from what some analysts call the shadow welfare state.[42] These are the social benefits that private employers offer to their workers: medical insurance and pensions, for example. The federal government subsidizes such benefits by not taxing the payments that employers and employees make for health insurance and pensions. These **tax expenditures**, as they are called, are an important way the federal government helps ensure the social welfare of the middle class. (Such programs are called "tax expenditures" because the federal

tax expenditures government subsidies provided to employers and employees through tax deductions for amounts spent on health insurance and other benefits

government helps finance them through the tax system rather than by direct spending.) Another key tax expenditure that helps the middle class is the tax exemption on mortgage interest payments: taxpayers can deduct the amount they have paid in interest on a mortgage from the income they report on their tax return. By not taxing these payments, the government makes home ownership less expensive.

People often don't think of these tax expenditures as part of social policy because they are not as visible as the programs that provide direct payments or services to beneficiaries. But tax expenditures represent a significant federal investment: they cost the national treasury some $945 billion a year and make it easier and less expensive for working Americans to obtain health care, save for retirement, and buy homes.[43] These programs are very popular with the middle class, and Congress rarely considers reducing them. On the few occasions when public officials have tried to limit these programs—with proposals to limit the amount of mortgage interest that can be deducted, for example—they have quickly retreated. These programs are simply too popular among Americans whose power comes from their numbers at the polling booth.

The Working Poor

People who are working but are poor or are just above the poverty line receive only limited assistance from government social programs. This is somewhat surprising, given that Americans value work so highly. But the working poor are typically employed in jobs that do not provide pensions or health care; often they are renters because they cannot afford to buy homes. This means they cannot benefit from the shadow welfare state that subsidizes the social benefits enjoyed by most middle-class Americans. At the same time, however, they cannot get assistance through programs such as Medicaid and TANF, which are largely restricted to the nonworking poor.

Two government programs do assist the working poor: the Earned Income Tax Credit (EITC) and food stamps. The EITC was implemented in 1976 to provide poor workers some relief from increases in the taxes that pay for Social Security. As

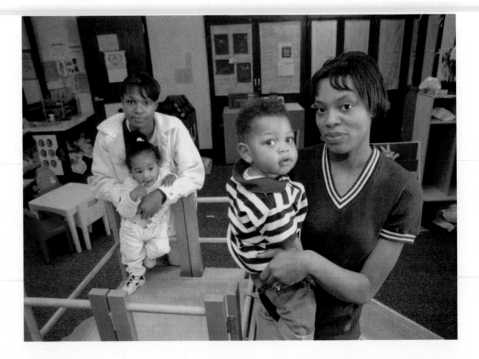

The poor and working poor (including many single mothers with children) have little influence on government. Although organized protests representing their interests occasionally do occur, they fail to have the impact of similar protests by other groups, such as senior citizens.

it has expanded, the EITC has provided a modest wage supplement for the working poor, allowing them to catch up on utility bills or pay for children's clothing.

Poor workers can also receive food stamps. These two programs help supplement the income of poor workers, but they offer only modest support. Because the wages of less-educated workers have declined significantly over the past fifteen years and minimum wages have not kept pace with inflation, the problems of the working poor remain acute.

Even though the working poor may be seen as deserving, they are not politically powerful because they are not organized. There is no equivalent to AARP for the poor. Nonetheless, because work is highly valued in American society, politicians find it difficult to cut the few social programs that help the working poor. In 1995, efforts to cut the EITC were defeated by coalitions of Democrats and moderate Republicans, although Congress did place new restrictions on food stamps and also reduced the level of spending on this type of aid.

The Nonworking Poor

The only nonworking, able-bodied poor people who receive federal cash assistance are parents who are caring for children. The primary source of cash assistance for these families was AFDC and now is the state-run TANF program, but they also rely on food stamps and Medicaid. Able-bodied adults who are not caring for children are not eligible for federal assistance other than food stamps. Many states provide small amounts of cash assistance to such individuals through programs called "general assistance," but in the past decade, many states have abolished or greatly reduced their general assistance programs in an effort to encourage these adults to work. Thus, the primary reason the federal government provides any assistance to able-bodied adults is that they are caring for children. Although Americans don't like to subsidize adults who are not working, they do not want to harm children.

AFDC was the most unpopular social spending program ever undertaken by the federal government; as a result, spending on it declined after 1980. Under TANF, states receive a fixed amount of federal funds, whether the welfare rolls rise or fall. Because the number of people on welfare has declined so dramatically since 1994—by over 50 percent—states have had generous levels of federal resources for the remaining welfare recipients. Many states, however, have used the windfall of federal dollars to cut taxes and indirectly support programs that benefit the middle class, not the poor.[44] Welfare recipients have little political power to resist cuts in their benefits. During the late 1960s and early 1970s, the short-lived National Welfare Rights Organization sought to represent the interests of welfare recipients. But keeping the organization in operation proved difficult because its members and its constituents had few resources and were difficult to organize.[45] Because welfare recipients are widely viewed as undeserving, and because they are not politically organized, they have played little part in recent debates about welfare.

Minorities, Women, and Children

Minorities, women, and children are disproportionately poor. Much of this poverty is the result of disadvantages that stem from the position of these groups in the labor market. African Americans and Latinos tend to be economically less well-off than the rest of the American population. In 2009, the poverty rate for African Americans was 24.6 percent, and for Latinos it was 23.2 percent. Both rates are more than double the poverty rate for non-Hispanic whites, which was 8.6 percent.[46] The median income for black households in 2008 was $34,218. For

for critical analysis

Two factors that seem to influence a particular group's ability to get what it wants from social policy are: (1) the perception that the group is deserving; and (2) the political organization and power of the group. How has each of these factors affected social policy in recent years?

Hispanics it was $37,913, whereas for non-Hispanic white households the median household income was $52,312.[47] Much of this economic inequality occurs because minority workers tend to have low-wage jobs. Minorities are also more likely to become unemployed and to remain unemployed for longer periods of time than are white Americans. African Americans, for example, typically have experienced twice as much unemployment as other Americans have. The combination of low-wage jobs and unemployment often means that minorities are less likely to have jobs that give them access to the shadow welfare state. They are more likely to fall into the precarious categories of the working poor or the nonworking poor.

In the past several decades, policy analysts have begun to talk about the "feminization of poverty," or the fact that women are more likely than men to be poor. This problem is particularly acute for single mothers, who are more than twice as likely to fall below the poverty line than the average American (see Figure 17.4). When the Social Security Act was passed in 1935, the main programs for poor women were Aid to Dependent Children (ADC) and survivors' insurance for widows. The framers of the act believed that ADC would gradually disappear as more women became eligible for survivors' insurance. The social model behind the Social Security Act was that of a male breadwinner with a wife and children. Women were not expected to work, and if a woman's husband died, ADC or survivors' insurance would help her stay at home and raise her children. The framers of Social Security did not envision today's large number of single women heading families. At the same time, they did not envision that so many women with children would also be working. This combination of changes helped make AFDC (the successor program to ADC) more controversial. Many people asked, Why shouldn't welfare recipients work, if the majority of women who are not on welfare work? Such questions

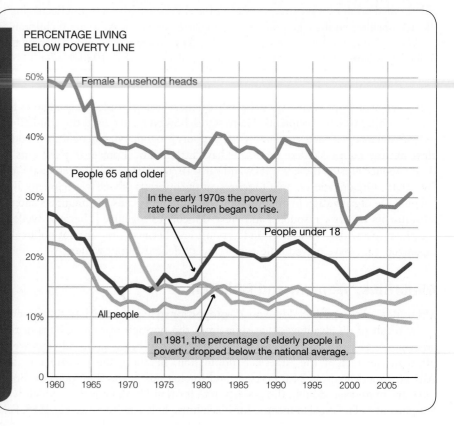

FIGURE 17.4

Poverty Level in the United States, 1960–2008

Poverty among all Americans has declined markedly since 1960. However, the rate of progress has varied significantly across groups. Female-headed households have made the slowest progress, although poverty rates for this group have dropped sharply since 1994. Which group has seen the greatest reduction in its poverty level since 1960?

SOURCE: U.S. Census Bureau, Current Population Survey, Annual Social and Economic (ASEC) Supplement, "POV01: Age and Sex of All People, Family Members and Unrelated Individuals Iterated by Income-to-Poverty Ratio and Race: 2008," www.census.gov; "POV02. People in Families by Family Structure, Age, and Sex, Iterated by Income-to-Poverty Ratio and Race," www.census.gov (accessed 3/14/10).

PERCENTAGE LIVING BELOW POVERTY LINE

Female household heads

People 65 and older

In the early 1970s the poverty rate for children began to rise.

People under 18

All people

In 1981, the percentage of elderly people in poverty dropped below the national average.

Take an Active Stance on Social Problems

In June 2008, a small group of young people from across the country went to Washington, D.C., for a two-day "Youth Entitlement Summit." These young men and women spent their days in congressional hearing rooms, conducting their own hearings, where they questioned leading experts about the current and future state of Social Security, the health care crisis, and the underrepresentation of youth voices in current debates. At the end of the summit, they had developed a series of policy statements on these key issues—and a blueprint for continuing to educate themselves and others. Their goal was to help shape the debate rather than simply react to the plans offered by elected officials or other organizations.

As this chapter illustrates, social policy affects all aspects of our lives. The decisions we make as a society concerning issues such as these reflect our national values. So, when we increase spending on federal grants for higher education we make a commitment to expand access to college for low- and middle-income students. When we require welfare recipients to move to work or risk losing their benefits, we emphasize our commitment to self-reliance. And if we allow individuals to invest some of their Social Security taxes in the private market, we underscore our faith in liberty and choice.

Social policy also reflects what we believe about responsibility. It illustrates what we think about our responsibility to each other and what we are willing to do for each other as members of a shared polity. With so many issues (and with limits on our ability to fund everything), it may be hard to decide what to support or what you want the government to do. Certainly, many people feel so overwhelmed or intimidated that they opt out of the debate altogether. But others, like the young people at the YES summit, decide to educate themselves about the issues and take an active role in the national conversation. You can do so as well.

- You can start by thinking through debates over major social policies and finding out where you fit. Two issues that have been debated recently are health care reform and immigration. A good place to start developing a deeper understanding of these issues is the Public Agenda Foundation (www.publicagenda.org/issues/issue-home.cfm), which provides background on various issues.

- Many people across the political spectrum see an important role for nonprofit organizations, including faith-based groups, to work with (or instead of) government in providing key services to those in need. The Roundtable on Religion and Social Policy (from SUNY Rochester), www.religionandsocialpolicy.org/, provides independent analysis of this phenomenon. The Web site includes an overview of what faith-based initiatives mean, an analysis of their effectiveness in addressing social problems, and insight into key state initiatives.

- Immigration reform is a perennial issue in American politics. As much as we like to think of ourselves as the proverbial "melting pot," the influx of immigrants, many of whom are here illegally, challenges our embrace of diversity. By working through a campus organization (student government, campus Democrats or Republicans, etc.), you might consider staging a debate with experts on both sides of the issue. Groups that you might consider contacting for speakers include the American Civil Liberties Union (www.aclu.org), American Conservative Union (www.conservative.org), National Council of La Raza (www.nclr.org), and the Asian American Legal Defense and Education Fund (www.aaldef.org).

led to the welfare reform of 1996, which created TANF, specifically meant as a means of temporary assistance to families.

The need to combine work and child care is a problem for most single parents. This problem is more acute for single mothers than for single fathers, because on average, women still earn less than men, and because working creates new expenses such as child-care and transportation costs. Many women working in low-wage jobs do not receive health insurance as a benefit of their jobs; they must pay the cost of such insurance themselves. As a result, many poor women found that once they were working, the expenses of child care, transportation, insurance, and other needs left them with less cash per month than they would have received if they had not worked and had instead collected AFDC and Medicaid benefits. These women concluded that it was not "worth it" for them to leave AFDC and work. Some states are now experimenting with programs to encourage women to work by allowing them to keep some of their welfare benefits even when they are working. Although Americans want individuals to be self-sufficient, research suggests that single mothers with low-wage jobs are likely to need continuing assistance to make ends meet.[48]

One of the most troubling issues related to American social policy is the number of American children who live in poverty. The rate of child poverty in 2008 was 19 percent—5.8 percent higher than that of the population as a whole. These high rates of poverty stem in part from the design of American social policies. Because these policies do not generously assist able-bodied adults who aren't working, and because these policies offer little help to the working poor, the children of these adults are likely to be poor as well.

As child poverty has grown, several lobbying groups have emerged to represent children's interests; the best-known of these is the Children's Defense Fund. But even with a sophisticated lobbying operation and although their numbers are large, poor children do not vote and therefore cannot wield much political power.[49]

● Thinking Critically about Social Policy and Equality

The development of social policy in the United States reflects shifts in our views about how government can best help accomplish fundamental national goals. Until the 1930s, the federal government did very little in the domain of social policy. The country's major social policy was free public education, which was established by the states and administered locally. Americans placed especially strong emphasis on education because an educated citizenry was seen as an essential component of a strong democracy.[50] Given the strength of these beliefs, it is not surprising that free public education was available in the United States well before European nations established public education systems.

Other public social policies, established from the 1930s on, have stirred up much more controversy. Liberals often argue that more generous social policies are needed if America is to truly ensure equality of opportunity. Some liberals have argued that the government needs to go beyond simply providing opportunity and should ensure more equal conditions, especially where children are concerned. Conservative critics, on the other hand, often argue that social policies that offer income support take the ideal of equality too far and, in the process, do for individuals what they should be doing for themselves. From this perspective, social policies make the government too big, and big government is seen as a fundamental threat to Americans' liberties.

for critical analysis

Critics of American social policy argue that social policy does more harm than good. What negative consequences of social policy do they point to? Do you agree with their arguments?

Where do average Americans fit in these debates? Americans are often said to be philosophical conservatives and operational liberals.[51] When asked about government social policy in the abstract, they say they disapprove of activist government—a decidedly conservative view. But when they must evaluate particular programs, Americans generally express support—a more liberal perspective. Some programs, of course, are preferred over others. Policies in which the recipients are regarded as deserving, such as programs for the elderly, receive more support than those that assist working-age people. Programs that have a reputation for effectiveness and programs that require people to help themselves through work are also viewed favorably.[52]

In sum, most Americans take a pragmatic approach to social welfare policies: they favor programs that work, and they want to reform those that seem not to work. By rejecting the policy extremes, Americans signal their awareness of the tensions that social policies generate among their most deeply held values of liberty, equality, and democracy. Political debates about social policy connect most closely with the public when they consider which mix of policies represents the appropriate balance among these three ideals, rather than when they ask the public to choose among them.

studyguide

Practice Quiz

Find a diagnostic Web Quiz with 35 additional questions on the StudySpace Web site: www.wwnorton.com/we-the-people

The Welfare State

1. Prior to 1935, the private welfare system in the United States made a distinction between *(p. 655)*
   a) contributory and noncontributory programs.
   b) citizens and recent immigrants.
   c) the deserving poor and the undeserving poor.
   d) religious and secular assistance.

2. Which of the following is *not* an example of a contributory program? *(pp. 655–56)*
   a) Social Security
   b) Medicare
   c) food stamps
   d) All of the above are examples of contributory programs.

3. America's welfare state was constructed initially in response to *(p. 655)*
   a) World War II.
   b) political reforms of the Progressive era.
   c) the Great Depression.
   d) the growth of the military-industrial complex.

4. Means testing requires that applicants for welfare benefits show *(p. 656)*
   a) that they are capable of getting to and from their workplace.
   b) that they have the ability to store and prepare food.

   c) some definite need for assistance plus an inability to provide for it.
   d) that they have the time and resources to take full advantage of federal educational opportunities.

5. In 1996, as part of welfare reform, Aid to Families with Dependent Children was abolished and replaced by *(p. 656)*
   a) the Earned Income Tax Credit.
   b) Aid to Dependent Children.
   c) Supplemental Security Income.
   d) Temporary Assistance to Needy Families.

6. Which of the following are examples of in-kind benefits? *(p. 658)*
   a) Medicaid and food stamps
   b) Social Security payments and cost-of-living adjustments
   c) Medicare and unemployment compensation
   d) none of the above

7. Government benefits to individuals that *cannot* be taken away without due process of the law are called *(p. 658)*
   a) cost-of-living adjustments.
   b) entitlement programs.
   c) indexing programs.
   d) tax expenditure programs.

Opening Opportunity

8. Which of the following is *not* aimed at breaking the cycle of poverty? *(pp. 664–73)*
   a) drug policies
   b) education policies
   c) employment training programs
   d) health policies

9. What event prompted the federal government to enter the field of elementary education? *(p. 664)*
   a) the Great Depression
   b) World War II
   c) the Soviet Union's launching of *Sputnik*
   d) the Civil Rights movement

10. Which of the following was *not* part of the No Child Left Behind Act of 2001? *(pp. 664–66)*
    a) a provision allowing parents whose child is attending a failing school to transfer the child to a better school
    b) a requirement that schools show positive results for all subcategories of students and not just positive overall averages
    c) a requirement that a national test be used to evaluate every student around the country
    d) a requirement that every child in grades 3 through 8 be tested yearly for proficiency in math and reading

11. A charter school is *(p. 665)*
    a) a publicly funded school that is free from the rules and regulations of local school districts.
    b) a privately funded school that is subject to the rules and regulations of local school districts.
    c) a privately funded school that is free from the rules and regulations of local school districts.
    d) a school created by the GI Bill of Rights of 1944.

Who Gets What from Social Policy?

12. In terms of receiving benefits of social policies, what distinguishes the elderly from the working poor? *(pp. 674–77)*
    a) The elderly are perceived as deserving, whereas the working poor are not.
    b) There is no significant difference between these two groups.
    c) The elderly are more organized and more politically powerful than are the working poor.
    d) The elderly are less organized and less politically powerful than are the working poor.

13. Who are the chief beneficiaries of the "shadow welfare state"? *(p. 678)*
    a) the rich
    b) the nonworking poor
    c) the working poor
    d) the middle class

14. Which two government programs provide direct assistance to the working poor? *(p. 676)*
    a) Medicaid and the Earned Income Tax Credit
    b) Temporary Assistance to Needy Families and food stamps
    c) Temporary Assistance to Needy Families and the Earned Income Tax Credit
    d) Food stamps and the Earned Income Tax Credit

15. Which of the following statements best describes the poverty level in the United States since 1960? *(p. 678)*
    a) It has declined equally among all groups.
    b) It has declined overall but has fallen at different rates for different groups.
    c) It has increased equally among all groups.
    d) It has increased overall but has risen at different rates for different groups.

Chapter Outline

Find a detailed Chapter Outline on the StudySpace Web site: www.wwnorton.com/we-the-people

Key Terms

Find Flashcards to help you study these terms on the StudySpace Web site: www.wwnorton.com/we-the-people

contributory programs *(p. 655)*
cost-of-living adjustment (COLA) *(p. 656)*
entitlement *(p. 658)*
equality of opportunity *(p. 664)*
food stamps *(p. 657)*

indexing *(p. 656)*
in-kind benefits *(p. 658)*
means testing *(p. 656)*
Medicaid *(p. 657)*
Medicare *(p. 656)*

noncontributory programs *(p. 656)*
Social Security *(p. 655)*
tax expenditures *(p. 675)*

For Further Reading

Campbell, Andrea Louise. *How Policies Make Citizens: Senior Political Activism and the American Welfare State*. Princeton, NJ: Princeton University Press, 2005.

Hacker, Jacob S. *The Great Risk Shift: Why American Jobs, Families, Health Care, and Retirement Aren't Secure—and How We Can Fight Back*. New York: Oxford University Press, 2006.

Howard, Christopher. *The Welfare State Nobody Knows: Debunking Myths about U.S. Social Policy*. Princeton, NJ: Princeton University Press, 2007.

Katz, Michael. *In the Shadow of the Poorhouse: A Social History of Welfare in America*. New York: Basic Books, 1986.

Katznelson, Ira, and Margaret Weir. *Schooling for All: Race, Class, and the Democratic Ideal*. New York: Basic Books, 1985.

Light, Paul. *Artful Work: The Politics of Social Security Reform*. New York: Random House, 1985.

Mettler, Suzanne. *Soldiers to Citizens: The GI Bill and the Making of the Greatest Generation*. New York: Oxford University Press, 2005.

Murray, Charles. *Losing Ground: American Social Policy, 1950–1980*. New York: Basic Books, 1984.

Patterson, James T. *America's Struggle against Poverty in the Twentieth Century*. Cambridge, MA: Harvard University Press, 2000.

Rank, Mark Robert. *One Nation, Underprivileged: Why American Poverty Affects Us All*. New York: Oxford University Press, 2004.

Skocpol, Theda. *The Missing Middle: Working Families and the Future of American Social Policy*. New York: Norton, 2000.

Weir, Margaret, Ann Orloff, and Theda Skocpol, eds. *The Politics of Social Policy in the United States*. Princeton, NJ: Princeton University Press, 1988.

Recommended Web Sites

Center on Budget and Policy Priorities
www.cbpp.org

The Center on Budget and Policy Priorities is a nonpartisan, liberal-leaning, nonprofit organization that provides timely data and analysis of social programs that serve low-income Americans. It also studies economic and social changes that affect the well-being of low-income people. Areas of research include the Earned Income Tax Credit, Food Assistance, Social Security, and climate change. It focuses on national programs as well as state and local policies.

Center for Retirement Research
http://crr.bc.edu/index.php

Americans pay for their retirement with a mix of Social Security, employer-sponsored savings plans, and private savings. This Web site provides analyses of the challenges that face all aspects of the current arrangements and includes a downloadable "Social Security Fix-It Book."

Libertarian Party
www.lp.org

Contrary to many other Americans, libertarians believe that social programs pose a threat to personal freedom and should be eliminated. Go to the Libertarian Party's Web site to read the organization's opinions and positions on most current social policies.

Medicare
www.medicare.gov

Health care is one of the largest and most controversial social programs in the United States. At the Medicare Web site, find out what services the Department of Health and Human Services provides.

Modern American Poetry: The Great Depression
www.english.uiuc.edu/maps/depression/depression.htm

The Great Depression changed American opinion about the causes of and responsibility for poverty. This Web site, by Carey Norton at the University of Illinois at Urbana-Champaign, provides information, statistics, and photos of this historical period as well as analysis of poems by Depression-era writers.

Poverty.com
www.poverty.com

Poverty is a problem that exists in the United States and around the world. Read about how poverty, hunger, and related problems affect people in other areas of the globe.

Public Agenda
www.publicagenda.com

Public Agenda is a nonpartisan organization that tries to bridge the gap between American leaders and public opinion on current social, domestic, and foreign-policy issues.

U.S. Department of Education
www.ed.gov

The U.S. Department of Education is dedicated to providing equal access to education and improving academic programs throughout America. At the department's Web site, you can learn about the No Child Left Behind Act and other policies.

Foreign policy often involves finding a balance between cooperation and promoting U.S. interests. Here, President Obama meets with President Hamid Karzai of Afghanistan to discuss the ongoing war there.

Foreign Policy and Democracy

WHAT GOVERNMENT DOES AND WHY IT MATTERS Ever since George Washington, in his Farewell Address, warned the American people "to have...as little political connection as possible" with foreign nations and to "steer clear of permanent alliances," Americans have been distrustful of foreign policy. But, despite their distrust, the United States has been forced to pursue its national interests in the world through a variety means, including diplomacy, economic policy, and precisely the sorts of entangling alliances with other nations and involvements with international organizations that would have troubled Washington.

America has also fought a large number of wars. Though Americans like to regard themselves as a peaceful people, since our own Civil War, American forces have been deployed abroad on hundreds of occasions for major conflicts as well as minor skirmishes. Writing in 1989, historian Geoffrey Perret commented that no other nation, "has had as much experience of war as the United States."[1]

focusquestions

- What are the major goals of foreign policy?
- Who makes foreign policy?
- What are the instruments of foreign policy?
- Why does foreign policy sometimes conflict with American ideals?

America has not become less warlike in the years since Parret published his observation. Between 1989 and the present, American forces have fought two wars in the Persian Gulf and a war in Afghanistan, while engaging in lesser military actions in Panama, Kosovo, Somalia, and elsewhere. Every year, of course, America's military arsenal and defense budget dwarfs those of other nations. America currently spends more than $600 billion per year on its military and weapons programs—a figure that represents more than one-third of the world's total military expenditure and nearly ten times the amount spent by the Chinese People's Republic, the nation that currently ranks second to the United States in overall military outlays.

An old American adage asserts that "politics stops at the water's edge." The point of this saying is that if we fail to work together to protect our nation's political, economic, and security interests in the wider world, we will all suffer. In today's world, however, the water's edge does not neatly demarcate the difference in interests between "us" and "them." As the 2009 global economic crisis revealed, "our" economic interests and "their" economic interests are intertwined. Environmental concerns are global, not national. And even in the realm of security interests, some risks and threats are shared and require international rather than national responses. Our national government, created to further our national interests, must find ways of acting internationally and striking the right balance between competition and cooperation in the international arena. Writing in the 1830s, Alexis de Tocqueville declared that democracies are not well suited to successfully pursue foreign-policy goals. "A democracy can only with great difficulty regulate the details of an important undertaking, persevere in a fixed design, and work out its execution in spite of serious obstacles. It cannot combine its measures with secrecy or await their consequences with patience."[2] Let us see if Tocqueville's assessment is still true today.

chapter contents

The Nature of Foreign Policy

The term *foreign policy* refers to the programs and policies that determine America's relations with other nations and foreign entities. Foreign policy includes diplomacy, military and security policy, international human rights policies, and various forms of economic policy, such as trade policy and international energy policy. Of course, foreign policy and domestic policy are not completely separate categories but are instead closely intertwined. Take security policy, for example. Defending the nation requires the design and manufacture of tens of billions of dollars worth of military hardware. The manufacture and procurement of this military equipment involves a host of economic policies, and paying for it shapes America's fiscal policies.

Many of the basic contours of the foreign-policy arena are similar to those of America's other policy domains. The nation's chief foreign-policy makers are the president, Congress, and the bureaucracy. Just as in economic and social policy, battles over foreign policy often erupt between and within these institutions as competing politicians and a variety of organized groups and rival political forces pursue their own versions of the national interest or their own narrower purposes which they seek to present as the national interest. In the foreign-policy arena, the institutional powers of the presidency give presidents and their allies an advantage over political forces based in Congress, although Congress is not without resources of its own through which to influence the conduct of foreign policy. Moreover, like domestic-policy matters, foreign-policy issues often figure prominently in public debate and national election campaigns as competing forces seek to mobilize popular support for their positions, or at least to castigate the opposition for the putative shortcomings of its policies.

In this chapter, we will first examine the main goals and purposes of American foreign policy. We will then discuss the actors and institutions that shape foreign policy. Next, we will analyze the instruments that policy makers have at their disposal to implement foreign policy.

Foreign policy often intersects with domestic policy. As the government has taken steps to protect Americans from foreign terrorists, such as monitoring borders more closely, this has also affected domestic-level debates about issues like immigration. Here, a Homeland Security official watches video feeds of the U.S.-Canadian border.

The Goals of Foreign Policy

Although U.S. foreign policy has a number of purposes, three main goals stand out. These are security, prosperity, and the creation of a better world. These goals are, of course, closely intertwined and can never be pursued fully in isolation from each other.

Security

To many Americans, the chief purpose of the nation's foreign policy is protection of America's security in an often hostile world. Traditionally, the United States has been concerned about threats that might emanate from other nations, such as Nazi Germany during the 1940s and then Soviet Russia until the Soviet Union's collapse in the late 1980s. Today, American security policy is concerned not only with the actions of other nations but also with the activities of terrorist groups and other hostile **non-state actors**.[3] To protect the nation's security from foreign threats, the United States has built an enormous military apparatus and a complex array of intelligence-gathering institutions, such as the Central Intelligence Agency (CIA), charged with evaluating and anticipating challenges from abroad.[4]

Security is, of course, a broad term. Policy makers must be concerned with Americans' physical security. The 9/11 terrorist attacks killed and injured thousands of Americans, and the government constantly fears that new attacks could be even more catastrophic. Policy makers must also be concerned with such matters as the security of America's food supplies, transportation infrastructure, and energy supplies. Many of our efforts in the Middle East, for example, are aimed at ensuring continuing American access to vital oil fields. In recent years, cyberspace has become a new security concern. The nation's dependence on computers means that the government must be alert to efforts by hostile governments, groups, or even individual "hackers" to damage computer networks.

During the eighteenth and nineteenth centuries, the United States believed that its security was based on its geographic isolation. We were separated by two oceans from European and Asian powers, and many Americans thought that our security would be best preserved by remaining aloof from international power struggles. This policy was known as **isolationism**. In his 1796 farewell address, President George Washington warned Americans to avoid permanent alliances with foreign powers, and in 1823, President James Monroe warned foreign powers not to meddle in the Western Hemisphere. Washington's warning and what came to be called the Monroe Doctrine were the cornerstones of U.S. foreign policy of isolationism until the end of the nineteenth century. The United States saw itself as the dominant power in the Western hemisphere and, indeed, believed that its "manifest destiny" was to expand from sea to sea. The rest of the world, however, should remain at arm's length.

In the twentieth century, technology made oceans less of a barrier to foreign threats, and the world's growing economic interdependence meant that the United States could no longer ignore events abroad. At the beginning of the twentieth century, despite its isolationist sentiments, the United States entered World War I on the side of Great Britain and France when the Wilson administration concluded that America's economic and security interests would be adversely affected by a German victory. In 1941, America was drawn into World War II when Japan attacked the U.S. Pacific fleet anchored at Pearl Harbor, Hawaii. Even before the Japanese attack forced America to fight, the Roosevelt administration had already concluded that the

non-state actors groups other than nation-states that attempt to play a role in the international system. Terrorist groups are one type of non-state actor

isolationism desire to avoid involvement in the affairs of other nations

United States must act out to prevent a victory by the German-Japanese-Italian Axis alliance. Until the Japanese attack, however, President Roosevelt had not been able to overcome proponents of American isolationism, who declared that our security was best served by leaving foreigners to their own devices. With their attack, the Japanese proved that the Pacific Ocean could not protect the United States from foreign foes and effectively discredited isolationism as a security policy.

In the aftermath of World War II, the United States developed a new security policy known as **deterrence**, designed to "contain" the growing power of the Soviet Union. By the end of the 1940s, the Soviets had built a huge empire and enormous military forces. Most threatening of all, the Soviet Union had built nuclear weapons and intercontinental bombers capable of attacking the United States. Some Americans argued that we should attack the Soviets before it was too late. This policy is known as **preventive war**. Others said that we should show our peaceful intentions and attempt to placate the Soviets. This policy is called **appeasement**.

The policies that the United States actually adopted, deterrence and containment, could be seen as midway between preventive war and appeasement. A nation pursuing a policy of deterrence, on the one hand, signals its peaceful intentions, but on the other hand indicates its willingness and ability to fight if attacked. Thus, during the era of confrontation with the Soviet Union, known as the **Cold War**, the United States frequently asserted that it had no intention of attacking the Soviet Union. At the same time, however, the United States built a huge military force, including an arsenal of nuclear weapons and intercontinental missiles, and frequently asserted that in the event of a Soviet attack, it had the ability and will to respond with overwhelming force. The Soviet Union announced that its nuclear weapons were also intended for deterrent purposes. Eventually the two sides possessed such enormous arsenals of nuclear missiles that each potentially had the ability to destroy the other in the event of war. This heavily armed standoff came to be called a posture of mutually assured destruction. During the 1962 "Cuban missile crisis," the United States and the USSR came to the brink of war when President Kennedy declared that the Soviet Union must remove its nuclear missiles from Cuba and threatened to use force if the Soviets refused. After an extremely intense several weeks, the crisis was defused by a negotiated compromise in which the Soviets agreed to remove their missiles in exchange for a U.S. guarantee that it would not invade Cuba. The two superpowers had come so close to nuclear war that the leaders of both nations sought ways of reducing tensions. This effort led to a period of "détente" in which a number of arms control agreements were signed and the threat of war was reduced.

A policy of deterrence not only requires the possession of large military forces but also requires that the nation pursuing such a policy convince potential adversaries that it is willing to fight. France had a large army in the 1930s, but Nazi Germany was not deterred from pursuing its expansionist goals in Europe because the German chancellor, Adolf Hitler, did not believe that the French were actually willing to fight. Thus, as part of its policy of deterrence, the United States engaged in wars in Korea, Vietnam, and elsewhere in response to what it believed to be Soviet aggression. Though the United States had no particular interests in Korea or Vietnam, American policy makers believed that if

deterrence the development and maintenance of military strength as a means of discouraging attack

preventive war policy of striking first when a nation fears that a foreign foe is contemplating hostile action

appeasement effort to forestall war by giving in to the demands of a hostile power

Cold War the period of struggle between the United States and the former Soviet Union between the late 1940s and about 1990

During the Cold War, the United States and the Soviet Union engaged in an arms race, each acquiring nuclear weapons to deter the other from attacking.

the United States did not fight in these areas, the Soviets would be emboldened to pursue an expansionist policy elsewhere, thinking that the Americans would not respond. Interventions in Korea and Vietnam were also justified by the so-called Truman Doctrine, which called for American assistance to any nation threatened by the Soviet Union and its allies.

The dissolution of the Soviet Union began in 1985, and the final collapse occurred in 1991, partly because its huge military expenditures undermined its creaky and inefficient centrally planned economy. The new Russia, though still a formidable and sometimes unfriendly power, seemed to pose less of a threat to the United States. Americans celebrated the end of the Cold War and believed that the enormous expense of America's own military forces might be reduced. Within a few years of the Soviet collapse, however, a new set of security threats emerged, requiring new policy responses. The September 11 terrorist attacks demonstrated a threat against which some security scholars had long warned. The threat was that non-state actors and so-called rogue states might acquire significant military capabilities, including nuclear weapons, and would not be affected by America's deterrent capabilities.

A policy of deterrence assumes certainty and rationality. Certainty means that a potential adversary must know for sure that the United States will reply with force if attacked. Rationality means that, to be deterred, a potential adversary must be capable of rationally assessing the risks and costs of aggression against the United States. These two assumptions, which were valid when we faced the Soviet Union, may not be appropriate in the face of contemporary security threats. Unlike **nation-states**, countries with governments and fixed borders, terrorist groups are non-state actors having no fixed geographic location that can be attacked. Terrorists may believe that they can attack and melt away, leaving the United States with

nation-state a political entity consisting of a people with some common cultural experience (nation) who also share a common political authority (state), recognized by other sovereignties (nation-states)

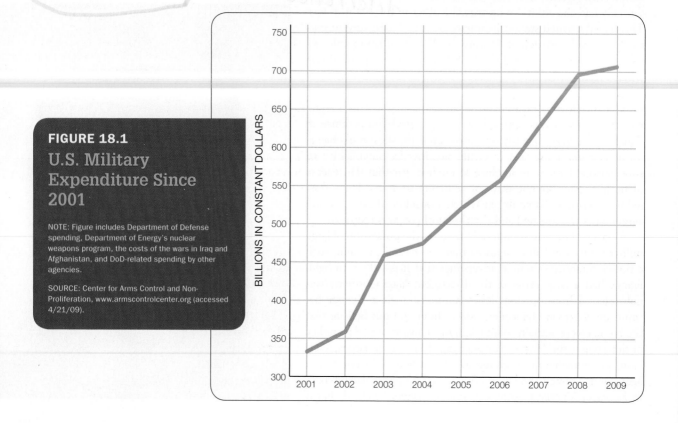

FIGURE 18.1

U.S. Military Expenditure Since 2001

NOTE: Figure includes Department of Defense spending, Department of Energy's nuclear weapons program, the costs of the wars in Iraq and Afghanistan, and DoD-related spending by other agencies.

SOURCE: Center for Arms Control and Non-Proliferation, www.armscontrolcenter.org (accessed 4/21/09).

The U.S. invasion of Iraq was an example of preemptive war. The Bush administration argued that it had to strike Iraq first, before Iraq used weapons of mass destruction to attack American interests.

no one against whom to retaliate. Hence, the threat of massive retaliation does not deter them. Rogue states are nations with unstable and erratic leaders who seem to pursue policies driven by ideological or religious fervor rather than careful consideration of economic or human costs. The United States considers North Korea and Iran to be rogue states.

To counter these new security threats, the George W. Bush administration shifted from a policy of deterrence to one of **preemption**. Preemption is often used as another name for preventive war or willingness to strike first in order to prevent an enemy attack. The United States declared that it would not wait to be attacked but would, if necessary, take action to disable terrorist groups and rogue states before they could do us harm. The Bush administration's "global war on terror" is an expression of this notion of preemption, as was the U.S. invasion of Iraq. The United States has also refused to rule out the possibility that it would attack North Korea or Iran if it deemed those nations' nuclear programs to be an imminent threat to American security interests. Accompanying this shift in military doctrines has been an enormous increase in overall U.S. military spending (see Figure 18.1). It remains to be seen whether America's doctrine of preemption will successfully counter threats. The Obama administration declared that it would endeavor to establish constructive dialogues with North Korea, Iran, and other hostile states. However, Obama did not necessarily renounce the Bush Doctrine for those states that declined to become constructively engaged.

preemption the principle that allows the national government to override state or local actions in certain policy areas. In foreign policy, the willingness to strike first in order to prevent an enemy attack

Economic Prosperity

A second major goal of U.S. foreign policy is promoting American prosperity. America's international economic policies are intended to expand employment opportunities in the United States, to maintain access to foreign energy supplies at a reasonable cost, to promote foreign investment in the United States, and to lower the prices Americans pay for goods and services.

Among the most visible and important elements of U.S. international economic policy is trade policy. The promotion and advertising of American goods and services abroad is a long-standing goal of U.S. trade policy, and it is one of the major obligations of the Department of Commerce. Yet modern trade policy involves a complex arrangement of treaties, tariffs, and other mechanisms of policy formation. For example, the United States has a long-standing policy of granting **most favored nation status** to certain countries—that is, the United States offers to another country the same tariff rate it already gives to its most favored trading partner, in return for trade (and sometimes other) concessions. In 1998, to avoid any suggestion that "most favored nation" implied some special relationship with an undemocratic country (China, for example), President Clinton changed the term from "most favored nation" to "normal trade relations."[5]

The most important international organization for promoting trade is the **World Trade Organization (WTO)**, which officially came into being in 1995. The WTO grew out of the **General Agreement on Tariffs and Trade (GATT)**. Since World War II, GATT had brought together a wide range of nations for regular negotiations designed to reduce barriers to trade. Such barriers, many believed, had contributed to the breakdown of the world economy in the 1930s and had helped to cause World War II. The WTO has 151 members worldwide, including the United States. Similar policy goals are pursued in regional arrangements, such as the **North American Free Trade Agreement (NAFTA)**, a trade treaty among the United States, Canada, and Mexico.

Working toward freer trade has been an important goal of each presidential administration since World War II. Yet as globalization has advanced, concerns about free trade and about the operation of the WTO, in particular, have grown. The WTO meetings held in Seattle in 1999 provoked unprecedented protests by groups that included environmentalists and labor unions. Tens of thousands

most favored nation status agreement to offer a trading partner the lowest tariff rate offered to other trading partners

Word Trade Organization (WTO) international promoting free trade that grew out of the General Agreement on Tariffs and Trade

General Agreement on Tariffs and Trade (GATT) international trade organization, in existence from 1947 to 1995, that set many of the rules governing international trade

North American Free Trade Agreement (NAFTA) trade treaty among the United States, Canada, and Mexico to lower and eliminate tariffs among the three countries

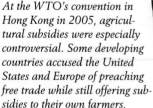

At the WTO's convention in Hong Kong in 2005, agricultural subsidies were especially controversial. Some developing countries accused the United States and Europe of preaching free trade while still offering subsidies to their own farmers.

of protesters denounced the undemocratic decision-making process of the WTO, which, they charged, was dominated by the concerns of business. These critics believe that the WTO does not pay sufficient attention to the concerns of developing nations and to such issues as environmental degradation, human rights, and labor practices, including the use of child labor in many countries. The Seattle meetings were adjourned with no agreement having been reached. Since the Seattle meetings, the major problem in WTO negotiations has been conflicts between poor, developing nations and rich, developed countries. Countries in the developing world accuse the United States and Europe of hypocrisy, preaching free trade but then using patents and subsidies to protect their own markets. There have been some successes on these issues, notably new WTO guidelines that allow poor countries to override expensive patents. Such patents make desperately needed drugs unavailable to most of the developing world. It has been more difficult to reach agreement on agricultural subsidies. Both the United States and Europe provide massive subsidies to their own agricultural industries. The prospects for resolving this issue are dim. The developed world has been reluctant to confront the economic dislocations and political costs of reducing the subsidies.

For over a half century, the United States has led the world in supporting free trade as the best route to growth and prosperity. Yet the American government, too, has sought to protect domestic industry when it is politically necessary. Subsidies, as we have seen, have long boosted American agriculture, artificially lowering the price of American products on world markets. In 2002 President George W. Bush, a vocal advocate of free trade, angered the rest of the world when he imposed protective tariffs on imported steel. Accused of hypocrisy and faced with retaliation from trading partners, the administration defended its actions by pointing to the damage that imports were doing to the domestic steel industry. When the WTO ruled that the steel tariffs violated WTO rules, Bush faced an unhappy choice. He could allow the European Union to retaliate by imposing tariffs, many of them on goods produced in politically important states, or he could lift the tariffs, thus angering steel producers and workers. The president chose to lift the steel tariffs.

Trade was also an issue in the 2008 election. During their third debate, John McCain accused Barack Obama of promoting protectionist policies, while Obama said Republicans had exported American jobs abroad and allowed an enormous trade deficit to develop. The U.S. trade deficit was projected to reach $60 billion (see Figure 18.2), and jobs growth in the United States had been low for several years. Analysts predicted that many of the 2.8 million manufacturing jobs lost in the recession of the early 2000s would never return to the United States. Moreover, outsourcing—the practice of moving jobs to other countries—began to hit the white-collar workforce, as jobs for workers such as call center operators and computer programmers moved to India and other countries with cheaper labor forces. In 2010, the United States accused China of manipulating trade rules to its own advantage, and China, in return, accused the United States of mismanaging its own economy. Trade creates both economic interdependence and political friction.

International Humanitarian Policies

A third goal of American policy is to make the world a better place for all its inhabitants. The main forms of policy that address this goal are international environmental policy, international human rights policy, and international peacekeeping.

for critical analysis

What are the arguments in favor of free trade (versus restrictions on trade)? Do the advocates of restrictions on trade always favor narrow special interests, or can they, too, be seen as favoring the public interest?

The United States and the World Trade Organization

The United States has been the strongest proponent of free trade on the world stage for more than half a century. The American government played a central role in creating international institutions, designed to reduce barriers to trade, including the World Trade Organization. Formed in 1995, the WTO is a forum for enforcing international rules to promote free trade. Member countries can appeal to the WTO when they believe another nation is violating international rules by imposing excessive tariffs or protective subsidies. If the WTO decides in favor of the challengers, it allows them to retaliate by imposing their own tariffs on the offending country.

One of the most controversial areas of trade liberalization is agriculture. Since 2001, the WTO trade talks—called the Doha Round because they began in Doha, Qatar in 2001—have especially focused on reducing trade barriers in agriculture. Since the formation of the WTO, the United States has pressured the develop-

ing world to reduce trade barriers. At the same time, however, the United States and Europe have offered heavy subsidies to their own agricultural industries. Such subsidies keep the prices of commodities high, helping to ensure that farmers make a profit. Developing countries have long imposed tariffs to limit the entry of these artificially cheap products, which would otherwise destroy their agricultural sector. During the Doha Round, the developing world charged the richer nations with hypocrisy for demanding that poor countries lower tariffs while the rich

countries refused to reduce their agriculture subsidies.

Both the United States and Europe have been reluctant to reduce subsidies and tariffs because farmers are important political constituencies. During the mid-1990s, the United States began to cut agricultural subsidies, but in the lead-up to the 2002 elections, President Bush signed a very generous farm bill that reinstated many of these subsidies. By 2006, American farm subsidies neared record highs. U.S. trade officials have sought to persuade American farmers that the costs of reduced subsidies will be far outweighed by the benefits gained from opening new markets for their products.

American farmers are not the only constituency blocking more liberalized trade in agricultural products. European nations also have highly subsidized agricultural industries. Despite years of trade talks on the issue, by 2005 the European Union (EU) continued to resist making substantial changes in its tariff levels.

In July 2006, the Doha Round of trade talks finally collapsed. The deep conflicts over liberalizing agricultural trade underscore the high stakes involved in promoting free trade. The United States and the rest of the developed world must be willing to bear the domestic economic and political costs of reducing trade barriers if world trade is to occur on a more level playing field.

for critical analysis

1. What is the role of the World Trade Organization? What have been some of the obstacles to promoting open markets around the world?

2. Why do agricultural protections pose a particularly difficult problem for advocates of liberalizing world trade? Why have the richer countries, which espouse free trade, been so reluctant to reduce protections for their own agricultural sectors?

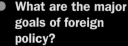
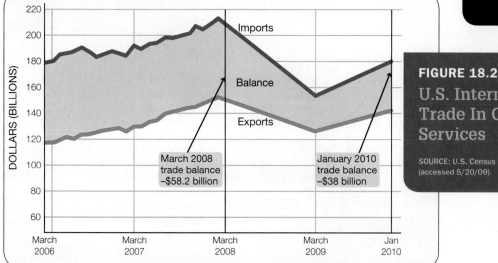

FIGURE 18.2

U.S. International Trade In Goods And Services

SOURCE: U.S. Census Bureau, www.census.gov (accessed 5/20/09).

The United States also contributes to international organizations such as the World Health Organization that work for global health and against hunger. These policies are often seen as secondary to the other goals of American foreign policy, forced to give way if they interfere with security or foreign economic policy. Moreover, although the United States spends billions annually on security policy and hundreds of millions on trade policy, we spend relatively little on environmental, human rights, and peacekeeping efforts. Some critics charge that America has the wrong priorities, spending far more to make war than to protect human rights and the global environment. Nevertheless, a number of important American foreign-policy efforts are, at least in part, designed to make the world a better place.

In the realm of international environmental policy, the United States supports a number of international efforts to protect the environment. These include the United Nations Framework Convention on Climate Change, an international agreement to study and ameliorate harmful changes in the global environment, and the Montreal Protocol, an agreement signed by more than 150 countries to limit the production of substances potentially harmful to the world's ozone layer. Other nations have severely criticized the United States for withdrawing from the 1997 Kyoto Protocol, an agreement setting limits on emissions of greenhouse gases from industrial countries. The United States has asserted that the Kyoto Protocol would be harmful to American economic interests. Although the United States is concerned with the global environment, national economic interests took precedence in this case. In preparation for the 2012 expiration of the Kyoto agreement, world leaders gathered in Copenhagen, Denmark, in 2009 to begin the process of negotiating a new climate treaty. The "Copenhagen Climate Summit," however, failed to produce a binding international agreement and ended with the United States, Europe, and China blaming one another for the lack of concrete results.

The same national priorities seem apparent in the area of human rights policy. The United States has a long-standing commitment to human rights and is a party to most major international agreements concerning human rights. These include the International Covenant on Civil and Political Rights, the International Convention against Torture, the Convention on the Elimination of All Forms of Racial

Many Americans believe that protecting human rights around the world should be a goal of U.S. foreign policy. These protesters called for U.S. government action to stop human-rights abuses by China in Tibet. However, humanitarian goals in foreign policy sometimes conflict with other political and economic goals.

Discrimination, and various agreements to protect children. The State Department's Bureau of Democracy, Human Rights, and Labor works cooperatively with international organizations to investigate and focus attention on human-rights abuses. In 1998, the United States enacted the International Religious Freedom Act, which calls on all governments to respect religious freedom. The act lists a number of sanctions that the United States and other signatories may employ to punish nations found to be in violation.

Although the United States is committed to promoting human rights, this commitment has a lower priority in American foreign policy than the nation's security concerns and economic interests. Thus, the United States is likely to overlook human rights violations by its major trading partners, such as China, and remain silent in the face of human rights violations by such allies as Saudi Arabia. Nevertheless, human rights concerns do play a role in American foreign policy. For example, beginning in 2007, the United States has made available several million dollars annually in small grants to pay medical and legal expenses incurred by individuals who have been the victims of retaliation in their own countries for working against their governments' repressive practices. In this small way, the United States is backing its often-asserted principles.

Another form of U.S. policy designed to improve the condition of the world is support for international peacekeeping efforts. At any point in time, a number of border wars, civil wars, and guerrilla conflicts flare somewhere in the world, usually in its poorer regions. These wars often generate humanitarian crises in the form of casualties, disease, and refugees. In cooperation with international agencies and other nations, the United States funds a number of efforts to keep the peace in volatile regions and to deal with the health-care and refugee problems associated with conflict. In 2007, the United States provided more than $1 billion in funding for United Nations peacekeeping operations in Bosnia, Kosovo, Sierra Leone, Lebanon, the Democratic Republic of Congo, and East Timor. As the world's wealthiest nation, the United States also recognizes an obligation to render assistance to nations facing crises and emergencies. In 2010, for example, the United States sent medical aid, food relief, and rescue teams to Haiti when that impoverished island nation was struck by a devastating earthquake.

America's humanitarian policies are important. Without American efforts and funding, many international humanitarian programs would be far less successful than they are today. In general, though, security and economic interests take precedence in the eyes of U.S. policy makers over humanitarian concerns. The U.S. government is far more likely to decry abuses of religious freedom in Iran—an adversary—than in Saudi Arabia—an ally.

● Who Makes American Foreign Policy?

As we have seen, domestic policies are made by governmental institutions and influenced by a variety of interest groups, political movements, and even the mass media. The same is true in the realm of foreign policy. The president and his chief advisers are the principal architects of U.S. foreign policy. However, Congress, the bureaucracy, the courts, political parties, interest groups, and trade associations also play important roles in this realm. Often, the president and Congress are at odds over foreign policy. When the Democrats took control of Congress in 2006, they vowed to force President Bush to end the war in Iraq. The president vowed to resist the Democrats' efforts and generally prevailed. Ethnic lobbies such as the pro-Israel lobby and the Armenian lobby also seek to affect foreign policy. In 2007, the Armenian lobby persuaded Congress to condemn Turkey's actions in 1915 that led to the deaths of more than one million Armenians. The president feared that Turkey, an important U.S. ally, would be offended and blocked the effort. Let us examine the major institutions and forces shaping American foreign policy.

Managing relations with China has been an important part of the Obama administration's foreign policy. In 2010, President Obama met with Chinese president Hu Jintao in Washington as part of the nuclear security summit.

The President

Most American presidents have been domestic politicians who set out to make their place in history through achievements in domestic policy. A standard joke during Bill Clinton's 1992 campaign, extending well into his first year, was that he had learned his foreign policy at the International House of Pancakes. Thus, it was not unusual that President George W. Bush had virtually no foreign-policy preparation prior to taking office. He had traveled very little outside the United States, and he had had virtually no foreign experience as governor of Texas.

Nonetheless, Bush was decisive in the initiatives he took to define America's national interest for his administration. Examples include revival of the controversial nuclear missile shield ("Star Wars"); his abandonment of the Anti-Ballistic Missile (ABM) treaty, which alienated Russia; changes in policy priorities away from humanitarian and environmental

The White House and Congress have often looked to military commanders for information and advice. General Stanley McChrystal, pictured here, commanded U.S. forces in Afghanistan in 2009 and 2010. He was removed from his post after he made derisive remarks about the Obama administration in a Rolling Stone *article*.

Bush Doctrine foreign policy based on the idea that the United States should take preemptive action against threats to its national security

goals with a far stronger emphasis on goals more specifically within the realm of national security; and turning America's concerns (by degree or emphasis) away from Europe toward an "Asia-first" policy.

September 11 and its aftermath immensely accentuated the president's role and his place in foreign policy.[6] By 2002, foreign policy was the centerpiece of the Bush administration's agenda. In a June 1 speech at West Point, the **"Bush Doctrine"** of preemptive war was announced. Bush argued that "our security will require all Americans . . . to be ready for preemptive action when necessary to defend our liberty and to defend our lives." Bush's statement was clearly intended to justify his administration's plans to invade Iraq, but it had much wider implications for international relations, including the central role of the American president in guiding foreign policy.

In 2008, John McCain, the Republican presidential candidate, was an exception to the usual rule emphasizing domestic priorities. McCain had specialized in foreign-policy matters in the Senate. During the presidential race, McCain emphasized his foreign-policy expertise. Obama countered by naming Senator Joseph Biden, chairman of the Senate Foreign Relations Committee, as the vice-presidential candidate. After his election, President Obama surrounded himself with experienced foreign-policy advisers such as General James Jones, appointed to serve as national security adviser, and Robert Gates, asked to stay on as defense secretary. In October 2010, Jones announced his resignation and was replaced by his deputy, Thomas E. Donilon.

By 2010, Obama had put his own stamp on American foreign policy, altering the conduct of America's war in Afghanistan and seeking to compel the Israelis and Palestinians to accept a Middle East peace deal. Obama also sought to more fully engage America's allies who had been miffed by the previous administration's tendency to engage in unilateral action.

The Bureaucracy

The major foreign-policy actors in the bureaucracy are the secretaries of the departments of State, Defense, and the Treasury; the Joint Chiefs of Staff (JCS), especially the chair of the JCS; and the director of the Central Intelligence Agency (CIA). Since 1947, a separate unit in the White House has overseen the vast foreign-policy establishment for the purpose of synthesizing all the messages arising out of the bureaucracy and helping the president make his own foreign policy. This is the National Security Council (NSC). It is a "subcabinet" made up of the president, the vice president, the secretary of defense, and the secretary of state, plus others each president was given the authority to add. Since the profound shake-up of September 11, two additional key players have been added. The first of these was the secretary of the new Department of Homeland Security (DHS), composed of twenty-two existing agencies relocated from all over the executive branch on the theory that their expertise could be better coordinated, more rational, and more efficient in a single organization designed to fight international terrorism and domestic natural disasters. The second was imposed at the top as the war in Iraq was becoming a quagmire: a director of national intelligence, to collate and coordinate intelligence coming in from multiple sources and to report a synthesis of all this to the president, on a daily basis.

Since the creation of the CIA and the Department of Defense in 1947, the secretary of defense and the director of the CIA have often been rivals engaged in power struggles for control of the intelligence community.[7] For the most part, secretaries of defense have prevailed in these battles, and the Defense Department today controls more than 80 percent of the nation's intelligence capabilities and funds. The creation of the position of director of national intelligence in 2005 to coordinate all intelligence activities set off new Washington power struggles as the "intelligence czar" faced opposition from both the CIA and the Department of Defense. As of 2010, the Defense Department has continued to resist cooperating with civilian intelligence agencies and moved to expand its own intelligence capabilities at their expense.

In addition to these top cabinet-level officials, key lower-level staff members have policy-making influence as strong as that of the Cabinet secretaries. Some may occasionally exceed Cabinet influence. These include the two or three specialized national security advisers in the White House, the staff of the NSC (headed by the national security adviser), and a few other career bureaucrats in the departments of State and Defense whose influence varies according to their specialty and to the foreign-policy issue at hand. A few civilian intelligence agencies are also involved in foreign-policy and national security, the most important of which are the Federal Bureau of Investigation (FBI), the U.S. Citizenship and Immigration Services, and the Internal Revenue Service (IRS).

In the wake of 9/11, military and law enforcement agencies have increased their role in America's foreign-policy making.[8] To a significant extent, American foreign policy is driven by military and antiterrorist concerns, and the agencies deemed capable of addressing these concerns are coming to play a larger and larger role in American foreign policy. For example, in recent years, American ambassadors have complained that they have been relegated to secondary status as the White House has looked to military commanders for information, advice, and policy implementation. For every region of the world, the U.S. military has assigned a "combatant commander," usually a senior general or admiral, to take charge of operations in that area. In many instances, these combatant commanders, who control troops, equipment, and intelligence capabilities, have become the real eyes, ears, and spokespersons for American foreign policy in their designated regions.

Congress

Although the Constitution gives Congress the power to declare war (see Table 18.1), Congress has exercised this power on only five occasions: the War of 1812, the Mexican War (1846), the Spanish-American War (1898), World War I (1917), and World War II (1941). For the first 150 years of American history, Congress's role was limited because the United States' role in world affairs was limited. During this time, the Senate was the only important congressional foreign-policy player because of its constitutional role in reviewing and approving treaties. The treaty power is still the primary entrée of the Senate into foreign-policy making. But since World War II and the continual involvement of the United States in international security and foreign aid, Congress as a whole has become a major foreign-policy maker because most modern foreign policies require financing, which requires action by both the House of Representatives and the Senate. For example, Congress's first act after September 11 was to authorize the president to use "all necessary and

TABLE 18.1

Principal Foreign-Policy Provisions of the Constitution

| | POWERS GRANTED | |
	PRESIDENT	CONGRESS
War power	Commander in chief of armed forces	Provide for the common defense; declare war
Treaties	Negotiate treaties	Ratification of treaties by two-thirds majority (Senate)
Appointments	Nominate high-level government officials	Confirm president's appointments (Senate)
Foreign commerce	No explicit powers, but treaty negotiation and appointment powers pertain	Explicit power "to regulate foreign commerce"
General powers	Executive power; veto	Legislative power; power of the purse; oversight and investigation

appropriate force," coupled with a $40 billion emergency appropriations bill for homeland defense. And although President Bush believed he possessed the constitutional authority to invade Iraq, he still sought congressional approval, which he received in October 2002. After the Democrats took control of Congress in 2007, the Democratic leadership proposed a new resolution opposing President Bush's policies in Iraq. The president asserted that he would not be bound by such a vote. After a battle with the president, it was Congress that was forced to withdraw, and in May 2007, Congress acceded to Bush's demands.

Not only does the president need Congress to provide funding for foreign and military policy initiatives but, under the Constitution, many presidential agreements with foreign nations also have to be approved by Congress. Article II, Section 2, of the Constitution declares that proposed treaties with other nations must be submitted by the president to the Senate and approved by a two-thirds vote. Because this "supermajority" is usually difficult to achieve, presidents generally prefer a different type of agreement with other nations called an **executive agreement**. An executive agreement is similar to a treaty and has the force of law but usually requires only a plurality vote (that is, 50 percent plus one) in both houses of Congress for approval.

Another aspect of Congress's role in foreign policy is the Senate's power to confirm the president's nominations of Cabinet members, ambassadors, and other high-ranking officials (such as the director of the CIA, but not the director of the NSC). A final constitutional power of Congress is the regulation of "commerce with foreign nations."

Other congressional players are the foreign-policy, military-policy, and intelligence committees: in the Senate, these are the Foreign Relations Committee, the Armed Services Committee, and the Homeland Security and Governmental Affairs Committee; in the House, these are the Foreign Affairs and Homeland Security Committee and the Armed Services Committee. Usually, a few members

executive agreement an agreement, made between the president and another country, that has the force of a treaty but does not require the Senate's "advice and consent"

of these committees who have spent years specializing in foreign affairs become trusted members of the foreign-policy establishment and are influential makers of foreign policy. In fact, several members of Congress have left the legislature to become key foreign-affairs cabinet members. After September 11, congressional committees conducted hearings on the failure of the intelligence agencies, but at the time most members of Congress were reluctant to take on these agencies or a popular president. In 2007, though, with Congress under Democratic control and the president's popularity fading, a number of congressional committees launched inquiries into the conduct of the war in Iraq and the more general operations of the intelligence and defense communities. Within weeks, congressional testimony revealed flaws in military procurement procedures, military planning, and other aspects of the administration's programs and policies. Congressional investigations and the publicity they generate are weapons Congress frequently uses to blunt presidential power. Since 2009, Congress's Democratic leadership has been generally cooperative with the Obama administration's foreign-policy initiatives, though liberal Democrats sometimes accuse the president of not doing enough to end the war in Afghanistan or to promote humanitarian foreign-policy goals.

Interest Groups

Although the president, the executive-branch "bureaucracy," and Congress are the true makers of foreign-policy, the "foreign-policy establishment" is a much larger arena, including what can properly be called the shapers of foreign policy—a host of unofficial, informal players, people who possess varying degrees of influence, depending on their prestige, their reputation, their socioeconomic standing, and—most important—the party and ideology that are dominant at a given moment.

By far the most important category of nonofficial player is the interest group—that is, the interest group to which one or more foreign-policy issues are of longstanding and vital relevance. The type of interest group with the reputation for the most influence is the economic interest group. Yet the myths about its influence far outnumber and outweigh the realities. The actual influence of organized economic interest groups in foreign policy varies enormously from issue to issue and year to year. Most of these groups are "single-issue" groups and are therefore most active when their particular issue is on the agenda. On many of the broader and more sustained policy issues—such as the North American Free Trade Agreement (NAFTA) or the general question of American involvement in international trade—the larger interest groups, sometimes called peak associations, find it difficult to maintain tight enough control of their many members to speak with a single voice. The most systematic study of international trade policies and their interest groups concluded that the leaders of these large economic interest groups spend more time maintaining consensus among their members than they do lobbying Congress or pressuring major players in the executive branch.[9] The more successful economic interest groups, in terms of influencing foreign policy, are the narrower,

Members of Amnesty International asked the U.S. government to take action to end the violence in the Darfur region of Sudan. Interest groups like Amnesty International may influence foreign policy by lobbying the government directly and by raising public awareness of certain issues.

single-issue groups such as the tobacco industry, which over the years has successfully kept American foreign policy from putting heavy restrictions on international trade in and advertising of tobacco products; and the computer hardware and software industries, which have successfully hardened the American attitude toward Chinese piracy of intellectual property rights.

Another type of interest group with a well-founded reputation for influence in foreign policy is made up of people with strong attachments to and identification with their country of national origin. The interest group with the reputation for the greatest influence is Jewish Americans, whose family and emotional ties to Israel make them one of the most alert and active interest groups in the whole field of foreign policy. In 2010, a dispute between Israel and the Obama administration over Israel's construction of new Jewish housing in Jerusalem led to an intense effort by American Jews to generate congressional support for Israel's position. Similarly, Americans of Irish heritage, despite having lived in the United States for two, three, or four generations, still maintain vigilance about American policies toward Ireland and Northern Ireland; some even contribute to the Irish Republican Army. Many other ethnic and national interest groups wield similar influence over American foreign policy.

These ethnic or national-origin interest groups are more influential than their counterparts in other democratic countries. This is a kind of dual loyalty that Americans generally welcome as a worthy sentiment. But there are limits, especially when national origin is coupled with or tied to countries in which a single religion is dominant. For example, Jews with strong ties to Israel and Catholics with connections to Ireland have on occasion been blocked from group influence on foreign policy because "dual loyalty" can be taken by other groups as "doubtful loyalty."[10] Nevertheless, Irish and Jewish groups, as well as a variety of other ethnic American interest groups, are vigorously involved in salient aspects of foreign policy, and it is an irrational or nonrational elected politician who disregards their signals. It is quite possible that the "electoral connection"[11] and the politics of representation in Congress (and the White House) are at their most intense when national origin is linked to a foreign-policy issue. Many will argue that the rationality principle "need not . . . be equated with such narrowly self-serving actions."[12] However, the nationality interest is often the strongest electoral connection.

A third type of interest group, one with a reputation that has been growing in the past two decades, is devoted to human rights. Such groups are made up of people who, instead of having self-serving economic or ethnic interests in foreign policy, are genuinely concerned about the welfare and treatment of people throughout the world—particularly those who suffer under harsh political regimes. A relatively small but often quite influential example is Amnesty International, whose exposés of human-rights abuses have altered the practices of many regimes around the world. In recent years, the Christian right has been a vocal advocate for the human rights of Christians who are persecuted in other parts of the world, most notably in China, for their religious beliefs. For example, the Christian Coalition joined groups such as Amnesty International in lobbying Congress to restrict trade with countries that permit attacks against religious believers.

A related type of group with rapidly growing influence is the ecological or environmental group, sometimes collectively called "greens." Groups of this nature often depend more on demonstrations than on the usual forms and strategies of influence in Washington, such as lobbying and using electoral politics, for example. In recent years environmental activists staged major protests, at the 2009 London and 2010 Toronto international economic summits.

The Media

Each part of the media has its own character and mode of operations, and as a consequence each may represent a different source of anguish and a different source of opportunity in making and implementing foreign policy. This makes the media a very special problem for every president because—as George Washington warned—once we become "entangled" with other nations, the media have to be "managed" to a certain extent, or persuaded to present a single, national voice. And managing can come close to a violation of the First Amendment's guarantee of freedom of the press. Such management, then, becomes an overwhelming problem during times of war, cold war, or any other sustained threat to national security, including these years following September 11, 2001.

The balancing of security against freedom of the press has become increasingly difficult with the increased power of the media that has resulted from significant developments in communications and information technology. Iraq is of course a compelling case in point. During the first few weeks of the invasion in 2003, nearly 600 embedded journalists (plus a number of "free-floating" U.S. and non-U.S. journalists) provided the most intensive coverage in the history of war, and without any question for the first time the coverage was instantaneous, visual, annotated, and in color—not only on television but on the front pages of the major newspapers and online as well.

Take special note of the word *embedded*. No matter how delicately put, embedding involved the management of the journalists in a deal to provide access and protection in return for "responsible" reporting, a deal that led to the widespread suspicion and fear that not only the journalists but also the news itself was being managed. The suspicion grew as the war changed after the regime of Saddam Hussein was deposed, the Iraqi armed forces dispersed, and the entire civil government that had been dominated by Saddam Hussein's Baath Party was decommissioned. Quite simply, the situation changed from a conventional, organized war to an ambiguous, insurgent war. This was the end of any practice of embedding and the beginning of fewer but freer-floating journalists, a change that also meant the expansion of dissent and open criticism accompanying the reports. "News management" to any degree was no longer possible.

Putting It Together

What can we say about who really makes American foreign policy? First, except for the president, the influence of players and shapers varies from case to case—this is a good reason to look with some care at each example of foreign policy in this chapter. Second, because the one constant influence is the centrality of the president in foreign-policy making, it is best to evaluate other actors and factors as they interact with the president.[13] Third, the reason influence varies from case to case is that each case arises under different conditions and with vastly different time constraints: for issues that arise and are resolved quickly, the opportunity for influence is limited. Fourth, foreign-policy experts will usually disagree about the level of influence any player or type of player has on policy making.

Let's make a few tentative generalizations to frame the remainder of this chapter. First, when an important foreign-policy decision has to be made under conditions of crisis—where time is of the essence—the influence of the presidency is at its strongest. Second, within those time constraints, access to the decision is limited almost exclusively to the narrowest definition of the foreign-policy establishment.

Obama's appointment of Hillary Clinton—one of the most prominent politicians in the country—as secretary of state reflected his commitment to diplomacy. Here, Clinton meets with Palestinian Prime Minister Salam Fayyad.

The arena for participation is tiny; any discussion at all is limited to the officially and constitutionally designated players. To put this another way, in a crisis, the foreign-policy establishment works as it is supposed to.[14] As time becomes less restricted, even when the decision to be made is of great importance, the arena of participation expands to include more government players and more nonofficial, informal players—the most concerned interest groups and the most important journalists. In other words, the arena becomes more pluralistic and, therefore, less distinguishable from the politics of domestic policy making. Third, because there are so many other countries with power and interests on any given issue, there are severe limits on the choices the United States can make. That is, in sharp contrast to domestic politics, U.S. policy makers in the foreign-policy realm are engaged not only in infighting but also in strategic interaction with policy makers in other nations; their choices are made both in reaction to and in anticipation of these strategic interactions. As one author concludes, in foreign affairs, "policy takes precedence over politics."[15] Thus, even though foreign-policy making in noncrisis situations may closely resemble the pluralistic politics of domestic-policy making, foreign-policy making is still a narrower arena with fewer participants.

● The Instruments of Modern American Foreign Policy

Any government has at hand certain instruments, or tools, to use in implementing its foreign policy. An instrument is neutral, capable of serving many goals. There have been many instruments of American foreign policy, and we can deal here only with those instruments we deem to be most important in the modern epoch: diplomacy, the United Nations, the international monetary structure, economic aid, collective security, and military deterrence. Each of these instruments will be evaluated in this section for its utility in the conduct of American foreign policy, and each will be assessed in light of the history and development of American values.

Diplomacy

diplomacy the representation of a government to other governments

We begin this treatment of instruments with diplomacy because it is the instrument to which all other instruments should be subordinated, although they seldom are. **Diplomacy** is the representation of a government to other foreign governments. Its purpose is to promote national values or interests by peaceful means. According to Hans Morgenthau, "a diplomacy that ends in war has failed in its primary objective."[16]

The first effort to create a modern diplomatic service in the United States was made through the Rogers Act of 1924, which established the initial framework for a professional foreign-service staff. But it took World War II and the Foreign Service Act of 1946 to forge the foreign service into a fully professional diplomatic corps.

Diplomacy, by its very nature, is overshadowed by spectacular international events, dramatic initiatives, and meetings among heads of state or their direct personal representatives. The traditional American distrust of diplomacy continues today, albeit in weaker form. Impatience with or downright distrust of diplomacy has been built not only into all the other instruments of foreign policy but also into the modern presidential system itself.[17] So much personal responsibility has been heaped on the presidency that it is difficult for presidents to entrust any of their authority or responsibility in foreign policy to professional diplomats in the State Department and other bureaucracies.

Distrust of diplomacy has also produced a tendency among all recent presidents to turn frequently to military and civilian personnel outside the State Department to take on a special diplomatic role as direct personal representatives of the president. As discouraging as it is to those who have dedicated their careers to foreign service to have personal appointees chosen over their heads, it is probably even more discouraging when they are displaced from a foreign-policy issue as soon as relations with the country they are posted in begin to heat up. When a special personal representative is sent abroad to represent the president, that envoy holds a status higher than that of the local ambassador, and the embassy becomes the envoy's temporary residence and base of operation. Despite the impressive professionalization of the American foreign service—with advanced training, competitive exams, language requirements, and career commitment—this practice of displacing career ambassadors with political appointees and with special personal presidential representatives continues. For instance, when President Clinton in 1998 sought to boost the peace process in Northern Ireland, he called on George Mitchell, a former senator from Maine. Mitchell received almost unanimous praise for his skill and patience in chairing the Northern Ireland peace talks. The caliber of his work in Northern Ireland led to Senator Mitchell's becoming involved in another of the world's apparently unsolvable conflicts, that between the Israelis and the Palestinians.

In 2008, both parties' presidential candidates criticized the Bush administration for having failed to use diplomacy to secure greater international support for the Iraq war. Both promised to revitalize American diplomacy. President Obama appointed Hillary Clinton secretary of state, in part to underline the importance he attached to diplomacy by choosing such a prominent figure as America's chief diplomat.

The significance of diplomacy and its vulnerability to politics may be better appreciated as we proceed to the other instruments. Diplomacy was an instrument more or less imposed on Americans as the prevailing method of dealing among nation-states in the nineteenth century. The other instruments to be identified and assessed below are instruments that Americans self-consciously crafted for themselves to take care of their own chosen place in the world affairs of the second half of the twentieth century and beyond. They therefore better reflect American culture and values than diplomacy does.

The United Nations

The utility of the **United Nations (UN)** to the United States as an instrument of foreign policy can be too easily underestimated because the United Nations is a very large and unwieldy institution with few powers and no armed forces to implement its rules and resolutions. Its supreme body is the UN General Assembly, comprising one representative of each of the 192 member states; each member representative has one vote, regardless of the size of the country. Important issues require a two-thirds majority vote, and the annual session of the General Assembly

United Nations (UN) an organization of nations founded in 1945 to be a channel for negotiation and a means of settling international disputes peaceably. The UN has had frequent successes in providing a forum for negotiation and on some occasions a means of preventing international conflicts from spreading. On a number of occasions, the UN has been a convenient cover for U.S. foreign-policy goals

The United Nations is not always but can be an important instrument of American foreign policy. In trying to build international support for the U.S. case against Iraq, President Bush went before the General Assembly and urged the United Nations to compel Iraq to disarm. Two months later, the UN Security Council gave its qualified support to Bush's position.

runs only from September to December (although it can call extra sessions). It has little organization that can make it an effective decision-making body, with only six standing committees, few tight rules of procedure, and no political parties to provide priorities and discipline. Its defenders are quick to add that although it lacks armed forces, it relies on the power of world opinion—and this is not to be taken lightly. The powers of the United Nations devolve mainly to its "executive committee," the UN Security Council, which alone has the real power to make decisions and rulings that member states are obligated by the UN Charter to implement. The Security Council may be called into session at any time, and each member (or a designated alternate) must be present at UN Headquarters in New York at all times. It is composed of fifteen members: five are permanent (the victors of World War II), and ten are elected by the General Assembly for two-year, nonrepeatable terms. The five permanent members are China, France, Russia, the United Kingdom, and the United States. Each of the fifteen members has only one vote, and a nine-vote majority of the fifteen is required on all substantive matters. But each of the five permanent members also has a negative vote, a "veto," and one veto is sufficient to reject any substantive proposal.

The UN can serve as a useful forum for international discussions and an instrument for multilateral action. Most peacekeeping efforts to which the United States contributes, for example, are undertaken under UN auspices.

The International Monetary Structure

Fear of a repeat of the economic devastation that followed World War I brought the United States together with its allies (except the USSR) to Bretton Woods, New Hampshire, in 1944 to create a new international economic structure for the postwar world. The result was two institutions: the International Bank for Reconstruction and Development (commonly called the World Bank) and the International Monetary Fund.

The World Bank was set up to finance long-term capital. Leading nations took on the obligation of contributing funds to enable the World Bank to make loans to capital-hungry countries. (The U.S. quota has been about one-third of the total.)

Popular Culture and America's Reputation Abroad

In the past few years, scholars and journalists have been discussing America's "image problem" across the globe. In Chapter 16 we looked at how foreign-policy decisions were affecting the global marketplace and consumption of American brands. But how does American popular culture itself contribute to the image of what America is like and who Americans are as people? Does American popular culture help or hurt perceptions of America around the globe?

Although perceptions of American foreign policy may be negative in numerous countries, appreciation for America's popular culture has remained relatively high. Andrew Kohut of the Pew Global Attitudes Project reports that in countries with large Muslim populations, where U.S. foreign policy is often seen unfavorably, appreciation for American popular culture is greater than one might expect. In Lebanon, for example, approval of U.S. foreign policy is particularly low, and yet 65 percent of the population still reports liking American films, television, and music.

However, some scholars and researchers are concerned about the potentially negative impact of American popular culture on global perceptions of the United States. The humanities scholar Martha Bayles is a critic of the export of American culture abroad due to the impression that violent and sexually explicit content may make on foreign viewers of American media. "Along with worrying about what popular culture is teaching our children about life," writes Bayles, "we need also to worry about what it is teaching the world about America."[a] One set of studies directly addressed the question of what impact American media may have on the international community's opinions of American culture. Through surveys administered to high school students in twelve countries, the authors determined that perceptions of Americans as violent, criminal, and sexually immoral were significantly influenced by the violent and sexual images that bombarded them through American media."[b]

Interestingly, television programmers in international markets report that the violence in American media is often what international television viewers want the most. Klaus Hallig, who purchases American media for various Eastern European television markets, explained to *the Washington Post* that Central Europeans want big, violent television. "They want cars to be exploded fourteen stories high—blow 'em up, kill 'em, stab 'em."[c]

Some researchers have observed that positive aspects of American television and film speak to global audiences. The quintessentially American narrative of the underdog protagonist who triumphs over hardship has broad appeal. The sociologist Todd Gitlin stated in a *Washington Post* interview that the United States is particularly skilled at "producing themes and story lines that appeal to a global sensibility: freedom, freedom of movement, freedom from family, from place, from earth, from roles."[d]

[a]M. Bayles, "Now Showing: The Good, the Bad and the Ugly Americans," *Washington Post*, August 28, 2005, p. B1.
[b]M. DeFleur and M. DeFleur, *Learning to Hate Americans: How the U.S. Media Shape Negative Attitudes among Teenagers in Twelve Countries* (Spokane, WA: Marquette Books, 2003).
[c]P. Farhi and M. Rosenfeld, "American Pop Penetrates Worldwide," *Washington Post*, October 25, 1998, p. A1.
[d]Farhi and Rosenfeld, "American Pop Penetrates Worldwide."

for critical analysis

1. Do you think that American popular culture contributes to positive or negative opinions of America abroad? Should the government try to regulate or influence the image of the United States that is conveyed through popular culture?

2. Why do you think that American popular culture remains fairly popular in countries where American foreign policy is distinctly unpopular?

International Monetary Fund (IMF) an institution established in 1944 that provides loans and facilitates international monetary exchange

The **International Monetary Fund (IMF)** was set up to provide for the short-term flow of money. After the war, the U.S. dollar replaced gold as the chief means by which the currencies of one country would be "changed into" currencies of another country for purposes of making international transactions. To permit debtor countries with no international balances to make purchases and investments, the IMF was set up to lend dollars or other appropriate currencies to needy member countries to help them overcome temporary trade deficits. For many years after World War II, the IMF, along with U.S. foreign aid, in effect constituted the only international medium of exchange.

During the 1990s, the IMF returned to a position of enhanced importance through its efforts to reform some of the largest debtor nations and formerly communist countries, to bring them more fully into the global capitalist economy. For example, in the early 1990s, Russia and thirteen other former Soviet republics were invited to join the IMF and the World Bank with the expectation of receiving $10.5 billion from these two agencies, primarily for a currency-stabilization fund. Each republic was to get a permanent IMF representative, and the IMF increased its staff by at least 10 percent to provide the expertise necessary to cope with the problems of these emerging capitalist economies.[18]

The IMF, with tens of billion of dollars contributed by its members, has more money to lend poor countries than does the United States, Europe, or Japan (the three leading IMF shareholders) individually. It makes its policy decisions in ways that are generally consonant with the interests of the leading shareholders.[19] Two weeks after September 11, 2001, the IMF had approved a $135 million loan to economically troubled Pakistan, a key player in the war against the Taliban government of Afghanistan because of its strategic location. Turkey, also because of its strategic location in the Middle East, was likewise put back in the IMF pipeline.[20] The future of the IMF, the World Bank, and all other private sources of international investment will depend in part on extension of more credit to the Third World and other developing countries, because credit means investment and productivity. But the future may depend even more on reducing the debt that is already there from previous extensions of credit.

Economic Aid and Sanctions

Every year, the United States provides nearly $30 billion in economic assistance to other nations. Some aid has a humanitarian purpose, such as helping to provide health care, shelter for refugees, or famine relief. A good deal of American aid, however, is designed to promote American security interests or economic concerns. For example, the United States provides military assistance to a number of its allies in the form of advanced weapons or loans to help them purchase advanced weapons. Such loans generally stipulate that the recipient must purchase the designated weapons from American firms. In this way, the United States hopes to bolster its security and economic interests with one grant. The two largest recipients of American military assistance are Israel and Egypt, American allies that fought two wars against one another. The United States believes that its military assistance allows both to feel sufficiently secure to remain at peace with one another.

Aid is an economic carrot. Sanctions are an economic stick. Economic sanctions that the United States employs against other nations include trade embargoes, bans on investment, and efforts to prevent the World Bank or other international institutions from extending credit to a nation against which the United States has

for critical analysis

There has been a good deal of debate about whether economic sanctions can convince North Korea or Iran to halt their nuclear weapons programs. What factors might help to determine the effectiveness of economic sanctions?

Who Are Americans in the Eyes of the World?

Percentage of Population with a Favorable View of the United States

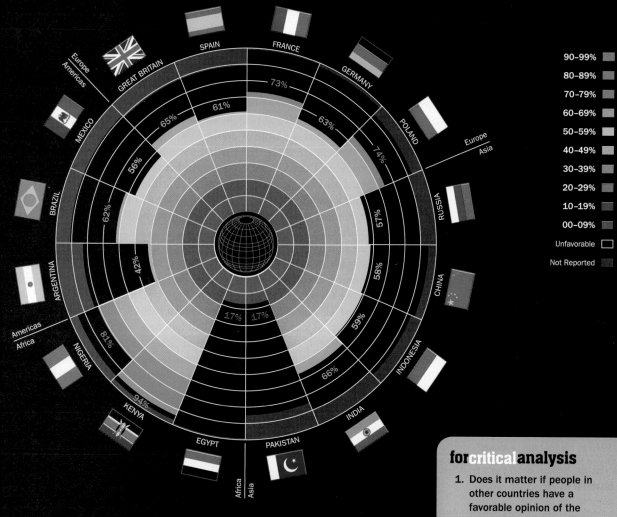

Legend:
- 90–99%
- 80–89%
- 70–79%
- 60–69%
- 50–59%
- 40–49%
- 30–39%
- 20–29%
- 10–19%
- 00–09%
- Unfavorable
- Not Reported

Chart values: SPAIN 61%, FRANCE 73%, GERMANY 63%, GREAT BRITAIN 65%, POLAND 74%, MEXICO 56%, RUSSIA 57%, BRAZIL 62%, CHINA 58%, ARGENTINA 42%, INDONESIA 59%, NIGERIA 81%, INDIA 66%, KENYA 94%, EGYPT 17%, PAKISTAN 17%

While American foreign policy is often shaped by the realities of pursuing the country's interests in the international arena, many Americans believe that the United States should also take a benevolent leadership role in the world, in keeping with the political values of liberty, equality, and democracy. Do people in other countries see America as a potential force for good in the world?

SOURCE: The Pew Global Attitudes Project, "Obama More Popular Abroad Than At Home, Global Image of U.S. Continues to Benefit," June 17, 2010.

for critical analysis

1. Does it matter if people in other countries have a favorable opinion of the United States? How could international opinions affect American foreign policy?

2. Which regions or types of countries have the most favorable opinion of the United States? Which have the least favorable? Can you think of some possible reasons for these patterns?

a grievance. Sanctions are most often employed when the United States seeks to weaken what it considers a hostile regime or when it is attempting to compel some particular action by another regime. Thus, for example, in order to weaken the Castro government, the United States has long prohibited American firms from doing business with Cuba. In recent years, the United States has maintained economic sanctions against Iran and North Korea in an effort to prevent those nations from pursuing nuclear-weapons programs.

Unilateral sanctions by the United States usually have little effect, since the target can usually trade elsewhere, sometimes even with foreign affiliates of U.S. firms. If, however, the United States is able to convince its allies to cooperate, sanctions have a better chance of success. International sanctions that were applied to Libya, for example, played a role in the regime's decision to enter into negotiations with the United States over Libyan responsibility for a number of terrorist attacks.

Collective Security

In 1947, most Americans hoped that the United States could meet its world obligations through the United Nations and economic structures alone. But most foreign-policy makers recognized that was a vain hope even as they were permitting and encouraging Americans to believe it. They had anticipated the need for military entanglements at the time of drafting the original UN Charter by insisting on language that recognized the right of all nations to provide for their mutual defense independent of the United Nations. And almost immediately after enactment of the Marshall Plan, designed to promote European economic recovery, the White House and a parade of State and Defense Department officials followed up with an urgent request to the Senate to ratify, and to both houses of Congress to finance, mutual defense alliances.

At first quite reluctant to approve treaties providing for national security alliances, the Senate ultimately agreed with the executive branch. The first collective security agreement was the Rio Treaty (ratified by the Senate in September 1947), which created the Organization of American States (OAS). This was the model treaty, anticipating all succeeding collective security treaties by providing that an armed attack against any of its members "shall be considered as an attack against all the American States," including the United States. A more significant break with U.S. tradition against peacetime entanglements came with the North Atlantic Treaty (signed in April 1949), which created the **North Atlantic Treaty Organization (NATO)**. ANZUS, a treaty tying Australia and New Zealand to the United States, was signed in September 1951. Three years later, the Southeast Asia Treaty created the Southeast Asia Treaty Organization (SEATO).

In addition to these multilateral treaties, the United States entered into a number of **bilateral treaties**—treaties between two countries. As one author has observed, the United States has been a *producer* of security, whereas most of its allies have been *consumers* of security.[21]

This pattern has continued in the post–Cold War era, and its best illustration is in the Persian Gulf War, where the United States provided the initiative, the leadership, and most of the armed forces, even though its allies were obliged to reimburse over 90 percent of the cost.

It is difficult to evaluate collective security and its treaties, because the purpose of collective security as an instrument of foreign policy is prevention, and success of this kind has to be measured in terms of what did *not* happen. Critics have argued that U.S. collective security treaties posed a threat of encirclement to the

North Atlantic Treaty Organization (NATO) a treaty organization, comprising the United States, Canada, and most of Western Europe, formed in 1948 to counter the perceived threat from the Soviet Union

bilateral treaty a treaty made between two nations

Soviet Union, forcing it to produce its own collective security, particularly the Warsaw Pact.[22] Nevertheless, no one can deny the counterargument that more than sixty years have passed without a world war.

In 1998, the expansion of NATO took its first steps toward former Warsaw Pact members, extending membership to Poland, Hungary, and the Czech Republic. Most of Washington embraced this expansion as the true and fitting end of the Cold War, and the U.S. Senate echoed this with a resounding 80-to-19 vote to induct these three former Soviet satellites into NATO. The expansion was also welcomed among European member nations, who quickly approved the move, hailing it as the final closing of the book on Yalta, the 1945 treaty that divided Europe into Western and Soviet spheres of influence after the defeat of Germany. Expanded membership seems to have made NATO less threatening and more acceptable to Russia. Russia became a partner when the NATO-Russia Council was formed in 2002. Finally, although the expanded NATO membership (twenty-eight countries in 2009) reduces the threat to Russia, it also reduces the utility of NATO as a military alliance. The September 11 attack on the United States was the first time in its in its more than fifty-year history that Article 5 of the North Atlantic Treaty had to be invoked; it provides that an attack on one country is an attack on all the member countries. In fighting the war on terror, the Bush administration recognized that no matter how preponderant American power was, some aspects of its foreign policy could not be achieved without multilateral cooperation. On the other hand, the United States did not want to be constrained by its alliances. The global coalition initially forged after September 11 numbered over 170 countries. Not all joined the war effort in Afghanistan, but most if not all provided some form of support for some aspect of the war on terrorism, such as economic sanctions and intelligence. The war in Iraq, however, put the "coalition of the willing" to a test. The Bush administration was

Military force is the most visible instrument of foreign policy. The use of such force, however, almost always engenders unanticipated consequences and problems, as America's experience in Iraq has shown.

determined not to make its decision to go to war subject to the UN or NATO or any other international organization. The breadth of the United States' coalition was deemed secondary to its being nonconstraining. As a result, other than the British government, no major power supported the United States' actions.

Military Force

The most visible instrument of foreign policy is, of course, military force. The United States has built the world's most imposing military, with army, navy, marine, and air force units stationed in virtually every corner of the globe. The United States spends nearly as much on military might as the rest of the world combined (Figure 18.3). The famous Prussian military strategist Carl von Clausewitz called war "politics by other means." By this he meant that nations used force not simply to demonstrate their capacity for violence. Rather, force or the threat of force is a tool nations must sometimes use to achieve their foreign-policy goals. Military force may be needed to protect a nation's security interests and economic concerns. Ironically, force may also be needed to achieve humanitarian goals. For example, without international military protection, the Africans who have taken refuge in Darfur camps would be at the mercy of the violent Sudanese regime.

Though force is sometimes necessary, military force is generally seen as a last resort and avoided if possible because of a number of problems commonly associated with its use. First, the use of military force is extremely costly in both human and financial terms. In the past fifty years, tens of thousands of Americans have been killed and hundreds of billions of dollars spent in America's military operations. Before they employ military force to achieve national goals, policy makers must

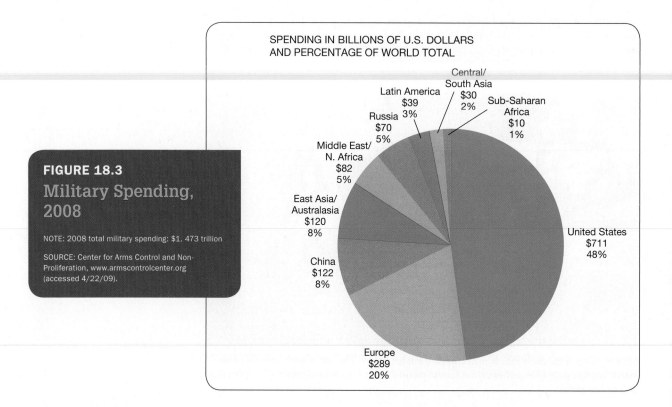

FIGURE 18.3
Military Spending, 2008

NOTE: 2008 total military spending: $1. 473 trillion

SOURCE: Center for Arms Control and Non-Proliferation, www.armscontrolcenter.org (accessed 4/22/09).

SPENDING IN BILLIONS OF U.S. DOLLARS AND PERCENTAGE OF WORLD TOTAL

Central/South Asia $30 2%
Latin America $39 3%
Sub-Saharan Africa $10 1%
Russia $70 5%
Middle East/N. Africa $82 5%
East Asia/Australasia $120 8%
China $122 8%
United States $711 48%
Europe $289 20%

be certain that achieving these goals is essential and that other means are unlikely to succeed.

Second, the use of military force is inherently fraught with risk. However carefully policy makers and generals plan for military operations, results can seldom be fully anticipated. Variables ranging from the weather to unexpected weapons and tactics deployed by opponents may upset the most careful calculations and turn military operations into costly disasters or convert maneuvers that were expected to be quick and decisive into long, drawn-out, expensive struggles. For example, American policy makers expected to defeat the Iraqi army quickly and easily in 2003—and they did. Policy makers did not anticipate, however, that American forces would still be struggling years later to defeat the insurgency that arose in the war's aftermath.

Finally, in a democracy, any government that chooses to address policy problems through military means is almost certain to encounter political difficulties Generally speaking, the American public will support relatively short and decisive military engagements. If, however, a conflict drags on, producing casualties and expenses with no clear outcome, the public loses patience and opposition politicians point to the government's lies and ineptitude. Korea, Vietnam, and Iraq are all examples of protracted conflicts whose domestic political repercussions brought down the governments that decided military force was needed.

Thus, military force remains a major foreign-policy tool, and the United States currently possesses a more powerful and effective set of military forces than any other nation. Nevertheless, even for the United States, the use of military force is fraught with risk and is not to be undertaken lightly.

Arbitration

The final foreign-policy tool we shall consider is dispute arbitration. Arbitration means referring an international disagreement to a neutral third party for resolution. Arbitration is sometimes seen as a form of "soft power" as distinguished from military force, economic sanctions, and other coercive foreign-policy instruments. The United States will occasionally turn to international tribunals to resolve disputes with other countries. For example, in February 2008, the U.S. government asked the International Court of Justice to resolve a long-standing dispute with Italy over American property confiscated by the Italian government more than forty years ago. To take another example, in 1981 the United States and Iran established an arbitral tribunal to deal with claims arising from Iran's seizure of the U.S. embassy in Tehran in 1979.

More important, the United States relies heavily on the work of arbitral panels to maintain the flow of international trade on which America's economy depends. American firms would be reluctant to do business abroad if they could not be certain that their property and contractual rights would be honored by other nations. Arbitration helps produce that certainty. Almost every international contract contains an arbitration clause requiring that disputes between the parties will be resolved not by foreign governments but by impartial arbitral panels accepted by both sides. By the terms of the New York Convention, virtually every nation in the world has agreed to accept and enforce arbitral verdicts. The United States has incorporated the terms of the New York Convention into federal law, and U.S. courts vigorously enforce arbitral judgments. The United States may not be happy with the outcome of every arbitral proceeding, but the arbitral system is essential to America's economic interests.

Thinking Critically about America's Role in the World Today

The nineteenth-century British statesman Lord Palmerston famously said, "Nations have no permanent friends or allies; they only have permanent interests." Palmerston's comment illustrates what is sometimes known as the "realist" view of foreign policy. The realist school holds that foreign policies should be guided by the national interest—mainly security and economic interest—and that policy makers should steel themselves to the necessity of making decisions that might be viewed from the outside as cold and ruthless if they serve the nation's interests. Although many public officials have denounced such views in public—especially if they were running for office—many have become realists once in power. Every one of America's post–World War II presidents, liberals and conservatives, Democrats and Republicans alike, have been willing to order young Americans into battle and to visit death and destruction on the citizens of foreign states if they believed the national interest required it.

The harsh rationality of foreign policy often clashes with America's history and ideals. Our democratic and liberal traditions lead us to hope for a world in which ideals rather than naked interests govern foreign policy and in which our leaders pay heed to ideals. The ideals that Americans have historically espoused (though not always lived by) assert that our foreign policies should have a higher purpose than the pursuit of interest and that America is to use force only as a last resort. Since the realities of our foreign policy often clash with these historic ideals, our policy makers often struggle to explain their actions and avoid admitting to motivations that don't embody those ideals.

"I have previously stated and I repeat now that the United States plans no military intervention in Cuba." said President John F. Kennedy in 1961 as he planned military action in Cuba. "As president, it is my duty to the American people to report that renewed hostile actions against United States ships on the high seas in the Gulf of Tonkin have today required me to order the military forces of the United States to take action in reply," said President Lyndon Johnson in 1964 referring to a fabricated incident used to justify expansion of American involvement in Vietnam. "We did not, I repeat, did not trade weapons or anything else [to Iran] for hostages, nor will we," said President Ronald Reagan in November 1986, four months before admitting that U.S. arms had been traded to Iran in exchange for Americans being held hostage there. "Simply stated, there is no doubt that Saddam Hussein now has weapons of mass destruction," said Vice President Dick Cheney in 2002. When it turned out that these weapons did not exist, Assistant Defense Secretary Paul Wolfowitz explained, "For bureaucratic reasons, we settled on one issue, weapons of mass destruction [as justification for invading Iraq] because it was the one reason everyone could agree on."[23] These false statements may hide discrepancies between our historic ideals and rationality, but they do not resolve them.

The ever-present conflicts between ideals and harsh realities manifested themselves again in 2009. As a candidate for the presidency, Barack Obama was praised for denouncing the Bush administration's treatment of enemy combatants. Obama was especially critical of the Guantánamo detention facility, where some alleged enemy combatants were incarcerated, and the creation of military tribunals, outside the regular court system, to hear their cases. Once in office, however, Obama did not rush to close the Guantánamo facility—though he continued to plan for

for critical analysis

In what ways do America's ideals affect the nation's foreign policies? Should foreign policies be guided by ideals or determined by national interests?

Make Your Voice Heard in Foreign Policy

On April 4, 2008, a group of students at the University of Utah staged a "die-in" to raise awareness about the genocide in Darfur, Sudan. Following in the footsteps of thousands of students nationwide, these young men and women spent five minutes lying in silence to symbolize the victims who have died or been displaced since the conflict began. The students were part of a local chapter of STAND, an acronym for "Students Taking Action NOW: Darfur." Formed in 2004, the antigenocide student-run organization has chapters in over 600 colleges and high schools throughout the United States. These students have been motivated to action by stories of the hundreds of thousands of Sudanese who have died from violence, disease, and starvation, as well as the 2.5 million refugees who have fled their homes since the conflict began.

The students in STAND fall in line with a history of student activism that is associated with divestment strategies. In the 1980s, college students nation-wide, horrified by the apartheid system in South Africa, urged their colleges and universities to divest from the country—and pushed for U.S. sanctions against the South African government. Just like the STAND activists, anti-apartheid groups educated their fellow students about the issue, staged protests, and lobbied policy makers. Some even lived in make-shift shanties on campus quads, to serve as symbols of the conditions of blacks under apartheid.

You may feel you do not know enough about U.S. foreign policy to get involved in the debate. Fortunately, there are many easily accessible resources available to help you learn and, once you've educated yourself, many outlets for action.

- *Take the test.* You can test your own geographic knowledge by taking a quiz from National Geographic at www.nationalgeographic.com/roper2006/. You can see how well you do—and how you compare to other young adults worldwide.

- *Educate yourself.* The Council on Foreign Relations (www.cfr.org) is a nonpartisan, nonprofit organization that has numerous resources for educating yourself about the key issues in U.S. foreign policy. You can link to background materials to learn about the key issues facing the nation and the world.

- *Join an advocacy group.* As you learn more about key issues, you may find yourself developing support for a particular perspective or side in the debate. There are groups working to influence public policy from every perspective. Visiting their Web sites and taking advantage of their educational materials, as well as the opportunities they offer to get more involved, will provide you a means of adding your voice to others who share your values. For example, if you are concerned about the war in Iraq, you can check out the National Youth & Student Peace Coalition (www.nyspc.org). Or, if you think U.S. foreign policy should be more oriented toward reflecting key American values of equality and justice, then you can read the materials and sign the petitions at www.justforeignpolicy.org. Finally, if you want to work to ensure that the American troops in Afghanistan and Iraq receive the support they need, look into www.moveamericaforward.org.

- *Educate your fellow students.* You may find that you are so moved by some of the foreign-policy issues that you want to share your knowledge with other students. Many of the national organizations have resources to help students start campus chapters. STAND, for example, will provide you with training in establishing a group on campus, instructions on how to advocate effectively, and even help you to find speakers to bring to campus.

the facility's eventual closure. As for the tribunals, the Obama administration indicated in 2010 that it might employ them in some cases after all, not wishing to bring the most important enemy combatant cases to the regular courts. Ideals seemed to have given way to interests again.

Must America always choose between its ideals and its interests? The founders of the republic believed that America would be different from other nations. They believed that its ideals would be its source of power; that its ideals would allow it to inspire and lead others as a "shining beacon." If, in the interest of national power and security, our political leaders always choose narrow interests over transcendent ideals, might they be robbing America of its true source of international power and global security?

studyguide

Practice Quiz

Find a diagnostic Web Quiz with 31 additional questions on the StudySpace Web site: www.wwnorton.com/we-the-people

The Goals of Foreign Policy

1. Which of the following terms best describes the American posture toward the world prior to the middle of the twentieth century? (p. 688)
   a) interventionist
   b) isolationist
   c) appeasement
   d) none of the above

2. The "Cold War" refers to the (p. 689)
   a) competition between the United States and Canada over Alaska.
   b) the years between World War I and World War II when the United States and Germany were hostile to one another.
   c) the period of struggle between the United States and the Soviet Union between the late 1940s and the late 1980s.
   d) the economic competition between the United States and Japan today.

3. Which of the following terms describes the idea that the development and maintenance of military strength discourages attack? (p. 689)
   a) deterrence
   b) containment
   c) "Minuteman" theory of defense
   d) détente

4. If the United States has granted most favored nation status to a country it means that (p. 692)
   a) the United States has offered that country the lowest tariff rate it already offers to other countries.
   b) the United States has agreed to give foreign aid to that country.
   c) the United States has signed a bilateral treaty with that country.
   d) the United States has offered to eliminate tariffs for that country.

5. Which of the following statements about the General Agreement on Tariffs and Trade is not true? (p. 692)
   a) It set many of the rules governing international trade.
   b) It was the precursor to the World Trade Organization.
   c) It was designed to reduce barriers to trade.
   d) It was in existence from 1791 to 1947.

Who Makes American Foreign Policy?

6. The Bush Doctrine refers to (p. 698)
   a) the idea that the United States should not allow foreign powers to meddle in the Western Hemisphere.
   b) the idea that the United States should avoid future wars by giving in to the demands of hostile foreign powers.

c) the idea that the United States should take preemptive action against threats to its national security.

d) the idea that the United States should never take preemptive action against threats to its national security.

7. The Constitution assigns the power to declare war to *(p. 699)*
   a) the president.
   b) Congress.
   c) the secretary of defense.
   d) the chief justice of the United States.

8. An agreement made between the president and another country that has the force of a treaty but requires only a plurality vote in both houses of Congress for approval is called *(p. 700)*
   a) an executive order.
   b) an executive agreement.
   c) a diplomatic decree.
   d) arbitration.

9. The making of American foreign policy is *(p. 701)*
   a) dominated entirely by the president.
   b) dominated entirely by Congress.
   c) dominated entirely by interest groups.
   d) highly pluralistic, involving a large mix of both official and unofficial players.

The Instruments of Modern American Foreign Policy

10. Which of the following was not an important international economic institution created in the 1940s? *(p. 708)*
    a) the Federal Reserve
    b) the World Bank
    c) the International Monetary Fund
    d) All three are important international economic institutions created in the 1940s.

11. Which of the following was dedicated to the relief, reconstruction, and economic recovery of Western Europe? *(p. 710)*
    a) the Marshall Plan
    b) the Lend-Lease Act
    c) the General Agreement on Tariffs and Trade
    d) the North American Free Trade Agreement

12. The North Atlantic Treaty Organization was formed in 1949 by the United States, *(p. 710)*
    a) Canada, and most of Eastern Europe.
    b) Canada, and Mexico.
    c) Canada, and most of Western Europe.
    d) Canada, and the United Kingdom.

13. Which statement best describes the United States' military spending compared to other countries? *(p. 712)*
    a) The United States spends significantly more than any other country in the world.
    b) The United States spends significantly more than any other country in the world except for China.
    c) The United States spends significantly less than any other country in the world.
    d) The United States spends about the same as most other countries in the world.

14. Which of the following statements about the United Nations is *not* true? *(p. 713)*
    a) It gives every country one vote in the General Assembly.
    b) It has a powerful army to implement its decisions.
    c) It was founded in 1945.
    d) It was designed to be a channel for negotiation and a means of settling international disputes peaceably.

Thinking Critically about America's Role in the World Today

15. The "realist" school of thought on foreign policy says *(p. 714)*
    a) a country's foreign policy should be guided by the preferences of their closest allies.
    b) a country's foreign policy should be guided by public opinion.
    c) a country's foreign policy should be guided by humanitarian concerns rather than by its own security and economic interests.
    d) a country's foreign policy should be guided by their security and economic interests even if this leads to decisions that may be viewed from the outside as ruthless and cold.

Chapter Outline

Find a detailed Chapter Outline on the StudySpace Web site: www.wwnorton.com/we-the-people

Key Terms

Find Flashcards to help you study these terms on the StudySpace Web site: www.wwnorton.com/we-the-people

appeasement *(p. 689)*
bilateral treaty *(p. 710)*
Bush Doctrine *(p. 698)*
Cold War *(p. 689)*
deterrence *(p. 689)*
diplomacy *(p. 704)*
executive agreement *(p. 700)*
General Agreement on Tariffs and Trade (GATT) *(p. 692)*

International Monetary Fund (IMF) *(p. 708)*
isolationism *(p. 688)*
most favored nation status *(p. 692)*
nation-state *(p. 690)*
non-state actors *(p. 688)*
North American Free Trade Agreement (NAFTA) *(p. 692)*

North Atlantic Treaty Organization (NATO) *(p. 710)*
preemption *(p. 691)*
preventive war *(p. 689)*
United Nations (UN) *(p. 705)*
World Trade Organization (WTO) *(p. 692)*

For Further Reading

Art, Robert. *The Use of Force: Military Power and International Politics*. New York: Rowman and Littlefield, 2009.

Bacevich, Andrew. *The New American Militarism: How Americans Are Seduced by War*. New York: Oxford University Press, 2006.

———. *The Limits of Power: The End of American Exceptionalism*. New York: Metropolitan Books, 2008.

Daalder, Ivo H., and James M. Lindsay. *American Unbound—The Bush Revolution in Foreign Policy*. Washington, DC: Brookings Institution Press, 2003.

Drezner, Daniel. "The Realist Tradition in American Public Opinion." *Perspectives on Politics* (March 2008), 51–70.

Fisk, Robert. *The Great War for Civilization: The Conquest of the Middle East*. New York: Knopf, 2005.

Gaddis, John L. *The Cold War: A New History*. New York: Penguin, 2005.

Jentleson, Bruce W. *American Foreign Policy—The Dynamics of Choice in the 21st Century*. 4th ed. New York: Norton, 2010.

Johnson, Chalmers. *The Sorrows of Empire*. New York: Henry Holt, 2004.

Kagan, Robert. *Dangerous Nation*. New York: Knopf, 2006.

Kaufman, Joyce. *A Concise History of U.S. Foreign Policy*. New York: Rowman and Littlefield, 2010.

Kennan, George F. *Around the Cragged Hill: A Personal and Political Philosophy*. New York: Norton, 1993.

Mandelbaum, Michael. *The Case for Goliath: How America Acts as the World's Government in the 21st Century*. Washington, DC: Public Affairs Press, 2005.

Renshon, Stanley. *National Security in the Obama Administration*. New York: Routledge, 2009.

Recommended Web Sites

American Israel Public Affairs Committee
www.aipac.org

Interest groups are some of the main shapers of foreign policy. One of the top lobbies in the nation, the American Israel Public Affairs Committee (AIPAC) works to strengthen the U.S.–Israel relationship.

Foreign Policy Association
www.fpa.org

This nonprofit organization tries to generate interest in and draw attention to global issues and policies.

International Monetary Fund
www.imf.org

World Trade Organization
www.wto.org

The International Monetary Fund (IMF) and the World Trade Organization (WTO) have been considered instruments of modern American foreign policy. Read about how these organizations are trying to promote capitalism, free trade, and economic development.

National Security Council
www.whitehouse.gov/nsc/

The National Security Council was formed in 1947 and consists of senior advisers and Cabinet officials who keep the president informed on all matters of national security and foreign policy.

Peterson Institute for International Economics
www.iie.com

The Peterson Institute for International Economics is dedicated to analyzing international economic policy. Take a minute to review some of the studies that have influenced the policies of such international organizations as NAFTA, the WTO, and the IMF.

United Nations
www.un.org

Founded in 1945, the United Nations (UN) promotes international peace and security. Visit the UN Web site for information on the General Assembly, the Security Council, economic and social development, and humanitarian issues.

U.S. Department of State
www.state.gov

The U.S. Department of State is the primary bureaucratic department for American diplomacy and national security.

U.S. Senate: Treaties
http://senate.gov/pagelayout/legislative/d_three_sections_with_teasers/treaties.htm

The most important foreign policy task of the Senate is reviewing and approving treaties. Learn more about the Senate's treaty-making powers and find information about treaty action at this U.S. Senate Web site.

In some ways, state-level politics in Texas resemble national politics, but in other ways Texas's political culture is quite distinctive.

The Political Culture, People, and Economy of Texas

WHAT GOVERNMENT DOES AND WHY IT MATTERS Legends die. Eras come to an end. Sometimes both happen at the same time.

On June 20, 1999, the former lieutenant governor Bob Bullock was laid to rest in the historic Texas State Cemetery in Austin. Bullock was a towering figure in Texas politics, almost larger than life, for over forty years. He was born on July 10, 1929, in Hillsboro, a small town near Waco in central Texas. As a student at Baylor University Law School, he was elected to the Texas House of Representatives in 1957 as a Democrat. He quit before the end of his second term in order to practice law. Bullock returned to state government in the mid-1960s as an assistant to Governor Preston Smith. Later, he was appointed secretary of state by Governor Smith. In 1974, Bullock

focusquestions

- What are the defining characteristics of political culture in Texas?

- What are the major geographic regions in Texas?

- What are the major economic changes that have defined the Texas political economy?

- How has Texas's demography evolved?

- What does it mean to say that Texas has become an urbanized state?

was elected state comptroller. After sixteen years as comptroller, Bullock was elected lieutenant governor, a position from which he dominated state politics for the next ten years.

Like his public career, Bullock's private life was sensational. He was divorced four times, married five. Early in his political career he had been a heavy drinker, often holding political court in one of Austin's many bars. Although he gave up alcohol for abstinence in the early 1980s, he never stopped holding court. His fierce temper was legendary, as was his willingness to use power to accomplish his objectives. He dominated people in Texas politics more than anyone else in his generation. As the political columnist Molly Ivins explained at his retirement, "Not since Lyndon B. Johnson has there been another pol who could so dominate everyone around him by sheer force of personality."[1]

Bullock was in many ways a throwback to an earlier time. When he entered politics, the state had been dominated by a Democratic Party establishment for over eighty years. To be a successful politician, one had to be white, male, and a conservative Democrat. By the time he left politics, minorities, women, and Republicans had come to play crucial roles in the state.

The 2010 elections signal a new crossroads in Texas politics but one whose ultimate destination may be unclear until well into the next legislative session. Long-term demographic pressures appear to favor the Democrats. But conservatives in the Republican Party in Texas have been revitalized at the grassroots level by the Tea Party movement. The political culture in Texas appears to be undergoing a dramatic shift.

chaptercontents

● Texas Political Culture

At the beginning of the twenty-first century, Texas finds itself at the start of a new era. Certain myths continue to define Texas in the popular imagination. An unpopulated rural land that rolls on forever, an arid countryside that challenges the hardiest of souls, undeveloped prairies that rise up into mountains, and a coastal region of inhospitable heat and humidity—such are the myths of the land that is Texas. The cowboy who challenges both Indian and Mexican rule, the rancher and farmer who cherish their economic independence, the wildcatter who is willing to risk everything for one more roll of the dice, and the independent entrepreneur who fears the needless intrusion of government into his life—such are the myths about the people. But the reality of the land and the people of Texas is a far cry from the myth.

Studies of Texas politics often begin with a discussion of the **political culture** of the state. Though the concept is somewhat open ended, states do often exhibit a distinctive culture that is the "product of their entire history." Presumably the political culture of a state has an effect on how people participate in politics and how individuals and institutions interact.[2] Daniel Elazar has created a classification scheme for state political cultures that is used widely. He uses the concepts of moralistic, individualistic, and traditionalistic to describe such cultures. These three state political cultures are contemporary manifestations of the ethnic, socioreligious, and socioeconomic differences that existed among the original thirteen colonies.[3]

According to Elazar, **moralistic political cultures** were rooted in New England, where Puritans and other religious groups sought to create the Good Society. In such a culture, politics is the concern of everyone and government is expected to be interventionist in promoting the public good and in advancing the public welfare. Citizen participation in politics is viewed as positive; people are encouraged to pursue the public good in civic activities.

Individualistic political cultures, on the other hand, originated in the middle states, where Americans sought material wealth and personal freedom through commercial activities. A state with an individualistic political culture generally places a low value on citizen participation in politics. Politics is a matter for professionals rather than for citizens, and the role of government is strictly limited. Government's role is to ensure stability so that individuals can pursue their own interests.

Traditionalistic political culture developed initially in the South, reflecting the values of the slave plantation economy and its successor, the Jim Crow era. Rooted in preindustrial values that emphasize social hierarchy and close interpersonal, often familial, relations among people, traditional culture is concerned with the preservation of tradition and the existing social order. In such states, public participation is limited and government is run by an established **elite**. Public policies disproportionately benefit the interests of those elites.

States can, of course, have cultures that combine these concepts. One book classified Colorado, for example, as having a "moralistic" political culture. California was classified as having a "moralistic individualistic" political culture and New York an "individualistic

political culture broadly shared values, beliefs, and attitudes about how the government should function. American political culture emphasizes the values of liberty, equality, and democracy

moralistic political culture the belief that government should be active in promoting the public good and that citizens should participate in politics and civic activities to ensure that good

individualistic political culture the belief that government should limit its role to providing order in society, so that citizens can pursue their economic self-interests

traditionalistic political culture the belief that government should be dominated by political elites and guided by tradition

elite a small group of people that dominates the political process

Although he was a Democrat, former lieutenant governor Bob Bullock supported George W. Bush's re-election as governor in 1998, saying that he thought Bush was the better candidate.

moralistic" culture. New Jersey was classified as "individualistic" and Georgia "traditionalistic." Florida and Kentucky were seen as "traditionalistic individualistic."

Often Texas is categorized as having a "traditionalistic individualistic" political culture.[4] Taxes are kept low, and social services are minimized. Political elites, such as business leaders, have a major voice in how the state is run. In spite of the difficulty in measuring the concept of political culture in any empirical way, it is a concept widely regarded as useful in explaining fundamental beliefs about the state and the role of state government.

Yet, the political culture of a state can change over time. Texas is undergoing dramatic changes, including some change in the state's political culture. It is also difficult to classify the political culture of a state as large and as diverse as Texas in any one category. In fact, Texas has many different political cultures or subcultures within its borders. In 2008, Texas was estimated to have 24.3 million people. Whites were estimated to comprise 47.4 percent of the population, Hispanics 36.5 percent, African Americans 11.3 percent, and Asian Americans 3.3 percent.[5] These people reside in a state that is larger in area than the combined area of the fifteen smallest states. Texarkana, in the far northeastern corner of the state, is actually closer to Chicago than it is to El Paso. El Paso is closer to the Pacific Ocean than it is to the eastern boundary of Texas, and the eastern boundary is closer to the Atlantic Ocean than it is to El Paso. One can drive in a straight line for over 800 miles without leaving Texas—almost the same distance as from New York City to St. Louis.

Three long-lasting patterns in Texas politics seem to indicate a "traditionalistic individualistic" state political culture. These patterns relate to a domination of the state by political elites interested in limited government with low taxes and few social services. It is also the case that at least some of these lasting characteristics of state politics are undergoing rapid change. These three patterns of state politics are described below.

The One-Party State

For over 100 years, Texas was dominated by the Democratic Party. Winning the Democratic Party primary was tantamount to winning the general election. As we will see in later chapters, this pattern no longer holds. During the 1990s, substantial competition emerged between the parties for control of the state legislature. Following redistricting in 2002, the Republicans secured a seven-vote majority in the state Senate and a twenty-four-vote majority in the state House. Between 2002 and 2010, all major statewide elected offices were controlled by Republicans. The question today is not whether the political culture of Texas will continue to be defined by a powerful Democratic Party but how that culture will be redefined by two forces: a powerful Republican Party in most suburban and rural areas and a resurgent Democratic Party in Texas's most urban counties.

Provincialism

A second pattern that has defined Texas political culture is **provincialism**, a narrow view of the world that is often associated with rural values and Jeffersonian notions of limited government. The result often was an intolerance of diversity and a notion of the public interest that dismissed social services and expenditures for education. Some of the more popular politicians in Texas have stressed corn pone, intolerance, and a narrow worldview rather than policies that might offer advantages to the state as it competes with other states and with other nations. Like the

provincialism a narrow, limited, and self-interested view of the world

The Lone Star is the symbol of Texas and reflects its individualistic political culture.

Ties between business and political leaders in Texas have always been strong. Here, Governor Rick Perry appears with Ralph Babb, the chief executive of Comerica Bank, to announce that Comerica would move its corporate headquarters to Dallas.

one-party Democratic state, Texas provincialism has faded as a defining feature of the political culture. The growing influence of minorities, women, and gays in state politics and the ongoing urbanization of the state have undercut provincialism.

Business Dominance

A third, continuing pattern that has helped to define Texas's political culture is its longtime dominance by business. Labor unions are rare in Texas except in the oil-refinery areas around Beaumont–Port Arthur. Other groups that might offer an alternative to a business perspective, such as consumer interests, are poorly organized and funded. Business groups are major players in Texas politics, in terms of campaign contributions, organized interest groups, and lobbyists.

This chapter will investigate the economic, social, and demographic changes that transformed Texas's political culture during the twentieth century. These changes shook Texas government and politics in the 1990s and have continued to shape them in the first decade of the twenty-first century.

● The Land

Much of Texas's history has been shaped by the relationship forged between its people and the land. Texas is the second largest state in size, next to Alaska, comprising 267,000 square miles. The longest straight-line distance across the state from north to south is 801 miles; the longest east-west distance is 773 miles. To

FIGURE 19.1

The Physical
Regions of Texas

SOURCE: Dallas Morning News, *Texas
Almanac 2000–2001* (Dallas: Dallas Morning
News, 1999), 55.

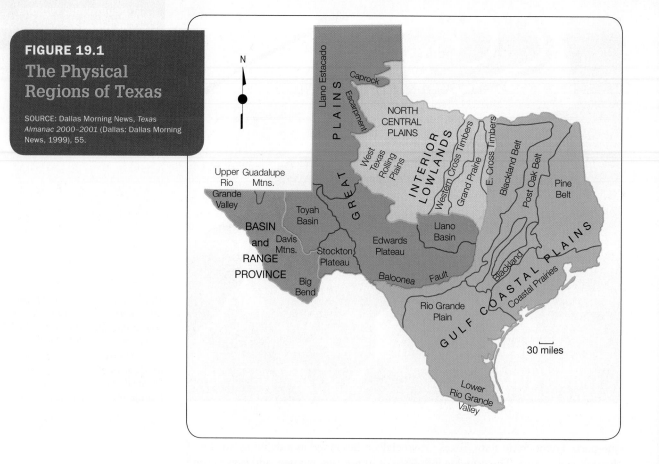

put this into perspective, the east-west distance from New York City to Chicago is 821 miles, cutting across five different states. The north-south distance between New York City and Charleston, South Carolina, is 763 miles, cutting across six different states.

Distances alone do not tell the whole story of the diverse geography found in Texas. There are four distinct physical regions in Texas: the Gulf Coastal Plains, the Interior Lowlands, the Great Plains, and the Basin and Range Province (see Figure 19.1).[6]

The Gulf Coastal Plains

The Gulf Coastal Plains extend from the Louisiana border and the Gulf of Mexico, along the Rio Grande up to Del Rio, and northward to the line of the Balcones Fault and Escarpment. As one moves to the west, the climate becomes increasingly arid. Forests become less frequent as post oak trees dominate the landscape until they too are replaced by the prairies and brush lands of Central Texas.

The eastern portion of the Gulf Coastal Plains—so-called East Texas—is characterized by hilly surfaces covered by forests of pine and hardwoods. Almost all of Texas's timber production takes place here. It is also the home of some of Texas's most famous oil fields. To the west is the Blackland Belt. A rolling prairie soil made the Blackland Belt a prime farming area during the late nineteenth and early twentieth centuries. It was a major center of cotton production in Texas. Today it is the most densely populated area of the state and has a diversified manufacturing base.

The Coastal Prairies around Houston and Beaumont were the center for the post–World War II industrial boom, particularly in the petrochemical industry. Winter-vegetable and fruit production play a major role in the Lower Rio Grande Valley, while livestock is important in the Rio Grande Plain, an area that receives less than twenty-four inches of rainfall on average every year and during the summer months experiences rapid evaporation.

● What are the major economic changes that have defined the Texas political economy?

The Interior Lowlands

The Interior Lowlands region is an extension of the interior lowlands that run down from Canada. They are bordered by the Balcones Escarpment on the east and south and the Caprock Escarpment on the west. Beginning to the west of Fort Worth, the eastern edge of the Interior Lowlands has predominantly an agricultural economy and a rural population. The western portion, meanwhile, rises from 750 to 2,000 feet in elevation. The West Texas Rolling Plains contain much level, cultivable land, and is the home to a large cattle-raising industry. Many of the state's largest ranches are located here.

for critical analysis
How has the diverse geography of Texas affected its development?

The Great Plains

Pushing down into northwest Texas from the Rocky Mountains to the Balcones Fault, the Great Plains define the terrain in much of western Texas, rising from 2,700 feet in the east to more than 4,000 feet along the New Mexico border. The major city on the northern plains is Amarillo. Ranching and petroleum production dominate the economy. The southern plains economy centers around agriculture and cotton production, with Lubbock as the major city. Large-scale irrigation from underwater reservoirs, particularly the Ogallala Aquifer, has played a major role in the economic development of this region. A major concern of policy makers is that pumping out of the aquifer exceeds replenishment, raising questions of the viability of basing future growth on the irrigation practices of the past.[7]

The Basin and Range Province

The fourth geographic region in Texas is the Basin and Range Province. Here one finds Texas's true mountains in the Guadalupe Range along the border with New Mexico, which includes Guadalupe Peak (8,749 feet) and El Capitan (8,085 feet). To the southeast is Big Bend country, so named because the Rio Grande River surrounds it on three sides as the river makes its southward swing. Rainfall and population are sparse in this region.

● Economic Change in Texas

The famous twentieth-century economist Joseph Schumpeter characterized the capitalist economic system as being a process of "creative destruction."[8] By this he meant that capitalism was an economic system that underwent periodic waves of transformation fueled by technological innovations in production and distribution. These waves of technological transformation were put into place by entrepreneurs who had visions of new ways of producing and distributing goods and services and who were willing to act on those visions. The capitalist process of creative destruction not only creates a new economic and social world, it destroys old ones. The world of railroads, steam, and steel transformed American economic and social life by nationalizing the market and making new opportunities available to businesses and individuals during the late nineteenth century. It also destroyed the local markets that had defined rural American communities since the Founding. Similarly, the technological innovation tied to gasoline combustion engines, electricity, and radio restructured the American economy again in the 1920s, leaving in its wake a society and economy that would never be the same.

Schumpeter's theory of creative destruction provides a useful way to think about the economic changes that have shaped and reshaped the Texas economy since the days of the Republic. Three great waves of technological change have helped to define and redefine the Texas political economy over the last 150 years. The first centered on the production of cotton and cattle and their distribution by an extensive railroad system. The second grew out of the oil industry. The third and most recent is tied to the development of the high-tech economy.

Cotton

Cotton is one of the oldest crops grown in Texas.[9] Missions in San Antonio in the eighteenth century are reported to have produced several thousand pounds of cotton annually, which were spun and woven by local artisans. Serious cultivation of cotton began in 1821 with the arrival of Anglo Americans. Political independence, statehood, and the ongoing removal of the Native American "threat" in the years before the Civil War promoted the development of the cotton industry. By the mid-nineteenth century, cotton production in Texas soared, placing Texas eighth among the top cotton-producing states in the Union. Although production fell in the years following the Civil War, by 1869 it had begun to pick up again. By 1880, Texas led all states in the production of cotton in most years.

A number of technological breakthroughs further stimulated the cotton industry in Texas. In the 1870s, barbed wire was introduced, enabling farmers to cordon off

During the late nineteenth century, in most years Texas produced more cotton than any other state. But although one-quarter of the cotton produced in the United States still comes from Texas, the state's cotton industry has been in decline since the 1920s. This photo shows land and machinery once used to farm cotton.

their lands and protect their cash crop from grazing cattle. Second, the building of railroads brought Texas farmers into a national market. Finally, a newly designed plow made it easier to dig up the prairie soil and significantly increase farm productivity.

Throughout the 1870s, immigrants from the Deep South and Europe flooded the prairies of Texas to farm cotton. Most of these newly arrived Texans became tenant farmers or sharecroppers. Tenants lived on farms owned by landowners, providing their own animals, tools, and seed. They generally received two-thirds of the final value of the cotton grown on the farm, while the landlords received the other third. Sharecroppers furnished only their labor but received only one-half of the value of the final product. Almost half of the state farmers were tenants by the turn of the century.[10]

Two important consequences resulted from the tenant and sharecropping system. First, it created a system of social and economic dependency that trapped many Texans in the rural areas. The notorious "crop-lien" system was developed to extend credit to farmers in exchange for liens on their crops. The result often was to trap farmers in a debt cycle from which they could not escape. Second, the tenant and sharecropping system helped to fuel radical political discontent in rural areas, sparking both the Grange and Populist movements. These movements played a major role in defining the style of Texas politics throughout much of the late nineteenth and early twentieth centuries.

Cotton production cycled up and down as farmers experienced a series of crises and opportunities during the late nineteenth and early twentieth centuries, ranging from destructive boll weevils to an increased demand brought on by World War I to a collapse in prices following the war. Although some sharecroppers returned to the farm during the Great Depression in the 1930s, the general decline of the cotton culture continued after World War II. The production of cotton also shifted from East and Central Texas to the High Plains and Rio Grande Valley.[11]

Cattle Ranching

The history of ranching and the cattle industry parallels that of cotton in many ways.[12] Its origins extend back to the late seventeenth century, when the Spanish brought livestock to the region to feed their missionaries, soldiers, and civilians. Ranching offered an attractive alternative to farming for immigrants during the periods of Mexican and Republican rule. In the 1830s, traffic in cattle was limited to local areas. This began to change as cattle drives and railroads began opening up new markets in the East.

Following the Civil War, the cattle industry took off, expanding throughout the state. As with cotton, the invention of barbed wire helped to close off the lands used for grazing. By the end of the nineteenth century, ranch lands had been transformed from open range to fenced pasturing. As a result, conflicts over land often broke out between large and small ranchers, as well as between ranchers and farmers. As cattle raising became a more specialized and rationalized business, periodic conflicts broke out between employers and employees. Throughout the twentieth century, ranching remained a cyclical industry, struggling when national and international prices collapsed and thriving during upturns in the economy.

Ranching and cotton production still remain important industries in the state, although increasingly dominated by big agribusiness companies. As in the past, in 2008 Texas continued to lead the nation in livestock production. Similarly, it leads all other states in cotton production. Approximately one-quarter of the total cotton production in the United States comes from Texas. In 2008, the annual

Cattle ranching is another of Texas's dominant industries. The most famous ranch in Texas is the King Ranch, shown here in 1950. Currently covering almost thirteen hundred square miles, it is larger than the state of Rhode Island.

cotton crop was 4.6 million bales, down from a peak in 2005 of 8.4 million bales. The decline was in large part due to a severe drought.[13]

Neither cotton production nor ranching drives the Texas political economy as in the past. The number of people making a living from agriculture has dropped significantly over the last fifty years as agribusiness has pushed out the family farm and ranch. In 1940, 23 percent of the population worked on farms and ranches. Seventeen percent were suppliers to farms and ranches or helped to assemble, process, or distribute agricultural products. In 2008, less than 2 percent of the population lived on farms and ranches, with an additional 15 percent of the population providing support, processing, or distribution services to agriculture in Texas.

A new set of technological breakthroughs challenged the nineteenth-century dominance of cotton and cattle in the early twentieth century. These breakthroughs focused not on what grew on the land, but what lay beneath it.

Oil in the Texas Economy

Oil was first sighted in the mid-seventeenth century by Spanish explorers.[14] There was no market or demand for the product, and nothing was done to develop this natural resource. Over a century later, encouraged by a growing demand for petroleum products following the Civil War, a scattering of entrepreneurs dug wells, although they were not commercially viable. The first economically significant oil discovery in Texas was in 1894 in Navarro County near Corsicana. By 1898, the state's first oil refinery was operating at the site. Although production peaked in 1900, the economic viability of oil production had been proven.

What catapulted Texas into the era of oil and gas was the discovery at Spindletop on January 10, 1901. Located three miles south of Beaumont along the Gulf Coast, the Spindletop discovery produced Texas's first oil boom. The success of Spindletop encouraged large numbers of speculators and entrepreneurs to try their luck in the new business. Within three years, three major oil fields had been discovered within 150 miles of Spindletop.

Oil fever spread throughout Texas over the next decade. In North Central Texas, major discoveries took place at Brownwood, Petrolia, and Wichita Falls. In the teens, major discoveries were made in Wichita County, Limestone County near Mexia, and once again in Navarro County. In 1921, oil was found in the Panhandle, and by the end of the decade major oil fields were being developed all across the state. The biggest oil field in the state was found in October 1930 in East Texas. As Mary G. Ramos notes, "By the time the East Texas field was developed, Texas's economy was powered not by agriculture, but by petroleum."[15]

The oil and gas industry transformed the social and economic fabric of Texas in a number of important ways. By providing cheap oil and gas, the industry made possible a new industrial revolution in twentieth-century America that was fueled by hydrocarbons. Cheap oil provided a new fuel for transportation and manufacturing. Railroads and steamships were able to convert from coal to oil. Manufacturing plants and farms were able to operate more efficiently with a new cheap source of energy, encouraging individuals to migrate to cities away from farms. Automobile production was encouraged, as was the building of roads. The Interstate Highway System that was built during the 1950s and 1960s changed fundamentally the transportation patterns that shaped the movements of people and goods in Texas. The triangle formed by I-35 from San Antonio to Dallas–Fort Worth, I-45 from Dallas–Fort Worth to Houston, and I-10 from Houston to San Antonio became the heartland of the Texas economy and the location of an increasing percentage of the state's population (see Figure 19.2).

The oil and gas industry also sparked a rapid industrialization of the Gulf Coast region. Among the companies developing the Gulf Coast oil fields were Gulf Oil,

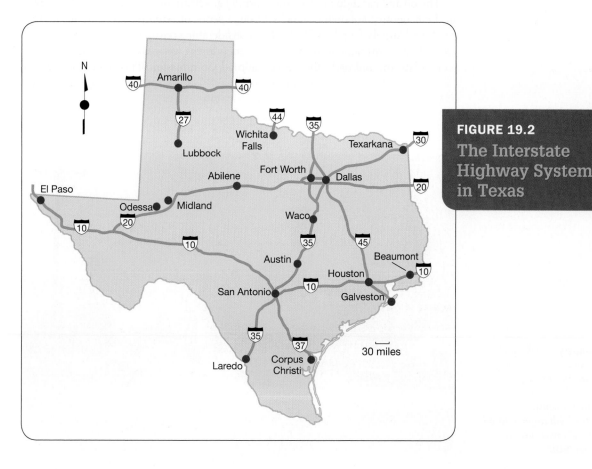

FIGURE 19.2

The Interstate Highway System in Texas

Sun Oil, Magnolia Petroleum, the Texas Company (later Texaco), and Humble Oil (which later became Esso, then Exxon, and finally ExxonMobil). The refineries, pipelines, and export facilities laid the foundations for the large-scale industrialization that would take place along the Gulf Coast in the Houston–Beaumont–Port Arthur region. By 1929 in Harris County, for example, 27 percent of all manufacturing employees worked in refineries. By 1940, the capacity of all the refineries had increased fourfold.[16] The petrochemical industry continued to flourish throughout the 1960s when demand for its products grew at the rate of 10 percent a year.

One important effect of the oil and gas boom in Texas was the development of a new rhythm to economic life in the state. There had been a natural pace to the economy when it was tied to the production of cotton and cattle. Prices of products could rise and fall, bringing prosperity or gloom to local economies. But there was a bond between the land and the people and the communities that formed around them. Oil and gas, on the other hand, introduced a boom-and-bust mentality that carried over into the communities that sprang up around oil and gas discoveries. Rural areas were often unprepared for the population explosion that followed an oil or gas strike. Housing was often inadequate or nonexistent. Schools quickly became overcrowded. General living conditions were poor as people sought to "make it big." The irony of the oil and gas business was that a major discovery that brought large amounts of new oil and gas to market could lead to a sudden collapse in prices. Prosperous economic times could quickly turn into local depressions. And when particular fields were tapped out, boom towns could quickly become ghost towns.

The oil and gas industry also transformed government and the role that it played in the economy. Following the Civil War, a series of attempts to regulate the railroads had largely failed. In 1890, after considerable controversy fueled by Populist antirailroad sentiment, a constitutional amendment was passed to create an agency to regulate the railroads, the Texas Railroad Commission. This regulatory agency

The oil industry transformed the social and economic fabric of Texas, leading to, among other things, the creation of boom towns—hastily constructed communities built around the oil fields in rural areas such as the Permian Basin.

TABLE 19.1

Oil Production in Texas

YEAR	PRODUCTION	VALUE	AVERAGE PRICE PER BARREL
1915	24,943,000	$13,027,000	$0.52
1945	754,710,000	$914,410,000	$1.21
1955	1,053,297,000	$2,989,330,000	$2.84
1965	1,000,749,000	$2,962,119,000	$2.96
1975	1,221,929,000	$9,336,570,000	$7.64
1980	977,436,000	$21,259,233,000	$21.75
1985	860,300,000	$23,159,286,000	$26.92
1990	672,081,000	$15,047,902,000	$22.39
1995	503,200,000	$8,177,700,000	$16.25
2000	348,900,000	$10,037,300,000	$28.77
2001	325,500,000	$7,770,500,000	$23.87
2002	335,600,000	$8,150,400,000	$24.29
2003	333,300,000	$9,708,600,000	$29.13
2004	327,910,000	$12,762,650	$38.92
2005	327,600,000	$12,744,600	$38.90
2006	314,600,000	$19,353,500	$61.52
2007	311,830,000	$21,341,100	$57.00
2008	315,896,000	$30,409,170	$79.12

SOURCE: Dallas Morning News, *Texas Almanac 2010–2011*. (Dallas: Dallas Morning News, 2010), 635.

was extended in 1917 to regulate energy. The Railroad Commission was empowered to see that petroleum pipelines were "common carriers" (that they transported all producers' oil and gas) and to promote well-spacing rules. In an attempt to bring stability to world oil prices brought on by the glut of oil on world markets in the 1930s, the commission won the authority to prorate oil and determine how much every oil well in Texas might produce. Through the late 1960s, the Texas Railroad Commission was one of the most important regulatory bodies in the nation. It was also one of the few democratically elected agencies.

Helping to expand the power of state government in the economy through the Railroad Commission was only one effect of the oil and gas industry in Texas. It also had an important fiscal effect on state government. Beginning in 1905, the state collected oil-production taxes. These rose from $101,403 in 1906 to over $1 million in 1919 and almost $6 million in 1929. By 2008, oil production taxes, or severance taxes, contributed $1.44 billion to the state budget. Natural gas production taxes added another $2.9 billion to the state budget.[17]

Much like the state coffers, higher education in Texas has benefited from the oil and gas industry. What many thought was worthless land at the time had been set aside by the state constitution of 1876 and the state legislature in 1883 to support higher education (the Permanent University Fund). As luck would have it, oil was discovered in the West Texas Permian Basin in 1923 on university lands. Soon seventeen wells were producing oil on university lands, sparking a building boom at the University of Texas. In 1931, the income of the Permanent University Fund was split between the University of Texas at Austin and Texas A&M University, with the former receiving two-thirds and the latter one-third. In 1984, the income was opened up to all University of Texas and Texas A&M schools. Along with the royalties from other natural resources on university land, oil and gas royalties created one of the largest university endowments in the world. In August 2009, the Net Asset Value of the Permanent University Fund was calculated to be $9.674 billion.[18]

The oil and gas industry had one other effect on life in Texas that is worth noting. Fortunes were made in the industry that paved the way for an expansion of private philanthropy that would have a major influence in shaping Texas's culture. Among the most famous of these were the Meadows Foundations, established in 1948 to promote programs in health, education, visual arts, social services, and historical preservation. The Sid W. Richardson Foundation was founded in 1947 and supported health and education programs, as well as the development of the arts in Fort Worth. The Bass Performance Hall, which opened in May 1998, was funded by the Bass brothers, grandnephews of the independent oilman Sid Richardson.

One can trace the rise and decline of the oil and gas industry in Texas through production figures (see Table 19.1). By the end of the twentieth century, oil and gas remained significant industries in the Texas economy, but they were becoming increasingly less important. As the 1980s slipped into the 1990s, the Texas economy continued to diversify. As Texas oil fields were drained, other industries and technologies began to assume significant roles in plotting the state's economic future. Among the most important of these was the burgeoning high-tech industry.

The Emergence of the High-Tech Economy

The movement out of the era of oil and gas and into that of high tech was not an easy one.[19] World oil prices rose in 1981 to almost $35 per barrel. At the time, oil-related businesses accounted for 26 percent of the gross state product. From 1971 to 1981, the average rate of economic growth was 4.4 percent. Fueled by a booming oil-based economy and a rapidly increasing population, real estate prices shot up in urban areas such as Houston and Dallas. Projections were made that as oil prices rose, perhaps to $70 or $80 per barrel on the world market, future prosperity was inevitable. Indeed, there was some talk that Texas's oil-driven economy had become recession-proof. Such talk proved to be premature, to say the least.

World oil prices began to collapse in 1982, bottoming out on March 31, 1986, at $10 per barrel. Other sectors of the economy began to suffer as the price of oil fell. Real estate deals fell through, and construction projects slowed and then shut down. Speculators defaulted on their loans, and banks began to fail. Throughout the 1980s, 370 banks went under in Texas. At the same time, the state went through two major recessions, one in 1982 and another in 1986–87. The average annual economic growth slowed to 1.7 percent, the worst since World War II.

In the 1990s, Texas emerged as a leader in high-tech industries. In 2009, computer and electronic products accounted for $35.2 billion in exports from Texas. This photo shows product testing being done at a Dell Computer plant in Austin.

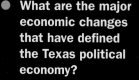

● What are the major economic changes that have defined the Texas political economy?

Texas emerged from the economic malaise of the eighties with a transformed state economy. Though remaining an important sector in the economy, the oil and gas business was no longer the primary driving force. By 1992, the production of oil had fallen to 642 million barrels worth only $11.8 billion. Production continued to fall until 2000 to just under 349 million barrels worth a little over $10 billion. Over 146,000 jobs had been lost in the oil industry throughout the 1980s. By the early 1990s, oil accounted for only about 12 percent of the gross state product.

In contrast to the 1980s, the 1990s was a period of rapid growth. Unlike early periods of speculative booms, such as the 1970s, the economy's growth was grounded in a rapidly diversifying economy. At the heart of this boom was a fast-growing manufacturing sector tied to high tech. In the 1990s, Texas went from seventh in the nation in total manufacturing employment to second. By 2008, 13 percent of the $160.8 billion gross state product came from manufacturing.[20]

Two metropolitan areas stand out as national centers for the rapidly evolving high-tech industry. The Austin–San Marcos metropolitan area has become a production center for computer chips, personal computers, and other related computer hardware. Seven of the area's largest employers are part of the computer or semiconductor industry. The Dallas metropolitan area, particularly north of the city, is the home of a number of important electronic and electronic-equipment companies.

NAFTA

Another defining feature of the Texas economy in the 1990s was the **North American Free Trade Agreement (NAFTA)**. Signed on December 17, 1992, by Prime Minister Brian Mulroney of Canada, President Carlos Salinas de Gortari of Mexico, and President George H. W. Bush of the United States, NAFTA sought to create a free-trade zone in North America that was the largest of its kind in the world. Considerable controversy surrounded the passage of NAFTA, with many groups arguing that free trade would hurt American workers and companies because of the cheap labor available in Mexico. After fourteen years, it appears that the trade

North American Free Trade Agreement (NAFTA) trade treaty among the United States, Canada, and Mexico to lower and eliminate tariffs among the three countries

The signing of NAFTA in 1992 created a free-trade zone in North America. Although many Texas workers were adversely affected by the availability of cheaper labor in Mexico, NAFTA appears to have had a beneficial effect on the state's economy as a whole. Here, President George H. W. Bush stands between President Carlos Salinas de Gortari of Mexico and Prime Minister Brian Mulroney of Canada at the signing ceremony.

Texas was not hit as hard as other states by the recession that started in 2007 and deepened in 2008. However, some Texans—including these Tea Party protesters—were alarmed by the massive spending involved in the national government's stimulus efforts.

agreement has had both negative and positive impacts on Texas.

One study found that NAFTA was responsible for approximately 25 percent of the increase in exports from Texas to Mexico and a third of those going to Canada between 1993 and 2000. According to a report from the U.S. Department of Labor, 27,676 workers in Texas were certified as being negatively affected by NAFTA between November 4, 2002, and September 30, 2007.[21] Such workers generally lost their jobs because of the stiffer competition from low-wage businesses in Mexico or because plants had been relocated to Mexico. (Under federal law such workers are entitled to additional unemployment compensation.)

Although there were some losers in the movement toward free trade with Mexico and Canada, there were also big winners. According to a Texas Public Policy Foundation report, conservative estimates are that Texas increased exports to Canada and Mexico by over $10 billion in the first five years of NAFTA. Of the thirty-two industries in Texas that export to Mexico, twenty-four had double-digit gains. Meanwhile, twenty-seven of the thirty-one industries that exported to Canada showed gains as well. Studies by the Department of Commerce and the Council of the Americas put the total number of jobs added to Texas's economy by NAFTA at 190,000 or higher. A few statistics put the importance of Texas's international trade, particularly with Mexico and Canada, into perspective.[22] In 2008,

- Texas exports totaled $192.1 billion, a $23.9 billion increase from 2007. This ranked Texas number one, among states for exports.
- The North American market (Mexico and Canada) was the destination for 41.9 percent of these exports.
- Mexico was the top importer at $62.08 billion.
- Canada imported $19.28 billion worth of goods, second to Mexico.

It is important to stress that Texas is only at the beginning of the era of high tech and NAFTA. The state is just starting to feel the effects of the movement into the information age and the global economy. It is impossible to say exactly what the state's economy will look like in twenty years, or which companies will become the Texacos or ExxonMobils of the information age. We can say, however, that it will be an economy as different from that of the oil and gas era as the oil and gas era was from the era of cotton and cattle.

Texas in the Great Recession

In December 2007, the nation entered what some have called "the Great Recession," a time of chronic economic problems that drew analogies to the Great Depression of the 1930s. A speculative bubble in the housing market fueled by cheap credit and poor business practices culminated in a credit crisis that brought some of America's largest banks and investment houses to their knees. Only the massive intrusion of the Federal Reserve System into credit markets in the fall of 2008 prevented the banking system from melting down. The Federal Reserve reported that between November 2007 and March 2009, 86 percent of American industries cut back production. The GNP dropped 1.7 percent and household net worth fell $11 trillion or 18 percent during the recession.[23]

Compared to the rest of the nation, Texas weathered the Great Recession relatively well. The housing market declined much less severely in Texas than in the rest of the nation. Most of Texas did not experience the surge in real estate values found in other states like California, Nevada, Florida, and Arizona. While foreclosure rates throughout the country increased sixfold between 2005 and 2009, in Texas they rose only marginally. Texas's banking industry also appeared to have weathered the storm better than its counterparts in other states. Article XVI of the Texas Constitution, as amended in 1997, forbids consumers from using home-equity loans for credit that exceeds 80 percent of the mortgage, and this probably provided a cushion against the credit crunch.[24]

Texas was one of the last states to enter the Great Recession and seemed likely to be one of the first to exit. In spring 2010, jobs were being added to the state's economy, and unemployment stood well below the national rate. Housing starts and exports were also up, as were other leading economic indicators in the state. However, Texas faces huge budget shortfalls that have no easy solution. A diversified economy has helped Texas weather the economic storm to a considerable degree on, but there are no guarantees that the Great Recession is over.[25]

The People: Texas Demography

The population in Texas has grown rapidly since the early days of the Republic. In 1850, the population stood at a little over 210,000 people, over one-quarter of whom were African American slaves. Texas in 1850 also was an overwhelmingly rural state. Only 4 percent of the population lived in urban areas. By 1900 the population had increased to over 3 million people, with 83 percent continuing to live in rural areas. The 1980s began as boom years for population growth, with increases running between 2.9 percent and 1.6 percent per year from 1980 through 1986. With the collapse of oil prices, however, population growth slowed significantly between 1987 and 1989 to less than 1 percent.[26]

With a recovering economy, however, population growth surged forward in the 1990s (see Table 19.2). In 1990, 17 million people resided in the state. By 2009, the number of people was estimated to be 24.8 million. Slightly less than 47 percent of the population were Anglo American in 2009, down from 61 percent in 1990. Twelve percent were African American. Thirty-seven percent were Hispanic, up from 25 percent in 1990.

Three factors account for the population growth in Texas in the 1990s: natural increase due to the difference between births and deaths; international immigration, particularly from Mexico; and domestic immigration from other states. The makeup of the growth in population shifted in significant ways over the course of the decade. In 1991, almost two-thirds of population growth was accounted for by natural increases. A little over 20 percent was due to international immigration, while under 14 percent was due to domestic immigration. By 2006, natural increases accounted for only a little over half of the population growth, while international immigration accounted for 20 percent and domestic immigration for 30 percent. Interestingly, estimates were that between 120,000 and 160,000 people moved to Texas from Louisiana after Hurricane Katrina.[27] In the early years of the twenty-first century, Texas was being redefined not by native-born Texans but by individuals coming to Texas to share in and contribute to the state's high-tech economic boom.

TABLE 19.2

The Changing Face of Texas, 1850–2008

The population of Texas grew especially quickly during the 1990s, and continued to grow after 2000. Which group grew the most between 1990 and 2008?

	1850	1900	1950	1990	2009
Population	213,000	3,050,000	7,710,000	17,000,000	24,782,000
Anglo	72%	80%	87%	61%	47%
African American	28%	20%	13%	12%	12%
Hispanic	n/a	n/a	n/a	25%	37%
Other	n/a	n/a	n/a	2%	5%

n/a = not available

SOURCES: *Statistical Abstract of the United States: 1994* (Washington, DC: U.S. Department of Commerce, Bureau of the Census, 1994); Dallas Morning News, *Texas Almanac 2004–2005* (Dallas: Dallas Morning News, 2004), 10; Dallas Morning News, *Texas Almanac 2010–2011* (Dallas: Dallas Morning News, 2010), 395, 396; and U.S. Census Bureau, http://quickfacts.census.gov/qfd/states/48000.html (accessed 11/4/10).

Anglos

For most of the nineteenth and twentieth centuries, the dominant ethnic group was white, or Anglo. Anglos in Texas comprise a wide range of European ethnic groups, including English, Germans, Scots, Irish, Czechs, and European Jews. The first wave of Anglos came to Texas before the break with Mexico. Encouraged by impresarios such as Moses Austin and his son Stephen F. Austin, who were authorized by the Spanish and later the Mexican leaders to bring people to Texas, these Anglos sought inexpensive land. But they brought along a new set of individualistic attitudes and values about democratic government that paved the way for

Prior to statehood, many of Texas's Anglos were European immigrants. For instance, in 1844 close to 5,000 Germans arrived and soon thereafter established the towns of New Braunfels and Fredericksburg. This painting from the 1850s shows a German American family from Fredericksburg "going visiting."

FIGURE 19.3
Anglo Population in Texas Counties, 2000

SOURCE: Data are drawn from the 2000 census. Texas State Data Center, http://txsdc.utsa.edu/maps/thematic/cnty_anpop.php (accessed 3/28/08).

Anglo Population

- 0–1,000 persons (n = 15)
- 1,001–10,000 persons (n = 108)
- 10,001–100,000 persons (n = 110)
- 100,001–1,456,811 persons (n = 21)

the Texas Revolution. Following the Revolution, a new surge of Anglo immigrants came from the Deep South. Like their predecessors, they sought cheap land. But they brought with them new cultural baggage: slavery. By the time of the American Civil War, this group had come to dominate the political culture of the state. Although most Texas farmers did not own slaves themselves, the vast majority supported the institution as well as secession from the Union.

Defeat in the Civil War shattered the hegemony of the traditional Anglo power structure in the state. By the end of Reconstruction, however, it had reasserted itself, establishing the three patterns that defined Texas politics for the next hundred years: the one-party Democratic state, provincialism, and business dominance. Anglos continued to dominate and define Texas's political culture throughout much of the twentieth century. By the end of the century, however, much had changed. As a percentage of the population, Anglo influence peaked in 1950, when 74 percent of the population was officially categorized as Anglo. This percentage began to fall, reaching 46.7 percent in 2009, and will likely continue to fall.

Numbers alone do not tell the whole story. Anglos living in Texas at the end of the twentieth century were not cut from the same cloth as those who had preceded them. A new wave of Anglo immigration into Texas over the past forty years has redefined what it means to be an Anglo in Texas. No longer can one say that an Anglo lives on a farm, holds culturally conservative values, and is firmly tied to the Democratic Party. On the contrary, he or she may be an urbanite or suburbanite who wasn't born in Texas and votes Republican (see Figure 19.3).

Hispanics

Most Hispanics in Texas are people of Mexican descent.[28] Prior to independence from Spain, this included people born of Iberian (Spanish) parents as well as mestizos (people of mixed Spanish and Native American ancestry). In the early nineteenth century, approximately 5,000 people of Mexican descent were living in Texas. Although this number fluctuated considerably over the years, by 1850 it was estimated that 14,000 Texans were of Mexican origin. Texas became for many a refuge from the political and economic instability that troubled Mexico from the late 1850s to the 1920s. Despite periodic attempts to curtail the growth of the Mexican American population in Texas, it grew from an estimated 700,000 in 1930 to 1,400,000 in 1960. The 2000 census counted 5.1 million Mexican Americans living in Texas. By current estimates there are now more than 9.1 million Hispanics residing in Texas.[29]

Up until 1900, Hispanics constituted a majority in south Texas along the border with Mexico and in certain border counties of West Texas. During the first few decades of the twentieth century, Hispanics migrated to northwest Texas and the Panhandle to work as laborers in the newly emergent cotton economy. Labor segregation limited the opportunities available to many Hispanics before World War II. After World War II, however, many Hispanics left agricultural work and took jobs in the rapidly growing urban areas of Texas. By the end of the century, Hispanics comprised majorities in the cities of San Antonio and El Paso and sizable minorities in Houston, Dallas, Austin, and Fort Worth (see Figure 19.4).

Most Hispanics in Texas are Mexican American. During the first half of the twentieth century, Mexicans immigrated to Texas to work in the emerging cotton industry. This 1939 photo shows cotton pickers laboring in the sun over rows of white cotton.

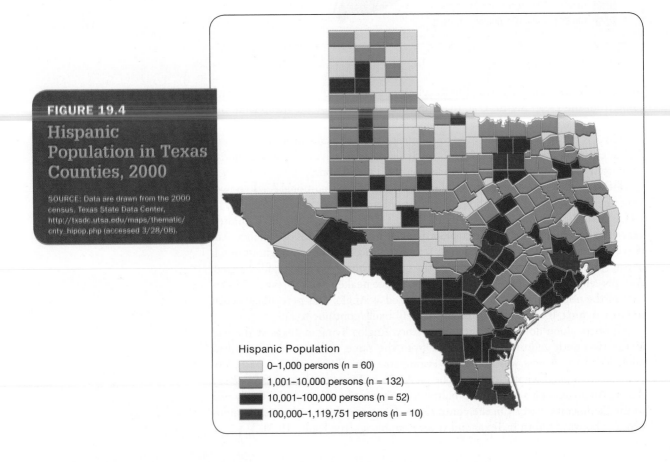

FIGURE 19.4

Hispanic Population in Texas Counties, 2000

SOURCE: Data are drawn from the 2000 census, Texas State Data Center, http://txsdc.utsa.edu/maps/thematic/cnty_hipop.php (accessed 3/28/08).

Hispanic Population

- 0–1,000 persons (n = 60)
- 1,001–10,000 persons (n = 132)
- 10,001–100,000 persons (n = 52)
- 100,000–1,119,751 persons (n = 10)

The political status of Hispanics in Texas has changed considerably over the past hundred years. In the nineteenth century, numerous obstacles limited their participation in the political life of the state. Voting, particularly among the lower classes, was discouraged or tightly controlled. The white primary and the poll tax actively discouraged voting by Hispanics. Only after World War II were Hispanic politicians able to escape some of the strictures that had been imposed on them by the dominant Anglo political culture of the time. A more tolerant atmosphere in the growing urban areas enabled Hispanic politicians to assume positions of importance in the local political community. In 1956, Henry B. Gonzalez became the first Mexican American to be elected to the Texas Senate in modern times. In the mid-1960s a political movement emerged in the Raza Unida Party, which sought to confront many of the discriminatory practices that isolated Texas Hispanics from the political and economic mainstream. By the 1980s, Hispanic political leaders were playing a growing role in state politics, and Hispanic voters were courted heavily by both political parties. The number of Hispanics elected to public office rose from 1,466 in 1986 to 2,294 in 2008. After the 2008 elections, the National Association of Latino Elected and Appointed Officials Education Fund reported that six Hispanics represented Texas in the U.S. House of Representatives; six Hispanics were in the Texas State Senate; and thirty-one Hispanics were elected to the Texas House of Representatives.[30]

African Americans

People of African descent were among the earliest explorers of Texas.[31] Most African Americans, however, entered Texas as slaves. Anglo Americans from the upper and lower South brought slaves with them to Texas. At first, antislavery attitudes among Spanish and Mexican authorities kept the slave population down. However, independence from Mexico lifted the restrictions on slavery, creating an incentive for southerners to expand the system of slavery westward. The number of slaves in Texas rose from 5,000 in 1830 to 11,000 in 1840 to 58,000 in 1850. By the Civil War, over 182,000 slaves lived in Texas, approximately one-third of the state's entire population.

Emancipation for African Americans living in Texas came on June 19, 1865. Emancipation, however, did not bring anything approaching equality. Between

As in most former slave states, there was initial resistance to the civil rights movement in Texas. These signs appeared in Fort Worth's Riverside section in September of 1956 during a protest over a black family's moving into a previously all-white block of homes.

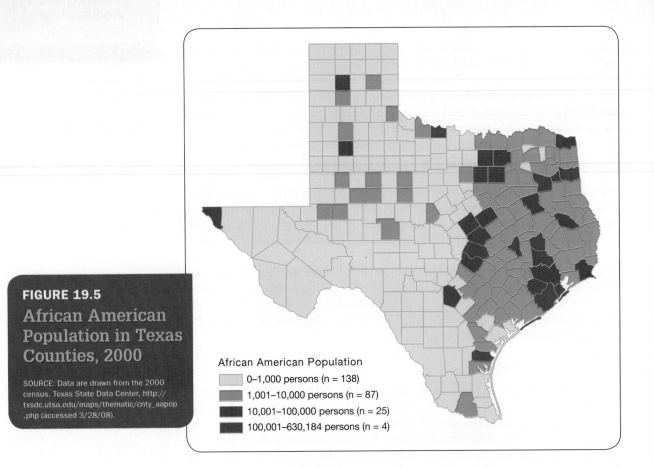

FIGURE 19.5

African American Population in Texas Counties, 2000

SOURCE: Data are drawn from the 2000 census. Texas State Data Center, http://txsdc.utsa.edu/maps/thematic/cnty_aapop.php (accessed 3/28/08).

African American Population

- 0–1,000 persons (n = 138)
- 1,001–10,000 persons (n = 87)
- 10,001–100,000 persons (n = 25)
- 100,001–630,184 persons (n = 4)

1865 and 1868, a series of Black Codes were passed by the state legislature and various cities that sought to restrict the rights of former slaves. Military occupation and congressional reconstruction opened up new opportunities for former slaves, who supported the radical wing of the Republican Party. Ten African American delegates helped to write the Texas constitution of 1869. Forty-three served as members of the state legislature between 1868 and 1900. The end of Reconstruction and the return to power of the Democratic Party in the mid-1870s reversed much of the progress made by former slaves in the state. In 1900, over 100,000 African Americans voted in Texas elections. By 1903, the number had fallen to under 5,000, largely due to the imposition of the poll tax in 1902 and the passage of a white-primary law in 1903. Segregation of the races became a guiding principle of public policy, backed by the police power of the state and reinforced by lynchings and race riots against African Americans. For all intents and purposes, African Americans had become second-class citizens, disenfranchised by the political system and marginalized by the political culture.

Federal court cases in the 1940s and 1950s offered some hope of relief to African Americans living in Texas. The white primary was outlawed in 1944 in the Supreme Court decision in *Smith v. Allwright*. In 1950, African Americans were guaranteed admission to Texas's graduate and professional schools in *Sweatt v. Painter*. Finally, the segregation of public schools was outlawed by the Supreme Court in *Brown v. Board of Education* in 1954.

Political progress was much slower. The Civil Rights Act of 1964 and the Voting Rights Act of 1965 helped to open up the political system in Texas to African

Americans. In 1966, a small number of African American candidates actually began to win political office in the state. In 1972, Barbara Jordan became the first African American to be elected to the United States House of Representatives from Texas.

Today the African American population is concentrated in East Texas, where the southern plantation and sharecropping systems were dominant during the nineteenth century. Large numbers of African Americans had also migrated to form sizable minorities in the urban and suburban areas of Houston and Dallas (see Figure 19.5). African American political leaders have come to play major roles in these areas as members of Congress, the state legislature, and city councils. African Americans were also elected mayors of Houston and Dallas in the late 1990s. The political influence of African Americans in Texas has not been extended to West Texas, where few African Americans live.

Age

When compared with the rest of the nation, the population of Texas is relatively young. In 2009, 27.8 percent of the population was under eighteen years old, compared with 24.3 percent nationally. In addition, only 10.2 percent of the population in Texas was sixty-five years of age or older, compared to 12.9 percent nationally. Having a relatively young population compared with those of other states presents Texas with a variety of problems and opportunities, as we shall see in later chapters.[32]

Poverty and Wealth

Younger populations tend to be poorer, as income and poverty statistics bear out. As noted above, the 1990s were a period of rapid economic growth in Texas. Between 1990 and 2000, personal income per capita in constant 1996 dollars rose from $20,388 to $25,363. Despite these gains, however, Texas continued to lag behind the nation as a whole (see Table 19.3). At the national level during the same period, personal per capita income rose from $22,870 to $27,269. By 2009, Texas ranked only twenty-ninth among the states in per capita income, up from thirty-second in 1990.

The percentage of the population in Texas living below the poverty level—a level established by the federal government, which will be discussed in more detail in Chapter 27—fell from 15.7 percent to 14.9 percent between 1990 and 2004,

for critical analysis

How did the population of Texas change during the 1990s? What is its racial and ethnic composition? How do these changes complicate the idea of the "typical" Texan?

TABLE 19.3

Per Capita Income in Texas and the United States, 1990–2009 (in Nominal Nonadjusted Dollars)

	1990	1995	2006	2009
USA	$19,477	$23,076	$36,276	$39,138
Texas	$17,421	$21,033	$34,257	$36,484

SOURCE: U.S. Department of Commerce, www.bea.gov/newsreleases/regional/spi/2007/spi0307.htm (accessed 3/28/08); Bureau of Economic Analysis: www.bea.gov (accessed 7/7/10).

rose to 16.9 percent in 2006, and fell to 15.8 percent in 2008. During the same period, the national poverty rate fell from 13.5 percent to 11.7 percent, rose to 13.3 percent in 2006, and fell to 13.2 percent in 2008.[33]

● Urbanization

urbanization the process by which people move from rural areas to cities

Urbanization is the process by which people move from rural to urban areas. Suburbanization is the process by which people move out of central city areas to surrounding suburban areas. Much of Texas's history is linked to ongoing urbanization. By the end of the twentieth century, this process was largely complete, as 88 percent of the population now resides in urban areas (see Table 19.4). Suburbanization, however, continues as city populations spill over into surrounding suburban areas.

Urbanization in Texas owes little to Native American civilization.[34] Most Texas cities are the result of European settlement and culture. The Spanish influence on urban life in Texas grew out of efforts to extend territorial control northward out of Mexico through a series of presidios (garrisons), missions (churches), and pueblos (towns). The physical organization and planning of the towns reflected this imperial mission. For example, the largest Spanish settlement was San Antonio. It was initially established as a supply depot to missions in East Texas. Later it expanded as missions were established to convert local Native Americans to Christianity and farms were cultivated to feed the local population. By the early nineteenth century, San Antonio's population had reached 2,500. Other smaller settlements were located in East Texas, along the border with French and, later, American territory.

Anglo American influence began with the arrival of Moses Austin in 1820 in San Antonio. Soon his son Stephen F. Austin followed. The Spanish offered the Austins and other impresarios grants of land to encourage the inflow of Americans into underpopulated regions of Texas. Small towns emerged as administrative units for impresario grants. There was considerably more freedom and dynamism in Anglo American urban areas than in Spanish ones. Americans brought with them a host of new interests and ideas that would transform urban life in Texas, including a new language, slavery, Protestantism, and a commitment to free enterprise and democracy. The courthouse became a central feature of many Anglo American towns, often located in the center of the town surrounded by shops.

TABLE 19.4

Urbanization in Texas, 1850–2008

	1850	1900	1950	2008*
Urban	4%	17%	63%	88%
Rural	96%	83%	37%	12%

SOURCES: *Statistical Abstracts of the United States: 1994* (Washington, DC: U.S. Department of Commerce, Bureau of the Census, 1994); Dallas Morning News, *Texas Almanac 2001-2002* (Dallas: Dallas Morning News, 2001); and U.S. Department of Agriculture, www.ers.usda.gov/StateFacts/TX.htm (accessed 3/28/08); Dept. of Agriculture, ers.usda.gov (accessed 7/7/10).
*estimated

How Is the Texas Population Changing?

The face of Texas is changing rapidly and will continue to change well into the future. The figures below show projections of how the Texas population will change over the next 30 years. The state's population will continue to grow quickly, especially as the number of Hispanic Texans increases. Further, most of the population growth in the state will happen in metropolitan areas—Dallas-Fort Worth, Houston, San Antonio, and Austin.

Race and Total Population

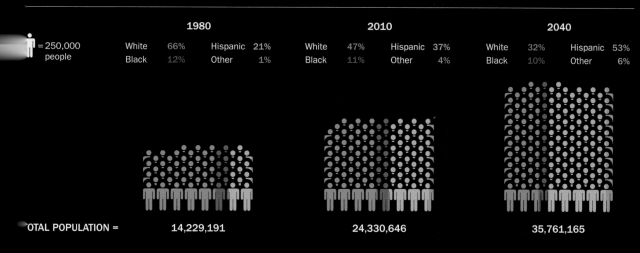

	1980			2010			2040	
White	66%	Hispanic 21%	White	47%	Hispanic 37%	White	32%	Hispanic 53%
Black	12%	Other 1%	Black	11%	Other 4%	Black	10%	Other 6%

= 250,000 people

TOTAL POPULATION =	14,229,191	24,330,646	35,761,165

Geography   Projected Population Growth from the year 2000, by Metropolitan Area

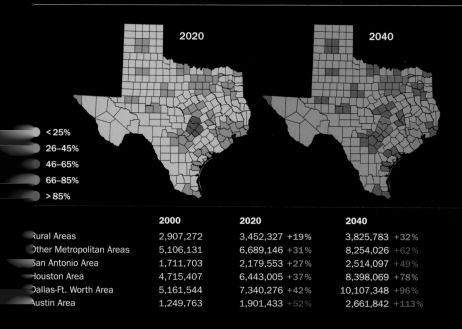

2020   2040

- < 25%
- 26–45%
- 46–65%
- 66–85%
- > 85%

	2000	2020		2040	
Rural Areas	2,907,272	3,452,327	+19%	3,825,783	+32%
Other Metropolitan Areas	5,106,131	6,689,146	+31%	8,254,026	+62%
San Antonio Area	1,711,703	2,179,553	+27%	2,514,097	+49%
Houston Area	4,715,407	6,443,005	+37%	8,398,069	+78%
Dallas-Ft. Worth Area	5,161,544	7,340,276	+42%	10,107,348	+96%
Austin Area	1,249,763	1,901,433	+52%	2,661,842	+113%

SOURCES: Texas State Data Center; Office of State Demographer.

for critical analysis

1. How do you think the increase in the Hispanic portion will change the nature of Texas politics? Will it change the issues that our state government focuses on? Will it have an impact on what party wins elections in Texas?

2. Texas is traditionally associated with images of farming, ranching, and other elements of rural life. How do you think the growth of the urban population will change the image of Texas?

The expansion of Anglo American urban life initially began along the Gulf Coast and gradually expanded east to west, particularly along rivers. New technologies transformed the urban landscape of Texas. Dredging technologies helped to stimulate the growth of port cities such as Houston, Galveston, Corpus Christi, and Brownsville. Railroad construction in the second half of the nineteenth century opened up new lands, which had been difficult for populations to reach, to urban development. In 1880, there were only eleven towns of 4,000 or more people in all of Texas. Following the rapid expansion of the railroads in the 1880s and 1890s, the number rose to thirty-six. By 1910, when the railroad network of 13,110 miles was completed, Texas had forty-nine towns with a population of 4,000 or more. By 1920, five cities—Dallas, El Paso, Fort Worth, Houston, and San Antonio—had populations of over 50,000. Later technological breakthroughs in transportation, such as cars and air travel, would reinforce the population grid laid out by the railroads.

The Urban Political Economy

political economy the complex interrelations between politics and the economy, as well as their effect on one another

Understanding the complexity of the **political economy** of Texas today demands having some sense of how Texas's three major metropolitan areas compare with each other (see Tables 19.5 and 19.6).

Houston Houston, located in Harris County, is the largest city in Texas and the fourth largest city in the United States—with a population of over 2 million—behind New York, Los Angeles, and Chicago. Its consolidated metropolitan area encompasses eight counties, with an estimated population of almost 5.7 million in 2008.

The city originated in 1836 out of the entrepreneurial dreams of two brothers, Augustus Chapman Allen and John Kirby Allen, who sought to create a "great interior commercial emporium of Texas."[35] The town was named after Sam Houston, the leader of Texas's army during its war of independence from Mexico. Early settlers came from the South, bringing with them the institution of slavery. As a consequence, segregation was built into the social structure from the outset. For the first half of the twentieth century, African Americans were either denied or given limited access to a variety of public services such as parks, schools, buses, restrooms, and restaurants. Although not enforced legally, residential segregation

TABLE 19.5

Populations of the Largest Cities in Texas (2009 Estimates)

Houston (Harris County)	2,254,690
San Antonio (Bexar County)	1,363,612
Dallas (Dallas County)	1,278,484
Austin (Travis County)	786,481
Fort Worth (Tarrant County)	717,136
El Paso (El Paso County)	618,251

SOURCE: Texas State Data Center, Office of the State Demographer, http://txsdc.utsa.edu (accessed 7/7/10).

TABLE 19.6

Ethnic Breakdown of Largest Texas Counties (2008 Estimates)

COUNTY	POPULATION (IN MILLIONS)	WHITE	BLACK	HISPANIC	OTHER
Harris	3.98	36%	18.7%	39.3%	6.5%
Dallas	2	45	20.5	29.9	4.7
Tarrant	1.4	62.8	13	19.7	4.5
Bexar	1.4	36.3	7.2	54.4	2.1
Travis	.8	57.3	9.4	28.2	5.1
El Paso	.7	17.4	2.9	78.2	1.4
Collin	.5	77.1	5	10.3	7.6

NOTE: This table is based on the U.S. Bureau of the Census 2000 survey.
SOURCE: Dallas Morning News, *Texas Almanac 2008–2009*.

divided the city into a number of distinct racially divided neighborhoods for much of the twentieth century.

In the late nineteenth century, Houston's economic well-being depended on cotton and commerce. Railroads played an integral role in placing Houston at the hub of the Texas economy. The opening of the Houston Ship Channel further enhanced Houston's place in the state economy by helping to turn it into the second or third (depending on whose ranking is used) deep-water port in the United States. But it was oil that fundamentally transformed the Houston area in the twentieth century. Oil refineries opened along the Ship Channel and a petrochemical industry emerged, making Houston one of the leading energy centers in the world. Today it continues to rank first in the nation in the manufacture of petroleum equipment.

By 1930, Houston had become the largest city in Texas, with a population of around 292,000 people. Population continued to expand throughout the 1940s, 1950s, and 1960s, assisted by a liberal annexation policy that enabled the city to incorporate into itself many of the outlying suburban areas. Although the oil bust in the mid-1980s slowed down the city's growth, it continued in the 1990s, extending into suburban areas such as Clear Lake City and other urban areas such as Galveston.

Of the 1.95 million people living in the city at the time of the 2000 census, 30.8 percent of the population was white non-Hispanic, 25.3 percent was black, and 5.3 percent was Asian. Hispanics (who may designate themselves as either white or black), meanwhile, counted for 37.4 percent of the overall population.

Dallas–Fort Worth The Metroplex is an economic region encompassing the cities of Dallas and Fort Worth, as well as a number of other suburban cities, including Arlington (population 355,641), Mesquite (145,798), Garland (234,003), Richardson (102,331), Irving (204,806), Plano (259,305), Carrollton (121,256), Grand Prairie (172,747), Denton (15,022), and Frisco (104,826).[36] The major counties in

for critical analysis

Based on the population growth, urbanization, and economic change of the last two decades, what do the next two decades hold for Texas? Which areas will grow in population, and will government be ready for that growth? What can/should government do to maintain and strengthen the economy of Texas?

In some areas of Texas, Asian immigrants are a growing force. The signs at this shopping center in Houston attest to the changing demographic landscape of Texas.

the area are Dallas, Tarrant, and Collin. The Metroplex is joined together by a number of interlocking highways running north-south and east-west, and a major international airport that is strategically located in the national air system.

Dallas was founded as a trading post in 1841, near where two roads were to be built by the Republic.[37] By the 1850s, it had become a retail center servicing the rural areas. By 1870, the population had reached 3,000 people. The coming of the Houston and Texas Central Railroad in 1871 and the Texas and Pacific Railroad in 1873 made Dallas the first rail crossroads in Texas and transformed forever its place in the state's economy. Markets now beckoned east and north, encouraging entrepreneurs and merchants to set up shop. Cotton became a major cash crop, and the population expanded over threefold to more than 10,000 people in 1880. By the turn of the twentieth century, the city had grown to over 42,000 people.

As with Houston, the oil economy changed the direction and scope of the city's economic life. With the discovery of oil in East Texas in 1830, Dallas became a major center for petroleum financing. By the end of World War II, the economy had diversified, making Dallas a minor manufacturing center in the nation. In the 1950s and 1960s, technology companies such as Ling-Temco-Vought (LTV) and Texas Instruments were added to the industrial mix, transforming Dallas into the third-largest technology center in the nation. The high-tech boom of the 1990s built off the corporate infrastructure laid down in the 1950s and 1960s.

Dallas grew from 844,401 people in 1970 to 904,078 in 1980 to an estimated 1,278,484 in 2009. According to the 2000 census, 34.6 percent of the population was white non-Hispanic, 25.9 percent was black, 35.6 percent was Hispanic, and 2.2 percent was Asian.

Although they are locked together in important ways economically, Dallas and Fort Worth are as different as night and day. Whereas Dallas looks to the East and embodies a more corporate white-collar business culture, Fort Worth looks to the West. It is where the West begins in Texas.

Fort Worth originated as an army post in 1849.[38] By 1853, the post had been abandoned as new forts were located to the west. Although settlers took the fort over, population growth was slow through the early 1870s. The spark that enabled the town to begin to prosper was the rise of the cattle industry. Fort Worth was a convenient place for cowboys to rest on their cattle drives to Kansas. Cattle buyers established headquarters in the city. Gradually other businesses grew up around these key businesses. Transportation and communication links improved with the establishment of stage lines to the west and railroad lines to the north and east.

By 1900, Fort Worth was served by eight different railroad companies, many of them transporting cattle and cattle-related products to national markets. The two world wars encouraged further economic development in Fort Worth. Over 100,000 troops were trained at Camp Bowie during World War I. World War II brought an important air force base and, along with it, the aviation industry. The Consolidated Vultee Aircraft Corporation, which was later bought by General Dynamics, became the largest manufacturing concern in the city. Between 1900 and 1950, the population grew from 26,668 to 277,047. It was estimated to be 717,136 in 2009. The overall metropolitan area of Dallas–Fort Worth included 6.3 million people as of 2008.

San Antonio San Antonio is located in Bexar County, the fourth-largest county in Texas today. San Antonio grew out of the Spanish presidio San Antonio de Bexar, which was founded in 1718.[39] In 1773, it became the capital of Spanish Texas, with a population of around 2,100 people. Because of the threats posed by Native Americans and Mexicans after the Texas Revolution, the population declined to about 800 people by 1846. On Texas's entry into the Union, however, the population took off, reaching 3,488 in 1850 and 8,235 in 1860. By the Civil War, San Antonio was the largest city in Texas.

Following the Civil War, San Antonio grew rapidly, stimulated by the building of the San Antonio Railroad in 1877. By 1880, the population had reached over 20,000 people, most being Anglo Americans from southern states. The population continued to grow through the first two decades of the twentieth century, reaching 161,000 by 1920. Mexican immigration increased significantly following the Mexican Revolution of 1910 and the building of a city infrastructure that provided paved roads, utilities, water, telephones, and hospitals. By midcentury, San Antonio had become a unique blend of Hispanic, German, and southern Anglo American cultures. Population growth slowed down in the 1930s but picked up again during World War II, reaching over 408,000 in 1950. Major military bases came to dot the landscape around San Antonio. By 1960, the population topped 587,000 people.

Today, San Antonio is Texas's second-largest city. The population of the city was estimated to be 1,363,612 in 2009, and the San Antonio metropolitan area as a whole had a population estimated to be 2,031,000 in 2008, making it the twenty-seventh largest metropolitan area in the country. San Antonio's population has become increasingly Hispanic. Approximately 62.6 percent of the people are Hispanic, 29 percent are Anglo American, and 6.2 percent are African American.[40]

Unlike Houston or Dallas, San Antonio lacks high-paying manufacturing jobs, and average metropolitan income is lower than in Houston and Dallas. The economy rests on four legs: national military bases, educational institutions, tourism, and a large medical research complex.

● Conclusion: Liberty, Equality, and Democracy in Texas

In this chapter, we have studied the political culture of Texas and seen how the state has been transformed by economic and demographic shifts over the past hundred years. Three great technological revolutions have reshaped the economic life of the state. The first—based on the production of agricultural products such cotton and cattle and on the newly built railroad system—defined economic life in the latter decades of the nineteenth and early twentieth centuries. The second—based on the production of oil and the industries that cheap oil made possible—dominated the economy well into the second half of the twentieth century. The third—the era of high tech—has transformed the state by diversifying its economy and tying it closely to the growing international economy. Accompanying and fueling these economic revolutions has been ongoing demographic change, which has redefined who the "typical" Texan is and where this person lives. No longer can it be said that a "typical" Texan is simply an extension of an Anglo American culture rooted in southern tradition. No longer does this person reside in a small town, living life close to the land much as his or her ancestors did. Like the economy, the people of Texas have been diversified. Increasing numbers of Hispanics from Mexico and Anglo Americans from other parts of the United States have created a new melting pot of cultures and concerns throughout the state. These cultures have come together in the big metropolitan areas across Texas.

The chapters that follow will analyze the way specific aspects of Texas politics and government work. In the process, we will explore the meaning of liberty, equality, and democracy in Texas and how these ideas are influencing Texas politics and government today. One of our central concerns will be to see how the ideas of liberty, equality, and democracy often play out very differently in Texas than they do in the nation as a whole.

As we have seen in this chapter, the majority of Texans today continue to view liberty through the lens of a political culture dominated by both traditionalistic and individualistic values. There is a tendency in the political culture to defer to leaders in positions of authority. But this deferential politics is checked by a healthy suspicion of giving too much power to those in authority. As a result, in Texas, govern-

In 2006, an estimated half million people marched in Dallas to demand fairer treatment for immigrants. As immigration changes the demographic profile of Texas, it has also given rise to numerous political debates.

● What does it mean
  to say that Texas
  has become an
  urbanized state?

ment is often perceived as something that gets in the way of our individual liberty rather than something through which we accomplish collective objectives.

Two notions of equality also play important roles in Texas political life. First, there is the idea of equality of opportunity. This aspect of equality is deeply rooted in Texas's traditional individualistic political culture. The job of government is to treat individuals fairly and to ensure them a fair chance to make it on their own through their own skills and initiative. Few Texans believe that it is the task of state government to redistribute resources from the rich to the poor, ensuring some equality of result.

In addition to equality of opportunity, political equality has been an issue in Texas politics, with the growing importance of African American and Hispanic minorities in the state. Much of the history of Texas from 1950 to the present represents an effort to expand the political rights of these groups. Additionally, debates over the meaning of equal participation and representation at all levels of state government have reshaped the broad contours of political life in Texas and given rise to one of the bitterest and most controversial issues to face the state legislature in recent decades: congressional and legislative redistricting.

Like liberty and equality, the ideals of democratic self-government are enshrined in various constitutions under which Texas has operated since the days of the Republic. The people are formally given a number of important roles to play in the political process, including choosing the members of all three branches of government and approving constitutional amendments. As we will see, however, the actual operations of state government and politics tend to work in seemingly undemocratic ways. Arcane rules in the legislature and executive branches allow power to concentrate in the hands of a few individuals. Elections of judges politicize the selection of judges in a way unimaginable in national politics. Well-funded special-interest groups have been able to exert their influence on elections in Texas and to penetrate the legislative process. The rise to power of the Republican Party in the state may be best understood as the triumph of a new set of interests that have successfully displaced those attached to the traditional Democratic Party.

Texans in general and Texas political leaders in particular may be committed to the idea of democracy. The Texas Constitution may enshrine the values of democratic self-government. As we will see, however, the actual operations of Texas politics and government raise serious questions about what kind of democracy our state really is. The tension between the ideal and reality of democracy in Texas may come to play an important role in restructuring the political system as it responds to ongoing economic and demographic change in the state.

for critical analysis

In Texas political culture, governmental power is often seen as a threat to individual liberty. However, Texans also tend to value equality of opportunity and political equality for all citizens. To what extent should the Texas state government use its power to ensure equality?

studyguide

Practice Quiz

 Find a diagnostic Web Quiz with 20 additional questions on the StudySpace Web site: www.wwnorton.com/we-the-people

1. In terms of area, how does Texas rank among the fifty states? *(p. 724)*
   a) first
   b) second
   c) fifth
   d) seventh

2. *Provincialism* refers to *(p. 724)*
   a) a narrow view of the world.
   b) a progressive view of the value of diversity.
   c) a pro-business political culture.
   d) all of the above.

3. Which of Texas's physical regions is characterized by the presence of many of the state's largest ranches? *(p. 726)*
   a) Gulf Coastal Plains
   b) Great Plains
   c) Interior Lowlands
   d) Basin and Range Province

4. Which of Texas's physical regions is found in West Texas? *(p. 727)*
   a) Gulf Coastal Plains
   b) Great Plains
   c) Interior Lowlands
   d) Basin and Range Province

5. Creative destruction *(p. 727)*
   a) destroys both old and new economies.
   b) creates new economies and destroys old ones.
   c) maintains old economies and creates new ones.
   d) creates and maintains old and new economies.

6. Land and land use gave rise to which three economies? *(pp. 728–30)*
   a) railroads, transportation, and high technology
   b) cotton, cattle, and oil
   c) oil, cattle, and transportation
   d) insurance, computers, and electronics

7. Which industry controlled the politics and economy of Texas for most of the twentieth century? *(p. 730)*
   a) cotton
   b) cattle
   c) railroad
   d) oil

8. Which of the following statements is true? *(pp. 730–34)*
   a) Oil production no longer plays an important role in the state's economy.
   b) Oil production has declined in Texas in the early twenty-first century.
   c) The DFW region has become a major producer of oil in the early twenty-first century.
   d) Oil production in Texas is predicted to accelerate significantly in the next twenty years.

9. The Texas economy of the twenty-first century is centered on *(p. 735)*
   a) computers, electronics, and other high-tech products.
   b) transportation, oil and natural gas, and banking.
   c) insurance, construction, and banking.
   d) education, the military, and agriculture.

10. NAFTA refers to *(p. 735)*
    a) an oil company.
    b) an independent regulatory commission.
    c) an interstate road network.
    d) none of the above.

11. What is meant by the "Great Recession"? *(p. 736)*
    a) the post–Vietnam War era in the mid 1970s when housing prices rose
    b) the period of high inflation during the early 1980s
    c) a time of chronic economic problems beginning in late 2007 that drew analogies to the Great Depression of the 1930s
    d) the time when Democrats lost control of the Texas House for the first time since Reconstruction

12. Which of the following accounts for most of Texas's population growth? *(p. 737)*
    a) immigration
    b) the positive difference between births and deaths
    c) domestic immigration
    d) movement from rural to urban areas

13. Which of the following is *not* true? *(pp. 740–41)*
    a) Hispanics are increasing as a percentage of the population in Dallas.
    b) More African Americans live in East Texas than West Texas.

c) San Antonio has a larger Anglo population than Hispanic.

d) Houston's largest minority population is Hispanic.

14. *Urbanization* refers to a process in which *(p. 744)*
   a) people move from rural to urban areas.
   b) people from the north and west move to Texas.
   c) people move out of urban centers to the suburbs.
   d) minorities assume political control of a city.

15. The three major metropolitan areas in Texas are *(p. 746)*
   a) Houston, Dallas–Fort Worth, and San Antonio.
   b) Houston, Dallas–Fort Worth, and El Paso.
   c) El Paso, Houston, and Austin.
   d) San Antonio, El Paso, and Brownsville-Harlingen-McAllen.

Chapter Outline

Find a detailed Chapter Outline on the StudySpace Web site: www.wwnorton.com/we-the-people

Key Terms

Find Flashcards to help you study these terms on the StudySpace Web site: www.wwnorton.com/we-the-people

elite *(p. 723)*
individualistic political culture *(p. 723)*
moralistic political culture *(p. 723)*
North American Free Trade Agreement (NAFTA) *(p. 735)*

political culture *(p. 723)*
political economy *(p. 746)*
provincialism *(p. 724)*

traditionalistic political culture *(p. 723)*
urbanization *(p. 744)*

Recommended Web Sites

Business QuickFacts
http://quickfacts.census.gov/qfd/states/48000.html

Federal Reserve Bank of Texas
http://dallasfed.org/index.cfm

Handbook of Texas
www.tshaonline.org/handbook/online/

Office of the Governor, Economic Development and Tourism, Business and Industry Data Center
www.governor.state.tx.us/ecodev/divisions/bidc/

Texas Almanac
www.texasalmanac.com

Texas State Data Center and Office of the State Demographer
www.txsdc.utsa.edu

The Texas Constitution has been amended 467 times. An example of a recent amendment is Proposition 15, approved by voters in 2007. Here, Lance Armstrong, cycling champion and cancer survivor, campaigns in support of Proposition 15.

The Texas Constitution

WHAT GOVERNMENT DOES AND WHY IT MATTERS Every few years, the Texas legislature presents to the voters a list of proposed amendments to the state constitution. Voter approval is necessary for the amendments to take effect. In 2009, eleven amendments were proposed, among them an amendment protecting private property from some property takings involving eminent domain, an amendment establishing a National Research University Fund, and an amendment allowing members of emergency services districts to serve for four years. In 2007, sixteen amendments were put forward spanning a wide range of matters. Some amendments grapple with essential problems of constitutional government and public policy. Others are more technical, reflecting efforts to clean up specific language in the state constitution. Some have an air of whimsy about them that belie a deadly seriousness that the current state constitution is a clumsy document and is, in many respects, out of date. Such is the case with Proposition 10, an amendment proposed in 2007 to abolish the constitutional authority of the county Office of the Inspector of Hides and Animals.[1]

In 1871 the state legislature established the office for the inspection of the brands on all hides and animals that were shipped out of a county.[2] Over time, the need for inspectors declined. By 1945, only about one-third of Texas counties still had an inspector of hides and animals. Nonetheless, under constitutional amendments passed in 1954 and 1958, the office acquired constitutional status. By the 1990s, few counties still had an inspector of hides and animals, and in those that did, the office was not taken all that seriously.

In Fort Bend County, Jeff McMeans served as the inspector for seventeen years, after running for the position initially as a joke in 1986. "It was the perfect office," McMeans told a *Dallas Morning News* reporter. "No pay, no office, no responsibility, no nothing." Glenn Maxey was elected inspector of hides and animals in Travis County in 1986. Before he could file as a candidate, he had to convince the county clerk in Travis County that there really was such an office. Running unopposed, Maxey was elected, but he refused to take the oath of office, noting that his objective in running was not to win but to abolish a useless county office.

The demise of the office of inspector of hides and animals took place eventually in 2003 when the legislature changed the Agricultural Code. But the language in the constitution remained unchanged. Finally, during the 2007 session, the legislature passed a proposed amendment to the constitution (Proposition 10) that would delete any reference to the office in the constitution itself. Although there was no serious opposition to Proposition 10, some used it to draw attention to the fact that the amendment process and the state constitution itself were seriously flawed. A group of Austin Community College students rallied against Proposition 10, to show that the constitution was woefully out of date and that piecemeal amendments such as Proposition 10 only made matters worse. Not surprisingly, the proposition passed.

Efforts have been made in the past to rethink the constitutional foundations of political life in Texas. In spite of reform efforts, the Texas Constitution remains a document much disparaged and not well understood by the population as a whole. However, the Texas Constitution probably has a greater immediate impact on the lives of Texans than does the U.S. Constitution.

chapter contents

The Role of a State Constitution

What are the similarities and differences between the U.S. and Texas constitutions?

State **constitutions** perform a number of important functions. They legitimate state political institutions by clearly explaining the source of their power and authority. State constitutions also delegate power, explaining which powers are granted to particular institutions and individuals and how those powers are to be used. They prevent the concentration of political power by providing political mechanisms that check and balance the powers of one political institution or individual office-holder against another. Finally, they mark out the limits of political power. Through declarations of rights, state constitutions explicitly forbid the intrusion of certain kinds of governmental activities into the lives of individuals.

constitution the legal structure of a government, which establishes its power and authority as well as the limits on that power

From its first constitution, the idea of constitutional government in Texas has been heavily indebted to the larger American experience (see Chapter 2). Five ideas unite the U.S. and Texas constitutional experiences. First, political power in both is ultimately derived from the people. Political power is something that is artificially created through the constitution by a conscious act of the people. Second, political power is divided into three separate parts and placed in separate branches of government. The legislative, executive, and judicial branches of government have their own unique powers and corresponding duties and obligations. Third, the U.S. and Texas constitutions structure political power in such a way that the power of one branch is checked and balanced by the power of the other two branches. The idea of checks and balances reflects a common concern among the framers of the U.S. Constitution and the authors of Texas's various constitutions that the intent of writing a constitution was not just to establish effective governing institutions. Its purpose was also to create political institutions that would not tyrannize the very people who established them. The concern for preventing the emergence of tyranny is also found in a fourth idea that underlies the U.S. and Texas constitutions: the idea of individual rights. Government is explicitly forbidden to violate a number of particular rights that the people possess.

The final idea embodied in both the U.S. and Texas constitutions is that of **federalism**. Federalism is the dividing up of government into a central government and a series of regional governments (see Chapter 3). Both governments exercise direct authority over individual citizens of the United States and of each particular state. Article IV, Section 4, of the U.S. Constitution guarantees that every state in the Union will have a "Republican Form of Government." Curiously, no attempt is made to explain what exactly a "Republican Form of Government" entails. The Tenth Amendment to the U.S. Constitution also recognizes the importance of the idea of federalism to the American political system. It reads: "The powers not delegated to the United States by the Constitution, nor prohibited by it to the States, are reserved to the States respectively, or to the people." According to the U.S. Constitution, enormous reservoirs of political power are thus derived from the people who reside in the states themselves.

federalism a system of government in which power is divided, by a constitution, between a central government and regional governments

However, some important differences distinguish the constitutional experience of Texas from that of the United States. Most important is the subordinate role that Texas has in the federal system. Article VI of the U.S. Constitution contains the famous **supremacy clause**, declaring the Constitution and the laws of the United States to be "the supreme Law of the Land." It requires all judges in every state to be bound by the U.S. Constitution, notwithstanding the laws or constitution of their particular state. In matters of disagreement, the U.S. Constitution thus takes precedence over the Texas Constitution.

supremacy clause Article VI of the U.S. Constitution, which states that the Constitution and laws passed by the national government and all treaties are the supreme law of the land and superior to all laws adopted by any state or any subdivision

One of the major issues of the Civil War was how the federal system was to be understood. Was the United States a confederation of autonomous sovereign states that were ultimately independent political entities capable of withdrawing (much like the current European Union)? Was the United States a perpetual union of states that were ultimately in a subordinate relationship to the central government? The results of the war and the passage of the Fourteenth Amendment in 1868 ultimately resolved this question in terms of the latter. The idea that the United States was a perpetual union composed of subordinate states would have profound implications for constitutional government in Texas throughout the late nineteenth and twentieth centuries. The incorporation of the Bill of Rights through the Fourteenth Amendment, which made much of the Bill of Rights apply to the states, became a dominant theme of constitutional law in the twentieth century. The Fourteenth Amendment effectively placed restrictions on Texas government and public policy that went far beyond those laid out in Texas's own constitution.

Another major difference between the U.S. and Texas constitutions lies in the **necessary and proper clause** of Article I, Section 8. Section 8 begins by listing in detail the specific powers granted to Congress by the Constitution. The Founders apparently wanted to limit the scope of national government activities. But Section 8 concludes by granting Congress the power that is needed to accomplish its constitutional tasks. The net effect of this clause was to provide a constitutional basis for an enormous expansion of central government activities over the next 200 years.

Drafters of Texas's various constitutions generally have been unwilling to grant such an enormous loophole in the exercise of governmental power. Although granting state government the power to accomplish certain tasks, Texas constitutions have generally denied officeholders broad grants of discretionary power to accomplish their goals.

necessary and proper clause
Article I, Section 8, of the U.S. Constitution; it provides Congress with the authority to make all laws "necessary and proper" to carry out its expressed powers

● The First Texas Constitutions

Texas has had six constitutions. Each was shaped by historical developments of its time and, following the first constitution, attempted to address shortcomings of each previous constitution.

The Constitution of Coahuila y Tejas, 1827 Despite the growing fears of American expansionism following the Louisiana Purchase, in 1803 Spanish Texas was still sparsely populated. In 1804, the population of Spanish Texas was estimated to be 3,605. In 1811, Juan Bautista de las Casas launched the first revolt against Spanish rule in San Antonio. The so-called Casas Revolt was successfully put down by the summer of 1811. The next year, a second challenge to Spanish rule took place along the border between Texas and the United States. After capturing Nacogdoches, La Bahia, and San Antonio, rebel forces under José Bernardo Gutiérrez de Lara issued a declaration of independence from New Spain and drafted a constitution. By 1813, however, this revolt had also been put down, and bloody reprisals had depopulated the state. Texas remained part of New Spain until the Mexican War of Independence.[3]

The Mexican War of Independence grew out of a series of revolts against Spanish rule during the Napoleonic Wars. Burdened by debts brought on by a crippling war with France, Spain sought to extract more wealth from its colonies. The forced

This 1844 cartoon satirized congressional opposition to the annexation of Texas. Personified as a beautiful young woman, Texas is holding a cornucopia filled with flowers. Though James K. Polk, elected to the presidency in 1844, welcomes Texas, the Whig Party leader Senator Henry Clay, with arms folded, warns, "Stand back, Madam Texas! For we are more holy than thou! Do you think we will have anything to do with gamblers, horse-racers, and licentious profligates?"

abdication of Ferdinand VII in favor of his brother Joseph in 1808 and an intensifying economic crisis in New Spain in 1809 and 1810 undermined the legitimacy of Spanish rule. Revolts broke out in Guanajuato and spread throughout Mexico and its Texas province. Although these rebellions were initially put down by royalist forces loyal to Spain, by 1820 local revolts and guerrilla actions had helped to weaken continued royal rule from Spain. On August 24, 1821, Mexico was formally granted independence by Spain.

Because Texas was part of Mexico, the first federal constitution that it operated under was the Mexican Constitution. At the national level, there were to be two houses of Congress. The lower house was composed of deputies serving two-year terms. In the upper house, senators served four-year terms and were selected by state legislatures. The president and vice president were elected for four-year terms by the legislative bodies of the states. There was a supreme court, composed of eleven judges, and an attorney general. Although the Mexican Constitution mandated separate legislative, executive, and judicial branches, no attempt was made to define the scope of state rights in the Mexican confederation. Local affairs remained independent of the central government. Although the Mexican Constitution embodied many of the ideas found in the U.S. Constitution, there was one important difference: Catholicism was established as the state religion and was supported financially by the state.[4]

Under the Mexican Constitution, the state of Coahuila and the sparsely populated province of Texas were combined together into the state of Coahuila and Texas. Saltillo, Mexico, was the capital. More than two years were spent drafting a constitution for the new state. It was finally published on March 11, 1827.

The state was formally divided into three separate districts, with Texas composing the District of Bexar. Legislative power for the state was placed in a **unicameral** legislature composed of twelve deputies elected by the people. The people of the District of Bexar (Texas) elected two of these. Along with wide-ranging legislative powers, the legislature was also empowered to elect state officials when no majority

unicameral comprising one body or house, as in a one-house legislature

emerged from the popular vote, to serve as a grand jury in political and military matters, and to regulate the army and militia. Executive power was vested in a governor and a vice governor, each elected by the people for a four-year term. Judicial power was placed in state courts. Although these courts could try cases, they were not supposed to interpret the law.

The Constitution of 1827 formally guaranteed citizens the right to liberty, security, property, and equality. Language in the Constitution also supported efforts to curtail the spread of slavery, an institution of vital importance to planters who were immigrating from the American South. The legislature was ordered to promote education and freedom of the press. As in the Mexican federal constitution, Catholicism was the established state religion.[5]

The Constitution of the Republic of Texas, 1836

Texas's break with Mexico was in large part a constitutional crisis that culminated in separation. Political conventions held in San Felipe de Austin in 1832 and 1833 reflected a growing discontent among Texans over their place in the Mexican federal system. Along with other demands for a more liberal immigration policy for people from the United States and for the establishment of English- and Spanish-speaking primary schools, calls for separate statehood for Texas emerged from the conventions. The 1833 convention actually drafted a constitution for this newly proposed state modeled on the Massachusetts Constitution of 1780. Stephen F. Austin's attempt to bring the proposed constitution to the attention of the central government in Mexico City led to his imprisonment, which, in turn, pushed Texas closer to open rebellion against the central Mexican government.

On November 7, 1835, a declaration was adopted by a meeting of state political leaders at San Felipe, which stated the reasons Texans were beginning to take up arms against the Mexican government. The declaration proclaimed that Texas was rising up in defense of its rights and liberties as well as the republican principles articulated in the Mexican Constitution of 1824. This declaration was but a prelude to the formal Texas Declaration of Independence that emerged out of the convention of 1836 held at Washington-on-the-Brazos.

Of the fifty-nine delegates attending the Convention of 1836, only ten had lived in Texas prior to 1830. Two had arrived as late as 1836. Thirty-nine of the delegates were from southern slave states, six were from the border state of Kentucky, seven were from northern states, three were from Mexico (including two born in Texas), and four were from other English-speaking lands.[6] The final products of the convention—the Texas Declaration of Independence and the Constitution of 1836—reflected the interests and values of these participants.

In their own Declaration of Independence, delegates to the convention proclaimed that the federal constitutional regime they had been invited to live under by the rulers of Mexico had been replaced by a military tyranny that combined a "despotism of the sword and the priesthood." Echoing the American Declaration of Independence, they presented a long list of grievances against the central government, including the failure to provide freedom of religion, a system of public education, and trial by jury.

The Texas Declaration of Independence Like the Founders during the American Revolution, leaders of the Texas Revolution felt they needed to justify their actions in print. Written by George C. Childress and adopted by the general convention at Washington-on-the-Brazos on March 2, 1836, the Texas Declaration of

UNANIMOUS

DECLARATION OF INDEPENDENCE,

BY THE

DELEGATES OF THE PEOPLE OF TEXAS,

IN GENERAL CONVENTION,

AT THE TOWN OF WASHINGTON.

ON THE SECOND DAY OF MARCH, 1836.

The Texas Declaration of Independence was written by George C. Childress and adopted at the Convention of 1836. Childress modeled the document on the American Declaration of Independence.

Independence stated why it was necessary to separate from Mexico and create an independent republic. Not surprisingly, the document draws heavily on the ideas of John Locke and Thomas Jefferson for inspiration. The description of the role of the government, "to protect the lives, liberty, and property of the people," repeated verbatim Locke's litany of the primary reasons for establishing government. Like Jefferson's Declaration, Texas's declaration catalogues a list of grievances against the Mexican regime. According to the declaration, the existing government had abdicated its duties to protect the governed and broken the trustee relationship that binds a people to those in authority. By dissolving civil society into its original elements, the government had forced the people to assert their inalienable right of self-preservation and to take political affairs into their own hands again. The "melancholy conclusion" of the declaration echoed ideas that Locke and Jefferson would have understood well: any government that stripped a people of their liberty was unacceptable to those raised on principles of self-government. Self-preservation demanded "eternal political separation" from the very state that had invited them to settle in Texas.

After declaring Texas a separate republic independent from Mexico, the convention proceeded to draft and pass a new constitution reflecting these republican sentiments. Resembling the U.S. Constitution in being brief and flexible (fewer than 6,500 words), the 1836 Constitution established an elected chief executive with considerable powers, a **bicameral** legislature, and a four-tiered judicial system composed of justice, county, district, and supreme courts.[7] Power was divided among these three branches, and a system of checks and balances was put into place. Complicated procedures were included for amending the constitution, and a bill of rights was elaborated.

A number of important provisions from Spanish-Mexican law were adapted for the Texas Republic in the constitution, including the idea of community property, homestead exemptions and protections, and debtor relief. The values of American democracy percolated through the document. White male suffrage was guaranteed. Ministers and priests were ineligible for public office. But one of the most important aspects of the Constitution of 1836, at least from the perspective of newly immigrated Americans from the South, may have been the defense of slavery as an institution.

The Constitution of Coahuila y Tejas of 1827 had challenged, albeit unsuccessfully, the existence of slavery as an institution. Although the 1836 Constitution of the Republic of Texas outlawed the importation of slaves from Africa, it guaranteed that slaveholders could keep their property and that new slaveholding immigrants could bring their slaves into Texas with them. The results of this constitutional protection were monumental. In 1836, Texas had a population of 38,470, including 5,000 slaves. By 1850, the slave population had grown to 58,161, over one-quarter of the state's population. By 1860, there were over 182,566 slaves, accounting for over 30 percent of the state's population.[8] To all intents and purposes, the Constitution of 1836 not only saved slavery as an institution in Texas but also provided the protections needed for it to flourish.

bicameral having a legislative assembly composed of two chambers or houses; opposite of unicameral

The lowering of the Republic flag marked Texas's annexation to the Union on March 1, 1845. A state constitution was drafted shortly thereafter to reflect Texas's new role.

It was one thing to declare independence from Mexico, but quite another to win independence. Only after the Battle of San Jacinto, where on April 21 Sam Houston's force of 900 men overran the 1,300-man force of Santa Anna and captured Santa Anna himself, did Texas become an independent state.[9]

● How do the pre-1876 Texas constitutions differ from one another?

The Texas State Constitution of 1845

Although the 1836 Constitution called for annexation by the United States, Texas remained an independent republic for nine years. There were concerns in the United States that if Texas were admitted to the union, it would be as a slave state. Texas's admission to the Union could alter the delicate balance between slave and free states and further divide the nation over the sensitive subject of slavery. Additionally, it was feared that annexation by the United States would lead to war with Mexico. Santa Anna—the Mexican general and dictator whom Sam Houston had defeated at the battle of San Jacinto—had repudiated the Treaty of Velasco, which had ended the war between Texas and Mexico. Still claiming Texas as part of its own territory, Mexico undoubtedly would have gone to war to protect what it felt to be rightfully its own.

Hesitation over admitting Texas to the Union was overcome by the mid-1840s. On March 1, 1845, the United States Congress approved a resolution that would bring Texas into the Union as a state. The annexation resolution had a number of interesting provisions. First, the Republic of Texas ceded to the United States all military armaments, bases, and facilities pertaining to public defense. Second, Texas retained a right to all "its vacant and unappropriated lands" as well as to its public debts. This was no small matter, because Texas claimed an enormous amount of land that extended far beyond its present state boundaries. These issues were not resolved until the passage of the Compromise of 1850. Finally, Texas was given permission to break up into four additional states when population proved adequate.

On July 4, 1845, a convention was called by President Anson Jones to draft a state constitution in Austin. Drafters of the constitution relied heavily on the Constitution of 1836, although the final document ended up being almost twice as long. The familiar doctrines of separation of powers, checks and balances, and individual rights defined the basic design of government.

Under the Constitution of 1845, the legislature was to be composed of two houses. The House of Representatives would have between forty-five and ninety members, elected for two-year terms. Members would have to be at least twenty-one years of age. The Senate was to be composed of between nineteen and thirty-three members, elected for four-year terms. Half of the Senate would be elected every two years. As in the U.S. Constitution, revenue bills were to originate in the House. Executive vetoes could be overturned by a two-thirds vote of each house. In a separate article on education, the legislature was ordered to establish a public school system and to set aside lands to support a Permanent School Fund. Another interesting power granted to the legislature was the power to select the treasurer and comptroller in a joint session.

This constitution provided for an elected governor and lieutenant governor. The governor's term was set at two years. He could serve only four years as governor in any six-year period. Among the executive powers granted to the governor were the powers to convene and adjourn the legislature, to veto legislation, to grant pardons and reprieves, and to command the state militia. The governor also had the power to appoint the attorney general, secretary of state, and district and supreme court judges, subject to the approval of the Senate.

The Constitution of 1845 established a judicial branch consisting of a supreme court composed of three judges, district courts, and lower courts deemed necessary by the legislature. Judges on the higher courts were to be appointed to six-year terms and could be removed from office subject to a two-thirds vote of both houses of the legislature.

Amending the Constitution of 1845 was difficult. After being proposed by a two-thirds vote of each house, amendments had to be approved by a majority of the voters. In the next legislature, another two-thirds vote of each house was necessary for ratification. Only one amendment was ever made to the Constitution of 1845. In 1850, an amendment was added to provide for the election of state officials who were originally appointed by the governor or by the legislature.[10]

This constitution contained some unusual provisions. Consistent with the terms of annexation, Texas could divide itself into as many as five states. Texas itself had to pay its foreign debt. It would retain title to its public lands, which could be sold to pay its debt. There was even a provision allowing Texas to fly its flag at the same height as the U.S. flag.

The Constitution of 1861: Texas Joins the Confederacy

The issue of slavery had delayed Texas's admission into the United States for nine years until 1845. It drove Texas from the Union in 1861. By 1860, slavery had become a vital institution to the Texas economy. Concentrated in east Texas and along the Gulf Coast, slaves had come to constitute 30 percent of the population. However, in large sections of the state, particularly in the north and west, the economy was based on ranching or corn and wheat production rather than cotton. There slavery was virtually nonexistent. The question of whether Texas should secede was a controversial one that divided the state along regional and ethnic as well as party lines.

Pressure to secede mounted following the presidential election of Abraham Lincoln in November 1860. A staunch Unionist, Governor Sam Houston refused to convene a special session of the legislature to discuss secession. Seeking to bypass Houston, a number of influential political leaders in the state, including the chief justice of the Texas Supreme Court, called for a special convention in January 1861 to consider secession. Giving in to the pressure, Houston called a special session of the legislature in the hopes of undercutting the upcoming secession convention. The legislature, however, had other ideas, validating the call for the convention and turning its chambers over to the convention.

Lawyers and slaveholders dominated the secession convention. Lawyers composed 40 percent of the delegates; slaveholders composed 70 percent. The Texas Ordinance of Secession, produced by the convention on February 2, 1861, reflected this proslavery membership. In striking language, it proclaimed that the northern states had broken faith with Texas, particularly regarding the institution of slavery. Northerners had violated the very laws and constitution of the federal Union by appealing to a "higher law" that trampled on the rights of Texans. In language that people living in the twenty-first century find hard to understand, the Ordinance of Secession proclaimed

Prior to the Civil War, Governor Sam Houston opposed secession from the Union and attempted to block efforts by those wishing to secede.

We hold as undeniable truths that the governments of the various States, and of the confederacy itself, were established exclusively by the white race, for themselves and their posterity; that the African race had no agency in their establishment; that they were rightfully held and regarded as an inferior and dependent race, and in that condition only could their existence in this country be rendered beneficial and tolerable.[11]

● How do the pre-1876 Texas constitutions differ from one another?

Texas voters approved secession from the Union on February 23, 1861. The secession convention reconvened to enact a new constitution to guide the state as it entered the **Confederacy**. There were surprisingly few changes in the final document. This constitution was similar to the Constitution of 1845 except that references to the United States of America were replaced with references to the Confederate States of America. Public officials had to declare allegiance to the Confederacy, and slavery and states' rights were defended. A clause in the 1845 Constitution that provided for the emancipation of slaves was eliminated, and freeing slaves was declared illegal. But for the most part, the document accepted the existing constitutional framework. Controversial proposals, such as resuming the African slave trade and taking a strong states' rights position, were rejected. The move out of the Union into the Confederacy may have been a radical one, but the new constitution was conservative insofar as it reaffirmed the existing constitutional order in the state.[12]

Confederacy the Confederate States of America, those southern states that seceded from the United States in late 1860 and 1861 and argued that the power of a government is based in its states

The Constitution of 1866: Texas Rejoins the Union

Defeat in the Civil War led to the institution of another state constitution in 1866. The provisional governor, Andrew Jackson Hamilton, called a constitutional convention on November 15, 1865, a little over six months after the surrender of Lee's army in Virginia. Delegates were elected on January 8, 1866, and the convention was held February 7. Few former secessionists were excluded from voting, with the result that there were strong Unionist and secessionist factions at the convention.

A number of actions were taken to bring the state into compliance with President Andrew Johnson's policy of Reconstruction, including the rejection of the right to secession, a repudiation of the war debt incurred by the state, and an acceptance of the abolition of slavery. The convention granted freedmen fundamental rights to their persons and property and gave them the right to sue and be sued as well as the right to contract with others. However, there was little support for extending suffrage to blacks, and they were banned from holding public office. The convention also made a few changes to the existing constitutional system in Texas. These changes came to be known as the Constitution of 1866.

As in the two previous constitutions, the size of the House was set between forty-five and ninety, and that of the Senate between nineteen and thirty-three. Terms of office remained the same as under the 1845 and 1861 constitutions, although salaries were increased. Reapportionment was to be based on the number of white male citizens, who would be counted in a census every ten years.

The governor's salary was also increased, and the term was extended to four years, with a limit of eight years in any twelve-year period. The governor was also granted, for the first time, a line-item veto on appropriations. The comptroller and the treasurer were to be elected by the voters for four-year terms.

Under the new constitution, the state supreme court was expanded from three to five judges and terms were increased to ten years. Salaries also were increased. The chief justice was to be selected from the five judges on the supreme court. District court judges were to be elected for eight-year terms, and the attorney general for a four-year term.

Voters ratified the Constitution of 1866 in June in a relatively close referendum, 28,119 to 23,400. The close vote was attributed to a widespread unhappiness with the increase in salaries of the various state officers.[13]

The Reconstruction Constitution of 1869

In 1869, Texas wrote still another constitution to meet the requirements of the Congressional Reconstruction Acts of 1867. A vote calling for a constitutional convention was ordered by General Winfield Scott Hancock, the commander of the Texas and Louisiana military district, in early 1868. Although Democrats were opposed to the convention, **Radical Republicans** easily won by 44,689 to 11,440. Of the ninety delegates to the convention, only six had served in the previous constitutional convention. Ten were blacks. The vast majority represented the interests of various wings in the Republican Party. The convention was a rancorous affair as delegates argued over a wide range of issues, including railroad charters, lawlessness in the state, and whether laws passed during the war years were legal. In the final days of the convention, delegates finally got down to the constitutional matters and the problems of accepting the Thirteenth and Fourteenth amendments. Although delegates never completed their task of reworking the Constitution of 1866, their efforts were published under orders by military officials and became the Constitution of 1869.

A number of features of the Constitution of 1869 stand out.[14] The U.S. Constitution was declared to be the supreme law of the land. Slavery was forbidden, and blacks were given the right to vote. Fourteenth Amendment guarantees of equality before the law were recognized. Additionally, the constitution altered the relationship among the three branches of government.

The House of Representatives was set at ninety and the Senate at thirty members. Senatorial terms were extended to six years, with one-third of the seats to be elected every biennium. Legislative sessions were to be held annually.

The most critical changes were in the executive branch and the courts. The powers of the governor were vastly expanded. Among other things, the governor was given wide-ranging appointment powers that included the power to appoint judges. The state supreme court was reduced from five to three judges. The term of supreme court judges was also lowered to nine years, with one new judge to be appointed every three years. Salaries for state officials were increased.

A Republican affiliated with the Radical faction of the party and a former Union general, Edmund Davis, governed under this constitution. Davis had vast authority, since the constitution had centralized power in the executive while reducing local governmental control. Varying interpretations exist of the government provided by Davis, though the popular perception at the time was that Davis presided over a corrupt, extravagant administration that eventually turned to the state police and the militia to attempt to maintain its regime.

In 1872, the Democrats regained control of the state government and in 1873, the Democrat Richard Coke was elected governor. Davis attempted to maintain control over the governor's office by having his handpicked Supreme Court invalidate Coke's election. Davis refused to give up his office and surrounded himself with state police in the capitol. However, when Democrats slipped past guards and gathered upstairs in the capitol building to organize a government, Davis was unable to obtain federal troops to retain him in office. Democrats were able to form a government, and Davis left office.

Radical Republicans a bloc of Republicans in the U.S. Congress who pushed through the adoption of black suffrage as well as an extended period of military occupation of the South following the Civil War

The former Union general Edmund Davis governed Texas under the Constitution of 1869. The constitution granted Davis vast unchecked powers, and he was perceived as presiding over a corrupt administration.

The example of Davis's reign motivated the revision of executive branch power in the Constitution of 1876. The framers of that constitution sought popular control of state government in order to limit the appointment powers of the governor as provided by the Constitution of 1869.

The Constitution of 1876

To prevent another government such as Davis's, efforts were made to write a new constitution. In 1874, a constitution was proposed and later rejected by a sitting legislature.[15] Finally in 1875, a constitutional convention was called. Three delegates were selected by popular vote from each of the thirty senatorial districts. The final composition of the convention included seventy-five Democrats and fifteen Republicans, six of whom were black. Not one of the elected delegates had participated in the constitutional conventional of 1868–69. Forty of the delegates were farmers, and forty were members of the **Grange**, a militant farming organization that had emerged to improve the plight of farmers.

These framers were committed to a constitution with four major themes. First, they wanted strong popular control of state government. Second, they believed that a constitution should seriously limit the power of state government. Third, they sought economy in government. Fourth, the framers sought to promote agrarian interests, particularly those of small farmers, who formed the basis of support for the Grange movement.

Popular control of state government meant that the governor's vast appointment powers were to be limited by having public officials subject to election. Judges and other officials who had been appointed by the governor under the 1869 Constitution were now independently elected officials. But popular control of the government did not mean that all the electorate voted. When the framers of the

Grange a militant farmers' movement of the late nineteenth century that fought for improved conditions for farmers

1876 Constitution thought of popular control of state government, they thought of control by white males.

In an era of agriculture when prices and incomes were low and when little was demanded or expected from government, much in the Constitution of 1876 made sense. However, one might question whether a constitution designed by white males primarily for whites in a rural agrarian society—and for the purpose of keeping the likes of Edmund Davis from ever controlling the state again—is workable in the modern era.

State government was to be a government of limited powers. Executive authority would be diffused among numerous officeholders to prevent any future governor from wielding the vast powers held by Governor Davis. Although this provision subsequently changed by constitutional amendment, the governor initially was further limited in powers by serving only a two-year term. The legislature would be part-time, ordinarily sitting for a limited time period every other year. This was in contrast to the 1869 Constitution, which provided that the legislature meet in annual sessions. Additionally, legislators would not be highly paid. The judicial branch would be elected, rather than appointed, to limit further gubernatorial power. The constitution would place great restrictions on the actions of government, restrictions that would have to be modified through a complex constitutional amendment process.

The constitution would restrict the extent of government debt and of government's power to tax. To emphasize that Texas government was economical, there were even limits on the salaries of state officials, especially legislators. A major economic depression had begun in 1873, and many Texans were experiencing economic hardship. One way money was saved was to decentralize public education. Schools were segregated, and compulsory education laws were eliminated. By having local control over education, white landowners could avoid paying taxes for the education of black students.

Texas at that time was an agricultural state, and many of the framers of the Constitution of 1876 were farmers, often involved with the Grange, a political organization of mostly small farmers. The framers wished to protect agrarian interests and wrote into the constitution provisions protecting homesteads and restricting institutions that, at that time, were perceived to be harmful to farmers, such as banks and railroads. Greater responsibility was placed on local instead of state officials. There were also detailed regulations on railroad competition, freight and passenger rates, and railroad construction incentives.

Even in its earliest stages, the Texas Constitution of 1876 was a detailed document that included numerous restrictions on government power. In the U.S. Constitution, much had been left unsaid so that the document was short and flexible, and it allowed lawmaking to be done by statute. With the Texas Constitution, the standard was different. It was to be lengthy, rigid, and detailed. Regulations were placed, not in statutes, but in the body of the constitution. The idea was that the Radical Republicans and Edmund Davis would never again be able to reign and spend in Texas. They, of course, never did, although over the years the constitution became an increasingly unwieldy document.

● The Constitution of Texas Today

The United States Constitution has two great virtues: brevity and flexibility. Neither of these virtues can be said to characterize the Texas Constitution. The U.S. Constitution is limited to seven short articles and twenty-seven amendments, and

TABLE 20.1

The Texas Constitution: An Overview

Article I: The Bill of Rights

Article II: Separation of Powers in State Government

Article III: The State Legislature

Article IV: The Plural Executive

Article V: The Judicial Department

Article VI: Suffrage in Texas

Article VII: Public Education in Texas

Article VIII: Taxation and State Revenues

Article IX and XI: Concerning Local Government, including Counties and Municipal Corporations

Article X: Empowering the State to Regulate Railroads and to Create the Texas Railroad Commission

Article XII: Empowering the State to Create General laws for Corporations

Article XIII: Concerning Spanish and Mexican Land Titles, Now Deleted from the Constitution

Article XIV: Creates the General Land Office to Deal with Registering Land Titles

Article XV: Impeachment Provisions

Article XVI: General Provisions Covering a Wide Range of Topics

Article XVII: Amendment Procedures

takes up only eight pages of the *World Almanac.* In contrast, in 2009 the Texas Constitution contains sixteen articles and has been amended 467 times (see Table 20.1). Although the table above shows seventeen articles, Article XVI, dedicated to Spanish and Mexican land grants, was repealed in 1969. Many of the articles are lengthy, complex affairs, taking up over sixty-seven pages of text in one edition of the *Texas Almanac.* But it is not just the length that differentiates the two constitutions. There is a difference in tone. The Texas Constitution clearly reflects the writers' fears of what government could do if the principle of **limited government** was not clearly established.

The Texas Constitution severely curtails executive power by limiting the power granted to the governor and decentralizing executive authority in ways unimagined by the writers of the U.S. Constitution. It also addresses a number of specific policy problems directly in the text, turning what might appear to be matters of public policy into issues of constitutional authority. By granting a variety of boards and districts a special place in the constitution, the constitution set out additional checks and balances that make it difficult for government to exercise power effectively without being able to maintain extraordinary majorities in a variety of political arenas. Quite unintentionally, the Texas Constitution became a place where special interests could seek to promote and protect their own agendas, even in the face of considerable political opposition.

The U.S. Constitution was written to overcome the liabilities of the Articles of Confederation and create a government that could act effectively in the public

limited government a principle of constitutional government; a government whose powers are defined and limited by a constitution

welfare in a variety of policy areas. The Texas Constitution was written to prevent the expansion of governmental authority and the return of a system of political power that acted against the interests of the people.

The Preamble

The preamble to Texas's Constitution is surprisingly short: "Humbly invoking the blessings of Almighty God, the people of the State of Texas do ordain and establish this Constitution." This brevity is more than made up for in what follows.

Article I: Bill of Rights

Article I of the U.S. Constitution establishes and delegates power to the legislative branch of government. One of the overriding concerns of the Founders was to create a legislature that could act effectively in public affairs. What came to be known as the Bill of Rights—the first ten amendments to the Constitution—was added after the original Constitution was drafted and approved.

In contrast, the Texas Constitution puts its Bill of Rights up front as Article I, well before any discussion of the legislature, the executive, or the courts. From the beginning, the purpose of the Texas Constitution was not simply to create a set of institutions that could wield political power. It was to limit the way political power is used and to prevent it from being abused.

The Bill of Rights embodies certain ideas captured in the U.S. Bill of Rights. All "free men" are declared to have free and equal rights that cannot be denied or abridged because of sex, race, color, creed, or national origin. Freedom of religious worship is guaranteed, and there will be no religious test for office. Liberty of speech and press are guaranteed. Individuals are protected from unreasonable search and seizure, from excessive bail, bills of attainder or ex post facto laws, and from double jeopardy. Article I also guarantees an individual a right to trial by jury and the right to bear arms "in the lawful defense of himself or the State; but the Legislature shall have the power, by law, to regulate the wearing of arms, with a view to prevent crime" (Article I, Section 23).

republican government a representative democracy, a system of government in which power is derived from the people

Article I also contains some ideas that move beyond those guaranteed by the first ten amendments to the U.S. Constitution. The right to **republican government**, something clearly stated in the main body of the Constitution but not in the U.S. Bill of Rights, is powerfully articulated in the first two sections of Article I. According to Article I of the Texas Constitution, all political power is inherent in the people, and the people of Texas have at all times the "inalienable right to alter, reform or abolish their government in such manner as they may think expedient" (Article I, Section 2).

The differences between the Texas Bill of Rights and the U.S. Bill of Rights are not simply matters of where best to articulate a philosophy of republican government. They also involve very concrete matters of public policy. Section 26, for example, forbids monopolies that are contrary to the public interest, and states that the law of primogeniture and entail (a law designed to keep large landed properties together by restricting inheritance to the firstborn) will never be in effect in the state. Although monopolies remain a public concern today, primogeniture and entail do not. Section 11 grapples with the complicated issue of bail and under what specific circumstances an individual can be denied bail. Significantly, Section 11 has been the subject of three major constitutional revisions: in 1955, 1977, and

1993. Section 30, adopted in 1989, provides a long list of the "rights of crime victims," including the right to be treated fairly and with dignity, the right to be protected from the accused, and the right to restitution. Although these are important matters of public policy for Texas today, they could hardly be considered proper material for the U.S. Constitution.

Article II: The Powers of Government

Like the U.S. Constitution, Article II divides the power of government in Texas into three distinct branches: the legislative, the executive, and the judicial (see Figure 20.1). It also stipulates that no one in any one branch shall be attached to either of the other branches, except where explicitly permitted (as in the case of the lieutenant governor's role in the Senate). The article—one short paragraph of text—assures that a version of the **separation of powers** doctrine found in the U.S. Constitution will be embodied in Texas institutions.

separation of powers the division of governmental power among several institutions that must cooperate in decision making

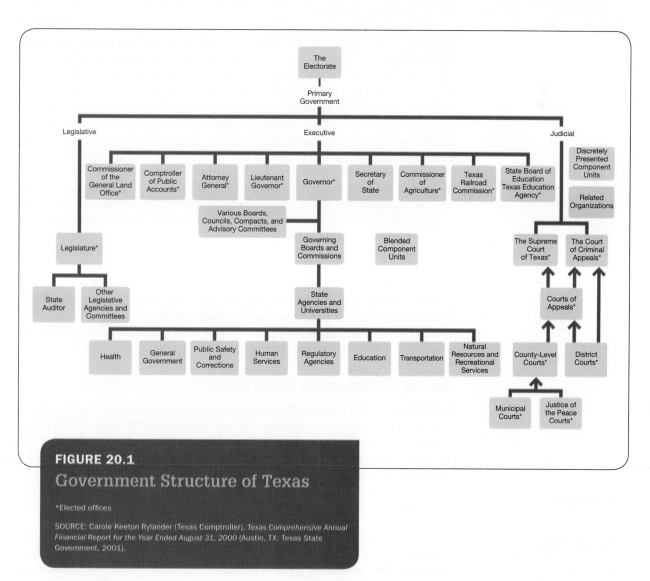

FIGURE 20.1

Government Structure of Texas

*Elected offices

SOURCE: Carole Keeton Rylander (Texas Comptroller), *Texas Comprehensive Annual Financial Report for the Year Ended August 31, 2000* (Austin, TX: Texas State Government, 2001).

Article III: Legislative Department

Article II is one of the shortest articles in the Texas Constitution. Article III is the longest, comprising almost one-third of the text. Like Article I of the U.S. Constitution, Article III of the Texas Constitution vests legislative power in two houses: a Senate of 31 members and a House of Representatives of no more than 150 members. It stipulates the terms of office and qualifications. House members serve two-year terms, whereas senators serve four-year terms, half being elected every two years. House members must be citizens of the United States, must be at least twenty-one years of age, and must have resided in the state for two years and in their district for one year. Senators must be citizens of the United States, must be at least twenty-six years old, and must have resided in the state for five years and in their districts for one year. In addition, Article III provides for the selection of officers in both houses of the legislature, states when and for how long the legislature shall meet (Section 5), and explains how the legislative proceedings will be conducted (Sections 29–41) and how representative districts will be apportioned (Sections 25, 26, and 28).

Like Article I, Texas's Bill of Rights, Article III moves well beyond the U.S. Constitution, putting limits on what the legislature can do. For example, it puts limits on what legislators may receive in salary and makes it difficult to increase that salary. Article III also creates a bipartisan Texas Ethics Commission whose job is to recommend salary increases for members of the legislature and to set per diem rates for legislators and the lieutenant governor. Significantly, even the commission's recommendations are subject to approval by the people in a referendum, something that has proven difficult to achieve. Article III, Section 49(a), also subjects the legislature to the actions of the comptroller of public accounts, whose duty is to prepare a report prior to the legislative session on the financial condition of the state treasury and to provide estimates of future expenditures by the state. This provision of the Constitution effectively limits the state legislature to the financial calculations and endorsements of the comptroller, a check on the legislature all but unimaginable to the writers of the U.S. Constitution.

Putting constraints on certain legislative actions is only part of the story. The largest portion of Article III (Sections 47–64) is dedicated to addressing a variety of policy problems, including lotteries, emergency service districts, the problem of debt creation, problems surrounding the Veterans' Land Board and the Texas Water Development Board, Texas park development, the creation of a state medical education board, and even the establishment of an economic development fund in support of the now defunct superconducting supercollider.

Article IV: Executive Department

Article II of the U.S. Constitution concentrates executive power in the presidency. The desire was to create a more effective and more responsible executive than had been possible under the Articles of Confederation. In contrast, Article IV of the Texas Constitution states that the executive shall consist of six distinct offices: the governor, who serves as the chief executive; the lieutenant governor, who serves as the president of the Senate; the secretary of state, who keeps the official seals of the state; the comptroller of public accounts; the commissioner of the General Land Office; and the attorney general, who acts as the state's chief legal officer. With the exception of the secretary of state, who is appointed by the governor and approved by the Senate, all other offices are elected by qualified voters every four years. Besides creating a **plural executive**, Article IV guarantees its members

plural executive an executive branch in which power is fragmented because the election of statewide officeholders is independent of the election of the governor

will have independent political bases in the electorate. This provides an additional check against any concentration of powers in the hands of any one person.

● Why has it proven so difficult to rewrite the Texas Constitution?

Article V: Judicial Department

Article III of the U.S. Constitution succinctly provides for a Supreme Court and empowers Congress to create any necessary lower courts. Nothing could be further from the detailed discussion of the state courts found in Article V of the Texas Constitution. Besides creating one supreme court to hear civil cases and one court of criminal appeals to hear criminal cases, Article V provides for such lesser courts as courts of appeal, district courts, commissioner's courts, and justice of the peace courts, and empowers the legislature to establish other courts as deemed necessary. It also goes into such details as the retirement and compensation of judges, the jurisdictions of the various courts, and the duties of judges; it states what to do in the case of court vacancies, and includes a series of discussions on particular issues involving the lower courts.

An even greater difference between the federal Constitution and the Texas Constitution is the crucial role the latter gives to elections. Federal judges are appointed by the executive and approved by the Senate. In Texas, the people elect state judges. Nine supreme court and nine court of criminal appeals judges are elected at large in the state. Lower court positions are elected by voters in their relevant geographic locations. Much like the U.S. Constitution, the Texas Constitution seeks to create an independent judiciary that can check and balance the other two branches of government. But it seeks an additional check as well. It wants the people to watch over the courts.

Article VI: Suffrage

Article VI contains a short but detailed discussion about who may vote in Texas. It also empowers the legislature to enact laws regulating voter registration and the selection of electors for president and vice president.

Article VII: Education

The concerns found in the Texas Declaration of Independence over the need for public schools to promote a republican form of government are directly addressed in Article VII. Section 1 makes it a duty of the state legislature to support and maintain "an efficient system of public free schools." The Texas Supreme Court's interpretation of this provision as applying to school funding in the state has led to the current political battles over school finance. Sections 2–8 provide for their funding and the creation of a State Board of Education to oversee the operations of elementary and secondary education in the state. State universities are the subject of over half of Article VII, where detailed discussions of the funding and operations of particular state institutions are put directly into the text.

Article VIII: Taxation and Revenue

The complex issue of taxation is the subject of Article VIII. Once again we find a highly detailed account of several important policy issues built directly into the text of the constitution. One of the most controversial sections of the Texas Constitution centers around the issue of the income tax. Section 1 enables the legislature to tax the income of individuals and businesses. This power, however, is subject to Section 24, which was passed by the 73rd legislature in 1993. Section 24 requires that the registered voters in the state approve a personal income tax and that the proceeds from this tax be dedicated to education and tax relief. As with other portions of the constitution, the net effect of these provisions is to curtail severely what the state legislature can do and how it is to do it. If Section 24 of Article VIII is any indication, the public fear of unresponsive and potentially tyrannical government was as alive during the 1990s as it was in 1876.

Articles IX and XI: Local Government

These articles provide highly detailed discussions of the creation, organization, and operation of counties and municipal corporations.

Articles X, XII, XIII, and XIV

These heavily revised articles deal with a series of specific topics: the railroads (X), private corporations (XII), Spanish and Mexican Land Titles (XIII), and public lands (XIV). Article X empowers the state to regulate railroads and to establish the Railroad Commission. Article XII empowers the state to create general laws creating private corporations and protecting the public and individual stockholders. Article XIII, now entirely deleted from the constitution, dealt with the nineteenth-century issue of Spanish and Mexican land titles. Article XIV created a General Land Office to deal with the registration of land titles.

Article XV: Impeachment

impeachment Under the Texas Constitution, the formal charge by the House of Representatives that leads to trial in the Senate and possible removal of a state official

Impeachment is, in the U.S. Constitution, one of the major checks Congress holds against both the executive and judicial branches of government. The House of Representatives holds the power to impeach an individual; the Senate is responsible for conducting trials. A two-thirds vote in the Senate following impeachment by the House leads to the removal of an individual from office.

A similar process is provided for in Article XV of the Texas Constitution. The House has the power to impeach. The Senate has the power to try the governor, lieutenant governor, attorney general, land-office commissioner, and comptroller, as well as judges of the supreme court, the courts of appeal, and district courts. Conviction requires a two-thirds vote of the senators present. In contrast to the U.S. Constitution, the Texas Constitution rules that all officers against whom articles of impeachment are proffered are suspended from their office. The governor is empowered to appoint a person to fill the vacancy until the decision on impeachment is reached.

Despite these similarities to the impeachment procedures in the U.S. Constitution, the Texas Constitution has its own caveats. Most notable, the Texas Constitution does not explicitly define impeachable offenses in terms of "Treason, Bribery, or other high Crimes and Misdemeanors," as the U.S. Constitution does. The House and Senate (and the courts) decide what constitutes an impeachable offense.[16] In addition, the supreme court has original jurisdiction to hear and determine whether district court judges are competent to discharge their judicial duties. The governor may also remove judges of the supreme court, courts of appeal, and district courts when requested by the two-thirds vote of each legislature. Significantly, the reasons for removing a judge in this case need not rise to the level of an impeachable offense, but only involve a "willful neglect of duty, incompetence, habitual drunkenness, oppression in office, or other reasonable cause" (Article XV, Section 8). The barriers to removing a judge by political means are thus, at least on paper, much lower in Texas than in national government.

In 1980, Section 9 was added to Article XV, providing a new way to remove officials appointed by the governor. With the advice and consent of two-thirds of the members of the senate present, a governor may remove an appointed public official. If the legislature is not in session, the governor is empowered to call a special two-day session to consider the proposed removal.

Article XVI: General Provisions

Article XVI is one of the lengthiest in the Texas Constitution and has no parallel in the U.S. Constitution. It is literally a catchall article tackling a variety of issues ranging from official oaths of office to community property to banking corporations and stock laws to the election of the Texas Railroad Commission to the state retirement systems. Here, perhaps more than anywhere else, we see the complexity and confusion of the philosophy reflected in Texas's Constitution.

Article XVII: Amending the Constitution

Like the U.S. Constitution, the Texas Constitution explicitly delineates how it can be amended. Essentially, amendments undergo a four-stage process: First, the legislature must meet either in regular or special session and propose amendments.

TABLE 20.2

Amending the Texas Constitution

The Constitution of Texas has been amended 467 times since its inception in 1876.

YEARS	NUMBER PROPOSED	NUMBER ADOPTED	AVERAGE NUMBER ADOPTED PER SESSION
1879–1900	31	17	1.62
1901–20	55	21	2.10
1921–40	91	47	4.70
1941–60	78	59	5.90
1961–80	151	98	9.80
1981–97	163	135	15.0
1998–2002	37	33	16.0
2003	22	22	22
2005	9	7	7
2007*	1	1	NA
2007†	16	16	16
2009	11	11	11
Totals	665	467	

*May 2007 election.
†November 2007 election.

SOURCE: Texas Legislative Reference Library.

Second, these amendments must be approved by a two-thirds vote of all the members elected to each house. Third, a brief statement explaining the amendments must be published twice in each recognized newspaper in the state that meets the publication requirements for official state notices. Finally, the amendments must be approved by a majority of the state voters.

● Recent Attempts to Rewrite the Texas Constitution

Given the difficulty of amending the state constitution, a surprising number of amendments have been proposed since 1876. A considerable number of these have been turned down in the popular vote. As Table 20.2 shows, demands for amending the Constitution have intensified in recent years, as legislators have dealt with the problem of making changes in public policy while being constrained by an unwieldy constitutional document.

Sharpstown and the Failed Constitutional Reforms of 1974

A drive to rewrite the Texas Constitution grew out of a major stock fraud that broke in the early 1970s, involving the Sharpstown State Bank and the National Bankers Life Insurance Corporation. Following the 1970 elections, which had been dominated, as generally was the case, by the conservative wing of the Democratic Party, a suit was filed in Dallas federal court. Attorneys for the Securities and Exchange Commission alleged that a number of influential Democrats, including Governor

The Sharpstown State Bank scandal led to a demand for a new constitution to replace the outmoded 1876 document. This cartoon, which shows Governor Dolph Briscoe regally proclaiming, "This baby has a wart . . . off with his head!" satirizes Briscoe's stance against the new constitution.

— By BOB TAYLOR, Times Herald Staff Cartoonist

"This baby has a wart...off with his head!"

● Why has it proven
so difficult to
rewrite the Texas
Constitution?

Preston Smith, the state Democratic chairman and state banking board member Elmer Baum, Speaker of the House Gus Mutscher, and others, had been bribed. By the fall of 1971, Mutscher and two of his associates had been indicted. On March 15, 1972, they were convicted and sentenced to five years' probation.

The convictions fueled a firestorm in the state to "throw the rascals out." During the 1972 elections, "reform" candidates dominated the Democratic primary and the general election. The conservative rancher-banker Dolph Briscoe became governor, but only by a plurality, making him the first governor in the history of the state not to receive a majority of the popular vote. Other reform-minded candidates such as William P. Hobby, Jr., and John Hill were successful. Hobby won the lieutenant governor's race, while Hill became attorney general, defeating the three-term Democratic incumbent Crawford C. Martin. When the smoke had cleared, half of the House seats were occupied by new members, and the Senate had witnessed a higher than normal rate of turnover. The elections had one other outcome: an amendment was passed empowering the legislature to sit as a constitutional convention whose task would be to rewrite the Constitution.[17]

The constitutional convention met on January 8, 1974, in Austin. The idea was for the convention to draft a new constitution that would then be presented to the voters of the state for ratification. Originally scheduled to last 90 days, the convention was extended to 150 days. Even so, it did not have enough time. Bitter politics, coupled with the intense demands of highly mobilized special interests, made it impossible to reach the necessary agreement. In the end, proponents of a new constitution failed to achieve a two-thirds majority by three votes (118–62, with 1 abstention).

The movement to rewrite the constitution did not die at the convention. During the next session of the legislature, eight constitutional amendments were passed that effectively would have rewritten the Constitution through the normal amendment process. Each proposal, however, was turned down by the electorate in a special election on November 4, 1975. The Constitution of 1876 remained alive, if not well.

The 1999 Ratliff-Junell Proposal

For the first time since the unsuccessful effort to revise the Constitution in the mid-1970s, state senator Bill Ratliff and state representative Rob Junell, both powerhouses in the state legislature, proposed a new constitution for Texas in 1999. Ratliff argued, "It's time for Texas to have a constitution that's appropriate for the twenty-first century." They were concerned that the 1876 Constitution was too restrictive and cumbersome for modern government. It is lengthy, cluttered, and disorganized. The document had become so chaotic that in both 1999 and 2001, constitutional amendments were approved "to eliminate duplicative, executed, obsolete, archaic, and ineffective provisions" in the Constitution.

Among the major Ratliff-Junell proposals were that the governor would be given the authority to appoint several state officeholders who are now elected. Additionally, the executive branch would be reorganized so that the governor would have an appointed cabinet of department heads, subject to senate confirmation, much as the U.S. president does. With their proposal, only the lieutenant governor, the attorney general, and the state comptroller would be elected.

The governor would also be given the power to appoint all appellate and district judges. Afterward, the judges would be subject to voter approval in retention elections—where they have no opponent on the ballot, but where voters are asked if they wish to retain the appointed judge in office for a specified time period.

for critical analysis

What was the rationale for attempting to rewrite the constitution in 1974 and 1999? What changes were proposed? Why did these attempts fail?

In 1999 State Senator Bill Ratliff and State Representative Rob Junell proposed a rewriting of the Texas constitution that would make the executive branch more accountable. The proposal failed.

Ratliff argued that the changes would make the governor more accountable for how state government works.

The legislature would remain part time and would continue to meet in regular session every other year. It would also convene in a special fifteen-day "veto session," in order to consider overriding any gubernatorial vetoes from previous sessions. State senators now serve four-year terms and state representatives two-year terms. Under the proposed constitution, these terms would be increased to six years for state senators and four years for state representatives. For the first time, there would also be term limits so that representatives' service would be limited to eight regular sessions in the House or sixteen years in office, and senators' service could not exceed nine regular sessions in the Senate or eighteen years in office.

Although county government would remain as it is today, local voters would be given the authority to abolish their own county's obsolete offices without statewide approval through constitutional amendments.

Even as it was proposed, its sponsors realized that the proposed constitution would be tough to pass. And they were right—it did not pass, but suffered the fate of earlier efforts to change the 1876 Constitution.

The 2009 Amendments

In the 2009 constitutional amendment elections, voters were asked to consider eleven proposed amendments. All amendments passed, although only approximately 8.2 percent of registered voters bothered to vote. One thing that is clear about elections that deal with constitutional amendments is that voting participation is invariably low. Table 20.3 compares the percentage turnout of registered voters in November special elections on constitutional amendments with the percentage turnout in presidential elections (which tend to produce the highest turnout). There are two likely reasons for the low voter turnout in constitutional amendment elections: (1) Constitutional amendment elections are held in "off" years when there are no elections with candidates on the ballot. Since the elections are off year and without candidates, the political parties take a less active role in getting out the vote, and there are no candidates to generate voter turnout. As a result, advertising campaigns to get out the vote are frequently limited only to the activities of interest groups that support or oppose the issues on the ballot. (2) The second reason that voter participation is so low in these elections is that many of the amendments are relatively insignificant to most voters. The 2009 proposed constitutional amendments listed in Box 20.1 were largely uncontroversial. All propositions passed with support levels ranging between 55.2 percent for Proposition 1, which authorized local financing to buy buffer areas near military installations, to 81.01 percent for Proposition 11, which limited the power of eminent domain. Not surprising, the turnout rate for the election was low compared with that of other elections. Sometimes controversial amendments spark higher turnout.

In 2003, Proposition 12 authorized the legislature to limit noneconomic damages assessed against a provider of medical or health care. After January 1, 2005, the legislature could place limits on awards in other types of cases as well. The proposition was a major change in the state's tort law, and it probably accounts for the increase in voter participation in the 2003 constitutional amendment election

Why Is the Texas Constitution So Long?

State Constitution Length (estimated)

- < 19,999 words
- 20,000 – 39,999 words
- 40,000 – 59,999 words
- 60,000 – 79,999 words
- > 79,999 words

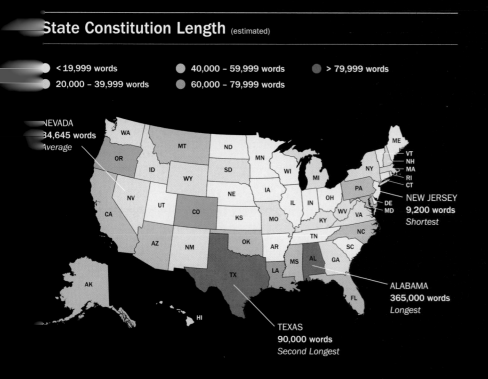

NEVADA
34,645 words
Average

NEW JERSEY
9,200 words
Shortest

ALABAMA
365,000 words
Longest

TEXAS
90,000 words
Second Longest

The Texas constitution is the second longest state constitution in the United States. The framers of the Texas constitution gave the state government very specific powers so that the government could not use ambiguity to expand its powers. As a result, the Texas constitution requires frequent amendments to address situations not covered specifically in the original constitution. The Texas constitution has been amended 456 times as of 2008, fourth most of any state.

Amendments Added to Constitution

- < 75 amendments
- 75 – 149 amendments
- 150 – 224 amendments
- 225 – 300 amendments
- > 300 amendments

IDAHO
.11
amendments
Average

SOUTH CAROLINA
10 amendments
Lowest

ALABAMA
807 amendments
Highest

TEXAS
456 amendments
Fourth Highest

for critical analysis

1. How would such a long and detailed state constitution achieve the framers' goal of limiting the scope and power of government in Texas?

2. The U.S. Constitution is a much shorter document than the Texas constitution and has only 27 amendments. Why would a shorter constitution lead to fewer amendments?

TABLE 20.3

Voter Turnout in Texas Constitutional Amendment Elections Compared with Texas Turnout for Presidential Elections

ELECTION	% TURNOUT OF REGISTERED VOTERS
2009 constitutional amendment	8.2
2008 presidential	59.5
2007 constitutional amendment (November)	8.4
2007 constitutional amendment (May)	7.1
2005 constitutional amendment	17.97
2004 presidential	56.6
2003 constitutional amendment	12.2
2001 constitutional amendment	6.9
2000 presidential	51.8
1999 constitutional amendment	8.38
1997 constitutional amendment (August)	6.94
1997 constitutional amendment (November)	10.6
1996 presidential	52.24
1995 constitutional amendment	7.86
1993 constitutional amendment	12.59
1992 presidential	72.92
1991 constitutional amendment	26.25

SOURCE: Texas Secretary of State.

over the 2001 election. Indeed, turnout in the 2003 election was the highest for such an election since 1993.[18]

Approved with only about 51 percent support of the voters, Proposition 12 inspired the costliest battle ever waged in Texas over a proposed state constitutional amendment. Donations to support the amendment came largely from doctors, hospitals, medical groups, insurance companies, and businesses. Amendment supporters spent $7.8 million in the campaign to get the amendment approved. Opponents of the amendment spent $9.3 million, with most of the money coming from lawyers and law firms.[19] Much of the campaign focused on the caps of noneconomic damages for medical malpractice awards. Supporters argued that huge medical malpractice awards were driving doctors from medical practice and reducing the availability of medical care for Texans. Opponents, on the other hand, claimed that the proposal reduced access to the courts for Texans and provided no control over the underlying problem of medical malpractice. And although the immediate consequence of the battle was a reduction in the amount of noneconomic damages that could be awarded in medical malpractice cases, the language of the amendment allows for reduction of damage awards in other types of cases in the near future. It was a close vote, but a victory for the new Republican-controlled Texas government, which was sympathetic to tort reform efforts. At the same time, it was a defeat for Democrats who had been unsympathetic toward tort reform, and it was a real blow for trial lawyers—once a mighty interest group in Texas politics but now left with only a fraction of its former political influence.[20]

Most of the 2005 proposed constitutional amendments were, like the previously discussed propositions, of significance only to a narrow group of people. For example, one of the nine proposed amendments provided for clearing land titles in Upshur and Smith counties. Another proposition authorized the addition of a public member and constitutional county court judge to the State Commission on Judicial Conduct. Still another authorized the legislature to provide for a six-year term for a board member of a regional mobility authority. Yet the turnout in this election was much higher than is typically seen in constitutional amendment elections. The

● Why has it proven so difficult to rewrite the Texas Constitution?

BOX 20.1

Passed Constitutional Amendments November 3, 2009

Proposition 1 (H.J.R. 132). The constitutional amendment authorizing the financing, including through tax increment financing, of the acquisition by municipalities and counties of buffer areas or open spaces adjacent to a military installation for the prevention of encroachment or for the construction of roadways, utilities, or other infrastructure to protect or promote the mission of the military installation. In Favor: 580,030; Against: 470,746

Proposition 2 (H.J.R. 36-1). The constitutional amendment authorizing the legislature to provide for the ad valorem taxation of a residence homestead solely on the basis of the property's value as a residence homestead. In Favor: 722,427; Against: 336,559

Proposition 3 (H.J.R. 36-3). The constitutional amendment providing for uniform standards and procedures for the appraisal of property for ad valorem tax purposes. In Favor: 691,294; Against: 363,703

Proposition 4 (H.J.R. 14-2). The constitutional amendment establishing the national research university fund to enable emerging research universities in this state to achieve national prominence as major research universities and transferring the balance of the higher education fund to the national research university fund. In Favor: 593,773; Against: 453,319

Proposition 5 (H.J.R. 36-2). The constitutional amendment authorizing the legislature to authorize a single board of equalization for two or more adjoining appraisal entities that elect to provide for consolidated equalizations. In Favor: 631,365,; Against: 390,080

Proposition 6 (H.J.R. 116). The constitutional amendment authorizing the Veterans' Land Board to issue general obligation bonds in amounts equal to or less than amounts previously authorized. In Favor: 672,285; Against: 351,036

Proposition 7 (H.J.R. 127). The constitutional amendment to allow an officer or enlisted member of the Texas State Guard or other state militia or military force to hold other civil offices. In Favor: 764,944; Against: 281,855

Proposition 8 (H.J.R. 7). The constitutional amendment authorizing the state to contribute money, property, and other resources for the establishment, maintenance, and operation of veterans hospitals in this state. In Favor: 789,703; Against: 265,627

Proposition 9 (H.J.R. 102). The constitutional amendment to protect the right of the public, individually and collectively, to access and use the public beaches bordering the seaward shore of the Gulf of Mexico. In Favor: 805,362; Against: 241,522

Proposition 10 (H.J.R. 85). The constitutional amendment to provide that elected members of the governing boards of emergency services districts may serve terms not to exceed four years. In Favor: 759,059; Against: 279,566

Proposition 11 (H.J.R. 14-1). The constitutional amendment to prohibit the taking, damaging, or destroying of private property for public use unless the action is for the ownership, use, and enjoyment of the property by the State, a political subdivision of the State, the public at large, or entities granted the power of eminent domain under law or for the elimination of urban blight on a particular parcel of property, but not for certain economic development or enhancement of tax revenue purposes, and to limit the legislature's authority to grant the power of eminent domain to an entity. In Favor: 848,651; Against: 198,822

SOURCE: Texas Secretary of State.

reason was Proposition 2, which defined marriage in Texas as the union of one man and one woman. The proposition also prohibited the state or any political subdivision of the state from creating or recognizing any legal status identical to or similar to marriage. The proposition generated a strongly favorable vote—1,723,782 in favor versus 536,913 against. Unlike Proposition 12 in 2003, this was not an economic battle involving interests concerned with tort law; rather, this was an issue pitting social conservative against those more sympathetic to gay rights. The strength of the social conservative vote in the state was, of course, remarkable, since the amendment carried by more than a 3 to 1 margin. Many churches and religious organizations strongly supported the proposed amendment. Their activities probably generated the relatively high voter turnout. The proposition was unusual in that people felt it was important to their lives because it affected their value systems. Although it is doubtful the amendment was necessary to support the traditional concept of marriage and although the ambiguity of the provision rejecting any legal status similar to marriage is disturbing, a significant part of the voting population apparently believed that it was important to vote their moral values, even if the proposal was largely symbolic.

In 2005, social conservatives urged Texans to vote in favor of Proposition 2, which defined marriage in Texas as the union of one man and one woman. This appeal to moral values contributed to relatively high turnout, and Proposition 2 passed by more than a 3-to-1 margin.

Box 20.2 identifies some of those constitutional amendments like Proposition 12 in 2003 or Proposition 2 in 2005 that had great significance in the public policy of the state. Most but not all of the amendments are not of great importance, but some, such as in Box 20.2, have had enormous significance.

● Conclusion: Thinking Critically about the Texas Constitution

In this chapter, we explored the history of constitutional government in Texas. We analyzed the seven constitutions under which Texas has been governed and explained the similarities and differences between the U.S. Constitution and Texas's current constitution (the Constitution of 1876). We also discussed attempts over the past thirty years to replace this constitution with a new one. The ideas of liberty and equality are enshrined in the Texas Constitution as they are in the U.S. Constitution. In some ways, the Texas Constitution does a better job of protecting liberty and providing for equality than does the U.S. Constitution. Where the Texas Constitution most fundamentally differs from the U.S. Constitution is in its view of democracy. Although championing democratic forms of government, the writers of the Texas Constitution were even more suspicious of centralized institutions of power than were the Founders of the United States. The Texas Constitution places serious constraints on the Texas legislature's ability to act as an independent body. It creates a weak plural executive, where executive power is limited and decentralized. And, finally, the Constitution subjects the courts to periodic elections. In Texas, the institutions of democracy were never supposed to be too far removed from the guiding hand of the people.

A number of additional themes were emphasized in this chapter. First, Texas's current constitution is far more complex than its predecessors or the U.S. Constitution. Matters that are considered public policy in most other states often must be addressed as constitutional issues in Texas. Second, the Texas Constitution is based on a general distrust of politicians and political power. It was originally written to prevent the expansion of political power that had taken place during Reconstruction and to make sure that political power could not be centralized in such a way that it might hurt the liberties and civil rights of the people. By limiting and decentralizing power, the Texas Constitution makes it difficult to exercise power effectively without being able to maintain extraordinary majorities in a variety of political arenas. Third, the Texas Constitution has been a difficult document to replace. Although amended 467 times, it has not been replaced by a new constitution and will probably not be replaced in the future. One reason for this is that mobilizing support for a wholesale reworking of the constitution has proven to be difficult. Another is that the general distrust of government and political power that gave birth to the Constitution of 1876 continues to hold sway among the citizenry.

BOX 20.2

Some Important Constitutional Amendments

In 1894, Texans strongly supported an amendment providing for the election of railroad commissioners. In later years, when Texas became a major oil producer, the railroad commission gained the authority to regulate oil production and became the most powerful elected regulatory agency in the country.

In 1902, Texans by a huge majority backed an amendment "requiring all persons subject to a poll tax to have paid a poll tax and to hold a receipt for same before they offer to vote at any election in this state, and fixing the time of payment of said tax." The poll tax required a payment of money prior to voting. The effect was to reduce the size of the electorate, limiting the opportunity of those with lower incomes to vote.

In 1919, the same year the national prohibition amendment was ratified, Texas ratified a state prohibition amendment.

1935 saw Texans repeal statewide prohibition. In its place was a local option whereby local communities chose whether alcohol would be sold in those communities. This was two years after repeal of national prohibition.

In 1954, Texans passed an amendment requiring women to serve on juries. Previous to that, women were exempt on the grounds that they were needed at home as the center of home life.

In 1966, Texans repealed the poll tax as a voting requirement in the face of pressures from the U.S. Supreme Court and from a national constitutional amendment that eliminated the poll tax in national elections.

In 1972, Texans overwhelmingly passed a constitutional amendment "to provide that equality under the law shall not be denied or abridged because of sex, race, color, creed or national origin." This amendment was primarily seen as an equal rights amendment banning sex discrimination, since federal civil rights statutes largely dealt with discrimination on other grounds. It was the state version of a proposed sexual equal rights amendment that was never ratified and made part of the U.S. Constitution.

2003 saw the passage of a constitutional amendment promoting the tort reform agenda that placed limitations on lawsuits. In "civil lawsuits against doctors and health care providers, and other actions," the legislature was authorized "to determine limitations on non-economic damages."

In 2005, a constitutional amendment was passed "providing that marriage in this state consists only of the union of one man and one woman and prohibiting this state or a political subdivision of this state from creating or recognizing any legal status identical or similar to marriage." The amendment was passed in response to the movement toward the recognition of civil unions and same-sex marriage in some states.

2009 saw Texas support an amendment establishing "the national research university fund to enable emerging research universities in this state to achieve national prominence as major research universities. . . . The amendment was a recognition that the Texas economy would benefit by the development of nationally recognized research universities in the state.

In 2009, in reaction to a U.S. Supreme Court decision involving eminent domain—the taking of private property for public use—that was seen as unsympathetic to property rights, Texans passed an amendment "to prohibit the taking, damaging, or destroying of private property for public use unless the action is for the ownership, use, and enjoyment of the property by the State, a political subdivision of the State, the public at large, or entities granted the power of eminent domain under law or for the elimination of urban blight on a particular parcel of property, but not for certain economic development or enhancements of tax revenue purpose."

Many people see some desirable features in the Texas Constitution. Like many state constitutions, the Texas Constitution has a Bill of Rights. Nor are all the rights in the Texas Bill of Rights merely a duplication of the rights in the U.S. Constitution. To some extent, the Texas Bill of Rights provides more constitutional protections than does the U.S. Constitution. State constitutions may do this under the doctrine of independent state grounds. That is, although a state constitution may provide more rights than the U.S. Constitution, it may not take away rights granted by the U.S. Constitution. One may think of the U.S. Constitution as a baseline to which states can add, but not subtract, protections. One of the most interesting Texas rights is an amendment adopted in 1972. It states, "Equality under the law shall not be denied or abridged because of sex, race, color, creed, or national origin. This amendment is self-operative." Although the amendment is not the subject of much litigation, note that it provides explicit protection from sex discrimination, something that is not mentioned in the U.S. Constitution. It is, in fact, a state version of the federal Equal Rights Amendment, which was almost ratified in the 1970s, but which never quite received sufficient support from the states to become a part of the U.S. Constitution.

Still, in spite of its positive aspects, the Texas Constitution is a lengthy, confusing, and highly restrictive document. Yet efforts to drastically change the document seem doomed to failure. There is little public outcry over the large numbers of amendments on which voters regularly must cast ballots. Additionally, the Constitution provides protections for the interests of key groups in Texas society, groups that are reluctant to give up those protections in exchange for a more flexible document.

for critical analysis

How does the supremacy clause of the U.S. Constitution affect Texas government?

studyguide

Practice Quiz

Ⓢ Find a diagnostic Web Quiz with 20 additional questions on the StudySpace Web site: www.wwnorton.com/we-the-people

1. Which idea is contained in both the U.S. and Texas Constitutions? *(p. 757)*
   a) a supremacy clause
   b) federalism
   c) laissez-faire economics
   d) *Rebus sic stantibus*

2. Which of the following is *not* an important function of a state constitution? *(p. 757)*
   a) prevents the concentration of political power
   b) delegates power to individuals and institutions
   c) allows government to intrude in the lives of businesses and individuals
   d) legitimizes political institutions

3. Which part of the U.S. Constitution reserves power to the states? *(p. 757)*
   a) Article I
   b) Article VI
   c) First Amendment
   d) Tenth Amendment

4. Under the U.S. Constitution, the government of Texas is most limited by *(p. 758)*
   a) Article IV of the U.S. Constitution.
   b) the implied powers clause and the Tenth Amendment.
   c) the Fourteenth Amendment.
   d) its own sense of self-importance.

5. The Constitution of 1861 was *(p. 764)*
   a) opposed by Sam Houston.
   b) guided Texas's entry into the Confederate States of America.
   c) supported slavery.
   d) all of the above

6. A unique feature of the Constitution of 1869 was that *(p. 766)*
   a) fewer than 1 percent of voters opposed it.
   b) it was less than four pages long.
   c) it was never submitted to the voters.
   d) it is considered the best of Texas's constitutions.

7. A new Texas constitution was written (p. 767)
   a) when Reconstruction ended.
   b) when the Compromise of 1850 was adopted.
   c) at the start of World War I.
   d) in 1999.

8. The present Texas constitution (p. 767)
   a) is well organized and well written.
   b) is considered to be one of the best of the fifty state constitutions.
   c) delegates a great deal of power to the governor.
   d) severely limits the power of the governor and other state officials.

9. The Constitution of 1876 was a reaction to the Reconstruction Constitution of 1869 because (p. 767)
   a) the 1869 Constitution was too short.
   b) the 1869 Constitution forbade slavery.
   c) the 1869 Constitution increased state officials' salaries.
   d) the 1869 Constitution was seen as giving the governor too much power.

10. Those who wrote the Constitution of 1876 wanted to return control of government to the people. By "the people" they meant (p. 768)
    a) all adult citizens of Texas.
    b) all adult male citizens of Texas.
    c) all adult white male citizens of Texas.
    d) all citizens except carpetbaggers and scalawags.

11. Article I of the Texas Constitution (p. 770)
    a) contains the Texas Bill of Rights.
    b) renounces the use of the death penalty.

c) recognizes the supremacy of the national government.
d) accepts the principle of rapprochement.

12. The Texas Bill of Rights (p. 770)
    a) guarantees some rights not found in the U.S. Bill of Rights.
    b) duplicates the U.S. Bill of Rights.
    c) is unusual, since state constitutions generally do not have Bills of Rights.
    d) guarantees gay marriage.

13. The Texas Constitution requires that Texas judges (p. 773)
    a) be appointed by the governor.
    b) be senior lawyers.
    c) be elected by the people.
    d) cannot receive campaign contributions.

14. A new constitution for Texas (p. 777)
    a) is unlikely to be ratified before 2012.
    b) is scheduled for a vote in 2010.
    c) has a 50–50 chance of being ratified.
    d) has a very small chance of being ratified.

15. Voter turnout for constitutional amendment elections could be improved if (p. 778)
    a) they were held at the same time as presidential elections.
    b) there were more voter awareness of the proposed amendments.
    c) the amendments involved significant issues for voters.
    d) all of the above

Chapter Outline

Find a detailed Chapter Outline on the StudySpace Web site: www.wwnorton.com/we-the-people

Key Terms

Find Flashcards to help you study these terms on the StudySpace Web site: www.wwnorton.com/we-the-people

bicameral (p. 762)
Confederacy (p. 765)
constitution (p. 757)
federalism (p. 757)
Grange (p. 767)

impeachment (p. 774)
limited government (p. 769)
necessary and proper clause (p. 758)
plural executive (p. 772)
Radical Republicans (p. 766)

republican government (p. 770)
separation of powers (p. 771)
supremacy clause (p. 757)
unicameral (p. 759)

Recommended Web Sites

Handbook of the State of Texas
www.tshaonline.org/handbook/online/

Texas Constitution
www.constitution.legis.state.tx.us/

Texas Constitutions 1824–1876
http://tarlton.law.utexas.edu/constitutions/

In 2010, Kay Bailey Hutchison, a U.S. senator from Texas, challenged Governor Rick Perry in the Republican primary elections. Hutchison hoped to win the support of Republicans who were unhappy with some of Perry's recent decisions. However, growing anti-Washington sentiment among Texas Republicans helped Perry defeat Hutchison.

Parties and Elections in Texas

WHAT GOVERNMENT DOES AND WHY IT MATTERS In 2009, Senator Kay Bailey Hutchison announced that she would run for governor of Texas in 2010. Few doubted at the outset that she would be successful. She had amassed a campaign chest that was the envy of many. She had the support of major party leaders who were willing to back her publicly, even if it meant coming out against the sitting governor, Rick Perry.

In the summer of 2009, Perry appeared vulnerable in the state. A number of apparent missteps in the previous term seemed to have undermined his hold on power. Perry's handling of the evacuation of Houston and Galveston during Hurricane Rita and his attempt to mandate the vaccination of young girls against HPV (human papilloma virus), the virus that causes cervical cancer, led some supporters to question his political judgment on certain issues. His support for the Trans Texas Corridor and his

focusquestions

- How do political parties organize elections and the electorate in Texas?

- What does it mean to be a "one-party state"?

- Why is it difficult to be elected as an independent in Texas?

- What are the types of elections held in Texas?

- Why do so few Texans vote?

- Why are political campaigns so expensive in Texas?

desire to gain control of institutions of higher education through the appointment of his own political cronies to various boards of regents led many opinion makers to raise concerns over Perry's ongoing accumulation of power. The governor's office, many thought, was Hutchison's for the taking.

By December of 2009, however, the "inevitable" Hutchison victory began to unravel. Opposition to the Obama administration was growing across the nation and within Texas. A grassroots movement dubbed the Tea Party movement challenged many of the ideological assumptions of the Obama administration and urged Republicans toward cultural conservatism and an anti-Washington stance.

Perry embraced the anti-Washington rhetoric that was taking hold among many Republicans at the local level. He positioned himself as a conservative sensitive to the concerns of the Tea Party movement, even tipping his hat to secession as a possible solution to an unresponsive central government. Perry painted Hutchison as a Washington insider who might have lost touch with the conservative core of the Republican Party in Texas.

Perry's message struck a chord in the hearts of conservative Republicans across the state. Polls showed support for Perry building throughout early 2010. Meanwhile, Hutchison's campaign floundered throughout the winter months and was never able to offer a convincing argument for why she was not just another Washington insider. The popular senator from Texas found herself to be another victim of the growing conservative backlash to the Obama administration. Hutchison lost the Republican gubernatorial primary in the early spring to Perry, who then rode his anti-Washington rhetoric to victory in the November 2010 election.

In this chapter, we will examine the roles that political parties and elections play in Texas politics.

chaptercontents

● How do political
parties organize
elections and the
electorate in Texas?

● The Role of Political Parties in Texas Politics

Elections are the most important vehicles by which the people express themselves in the democratic process in Texas. Political parties help candidates win elections and assist voters in making their electoral choices. At the national level, elections are limited to the selection of the president and vice president and members of Congress. In Texas, however, voters select candidates for various offices in all three branches of government. In theory, such elections are meant to enable the people to exercise some direct control over each branch. In practice, however, one-party dominance and low levels of voter participation have often told a different story, leaving the government exposed to special interests and big money.

Perhaps the most important function of parties in Texas is that they provide a label under which candidates can run and with which voters can identify. Since Texas elects very large numbers of officeholders, it is unlikely that voters will be familiar with the views or the qualifications of every candidate. However, Texas voters overwhelmingly identify with or lean toward either the Republican Party or the Democratic Party.[1] Those voters will use the party affiliation of the candidates as a way of deciding for whom to vote. Thus, for many voters, without other information, the party label becomes the standard they apply in casting a ballot for a candidate. Voters often use the party label as a cue to the ideology of candidates. A voter may assume that, for example, a Republican candidate is a "conservative" and may vote for or against that candidate because of the ideology that a party affiliation implies.[2]

Parties to some extent help in raising money for candidates' campaigns and in assisting candidates with legal requirements and with training for a campaign. They sometimes recruit candidates for political races, although in Texas any candidate may run in a party primary, and, if victorious in the primary, will become the party nominee. Parties also assist in "getting out the vote" for candidates through phone banks, door-to-door contacts, and other efforts.

Once a candidate is elected to office, party affiliation helps in organizing the government. Governors will usually appoint people who are members of their own

Parties select candidates to run for office under the party label. In 2010, the Democrats chose Bill White to run for governor. White had previously served as mayor of Houston.

party. Increasingly, the Texas legislature is divided by party. Public officials may also feel a greater sense of loyalty and cooperation toward other public officials of their party. After all, they often campaign together and make appearances at the same political events, and their fortunes often rise and fall together based on the popularity of the party. In that sense, the banding together of officeholders with the same party affiliation provides voters an opportunity to hold the party accountable for its policies or its failures.

Party Organization

Although it is common for Texans to proclaim that they are "registered Republicans" or "registered Democrats," Texas does not have a system of party registration. Registered voters may vote in either the Democratic or Republican primary. When they do vote in a primary, their voter registration card will be stamped "Democrat" or "Republican" to prevent them from voting in the other primary as well.

One of the most important functions of political parties is to select candidates to run for office under the party label. Today that is done through primary elections. If several candidates are running for the party nomination in a primary election, it may be that none receives a majority vote. In that case, the party will hold a run-off election to determine who will be nominated. Primaries were not always used to select the party nominee. During the nineteenth century, candidates were nominated at party conventions, but early in the twentieth century the state moved to the primary as a way of selecting candidates.

To understand how the parties are organized, think first in terms of the permanent organization of the party and then in terms of the temporary (campaign) organization (see Figure 21.1). In each election **precinct**, a **precinct chair** will be elected in the party primary. The precinct chair will head the precinct convention and will also serve on the party's **county executive committee**. In the primary, the **county chair** will also be elected. The county chair will head the county executive

precinct a local voting district

precinct chair the local party official, elected in the party's primary election, who heads the precinct convention and serves on the party's county executive committee

county executive committee the party group, made up of a party's county chair and precinct chairs, that is responsible for running a county's primary elections and planning county conventions

county chair the county party official, who heads the county executive committee

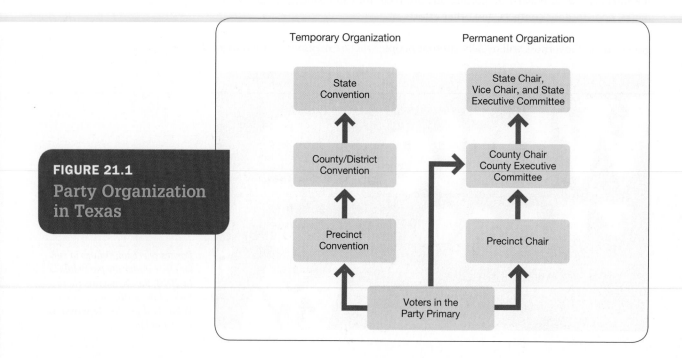

FIGURE 21.1
Party Organization in Texas

committee, which is composed of the chair and the precinct chairs. The main responsibility of the county executive committee is to run the county primary and plan the county conventions. There may be other district committees as well for political divisions that do not correspond to the county lines.

At the state level, there is a **state executive committee**, which includes a **state chair and vice chair**. These officers are selected every two years at the state party conventions. The state executive committee accepts filings by candidates for statewide office. It helps raise funds for the party, and it helps establish party policy. Both the Democratic and Republican parties also employ professional staff to run day-to-day operations and to assist with special problems that affect the party.

The temporary organization of the party includes the **precinct conventions**. The main role of the precinct conventions is to select delegates to the **county convention** and possibly to submit resolutions that may eventually become part of the party platform.

Delegates chosen by the precinct convention then go to the county conventions (or in urban areas, district conventions). These conventions will elect delegates to the **state convention**. Both the Democratic and Republican parties hold state conventions every other year. These conventions certify the nominees of the party for statewide office; adopt a platform; and elect a chair, vice chair, and a state executive committee. In presidential election years, the state conventions select delegates for the national party conventions; elect delegates for the national party committee; and choose presidential electors, who, if the party's choice for president carries the state in the election, will formally cast the state's electoral votes for the president in the electoral college.

Battles for control of a state party have often been fought in Texas politics, where rival ideological and other interest groups have struggled to control precinct, county, and state conventions and to elect their candidates for precinct chair, county chair, and state executive committee. In the 1950s, when loyal and liberal Democrats battled the Shivercrats for control of the Democratic Party, struggles for control of the party organization were fierce. There have also been calmer times in Texas politics, where involvement in the parties has been minimal and battles have been few. Sometimes, apathy has been so great that precinct conventions have been sparsely attended and offices such as precinct chair have gone unfilled.

state executive committee the committee responsible for governing a party's activities throughout the state

state chair and vice chair the top two state-level leaders in the party

precinct convention a meeting held by a political party to select delegates for the county convention and to submit resolutions to the party's state platform; precinct conventions are held on the day of the party's primary election and are open to anyone who voted in that election

county convention a meeting held by a political party following its precinct conventions, for the purpose of electing delegates to its state convention

state convention a party meeting held every two years for the purpose of nominating candidates for statewide office, adopting a platform, electing the party's leadership, and in presidential election years selecting delegates for the national convention and choosing presidential electors

● Texas's History as a One-Party State

With the defeat of the Republican governor Edmund J. Davis in 1873, Texas entered a period of Democratic dominance that would last for over a century. Often the Republican Party would not contest major state offices, and other parties—such as the Populist or People's Party—though having some influence for brief periods, did not have staying power. In general elections, it was a foregone conclusion that the Democratic nominee would win. If there was a meaningful election contest, it was in the Democratic Party primary.

Republicans tended to have a limited role in Texas politics. Most commonly, people remained Republicans in the hope of gaining political patronage (usually local postmaster or rural mail carrier positions) when Republican presidents were in office. Some Republicans were business people unhappy with the liberal policies of Democratic presidents such as Franklin D. Roosevelt or Harry Truman. However, the Republican Party was not a threat to Democratic dominance in the state. Indeed,

Republicans interested in patronage from the national government may have had an incentive to keep the Republican Party small, since the fewer the Republicans, the less the competition for patronage positions. When the father of the late senator Lloyd Bentsen first moved to the Rio Grande Valley, he visited with R. B. Creager, who was then state chairman of the Republican Party. Lloyd Bentsen, Sr., told Creager that he wanted to get involved in the Republican Party because his father had been a devoted Republican in South Dakota. Rather than welcoming Bentsen into the Republican Party, Creager told Bentsen, "You go back to Mission [Texas] and join the Democratic Party, because what's best for Texas is for every state in the union to have a two-party system and for Texas to be a one-party state. When you have a one-party state, your men stay in Congress longer and build up seniority.[3]

In 1952 and in 1956, however, the Democratic governor Allan Shivers led a movement often known as the **Shivercrat movement**, which presaged a dramatic change in party alignments a quarter-century later. Governor Shivers was a conservative Democrat and widely regarded as one of the most able Texas governors of the twentieth century. He supported the candidacy of the Republican Dwight Eisenhower for the presidency against the Democratic nominee, Adlai Stevenson. Stevenson opposed the Texas position on the Tidelands, offshore lands claimed by both Texas and the national government, which were believed to contain oil. Additionally, Stevenson was much more liberal than Shivers, and Eisenhower was a famous and popular hero of World War II. Governor Shivers not only supported Eisenhower for the presidency, he and all statewide officeholders except the agriculture commissioner, John White, ran on the ballot as Democrats *and* Republicans. It was an act of party disloyalty condemned by loyal Democrats such as Speaker of the U.S. House of Representatives Sam Rayburn, and it led to much tension in the Democratic Party between liberal and conservative Democrats as well as between party loyalists and the Shivercrats.

The Shivercrat movement sent a strong message that many conservative Democrats were philosophically opposed to the national Democratic Party and, although they were unwilling to embrace the Republican Party fully, they found the Republican Party more compatible to their views. A pattern in voting known as **presidential Republicanism** was strengthening, whereby conservative Texas voters would vote Democratic for state offices, but vote Republican for presidential candidates. With the Shivercrat movement, those conservatives were more numerous and more closely aligned with the Republican Party.

Still, in state elections, the Democratic Party was overwhelmingly the dominant party. There might be pockets of the state where Republicans showed strength. Traditionally, in the post–Civil War era, the "German counties" in the Texas Hill Country, which were settled by German immigrants, showed Republican leanings. Dallas County, whose voters were influenced by a powerful group of conservative businesspeople and a conservative newspaper, the *Dallas News*, showed early Republican strength, electing a very conservative Republican congressman in the 1950s. However, for the most part, the Democratic Party was so dominant in state elections that the Republican Party did not field opponents to the Democratic nominees.

During this era, the Democratic Party was an umbrella party that held a variety of groups and interests. Liberals and conservatives belonged to the party, as did members of labor unions and businesspeople, farmers and citydwellers. Often liberals and conservatives within the party battled for control of the party and its offices. But when liberals and conservatives were not engaged in periodic intraparty

Shivercrat movement a movement, led by the Texas governor Allan Shivers during the 1950s, in which conservative Democrats in Texas supported Republican candidates for office because many of them believed that the national Democratic Party had become too liberal

presidential Republicanism a voting pattern in which conservatives vote Democratic for state offices, but Republican for presidential candidates

Although the Democratic Party dominated state politics for much of the twentieth century, by the 1950s it faced internal divisions between liberal and conservative Democrats. Governor Allen Shivers (third from left) was a conservative Democrat and encouraged his supporters to vote for Republican candidates when they felt that the Democratic candidates were too liberal.

battles, battles that occurred with considerable regularity, what political organization existed tended to be based on personal ties and personal popularity of individual candidates.

With the imposition of the poll tax and the white primary at the beginning of the twentieth century (discussed later in this chapter), stable factions ceased to exist in the Democratic Party. Earlier factions in Texas politics reflected "have" and "have-not" economic interests. Until about the 1940s, Texas politics was often chaotic and confused. By about the mid-1940s, however, a split between liberals and conservatives developed in the Democratic Party that focused on New Deal economic policies and civil rights measures. This liberal-conservative split became a characteristic division within the Democratic Party, and liberals and conservatives battled in the party primaries. Between the mid-1940s and the mid-1970s, the victor in these primary squabbles would then go on to win the general election. However, by the late 1970s, the winner of the Democratic primary had to face a significant conservative challenge from Republicans in the general election.[4]

The Growth of the Republican Party

One of the most important developments in Texas politics has been the growth of the Republican Party. In the 1950s, more than 60 percent of Texans identified with the Democratic Party and fewer than 10 percent identified themselves as Republicans. The remainder considered themselves independents. In the 1960s, Republican identification in Texas rose above 10 percent; Democratic identification remained above 60 percent; and identification with independents dropped slightly. The 1970s saw a decline in Democratic affiliation and an increase in Republican affiliation. That pattern of increase of Texans who identified themselves as Republicans and decline among those who identified themselves as Democrats accelerated during the 1980.[5] In 2008, Texans who identified themselves as Republicans saw a drop from 37 percent in 2004 to 33 percent, whereas Democratic Party affiliation remained steady at 30 percent.[6] A 2009 gallup poll study identified Texas as being a competitive state with Republican leanings.[7] However, there is a difference between potential voters who respond to surveys and actual voters. Among actual voters, Texas is strongly Republican in statewide elections.

In the first quarter of the twentieth century, the Republican Party was only a token party. In the state legislature, for example, Republicans never held more than one seat in the Texas Senate and never more than two seats in the Texas House from 1903 to 1927. From 1927 to 1951, there were no Republicans in the Texas legislature, and then a lone Republican was elected from Dallas to serve only one term in the Texas House. It was another decade before Republicans were again elected to the legislature, when two served in the Texas House. Then in 1962, six Republicans were elected to the House from Dallas County and one from Midland County. By 1963, there were ten Republicans in the Texas House and none in the Texas Senate.[8]

As Table 21.1 shows, as late as 1974, there were not many more than seventy-five Republican officeholders in the entire state of Texas. One of those officeholders was U.S. Senator John Tower, and there were two Texas Republicans in the U.S. House of Representatives. No Republicans were elected to state office in statewide elections. There were only three Republicans in the Texas Senate and only sixteen Republicans in the Texas House of Representatives. By contrast, in 2010 both U.S. senators from Texas were Republican and twenty-four Texas members of the U.S.

TABLE 21.1

Growth of the Republican Party in Texas

YEAR	U.S. SENATE	OTHER STATEWIDE	U.S. HOUSE	TEXAS SENATE	TEXAS HOUSE	COUNTY OFFICE	DISTRICT OFFICE	SCHOOL BOARD	TOTAL
1974	1	0	2	3	16	53			75+
1976	1	0	2	3	19	67			92+
1978	1	1	4	4	22	87			119+
1980	1	1	5	7	35	166			215+
1982	1	0	5	5	36	191	79		317
1984	1	0	10	6	52	287	90		446
1986	1	1	10	6	56	410	94		578
1988	1	5	8	8	57	485	123	5	692
1990	1	6	8	8	57	547	170	5	802
1992	1	8	9	13	58	634	183	5	911
1994	2	13	11	14	61	734	216	8	1059
1996	2	18	13	17	68	?938	278	9	1343
1998	2	27	13	16	72	1108	280	9	1527
2000	2	27	13	16	72	1233	336	10	1709
2002	2	27	15	19	88	1443	362	10	1966
2004	2	27	21	19	87	1608	392	10	2166
2006	2	27	19	20	82	1814	379	10	2353
2008	2	27	20	18	75	1820	383	10	2355
2010	2	27	24	19	99	NA	NA	NA	NA

SOURCE: Derek Ryan, Republican Party of Texas, e-mail to authors; Republican Party of Texas Web site.

● Why is it difficult
to be elected as
an independent in
Texas?

House of Representatives were Republican. A majority of the Texas Senate, nineteen of the thirty-one members, and the Texas House of Representatives, ninety-nine of the 150 members, was Republican.

It was a record of remarkable Republican growth and Democratic decline. By 1998, every statewide elected official was Republican. (This remained true in 2010 as well.) That included the governor, the lieutenant governor, the attorney general, the comptroller, land commissioner, agriculture commissioner, all three members of the Texas Railroad Commission, and all nine members of both the Texas Supreme Court and the Texas Court of Criminal Appeals. Only twenty years earlier, William Clements was the first statewide official elected as a Republican since Reconstruction.

● Issues in Texas Party Politics

Running as an Independent

It is unusual for a candidate to run for office in Texas as an independent. One reason is that there are substantial requirements for getting one's name on the ballot. Additionally, an independent candidate lacks the political support of party organizations and the advantage of having a party label on the ballot. In 2006, however, Texas had two independent candidates for governor. One was the musician and humorist Kinky Friedman. The other was Carole Keeton Strayhorn, the state comptroller, who had been elected to that office as a Republican.

Both candidates were obviously hoping that an independent candidacy would attract the votes of Democrats who believed that a Democratic candidate for governor could not win in such a strongly Republican state. They also were hoping

Independent candidates face considerable challenges in elections. Although the musician and writer Kinky Friedman's 2006 candidacy for governor attracted major media attention, Friedman received only 12.4 percent of the vote.

to get substantial votes from Republicans disaffected with the policies and performance of the Republican governor, Rick Perry. Strayhorn, in particular, seemed to have strong appeal to Democrats who usually contributed large sums to Democratic nominees. One study of Strayhorn's contributions from July through December of 2005, for example, found that 52 percent of her campaign funds were from people who had given exclusively or almost exclusively to Democrats over the past five years.[9]

In general, however, independents have a hard time getting on the ballot in Texas. For Friedman and Strayhorn to get on the ballot, for example, they had to meet the following requirements:

1. The candidates must obtain signatures on a petition from registered voters. The signatures must equal 1 percent of the total votes in the last governor's race. This meant that Friedman and Strayhorn each had to obtain 45,540 signatures.

2. The signatures must come from registered voters who did not participate in any political party primary election.

3. Signature collection cannot begin until the day after the last primary election. In 2006, this was March 8.

4. Voters may sign only one candidate's petition. If they sign both, only the first signature provided will count.[10]

Making it difficult for independents to get their names on the ballot helps to ensure that the two major political parties will continue to dominate politics in the state well into the future. Elections may be open in Texas, but they work through the dominant political parties, helping to solidify their control over the political process and the major political offices in the state. The electoral performances of Friedman and Strayhorn also point to the difficulties of independent candidacies. Friedman received only 12.4 percent of the vote and Strayhorn got only 18.1 percent.

Party Unity and Disunity

All groups have factions within them, and political parties are no exception. When a party becomes dominant in a state, however, these factional battles become particularly important because the stakes are higher for the factions of the dominant party.

When the Democratic Party was the dominant party in Texas, factional battles were common between liberals and conservatives in the party. These conflicts in the Democratic Party were especially notable during the 1950s in the struggles between the pro-Eisenhower conservative Democrats, led by Allan Shivers, and the pro-Stevenson liberal and loyalist Democrats, led by Sam Rayburn, Lyndon Johnson, and Ralph Yarborough. Now that the Republican Party is the dominant party in Texas, major factional battles have occurred for control of the Republican Party. One faction is the religious right. This group includes religious conservatives who are especially concerned with social issues such as abortion, prayer in public schools and at school events, the teaching of evolution in public schools, and the perceived decline in family values. The other major segment of the party is composed of economic conservatives. This group is primarily concerned with reduced government spending, lower taxes, and greater emphasis on free enterprise.

● Why is it difficult
to be elected as
an independent in
Texas?

In the 2006 primary, some Republicans, including two of the party's largest contributors in Texas, spent money to try to defeat Republicans in the Texas House who they believed were too moderate.[11] At least six Republican incumbents were aided by last-minute contributions from a political action committee that poured about $300,000 into their campaigns to help protect them from Republican challengers. Nevertheless, two of the six incumbents were defeated and one was thrown into a runoff.[12]

The important thing for the Republican Party is to keep these factional disputes within the party. For years, the Democratic Party battles between its liberal and conservative wings were kept inside the party because there was no rival party where one of the factions could go. Eventually, however, the Republican Party emerged as a home where many conservative Democrats felt comfortable. Conceivably, the factional disputes in the Republican Party could lead one of the factions—most likely the more moderate Republicans—to move to the Democratic Party.

Hispanics and the Future of Party Politics in Texas

In the media coverage of the 2000 presidential election, one little judicial race in Dallas County was almost overlooked. Only one puzzled article on the race's results appeared in the *Dallas Morning News*.[13] A three-time Republican judge, Bill Rhea, won re-election against a first-time Democratic candidate, Mary Ann Huey. That should have been no surprise. By the late 1980s, the only Democrat who could win a judicial race in Dallas County was Ron Chapman, a Democratic judge who happened to share the name of the most popular disk jockey in the county.[14] In the early 1980s, there had been a wholesale rush of incumbent Democratic judges to the Republican Party. Although varying explanations were given by the party switchers, perhaps the most honest and straightforward was by Judge Richard Mays: "My political philosophy about general things has nothing to do with me [*sic*] being a judge. . . . That's not the reason I'm switching parties. The reason I'm switching is that to be a judge in Dallas County you need to be a Republican." With Mays's switch in August 1985, thirty-two of the thirty-six district judges in Dallas County were Republicans, though none were Republicans before 1978.[15] It would, of course, not take long until all judges in Dallas County were Republican.[16]

So what was remarkable about that one district court race between a Democratic challenger and a longtime Republican incumbent, other than the fact that a Democrat had the temerity to challenge an incumbent in a Republican bastion such as Dallas County? Out of 560,558 votes cast, only 4,150 votes separated the two candidates. In other words, a three-term Republican judge with no scandal or other controversy surrounding his name won with only 50.3 percent of the vote. It is no wonder that the judge commented, "I'm thrilled to be serving again and duly humbled by the vote count."[17] Even more astounding, Judge Rhea's Democratic opponent, Mary Ann Huey, had run with no money, no political experience, and no support from the legal community. She ran in the same year that George W. Bush was the presidential nominee, with no other Democratic judicial candidates on the ballot at the county level, and with little more than chutzpah on her side.

Judge Rhea's humbling experience, of course, was not caused by his judicial performance but rather by demographic changes. The Republican base in Dallas County has moved to places such as Collin, Denton, and Rockwall counties. That suburban growth has changed those traditionally Democratic counties into Republican

forcritical**analysis**

What is the significance of Hispanic population growth to parties and elections in Texas?

State Senator Leticia Van de Putte, of San Antonio, is one of a growing number of influential Hispanics in the Democratic Party in Texas. Here, she makes an announcement about helping indentured servants, who are brought over the border and then forced to work, often under harsh conditions, to pay off their "debt" to the traffickers who brought them over.

counties, but the old Republican base—Dallas—is left with a larger African American and Hispanic population and has returned to the Democratic column that it left a little over twenty years ago.

In the 2004 elections, George W. Bush carried Dallas County by fewer than 10,000 votes (50.72 percent), and Dallas County elected Democrats as sheriff and four countywide elected judges. The 2006 elections in Dallas County were truly a watershed in the county's politics. A Democrat was elected county judge, a Democrat was elected district attorney, and all forty-two Democrats who ran for Dallas County judgeships were elected. Democrats continued their sweep of countywide elections in 2008 and 2010.

In 2008, Harris County dramatically shifted to the Democratic column, electing a large number of Democrats to county office. It seemed to be following in Dallas County's footsteps. However, the 2010 elections moved Harris County back into the Republican column.

The 2002 elections, however, raised serious questions about how soon the Hispanic vote would transform politics in Texas. In an attempt to break the lock that the Republicans had on statewide offices, the Democratic Party put forward a "Dream Team" with Tony Sanchez, a wealthy Hispanic businessman, running for governor alongside Ron Kirk (a former mayor of Dallas who is African American) running for the U.S. Senate and John Sharp (a former state comptroller and white conservative Democrat) running for lieutenant governor. The idea was to mobilize minority voters to vote for the Democratic ticket while holding traditional white voters. The strategy failed dismally as Sanchez lost to the Republican candidate Perry (40 percent to 58 percent), Kirk lost to the Republican Cornyn (43 percent to 55 percent), and Sharp to the Republican Dewhurst (46 percent to 52 percent). Especially disappointing since Sanchez was the first major party nominee

How Did Texans Vote in 2008?

	Race	pop.%	🫏 = Obama	🐘 = McCain		

National

Race	pop.%		Obama	McCain
White	74%		43%	55%
Black	13%		95%	4%
Hispanic	9%		67%	31%
Asian	2%		62%	35%
Other	3%		66%	31%

Texas

Race	pop.%		Obama	McCain
White	63%		26%	73%
Black	13%		98%	2%
Hispanic	20%		63%	35%
Asian	2%			
Other	2%			

Note: Data on Asian American voters and other groups were not available from Texas exit polls.

California

Race	pop.%		Obama	McCain
White	63%		52%	46%
Black	10%		94%	5%
Hispanic	18%		74%	23%
Asian	6%		64%	35%
Other	3%		55%	41%

Voters in Texas are known for their conservatism and their support of the Republican Party. In 2008, while the country voted for Barack Obama over John McCain by a 53%–46% margin, Texas went for McCain 55–44.

In Texas, exit polls showed that McCain won in large part because he won an overwhelming share of white voters. Obama won among African American and Hispanic voters in Texas by similar numbers to what he won nationally. McCain won 73% of white votes in Texas, 18 points better than the 55% of white voters he won nationally. Compare this to California, a state with similar demographics to Texas; McCain won only 46% of California's white voters.

for critical analysis

1. Why do you think McCain appealed to white Texans more than he appealed to white voters in the rest of the country? How distinct does this make Texans?

2. As discussed in Chapter 19, the Hispanic population of Texas is growing rapidly. How might this growth change the outcomes of future elections in Texas?

for governor who was Hispanic, Hispanic voter turnout was only 32.8 percent. The Democratic "Dream Team" became a nightmare. Sanchez had money and spent it with abandon, but he was a poor campaigner who could not even mobilize the Hispanic vote.

Additionally, Democrats didn't anticipate the grassroots get-out-the-vote effort put forth by the Republicans. Republican straight-ticket voting in key urban and suburban counties across the state appeared to have outdistanced Democratic straight-ticket voting. Further, it appeared that the negative campaigning, particularly that directed at Tony Sanchez, may have undercut support for the Democratic ticket among traditional white conservative voters. Bob Stein, a political science professor at Rice University, estimates that 15 percent of Democrats abandoned Sanchez because of questions raised by his involvement in a failed savings and loan bank that was accused of laundering money for Mexican drug kingpins.

The 2010 election has been described as a Republican tsunami running throughout the nation. Texas experienced this wave in three important ways. First, four Democratic incumbents were defeated. Second, Republicans maintained their monopoly over state-wide elected offices. Third, Republicans gained twenty-two seats in the Texas House. A conservative majority reasserted itself in Texas politics.

Despite the final results of the 2008 and 2010 elections, few commentators were willing to dismiss the growing importance of the Hispanic vote in the state. One indication of that importance is that in 2010, it was estimated that Hispanic make up about 20 percent of the registered voters in Texas.[18]

However, Hispanics have not fully realized their potential voting strength. Table 21.2 shows Hispanic voting in comparison to other racial and ethnic groups, comparing the group's share of the population with its share of voters in the 2008 election. It does seem likely that Hispanics will at some point significantly increase their share of the vote in Texas, although one obstacle may be that large numbers are not citizens and are ineligible to vote.[19] When Hispanic voting does increase, the key question will be whether Republicans can make inroads into the Hispanic vote to the extent necessary to keep the Democratic Party from emerging as a dominant party in Texas once again. As of now, Hispanics comprise 37 percent of the Texas population and 25 percent of the eligible voters; yet they are only 20 percent of registered voters and only 12–14 percent of actual voters.[20]

TABLE 21.2

Racial/Ethnic Groups' Share of Texas's Population and the State's 2008 Vote

GROUP	% SHARE OF POPULATION	% SHARE OF ELIGIBLE VOTERS
White	50.5	61.5
Hispanic	37.4	25.5
African American	12	13

SOURCE: Pew Hispanic Center, "Hispanics in the 2008 Election: Texas," February 20, 2008.

● Elections in Texas

Elections are the mechanisms people use to select leaders, authorize actions by government, and borrow money on behalf of government. In Texas, there are a multitude of elections: primary elections, general elections, city elections, school board elections, special elections, elections for community college boards of regents and the boards of directors for many special districts, and bond elections for city, county, and state governments.

Primary Elections

Primary elections are the first elections held. In Texas, they are held on the second Tuesday in March of even-numbered years. Primary elections determine the party's nominees for the general election. They are conducted by the political party and funded jointly by the party and the state. Essentially, parties collect filing fees from those seeking nomination and use these funds to pay for their share of holding the primary election.

Both parties conduct primaries in all of Texas's 254 counties. Within each county, voters cast ballots in precincts. The number of voting precincts varies depending on the population of the county. Less-populated counties such as Loving and Kenedy have as few as 6 precincts, whereas Harris County contains more than 1,000 voting precincts.[21]

Republicans seeking their party's nomination file papers and pay a filing fee to the Republican Party. Likewise, Democrats file papers and pay a filing fee to the Democratic Party. If several Republicans (or Democrats) seek the office of governor, they will campaign against each other and one will be chosen to run in the general election. Winning the primary election requires an absolute majority. The party's nominees must have more votes than all opponents combined. If no candidate receives an absolute majority, there is a **runoff primary** held the second Tuesday in April between the two candidates receiving the most votes. Voters who participate in the Republican Party primary cannot vote in a Democratic runoff; likewise, anyone who voted in the Democratic Party primary cannot vote in a Republican runoff. However, those who vote in neither the Democratic nor Republican primary can vote in either the Republican or Democratic runoff primary.

An **open primary** allows any registered voter to cast a ballot in either, but not both, primaries. There are no party restrictions. One can consider oneself a Republican and vote in the Democratic primary or can leave home intending to vote in the Democratic primary, change one's mind, and vote in the Republican primary.

The Texas Constitution and election laws call the Texas system a **closed primary**, since one must declare one's party affiliation before voting, but in practice it is an open primary. Before receiving a primary ballot, the voter signs a roll sheet indicating eligibility to vote and pledging to support the party's candidates. By signing the roll sheet, the voter makes a declaration of party affiliation prior to voting. However, since the voter declares a party affiliation only a few moments prior to voting in the primary, the primary is closed only in the narrowest sense of the term.

primary elections elections held to select a party's candidate for the general election

runoff primary where no candidate received a majority, a second primary election is held between the two candidates who received the most votes in the first primary election

open primary a primary election in which the voter can wait until the day of the primary to choose which party to enroll in to select candidates for the general election

closed primary a primary election in which voters can participate in the nomination of candidates, but only of the party in which they are enrolled for a period of time prior to the primary day

General Election

general election a decisive election that determines who is elected to office

The **general election** is held the first Tuesday following the first Monday in November of even-numbered years. The Democratic Party's nominee runs against the nominee of the Republican Party. It is possible that independent and minor party candidates will also appear on the general election ballot.

Major state officials (governor, lieutenant governor, comptroller of public accounts, attorney general, and so on) are elected in nonpresidential election years. This seeks to prevent popular presidential candidates from influencing the outcomes of Texas races. For example, it is possible that a popular Republican presidential candidate might draw more than the usual number of Republican votes, and an unusually large Republican presidential vote might swing the election for statewide candidates running under the Republican banner. Likewise, it prevents an uncommonly popular statewide candidate from influencing the presidential election. If statewide elections were held in presidential election years, a Democratic candidate for governor might influence Texas's presidential voting by increasing the number of votes for Democratic candidates in general.

General elections are held in November to select national and state officeholders. Members of city councils, school boards, and other local government entities are also selected by general elections; however, these elections usually take place outside the traditional early November time period.

Special Elections

special elections an election that is not held on a regularly scheduled basis; in Texas, a special election is called to fill a vacancy in office, to give approval for the state government to borrow money, or to ratify amendments to the Texas Constitution

In Texas, **special elections** are used to fill vacancies in office, to give approval to borrow money, or to ratify amendments to the Texas Constitution. The dates for special elections are specified by the Texas legislature. If a Texas senator resigns, for example, the governor will call a special election to fill the vacancy.

Laws require voter approval before any governmental agency can borrow money and undertake long-term debt. If the local school district wants to borrow money to build a new high school and repair three elementary schools, a special elec-

Some blame the relatively low voter turnout for Texas elections on the frequency of elections and the large number of candidates. Also, state officials are not elected in presidential election years, when voter participation tends to be highest.

tion must be held. During the election, voters decide whether they will allow the school board to borrow the money.

The legislature proposes amendments to the Texas Constitution and they are ratified by the voters in a special election.

● Participation in Texas Elections

We will now focus on voting in Texas. Issues include who can vote, how easy it is to register to vote, and why few Texans vote.

Earlier Restrictions on the Franchise

For much of the period of one-party Democratic control that began in the late nineteenth century, there were restrictions on the franchise.

Women Women were allowed to vote in primaries and party conventions in Texas in 1918 and obtained the right to vote in all elections as a result of the Nineteenth Amendment to the U.S. Constitution in 1920. However, some of the most influential politicians in the state were opposed to the franchise for women. Joseph Weldon Bailey, for example, who had been Democratic leader in the U.S. House of Representatives and later the informal Democratic leader in the U.S. Senate, was an eloquent opponent of women's suffrage, arguing that women could not vote because they could not perform the three basic duties of citizenship: jury service, *posse comitatus* service (citizens who are deputized to deal with an emergency), and military service. He believed that women's morals dictated their beliefs and that women would force their beliefs on men. The result, he felt, would be prohibition.[22] Tinie Wells, the wife of Jim Wells, perhaps the most influential south Texas political leader of his day, was also an important and influential spokesperson for the anti-women's suffrage movement.[23] Governor "Farmer Jim" Ferguson was another opponent of women's suffrage, but when he was impeached, his successor, William P. Hobby, proved a key supporter of women's right to vote. It was Governor Hobby who called the legislature into special session in 1919 to consider the Nineteenth Amendment. Thus Texas became the ninth state and the first state in the South to ratify the women's suffrage amendment.[24]

Minority Groups Minorities had an even tougher time gaining access to the ballot in Texas. In the early part of the twentieth century, powerful political bosses such as Jim Wells and Archer Parr had economic power and personal influence over Hispanic voters. They used this power to support national politicians such as John Nance Garner. Garner represented a huge part of south Texas, which stretched from Laredo to Corpus Christi and then north almost to San Antonio. A lifelong Democrat, he began his service in the House of Representatives in 1903 and served until 1933. From 1931 to 1933, he was Speaker of the U.S. House of Representatives, and from 1933 to 1941, he was vice president of the United States. Garner was the first speaker from Texas and the first vice president from Texas. His south Texas political base was secured by votes that were controlled by the south Texas political bosses.[25]

Poll Tax One restriction on voting that affected poor people in general was the **poll tax**. Enacted in 1902, it required voters to pay a tax, presumably to cover the costs of elections. That tax was usually between $1.50 and $1.75. It was a small

poll tax a state-imposed tax on voters as a prerequisite for registration. Poll taxes were rendered unconstitutional in national elections by the Twenty-fourth Amendment, and in state elections by the Supreme Court in 1966

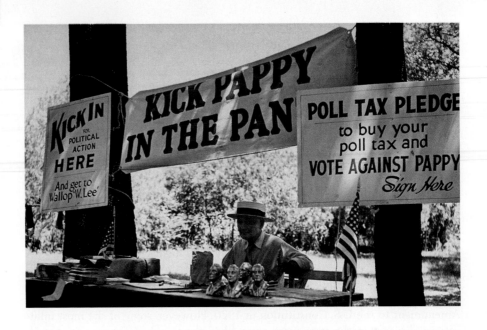

Participation in elections in Texas is low relative to that in other states. In the past, there were restrictions on the franchise. One such restriction that discouraged poor people from voting was the poll tax, which remained legal in Texas until 1966.

sum, but it had to be paid in advance of the election and, in the first third of the century, the tax could be one, two, or even more days' wages for a farmworker. Thus, it tended to disenfranchise poorer people.

The south Texas political bosses used the poll tax, however, to great advantage. They would purchase large numbers of poll tax receipts and provide those receipts to their supporters, who often depended on the bosses for jobs and other economic, legal, and political assistance, and who therefore would vote as the bosses wanted.

Although the poll tax was made illegal in federal elections in 1964 by the passage of the Twenty-fourth Amendment to the U.S. Constitution, it remained legal in state elections in Texas until 1966, when it was held unconstitutional.[26] After the elimination of the poll tax, Texas continued to require **early registration** for voting—registration more than nine months before the general election. Early registration was required on a yearly basis. This requirement effectively prevented migrant workers from voting. These provisions lasted until 1971, when they were voided by the federal courts.[27] Texas even allowed only property owners to vote in revenue bond and tax elections until the practice was stopped by federal courts.[28] Texas also required an unusually long period of residency. Voters had to have lived in the state for at least one year and to have lived in the county for at least six months prior to voting. This was another restriction on the franchise that was struck down by the federal courts.[29]

early registration the requirement that a voter register long before the general election; in effect in Texas until 1971

White Primary The most oppressive restriction on the franchise, however, was designed to minimize the political strength of African American voters. It was the **white primary**. For this restriction on the franchise to work, it was necessary for Texas to be a one-party state, where elections were decided in the party primary. In 1923, the Texas legislature flatly prohibited African Americans from voting in the Democratic primary. The effect in one-party Texas, of course, was to prevent African Americans from participating in the only "real" election contests. Texas was able to do this because of a 1921 U.S. Supreme Court decision, *Newberry v. United*

white primary primary election in which only white voters are eligible to participate

States, which dealt with a federal campaign-expenditures law. In interpreting the law, the Court stated that the primary election was "in no real sense part of the manner of holding the election."[30] This cleared the way for southern states, including Texas, to discriminate against African Americans in the primaries. In 1927, however, the Supreme Court struck down the Texas white primary law, claiming that the legal ban on black participation was a violation of the equal protection clause of the Constitution.[31] In response, the Texas legislature passed another law that authorized the political parties, through their state executive committees, to determine the qualifications for voting in the primaries. That law, of course, allowed the parties to create white primaries. The theory was that what a state could not do directly because of the Fourteenth Amendment, it could authorize political parties to do. However, in *Nixon v. Condon*, the U.S. Supreme Court held that the state executive committees were acting as agents of the state and were discriminating in violation of the Fourteenth Amendment.[32] As a result, the Texas Democratic Party convention, acting on its own authority and without any state law, passed a resolution that confined party membership to white citizens. That case was also appealed to the U.S. Supreme Court and, in *Grovey v. Townsend*, the Court held there was no violation of the Fourteenth Amendment. It is "state action" that violates the "equal protection of the laws" that the Fourteenth Amendment protects against. Since there was no state law authorizing the white primary, the Court believed there was no "state action," only discrimination by a private organization, the Democratic Party, which is not banned by the Fourteenth Amendment.[33] Thus, the Court upheld the white primary until 1944, when, in *Smith v. Allwright*, it decided that the operation of primary elections involved so much state action and so much public responsibility that the white primary did involve unconstitutional state action.[34] Even with the *Smith* decision, at least one Texas county held unofficial primaries by the Jaybird Party. This was a Democratic political organization that excluded African Americans. The winners in the Jaybird primary then entered the regular Democratic Party primary, in which they were never defeated for county office and where they seldom had opposition. In *Terry v. Adams*, the U.S. Supreme Court finally ruled that the Jaybird primary was an integral, and the only effective, part of the elective process in the county. Thus, the Fifteenth Amendment (which deals with the right to vote) was applicable, and the white "preprimary" primary of the Jaybird Party was ruled unconstitutional.[35]

Expanding the Franchise We can detect, at least since the 1940s, a gradual expansion of the franchise in Texas. Much of that expansion was brought about by litigation in the federal courts, often by African American and Hispanic civil rights organizations. Federal laws also played an important role in the expansion of the franchise. The most important of these laws was the 1965 Voting Rights Act, which applied to Texas as a result of Congressional amendments after 1975.

If Texas had had a competitive two-party system during this era instead of a one-party system, the state might have had a more difficult time imposing and maintaining these restrictions on the franchise. In a competitive two-party system, to obtain and retain power, both parties would have to search for ways of building and increasing their base of support in order to be the victorious party. In a one-party system, there is a greater incentive to restrict participation in the party in order to retain control over the party. Losers in a battle for control of a one-party system essentially have no place to go. If they cannot maintain a place in the dominant party's councils, then they have no other avenue for expressing their political views.

Qualifications to Vote

Today, meeting the qualifications to register to vote in Texas is relatively easy. A voter must be:

1. eighteen years of age
2. a U.S. citizen
3. a resident of Texas for thirty days
4. a resident of the county for thirty days

To be eligible to vote, one must be a registered voter for thirty days preceding the election and a resident of the voting precinct on the day of the election. Two groups of people cannot vote even if they meet all the above qualifications: felons and those judged by a court to be mentally incompetent.

About 69.3 percent of the state's voting-age population is registered to vote.[36] The **motor voter law**,[37] which allows individuals to register to vote when applying for or renewing driver's licenses, is one factor in increased registration. Public schools distribute voter registration cards as students turn eighteen. Cooperative efforts between the secretary of state's office and corporations such as Diamond Shamrock, Stop 'n' Go, and the Southland Corporation (which operates 7-Eleven stores) also increase the number of registered voters. In 2010, Texas had about 13 million registered voters out of a voting-age population of over 18.8 million.[38]

motor voter law a national act, passed in 1993, that requires states to allow people to register to vote when applying for a driver's license

Low Voter Turnout

In most elections, fewer than 50 percent of U.S. citizens vote.[39] Even fewer Texans exercise their right to vote. Historically, Texans rank in the bottom third in terms of voter participation. Table 21.3 provides data on the abysmal turnout of registered voters in the various types of recent Texas elections. Considering the ease of registration and the ability to vote early, voter participation should be higher. Why do so few Texans vote?

A more detailed analysis reminds us of several factors that may contribute to low participation rates:

1. low levels of educational attainment
2. low per capita income
3. high rate of poverty
4. ethnicity
5. residing in the South
6. young population
7. traditionalistic and individualistic political culture
8. weak political parties and interest groups
9. poor media
10. large numbers of undocumented persons and felons

Income and education are the two most important factors in determining whether someone votes.

Texas ranks fortieth among the fifty states in average per-pupil expenditures for public education.[40] It is estimated that 4 million adult Texans never graduated from high school.[41] Many Texans are not well educated, and this is reflected in their low levels of voting.

for critical analysis

Voter participation in Texas is among the lowest in the nation. What accounts for the state's low levels of participation? What can be done to increase voter participation in the short term? In the long term?

TABLE 21.3

Turnout by Registered Voters in Texas Elections

ELECTION	PERCENTAGE OF VOTING TURNOUT TO REGISTERED VOTERS
2000 Democratic Primary (Presidential)	6.8
2000 Republican Primary (Presidential)	9.7
2000 Democratic Runoff Primary	2.1
2000 Republican Runoff Primary	1.9
2000 General Election (Presidential)	**51.8**
2001 Special Election (Constitutional Amendments)	6.9
2002 Democratic Primary (Gubernatorial)	8.4
2002 Republican Primary (Gubernatorial)	5.1
2002 General Election (Gubernatorial)	**36.2**
2003 Special Election (Constitutional)	12.2
2004 Democratic Primary (Presidential)	6.8
2004 Republican Primary (Presidential)	5.6
2004 General Election (Presidential)	**56.6**
2005 Special Election (Constitutional Amendments)	18
2006 Democratic Primary (Gubernatorial)	4
2006 Republican Primary (Gubernatorial)	5.2
2006 General Election (Gubernatorial)	**33.6**
2007 November Special Election (Constitutional Amendments)	8.65
2008 General Election (Presidential)	**59.5**
2009 November Special Election (Constitutional Amendments)	8.18
2010 Democratic Primary (Gubernatorial)	5.2
2010 Republican Primary (Gubernatorial)	11.4

SOURCES: Texas Secretary of State; Christy Hoppe, "Primary Draws Lowest Turnout in Decades," *Dallas Morning News*, March 10, 2006, p. 3A.

The higher an individual's income, the more likely she is to vote. The lower her income, the less likely. About 15.8 percent of Texans lived in poverty in 2008. Texas's poverty rate is the eighth highest in the nation, with 3.7 million Texans below federal poverty guidelines.[42] Texas's high rate of poverty is another predictor of low voter participation.

In the southern states that comprised the Confederacy, individuals participate in smaller numbers than in other parts of the United States. Texas was part of the Confederacy, and its level of participation is consistent with lower levels of voting in the South. Young people vote in smaller numbers as well; the average age of Texans is less than the national average.

According to the political scientist Daniel Elazar (see Chapter 19), Texas's political culture is traditionalistic and individualistic. Low levels of voting characterize

Easier-to-use, automated voting machines may also bring more and younger Texans out to vote. In November 2002, Harris County became the first Texas county and the largest one in the country to switch completely to an electronic voting system.

these cultures. In a traditionalistic political culture, the political and economic elite discourages voting. People choose not to vote in individualistic cultures because of real or perceived corruption in government.

Interestingly, there are still other possible explanations for low voter participation in Texas. In keeping with the Texas tradition of decentralized government, there are so many elections in Texas and so many candidates for office that voters are simply overloaded with elections and candidates. Note that as shown in Table 21.3, voter participation was much higher in the general election than in the special constitutional election. If there were fewer elections, the ballot might be longer, but voter turnout would likely be higher, since more voters would be attracted to at least some races or issues on the ballot. Additionally, elections for major offices in Texas are scheduled not to coincide with the presidential election in order to keep the state election separate from the influence of the presidential candidates. However, there is a trade-off in having elections in nonpresidential election years, because the highest voter participation tends to occur for presidential elections. A third problem is that most elections in Texas involve very low-visibility offices. Voters likely know little about the candidates for these positions or the offices themselves, and such a lack of knowledge would naturally discourage voter participation. Efforts have been made in a number of states, most notably Washington, to increase voter knowledge by having the state provide biographical information about the candidates to voters, but Texas makes little effort to enhance voter knowledge of candidates.

Early Voting

early voting a procedure that allows voters to cast ballots during the two-week period before the regularly scheduled election date

Early voting is a procedure that increases the polling period from twelve hours on Election Day to an additional two weeks prior to the election. The legislature has allowed early voting in an effort to increase participation. It is designed for those who have trouble getting to the polls between 7 A.M. and 7 P.M. on Election Day. For most elections, early voting commences on the seventeenth day before the elections and ends four days prior to Election Day.

Voting early is basically the same as voting on Election Day. An individual appears at one of the designated polling places, presents appropriate identification, and receives and casts a ballot. Each general election has seen an increase in early voting, but overall turnout has increased only modestly. Those who normally vote on the official Election Day simply cast their ballots early.

Predictions that Democrats would benefit from early voting did not hold true after Texas moved strongly into the Republican column. Republican candidates for the highest office on the ballot get a much larger proportion of early votes than do the Democratic candidates. In 2004, for example, 63 percent of the early votes for President in Texas were cast for George W. Bush, compared with 37 percent of the early votes for John Kerry. In five of the seven elections examined, however, Republicans got a slightly smaller proportion of overall votes (votes cast in early voting plus Election Day voting) than early votes. And in four of the six elections, Democrats got a slightly larger proportion of overall votes than early votes. This

TABLE 21.4

Early Voting and Overall Voting by Party in Texas

YEAR	OFFICE	REPUBLICANS EARLY/ OVERALL VOTING %	DEMOCRATS EARLY/ OVERALL VOTING %
1994	Senate	62–61	37–38
1996	President	52–49	45–44
1998	Governor	68–69	32–31
2000	President	63–59	35–38
2002	Senator	57–55	42–43
2004	President	63–61	37–38
2006	Senator	56–56	44–44
2008	President	54–55	45–44

SOURCE: Texas Secretary of State.

suggests that early voting has been a bit more beneficial to Republicans than to Democrats, although the advantage has been very slight (see Table 21.4).

● Campaigns

Political campaigns are efforts of candidates to win support of the voters. The goal of the campaign is to attain sufficient support to win the primary election in March and the general election in November. Some campaigns last a year or more; however, the more accepted practice is to limit the campaign to a few weeks before the election. In Texas, campaigns to win the party primary begin in January and continue to the second Tuesday in March. Labor Day is the traditional start of the general election campaign, which lasts from early September to the first Tuesday following the first Monday in November. However, in recent elections statewide campaigns began months earlier than September.

In 2010, interestingly, the distinguishing feature of the race was the unimportance of state issues, including the pressing issue of the state budget. Republicans ran against the national Democratic administration, whereas, Democrats tried to distance themselves from President Obama and his policies.

Campaigns involve attempts to reach the voters through print and electronic media, the mail, door-to-door campaigning, speeches to large and small groups, coffee hours, and telephone solicitation. Costs are enormous. During the 1980s and 1990s, candidates for statewide races spent as much as $30 million. A new record for campaign spending was set in the 2002 gubernatorial race, when the Democrat Tony Sanchez and the Republican Rick Perry spent a total of $88 million. In 2006, the amount raised in the gubernatorial race fell to $53.4 million, 28.7 percent of which went to two independent candidates, the former Republican

TABLE 21.5

Amount Raised by All Candidates in Texas, 2006, Listed by Political Party

OFFICE	DEMOCRAT	REPUBLICAN	THIRD-PARTY
Governor	$7,639,588	$30,418,154	$15,374,328
Judicial	$197,912	$3,373,211	$0
Other Statewide	$565,948	$17,838,604	$756
House	$23,070,469	$42,316,941	$21,681
Senate	$10,556,094	$17,976,304	$11,317
Total	$42,078,663	$111,923,214	$15,408,081

SOURCE: Calculated from Institute on Money in State Politics.

comptroller Carole Keeton Strayhorn and the musician and author Kinky Friedman (see Table 21.5 and Table 21.6).

In some places in the United States, the parties have a major role in the running of political campaigns. That is not the case in Texas. Here the candidates have the major responsibility for campaign strategy, for running their campaigns, and for raising money. At times, party leaders will try to recruit individuals to run for office, especially if no candidates volunteer to seek an office or if the candidates appear to be weak ones. For the most part, the benefit of the party to a candidate in Texas is that the party provides the party label under which the candidate runs. That "Democratic" or "Republican" label is, of course, important to candidates because many voters use the party label in casting their votes, especially for low-visibility races. The party also contains numerous activists who the candidate can tap for campaign tasks such as manning phone banks, preparing mailings, and posting campaign ads. Additionally, the party does provide some support for the candidate, most commonly through campaigns to get out the vote for the party's candidates. Campaigning in Texas, however, is generally left up to the candidate, and in that effort, the parties take a secondary role.

Name recognition is essential for candidates. If voters do not recognize a candidate's name, she has little chance of winning. Incumbents hold a distinct advantage in this regard. The officeholder has many ways to get name visibility. She can mail out news releases, send newsletters to her constituents, appear on radio talk shows, and give speeches to civic clubs. Challengers have a more difficult time getting that crucial name visibility.

In 1978, William R. Clements was a political unknown. He spent thousands of dollars of his own fortune to gain name recognition. He leased hundreds of billboards throughout the state. Each had a blue background with white letters proclaiming "CLEMENTS." In the print media, early ads bore the simple message, "ELECT CLEMENTS." The unprecedented scale of this advertising effort made Clements's name better known among the voters in Texas. This, in turn, stimulated interest in his campaign's message. Clements won the race for governor, becoming the first Republican to hold that office in Texas since the end of Reconstruction.

TABLE 21.6

Campaign Contributions in Contested Statewide Executive Offices: Texas 2006

OFFICE	CANDIDATE	AMOUNT CONTRIBUTED	% VOTE*
Governor	Rick Perry (R)	$21,199,539	39.02
	Chris Bell (D)	$7,359,018	29.78
	Kinky Friedman (I)	$6,288,113	12.44
	Carole Keeton Strayhorn (I)	$9,084,635	18.11
Lieutenant Governor	David Dewhurst (R)	$10,204,273	58.19
	Maria Luisa Alvarado (D)	$50,991	37.44
Agriculture Commissioner	Todd Staples (R)	$2,207,927	54.77
	Hank Gilbert (D)	$97,923	41.79
Attorney General	Greg Abbott (R)	$6,855,483	59.51
	David Van Os (D)	$211,584	37.23
Comptroller	Susan Combs (R)	$4,621,504	59.47
	Fred Head (D)	$86,484	37.01
Land Commissioner	Jerry Patterson (R)	$1,049,490	55.13
	Valinda Hathcox (D)	$9,440	40.96
Railroad Commissioner	Elizabeth Ames Jones (R)	$2,160,588	54.03
	Henry Dale (D)	$47,748	41.73

*Numbers do not add to 100 percent due to the presence of third-party candidates.
SOURCES: Institute on Money in State Politics and Texas Secretary of State.

Running for statewide office is significantly different from seeking the office of state representative from an urban area. One obvious difference is the amount of money needed for the campaign, but there are others. The statewide candidate travels tens of thousands of miles across the state to seek votes. In a more localized race, candidates spend much time traveling, but there is a difference. The local candidate will walk from house to apartment to condominium complex. She will wear out more than one pair of shoes knocking on doors and visiting with potential voters. A statewide candidate flies from city to city, gives a speech, shakes a few hands, and climbs back into the plane for another campaign stop 200 miles away.

Media account for the greatest expense in most campaigns. In metropolitan areas, television, radio, and print advertising are very costly. Full-page ads in metropolitan newspapers can be as much as $40,000. Candidates for metropolitan districts in the Texas House of Representatives and Texas Senate need to reach only a small portion of the population, but they are forced to purchase ads in media sources that go to hundreds of thousands of people not represented. In rural areas, any individual ad is relatively inexpensive. However, candidates must advertise in dozens of small newspapers and radio stations, and costs mount.

Even more important, the campaigns must be well designed. A slipup in a well-funded campaign can do great harm, as David Dewhurst discovered in the early stages of his 2002 campaign for lieutenant governor. Dewhurst's personal wealth and his willingness to spend it had already pushed Bill Ratliff, the state senator elected by his colleagues to succeed Rick Perry as lieutenant governor, out of the race for the office. And Dewhurst was not remiss in spending money. He purchased a very expensive four-page ad in *Texas Monthly* that was intended to advertise his appointment by Governor Perry as the state's new chairman of the Governor's Task Force on Homeland Security. In the wake of the September 11, 2001, terrorist attacks, such an appointment might be turned into an important political asset. Indeed, Dewhurst listed "protecting the physical safety of all Texans" as the top issue in his campaign. In the ad, however, a military officer appears in dress uniform against a background of the American flag. Unfortunately for Dewhurst, the officer is not wearing an American military uniform, but the uniform of the German Luftwaffe with German military insignia and a name tag bearing a German flag. Alongside the picture is a plea from Dewhurst to support "the brave men and women of our armed forces." Such an ad can be a candidate's worst nightmare. Dewhurst had spent a substantial sum to show in a widely circulated, full-color magazine on glossy paper that the person in charge of homeland security for the state did not know the difference between an American officer and a German officer![43]

Some impressive but limited evidence indicates that television can be a very valuable tool for a Texas political candidate. On four occasions in the 1990s, Republican supreme court candidates were challenged in the primary by candidates with little if any organized support and minimal funding. Yet the insurgent candidates all showed great strength in areas where the established candidates did not run television ads. Of course, there may be additional explanations for the strength of established candidates in areas where ads were shown. Perhaps the candidates worked harder in those areas or were better organized. And in some areas, candidates may have had stronger name recognition than their opponents.[44]

The insurgent candidates did not have the resources to run television ads; only the established candidates did, and only in some media markets. It was the support the established candidates received in the areas where they ran television ads that led to their victories. It is important to note that since the data all relate to the Republican primary, the effect of the political party label is controlled. If we compare the percentage difference in votes for established candidates in areas where television ads were run with votes in areas where no ads were run, the difference is remarkable: established candidates received between 12 percent and 18.5 percent more votes in media markets where they bought television time.[45]

Given the myriad factors that may explain electoral success, we should beware of imputing victory in these judicial races solely to television ads. On the other hand, the general pattern of high margins of victory in areas where television was used is so powerful that it cannot be ignored.

● Conclusion

Political parties provide a structure through which candidates strive to win office. Moving through that structure, however, is a massive undertaking. The candidate must first run in a party primary; then, if the candidate does not receive a majority of the votes, he or she must run in a runoff primary. Ideally, the battles of primaries and runoff primaries will be forgotten and the party will come together in support of the nominee in order to win the election. However, what often happens is that the primaries and runoffs create enormous conflicts and divisions in the party that are not healed. The opposition then exploits those party divisions so that their candidate can win the election.

Texas is so large and diverse, and has so many media markets, that campaigns—especially statewide campaigns—are very expensive. For the most part, the candidates themselves must raise the money necessary to win an election. Gubernatorial campaigns can cost $40 million or more. One effect of the high cost of campaigns in Texas is that candidates are often very wealthy individuals willing to use their own money in their campaigns.

Although Texas once tried to narrow the franchise, primarily by limiting the right to vote through poll taxes and white primaries, in recent years it has tried to expand the franchise through the motor voter law and through early voting. Yet voter participation in Texas is quite low. That is probably because of the demographics of Texas voters, but it may also be due to the scheduling of elections in Texas, the vast number of elections, and the large number of low-visibility candidates for office.

One of the most striking developments in Texas politics over the past twenty to twenty-five years is that one-party Democratic dominance is gone from the Texas political scene. That decline in Democratic dominance corresponds to the rise of the Republican Party in Texas. In 2010, every statewide elected officeholder in Texas was a Republican.

Currently, the most dangerous division in the Republican Party is the split between religious conservatives who have a social agenda and economic conservatives who have a low-taxing, low-spending agenda. This split was strikingly revealed in the primary battle between Perry and Hutchison. Perry's victory in the primary may signal the triumph of the social conservatives and their increasingly powerful role in the state's politics. Republicans are not necessarily secure as the dominant party. It is important that they grow and expand their base of support. One of the Republican Party's great weaknesses is its lack of support among Hispanics, the fastest-growing ethnic group in Texas. If the Republicans are to continue their remarkable successes in Texas politics, they will have to make greater inroads with Hispanic voters.

Democrats still have a significant base of support in urban counties with large minority populations, and with older Texans, with native Texans, and with liberals. For Texas to be a competitive two-party state, the Democrats need to win some statewide elections. The party needs to regroup and redirect its appeal to Texans. Most important, if the Democratic Party is to do more than lose elections, it must do what parties have traditionally done in states that have political machines. That is, it must get out the vote. The key to success in future Texas elections is a party's ability to mobilize the Hispanic vote in the state.

studyguide

Practice Quiz

 Find a diagnostic Web Quiz with 20 additional questions on the StudySpace Web site: www.wwnorton.com/we-the-people

1. Providing a label that helps voters identify those seeking office is an important function of *(p. 790)*
   a) the state.
   b) political parties.
   c) interest groups.
   d) regional and subregional governments.

2. In the state of Texas, the highest level of temporary party organization is the *(p. 791)*
   a) state convention.
   b) state executive committee.
   c) governor's convention.
   d) civil executive committee.

3. The Shivercrat movement *(p. 792)*
   a) was a group of conservative Democrats in Texas who supported Republicans.
   b) was a group of liberal Democrats who supported equal rights for all Americans.
   c) was a group of conservative Republicans who rejected the Obama administration.
   d) none of the above

4. In Texas, the Republican Party became the dominant party in the *(p. 794)*
   a) 1960s.
   b) 1970s.
   c) 1980s.
   d) 1990s.

5. Which of the following is *not* true? *(p. 798)*
   a) Democrats are winning most local races in urban counties like Dallas and Harris County.
   b) Republicans are winning most local races in suburban counties like Collin County.
   c) It is difficult for an independent to win local elections in either an urban or a suburban country.
   d) All of the above are true.

6. Which demographic group has the largest percentage share of voters in Texas? *(p. 800)*
   a) white/Anglo
   b) Asian
   c) Hispanic
   d) African American

7. Officially, Texas has a *(p. 801)*
   a) joint primary.
   b) extended primary.

   c) open primary.
   d) closed primary.

8. In a primary election, *(p. 801)*
   a) voters choose all local officials who will hold office in the following year.
   b) voters select representatives to the state convention.
   c) voters select their party's candidate for a general election.
   d) none of the above

9. Which of the following is *not* a type of election found in Texas? *(pp. 801–02)*
   a) general
   b) primary
   c) distinguished
   d) special

10. The first Tuesday following the first Monday in November of even-numbered years is the day for which election? *(p. 802)*
    a) primary election
    b) runoff primary
    c) general election
    d) runoff for the general election

11. Which of the following is true? *(pp. 803–06)*
    a) Women acquired the right to vote in the original 1876 Texas Constitution.
    b) The Poll Tax restricted the participation of poor people in the general election.
    c) You do not have to be a resident of Texas to vote in Texas.
    d) None of the above is true.

12. In which of the following elections is voter turnout the highest? *(p. 808)*
    a) presidential elections
    b) gubernatorial general elections
    c) off-year congressional elections
    d) none of the above

13. The two most important factors in determining whether someone will vote are *(p. 806)*
    a) income and education.
    b) education and family history of voting.
    c) income and gender.
    d) party membership and gender.

14. Who has benefited the most from early voting? *(p. 808)*
 a) Republicans
 b) Democrats
 c) All parties have benefitted equally.
 d) Independents

15. The most costly item for most political campaigns is *(p. 811)*
 a) travel.
 b) security.
 c) fund-raising.
 d) media.

Chapter Outline

Find a detailed Chapter Outline on the StudySpace
Web site: www.wwnorton.com/we-the-people

Key Terms

Find Flashcards to help you study these terms on the
StudySpace Web site: www.wwnorton.com/we-the-people

closed primary *(p. 801)*
county chair *(p. 790)*
county convention *(p. 791)*
county executive committee *(p. 790)*
early registration *(p. 804)*
early voting *(p. 808)*
general election *(p. 802)*
motor voter law *(p. 806)*

open primary *(p. 801)*
poll tax *(p. 803)*
precinct *(p. 790)*
precinct chair *(p. 790)*
precinct convention *(p. 791)*
presidential Republicanism *(p. 792)*
primary elections *(p. 801)*
runoff primary *(p. 801)*

Shivercrat movement *(p. 792)*
special election *(p. 802)*
state chair and vice chair *(p. 791)*
state convention *(p. 791)*
state executive committee *(p. 791)*
white primary *(p. 804)*

Recommended Web Sites

Libertarian Party of Texas
www.tx.lp.org

Republican Party of Texas
www.texasgop.org

Texas Democrats
www.txdemocrats.org

Texas Secretary of State
www.sos.state.tx.us/

The highway construction industry had a strong interest in the Trans-Texas Corridor project and attempted to forward that interest through lobbying and campaign contributions. Here, construction company executives appear with Governor Perry and transportation officials after signing a contract related to the proposed project.

Interest Groups and Lobbying

WHAT GOVERNMENT DOES AND WHY IT MATTERS In 2002, Governor Rick Perry proposed the Trans-Texas Corridor. It was to be the largest privatized tollway in the United States, consisting of 4,000 miles of state roads at a cost of $175 billion. The idea of privatized roads was nothing new. Indiana, for example, has a 157-mile toll road that has been leased to a private entity since 2006 and Chicago has leased its eight-mile Skyway since 2004. It was the massive size of the Trans-Texas Corridor, however, that made Governor Perry's proposal so extraordinary.

In June 2003, Governor Perry signed legislation that authorized the Trans-Texas Corridor and expanded the powers of the Texas Department of Transportation to include road privatization. The creation of such a vast new highway system would be an enormous boon to the highway construction industry, and they tried to forward their interests in the highway system through campaign contributions to key politicians. Prior to Governor Perry's announcement of his highway plan, three major construction industry companies (Zachry Construction, Pate Engineers, and Othon) had made political

focusquestions

● **What are the roles of interest groups in Texas politics?**

● **What role do political action committees play in interest group politics?**

● **What are the difficulties facing individual citizens who seek to influence the legislature?**

contributions totaling $113,280 from 1999 to 2000. In the 2002 election cycle after Governor Perry announced his construction plans, these three companies tripled their contributions. The same occurred with the construction companies Williams Brothers, Ballenger Construction, Parsons Corporation, and Klotz Associates. Contractors were particularly interested in contributing to Lt. Governor David Dewhurst who possesses significant power in the Texas Senate. Governor Perry also received large contributions, as did state senators who sit on the Senate Transportation Committee. The Trans-Texas Corridor contractors also spent somewhere between $2,770,000 and $6,130,000 (Texas reporting laws provide for huge ranges in lobbying contracts and so exact amounts cannot be known) on 163 different contracts with lobbyists.

As the size of the project sank into the public consciousness, opposition emerged, most notably from the landowners who became aware of the massive acreage that would be condemned for the Corridor. A U.S. Supreme Court decision in 2005, *Kelo v. City of New London*,[1] had angered property owners in upholding the condemnation of private property in order to enhance city revenues. That led to public outcry in Texas (and to a considerable degree nationwide) favoring private property rights over the taking of property for questionable public uses. The public outcry increased when estimates were made that these privatized roads could still cost Texans billions of dollars. By 2008, the Trans-Texas Corridor seemed to be dead.

The case of the Trans-Texas Corridor is a classic example of interest group politics, a topic we will explore in more detail in this chapter.

chapter contents

● Interest Groups in the Political Process

It is probably true that all of us have political interests, goals, or objectives that can be achieved with governmental intervention. Many of us, however, will never act to achieve those goals. A few of us may speak privately to a legislator or other official. However, some of us will join with others to try to convince the government to help us in achieving our interests. When we do that, we have formed an **interest group**.

It has often been claimed that business-oriented interest groups dominated the Texas legislature. Using campaign contributions, political pressure, and sometimes corruption, "The Lobby," as pro-business groups were called, was once purported to run Texas government. Some of the most influential business leaders of the state belonged to the "8F Crowd." 8F was the number on a suite of rooms at the Lamar Hotel in Houston, where George R. Brown held court. Brown was a founder of Brown & Root, one of the world's largest construction firms and until April 2007 part of the even larger Halliburton Company. He met regularly with other fabulously wealthy Texans such as Jesse Jones of Texas Commerce Bank and Tenneco, Gus Wortham of American General Insurance, and James Elkins of the Vinson & Elkins law firm. These men socialized together and worked together to promote their political interests. For forty years they were considered the kingmakers in Texas politics who determined much of the important policy of state government.[2]

The "8F Crowd" was, of course, an interest group—an elite, wealthy, powerful, pro-business interest group. Although the "8F Crowd" is long gone from the Texas political scene, much of what they did is still done in Texas politics by other interest groups, though no modern-day group is ascribed the influence that was alleged to be held by the "8F Crowd."

interest group individuals who organize to influence the government's programs and policies

The influence of corporate money in Texas politics has come under some criticism, but there have been only modest attempts to regulate the lobbying industry. Editorial cartoonist Ben Sargent suggested that after the 2002 elections, with the Republicans in control of the House as well as the Senate, the influence of pro-business lobbies was likely to become even greater.

Nevertheless, Texas is known as a state that has long had powerful interest groups. During the Texas Constitutional Convention of 1875, an interest group played an important role. That was the Grange, a powerful farmers' organization, of which many of the framers were members. As Chapter 20 indicated, the Constitution of 1876 reflected many of the values of Grange members. It was a document for rural Texas that was pro–small farmer and opposed to a powerful state government.

With the development of a strong oil and gas industry in Texas in the first half of the twentieth century, the oil industry began playing an important role in state politics. In one-party states, interest groups often become powerful political actors, perhaps because one-party states tend to have a small number of important sectors in their economies and limited economic development. However, as Chapter 21 showed, Texas has in the past twenty years moved from a Democratic one-party system to a competitive two-party system to a Republican-dominated system. And with an expanding Hispanic vote, it may soon become a more competitive two-party system again. It also now has a strong and diversified economy. Yet interest groups maintain great influence.[3]

Interest Groups and Policy Makers

Interest groups want something from policy makers: they want policy that is beneficial for their groups. On the other hand, policy makers benefit from developing relationships with interest groups. From those groups, the policy maker gains information, since the interest groups can provide substantial expertise in areas that are of special concern to the group. Additionally, interest groups can provide campaign funds to the policy maker. In a state as large as Texas, with numerous media markets and with somewhat competitive parties, considerable campaign funds are necessary to run and win elections. An interest group can help raise money from its membership for a candidate sympathetic to the interest group's goals. Also, interest groups can supply votes to the policy maker. They can assist in mobilizing their own groups, and they can supply campaign workers to distribute campaign leaflets and to operate phone banks to get out the vote. Interest groups can also publicize issues through press conferences, press releases, publications, conferences, hearings, and even by filing lawsuits. Finally, interest groups can engage in research and education programs. It has become increasingly common for interest groups to engage in public education programs by running advertisements in the Texas media explaining why their particular approaches to a public policy problem would be more beneficial to Texans in general.

Unlike a private citizen interested in and involved in politics, larger or better-funded interest groups have several advantages: (1) time; (2) money; (3) expertise; and (4) continuity.

Although concerned citizens do have an impact on public policy in Texas, organized and well-funded interest groups have an advantage in affecting the policy process. It is difficult for a concerned citizen from Houston to spend time in Austin developing relationships with policy makers and trying to convince those policy makers of the desirability of public policies that are compatible with the individual's goals. On the other hand, if that individual joins with like-minded people to create an organized interest group, the group may have a greater likelihood of achieving policy goals. It might be possible to fund an office in Austin and pay a staff that could, on a daily basis, monitor events in state government, and develop relationships with key policy makers. Additionally, although some individuals in

Texas do have the money to provide substantial campaign support to policy makers, even those individuals can get more "bang for the buck" if they join with like-minded individuals in **bundling** their contributions into a larger contribution from the interest group. The creation of an organized interest group also allows for the development of a staff. The staff can gain in-depth knowledge of an area of policy far greater than could be gained by most individuals working alone. Also, an individual may be intensely concerned with an issue in one legislative session, but may find it difficult to sustain that interest over a period of many legislative sessions. The larger, better-funded, more successful organized interest groups have continuity. They are in Austin, developing relationships with policy makers and presenting the views of the organization day in and day out, year in and year out. The result is that legislators and other policy makers can develop long-standing relationships with the interest groups and the groups' representatives in Austin.

We can get an idea of the importance of relationships between interest groups and legislators by examining one day's busy and overlapping schedule for one state representative—Melissa Noriega. The schedule is for January 25, 2005 (and is still typical for a Texas legislator).

bundling the interest-group practice of combining campaign contributions from several individuals into one larger contribution from the group, so as to increase the group's impact on the candidate

> 7–8 A.M.: Members' Prayer Group
>
> 7:45–9 A.M.: United Methodist Women of Texas breakfast
>
> 10–11 A.M.: House session
>
> 11:30 A.M.–3:30 P.M.: Texas Association of Insurance and Financial Advisers lunch
>
> 12–12:30 P.M.: Students' wagon-train event
>
> 4:30–5 P.M.: Mexican American Legislative Caucus meeting
>
> 5–8 P.M.: Texas Chiropractors Association reception-dinner
>
> 5–7 P.M.: TXU Corp. event
>
> 6–8 P.M.: Mexican American Bar Association legislative reception

Five of Noriega's scheduled activities appear to involve interest groups: the United Methodist Women of Texas, the Texas Association of Insurance and Financial Advisers, the Texas Chiropractors Association, TXU, and the Mexican American Bar Association. It is a busy schedule in which more time in the day involves interaction with interest groups than any other activity, including legislating.[4]

Types of Interest Groups and Lobbyists

Interest groups strive to influence public opinion, to make their views known to policy makers, and to elect and support policy makers who are friendly to their points of view. To do those things, interest groups usually maintain **lobbyists** in Austin who will try to gain access to policy makers and communicate their objectives to those policy makers. There are several different types of lobbyists. Some interest groups have full-time staffs in Austin whose members work as lobbyists. One form of interest group is, of course, a corporation, and companies often have government relations departments that lobby for the companies' interests. Lobbyists may be employed by an interest group to deal with one issue, or they may be employed by an interest group on a regular basis. Some lobbyists represent only one client; others will represent large numbers of clients. All lobbyists, however, must be able to reach and communicate with policy makers. Corporate interest

lobbyist an individual employed by an interest group who tries to influence governmental decisions on behalf of that group

groups tend to use either government relations departments or law firms to represent their interests in Austin. Often industries have broad interests that need representation. For example, an insurance company may have one specific interest it wishes to have represented. However, the insurance industry as a whole also has a wide range of issues that need representation, and thus it will form an industry-wide interest group.

Interest groups may also represent professional groups. One of the most influential professional groups in Austin is the Texas Medical Association, which represents the interests of doctors in state government. Other professional groups represent accountants, chiropractors, opticians, dentists, and teachers.

That teachers are an important interest group suggests still another type of interest group—public-employee interest groups. Public school teachers may be the largest and most effective of these groups, but firefighters, police officers, and even justices of the peace and constables all are represented in Austin.

Some interest groups are concerned with a single issue. For example, an interest group may be concerned about the regulation of abortion or school vouchers or tort reform or the environment. Other interest groups are concerned with multiple issues that affect the groups. Public school teachers, for example, are concerned about job security, qualifications of teachers, health insurance, pensions, salaries, and other matters that affect the lives of their members.

Civil rights groups such as the National Association for the Advancement of Colored People, the League of United Latin American Citizens, or the Mexican American Legal Defense Fund are concerned about civil rights issues affecting the lives primarily of African Americans and Latinos. Interestingly, not only do these groups often try to influence public opinion and the legislature, but they have had notable success in representing their groups' interests through litigation, especially in the federal courts.

Other public-interest groups try to promote consumer, environmental, and general public issues. Examples of these groups are Public Citizen, the Sierra Club, and Common Cause. Groups such as the Sierra Club work to promote environmental interests, whereas groups such as Public Citizen and Common Cause tend to have broader interests and work to promote more open government. These groups rarely have much funding, but they often can provide policy makers with information and expertise. In addition, they can mobilize their membership to support or oppose bills, and they can publicize matters that are important to their goals.

Getting Access to Policy Makers

It is important for the interest groups' representatives, the lobbyists, to communicate with policy makers, and that need for communication means lobbyists must gain access to policy makers. Gaining access to policy makers, of course, imposes on the time of legislators, so lobbyists will often spend significant sums entertaining them. That entertainment is one of the most criticized aspects of lobbying, but from the lobbyists' perspective, entertainment of a legislator provides the lobbyist access and puts the policy maker in a congenial frame of mind. Entertainment by lobbyists can involve expensive dinners, golfing, and other activities. Lobbyists for Texas utilities for example, bought a $300 saddle for one state representative and a $200 bench for another. A state senator was treated to a trip to the Masters golf tournament by TXU lobbyists, who also picked up a dinner tab for the senator. A House member received a gun as a gift, another received a jacket, and several got "deer-processing" costs paid for by these lobbyists.[5]

● What are the roles
of interest groups in
Texas politics?

When Governor Perry wanted to go to the Rose Bowl game, the trucking lobby picked up the costs of a private jet for $14,580. The former Texas Motor Transportation Association president who arranged the trip said, "Let's face it, if you have a way to help the sitting governor get somewhere he wants to be and to help our industry get where it needs to be, to me it becomes a no-brainer."[6]

Texas lawmakers receive only $600 per month plus $120 a day per session allowance when on legislative business, but lawmakers are permitted to use campaign contributions for expenses associated with holding office. This allows interest groups to fund significant lavish benefits for lawmakers. Indeed, about one-third of the spending of North Texas lawmakers—about $3.4 million of roughly $10 million in 2007–2009—has gone to fund things other than campaign expenditures. Senator Florence Shapiro, for example, has used her contributions to fund a car lease for a Mercedes Benz and to pay for conference stays at the Ritz-Carlton in Palm Beach, the Venetian in Las Vegas, and the Hay-Adams in Washington D.C., thirty-six North Texas lawmakers spent nearly $560,000 on travel and entertainment, $470,000 on Austin living expenses, and $290,000 on food. The bulk of this money was for charitable contributions, gifts, and campaign contributions.[7]

Sometimes lobbyists have long-standing personal ties to policy makers, and those bonds can be invaluable to the lobbyists' clients. Access to policy makers may also be gained by building support for an issue among their constituents. Constituents may be encouraged, for example, to write or call legislators about a bill and offer their opinions. Essentially, the interest group tries to mobilize interested voters to get involved in the political process on behalf of the groups' goals.

One important way of gaining access to those in government is to employ former officials as lobbyists. A lobbyist who is a former legislator often has friends in the legislature and can use that friendship to gain access. Additionally, a former legislator often is in an exceptionally good position to understand the personal relationships and informal power centers that must be contacted to accomplish a legislative objective. As a result, some of the best-paid lobbyists in Austin are former Texas state officials and often are former legislators.

Lobbying, derided by some as "Austin's oldest profession," is big business in Texas. While the legislature is in session, many lobbyists can be spotted chatting with legislators or talking on cell phones. While the legislature is not in session, lobbyists are often busy with election campaigns.

Ten recently retired lawmakers were lobbyists in the 2009 legislative session. The ten had a total of sixty-eight lobbying contracts allowing them to generate between $2,025,000 and $3,890,000 in fees. One gets a sense of the value of these ex-legislators turned lobbyists from the explanation Representative Jim Pitts gave for sponsoring an amendment that was pushed by an AT&T lobbyist and former legislator, Pat Heggerty. The amendment would have forced the state to pay for rerouting phone lines for road projects. Said Representative Pitts of the amendment, "I was just trying to help Pat out."[8] The amendment later failed to pass.

One former legislator turned lobbyist actually reversed course and went back into the legislature. Todd Hunter had served in the legislature from 1989–97. An active lobbyist as late as 2007, Hunter was elected to the Texas House in 2008.[9] The issue of lobbying by former officials and their staffs is a significant one, since there is concern that policy decisions may be made with an eye toward future lucrative lobbying jobs.

In 2009, there were 1,861 registered lobbyists in Texas.[10] This is an increase over the 1,525 registered lobbyists in 2005. An analysis of lobbying reports in 2005 found that these lobbyists had 2,471 clients. In 2009, the lobbyists had 3,061 clients.[11] Due to the loose nature of the Texas reporting laws, it is unclear what these lobbyists were paid, but it was as much as $348 million in 2007.[12] Over the past ten years, lobbyists in Texas have been paid as much as $2.4 billion. Some Texas lobbyists make enormous sums. Twenty-eight of them reported maximum lobbying incomes of $1.5 million. Depending on how the data are analyzed, Texas ranked fourth in the nation in the amount of money that was spent on lobbying.[13]

Once lobbyists obtain access to policy makers, they provide information that may be useful. For example, they may explain how a bill benefits a legislator's district, or how it benefits the state, or how it is perceived as being unfair. Since the staffs of Texas legislators are small, lobbyists perform useful functions by explaining what numerous bills are intended to do. They may even write bills to be introduced by friendly legislators or write amendments to bills. Almost certainly, if a bill affects the interests of a lobbyist's client and reaches a point in the process where hearings are held on the bill, the lobbyist will arrange for testimony to be given at the hearing explaining the interest group's viewpoint on the proposed legislation.

Lobbyists do not limit their activities to the legislative process, of course. Rules proposed by the bureaucracy or the courts can affect the interests of lobbyists' clients. Lobbyists will testify at hearings on rules and try to provide information to administrators in face-to-face meetings as well.

There is always a concern that lobbyists may corrupt policy makers by bribing them in order to accomplish the interest groups' policy objectives. Early in the twentieth century, Sam Rayburn, later a famed U.S. congressman and Speaker of the House, served in the Texas House of Representatives for six years. At that time, he was especially concerned with corruption and refused to accept free meals and entertainment from lobbyists. He called some of his fellow legislators "steak men." By that he meant that the legislators would sell their votes on a bill for a steak dinner at the Driskill Hotel in Austin. "Steak men" (and women) may still exist in Texas politics, but, for the most part, lobbyists provide information, campaign contributions, and political support (or opposition) rather than bribes.

Still, from time to time lobbying does stoop to very low levels. In 1989, "Bo" Pilgrim, a large poultry producer, distributed $10,000 checks to state senators in the capitol while he was lobbying them on workers' compensation reform. Perhaps even more troubling, some senators accepted the checks until media attention

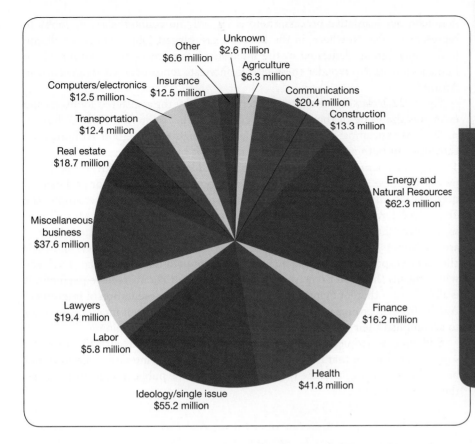

Other $6.6 million
Unknown $2.6 million
Agriculture $6.3 million
Computers/electronics $12.5 million
Insurance $12.5 million
Communications $20.4 million
Construction $13.3 million
Transportation $12.4 million
Real estate $18.7 million
Energy and Natural Resources $62.3 million
Miscellaneous business $37.6 million
Lawyers $19.4 million
Finance $16.2 million
Labor $5.8 million
Health $41.8 million
Ideology/single issue $55.2 million

FIGURE 22.1

Lobbying Expenditures, 2009

NOTE: Expenditures are the maximum values on the broad range of amounts in the lobbying report forms. Amounts are only for direct lobbying of government officials and do not include money for grassroots lobbying or media campaigns. The amounts in the figure are rounded. The Communications category includes Communications and Electronics. The Lawyer category is the category for Lawyers and Lobbyists.

SOURCE: Texans for Public Justice, *Austin's Oldest Profession* (2010).

forced them to reconsider. Yet this practice of offering $10,000 while asking for a senator to vote on a specific bill was not illegal. A year later, the Speaker of the Texas House of Representatives, "Gib" Lewis, got in trouble for his close relationship with a law firm that specialized in collecting delinquent taxes for local governments. In 1991, Speaker Lewis was indicted for receipt of an illegal gift from the law firm. Ultimately, Lewis plea-bargained and received a minor penalty. The result of these scandals, however, was legislation that created a state ethics commission. The legislation also imposed additional lobbying reporting requirements and restrictions on speaking fees that interest groups paid legislators and pleasure trips that lobbyists provided. By no means was the law a major regulation of or restriction on lobbying practices, but it did put some limits on lobbying behavior.

Texas has only weak laws dealing with lobbying by former government officials. A former member of the governing body or a former executive head of a regulatory agency cannot lobby the agency for two years after leaving office. Senior employees or former officers of Texas regulatory agencies cannot ever lobby a government entity on matters they were involved in when employed by the government. However, there are no legal restrictions on lobbying by a former governor, former lieutenant governor, former legislator, or any former aides to these officials.[14]

Who Represents Bubba?

Another problem with lobbying was well described by the director of a public-interest lobby, Craig McDonald: "Legislators are rubbing shoulders with . . . lobbyists, almost all of whom hustle for business interests. While corporate interests dominate our legislative process, there is virtually no counterbalancing lobby to represent Bubba. Nowhere on the list of Texas' biggest lobby spenders will you find a single group dedicated to the interests of consumers, the environment or human services. No wonder these citizen interests repeatedly get steamrolled in Austin."[15]

Figure 22.1 classifies the interests represented by the registered lobbyists and estimates the value of those lobbying contracts. The "Who Are Texans?" box on p. 827 looks at campaign contributions to Texas legislators in 2008. Although the categories in both are very broad, it is clear that business interests dominate in Texas government. Of course, many issues considered by Texas government may pit one business interest against another, and sometimes a business or professional organization may find itself aligned with consumer interests. For example, the Texas Trial Lawyers Association, an organization of plaintiffs' lawyers in Texas, frequently allies with consumer interests. Many of the clients of these lawyers are consumers who sue large businesses. The interests of these lawyers and their clients are especially close, since the lawyers are paid on a contingent fee basis, which means they don't receive payment unless their clients receive payment. It is also the case that lobbying is not all there is to the representation of interests in Austin. Interest groups without money may still mobilize their members in order to accomplish their objectives, or they may influence public opinion.

Still, there is no question that money does help in politics. Figure 22.1 provides support for concern that in this battle of mostly business interests, there may not be an objective voice, or at the very least a voice, for the public interest that reaches the ears of legislators.

● Another Side to Lobbying

Lobbyists in Texas represent mostly business interests, and they are active in trying to gain access to government officials and inform them of the legislative desires of their clients. But interest groups are not simply information channels between business and government. They also promote the political interests of elected officials who support their viewpoints and oppose the interests of those who do not. One major way that interest groups engage in this activity is by making campaign contributions. Interest groups may encourage individual members to make contributions to candidates, or they may collect funds from their members, bundling those funds as a donation from the interest group. When this is done, the interest group creates a **political action committee (PAC)** to make the contribution.

political action committee (PAC) a private group that raises and distributes funds for use in election campaigns

There are numerous reasons for forming a political action committee. A candidate is more likely to notice a substantial contribution from a PAC than many small contributions from individual members of an interest group. Additionally, the lobbyist who delivers a substantial PAC check to a candidate can more likely gain access to a politician than can a lobbyist who simply asks members of the interest group to mail individual small contribution checks.

The PAC becomes a way for the interest groups to send a message to the candidate that its members support the goals of the interest group strongly enough that they are prepared to back those goals with money. In some cases, a PAC can even serve as an intermediary to provide money to candidates that the PAC's members might not want to support publicly.

Whose Interests Are Represented in Texas Politics?

Interest groups try to achieve favorable policies not only by lobbying members of the Texas legislature directly but also by influencing who becomes members of the legislature in the first place by donating to the election campaigns of favored candidates. The chart below breaks down contributions from employees of different industries by party in 2008.

Contributions to Texas Legislature Candidates in 2008

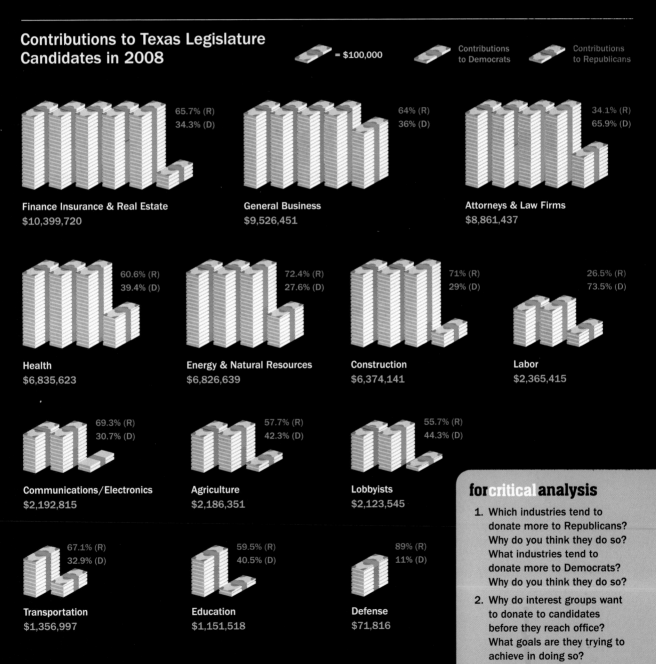

= $100,000   Contributions to Democrats   Contributions to Republicans

Finance Insurance & Real Estate
$10,399,720
65.7% (R)
34.3% (D)

General Business
$9,526,451
64% (R)
36% (D)

Attorneys & Law Firms
$8,861,437
34.1% (R)
65.9% (D)

Health
$6,835,623
60.6% (R)
39.4% (D)

Energy & Natural Resources
$6,826,639
72.4% (R)
27.6% (D)

Construction
$6,374,141
71% (R)
29% (D)

Labor
$2,365,415
26.5% (R)
73.5% (D)

Communications/Electronics
$2,192,815
69.3% (R)
30.7% (D)

Agriculture
$2,186,351
57.7% (R)
42.3% (D)

Lobbyists
$2,123,545
55.7% (R)
44.3% (D)

Transportation
$1,356,997
67.1% (R)
32.9% (D)

Education
$1,151,518
59.5% (R)
40.5% (D)

Defense
$71,816
89% (R)
11% (D)

for critical analysis

1. Which industries tend to donate more to Republicans? Why do you think they do so? What industries tend to donate more to Democrats? Why do you think they do so?

2. Why do interest groups want to donate to candidates before they reach office? What goals are they trying to achieve in doing so?

SOURCE: National Institution on State Money in Politics, www.followthemoney.org (accessed 9/7/10).

issue advocacy independent spending by individuals or interest groups on a campaign issue but not directly tied to a particular candidate

PACs may give money directly to the candidate, or they may engage in **issue advocacy** that is supportive of the candidate but is independent of the candidate's control. The candidate does not report these independent expenditures on contribution disclosure statements. PACs may also spend money to support an issue rather than a specific candidate or to support such activities as "get-out-the-vote" campaigns. In 2008, about 55 percent of the money given to Democratic and Republican legislative candidates was given by PACs. About 45 percent of the money was given by individuals.[16]

Campaign contributions can be, to a considerable degree, divided in terms of the economic interests represented by the contributors. The Who Are Texans section in this chapter shows that the largest contributor was the finance, insurance, and real estate sector. This sector is a major part of the Texas economy and is subject to significant state regulation. That is also true of general business, energy, and natural resources, construction, and health, other economic groups that were also major contributors in the 2008 Texas elections. In contrast to business, political parties, agriculture, and even candidates providing funds to their own campaigns, labor represents a small amount of campaign spending.

Getting Out the Vote

The Texas Medical Association constructed a grassroots campaign in 1988 to elect its slate of candidates to the Texas Supreme Court. Physicians were encouraged to give to TEXPAC, the medical association PAC. They were also encouraged to make individual contributions to certain candidates. Additionally, physicians were given slate cards with recommended candidates, literature endorsing candidates, and even expensively produced videotapes. They were asked not only to encourage families and friends to vote for the candidates endorsed by the medical association but also to encourage their patients to vote for them. The effort by the medical association was remarkable for its fund-raising success and for its reaching and mobilizing the grass roots.[17] It was probably the most successful get out the vote campaign ever run by an interest group in Texas.

Most efforts by interest groups, however, are far less sophisticated than the classic involvement of physicians in Texas Supreme Court races. Generally, interest groups' political action committees contribute to candidates by providing resources for the candidates to get out the vote. Unfortunately for the interest groups, sometimes they misjudge the political viability of the candidates they support. This results in a waste of funds by the interest groups and the likely alienation of the candidate who defeated the candidate backed by the interest group. In the 2010 primary campaign, Texans for Lawsuit Reform, the pro-business and pro–tort reform interest group that has had spectacular successes in forwarding its agenda over the past fifteen years, suffered a remarkable failure. Although it had contributed $602,290 to twenty-eight candidates in primaries in 2010, 53 percent of this money was spent on four candidates who lost their primaries, and another 28 percent of their money was spent on three candidates who were forced into a runoff election. Obviously, Texans for Lawsuit Reform thought these candidates were important for achieving its agenda, but it is questionable how desirable it is for an interest group to pump huge amounts of money into the campaigns of incumbent candidates who do not have the political strength even to win in their own party primary elections. And the high degree of financial support for candidates can be hurtful to the candidate. The winning candidate's main issue in defeating the incumbent in one of these races was that she had received money from an organization known for giving huge sums to Republican

The Texas Freedom Network is an interest group that opposes what they see as the religious right's attempts to infringe on individual liberty. In this photo, they hold a press conference to argue against censorship of biology textbooks that teach evolution.

candidates, and this was proof that the incumbent Democrat was not a real Democrat but a Republican with a Democratic label.[18]

Defeating Opponents

Generally, incumbents have a huge advantage over challengers in an election. Since they are officeholders, they usually have greater name recognition than challengers, and it is easy for incumbents to get publicity by holding town hall meetings, by announcing the relocation of new businesses to the district, or simply by attending community events. Additionally, they usually have an established network of supporters who helped them get into office at least once previously. There are two great exceptions to incumbency advantage: (1) scandal can destroy incumbency advantage, and (2) redistricting can ruin the political base of incumbents.

Except in cases of scandal or redistricting, however, it is far safer for interest groups to try to work with incumbents. Campaign money, for example, overwhelmingly goes to incumbents. In the 2010 campaign for the Texas House of Representatives, as Table 22.1 shows, incumbents raised three times the amount raised by challengers, and in the Texas Senate incumbents raised eight times the amount raised by challengers. Incumbents win elections to an overwhelming degree.[19]

Of course, sometimes an interest group does not want to help a candidate or even pressure a candidate; it wants to defeat that candidate. This can be a risky strategy because the candidate might win, and then the interest group will be faced with not only an unfriendly public official, but also one angry at the interest group for its opposition. When that happens, the interest group will often "get well" or "get on the late train." This means that the interest group will make a substantial political contribution to the candidate it opposed who won. Often, winning candidates have significant campaign debts after a grueling election battle, and they

TABLE 22.1

Average Dollars Raised by Incumbents and Challengers for the Texas Legislature (2010)

OFFICE	INCUMBENTS	CHALLENGERS
House	$207,958	$71,585
Senate	$331,114	$42,357

SOURCE: National Institute on Money in State Politics.

appreciate the late contributions of former enemies, which are offered as a way of making amends. About 9 percent of the roughly $2.82 million contributed to the three successful candidates for the Texas Supreme Court in 2008 was "late train" money, or at least money donated after the general election.[20]

Commonly, candidates are especially loyal to those supporters who backed them early; without support at the very beginning of a campaign, it is hard for a candidate to build an organization and get the support necessary to make a decent campaign start. That is why early supporters are so valuable. The best lobbyists start early in trying to develop relationships with candidates and with new legislators. Legislators remember who was with them at the beginning of their political careers—and this can be immensely beneficial to the lobby that developed an early relationship.[21] A national PAC, EMILY's List (EMILY stands for Early Money Is Like Yeast), provides early campaign funding to female candidates. EMILY's List is funded by women on behalf of female candidates. However, though "late train" contributors may never merit the loyalty that politicians reserve for their earliest supporters, at least those debt-paying late contributions will make the official feel somewhat more positive about the interest groups and their goals.

Sometimes PACs will even give to both candidates as a way to avoid alienating either one, though the possibility remains that such dual giving will wind up alienating both. At other times, interest groups simply don't care if they alienate a candidate. The 2010 Democratic primary election between State Representatives Tara Rios Ybarra and Jose Manuel Lozano highlighted the lines that can clearly separate interest groups during a campaign. Texans for Lawsuit Reform, a pro-business and pro–tort reform interest group, contributed $256,610 to Ybarra, which was 56 percent of her campaign funds. Ybarro lost to Lozano, who was backed by trial lawyers who were not the least bit sympathetic to the goals of Texans for Lawsuit Reform.[22]

When an interest group is convinced that it cannot work with a public official, the interest group may undertake an all-out effort to defeat that official. But spending money by no means guarantees success. Dr. James Leininger is one of the biggest contributors to Republican candidates. In the 2006 election cycle, he gave over $5 million to Republican candidates in Texas, either through individual contributions or by giving to PACs that then made contributions. Leininger and some of the PACs he supports are strong supporters of school vouchers. Much of this money backed challengers to Republican incumbents who were unfavorable to vouchers. The effort was unsuccessful and the result, according to Texans for Public Justice, is a legislature "even less receptive to vouchers than its predecessor."[23]

Former governor Ann Richards received support from the PAC EMILY's List early in her career. EMILY's List is a national organization that provides campaign funding to female candidates.

Individuals as Lobbyists

- **What are the difficulties facing individual citizens who seek to influence the legislature?**

Sometimes ordinary individuals can have a remarkable impact on public policy, although interest groups clearly have an advantage in influencing the legislative process. Nevertheless, a persistent individual with a well-reasoned argument can make a difference. For example, Tyrus Burks lost his wife and two children in a late-night electrical fire in West Dallas. Tyrus did not awaken in time to save them because he is deaf and did not hear the audible smoke alarm. Texas's state property code required the installation of audible smoke alarms but not visual alarms. In 2009, Tyrus became an advocate for a bill that would require property managers to buy and install visual smoke alarms if hearing-impaired tenants requested them and to put the alarms in visible locations such as bedrooms. Enlisting the support of State Senator Royce West, the Sephra Burks Law, named for Tyrus's wife who was also deaf and who died in the fire, went into effect at the start of 2010. Tyrus was an active lobbyist for the bill and gave legislative testimony, with the aid of a sign language interpreter, in favor of the bill.

Tyrus's efforts benefited from the support of the Texas Apartment Association, a major organized interest group representing apartment property interests, who backed the bill. Tyrus's story was tragic, and it would have been difficult for opposition to emerge against such a proposal. Still, Tyrus's efforts resulted in a major victory for the deaf, who are protected by such a law requiring visual smoke alarms in only three other states and the District of Columbia.[24]

Of course, Tyrus Burks is an exceptionally dedicated person who had a compelling argument. In obtaining legislation he wanted, he did not have to struggle against powerful, organized interest groups to achieve his objective. However, this success shows that at least sometimes, an individual can be a successful lobbyist.

Occasionally, ordinary individuals can have a direct influence on policy. Barbara Brown, of Plano, lobbied local government and the state legislature to get better bicycle safety laws and programs passed. Brown's son was killed in an accident while riding his bicycle.

● Conclusion

Interest groups play an important role in Texas politics even though Texas is no longer a one-party state with limited economic development. Even with two major political parties and a diverse economy, Texas politics cannot be understood without also examining the role of interest groups. Interest groups in Texas have a notable pro-business tinge. Labor is weak in Texas, and its role in the political process is quite limited. Trial lawyers are an especially wealthy and important interest group that promotes liberal policies in Texas, but with the growth of the Republican Party and tort reform interest groups, the influence of the trial lawyers has waned.

Though no single interest group or coalition of interest groups dominates Texas politics, by far most lobbyists represent business interests, and the bulk of PAC money comes from business interests. Often, of course, businesses are pitted against businesses in the political process. Also, public interest, civil rights, consumer, and environmental groups may still be successful by mobilizing public opinion and influencing the media. However, there are only a few interest groups that offer alternatives to business perspectives on policy issues. Less frequently, ordinary individuals are able to influence public policy. Although they tend to be at a disadvantage in terms of money and other resources, dedicated individuals with a compelling argument sometimes succeed in lobbying for specific legislation. This is especially true when they are pursuing goals that do not put them in conflict with well-organized and well-funded interest groups.

studyguide

Practice Quiz

Find a diagnostic Web Quiz with 20 additional questions on the StudySpace Web site: www.wwnorton.com/we-the-people

1. The goals of interest groups include all *except* (p. 819)
   a) electing people to office in order to control the government.
   b) influencing those who control government.
   c) educating the public and members about issues of importance to the group.
   d) maintaining a heterogeneous membership.

2. The "8F Crowd" (p. 819)
   a) was a group of legislators who failed the eighth grade.
   b) was a group of extremely wealthy Texans who met in Suite 8F of the Lamar Hotel in Houston and controlled Texas politics for more than forty years.
   c) were twenty-five legislators who boycotted the eighth session of the legislature in order to prevent the legislators from taking any action because it lacked a quorum.
   d) were the eight most powerful officials in the state who met in Suite F of the Austin State Office Building.

3. Interest groups supply public officials with all the following *except* (p. 820)
   a) information.
   b) money.
   c) media coverage.
   d) committee assignments.

4. When PACS combine small contributions from many people to form one large contribution it is called (p. 821)
   a) bundling.
   b) compacting.
   c) cracking.
   d) packing.

5. Lobbyists are (p. 821)
   a) corrupt.
   b) unethical.
   c) important sources of information for legislators.
   d) harmful to the democratic process.

6. The most important thing interest groups need to be effective is *(p. 821)*
   a) office space in Austin.
   b) a variety of issues on which to lobby.
   c) a large, paid staff.
   d) access to politicians.

7. Interest groups have an advantage over individuals in influencing policy because interest groups usually have *(p. 823)*
   a) more time to influence officials.
   b) greater expertise than individuals.
   c) more money to influence elections.
   d) all of the above

8. Interest groups often hire former legislators as lobbyists to *(p. 824)*
   a) gain greater access to current legislators.
   b) benefit from the policy expertise of former legislators.
   c) benefit from the personal "insider" knowledge of the former legislator.
   d) all of the above

9. Trial lawyers are which type of interest group? *(p. 826)*
   a) professional group
   b) public employee group
   c) single-issue group
   d) consumer group

10. Lobbying takes place in the *(p. 826)*
    a) legislative branch only.
    b) legislative and executive branches only.
    c) executive and judicial branches.
    d) legislative, executive, and judicial branches.

11. PACs are used to *(p. 826)*
    a) stir the public's interest in politics.
    b) elect officers of the interest group.

c) raise money from individuals, which is then bundled and given to candidates.
d) create media campaigns to influence the course of government.

12. One of the most important grassroots tactics of interest groups is *(p. 828)*
    a) to get out the vote.
    b) to form political alliances with executive and legislative leaders.
    c) to lobby the judicial branch of national and state government.
    d) to interpret the needs of their members.

13. Individuals have the best chance to influence public policy when they *(p. 828)*
    a) are not opposed by organized interest groups.
    b) are polite.
    c) entertain legislators.
    d) vote.

14. Interest groups have a hard time defeating incumbent legislators unless *(p. 829)*
    a) the legislator is involved in scandal.
    b) the legislator has been redistricted.
    c) the legislator's positions have generated overwhelming opposition in the district.
    d) all of the above

15. In Texas, the most powerful interest groups represent which interests? *(p. 832)*
    a) consumer
    b) civil rights
    c) business
    d) public employee

Chapter Outline

 Find a detailed Chapter Outline on the StudySpace Web site: www.wwnorton.com/we-the-people

Key Terms

 Find Flashcards to help you study these terms on the StudySpace Web site: www.wwnorton.com/we-the-people

bundling *(p. 821)*
interest group *(p. 819)*
issue advocacy *(p. 828)*

lobbyist *(p. 821)*
political action committee (PAC) *(p. 826)*

Recommended Web Sites

Like the U.S. Congress, the Texas legislature is bicameral, with two chambers: a house of representatives and a senate. Here, members of the Texas House of Representatives vote on a bill.

23

The Texas Legislature

WHAT GOVERNMENT DOES AND WHY IT MATTERS The story of Tom Craddick's time as speaker of the Texas House of Representatives highlights the partisan nature of legislative politics in Texas in recent years. The Craddick years were supposed to be years of triumph for the Republican Party in Texas. Following the 2002 election, Republicans seized control of the House for the first time in over 100 years with an 88–62 majority. They elected Tom Craddick, a conservative businessman from

Midland to lead them. A Republican stalwart since 1968 when he was first elected to the Texas House, Craddick had long pushed a partisan agenda. Assuming power in the midst of a fiscal crisis that gripped the state, Craddick began pushing a conservative Republican agenda that included lawsuit limitations, private school vouchers, pro-business legislation, and congressional redistricting. By the end of the term, over fifty Democratic members of the House had fled the state for Oklahoma, seeking to deny the Speaker a quorum and an inevitable Republican victory on redistricting. Although redistricting was passed during a special session in the summer,

focusquestions

● How does the Texas legislature differ from the U.S. Congress?

● What are the consequences of having a legislature that meets for only a limited number of days every two years?

● What powers does the state legislature have?

● How does a bill become a law in Texas?

● In addition to legislators, who else is involved in the legislative process?

● Who are the leaders in the Texas House and Senate?

● Do private citizens have an opportunity to influence the legislative process?

bad blood continued to exist between many Democrats and the aggressive Republican Speaker.

In 2008, the bad blood in the House spilled over into the Republican Party as a bitter fight broke out between the Speaker and disgruntled Republicans. Failing to defeat Craddick's re-election to a third term as Speaker at the beginning of the session, opponents tried to remove him from office at the end of the session by a motion on the House floor. By January 2009, a makeshift coalition of seventy-two Democrats and sixteen Republicans had signed pledges to back Representative Joe Straus, a moderate Republican from San Antonio, to replace Craddick as Speaker. Socially conservative Republicans tried to mobilize against Straus's candidacy, but their efforts failed as the coalition of Democrats and insurgent Republicans held fast, ushering in a new era of moderate Republican leadership in the House.

The 2010 election, however, clearly pushed the legislature in a right direction. Conservative policies, such as drastic spending cuts, anti-immigration policies, and conservative policies on abortion and gay marriage, returned to the forefront. Speaker Joe Straus, facing conservative opposition in the aftermath of the 2010 election, claimed to have the votes necessary for re-election as Speaker, but his continued moderate power base was by no means certain.[1]

chaptercontents

Structure of the Texas Legislature

● How does the Texas legislature differ from the U.S. Congress?

The Texas state legislature is the most important representative institution in the state. Members share many of the duties and responsibilities that are taken up at the national level by members of the U.S. Congress. Like members of Congress, the members of the Texas House and Senate are responsible for bringing the interests and concerns of their constituencies directly into the democratic political processes. But the important constitutional and institutional differences between the U.S. Congress and the Texas state legislature must be taken into account if we are to understand the role that the state legislature plays in democracy in Texas.

Bicameralism

Like the U.S. Congress and all the states except Nebraska, Texas has a **bicameral** legislature, with two chambers: the Texas House of Representatives and the Texas Senate. Its 31 senators and 150 House members meet in regular session for 140 days every odd-numbered year. Senators serve four-year terms and House members serve for two years. Each represents a single-member district. Members of the Texas House represent approximately 169,000 people. Senators represent about nearly 819,000 constituents. A state senator now represents more people than does a member of the U.S. House of Representatives. Elections are held in November of even-numbered years, and senators and House members take office in January of odd-numbered years.

Bicameralism creates interesting dynamics in a legislature. For one thing, it means that before a law is passed, it will be voted on by two deliberative bodies representing different constituencies. In 2009, for example, the Texas Senate passed legislation to allow college students and faculty with concealed handgun licenses to carry their firearms on campus. That legislation, however, was killed in the Texas House of Representatives.[2] It also means that if a bill cannot be killed in one house, it is possible that interest groups can kill or modify the bill in the other body.

One effect of bicameralism in Texas is that the author of a bill in one house whose bill has been amended in the other body has the option of accepting the amended bill. In that case, the bill moves forward. If, however, the author rejects the amendment, the bill is killed.

Bicameralism also means that a member of one legislative body can retaliate against a member of the other body for not cooperating on desired legislation. A "local and consent" calendar in the House is usually reserved for uncontroversial bills or bills limited to a localized problem. In order for a bill to be passed from that calendar, it has to pass without the objection of any member of the House. That requirement provides a perfect opportunity for members to retaliate against other members for perceived slights.[3]

Membership

The constitutional requirements for becoming a member of the Texas legislature are minimal. A senator must be a U.S. citizen, a qualified voter, and a resident of the state for at least five years and of the district for at least one year. Additionally, the senator must be at least twenty-six years of age. Members of the House must be at least twenty-one, U.S.

bicameral having a legislative assembly composed of two chambers or houses

Before a law is passed in Texas, it is voted on by the two chambers of the legislature—the House and the Senate. Here, state senator Jeff Wentworth casts a vote; raising one finger means "yes" and two fingers mean "no."

Although the "typical" member of the Texas state legislature is white and male, women and minority groups have increased their representation in recent years. In 2003, Democratic senators charged that the Republicans' plan to redraw electoral districts would reduce minority representation dramatically.

citizens, qualified voters, and residents of the state for two years and of the district for one year. These requirements are in keeping with the political philosophy of those who wrote the Constitution of 1876. They believed holding public office required little or no formal training and should be open to most citizens.

In Texas, the typical legislator is white, male, Protestant, college-educated, and affluent, and has a professional or business occupation. These characteristics do not mean that a poor high school dropout who is a day laborer cannot be elected to the state legislature, but they do indicate that individuals with most of these informal characteristics have a distinct advantage. Members of the legislature must have jobs that allow them the flexibility to campaign for office and to work in the legislature for 140 days every other year, as well as in special legislative sessions and meetings of committees when the legislature is not in session. Thus, about one-third of the members of the legislature are attorneys. The legal profession is one of the few careers that pays well and also offers the necessary degree of time flexibility a legislator needs. Lawyers who serve in the legislature may even gain increased legal business either from interests with legislative concerns or because of the enhanced visibility of a lawyer-legislator.[4]

Legislators in Texas cannot expect to live on their legislative salaries. In keeping with the Texas constitutional tradition of a low-cost, part-time legislature, Texas representatives receive a salary of only $7,200 a year. Legislators also receive a payment of $139 a day when the legislature is in session. When the legislature is not in session, legislators may claim up to twelve days per month of per diem pay if they are in Austin on official business, or sixteen days if they are committee chairs. The legislators themselves determine what is official business. It is common to pay expenses from officeholder expense accounts and to pocket the per diem so that it becomes a salary supplement.

Originally, per diem rates were set by the Texas Constitution, and a constitutional amendment was necessary to change this. In 1991, Texans adopted an amendment allowing the Texas Ethics Commission to propose changes in legislative salaries, which then require voter approval. To date, the commission has not

Who Are the Members of the Texas Legislature?

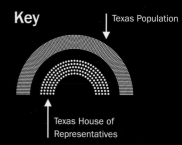

Texas Population

Texas House of
Representatives

Gender

	TX Pop.	TX House
Female	50%	24%
Male	50%	76%

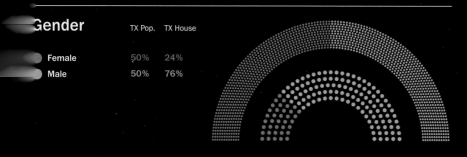

The Texas legislature is designed to be a representative body, which looks and sounds like the state as a whole. How well does the legislature represent Texas? In many ways, the legislature does not look like Texas. The data to the left are for the Texas House in 2009-2010. While the state has no ethnic majority in its population, two-thirds of Texas House members are white. The state is evenly split between men and women, while the legislature is over three-quarters male. Perhaps the biggest differences, though, regard socioeconomic status. Over half of the members of the Texas House hold graduate degrees, while only 8.2% of the state's population does.

Race

	TX Pop.	TX House
White	48%	69%
Black	12%	9%
Hispanic	36%	20%
Asian	3%	1%

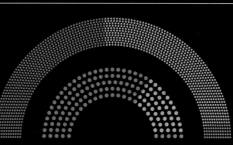

Education

	TX Pop.	TX House
< High school	21%	—
High school grad	27%	14%
Associate's degree	6%	1%
Bachelor's degree	17%	35%
Masters degree	8%	50%
Doctorate	<1%	5%

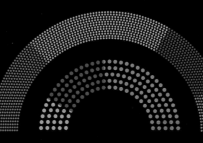

for critical analysis

1. How much do you think the racial, gender, and socio-economic makeup of the Texas legislature matter to the type of laws that the legislature passes? If the legislature had more people of color, more women, or more middle class members, would they pass different policies?

2. Why do you think that members of the Texas legislature come from the more educated, higher socioeconomic groups? Does the structure of the Texas legislature encourage or discourage people from particular occupations to run?

Occupation

Members of the Texas House of Representatives

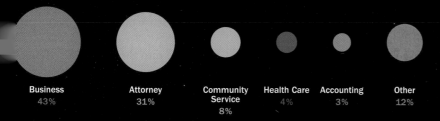

Business	Attorney	Community Service	Health Care	Accounting	Other
43%	31%	8%	4%	3%	12%

SOURCES: For Texas House, 2009-2010, numbers calculated by author based on data from the online version of the Texas State Directory, http://www.txdirectory.com/. State demographic data calculated from the U.S. Census Bureau American Community Survey, 2006-2008.

TABLE 23.1

Gender and Minority Membership in the Texas Legislature

	% OF TEXAS POPULATION	% OF 2009 TEXAS HOUSE MEMBERSHIP	% OF 2009 TEXAS SENATE MEMBERSHIP
Men	50	76	81
Women	50	24	19
African American	12	9	6
Anglo	48	69	74
Hispanic	36	20	19
Asian	3	1	0

SOURCES: For Texas House, numbers calculated by author based on data from the online version of the Texas State Directory, http://www.txdirectory.com/. State demographic data calculated from the U.S. Census Bureau American Community Survey, 2006-2008.

recommended a salary increase. At the start of each regular session, the Ethics Commission sets the legislative per diem.

Table 23.1 shows the proportions of minorities and women serving in the legislature. Although those numbers have increased over the years, they are not in proportion to their strength in the population of Texas. Civil rights laws have increased voting by minorities, and those laws provide protection for minority political districts. Thus, more minority officeholders have been elected and, as the Hispanic population in Texas increases, additional Hispanic legislators will be elected. Women have also had an increased role in politics, especially since the 1970s, and as a result, it is likely that additional women will be elected to legislative office as well.

● Sessions of the Legislature

Regular Sessions

regular session the 140-day period during which the Texas legislature meets to consider and pass bills; occurs only in odd-numbered years

biennial occurring every two years

The Texas Constitution specifies that **regular sessions** of the Texas legislature be held for 140 days in odd-numbered years. The idea of **biennial** legislative sessions grew from the nineteenth-century idea that legislative service is a part-time job and a belief that short, biennial sessions would limit the power of the legislature. For a few years, legislators were encouraged to end their work early by being paid for only 120 days of service.

Thousands of bills and resolutions are introduced into the legislature during a regular session, and the 140-day limitation places a considerable restriction on the legislature's ability to deal with this workload. Hundreds of bills pass in the last hours of a legislative session, most with little or no debate. More die in the end-of-session crush of business because there isn't time to consider them.

Special Sessions

If the legislature does not complete its agenda before the end of the legislative session or if problems arise between regular sessions, the governor may call a **special session**. Special sessions last no more than thirty days, and the governor sets their agenda. Texas has averaged one special session a year since 1876, although years may go by with no special session, whereas in some years there may be three or four sessions.

The governor's ability to set the agenda of a special session provides him or her with control over which issues are discussed and what bills are passed. In many instances, the governor, the Speaker of the Texas House, the lieutenant governor, and various committee chairs will meet to decide what will be done to solve the problem at hand. Once the leaders address the issue and develop solutions, the governor calls the special session.

Once the session begins, the governor can open it to different issues. At times, the governor bargains for a legislator's vote in return for adding to the special session agenda an issue of importance to that legislator. In 2003, Governor Perry called three special sessions of the legislature to address congressional redistricting. In 2004, a fourth special session was called to address school finance. In 2005, in addition to the regular session, two special sessions addressed school finance. There was also a special session in 2006 and one in 2009.

Between legislative sessions, members serve on interim committees that may require a few days of their time each month. Legislators are also frequently called on to present programs to schools, colleges, and civic clubs. They supervise the staff of their district offices and address the needs of their constituents. Special sessions, interim committee meetings, speeches, and constituent services require long hours, with little remuneration. Many members devote more than forty hours a week to legislative business in addition to maintaining their full-time jobs.

When Texas was a rural, predominantly agricultural state, biennial sessions worked well; however, Texas has moved beyond this description. In the twenty-first century, Texas is a modern state with more than 80 percent of its population living in metropolitan areas. Population growth continues at a rapid rate. Texas is home to many high-tech and biotech corporations. It is a center for medical research, and Texas hosts the headquarters for NASA and the Lyndon Johnson Space Center. The state's gross domestic product exceeds that of many nations. Part-time legislators serving biennial 140-day sessions may not work well anymore in allowing the state to respond quickly and effectively to problems that arise.

● Powers of the Legislature

The Texas legislature sets public policy by passing bills and resolutions, but it also supervises the state bureaucracy through the budgetary process and the Sunset Act. This is achieved using legislative and nonlegislative powers. Legislative powers consist of passing bills and resolutions. Nonlegislative powers are those functions falling outside the lawmaking function.

Legislative Powers

Bills Revenue bills must begin in the House of Representatives. All other bills may start in either the House or the Senate. For decades, a **bill** would be introduced in either the House or the Senate and work its way through the legislative process

● **What are the consequences of having a legislature that meets for only a limited number of days every two years?**

special session a legislative session called by the governor that addresses an agenda set by him or her and that lasts no longer than thirty days

for critical analysis
Texas is the second largest state and the second most populous state. Can a legislature that meets only 140 days every other year meet the needs of this modern, urban state? Will changes in the economy make a full-time legislature necessary?

bill a proposed law that has been sponsored by a member of the legislature and submitted to the clerk of the House or Senate in that chamber. A bill introduced in the Senate would be passed by the Senate prior to going to the House. Today, it is customary for a bill to be introduced into the House and the same bill, a companion bill, to be introduced into the Senate at the same time. This simultaneous consideration of bills saves time in the legislature.

There are three classifications of bills in the Texas legislature: (1) local bills; (2) special bills; and (3) general bills. **Local bills** affect only units of local government such as a city, a county, special districts, or more than one city in a county. A local bill, for example, might allow a county to create a sports authority or to establish a community college. **Special bills** give individuals or corporations an exemption from state law. A special bill could grant compensation to an individual wrongly convicted and sentenced to prison. **General bills** apply to all people and/or property in the state. General bills define criminal behavior; establish standards for divorce, child custody, or bankruptcy; and address other matters affecting people and property throughout the state.

Resolutions There are three types of **resolutions** in the Texas legislature: (1) concurrent resolutions; (2) joint resolutions; and (3) simple resolutions. **Concurrent resolutions** must pass both the House and Senate, and except for resolutions setting the time of adjournment, they require the governor's signature. These resolutions involve issues of interest to both chambers. They may request information from a state agency or call on Congress for some action. Senate Concurrent Resolution 6 might, for example, call on Congress to propose an amendment requiring a balanced federal budget.

Joint resolutions require passage in both the House and Senate but are not sent to the governor. The most common use of joint resolutions is to propose amendments to the Texas Constitution or to ratify amendments to the U.S. Constitution. Resolutions that propose amendments to the Texas Constitution require a two-thirds vote of the membership of both houses of the state legislature. Ratification of amendments to the U.S. Constitution requires a majority vote in both the Texas House and Senate.

Simple resolutions concern only the Texas House or the Senate, and they do not require the governor's signature. They are used to adopt rules, to request opinions from the attorney general, to appoint employees to office in the House or Senate, or to honor outstanding achievements by Texas residents. For example, SR 27 could recognize the achievements of a Nobel Prize winner or the San Jacinto College baseball program for accomplishments in the National Junior College Athletic Association.

Resolutions of honor or recognition are acted on without debate and without requiring members to read the resolution. Resolutions are mostly symbolic acts that are designed to promote goodwill with voters. However, at times these simple symbolic acts can go terribly wrong. A Fort Worth doctor was twice honored by the Texas House of Representatives as the "doctor of the day." It was then, to the embarrassment of the House and the legislators who introduced him to the House, reported that the doctor was a registered sex offender who had been convicted of having a sexual relationship with a seventeen-year-old female patient.[5]

Nonlegislative Powers

Nonlegislative powers include constituent powers, electoral powers, investigative powers, directive and supervisory powers, and judicial powers. The functions of these powers fall outside the scope of passing bills and resolutions; however, the passage of legislation may be necessary to exercise these powers.

local bill a bill affecting only units of local government, such as a city, county, or special district

special bill a bill that gives an individual or corporation a special exemption from state law

general bill a bill that applies to all people and/or property in the state

resolution a proposal, made by a member of the legislature, that generally deals with the internal workings of the government; a resolution is similar to a bill, but it has a more limited scope and lacks the force of public law

concurrent resolution a resolution of interest to both chambers of the legislature and which must pass both the House and Senate and generally be signed by the governor

joint resolution a resolution, commonly a proposed amendment to the Texas Constitution or ratification of an amendment to the U.S. Constitution, that must pass both the House and Senate but which does not require the governor's signature

simple resolution a resolution that concerns only the Texas House or Senate, such as the adoption of a rule or the appointment of an employee, and which does not require the governor's signature

Constituent powers are those things done for or in the name of **constituents**. Efforts on behalf of constituents may involve legislative activity, such as introducing a bill or voting on a resolution. Often, however, working on behalf of constituents involves nonlegislative activity, such as arranging an appointment for a constituent with a government agency that regulates some aspect of the constituent's life, writing a letter of recommendation for a constituent, or giving a speech to a civic group in the legislator's district.

Electoral powers of the legislature consist of formally counting returns in the elections for governor and lieutenant governor. This is accomplished during a joint session of the legislature when it is organized for the regular session.

Investigative powers can be exercised by the House of Representatives, the Senate, or jointly by both bodies. The legislature can undertake to investigate problems facing the state, the integrity of a state agency, or almost anything else it wishes. A special investigative committee is established by a simple resolution creating the committee, establishing the jurisdiction of the committee, and explaining the need for the investigation. If the special committee is formed in the House, the Speaker appoints the members of the committee. The lieutenant governor appoints members for special committees in the Senate. The Speaker and the lieutenant governor share appointments if it is a joint investigation.

Directive and supervisory powers enable the legislature to have considerable control over the executive branch of government. The legislature determines the size of the appropriation each agency has to spend for the next two years. The amount of money an agency has determines how well it can carry out its goals and objectives. A review of each agency of state government takes place each twelve years.

Judicial powers include the ability of the House to impeach members of the executive and judicial branches of state government. On **impeachment**, a trial takes place in the Senate. A majority vote of the House is required to bring charges, and a two-thirds vote of senators attending is necessary to convict an individual of the impeachment charges. Unlike the U.S. Constitution, the Texas Constitution does not explicitly define what constitutes an impeachable offense. This will be determined by the House and Senate in the impeachment process itself.[6]

Each body can compel attendance at regular and special sessions. More than once, Texas Rangers have handcuffed absent members and brought them to the legislature. On rare occasions, a chamber will punish nonmembers who disrupt proceedings by imprisoning them for up to forty-eight hours. The House and Senate judge the qualifications of members and can expel a member for cause.

constituent powers efforts made by a member of a legislature on behalf of his or her constituency

constituent a person living in the district from which an official is elected

electoral powers the legislature's mandated role in counting returns in the elections for governor and lieutenant governor

investigative powers the power, exercised by the House, the Senate, or both chambers jointly, to investigate problems facing the state

directive and supervisory powers the legislature's power over the executive branch; for example, the legislature determines the size of appropriations for state agencies

judicial powers the power of the House to impeach and of the Senate to convict members of the executive and judicial branches of state government

impeachment according to the Texas Constitution, the formal charge by the House of Representatives that leads to a trial in the Senate and possible removal of a state official

● How a Bill Becomes a Law in Texas

Anyone can write a bill, but only members of the legislature can introduce a bill. Bills may be written by members of the executive branch, by lobbyists, by constituents, or by local governmental entities. Legislators may also write bills, often with the help of a legislative staff expert in drafting legislation. There are, of course, innumerable reasons for drafting and introducing a bill.

Revenue bills must start in the House of Representatives. Other bills can start in either the House or Senate. During the 81st Legislature regular session that met in 2009, a total of 7,419 bills were introduced in the legislature. Of this number, 1,459 passed the legislature, and the governor vetoed 36 of them.[7]

Figure 23.1 shows the flow of a bill from the time it is introduced in the Texas House of Representatives to final passage and submission to the governor. A bill introduced in the Senate would follow the same procedure in reverse. Examining this figure suggests that the process of how a bill becomes law is long, detailed, and cumbersome. However, when the process is distilled to its basic parts, there are only six steps in how a bill becomes law. For a bill that starts in the House these steps are (1) **introduction**; (2) **referral**; (3) **consideration by standing committee**; and (4) **floor action**. Steps (1) through (4) are repeated in the Senate. Step (5) is action by a **conference committee** and, finally, (6) is **action by the governor**.

Introduction in the House

A legislator introduces a bill by placing copies of the bill with the clerk of the House. In the Senate, the secretary of the Senate receives the bill. The clerk or secretary numbers the bill and enrolls it by recording its number, title, caption, and sponsor in a ledger. Similar information is entered into a computer.

Rules of the legislature require the bill be read on three separate occasions. After enrollment, the bill is read for the first time by its number, title, and caption. There is great variation in the number of bills introduced by various members of the legislature. Senator John Whitmire of Houston, for example, introduced five bills in one legislative session; Senator Eliot Shapleigh of El Paso filed nearly one hundred bills. The variation is related, in part, to the political philosophy of the legislators. Whitmire, for example, believes his constituents think there are already too many laws and that his job is to look at legislation that ought to be killed or opposed. Others believe that constituents judge them on the number of bills they introduce. Still others think it is important to represent the views of their constituents by introducing the bills their district wants. Still others file bills they know will be defeated, simply to make a point.[8]

Referral

After undergoing first reading, the bill is assigned to a standing committee by the Speaker. In the Senate, the lieutenant governor assigns it to a committee. Since committees in the Texas legislature have overlapping jurisdictions, the Speaker and lieutenant governor can assign a bill to a friendly committee or an unfriendly one. The committee to which a bill is assigned can determine whether the bill survives or dies in committee.

Committee Action

Every bill introduced in the Texas legislature is assigned to a **standing committee**, and the vast majority of bills die in committee. The chair of the committee kills most by pigeonholing. **Pigeonholing** means that the committee chair sets the bill aside and never brings it before the committee.

Standing committees are considered the "workhorses" of the legislature (see Box 23.1). If the bill does not die, it most likely is amended. Few bills leave the committee in the same form as they arrived. Parts of several bills can also be combined to form a single bill. Changes are made to make the bill more acceptable to the entire legislature or to meet the political desires of the leadership or members of the committee. Hearings can take place to allow experts and the public to educate committee members on the good and bad points of the bill. In the Senate, all bills reported by the committee must have a public hearing.

introduction the first step in the legislative process, during which a member of the legislature gets an idea for a bill and files a copy of it with the clerk of the House or secretary of the Senate

referral the second step in the legislative process, during which a bill is assigned to the appropriate standing committee by the Speaker (for House bills) or the lieutenant governor (for Senate bills)

consideration by standing committee the third step in the legislative process, during which a bill is killed, amended, or heard by a standing committee

floor action the fourth step in the legislative process, during which a bill referred by a standing committee is scheduled for floor debate by the Calendars Committee

conference committee a joint committee created to work out a compromise on House and Senate versions of a piece of legislation

action by the governor the final step in the legislative process, during which the governor either signs, vetoes, or refuses to a bill

standing committee a permanent committee with the power to propose and write legislation that covers a particular subject, such as finance or agriculture

pigeonholing a step in the legislative process during which a bill is killed by the chair of the standing committee to which it was referred, as a result of his or her setting the bill aside and not bringing it before the committee

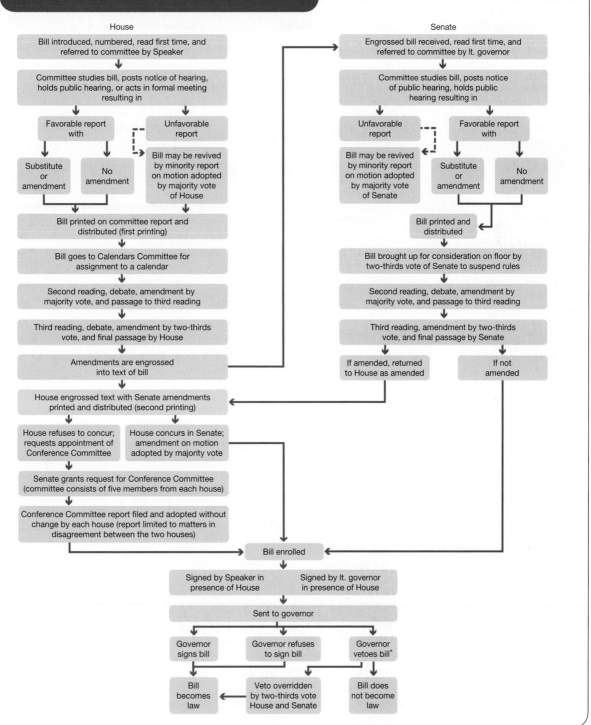

FIGURE 23.1

How a Bill Becomes a Law in Texas
(if introduced in the House)

*The governor may also veto a portion of the bill through a line-item veto.
SOURCE: Texas Staxe Senate, Citizen Handbook.

BOX 23.1

Standing Committees of the Texas Senate and House (81st Legislature)

SENATE COMMITTEES

Administration	Finance	Jurisprudence
Agriculture & Rural Affairs	Government Organization	Natural Resources
Business & Commerce	Health & Human Services	Nominations
Criminal Justice	Higher Education	State Affairs
Economic Development	Intergovernmental Relations	Transportation & Homeland Security
Education	International Relations & Trade	Veteran Affairs & Military Installations

HOUSE COMMITTEES

Agriculture & Livestock	Environmental Regulation	Pensions, Investments & Financial Services
Appropriations	General Investigating & Ethics	Public Education
Border & Intergovernmental Affairs		Public Health
		Public Safety
Business & Industry	Higher Education	Redistricting
Calendars	House Administration	Rules & Resolutions
Corrections	Human Services	State Affairs
County Affairs	Insurance	Technology, Economic Development & Workforce
Criminal Jurisprudence	Judiciary & Civil Jurisprudence	Transportation
Culture, Recreation & Tourism	Land & Resource Management	Urban Affairs
Defense & Veterans' Affairs	Licensing & Administrative Procedures	Ways & Means
Elections	Local & Consent Calendars	
Energy Resources	Natural Resources	

Floor Action

In the House, bills referred by a standing committee go next to the Calendars Committee, which, after consulting the Speaker, schedules bills for debate. In the Senate, the lieutenant governor controls the agenda and decides when a bill will be considered.

The Speaker determines the length of debate in the House. Customarily, each member is allowed ten minutes of debate. Early in the session when the agenda is uncrowded, debate may last longer. Later in the session when there is a crush of legislative business, debate will be more limited. Some bills will be voted on without debate; however, important or controversial bills are usually allocated adequate

of the Speaker and lieutenant governor are chosen. In 2009, six of the eighteen standing committee chairs in the senate were Democrats. Fifteen of the thirty-four standing committee chairs in the House were Democrats.

Not only do the Speaker and the lieutenant governor have vast committee assignment powers, but committees in the Texas legislature also have overlapping jurisdiction. Although each bill must be assigned to a committee, it can be assigned to more than one committee. Since the Speaker and the lieutenant governor assign bills to committees in their respective chambers, they use the bill assignment power to influence the fate of the bill. They can, for example, assign bills they oppose to committees they believe hostile to the bill and those they support to committees they believe will favor the bill.

Since bills must pass the House and Senate in exactly the same form, the Speaker and the lieutenant governor can exercise still another important influence on policy through their power to appoint conference committees. As we have seen, if any differences exist in a bill passed by both the House and the Senate, the bill goes to a conference committee that works out the differences in the House and Senate versions. By appointing the conference committee members, the Speaker and lieutenant governor can affect the language and even the fate of the bill.

Redistricting

One of the most controversial and partisan issues is redistricting—the redrawing of district lines for the Texas House, the Texas Senate, and the U.S. House of Representatives, which must be done at least every ten years, after the federal census.

There are 150 Texas House districts and thirty-one Texas Senate districts. One senator or one member of the House represents each district. This is called representation by **single-member districts**.

After each census, the legislature draws new boundaries for each district. Drawing new boundaries for Texas House and Senate districts is called **redistricting**. Newly drawn districts must contain an almost equal number of people in order to ensure equal representation. It guarantees that each person's vote counts the same whether the vote is cast in Houston, Big Lake, El Paso, Presidio, Brownsville, or Commerce.

For almost fifty years, Texas and other states failed to draw new boundaries, and even after U.S. Supreme Court decisions, Texas did not do so willingly.

Not until the U.S. Supreme Court's decisions in *Baker v. Carr* and *Reynolds v. Sims*, compelling the legislature to draw new districts, were boundaries drawn that represented the population fairly.[16] These and subsequent decisions meant that Texas had to draw legislative districts of roughly equal populations—a concept known as the **one-person, one-vote principle**.

Congressional redistricting is also a responsibility of the legislature. Once the U.S. Congress apportions itself, the Texas legislature divides Texas into the appropriate number of congressional districts. According to the 1964 Supreme Court case *Wesberry v. Sanders*, each state's congressional districts must be equal in population.[17] Depending on how the districts are drawn, the representation of the two political parties in the U.S. House of Representatives can be significantly changed. Indeed, reapportionment can so change the division of the parties that control of the U.S. House of Representatives can be affected. Thus, maneuvering over redistricting is highly partisan.

If the legislature fails to redistrict the Texas House or Texas Senate at the first regular session after the census, the task falls to the Legislative Redistricting Board

single-member district an electorate that is allowed to select only one representative from each district

redistricting the process of redrawing election districts and redistributing legislative representatives. This happens every ten years to reflect shifts in population or in response to legal challenges in existing districts

one-person, one-vote principle the principle that all districts should have roughly equal populations

(LRB). The LRB has five *ex officio* members: the lieutenant governor, the Speaker of the House, the attorney general, the commissioner of the General Land Office, and the comptroller of public accounts.

When the legislature adjourns without redistricting, either the House, the Senate, or both, the LRB comes into existence. It must meet within ninety days of legislative adjournment and complete its responsibilities within another sixty days. Even here, the influence of the Speaker and the lieutenant governor is clearly visible.

Partisan differences in the state legislature resulted in the failure to pass a redistricting plan in 2001 during its regular session, transferring the responsibility to the Republican-dominated LRB. On a split vote, the board developed redistricting plans that appeared to favor the Republican Party. The board's decision, in turn, was appealed to the federal courts. A three-judge panel, composed of two Democrats and one Republican, approved the lines drawn for the state Senate, noting that the U.S. Justice Department had determined that the plan did not violate the Voting Rights Act. However, the court modified the board's plan for the House, arguing that the Department of Justice had rejected the plan because it was seen as diluting Hispanic voting strength in three areas of the state. The court felt that its role in the entire redistricting process was constrained. In their decision, the judges commented that "federal courts have a limited role in considering challenges to pre-cleared, legislatively adopted redistricting plans."[18]

The final plan approved by the court appeared to be a great victory for the Republican Party. Twenty-seven incumbent Democrats found themselves placed in districts with other Democratic incumbents. Four Democrats who chaired key committees announced that they would not seek reelection. Many observers felt that redistricting would make the Republicans the majority party in the House and would maintain their majority status in the Senate. And many doubted that the Speaker of the House, Democrat Pete Laney, would be able to mobilize the votes needed for reelection to the speakership in the next session. After the 2002 elections, these observers were proven correct.[19]

Power and Partisanship in the Redistricting Battle

Republican control of the Texas House and Senate in 2002 heralded more than simply a shift in party control of the legislature. With Republican control came a significant decline in the harmonious, bipartisan spirit that had largely governed the Texas legislature. The Republican leadership, especially House Speaker Tom Craddick, chose to govern in a more partisan fashion. Additionally, a number of Democrats in the House who saw their power slipping away chose a rebellious course. They worked to make Craddick's speakership a difficult one, obstructing Republican legislative efforts as much as possible.

This new partisan tension in the Texas legislature rose to a fever pitch in 2003 when Republicans, with the support of the Republican majority leader Tom DeLay, sought to alter the Texas congressional districts for partisan advantage. The Republican goal was to increase Republican representation in the Texas congressional delegation and, in so doing, help ensure a continuing Republican majority in the U.S. House of Representatives. The Republican effort was unconventional in that it occurred in mid-cycle—that is, it was the second redistricting after the 2000 census. As a rule, redistricting occurs only once after each decennial census, although there is no legal requirement that this be the case.

After the 2000 census, the Texas legislature could not agree on redistricting, and a federal court devised a plan. The 2000 congressional redistricting gave the Democrats an advantage. With control of the state legislature, however, Republicans argued that the existing redistricting plan was unsatisfactory because it reflected a Democratic majority that no longer existed. Republicans wanted a plan that more clearly reflected Republican voting in Texas.[20] In 2000, Democrats won seventeen congressional seats and Republicans won thirteen, even though Republicans won 59 percent of votes in the state and Democrats received only 40 percent. In 2002, Democrats got only 41 percent of the statewide vote, but they won seventeen seats to fifteen for the Republicans. In fact, since 1996, Republicans had never received less than 55 percent of the statewide vote, and Democrats never won more than 44 percent, yet Republicans were a minority in the Texas congressional delegation. With the new redistricting plan in 2004, Republicans got 58 percent of the statewide vote and elected twenty-one members of Congress from Texas. Democrats got 41 percent of the statewide vote and elected eleven members of Congress from Texas.[21]

The Republican congressional redistricting plan was not enacted without political turmoil, however. At the end of 2003, fifty-one Democrats from the state legislature walked out and gathered in Ardmore, Oklahoma, where the Texas state police did not have jurisdiction to bring them back to the state capitol. The result was that a quorum could not be reached to pass the plan. The Democratic legislators did not return to Austin until redistricting was taken off the agenda. A special legislative session was called to deal with redistricting, but the two-thirds rule in the state Senate prevented the bill from being passed. In a second special session that was called to deal with redistricting, eleven of the twelve Democratic members of the Senate fled to Albuquerque in order to prevent a Senate vote. Finally, a third special session produced a plan that passed both houses of the legislature.[22]

Although the Texas legislature is not as susceptible to partisan squabbling as the U.S. Congress, flare-ups between the Democrats and Republicans do occur. For example, in this photo, Texas House Democrats celebrate after returning to Texas on May 15, 2003, after spending four days in Ardmore, Oklahoma, to kill a GOP-produced congressional redistricting plan.

In 2006, the United States Supreme Court upheld most of the new boundaries drawn in the Republicans' controversial redistricting but found that some of the redrawn districts failed to protect minority voting rights. Here, Governor Perry displays the new redistricting map.

Most notable about the 2004 redistricting was that seven incumbent congressional Democrats were targeted for defeat. A lawsuit that challenged the redistricting on the grounds that it diluted minority votes stressed that the Democrats had been elected with minority support. The lawsuit also pointed out that these seven Democrats had either been paired so that they had to run against another incumbent or had been given a more Republican district.[23] A case before the U.S. Supreme Court challenged the extreme partisan gerrymandering of the Texas redistricting, its reduction of the strength of minority voters, and its use of the now outdated 2000 census. The Court did find that there had been a reduction in the strength of minority voters. However, the extreme partisan gerrymander and the mid-decennial redistricting using the 2000 census were upheld. For the most part, Republicans were successful in reshaping the partisan composition of the Texas delegation to the U.S. House of Representatives. However, the 2006 election led to Democratic control of the U.S. House and to a Texas Congressional delegation with vastly weakened power due to the loss of key Democrats in the redistricting.[24] The consequence of this redistricting is also that the bipartisan spirit that had been the hallmark of the Texas legislature will never be the same.

The 2010 census will lead to another redistricting of districts for the Texas legislature and the U.S. House of Representatives. There is no doubt that the result will be another partisan battle. As a result, the 2010 elections to the Texas legislature are especially important, since those legislators will determine the composition of state and U.S. congressional legislative districts and, in the process, determine the partisan composition of those legislative bodies.

● Conclusion

The Texas Legislature has undergone great changes and continues to do so. Perhaps the most significant change has been the increasing partisanship. The Texas legislature is less partisan than the U.S. Congress, but the party divide was especially notable under Speaker Tom Craddick, during the redistricting battles of 2003, and during the battles over a voter identification law in 2009. The revolt against Speaker Craddick and his replacement with Joe Straus represented a somewhat more harmonious period in the Texas legislature, but it is likely that partisan battles will break out again in the aftermath of the 2010 election.

Increasingly, as well, the two-thirds rule in the Texas Senate is under attack. That rule requires considerable consensus to pass legislation from that body. If the two-thirds rule is reduced to a three-fifths rule or even majority rule, there will be renewed partisanship and rancor in the Texas Senate.

The Texas legislature seems in some ways like an archaic institution. Unless there are special sessions, it meets once every two years and is a part-time body with very limited compensation for its members. The structure of the legislature, however, has survived since the 1876 Constitution, and there seems little likelihood that the structure will soon change.

Especially notable regarding the legislature is the vast power held by the Speaker and the lieutenant governor. The 1876 Constitution showed its distrust of a powerful governor, and the result is that in Texas the governor must share political influence with two other major powers in Texas government—the Speaker and the lieutenant governor, over whom the governor exerts no formal control. Still, the revolt against Speaker Craddick does remind us that it is perilous for the Speaker to try to exert so much power that he becomes subject to rebuke from a constituency whose views he ultimately must reflect—the views of a majority of the members of the Texas House.

● Do private citizens have an opportunity to influence the legislative process?

studyguide

Practice Quiz

Ⓢ Find a diagnostic Web Quiz with 20 additional questions on the StudySpace Web site: www.wwnorton.com/we-the-people

1. There are _____ members of the Texas Senate, and state senators serve a _____ year term. (p. 837)
   a) 31/4
   b) 100/6
   c) 150/2
   d) 435/2

2. The Texas legislature meets in regular session (p. 837)
   a) 90 days every year.
   b) 180 days every year.
   c) 140 days each odd-numbered year and 60 days each even-numbered year.
   d) 140 days each odd-numbered year.

3. Texas House members differ from Texas Senate members because (p. 837)
   a) House members represent small districts and are subject to more frequent elections.

   b) House members represent people and senators represent counties.
   c) House members are elected from single-member districts and senators from multimember districts.
   d) House members have term limits and senators do not have term limits.

4. The agenda for a special session of the Texas legislature is set by the (p. 841)
   a) lieutenant governor and the Speaker of the House.
   b) governor.
   c) Texas Supreme Court.
   d) chair of the Joint committee on Special Sessions.

5. If a bill fails to pass the Texas House and Texas Senate in exactly the same form, the bill (p. 847)
   a) dies.
   b) is returned to the standing committee in the House or Senate that originally considered the bill.

c) is sent to a conference committee.

d) is sent to the governor, who decides which version of the bill will be signed.

6. The ability of the lieutenant governor and the Speaker of the House to control the final outcome of legislation comes from their power to *(p. 847)*

   a) appoint members of conference committees.

   b) refuse to approve the work of standing committees.

   c) exercise the legislative line-item veto.

   d) change up to three lines in any bill.

7. The _____ provides the governor with a powerful tool with which to bargain with the legislature. *(p. 848)*

   a) ability to introduce five bills in a regular session

   b) post-adjournment veto

   c) pocket veto

   d) message power

8. Which state official, in large part, determines the amount of money the legislature may appropriate? *(p. 849)*

   a) governor

   b) comptroller of public accounts

   c) lieutenant governor

   d) attorney general

9. The two most powerful political figures in the Texas legislature are the *(p. 851)*

   a) governor and the lieutenant governor.

   b) governor and the attorney general.

   c) Speaker of the House and the governor.

   d) Speaker of the House and the lieutenant governor.

10. The Speaker of the Texas House is chosen *(p. 851)*

    a) in a statewide election.

    b) in a party-line vote by members of the Texas House.

c) by of majority of the members of the House whether Democrat or Republican.

d) by seniority in the House.

11. The lieutenant governor is the presiding officer of *(p. 852)*

    a) the Texas Senate.

    b) the governor's cabinet.

    c) the Texas legislature.

    d) the Legislative Conference committees.

12. In recent years, the Texas Legislature has *(p. 853)*

    a) become more partisan.

    b) become more experienced in lawmaking.

    c) been more inclined to let the governor make policy.

    d) been more respectful of county officials.

13. The chairs of the Texas House committees are *(p. 854)*

    a) of the same party as the Speaker.

    b) selected on the basis of seniority.

    c) chosen because of their experience.

    d) both Democrats and Republicans.

14. An important issue for the legislature at least every ten years is *(p. 855)*

    a) adopting a budget.

    b) deciding the order of succession to the office of governor.

    c) impeaching the lieutenant governor.

    d) redistricting.

15. Republicans are a majority in *(p. 856)*

    a) the Texas House.

    b) the Texas Senate.

    c) both the Texas House and Senate.

    d) neither the Texas House nor the Texas Senate.

Chapter Outline

Find a detailed Chapter Outline on the StudySpace Web site: www.wwnorton.com/we-the-people

Key Terms

Find Flashcards to help you study these terms on the StudySpace Web site: www.wwnorton.com/we-the-people

action by the governor *(p. 844)*

bicameral *(p. 837)*

biennial *(p. 840)*

bill *(p. 841)*

concurrent resolution *(p. 842)*

conference committee *(p. 844)*

consideration by standing committee *(p. 844)*

constituent *(p. 843)*

constituent powers *(p. 843)*

directive and supervisory powers *(p. 843)*

electoral powers *(p. 843)*

filibuster *(p. 847)*

floor action *(p. 844)*

general bill *(p. 842)*
impeachment *(p. 843)*
introduction *(p. 844)*
investigative powers *(p. 843)*
joint resolution *(p. 842)*
judicial powers *(p. 843)*
line-item veto *(p. 848)*
local bill *(p. 842)*

one-person, one-vote principle *(p. 855)*
pigeonholing *(p. 844)*
post-adjournment veto *(p. 848)*
recognition *(p. 853)*
redistricting *(p. 855)*
referral *(p. 844)*
regular session *(p. 841)*
resolution *(p. 842)*

simple resolution *(p. 842)*
single-member district *(p. 855)*
Speaker *(p. 851)*
special bill *(p. 842)*
special session *(p. 841)*
standing committee *(p. 844)*
veto *(p. 847)*

Recommended Web Sites

Chron.com—*Houston Chronicle*
www.chron.com/new/politics/

Speaker of the Texas House of Representatives
www.house.state.tx.us/speaker/welcome.htm

Texas Legislative Council
www.tlc.state.tx.us

Texas Legislature Online
www.capitol.state.tx.us

Texas Lieutenant Governor
www.senate.state.tx.us/75r/LtGov/Ltgov.htm

Window on State Government (Comptroller of Public Accounts)
www.window.state.tx.us

Although the governor is the most visible leader in Texas politics, Texas governors have fewer powers than governors in other states. This is in keeping with Texans' mistrust of excessive governmental power. Like other Texas governors before him, Governor Rick Perry has frequently been checked by the legislature.

The Texas Executive Branch

Candidates for the governorship in Texas can pursue several electoral strategies when seeking office. For example, they can try to direct attention to state issues, emphasizing their special abilities to address the concerns and problems facing Texans today. Alternatively, an unpopular presidential administration can drive state and local candidates to focus on their differences with national leaders and why they are better able to address the needs of the state. Or, candidates can embrace a popular presidential administration and try to identify themselves with its larger vision of where the state and nation must go. By nationalizing the election, candidates seek to move the electorate's attention away from state politics to those of the nation.

The Texas Constitution limits the intrusion of national politics into state elections by scheduling the election of its governor and other executive officers every four years on "off-presidential years." Holding elections in off-presidential years, however, does not guarantee that national politics do not intrude into state-wide elections during these off-presidential

focusquestions

- **What factors account for the weakness of the Texas governor?**

- **How does the plural executive work in Texas?**

- **What roles are played by boards, commissions, and regulatory agencies in state government?**

years. Indeed, the 2010 election was a classic example of how gubernatorial elections can be nationalized.

As noted in the introduction to Chapter 21, with support from the Tea Party movement in the state, Governor Rick Perry rode anti-Washington sentiment to victory in the 2010 Republican primary, and carried these anti-Washington themes into the general election campaign. Perry portrayed himself as a leader who would protect Texas from the excesses of the Obama administration. Although Perry's legislative accomplishments in two and a half terms as governor were modest at best, his popularity rose as his anti-Washington, anti-Democrat, anti-Obama message intensified.

Perry refused to debate his Democratic opponent Bill White on television, citing his opponent's failure to release certain tax returns as a reason. Commentators from the press were highly critical of this decision, bemoaning the fact that the key issues facing the state would never be discussed in an open forum. Conversation about the issues that ensued was largely one-sided, either between the press and one candidate or across campaign ads. One of the most important consequences of this limited debate over the issues was that Perry was able to side-step discussing the most difficult issue that was facing the state—a burgeoning budget deficit.

Perry's strategy of nationalizing the 2010 gubernatorial race was highly successful. The week following the election, he published his first book *Fed Up! Our Fight to Save America from Washington*. The book reads less like a conclusion to a race for the governorship than it does a preface to a future campaign for national office. Its anti-Washington theme is typical of Perry's 2010 campaign which focused not on state issues—even as pressing as a gargantuan budget deficit—but on the evils of Washington and national power. But as Perry moved into his third term, the budget deficit and other serious issues confronted Texas's government.

chapter contents

● What factors
account for the
weakness of the
Texas governor?

● The Governor

At the national level, the president represents and is responsible to the people as a whole. The president is the spokesperson for the government and the people in national and international affairs. Throughout the twentieth century, various presidents parlayed the powers granted them by the U.S. Constitution into what some commentators call the "imperial presidency." The governorship in Texas is not an analogous, imperial one. Compared with the president, the governor of Texas is weak. Executive power in Texas is divided among a number of separately elected officials, all of whom are elected by and responsible to the people as a whole. This plural executive has important implications for democratic life in the Lone Star State.

Although the governor of Texas is the most visible state official, Texas's governor has far less formal power than most governors. In 1983, a study done of the appointment, budget, removal, and organizational powers of governors ranked Texas's governor forty-ninth in the nation, ahead only of the governor of South Carolina.[1] In 1990, a study was done of gubernatorial authority in the nation that also ranked Texas's governor forty-ninth, ahead of the governor of Rhode Island.[2] To understand the restrictions placed on the office, it is necessary to remember that the Constitution of 1876 was a reaction to the Reconstruction government that existed in Texas following the Civil War. The governor during Reconstruction was very powerful, and state government was regarded as oppressive and corrupt. When a new constitution was drafted at the end of the Reconstruction era, Texans did their best to ensure that no state official had extensive power. The Texas Constitution of 1876 placed strict limits on the governor's ability to control the people appointed to office and almost eliminated the possibility that appointees to office could be removed. Power was further fragmented among other officeholders, who are collectively known as the plural executive. Each of these officeholders is elected and has separate and distinct responsibilities. Members of major state boards, such as the Railroad Commission and the State Board of Education, are also elected and are largely outside the control of the governor.

Governors who are successful in pushing their programs through the legislature and seeing them implemented by the bureaucracy are able to use the limited formal powers available to them, exercise their personal political power, exploit the prestige of the office of governor, and marshal various special interests to their cause. One political writer likens the office of governor to a bronco that breaks most men and will be successfully ridden by very few. In short, successful governors are successful politicians.[3]

Former state representative Brian McCall has recently written about the modern Texas governorship, arguing that Texas governors can be quite powerful in spite of the weaknesses of the office that are inherent in the Texas Constitution. He points out that governors who develop a collaborative relationship with the legislature can realize many of their goals if they are flexible, have a vision, are willing to motivate others to achieve that vision, and will work cooperatively with the legislature. McCall notes that when former governor Allan Shivers was asked about the weak governorship of Texas, he responded, "I never thought it was weak. I had all the power I needed." McCall, in stressing that the Texas governorship can be parlayed into a position of power by capable individuals, noted that the governor has the only power to call special sessions of the legislature. The governor can pardon criminals and can permit fugitives to be extradited to other states. The governor appoints people to state governing boards and commissions. Only the governor can declare martial law. Only the governor can veto acts of the legislature. Through the

for critical analysis

What can governors do to overcome the inherent weakness of the position? What are the implications for democratic government of a weak chief executive?

traditional State of the State address that the governor gives at the beginning of every legislature session, he or she can outline state priorities and convince others of the importance of those priorities. Governors can be a major persuasive force in mobilizing interest groups, editorial boards of newspapers, and opinion leaders behind his or her agenda.

Not all governors have the personal skills to turn the office into a powerful one. Some have been unable to develop a collaborative relationship with the legislature. Others have not had the interest or the ability to develop their own vision and political agenda. Still others have been unable to accomplish their goals because of economic downturns that have limited the resources that they have had. However, McCall argues that modern governors such as John Connally, Ann Richards, and George Bush have had the persuasive skills that have enabled them to achieve major political objectives in spite of the constitutional limitations on the powers of the office.[4]

Qualifications

Only three formal constitutional qualifications are required to become governor of Texas. Article IV of the Texas Constitution requires the governor to (1) be at least thirty years of age; (2) be a U.S. citizen; and (3) live in Texas five years immediately before election. Texas governors have tended to be male, white, Democratic, politically moderate or conservative, either personally wealthy or with access to wealth, Protestant, and middle-aged, and they have had considerable prior political experience.

Women compose more than 50 percent of the population of the United States and Texas, but only two women—Miriam Ferguson (1925–27, 1933–35) and Ann Richards (1991–95)—have served as governor of Texas.

William Clements's victory over John Hill in the gubernatorial campaign of 1978 was the first time since Reconstruction that a Republican had won the office. George W. Bush was the second Republican elected governor and the first individual elected for two consecutive four-year terms.

Gubernatorial campaigns in Texas are expensive. In 2002, Tony Sanchez spent tens of millions of dollars of his own money but still lost the race to Rick Perry.

Access to money is important because running for governor is inordinately expensive. A campaign for the governorship can cost tens of millions of dollars, and few Texans have that kind of money available. The 2002 gubernatorial campaigns set a record, costing about $87 million. Tony Sanchez, the Democratic nominee for governor in 2002, spent over $66 million in that campaign. About $60 million of those funds came from his family's fortune in a losing effort for the governor's mansion.

Sam Kinch, a former editor of *Texas Weekly*, suggests that prior political experience is an important consideration in selecting a governor. Kinch maintains that although experience may not mean that someone will be a better governor, it does mean he or she is more likely to know how to handle the pressures of the office.[5]

Election and Term of Office

Before 1974, Texas governors served two-year terms, with most being elected to a maximum of two consecutive two-year terms. As Table 24.1 shows, there have been exceptions, such as Coke

TABLE 24.1

Governors of Texas and Their Terms of Office since 1874

Richard Coke	1874–76	Miriam Ferguson	1933–35
Richard B. Hubbard	1876–79	James V. Allred	1935–39
Oran M. Roberts	1879–83	W. Lee O'Daniel	1939–41
John Ireland	1883–87	Coke Stevenson	1941–47
Lawrence S. Ross	1887–91	Beauford H. Jester	1947–49
James S. Hogg	1891–95	Allan Shivers	1949–57
Charles A. Culberson	1895–99	Price Daniel	1957–63
Joseph D. Sayers	1899–1903	John Connally	1963–69
S. W. T. Lanham	1903–07	Preston Smith	1969–73
Thomas M. Campbell	1907–11	Dolph Briscoe	1973–79*
Oscar B. Colquitt	1911–15	William Clements	1979–83
James E. Ferguson	1915–17	Mark White	1983–87
William P. Hobby	1917–21	William Clements	1987–91
Pat M. Neff	1921–25	Ann Richards	1991–95
Miriam Ferguson	1925–27	George W. Bush	1995–2000†
Dan Moody	1927–31	Rick Perry	2000–
Ross Sterling	1931–33		

*Term changed to four years with the 1974 general election.
†Resigned to become president of the United States.
SOURCE: Dallas Morning News, *Texas Almanac and State Industrial Guide 1998–99* (Dallas: A. H. Belo, 1999).

Stevenson, Price Daniel, and John Connally, who each served for six years, or Allan Shivers, who served for eight years. In 1972, Texas voters adopted a constitutional amendment changing the governor's term to four years. In 1974, Dolph Briscoe was the first governor elected to a four-year term of office.

Gubernatorial elections are held in off-years (election years in which a president is not elected) to minimize the effect of presidential elections on the selection of the Texas governor. The Texas legislature, controlled at the time by Democrats, designed the off-year system to eliminate the possibility that a popular Republican presidential candidate would bring votes to a Republican candidate for governor. Likewise, party leaders wanted to negate the chances of an unpopular Democratic presidential candidate costing a Democratic gubernatorial candidate votes in the general election. Unfortunately, because of this timing, voter turnout in gubernatorial contests is relatively low.

Campaigns

Campaigns for governor of Texas last at least ten months. Candidates hit the campaign trail in January of an election year to win their party's primary election in March, then continue campaigning until the November general election. Successful

Governor Rick Perry spent millions of dollars on his 2010 campaign for re-election, as he first fended off a serious challenge from Kay Bailey Hutchison in the Republican primary election and then campaigned in the general election.

candidates spend thousands of hours and millions of dollars campaigning. The money goes to pay staff salaries and for travel, opinion polls, telephone banks, direct mailings, and advertisements in print and broadcast media. Texas is so large that statewide candidates must purchase print and electronic advertisements in nineteen media markets to reach every corner of the state.

In the 2010 Republican primary, Kay Bailey Hutchison spent over $14 million in her losing battle against Rick Perry. Perry spent nearly $13 million in the primary. Overall, Perry spent about $40,000,000 and Bill White spent about $25,000,000 in their campaigns. That is $14.58 for every vote Perry received and $11.76 for every vote White received. High-priced campaigns illustrate that successful candidates need personal wealth or access to wealth.

Removal of a Governor

In Texas, the only constitutional method of removing a governor from office is by **impeachment** and conviction. "To impeach" means to accuse or to indict, and impeachment is similar to a true bill (indictment) by a grand jury. The Texas Constitution notes that the governor may be impeached but does not give any grounds for impeachment. Possible justifications for impeachment are failure to perform the duties of governor, gross incompetence, or official misconduct.

Impeachment begins in the Texas House of Representatives. A majority vote of the Texas House is required to impeach, or to bring charges. If the House votes for impeachment, the trial takes place in the Texas Senate. One or more members of the Texas House prosecute the case, and the Chief Justice of the Supreme Court of Texas presides over the impeachment proceedings. A two-thirds vote of the senators present and voting is necessary to convict. If convicted, the governor is removed from office and disqualified from holding any other state office.

Any member of the executive or judicial branch may be impeached. Once the House votes for impeachment charges against an official, that individual is suspended from office and cannot exercise any of his duties. Governor James Ferguson was the only Texas governor to be impeached and convicted.

Succession

The Texas Constitution provides for the lieutenant governor to become governor if the office becomes vacant through impeachment and conviction, death, resignation, or the governor's absence from the state.

In December 2000, a succession occurred when Governor George W. Bush became president-elect of the United States and resigned as governor. Lieutenant Governor Rick Perry immediately took the oath to become governor of Texas. According to the *Houston Chronicle*, Rick Perry is "a politician who so looks the part that it's been joked that he was ordered straight from central casting."[6] Perry, a

impeachment the formal charge by the House of Representatives that leads to a trial in the Senate and the possible removal of a state official

Who Re-Elected Governor Perry in 2010?

Rick Perry is from Paint Creek, Texas, a rural community in Haskell County. Bill White served as mayor of Houston, Texas's largest city. The results of the 2010 governor's election reflect this urban/rural divide between the two candidates. Perry did best in rural counties, especially in his native West Texas. Outside of the Rio Grande Valley, White did best in the urban counties.

2010 Election Results, by County

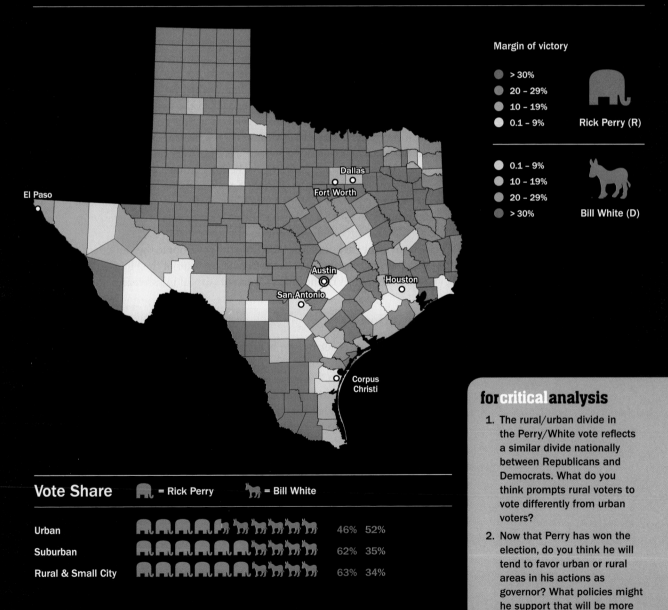

Margin of victory

- \> 30%
- 20 – 29%
- 10 – 19%
- 0.1 – 9%   **Rick Perry (R)**

- 0.1 – 9%
- 10 – 19%
- 20 – 29%
- \> 30%   **Bill White (D)**

El Paso · Dallas · Fort Worth · Austin · Houston · San Antonio · Corpus Christi

Vote Share   = Rick Perry   = Bill White

		Perry	White
Urban		46%	52%
Suburban		62%	35%
Rural & Small City		63%	34%

SOURCE: Texas Secretary of State

for critical analysis

1. The rural/urban divide in the Perry/White vote reflects a similar divide nationally between Republicans and Democrats. What do you think prompts rural voters to vote differently from urban voters?

2. Now that Perry has won the election, do you think he will tend to favor urban or rural areas in his actions as governor? What policies might he support that will be more favorable to rural areas?

former state legislator from Haskell, was a conservative Democrat who switched to the Republican Party in 1990 and ran successfully for commissioner of agriculture. His six years in the Texas House, eight years as head of a major state agency, and two years as lieutenant governor and president of the Texas Senate provided him with a great deal more experience than any other governor of the last three decades.[7]

Should the governor leave the bounds of the state, the lieutenant governor becomes acting governor. If the governor is impeached, the lieutenant governor serves as acting governor before and during the trial. While serving as acting governor, the lieutenant governor earns the governor's daily salary of $316, which is far better than the $20 earned as lieutenant governor. (However, the governor does not forfeit his salary if he is absent from the state. Both the governor and the lieutenant governor earn $316 for every day the governor is out of the state.)

When out of the state, the governor is legally entitled to Department of Public Safety protection. George W. Bush spent part of 1999 and 2000 campaigning to be president of the United States. During fiscal year 1999, it cost Texans an additional $2,365,000 to provide protection for the governor while he was on the presidential campaign trail.[8] In 1992, Governor Ann Richards was often out of the state campaigning for Bill Clinton, and the Texas taxpayers picked up the cost of her security detail.

Constitutionally, the governor's office is weak. Former lieutenant governor Bill Hobby noted that about the only way he knew when he was acting governor was by a note his secretary left on his daily calendar.[9] In the first three months of 2000, Rick Perry, then lieutenant governor, served as acting governor more days than Bush was in the state to serve as governor. Perry's press secretary commented that the added duties of being acting governor were not very noticeable and that those duties made little difference in Perry's schedule.[10] State government takes little notice of the governor's absences. Former Speaker of the Texas House Pete Laney has said that the governor's office is "holding court and cutting ribbons" and in 2000 commented on Governor Bush's out-of-state campaigning by saying, "I guess we've been doing pretty well without one [a governor]."[11]

Legislation further defines succession from the governor to the lieutenant governor, to the president *pro tempore* of the Texas Senate, Speaker of the House, attorney general, and the chief judges of the Texas Courts of Appeal in ascending order.

Compensation

The governor's salary is set by the legislature. Texas pays its governor $115,345 annually. In addition to this salary, the governor receives use of an official mansion near the capitol grounds. Governors and the legislature often squabble about the amount of money needed for upkeep of the mansion and its grounds. The governor also receives use of a limousine, a state-owned aircraft, and a personal staff.

Staff

The governor's staff consists of more than 200 individuals. This includes a chief of staff, a deputy chief of staff, a general counsel, and a press secretary. A scheduler coordinates the governor's appointments, personal appearances, and work schedule.

The staff keeps the governor informed about issues and problems facing the state, and it may suggest courses of action. In addition, during a four-year term, a governor makes several thousand of appointments to various state posts. It is impossible for a governor to be acquainted personally with each appointee. Part of the staff finds qualified individuals for each post and recommends them to the governor. Other staff members track legislation. They talk with legislators, especially key people such as committee chairpersons. The staff lets the governor know when his or her personal touch might make a difference in the outcome of legislation. For each bill that passes the legislature, a staff member prepares a summary of the bill with a recommendation that the governor sign or veto the bill.

Recent governors have used their staffs to be more accessible to the public. Governor Perry, like his immediate predecessors, wants his staff to be no more than a phone call away from those who need assistance. In theory, individuals need only call a member of the governor's staff to receive help or find out where to go for help. The Office of the Governor has a Citizen's Assistance Hotline that handles more than 10,000 calls each year from Texans needing assistance with their problems with state government.

Executive Powers of the Governor

Texas has a board or agency form of government. Approximately 200 state boards, commissions, and agencies make up the executive branch of Texas government. Agencies may be as obscure as the Texas Funeral Commission or the State Preservation Board or as well-known as the Public Utilities Commission of Texas or the Texas Department of Human Services, but each is important to its constituents. These multimember boards are the policy-making bodies for their agencies. They employ and oversee the people who operate the agencies on a daily basis.

Appointment Power The governor's power of **appointment** is the most significant executive power. It allows a degree of control over about 200 state agencies. During a typical four-year term, a governor will make around 3,000 appointments.

The power of appointment enables the governor to exercise the power of **patronage**. It permits the governor to reward supporters by appointing them to office. Most of the offices pay very little, but they do offer supporters some prestige. The governor can also use the appointment power to repay political favors by appointing friends and associates of legislators to office as well as to garner political IOUs from politicians. Most important, a governor can use the appointment power to influence agency policy. To a great degree, the effectiveness of a governor's use of the appointment power will determine the governor's success in office.

A governor, however, must exert some care in appointments. In 2007, there was a scandal within the Texas Youth Commission, which has authority over institutionalized juveniles. It became clear that not only was there a widespread pattern of physical and sexual abuse of juveniles in the facilities, but authorities tried to cover up the abuse. As a result, Governor Perry's appointees had to resign from the commission and it was necessary to reorganize the agency.

The governor appoints people to office, but the Texas Senate must also confirm them. However, since the Senate may not meet for almost two years, the appointee takes office immediately and does not wait for Senate confirmation. An important limitation on the power of the governor to appoint

appointment the power of the chief executive, whether the president of the United States or the governor of a state, to appoint persons to office

patronage the resources available to higher officials, usually opportunities to make partisan appointments to offices and to confer grants, licenses, or special favors to supporters

One of the governor's most important powers is the power to appoint people to various positions in state government. For example, in 2010, Rick Perry appointed Eva Guzman to the Texas Supreme Court.

senatorial courtesy the practice whereby the president, before formally nominating a person for a federal judgeship, seeks the indication that senators from the candidate's own state support the nomination; in Texas, the practice whereby the governor seeks the indication that the senator from the candidate's home supports the nomination

persons to office is the requirement that the individual's state senator must approve the appointment. This is known as **senatorial courtesy** and applies regardless of the party affiliation of the governor, senator, or appointee. Usually, if the appointee's senator concurs in the appointment, the remainder of the Senate will agree. However, if the appointee's senator opposes the appointment, the remainder of the Senate will also oppose the appointment.

The process for removing someone is also complicated. A governor cannot remove an appointee who refuses to resign unless the governor can show cause and get two-thirds of the Texas Senate to approve.[12] This complex procedure for the termination of members of boards and commissions, along with the practice of senatorial courtesy, can be a significant limitation on the governor's power to influence the policies of state agencies.

Budgetary Power Officially, the Texas governor is the state's chief budget officer. As such, governors are required to submit an **executive budget** to the legislature. This budget suggests a plan for revenue and expenditure for Texas, but more important, it indicates the governor's priorities for the state in the next biennium.

executive budget the state budget prepared and submitted by the governor to the legislature, which indicates the governor's spending priorities. The executive budget is overshadowed in terms of importance by the legislative budget

In 1949, in an effort to gain more control over the state's budget, the legislature established the Legislative Budget Board (LBB), which is responsible for preparing a **legislative budget**. Thus, two budgets are prepared and submitted to the legislature: an executive budget by the governor and a legislative budget by the LBB. As a creation of the legislature, the LBB's budget proposal receives more consideration by the House and Senate than the governor's recommendations, and in recent years the governor's budget has fallen into disuse. Legend has it that the governor's budget has been used as a doorstop and a paperweight, and one diminutive legislator used two copies as a booster in his office chair. In 1989, Governor Clements recognized the futility of submitting an executive budget and simply endorsed the recommendations of the LBB. Ann Richards followed Clements's precedent, but Governor George Bush took a more active role in budget preparation.

legislative budget the state budget that is prepared and submitted by the Legislative Budget Board (LBB) and that is fully considered by the House and Senate

The governor has some control over the final appropriations bill through the use of the line-item veto; however, the governor cannot impound funds or transfer funds from one agency to another, even if circumstances change from the time the money was appropriated. Overall, the budgetary process does not provide the governor with an effective means of controlling state agencies.

In the mid-1980s, then comptroller of public accounts Bob Bullock notified Governor Mark White that due to a decline in the price of oil, state revenues would fall 13 percent (about $1 billion) below projections. In an effort to avert a fiscal crisis, Governor White called on all state agencies to reduce expenditures, but he had no legal way to back the request. In order to meet the revenue shortfall, the governor had to call a special session of the legislature.

for critical analysis

What are the governor's formal powers? How does the governor exercise these powers?

Military Power The governor is commander in chief of the state's National Guard units when they are not under presidential orders. These units are headed by the adjutant general, who is appointed by the governor. The governor can declare martial law, which suspends most civil authority and imposes military rule over an area. Martial law can be declared in the event of a riot, flood, hurricane, tornado, or other disaster to protect lives and property.

Police Power In Texas, law enforcement and police power are primarily a local responsibility, and the governor has few responsibilities in this area. The governor appoints, with Senate approval, the three-member Public Safety Commission that

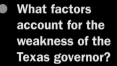

● **What factors
account for the
weakness of the
Texas governor?**

*Deployment of the state's
national guard in times of
emergency is one aspect of the
governor's military power. Here,
Texas National Guard troops
deliver relief supplies after
Hurricane Ike in 2009.*

directs the work of the Department of Public Safety (DPS). The DPS is responsible for highway traffic enforcement (highway patrol), drivers' licensing, motor vehicle inspection, truck weighing stations, and the Texas Rangers. When circumstances warrant, the governor can assume command of the Rangers, an elite, highly trained force of about one hundred officers. If there is evidence of ongoing violence or corruption, the governor can use informal powers, the prestige of the governor's office, and appeals to the media to compel appropriate action from local law enforcement officials.

Legislative Powers of the Governor

The governor's legislative powers include message power, power of the veto, and the authority to call special sessions and set their agendas. If a governor uses these powers effectively, he or she can have considerable control over the state's legislative business, but they do not enhance his or her ability to control the executive branch of state government.

Message Power Any communication between the governor and the legislature is part of the message power. Early in each regular session, the governor delivers a State of the State message. In this speech to a joint session of the legislature, the governor explains his or her plan for the state in the coming two years. The governor may propose specific programs or simply set general goals for the state. The speech is covered by most news media, and it is often broadcast on public television and radio stations.

If the governor submits an executive budget, he or she may address the legislature on the important items in the proposed plan of spending and revenue. At the very least, the budget proposal is forwarded to the legislature with a letter briefly explaining the budget.

Lobbying by governors is part of the message power. Governors try to pass or defeat bills important to them. For example, early in 1991, Governor Ann Richards successfully lobbied for legislation that would expand higher educational opportunities in the Rio Grande Valley and that resulted in the creation of the University of Texas at Brownsville.

Although Governor Bill Clements personally lobbied the legislature, he preferred to use his five full-time paid lobbyists to influence the legislature. Although not exactly part of the governor's message power, the use of lobbyists is an effective way for a governor to communicate with and influence the legislature.

Veto Power Governors of Texas can sign or **veto** legislation—but in most cases they sign legislation. In the 81st Legislature, Governor Perry vetoed 3.5 percent of the 1,658 bills that were passed.

When the governor vetoes a bill after the legislature adjourns, it is called a **post-adjournment** or strong veto. This veto is absolute, since the legislature that passed the vetoed bills no longer exists. As a result, if the governor decides to veto a bill, it stays vetoed.

Texas governors possess the **line-item veto**, which is the ability to veto individual parts of an appropriation bill. The governor signs the bill but strikes out particular lines in the bill. Items struck from the bill do not become law, but the remainder of the appropriations bill does.

In 2007, Governor Perry used the line-item veto to cut $646.5 million from the total state budget. One of his most controversial vetoes was for group insurance contributions for community and junior colleges that came to $153 million. He cut another $36 million in special-item funding for higher education, such as $2 million for obesity research at the Texas Cooperative Extension and $5 million for public health programs at the University of Texas Health Science Center at Houston.[13]

In 2009, Perry exercised the line-item veto to reduce the state's two-year budget by $97.2 million in general revenue and $288.0 from all funding sources.[14]

Special Sessions Special sessions of the Texas legislature are called by the governor, last for no more than thirty days, and may consider only those items placed on the agenda by the governor. **Special sessions** are called to address critical problems that have arisen since the last regular session. The nature of special sessions allows the legislature to focus attention on specific issues.

From 1989 to 2009, the legislature met in eighteen special sessions. These sessions considered the complicated and divisive issues of reform of workers' compensation laws, public school finance, reapportionment, and voter identification. The sessions ranged from thirty days to two days, with six of the sessions occurring in 1989–90 and only four occurring from 2005 to 2009.[15]

Judicial Powers of the Governor

Texas elects each of its state court judges, but when vacancies occur due to the death, resignation, or retirement of the incumbent, or as a result of creation of new courts, the governor is responsible for appointing individuals to fill these vacancies.

Once appointed to office, judges tend to remain in office. More than 95 percent of incumbents win reelection. Through this power to appoint judges, the governor has considerable influence over the Texas judicial system.

Clemency normally includes the power to issue pardons, grant paroles, and issue reprieves. The governor's power in this area is severely limited because of abuses of previous governors. Pardons can be granted only on the recommendation of the Board of Pardons and Paroles. Texas governors can neither grant nor deny paroles. Governors have the ability to grant each person condemned to death one thirty-

veto the governor's power to turn down legislation; can be overridden by a two-thirds vote of both the House and Senate

post-adjournment veto a veto of a bill that occurs after the legislature adjourns, thus preventing the legislature from overriding it

line-item veto the power of the executive to veto specific provisions (lines) of an appropriation bill passed by the legislature

special session a legislative session called by the governor that addresses an agenda set by him or her and that lasts no longer than thirty days

day reprieve. Additional reprieves and any other act of clemency must be recommended by the Board of Pardons and Paroles.

The Office and Its Occupants

People often expect governors to be able to do things they are not equipped to do. They are expected to be chief executives in more than name only despite being granted little in the way of formal power. Constitutionally and statutorily, the governor is ill-equipped to exert control and direction over the Texas bureaucracy.

John Connally was regarded as a strong governor, whereas Dolph Briscoe was regarded as weak. In part, the difference was that Connally actively sought to lead. As governor, he had a dynamic personality, whereas Briscoe was more retiring in his personal style and did not seek to have the impact Connally had. Allan Shivers was an imperial governor, as Richard Nixon was called an imperial president. Preston Smith was described as one of the most ordinary people ever to serve as governor. Smith is seldom given credit for doing anything as governor, yet he established the first actual planning organization in Texas government.

In large part, the office of governor is what the person holding the position makes it. Whether the governor is viewed as strong or weak depends on how the governor conducts himself or herself in office, makes use of the position's formal power, and exercises political influence.

The Plural Executive

When Texans drafted a constitution in 1876, they chose to limit executive power and disperse it through several elected officials called the **plural executive**. Texans elect six of the seven people who make up the plural executive: the governor, lieutenant governor, attorney general, comptroller of public accounts, commissioner of the General Land Office, and commissioner of agriculture (see Table 24.2

plural executive an executive branch in which power is fragmented because the election of statewide officeholders is independent of the election of the governor

TABLE 24.2

State Executive Office Holders, 2010

Governor	Rick Perry (Republican)
Lieutenant Governor	David Dewhurst (Republican)
Attorney General	Greg Abbott (Republican)
Comptroller of Public Accounts	Susan Combs (Republican)
Commissioner of the General Land Office	Jerry Patterson (Republican)
Commissioner of Agriculture	Todd Staples (Republican)
Railroad Commissioners	Michael Williams (Republican) David Porter (Republican) Elizabeth Jones (Republican)
Secretary of State (appointed)	Hope Andrade (Republican)

TABLE 24.3

Elected Officials in Texas with Executive Responsibilities

SINGLE ELECTED EEXCUTIVES	MULTI-ELECTED EXECUTIVES
Governor	Railroad Commission (3 members)
Lieutenant Governor	
Attorney General	
Land Commissioner	State Board of Education (15 members)
Agriculture Commissioner	
Comptroller	

for critical analysis

What are the effects of a plural executive on accountability in state government?

and Table 24.3). The governor appoints the seventh person, the secretary of state. Except for the lieutenant governor, who receives the same salary as a legislator, salaries of members of the plural executive are set by the legislature. Additionally, two major regulatory agencies, the Railroad Commission of Texas and the State Board of Education, are run by officials who are independently elected. The result is vast fragmentation of responsibility for public policy in the state.

Elections are partisan, and each member of the plural executive may choose to operate independently of the others. At times, members of the plural executive may be in competition with each, often due to conflicting personal ambitions. That occurred when John Hill was attorney general and sought to take the governorship from Dolph Briscoe, and when Mark White was attorney general and sought the governorship from Bill Clements. Champions of the plural executive believe that it limits the power of executive officials and makes these officers more accountable to the public. Opponents assert the plural executive is inefficient and does not promote good government. The governor is a member of the plural executive, but this multipart executive limits the governor's control of the executive branch because he or she has little authority over this group.

One can get a sense of the importance of the various positions in the plural executive simply by looking at the campaign contributions received by winning candidates for these offices in the 2010 elections. Table 24.4 shows the contributions received by both the Democratic and the Republican nominees in 2010. Governor Rick Perry, the incumbent Republican, received over $28 million in contributions through November 5, 2010. In contrast, his Democratic opponent, Bill White, received much less. The incumbent Republican lieutenant governor David Dewhurst had over $6 million in contributions, compared with only about $790,000 in contributions for his opponent. The winning candidate for attorney general had over $5 million in contributions, the winning candidate for comptroller over $2 million in contributions even though she had no Democratic opponent. The agriculture commissioner had over $1.2 million, and the land commissioner had over $572,000. Two things are especially notable about these figures. One is the enormous amounts of money that are contributed to candidates for the plural executive offices. The other is how lopsided the contributions are in favor of the Republican candidates. It is a sign of the strength of the Republican Party in Texas statewide elections and the weakness of the Democratic Party that Republican candidates raise so much more money for their campaigns than do Democratic candidates.

Secretary of State

Strangely, given Texas's fragmentation of power, the governor does appoint the Texas **secretary of state**, even though this office is an elective one in thirty-seven states.[16] Though once considered a "glorified keeper of certain state records," the secretary of state is now an important officer.[17] The secretary of state has myriad responsibilities, and the appointment of a secretary of state is one of the governor's most important tasks.

secretary of state state official, appointed by the governor, whose primary responsibility is administering elections

As Texas's chief election official, the secretary of state conducts voter registration drives. His or her office works with organizations such as the League of Women Voters to increase the number of registered voters. The secretary of state's office also collects election-night returns from county judges and county clerks and makes the results available to the media. This service provides media and voters with a convenient method of receiving the latest official election returns in Texas.

All debt and Uniform Commercial Code filings are placed with the secretary of state's office. When any individual borrows money from a financial institution, a copy of the loan agreement is placed in the secretary of state's office.

Lieutenant Governor

The **lieutenant governor** is a member of the plural executive and has executive responsibilities, such as serving as acting governor when the governor is absent from the state or replacing a governor who is unable to perform his or her duties.

lieutenant governor the second-highest elected official in the state and president of the state Senate

---

TABLE 24.4

Campaign Contributions in 2010 and the Plural Executive

OFFICE	LOSING CANDIDATE	CONTRIBUTIONS TO LOSER	WINNING CANDIDATE	CONTRIBUTIONS TO WINNER
Governor	B. White (Dem.)	$21,351,029	R. Perry (Rep.)	$28,305,344
Lieutenant Governor	L. Chavez-Thompson (Dem.)	$789,946	D. Dewhurst (Rep.)	$6,397,416
Attorney General	B. Radnotsky (Dem.)	$1,098,792	G. Abbott (Rep.)	$5,097,018
Comptroller	(No Dem. candidate)	$0	S. Combs (Rep.)	$2,011,900
Agriculture Commissioner	P. Gilbert (Dem.)	$317,616	T. Staples (Rep.)	$1,209,289
Land Commissioner	H. Uribe (Dem.)	$90,050	J. Patterson (Rep.)	$572,705

SOURCE: National Institute on Money in State Politics, (Contributions reported through 11-05-2010).

Republican David Dewhurst was re-elected as lieutenant governor of Texas in 2010. The lieutenant governor's most important powers derive from his or her role in the legislature.

forcritical**analysis**

How does the power of the lieutenant governor differ from that of the governor?

The lieutenant governor also succeeds the governor on resignation from office. The real power of the office, however, is derived from its place in the legislative process.

The Texas constitution names the lieutenant governor as the "Constitutional President of the Senate" and gives him or her the right to debate and vote on all issues when the Senate sits as a "Committee of the Whole." It also grants the lieutenant governor the power to cast a deciding vote in the Senate when there is a tie. Like the Speaker of the House, the lieutenant governor signs all bills and resolutions. The constitution names the lieutenant governor to the Legislative Redistricting Board, a five-member committee that apportions the state into senatorial and House districts if the legislature fails to do so following a census. Other powers of the lieutenant governor are derived from various statutes passed by the legislature. For example, the lieutenant governor is a member of a number of boards and committees, including the Legislative Budget Board (of which he or she is the chair), the Legislative Audit Committee, the Legislative Education Board, the Cash Management Committee, and the Bond Review Board.

The Texas constitution grants the Senate the power to make its own rules, and lieutenant governors traditionally have been granted significant legislative power by the Senate itself. The Senate rules empower the lieutenant governor to decide all parliamentary questions and to use his or her discretion in following Senate procedural rules. The lieutenant governor is also empowered to set up standing and special committees, to appoint committee members and individual chairs of the committees, and to set the order in which bills were considered by the legislature. The Senate rules, and not just the Texas Constitution, make the lieutenant governor one of the most powerful political leaders in the state. New Senate rules passed by a future Senate could, of course, substantially alter the power possessed by the lieutenant governor.

Political Style of Lieutenant Governors Bob Bullock served as lieutenant governor of Texas from 1991 to 1999. A force in Texas politics for over forty years, he was one of the strongest and most effective lieutenant governors Texas politics had ever seen. He took a bluff, rough, tough, head-knocking approach to leadership. He was feared and respected by friends and foes alike.

His successor, Rick Perry, brought a very different style to the office. The first Republican elected lieutenant governor in over one hundred years, Perry had served two terms as Texas Commissioner of Agriculture from 1985 to 1991. Prior to that, he served in the Texas House of Representatives, representing a rural west Texas district as a Democrat. His switch to the Republican Party reflected the broader movement of rural conservatives in the 1980s and 1990s. Expectations for Perry were low when he assumed office. In contrast to Bullock, Perry had a low-key style. But his style was appreciated by senators long under the demanding eye of Bob Bullock. Perry compared himself with a football player following in the footsteps of the Heisman Trophy winner Ricky Williams from the University of Texas. Like a running back imagining himself scoring a touchdown, Perry actually practiced banging a gavel in the empty Senate chamber. Perry's situation was also made more difficult by the fact that then incumbent governor Bush was actively pursuing the presidency, leaving additional jobs and uncertainties on Perry's shoulders.

The House Democrat John Whitmire, whom Perry had removed as chairman of the Senate Criminal Justice Committee, may have offered the best evaluation of Perry's leadership ability when commenting on a newspaper article that claimed Perry had lost control of the Senate during the debate over hate-crime legislation. Whitmire said, "I don't know how in the hell you say he lost control of the Senate. Was it a major difference in the way Bullock would have done it? Yeah. Serious difference. But I think members kind of appreciated the fact he didn't use his position as lieutenant governor to strong-arm members into positions that were contrary to their districts. Do I agree with all his decisions or operations, philosophy? Of course not. Essentially he was a freshman. . . . I'm sure he would be the first to tell you he learned by doing. No one's ever tried to govern us while the governor's been running for president. He had a good session."[18]

When George W. Bush became president and Lieutenant Governor Rick Perry became governor, the Senate elected one of its members to serve as lieutenant governor. That person was Bill Ratliff, a Republican from Mount Pleasant who was chairman of the powerful Senate Finance Committee. Ratliff had been in the Senate since 1989. A civil engineer, Ratliff was a strong believer in bipartisanship and was fascinated by the policy-making process. Known for his candor and moderation, he quickly alienated conservatives in his party when he named the Democratic senator Rodney Ellis of Houston as his replacement as chairman of the Finance Committee. As the presiding officer of the Senate, Ratliff oversaw a legislative session with considerable accomplishments, such as passage of a state-wide teacher health plan and the extension of Medicaid coverage to hundreds of thousands of poor children.

One poll showed Ratliff the leader in a Republican primary for lieutenant governor, and so he announced he would seek the office in the next election. However, one of his opponents was Land Commissioner David Dewhurst, who claimed he would spend tens of millions of dollars of his own money in the race. Ratliff soon ran into trouble with Republican contributors whom he needed in order to counteract Dewhurst's money. Ratliff quickly discovered that his political moderation was not favored by many contributors and, with a love for policy but a distaste for politics, Ratliff concluded he should withdraw and not be a candidate for the office. One of his advisers suggested that Ratliff claim he was dropping out of the race because of a fatal disease. The fatal disease, noted Ratliff, was "independence and moderation."[19]

Dewhurst successfully ran for lieutenant governor in 2002, was re-elected in 2006 and in 2010. As lieutenant governor, Dewhurst is in very different political circumstances from his two Republican predecessors, Perry and Ratliff. Republicans held a majority in the Senate throughout the Dewhurst years. Though Dewhurst pledged to work with state Democrats and appointed some as committee chairmen, partisanship became an increasingly divisive force in the state Senate under Dewhurst.

Attorney General

The **attorney general** (AG) is elected to a four-year term. The AG acts as the chief lawyer for the state of Texas. He or she is, in effect, head of Texas's civil law firm.

The AG's office is concerned primarily with civil matters. When a lawsuit is filed against the state or by the state, the AG manages the legal activities surrounding that lawsuit. Any time a state agency needs legal representation, the AG's office

attorney general elected state official who serves as the state's chief civil lawyer

The General Land Office is influential in large part because it awards oil and gas exploration rights for publicly owned lands. Land Commissioner Jerry Patterson was re-elected in 2010.

land commissioner elected state official who is the manager of most publicly owned lands

represents the agency. In any lawsuit to which Texas is a party, the AG's office has full responsibility to resolve the case and can litigate, compromise, settle, or choose not to pursue the suit.

One of the more important powers of the AG's office comes from the opinion process. Any agency of state or local government can ask the AG's office for an advisory opinion on the legality of an action. The AG's office will rule on the question, and the ruling has the force of law unless overturned by a court or the legislature.

Probably the most controversial and criticized aspect of the work of the office of attorney general is child support collection. Almost one-half of the attorney general's 3,900 employees are involved in collecting child support, and they collect more than $2 billion a year. However, this program is the subject of intense criticism because much child support remains uncollected.

The AG's office has little responsibility in criminal law but may appoint a special prosecutor if a local district attorney asks the AG for assistance. This can happen when there is a conflict of interest with the district attorney. The DA may not want to prosecute one of his local officials if he is a friend of or works with the official under investigation.

Generally, criminal cases in Texas are prosecuted by district or county attorneys elected in each county. The county is usually responsible for the costs of the trial and for all appeals in state court. If a criminal case is appealed to the federal courts, the attorney general's office assumes responsibility.

Commissioner of the General Land Office

The Land Office is the oldest state agency in Texas. Historically the **land commissioner** gave away land. Today, the General Land Office (GLO) is the land manager for most publicly owned lands in Texas. Texas owns or has mineral interest in 20.3 million acres of land in the state, plus all submerged lands up to ten miles into the Gulf of Mexico. The GLO also awards grazing and oil and gas exploration rights on this land. All but 28 of Texas's 254 counties have some of these public lands; however, 8 million acres are located west of the Pecos River, and 4 million acres are found along the Texas coast.

Thousands of producing oil and gas wells are found on state-owned land and are managed by the GLO. A significant portion of royalties on oil and natural gas produced by these wells goes to the Permanent School Fund and the Permanent University Fund.

The commissioner also manages the Veterans' Land Program, through which the state makes low-cost loans to Texas veterans. The program includes loans for land, housing, and home improvements. Recently, the GLO was given authority over some environmental matters. The land commissioner is responsible for environmental quality on public lands and waters, especially along the Texas coast. Submerged lands on the coast of Texas are owned by the state and managed by the Land Office. Additionally, all of Texas's Gulf Coast beaches are publicly owned and under the jurisdiction of the GLO.

The commissioner of the GLO is influential because he or she is the person primarily responsible for awarding the right to explore for and produce oil and natural gas on state-owned land and is responsible for more than 18,000 producing wells.[20]

Commissioner of Agriculture

The **agricultural commissioner** is primarily responsible for enforcing agricultural laws. These include administration of animal quarantine laws, inspection of food, and enforcement of disease- and pest-control programs. Enforcement of the state's laws helps to ensure that Texas's farm products are of high quality and are disease free.

The Department of Agriculture checks weights and measures. Each year a representative of the department checks each motor fuel pump to make sure that it dispenses the correct amount of fuel. Scales used by grocery stores and markets are checked to guarantee that they weigh products correctly.

Farming and ranching are big business in Texas. Although a large number of small family farms exist in the state, large corporate farms increasingly dominate Texas agriculture. These large agribusinesses are greatly affected by the decisions of the commissioner. Such decisions can increase or decrease the cost of production. Changes in production costs affect the profit margins of these agribusinesses and ultimately the price consumers pay for food products.

agricultural commissioner elected state official who is primarily responsible for enforcing agricultural laws

Comptroller of Public Accounts

The **comptroller** is a powerful state official because he or she directs the collection of tax and nontax revenues and issues an evaluation and estimate of anticipated state revenues before each legislative session. Tax collection is the most visible function of the comptroller. The taxes collected by the comptroller include the general sales tax, severance tax on natural resources, motor fuel tax, inheritance tax, most occupational taxes, and many minor taxes.

Although collecting billions in revenue is important, estimating revenues provides the comptroller with more power. These estimates, issued monthly during legislative sessions, are vital to the appropriations process because the legislature is prohibited from spending more than the comptroller estimates will be available. Final passage of any appropriations bill is contingent on the comptroller's certifying that revenues will be available to cover the monies spent in the appropriation. Since most bills require the expenditure of monies, this certification function provides the comptroller with significant power over the legislative process. If the comptroller is unable to certify that monies are available to pay for the appropriation, the legislature must reduce the appropriation or increase revenues. More than just an auditor, accountant, and tax collector, the comptroller is a key figure in the appropriations process.

In 1996, the office of state treasurer was eliminated, and the comptroller of public accounts assumed the duties of that office. Originally the state treasurer and now the comptroller of public accounts is the official custodian of state funds and is responsible for the safety of the state's money and for investing that money.

To ensure the safety of Texas's money, funds are deposited only in financial institutions designated by the State Depository Board as eligible to receive state monies. Deposits are required to earn as much money as possible because not all money earned in this fashion does not have to be made up in tax dollars. The more money earned for Texas, the fewer tax dollars needed.

An interesting responsibility of the comptroller is returning abandoned money and property to its rightful owners. In October of each year, the comptroller publishes a list of individuals with unclaimed property. One list included $117,000

comptroller elected state official who directs the collection of taxes and other revenues

in a forgotten savings account, a certificate of deposit for $104,000, gold coins, diamond rings, family photos, and rare baseball trading cards. Money that remains unclaimed goes to the state.

Accountability of the Plural Executive

Except for the secretary of state, each member of the plural executive is directly accountable to the people of Texas through elections. The plural executive is accountable to the legislature in three ways: the budgetary process, Sunset review, and the impeachment process. The amount of money appropriated to an agency by the legislature can be an indication of the quality of work done by a department. A significant increase in appropriations indicates an agency in good standing with the legislature, whereas little or no increase in funds is an indication of legislative displeasure.

The Texas Constitution, not the legislature, creates most agencies of the plural executive. Therefore, they would not cease to exist under the Sunset process, which will be discussed later. However, the Sunset review allows the legislature to examine the quality and nature of the work of each agency and to seek ways for that agency to serve better the people of Texas. Impeachment and conviction is the ultimate check on an elected official. The Texas House of Representatives can impeach an official for such things as criminal activity or gross malfeasance in office. The Texas Senate then tries the official. If convicted by the Senate, the official is removed from office.

The Plural Executive and the Governor

The plural executive dilutes the ability of the governor to control state government. The governor appoints the secretary of state, but has no control over other members of the plural executive. Officials are elected independently, and they do not run as a slate. They do not answer to the governor, and they do not serve as a cabinet. They tend to operate their offices as independent fiefdoms, and they jealously guard their turf. The plural executive can make state government appear as if it is going in several different directions at once. It is common for members of the plural executive to be political rivals. For example, widely publicized tensions between Governor Rick Perry and Comptroller Carole Strayhorn led to Strayhorn's unsuccessful campaign as an independent against Perry in 2006.

With each member of the plural executive having separate and distinct responsibilities, state government and statewide planning lack cohesiveness. However, the plural executive is a product of Texas's history and environment. Like much of Texas government, it was a result of the public's negative reaction to Governor Edmund J. Davis at the close of Reconstruction.

● Boards, Commissions, and Regulatory Agencies

The state **bureaucracy** in Texas has approximately 200 state boards and commissions as well as major agencies within the plural executive. In addition to the agencies under the direct control of the single executives who are elected by the people and who are part of the plural executive, there are also (1) agencies run

bureaucracy the complex structure of offices, tasks, rules, and principles of organization that are employed by all large-scale institutions to coordinate the work of their personnel

by multimember boards appointed by the governor and confirmed by the Senate; (2) agencies with single executives appointed by the governor and confirmed by the Senate; and (3) agencies run by multimember boards elected by the people.

Governor Perry's lengthy service has given him enormous influence throughout state government, since he is the only Texas governor in modern history to have made every appointment in state government that a governor can make—and he has also made numerous appointments to vacancies in office such as the Texas appellate courts and scores of district judgeships. State law usually sets the terms of persons on state boards at four or six years. As a result, each new governor spends a great deal of time replacing holdover appointments from previous governors. With Perry's lengthy service as governor, however, those holdover appointments are long gone. The result, according to Brian McCall, a former state representative and author of a book on Texas governors, is that "In this regard, he [Perry] is by far the most powerful governor in Texas history. No governor has been able to do what he has done."

Perry has placed many of his closest advisers in key positions, which has spread not only his personal influence but also his personal political philosophy of a pro-business state government. In an effort to compare Perry's influence with previous governors, McCall noted that Governor Preston Smith in 1969 was able to appoint the entire board of regents at Texas Tech by getting an amendment inserted into a minor bill that changed the name of Texas Technological to Texas Tech University. When the name change took effect, the entire board of regents lost their positions and Smith was able to appoint the board. Perry has appointed the entire boards of seventeen public colleges and universities and has had a voice in picking the chancellors of those universities.[21]

Perry has also been willing to discipline board members who have displeased him. For example, he refused to reappoint three members of the Texas Forensic Science Board two days before they were going to examine a flawed arson investigation, and he appointed a new chair of the commission, who abruptly canceled the meeting of the commission.[22] A Texas Tech regent who was a Perry appointee claimed that a former Perry staff member had told him to resign from the Board of Regents because he had endorsed Kay Bailey Hutchison in the Republican primary for governor.[23]

On occasion, Perry's nominees have not been approved by the overwhelmingly Republican state senate, so he has not had a completely free pass in making his appointments. His nominee for the Board of Pardons and Paroles, best-known for her political activism and opposition to sex-toy parties in the Burleson, Texas area, was turned down by the senate with an overwhelming 27–4 vote against her confirmation. State Senator John Whitmire, a Democrat and the chair of the Senate Criminal Justice Committee, argued that she was turned down not because the issue was a partisan one but simply because she was not qualified for a position that considers "life and death matters."[24]

Multimember Appointed Boards

Most boards and commissions in Texas are headed by members appointed by the governor and confirmed by the Senate. Multimember commissions with heads appointed by the governor include innocuous agencies, such as the Bandera County River Authority, the State Seed and Plant Board, the Caddo Lake Compact Commission, and the Texas Funeral Commission. There are also better-known agencies, such as the Texas Alcoholic Beverage Commission, the Department of Parks and

Regulatory commissions, such as the Public Utility Commission or Texas Alcoholic Beverage Commission, have a big impact on the lives of all Texans. The TABC, for example, protects against underage drinking and driving through its education program. This photo shows a "Shattered Dreams" presentation at Pharr High School. The presentation includes the dramatization of an alcohol-related crash.

Wildlife, the Texas Youth Commission, and the Texas Department of Corrections. Except in the case of a major controversy such as the sexual abuse scandal that embroiled the Texas Youth Commission in 2007, these agencies work in anonymity, although several of them have a direct effect on the lives of Texans. One such example is the Public Utilities Commission.

Public Utilities Commission (PUC) More than any other agency, the PUC has a direct effect on consumers' pocketbooks. Before 1975, cities in Texas set utility rates. The Public Utilities Commission was established in 1975, in part, to protect consumers and to curb the rate at which utility costs were increasing. The commission is responsible for setting local telephone and some electric rates.

The PUC sets all local telephone rates. Rates vary from one part of Texas to another, but all rates in a service area are the same. The commission also determines the maximum charge for pay telephones and approves additional services such as caller ID, call waiting, and call forwarding. A rule that took effect in September 1999 prohibits an individual's local service from being disconnected for nonpayment of long-distance bills. Another regulation established by the PUC requires all calls to information to be answered by a person, not a recording with a menu. The personal touch is not yet a complete casualty of the computer age.

With the introduction of retail competition to the electric industry, the PUC has had a major role in providing information to consumers and in setting requirements for providers of electric services.

Appointed Single Executives

The Texas Department of Insurance Whereas the Public Utilities Commission is run by a multimember body appointed by the governor and confirmed by the Texas Senate, the Texas Department of Insurance is run by one commissioner appointed by the governor for a two-year term and confirmed by the Senate. This single-member appointive system has been in effect since 1993, when governance of the agency by a three-member appointed board was abandoned in favor of single-member governance. The purpose of the Department of Insurance is to regulate the insurance market in Texas, a complicated task that affects most Texans.[25]

In the early 2000s Texas was faced with huge increases in the cost of homeowners' insurance brought on at least in part by major increases in insurance claims, most notably for mold damage. From the first quarter of 2000 to the fourth quarter of 2001, the number of mold claims increased from 1,050 to 14,706. Additionally, the costs of these claims increased significantly to the point that insurance payments became greater than insurance premiums. And with a declining economy during this period, insurance companies were no longer making substantial profits on their investment of insurance premiums. Homeowner premiums increased rapidly. Between 2001 and 2002, homeowners' premiums rose 21.8 percent. Some companies chose not to write any new homeowners' policies; other companies simply pulled out of the Texas market. In 1997, 166 companies were writing homeowners' policies in Texas; by 2003, only 101 companies were writing policies.

In response, the Texas Department of Insurance began to deregulate insurance coverage so that, for example, policies could be written that charged more for mold coverage, less for reduced mold coverage, and significantly less for no mold coverage.

The legislature also stepped into the homeowners' insurance cost issue, which by 2002–03 was reaching crisis proportions. One effect of the legislature's involvement was a "file and use" regulatory system that was implemented at the end of 2004. This system allowed insurers to institute new rates immediately after filing them with the Texas Department of Insurance. The commissioner of insurance can then disapprove of the new rates and may force the company to issue rebates to policyholders.[26] Thus, the commissioner of insurance appears to wield great power over insurance rates but only after those rates have gone into effect.

In 2007, Insurance Commissioner Mike Geeslin canceled Allstate's 5.9 percent rate hike, but Allstate got a court order allowing it to keep charging higher rates, at least temporarily. State Farm has been battling the Department of Insurance for years after ignoring an order from the commissioner to cut its rates by 12 percent.

State Farm's battle with the Texas Insurance Commission has taken on the characteristics of a marathon. The company has shown no sign of compromising with the state in its legal battle over the state's claim that it overcharged homeowners. Additionally, in 2009–10 it twice filed to increase its insurance rates and ignored the Insurance Commissioner's claim that customers deserved a break from increases. It has also successfully sued the Texas Department of Insurance to keep the agency from publicizing documents related to its rate increases.[27]

Although insurance companies advocate less regulation, consumer groups argue that the insurance commissioner has inadequate powers to deal with insurance companies. Additionally, while these battles are going on with Allstate and State Farm, insurance companies have been reducing coverage of homes on the Texas coast out of fear that a hurricane could cause them major losses.[28]

Although the insurance commissioner is a single appointed official who has regulatory power over the insurance industry in Texas, it is doubtful that he has sufficient power to force an uncooperative insurer to comply with his decisions. The commissioner is also faced with a seemingly intractable problem of keeping rates low and coverage available in hurricane-prone areas to which more and more people are moving.

Multimember Elected Boards

Members of two state agencies are elected by the voters: the Railroad Commission of Texas (RRC) and the State Board of Education (SBOE). The RRC has three members elected statewide to six-year terms of office. One of the three members is elected every two years. The SBOE is a fifteen-member board elected to four-year terms from single-member districts.

Railroad Commission of Texas (RRC) At one time, the Railroad Commission was one of the most powerful state agencies in the nation. It regulated intrastate railroads, trucks, and bus transportation, and supervised the oil and natural gas industry in Texas. For most of its life, regulation of the oil and gas industry was the primary focus of the RRC.

Today, the RRC is a shadow of its former self. Court decisions, deregulation of the transportation industry, other state and federal legislation, and the decline in the nation's dependence on Texas's crude oil production have diminished the power of the commission. In 2005 its limited authority over railroads was transferred to the Texas Department of Transportation, so it now has no authority over what was once its major reason for existence. The railroad commission's heyday was when Texas was a major oil producer. During that time it limited oil production to conserve oil and to maintain prices. Because it restricted oil production, the commission was one of the most economically significant governmental bodies on the national and international stage. As oil production shifted to the Middle East, the RRC became the model for OPEC, the Organization of Petroleum Exporting Countries, which also seeks to limit oil production to maintain prices. At one time, members of the Texas Railroad Commission wielded such vast economic power that they were among the state's most influential politicians. As the power of the office has been weakened through declining oil production and decreasing dependence on Texas oil, it has become increasingly difficult for railroad commissioners to move into higher offices, and their political visibility has waned.

State Board of Education (SBOE) Policy for public education (pre-kindergarten to twelfth grade programs supported by the state government) in Texas is set by the SBOE. The education bureaucracy under the SBOE is called the Texas Education Agency (TEA). It enforces rules and regulations affecting pre-kindergarten through twelfth grade in Texas. Together these two bodies control public education in Texas by determining licensing requirements for public school teachers, setting minimum high school graduation criteria for recommended or advanced curriculum, establishing standards for accreditation of public schools, and adopting public school textbooks.

Texas spends millions of dollars each year purchasing textbooks, and the state furnishes these books without charge to students. Books must meet stringent criteria, and because the state buys so many textbooks, publishers print books especially for students in Texas. Often states that spend less money on textbooks than Texas does must purchase those originally printed for Texas.

The commissioner of education is appointed by the governor from a list of candidates submitted by the SBOE. He or she is administrative head of the TEA and serves as adviser to the State Board of Education. The commissioner of education is at the apex of the public education bureaucracy in Texas.

● What roles are
played by boards,
commissions,
and regulatory
agencies in state
government?

In 2010, the Texas State Board of Education made national headlines when it proposed controversial changes in the guidelines for American history courses taught in Texas public schools.

In recent years, the Texas State Board of Education has become an ideological battleground. In 2009, that conflict led the board to review how evolution was taught. In what was a partial defeat for the social conservatives, no longer would teachers be required to teach "strengths and weaknesses" of evolution, although they would be encouraged to teach "all sides." Other battles have broken out over other aspects of educational policy. For example, one policy goal was that high school students were to learn how the cultural contributions of "people from various racial, ethnic, gender, and religious groups shape American culture." One amendment from the one of the leading social conservatives on the board proposed that the words "from various racial, ethnic, gender, and religious groups" be deleted. That suggested, of course, that teaching would not focus on the role of those specific groups in shaping American culture. Another amendment proposed that students be required to evaluate the contributions of significant Americans— Thurgood Marshall, Billy Graham, Newt Gingrich, William F. Buckley, Jr., Hillary Rodham Clinton, and Edward Kennedy. All passed the board except for Edward Kennedy. Other issues involve whether César Chávez is significant enough to be in social studies textbooks and whether greater emphasis should be placed on Christianity in the founding of the nation. The battles fought within the board are not well known to many Texas voters, but they are important not only because they affect how Texas school children are educated but also because the textbook market is so large in Texas that the content of the textbooks used in the state sets the tone for textbook content in other states that are less populous and therefore have smaller markets for texts.[29]

Making Agencies Accountable

In a democracy, elected officials are ultimately responsible to the voters. Appointed officials are indirectly accountable to the people through the elected officials who appointed them. Both are responsible to legislatures that determine responsibilities and appropriate money to carry out those responsibilities. In Texas, the plural executive is responsible to the legislature for its biennial funding and to the voters

Sunset Advisory Commission (SAC) a commission created in 1975 for the purpose of reviewing the effectiveness of state agencies

for re-election. The myriad state agencies look to the legislature for funding, and once each twelve years they must justify their existence to the **Sunset Advisory Commission** (SAC).

The twelve-member Sunset Advisory Commission has five members from the Texas Senate and one public member appointed by the lieutenant governor. Five members from the Texas House and one public member are appointed by the Speaker of the Texas House.

The Sunset Review Act created the Sunset Advisory Commission in 1977. It establishes specific criteria to be considered in evaluating the continuing need for an agency. One of several laws enacted in the mid-1970s to bring more openness and accountability to Texas government, the Sunset process establishes a date on which an agency is abolished unless the legislature passes a bill for the agency to continue in operation.

During its Sunset review, an agency must, among other things, document its efficiency, the extent to which it meets legislative mandates, and its promptness and effectiveness in handling complaints, and it must establish the continuing need for its services. The review process is lengthy, lasting almost two years.

After a thorough study of an agency, the SAC recommends one of three actions to the legislature: (1) the agency continues as is, with no change in its organization or functions; (2) the agency continues but with changes (reorganization, a new focus for the agency, or merger with other agencies); or (3) the agency is abolished.

If option 1 or 2 is recommended, specific action by the legislature is required before the date of the agency's abolition. Option 1 requires specific legislation to re-create the agency in its existing form. The second option requires the legislature to re-create the agency with some or all of the changes recommended by the SAC. If the legislature agrees the agency should be abolished, no action is necessary. It will die at the Sunset deadline; the sun sets and the agency is no more.

Each state agency has been through the Sunset process. The legislature has allowed the sun to set on more than fifty-eight agencies; twelve agencies have been merged with existing bodies. Since 1977, the legislature has accepted the majority of recommendations of the Sunset Commission.

for critical analysis

What is the source of power of Texas bureaucratic agencies? How are these agencies held accountable to other elected public officials or the public?

● Conclusion: Democracy and the Executive in Texas

At the national level, the president is elected, through the Electoral College, by the people as a whole. The president is the spokesperson for the nation in the world and is the commander in chief of the armed forces. When there is a national crisis, the people look to the president for leadership. As we saw in Chapter 13, throughout the twentieth century, the power and authority of the presidency increased significantly, often at the expense of Congress. American democracy has become an executive-led system, with a weak Congress and a partially demobilized electorate.

Such is not the case in Texas. The fear of a strong executive who could ignore the wishes of either the legislature or the people, as was the case during Reconstruction in Texas, led in 1876 to a constitution that created a plural executive. The governor is the chief executive officer in the state, elected directly by the popular vote of all the people of Texas. People turn to the governor for leadership and direction during times of crisis. But compared with that of the president, the power of the Texas governor is seriously circumscribed. Many key executive officials, including the lieutenant governor, the attorney general, the comptroller, and the land commissioner, are elected—like the governor—directly by the people. These members of the plural executive, along with other popularly elected statewide boards and commissions, possess power and authority that under other constitutional arrangements the governor might possess. In some arenas of power, such as the state legislature, the governor might be considered one of the weakest members of the executive branch.

The existence of a weak governor and a plural executive has a number of important implications for democracy in Texas. First, because power and authority are divided among a number of distinct officers, no one individual is fully responsible for executive initiatives in the state. Indeed, executive officials can struggle for power as they seek to move the state government in different directions. Partisanship can exacerbate the natural conflict built into the executive branch in Texas. A Democratic lieutenant governor may or may not be willing to work closely with a Republican governor. But the worst clashes may be among executive officials of the same party. The fight between Governor Rick Perry and Comptroller Caroline Strayhorn, both Republicans, culminating in Strayhorn's running against the incumbent governor as an independent in 2006, is only the latest example of a fundamental truth in Texas politics: the executive does not have to speak with one voice or in harmony with itself.

A second consequence of the plural executive for democracy in Texas is that it has given rise to a powerful executive officer in the state legislature, outside the office of the governor. The lieutenant governor has become, along with the Speaker of the House, one of the two most important officials in the state legislature. The lieutenant governor, not the governor, runs the Senate. The lieutenant governor, not the governor, is the executive branch's chief legislative official.

The dispersal of power and authority among a number of different executive offices in the state has a third consequence for democracy in the state. Additional points of access are created for interest groups seeking to influence government and public policy, making it easier for special interests to impose their will on the policy-making process. The 2010 elections have solidified the Republican Party's firm hold over the plural executive and will have major consequences for policy and politics in Texas.

> ● **What roles are played by boards, commissions, and regulatory agencies in state government?**

The governor's powers are checked by those of the legislature. In 2006, Governor Perry issued an executive order to deliver HPV vaccines to sixth grade girls, but the legislature passed a bill blocking officials from following Perry's order.

studyguide

Practice Quiz

 Find a diagnostic Web Quiz with 20 additional questions on the StudySpace Web site: www.wwnorton.com/we-the-people

1. Which of the following is *not* a qualification to become governor of Texas? *(p. 865)*
   a) A candidate must be thirty years of age.
   b) A candidate must have lived in Texas for five years.
   c) A candidate must be a U.S. citizen.
   d) A candidate must be literate.

2. The election for governor of Texas is held in an off-year in order to *(p. 867)*
   a) increase voter participation in elections in odd-numbered years.
   b) influence the presidential vote in Texas.
   c) prevent the presidential vote in Texas from influencing the election of state officials.
   d) decrease the likelihood of voter fraud.

3. The only constitutional method of removing the governor is *(p. 868)*
   a) *quo warranto* proceedings.
   b) *ex post facto* removal.
   c) impeachment.
   d) impeachment and conviction.

4. The governor's most effective power in controlling the executive branch of state government is the power *(p. 871)*
   a) of appointment.
   b) of removal.
   c) of judicial review.
   d) to create a state budget.

5. The governor's veto is absolute when it is a *(p. 874)*
   a) line-item veto.
   b) special veto.
   c) post-adjournment veto.
   d) select veto.

6. The governor can grant *(p. 874)*
   a) pardons.
   b) suspended sentences.
   c) probation.
   d) parole.

7. Which member of the plural executive is appointed? *(p. 875)*
   a) secretary of state
   b) lieutenant governor
   c) comptroller of public accounts
   d) attorney general

8. Members of the plural executive are accountable to the *(p. 875)*
   a) voters and the governor.
   b) legislature.
   c) legislature and voters.
   d) constitution.

9. The attorney general is *(p. 879)*
   a) part of the governor's Cabinet.
   b) the governor's lawyer.
   c) elected independently of the governor.
   d) chosen by the State Bar of Texas.

10. The Commissioner of the General Land Office *(p. 880)*
    a) heads the oldest state agency in Texas.
    b) is the land manager for most publicly owned land in Texas.
    c) manages the Veterans' Land Program.
    d) all of the above

11. Which agency investigates the performance of state agencies and recommends whether an agency should be abolished, continued as is, or continued with changes? *(p. 882)*
    a) Legislative Budget Board
    b) Legislative Research Bureau
    c) Texas Research League
    d) Sunset Advisory Commission

12. The Railroad Commission of Texas *(p. 886)*
    a) is responsible for the safety of the state's railroads.
    b) issues bonds to support the state's transportation needs.
    c) regulates oil and gas production in Texas.
    d) approves mergers of railroads.

13. The State Board of Education *(p. 886)*
    a) has a major role in determining the books used in Texas public schools.
    b) is appointed by the legislature.
    c) is responsible for school property tax rates.
    d) governs local boards of education.

14. Who runs Texas state government? *(p. 889)*
    a) the governor alone
    b) the governor and the plural executive
    c) the executive directors of various state agencies
    d) numerous elected and appointed officials

15. The lieutenant governor of Texas *(p. 889)*
    a) has a major role in both the executive and legislative branches.
    b) serves as governor in the event of the governor's death or resignation.
    c) serves as governor when the governor is out of the state.
    d) all of the above

Chapter Outline

Find a detailed Chapter Outline on the StudySpace Web site: www.wwnorton.com/we-the-people

Key Terms

Find Flashcards to help you study these terms on the StudySpace Web site: www.wwnorton.com/we-the-people

agricultural commissioner *(p. 881)*
appointment *(p. 871)*
attorney general *(p. 879)*
bureaucracy *(p. 882)*
comptroller *(p. 881)*
executive budget *(p. 872)*
impeachment *(p. 868)*

land commissioner *(p. 880)*
legislative budget *(p. 872)*
lieutenant governor *(p. 877)*
line-item veto *(p. 874)*
patronage *(p. 871)*
plural executive *(p. 875)*
post-adjournment veto *(p. 874)*

secretary of state *(p. 877)*
senatorial courtesy *(p. 872)*
special session *(p. 874)*
Sunset Advisory Commission (SAC)
   (p. 888)
veto *(p. 874)*

Recommended Web Sites

Attorney General of Texas
www.oag.state.tx.us/

Lieutenant Governor of Texas
www.ltgov.state.tx.us/

Office of the Governor
www.governor.state.tx.us/

Railroad Commission of Texas
www.rrc.state.tx.us/

Sunset Advisory Commission
www.sunset.state.tx.us/

Texas Department of Agriculture
www.agr.state.tx.us/

Texas General Land Office
www.glo.state.tx.us/

Texas Secretary of State
www.sos.state.tx.us/

Window on State Government (Comptroller's Office)
www.window.state.tx.us/

Some opponents of the death penalty argue that Texas's system of electing judges and prosecutors leads to more executions, as elected officials try to show voters that they are tough on crime. Texas executes more people than any other state.

The Texas Judiciary

WHAT GOVERNMENT DOES AND WHY IT MATTERS The presiding judge of the Texas Court of Criminal Appeals, Sharon Keller, has cultivated a "tough on crime" image. Her campaign literature, for example, has shown a figure behind bars with the headline, "He won't be voting for Judge Sharon Keller."

However, Keller may have crossed the line in terms of her harshness toward criminal defendants on September 25, 2007. That evening, Michael Richard was scheduled to die by lethal injection. Earlier that day, the Supreme Court of the United States had agreed to hear a challenge to the constitutionality of death by lethal injection. Ordinarily, that would lead to a petition to the Court of Criminal Appeals for a stay of execution, in order to wait for the decision of the U.S. Supreme Court.

Things went terribly wrong. The lawyers for Michael Richard were working against a tight deadline for their petition and they claimed they experienced computer problems that created a delay in preparing their documents. They called the Court of Criminal Appeals and asked that the Court stay open an extra twenty minutes so that the stay of execution request could be filed. Judge Keller refused to keep the Court open. In making this decision, she did not consult with other judges on the court, some of whom were working in the same building. Other judges on the court have stated that they would have stayed late to hear

focusquestions

- How is the Texas court system organized?

- What are the major differences between criminal and civil law?

- Does the process for selecting judges in Texas successfully hold judges accountable for their actions?

- How do courts in Texas have an important impact on the lives of all Texans?

the appeal if they had known about it. Michael Richard was executed that evening.

Complaints were filed against Judge Keller with the State Commission on Judicial Conduct. The hearing officer, known as a special master, found plenty of blame to go around in this case. He found that the Texas Defender Service, which provided legal representation for Michael Richard, was unable to show that it actually had computer problems that made it unable to file the claim on time. In fact, Texas Defender Service did not even contemplate filing a lethal injection claim until over two hours after the Supreme Court had agreed to hear a lethal injection case, and then it assigned a junior attorney to prepare documents, the first of which was not ready until 4:45 P.M. and all of which were not completed until 5:56 P.M. that day. Nor did the Court of Criminal Appeals escape criticism. And though Judge Keller's behavior did not, according to the special master, justify removal from office or reprimand, it "was not exemplary of a public servant." He stated, "Although [Judge Keller] says that if she could do it all over again she would not change any of her actions, this cannot be true. Any reasonable person, having gone through this ordeal, surely would realize that open communication, particularly during the hectic few hours before an execution, would benefit the interests of justice. Further, her judgment in not keeping the clerk's office open past 5:00 to allow the TDS to file was highly questionable. In sum, there is a valid reason why many in the legal community are not proud of Judge Keller's actions."[1] Interestingly, in the fall of 2010, a special court of review dismissed the public warning against Keller on the grounds that a warning cannot be a penalty following a formal proceeding against a judge.

This episode highlights some notable characteristics of the Texas judiciary: (1) Texas judges are elected, which encourages judges and judicial candidates to behave in ways that may cultivate the favor of voters even as the judges seem to sidestep notions of justice; and (2) one reason that Texas is the death penalty capital of the nation may be that it has a partisan election system for selecting not only judges but also the district attorneys, who prosecute crimes.

chaptercontents

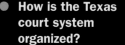

● Court Structure

Like the federal courts, the state and local courts in Texas are responsible for securing liberty and equality under the law. However, the democratic mechanisms put into place in Texas to select judges and to hold them accountable for their actions are quite different from those at the national level. Federal judges are appointed by the president and confirmed by the Senate. They have lifetime appointments. This means that federal judges, subject to good behavior in office, are free from the ebb and flow of democratic politics. They do not have to cater to public opinion and are empowered to interpret the law as they see fit, without fear of reprisal at the polls. In Texas, however, judges are elected to office. Although they may initially be appointed to their offices, sooner or later they are responsible to the people for their decisions in office. Election of judges brings not only the people but also interest groups into the selection and retention of judges. The influence of special interest money in judicial campaigns raises important questions about the relationship between the rule of law and the nature of democratic politics.

Texas has a large and complex court structure consisting of a hodgepodge of courts with overlapping jurisdiction (see Figure 25.1). Additionally, some courts have specialized jurisdiction, whereas others have broad authority to handle a variety of cases. At the highest level for civil cases is the **Texas Supreme Court**, which consists of nine justices, including a chief justice. This court hears civil cases only. The only requirements for being a Texas Supreme Court justice are that one must be a citizen of the United States and a resident of Texas, be at least thirty-five years of age, and have been either a practicing lawyer or judge for at least ten years. The term of a justice is six years, with at least three justices being elected every two years.

The **Texas Court of Criminal Appeals** is the highest court in the state for criminal cases. This court also has nine judges, including a presiding judge. The pay, terms, and qualifications of Court of Criminal Appeals judges are the same as for the Texas Supreme Court. Perhaps the most important task of the Court of Criminal Appeals is its jurisdiction over automatic appeals in death penalty cases.

Texas Supreme Court the highest civil court in Texas; consists of nine justices and has final state appellate authority over civil cases

Texas Court of Criminal Appeals the highest criminal court in Texas; consists of nine justices and has final state appellate authority over criminal cases

Texas has two supreme courts: The Texas Supreme Court (whose justices are shown here) is the highest civil court in Texas, while the Texas Court of Criminal Appeals is the highest court in the state for criminal cases.

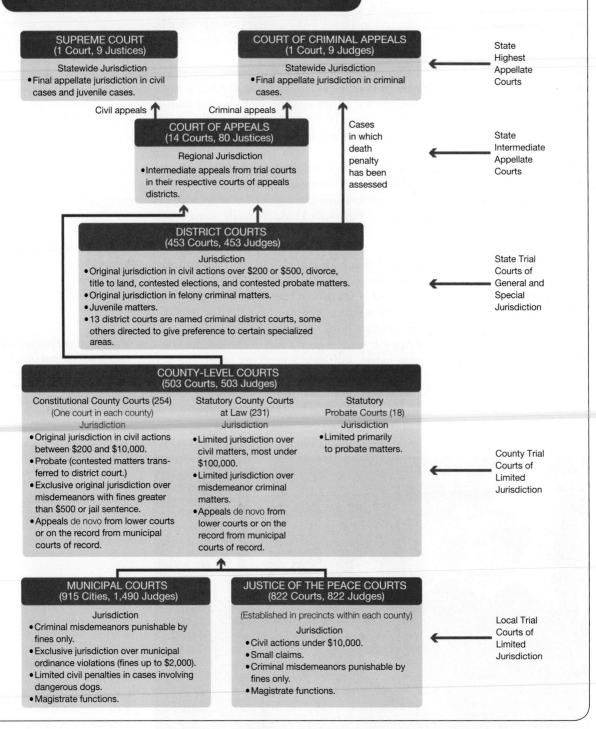

FIGURE 25.1
The Structure of the Texas Court System

SOURCE: Texas Office of Court Administration.

SUPREME COURT
(1 Court, 9 Justices)

Statewide Jurisdiction
• Final appellate jurisdiction in civil cases and juvenile cases.

COURT OF CRIMINAL APPEALS
(1 Court, 9 Judges)

Statewide Jurisdiction
• Final appellate jurisdiction in criminal cases.

State Highest Appellate Courts

Civil appeals   Criminal appeals

COURT OF APPEALS
(14 Courts, 80 Justices)

Regional Jurisdiction
• Intermediate appeals from trial courts in their respective courts of appeals districts.

Cases in which death penalty has been assessed

State Intermediate Appellate Courts

DISTRICT COURTS
(453 Courts, 453 Judges)

Jurisdiction
• Original jurisdiction in civil actions over $200 or $500, divorce, title to land, contested elections, and contested probate matters.
• Original jurisdiction in felony criminal matters.
• Juvenile matters.
• 13 district courts are named criminal district courts, some others directed to give preference to certain specialized areas.

State Trial Courts of General and Special Jurisdiction

COUNTY-LEVEL COURTS
(503 Courts, 503 Judges)

Constitutional County Courts (254) (One court in each county) Jurisdiction	Statutory County Courts at Law (231) Jurisdiction	Statutory Probate Courts (18) Jurisdiction
• Original jurisdiction in civil actions between $200 and $10,000. • Probate (contested matters transferred to district court.) • Exclusive original jurisdiction over misdemeanors with fines greater than $500 or jail sentence. • Appeals de novo from lower courts or on the record from municipal courts of record.	• Limited jurisdiction over civil matters, most under $100,000. • Limited jurisdiction over misdemeanor criminal matters. • Appeals de novo from lower courts or on the record from municipal courts of record.	• Limited primarily to probate matters.

County Trial Courts of Limited Jurisdiction

MUNICIPAL COURTS
(915 Cities, 1,490 Judges)

Jurisdiction
• Criminal misdemeanors punishable by fines only.
• Exclusive jurisdiction over municipal ordinance violations (fines up to $2,000).
• Limited civil penalties in cases involving dangerous dogs.
• Magistrate functions.

JUSTICE OF THE PEACE COURTS
(822 Courts, 822 Judges)

(Established in precincts within each county)
Jurisdiction
• Civil actions under $10,000.
• Small claims.
• Criminal misdemeanors punishable by fines only.
• Magistrate functions.

Local Trial Courts of Limited Jurisdiction

Both the Supreme Court and the Court of Criminal Appeals have appellate jurisdiction. This means that they have the authority to review the decisions of lower courts to determine whether legal principles and court procedures were followed correctly. This authority also provides the power to order that a case be retried if mistakes were made. Texas has fourteen other appellate courts, located in various parts of the state, which have both criminal and civil jurisdiction. These courts are intermediate appellate courts and hear appeals from the trial courts. Usually, before the Supreme Court or the Court of Criminal Appeals hears a case, the initial appeal has been heard by one of the **courts of appeal**. Presently, there are eighty judges who serve on the fourteen courts of appeal, which range in size from three to thirteen judges. Although there are occasions when every judge on a court of appeal will hear a case, mostly appeals at this level are heard by panels of three judges. The requirements for a court of appeals justice are the same as those for justices of the higher courts. Each of the fourteen courts has one chief justice.

The major trial courts in Texas are the **district courts**. Each county has at least one district court, although rural parts of Texas may have several counties that are served by one district court. Three hundred fifty-six districts are in one county; ninety-seven are in more than one county. In contrast, urban counties have many district courts. Harris County (Houston), for example, has sixty district courts. District courts usually have general jurisdiction, meaning that they hear a broad range of civil and criminal cases. However, in urban counties, some district courts with specialized jurisdiction hear only civil, criminal, juvenile, or family law matters. Those district courts having general jurisdiction would hear felonies, divorces, land disputes, election contests, and civil lawsuits. Currently, there are 453 district judges, nine State Supreme Court judges, nine court of criminal appeals judges, and eighty court of appeals judges.

Texas is unusual in having the office of **county judge** in each of its 254 counties. Not only does the county judge preside over the county commissioners court and thus have responsibilities for administration of county government, but the county judge also presides over the county court. Often these **county courts** have jurisdiction over probate cases and over the more serious misdemeanor criminal offenses as well as over civil cases where the amounts in dispute are relatively small. The county court may also hear appeals from municipal courts or from justice of the peace courts. Thus, the county judge combines political-administrative functions with some judicial functions. However, in the more populated counties, there are county courts at law and sometimes probate courts. As a result, in the larger counties most, and sometimes all, of the county judges' judicial duties are now performed by other courts.

In larger counties, there are **statutory county courts at law**. Since the county courts at law were created by statute, often at widely different times, the jurisdiction of these courts varies significantly. Usually, the county courts at law hear appeals from justices of the peace and from municipal courts. In civil cases, they usually hear cases involving sums greater than would be heard by a justice of the peace court, but less than would be heard by district courts. In comparison to the district courts, the county courts at law would hear less serious criminal offenses.

Some of the county courts at law have specialized jurisdiction; most commonly these are in the most urban counties, where some of the courts will have only civil jurisdiction and others only criminal jurisdiction. Currently there are 231 county court at law judges.

In the most urban areas of the state, the legislature has created courts known as **statutory probate courts**. These courts are highly specialized, as their primary

courts of appeal the fourteen intermediate-level appellate courts that hear appeals from district and county courts to determine whether the decisions of these lower courts followed legal principles and court procedures

district courts the major trial courts in Texas, which usually have general jurisdiction over a broad range of civil and criminal cases

county judge the person in each of Texas's 254 counties who presides over the county court and the county commissioners court, with responsibility for the administration of county government; some county judges carry out judicial responsibilities

county courts the courts that exist in some counties that are presided over by county judges

statutory county courts at law courts that tend to hear less serious cases than those heard by district courts

statutory probate courts specialized courts whose jurisdiction is limited to probate and guardianship matters

activity involves probate matters that relate to the disposition of property of deceased persons. They may also deal with matters relating to guardianship of people unable to handle their own affairs, and they may handle mental-health commitments. In other parts of the state, depending on the statute, probate matters may be heard by the county court, the county court at law, or the district court. Currently, there are eighteen statutory probate court judges.

Each county in Texas has between one and eight justice of the peace precincts, depending on population, although large urban counties have more than one justice in each precinct. Harris County, for example, has two in each of eight precincts. Within each precinct are **justice of the peace courts**. There are 822 justice of the peace courts in Texas. These courts hear class C misdemeanors, which are less serious crimes. They also have jurisdiction over minor civil matters, and they function as small claims courts. Justices may issue search and arrest warrants. In counties without medical examiners, justices may fulfill the administrative functions of coroners.

Justices of the peace mostly handle traffic misdemeanors. Of the more than 3 million criminal cases disposed of by justice of the peace courts in the year ending August 31, 2009, nearly 2.1 million were traffic misdemeanors. In contrast, justice of the peace courts heard only about 379,000 civil cases.[2]

Justices of the peace have faced considerable criticism in recent years. In Dallas County, an auditor discovered 22,000 unprocessed traffic cases. The justice of the peace had failed to collect as much as $2 million in fines. Unlike any other judge in Texas except for the county judge (who is often an administrator rather than a judge), 93 percent of the 822 justices of the peace in Texas are non-lawyers, and the lack of justices' legal credentials has led to considerable debate in the state.[3] The office has its origins in medieval England and has existed in Texas since 1837, even before statehood. In the days of the frontier, justices of the peace provided legal authority where no other existed. Indeed, the famed Judge Roy Bean was a justice of the peace. The initial idea was that a justice of the peace would be a respected person in the community who was chosen for ability, judgment, and integrity. Today, as the former State Bar president Frank Newton has pointed out, "In almost every

justice of the peace courts
local trial courts with limited jurisdiction over small claims and very minor criminal misdemeanors

The boxes of evidence that the State of Texas prepared for the trial against tobacco companies in 1997 occupied an entire gym in Texarkana. In a civil case, the plaintiff bears the burden of proof and must demonstrate that the defendant is more than likely responsible for the harm suffered by the plaintiff.

large metropolitan area, there are some JPs who do virtually nothing and sort of get lost in the shuffle. People don't tend to get all excited about JP elections. Most people don't know what a JP does. JP is not a very prestigious job."[4]

Municipal courts have been created by the legislature in each of the incorporated cities of the state. There are 915 cities and towns in Texas that have these courts; larger cities have multiple courts. There are 1,490 municipal courts in the state. Municipal courts have jurisdiction over violations of city **ordinances** and, concurrent with justice of the peace courts, have jurisdiction over class C misdemeanors, for which the punishment for conviction is a fine. Municipal judges may issue search and arrest warrants, but they have only limited civil jurisdiction.[5] Municipal courts, like justice of the peace courts, function primarily as traffic courts. In the year ending August 31, 2009, municipal courts disposed of almost 7 million cases. About 5.1 million of these cases were non-parking traffic misdemeanors; another 783,704 were parking cases.[6]

● What are the major differences between criminal and civil law?

municipal courts local trial courts with limited jurisdiction over violations of city ordinances and very minor criminal misdemeanors; municipal courts are located in each of Texas's incorporated cities and towns

ordinance a regulation enacted by a city government

● The Legal Process

Just as the Texas Supreme Court hears civil cases and the Texas Court of Criminal Appeals hears criminal cases, it is useful to think of the law as divided into these parts. **Civil law** involves a dispute, usually between private individuals over relationships, obligations, and responsibility. Though there are exceptions with a violation of the civil law, the remedy is often for the offending party to pay compensation to the injured party.

In contrast, **criminal law** involves the violation of concepts of right and wrong as defined by criminal statutes. In criminal law, the state accuses individuals of violations and, if found guilty, the violator is subject to punishment. In some cases, that punishment may involve loss of liberty or even loss of life.

In civil law, an aggrieved person will usually obtain a lawyer and file a petition that details the **complaint** against the person accused of causing the harm. The petition is filed with the clerk of court, who issues a citation against the defendant. The defendant will usually file an **answer** explaining why the allegations are not valid. Depending on the issue, the amounts of money that may be awarded as damages, and the probability of success, the aggrieved person may be able to obtain the services of a lawyer on a **contingent fee** basis. This means that the lawyer will not charge the individual if the case is lost but will obtain a portion of the damages awarded if the case is won. It is not unusual for such contingent fee arrangements to involve one-third or more of the damages award plus expenses. Lawyers who handle cases on contingent fee agreements often handle personal-injury cases and are known as trial lawyers. Traditionally, these lawyers will contribute money to judicial candidates who are sympathetic to plaintiffs. The reason is that they make money only if they win, so they have a strong economic interest in supporting the election efforts of judicial candidates who are sympathetic to plaintiffs and to the award of large damages.

The person being sued will either have to hire an attorney on his or her own or, if insured, will be represented by an attorney paid for by the insurance company. Fee arrangements vary for civil defense lawyers, but often they are paid by the hour. Civil defense lawyers also like to win cases, of course, but since they are often paid by the hour whether they win or lose a case, they may not have the same economic incentives to contribute money to judicial campaigns.

civil law a branch of law that deals with disputes that do not involve criminal penalties

criminal law the branch of law that regulates the conduct of individuals, defines crimes, and specifies punishment for criminal acts

complaint the presentation of a grievance by the plaintiff in a civil case

answer the presentation of a defendant's defense against an allegation in a civil case

contingent fee a fee paid to the lawyer in a civil case and which is contingent on winning the case

In 2008, members of the Fundamentalist Church of Jesus Christ of Latter Day Saints appealed to the Texas courts after Child Protective Services took more than 400 children from the polygamist compound into custody. The Texas Supreme Court affirmed a lower-court ruling that state officials had acted improperly.

The court to which a civil case is taken depends on the type of case and the amount of money involved. Most commonly, a civil case will be settled, meaning the dispute is resolved without going to court. Settlements may, however, occur during trial, sometimes immediately before a jury renders its decision. If a case is not settled and goes to trial, it may be heard by either a judge or, if requested by either side, by a jury. Although civil jury cases do not have to be unanimous in Texas, the burden of proof is on the plaintiff. The standard of proof that the plaintiff must meet is **preponderance of the evidence**. That means that the plaintiff must show that it is more likely than not that the defendant is the cause of the harm suffered by the plaintiff.

Civil cases may involve tiny amounts of damages or they may involve billions of dollars, which have the potential of breaking huge corporations, such as happened in the 1980s when Pennzoil successfully sued Texaco in a dispute over the takeover of the Getty Oil Company.[7]

Civil case verdicts may, of course, be appealed. Appeals are usually from the trial court to the intermediate court of appeal and perhaps further to the state supreme court. Given the cost of appeals and the delay that is involved, it is not unusual for some settlement to be reached after the verdict, but before the case goes through the appellate process. For example, a plaintiff might agree to settle for much less than the verdict in the case to avoid the expense and delay of further appeals.

In criminal cases, the state alleges a violation of a criminal law and is usually represented in court by a prosecutor. Some prosecutors are career prosecutors with vast trial experience. These people will often prosecute the most difficult and complex cases, such as felonies and **capital cases.** However, because the pay of prosecutors is often much lower than that of lawyers who do litigation in the private sector, it is common for most prosecutors to be quite young and inexperienced. Once they gain trial experience, prosecutors commonly move into the private sector.

Defendants may hire criminal defense attorneys, who usually charge a flat fee to handle the case. Criminal defense lawyers, of course, do not work on a contingent fee basis. Since most criminal defendants are found guilty, criminal defense lawyers often prefer to obtain as much of their fee as possible in advance of the verdict.

Some parts of Texas have public defender offices where salaried lawyers provide at least some adult indigent criminal defense services in a county. Bexar County has established the first public defender office for indigent criminal appeals. Travis County has a public defender office representing only indigents with mental impairments.[8] A public defender office represents indigents in capital cases in West Texas.[9]

In Texas, indigent criminal defendants are more commonly represented by court-appointed lawyers. These are lawyers appointed by the judge to represent a defendant. Usually, these government-paid fees are less than would be charged to nonindigent defendants. Thus, some lawyers are reluctant to fulfill court appointments; others may not put the time and energy into a court-appointed case that they would if they were privately paid; others take court appointments because they have a limited number of paying clients; and still others take court appointments to gain experience. Concern over the poor quality of legal representation provided indigent criminal defendants, especially in capital cases, led to legislation in 2001 to increase the pay and qualifications of court-appointed lawyers.

Serious crimes are **felonies**. In those cases, as well as many lesser offenses known as **misdemeanors**, prior to the trial there will be an indictment by a grand jury. In Texas, a **grand jury** consists of twelve persons who sit for two to six months. Depending on the county, a grand jury may meet only once or twice, or it may meet several times a week. Although sometimes grand juries are selected randomly from a pool of qualified citizens, mostly Texas grand jurors are chosen by a commissioner system. A district judge will appoint several grand jury commissioners, who will then select fifteen to twenty citizens of the county. The first twelve who are qualified become the grand jury.[10]

Grand juries can inquire into any criminal matter but usually spend most of their time on felony crimes. They work in secret and rely heavily on the information provided by the prosecutor, though in some cases grand juries will work quite independently of the prosecutor. These grand juries are called runaway grand juries because the prosecutor has lost control of them, but such cases are very rare. If nine of the grand jurors decide a trial is warranted, they will indict a suspect. An **indictment** is also known as a "true bill." On the other hand, sometimes a grand jury does not believe a trial is warranted. In those cases, the grand jury issues a "no bill" decision.

Although a suspect has the right to trial by jury, he or she may waive that right and undergo a **bench trial** before the judge only. Most commonly, the suspect will engage in a **plea bargain**. With plea bargaining, a suspect agrees to plead guilty in exchange for a lighter sentence than might be imposed if the suspect were found guilty at trial. Approximately 97 percent of criminal convictions in Texas are the result of plea bargains.[11] If the suspect does choose trial by jury, felony juries will have twelve members; misdemeanor juries will have six members. There must be a unanimous verdict of guilty or not guilty. If the jurors are not unanimous, the result is a hung jury and a mistrial is declared. The prosecutor may then choose to retry the suspect. In addition to the requirement of unanimity in jury decisions, another important difference between civil and criminal cases is the standard of proof. In criminal cases, rather than the standard of preponderance of the evidence, the standard is **beyond a reasonable doubt**. This means that the prosecutor must prove the charges against the defendant, and they must be proven to a very high standard so that a reasonable doubt of innocence does not exist.

If a guilty verdict is returned, there will be a separate hearing on the sentence, which in Texas is sometimes also determined by the jury. At the sentencing hearing, factors such as prior record and background will be considered, even though it is likely these factors could not be considered at the trial portion of the proceeding.

Of course a defendant may also appeal a verdict. Usually the appeals are by a convicted defendant who alleges that an error in the trial may have affected the case's outcome. In rare cases, a prosecutor may also appeal. For the most part, however, criminal defendants will appeal their convictions to an intermediate appeals court and perhaps further to the Texas Court of Criminal Appeals. In capital cases, however, the appeal will be directly to the Texas Court of Criminal Appeals.

indictment a written statement issued by a grand jury that charges a suspect with a crime and states that a trial is warranted

bench trial a trial held without a jury and before only a judge

plea bargain negotiated agreement in a criminal case in which a defendant agrees to plead guilty in return for the state's agreement to reduce the severity of the criminal charge or prison sentence the defendant is facing

beyond a reasonable doubt the legal standard in criminal cases, which requires the prosecution to prove that a reasonable doubt of innocence does not exist

● How Judges Are Selected

Although there are still generalist lawyers who handle all sorts of cases, much of the practice of law is very specialized. Thus, in the civil process trial lawyers and civil defense lawyers tend to back opposing candidates for judgeships. It is not unusual for trial lawyers to support one candidate, often the Democrat, who is more likely to be the more liberal, or pro-plaintiff candidate, and for the civil defense lawyers to support the Republican, who is more likely to be the conservative, or pro-defendant candidate. The civil defense lawyers will often align themselves with business groups and with professional groups, such as medical doctors, to support judges inclined to favor the civil defense side.

Is justice for sale in Texas? Because statewide judicial races have been increasingly expensive, candidates for judgeships have been forced to raise more money. This, in turn, has led to criticism that judicial decisions are, in effect, being bought.

for critical analysis

What is the most important feature of how judges are selected in Texas? What does this feature reveal about Texas politics more broadly?

In the criminal process, it is sometimes possible to see criminal defense lawyers backing one candidate and prosecutors backing the other. Some prosecutors' offices are quite political, and the prosecutors will publicly support pro-prosecution judicial candidates. They will often be aligned with victims' rights groups. Criminal defense lawyers, on the other hand, will often back one of their own in contested criminal court races.

One big difference in the campaigns of civil court judges versus criminal court judges is the amount of money involved. Enormous amounts can be involved in civil cases, and so it is worth lots of money to trial lawyers and civil defense interests to elect candidates favorable to their point of view. On the other hand, with the exception of a relatively few highly paid criminal defense lawyers, the practice of criminal law is not very lucrative. Prosecutors are on salary, and usually the salaries are not large. Criminal defense lawyers often represent clients with little money. And most criminal cases are plea-bargained. The economic incentives to contribute large sums to criminal court races don't exist. The result is that a strong candidate for the Texas Supreme Court may raise in the neighborhood of $1,000,000 for a campaign, whereas a strong candidate for the Texas Court of Criminal Appeals may raise $100,000.

Initial Appointment of Judges by the Governor

A notable aspect of the Texas judiciary is that with the exception of municipal judges, who tend to be appointed by local governments, all judges are elected in partisan elections. Still, because the governor appoints district and appellate judges to the bench to fill vacancies prior to an election or to fill judgeships on new courts, large percentages of judges initially get on the bench through appointment. Although there has been some controversy over the relatively small number of appointments of minorities made by some governors, gubernatorial appointment has generated little additional controversy.[12] Table 25.1 shows the percentage of district and appellate judges who have initially gained their seats through appointment

TABLE 25.1

Percentage of Judges Obtaining Their Position Initially through Appointment

YEAR	TRIAL COURTS[a]	APPELLATE COURTS[b]
1962	57%	50%
1984	67	51
1998	46	40
2001	34	38
2003	43	43
2006	43	50
2009	36	51

a. Trial courts are the district and criminal district courts.
b. Appellate courts are the supreme court, the court of criminal appeals, and the courts of appeal.
SOURCES: Anthony Champagne, "The Selection and Retention of Judges in Texas," *Southwestern Law Journal* 40 (May 1986): 66; and Texas Office of Court Administration, "Profile of Appellate and Trial Judges" as of September 1, 1998, 2001, 2003, 2006, and 2009

by the governor. Currently, about 51 percent of appellate judges and 36 percent of the trial judges initially got on the bench through appointment.[13] Still, the controversial issue in Texas judicial politics deals with how the remaining judges obtained their seats and how all judges retain their seats if they wish to remain in office. That controversy involves the partisan election of judges in Texas.

The Elections Become Highly Partisan

Until 1978, the selection of judges in partisan elections did not create much concern. Texas was overwhelmingly a Democratic state, and judges were elected as Democrats. The only real competition occurred in the Democratic primary, and with the political advantage of incumbency, judges were rarely defeated even in the primary. The only real competition in judicial races occurred in those relatively rare cases where there was an open seat in which no incumbent sought office. Beginning in 1978, however, changes began to occur in Texas judicial politics. William Clements, the first Republican governor since Reconstruction, was elected. The governor has the power to appoint judges to the district and higher courts when new courts have been created or when a judicial vacancy occurs as a result of death, resignation, or retirement. Unlike the previous Democratic governors, who appointed members of the Democratic Party, Clements began appointing Republicans. With that advantage of incumbency, some of the Republican judges began to win re-election.

Helped by the popularity of Ronald Reagan in Texas, other Republicans began seeking judicial offices and winning. Thus, by the early 1980s, in statewide elections and in several counties in Texas, competition began to appear in judicial races. With that competition, incumbent judges began to be defeated. Sensing the growth of Republican strength, a number of Democratic judges changed to a Republican Party affiliation. From 1980 through July 24, 1985, thirteen district and appellate judges changed from the Democratic to the Republican Party; eleven county court judges switched; and five justices of the peace changed parties. Judge Don Koons

Despite the increase in campaign spending and advertising in judicial races, many voters are still unaware of most candidates for office. District Judge Bill Moody and his supporters tried to get voters' attention during his 2006 campaign by walking across the state of Texas.

switched parties in early 1985 and explained his move to the Republican Party by saying: "I ran as a Democrat in 1982. It was a long, tough year, but we won. On the other hand, it cost a lot more money and time away from the bench to run as a Democrat. The work suffers some, and you've got to be always hustling money."[14] Koons apparently believed that with the emerging strength of the Republican Party, a switch in party affiliation would make his job more secure.

Judicial elections became more expensive because judicial candidates needed money to run meaningful campaigns. In particular, campaigns that used television advertising became very expensive because of high media costs.

Judicial candidates needed money because judicial races tend to have low-visibility campaigns in which voters are unaware of the candidates. The races tend to be overshadowed by higher-visibility races, such as the race for governor or U.S. senator. Money was needed to give judicial candidates some degree of name visibility by voters. However, in general, Texas voters do not give much money to judicial campaigns. Instead, it is lawyers, interest groups, and potential litigants who tend to be donors in judicial races.[15] That has raised concerns about the neutrality of Texas judges who are deciding cases that involve the financial interests of persons who have given them campaign funds. A recent Texas poll found that 83 percent of the public thought that judges were strongly or somewhat influenced by contributions in their decisions. Ninety-nine percent of lawyers believed that campaign contributions have at least some influence on judges. Perhaps even more striking, 86 percent of judges reported that they believed campaign contributions had at least some influence on judicial decisions.[16]

Contributions for judicial races in Texas can sometimes amount to several hundred thousand dollars, especially for hotly contested district court races or appellate races. In general, however, the most expensive races are for the Texas Supreme Court. When races are contested between Democratic and Republican candidates, a candidate can raise well over $1 million. That is because these are statewide races and because this court sets the tone of tort law throughout the state, so a great deal of money is needed and a great deal can be raised. Table 25.2 shows the average

TABLE 25.2

Average Contributions to Texas Supreme Court Candidates[a]

YEAR	AVERAGE FOR ALL CANDIDATES	AVERAGE FOR WINNING CANDIDATES
1980	$155,033	$298,167
1982[b]	$173,174	$332,998
1984[b]	$967,405	$1,922,183
1986	$519,309	$1,024,817
1988	$859,413	$842,148
1990	$970,154	$1,544,939
1992	$1,096,001	$1,096,687
1994	$1,499,577	$1,627,285
1996	$656,190	$1,277,127
1998	$521,519	$829,794
2000	NA[c]	$584,719[d]
2002[e]	$425,474	$568,430
2004[b]	$394,906	$548,685
2006[b]	$995,218	$1,792,523
2008	$654,819	$910,973
2010[f]	$366,825	$654,454

a. Averages are reported for candidates from contested races featuring both a Republican and Democratic candidate.
b. The 1982, 1984, 2004, and 2006 elections each featured only one contested race with both a Democratic and Republican candidate.
c. No Democrats ran in the three Supreme Court elections in 2000.
d. Average campaign contributions for the three victorious Republicans; none had a Democratic opponent.
e. Chief Justice Tom Phillips ran for re-election and refused to accept any campaign contributions beyond his cash on hand, which amounted to $19,433. His Democratic opponent, however, raised almost no funds—$12,815. Phillips was the victor in this race, which lowers the average contributions for this year.
f. 2010 contributions are Through November 5, 2010.
SOURCES: Kyle Cheek and Anthony Champagne, *Judicial Politics in Texas* (New York: Peter Lang, 2005), 38; Institute on Money in State Politics.

contribution to Texas Supreme Court candidates for each election period from 1982 through 2010. The contribution data are reported for those races that were contested by both a Republican and a Democratic candidate. In the 2000 Supreme Court elections, the Republicans were so strong that no Democrat even bothered to run for any position on the Texas Supreme Court.

In spite of judicial campaigns, however, voters often know little about judicial candidates. As a result, they vote not for the best-qualified person to be a judge, but for the party label. As the Republican Party has become increasingly dominant in statewide races, it is the Republican label, rather than the qualifications or experience of judicial candidates, that has determined the outcome of judicial races. Related to the importance of party label in judicial races is the effect of top-of-the-ticket voting. In 1984, the popularity of Ronald Reagan seemed to help Texas judicial candidacies as many voters cast straight or almost straight Republican ballots.

In that year, Reagan received nearly 64 percent of the presidential vote in Texas. All four Republican incumbent district judges who were challenged by Democrats won. Sixteen Democratic incumbent district judges were challenged by Republicans. Only three of those Democrats won. In contrast, in 1982, U.S. Senator Lloyd Bentsen ran for re-election. Bentsen was a very popular senator and a Democrat. His candidacy on the Democratic ballot seems to have encouraged voters to cast ballots for Democrats further down on the ticket. Bentsen received slightly more than 59 percent of the vote in Texas. In that year, twenty-six Republican incumbent district judges faced Democratic opposition; only fourteen won. Yet sixteen Democratic district judges faced opposition, and fourteen won.[17]

Even voters who try to make a serious effort to learn about judicial candidates can have a hard time. In Houston, for example, voters are faced with ballots loaded with so many judicial candidates that it becomes nearly impossible to be an informed voter. In 1994, one of the most extreme examples of a long judicial ballot occurred in Harris County, where voters were faced with forty-five judicial elections that were primary elections and then eight runoff primary elections. In the general election, there were fifty-nine contested judicial elections and sixteen more elections where the judicial candidate was unopposed. In 2010, Harris County voters cast ballots in ten contested appellate court races and thirty-six contested district court races.

The Name Game

In 1994, Cathy Herasimchuk ran for the Texas Court of Criminal Appeals. In a three-way Republican primary she won only 26 percent of the statewide vote. The candidates in the Democratic and Republican primaries who did make the runoff for that seat all had simple, easy-to-spell and easy-to-pronounce names. Herasimchuk was appointed to the Court of Criminal Appeals in 2001, but in running for election to the court in 2002, she realized she had a problem with her name. As she said, "Everybody told me you couldn't win city dog catcher with the name Herasimchuk, and they all turned out to be accurate." Herasimchuk's problems getting elected certainly had nothing to do with her credentials. She has been a Harris County prosecutor, a criminal defense lawyer, an adviser to then governor Bush, and a law school lecturer. When she ran in 2002, she did so under the name Cathy Cochran.[18]

There has also been scholarly research on name recognition of judges. One 1991 study consisted of telephone interviews with one thousand Dallas County voters. The voters were asked if they recognized the names of a list of public officials. At the time, Lloyd Bentsen was a U.S. senator from Texas, and Annette Strauss was the mayor of Dallas. Raul Gonzalez was a justice on the Texas Supreme Court. The other persons were district court judges in Dallas County.

Lloyd Bentsen had very high name recognition, as did Mayor Annette Strauss. Justice Gonzalez had moderately high recognition, as did Larry Baraka, who at the time had been involved in a visible and controversial case that had been the subject of a movie. Jack Hampton, a district judge at the time, also had moderately high name recognition. He had been the subject of nationwide controversy over remarks he had made about gay murder victims in a trial he had conducted. No other district court judge had high name recognition except for Ron Chapman, who had remarkably high name recognition, almost as high as Lloyd Bentsen and Annette Strauss and far higher than any other judge. The voters were then asked to recall the "public office" that these individuals held. Overwhelmingly in reference to Ron Chapman, the respondents stated that Chapman's public office was "disk jockey." At the time, another Ron Chapman *was* a disk jockey and was the most popular

ow Do Texans Choose Their Judges?

s elect many, many judges. Most voters know little about the individual judicial candidates, and use the party
ions of the candidates to fill in the gaps about who the candidate is and what type of judge he or she will be. As
lt, voters often vote "straight party," punching one place on the ballot to vote for all the nominees of their party.

sults of the 2008 election show how closely the results of district judge elections track straight ticket voting.
aphs below compare the percentage of the vote won by the average district court judicial candidate to the
ntage of straight ticket votes in Texas's five largest counties.

Share, 2008

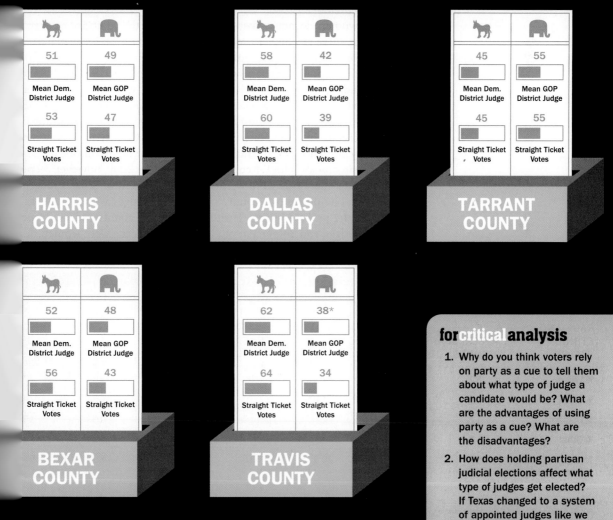

HARRIS COUNTY
Mean Dem. District Judge 51 · Mean GOP District Judge 49
Straight Ticket Votes 53 · Straight Ticket Votes 47

DALLAS COUNTY
Mean Dem. District Judge 58 · Mean GOP District Judge 42
Straight Ticket Votes 60 · Straight Ticket Votes 39

TARRANT COUNTY
Mean Dem. District Judge 45 · Mean GOP District Judge 55
Straight Ticket Votes 45 · Straight Ticket Votes 55

BEXAR COUNTY
Mean Dem. District Judge 52 · Mean GOP District Judge 48
Straight Ticket Votes 56 · Straight Ticket Votes 43

TRAVIS COUNTY
Mean Dem. District Judge 62 · Mean GOP District Judge 38*
Straight Ticket Votes 64 · Straight Ticket Votes 34

for critical analysis

1. Why do you think voters rely on party as a cue to tell them about what type of judge a candidate would be? What are the advantages of using party as a cue? What are the disadvantages?

2. How does holding partisan judicial elections affect what type of judges get elected? If Texas changed to a system of appointed judges like we have for federal courts, would a different type of judge be selected? If so, why?

: Data are from the appropriate County Clerk office.

rcentages are all two-party vote share. "Mean GOP (or Dem.) District Judge" is the mean vote share for all
an (or Democrat) district judge candidates in that county.

ounty had one state district judge race which was contested.

radio personality in Dallas County. Judge Ron Chapman seemed to be benefiting from the high name recognition created by the disk jockey Ron Chapman. That probably explains why Chapman was able to win re-election to his Dallas County trial court when other Democrats were being soundly defeated.[19]

The name game continued in the 2008 elections for judges in Harris County. Most Republican judges in that county were swept out of office, but four Republicans survived. They had all been challenged by Democrats with unusual names. As a result, the incumbent Republican judge Sharon McCally was able to defeat the Democratic challenger Ashish Mahendru; Republican judge Mark Kent Ellis defeated Democrat Mekisha Murray; Judge Patricia Kerrigan, a Republican, defeated the Democrat, Andres Pereira; and Judge Joseph Halback defeated his Democratic challenger, Goodwille Pierre.[20]

Minority Representation in the Texas Judiciary

Minority groups have been concerned that countywide and larger partisan judicial races make it difficult for minorities to get elected to judgeships—and that Texas judges do not reflect the diversity of the state. Table 25.3 lists the ethnicity of Texas judges as of September 1, 2009.

Although women do not make up 50 percent of the judiciary as they do in the population, there is a higher proportion of women in the Texas judiciary than minorities. Women were at one time a great rarity on the bench. In 1970, only 1 percent of the nation's judiciary was female. As late as 1979 only 4 percent of the nation's judges were women.[21] In Texas, the first woman to serve as a state judge was Sarah Hughes, who was appointed in 1935 and who served as a district judge until 1961, when she was appointed to the federal bench. Famous for a number of her decisions, including one that forced Dallas County to build a new jail, she is probably best known as the judge who swore in Lyndon Johnson as president after the assassination of John F. Kennedy. In September 2009, however, 39 percent of appellate judges in Texas were women, and 28 percent of district judges were women. Thirty-one percent of county court-at-law judges were female, as were 28 percent of the probate judges. Thirteen percent of county judges, 34 percent of municipal judges, and 34 percent of justices of the peace were women.[22]

TABLE 25.3

Race and Ethnicity of Texas Judges 2009

RACE AND ETHNIC STATUS	APPEALS COURTS	DISTRICT COURTS	COUNTY COURTS AT LAW	PROBATE COURTS	COUNTY COURTS	MUNICIPAL COURTS	JP COURTS
% White	82	77	73	81	89	77	77
% Black	4	5	4	0	1	5	4
% Hispanic	12	17	22	19	10	15	19
% Other	1	2	1	0	0	3	0
Total Number of Responding Judges	97	415	205	16	236	1,089	654

SOURCE: Texas Office of Court Administration, "Profile of Appellate and Trial Judges."

Different interpretations have been offered for the low numbers of minorities on the bench. The lack of racial and ethnic diversity on the bench is a nationwide problem. Ninety-two percent of the state judges in the nation are white.[23] Civil rights groups in several states with elective judiciaries, including Texas, have argued that white voters dominate countywide and larger districts and will vote against minority judicial candidates. Civil rights organizations representing Hispanics and African Americans have argued that for minorities to get elected to office, there must be smaller judicial districts where minority voters make up the majority.

An alternative argument is that minority candidates in Texas, like minority voters, tend to be Democrats at a time when Republicans increasingly are winning judicial races. Thus, minorities do not get elected to judicial office because they run as Democrats.[24] Still another argument is that there are few minority judges because there are few minority lawyers and, with the exception of county judges and justices of the peace, judges in Texas must be lawyers.

The issue of minority representation on the bench has been the subject of major concern by minority and civil rights leaders in Texas. It was also the subject of prolonged federal litigation. In 1989, a case was tried in federal court in Midland. The case, *League of United Latin American Citizens v. Mattox*, was a suit against countywide election of judges in ten of the larger counties in Texas.[25] The suit, filed by minority plaintiffs, argued that countywide election of judges diluted the strength of minority voters and violated the Voting Rights Act. The trial judge agreed with the plaintiffs and, after a political solution failed, ordered that judges be elected in nonpartisan elections from smaller judicial districts. The trial court order, however, was blocked by the Fifth Circuit, which is the federal court of appeals for the region that includes Texas.[26] The case was then appealed to the U.S. Supreme Court, along with a Louisiana case; the Supreme Court held that the Voting Rights Act did apply to judicial elections.[27] The case was then returned to the Fifth Circuit to examine whether minority voting strength was diluted and to determine the state's interest in maintaining countywide elections. Ordinarily, the federal courts of appeal do not preside as an entire group to hear cases; instead, they hear cases in panels of three judges. Such a panel decided in favor of the minority plaintiffs, and a settlement seemed to be reached with the state to have elections of judges from smaller districts in the larger counties. However, in important cases, it is sometimes possible to appeal a decision of a panel of three judges to the entire court of appeal. When this happens, the court is said to sit *en banc*. That happened when some of the defendants in the suit were unhappy with the settlement, and the entire Fifth Circuit ruled in 1993 that party affiliation of minority candidates explained the failure of minority judicial candidates to win election rather than the candidates' minority status. Thus, countywide election of judges was not illegal, and there was no legal need to reduce the size of districts from which judges were elected.[28]

Since that decision, minority leaders and minority groups have continued to express concerns about the small numbers of minority judges, but any solution that would involve smaller districts would have to result from an act of the legislature rather than the actions of a federal court. One of the most influential minority leaders is State Senator Rodney Ellis, a Democrat from Houston. Ellis argued that the *en banc* decision of the Fifth Circuit "radically reinterpreted voting rights law to fit its need. In order to preserve the status quo," Ellis wrote, "the court eviscerated the meaning and intent of the Voting Rights Act."[29] In contrast, David Godbey, one of the attorneys for a defendant in the litigation and now a federal district judge in Dallas, wrote that the reason the Fifth Circuit decided as it did was that there was

● **Does the process for selecting judges in Texas successfully hold judges accountable for their actions?**

for critical analysis

Few minorities hold judicial office in Texas. Although African Americans and Hispanics make up over 40 percent of the Texas population, relatively few Texas judges belong to these groups. Offer at least three suggestions, including alternative election methods, to increase the number of minorities holding judicial office in Texas.

en banc referring to an appellate hearing with all judges participating

no proof of violation of the Voting Rights Act. The plaintiffs, Godbey wrote, "failed to prove racial discrimination in voting. The evidence for Dallas County showed simply that Republican candidates usually win—whether they are white, black or brown—and that most African-American voters prefer Democratic candidates. The Fifth Circuit ruled that losing elections because of partisan politics, rather than race, does not establish a Voting Rights Act violation and that the people of Texas are entitled to continue electing their judges free from federal interference."[30]

Judicial reform bills in the legislature since this decision have included provisions for smaller judicial districts, but those bills have not passed. Perhaps the strongest judicial reform bill was one backed by the lieutenant governor at the time, Bob Bullock, who created a task force to try to develop an acceptable compromise on the judicial selection issue. The proposed constitutional amendment designed by the task force passed the Texas Senate in 1995 but failed to pass the Texas House. Under the plan, all appellate judges would be appointed by the governor. District judges, on the other hand, would be chosen from county commissioner precincts in nonpartisan elections. After serving for a time, they would run countywide in **retention elections**, in which there would be a "yes" or "no" vote on their retention in office and where they would face no opponent on the ballot.

On the surface, the compromise seemed to offer something for almost everyone. Because the governor appointed appellate judges, judges would have greater career security and no worries about campaign funding. The business community, recognizing that Texas tended to elect conservative governors and was increasingly likely to elect conservative Republican governors, got appointed appellate judges. Nonpartisan elections would protect trial judges from party sweeps in which judges are voted out of office solely because of their party affiliation. Minorities would get smaller judicial districts for the major trial courts. But what looked like a great compromise fell through. Although African Americans supported the compromise, Hispanics did not. The two largest counties in Texas—Harris and Dallas—elected a total of 96 of the 386 district judges then chosen in Texas. Under the compromise, one-fourth of Harris and Dallas county judges would be elected from each of the county commissioners' precincts in that county. Both Dallas and Harris counties had three white county commissioners and one African American. Hispanics, on the other hand, elected no county commissioner and believed that the compromise would not promote the election of more Hispanic judges. They believed that to elect Hispanic judges, considerably smaller districts were needed. As a result, much Hispanic support was not forthcoming. Further, the political parties opposed the compromise. Nonpartisan elections might protect the interests of judges, but they weakened the political parties. Additionally, an appointive system for appellate judges reduced the number of elective offices, thereby reducing the role of the political parties. Although his powers would have increased with an appointed appellate judiciary, Governor George W. Bush opposed the compromise, probably because he did not want to oppose the Republican Party. Because the plan had the support of Lieutenant Governor Bob Bullock and because he gave the legislation priority on his legislative agenda that year, it passed the senate. However, the proposal died in the Texas House. The Bullock proposal was probably the best hope for judicial change for a long time to come.[31]

One of the business community's underlying concerns about smaller districts seemed to be a fear that small districts might create a narrower electorate for judges. That narrow electorate might in some areas prove unduly sympathetic to plaintiffs who file suit against businesses. Also, at a time when the Republican Party is quite successful in judicial races, smaller judicial districts might increase

retention election an election in which voters decide "yes" or "no" regarding whether to keep an incumbent in office

the strength of the Democratic Party. Although Republicans, at least until very recently, can win elections countywide in areas such as Harris County, for example, they cannot win all elections when the political boundaries are less than county-wide, such as those based on county commissioner precincts, state representatives' districts, or justice of the peace precincts. Indeed, David Godbey claimed that the Republican judge Harold Entz, his client in the litigation by civil rights lawyers to create smaller judicial districts, intervened in the case as a defendant because he feared that the attorney general, a Democrat, would not defend the case ably and would try to settle it in ways that would create smaller judicial districts that would be more advantageous to Democrats.[32]

Whatever the cause of the low number of minority judges, the lack of diversity on the bench, the role of money in judicial races, the defeat of incumbents, the importance of party label, top-of-the-ticket voting, and the "name game" have all created support for alternative judicial selection systems.

Alternative Means of Selection

Judges are selected in the United States by a variety of ways. One way is through appointment by the governor and approval by the state senate. This method is used in Texas to select judges to new courts or courts where there has been a death, resignation, or retirement during a judicial term. It is also similar to the system for selecting federal judges, who are appointed by the president and con-firmed by vote of the U.S. Senate. However, this method of judicial selection is contrary to Texas's traditional distrust of a powerful chief executive. At a time when Texas governors are Republicans, it also is not a system that Democrats tend to favor.

Another system for selecting judges is nonpartisan election. Such a system for selecting judges in Texas would eliminate much of the partisan politics, but, at the same time, it would make it more difficult for candidates to reach voters. This is because in a truly nonpartisan election, judicial candidates would have to run for office without the benefit of political parties. In some states that have ostensibly nonpartisan elections, such as Ohio, the parties continue to take an active role to the point that it is difficult to distinguish that type of nonpartisan system from a partisan election system. If Texas instituted a truly nonpartisan system, however, candidates would require even more campaign money to reach voters they could no longer reach though the mechanisms of the political parties.

Most commonly, however, judicial reformers argue for a sys-tem of judicial selection that is commonly called **merit selection** of judges. In this system, a blue-ribbon committee consisting of lawyers and lay people supplies to the governor the names of a small number of candidates for a judgeship. The governor makes the judicial appointment from this list, and after the judge serves for a brief time, he or she runs in a retention election. In a reten-tion election, the incumbent does not have an opponent. Instead voters are asked whether the incumbent should be retained for another term of office. The voters then vote "yes" or "no" on the judge's retention. As might be expected in an election where one does not have an opponent, the incumbent usually wins. One study of retention elections found that only 1.6 percent of incum-bent judges were defeated in retention elections.[33] Yet from time

merit selection a judicial reform under which judges would be nominated by a blue-ribbon committee, appointed by the governor, and, after a brief period in office, would run in a retention election

Although Texas judges are often elected, the governor appoints district and appellate judges if there is a vacancy before an election. In 2006, Rick Perry appointed Philip Johnson to the state supreme court after one of the justices left to become a federal judge.

to time, interest groups will organize against a judge in a retention election and spend a great deal of money trying to defeat him or her; sometimes those efforts have been successful. One of the great concerns about merit selection is the nature of the merit selection commission, since those commissioners filter out all but a handful of prospective judges. Some are quite fearful of this centralized method of determining who should be judges, and although there is much support for merit selection in Texas, there is also much opposition.[34]

In recent years, one of the most popular reform proposals has been a system known as "appoint-elect-retain." Under this system, the governor would appoint a judge with confirmation by two-thirds of the state senate. The governor-appointed nominee would not assume office until confirmed by the senate, which would meet year-round for the purpose of dealing with judicial confirmations. In the first election thereafter, the judge would run in a contested nonpartisan election and subsequently in retention elections. This is, of course, a hybrid plan that encompasses aspects of gubernatorial appointment, nonpartisan election, and merit selection.

Another popular reform plan would have appellate vacancies filled by gubernatorial appointment with senatorial confirmation. The appellate judges would then run in nonpartisan elections followed by retention elections. In Dallas, Tarrant, and Bexar counties, district court judges would be elected from county commissioner precincts rather than from one district encompassing the entire county. Additionally, in Harris County, district judges would be elected from smaller geographic regions than county commissioner precincts. Supporters of this plan tend to believe that it would increase the number of minority judges, especially trial court judges in urban areas. Of course, this is also a hybrid plan designed to combine various reform proposals in order to gain sufficient support to become the new way Texas selects its judges.

At least for the time being, however, it seems likely that not much will change in the way Texas selects its judges. Restructuring the system would be a major change, and these are always difficult to initiate. Changing might upset many voters, who like being able to vote for judges, and it would surely upset the political parties, which like having large numbers of judicial candidates running under their party label. It might also upset lawyers accustomed to the traditional ways of selecting judges and even judges who have benefited from the present system. That has led some to argue that judicial reform needs to be less drastic and more incremental. These reformers have suggested lengthening judicial terms of office on the grounds that longer terms mean fewer election contests and therefore less need for campaign money, less of a chance for defeat of incumbents, and less involvement of judges in politics. Another proposed incremental reform is to remove judges from the straight party vote. This means that a voter would actually have to cast a ballot for the judicial candidate rather than simply voting for everyone on the Republican or Democratic column by casting a straight party vote. Such a reform would remove judicial candidates from the effects of top-of-the-ticket voting. It would, of course, also reduce the votes that judges receive and lessen their dependence and reliance on the political parties. Still another suggested reform is to increase the levels of experience needed to serve on the bench. The idea is that even if judicial races are subject to the whims of voters, high qualifications for judges would mean that there would be experienced judges on the bench rather than highly inexperienced judges who won simply because they were good campaigners or because they had the right party affiliation in that election year.

Judicial Campaign Fairness Act
a judicial reform under which campaign contributions are limited by the amount that a judicial candidate can receive from donors

Perhaps the most significant judicial reform in Texas is the **Judicial Campaign Fairness Act**. Texas is the only state with a campaign finance regulation of this type.

Among the most important aspects of compliance with the act are campaign contribution limitations. For example, statewide judicial candidates limit themselves to contributions of no more than $5,000 from any individual in any election. Additionally, statewide candidates can receive no more than $30,000 per election from any law firm. Although the amounts of money that can be donated are still quite high, there has been a significant reduction from contribution amounts in the 1980s when, prior to the act, some donors would give candidates $25,000, $50,000, and even more in campaign contributions. A recent strengthening of campaign contribution limits requires that if a judge receives campaign contributions from a party to a lawsuit, or if the party's lawyer had made contributions in excess of the limits in the Judicial Campaign Fairness Act, the judge would recuse him- or herself from the case.[35]

For many, the role of money in judicial campaigns is the most troubling issue in Texas judicial politics. In November 1999, a *Frontline* television show titled "Justice for Sale" was broadcast by PBS. The program focused on judicial politics, especially fund-raising, in Pennsylvania, Louisiana, and Texas. One of the major themes of the broadcast was that campaign fund-raising by judges created at least the appearance of impropriety; in some cases, campaign contributions suggested that judicial decisions were being bought. An alternative viewpoint, however, is that money is necessary if judges campaign for office in order to enhance their visibility to voters. What judicial campaign contributors are doing is contributing money to present those candidates to voters whose judicial philosophies are most compatible with the philosophies of the contributors. That, it can be argued, is what free speech and the democratic process are about. Nevertheless, the concern remains that there is something questionable about the contribution of money to judges who then decide cases of interest to contributors. As long as judges are elected, however, money will be necessary to run judicial campaigns, and where elections are competitive, a great deal of campaign money will be necessary.

● Does the process for selecting judges in Texas successfully hold judges accountable for their actions?

● The Importance of the Texas Courts

The Texas courts have an important impact on the lives of Texans in all sorts of ways, whether it involves the adjudication of a traffic accident, determination of child support, imposition of a jail sentence, or imposition of the most serious punishment of all, the death penalty. (Other aspects of criminal justice, especially sentencing and prison policy issues are found in Chapter 27.)

The Death Penalty

The most serious aspect of the judicial system in Texas, and one of the most controversial, is the death penalty. One study of the death penalty found that, nationwide, 68 percent of death penalty appeals were successful between 1973 and 1995, but Texas appeals were only successful 52 percent of the time. Another study found that after Texas created a new and faster system for handling death penalty appeals in 1995, only 8 of 278 cases were overturned by the Texas Court of Criminal Appeals.[36] Another reason for the lack of success of defendants in death penalty cases has to do with the quality of legal representation defendants receive if they have a court-appointed lawyer. One study found that more than one hundred death-row inmates in Texas have been represented by court-appointed attorneys with troubled histories whose performance became an issue on appeal. In one case, for example, a lawyer with no permanent license to practice law and no background in capital murder cases was appointed to handle a death penalty appeal even though he had practiced law less than two years. And the Texas Court of Criminal Appeals let him stay on the case even when he asked the court to delay the appeal so that he could take an introductory course in death penalty defense. When that lawyer did get an extension to take his class, he still missed a filing deadline and only filed his brief after the court threatened him with jail for contempt. When it came time for him to argue the case before the court, he did not show. The court left him on the case and denied the appeal, noting that six of his eleven arguments were inadequately briefed and presented nothing for review. That lawyer was paid $8,647 by Smith County for his work on the case and subsequently lost his probationary law license when he bounced checks for state bar dues and occupational taxes and failed to appear at a board hearing to defend himself. The board expressed concern that if he continued to practice law, there was a "likelihood that he would harm a client, obstruct the administration of justice, or violate [state bar rules]."[37]

Texas has led the nation in the number of executions since the death penalty was reinstated in 1976. Since 1977, lethal injection has been the means for execution in Texas. The first execution by lethal injection was on December 7, 1982. Beginning in 1923, the state ordered that executions be carried out in Huntsville by electrocution. Prior to that time, each county was responsible for carrying out executions.[38]

Texas executed 451 people from December 7, 1982, through March 11, 2010. As of March 16, 2010, there were 331 people on death row.[39]

In Texas, one is subject to the death penalty for the murder of a public safety officer, fireman, or correctional employee; murder during commission of a kidnapping, burglary, robbery, aggravated rape, or arson; murder for hire; multiple murders; murder during a prison escape; murder by a prison inmate serving a life sentence; or murder of a child under the age of six.

Texas has made greater use of the death penalty than other states, but opponents argue that the legal system does not do enough to protect defendants in death penalty cases. In 2007, Johnny Ray Conner became the 400th person to be executed under the death penalty in Texas. His family and death penalty opponents demonstrated outside the prison.

A stay on death row can be a lengthy one, even in Texas. The average time spent on death row prior to execution is 10.26 years, although the time varies considerably. One inmate under a death sentence waived his appeals and spent only a little more than eight months on death row prior to execution. On the other hand, Robert Excell White, who was executed in March 1999, had been convicted of murdering three men in 1974.[40] A death sentence carried out in February 1998, however, initiated the greatest controversy over the death penalty. The case of Karla Faye Tucker, a convicted ax murderer, generated national demands for clemency. Tucker was widely believed to have undergone a religious conversion after her 1983 conviction. She was also attractive and articulate and was the first woman in modern times condemned to be executed in Texas. Supporters of her execution argued that her gender, appearance, articulateness, and possible religious conversion were irrelevant to the fact that she was a convicted murderer who should be treated like others in similar situations.

One of the issues involving the death penalty is whether all offenders are treated in the same way. There is a racial/ethnic disparity such that minorities, especially African Americans, are disproportionately represented on death row. As of March 16, 2010, there were 128 African Americans on death row, 99 Hispanics, 100 whites, and 4 of "other" racial/ethnic classifications. Since 1982, 208 whites have been executed, 167 African Americans, 74 Hispanics, and 2 of "other" racial/ethnic groups. It may be that there is a bias in the criminal justice system such that minorities are disproportionately subject to the death penalty. There has been considerable argument at the national level that minorities are unfairly subjected to the death penalty more than are whites; however, the U.S. Supreme Court has refused to strike down the death penalty on the basis of statistical generalizations.[41]

The Texas Board of Pardons and Paroles votes on clemency to death-row inmates. Both a federal and a state judge have been highly critical of this process.[42] This board was originally considered to be a remedy for possible corruption in clemency granted by the governor. Prior to 1936, the governor essentially had unlimited power to grant clemency. This power was often abused, especially by Governor Miriam Ferguson, who granted 4,000 requests for commutations of sentences in

DNA evidence has been at the center of numerous recent legal controversies in Texas. In Dallas, new DNA technology led to the exonerations of 20 men who had been wrongfully convicted. Larry Fuller (right) served 25 years in prison before he was proven innocent by DNA testing and exonerated in 2006.

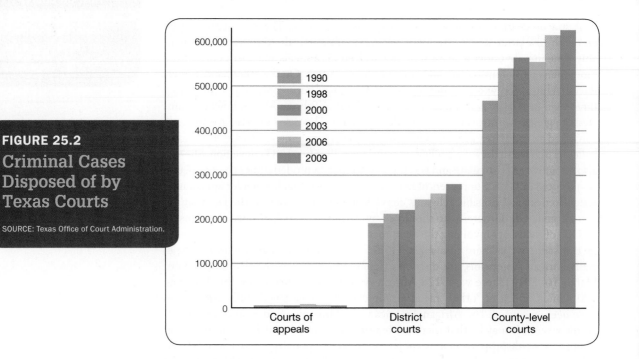

FIGURE 25.2

Criminal Cases Disposed of by Texas Courts

SOURCE: Texas Office of Court Administration.

1922 alone. It was widely believed that payments were made for many of these acts of executive clemency. In reaction, a constitutional amendment was passed in 1936 that charged the board with giving the governor recommendations on clemency. Without such a recommendation, the governor can only grant a single thirty-day reprieve. No other state so limits the powers of the governor.

In August 2007, the board recommended commutation of Kenneth Foster's sentence to be executed—only seven hours before Foster was scheduled to die. Governor Perry commuted Foster's sentence to life imprisonment about one hour later.[43] Fosters' much-publicized case seemed to challenge two aspects of the death penalty in Texas: (1) Foster had been tried simultaneously with the other capital defendants rather than getting a separate trial; and (2) he was the getaway driver in the crime and not the actual shooter in the robbery and murder.

Other Criminal Punishments

Although the death penalty is the most significant punishment that can be imposed, the Texas courts impose other deprivations of liberty as well.

Texas had 12.2 percent of the nation's total state prison population in January 1, 2010. Only the federal system had more prisoners under their jurisdiction.[44] Figure 25.2 shows the numbers of criminal cases disposed of by the courts of appeal and by the trial courts in 1990, 1998, 2000, 2003, 2006, and 2009. As can be seen from the figure, Texas judges dispose of large numbers of criminal cases, a caseload that is increasing over time.

The Integrity of the Texas Criminal Justice System

In recent years, Texas has been more aggressive than any other state in imposing the death penalty. Yet as Texas continues to execute people, in 2000 Illinois suspended the death penalty after revelations of a number of wrongful convictions. New Jersey, North Carolina, and California are all considering moratoriums on the death penalty. Since 1989, 251 people wrongfully convicted of crimes in 34 states have been cleared as a result of DNA testing, including 17 people who served time on death row. The average prison time served by an exoneree was thirteen years.[45] In the summer of 2005, Supreme Court Justice John Paul Stevens publicly noted that DNA evidence had shown that a number of death sentences had been erroneously imposed.[46]

This concern about the death penalty has even affected the internal dynamics of the Texas Court of Criminal Appeals, which is the state's court of last resort for death penalty appeals. Judge Tom Price challenged Presiding Judge Sharon Keller in the Republican primary in 2006 in part because he thought Judge Keller was too strict in her support of the decisions of trial courts in death penalty and other criminal cases. The Price-Keller primary battle reflects an emerging concern in Texas that the state has been too free in its imposition of the death penalty and too unquestioning of the evidence that leads to the imposition of criminal punishments.

Six other widely publicized matters, however, have also contributed to the questions raised about the adequacy of the Texas criminal justice system in protecting the innocent. One of those matters in particular became a national scandal—drug arrests in 1999 in Tulia, Texas. An undercover narcotics officer was responsible for the arrests of forty-seven persons in Tulia, thirty-eight of whom were black and made up about 20 percent of the black adults in the town. The defendants were zealously prosecuted. Though they were charged with possessing only small amounts of cocaine, the defendants, including those with no prior records, received long sentences—including one as long as 361 years. The undercover officer was supported by local authorities even as questions about his veracity mounted, and he was even named Officer of the Year in Texas. Doubts about the arrests and convictions, however, did not die. The officer never wore a wire, never videotaped his alleged drug buys, and was never observed by another officer. Indeed, most of his alleged drug buys had no corroboration at all.

Two and a half years after the last trials of the Tulia defendants, the undercover officer had been fired from two later narcotics assignments. It became clear that he had no undercover narcotics experience prior to coming to Tulia and that he had left jobs as a deputy sheriff in two other towns, leaving behind significant unpaid debts. One of the sheriffs who had employed him had filed criminal charges against him, which meant that he was indicted while working undercover in Tulia. Accusations were also made against him that he had racist attitudes as well as difficulties with telling the truth.

It eventually became clear that the Tulia drug busts were a massive miscarriage of justice. Thirty-five of the forty-seven defendants were pardoned by the governor; nine had their charges dismissed prior to trial or were placed on deferred adjudication. One was a juvenile at the time of his alleged crime and so will not have an adult criminal record. The remaining two were sent to prison on probation violations. The disturbing factor is that without the efforts of a small number of concerned citizens, lawyers, and the press, this gross abuse of the criminal justice process would have remained undetected and unresolved.[47]

Nor was the Tulia affair the only major problem with drug arrests. In 2001, the Dallas police department agreed to pay an informant one thousand dollars per kilogram of confiscated drugs. Although the informant did know actual drug dealers, he realized they were dangerous, so he found harmless persons—Mexican immigrants and legal residents—on whom he could plant drugs. Apparently the informant also realized he could make more money with less risk if he passed off gypsum as cocaine. (Gypsum is a substance found in billiard-cue chalk.) Convictions on dozens of drug

● How do courts in Texas have an important impact on the lives of all Texans?

for critical analysis

During 1999 and 2000, Governor George W. Bush issued pardons to six prison inmates who were cleared by DNA testing. In June of 2000, State Attorney General John Cornyn reported that at least six death-row inmates were sentenced to death on the basis of racially biased testimony. What can the state do to ensure that Texans receive equal treatment under the law? Can the judicial system ever ensure that only the guilty are convicted? Explain.

cases were obtained without even testing to see if the seized material contained real drugs. The informant was the Dallas Police Department's highest paid in 2001, earning more than $210,000 for the seizure of nearly one thousand pounds of cocaine and amphetamines that turned out to be fake drugs. Twenty fake drug cases were multi-kilo seizures, and two were the largest busts in the history of the Dallas police. Yet nothing seemed to arouse the suspicions of the police about the arrests. This scandal reached deep into the police department, where there was a lack of supervision of undercover officers and an extreme push for numbers in both terms of amounts of drugs seized and number of arrests. The implausibility of some of the arrests is amazing: a lone mechanic working under his car, with no guns or cash seized; a credit drug buy, according to the uncorroborated word of a confidential informant; and a seizure of 25 kilos of fake cocaine, for example. Nor did the district attorney's office escape blame: their policy was not to test seized drugs unless plea bargains failed and a case went to trial. When more than eighty of the drug cases were dismissed, Dallas District Attorney Bill Hill went on television and insisted that many of those who were released were guilty. Were it not for the efforts of some criminal defense attorneys who were suspicious of the drug seizures, the Dallas Police Department might well still be seizing huge quantities of gypsum and paying its informant. The Dallas County District Attorney might be sending innocent men and women to prison.[48]

In 2002 the Houston Police Department Crime Laboratory was closed. An independent audit of the lab's DNA section had identified enormous problems. Analysts did not know how to do their jobs, and supervisors were also incompetent. There was no quality control system and few standardized procedures. Other sections of the lab had problems as well, but the most serious were in the DNA section. Harris County sends more people to death row than any other county in America, and it had done thousands of other tests in non-death-penalty cases. All these tests were now placed in doubt. One of the first retests of the lab's work showed that a man who had been convicted of rape in 1998 at the age of sixteen and had been given a twenty-five-year sentence largely on the basis of DNA evidence was

The case of Cameron Todd Willingham raises serious questions about the Texas justice system. Both before and after Willingham's execution for murder, experts found reason to doubt the evidence presented by the prosecution.

● How do courts
in Texas have an
important impact
on the lives of all
Texans?

actually innocent. The problem with the lab was that as DNA technology changed, the analysts got no training in new methods, were overworked, and were following procedures inconsistently. Additionally, the lab was never inspected by an outside agency and did not seek accreditation. Nor were judges, prosecutors, and defense attorneys able to spot the lab's sloppy work—they had not kept up with DNA technology either. The lab's facilities were not conducive to good forensic science. The roof leaked over the DNA section of the crime lab, and the leaks were never patched. In 2001, when Tropical Storm Allison hit Houston, water poured through the roof and DNA evidence in three dozen murder and rape cases was soaked. Bloody water was seen seeping out of evidence boxes.[49] DNA is often seen as the definitive proof of guilt or innocence in many serious crimes, but it is hardly definitive when the facilities are defective and the analysts are incompetent.

Texas is the home of more verified wrongful convictions than any other state. Forty-two exonerations have occurred in Texas as a result of DNA testing.[50] Dallas County has emerged as the national leader in DNA exonerations of wrongfully convicted men. By early 2010 twenty men in Dallas County were exonerated by DNA evidence, almost half the DNA exonerations in the entire state of Texas.[51] One reason for the large number of DNA exonerations is simply that Dallas County has a policy of preserving physical evidence for lengthy periods of time, but others point to pattern of convictions based on eyewitness identification with little or questionable forensic evidence. Many of the wrongfully convicted were prosecuted during the administration of District Attorney Henry Wade, whose office was known for high conviction rates. Critics claimed his office prized those high conviction rates above all else.[52]

The case of Cameron Todd Willingham raises serious questions about whether an innocent man was executed for the arson murders of his three children. In 1991, Willingham's three girls were killed in a fire at their home shortly before Christmas. Willingham was convicted of starting the fire that killed them. Even though he was offered a plea bargain of a life sentence, he refused the plea, claiming that he was innocent. Willingham was executed in 2004. His conviction was largely based on expert testimony that the fire was arson. To a great extent, that testimony was based on the opinion that the fire had burned so hot that a fire accelerant must have been used to start the fire. Additionally, forensic tests had found evidence of an accelerant on the front porch of the house. However, before Willingham was executed a noted arson expert examined the case and prepared a report that showed that the fire patterns that were relied upon by the forensic experts who testified for the prosecution could have occurred without the presence of an accelerant and that the prosecution experts were relying on outdated information about the behavior of fire to reach their conclusions. That report was submitted to the Board of Pardons and Paroles, but the board rejected the plea for clemency.

After Willingham's execution, reporters for the *Chicago Tribune* investigated the case and asked three fire experts to examine the evidence. They concluded that the fire was not arson. Later, the Innocence Project, an organization that works on claims of innocence of those who have been imprisoned, asked four fire experts to review the Willingham case. They all agreed that the fire was not arson.

In 2005, Texas created a commission, the Texas Forensic Science Commission, to investigate claims of error or misconduct by forensic scientists. A fire scientist was hired by the commission to investigate the Willingham case and he, too, concluded there was no evidence the fire was arson.[53] In September 2009, forty-eight hours prior to the review of the report by the Texas Forensic Science Commission, Governor Perry replaced the head of the commission and two of its members. The meeting of the commission was canceled as a result. Earlier, Governor Perry had expressed confidence in Willingham's guilt, called the critics of the original arson investigation "supposed experts," and said that he had not "seen anything that would cause me to think that the decision [to execute Willingham] was not correct."[54] The commission, however, has not dropped the Willingham case, which remains under their review. The question remains: Did Texas execute an innocent man based on bad forensic science?

Another area of concern is the use of dog scent evidence to convict persons accused of crimes. Some prosecutors have claimed this evidence is as powerful as DNA evidence in supporting a conviction. This technique is not following a scent or picking out a package of drugs by trained dogs. Instead, it involves distinguishing different odors among people, identifying one odor, and then matching that odor to evidence obtained from a crime scene. A dog will be introduced to a scent sample collected at a crime scene. It will then be presented with a series of containers with similar scents—one taken from a suspect and others taken from other people matching the general description of the suspect. The dog will communicate to its handler if the first scent matches one of the scents in the containers. The handler will then testify that the dog accurately picked out the scent of a particular person or suspect. It is called a "scent lineup" and it has become a fairly widespread prosecution tool in Texas. The problem is that "scent lineups" are not reliable scientific evidence. Though prosecutors in Texas have used them since the mid-1990s, defense lawyers have only recently successfully challenged them. The result is that the Innocence Project of Texas is now trying identify persons in Texas who were convicted on the basis of "scent lineups" in the belief that this evidence is invalid and that those prisoners can be exonerated.[55]

Perhaps the criminal justice system in Texas works well. Overall, the previous examples may be exceptions to the rule. However, the Tulia drug arrests, the Dallas fake-drugs scandal, the Houston DNA lab's failures, and the Dallas DNA exonerations do cast doubt on whether the criminal justice system in Texas is working as well as it should.

Civil Cases

Figure 25.3 shows the numbers of civil cases disposed of by the courts of appeal and the trial courts in 1990, 1998, 2000, 2003, 2006, and 2009. The Texas court system is overloaded and would not be able to function adequately without the aid of visiting judges, retired or defeated judges who continue hearing cases in order to assist with the growing caseloads.

The Texas Supreme Court sets the tone for civil cases throughout the state. Most important of those types of cases, because of the large amounts of money involved, is tort law. In the early to mid-1980s, the court tended to be sympathetic to the plaintiffs' positions in tort cases. That is, they tended to support the side in a case that was suing businesses, professionals, and insurance companies. However, in 1988, more justices began to be elected who favored the defendants in civil lawsuits. One reason for this change was that in 1988, Republican justices began to be elected, and they were more conservative than many of the previous justices, who were Democrats. Another explanation is that interest groups that were harmed by the pro-plaintiff tendencies of the court began to organize, raise and spend money, and elect justices more sympathetic to their perspective. In the 1980s, plaintiffs' lawyers—lawyers who sue businesses, professionals, and insurance companies—had worked to elect pro-plaintiff justices. The tide turned, and business, professional, and insurance interests were now electing pro-defense justices. In 1996–97, civil defendants won three-fourths of the time, and insurance companies won almost all their substantive cases. Physicians, hospitals, and pharmaceutical companies won

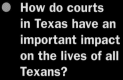
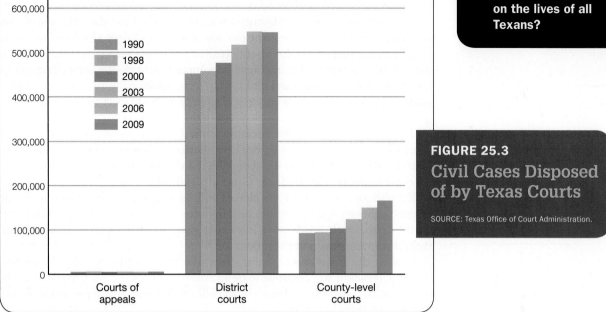

FIGURE 25.3

Civil Cases Disposed of by Texas Courts

SOURCE: Texas Office of Court Administration.

all seven of their cases before the Texas Supreme Court. In 1997–98, civil defendants won 69 percent of the time.[56] However, by 1998–99, the court was not as strongly pro-defendant, perhaps because of several new justices on the court who were regarded as somewhat moderate in their judicial philosophy. In insurance cases, defendants won 40 percent of the time; plaintiffs 40 percent of the time; and the decision of the court was a split decision 20 percent of the time. Defendants in medical cases, however, still won 100 percent of the time.[57] Most recently, the court seems to have shifted strongly in favor of civil defendants. A study of the decisions of the Texas Supreme Court in tort cases found that defendants won 87 percent of the time.[58] It is this power of the Texas Supreme Court to set the tone in civil cases that makes that court a political battleground, since millions—even billions—of dollars can be at stake as a result of the court's decisions.

Conclusion

Texas elects its judges in partisan judicial elections. For many years, when the Democratic Party was dominant, Texas judicial elections were staid, low-budget, noncompetitive events. However, with the growth of the Republican Party, judicial elections became highly political, and large amounts of money have been raised for judicial candidates, especially in Texas Supreme Court races. Often these judicial races pitted business interests against candidates backed by the plaintiffs' bar because the Supreme Court sets the tone of tort law in the state. These elections have calmed down in recent years as the Democratic Party has weakened and, at least in statewide races, judicial elections have become less competitive.

There have been problems in Texas judicial races, in large part because voters often don't know much about judicial candidates. As a result, voters often decide on the basis of the candidate's party affiliation or the candidate's name appeal. The result has been the election of several judicial candidates who lacked significant qualifications for the job.

Numerous efforts have been proposed to change the way judges are selected in Texas. There have been efforts to change the system of selection to "merit selection" and to nonpartisan election. Minority groups have pushed to reduce the size of judicial districts in order to increase the election of minority judges. However, no change so far has been successful. No majority coalition can agree on appropriate changes in the judicial selection system, and significant opposition to change comes from groups such as the political parties and business interests. Additionally, Texans seem satisfied with the current system of selection and seem to prefer to elect their judges.

Texas courts handle large caseloads of both civil and criminal cases. The highest civil court in the state is the Texas Supreme Court, currently an all-Republican court elected with strong support from business interests. The court has been severely criticized for being too sympathetic to those interests. The highest criminal court in the state is the Texas Court of Criminal Appeals. That court is also an all-Republican court, which was elected with strong support from prosecutors and victims' rights groups. Perhaps its most important function is as the appellate court for the death penalty in the state. It is a strongly pro-death-penalty court, and Texas ranks first in the nation in executions.

Because the Texas court system affects the liberty and especially the pocketbooks of Texans, it will continue to be an area of concern and controversy. And the most controversial area of Texas justice will continue to be the process by which judges are selected.

studyguide

Practice Quiz

Find a diagnostic Web Quiz with 20 additional questions on the StudySpace Web site: www.wwnorton.com/we-the-people

1. The highest criminal court in the state of Texas is the *(p. 895)*
   a) Texas Supreme Court.
   b) Texas Court of Appeals.
   c) Texas Court of Criminal Appeals.
   d) district court.

2. To reduce the caseload of county courts, the legislature created *(p. 897)*
   a) justice of the peace courts.
   b) regional courts.
   c) district courts.
   d) statutory county courts.

3. Which of the following judges do not have to be lawyers? *(p. 898)*
   a) Texas Supreme Court justices
   b) district judges
   c) justices of the peace
   d) none of the above

4. On conviction, the criminal's punishment is determined *(p. 901)*
   a) by the Grand Jury.

   b) in a separate hearing by the jury that determined the person's guilt.
   c) by the prosecuting attorney.
   d) by the prosecuting and defense attorneys.

5. In civil cases, defense lawyers often align themselves with *(p. 901)*
   a) business and industry.
   b) labor groups.
   c) groups that support workers.
   d) judges supported by the Democratic Party.

6. Grand juries *(p. 901)*
   a) determine the guilt of defendants.
   b) decide whether a trial of an accused is warranted.
   c) agree to plea bargains.
   d) recommend that defendants undergo bench trials.

7. Texas's movement from being a Democratic to a Republican state led to *(p. 903)*
   a) defeats of large numbers of incumbent judges.
   b) party switching by incumbent judges.
   c) large campaign contributions to judges.
   d) all of the above

8. In Texas, which event marked the rise of the Republican Party and partisan judicial elections? *(p. 906)*
   a) the election of President Ronald Reagan
   b) the impeachment of William Jefferson Clinton
   c) the appointment of Tom Phillips as Chief Justice of the United States
   d) the election of Bill Clements as governor of Texas

9. Which of the following groups has the largest number of judges? *(p. 908)*
   a) African American
   b) Asian American
   c) female
   d) Hispanic

10. Elections lost due to party membership rather than race or ethnicity do not violate *(p. 909)*
    a) the Fifth Amendment to the U.S. Constitution.
    b) Article I of the Texas Constitution.
    c) *Clements v. Maddox.*
    d) the Voting Rights Act.

11. How likely is Texas to change its method of selecting judicial candidates? *(p. 911)*
    a) Texas is scheduled to change to the Missouri Plan in January 2009.
    b) extremely likely in the next two decades
    c) likely in the next decade
    d) unlikely

12. Which of the following sets campaign contribution limits for judicial candidates in Texas? *(p. 912)*
    a) Judicial Campaign Fairness Act
    b) Judicial Campaign Act
    c) Voting Rights Act
    d) Civil Rights Act

13. In Texas, a person is subject to the death penalty for all except *(p. 914)*
    a) commission of a felony.
    b) murder of a fireman.
    c) murder for hire.
    d) murder of a child under the age of six.

14. Which of the following does not lead to questions about the integrity of the Texas criminal justice system? *(p. 919)*
    a) the large number of exonerations of people imprisoned in Texas
    b) the drug scandal in Tulia, Texas
    c) the Dallas fake-drug scandal
    d) none of the above

15. Philosophically, in the past few years, Texas courts became *(p. 922)*
    a) less likely to impose the death penalty.
    b) more liberal.
    c) more concerned with civil rights.
    d) more conservative.

Chapter Outline

(S) **Find a detailed Chapter Outline on the StudySpace Web site: www.wwnorton.com/we-the-people**

Key Terms

(S) **Find Flashcards to help you study these terms on the StudySpace Web site: www.wwnorton.com/we-the-people**

answer *(p. 899)*
bench trial *(p. 901)*
beyond a reasonable doubt *(p. 901)*
capital case *(p. 900)*
civil law *(p. 899)*
complaint *(p. 899)*
contingent fee *(p. 899)*
county courts *(p. 897)*
county judge *(p. 897)*
courts of appeal *(p. 897)*

criminal law *(p. 899)*
district courts *(p. 897)*
en banc *(p. 909)*
felony *(p. 900)*
grand jury *(p. 900)*
indictment *(p. 901)*
Judicial Campaign Fairness Act *(p. 912)*
justice of the peace courts *(p. 898)*
merit selection *(p. 911)*
misdemeanor *(p. 900)*

municipal courts *(p. 899)*
ordinance *(p. 899)*
plea bargain *(p. 901)*
preponderance of the evidence *(p. 900)*
retention election *(p. 910)*
statutory county courts at law *(p. 897)*
statutory probate courts *(p. 897)*
Texas Court of Criminal Appeals *(p. 895)*
Texas Supreme Court *(p. 895)*

Recommended Web Sites

The Supreme Court of Texas
www.supreme.courts.state.tx.us/

Texans for Public Justice
www.tpj.org

Texas Court of Criminal Appeals
www.cca.courts.state.tx.us/

Texas Courts Online: Texas Court Structure
www.courts.state.tx.us/

Recent scandals involving the Dallas County constables—including the high number of traffic tickets issued and the high number of cars impounded by constables—have raised questions about local government in Texas.

26

Local Government in Texas

WHAT GOVERNMENT DOES AND WHY IT MATTERS Local government is generally praised for being closer to the people it serves and, therefore, being more responsive to those people than the state or national governments can be. The problem is that sometimes local governmental officials work in relative obscurity, avoiding media and public scrutiny. This means that if they abuse their power, their behavior often takes longer to come to light. One example has been a recent scandal involving two of the five constables in Dallas County. Traditionally in Texas, the office of constable has been an elective office with limited duties. Constables have served civil court papers and have provided bailiffs for justices of the peace. However, some constables, such as those in Dallas County, transformed their offices into full-fledged police departments. Dallas County constables, for example, developed a traffic enforcement role. In Dallas County, in 1995, no deputy constable positions were devoted to traffic enforcement; in 2010 seventy-six deputy constables in that county did traffic enforcement. Constables also formed heavily armed, tactical units. They patrolled high-crime areas, shut down drug houses,

focusquestions

- What are the main types of public offices at the county level?

- Why is city government important to democratic governance at the local level?

- How do special districts differ from other forms of local government?

arrested parents who are behind on child support, and cracked down on drug dealers selling "cheese" heroin to students. County commissioners not only approved some of the expanded activities of constables, but also implemented new legal strategies to expand their law enforcement functions. Since constables are elected officials, they are not subject to much oversight and instead function as law enforcement fiefdoms in larger counties in Texas.

In two constables' precincts in Dallas County, there have been problems with vehicles being impounded. These constables have impounded thousands of vehicles without requiring that the towing companies account for what happened to the vehicles. Subsequent investigations of the two constables have also identified issues such as complaints that deputy constables have been forced to work on unpaid security details and to sell raffle tickets to raise money for constables' re-election campaigns.[1] These problems, going on for years, have only recently caused county commissioners to reconsider the expanded role of constables.

Sadly, it is not only the office of constable that shows problems at the local governmental level. Recent scandals in Dallas involving city council members show still other disturbing aspects of local government in Texas. Former mayor pro tem Don Hill and a number of associates were accused of taking bribes from low-income housing developers in exchange for political support for their projects. The corruption probe first became public in 2005, but did not result in convictions until toward the end of 2009. Hill was convicted of selling his votes in a bribery and extortion scheme that involved pressuring low-income housing developers for kickbacks.[2]

The cases of the constables and Don Hill show that while local government provides many of the services people depend on, the fact that few people pay close attention to local government means there is room for abuses of power and action that go against the interests of the public. In this chapter, we will take a closer look at the main features of local government in Texas.

chapter contents

● County Government in Texas

Local government institutions play a major role in Texas. In late 2007 there were 4,835 local governments, an average of 19.1 per county. Of these, 1,462 were *general purpose* governments, including 254 county governments and 1,209 municipal governments. There were also 3,373 *special purpose* governments, including 1,082 public school systems and 2,291 special district governments.[3] Local government is everywhere in Texas, providing water, electricity, and sewer services, as well as police protection and public education.

All but two states have governmental units known as counties (or parishes), but Texas has 254 counties, more than any other state.[4] County government in Texas is primarily a way of governing rural areas. Because Texas is so vast, with huge areas that are sparsely populated, county government remains an important aspect of local government. As was discussed in previous chapters, the Texas Constitution places numerous restrictions on government, and numerous provisions of the constitution place restrictions on counties. Indeed, in Texas, counties have very constricted governmental powers. Unlike city governments, they usually do not have powers to legislate. Because they lack much of the power of self-government, they often function primarily as an administrative arm of the state government.

Texas counties have their origins in the "municipality," which was the local governmental unit under Spanish and Mexican rule. These municipalities were large and included settlements and surrounding rural territories. In 1835, Texas was divided into three departments and twenty-three municipalities. With the Republic of 1836, the twenty-three municipalities became counties. By the time Texas became a state in 1845, there were thirty-six counties, and when Texas entered the Confederacy in 1861, there were 122 counties. The number of counties increased steadily until 1921, when the 254th county was created. The initial idea behind counties was that each citizen could travel to the county seat—on horseback, of course—and return home in a day. Given the sparse population of west Texas, in particular, that initial idea for county organization was eventually rejected, but it does show that Texans believed that the local center of government, the county seat, should be accessible to the people.[5]

Numerous County Offices: Checks and Balances or Built-In Problems?

As with the state government, one of the characteristics of county government in Texas is a multiplicity of elected governmental officials. Some argue that the large number of public officials at the county level is desirable because it creates a strong system of checks and balances, allowing no one official to dominate county government.[6] However, that system of checks and balances comes at a high price. There are problems of coordination of governmental activity, much as at the state level. One of the most important bodies of county elected officials is the **county commissioners court,** which is the main governing unit in the county. Although the commissioners court is not really a judicial court, it may have gotten its name from the Republic of Texas Constitution (1836–45), in which the county governing unit consisted of the chief justice of the county court and the justices of the peace within the county.[7]

county commissioners court
the main governing body of each county; has the authority to set the county tax rate and budget

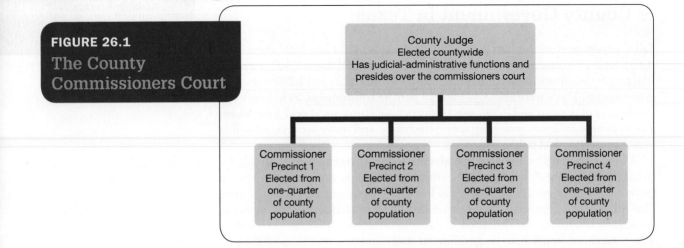

FIGURE 26.1
The County
Commissioners Court

County Judge
Elected countywide
Has judicial-administrative functions and
presides over the commissioners court

| Commissioner Precinct 1 Elected from one-quarter of county population | Commissioner Precinct 2 Elected from one-quarter of county population | Commissioner Precinct 3 Elected from one-quarter of county population | Commissioner Precinct 4 Elected from one-quarter of county population |

county judge the person in each of Texas's 254 counties who presides over the county court and county commissioners court, with responsibility for the administration of county government; some county judges carry out judicial responsibilities

county commissioner government official (four per county) on the county commissioners court whose main duty is the construction and maintenance of roads and bridges

The structure of the current arrangement for the county commissioners court, shown in Figure 26.1, consists of a **county judge** and four commissioners. The county judge is elected countywide and serves for four years. He or she presides over the meetings of the commissioners court and has administrative powers as well as judicial powers in rural counties. In those counties, the county judge hears minor criminal cases and handles some civil matters such as probate matters. In larger counties, the county judge is an administrator only, with the judicial duties of the office removed by the creation of judgeships, such as probate judgeships and county court-at-law judgeships.

Each commissioners court also has four **county commissioners**; each of these officials is elected from a precinct that encompasses roughly one-fourth the population of the county. In the late 1960s, one of the great issues in constitutional law involved the issue of malapportionment, the allegation that election districts did not represent equal population groupings but other types of groupings such as equal land areas. The malapportionment of Texas's county commissioners courts became an important case before the U.S. Supreme Court because the commissioners precincts tended to be drawn to represent fairly equal land areas within the county rather than equal population groupings. In *Avery v. Midland County* (1968), the U.S. Supreme Court held that the principle of "one person, one vote" applies to commissioners courts just as it applies to legislative districts. The result was that commissioners precincts must now be drawn to reflect equal population groupings within counties.[8]

The main duty of county commissioners is the construction and maintenance of roads and bridges; usually each commissioner provides for roadwork within his or her precinct. That aspect of a commissioner's work is, of course, very important to rural residents and can be politically controversial and sometimes tinged with corruption. In 1980, a federal probe of county commissioners began over the issue of kickbacks on road and bridge supplies. The investigation centered on roughly eight counties in east Texas, but when news of the federal investigation surfaced, prices paid for road and bridge supplies in some Texas counties suddenly dropped as much as 20 percent at a time when inflation was running at about 12 percent.[9]

The commissioners court also sets the county tax rate and the county budget. Related to its taxing and budgeting powers is its power to make contracts and

The county commissioners court is the main governing unit at the county level, with control over the county budget and the construction of bridges and roads in the county. Here, Travis County Commissioner Ron Davis, left, appears with business leaders to announce a major new construction project in Austin.

pay bills. Perhaps the most important expenditure of most county commissioners courts, other than road and bridge expenditures, is the cost of building and maintaining county jail facilities. Indigent health care can be a significant cost for counties as well, along with, in some cases, fire protection and sanitation. Some counties also have costs associated with the maintenance of libraries and hospitals and costs for emergency welfare expenditures, such as those brought on by natural disasters or fires. The commissioners court can appoint certain county officials, and it can hire personnel as well as fill vacancies in county offices. It also administers elections in the county.

However, as noted earlier, there are numerous elected officials in Texas counties, each with an independent power base. It seems nearly inevitable that tensions would develop between the budgetary powers of the commissioners courts and the needs and desires of other elected county officials.

As pointed out in Table 26.1, other officeholders are elected at the county level and still others at the precinct level of the county. There is some variation in the numbers of officeholders, depending on the county. For example, larger counties will have more justices of the peace and more **constables** than smaller ones. In some counties, constables serve legal papers; in others, constables not only serve legal papers but also have a law-enforcement role with the authority to patrol, give tickets, and make arrests. Some counties use constables to check on truants from school, having found a niche area that others in law enforcement do not seem to want.

Larger counties may have probate judges, numerous district judges, and county court-at-law judges. Smaller counties may not have probate judges or even county court-at-law judges. Some of the smaller counties may share district judges and district attorneys with other counties. Laws setting up different offices often vary from county to county as well. As a result, some counties have county attorneys

constable precinct-level county official involved with serving legal papers and, in some counties, enforcing the law

TABLE 26.1

Countywide and Precinct-Level Elected Officials

COUNTYWIDE OFFICIALS	PRECINCT-LEVEL OFFICIALS
County judge	County commissioners
Possibly county court-at-law judges, possibly probate judges, and district judges	Justices of the peace
County, criminal district, or district attorney	Constables
Sheriff	
County and district clerk	
Possibly county treasurer	
Tax assessor collector	
Possibly county surveyor	

and others have criminal district attorneys. Some counties have county clerks and district clerks; smaller counties may combine the offices in one person. Some counties have county treasurers; others do not have such an office.

Are Some Counties Too Small?

The reason for the variation in offices is not simply that laws were passed at different times, thus sacrificing uniformity among counties. It is also the case that Texas is a large, diverse state with great variation among its counties. The result is great variation in the numbers of government officials, the duties of officials, and the services provided by the different county governments. Brewster County has a population of only 9,271, but it has 6,193 square miles of territory, about the size of Connecticut and Rhode Island combined. Rockwall County, in contrast, has only 149 square miles and a population of 78,088. Although Harris County has a population of 3,984,349, Loving County has a population of only 57; yet Loving County covers a huge land area—nearly 677 square miles. That West Texas county experienced a 14.92 percent decrease in population since 2000.[10] As the county sheriff (who is also the tax assessor and the voting registrar) put it, "It doesn't surprise me. There's not much work here and some people have moved out." For the residents of Loving County, the leading employer is the Loving County government. Indeed, most of the people living in the county also work for the county. The fact that county government is the major employer in the county may be the main justification for Loving County's continuing existence as a governmental unit—although people with taxable property may also prefer the Loving County tax structure to that of another governmental unit.[11]

One of the medium-sized Texas counties is Jasper County in East Texas, which has a population of 35,401. Although a small population may create a sense of community and closeness to local government, citizens of Jasper County have learned that when unusual events occur in a small county, it can place a terrific strain on county resources. Jasper County had huge costs as a result of the capital murder trials of three men accused in the 1998 dragging death of James Byrd, Jr. Two of the three men were sentenced to death; the third got life in prison. Costs associated with the trial came to over $1.02 million. The result was such a strain on the $10 million annual county budget that the county was forced to increase property taxes by 6.7 percent over two years to pay for the trial. Only a massive flood in the county in the late 1970s had come close to creating a financial burden similar to that of the trial.

Jasper County is not the only one struggling with a huge financial burden from capital murder trials. Just prosecuting a capital case costs an average of $200,000 to $300,000, and that does not include the costs of indigent-defense lawyers, appeals, and trial transcripts.

The burden of the capital case on Jasper County convinced Texas lawmakers to expand a program to assist counties in paying the "extraordinary costs" of prosecuting capital murder cases. That aid program was motivated by a fear that smaller counties would pursue lesser charges than those carrying the death penalty to avoid incurring financial hardship. One of the sponsors of the legislation, for example, said that he had often heard concerns expressed over the cost pressures of capital trials from officials in the seventeen rural counties he represented.

Most recently, Polk County in East Texas (population about 46,175) estimated that it had unanticipated costs of $200,000 when the U.S. Supreme Court overturned the sentence of Johnny Paul Penry, who was convicted in the stabbing death of a woman in 1979, and sent the case back for another trial. Even with $100,000 in aid from the state to help pay the bill, the costs of one trial can tremendously burden such a small county.[12]

Franklin County Commissioners were recently told by the district attorney that they would need to come up with a minimum of $250,000 for a murder trial. The problem for Franklin County was that the commissioners had no money budgeted for such an expense, since capital murder cases were so rare in the county. For a small county such as Franklin (pop. 10,533), such an expense requires either major cuts in other budget items or a tax increase.[13]

One hundred sixty Texas counties have populations of fewer than 30,000, and 132 of those counties have populations of fewer than 20,000. One recent study found that Texas has wide variations in its counties' application of capital punishment, perhaps because of the costs of death penalty cases to smaller counties. Between 1976, when the U.S. Supreme Court reinstated capital punishment, and December 2008, Texas sent just over 1,000 inmates to death row. Harris County, the county in Texas with the largest population, accounted for 280 or 28 percent of the death sentences. Remarkably, even though Texas has 254 counties, a single county accounted for 280 of the death-sentenced inmates. If one adds three other heavily populated counties in Texas—Bexar, Dallas, and Tarrant counties—one finds that 510 of the state's death sentences since 1976 came from four of the counties in Texas with the largest populations. In contrast, 130 Texas counties with relatively small populations have not sent an inmate to death row in the last three decades.[14]

One of the duties of the county commissioners court is to construct and maintain roads and bridges, such as this one near Austin.

Counties exist as they do for a variety of reasons. One reason commonly given, but which offers only a partial explanation, is that, as we have seen, counties were intended to be compact enough that people could ride a horse to the county seat and back in one day. Whatever value that reason had for the development of counties is, of course, long gone. Other reasons are political. For example, wealthy landowners may have urged the legislature to create counties so that they could control county government and hence the amount of property taxes they might pay. Still, we must wonder if so many small counties are needed. The Jasper County situation suggests that even moderate-size counties by Texas standards may be too small to function adequately in unusual situations.

The Functions of County Government

What, then, are the main functions of Texas county government? Table 26.2 lists them. Like most other aspects of county government in Texas, these five primary functions are performed with great variation among the counties.

County road and bridge construction and maintenance have traditionally been such important functions of the commissioners court that often county commissioners are called "road commissioners." County commissioners maintain more than one-half of the roads in the state.[15] Although a 1947 law allowed counties to place the road system under the authority of a county engineer, in most counties roads and bridges remain one of the most important responsibilities of the commissioners.

Law enforcement is another important responsibility of county government. This job is undertaken by constables and by the sheriff. The sheriff is the chief law-enforcement officer within county government. In rural counties with few city police departments, the sheriff may be the major law-enforcement official in the county. In addition to law enforcement and the provision of deputies for

TABLE 26.2

Primary Functions of County Government

- Construction and maintenance of roads and bridges
- Law enforcement
- Dispute resolution
- Record keeping
- Social services

County governments are also important for law enforcement. Here, a captain from the McLennan County sheriff's office discusses the procedures for a protest with Cindy Sheehan. After Sheehan's son died in Iraq, she and her supporters demonstrated against the Iraq War outside of President Bush's Texas ranch.

In rural parts of Texas, county courts are where civil and criminal cases are heard. This photo shows the Jasper County Courthouse during the capital murder case of the men accused of the 1998 dragging death of James Byrd, Jr.

the district and county courts, sheriffs are responsible for the county jail. In many counties, operating a county jail is an expensive and major undertaking. In early 2010, for example, Harris County was guarding and supervising 9,406 inmates in its county jail, Dallas County had 6,433 inmates in its jail, and Tarrant County had 2,902. On the other hand, fifteen counties had no jails. Glasscock County had room for twelve inmates in its jail, but no residents; Sterling County had room for five inmates, but no residents. Real County had a jail capacity of three with one inmate, and Terrell County had a capacity of eight and six inmates.[16]

Although the law-enforcement budget is approved by the county commissioners court, sheriffs often have considerable influence in county government and develop their own law enforcement styles. The sheriff of Smith County, for example, has not only a SWAT team but two armored personnel carriers, each of which weighs thirteen tons, moves on tracks, can float, can move up 60-degree grades, and can go forty miles per hour.[17]

County and **district attorneys** also perform a law-enforcement role by prosecuting criminal cases. Usually, the district attorneys prosecute the more serious criminal cases in the district courts, whereas the county attorneys prosecute the lesser criminal cases in the county courts.

Record keeping is an important function of county government. **County clerks** keep vital statistics for the county and issue licenses; they maintain records for the commissioners court and the county courts. Most important, the county clerk is responsible for records relating to property transactions. Sometimes the county clerk maintains election and voting records. If there is a **district clerk**, he or she maintains records for the district courts, though in small counties this office is combined with the office of the county clerk. Tax records are maintained by the **county tax assessor-collector**, who also collects taxes, though in the smaller

county attorney county official who prosecutes lesser criminal cases in the county court

district attorney public official who prosecutes the more serious criminal cases in the district court

county clerk public official who is the main record-keeper of the county

district clerk public official who is the main record-keeper of the district court

county tax assessor-collector public official who maintains the county tax records and collects the taxes owed to the county

counties the sheriff often performs this job. Although constitutional amendments have eliminated the office of county treasurer in many counties, where the office does exist, the treasurer is responsible for receiving and expending county funds. The **county auditor** now does much of the work of the county treasurer. There are now about 200 county auditors in Texas. Auditors are not elected; they are appointed by the county's district judges. Not only do they audit the county's funds, but in large counties they will often prepare the county budget for the commissioners court.

Counties also have an important role in dispute resolution through their court system. Civil law is a way of resolving disputes between people, and the justice of the peace court and the county and district courts deal with large numbers of civil disputes as well as criminal matters. County and district attorneys may also represent the interests of the county or state in disputes that involve governmental interests.

Finally, counties may perform a social service function. The social services provided will vary from county to county. However, the most important social services will be emergency welfare assistance to individuals. This may include the provision of food, housing, rental assistance, or shelter to needy individuals. Larger counties have health departments to work on the prevention and control of communicable diseases. Some counties operate mental health services. Some counties provide parks, airports, fire protection, and sanitation facilities. One of the most important social services provided by counties is the provision of indigent health care.

County Government in Perspective

County government occupies an important role in Texas local government, although the powers of county government are greatly restricted by the Texas legislature. One of the most notable features of Texas counties is their great variation in geographical size, population, and even in county offices, duties of county officials, and services provided by county government. Additionally, like state government, county government has a large number of elected county officials. Although this may limit the power of any one county official, it also produces disagreement, conflict, and difficulty in accomplishing objectives.

Many of Texas's counties are very small, possibly too small to meet the needs of Texans in the twenty-first century, although there is no serious effort to change the current structure of counties. Counties perform important and often expensive functions. Some of those functions of county government and the costs associated with them—for example, road and bridge construction and maintenance, jail construction and operation, and indigent health care—are likely to increase significantly in the future.

● City Government in Texas

There are 1,209 municipal governments incorporated in Texas, ranging in size from 31 residents to over 2.1 million (see Table 26.3). Like county governments, municipal governments are creations of the state of Texas. In the early years of the Republic of Texas, the Texas Congress was responsible for enacting laws that incorporated cities. The number of urban areas grew in the state in the late nineteenth and early twentieth centuries, making the management of local affairs a growing

TABLE 26.3

Municipal Governments in Texas

SIZE	NUMBER
100,000 or more	28
50,000–99,999	29
10,000–49,999	148
5,000–9,999	122
Fewer than 5,000	882
Total	**1,209**

SOURCE: Calculated from *Texas Almanac 2008-2009* (Dallas: *Dallas Morning News*, 2008). 8, 498

TABLE 26.4

The Largest Home-Rule Cities (January 2009 estimates)

NAME	POPULATION	FORM OF GOVERNMENT	FIRST CHARTER	PRESENT FORM ADOPTED
Houston	2,254,690	Mayor-council	1905	1994
San Antonio	1,363,612	Council-manager	1914	1951
Dallas	1,278,484	Council-manager	1889	1907
Austin	786,484	Council-manager	1919	1994
Fort Worth	717,136	Council-manager	1924	1985
El Paso	618,251	Mayor-council	1873	1907
Arlington	376,314	Council-manager	1920	1990
Corpus Christi	288,241	Council-manager	1926	1993
Plano	285,750	Council-manager	1961	1993
Lubbock	223,432	Council-manager	1909	1917

SOURCES: Compiled from *Texas Almanac 2006–2007* (Dallas: *Dallas Morning News*, 2006), 340–64; and *Texas Almanac 2008–2009* (Dallas: *Dallas Morning News*, 2008), 8; Texas State Data Center.

burden on the state legislature. In 1912, the legislature passed a constitutional home-rule amendment that enabled cities of more than 5,000 inhabitants to adopt home-rule charters with a majority vote of qualified voters.

Home-rule charters essentially lay down the rules under which a city will operate.[18] They provide for the form of government that operates in the city and specify the number of members serving on the city's governing body. They also may grant the governing body the power to annex land adjacent to the city as well as to set property tax rates up to $2.50 per $100 valuation. Home-rule cities are also constitutionally authorized to borrow money in ways not available to smaller municipal entities. Home-rule charters must be consistent with the state constitution and any other relevant statutory provisions. For example, the state has mandated that most city elections take place on a date provided by the Texas Election Code. City elections must be conducted under the general guidelines set by the state. Nevertheless, home rule in Texas has delegated enormous power to local city governments. According to a report by the Advisory Commission on Intergovernmental Relations, the Texas Constitution leaves cities more "home rule" than does any other state. There are now 335 home-rule cities in Texas.[19] Table 26.4 lists the ten largest of these.

Cities and towns of fewer than 5,000 people are chartered by general statute, as was the case for all cities and towns prior to the passage of the Home-Rule Charter Amendments in 1912. These "general-law" cities and towns may act or organize themselves only as explicitly permitted by statutory law passed by the state legislature. The constitution also limits what they can do. For example, general-law cities may levy, assess, and collect taxes as authorized by statute. But the constitution sets

home-rule charter the rules under which a city operates

a maximum property tax rate of $1.50 per $100 valuation, compared with $2.50 per $100 valuation for home-rule cities.

Politics at the local level is often politics at its most basic. Unlike in presidential elections, in which the issues may well involve questions of war and peace, or state elections, in which issues may involve such things as whether a state should have an income tax, in local elections the most pressing issue may well be potholes in the city streets. Unlike most other city services such as parks, libraries, or police and fire protection, the condition of city streets is experienced by almost every city resident and thus it becomes a prime issue for discussion among candidates. Although pothole repair may not seem earthshaking in the hierarchy of political issues, it is exactly such an issue that most directly and routinely affects most people's lives. As mundane as such concerns are, these are the fundamental issues in most local elections because they reflect the needs and expectations that residents have of local government.

Forms of Government in Texas Cities

Texas home-rule cities have had three major forms of city government: the mayor-council form, the commissioner form, and the council-manager form. The **mayor-council form of government** is the oldest. It consists of an elected mayor and city council. The mayor is elected from the city at large. The council may be elected either at large or from a series of **single-member districts**, or a mixture of the two. In the mayor-council form of government, the mayor is the chief executive officer of the city. He or she presides over council meetings and has a variety of appointment powers. The city council, meanwhile, serves as the legislative body in the city, passing local laws and watching over the executive departments.

There have been both strong mayor-council systems and weak ones, depending on the powers given to the mayor by the city charter or state statute. In the *strong mayor–council* variation, various executive powers, such as appointive and removal powers to boards and departments or veto powers, are strong. These powers enable the mayor to establish effective control over various executive departments in the city and to control the legislative agenda of the city council. In the *weak mayor–council* variation, these executive powers are much more limited, fragmenting power between the mayor and other elected or appointed officials.

In the 1990s, the mayor-council form of government was the dominant form of government in most of the incorporated cities in Texas, particularly among general-law cities. However, among home-rule cities the mayor-council government was not popular. According to a 1995 survey of 284 home-rule cities conducted by the *Texas Almanac*, only thirty-one had adopted the mayor-council form of government.

A second form of city government found in Texas is the **commissioner form of government**.[20] Under the commissioner system, the city is run by a small commission, composed of between five and seven members generally elected on an at-large basis. The commission acts in both a legislative and an executive capacity. As a group, commissioners enact laws for the city. As individuals, commissioners are in charge of one of a variety of departments. One commissioner is also designated as the mayor to preside at meetings.

The commission plan was developed as a response to the devastating hurricane that hit Galveston in 1900, claiming an estimated 6,000 lives. It reflected a desire to bring good business practices to city government that would somehow escape

mayor-council form of government a form of city government in which the mayor is the chief executive and the city council is the legislative body; in the *strong mayor–council* variation, the mayor's powers enable him or her to control executive departments and the agenda of the city council; in the *weak mayor–council* variation, the mayor's power is more limited

single-member district voters within a district elect only one representative to represent that district

commissioner form of government a form of city government in which the city is run by a small group of elected commissioners who act in both legislative and executive capacities

the squabbles and inefficiency of traditional local government found in the mayor-council form. The commission plan was adopted by Houston in 1905 and by a number of other Texas cities in 1907, including Dallas, Fort Worth, and El Paso. Republicans and Democratic Progressives across the country supported the plan and other reform principles often integrated with it, including nonpartisan elections, merit selection of employees, and such direct democracy techniques as the initiative, referendum, and recall. At its peak in 1918, the commission form was used by approximately 500 cities across the country and 75 cities in Texas. Following World War I, the number of commission-form cities decreased. By 2000, no city in Texas had a pure commission form of government, although twenty-six still claimed to have some variation of a commission-manager form of government.[21] In practice, none of the "commissioners" in these cities exercised executive control over specific city departments as envisioned in the original commission system. Instead, they functioned more like council members under the council-manager form of city government.[22]

The third form of city government found in Texas is the **council-manager form of government**.[23] As originally envisioned, a city council elected in an **at-large election** was to be the policy-making body. Council members generally received little or no pay and were intended to be publicly motivated citizens interested in serving the public good, rather than professional politicians. A mayor was selected from among the council members. The city manager was to be the chief executive and administrative official in the city. As in the commissioner form of government, the goal of the council-manager form of government was twofold: to free local government from the seamier side of politics and to bring administrative expertise to local government.

In 1913, Amarillo was the first city to abandon the commissioner form of government for the council-manager system. In 1914, Taylor and Denton followed suit. By 1947, there were 47 council-manager systems in Texas. By the mid-1990s, 251 of the home-rule cities had council-manager systems. Across the United States, it has become the most popular form of government for cities of over 10,000 residents.

The commissioner form of government was developed as a response to the devastating hurricane that hit Galveston in 1900.

council-manager form of government a form of city government in which public policies are developed by the city council and executive and administrative functions are assigned to a professional city manager

at-large election an election in which officials are selected by voters of the entire geographical area, rather than from smaller districts within that area

Today, council-manager systems vary across the state in a number of ways. The desire for professional administration of local government remains high. Most city managers have graduate degrees and are paid high salaries like other executive officers in the private sector. But a desire for more political accountability through traditional democratic processes has introduced some changes. The growing ethnic and racial diversity of some Texas cities has forced many political leaders to question the wisdom of freeing local government too much from democratic controls. In most cities, mayors now are elected at large from the population as a whole, rather than from just the council. Many cities also elect council members from single-member districts rather than just at-large districts. Many see at-large districts as undercutting minority representation by diluting minority votes. Only when Dallas moved from an at-large council to a council elected from single-member districts in 1991 did minorities come to play a major role in the decision-making processes of city government. But most cities and towns under the council-manager system continue to view local political offices as part-time jobs. Mayoral and council salaries remain low. A few cities, such as Austin, offer considerably higher salaries. The demand for more democratic accountability in local government will likely continue to lead to more changes in the council-manager system of government across Texas. Balancing an efficient city government run by professionals with democratic political processes will continue to be a problem as Texas's metropolitan areas grow and diversify in the early twenty-first century.

city controller the chief financial officer of a city

A Tale of Three Cities

Houston is the largest city in Texas, with over 2.2 million people. It has a strong mayor-council form of government. There are sixteen elected officials in the city serving concurrent two-year terms, including a mayor, a controller, and fourteen council members. The mayor serves as the chief executive official in the city and is the city's chief administrator and official representative. Much of his power stems from his authority to appoint department heads and people serving on advisory boards, subject to council approval. The mayor also presides over the city council with voting privileges. The fourteen-member council is a legislative body composed of five at-large seats and nine single-member district seats.

Annise Parker is the current mayor of Houston. She previously served as a member of the city council and as city controller.

Unlike in most other cities, the city controller in Houston is an elected official.[24] The **city controller**, currently Ronald Green, is the city's chief financial officer. Besides investing city funds, conducting internal audits of city departments, and operating the city's financial management system, the controller is also responsible for certifying the availability of funds for city council initiatives. In the end, the office of the controller is both a professional position and a political position. Not surprisingly, the controller often comes into conflict with the mayor and the council over important policy issues.

Although local politics in Houston is nominally nonpartisan, in recent years it has taken on a partisan flavor. Houston's current mayor is Annise Parker, who serves as executive officer of the city.

Until recently, Dallas was the second largest city in Texas, but San Antonio has now overtaken Dallas. Dallas operates under a council-manager form of government. For years, city politics had been dominated by the white business community. At-large nonpartisan elections tended to elect a council that was relatively united in its understanding of the problems facing the city and its vision of where the city should go. A bitter struggle in the late 1980s and early 1990s over rewriting the city charter divided the city along racial lines. The new charter, which went into effect in 1991, called for a fourteen-member council elected from single-member districts and a mayor elected at large. Members are limited to serving four two-year terms consecutively. Under the new charter, membership on the council was transformed as a significant number of African Americans and Hispanics were elected to the council.

As in other council-manager systems, the power of the mayor in Dallas is weak. The mayor—currently Tom Leppert—presides over council meetings, creates council committees, and appoints members, chairs, and co-chairs. In many ways, however, the mayor is only first among equals on the council. The council as a whole is the legislative body for the city, approving budgets, determining the tax rate, and appointing key public officials, including the city manager, city attorney, city auditor, city secretary, municipal court judges, and various citizen boards and commissions. The city manager serves at the will of the council and is removable by a two-thirds vote of the council. As in San Antonio, the city manager's pow-

Mayor Tom Leppert of Dallas, right, speaks with Mexican president Felipe Calderon. Prior to his election as mayor in 2007, Leppert was the CEO of Turner Construction, the largest commercial builder in the United States.

ers in Dallas are great. As the chief administrative officer, the city manager has the power to appoint and remove all heads of departments and subordinate officers and employees in the city, subject to civil service provisions. Despite the attempt to remove the city manager from the pressures of political life in Dallas, recent city managers have found themselves forced to accommodate the reality of an increasingly politicized city council. The political pressures emerging from Dallas's single-member district council may ultimately compel the city to reexamine the wisdom of retaining a council-manager system. As Dallas learned in the 1990s, efficient government and democratic governance are not as easy to balance as advocates of the council-manager system once thought.

San Antonio has a council-manager form of government. The council is composed of members elected from ten single-member districts on a nonpartisan basis. The mayor, currently Julián Castro, is the eleventh member of the council and is selected at large. All members of the council serve for two-year terms and receive largely honorific salaries. The mayor's salary is a paltry $3,000 per year in addition to payment as a council member; other council members are paid $20 per meeting, not to exceed $1,040 per year. Members are subject to recall if 10 percent of the qualified voters in a district sign a petition of recall and a recall election is successful. The city charter also provides for initiatives and referendums that emerge from the voters.

The city manager in San Antonio serves at the pleasure of the council as the chief executive and administrative official in the city. He or she has wide-ranging appointment and removal authority over officers and employees in the administrative service of the city. The city manager is Sheryl Sculley. Prior to becoming city manager, she was assistant city manager of Phoenix. She supervises the activities of all city departments, a budget of $2 billion, and 12,000 employees.

San Antonio mayor Julian Castro, elected in 2009, previously served as a member of the city council.

One illustration of the push for change is that in 2001–02, each of the three major candidates for mayor suggested that the structure of city government needs reexamining. One of the mayoral candidates publicly commented on the need for more power to be in the hands of the mayor. A city council member argued that council members have so little power to set spending priorities or influence city staff that individual citizens do not see city government as a way of influencing their lives. There has even been some discussion of the value of partisan elections in city races.

● Special Districts

special district a unit of local government that performs a single service, such as education or sanitation, within a limited geographical area.

A **special district** is a unit of local government that performs a single service in a limited geographical area. These governments solve problems that cross borders of existing units of government. Special districts can be created to serve an entire county, part of a county, all of two or more counties, or parts of two or more counties. The number of special districts has increased dramatically in the last fifty years. In the United States, the number increased by 400 percent.[25] In Texas, the number increased by more than 600 percent.[26] By the year 2002, there were more special districts than any other form of local government.

Districts can be created to do almost anything that is legal. Some districts are formed to provide hospital care, others to furnish pure water to cities that, in turn, sell it to their residents. Mosquito control, navigation, flood control, sanitation, drainage, and law enforcement are a few more examples of special districts.

Types of Special Districts

school district a specific type of special district that provides public education in a designated area

There are two types of special districts in Texas. The first is the **school district**, which consists of independent school districts in the state. These districts offer public education from pre-kindergarten through twelfth grade. Almost all school districts offer the full range of educational opportunities; however, some small, rural schools provide education only through the eighth grade. Others limit their programs to the sixth grade, and still others end with the fourth grade. Those with limited offerings contract with nearby districts to complete the education of their students.

The second classification of special districts is the **nonschool special district**. Everything except the school districts is included in this category. Municipal utility districts (MUDs), economic development corporations, hospital districts, and fire-prevention districts are the most common examples.

School Districts

Every inch of land in Texas is part of a school district, and the state contains slightly more than 1,000 school districts. Some districts in East and West Texas cover an entire county. In metropolitan counties, there may be a dozen or more districts. Each is governed by an elected board of trustees composed of five to nine members. The board employs a superintendent to oversee the daily operation of the district. On the recommendation of the superintendent, the trustees

- set overall policy for the school district.
- adopt the budget for the district.
- set the tax rate for the district. (The maximum tax rate for a district is $1.04 for each $100 the property is worth. A rate higher than $1.04 requires voter approval.)
- adopt textbooks for classroom use.
- hire principals, faculty, and support staff.
- set the school calendar.
- determine salaries and benefits for employees.

Educating millions of students is a daunting task. By localizing public education, the state places much of the burden on the local school districts. This allows local residents to participate in governing the school districts. Unfortunately, few people vote in elections to select members of the board of trustees. Even fewer individuals attend meetings of the school board.

Nonschool Special Districts

Municipal Utility Districts Municipal utility districts (MUDs) offer electricity, water, sewer, and sanitation services outside the city limits. These governments might offer all utility services or only one or two, depending on the needs of the special district. Though located throughout Texas, the vast majority are found in the Houston metropolitan area.

MUDs can be a financial blessing for developers. Entrepreneurs who build housing additions outside the city limits must furnish utilities to the homes they build, but few developers can afford to do this over a long period of time.

Banks and finance companies, legislators, and land developers maintain a warm and snug relationship with each other. Banks and finance companies willingly lend land developers millions of dollars to establish residential subdivisions, build new homes, and run water and sewer services to these houses.

When a few houses are sold, the developer asks the residents to establish a municipal utility district. The enabling legislation is seldom a problem because of the close relationship between developers and local legislators.

● How do special districts differ from other forms of local government?

nonschool special district any special district other than a school district; examples include municipal utility districts (MUDs) and hospital districts

municipal utility district (MUD) a special district that offers services such as electricity, water, sewage, and sanitation outside the city limits

Once the MUD is up and running, the board of directors sets a tax rate and determines how much to charge residents for its services. One of its first activities is to borrow money by issuing bonds. The bond proceeds are used to purchase the utilities from the developer, often at a premium. Using the proceeds from the sale of the utilities, the developer is able to repay loans. By establishing the MUD, residents agree to pay a property tax to retire the bonded indebtedness. In addition to the property tax, residents pay a monthly fee for the water, sewer, and sanitation services.

Flood-Control Districts Flooding is seldom confined to a single county, and a flood-control district can be created to solve a multicounty flood-control problem.

Community College Districts Community college districts are classified as non-school special districts because they do not offer public education from pre-kindergarten through grade twelve. Community colleges offer postsecondary academic and vocational programs. They are governed by an elected board of regents. Residents of the district pay a property tax to the district. In return, residents pay lower tuition. The board employs a president or chancellor, who operates the college on a daily basis. The regents set policy on the recommendation of the president/chancellor. Among the regents' responsibilities are to

- set overall policy for the district.
- set the tax rate.
- set the cost of tuition and fees.
- build new buildings and repair older ones.
- hire teachers, counselors, administrators, and nonprofessional staff.
- set the school calendar.
- determine salaries and benefits for employees.

Creating a Special District Special districts are created by voters of the area to be served. Creating a special district requires

- a petition signed by the residents of the area to be served, requesting the legislature to authorize an election to create a special district.
- enabling legislation in the form of a law that authorizes a special election to create the district.
- a positive vote of those voting in the special election.

Governing a Special District Most special districts are governed by boards elected by the voters of the district. The board of a school district is called the board of trustees, the governing board of a community college is the board of regents, and the governing boards of other special districts are known as boards of directors. Each board is the policy-making group for its district. The directors set the tax rate and establish rules and policy for the operation of the district. It employs an individual who runs the district on a day-to-day basis.

Revenues Property taxes are the primary source of revenue for special districts; the second largest source of income is **user fees**. For some districts the property

property tax a tax based on an assessment of the value of one's property, which is used to fund the services provided by local governments, such as education

user fee a fee paid for public goods and services, such as water or sewage service

tax comprises as much as 90 percent of revenues. In 1949, school districts received 80 percent of their income from the state, and the school district furnished 20 percent of necessary funds, primarily from property taxes. Today, the largest source of revenue for most districts is the property tax, with state and federal aid furnishing the remainder.

Property tax rates and actual user fees are set by governing boards. User fees are raised from providing goods and services. Water districts, for example, sell water, sewer, and possibly sanitation services.

Hospital districts set fees for room occupancy, medicine dispensed, use of surgical suites, X-rays taken and evaluated, nursing and laboratory service, and myriad other charges. The board of trustees of a school district sets the local property rate for taxes, which fund pre-kindergarten through twelfth grade education. Tuition paid by in-district and out-of-district students, building fees, student fees, and technology and lab fees are determined by the board of regents of a community college district.

Hidden Governments There are more special districts than any other form of local government. Everyone in Texas lives in a least one special district, the school district. Most people live in several, have the opportunity to vote for people to represent them on the governing board of each district, and pay property taxes to these agencies of government. Yet few people are aware these agencies exist, thus their reputation as "**hidden governments.**"

Special districts provide needed services in specific geographic areas. Existing governments may lack authority to provide the service or the necessary funds to finance the project. In a special district, recipients of the services pay for them through property taxes and user fees. Special districts are an example of democracy working. Districts are created by a vote of the residents of the area to be served. The boards are elected by the voters. Decisions on policy, taxing, and fees are made by the board, in an open meeting attended by interested residents. Although special districts are democratic in theory, fewer than 10 percent of eligible voters cast ballots in special district elections. Fewer than 1 percent of district residents ever attend a board meeting.

hidden government a term that refers to special districts of which many citizens are unaware

Problems with Special Districts There is a potential for abuse in the creation of special districts. In 2001, a major investigation of the creation of special districts by developers in Dallas found some unusual and questionable practices. Some developers drew district boundaries to exclude existing residents of an area. Then the developers moved people into rent-free mobile homes shortly before the special district election. These people were the only ones eligible to vote in the election. After the election, the voters for the new district would often move away after approving large bond sales for the construction of roads, water lines, and sewers. Future homeowners in the area were then expected to pay for the bonds with property taxes on their homes. Sometimes a single voter—and always fewer than ten voters—were found to approve the bonded indebtedness that helped the developers create an infrastructure for their properties. In the Lantana subdivision near Flower Mound, for example, a family of three voted to authorize $277 million in bond sales by two water districts. That bond proposition rivals the biggest bond proposals by the city of Dallas.[27]

In 2006, developers in Denton County set up six people on property to be developed. They charged these people less than market rents so that they would vote in a special tax-district election that would affect the taxation of thousands of people who will one day live there. Once the districts are formed, developers can issue bonds to pay for roads, water, sewers, and other improvements. These bonds will be paid by the homeowners through the special-district taxes. Creation of such special districts has been especially prevalent in recent years in Travis, Harris, and Denton counties. Similar schemes in the 1980s in Harris County led to defaults on bond issues after a housing bust.[28]

The pervasiveness of these government bodies is shown by one study of Texas special districts that address water issues. The study found that about 1,000 MUDs (Municipal Utility Districts) were engaged in supplying water; forty-eight special districts existed to deal with water drainage issues; sixty-six special districts existed solely to supply fresh water. Others had these purposes: ninety-one to conserve groundwater, twenty-five for irrigation, forty-six to improve levees, forty-two to manage municipal water, twenty-six to deal with navigation, thirty-one to deal with rivers. Fifty-five special utility districts dealt with general water issues, 221 were water control and improvement districts; and eighteen were water improvement districts. Of course, this hodgepodge of special districts dealing with all aspects of water makes a coherent approach to statewide water policy a virtual impossibilty.[29]

The creation of special districts by developers has sometimes been controversial. Recent investigations have charged developers with abusing the process in order to circumvent inconvenient laws and to give the developers greater control over taxes and other government functions in the district.

Who Represents Texans at the Local Level?

Texas has many local governments, and as a result Texans have many elected representatives in different local governments. The charts show all of the local elected officials for two places in the state—the West Campus neighborhood in Austin and the Woodcreek neighborhood in North Harris County. Between county, city, school district, and community college district officials, Texans have many, many people serving them in local government.

AUSTIN—WEST CAMPUS AREA

COUNTY

County Judge, Sam Biscoe
County Commissioner, Precinct 2, Sarah Eckhardt
District Attorney, Rosemary Lehmberg
County Attorney, David Escamilla
County Sheriff, Greg Hamilton
County Tax Assessor-Collector, Nelda Wells Spears
District Clerk, Amalia Rodriguez-Mendoza
County Clerk, Dana DeBeauvoir
County Treasurer, Dolores Ortega Carter
County Constable, Precinct 5, Bruce Elfant
Justice of the Peace, Precinct 5, Herb Evans

CITY

Mayor, Lee Leffingwell
Council, Place 1, Chris Riley
Council, Place 2, Mike Martinez
Council, Place 3, Randi Shade

CITY (continued)

Council, Place 4, Laura Morrison
Council, Place 5, Bell Spelman
Council, Place 6, Sheryl Cole

SCHOOL DISTRICT

Austin ISD, District 5, Mark Williams

COMMUNITY COLLEGE DISTRICT

Austin CC, Place 1, Tim Mahoney
Austin CC, Place 2, John-Michael Cortez
Austin CC, Place 3, Nan McRaven
Austin CC, Place 4, Jeffrey Richard
Austin CC, Place 5, Victor Villareal
Austin CC, Place 6, Guadalupe Sosa
Austin CC, Place 7, Barbara Mink
Austin CC, Place 8, James McGuffie
Austin CC, Place 9, Allen Kaplan

NORTH HARRIS COUNTY—WOODCREEK AREA

COUNTY

County Judge, Ed Emmett
County Commissioner, Precinct 4, Jerry Eversole
District Attorney, Pat Lyons
County Attorney, Vince Ryan
County Sheriff, Adrian Garcia
County Tax Assessor-Collector, Leo Vasquez
District Clerk, Loren Jackson
County Clerk, Beverly Kaufman
County Treasurer, Orlando Sanchez
County Constable, Precinct 4, Ron Hickman
Justice of the Peace, Precinct 5, J. Kent Adams
School Trustee, Position 2, Tom Lawrence
School Trustee, At Large, Angie Chesnut
School Trustee, Position 7, Jim Henley
School Trustee, Position 5, Debra Kerner
School Trustee, Position 3, Michael Wolfe

SCHOOL DISTRICT

Board, Position 1, Rick Ogden
Board, Position 2, Marine Jones
Board, Position 3, Rose Avalos
Board, Position 4, Merlin Griffs
Board, Position 5, Steve Mead
Board, Position 6, Alton Smith
Board, Position 7, Violet Garcia

COMMUNITY COLLEGE DISTRICT

Board, Position 1, David Holsey
Board, Position 2, Chris Daniel
Board, Position 3, Stephanie Marquard
Board, Position 4, Robert Adam
Board, Position 5, David Vogt
Board, Position 6, Bob Wolfe
Board, Position 7, Linda Good
Board, Position 8, Randy Bates
Board, Position 9, Priscilla Kelley

for critical analysis

1. Why would there be so many local elected officials? What are the advantages of having many elected officials? How does this system promote democratic values?

2. Think of your own local school board. Do you know the elected officials who serve on it? How many people in your community do you think know all their local elected officials? If people do not know who is in office, can they evaluate the job their officials are doing at election time?

One of the most creative uses of special districts is a proposal by T. Boone Pickens to form a special district that would allow him to send groundwater and wind-generated electricity to North Texas from the Texas Panhandle. With a special district, it would be possible to bury 300 miles of water pipe and electrical transmission lines through a dozen counties and across private property. This is because the special districts have the power of eminent domain even outside the special district boundaries and can take private property for the district's purposes, even over the objection of landowners, as long as just compensation is provided.

Pickens's water and electricity plan is not a certainty, but there are efforts to create such special districts in Roberts and Kaufman counties. All that is needed is for one such special district to be created.[30]

Special districts are among the least studied areas of Texas politics, but their use as an instrument of private gain and their use by developers as a way of minimizing their financial risks suggest the need for much greater scrutiny. Of course, developers may defend this system as a way of improving property and enhancing the tax base of communities. On the other hand, the extent of enlistment of governmental taxing powers with little public scrutiny or accountability is disturbing. And if the huge bond issues floated by these entities default, thousands of people could suffer the financial consequences.

Councils of Government (COGs)

One of the greatest problems facing local governments in Texas today is coordination across legal boundaries. The Regional Planning Act of 1965 initially provided for the creation of regional **councils of government (COGs)** to promote coordination and planning across all local governments in a particular region. There are twenty-four regional councils in Texas today, each with its own bylaws or articles of agreement. The governing body of a regional council must consist of at least two-thirds of local elected officials of cities and counties, and may include citizen members and representatives of other groups.

The basic responsibilities of regional councils include planning for the economic development of an area, helping local governments carry out regional projects, contracting with local governments to provide certain services, and reviewing applications for state and federal financial assistance. Originally, COGs focused considerable attention on meeting federal mandates for water and sewer provision, open space, and housing planning. More recently, activities have focused on comprehensive planning and service delivery in such policy areas as aging, employment and training, criminal justice, economic development, environmental quality, and transportation.[31]

council of government (COG) a regional planning board composed of local elected officials and some private citizens from the same area

● Conclusion

In this chapter, we have investigated the role of local government in Texas government and politics. In many ways, local government affects the average citizen's life much more than either the federal or the state government. Sadly, local government may not be functioning as well as we might hope. Part of the problem may lie in the conflicting demands we have come to place on it. On the one hand, Texans want local government of all kinds to provide an efficient delivery of services to all in a fair and equitable manner. On the other hand, Texans also want to keep local government under some sort of democratic control. But what sort of local controls are the best? The demands of efficiency and democracy are not easily balanced. The social, political, and economic changes of the last twenty years may spark a rethinking of local government in Texas for the first time since the early decades of the twentieth century.

● **How do special districts differ from other forms of local government?**

studyguide

Practice Quiz

Ⓢ **Find a diagnostic Web Quiz with 20 additional questions on the StudySpace Web site: www.wwnorton.com/we-the-people**

1. Which of the following is *not* a type of local government found in Texas? *(p. 927)*
   a) city
   b) council of government
   c) county
   d) special district

2. The basic governing body of a county is known as *(p. 927)*
   a) a council of government.
   b) a county council.
   c) a county commissioners court.
   d) a county governing committee.

3. How many counties are there in Texas? *(p. 927)*
   a) 25
   b) 56
   c) 110
   d) 254

4. All county commissioner's precincts must be equal in population according to *(p. 928)*
   a) the Civil Rights Act of 1964.
   b) the Voting Rights Act of 1975.
   c) *Avery v. Midland County.*
   d) *Marbury v. Madison.*

5. A county judge *(p. 928)*
   a) only hears appellate cases from JP courts.
   b) is an appointive position from the governor.
   c) presides over the county court and the county commissioner's court.
   d) implements all the decisions of the Supreme Court affecting the country.

6. Which county officials are responsible for the jail and the safety of the prisoners? *(p. 929)*
   a) sheriff
   b) county council
   c) county commissioners court
   d) council of mayors

7. To adopt a home-rule charter, a city must have a minimum population of *(p. 935)*
   a) 201.
   b) 5,000.
   c) 10,000.
   d) 50,000.

8. The two legal classifications of Texas cities are *(p. 936)*
   a) local and regional.
   b) general law and home rule.
   c) tax and nontax.
   d) charter and noncharter.

9. The form of city government that allows the mayor to establish control over most of the city's government is called the (p. 936)
   a) commissioner form of city government.
   b) council-manager form of city government.
   c) council of government form of city government.
   d) strong mayor–council form of city government.

10. A city controller (p. 938)
    a) controls and manages the election in a city.
    b) is a city's chief elected official who presides over the city council.
    c) is independent of all political control in a small statutory city.
    d) is a city's chief financial officer.

11. Which local government provides a single service not provided by any other local government? (p. 940)
    a) special district
    b) council of government
    c) city
    d) county

12. What are the two types of special districts found in Texas? (p. 940)
    a) school and nonschool
    b) home rule and general law
    c) tax and nontax
    d) statutory and constitutional

13. A special district (p. 940)
    a) must be limited to under 150,000 people.
    b) covers the entire state to provide a particular service.
    c) is a unit of local government that provides a special service to a limited geographic area.
    d) temporarily combines two congressional districts.

14. A MUD (p. 941)
    a) serves the needs of developers.
    b) is generally opposed by banks and real estate developers as being too expensive.
    c) Provides ambulance service inside a city's geographic limits.
    d) delegates the setting of tax rates to the state legislature in a particular geographic area.

15. Comprehensive planning and service delivery in a specific geographic area is the function of a (p. 946)
    a) special district.
    b) council of government.
    c) city.
    d) county.

Chapter Outline

Find a detailed Chapter Outline on the StudySpace Web site: www.wwnorton.com/we-the-people

Key Terms

Find Flashcards to help you study these terms on the StudySpace Web site: www.wwnorton.com/we-the-people

at-large election (p. 937)
city controller (p. 938)
commissioner form of government (p. 936)
constable (p. 929)
council-manager form of government (p. 937)
council of government (COG) (p. 946)
county attorney (p. 933)
county auditor (p. 934)

county clerk (p. 933)
county commissioner (p. 928)
county commissioners court (p. 927)
county judge (p. 928)
county tax assessor-collector (p. 933)
district attorney (p. 933)
district clerk (p. 933)
hidden government (p. 943)
home-rule charter (p. 935)

mayor-council form of government (p. 936)
municipal utility district (MUD) (p. 941)
nonschool special district (p. 941)
property tax (p. 942)
school district (p. 940)
single-member district (p. 936)
special district (p. 940)
user fee (p. 942)

Recommended Web Sites

Individual State Descriptions
www.census.gov

Texas Association of Counties
www.county.org

Texas Local Government Code
www.statutes.legis.state.tx.us/

U.S. Census Bureau, State and County QuickFacts
http://quickfacts.census.gov/qfd/

Immigration policy has been controversial in Texas. In the 2010 elections, state and local policies on immigration were an issue. These protesters in Dallas called for greater rights and protections for immigrants.

Public Policy in Texas

WHAT GOVERNMENT DOES AND WHY IT MATTERS Like other states, Texas is involved in a broad range of public-policy initiatives. Some of these activities, such as crime prevention and corrections or public education, are largely state responsibilities. Although the national government may contribute some funds and regulate various aspects of these public-policy areas, they remain for the most part the duty and responsibility of the state of Texas. Other public-policy areas, however, have involved considerable intermingling of state and federal government responsibilities. The balance of power between the state and federal governments in these areas has shifted over time.

Throughout the first decade of the twenty-first century, state policy makers in Texas waded through a variety of policy problems, including tax reform, educational testing, and criminal incarceration. Republican domination of both houses of the state legislature and the executive offices in the state insured that a new conservative agenda would dominate policy debates across a variety of issues. Perhaps nothing captured this ideological orientation in

focusquestions

- **What does it mean to say Texas is a "low-tax, low-service" state?**

- **What are the major problems that have plagued corrections public policy in Texas?**

- **How have Texas constitutions shaped education policy in Texas?**

- **How has welfare policy evolved in Texas?**

public policy better than a new law that was passed during the 2007 session of the state legislature: the Religious Viewpoints Antidiscrimination Act.[1]

The law, which many claimed simply codified existing constitutional rulings by the federal courts, required Texas school districts to adopt a number of policies that would protect religious speech on campus. School districts were ordered to develop a neutral method for choosing student speakers at school events and graduation ceremonies, to ensure that religious-oriented clubs had the same access to school facilities as secular-oriented clubs, and to protect students who wished to express their religious beliefs in classroom assignments. The legislation did more than just give students permission to express their religious views in public schools; it also mandated the creation of a "limited public forum" for student speakers at public events that wouldn't discriminate against expressions of faith.

Social conservatives were ecstatic about the Religious Viewpoints Antidiscrimination Act, claiming that, at last, individual religious expression would be protected in the schools. Professional educators were somewhat hesitant in their praise for the bill, citing concerns about how the bill would be implemented and what it might mean for members of religious minorities.[2]

The Religious Viewpoints Antidiscrimination Act brings out two important truths about public policy in Texas. First, what goes on in Austin matters. The state legislature plays a major role in defining how public policy is conducted in the state. Second, public policy involves more than just introducing a bill in the legislature, passing it, and getting it signed. Laws also must be implemented. Implementation of policy by state agencies such as school boards is where the rubber meets the road in political life.

chaptercontents

● Taxing and Spending in Texas

Texas has a reputation of being a "low-tax, low-service" state that seeks to maintain a favorable environment for business. For the most part, this reputation is well earned. Texas is one of four states that still do not have a personal income tax. There is a high sales tax in Texas of 6.25 percent, the tenth highest in the nation. Combined state and local sales taxes in the state are 8.25 percent.[3] State taxes per capita in 2007 were $1,704, ranking Texas forty-eighth among the fifty states.

Although Texas state taxes are low compared with other states' taxes, local taxes are a slightly different story. In 2006, Texas ranked thirteenth among the states in terms of property taxes paid per capita at $1,405.

When state and local taxes are taken together, however, Texas remains a low-tax state. Combined state and local taxes were $3,580 per capita in 2008, ranking Texas thirty-second in the nation. A 2009 study conducted by the Tax Foundation concluded that Texas had the seventh most business-friendly tax system.[4]

The 1970s and early 1980s were boom years for the Texas economy. Rising inflation coupled with high oil prices and rapid economic growth drove the economy forward.[5] Tax increases were unnecessary as tax revenues soared. The problem facing the legislature was not how to balance the budget, but how to spend revenue windfalls. There were no tax increases in Texas during this time.

The collapse of oil prices and a sputtering state economy in the mid-1980s, particularly severe in real estate and construction, brought on a serious budget crisis. As projected deficits mounted, tax increases became commonplace. Between 1985 and 1986, state tax collections fell. Income from the oil severance tax alone dropped 28 percent. Tax rates were increased and the tax base was broadened in almost every year between 1984 and 1991. As the state's economy turned around in the early 1990s, the budgetary situation brightened considerably. However, renewed budget surpluses did not bring a return to the spending patterns of the pre–oil crash years. Business and political leaders from both parties expressed an ongoing concern that taxes were becoming burdensome, perhaps placing Texas at a disadvantage with other states in trying to create a favorable environment for business. Additionally, a growing concern that state government was expanding too fast sparked demands for making government more efficient. With the recession beginning in 2008, Texas has weathered the downturn far better than many other states, but declining state revenues suggest that cutbacks at state and local levels loom on the horizon.

The Constitution and the Budget

A number of constitutional factors affect the way the budget is made in Texas. First, the legislature is compelled to write a two-year, or **biennial**, budget because of the constitutional provision that the legislature may meet in regular session only once every two years. One of the effects of this restricted time frame is to force government agencies to project their budgetary needs well in advance of any clear understanding of the particular problems they may be facing during the biennium. Second, the legislature can meet for only 140 days in regular session. This seriously limits

biennial occurring every two years

The sales tax is the largest source of revenue for the state. Here, State Comptroller Susan Combs announces $14.3 billion in new revenue for the state's 2008–09 budget.

the amount of time that the legislature can spend analyzing the budget or developing innovative responses to pressing matters of public importance.

Third, a large portion of the biennial budget is dedicated for special purposes by federal law or by the Texas Constitution or state statute. These **dedicated funds** include federal monies earmarked for financing health care for the poor (Medicaid), as well as state funds for highways, education, teachers' retirement, and numerous other purposes. The purpose of dedicated funds is not difficult to understand. Supporters of particular programs want to create a stable revenue source for priority programs. But in protecting their own programs, supporters encourage other interests to do likewise, with the result that the legislature loses control of a large portion of the budget.

Fourth, a number of specific constitutional provisions constrain the legislature's control of the budget.[6]

The Pay-as-You-Go Limit Article III, Section 49a, requires the state to maintain a balanced budget. All bills that get as far as **appropriations** in the legislative process must be sent to the comptroller of public accounts so the comptroller can certify that they are within available budget limit projections. One of the most important consequences of the **pay-as-you-go limit** is to put the comptroller at the heart of the budget process.

The Welfare Spending Limit Article III, Section 51a, provides that the amount of money the state pays for assistance to or on behalf of needy dependent children and their caretakers shall not exceed 1 percent of the state budget in any biennium. This article sets a constitutional limit on the amount of money that the state may pay out to welfare beneficiaries under the Temporary Assistance for Needy Families program. This restriction has not been particularly important in recent years.

The Limit on the Growth of Certain Appropriations Article VIII, Section 22, limits the biennial rate of growth of appropriations from state revenue not dedicated by the Constitution to the estimated growth of the state's economy.

The state of Texas collects a tax of 20 cents per gallon on motor fuels. The federal government collects an additional 18.4 cents per gallon, but Texans still pay less tax on gasoline than residents of most other states.

Limitation on Debt Payable from the General Revenue Fund Under a 1997 amendment to Article III of the Texas Constitution, the legislature is prohibited from authorizing additional state debt if the resulting **debt service** from the general revenue exceeded 5 percent of the average amount of the General Revenue Fund revenue for the three preceding fiscal years.

The Budgetary Process

In theory, Texas has a "dual-budget" system. This means that responsibility for preparing an initial draft of the budget is shared by the governor and the legislature. In practice, the budget is the responsibility of the legislature.

Before 1949, there was little coordination in public budgeting. Financial procedures varied, and state agencies were funded by individual appropriations. In 1949, a law was enacted to establish a ten-member Legislative Budget Board (LBB) whose primary job would be to recommend appropriations for all agencies of state government. The board is chaired by the lieutenant governor. The vice chair is the Speaker of the House. Other members include the chairs of the House Appropriations Committee, the House Committee on Ways and Means, the Senate Finance Committee, and the Senate State Affairs Committee. Two additional members from the Senate and the House are chosen by the lieutenant governor and the Speaker, respectively.

The Legislative Budget Board appoints a budget director, who brings together budgeting requests from the various state agencies and prepares appropriation bills for them. Since 1973, the Legislative Budget Board has also been responsible for evaluating agency programs and developing estimates of the probable costs of implementing legislation introduced in a legislative session. The LBB's draft budget, not the governor's, is the basis for final legislation.

The budgetary process involves two stages.[7] In the first stage, the Legislative Budget Board develops a draft budget based on requests supplied by state agencies. Hearings are conducted well before the legislature goes into session. Since 1992, each agency has been required to develop a five-year plan that includes goals, objectives, strategies, and performance measures. This information provides the basis for LBB funding recommendations for each agency.

While the draft budgets are being prepared, the comptroller's office prepares the Biennial Revenue Estimate (BRE). The BRE is a detailed forecast of the total revenue that the state is expected to take in over the next biennium. The comptroller effectively sets a ceiling on what the state legislature may spend. Although the legislature can override the comptroller's estimates with a four-fifths vote of each house, this has never happened. The BRE is updated when economic conditions change significantly and for special sessions of the legislature.

The second stage of the budget process involves the legislative process. Budgets are submitted to the House Appropriations Committee and the Senate Finance Committee. They then work their way through the committee system and are subject to hearings, debates, and revisions. Final versions of the budget are prepared by the House Appropriations Committee and the Senate Finance Committee. Differences are reconciled in a conference committee.

The comptroller then formally certifies the budget. "Certification" means that the comptroller's office has analyzed the budget and concluded that it is within the current revenue estimates. After certification, the budget moves on to the governor, who decides whether to veto certain items.

> ● **What does it mean to say Texas is a "low-tax, low-service" state?**

debt service the amount of a budget spent by a government on paying interest on its debt

Revenue in Texas

Government and public policy in Texas is funded from a variety of sources, including sales tax, severance taxes on oil and natural gas produced in the state, licensing income, interest and dividends, and federal aid. In 2009, 44.9 percent of government revenues came from taxes of one sort or another. Many of these taxes are based on complex formulas. People often are unaware that they are paying them. But they are important sources of state revenue (see Table 27.1).

Sales and Use Tax The most important single tax financing Texas government is the sales tax. Today, the sales tax in Texas is 6.25 percent of the retail sales price of tangible personal property and selected services. Together county, city, and metropolitan transit authorities are authorized to impose an additional 2 percent sales and use tax. In 2009, the 6.25 percent sales and use tax accounted for 24.9 percent of state revenues.

Oil Production and Regulation Taxes The oil severance tax is 4.6 percent of the market value of oil produced in the state. As late as 1980, the state took in $786 million in oil production taxes, over 6 percent of total state revenues. By 1999, this once vital revenue source had fallen to $211 million, only .44 percent of state revenues. Although revenues produced by the oil severance tax increased to $884,510,773 in 2009, there is little likelihood that this revenue source will ever become as important as it once was.

TABLE 27.1

Texas Revenue by Source for Fiscal Year 2009

TAX COLLECTIONS BY MAJOR TAX

MAJOR TAXES	AMOUNT	PERCENT OF TOTAL	PERCENT CHANGE FROM 2008
Sales Tax	$21,014,065,089	24.9%	2.7%
Motor Vehicle Sales/Rental	$2,600,939,347	3.1%	22.2%
Motor Fuels Taxes	$3,032,770,482	3.6%	2.2%
Franchise Tax	$4,250,332,029	5%	4.5%
Insurance Taxes	$1,257,314,168	1.5%	13.3%
Natural Gas Production Tax	$1,407,739,109	1.7%	47.6%
Cigarette and Tobacco Taxes	$1,556,793,276	1.8%	7.6%
Alcoholic Beverage Taxes	$796,948,327	.9%	1.6%
Oil Production Tax	$884,510,773	1%	38.4%
Inheritance Tax	$2,004,064	0%	64.1%
Utility Taxes	$518,883,903	.6%	3%
Hotel Tax	$343,544,448	.4%	7.4%
Other Taxes	$156,607,998	.2%	11.2%
Total Taxes	**$37,822,453,013**	**44.9%**	**8.5%**

SOURCE: Texas Comptroller of Public Accounts.

● What does it
mean to say Texas
is a "low-tax,
low-service" state?

Natural Gas Production Tax There is a 7.5 percent tax on the market value of all natural gas produced in the state. As in the case of the oil production tax, revenues fell significantly from $734 million, or 6.9 percent of state revenues, in 1980 to $489 million, or a little over 1 percent of state revenues in 1997. In 2009, it accounted for $1,407,739,109 or 1.7 percent of the total revenue flowing to the state.

Motor Fuels Tax The motor fuels tax in Texas is 20 cents per gallon of gasoline and diesel fuel. There is a 15 cents per gallon tax on liquefied gas. In 2009, the motor fuels tax took in approximately $3,032,770,482, 3.6 percent of all state revenues.

Motor Vehicle Sales and Rentals and Manufactured Home Sales Tax There is a 6.25 percent tax on the sales price of all motor vehicles in the state. There is also a 10 percent tax on all rental vehicles up to thirty-five days and 6.25 percent thereafter. Newly manufactured homes are also taxed at 5 percent of 65 percent of the sales price. In 2009, these taxes took in $2,600,939,347, 3.1 percent of total state revenues.

Corporate Franchise Tax The franchise tax is imposed on all corporations in Texas. Corporations pay a tax based on net taxable capital or net taxable earned surplus (the net assets of a corporation minus its stated capital). In 2009, the corporate franchise tax took in $4,250,332,029, 5 percent of total state revenues.

Tobacco Taxes Texas imposes a variety of taxes on cigarettes and tobacco products. For example, every pack of twenty cigarettes has a 41-cent tax included in the purchase price. In 2009, $1,556,793,276 came to the state in the form of taxes on tobacco products.

Alcoholic Beverage Taxes As with tobacco, a variety of taxes are imposed on alcoholic beverages. For example, beer is taxed at the rate of $6.00 per 31-gallon barrel. Liquor is taxed at the rate of $2.40 per gallon. Mixed drinks are taxed at 14 percent of gross receipts. This tax took in $796,948,327 in 2009 and accounted for .9 percent of state revenues.

Insurance Occupation Taxes A complex schedule of tax rates is applied to insurance premiums. For example, life, health, and accident insurance are taxed at the rate of 1.75 percent on gross premium receipts. For life insurance premiums, a half-rate is applied to the first $450,000 in premiums. In 2009, insurance premium taxes came to $1,257,314,168, or 1.5 percent of state revenue.

Utility Taxes There is a tax of one-sixth of 1 percent on the gross receipts of public utilities. For gas, electric, and water utilities there is a tax on gross receipts ranging from .581 percent in towns of fewer than 2,500 people to 1.07 percent in cities of between 2,500 and 9,999 people to 1.997 percent in cities of 10,000 or more. There is also a tax on gas utility administration of one-half of 1 percent of the gross income of gas utilities.

Hotel and Motel Tax This state tax is 6 percent of the hotel and motel occupancy bill paid by the occupant. In 2009, $343,544,448 was collected through the hotel and motel tax, approximately 0.4 percent of total state revenues.

Inheritance Tax This state tax is equal to the amount of the federal credit that is imposed on the transfer of property at death. In 2009, the state inheritance

for critical analysis

Is the current tax system in Texas fair? Why or why not? How would the proposals for new forms of taxation affect the majority of Texans? What concerns should be kept in mind when proposing changes to the tax system?

tax accounted for only $2,004,064. This is a 64.1 percent reduction from 2008, brought on by changes in federal law.

The Question of the Income Tax in Texas

progressive/regressive taxation taxation that hits upper income brackets more heavily (progressive) or lower income brackets more heavily (regressive)

Many commentators have complained that the tax system in Texas is too **regressive**.[8] By this they mean that the tax burden in the state falls more heavily on lower-income individuals. Sales and use taxes such as those found in Texas are generally considered to be regressive. There have been occasional calls for the institution of a state income tax in Texas. Supporters argue that not only is the income tax a more reliable source of revenue for the state, it can also be made fairer. Unlike sales and use taxes, which are applied equally to everyone whatever their income, income taxes can be made **progressive**. With a progressive income tax, people with lower income pay a lower tax rate than people of higher income. Progressive income taxes thus place a higher tax burden on the rich than on the poor.

For the past forty years, few politicians were willing to support an income tax. One of the attractive features of Texas to business had always been the absence of an income tax. But in the early 1990s, the first serious attempt to put a state income tax in place was undertaken. Responding to mounting budgetary pressures, the retiring lieutenant governor, Bill Hobby, came out in favor of an income tax in late 1989. Bob Bullock, Hobby's successor, announced in early 1991 that he would actively campaign for an income tax. A blue-ribbon panel chaired by John Connally, a former governor, was charged with looking into new revenue sources for the state. The committee ended up recommending to the legislature both a corporate and a personal income tax but not without generating an enormous amount of controversy. Chairman Connally himself opposed the income-tax recommendations, as did Governor Ann Richards. By the 1993 legislative session, Lieutenant Governor Bullock was backing off. Bullock proposed a constitutional amendment requiring voter approval of any personal income tax. Moreover, it specified that funds raised under the personal income tax be used to support public education. The amendment quickly passed the 73rd legislature and was overwhelmingly approved by voters on November 2, 1993. Given the constitutional impediments, it is unlikely that Texans will have a personal income tax in the foreseeable future.[9]

Other State Revenue

matching funds federal monies given to a state to match the state's funding on a joint program

Next to taxes, the second-largest source of revenue for Texas is the federal government (see Table 27.2). Historically, Texas spends relatively little, compared with other states, for state-federal programs. As a result, the federal **matching funds** (federal monies going to a state based on state spending for a program) also have been relatively low. Nevertheless, federal aid to Texas skyrocketed in the 1980s because of the expansion of transportation and human-services programs. In recent years, the growth of federal dollars going into the state has slowed down as welfare caseloads have fallen and Medicaid (health care financing for the poor) has grown less than expected. In 2009, almost $23 billion came to Texas from Washington, D.C. Federal monies are concentrated in three areas: health care and human services, transportation, and education.

In addition to federal monies, there are a number of other revenue sources, including interest income, licenses and fees, the sales of goods and services provided by the state, and land income. Two other sources in recent years have had a major impact on monies flowing into the state budget. A state lottery was passed

What Are the Trade-Offs in Texas Public Policy?

The contemporary Texas government tends to pass conservative policies. The figures below show this in comparison to other states. Texas collects the lowest share of taxes of any state. But when government lacks revenue, it cannot spend money to address social problems, such as providing health insurance to those who cannot afford it.

State Taxes (as a percentage of gross state product)

Lowest Tax Rate
(3.51%)

Less ● ● ● ● ● More

Percent Uninsured

Highest % Uninsured
(24.4%)

Less ● ● ● ● ● More

State Taxation Compared to Percent Uninsured

	TAXES	UNINSURED		TAXES	UNINSURED		TAXES	UNINSURED
TX	3.51%	24.4%	OH	5.36%	11.0%	NJ	6.31%	15.2%
SD	3.57%	11.2%	AL	5.39%	13.9%	CA	6.37%	18.6%
NH	3.76%	10.5%	UT	5.58%	15.6%	WY	6.42%	14.3%
CO	3.90%	16.7%	IN	5.66%	12.3%	KY	6.51%	13.8%
TN	4.63%	13.9%	WA	5.70%	12.1%	OK	6.53%	18.2%
MO	4.67%	12.5%	MD	5.71%	13.6%	MT	6.77%	16.1%
DE	4.72%	11.8%	NY	5.72%	13.4%	ID	6.79%	14.7%
GA	4.76%	17.8%	SC	5.73%	16.5%	NM	6.92%	21.9%
IL	4.78%	13.7%	PA	5.78%	9.8%	MN	7.04%	8.5%
FL	4.82%	20.5%	NC	5.79%	16.6%	MS	7.30%	18.8%
NV	4.88%	17.9%	MA	5.87%	8.3%	ME	7.46%	9.5%
VA	4.94%	13.6%	KS	5.89%	11.8%	AK	7.67%	17.3%
OR	4.89%	16.8%	RI	5.92%	10.3%	AR	7.77%	17.5%
IA	4.98%	9.4%	CT	6.05%	9.9%	WV	8.04%	14.9%
AZ	5.04%	19.6%	WI	6.20%	8.8%	HI	8.21%	8.3%
NE	5.07%	12.0%	ND	6.25%	11.1%	VT	10.39%	11.0%
LA	5.24%	19.4%	MI	6.28%	10.8%			

SOURCES: The Tax Foundation, www.taxfoundation.org; Kaiser State Health Facts, www.statehealthfacts.org (accessed 10/6/10).

for critical analysis

1. How does the political culture and government structure of Texas contribute to conservative policy outcomes such as low taxes and lower spending on social programs?

2. What are the benefits of having such a low tax rate in the state? Do the benefits of a low tax rate outweigh the problems in your opinion?

TABLE 27.2

Federal Revenue by State Agency, 2009 (Millions of Dollars)

STATE AGENCY	
Texas Health and Human Services	$12,149
Texas Department of State Health Services	$913
Department of Public Safety	$155
Texas Education Agency	$3,834
Texas Department of Transportation	$3,250
Texas Workforce Commission	$877
Family and Protective Services	$330
Texas Rehabilitation Commission	$303
Texas Department of Housing and Community Affairs	$151
All Other Agencies	$291
Total All Agencies	**$22,253**

SOURCE: Texas Controller of Public Accounts, 2009 State of Texas Annual Cash Report.

by the state legislature in July 1991 and approved by the voters in November. Although the lottery was passed by voters overwhelmingly, attitudes about the appropriateness of using gambling as a source of state revenues are mixed. Some argue that the lottery unfairly takes money from people who can least afford to give it up by fooling them into thinking that they, too, can strike it rich if only they have a little luck. Large numbers of people from all social classes continue to play the lottery. In 2009, 42 percent of Texans claimed that they played a lottery game in the previous year. The average monthly dollar amount spent on any lottery game was $45.21.[10] Despite the lottery's popularity, revenues generated by it are still only 1.9 percent of total state revenue.[11] Actual lottery ticket sales in 2008 amounted to $3.671 billion.[12]

A second major source of nontax revenue is a result of the settlement the state reached with tobacco companies in 1999. Under the settlement, Texas would receive over $17.3 billion over the next twenty-five years, and an additional $580 million every year thereafter, from the tobacco industry. The largest payment—$3.3 billion—came up front, while the remainder was spread out over the remaining twenty-five years. Nationwide, states received a total of $246 billion in the final settlement reached with the tobacco industry. The annualized payout from the tobacco settlement in Texas equals about 2 percent of the budget, approximately the same amount collected by cigarette taxes.[13]

Expenditures in Texas

In 2009, Texas government spent $88.6 (see Table 27.3). The largest expenditure was on health and human services programs, which spent $33.5 billion, or 37.8

The lottery, approved by Texas voters in 1991, generates over $1 billion in state revenue every year.

percent, of the state budget. In addition, $33.1 billion, or 37.4 percent of the state budget, went to education programs. Transportation was the third largest expenditure, receiving over 6.7 or 7.6 percent of the state budget. Public safety and corrections programs were the fourth largest in terms of expenditures, taking up almost 5.1 billion, or 5.7 percent of the state budget.

The 2010 Budget Crisis in Texas

The financial crisis of 2008 and the accompanying Great Recession of 2009 sparked budget crises in state governments across the nation. Higher levels of unemployment and a slowing economy led to declining revenue from various tax sources and to increased demands on public services in health, welfare, and education. Some states, such as California, plunged into a serious political crises as state political leaders had difficulty reaching a consensus on how to balance the budget.

At first, Texas appeared to have escaped the budgetary woes of other states.[14] The economic slowdown in Texas did not appear to be as bad as in other states. The budget passed by the 2009 Texas legislature was a modest one built upon rosy assumptions about future trends. By 2010, concerns began to mount that the Texas budget was in trouble. Initial revenue projections for the 2010–2011 budget cycle were found to be too optimistic by up to $2 billion. Although some budgets cuts were put into place by state agencies in spring 2010, Comptroller Combs refused to alter revenue estimates made in January 2009. In May 2010, the chief budget writer for the Texas House, Representative Jim Pitts from Waxahachie, speculated that the budget deficit for the next two years might reach $15 to $18 billion. Pitts's projections were summarily rejected by Governor Perry as being "pulled out of the air." Leaders in neither party wanted to confront the intensifying budget crisis until after the election. The two gubernatorial candidates in 2010 seemed to offer little more than vague platitudes about how they would put into place either substantive spending cuts or tax increases to make up a growing budget deficit.

As the fall campaign progressed, it became increasingly difficult to ignore the intensifying budget problems. In early September 2010, the Democratic chairman

TABLE 27.3

Texas Net Expenditures by Function, Fiscal 2009 (All Funds, Excluding Trust)

GOVERNMENT FUNCTION	AMOUNT	PERCENT OF TOTAL	PERCENT CHANGE FROM PRIOR FISCAL YEAR
General Government			
Executive Departments	$2,475,671	28	15.4
Legislative	$141,750,457	.2	15.2
Judicial	$254,971,650	.3	4
Education	$33,120,732,460	37.4	7.6
Employee Benefits	$2,928,101,148	3.3	−1.7
Health and Human Services	$33,492,032,588	37.8	12.8
Public Safety and Corrections	$5,043,393,457	5.7	24.6
Transportation	$6,722,847,158	7.6	−12.3
Natural Resources/Recreation Services	$2,069,187,656	2.3	−1.6
Regulatory Services	$356,325,497	.4	18.2
Lottery Winnings Paid*	$491,322,426	.6	16.2
Debt Service	$1,005,304,449	1.1	3.4
Capital Outlay	$473,903,973	.5	1.2
TOTAL NET EXPENDITURES	$88,575,634,753	100	8.1

Totals may not sum due to rounding.
*Lottery Winnings Paid does not include payments made by retailers.
SOURCE: Texas Comptroller of Public Accounts.

of the House Ways and Means Committee, Representative Rene Olivera, warned of the disconnect between the budget and the state of the economy. The projected budget deficit was now estimated at $20.6 billion. On September 9, 2010, Perry finally conceded that the state was in trouble. "You'd have to be deaf, dumb, and blind not to understand that we have a major financial crisis on our hands," he told reporters. Yet he remained confident that the budget would be balanced without substantially raising taxes. His Democratic opponent Bill White criticized the Perry administration for financial mismanagement, but remained consistently unclear as to how White would cut the budget deficit if elected. In late October, state leaders were warned that the projected budget deficit had ballooned to almost $25 billion, about 25 percent of current spending. The gap was proportionally bigger than the one that California was experiencing.

There were many factors behind the budget crisis. On the revenue side, sales and business tax receipts were down, as were Medicaid matching funds from the federal government. On the expenditure side, state obligations were increasing as the demand for welfare, unemployment insurance, and healthcare intensified with the recession. The state's obligation to fund public schooling also rose.

Numerous proposals began to circulate for how to deal with the impending budget crisis in the 2011 legislative session. Among these were proposals to

- Tap the state's $9.0 billion rainy day fund
- Close loopholes in the sales tax
- Sell unused state land
- Eliminate various regulatory agencies involved with overseeing business and environmental regulations
- Eliminate various state agencies, including agriculture, the attorney general's office, Parks and Wildlife, and the Workforce Commission.
- Curtail various business and economic programs in the state
- Cut finding to elementary and secondary education
- Raise tuition at community colleges and state universities
- Curtail or even eliminate funds going to the poor through the Medicaid Program or the Temporary Assistance for Needy Families Program.

Significantly, no prominent political leader in the state called for any substantial tax increase prior to the 2010 election. Even after Election Day, triumphant Republican leaders remained quiet as to what might actually be proposed to addressed the yawning budget deficit in the upcoming legislative session. At least publicly, most were waiting for January 2011 when the comptroller would release her final budgetary projections. Only then would state leaders know the full extent of the budget crisis that was upon them and have to make the difficult and perhaps unpopular choices necessary to bring the budget into balance.

Crime and Corrections Policy

History of the Prison System

Shortly after Texas joined the Union, construction was authorized for a state penitentiary in Huntsville. The 225-cell facility opened in 1849. It confined prisoners in single cells at night and congregated inmates during the day to work in silence. From 1870 to 1883, the entire prison system was leased to private contractors who used the labor of inmates in exchange for providing maintenance and security for prisoners. After 1883, convicts in the Texas prison system were leased to railroads, planters, and others who provided the prisoners with food and clothing, and paid a stipend to the state. These leasing arrangements were abandoned in 1910 due to scandals and abuses of the system.[15]

Although Texas moved to a state-run system, abuses continued. In 1924, an investigation of the system found cruel and brutal treatment of prisoners, inefficient management, and inadequate care of inmates. That investigation led to the creation of a state prison board, which supervised the work of a general prison manager. Still, however, the abuses continued. By the mid-1940s, the Texas prison system was considered one of the worst in the United States. In 1974, the Joint Committee on Prison Reform submitted findings to the legislature that were very critical of the Texas prison system. It found fault with numerous aspects of the prison system's operation—from living and working conditions for inmates to classification of inmates to medical care to staff training. Still, nothing much happened.[16]

The event that had the most dramatic effect on the operation of the Texas prison system in modern times was a federal court case, *Ruiz v. Estelle*.[17] Lawsuits filed by prisoners are nothing new. During the tenure of W. J. Estelle, Jr., the prison director from 1973–83 and the defendant in the *Ruiz* case, prisoners filed 19,696 cases in the federal courts in Texas, a caseload amounting to about 20 percent of the federal court docket in Texas during that period.[18] However, the *Ruiz* case was exceptional. It was a class-action suit on behalf of inmates that began in 1972, and it focused on issues of crowding in the system, security and supervision, health care, discipline, and access to the courts. In 1980, the federal court concluded that inmates' constitutionally guaranteed rights had been violated. Texas joined several other states in having its prison system declared unconstitutional.

The result was the appointment by the court of a special master, a court officer, to oversee the Texas prison system to eliminate the constitutional problems such as overcrowding, improper supervision of inmates, and improper care of inmates. There was a massive reform of the system, one that had to be imposed from without—from the federal courts—since the state seemed unwilling or unable to reform its own prison system. Federal court supervision of the prison system ended in 2002.

For a long time, many in Texas government were resistant to federal court supervision of the prison system, arguing, for example, that the *Ruiz* decision involved federal court judicial activism and interfered with the rights of the state. In order to reduce the overcrowding in state prisons to comply with *Ruiz*, the state also encouraged the early release of prisoners, some of whom reentered society and committed further crimes. *Ruiz* did, however, help to turn the criminal justice system into a major public policy issue in Texas.

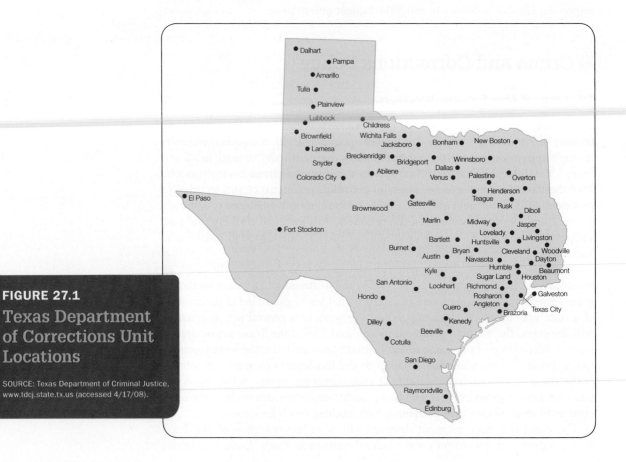

FIGURE 27.1

Texas Department of Corrections Unit Locations

SOURCE: Texas Department of Criminal Justice, www.tdcj.state.tx.us (accessed 4/17/08).

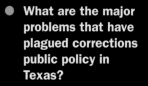
Texas Crime and Corrections

It has long been claimed that Texas does things in a big way. That is certainly true of its levels of crime and the way it deals with criminals. As of December 2008, 172,506 offenders were incarcerated in the state's correctional institutions.[19] These numbers exclude those incarcerated in municipal and county facilities. Texas keeps building more and more jails to house its criminal-offender population. In 2006, the Texas Department of Criminal Justice spent nearly $2.7 billion on the incarceration of criminals in 2007 and $2.9 billion 2008.[20] As noted in Figure 27.1, units of the Texas Department of Criminal Justice are now located throughout the state.[21]

There have been dramatic increases in the costs of prison construction and prison maintenance in Texas over time. Operating costs of Texas prisons rose from $147 million in 1982 to $609 million in 1990 to nearly $1.5 billion in 1996 and over $2.8 billion in 2008. Despite a steady increase in prison operating costs, prison construction costs have varied from year to year. In 1982, $126 million was spent on prison construction, but in 1990 only $24 million was spent. The greatest period of prison construction was from 1991 through 1995. During those years, nearly $1.4 billion was spent on prison construction.[22] In the wake of estimates in 2007 that Texas would need 17,000 new prison beds costing $1 billion by 2012, in 2007 the Texas legislature increased the capacity of prison alternatives such as drug treatment and halfway homes, much cheaper alternatives to prison.[23]

Until 2007, when the Texas legislature began to seriously address alternatives to prison, the state government had significantly increased the incarceration of offenders by building more prisons. From 1976 to 1990, the rate of property crime in Texas rose 38 percent, and the violent crime rate rose 113 percent. During the same time period, prison expansion did not keep up with the increase in the crime

forcritical**analysis**
What are the important issues and trends regarding the incarceration of criminals in Texas?

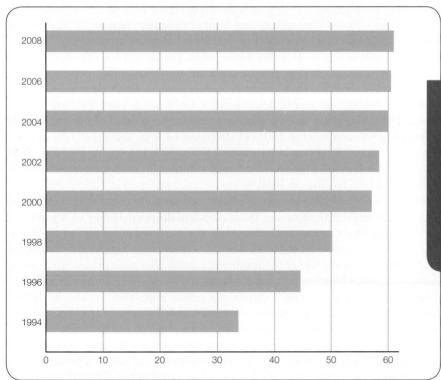

FIGURE 27.2

Percentage of Prison Sentence Served by Texas Inmates

SOURCES: Criminal Justice Policy Council, "Percentage of Prison Sentence Served for All Release Types, Fiscal Years 1994–2004"; Texas Department of Criminal Justice, Fiscal Year 2006 Statistical Report; Texas Department of Criminal Justice, Fiscal Year 2008 Statistical Report.

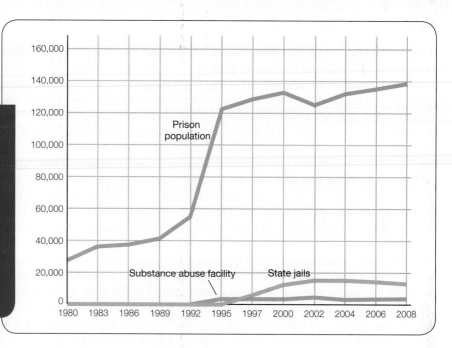

FIGURE 27.3

Texas Inmate
Population,
1980–2008

SOURCES: Associated Texans Against Crime
Annual Report, 1998; Texas Department
of Criminal Justice, "Fiscal Year 2004
Statistics"; Criminal Justice Policy Council,
"Texas Department of Criminal Justice State
Incarcerated Population, Fiscal Years
1988–2002"; and Texas Department of
Criminal Justice, 2006 and 2008 Statistical
Report.

rate. Instead, generous early-release policies were used to move prisoners out of jail to allow room for newly convicted inmates. With prison expansion, however, early-release polices were reduced. In 1990, for example, 38,000 prisoners were given early release from prison; however, even with a much larger prison population in 1997, only slightly more than 28,000 prisoners were given early release.[24] The steady lengthening of sentences is shown in Figure 27.2. In 1994, prisoners on average were released after serving one-third of their sentences. In 2008, prisoners were serving about 60 percent of their sentences before being released.[25]

As is shown in Figure 27.3, the Texas prison population has soared, especially since about 1992. In 1980, at the time of *Ruiz*, the Texas prison population consisted of fewer than 30,000 inmates. A decade later, in 1990, there were slightly more than 49,000 inmates in Texas prisons. Only seven years later, there were almost 130,000 inmates in state prisons. In 2000, the number of inmates in state prisons had jumped to over 150,000, dropping back to about 145,000 in 2002 but increasing to 132,000 in 2004 and to 139,134 in 2008. Put another way, there were over 4.5 inmates in state correctional facilities in 2008 for every inmate in state correctional facilities in 1980.[26]

For much of the 1980s, the rate of violent and property crime in Texas was very high. By the mid-1990s, however, those rates had dropped. It may be argued that the reduction in the crime rate is caused by the increased incarceration of offenders.[27] There may also be other causes, however. Others have suggested demographic change determines the size of the prison population. The most prison-prone group in society is males between the ages of twenty and twenty-nine. If that demographic group is large, then we would expect the prison population to also be large.[28] Indeed, 92 percent of Texas prisoners are male, and the average age of prisoners is only 37 years.[29] Of course, changes in laws and treatment practices also affect the crime rate and the incarceration rate. Long sentences for habitual criminals, for example, are relatively new, as are long sentences for the use of a firearm in the commission of a crime.[30] The number of prison inmates per 100,000 population

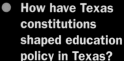
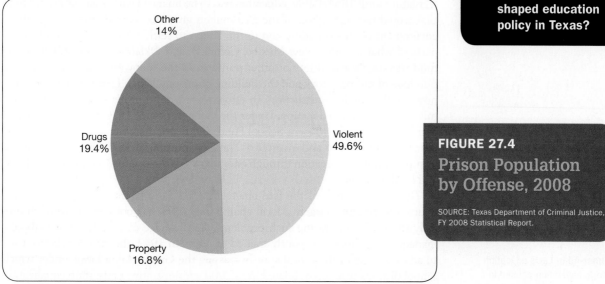

Other
14%

Drugs
19.4%

Violent
49.6%

Property
16.8%

FIGURE 27.4
Prison Population by Offense, 2008

SOURCE: Texas Department of Criminal Justice, FY 2008 Statistical Report.

in Texas in 2008 was 639. The national average was 504. California and New York, the closest states in population to Texas, incarcerate 467 per 100,000 population and 307 per 100,000, respectively.[31] Only Louisiana, Mississippi, and Oklahoma have a higher rate of incarceration than Texas.[32] In spite of its high rate of incarceration, Texas ranked high in crime. A study of crime rates nationwide found Texas ranked 37 in the United States in crime where a ranking of 1 is the least crime and 50 is the greatest crime ranking.[33]

As Figure 27.4 shows, Texas imprisons mostly violent offenders. In 2008, 49.6 percent of Texas inmates had been convicted of violent offenses and 16.8 percent had been convicted of property offenses. Nineteen percent of the inmate population was convicted of drug offenses.[34] Whether imprisonment for drug offenses is an appropriate remedy for the drug problem is, of course, debatable, but it is interesting that about one in five people in Texas prisons are there because of drugs.

During the administration of Governor Ann Richards, there was recognition that very large proportions of prisoners were involved with alcoholism, drug addiction, and drug-related crimes.[35] Some effort was made to create alcohol- and drug-abuse treatment programs within the prison system to help alleviate these problems, although the problems remain severe. In 2007, the Texas legislature again spent resources on prison alternatives, which have greatly reduced the need for prison construction. Indeed, those prison alternative programs have led to scrapping plans for three new prisons.[36]

Education Policy in Texas

The debate over public education in Texas extends back to the break with Mexico.[37] One of the indictments of the Mexican regime contained in the Texas Declaration of Independence was that the government had failed to establish a public system of education. Later, the Constitution of the Republic of Texas required a public system of education, but a bill actually establishing a public school system did not pass the legislature until 1854. Public education was to be financed with a special school fund that would use $2 million of the $10 million given to Texas by the United States government on Texas's admission to the Union to settle outstanding land claims in parts of what are now New Mexico, Colorado, and Oklahoma. Unfortunately, the fund was used for a variety of other purposes in the following years, including the purchase of railroad stock and the building of prisons. When Democrats returned to power following Reconstruction, an effort was made to protect the fund and commit its use solely to education. Under the Constitution of 1876, the Special School Fund became the Permanent School Fund, and restrictions were placed on how the money could be used and invested.[38] The Constitution of 1876 also had provisions to support public education through one-quarter of the occupation tax, a $1 poll tax, and local taxation.

Throughout much of the late nineteenth and early twentieth centuries, public education remained largely a local affair. Many of the school systems were chronically short of funds, facing such problems as a shortage of supplies and textbooks, inadequate facilities, and poorly trained teachers. In 1949, the state legislature tried to address some of these problems by passing the **Gilmer-Aikin Laws**, under which school districts were consolidated into 2,900 administrative units, state equalization funding was provided to supplement local taxes, teacher salaries were raised, and a minimum school year was established. In addition, the laws established the Texas Education Agency to supervise public education in the state.

The Gilmer-Aikin Laws also established bureaucratic institutions responsible for public education in the state. Previously, public education had been run by a State Board of Education, whose nine members were appointed by the governor for six-year terms, and an elected state superintendent of public instruction. This was replaced by an elected twenty-one-member board from each of the congressional districts in Texas. The State Board of Education became the policy-making body for public education in the state, adopting budgets, establishing regulations for school accreditation, executing contracts for the purchase of textbooks, and investing in the Permanent School Fund. The board also had the power to appoint a commissioner of education, subject to confirmation by the Texas Senate. The commissioner of education served a four-year term and became the chief executive officer for the State Department of Education, later renamed the Texas Education Agency (TEA). The TEA was responsible for setting standards for public schools, for supervising the public schools of the state, and for handling federal funds related to public education. For the next fifty years, educational policy in the state would work through the institutional framework established by the Gilmer-Aikin Laws.[39]

Since 1949, the State Board of Education has undergone occasional restructuring. Membership was expanded to twenty-four in 1973 and to twenty-seven in 1981. Following a special legislative session, the board became a fifteen-member appointed body in 1984. But in 1988, it reverted to an elected body composed of fifteen members serving four-year terms.

Three issues have played a major role in shaping educational policy over the last fifty years: desegregation, equity in funding, and the search for educational excellence.

Desegregation

Few issues have troubled educational policy in Texas as much as desegregation. Segregation of the races was provided for under the Texas Constitution of 1876. In *Plessy v. Ferguson* (1896), the U.S. Supreme Court upheld the validity of segre-

Gilmer-Aikin Laws education reform legislation passed in 1949 that supplemented local funding of education with state monies, raised teachers' salaries, mandated a minimum length for the school year, and provided more state supervision of public education

for critical analysis

What are the most important issues that have shaped education policy in Texas over the past fifty years? Have these issues been resolved?

gated schools through the now infamous "separate but equal" doctrine. In Texas, as elsewhere across the South, segregated schools may have been separate, but they were far from equal. In the 1920s and 1930s, for example, the length of the school term for black schools was only about four days shorter than that for white schools, but Texas spent an average of $3.39 less per student (about one-third less) on the education of African American students than on white students.[40]

The United States Supreme Court overturned *Plessy v. Ferguson* in the 1954 case *Brown v. Board of Education*, ruling that segregated schools violated the equal protection clause of the Fourteenth Amendment. School districts were ordered to desegregate their schools systems "with all deliberate speed." In some cases, "all deliberate speed" was quite quick. The San Antonio school district, for example, became one of the first school districts in the nation to comply with the Supreme Court's order. Other school districts in the state, such as Houston's, were much slower in implementing the Court's desegregation ruling.

The desegregation of public schools was hampered further by political opposition at both the local and state levels. In 1957, the Texas state legislature passed laws encouraging school districts to resist federally ordered desegregation, although the current governor, Price Daniel, Sr., chose to ignore such laws.[41] By the 1960s, legally segregated schools were a thing of the past. Nevertheless, **de facto** segregation remained a problem, particularly in urban areas with large minority populations. As in many other urban areas across the country, a large number of middle- and upper-income whites in Texas abandoned urban public school systems for suburban public schools or private schools.

de facto literally, "by fact"; practices that occur even when there is no legal enforcement, such as school segregation in much of the United States today

Equity in the Public School System

Federal court cases such as *Brown v. Board of Education* played a major role in shaping educational policy regarding the desegregation of schools. Two other important court cases have affected education policy and politics in Texas over the last thirty years: *Rodríguez v. San Antonio ISD* and *Edgewood ISD v. Kirby*.

Rodríguez v. San Antonio ISD *Rodríguez v. San Antonio ISD* was a landmark case involving the constitutionality of using property taxes to fund public schools.[42] At the heart of the case lay the question of the equitable funding of public schools. Lawyers for Rodríguez and seven other children in the poor Edgewood independent school district (ISD) argued that the current system of financing public schools in Texas was unfair. The Edgewood school district had one of the highest property tax rates in the country but could raise only $37 per pupil. Meanwhile the neighboring school district of Alamo Heights was able to raise $413 per pupil with a much lower property tax rate. The difference was that the value of the property subject to taxation in Alamo Heights far exceeded that in Edgewood. Equalizing educational funding would require Edgewood to tax at the rate of $5.76 per $100 property value while Alamo Heights could tax at a rate of $0.68 per $100 property value.

A three-judge federal district court was impaneled to hear the case in January 1969. The district court initially delayed action, giving the 1971 Texas legislature time to address the funding issue. When the legislature failed to act during its regular session, the court took action. On December 23, 1971, it ruled that the Texas school finance system was unconstitutional under the **equal protection clause** of the Fourteenth Amendment of the U.S. Constitution. However, on appeal to the U.S. Supreme Court, the decision was overturned. On March 21, 1973, the Supreme Court ruled 5–4 that states such as Texas were not required to subsidize

equal protection clause provision of the Fourteenth Amendment guaranteeing citizens "the equal protection of the laws." This clause has been the basis for the civil rights of African Americans, women, and other groups

The Edgewood *cases challenged the property tax–based funding system that made for inferior facilities and impoverished resources for schools in poor districts (such as the one shown here), while schools in wealthy districts thrived.*

poorer school districts under the equal protection clause of the Constitution. The question of equity in public school funding would have to be addressed later in terms of Texas's state constitution and in Texas courts.

Edgewood ISD v. Kirby The second landmark case involving the financing of public schools was *Edgewood ISD v. Kirby.* Unlike *Rodriguez, Edgewood* considered the equity of funding public schools by the existing property tax system in terms of the Texas state constitution. Much of the litigation over the next few years would center around Article VII, Section 1, of the 1876 Constitution, which read:

> A general diffusion of knowledge being essential to the preservation of the liberties and rights of the people, it shall be the duty of the Legislature of the State to establish and make suitable provision for the support and maintenance of an efficient system of free public schools.

A key constitutional issue would be exactly what constituted an "efficient system of free public schools."

On behalf of the Edgewood Independent School District, the Mexican American Legal Defense and Education Fund (MALDEF) sued William Kirby, the State Commissioner of Education, on May 23, 1984. Initially only eight districts were represented in the case. By the time the case was finally decided, sixty-seven other school districts had joined the original plaintiffs. The plaintiffs argued that the state's reliance on local property taxes to fund public education discriminated against poor children by denying them equal opportunities in education. A month after the original case was filed, the legislature passed House Bill 72, a modest reform measure that increased state aid to poor districts. In 1985, plaintiffs filed an amended lawsuit, arguing that the legislature's action was far from satisfactory.

The amended case was heard early in 1987 by a state district judge, who ruled on April 29, 1987, in favor of the plaintiffs. He found the state's system for financing public education unconstitutional, violating both the "equal protection" (Article I,

Section 3) and "efficient system" (Article VII, Section 1) clauses of the Texas Constitution. The judge called for the institution of a new system of public school funding by September 1989.

In a 2–1 vote, a state appeals court reversed this decision in December 1988, finding that the funding system was constitutional. Appealing this decision to the Texas Supreme Court, plaintiffs finally won on July 5, 1989. In a 9–0 decision, the Texas Supreme Court held that the funding system was, indeed, in violation of the state constitution. The court held that education was a fundamental right under the Texas Constitution and that the "glaring disparities" between rich and poor schools violated the efficiency clause of the constitution. In its ruling, the court did not demand "absolute equality" in per pupil spending. But it did require a standard of "substantially equal access to similar revenues per pupil at similar levels of tax effort."[43] It ordered the legislature to implement an equitable system by the 1990–91 school year.

The Texas Supreme Court's ruling touched off a political firestorm that swept through Texas politics throughout the early 1990s. The legislature failed to pass appropriate legislation in four special sessions called to address the funding problem. Finally, on June 1, 1990, a master appointed by the Texas Supreme Court announced an equity financing plan that would be implemented if the legislature failed to develop one of its own. Essentially, the plan called for wealthy school districts to transfer funds to poorer districts in order to equalize funds available to all public schools across the state. The so-called Robin Hood plan finally shook the legislature into action. During a sixth special session, the legislature passed Senate Bill 1 (SB 1), which, among other things, implemented funding adjustments to further assist poor school districts. Significantly, the bill did not restrict the ability of wealthier districts to enrich themselves through their higher property tax bases.

The new system of funding was found to be unconstitutional by a state district court in a case that came to be known as *Edgewood II*. The state supreme court upheld the lower court ruling, arguing that SB 1 failed to restructure the overall funding system. The court was particularly critical of the ability of wealthy school systems to accumulate funds outside the system and hinted that a solution might lie in the creation of consolidated countywide tax bases. The legislature responded by passing Senate Bill 351 (SB 351), creating 188 "county education districts," which would equalize wealth across districts by broadening the tax base. Property taxes funding schools were to be collected by both the county education district and the local school district.

This time wealthier districts challenged the legislative initiatives to settle the equity problem in public schools. In January 1992, the state supreme court held 7–2 in *Edgewood III* that SB 351 violated two constitutional provisions: first,

Another means of encouraging educational excellence has been to allow students to transfer from low-performing to high-performing schools, thus promoting competition among the schools and allowing parents more choices.

it had failed to get the required local voter approval of school property tax levies (Article VII, Section 3). Second, it had violated Article VII, Sections 1–3, which had prohibited a state property tax since 1980. Interestingly, the court did not rule on the nature of the tax itself or whether it adequately addressed the equity question. The state was given until June 1993 to devise a new system for funding public education that was equitable and constitutional.

The legislature met in special session and during regular session in an attempt to meet the court-imposed deadline. A constitutional amendment to allow for a statewide property tax was put before the voters on May 1, 1993, and soundly defeated. The legislature responded by quickly passing Senate Bill 7. The key difference between SB 7 and earlier attempts to address the equity issue was its equalization and recapture provisions. Seeking to redress the imbalance between wealthier and poorer districts, the bill set a $280,000 cap on the per student taxable property value base in all districts. Districts with property values exceeding this limit had to choose one of a variety of methods to reduce their taxable wealth. Among these methods were consolidating with a poorer district, ceding property tax base to another poorer district, writing a check to the state, partnering with a poorer district, and consolidating with one or more other districts.

Senate Bill 7 was challenged in *Edgewood IV*, but was upheld as being constitutional by the state supreme court. The court noted that additional work was still needed on equalizing and improving school facilities across the state. Unfortunately, not enough was done in a timely manner to address the problem. In November 2005, the Texas Supreme Court upheld a lower court ruling that the school districts lacked "meaningful discretion" in setting local maintenance and operation tax rates. In the Court's opinion, too many districts were being forced to set tax rates at the maximum $1.50 per $100 valuation. Essentially, this meant that the school system was being financed by an unconstitutional state property tax. The Court gave the legislature until June 1, 2006, to address the matter or it would enjoin the state from distributing funding to the public school system.

It took three special sessions of the state legislature to craft a compromise and finally put constitutional concerns over the financing of public schools brought on by Robin Hood to rest. The final proposal cut property taxes by a third and replaced lost revenues with money raised statewide by an expanded business tax and a new $1-per-pack tax on cigarettes. General revenues monies were now used to address some of the inequities of the property tax system.[44]

Discontent over the Robin Hood plan for financing public schools continued into the spring of 2006, when a special session was called to address the problem. The reforms adopted included modest property tax relief and new taxes, notably a $1.00 tax increase on a pack of cigarettes. Neither will likely solve the funding problem in education over the long run.

The struggle to rework the funding mechanism for public education was only one dimension of educational policy in Texas in the 1980s and 1990s. Concerns over the quality of education in the state and how best to promote educational excellence will continue to redefine educational policy in the early twenty-first century.

Educational Excellence and Accountability in Texas

The equity issue in public education had been touched off by litigation. Only when forced by the courts to rethink how schools were being funded was the legislature finally willing to act. A different set of factors has driven the debate over educational excellence and accountability.

Teachers' groups, such as the Texas Federation of Teachers, charged that recent school finance reforms passed in 2006 failed to address some important problems with Texas's education system. Education policy and school funding are likely to remain sources of debate in Texas politics in years to come.

The issue of education reform came to a head in the early 1980s in Texas. The Texas debate was actually part of a larger national debate over the state of education in the United States.[45] A 1983 report by the National Commission on Excellence in Education, *A Nation at Risk*, identified a number of crises that were beginning to grip the nation's educational system. Test scores were declining and functional illiteracy was on the rise. Students were simply not equipped with the intellectual skills that were required in the modern world. If something were not done soon to reform education in the United States, the report argued, the nation was at risk of falling behind other countries in the rapidly changing world of international competition.[46]

Educational reform was put on the state agenda when at the end of the 1983 regular session the legislature established the Select Committee on Public Education (SCOPE). Earlier in the session, the Democratic governor Mark White had hoped to appoint a commission concerned with the narrow issue of pay raises for teachers. What he got, as Clark D. Thomas has noted, was something very different. SCOPE was created as a twenty-two-member committee to which the governor would have only five appointments.[47] The remaining seats were filled by appointments made by the House and Senate leadership and by three members of the State Board of Education. The intent of the legislature in creating SCOPE was not just to figure out how to fund pay raises for teachers but to evaluate the entire system of public education in the state.

One of the most important decisions made by Governor White was appointing the Dallas businessman Ross Perot to chair the committee. Perot had supported White's opponent in the 1982 gubernatorial race. It was felt that his participation in the process would help broaden support for the committee across party lines as well as bringing in needed support from the business community. At the time of his selection, however, few knew how important Perot would be to the process of educational reform. To the surprise of many, Perot took an active role in SCOPE, mobilizing the committee in private and public to take on what he considered abuses in the public education system. Perot was particularly scornful of athletic programs and what he considered the misplaced priorities of the existing educational system. In the end, SCOPE presented 140 recommendations for reforming the Texas education system in its final report on April 19, 1984. Among the most controversial of the proposed reforms was "no pass, no play." Students who failed to earn a passing grade of 70, raised from 60, would be unable to participate in any extracurricular activities for the next grading period of six weeks. But "no pass, no play" was only the tip of the iceberg. Other reform proposals set new standards for students' attendance and performance; annual school performance reports and tighter accreditation standards, with schools that did not meet these higher standards losing state funds; a longer school year—from 175 to 180 days; and a professional career ladder for teachers, tying pay raises to performance.[48] Many of the reform proposals were put into place in a 266-page education reform bill and the necessary accompanying tax increases in early July 1984.

The so-called Perot reforms were but the first round in the debate over excellence and accountability in the public school system. A second round opened during the 1995 legislative session. There were some important differences in the reform package finally signed by Republican Governor George W. Bush. The Perot reforms had generally tended to centralize control over education policy in the state. The Bush reforms, in contrast, gave more discretion to local school districts to achieve the educational goals the state was mandating. Some of the reforms put through were symbolic. The controversial "no pass, no play" rule was relaxed, cutting the period of nonparticipation from six to three weeks and lifting a ban on practicing while on scholastic probation. But other changes were more substantive. Local control of public schools was increased by limiting the power of the Texas Education Agency. Local voters were empowered to adopt home charters that could free their school districts from many state requirements, including class-size caps at lower grades. The 1995 reforms also enabled students, under certain circumstances, to transfer from low-performing schools to high-performing schools in their districts, thus promoting competition among the schools by holding them accountable for the performance of their students.[49]

Education Policy in Perspective

It is difficult to judge whether the reforms instituted in the 1980s and 1990s have been successful in improving the overall equity and excellence of public education in Texas. Recent statistics suggest that the state still has a long way to go in turning its public school system into one of the best in the nation. Despite the efforts of recent administrations to raise them, teacher salaries and overall state and local spending on public education remained low compared with those in other states. In 2009, the high school graduation rate in Texas was 61 percent, thirty-sixth in the nation. The average reading SAT score in Texas was 486 and in math was 506, ranking Texas forty-sixth and thirty-eighth in the nation, respectively.[50] This compares to a national average in critical reading of 501 and a national average in math of 515. The dropout rate in grades seven through twelve, however, had declined throughout most of the 1990s, even though it is still high among minorities. Scores on standardized tests such as the TAAS (Texas Assessment of Academic Skills) test improved across the state, sparking calls for the development of new assessment tests to hold teachers and schools accountable. The TAKS (Texas Assessment of Knowledge and Skills) test replaced TAAS in 2003 and expanded the number of subjects assessed from grades three through eleven. Despite such efforts to increase oversight and accountability in the classroom, concerns were mounting that too

for critical analysis

In most categories of educational achievement, Texas's public schools rank poorly, despite the fact that the state budget allocates more for education than any other item. Call on your experience as a public or private school student, textbook readings, class discussion, and current events to propose a series of changes to enhance the state's educational system.

● How has welfare
policy evolved in
Texas?

much time was spent "teaching to the test." Reforms passed during the 2007 legislative session limited TAKS to grades three through eight. In high school TAKS will be replaced by new subject tests given at the end of a course. These tests are scheduled to go into effect beginning in 2012.[51] Reforming education with a concern for equity and excellence will continue to be a major policy issue in the state for many years to come.

● Welfare Policy

Poverty in Texas

Poverty has never been a popular subject in Texas. The idea that some individuals have trouble taking care of themselves or meeting the basic needs of their families seems to fly in the face of Texas's individualistic culture. Given the booming Texas economy of the late 1990s, we might hope that the poverty problem would go away. It hasn't. Between 1990 and 1999, the percentage of Texans living in poverty fell from 15.9 percent to 15.0 percent, rising again in 2008 to 15.8 percent. According to the U.S. Census Bureau, 3.76 million people in Texas lived in poverty in 2009. In January 2010, 2,918,958 people were enrolled in Medicaid, a federally financed, state-operated program providing medical services to low-income people.[52] Despite the economic boom fostered by the age of high tech, poverty remains one of the most intractable problems facing the state.

Policy makers define poverty in very specific terms. Poverty is the condition under which individuals or families do not have the resources to meet their basic needs, including food, shelter, health care, transportation, and clothing. The U.S. Department of Health and Human Services developed a "poverty index" in 1964.

The Texas Department of Public Welfare was established in 1939 during the New Deal. This photo shows farmers receiving support from the government at the time.

This index was revised in 1969 and 1980. The index calculates the consumption requirements of families based on their size and composition. The poverty index is adjusted every year to account for the rate of inflation. Although there is considerable controversy as to whether it adequately measures the minimal needs of a family, the poverty index is the generally accepted standard against which poverty is measured.

In 2009, the federal poverty guideline was $10,830 a year for one person and $3,740 a year for each additional person in the family. In 2008, Texas had 3.76 million people in poverty or 15.87 percent of its population compared to 13.2 percent of the population of the United States. Almost one out of four Hispanics in Texas are poor and between one in four and one in five African Americans are poor. Slightly over 12 percent of persons over sixty-five years of age in Texas are poor compared to 9.9 percent in the nation as a whole. Poverty among children, especially young children, is much higher than in the United States as a whole. Fifty-eight percent of poor families in Texas have a worker at the head of the family. Over one in four Texans (26.6 percent) are at 150 percent of the poverty level or less and 36.5 percent are at 200 percent of the poverty level or less. One hundred fifty percent of the poverty level is $26,400 a year for a family of three and 200 percent of the federal poverty level is $35,200 a year for a family of three.

Texas uses these federal poverty guidelines to determine eligibility for a variety of social programs. For example, a family of three is eligible for reduced price school meals if they are at no more than 185 percent of the poverty level. A family of three is eligible for free school meals if they are at no more than 130 percent of the poverty level and they are eligible for food stamps if they are at no more than 130 percent of the poverty level.[53]

Welfare in Texas, 1935–96

The origins of modern welfare policy lie in President Franklin D. Roosevelt's **New Deal**.[54] Prior to the 1930s, welfare was considered to be a state and local responsibility. The Great Depression overwhelmed many state and local welfare arrangements, causing the federal government to expand its role in addressing the needs of the poor and the unemployed. The Social Security Act of 1935 transformed the way in which welfare policy was implemented in the United States. Along with two social insurance programs (Old Age Insurance and Unemployment Insurance), the Social Security Act established a number of state-federal public assistance programs: Aid for Dependent Children (ADC, later **Aid to Families with Dependent Children** or AFDC), Old Age Assistance (OAA), and Aid for the Blind (AB). States administered and determined the benefit levels for these programs. In exchange for federal assistance in funding, state programs had to meet certain minimum federal guidelines.

The Department of Public Welfare was established in Texas in 1939 to run the state's various public assistance programs. It was to be supervised by a state board of welfare, composed of three members appointed by the governor for six-year terms. The board appointed an executive director who, in turn, was the chief administrative officer of the department.[55]

Through the early 1960s, the basic strategy adopted by welfare policy makers in Texas was to minimize the cost to the state while maximizing federal dollars. Some programs were expanded during these years. In 1950, ADC became AFDC as mothers were included in the program. Other new social-service programs were also added. Much of the initiative for the expansion of welfare came from the federal government. One of the major issues in Texas was the problem of the constitutional ceiling on welfare spending. This had to be raised from $35 million in 1945 to $52 million in 1961, and again to $60 million in 1963. Between 1945 and 1965, state AFDC expenditures rose from $1.495 million to $3.899 million. At the same time, federal expenditures in Texas rose from $1.242 million to $16.594 million.[56]

Welfare policy in Texas was transformed fundamentally in the 1960s. Federal court decisions between 1968 and 1971 effectively ended a series of practices such as man-in-the-house rules and residency requirements, which had been used by states to keep welfare rolls low. In 1965, Congress established **Medicaid**, a state-federal program to finance health care for the poor. President Lyndon Johnson's "War on Poverty" also expanded the number of social service programs available to the poor. Increasingly, it was argued, the solution to alleviating poverty was through an expanded federal control over welfare programs.

In 1965, the Department of Public Welfare was authorized to work with the federal government's new antipoverty programs. The welfare ceiling was raised to $80 million in 1969. Among the welfare programs administered by the Department were four public assistance programs: Aid to Families with Dependent Children, Aid for the Blind, Aid to the Permanently and Totally Disabled, and Old Age Assistance. The latter three programs were taken over by the federal government in 1972 in the form of the new national Supplemental Security Income program. Along with these programs the Department ran the Texas Medical Assistance Program (Medicaid), the national food stamp program, and a series of social-service programs.

In 1977, the Department of Public Welfare became the Department of Human Resources. It was renamed again in 1985 as the Texas Department of Human Services and to the Health and Human Services Commission in 2003. The name reflected an ongoing desire on the part of policy makers to think of the agency less as a welfare agency and more as a service agency to the poor. By 1980, the department was reorganized to focus on the major client groups it served: families with children and aged and disabled people. In 1981, the constitutional ceiling on welfare spending was replaced with a more flexible standard. Instead of a flat cap of $80 million, welfare expenditures could not exceed 1 percent of the total state budget. In 1989, the state board of welfare was expanded from three to six members.[57]

Between 1967 and 1973, participation rates and welfare expenditures in Texas exploded. The number of children on AFDC during this time rose from 79,914 to 325,244, while the number of families on AFDC went from 23,509 to 120,254. Rates leveled off in the late 1970s, but they began to push upward again in the 1980s. Liberal attempts to reform welfare by nationalizing AFDC (turning the state-federal program into a national program like Supplemental Security Income) failed throughout the 1970s. Conservative attempts to compel welfare recipients to participate in job-training programs, such as the Work Incentive Program of 1967, had limited success. A frustrating political stalemate set in. Few were happy with welfare policy as then conducted. But no consensus had emerged as to what would be a better alternative. Meanwhile, welfare rolls expanded and expenditures continued to increase in both Texas and the nation.

The Idea of Dependency and Welfare Reform

By the mid-1980s, a new critique of welfare programs had begun to emerge. At its heart lay the idea that the well-intentioned policies of the 1960s had backfired, creating a dysfunctional underclass of people dependent on welfare. Welfare programs such as AFDC may have helped people financially in the short run, but in

Medicaid a federally and state-financed, state-operated program providing medical services to low-income people

for critical analysis

In the past twenty years, what attempts have been made to reform the welfare system? How successful have these attempts been?

the long run they had robbed people of the character traits and the moral values that would enable them to succeed in a market economy.[58] Skyrocketing illegitimacy rates, particularly among minorities and the poor, were seen as the partial result of a perverse set of incentives put into place by the state supposedly to help the poor. Under the existing welfare system, the more children you had, the higher the welfare check. Because some states did not provide welfare to families with fathers in the home, fathers were actually being encouraged to abandon their families so that they might qualify for welfare. According to critics, the poor needed the encouragement and proper incentives to become independent workers rather than having a permanent source of income from the state.

At the national level, the deadlock over welfare reform was broken with the passage of the Family Support Act in 1988. In the attempt to stem the rising tide of illegitimacy rates and single-parent families among the poor, the act mandated two-parent coverage for all state AFDC programs. It also established a number of new "workfare" programs whose goals were to get people off welfare and into the workforce. New standards were also developed requiring parents to participate in these workfare programs or lose their benefits.[59]

Much hyperbole surrounded the passage of the Family Support Act. Although the act did break new ground in formulating programs to help people make the transition from welfare to work, it also was an important expansion of the existing AFDC system. Far from declining, welfare roll expansion was unabated in the early 1990s. In Texas, this expansion was especially rapid. By 1994, an average 786,400 people were receiving AFDC in Texas. Total federal and state expenditures rose from $188.3 million in 1984 to $544.9 million in 1994. Food stamp costs also rose rapidly during this period, from $664.9 million to $2.2 billion. But AFDC and food stamps were only part of the problem. Medicaid—the state-federal program to finance health care for the poor—was escalating at a rate of more than 20 percent a year. During the 1994–95 biennium, $18.6 billion in state and federal funds was being spent on Medicaid. This was 13 percent of the state budget, or $6.7 billion. Escalating costs of AFDC, food stamps, and Medicaid provided the backdrop to the welfare reforms that would be put into place by Texas policy makers in 1995.

Though poverty in Texas afflicts many different social groups, Hispanics currently make up the majority of Texans living below the poverty line. The border counties in West Texas are by far the poorest in the state.

● How has welfare
policy evolved in
Texas?

Growing discontent over welfare policy across the country encouraged many states to seek **waivers** from federal regulations so that they, too, might experiment with welfare reform.[60] Some states sought to modify AFDC rules to eliminate some of the perverse incentive structures in the welfare system. Other states set caps on benefits and how long one could continue to receive welfare. Welfare became a state issue during the 1994 elections. As governor of Texas, George W. Bush echoed the ideas of conservative critics of the welfare system, arguing that the existing system was robbing people of their independence. Among the changes that he called for were

waiver an exemption from a federal requirement

- strengthening child-support procedures and penalties.
- imposing a two-year limit on benefits for recipients able to work.
- requiring individuals receiving welfare to accept a state-sponsored job if after two years they were unable to find work.
- creating new child-care and job-training programs.
- requiring unwed mothers to live with their parents or grandparents.
- moving family support systems from the state to the local level.

Data released by the comptroller's office lent support to the Bush contention that there were serious problems with the existing system of welfare in Texas. Over one-quarter of all welfare recipients in 1993 were "long-term" recipients who had remained on the rolls for five years or more. The publication of *A Partnership for Independence: Welfare Reform in Texas*, by the office of the comptroller, John Sharp, a Democrat, helped to set the legislative agenda for the debate over welfare policy. Agreeing with other critics across the nation who were unhappy with the current state of welfare policy, the report documented how welfare often failed to help those most in need or to encourage those dependent on welfare to become independent of government largess. Among the report's one hundred proposals were many of the reforms that had been put into place by conservative reformers in other states or by the Bush gubernatorial administration.

A bipartisan legislative coalition ultimately supported major welfare reform in Texas. On May 26, 1995, the vote on House Bill 1863 in the House was 128 to 9 and in the Senate, 30 to 1. The law provided a number of "carrot and stick" incentives that sought to mold the character of welfare recipients in positive ways and wean them off welfare. Among the carrots were expanded education and job-training programs, as well as a select number of pilot studies involving transitional child care and medical benefits. Among the sticks were a limitation on benefits to thirty-six months, alimony for spouses who couldn't support themselves, and the institution of a five-year ban on reapplying for benefits once benefits ran out. To implement the state reforms, Texas secured a waiver from the federal government that freed the state from various federal regulations regarding welfare programs. In granting the waivers to Texas and other states, the Clinton administration hoped to stimulate innovative reforms that might be duplicated elsewhere.

Texas was ahead of the welfare reform curve in 1995. In 1996, President Bill Clinton signed into law the most important reform in federal welfare policy since the New Deal. The Personal Responsibility and Work Opportunity Reconciliation Act essentially rethought the assumptions that had guided the expansion of welfare programs for sixty years. Under the legislation, AFDC, JOBS (a work-related training program), and the Emergency Assistance Program were combined into one block grant entitled **Temporary Assistance for Needy Families (TANF)**. As with

Temporary Assistance for Needy Families (TANF) a federal block grant that replaced the AFDC program in 1996

the welfare reforms instituted in Texas and in other states across the country, the primary purpose of TANF was to make families self-sufficient by ending the cycle of dependency on government benefits. States such as Texas were given great flexibility in setting benefit levels, eligibility requirements, and other program details.

Today in Texas TANF provides temporary financial assistance to families with needy children when one or both of the parents are missing or disabled.[61] The one-time TANF program provides a $1,000 payment to individuals in certain crisis situations. To qualify, a recipient's income must be below 17 percent of the poverty income limit based on family size. In addition, the combined equity of the family may not exceed $2,000 ($3,000 for the elderly and disabled). People participating in TANF receive a monthly assistance payment based on the size of their family. They cannot receive benefits for more than thirty-six months. They are also eligible for Medicaid benefits, food stamps, and child day-care services. Unless legally exempt, recipients are also required to participate in an employment services program.

Evaluating Welfare Reform

The welfare reforms in Texas will probably be evaluated along two dimensions. First, they will be measured in terms of the number of people receiving welfare assistance from the state. Success will be determined by the degree to which the reforms help lower the number of welfare recipients in Texas. If the reforms do not decrease the welfare rolls, they likely will be considered a failure. A second measure of success will be the degree to which the reforms help to take people off welfare and move them into the workforce as productive, independent members of society.

Judged by changes in the number of people on welfare, the reforms appear to be a success. The average monthly number of people on welfare in Texas rose from a little over half a million in 1989 to a peak of more than three-quarters of a million in 1994 but then began to fall in 1995. Time limits and work requirements were put into place by the state legislature in 1995, one year before similar measures were passed nationally by the U.S. Congress. The decline in the number of people on welfare continued over the next decade, falling to 155,895 people in 2006 and to 109,915 in 2010.[62]

By the second measure—the number of people moving from welfare to work—preliminary indications are that the welfare reforms of 1995 are accomplishing their objectives. Texas ranks among the top ten states in moving families from welfare to work. The welfare rolls have decreased by 365,000 since 1995. There has been a caseload reduction of 68 percent.[63]

One qualifier must be made before we trumpet the success of welfare reform in the 1990s. Current reforms took place under conditions of a booming economy and a rising demand for all types of labor. Jobs seemed to be available for people who were willing and able to work. But how will the new welfare policies respond to the economic problems of the early years of the twenty-first century? Now that labor markets have tightened and jobs are difficult to find, will Texas policy makers be satisfied with the welfare reforms in place? How far will unemployment be allowed to go before policy makers demand that we reconsider the incentive structure created to get people off the public dole? These are questions that policy makers concerned with welfare reform will have to consider one day. Only then will we be able to have an exact evaluation of the welfare reforms of the mid-1990s.

Conclusion

In this chapter, we examined various aspects of public-policy making in Texas. We focused particular attention on the complex tax and spending issues surrounding the budget and the issues that have driven policy making in crime and corrections, public education, and welfare. In earlier chapters, we saw how the high-tech revolution transformed Texas's economy in the 1980s and 1990s. We also traced how social and political changes have restructured the political party system in the state and the increasing power of the Republican Party. In this chapter, we have seen how many of these shifts resulted in important changes in public policy in the 1990s. The reforms in budgetary policy as well as crime and corrections, public education, and welfare are part a larger shift in the Texas political economy away from an oil, cattle, and cotton economy into an era of computers, high technology, and globalization. We can't be sure exactly where public policy in Texas will go in the next decade. We can be sure that new solutions will be required as the Texas political system tries to meet the challenges and opportunities of the twenty-first century.

studyguide

Practice Quiz

Find a diagnostic Web Quiz with 20 additional questions on the StudySpace Web site: www.wwnorton.com/we-the-people

1. One result of the low taxes in Texas is that (p. 953)
   a) the state is continually in need of more money.
   b) it is also a low-service state.
   c) the state continually asks businesses to assess their taxes.
   d) citizens never lack for services.

2. The Texas Constitution (p. 955)
   a) severely limits the budgetary process.
   b) makes little mention of monetary concerns.
   c) places no restrictions on state spending for welfare.
   d) prohibits the state from receiving money from the federal government.

3. What is the major source of tax revenue for the state? (p. 956)
   a) federal funds
   b) selective sales tax on motor fuel
   c) selective sales tax on alcoholic beverages
   d) general sales tax

4. A progressive tax (p. 958)
   a) frees everyone from a state income tax.
   b) hits upper-income groups more heavily than lower-income groups.
   c) hits all income groups equally.
   d) none of the above

5. The most costly item in the Texas budget is (p. 960)
   a) public safety and corrections.
   b) public and higher education.
   c) transportation.
   d) human services.

6. What factors lie behind the 2010 Budget Crisis? (p. 961)
   a) slowing down economy
   b) increasing health care expenditures
   c) increasing education expenditures
   d) all of the above

7. The Texas prison system (p. 963)
   a) is considered a model of an effective and efficient state prison system.
   b) has space for at least 10,000 more inmates.
   c) is often overcrowded, fails to rehabilitate prisoners, and is subject to rising costs.
   d) is the most costly part of the state budget.

8. The *Ruiz* case was (p. 964)
   a) a class action suit brought on behalf of inmates in the federal Courts.
   b) a case that concluded state spending in education was unfair.
   c) a case that led to increased spending on AFDC.
   d) none of the above

9. Which of the following best describes corrections policy in Texas? *(p. 965)*
   a) Spare no expense to rehabilitate those in prison.
   b) Lock up some prisoners, then lock up some more prisoners, and build more prisons if necessary.
   c) Create as many drug and alcohol abuse rehabilitation and educational programs as are necessary.
   d) Place more emphasis on parole and probation and less on incarceration.

10. Public education in Texas is jointly controlled by *(p. 967)*
    a) the state and local school boards.
    b) local school boards and county government.
    c) county government and the state.
    d) the state and federal governments.

11. Which of the following is *not* one of the three most important education policy issues of the last fifty years? *(p. 968)*
    a) desegregation
    b) equity in funding
    c) no pass, no play
    d) excellence in education and accountability

12. The Gilmer-Aikin Laws *(p. 968)*
    a) amended the Texas Constitution and provided free public education to all children under the age of seventeen.
    b) established institutions responsible for public education in Texas.
    c) established the Medicaid program in Texas.
    d) none of the above

13. In *Edgewood v. Kirby (p. 969)*
    a) the Texas Supreme Court ordered the state legislature to implement an equitable public education system.
    b) the U.S. Supreme Court ended property tax funding of public school in Texas.
    c) The Texas Supreme Court eliminated the income tax as a way to fund higher education in Texas.
    d) none of the above

14. Which of the following statements is true about welfare policy in Texas? *(p. 975)*
    a) The New Deal programs from the 1930s have been expanded.
    b) In the 1990s, Texas abandoned all poverty programs.
    c) TANF has replaced the AFDC program.
    d) There are more people on welfare in Texas in 2005 than in 1995.

15. One of the effects of the welfare reforms of the late 1990s is that *(p. 977)*
    a) welfare rolls have doubled in size in Texas.
    b) welfare rolls have significantly decreased in size in Texas.
    c) welfare programs providing temporary income to poor people have been completely eliminated from Texas.
    d) none of the above

Chapter Outline

(S) **Find a detailed Chapter Outline on the StudySpace Web site: www.wwnorton.com/we-the-people**

Key Terms

(S) **Find Flashcards to help you study these terms or the StudySpace Web site: www.wwnorton.com/we-the-people**

Aid to Families with Dependent Children (AFDC) *(p. 976)*
appropriations *(p. 954)*
biennial *(p. 953)*
debt service *(p. 955)*
dedicated funds *(p. 954)*

de facto *(p. 969)*
equal protection clause *(p. 969)*
Gilmer-Aikin Laws *(p. 968)*
matching funds *(p. 958)*
Medicaid *(p. 977)*
New Deal *(p. 976)*

pay-as-you-go limit *(p. 954)*
progressive/regressive taxation *(p. 958)*
Temporary Assistance for Needy Families (TANF) *(p. 979)*
waiver *(p. 979)*

Recommended Web Sites

Texas Department of Criminal Justice
www.tdcj.state.tx.us

Texas Education Agency
www.tea.state.tx.us

Texas Health and Human Service Commission
www.hhsc.state.tx.us

Texas Workforce Commission
www.twc.state.tx.us

Window on State Government
www.window.state.tx.us

appendix

The Declaration of Independence

In Congress, July 4, 1776

The unanimous Declaration of the thirteen united States of America,

When in the Course of human events, it becomes necessary for one people to dissolve the political bands which have connected them with another, and to assume among the powers of the earth, the separate and equal station to which the Laws of Nature and of Nature's God entitle them, a decent respect to the opinions of mankind requires that they should declare the causes which impel them to the separation.

We hold these truths to be self-evident, that all men are created equal, that they are endowed by their Creator with certain unalienable Rights, that among these are Life, Liberty and the pursuit of Happiness.—That to secure these rights, Governments are instituted among Men, deriving their just powers from the consent of the governed.—That whenever any Form of Government becomes destructive of these ends, it is the Right of the People to alter or to abolish it, and to institute new Government, laying its foundation on such principles and organizing its powers in such form, as to them shall seem most likely to effect their Safety and Happiness. Prudence, indeed, will dictate that Governments long established should not be changed for light and transient causes; and accordingly all experience hath shewn, that mankind are more disposed to suffer, while evils are sufferable, than to right themselves by abolishing the forms to which they are accustomed. But when a long train of abuses and usurpations, pursuing invariably the same Object evinces a design to reduce them under absolute Despotism, it is their right, it is their duty, to throw off such Government, and to provide new Guards for their future security.—Such has been the patient sufferance of these Colonies; and such is now the necessity which constrains them to alter their former Systems of Government. The history of the present King of Great Britain is a history of repeated injuries and usurpations, all having in direct object the establishment of an absolute Tyranny over these States. To prove this, let Facts be submitted to a candid world.

He has refused his Assent to Laws, the most wholesome and necessary for the public good.

He has forbidden his Governors to pass Laws of immediate and pressing importance, unless suspended in their operation till his Assent should be obtained; and when so suspended, he has utterly neglected to attend to them.

He has refused to pass other Laws for the accommodation of large districts of people, unless those people would relinquish the right of Representation in the Legislature, a right inestimable to them and formidable to tyrants only.

He has called together legislative bodies at places unusual, uncomfortable, and distant from the depository of their public Records, for the sole purpose of fatiguing them into compliance with his measures.

He has dissolved Representative Houses repeatedly, for opposing with manly firmness his invasions on the rights of the people.

He has refused for a long time, after such dissolutions, to cause others to be elected; whereby the Legislative powers, incapable of Annihilation, have returned to the People at large for their exercise; the State remaining in the mean time exposed to all the dangers of invasion from without, and convulsions within.

He has endeavoured to prevent the population of these States; for that purpose obstructing the Laws for Naturalization of Foreigners; refusing to pass others to encourage their migrations hither, and raising the conditions of new Appropriations of Lands.

He has obstructed the Administration of Justice, by refusing his Assent to Laws for establishing Judiciary powers.

He has made Judges dependent on his Will alone, for the tenure of their offices, and the amount and payment of their salaries.

He has erected a multitude of New Offices, and sent hither swarms of Officers to harrass our people, and eat out their substance.

He has kept among us, in times of peace, Standing Armies without the Consent of our legislatures.

He has affected to render the Military independent of and superior to the Civil power.

He has combined with others to subject us to a jurisdiction foreign to our constitution, and unacknowledged by our laws; giving his Assent to their Acts of pretended Legislation:

For Quartering large bodies of armed troops among us:

For protecting them, by a mock Trial, from punishment for any Murders which they should commit on the Inhabitants of these States:

For cutting off our Trade with all parts of the world:

For imposing Taxes on us without our Consent:

For depriving us in many cases, of the benefits of Trial by Jury:

For transporting us beyond Seas to be tried for pretended offences:

For abolishing the free System of English Laws in a neighboring Province, establishing therein an Arbitrary government, and enlarging its Boundaries so as to render it at once an example and fit instrument for introducing the same absolute rule into these Colonies:

For taking away our Charters, abolishing our most valuable Laws, and altering fundamentally the Forms of our Governments:

For suspending our own Legislatures, and declaring themselves invested with power to legislate for us in all cases whatsoever.

He has abdicated Government here, by declaring us out of his Protection and waging War against us.

He has plundered our seas, ravaged our Coasts, burnt our towns, and destroyed the lives of our people.

He is at this time transporting large Armies of foreign Mercenaries to compleat the works of death, desolation and tyranny, already begun with circumstances of Cruelty & perfidy scarcely paralleled in the most barbarous ages, and totally unworthy the Head of a civilized nation.

He has constrained our fellow Citizens taken Captive on the high Seas to bear Arms against their Country, to become the executioners of their friends and Brethren, or to fall themselves by their Hands.

He has excited domestic insurrections amongst us, and has endeavoured to bring on the inhabitants of our frontiers, the merciless Indian Savages, whose known rule of warfare, is an undistinguished destruction of all ages, sexes and conditions.

In every stage of these Oppressions We have Petitioned for Redress in the most humble terms: Our repeated Petitions have been answered only by repeated injury. A Prince whose character is thus marked by every act which may define a Tyrant, is unfit to be the ruler of a free people.

Nor have We been wanting in attentions to our Brittish brethren. We have warned them from time to time of attempts by their legislature to extend an unwarrantable jurisdiction over us. We have reminded them of the circumstances of our emigration and settlement here. We have appealed to their native justice and magnanimity, and we have conjured them by the ties of our common kindred to disavow these usurpations, which, would inevitably interrupt our connections and correspondence. They too have been deaf to the voice of justice and of consanguinity. We must, therefore, acquiesce in the necessity, which denounces our Separation, and hold them, as we hold the rest of mankind, Enemies in War, in Peace Friends.

We, Therefore, the Representatives of the United States of America, in General Congress, Assembled, appealing to the Supreme Judge of the world for the rectitude of our intentions, do, in the Name, and by Authority of the good People of these Colonies, solemnly publish and declare, That these United Colonies are, and of Right ought to be Free and Independent States; that they are Absolved from all Allegiance to the British Crown, and that all political connection between them and the State of Great Britain, is and ought to be totally dissolved; and that as Free and Independent States, they have full Power to levy War, conclude Peace, contract Alliances, establish Commerce, and to do all other Acts and Things which Independent States may of right do. And for the support of this Declaration, with a firm reliance on the protection of divine Providence, we mutually pledge to each other our Lives, our Fortunes and our sacred Honor.

The foregoing Declaration was, by order of Congress, engrossed, and signed by the following members:

John Hancock

NEW HAMPSHIRE
Josiah Bartlett
William Whipple
Matthew Thornton

MASSACHUSETTS BAY
Samuel Adams
John Adams
Robert Treat Paine
Elbridge Gerry

RHODE ISLAND
Stephen Hopkins
William Ellery

CONNECTICUT
Roger Sherman
Samuel Huntington
William Williams
Oliver Wolcott

NEW YORK
William Floyd
Philip Livingston
Francis Lewis
Lewis Morris

NEW JERSEY
Richard Stockton
John Witherspoon
Francis Hopkinson
John Hart
Abraham Clark

PENNSYLVANIA
Robert Morris
Benjamin Rush
Benjamin Franklin
John Morton
George Clymer
James Smith
George Taylor
James Wilson
George Ross

DELAWARE
Caesar Rodney
George Read
Thomas M'Kean

MARYLAND
Samuel Chase
William Paca
Thomas Stone
Charles Carroll,
    of Carrollton

VIRGINIA
George Wythe
Richard Henry Lee
Thomas Jefferson
Benjamin Harrison
Thomas Nelson, Jr.
Francis Lightfoot Lee
Carter Braxton

NORTH CAROLINA
William Hooper
Joseph Hewes
John Penn

SOUTH CAROLINA
Edward Rutledge
Thomas Heyward, Jr.
Thomas Lynch, Jr.
Arthur Middleton

GEORGIA
Button Gwinnett
Lyman Hall
George Walton

Resolved, That copies of the Declaration be sent to the several assemblies, conventions, and committees, or councils of safety, and to the several commanding officers of the continental troops; that it be proclaimed in each of the United States, at the head of the army.

The Articles of Confederation

Agreed to by Congress November 15, 1777;
ratified and in force March 1, 1781

To all whom these Presents shall come, we the undersigned Delegates of the States affixed to our Names, send greeting. Whereas the Delegates of the United States of America, in Congress assembled, did, on the fifteenth day of November, in the Year of Our Lord One thousand Seven Hundred and Seventy seven, and in the Second Year of the Independence of America, agree to certain articles of Confederation and perpetual Union between the States of Newhampshire, Massachusetts-bay, Rhodeisland and Providence Plantations, Connecticut, New-York, New-Jersey, Pennsylvania, Delaware, Maryland, Virginia, North-Carolina, South-Carolina and Georgia in the words following, viz. "Articles of Confederation and perpetual Union between the states of Newhampshire, Massachusettsbay, Rhodeisland and Providence Plantations, Connecticut, New-York, New-Jersey, Pennsylvania, Delaware, Maryland, Virginia, North-Carolina, South-Carolina and Georgia.

Art. I. The Stile of this confederacy shall be "The United States of America."

Art. II. Each state retains its sovereignty, freedom and independence, and every Power, Jurisdiction and right, which is not by this confederation expressly delegated to the United States, in Congress assembled.

Art. III. The said states hereby severally enter into a firm league of friendship with each other, for their common defence, the security of their Liberties, and their mutual and general welfare, binding themselves to assist each other, against all force offered to, or attacks made upon them, or any of them, on account of religion, sovereignty, trade, or any other pretence whatever.

Art. IV. The better to secure and perpetuate mutual friendship and intercourse among the people of the different states in this union, the free inhabitants of each of these states, paupers, vagabonds and fugitives from Justice excepted, shall be entitled to all privileges and immunities of free citizens in the several states; and the people of each state shall have free ingress and regress to and from any other state, and shall enjoy therein all the privileges of trade and commerce, subject to the same duties, impositions and restrictions as the inhabitants thereof respectively, provided that such restriction shall not extend so far as to prevent the removal of property imported into any state, to any other state, of which the Owner is an inhabitant; provided also that no imposition, duties or restriction shall be laid by any state, on the property of the united states, or either of them.

If any Person guilty of, or charged with treason, felony, or other high misdemeanor in any state, shall flee from Justice, and be found in any of the united states, he shall, upon demand of the Governor or executive power, of the state from which he fled, be delivered up and removed to the state having jurisdiction of his offence.

Full faith and credit shall be given in each of these states to the records, acts and judicial proceedings of the courts and magistrates of every other state.

Art. V. For the more convenient management of the general interests of the united states, delegates shall be annually appointed in such manner as the legislature of each state shall direct, to meet in Congress on the first Monday in November, in every year, with a power reserved to each state, to recall its delegates, or any of them, at any time within the year, and to send others in their stead, for the remainder of the Year.

No state shall be represented in Congress by less than two, nor by more than seven Members; and no person shall be capable of being a delegate for more than three years in any term of six years; nor shall any person, being a delegate, be capable of holding any office under the united states, for which he, or another for his benefit receives any salary, fees or emolument of any kind.

Each state shall maintain its own delegates in a meeting of the states, and while they act as members of the committee of the states.

In determining questions in the united states, in Congress assembled, each state shall have one vote.

Freedom of speech and debate in Congress shall not be impeached or questioned in any Court, or place out of Congress, and the members of congress shall be protected in their persons from arrests and imprisonments, during the time of their going to and from, and attendance on congress, except for treason, felony, or breach of the peace.

Art. VI. No state without the Consent of the united states in congress assembled, shall send any embassy to, or receive any embassy from, or enter into any conference, agreement, or alliance or treaty with any King, prince or state; nor shall any person holding any office or profit or trust under the united states, or any of them, accept of any present, emolument, office or title of any kind whatever from any king, prince or foreign state; nor shall the united states in congress assembled, or any of them, grant any title of nobility.

No two or more states shall enter into any treaty, confederation or alliance whatever between them, without the consent of the united states in congress assembled, specifying accurately the purposes for which the same is to be entered into, and how long it shall continue.

No state shall lay any imposts or duties, which may interfere with any stipulations in treaties, entered into by the united states in congress assembled, with any king, prince or state, in pursuance of any treaties already proposed by congress, to the courts of France and Spain.

No vessels of war shall be kept up in time of peace by any state, except such number only, as shall be deemed necessary by the united states in congress assembled, for the defence of such state, or its trade; nor shall any body of forces be kept up by any state, in time of peace, except such number only, as in the judgment of the united states, in congress assembled, shall be deemed requisite to garrison the forts necessary for the defence of such state; but every state shall always keep up a well regulated and disciplined militia, sufficiently armed and accoutred, and shall provide and constantly have ready for use, in public stores, a due number of field pieces and tents, and a proper quantity of arms, ammunition and camp equipage.

No state shall engage in any war without the consent of the united states in congress assembled, unless such state be actually invaded by enemies, or shall have received certain advice of a resolution being formed by some nation of Indians to invade such state, and the danger is so imminent as not to admit of a delay, till the united states in congress asssembled can be consulted; nor shall any state grant commissions to any ships or vessels of war, nor letters of marque or reprisal, except it be after a declaration of war by the united states in congress assembled, and then only against the kingdom or state and the subjects thereof, against which war has been so declared, and under such regulations as shall be established by the united states in congress assembled, unless such state be infested by pirates; in which case vessels of war may be fitted out for that occasion, and kept so long as the danger shall continue, or until the united states in congress assembled shall determine otherwise.

Art. VII. When land-forces are raised by any state for the common defence, all officers of or under the rank of colonel, shall be appointed by the legislature of each state respectively, by whom such forces shall be raised, or in such manner as such state shall direct, and all vacancies shall be filled up by the state which first made the appointment.

Art. VIII. All charges of war, and all other expences that shall be incurred for the common defence or general welfare, and allowed by the united states in congress assembled, shall be defrayed out of a common treasury, which shall be supplied by the several states in proportion to the value of all land within each state, granted to or surveyed for any Person, as such land and the buildings and improvements thereon shall be estimated according to such mode as the united states in congress assembled, shall from time to time direct and appoint.

The taxes for paying that proportion shall be laid and levied by the authority and direction of the legislatures of the several states within the time agreed upon by the united states in congress assembled.

Art. IX. The united states in congress assembled, shall have the sole and exclusive right and power of determining on peace and war, except in the cases mentioned in the sixth article—of sending and receiving ambassadors—entering into treaties and alliances, provided that no treaty of commerce shall be made whereby the legislative power of the respective states shall be restrained from imposing such imposts and duties on foreigners, as their own people are subjected to, or from prohibiting the exportation of any species of goods or commodities whatsoever—of establishing rules for deciding in all cases, what captures on land or water shall be legal, and in what manner prizes taken by land or naval forces in the service of the united states shall be divided or appropriated—of granting letters of marque and reprisal in times of peace—appointing courts for the trial of piracies and felonies committed on the high seas and establishing courts for receiving and determining finally appeals in all cases of captures, provided that no member of congress shall be appointed a judge of any of the said courts.

The united states in congress assembled shall also be the last resort on appeal in all disputes and differences now subsisting or that hereafter may arise between two or more states concerning boundary, jurisdiction or any other cause whatever; which authority shall always be exercised in the manner following. Whenever the legislative or executive authority or lawful agent of any state in controversy with another shall present a petition to congress stating the matter in question and praying for a hearing, notice thereof shall be given by order of congress to the legislative or executive authority of the other state in controversy, and a day assigned for the appearance of the parties by their lawful agents, who shall then be directed to appoint by joint consent, commissioners or judges to constitute a court for hearing and determining the matter in question: but if they cannot agree, congress shall name three persons out of each of the united states, and from the list of such persons each party shall alternately strike out one, the petitioners beginning, until the number shall be reduced to thirteen; and from that number not less than seven, nor more than nine names as congress shall direct, shall in the presence of congress be drawn out by lot, and the persons whose names shall be so drawn or any five of them, shall be commissioners or judges, to hear and finally determine the controversy, so always as a major part of the judges who shall hear the cause shall agree in the determination: and if either party shall neglect to attend at the day appointed, without shewing reasons, which congress shall judge sufficient, or being present shall refuse to strike, the congress shall proceed to nominate three persons out of each state, and the secretary of congress shall strike in behalf of such party absent or refusing; and the judgment and sentence of the court to be appointed, in the manner before prescribed, shall be final and conclusive; and if any of the parties shall refuse to submit to the authority of such court, or to appear to defend their claim or cause, the court shall nevertheless proceed to pronounce sentence, or judgment, which shall in like manner be final and decisive, the judgment or sentence and other proceedings being in either case transmitted to congress, and lodged among the acts of congress for the security of the parties concerned: provided that every commissioner, before he sits in judgment, shall take an oath to be administered by one of the judges of the supreme or superior court of the state, where the cause shall be tried, "well and truly to hear and determine the matter in question, according to the best of his judgment, without favour, affection or hope of reward:" provided also, that no state shall be deprived of territory for the benefit of the united states.

All controversies concerning the private right of soil claimed under different grants of two or more states, whose jurisdictions as they may respect such lands, and the states which passed such grants are adjusted, the said grants or either of them being at the same time claimed to have originated antecedent to such settlement of jurisdiction, shall on the petition of either party to the congress of the united states, be finally determined as near as may be in the same manner as is before prescribed for deciding disputes respecting territorial jurisdiction between different states.

The united states in congress assembled shall also have the sole and exclusive right and power of regulating the alloy and value of coin struck by their own authority, or by that of the respective states—fixing the standard of weights and measures throughout the united states—regulating the trade and managing all affairs with the Indians, not members of any of the states, provided that the legislative right of any state within its own limits be not infringed or violated—establishing and regulating post-offices from one state to another, throughout all the united states, and exacting such postage on the papers passing thro' the same as may be requisite to defray the expences of the said office—appointing all officers of the land forces, in the service of the united states, excepting regimental officers—appointing all the officers of the naval forces, and commissioning all officers whatever in the service of the united states—making rules for the government and regulation of the said land and naval forces, and directing their operations.

The united states in congress assembled shall have authority to appoint a committee, to sit in the recess of congress, to be denominated "A Committee of the States," and to consist of one delegate from each state; and to appoint such other committees and civil officers as may be necessary for managing the general affairs of the united states under their direction—to appoint one of their number to preside, provided that no person be allowed to serve in the office of president more than one year in any term of three years; to ascertain the necessary sums of Money to be raised for the service of the united states, and to appropriate and apply the same for defraying the public expenses—to borrow money, or emit bills on the credit of the united states, transmitting every half year to the respective states an account of the sums of money so borrowed or emitted,—to build and equip a navy—to agree upon the number of land forces, and to make requisitions from each state for its quota, in proportion to the number of white inhabitants in such state; which requisition shall be binding, and thereupon the legislature of each state shall appoint the regimental officers, raise the men and cloath, arm and equip them in a soldier like manner, at the expense of the united states; and the officers and men so cloathed, armed and equipped shall march to the place appointed, and within the time agreed on by the united states in congress assembled: But if the united states in congress assembled shall, on consideration of circumstances judge proper that any state should not raise men, or should raise a smaller number than its quota, and that any other state should raise a greater number of men than the quota thereof, such extra number shall be raised, officered, cloathed, armed and equipped in the same manner as the quota of such state, unless the legislature of such state shall judge that such extra number cannot be safely spared out of the same, in which case they shall raise officer, cloath, arm and equip as many of such extra number as they judge can be safely spared. And the officers and men so cloathed, armed and equipped, shall march to the place appointed, and within the time agreed on by the united states in congress assembled.

The united states in congress assembled shall never engage in a war, nor grant letters of marque and reprisal in time of peace, nor enter into any treaties or alliances, nor coin money, nor regulate the value thereof, nor ascertain the sums and expenses necessary for the defence and welfare of the united states, or any of them, nor emit bills, nor borrow money on the credit of the united states, nor appropriate money, nor agree upon the number of vessels of war, to be built or purchased, or the number of land or sea forces to be raised, nor appoint a commander in chief of the army or navy, unless nine states assent to the same: nor shall a question on any other point, except for adjourning from day to day be determined, unless by the votes of a majority of the united states in congress assembled.

The congress of the united states shall have power to adjourn to any time within the year, and to any place within the united states, so that no period of adjournment be for a longer duration than the space of six Months, and shall publish the Journal of their proceedings monthly, except such parts thereof relating to treaties, alliances or military operations, as in their judgment require secrecy; and the yeas and nays of the delegates of each state on any question shall be entered on the Journal, when it is desired by any delegate; and the delegates of a state, or any of them, at his or their request shall be furnished with a transcript of the said Journal, except such parts as are above excepted, to lay before the legislatures of the several states.

Art. X. The committee of the states, or any nine of them, shall be authorised to execute, in the recess of congress, such of the powers of congress as the united states in congress assembled, by the consent of nine states, shall from time to time think expedient to vest them with; provided that no power be delegated to the said committee, for the exercise of which, by the articles of confederation, the voice of nine states in the congress of the united states assembled is requisite.

Art. XI. Canada acceding to this confederation, and joining in the measures of the united states, shall be admitted into, and entitled to all the advantages of this union: but no other colony shall be admitted into the same, unless such admission be agreed to by nine states.

Art. XII. All bills of credit emitted, monies borrowed and debts contracted by, or under the authority of congress, before the assembling of the united states, in pursuance of the present confederation, shall be deemed and considered as a charge against the united states, for payment and satisfaction whereof the said united states and the public faith are hereby solemnly pledged.

Art. XIII. Every state shall abide by the determinations of the united states in congress assembled, on all questions which by this confederation are submitted to them. And the Articles of this confederation shall be inviolably observed by every state, and the union shall be perpetual; nor shall any alteration at any time hereafter be made in any of them; unless such alteration be agreed to in a congress of the united states, and be afterwards confirmed by the legislatures of every state.

And Whereas it hath pleased the Great Governor of the World to incline the hearts of the legislatures we respectively represent in congress, to approve of, and to authorize us to ratify the said articles of confederation and perpetual union. Know Ye that we the undersigned delegates, by virtue of the power and authority to us given for that purpose, do by these presents, in the name and in behalf of our respective constituents, fully and entirely ratify and confirm each and every of the said articles of confederation and perpetual union, and all and singular the matters and things therein contained: And we do further solemnly plight and engage the faith of our respective constituents, that they shall abide by the determinations of the united states in congress assembled, on all questions, which by the said confederation are submitted to them. And that the articles thereof shall be inviolably observed by the states we respectively represent, and that the union shall be perpetual. In Witness whereof we have hereunto set our hands in Congress. Done at Philadelphia in the state of Pennsylvania the ninth day of July, in the Year of our Lord one Thousand seven Hundred and Seventy-eight, and in the third year of the independence of America.

The Constitution of the United States of America

We the People of the United States, in Order to form a more perfect Union, establish Justice, insure domestic Tranquility, provide for the common defence, promote the general Welfare, and secure the Blessings of Liberty to ourselves and our Posterity, do ordain and establish this Constitution for the United States of America.

Article I

SECTION 1

[LEGISLATIVE POWERS]
All legislative Powers herein granted shall be vested in a Congress of the United States, which shall consist of a Senate and House of Representatives.

SECTION 2

[HOUSE OF REPRESENTATIVES, HOW CONSTITUTED, POWER OF IMPEACHMENT]
The House of Representatives shall be composed of Members chosen every second Year by the People of the several States, and the Electors in each State shall have the Qualifications requisite for Electors of the most numerous Branch of the State Legislature.

No Person shall be a Representative who shall not have attained to the Age of twenty five Years, and been seven Years a Citizen of the United States, and who shall not, when elected, be an Inhabitant of that State in which he shall be chosen.

Representatives and *direct Taxes*[1] shall be apportioned among the several States which may be included within this Union, according to their respective Numbers, *which shall be determined by adding to the whole Number of free Persons, including those bound to Service for a Term of Years, and excluding Indians not taxed, three fifths of all other Persons.*[2] The actual Enumeration shall be made within three Years after the first Meeting of the Congress of the United States, and within every subsequent Term of ten Years, in such Manner as they shall by Law direct. The Number of Representatives shall not exceed one for every thirty Thousand, but each State shall have at Least one Representative; *and until such enumeration shall be made, the State of New Hampshire shall be entitled to chuse three, Massachusetts eight, Rhode-Island and Providence Plantations one, Connecticut five, New-York six, New Jersey four, Pennsylvania eight, Delaware one, Maryland six, Virginia ten, North Carolina five, South Carolina five, and Georgia three.*[3]

When vacancies happen in the Representation from any State, the Executive Authority thereof shall issue Writs of Election to fill such Vacancies.

The House of Representatives shall chuse their Speaker and other Officers; and shall have the sole Power of Impeachment.

SECTION 3

[THE SENATE, HOW CONSTITUTED, IMPEACHMENT TRIALS]
The Senate of the United States shall be composed of two Senators from each State, *chosen by the Legislature thereof,*[4] for six Years; and each Senator shall have one Vote.

Immediately after they shall be assembled in Consequence of the first Election, they shall be divided as equally as may be into three Classes. The Seats of the Senators of the first Class shall be vacated at the Expiration of the second Year, of the second Class at the Expiration of the fourth Year, and of the third Class at the Expiration of the sixth Year, so that one third may be chosen every second Year; *and if Vacancies happen by Resignation, or otherwise, during the Recess of the Legislature of any State, the Executive thereof may make temporary Appointments until the next Meeting of the Legislature, which shall then fill such Vacancies.*[5]

No Person shall be a Senator who shall not have attained to the Age of thirty Years, and been nine Years a Citizen of the United States, and who shall not, when elected, be an Inhabitant of that State for which he shall be chosen.

The Vice President of the United States shall be President of the Senate, but shall have no Vote, unless they be equally divided.

The Senate shall chuse their other Officers, and also a President pro tempore, in the Absence of the Vice President, or when he shall exercise the Office of President of the United States.

---

[1]Modified by Sixteenth Amendment.

[2]Modified by Fourteenth Amendment.

[3]Temporary provision.

[4]Modified by Seventeenth Amendment.

[5]Modified by Seventeenth Amendment.

The Senate shall have the sole Power to try all Impeachments. When sitting for that Purpose, they shall be on Oath or Affirmation. When the President of the United States is tried, the Chief Justice shall preside: And no Person shall be convicted without the Concurrence of two thirds of the Members present.

Judgment in Cases of Impeachment shall not extend further than to removal from Office, and disqualification to hold and enjoy any Office of honor, Trust or Profit under the United States: but the Party convicted shall nevertheless be liable and subject to Indictment, Trial, Judgment and Punishment, according to Law.

SECTION 4

[ELECTION OF SENATORS AND REPRESENTATIVES]

The Times, Places and Manner of holding Elections for Senators and Representatives, shall be prescribed in each State by the Legislature thereof; but the Congress may at any time by Law make or alter such Regulations, except as to the Places of chusing Senators.

The Congress shall assemble at least once in every Year, and such Meeting shall be on the first Monday in December, unless they shall by Law appoint a different Day.[6]

SECTION 5

[QUORUM, JOURNALS, MEETINGS, ADJOURNMENTS]

Each House shall be the Judge of the Elections, Returns and Qualifications of its own Members, and a Majority of each shall constitute a Quorum to do Business; but a smaller Number may adjourn from day to day, and may be authorized to compel the Attendance of absent Members, in such Manner, and under such Penalties as each House may provide.

Each House may determine the Rules of its Proceedings, punish its Members for disorderly Behaviour, and, with the Concurrence of two thirds, expel a Member.

Each House shall keep a Journal of its Proceedings, and from time to time publish the same, excepting such Parts as may in their Judgment require Secrecy; and the Yeas and Nays of the Members of either House on any questions shall, at the Desire of one fifth of those Present, be entered on the Journal.

Neither House, during the Session of Congress, shall, without the Consent of the other, adjourn for more than three days, nor to any other Place than that in which the two Houses shall be sitting.

SECTION 6

[COMPENSATION, PRIVILEGES, DISABILITIES]

The Senators and Representatives shall receive a Compensation for their Services, to be ascertained by Law, and paid out of the Treasury of the United States. They shall in all Cases, except Treason, Felony and Breach of the Peace, be privileged from Arrest during their Attendance at the Session of their respective Houses, and in going to and returning from the same; and for any Speech or Debate in either House, they shall not be questioned in any other Place.

No Senator or Representative shall, during the Time for which he was elected, be appointed to any civil Office under the Authority of the United States, which shall have been created, or the Emoluments whereof shall have been encreased during such time; and no Person holding any Office under the United States, shall be a Member of either House during his Continuance in Office.

SECTION 7

[PROCEDURE IN PASSING BILLS AND RESOLUTIONS]

All Bills for raising Revenue shall originate in the House of Representatives; but the Senate may propose or concur with Amendments as on other Bills.

Every Bill which shall have passed the House of Representatives and the Senate, shall, before it become a Law, be presented to the President of the United States: If he approve he shall sign it, but if not he shall return it, with his Objections to that House in which it shall have originated, who shall enter the Objections at large on their Journal, and proceed to reconsider it. If after such Reconsideration two thirds of that House shall agree to pass the Bill, it shall be sent, together with the Objections, to the other House, by which it shall likewise be reconsidered, and if approved by two thirds of that House, it shall become a Law. But in all such Cases the Votes of both Houses shall be determined by yeas and Nays, and the Names of the Persons voting for and against the Bill shall be entered on the Journal of each House respectively. If any Bill shall not be returned by the President within ten Days (Sundays excepted) after it shall have been presented to him, the Same shall be a Law, in like Manner as if he had signed it, unless the Congress by their Adjournment prevent its Return, in which Case it shall not be a Law.

Every Order, Resolution, or Vote to which the Concurrence of the Senate and House of Representatives may be necessary (except on a question of Adjournment) shall be presented to the President of the United States; and before the Same shall take Effect, shall be approved by him, or being disapproved by him, shall be repassed by two thirds of the Senate and House of Representatives, according to the Rules and Limitations prescribed in the Case of a Bill.

SECTION 8

[POWERS OF CONGRESS]

The Congress shall have Power

To lay and collect Taxes, Duties, Imposts and Excises, to pay the Debts and provide for the common Defence and general Welfare of the United States; but all Duties, Imposts and Excises shall be uniform throughout the United States;

To borrow Money on the credit of the United States;

---

[6]Modified by Twentieth Amendment.

To regulate Commerce with foreign Nations, and among the several States, and with the Indian Tribes;

To establish an uniform Rule of Naturalization, and uniform Laws on the subject of Bankruptcies throughout the United States;

To coin Money, regulate the Value thereof, and of foreign Coin, and fix the Standard of Weights and Measures;

To provide for the Punishment of counterfeiting the Securities and current Coin of the United States;

To establish Post Offices and post Roads;

To promote the Progress of Science and useful Arts, by securing for limited Times to Authors and Inventors the exclusive Right to their respective Writings and Discoveries;

To constitute Tribunals inferior to the supreme Court;

To define and punish Piracies and Felonies committed on the high Seas, and Offences against the Law of Nations;

To declare War, grant Letters of Marque and Reprisal, and make Rules concerning Captures on Land and Water;

To raise and support Armies, but no Appropriation of Money to that Use shall be for a longer Term than two Years;

To provide and maintain a Navy;

To make Rules for the Government and Regulation of the land and naval Forces;

To provide for calling forth the Militia to execute the Laws of the Union, suppress Insurrections and repel Invasions;

To provide for organizing, arming, and disciplining, the Militia, and for governing such Part of them as may be employed in the Service of the United States, reserving to the States respectively, the Appointment of the Officers, and the Authority of training the Militia according to the discipline prescribed by Congress;

To exercise exclusive Legislation in all Cases whatsoever, over such District (not exceeding ten Miles square) as may, by Cession of particular States, and the Acceptance of Congress, become the Seat of the Government of the United States, and to exercise like Authority over all Places purchased by the Consent of the Legislature of the State in which the Same shall be, for the Erection of Forts, Magazines, Arsenals, dock-Yards, and other needful Buildings;—And

To make all Laws which shall be necessary and proper for carrying into Execution the foregoing Powers, and all other Powers vested by this Constitution in the Government of the United States, or in any Department or Officer thereof.

SECTION 9

[SOME RESTRICTIONS ON FEDERAL POWER]
The Migration or Importation of such Persons as any of the States now existing shall think proper to admit, shall not be prohibited by the Congress prior to the Year one thousand eight hundred and eight, but a Tax or duty may be imposed on such Importation, not exceeding ten dollars for each Person.[7]

The Privilege of the Writ of Habeas Corpus shall not be suspended, unless when in Cases of Rebellion or Invasion the public Safety may require it.

No Bill of Attainder or ex post facto Law shall be passed.

No Capitation, or other direct, Tax shall be laid, unless in Proportion to the Census or Enumeration herein before directed to be taken.[8]

No Tax or Duty shall be laid on Articles exported from any State.

No Preference shall be given by any Regulation of Commerce or Revenue to the Ports of one State over those of another; nor shall Vessels bound to, or from, one State, be obliged to enter, clear, or pay Duties in another.

No Money shall be drawn from the Treasury, but in Consequence of Appropriations made by Law; and a regular Statement and Account of the Receipts and Expenditures of all public Money shall be published from time to time.

No Title of Nobility shall be granted by the United States: And no Person holding any Office of Profit or Trust under them, shall, without the Consent of the Congress, accept of any present, Emolument, Office, or Title, of any kind whatever, from any King, Prince, or foreign State.

SECTION 10

[RESTRICTIONS UPON POWERS OF STATES]
No State shall enter into any Treaty, Alliance, or Confederation; grant Letters of Marque and Reprisal; coin Money; emit Bills of Credit; make any Thing but gold and silver Coin a Tender in Payment of Debts; pass any Bill of Attainder, ex post facto Law, or Law impairing the Obligation of Contracts, or grant any Title of Nobility.

No State shall, without the Consent of the Congress, lay any Imposts or Duties on Imports or Exports, except what may be absolutely necessary for executing its inspection Laws: and the net Produce of all Duties and Imposts, laid by any State on Imports or Exports, shall be for the Use of the Treasury of the United States; and all such Laws shall be subject to the Revision and Control of the Congress.

No State shall, without the Consent of Congress, lay any Duty of Tonnage, keep Troops, or Ships of War in time of Peace, enter into any Agreement or Compact with another State, or with a foreign Power, or engage in War, unless actually invaded, or in such imminent Danger as will not admit of delay.

Article II

SECTION 1

[EXECUTIVE POWER, ELECTION, QUALIFICATIONS OF THE PRESIDENT]
The executive Power shall be vested in a President of the United States of America. *He shall hold his Office during the*

---

[7]Temporary provision.

[8]Modified by Sixteenth Amendment.

Term of four Years, and, together with the Vice President, chosen for the same Term, be elected, as follows[9]

Each State shall appoint, in such Manner as the Legislature thereof may direct, a Number of Electors, equal to the whole Number of Senators and Representatives to which the State may be entitled in the Congress: but no Senator or Representative, or Person holding an Office of Trust or Profit under the United States, shall be appointed an Elector.

The electors shall meet in their respective States, and vote by ballot for two Persons, of whom one at least shall not be an Inhabitant of the same State with themselves. And they shall make a List of all the Persons voted for, and of the Number of Votes for each; which List they shall sign and certify, and transmit sealed to the Seat of the Government of the United States, directed to the President of the Senate. The President of the Senate shall, in the Presence of the Senate and House of Representatives, open all the Certificates, and the Votes shall then be counted. The Person having the greatest Number of Votes shall be the President, if such Number be a Majority of the whole Number of Electors appointed; and if there be more than one who have such Majority, and have an equal Number of Votes, then the House of Representatives shall immediately chuse by Ballot one of them for President; and if no Person have a Majority, then from the five highest on the List the said House shall in like Manner chuse the President. But in chusing the President, the Votes shall be taken by States, the Representation from each State having one Vote; A quorum for this Purpose shall consist of a Member or Members from two thirds of the States, and a Majority of all the States shall be necessary to a Choice. In every Case, after the Choice of the President, the person having the greatest Number of Votes of the Electors shall be the Vice President. But if there should remain two or more who have equal Votes, the Senate shall chuse from them by Ballot the Vice President.[10]

The Congress may determine the Time of chusing the Electors, and the Day on which they shall give their Votes; which Day shall be the same throughout the United States.

No Person except a natural born Citizen, or a Citizen of the United States, at the time of the Adoption of this Constitution, shall be eligible to the Office of President; neither shall any Person be eligible to that Office who shall not have attained to the Age of thirty five Years, and been fourteen Years a Resident within the United States.

In Case of the Removal of the President from Office, or his Death, Resignation, or Inability to discharge the Powers and Duties of the said Office, the Same shall devolve on the Vice President, and the Congress may by Law provide for the Case of Removal, Death, Resignation or Inability, both of the President and Vice President, declaring what Officer shall then act as President, and such Officer shall act accordingly, until the Disability be removed, or a President shall be elected.

The President shall, at stated Times, receive for his Services, a Compensation, which shall neither be increased nor diminished during the Period for which he shall have been elected, and he shall not receive within that Period any other Emolument from the United States, or any of them.

Before he enter on the Execution of his Office, he shall take the following Oath or Affirmation:—"I do solemnly swear (or affirm) that I will faithfully execute the Office of President of the United States, and will to the best of my Ability, preserve, protect and defend the Constitution of the United States."

SECTION 2
[POWERS OF THE PRESIDENT]

The President shall be Commander in Chief of the Army and Navy of the United States, and of the Militia of the several States, when called into the actual Service of the United States; he may require the Opinion, in writing, of the principal Officer in each of the executive Departments, upon any Subject relating to the Duties of their respective Offices, and he shall have Power to grant Reprieves and Pardons for Offences against the United States, except in Cases of Impeachment.

He shall have Power, by and with the Advice and Consent of the Senate, to make Treaties, provided two thirds of the Senators present concur; and he shall nominate, and by and with the Advice and Consent of the Senate, shall appoint Ambassadors, other public Ministers and Consuls, Judges of the supreme Court, and all other Officers of the United States, whose Appointments are not herein otherwise provided for, and which shall be established by Law: but the Congress may by Law vest the Appointment of such inferior Officers, as they think proper, in the President alone, in the Courts of Law, or in the Heads of Departments.

The President shall have Power to fill up all Vacancies that may happen during the Recess of the Senate, by granting Commissions which shall expire at the End of their next Session.

SECTION 3
[POWERS AND DUTIES OF THE PRESIDENT]

He shall from time to time give to the Congress Information of the State of the Union, and recommend to their Consideration such Measures as he shall judge necessary and expedient; he may, on extraordinary Occasions, convene both Houses, or either of them, and in Case of Disagreement between them, with Respect to the Time of Adjournment, he may adjourn them to such Time as he shall think proper; he shall receive Ambassadors and other public Ministers; he shall take Care that the Laws be faithfully executed, and shall Commission all the Officers of the United States.

SECTION 4
[IMPEACHMENT]

The President, Vice President and all civil Officers of the United States, shall be removed from Office on Impeachment

---

[9]Number of terms limited to two by Twenty-second Amendment.

[10]Modified by Twelfth and Twentieth Amendments.

for, and Conviction of, Treason, Bribery, or other high Crimes and Misdemeanors.

Article III

SECTION 1

[JUDICIAL POWER, TENURE OF OFFICE]

The judicial Power of the United States, shall be vested in one supreme Court, and in such inferior Courts as the Congress may from time to time ordain and establish. The Judges, both of the supreme and inferior Courts, shall hold their Offices during good Behaviour, and shall, at stated Times, receive for their Services, a Compensation, which shall not be diminished during their Continuance in Office.

SECTION 2

[JURISDICTION]

The judicial Power shall extend to all Cases, in Law and Equity, arising under this Constitution, the Laws of the United States, and Treaties made, or which shall be made, under their Authority;—to all Cases affecting Ambassadors, other public Ministers and Consuls;—to all Cases of admiralty and maritime Jurisdiction;—to Controversies to which the United States shall be a Party;—to Controversies between two or more States;—*between a State and Citizens of another State;*—between Citizens of different States,—between Citizens of the same State claiming Lands under Grants of different States, *and between a State*, or the Citizens thereof, *and foreign States, Citizens or Subjects.*[11]

In all Cases affecting Ambassadors, other public Ministers and Consuls, and those in which a State shall be Party, the supreme Court shall have original Jurisdiction. In all the other Cases before mentioned, the supreme Court shall have appellate Jurisdiction, both as to Law and Fact, with such Exceptions, and under such Regulations as the Congress shall make.

The Trial of all Crimes, except in Cases of Impeachment, shall be by Jury; and such Trial shall be held in the State where the said Crimes shall have been committed; but when not committed within any State, the Trial shall be at such Place or Places as the Congress may by Law have directed.

SECTION 3

[TREASON, PROOF, AND PUNISHMENT]

Treason against the United States, shall consist only in levying War against them, or in adhering to their Enemies, giving them Aid and Comfort. No Person shall be convicted of Treason unless on the Testimony of two Witnesses to the same overt Act, or on Confession in open Court.

The Congress shall have Power to declare the Punishment of Treason, but no Attainder of Treason shall work Corruption of Blood, or Forfeiture except during the Life of the Person attainted.

Article IV

SECTION 1

[FAITH AND CREDIT AMONG STATES]

Full Faith and Credit shall be given in each State to the public Acts, Records, and judicial Proceedings of every other State. And the Congress may by general Laws prescribe the Manner in which such Acts, Records and Proceedings shall be proved, and the Effect thereof.

SECTION 2

[PRIVILEGES AND IMMUNITIES, FUGITIVES]

The Citizens of each State shall be entitled to all Privileges and Immunities of Citizens in the several States.

A Person charged in any State with Treason, Felony or other Crime, who shall flee from Justice, and be found in another State, shall on Demand of the executive Authority of the State from which he fled, be delivered up, to be removed to the State having Jurisdiction of the Crime.

No person held to Service or Labour in one State, under the Laws thereof, escaping into another, shall, in Consequence of any Law or Regulation therein, be discharged from such Service or Labour, but shall be delivered up on Claim of the Party to whom such Service or Labour may be due.[12]

SECTION 3

[ADMISSION OF NEW STATES]

New States may be admitted by the Congress into this Union; but no new State shall be formed or erected within the Jurisdiction of any other State; nor any State be formed by the Junction of two or more States, or Parts of States, without the Consent of the Legislatures of the States concerned as well as of the Congress.

The Congress shall have Power to dispose of and make all needful Rules and Regulations respecting the Territory or other Property belonging to the United States; and nothing in this Constitution shall be so construed as to Prejudice any Claims of the United States, or of any particular State.

SECTION 4

[GUARANTEE OF REPUBLICAN GOVERNMENT]

The United States shall guarantee to every State in this Union a Republican Form of Government, and shall protect each of them against Invasion; and on Application of the Legislature, or of the Executive (when the Legislature cannot be convened), against domestic Violence.

Article V

[AMENDMENT OF THE CONSTITUTION]

The Congress, whenever two thirds of both Houses shall deem it necessary, shall propose Amendments to this Constitution, or, on the Application of the Legislatures of two thirds of the

---

[11]Modified by Eleventh Amendment.

[12]Repealed by the Thirteenth Amendment.

several States, shall call a Convention for proposing Amendments, which, in either Case, shall be valid to all Intents and Purposes, as Part of this Constitution, when ratified by the Legislatures of three fourths of the several States, or by Conventions in three fourths thereof, as the one or the other Mode of Ratification may be proposed by the Congress; *Provided that no Amendment which may be made prior to the Year One thousand eight hundred and eight shall in any Manner affect the first and fourth Clauses in the Ninth Section of the first Article;*[13] and that no State, without its Consent, shall be deprived of its equal Suffrage in the Senate.

Article VI

[DEBTS, SUPREMACY, OATH]

All Debts contracted and Engagements entered into, before the Adoption of this Constitution, shall be as valid against the United States under this Constitution, as under the Confederation.

This Constitution, and the Laws of the United States which shall be made in Pursuance thereof; and all Treaties made, or which shall be made, under the Authority of the United States, shall be the supreme Law of the Land; and the Judges in every

State shall be bound thereby, any Thing in the Constitution or Laws of any State to the Contrary notwithstanding.

The Senators and Representatives before mentioned, and the Members of the several State Legislatures, and all executive and judicial Officers, both of the United States and of the several States, shall be bound by Oath or Affirmation, to support this Constitution; but no religious Test shall be required as a Qualification to any Office or public Trust under the United States.

Article VII

[RATIFICATION AND ESTABLISHMENT]

The Ratification of the Conventions of nine States, shall be sufficient for the Establishment of this Constitution between the States so ratifying the Same.[14]

Done in Convention by the Unanimous Consent of the States present the Seventeenth Day of September in the Year of our Lord one thousand seven hundred and Eighty seven and of the Independence of the United States of America the Twelfth. *In Witness* whereof We have hereunto subscribed our Names,

---

[13]Temporary provision.

[14]The Constitution was submitted on September 17, 1787, by the Constitutional Convention, was ratified by the conventions of several states at various dates up to May 29, 1790, and became effective on March 4, 1789.

G:⁰ WASHINGTON—
Presidt. and deputy from Virginia

NEW HAMPSHIRE
John Langdon
Nicholas Gilman

MASSACHUSETTS
Nathaniel Gorham
Rufus King

CONNECTICUT
Wm. Saml. Johnson
Roger Sherman

NEW YORK
Alexander Hamilton

NEW JERSEY
Wil: Livingston
David Brearley
Wm. Paterson
Jona: Dayton

PENNSYLVANIA
B Franklin
Thomas Mifflin
Robt. Morris
Geo. Clymer
Thos. FitzSimons
Jared Ingersoll
James Wilson
Gouv Morris

DELAWARE
Geo: Read
Gunning Bedford jun
John Dickinson
Richard Bassett
Jaco: Broom

MARYLAND
James McHenry
Dan of St Thos. Jenifer
Danl. Carroll

VIRGINIA
John Blair—
James Madison Jr.

NORTH CAROLINA
Wm. Blount
Richd. Dobbs Spaight
Hu Williamson

SOUTH CAROLINA
J. Rutledge
Charles Cotesworth Pinckney
Charles Pinckney
Pierce Butler

GEORGIA
William Few
Abr Baldwin

Amendments to the Constitution

Proposed by Congress and Ratified by the Legislatures of the Several States, Pursuant to Article V of the Original Constitution.

Amendments I–X, known as the Bill of Rights, were proposed by Congress on September 25, 1789, and ratified on December 15, 1791.

Amendment I

[FREEDOM OF RELIGION, OF SPEECH, AND OF THE PRESS]

Congress shall make no law respecting an establishment of religion, or prohibiting the free exercise thereof; or abridging the freedom of speech, or of the press; or the right of the people peaceably to assemble, and to petition the Government for a redress of grievances.

Amendment II

[RIGHT TO KEEP AND BEAR ARMS]

A well regulated Militia, being necessary to the security of a free State, the right of the people to keep and bear Arms, shall not be infringed.

Amendment III

[QUARTERING OF SOLDIERS]

No Soldier shall, in time of peace be quartered in any house, without the consent of the Owner, nor in time of war, but in a manner to be prescribed by law.

Amendment IV

[SECURITY FROM UNWARRANTABLE SEARCH AND SEIZURE]

The right of the people to be secure in their persons, houses, papers, and effects, against unreasonable searches and seizures, shall not be violated, and no Warrants shall issue, but upon probable cause, supported by Oath or affirmation, and particularly describing the place to be searched, and the persons or things to be seized.

Amendment V

[RIGHTS OF ACCUSED PERSONS IN CRIMINAL PROCEEDINGS]

No person shall be held to answer for a capital, or otherwise infamous crime, unless on a presentment or indictment of a Grand Jury, except in cases arising in the land or naval forces, or in the Militia, when in actual service in time of War or in public danger; nor shall any person be subject for the same offence to be twice put in jeopardy of life or limb; nor shall be compelled in any criminal case to be a witness against himself, nor be deprived of life, liberty, or property, without due process of law; nor shall private property be taken for public use, without just compensation.

Amendment VI

[RIGHT TO SPEEDY TRIAL, WITNESSES, ETC.]

In all criminal prosecutions, the accused shall enjoy the right to a speedy and public trial, by an impartial jury of the State and district wherein the crime shall have been committed, which district shall have been previously ascertained by law, and to be informed of the nature and cause of the accusation; to be confronted with the witnesses against him; to have compulsory process for obtaining witnesses in his favor, and to have the Assistance of Counsel for his defence.

Amendment VII

[TRIAL BY JURY IN CIVIL CASES]

In suits at common law, where the value in controversy shall exceed twenty dollars, the right of trial by jury shall be preserved, and no fact tried by a jury, shall be otherwise reexamined in any Court of the United States, than according to the rules of the common law.

Amendment VIII

[BAILS, FINES, PUNISHMENTS]

Excessive bail shall not be required, nor excessive fines imposed, nor cruel and unusual punishments inflicted.

Amendment IX

[RESERVATION OF RIGHTS OF PEOPLE]

The enumeration in the Constitution, of certain rights, shall not be construed to deny or disparage others retained by the people.

Amendment X

[POWERS RESERVED TO STATES OR PEOPLE]

The powers not delegated to the United States by the Constitution, nor prohibited by it to the States, are reserved to the States respectively, or to the people.

Amendment XI

[*Proposed by Congress on March 4, 1794;*
declared ratified on January 8, 1798.]

[RESTRICTION OF JUDICIAL POWER]

The Judicial power of the United States shall not be construed to extend to any suit in law or equity, commenced or prosecuted against one of the United States by Citizens of another State, or by Citizens or Subjects of any Foreign State.

Amendment XII

[*Proposed by Congress on December 9, 1803;*
declared ratified on September 25, 1804.]

[ELECTION OF PRESIDENT AND VICE PRESIDENT]

The Electors shall meet in their respective states and vote by ballot for President and Vice-President, one of whom, at least, shall not be an inhabitant of the same state with themselves; they shall name in their ballots the person voted for as President, and in distinct ballots the person voted for as Vice-President, and they shall make distinct lists of all persons voted for as President, and of all persons voted for as Vice-President, and of the number of votes for each, which lists they shall sign and certify, and transmit sealed to the seat of the government of the United States, directed to the President of the Senate;—the President of the Senate shall, in presence of the Senate and House of Representatives, open all the certificates and the votes shall then be counted;—The person having the greatest number of votes for President, shall be the President, if such number be a majority of the whole number of Electors appointed; and if no person have such majority, then from the persons having the highest numbers not exceeding three on the list of those voted for as President, the House of Representatives shall choose immediately, by ballot, the President. But in choosing the President, the votes shall be taken by states, the representation from each state having one vote; a quorum for this purpose shall consist of a member or members from two-thirds of the states, and a majority of all the states shall be necessary to a choice. And if the House of Representatives shall not choose a President whenever the right of choice shall devolve upon them, before the fourth day of March next following, then the Vice-President shall act as President, as in the case of the death or other constitutional disability of the President.—The person having the greatest number of votes as Vice-President, shall be the Vice-President, if such number be a majority of the whole number of Electors appointed, and if no person have a majority, then from the two highest numbers on the list, the Senate shall choose the Vice-President; a quorum for the purpose shall consist of two-thirds of the whole number of Senators, and a majority of the whole number shall be necessary to a choice. But no person constitutionally ineligible to the office of President shall be eligible to that of Vice-President of the United States.

Amendment XIII

[*Proposed by Congress on January 31, 1865;*
declared ratified on December 18, 1865.]

SECTION 1

[ABOLITION OF SLAVERY]

Neither slavery nor involuntary servitude, except as a punishment for crime whereof the party shall have been duly convicted, shall exist within the United States, or any place subject to their jurisdiction.

SECTION 2

[POWER TO ENFORCE THIS ARTICLE]

Congress shall have power to enforce this article by appropriate legislation.

Amendment XIV

[*Proposed by Congress on June 13, 1866;*
declared ratified on July 28, 1868.]

SECTION 1

[CITIZENSHIP RIGHTS NOT TO BE ABRIDGED BY STATES]

All persons born or naturalized in the United States, and subject to the jurisdiction thereof, are citizens of the United States and of the State wherein they reside. No State shall make or enforce any law which shall abridge the privileges or immunities of citizens of the United States; nor shall any State deprive any person of life, liberty, or property, without due process of law; nor deny to any person within its jurisdiction the equal protection of the laws.

SECTION 2

[APPORTIONMENT OF REPRESENTATIVES IN CONGRESS]

Representatives shall be apportioned among the several States according to their respective numbers, counting the whole number of persons in each State, excluding Indians not taxed. But when the right to vote at any election for the choice of electors for President and Vice-President of the United States, Representatives in Congress, the Executive and Judicial officers of a State, or the members of the Legislature thereof, is denied to any of the male inhabitants of such State, being twenty-one years of age, and citizens of the United States, or in any way abridged, except for participation in rebellion, or other crime, the basis of representation therein shall be reduced in the proportion which the number of such male citizens shall bear to the whole number of male citizens twenty-one years of age in such State.

SECTION 3

[PERSONS DISQUALIFIED FROM HOLDING OFFICE]

No person shall be a Senator or Representative in Congress, or elector of President and Vice-President, or hold any office, civil or military, under the United States, or under any State, who, having previously taken an oath, as a member of Congress, or as an officer of the United States, or as a member of any State legislature, or as an executive or judicial officer of any State, to support the Constitution of the United States, shall have engaged in insurrection or rebellion against the same, or given aid or comfort to the enemies thereof. But Congress may by a vote of two-thirds of each House, remove such disability.

SECTION 4
[WHAT PUBLIC DEBTS ARE VALID]
The validity of the public debt of the United States, authorized by law, including debts incurred for payment of pensions and bounties for services in suppressing insurrection or rebellion, shall not be questioned. But neither the United States nor any State shall assume or pay any debt or obligation incurred in aid of insurrection or rebellion against the United States, or any claim for the loss or emancipation of any slave; but all such debts, obligations and claims shall be held illegal and void.

SECTION 5
[POWER TO ENFORCE THIS ARTICLE]
The Congress shall have power to enforce, by appropriate legislation, the provisions of this article.

Amendment XV
[*Proposed by Congress on February 26, 1869;*
declared ratified on March 30, 1870.]

SECTION 1
[NEGRO SUFFRAGE]
The right of citizens of the United States to vote shall not be denied or abridged by the United States or by any State on account of race, color, or previous condition of servitude.

SECTION 2
[POWER TO ENFORCE THIS ARTICLE]
The Congress shall have power to enforce this article by appropriate legislation.

Amendment XVI
[*Proposed by Congress on July 2, 1909;*
declared ratified on February 25, 1913.]
[AUTHORIZING INCOME TAXES]
The Congress shall have power to lay and collect taxes on incomes, from whatever source derived, without apportionment among the several States, and without regard to any census or enumeration.

Amendment XVII
[*Proposed by Congress on May 13, 1912;*
declared ratified on May 31, 1913.]
[POPULAR ELECTION OF SENATORS]
The Senate of the United States shall be composed of two Senators from each State, elected by the people thereof, for six years; and each Senator shall have one vote. The electors in each State shall have the qualifications requisite for electors of the most numerous branch of the State legislatures.

When vacancies happen in the representation of any State in the Senate, the executive authority of such State shall issue writs of election to fill such vacancies: *Provided,* That the legislature of any State may empower the executive thereof to make temporary appointments until the people fill the vacancies by election as the legislature may direct.

This amendment shall not be so construed as to affect the election or term of any Senator chosen before it becomes valid as part of the Constitution.

Amendment XVIII
[*Proposed by Congress December 18, 1917;*
declared ratified on January 29, 1919.]

SECTION 1
[NATIONAL LIQUOR PROHIBITION]
After one year from the ratification of this article the manufacture, sale, or transportation of intoxicating liquors within, the importation thereof into, or the exportation thereof from the United States and all territory subject to the jurisdiction thereof for beverage purposes is hereby prohibited.

SECTION 2
[POWER TO ENFORCE THIS ARTICLE]
The Congress and the several States shall have concurrent power to enforce this article by appropriate legislation.

SECTION 3
[RATIFICATION WITHIN SEVEN YEARS]
This article shall be inoperative unless it shall have been ratified as an amendment to the Constitution by the legislatures of the several States, as provided in the Constitution, within seven years from the date of the submission hereof to the States by the Congress.[1]

Amendment XIX
[*Proposed by Congress on June 4, 1919;*
declared ratified on August 26, 1920.]
[WOMAN SUFFRAGE]
The right of citizens of the United States to vote shall not be denied or abridged by the United States or by any State on account of sex.

Congress shall have power to enforce this article by appropriate legislation.

---

[1]Repealed by the Twenty-first Amendment.

Amendment XX

[*Proposed by Congress on March 2, 1932; declared ratified on February 6, 1933.*]

SECTION 1

[TERMS OF OFFICE]

The terms of the President and Vice President shall end at noon on the 20th day of January, and the terms of Senators and Representatives at noon on the 3d day of January, of the years in which such terms would have ended if this article had not been ratified; and the terms of their successors shall then begin.

SECTION 2

[TIME OF CONVENING CONGRESS]

The Congress shall assemble at least once in every year, and such meeting shall begin at noon on the 3d day of January, unless they shall by law appoint a different day.

SECTION 3

[DEATH OF PRESIDENT-ELECT]

If, at the time fixed for the beginning of the term of the President, the President elect shall have died, the Vice President elect shall become President. If a President shall not have been chosen before the time fixed for the beginning of his term, or if the President elect shall have failed to qualify, then the Vice President elect shall act as President until a President shall have qualified; and the Congress may by law provide for the case wherein neither a President elect nor a Vice President elect shall have qualified, declaring who shall then act as President, or the manner in which one who is to act shall be selected, and such person shall act accordingly until a President or Vice President shall have qualified.

SECTION 4

[ELECTION OF THE PRESIDENT]

The Congress may by law provide for the case of the death of any of the persons from whom the House of Representatives may choose a President whenever the right of choice shall have devolved upon them, and for the case of the death of any of the persons from whom the Senate may choose a Vice President whenever the right of choice shall have devolved upon them.

SECTION 5

[AMENDMENT TAKES EFFECT]

Sections 1 and 2 shall take effect on the 15th day of October following the ratification of this article.

SECTION 6

[RATIFICATION WITHIN SEVEN YEARS]

This article shall be inoperative unless it shall have been ratified as an amendment to the Constitution by the legislatures of three-fourths of the several States within seven years from the date of its submission.

Amendment XXI

[*Proposed by Congress on February 20, 1933; declared ratified on December 5, 1933.*]

SECTION 1

[NATIONAL LIQUOR PROHIBITION REPEALED]

The eighteenth article of amendment to the Constitution of the United States is hereby repealed.

SECTION 2

[TRANSPORTATION OF LIQUOR INTO "DRY" STATES]

The transportation or importation into any State, Territory, or Possession of the United States for delivery or use therein of intoxicating liquors, in violation of the laws thereof, is hereby prohibited.

SECTION 3

[RATIFICATION WITHIN SEVEN YEARS]

This article shall be inoperative unless it shall have been ratified as an amendment to the Constitution by conventions in the several States, as provided in the Constitution, within seven years from the date of the submission hereof to the States by the Congress.

Amendment XXII

[*Proposed by Congress on March 21, 1947; declared ratified on February 27, 1951.*]

SECTION 1

[TENURE OF PRESIDENT LIMITED]

No person shall be elected to the office of President more than twice, and no person who has held the office of President or acted as President, for more than two years of a term to which some other person was elected President shall be elected to the office of the President more than once. But this Article shall not apply to any person holding the office of President when this Article was proposed by the Congress, and shall not prevent any person who may be holding the office of President, or acting as President, during the term within which this Article becomes operative from holding the office of President or acting as President during the remainder of such term.

SECTION 2

[RATIFICATION WITHIN SEVEN YEARS]

This article shall be inoperative unless it shall have been ratified as an amendment to the Constitution by the legislatures of three-fourths of the several States within seven years from the date of its submission to the States by the Congress.

Amendment XXIII

[Proposed by Congress on June 16, 1960;
declared ratified on March 29, 1961.]

SECTION 1

[ELECTORAL COLLEGE VOTES FOR THE DISTRICT OF COLUMBIA]
The District constituting the seat of Government of the United States shall appoint in such manner as the Congress may direct:

A number of electors of President and Vice President equal to the whole number of Senators and Representatives in Congress to which the District would be entitled if it were a State, but in no event more than the least populous State; they shall be in addition to those appointed by the States, but they shall be considered, for the purposes of the election of President and Vice President, to be electors appointed by a State; and they shall meet in the District and perform such duties as provided by the twelfth article of amendment.

SECTION 2

[POWER TO ENFORCE THIS ARTICLE]
The Congress shall have power to enforce this article by appropriate legislation.

Amendment XXIV

[Proposed by Congress on August 27, 1962;
declared ratified on January 23, 1964.]

SECTION 1

[ANTI-POLL TAX]
The right of citizens of the United States to vote in any primary or other election for President or Vice President, for electors for President or Vice President, or for Senator or Representative of Congress, shall not be denied or abridged by the United States or any State by reason of failure to pay any poll tax or other tax.

SECTION 2

[POWER TO ENFORCE THIS ARTICLE]
The Congress shall have power to enforce this article by appropriate legislation.

Amendment XXV

[Proposed by Congress on July 6, 1965;
declared ratified on February 10, 1967.]

SECTION 1

[VICE PRESIDENT TO BECOME PRESIDENT]
In case of the removal of the President from office or his death or resignation, the Vice President shall become President.

SECTION 2

[CHOICE OF A NEW VICE PRESIDENT]
Whenever there is a vacancy in the office of the Vice President, the President shall nominate a Vice President who shall take the office upon confirmation by a majority vote of both houses of Congress.

SECTION 3

[PRESIDENT MAY DECLARE OWN DISABILITY]
Whenever the President transmits to the President pro tempore of the Senate and the Speaker of the House of Representatives his written declaration that he is unable to discharge the powers and duties of his office, and until he transmits to them a written declaration to the contrary, such powers and duties shall be discharged by the Vice President as Acting President.

SECTION 4

[ALTERNATE PROCEDURES TO DECLARE AND
TO END PRESIDENTIAL DISABILITY]
Whenever the Vice President and a majority of either the principal officers of the executive departments, or of such other body as Congress may by law provide, transmit to the President pro tempore of the Senate and the Speaker of the House of Representatives their written declaration that the President is unable to discharge the powers and duties of his office, the Vice President shall immediately assume the powers and duties of the office as Acting President.

Thereafter, when the President transmits to the President pro tempore of the Senate and the Speaker of the House of Representatives his written declaration that no inability exists, he shall resume the powers and duties of his office unless the Vice President and a majority of either the principal officers of the executive department, or of such other body as Congress may by law provide, transmit within four days to the President pro tempore of the Senate and the Speaker of the House of Representatives their written declaration that the President is unable to discharge the powers and duties of his office. Thereupon Congress shall decide the issue, assembling within forty eight hours for that purpose if not in session. If the Congress, within twenty one days after receipt of the latter written declaration, or, if Congress is not in session, within twenty one days after Congress is required to assemble, determines by two-thirds vote of both Houses that the President is unable to discharge the powers and duties of his office, the Vice President shall continue to discharge the same as Acting President; otherwise, the President shall resume the powers and duties of his office.

Amendment XXVI

[Proposed by Congress on March 23, 1971;
declared ratified on July 1, 1971.]

SECTION 1
[EIGHTEEN-YEAR-OLD VOTE]
The right of citizens of the United States, who are eighteen years of age or older, to vote shall not be denied or abridged by the United States or by any State on account of age.

SECTION 2
[POWER TO ENFORCE THIS ARTICLE]
The Congress shall have power to enforce this article by appropriate legislation.

Amendment XXVII

[Proposed by Congress on September 25, 1789;
declared ratified on May 8, 1992.]

[CONGRESS CANNOT RAISE ITS OWN PAY]
No law varying the compensation for the services of the Senators and Representatives, shall take effect, until an election of representatives shall have intervened.

The Federalist Papers

No. 10: Madison

Among the numerous advantages promised by a well constructed Union, none deserves to be more accurately developed than its tendency to break and control the violence of
faction. The friend of popular governments never finds himself so much alarmed for their character and fate, as when he
contemplates their propensity to this dangerous vice. He will
not fail therefore to set a due value on any plan which, without violating the principles to which he is attached, provides
a proper cure for it. The instability, injustice, and confusion
introduced into the public councils have, in truth, been the
mortal diseases under which popular governments have everywhere perished, as they continue to be the favorite and fruit-
ful topics from which the adversaries to liberty derive their
most specious declamations. The valuable improvements made
by the American constitutions on the popular models, both
ancient and modern, cannot certainly be too much admired;
but it would be an unwarrantable partiality to contend that
they have as effectually obviated the danger on this side, as was
wished and expected. Complaints are everywhere heard from
our most considerate and virtuous citizens, equally the friends
of public and private faith and of public and personal liberty,
that our governments are too unstable, that the public good is
disregarded in the conflicts of rival parties, and that measures
are too often decided, not according to the rules of justice and
the rights of the minor party, but by the superior force of an
interested and overbearing majority. However anxiously we
may wish that these complaints had no foundation, the evidence of known facts will not permit us to deny that they are
in some degree true. It will be found, indeed, on a candid review of our situation, that some of the distresses under which
we labor have been erroneously charged on the operation of
our governments; but it will be found, at the same time, that
other causes will not alone account for many of our heaviest
misfortunes; and, particularly, for that prevailing and increasing distrust of public engagements and alarm for private rights
which are echoed from one end of the continent to the other.
These must be chiefly, if not wholly, effects of the unsteadiness
and injustice with which a factious spirit has tainted our public
administration.

By a faction I understand a number of citizens, whether
amounting to a majority or minority of the whole, who are
united and actuated by some common impulse of passion, or
of interest, adverse to the rights of other citizens, or to the permanent and aggregate interests of the community.

There are two methods of curing the mischiefs of faction:
the one, by removing its causes; the other, by controlling its
effects.

There are again two methods of removing the causes of
faction: the one, by destroying the liberty which is essential
to its existence; the other, by giving to every citizen the same
opinions, the same passions, and the same interests.

It could never be more truly said than of the first remedy,
that it is worse than the disease. Liberty is to faction what air
is to fire, an aliment without which it instantly expires. But it
could not be a less folly to abolish liberty, which is essential to
political life, because it nourishes faction, than it would be to
wish the annihilation of air, which is essential to animal life,
because it imparts to fire its destructive agency.

The second expedient is as impracticable, as the first would
be unwise. As long as the reason of man continues fallible, and
he is at liberty to exercise it, different opinions will be formed.
As long as the connection subsists between his reason and his
self-love, his opinions and his passions will have a reciprocal
influence on each other; and the former will be objects to
which the latter will attach themselves. The diversity in the
faculties of men, from which the rights of property originate,
is not less an insuperable obstacle to a uniformity of interests.
The protection of these faculties is the first object of Government. From the protection of different and unequal faculties
of acquiring property, the possession of different degrees and
kinds of property immediately results; and from the influence
of these on the sentiments and views of the respective proprietors, ensues a division of the society into different interests
and parties.

The latent causes of faction are thus sown in the nature
of man; and we see them everywhere brought into different
degrees of activity, according to the different circumstances
of civil society. A zeal for different opinions concerning religion, concerning Government, and many other points, as well
of speculation as of practice; an attachment to different leaders ambitiously contending for pre-eminence and power; or
to persons of other descriptions whose fortunes have been
interesting to the human passions, have in turn divided mankind into parties, inflamed them with mutual animosity, and
rendered them much more disposed to vex and oppress each
other, than to co-operate for their common good. So strong is
this propensity of mankind to fall into mutual animosities, that
where no substantial occasion presents itself, the most frivolous and fanciful distinctions have been sufficient to kindle

their unfriendly passions, and excite their most violent conflicts. But the most common and durable source of factions has been the various and unequal distribution of property. Those who hold and those who are without property have ever formed distinct interests in society. Those who are creditors, and those who are debtors, fall under a like discrimination. A landed interest, a manufacturing interest, a mercantile interest, a moneyed interest, with many lesser interests, grow up of necessity in civilized nations, and divide them into different classes, actuated by different sentiments and views. The regulation of these various and interfering interests forms the principal task of modern Legislation, and involves the spirit of party and faction in the necessary and ordinary operations of Government.

No man is allowed to be judge in his own cause, because his interest would certainly bias his judgment and, not improbably, corrupt his integrity. With equal, nay with greater reason, a body of men are unfit to be both judges and parties at the same time; yet what are many of the most important acts of legislation but so many judicial determinations, not indeed concerning the rights of single persons, but concerning the rights of large bodies of citizens; and what are the different classes of legislators but advocates and parties to the causes which they determine? Is a law proposed concerning private debts? It is a question to which the creditors are parties on one side and the debtors on the other. Justice ought to hold the balance between them. Yet the parties are, and must be, themselves the judges; and the most numerous party, or in other words, the most powerful faction must be expected to prevail. Shall domestic manufacturers be encouraged, and in what degree, by restrictions on foreign manufacturers? are questions which would be differently decided by the landed and the manufacturing classes, and probably by neither with a sole regard to justice and the public good. The apportionment of taxes on the various descriptions of property is an act which seems to require the most exact impartiality; yet there is, perhaps, no legislative act in which greater opportunity and temptation are given to a predominant party to trample on the rules of justice. Every shilling with which they overburden the inferior number is a shilling saved to their own pockets.

It is in vain to say that enlightened statesmen will be able to adjust these clashing interests and render them all subservient to the public good. Enlightened statesmen will not always be at the helm. Nor, in many cases, can such an adjustment be made at all without taking into view indirect and remote considerations, which will rarely prevail over the immediate interest which one party may find in disregarding the rights of another or the good of the whole.

The inference to which we are brought is that the *causes* of faction cannot be removed and that relief is only to be sought in the means of controlling its *effects*.

If a faction consists of less than a majority, relief is supplied by the republican principle, which enables the majority to defeat its sinister views by regular vote. It may clog the administration, it may convulse the society; but it will be unable to execute and mask its violence under the forms of the Constitution. When a majority is included in a faction, the form of popular government, on the other hand, enables it to sacrifice to its ruling passion or interest both the public good and the rights of other citizens. To secure the public good and private rights against the danger of such a faction, and at the same time to preserve the spirit and the form of popular government, is then the great object to which our enquiries are directed. Let me add that it is the great desideratum by which alone this form of government can be rescued from the opprobrium under which it has so long labored and be recommended to the esteem and adoption of mankind.

By what means is this object attainable? Evidently by one of two only. Either the existence of the same passion or interest in a majority at the same time must be prevented, or the majority, having such co-existent passion or interest, must be rendered, by their number and local situation, unable to concert and carry into effect schemes of oppression. If the impulse and the opportunity be suffered to coincide, we well know that neither moral nor religious motives can be relied on as an adequate control. They are not found to be such on the injustice and violence of individuals, and lose their efficacy in proportion to the number combined together, that is, in proportion as their efficacy becomes needful.

From this view of the subject it may be concluded that a pure Democracy, by which I mean a Society consisting of a small number of citizens, who assemble and administer the Government in person, can admit of no cure for the mischiefs of faction. A common passion or interest will, in almost every case, be felt by a majority of the whole; a communication and concert results from the form of Government itself; and there is nothing to check the inducements to sacrifice the weaker party or an obnoxious individual. Hence it is that such Democracies have ever been spectacles of turbulence and contention; have ever been found incompatible with personal security or the rights of property; and have in general been as short in their lives as they have been violent in their deaths. Theoretic politicians, who have patronized this species of Government, have erroneously supposed that by reducing mankind to a perfect equality in their political rights, they would at the same time be perfectly equalized and assimilated in their possessions, their opinions, and their passions.

A Republic, by which I mean a Government in which the scheme of representation takes place, opens a different prospect and promises the cure for which we are seeking. Let us examine the points in which it varies from pure Democracy, and we shall comprehend both the nature of the cure and the efficacy which it must derive from the Union.

The two great points of difference between a Democracy and a Republic are: first, the delegation of the Government, in the latter, to a small number of citizens elected by the rest; secondly, the greater number of citizens and greater sphere of country over which the latter may be extended.

The effect of the first difference is, on the one hand, to refine and enlarge the public views by passing them through the medium of a chosen body of citizens, whose wisdom may best discern the true interest of their country and whose patriotism and love of justice will be least likely to sacrifice it to temporary or partial considerations. Under such a regulation it may well happen that the public voice, pronounced by the representatives of the people, will be more consonant to the public good than if pronounced by the people themselves, convened for the purpose. On the other hand, the effect may be inverted. Men of factious tempers, of local prejudices, or of sinister designs, may, by intrigue, by corruption, or by other means, first obtain the suffrages, and then betray the interests of the people. The question resulting is, whether small or extensive Republics are most favorable to the election of proper guardians of the public weal; and it is clearly decided in favor of the latter by two obvious considerations.

In the first place it is to be remarked that however small the Republic may be, the Representatives must be raised to a certain number in order to guard against the cabals of a few; and that however large it may be they must be limited to a certain number in order to guard against the confusion of a multitude. Hence, the number of Representatives in the two cases not being in proportion to that of the Constituents, and being proportionally greatest in the small Republic, it follows that if the proportion of fit characters be not less in the large than in the small Republic, the former will present a greater option, and consequently a greater probability of a fit choice.

In the next place, as each Representative will be chosen by a greater number of citizens in the large than in the small Republic, it will be more difficult for unworthy candidates to practise with success the vicious arts by which elections are too often carried; and the suffrages of the people being more free, will be more likely to centre on men who possess the most attractive merit and the most diffusive and established characters.

It must be confessed that in this, as in most other cases, there is a mean, on both sides of which inconveniencies will be found to lie. By enlarging too much the number of electors, you render the representative too little acquainted with all their local circumstances and lesser interests; as by reducing it too much, you render him unduly attached to these, and too little fit to comprehend and pursue great and national objects. The Federal Constitution forms a happy combination in this respect; the great and aggregate interests being referred to the national, the local and particular to the State legislatures.

The other point of difference is the greater number of citizens and extent of territory which may be brought within the compass of Republican than of Democratic Government; and it is this circumstance principally which renders factious combinations less to be dreaded in the former than in the latter. The smaller the society, the fewer probably will be the distinct parties and interests composing it; the fewer the distinct parties and interests, the more frequently will a majority be found of the same party; and the smaller the number of individuals composing a majority, and the smaller the compass within which they are placed, the more easily will they concert and execute their plans of oppression. Extend the sphere and you take in a greater variety of parties and interests; you make it less probable that a majority of the whole will have a common motive to invade the rights of other citizens; or if such a common motive exists, it will be more difficult for all who feel it to discover their own strength and to act in unison with each other. Besides other impediments, it may be remarked, that where there is a consciousness of unjust or dishonorable purposes, communication is always checked by distrust in proportion to the number whose concurrence is necessary.

Hence, it clearly appears that the same advantage which a Republic has over a Democracy in controlling the effects of faction is enjoyed by a large over a small republic—is enjoyed by the Union over the States composing it. Does this advantage consist in the substitution of representatives whose enlightened views and virtuous sentiments render them superior to local prejudices and to schemes of injustice? It will not be denied that the representation of the Union will be most likely to possess these requisite endowments. Does it consist in the greater security afforded by a greater variety of parties, against the event of any one party being able to outnumber and oppress the rest? In an equal degree does the increased variety of parties comprised within the Union increase this security? Does it, in fine, consist in the greater obstacles opposed to the concert and accomplishment of the secret wishes of an unjust and interested majority? Here again the extent of the Union gives it the most palpable advantage.

The influence of factious leaders may kindle a flame within their particular States but will be unable to spread a general conflagration through the other States: a religious sect may degenerate into a political faction in a part of the Confederacy; but the variety of sects dispersed over the entire face of it must secure the national Councils against any danger from that source: a rage for paper money, for an abolition of debts, for an equal division of property, or for any other improper or wicked project, will be less apt to pervade the whole body of the Union than a particular member of it; in the same proportion as such a malady is more likely to taint a particular county or district than an entire State.

In the extent and proper structure of the Union, therefore, we behold a republican remedy for the diseases most incident to Republican Government. And according to the degree of pleasure and pride we feel in being republicans ought to be our zeal in cherishing the spirit and supporting the character of federalist.

PUBLIUS

No. 51: Madison

To what expedient, then, shall we finally resort, for maintaining in practice the necessary partition of power among the several departments as laid down in the constitution? The only answer that can be given is that as all these exterior provisions are found to be inadequate the defect must be supplied, by so contriving the interior structure of the government as that its several constituent parts may, by their mutual relations, be the means of keeping each other in their proper places. Without presuming to undertake a full development of this important idea I will hazard a few general observations which may perhaps place it in a clearer light, and enable us to form a more correct judgment of the principles and structure of the government planned by the convention.

In order to lay a due foundation for that separate and distinct exercise of the different powers of government, which to a certain extent is admitted on all hands to be essential to the preservation of liberty, it is evident that each department should have a will of its own; and consequently should be so constituted that the members of each should have as little agency as possible in the appointment of the members of the others. Were this principle rigorously adhered to, it would require that all the appointments for the supreme executive, legislative, and judiciary magistracies should be drawn from the same fountain of authority, the people, through channels having no communication whatever with one another. Perhaps such a plan of constructing the several departments would be less difficult in practice than it may in contemplation appear. Some difficulties, however, and some additional expense would attend the execution of it. Some deviations, therefore, from the principle must be admitted. In the constitution of the judiciary department in particular, it might be inexpedient to insist rigorously on the principle: first, because peculiar qualifications being essential in the members, the primary consideration ought to be to select that mode of choice which best secures these qualifications; second, because the permanent tenure by which the appointments are held in that department must soon destroy all sense of dependence on the authority conferring them.

It is equally evident that the members of each department should be as little dependent as possible on those of the others for the emoluments annexed to their offices. Were the executive magistrate, or the judges, not independent of the legislature in this particular, their independence in every other would be merely nominal.

But the great security against a gradual concentration of the several powers in the same department consists in giving to those who administer each department the necessary constitutional means and personal motives to resist encroachments of the others. The provision for defence must in this, as in all other cases, be made commensurate to the danger of attack. Ambition must be made to counteract ambition. The interest of the man must be connected with the constitutional rights of the place. It may be a reflection on human nature that such devices should be necessary to control the abuses of government. But what is government itself but the greatest of all reflections on human nature? If men were angels, no government would be necessary. If angels were to govern men, neither external nor internal controls on government would be necessary. In framing a government which is to be administered by men over men, the great difficulty lies in this: You must first enable the government to control the governed; and in the next place

oblige it to control itself. A dependence on the people is, no doubt, the primary control on the government; but experience has taught mankind the necessity of auxiliary precautions.

This policy of supplying, by opposite and rival interests, the defect of better motives, might be traced through the whole system of human affairs, private as well as public. We see it particularly displayed in all the subordinate distributions of power, where the constant aim is to divide and arrange the several offices in such a manner as that each may be a check on the other; that the private interest of every individual may be a sentinel over the public rights. These inventions of prudence cannot be less requisite in the distribution of the supreme powers of the State.

But it is not possible to give to each department an equal power of self-defense. In republican government, the legislative authority necessarily predominates. The remedy for this inconveniency is to divide the legislature into different branches; and to render them, by different modes of election and different principles of action, as little connected with each other as the nature of their common functions and their common dependence on the society will admit. It may even be necessary to guard against dangerous encroachments by still further precautions. As the weight of the legislative authority requires that it should be thus divided, the weakness of the executive may require, on the other hand, that it should be fortified. An absolute negative on the legislature appears, at first view, to be the natural defense with which the executive magistrate should be armed. But perhaps it would be neither altogether safe nor alone sufficient. On ordinary occasions it might not be exerted with the requisite firmness, and on extraordinary occasions it might be perfidiously abused. May not this defect of an absolute negative be supplied by some qualified connection between this weaker branch of the stronger department, by which the latter may be led to support the constitutional rights of the former, without being too much detached from the rights of its own department?

If the principles on which these observations are founded be just, as I persuade myself they are, and they be applied as a criterion to the several State constitutions, and to the federal Constitution, it will be found that if the latter does not perfectly correspond with them, the former are infinitely less able to bear such a test.

There are, moreover, two considerations particularly applicable to the federal system of America, which place that system in a very interesting point of view.

First. In a single republic, all the power surrendered by the people is submitted to the administration of a single government; and usurpations are guarded against by a division of the government into distinct and separate departments. In the compound republic of America, the power surrendered by the people is first divided between two distinct governments, and then the portion allotted to each subdivided among distinct and separate departments. Hence a double security arises to the rights of the people. The different governments will control each other, at the same time that each will be controlled by itself.

Second. It is of great importance in a republic not only to guard the society against the oppression of its rulers, but to guard one part of the society against the injustice of the other part. Different interests necessarily exist in different classes of citizens. If a majority be united by a common interest, the rights of the minority will be insecure. There are but two methods of providing against this evil: The one by creating a will in the community independent of the majority—that is, of the society itself; the other, by comprehending in the society so many separate descriptions of citizens as will render an unjust combination of a majority of the whole very improbable, if not impracticable. The first method prevails in all governments possessing an hereditary or self-appointed authority. This, at best, is but a precarious security; because a power independent of the society may as well espouse the unjust views of the major as the rightful interests of the minor party, and may possibly be turned against both parties. The second method will be exemplified in the federal republic of the United States. Whilst all authority in it will be derived from and dependent on the society, the society itself will be broken into so many parts, interests and classes of citizens, that the rights of individuals, or of the minority, will be in little danger from interested combinations of the majority. In a free government the security for civil rights must be the same as that for religious rights. It consists in the one case in the multiplicity of interests, and in the other in the multiplicity of sects. The degree of security in both cases will depend on the number of interests and sects; and this may be presumed to depend on the extent of country and number of people comprehended under the same government. This view of the subject must particularly recommend a proper federal system to all the sincere and considerate friends of republican government: Since it shows that in exact proportion as the territory of the Union may be formed into more circumscribed Confederacies, or States, oppressive combinations of a majority will be facilitated; the best security, under the republican form, for the rights of every class of citizens, will be diminished; and consequently the stability and independence of some member of the government, the only other security, must be proportionally increased. Justice is the end of government. It is the end of civil society. It ever has been and ever will be pursued until it be obtained, or until liberty be lost in the pursuit. In a society under the forms of which the stronger faction can readily unite and oppress the weaker, anarchy may as truly be said to reign as in a state of nature, where the weaker individual is not secured against the violence of the stronger: And as, in the latter state, even the stronger individuals are prompted, by the uncertainty of their condition, to submit to a government which may protect the weak as well as themselves: So, in the former state, will the more powerful factions or parties be gradually induced, by a like motive, to wish for a government which will protect all parties, the weaker as well as the more powerful. It can be little doubted that if the State of Rhode Island was separated from the Confederacy and left to itself, the insecurity of rights under the popular form of government within such narrow limits would be displayed by such reiterated oppressions of factious majorities that some power altogether independent of the people would soon be called for by the voice of the very factions whose misrule had proved the necessity of it. In the extended republic of the United States, and among the great variety of interests, parties, and sects which it embraces, a coalition of a majority of the whole society could seldom take place on any other principles than those of justice and the general good; and there being thus less danger to a minor from the will of the major party, there must be less pretext, also, to provide for the security of the former, by introducing into the government a will not dependent on the latter, or, in other words, a will independent of the society itself. It is no less certain than it is important, notwithstanding the contrary opinions which have been entertained, that the larger the society, provided it lie within a practicable sphere, the more duly capable it will be of self-government. And happily for the *republican cause*, practicable sphere may be carried to a very great extent by a judicious modification and mixture of the *federal principle*.

PUBLIUS

Presidents and Vice Presidents

	PRESIDENT	VICE PRESIDENT		PRESIDENT	VICE PRESIDENT
1	George Washington *(Federalist 1789)*	John Adams *(Federalist 1789)*	12	Zachary Taylor *(Whig 1849)*	Millard Fillmore *(Whig 1849)*
2	John Adams *(Federalist 1797)*	Thomas Jefferson *(Dem.-Rep. 1797)*	13	Millard Fillmore *(Whig 1850)*	
3	Thomas Jefferson *(Dem.-Rep. 1801)*	Aaron Burr *(Dem.-Rep. 1801)*	14	Franklin Pierce *(Democratic 1853)*	William R. D. King *(Democratic 1853)*
		George Clinton *(Dem.-Rep. 1805)*	15	James Buchanan *(Democratic 1857)*	John C. Breckinridge *(Democratic 1857)*
4	James Madison *(Dem.-Rep. 1809)*	George Clinton *(Dem.-Rep. 1809)*	16	Abraham Lincoln *(Republican 1861)*	Hannibal Hamlin *(Republican 1861)*
		Elbridge Gerry *(Dem.-Rep. 1813)*			Andrew Johnson *(Unionist 1865)*
5	James Monroe *(Dem.-Rep. 1817)*	Daniel D. Tompkins *(Dem.-Rep. 1817)*	17	Andrew Johnson *(Unionist 1865)*	
6	John Quincy Adams *(Dem.-Rep. 1825)*	John C. Calhoun *(Dem.-Rep. 1825)*	18	Ulysses S. Grant *(Republican 1869)*	Schuyler Colfax *(Republican 1869)*
7	Andrew Jackson *(Democratic 1829)*	John C. Calhoun *(Democratic 1829)*			Henry Wilson *(Republican 1873)*
		Martin Van Buren *(Democratic 1833)*	19	Rutherford B. Hayes *(Republican 1877)*	William A. Wheeler *(Republican 1877)*
8	Martin Van Buren *(Democratic 1837)*	Richard M. Johnson *(Democratic 1837)*	20	James A. Garfield *(Republican 1881)*	Chester A. Arthur *(Republican 1881)*
9	William H. Harrison *(Whig 1841)*	John Tyler *(Whig 1841)*	21	Chester A. Arthur *(Republican 1881)*	
10	John Tyler *(Whig and Democratic 1841)*		22	Grover Cleveland *(Democratic 1885)*	Thomas A. Hendricks *(Democratic 1885)*
11	James K. Polk *(Democratic 1845)*	George M. Dallas *(Democratic 1845)*	23	Benjamin Harrison *(Republican 1889)*	Levi P. Morton *(Republican 1889)*

	PRESIDENT	VICE PRESIDENT		PRESIDENT	VICE PRESIDENT
24	Grover Cleveland *(Democratic 1893)*	Adlai E. Stevenson *(Democratic 1893)*	34	Dwight D. Eisenhower *(Republican 1953)*	Richard M. Nixon *(Republican 1953)*
25	William McKinley *(Republican 1897)*	Garret A. Hobart *(Republican 1897)*	35	John F. Kennedy *(Democratic 1961)*	Lyndon B. Johnson *(Democratic 1961)*
		Theodore Roosevelt *(Republican 1901)*	36	Lyndon B. Johnson *(Democratic 1963)*	Hubert H. Humphrey *(Democratic 1965)*
26	Theodore Roosevelt *(Republican 1901)*	Charles W. Fairbanks *(Republican 1905)*	37	Richard M. Nixon *(Republican 1969)*	Spiro T. Agnew *(Republican 1969)*
27	William H. Taft *(Republican 1909)*	James S. Sherman *(Republican 1909)*			Gerald R. Ford *(Republican 1973)*
28	Woodrow Wilson *(Democratic 1913)*	Thomas R. Marshall *(Democratic 1913)*	38	Gerald R. Ford *(Republican 1974)*	Nelson Rockefeller *(Republican 1974)*
29	Warren G. Harding *(Republican 1921)*	Calvin Coolidge *(Republican 1921)*	39	James E. Carter *(Democratic 1977)*	Walter Mondale *(Democratic 1977)*
30	Calvin Coolidge *(Republican 1923)*	Charles G. Dawes *(Republican 1925)*	40	Ronald Reagan *(Republican 1981)*	George H. W. Bush *(Republican 1981)*
31	Herbert Hoover *(Republican 1929)*	Charles Curtis *(Republican 1929)*	41	George H. W. Bush *(Republican 1989)*	J. Danforth Quayle *(Republican 1989)*
32	Franklin D. Roosevelt *(Democratic 1933)*	John Nance Garner *(Democratic 1933)*	42	William J. Clinton *(Democratic 1993)*	Albert Gore, Jr. *(Democratic 1993)*
		Henry A. Wallace *(Democratic 1941)*	43	George W. Bush *(Republican 2001)*	Richard Cheney *(Republican 2001)*
		Harry S. Truman *(Democratic 1945)*	44	Barack H. Obama *(Democratic 2009)*	Joseph R. Biden, Jr. *(Democratic 2009)*
33	Harry S. Truman *(Democratic 1945)*	Alben W. Barkley *(Democratic 1949)*			

glossary

action by the governor the final step in the legislative process, during which the governor either signs or vetoes a bill

affirmative action government policies or programs that seek to redress past injustices against specified groups by making special efforts to provide members of these groups with access to educational and employment opportunities

agencies of socialization social institutions, including families and schools, that help to shape individuals' basic political beliefs and values

agency representation the type of representation in which a representative is held accountable to a constituency if he or she fails to represent that constituency properly. This is the incentive for good representation when the personal backgrounds, views, and interests of the representative differ from those of his or her constituency

agenda setting the power of the media to bring public attention to particular issues and problems

agricultural commissioner elected state official who is primarily responsible for enforcing agricultural laws

Aid to Families with Dependent Children (AFDC) a federally and state-financed program for children living with parents or relatives who fell below state standards of need. Replaced in 1996 by TANF

amendment a change added to a bill, law, or constitution

American political community citizens who are eligible to vote and who participate in American political life

amicus curiae literally, "friend of the court"; individuals or groups who are not parties to a lawsuit but who seek to assist the Supreme Court in reaching a decision by presenting additional briefs

answer the presentation of a defendant's defense against an allegation in a civil case

Antifederalists those who favored strong state governments and a weak national government and who were opponents of the Constitution proposed at the American Constitutional Convention of 1787

antitrust policy government regulation of large businesses that have established monopolies

appeasement effort to forestall war by giving in to the demands of a hostile power

appointment the power of the chief executive, whether the president of the United States or the governor of a state, to appoint persons to office

apportionment the process, occurring after every decennial census, that allocates congressional seats among the fifty states

appropriations the amounts of money approved by Congress in statutes (bills) that each unit or agency of government can spend

Articles of Confederation America's first written constitution; served as the basis for America's national government until 1789

at-large election an election in which officials are selected by voters of the entire geographical area, rather than from smaller districts within that area

attitude (or opinion) a specific preference on a particular issue

attorney general elected state official who serves as the state's chief civil lawyer

authoritarian government a system of rule in which the government recognizes no formal limits but may nevertheless be restrained by the power of other social institutions

autocracy a form of government in which a single individual—a king, queen, or dictator—rules

balance-of-power role the strategy whereby many countries form alliances with one or more countries in order to counterbalance the behavior of other, usually more powerful, nation-states

bandwagon effect a shift in electoral support to the candidate whom public opinion polls report as the front-runner

bench trial a trial held without a jury and before only a judge

benign gerrymandering attempts to draw district boundaries so as to create districts made up primarily of disadvantaged or underrepresented minorities

beyond a reasonable doubt the legal standard in criminal cases, which requires the prosecution to prove that a reasonable doubt of innocence does not exist

bicameral having a legislative assembly composed of two chambers or houses; opposite of unicameral

biennial occuring every two years

bilateral treaty a treaty made between two nations

bill a proposed law that has been sponsored by a member of Congress and submitted to the clerk of the House or Senate

Bill of Rights the first ten amendments to the U.S. Constitution, ratified in 1791; they ensure certain rights and liberties to the people

bill of attainder a law that declares a person guilty of a crime without a trial

block grants federal grants-in-aid that allow states considerable discretion in how the funds are spent

brief a written document in which attorneys explain, using case precedents, why the court should find in favor of their client

Brown v. Board of Education the 1954 Supreme Court decision that struck down the "separate but equal" doctrine as fundamentally unequal. This case eliminated state power to use race as a criterion of discrimination in law and provided the national government with the power to intervene by exercising strict regulatory policies against discriminatory actions

budget deficit amount by which government spending exceeds government revenue in a fiscal year

bundling the interest-group practice of combining campaign contributions from several individuals into one larger contribution from the group, so as to increase the group's impact on the candidate

bureaucracy the complex structure of offices, tasks, rules, and principles of organization that are employed by all large-scale institutions to coordinate the work of their personnel

Bush Doctrine foreign policy based on the idea that the United States should take preemptive action against threats to its national security

Cabinet the secretaries, or chief administrators, of the major departments of the federal government. Cabinet secretaries are appointed by the president with the consent of the Senate

campaign an effort by political candidates and their staffs to win the backing of donors, political activists, and voters in the quest for political office

capital case a criminal case that calls for the death penalty

categorical grants congressional grants given to states and localities on the condition that expenditures be limited to a problem or group specified by law

caucus (congressional) an association of members of Congress based on party, interest, or social group, such as gender or race

caucus (political) a normally closed meeting of a political or legislative group to select candidates, plan strategy, or make decisions regarding legislative matters

checks and balances mechanisms through which each branch of government is able to participate in and influence the activities of the other branches. Major examples include the presidential veto power over congressional legislation, the power of the Senate to approve presidential appointments, and judicial review of congressional enactments

chief justice justice on the Supreme Court who presides over the Court's public sessions

citizenship informed and active membership in a political community

city controller the chief financial officer of a city

civic engagement a sense of concern among members of the political community about public, social, and political life, expressed through participation in social and political organizations

civil law the branch of law that deals with disputes that do not involve criminal penalties

civil liberties areas of personal freedom with which governments are constrained from interfering

civil rights obligation imposed on government to take positive action to protect citizens from any illegal action of government agencies as well as of other private citizens

class-action suit a legal action by which a group or class of individuals with common interests can file a suit on behalf of everyone who shares that interest

"clear and present danger" test test to determine whether speech is protected or unprotected, based on its capacity to present a "clear and present danger" to society

closed caucus a presidential nominating caucus open only to registered party members

closed primary a primary election in which voters can participate in the nomination of candidates, but only of the party in which they are enrolled for a period of time prior to primary day

closed rule a provision by the House Rules Committee limiting or prohibiting the introduction of amendments during debate

cloture a rule allowing a majority of two-thirds or three-fifths of the members of a legislative body to set a time limit on debate over a given bill

coattail effect the result of voters casting their ballot for president or governor and "automatically" voting for the remainder of the party's ticket

Cold War the period of struggle between the United States and the former Soviet Union between the late 1940s and about 1990

collective goods benefits, sought by groups, that are broadly available and cannot be denied to nonmembers

commander in chief the role of the president as commander of the national military and the state national guard units (when called into service)

commerce clause Article I, Section 8, of the Constitution, which delegates to Congress the power "to regulate commerce with foreign nations, and among the several States and with the Indian tribes." This clause was interpreted by the Supreme Court in favor of national power over the economy

commissioner form of government a form of city government in which the city is run by a small group of elected commissioners who act in both legislative and executive capacities

committee markup session in which a congressional committee rewrites legislation to incorporate changes discussed during hearings on the bill

complaint the presentation of a grievance by the plaintiff in a civil case

comptroller elected state official who directs the collection of taxes and other revenues

concurrent powers authority possessed by *both* state and national governments, such as the power to levy taxes

concurrent resolution a resolution of interest to both chambers of the legislature, and that must pass both the House and Senate and generally be signed by the governor

Confederacy the Confederate States of America, those southern states that seceded from the United States in late 1860 and 1861 and argued that the power of a government is based in its states

confederation a system of government in which states retain sovereign authority except for the powers expressly delegated to the national government

conference a gathering of House Republicans every two years to elect their House leaders. Democrats call their gathering the caucus

conference committee a joint committee created to work out a compromise on House and Senate versions of a piece of legislation

conservative today this term refers to those who generally support the social and economic status quo and are suspicious of efforts to introduce new political formulae and economic arrangements. Conservatives believe that a large and powerful government poses a threat to citizens' freedom

consideration by standing committee the third step in the legislative process, during which a bill is killed, amended, or heard by a standing committee

constituency the residents in the area from which an official is elected

constituent powers efforts made by a member of a legislature on behalf of his or her constituency

constituent a person living in the district from which an official is elected

constitution the legal structure of a government, which establishes its power and authority as well as the limits on that power

constitutional government a system of rule in which formal and effective limits are placed on the powers of the government

constable precinct-level county official involved with serving legal papers and, in some counties, enforcing the law

contingent fee a fee paid to the lawyer in a civil case and which is contingent on winning the case

contracting power the power of government to set conditions on companies seeking to sell goods or services to government agencies

contributory programs social programs financed in whole or in part by taxation or other mandatory contributions by their present or future recipients

cooperative federalism a type of federalism existing since the New Deal era in which grants-in-aid have been used strategically to encourage states and localities (without commanding them) to pursue nationally defined goals. Also known as "intergovernmental cooperation"

cost-of-living adjustment (COLA) a change made to the level of benefits of a government program based on the rate of inflation

council of government (COG) a regional planning board composed of local elected officials and some private citizens from the same area

council-manager form of government a form of city government in which public policies are developed by the city council and executive and administrative functions are assigned to a professional city manager

county attorney county official who prosecutes lesser criminal cases in the county court

county auditor public official, appointed by the district judges, who receives and disburses county funds; in large counties, this official also prepares the county budget

county chair the county party official, who heads the county executive committee

county clerk public official who is the main record-keeper of the county

county commissioners court the main governing body of each county; has the authority to set the county tax rate and budget

county commissioner government official (four per county) on the county commissioners court whose main duty is the construction and maintenance of roads and bridges

county convention a meeting held by a political party following its precinct conventions, for the purpose of electing delegates to its state convention

county courts the courts that exist in some counties that are presided over by county judges

county executive committee the party group, made up of a party's county chair and precinct chairs, that is responsible for running a county's primary elections and planning county conventions

county judge the person in each of Texas's 254 counties who presides over the county court and county commissioners court, with responsibility for the administration of county government; some county judges carry out judicial responsibilities

county tax assessor-collector public official who maintains the county tax records and collects the taxes owed to the county

court of appeals a court that hears appeals of trial court decisions

courts of appeal (Texas) the fourteen intermediate-level appellate courts that hear appeals from district and county courts to determine whether the decisions of these lower courts followed legal principles and court procedures

criminal law the branch of law that regulates the conduct of individuals, defines crimes, and specifies punishment for criminal acts

debt service the amount of a budget spent by a government on paying interest on its debt

dedicated funds a portion of the state budget that is dedicated to mandatory spending on programs such as health care for the poor

de facto literally, "by fact"; practices that occur even when there is no legal enforcement, such as school segregation in much of the United States today

de jure literally, "by law"; legally enforced practices, such as school segregation in the South before the 1960s

defendant the one against whom a complaint is brought in a criminal or civil case

delegate a representative who votes according to the preferences of his or her constituency

delegated powers constitutional powers that are assigned to one governmental agency but that are exercised by another agency with the express permission of the first

delegates political activists selected to vote at a party's national convention

democracy a system of rule that permits citizens to play a significant part in the governmental process, usually through the election of key public officials

department the largest subunit of the executive branch. The secretaries of the fifteen departments form the Cabinet

deregulation a policy of reducing or eliminating regulatory restraints on the conduct of individuals or private institutions

deterrence the development and maintenance of military strength as a means of discouraging attack

devolution a policy to remove a program from one level of government by delegating it or passing it down to a lower level of government, such as from the national government to the state and local governments

diplomacy the representation of a government to other foreign governments

direct democracy a system of rule that permits citizens to vote directly on laws and policies

directive and supervisory powers the legislature's power over the executive branch; for example, the legislature determines the size of appropriations for state agencies

discretionary spending federal spending on programs that are controlled through the regular budget process

discrimination use of any unreasonable and unjust criterion of exclusion

dissenting opinion a decision written by a justice in the minority in a particular case in which the justice wishes to express his or her reasoning in the case

district attorney public official who prosecutes the more serious criminal cases in the district court

district clerk public official who is the main record-keeper of the district court

district courts the major trial courts in Texas, which usually have general jurisdiction over a broad range of civil and criminal cases

divided government the condition in American government wherein the presidency is controlled by one party while the opposing party controls one or both houses of Congress

double jeopardy the Fifth Amendment right providing that a person cannot be tried twice for the same crime

dual federalism the system of government that prevailed in the United States from 1789 to 1937, in which most fundamental governmental powers were shared between the federal and state governments

due process of law the right of every citizen against arbitrary action by national or state governments

early registration the requirement that a voter register long before the general election; in effect in Texas until 1971

early voting a procedure that allows voters to cast ballots during the two-week period before the regularly scheduled election date

economic expansionist role the strategy often pursued by capitalist countries to adopt foreign policies that will maximize the success of domestic corporations in their dealings with other countries

elastic clause Article I, Section 8, of the Constitution (also known as the necessary and proper clause), which enumerates the powers of Congress and provides Congress with the authority to make all laws "necessary and proper" to carry them out

electoral college the presidential electors from each state who meet after the popular election to cast ballots for president and vice president

electoral powers the legislature's mandated role in counting returns in the elections for governor and lieutenant governor

electoral realignment the point in history when a new party supplants the ruling party, becoming in turn the dominant political force. In the United States, this has tended to occur roughly every thirty years

elite a small group of people that dominates the political process

eminent domain the right of government to take private property for public use

en banc referring to an appellate hearing with all judges participating

entitlement a legal obligation of the federal government to provide payments to individuals, or groups of individuals according to eligibility criteria or benefit rules

equal protection clause provision of the Fourteenth Amendment guaranteeing citizens "the equal protection of the laws." This clause has been the basis for the civil rights of African Americans, women, and other groups

equal time rule the requirement that broadcasters provide candidates for the same political office equal opportunities to communicate their messages to the public

equality of opportunity a widely shared American ideal that all people should have the freedom to use whatever talents and wealth they have to reach their fullest potential

establishment clause the First Amendment clause that says that "Congress shall make no law respecting an establishment of religion." This law means that a "wall of separation" exists between church and state

ex post facto law a law that declares an action to be illegal after it has been committed

exclusionary rule the ability of courts to exclude evidence obtained in violation of the Fourth Amendment

executive agreement an agreement, made between the president and another country, that has the force of a treaty but does not require the Senate's "advice and consent"

executive budget the state budget prepared and submitted by the governor to the legislature, which indicates the governor's spending priorities. The executive budget is overshadowed in terms of importance by the legislative budget

Executive Office of the President (EOP) the permanent agencies that perform defined management tasks for the president. Created in 1939, the EOP includes the Office of Management and Budget, the Council of Economic Advisers, the National Security Council, and other agencies

executive order a rule or regulation issued by the president that has the effect and formal status of legislation

executive privilege the claim that confidential communications between a president and close advisers should not be revealed without the consent of the president

expressed powers specific powers granted by the Constitution to Congress (Article I, Section 8), and to the president (Article II)

fairness doctrine a Federal Communications Commission requirement for broadcasters who air programs on controversial issues to provide time for opposing views. The FCC ceased enforcing this doctrine in 1985

federal funds rate the interest rate on loans between banks that the Federal Reserve Board influences by affecting the supply of money available

Federal Reserve System a system of twelve Federal Reserve Banks that facilitates exchanges of cash, checks, and credit; regulates member banks; and uses monetary policies to fight inflation and deflation

federal system a system of government in which the national government shares power with lower levels of government, such as states

federalism a system of government in which power is divided, by a constitution, between a central government and regional governments

Federalist Papers a series of essays written by Alexander Hamilton, James Madison, and John Jay supporting the ratification of the Constitution

Federalists those who favored a strong national government and supported the Constitution proposed at the American Constitutional Convention of 1787

felony a serious criminal offense, punishable by a prison sentence or a fine

Fifteenth Amendment one of three Civil War amendments; guaranteed voting rights for African American men

fighting words speech that directly incites damaging conduct

filibuster a tactic used by members of the Senate to prevent action on legislation they oppose by continuously holding the floor and speaking until the majority backs down. Once given the floor, senators have unlimited time to speak, and it requires a vote of three-fifths of the Senate to end a filibuster. In Texas, Senate rules require that a senator stand upright at his/her desk and remain on topic while speaking. This is unlike the U.S. Senate, where it is not necessary to remain on topic.

fiscal policy the government's use of taxing, monetary, and spending powers to manipulate the economy

501c(4) committees nonprofit groups that also engage in issue advocacy. Under Section 501c(4) such a group may spend up to half its revenue for political purposes

527 committees nonprofit independent groups that receive and disburse funds to influence the nomination, election, or defeat of candidates. Named after Section 527 of the Internal Revenue Code, which defines and provides tax-exempt status for nonprofit advocacy groups

floor action the fourth step in the legislative process, during which a bill referred by a standing committee is scheduled for floor debate by the Calendars Committee

food stamps a debit card that can be used for food at most grocery stores; the largest in-kind benefits program

formula grants grants-in-aid in which a formula is used to determine the amount of federal funds a state or local government will receive

Fourteenth Amendment one of three Civil War amendments; guaranteed equal protection and due process

framing the power of the media to influence how events and issues are interpreted

free exercise clause the First Amendment clause that protects a citizen's right to believe and practice whatever religion he or she chooses

free riders those who enjoy the benefits of collective goods but did not participate in acquiring them

full faith and credit clause provision from Article IV, Section 1, of the Constitution, requiring that the states normally honor the public acts and judicial decisions that take place in another state

gender gap a distinctive pattern of voting behavior reflecting the differences in views between women and men

General Agreement on Tariffs and Trade (GATT) international trade organization, in existence from 1947 to 1995, that set many of the rules governing international trade

general bill a bill that applies to all people and/or property in the state

general election a decisive election that determines who is elected to office

general revenue sharing the process by which one unit of government yields a portion of its tax income to another unit of government, according to an established formula. Revenue sharing typically involves the national government providing money to state governments

gerrymandering apportionment of voters in districts in such a way as to give unfair advantage to one racial or ethnic group or political party

Gilmer-Aikin Laws education reform legislation passed in 1949 that supplemented local funding of education with state monies, raised teachers' salaries, mandated a minimum length for the school year, and provided more state supervision of public education

government institutions and procedures through which a territory and its people are ruled

government corporation a government agency that performs a service normally provided by the private sector

grand jury jury that determines whether sufficient evidence is available to justify a trial; grand juries do not rule on the accused's guilt or innocence

Grange a militant farmers' movement of the late nineteenth century that fought for improved conditions for farmers

grants-in-aid programs through which Congress provides money to state and local governments on the condition that the funds be employed for purposes defined by the federal government

grassroots mobilization a lobbying campaign in which a group mobilizes its membership to contact government officials in support of the group's position

Great Compromise the agreement reached at the Constitutional Convention of 1787 that gave each state an equal number of senators regardless of its population, but linked representation in the House of Representatives to population

Gross Domestic Product (GDP) the total value of goods and services produced within a country

habeas corpus a court order demanding that an individual in custody be brought into court and shown the cause for detention

hidden government a term that refers to special districts of which many citizens are unaware

Holy Alliance role a strategy pursued by a superpower to prevent any change in the existing distribution of power among nation-states, even if this requires intervention into the internal affairs of another country in order to keep a ruler from being overthrown

home rule power delegated by the state to a local unit of government to manage its own affairs

home-rule charter the rules under which a city operates

illusion of saliency the impression conveyed by polls that something is important to the public when actually it is not

impeachment the formal charge by the House of Representatives that a government official has committed "Treason, Bribery, or other high Crimes and Misdemeanors"; in Texas, the formal charge by the House of Representatives that leads to trial in the Senate and possible removal of a state official

implementation the efforts of departments and agencies to translate laws into specific bureaucratic rules and actions

implied powers powers derived from the necessary and proper clause of Article I, Section 8, of the Constitution. Such powers are not specifically expressed, but are implied through the expansive interpretation of delegated powers

in-kind benefits noncash goods and services provided to needy individuals and families by the federal government

incumbency holding a political office for which one is running

incumbent a candidate running for re-election to a position that he or she already holds

independent agency an agency that is not part of a Cabinet department

indexing periodic process of adjusting social benefits or wages to account for increases in the cost of living

indictment a written statement issued by a grand jury that charges a suspect with a crime and states that a trial is warranted

individualistic political culture the belief that government should limit its role to providing order in society, so that citizens can pursue their economic self-interests

inflation a consistent increase in the general level of prices

informational benefits special newsletters, periodicals, training programs, conferences, and other information provided to members of groups to entice others to join

inherent powers powers claimed by a president that are not expressed in the Constitution, but are inferred from it

institutional advertising advertising designed to create a positive image of an organization

interest group individuals who organize to influence the government's programs and policies

intermediate scrutiny test used by the Supreme Court in gender discrimination cases, which places the burden of proof partially on the government and partially on the challengers to show that the law in question is unconstitutional

International Monetary Fund (IMF) an institution established in 1944 that provides loans and facilitates international monetary exchange

introduction the first step in the legislative process, during which a member of the legislature gets an idea for a bill and files a copy of it with the clerk of the House or secretary of the Senate

investigative powers the power, exercised by the House, the Senate, or both chambers jointly, to investigate problems facing the state

iron triangle the stable, cooperative relationship that often develops among a congressional committee, an administrative agency, and one or more supportive interest groups. Not all of these relationships are triangular, but the iron triangle is the most typical

isolationism desire to avoid involvement in the affairs of other nations

issue network a loose network of elected leaders, public officials, activists, and interest groups drawn together by a specific policy issue

issue advocacy independent spending by individuals or interest groups on a campaign issue but not directly tied to a particular candidate

"Jim Crow" laws laws enacted by southern states following Reconstruction that discriminated against African Americans

joint committee a legislative committee formed of members of both the House and the Senate

joint resolution a resolution, commonly a proposed amendment to the Texas Constitution or ratification of an amendment to the U.S. Constitution, that must pass both the House and Senate but does not require the governor's signature

judicial activism judicial philosophy that posits that the Court should go beyond the words of the Constitution or a statute to consider the broader societal implications of its decisions

Judicial Campaign Fairness Act a judicial reform under which campaign contributions are limited by the amount that a judicial candidate can receive from donors

judicial powers the power of the House to impeach and of the Senate to convict members of the executive and judicial branches of state government

judicial restraint judicial philosophy whose adherents refuse to go beyond the clear words of the Constitution in interpreting its meaning

judicial review the power of the courts to review and, if necessary, declare actions of the legislative and executive branches invalid or unconstitutional. The Supreme Court asserted this power in *Marbury v. Madison*

jurisdiction the sphere of a court's power and authority

justice of the peace courts local trial courts with limited jurisdiction over small claims and very minor criminal misdemeanors

Keynesians followers of the economic theories of John Maynard Keynes, who argued that the government can stimulate the economy by increasing public spending or by cutting taxes

Kitchen Cabinet an informal group of advisers to whom the president turns for counsel and guidance. Members of the official Cabinet may or may not also be members of the Kitchen Cabinet

laissez-faire capitalism an economic system in which the means of production and distribution are privately owned and operated for profit with minimal or no government interference

land commissioner elected state official who is the manager of most publicly owned lands

legislative budget the state budget that is prepared and submitted by the Legislative Budget Board (LBB) and that is fully considered by the House and Senate

legislative initiative the president's inherent power to bring a legislative agenda before Congress

***Lemon* test** a rule articulated in *Lemon v. Kurtzman* that government action toward religion is permissible if it is secular in purpose, neither promotes nor inhibits the practice of religion, and does not lead to "excessive entanglement" with religion

libel a written statement made in "reckless disregard of the truth" that is considered damaging to a victim because it is "malicious, scandalous, and defamatory"

liberal today this term refers to those who generally support social and political reform; extensive governmental intervention in the economy; the expansion of federal social services; more vigorous efforts on behalf of the poor, minorities, and women; and greater concern for consumers and the environment

libertarian the political philosophy that is skeptical of any government intervention as a potential threat to individual liberty; one who favors minimal government and maximum individual freedom

liberty freedom from governmental control

lieutenant governor the second-highest elected official in the state and president of the state Senate

limited government a principle of constitutional government; a government whose powers are defined and limited by a constitution

line-item veto the power of the executive to veto specific provisions (lines) of a bill passed by the legislature

litigation a lawsuit or legal proceeding; as a form of political participation, an attempt to seek relief in a court of law

lobbying a strategy by which organized interests seek to influence the passage of legislation by exerting direct pressure on members of the legislature

lobbyist an individual employed by an interest group who tries to influence governmental decisions on behalf of that group

local bill a bill affecting only units of local government, such as a city, county, or special district

logrolling a legislative practice whereby agreements are made between legislators in voting for or against a bill; vote trading

loophole incentive to individuals and businesses to reduce their tax liabilities by investing their money in areas that the government designates

machines strong party organizations in late-nineteenth- and early-twentieth-century American cities. These machines were led by "bosses" who controlled party nominations and patronage

majority leader the elected leader of the majority party in the House of Representatives or in the Senate. In the House, the majority leader is subordinate in the party hierarchy to the Speaker of the House

majority-minority district a gerrymandered voting district that improves the chances of minority candidates by making selected minority groups the majority within the district

majority party the party that holds the majority of legislative seats in either the House or the Senate

majority rule, minority rights the democratic principle that a government follows the preferences of the majority of voters but protects the interests of the minority

majority system a type of electoral system in which, to win a seat in the parliament or other representative body, a candidate must receive a majority of all the votes cast in the relevant district

mandate a claim by a victorious candidate that the electorate has given him or her special authority to carry out promises made during the campaign

mandatory spending federal spending that is made up of "uncontrollables," budget items that cannot be controlled through the regular budget process

marketplace of ideas the public forum in which beliefs and ideas are exchanged and compete

matching funds federal monies given to a state to match the state's funding on a joint program

material benefits special goods, services, or money provided to members of groups to entice others to join

mayor-council form of government a form of city government in which the mayor is the chief executive and the city council is the legislative body; in the *strong mayor–council* variation, the mayor's powers enable him or her to control executive departments and the agenda of the city council; in the *weak mayor–council* variation, the mayor's power is more limited

means testing a procedure by which potential beneficiaries of a public-assistance program establish their eligibility by demonstrating a genuine need for the assistance

measurement error failure to identify the true distribution of opinion within a population because of errors such as ambiguous or poorly worded questions

Medicaid a federally and state-financed, state-operated program providing medical services to low-income people

Medicare a form of national health insurance for the elderly and the disabled

membership association an organized group in which members actually play a substantial role, sitting on committees and engaging in group projects

merit selection a judicial reform under which judges would be nominated by a blue-ribbon committee, appointed by the governor, and, after a brief period in office, would run in a retention election

merit system a product of civil service reform, in which appointees to positions in public bureaucracies must objectively be deemed qualified for those positions

midterm elections congressional elections that do not coincide with a presidential election; also called off-year elections

minority leader the elected leader of the minority party in the House or Senate

minority party the party that holds a minority of legislative seats in either the House or the Senate

Miranda rule the requirement, articulated by the Supreme Court in *Miranda v. Arizona*, that persons under arrest must be informed prior to police interrogation of their rights to remain silent and to have the benefit of legal counsel

misdemeanor a minor criminal offense, usually punishable by a small fine or a short jail sentence

mobilization the process by which large numbers of people are organized for a political activity

monetarists followers of economic theories that contend that the role of the government in the economy should be limited to regulating the supply of money

monetary policy an effort to regulate the economy through the manipulation of the supply of money and credit. America's most powerful institution in this area of monetary policy is the Federal Reserve Board

monopoly the existence of a single firm in a market that controls all the goods and services of that market; absence of competition

mootness a criterion used by courts to screen cases that no longer require resolution

moralistic political culture the belief that government should be active in promoting the public good and that citizens should participate in politics and civic activities to ensure that good

most favored nation status agreement to offer a trading partner the lowest tariff rate offered to other trading partners

motor voter law a national act, passed in 1993, which requires states to allow people to register to vote when applying for a driver's license

multiple-member district an electorate that selects all candidates at large from the whole district; each voter is given the number of votes equivalent to the number of seats to be filled

municipal courts local trial courts with limited jurisdiction over violations of city ordinances and very minor criminal misdemeanors; municipal courts are located in each of Texas's incorporated cities and towns

municipal utility district (MUD) a special district that offers services such as electricity, water, sewage, and sanitation outside the city limits

Napoleonic role a strategy pursued by a powerful nation to prevent aggressive actions against it by improving the internal state of affairs of a particular country, even if this means encouraging revolution in that country

nation-state a political entity consisting of a people with some common cultural experience (nation) who also share a common political authority (state), recognized by other sovereignties (nation-states)

national convention a national party political institution that nominates the party's presidential and vice-presidential candidates, establishes party rules, and writes and ratifies the party's platform

National Security Council (NSC) a presidential foreign-policy advisory council composed of the president; the vice president; the secretary of state; defense; and other officials invited by the president

necessary and proper clause Article I, Section 8, of the U.S. Constitution, it provides Congress with the authority to make all laws "necessary and proper" to carry out its expressed powers

New Deal President Franklin D. Roosevelt's 1930s program to stimulate the national economy and provide relief to victims of the Great Depression

New Federalism attempts by Presidents Nixon and Reagan to return power to the states through block grants

New Jersey Plan a framework for the Constitution, introduced by William Paterson, which called for equal state representation in the national legislature regardless of population

New Politics movement a political movement that began in the 1960s and 1970s, made up of professionals and intellectuals for whom the civil rights and antiwar movements were formative experiences. The New Politics movement strengthened public interest groups

nomination the process through which political parties select their candidates for election to public office

non-state actors groups other than nation-states that attempt to play a role in the international system. Terrorist groups are one type of non-state actor

noncontributory programs social programs that provide assistance to people on the basis of demonstrated need rather than any contribution they have made

nonschool special district any special district other than a school district; examples include municipal utility districts (MUDs) and hospital districts

North American Free Trade Agreement (NAFTA) trade treaty among the United States, Canada, and Mexico to lower and eliminate tariffs among the three countries

North Atlantic Treaty Organization (NATO) a treaty organization, comprising the United States, Canada, and most of Western Europe, formed in 1948 to counter the perceived threat from the Soviet Union

oligarchy a form of government in which a small group—landowners, military officers, or wealthy merchants—controls most of the governing decisions

one-person, one-vote principle the principle that all districts should have roughly equal populations

open caucus a presidential nominating caucus open to anyone who wishes to attend

open-market operations method by which the Open Market Committee of the Federal Reserve System buys and sells government securities, etc., to help finance government operations and to reduce or increase the total amount of money circulating in the economy

open primary a primary election in which the voter can wait until the day of the primary to choose which party to enroll in to select candidates for the general election

open rule a provision by the House Rules Committee that permits floor debate and the addition of new amendments to a bill

opinion the written explanation of the Supreme Court's decision in a particular case

oral argument stage in Supreme Court procedure in which attorneys for both sides appear before the Court to present their positions and answer questions posed by justices

ordinance a regulation enacted by a city government

original jurisdiction the authority to initially consider a case. Distinguished from appellate jurisdiction, which is the authority to hear appeals from a lower court's decision

oversight   the effort by Congress, through hearings, investigations, and other techniques, to exercise control over the activities of executive agencies

party activists   partisans who contribute time, energy, and effort to support their party and its candidates

party identification   an individual voter's psychological ties to one party or another

party organization   the formal structure of a political party, including its leadership, election committees, active members, and paid staff

party unity vote   a roll-call vote in the House or Senate in which at least 50 percent of the members of one party take a particular position and are opposed by at least 50 percent of the members of the other party

patronage   the resources available to higher officials, usually opportunities to make partisan appointments to offices and to confer grants, licenses, or special favors to supporters

pay-as-you-go limit   a rule in the Texas Constitution that requires the state to balance its budget

per curiam   a brief, unsigned decision by an appellate court, usually rejecting a petition to review the decision of a lower court

pigeonholing   a step in the legislative process during which a bill is killed by the chair of the standing committee to which it was referred, as a result of his or her setting the bill aside and not bringing it before the committee

plaintiff   the individual or organization that brings a complaint in court

platform   a party document, written at a national convention, that contains party philosophy, principles, and positions on issues

plea bargain   a negotiated agreement in a criminal case in which a defendant agrees to plead guilty in return for the state's agreement to reduce the severity of the criminal charge or prison sentence the defendant is facing

plural executive   an executive branch in which power is fragmented because the election of statewide officeholders is independent of the election of the governor

pluralism   the theory that all interests are and should be free to compete for influence in the government. The outcome of this competition is compromise and moderation

plurality system   a type of electoral system in which, to win a seat in the parliament or other representative body, a candidate need only receive the most votes in the election, not necessarily a majority of the votes cast

pocket veto   a presidential veto that is automatically triggered if the president does not act on a given piece of legislation passed during the final ten days of a legislative session

police power   power reserved to the state government to regulate the health, safety, and morals of its citizens

policy entrepreneur   an individual who identifies a problem as a political issue and brings a policy proposal into the political agenda

political action committee (PAC)   a private group that raises and distributes funds for use in election campaigns

political culture   broadly shared values, beliefs, and attitudes about how the government should function. American political culture emphasizes the values of liberty, equality, and democracy

political economy   the complex interrelations between politics and the economy, as well as their effect on one another

political efficacy   the ability to influence government and politics

political equality   the right to participate in politics equally, based on the principle of "one person, one vote"

political ideology   a cohesive set of beliefs that forms a general philosophy about the role of government

political participation   political activities, such as voting, contacting political officials, volunteering for a campaign, or participating in a protest, whose purpose is to influence government

political parties   organized groups that attempt to influence the government by electing their members to important government offices

political socialization   the induction of individuals into the political culture; learning the underlying beliefs and values on which the political system is based

politics   conflict over the leadership, structure, and policies of governments

poll tax   a state-imposed tax on voters as a prerequisite for registration. Poll taxes were rendered unconstitutional in national elections by the Twenty-fourth Amendment, and in state elections by the Supreme Court in 1966

popular sovereignty   a principle of democracy in which political authority rests ultimately in the hands of the people

pork barrel (or pork)   appropriations made by legislative bodies for local projects that are often not needed but that are created so that local representatives can win re-election in their home districts

post-adjournment veto   a veto of a bill that occurs after the legislature adjourns, thus preventing the legislature from overriding it

power   influence over a government's leadership, organization, or policies

precedent   a prior case whose principles are used by judges as the basis for their decision in a present case

precinct   a local voting district

precinct chair   the local party official, elected in the party's primary election, who heads the precinct convention and serves on the party's county executive committee

precinct convention   a meeting held by a political party to select delegates for the county convention and to submit resolutions to the party's state platform; precinct conventions are held on the day of the party's primary election and are open to anyone who voted in that election

preemption the principle that allows the national government to override state or local actions in certain policy areas. In foreign policy, the willingness to strike first in order to prevent an enemy attack

preponderance of the evidence the standard of proof in a civil jury case, by which the plaintiff must show that the defendant is more likely than not the cause of the harm suffered by the plaintiff

presidential Republicanism a voting pattern in which conservatives vote Democratic for state offices, but Republican for presidential candidates

preventive war policy of striking first when a nation fears that a foreign foe is contemplating hostile action

priming process of preparing the public to take a particular view of an event or political actor

primary elections elections held to select a party's candidate for the general election

prior restraint an effort by a governmental agency to block the publication of material it deems libelous or harmful in some other way; censorship. In the United States, the courts forbid prior restraint except under the most extraordinary circumstances

private bill a proposal in Congress to provide a specific person with some kind of relief, such as a special exemption from immigration quotas

privatization removing all or part of a program from the public sector to the private sector

privileges and immunities clause provision from Article IV, Section 2, of the Constitution, that a state cannot discriminate against someone from another state or give its own residents special privileges

probability sampling a method used by pollsters to select a representative sample in which every individual in the population has an equal probability of being selected as a respondent

progressive taxation taxation that hits upper income brackets more heavily

project grants grant programs in which state and local governments submit proposals to federal agencies and for which funding is provided on a competitive basis

property tax a tax based on an assessment of the value of one's property, which is used to fund the services provided by local governments, such as education

proportional representation a multiple-member district system that allows each political party representation in proportion to its percentage of the total vote

prospective voting voting based on the imagined future performance of a candidate

protest participation that involves assembling crowds to confront a government or other official organization

provincialism a narrow, limited, and self-interested view of the world

public good a good or service that is provided by the government because it either is not supplied by the market or is not supplied in sufficient quantities

public interest groups groups that claim they serve the general good rather than only their own particular interest

public opinion citizens' attitudes about political issues, leaders, institutions, and events

public-opinion polls scientific instruments for measuring public opinion

public policy a law, rule, statute, or edict that expresses the government's goals and provides for rewards and punishments to promote their attainment

public relations an attempt, usually through the use of paid consultants, to establish a favorable relationship with the public and influence its political opinions

purposive benefits selective benefits of group membership that emphasize the purpose and accomplishments of the group

push polling a polling technique in which the questions are designed to shape the respondent's opinion

Radical Republicans a bloc of Republicans in the U.S. Congress who pushed through the adoption of black suffrage as well as an extended period of military occupation of the South following the Civil War

random digit dialing a polling method in which respondents are selected at random from a list of ten-digit telephone numbers, with every effort made to avoid bias in the construction of the sample

recall procedure to allow voters an opportunity to remove state officials from office before their terms expire

recognition the Speaker of the House's power to control floor debate by recognizing who can speak before the House

redistribution a policy whose objective is to tax or spend in such a way as to reduce the disparities of wealth between the lowest and the highest income brackets

redistributive programs economic policies designed to control the economy through taxing and spending, with the goal of benefiting the poor

redistricting the process of redrawing election districts and redistributing legislative representatives. This happens every ten years to reflect shifts in population or in response to legal challenges in existing districts

redlining a practice in which banks refuse to make loans to people living in certain geographic locations

referendum the practice of referring a measure proposed or passed by a legislature to the vote of the electorate for approval or rejection

referral the second step in the legislative process, during which a bill is assigned to the appropriate standing committee by the Speaker (for House bills) or the lieutenant governor (for Senate bills)

regressive taxation taxation that hits lower income brackets more heavily

regular session   the 140-day period during which the Texas legislature meets to consider and pass bills; occurs only in odd-numbered years

regulated federalism   a form of federalism in which Congress imposes legislation on states and localities, requiring them to meet national standards

regulatory agencies   departments, bureaus, or independent agencies whose primary mission is to impose limits, restrictions, or other obligations on the conduct of individuals or companies in the private sector

representative democracy/republic   a system of government in which the populace selects representatives, who play a significant role in governmental decision making

republican government   a representative democracy, a system of government in which power is derived from the people

reserve requirement   the amount of liquid assets and ready cash that banks are required to hold to meet depositors' demands for their money

reserved powers   powers, derived from the Tenth Amendment to the Constitution, that are not specifically delegated to the national government or denied to the states

resolution   a proposal, made by a member of the legislature, that generally deals with the internal workings of the government; a resolution is similar to a bill, but it has a more limited scope and lacks the force of public law

responsible party government   a set of principles that idealizes a strong role for parties in defining their stance on issues, mobilizing voters, and fulfilling their campaign promises once in office

retention election   an election in which voters decide "yes" or "no" regarding whether to keep an incumbent in office

retrospective voting   voting based on the past performance of a candidate

revenue agencies   agencies responsible for collecting taxes. Examples include the Internal Revenue Service for income taxes, the U.S. Customs Service for tariffs and other taxes on imported goods, and the Bureau of Alcohol, Tobacco, and Firearms for collection of taxes on the sales of those particular products

right of rebuttal   a Federal Communications Commission regulation giving individuals the right to have the opportunity to respond to personal attacks made on a radio or television broadcast

right to privacy   the right to be left alone, which has been interpreted by the Supreme Court to entail free access to birth control and abortions

roll-call vote   a vote in which each legislator's yes or no vote is recorded as the clerk calls the names of the members alphabetically

runoff primary   where no candidate received a majority, a second primary election is held between the two candidates who received the most votes in the first primary election

salient interests   attitudes and views that are especially important to the individual holding them

sample   a small group selected by researchers to represent the most important characteristics of an entire population

sampling error   polling error that arises based on the small size of the sample

school district   a specific type of special district that provides public education in a designated area

secretary of state   state official, appointed by the governor, whose primary responsibility is administering elections

select committee   a (usually) temporary legislative committee set up to highlight or investigate a particular issue or address an issue not within the jurisdiction of existing committees

selection bias   polling error that arises when the sample is not representative of the population being studied, which creates errors in overrepresenting or underrepresenting some opinions

selective incorporation   the process by which different protections in the Bill of Rights were incorporated into the Fourteenth Amendment, thus guaranteeing citizens protection from state as well as national governments

senatorial courtesy   the practice whereby the president, before formally nominating a person for a federal judgeship, seeks the indication that senators from the candidate's own state support the nomination; in Texas, the practice whereby the governor seeks the support of the senator from the nominee's district. Failure to obtain that support will usually mean the Senate will not confirm the nominee

seniority   ranking given to an individual on the basis of length of continuous service on a committee in Congress

"separate but equal" rule   doctrine that public accommodations could be segregated by race but still be equal

separation of powers   the division of governmental power among several institutions that must cooperate in decision making

Shivercrat movement   a movement, led by the Texas governor Allan Shivers during the 1950s, in which conservative Democrats in Texas supported Republican candidates for office because many of them believed that the national Democratic Party had become too liberal

simple resolution   a resolution that concerns only the Texas House or Senate, such as the adoption of a rule or the appointment of an employee, and does not require the governor's signature

single-member district   an electorate that is allowed to select only one representative from each district; the normal method of representation in the United States

slander   an oral statement, made in "reckless disregard of the truth," which is considered damaging to the victim because it is "malicious, scandalous, and defamatory"

Social Security   a contributory welfare program into which working Americans contribute a percentage of their wages, and from which they receive cash benefits after retirement

socioeconomic status   status in society based on level of education, income, and occupational prestige

sociological representation   a type of representation in which representatives have the same racial, gender, ethnic, religious, or educational backgrounds as their constituents. It is based on the principle that if two individuals are similar in background, character, interests, and perspectives, then one could correctly represent the other's views

soft money   money contributed directly to political parties for political activities that is not regulated by federal campaign spending laws

solicitor general   the top government lawyer in all cases before the Supreme Court where the government is a party

solidary benefits   selective benefits of group membership that emphasize friendship, networking, and consciousness raising

sound bites   short snippets of information aimed at dramatizing a story rather than explaining its substantive meaning

Speaker of the House (or Speaker, in Texas)   the chief presiding officer of the House of Representatives. The Speaker is the most important party and House leader, and can influence the legislative agenda, the fate of individual pieces of legislation, and members' positions within the House

special bill   a bill that gives an individual or corporation a special exemption from state law

special district   a unit of local government that performs a single service, such as education or sanitation, within a limited geographical area

special election   an election that is not held on a regularly scheduled basis; in Texas, a special election is called to fill a vacancy in office, to give approval for the state government to borrow money, or to ratify amendments to the Texas Constitution

special session   a legislative session called by the governor that addresses an agenda set by him or her and that lasts no longer than thirty days

"speech plus"   speech accompanied by conduct such as sit-ins, picketing, and demonstrations; protection of this form of speech under the First Amendment is conditional, and restrictions imposed by state or local authorities are acceptable if properly balanced by considerations of public order

spot advertisement   a fifteen-, thirty-, or sixty-second television campaign commercial that permits a candidate's message to be delivered to a target audience

staff agency   a legislative support agency responsible for policy analysis

staff organization   a type of membership group in which a professional staff conducts most of the group's activities

standing   the right of an individual or organization to initiate a court case, on the basis of their having a substantial stake in the outcome

standing committee   a permanent committee with the power to propose and write legislation that covers a particular subject, such as finance or agriculture

stare decisis   literally, "let the decision stand." The doctrine that a previous decision by a court applies as a precedent in similar cases until that decision is overruled

state chair and vice chair   the top two state-level leaders in the party

state convention   a party meeting held every two years for the purpose of nominating candidates for statewide office, adopting a platform, electing the party's leadership, and in presidential election years selecting delegates for the national convention and choosing presidential electors

state executive committee   the committee responsible for governing a party's activities throughout the state

states' rights   the principle that the states should oppose the increasing authority of the national government. This principle was most popular in the period before the Civil War

statutory county courts at law   courts that tend to hear less serious cases than those heard by district courts

statutory probate courts   specialized courts whose jurisdiction is limited to probate and guardianship matters

strict scrutiny   test used by the Supreme Court in racial discrimination cases and other cases involving civil liberties and civil rights, which places the burden of proof on the government rather than on the challengers to show that the law in question is constitutional

subsidy   a government grant of cash or other valuable commodities, such as land, to an individual or organization; used to promote activities desired by the government, to reward political support, or to buy off political opposition

suffrage   the right to vote; also called franchise

Sunset Advisory Commission (SAC)   a commission created in 1975 for the purpose of reviewing the effectiveness of state agencies

superdelegate   a convention delegate position, in Democratic conventions, reserved for party officials

supply-side economics   posits that reducing the marginal rate of taxation will create a productive economy by promoting levels of work and investment that would otherwise be discouraged by higher taxes

supremacy clause   Article VI of the U.S. Constitution, which states that the Constitution and laws passed by the national government and all treaties are the supreme law of the land and superior to all laws adopted by any state or any subdivision

supreme court   the highest court in a particular state or in the United States. This court primarily serves an appellate function

tariff   a tax on imported goods

tax expenditures   government subsidies provided to employers and employees through tax deductions for amounts spent on health insurance and other benefits

Temporary Assistance for Needy Families (TANF)   a federal block grant that replaced the AFDC program in 1996

term limits legally prescribed limits on the number of terms an elected official can serve

Texas Court of Criminal Appeals the highest criminal court in Texas; consists of nine justices and has final state appellate authority over criminal cases

Texas Supreme Court the highest civil court in Texas; consists of nine justices and has final state appellate authority over civil cases

third parties parties that organize to compete against the two major American political parties

Thirteenth Amendment one of three Civil War amendments; abolished slavery

Three-fifths Compromise the agreement reached at the Constitutional Convention of 1787 that stipulated that for purposes of the apportionment of congressional seats, every slave would be counted as three-fifths of a person

totalitarian government a system of rule in which the government recognizes no formal limits on its power and seeks to absorb or eliminate other social institutions that might challenge it

town meeting a media format in which candidates meet with ordinary citizens. Allows candidates to deliver messages without the presence of journalists or commentators

traditionalistic political culture the belief that government should be dominated by political elites and guided by tradition

trial court the first court to hear a criminal or civil case

trustee a representative who votes based on what he or she thinks is best for his or her constituency

turnout the percentage of eligible individuals who actually vote

two-party system a political system in which only two parties have a realistic opportunity to compete effectively for control

tyranny oppressive government that employs cruel and unjust use of power and authority

uncontrollable a budgetary item that is beyond the control of budgetary committees and can be controlled only by substantive legislative action in Congress. Some uncontrollables, such as interest on the debt, are beyond the power of Congress, because the terms of payments are set in contracts

unfunded mandates regulations or conditions for receiving grants that impose costs on state and local governments for which they are not reimbursed by the federal government

unicameral comprising one body or house, as in one house legislature

Uniform Commercial Code code used in many states in the area of contract law to reduce interstate differences in judicial decisions.

unitary system a centralized government system in which lower levels of government have little power independent of the national government

United Nations (UN) an organization of nations founded in 1945 to serve as a channel for negotiation and a means of settling international disputes peaceably. The UN has had frequent successes in providing a forum for negotiation and on some occasions a means of preventing international conflicts from spreading. On a number of occasions, the UN has been a convenient cover for U.S. foreign policy goals

urbanization the process by which people move from rural areas to cities

user fee a fee paid for public goods and services, such as water or sewage service

values (or beliefs) basic principles that shape a person's opinions about political issues and events

veto the president's constitutional power to turn down acts of Congress. A presidential veto may be overridden by a two-thirds vote of each house of Congress; according to the Texas Constitution, the governor's power to turn down legislation; can be overridden by a two-thirds vote of both the House and Senate

Virginia Plan a framework for the Constitution, introduced by Edmund Randolph, which called for representation in the national legislature based on the population of each state

waiver an exemption from a federal requirement

War Powers Resolution a resolution of Congress that the president can send troops into action abroad only by authorization of Congress, or if American troops are already under attack or serious threat

whip a party member in the House or Senate responsible for coordinating the party's legislative strategy, building support for key issues, and counting votes

White House staff analysts and advisers to the president, often given the title "special assistant"

white primary primary election in which only white voters are eligible to participate

winner-take-all system a system in which all of a state's presidential nominating delegates are awarded to the candidate who wins the most votes, while runners-up receive no delegates

World Trade Organization (WTO) international trade agency promoting free trade that grew out of the General Agreement on Tariffs and Trade

writ of *certiorari* a decision of at least four of the nine Supreme Court justices to review a decision of a lower court; from the Latin "to make more certain"

writ of *habeas corpus* a court order that the individual in custody be brought into court and shown the cause for detention. *Habeas corpus* is guaranteed by the Constitution and can be suspended only in cases of rebellion or invasion

endnotes

Chapter 1

1. Gary Orren, "Fall from Grace: The Public's Loss of Trust in Government," in *Why People Don't Trust Government*, ed. Joseph S. Nye, Jr., Philip D. Zelikow, and David C. King (Cambridge, MA: Harvard University Press, 1997), 80–81.

2. Robert J. Blendon et al., "Changing Attitudes in America," in *Why People Don't Trust Government*, ed. Nye, Zelikow, and King, 207–8.

3. Michael A. Fletcher, "Trust and Interest in Government Soar on College Campuses," *Washington Post*, November 23, 2001, p. A3.

4. Amelia Gruber, "Public Finds Government Inefficient, Study Shows," GovExec.com, August 8, 2003.

5. CBS News, "CBS/New York Times Poll, June 12–16, 2009," www.cbsnews.com/htdocs/pdf/CBSPOLL_June09a_health_care.pdf (accessed 9/25/09).

6. CBS News, "CBS News Poll, March 12–15, 2009," www.cbsnews.com/htdocs/pdf/MAR09A-Banks.pdf (accessed 9/25/09).

7. CNN Political Ticker, "Poll: Let Carmakers Go Bankrupt, Say Americans," April 9, 2009, http://politicalticker.blogs.cnn.com/2009/04/09/poll-let-carmakers-go-bankruptsay-americans/ (accessed 9/25/09).

8. Joseph S. Nye, Jr., "Introduction: The Decline of Confidence in Government," in *Why People Don't Trust Government*, ed. Nye, Zelikow, and King, 4.

9. The Pew Research Center for the People and the Press, "Trends in Political Attitudes and Core Values, 1987–2009, May 21, 2009," http://people-press.org/reports/pdf/517.pdf (accessed 9/26/09).

10. This definition is taken from Norman H. Nie, Jane Junn, and Kenneth Stehlik-Barry, *Education and Democratic Citizenship in America* (Chicago: University of Chicago Press, 1996).

11. Freedom House, "Freedom in the World Report, 2009, Tables and Charts," www.freedomhouse.org/template.cfm?page=25&year=2009 (accessed 9/27/09).

12. See Eugen Weber, *Peasants into Frenchmen: The Modernization of Rural France, 1870–1914* (Stanford, CA: Stanford University Press, 1976), chap. 5.

13. See V. O. Key, *Politics, Parties, and Pressure Groups* (New York: Crowell, 1964), 201.

14. Harold Lasswell, *Politics: Who Gets What, When, How* (New York: Meridian Books, 1958).

15. Susan B. Carter, Scott Sigmund Gartner, Michael R. Haines, Alan L. Olmsted, Richard Sutch, and Gavin Wright, eds., *Historical Statistics of the United States: Millennial Edition Online*, Table Aa145-184, Population, by Sex and Race: 1790–1990 (New York: Cambridge University Press, 2006). 2009 data available at U.S. Census Bureau, www.census.gov (accessed 2/25/10).

16. Carter et al., *Historical Statistics of the United States*, Table Aa145-184, Population, by Sex and Race: 1790–1990.

17. Carter et al., *Historical Statistics of the United States*, Table Aa145-184, Population, by Sex and Race: 1790–1990; Table Aa2189-2215, Hispanic Population Estimates.

18. U.S. Census Bureau, www.census.gov; Claude S. Fischer and Michael Hout, *A Century of Difference: How America Changed in the Last One Hundred Years* (New York: Russell Sage Foundation, 2006), 36.

19. Carter et al., *Historical Statistics of the United States*, Table Aa22-35, Selected Population Characteristics.

20. Fischer and Hout, *A Century of Difference*, 24.

21. Michael B. Katz and Mark J. Stern, *One Nation Divisible: What America Was and What It Is Becoming* (New York: Russell Sage Foundation, 2006), 16.

22. Carter et al., *Historical Statistics of the United States*, Table Aa145-184, Population, by Sex and Race: 1790–1990.

23. U.S. Census Bureau, "Annual Estimates of the Resident Population by Sex, Race, and Hispanic Origin for the United States: April 1, 2000 to July 1, 2008," www.census.gov/popest/national/asrh/NC-EST2008-srh.html (accessed 9/28/09).

24. U.S. Census Bureau, "Population Profile of the United States: Dynamic Version," www.census.gov/popu-lation/pop-profile/dynamic/ForeignBorn.pdf (accessed 2/5/08).

25. Jeffrey S. Passel, "Size and Characteristics of the Unauthorized Migrant Population in the U.S.," Pew Hispanic Center, March 7, 2006, www.pewhispanic.org/files/reports/61.pdf (accessed 2/5/08).

26. Anthony Faiola, "States' Immigrant Policies Diverge," *Washington Post*, October 15, 2007, p. A1.

27. Fischer and Hout, *A Century of Difference*, 187; Pew Forum on Religion and Public Life, "Religious Demoraphic Profile: United States," www.pewforum.org/world-affairs/countries/?CountryID=222 (accessed 2/5/08).

28. The Pew Forum on Religion & Public Life, "U.S. Religious Landscape Survey, 2008: Affiliations," http://religions .pewforum.org/affiliations (accessed 9/28/09).

29. U.S. Census Bureau, "Annual Estimates of the Resident Population by Sex and Selected Age Groups for the United States: April 1, 2000 to July 1, 2008," www .census.gov/popest/national/asrh/NC-EST2008-sa.html (accessed 9/28/09).

30. Carter et al., *Historical Statistics of the United States*, Table Aa22-35, Selected Population Characteristics; Kevin Kinsella and Victoria A. Velkoff, *An Aging World: 2001* (November 2001), www.census.gov/prod/200pubs/p95-01-1.pdf (accessed 3/18/08).

31. Michael R. Haines, "Population Characteristics," in *Historical Statistics of the United States*, ed. Carter et al., 1–21.

32. Constitution of the United States of America, Article I, Section 2; Karen M. Mills, *Congressional Apportionment: Census 2000 Brief* (U.S. Census Bureau, 2001), www.census.gov/prod/2001pubs/c2kbr01-7.pdf (accessed 2/5/08).

33. Herbert McClosky and John Zaller, *The American Ethos: Public Attitudes toward Capitalism and Democracy* (Cambridge, MA: Harvard University Press, 1984), 19.

34. J. R. Pole, *The Pursuit of Equality in American History* (Berkeley: University of California Press, 1978), 3.

35. See Judith N. Shklar, *American Citizenship: The Quest for Inclusion* (Cambridge, MA: Harvard University Press, 1991).

36. Gardiner Harris, "Flavors Banned from Cigarettes to Deter Youths," *New York Times* September 22, 2009, www.nytimes.com/2009/09/23/health/policy/23fda .html (accessed 9/24/09).

37. See Rogers M. Smith, *Liberalism and American Constitutional Law* (Cambridge, MA: Harvard University Press, 1985), chap. 6.

38. The case was *San Antonio Independent School District v. Rodriguez*, 411 U.S. 1 (1973). See the discussion in Smith, *Liberalism and American Constitutional Law*, 163–64.

39. See the discussion in Eileen McDonagh, "Gender Political Change," in *New Perspectives on American Politics*, ed. Lawrence C. Dodd and Calvin Jillson (Washington, DC: Congressional Quarterly Press, 1994), 58–73. The argument for moving women's issues into the public sphere is made by Jean Bethke Elshtain, *Public Man, Private Woman* (Princeton, NJ: Princeton University Press, 1981).

40. Roger Lowenstein, "The Way We Live Now: The Inequality Conundrum," *New York Times Magazine*, June 10, 2007, p. 11.

41. Associated Press, "Obama: Tax Cuts Will Be Felt by April 1," February 21, 2009, www.msnbc.msn.com/id/29314485/ (accessed 9/28/09).

42. Reuters, "Obama to Allow Bush Tax Cuts to Expire on Schedule," February 21, 2009, www.reuters.com/article/topNews/idUSTRE51K1ZF20090221 (accessed 9/28/09).

43. Kevin Phillips, *Arrogant Capital: Washington, Wall Street, and the Frustration of American Politics* (Boston: Little, Brown, 1994).

44. United States Election Project, "Voter Turnout: Turnout 1980–2008," http://elections.gmu.edu/voter_turnout.htm (accessed 9/29/09).

45. Center for the Study of the American Electorate, "2008 Turnout Report: African-Americans, Anger, Fear and Youth Propel Turnout to Highest Level since 1960," News Release, December 17, 2008, www.american.edu/ia/cdem/csae/pdfs/2008pdfoffinaledited.pdf (accessed 9/29/09).

Chapter 2

1. Michael Kammen, *A Machine That Would Go of Itself* (New York: Vintage, 1986), 22.

2. The social makeup of colonial America and some of the social conflicts that divided colonial society are discussed in Jackson Turner Main, *The Social Structure of Revolutionary America* (Princeton, NJ: Princeton University Press, 1965).

3. George B. Tindall and David E. Shi, *America: A Narrative History*, 3rd ed. (New York: Norton, 1992), 194.

4. For a discussion of events leading up to the Revolution, see Charles M. Andrews, *The Colonial Background of the American Revolution* (New Haven, CT: Yale University Press, 1924).

5. See Carl Becker, *The Declaration of Independence* (New York: Knopf, 1942).

6. An excellent and readable account of the development from the Articles of Confederation to the Constitution will be found in Alfred H. Kelly, Winfred A. Harbison, and Herman Belz, *The American Constitution: Its Origins and Development*, 7th ed. (New York: Norton, 1991), vol. I, chap. 5.

7. Reported in Samuel E. Morrison, Henry Steele Commager, and William Leuchtenberg, *The Growth of the American Republic* (New York: Oxford University Press, 1969), vol. 1, 244.

8. Quoted in Morrison et al., *The Growth of the American Republic*, vol. 1, 242.

9. Charles A. Beard, *An Economic Interpretation of the Constitution of the United States* (New York: Macmillan, 1913).

10. Madison's notes, along with the somewhat less complete records kept by several other participants in the convention, are available in a four-volume set. See Max Farrand, ed., *The Records of the Federal Convention of 1787*, 4 vols., rev. ed. (New Haven, CT: Yale University Press, 1966).

11. Farrand, ed., *The Records of the Federal Convention of 1787*, vol. 1, 476.

12. Farrand, ed., *The Records of the Federal Convention of 1787*, vol. 2, 10.

13. Alexander Hamilton, James Madison, and John Jay, *The Federalist*, ed. E. M. Earle (New York: Modern Library, 1937), No. 71.

14. Hamilton et al., *The Federalist*, No. 62.

15. Hamilton et al., *The Federalist*, No. 70.

16. Max Farrand, *The Framing of the Constitution of the United States* (New Haven, CT: Yale University Press, 1962), 49.

17. Melancthon Smith, quoted in Herbert J. Storing, *What the Anti-Federalists Were For* (Chicago: University of Chicago Press, 1981), 17.

18. "Essays of Brutus," No. 1, in Herbert Storing, ed., *The Complete Anti-Federalist* (Chicago: University of Chicago Press, 1981).

19. Hamilton et al., *The Federalist*, No. 57.

20. "Essays of Brutus," No. 15, in Storing, ed., *The Complete Anti-Federalist.*

21. Hamilton et al., *The Federalist*, No. 10.

22. "Essays of Brutus," No. 7, in Storing, ed., *The Complete Anti-Federalist.*

23. "Essays of Brutus," No. 6, in Storing, ed., *The Complete Anti-Federalist.*

24. Storing, *What the Anti-Federalists Were For*, 28.

25. Hamilton et al., *The Federalist*, No. 51.

26. Quoted in Storing, *What the Anti-Federalists Were For*, 30.

27. See Marcia Lee, "The Equal Rights Amendment: Public Policy by Means of a Constitutional Amendment," in *The Politics of Policy Making in America*, ed. David Caputo (San Francisco: Freeman, 1977); Jane Mansbridge, *Why We Lost the ERA* (Chicago: University of Chicago Press, 1986); and Donald Mathews and Jane Sherron DeHart, *Sex, Gender, and the Politics of the ERA* (New York: Oxford University Press, 1990).

28. Hamilton et al., *The Federalist*, No. 10.

Chapter 3

1. Matt Richtel, "Not Driving Drunk, but Texting? Utah Law Sees Little Difference," *New York Times*, August 29, 2009, p.A1.

2. Kim Geiger, "Senate Bill Pushes Phone Driving Ban," *Los Angeles Times*, October 14, 2009, p. A16.

3. Adam Liptak, "Bans on Interracial Unions Offer Perspective on Gay Ones," *New York Times*, March 17, 2004, p. A.22.

4. National Conference of State Legislators, Same Sex Marriage, Civil Unions and Domestic Partnerships, Last Update: August, 2009, http://www.ncsl.org/IssuesResearch/HumanServices/SameSexMarriage/tabid/16430/Default.aspx; (accessed 10/16/09); "California Bill to Recognize Some Same-Sex Marriages," http://www.cnn.com/2009/US/10/12/california.samesex.marriage (accessed 10/16/09).

5. Ken I. Kersch, "Full Faith and Credit for Same-Sex Marriages?" *Political Science Quarterly* 112 (Spring 1997), 117–36; Joan Biskupic, "Once Unthinkable, Now under Debate," *Washington Post*, September 3, 1996, p. A1.

6. Barbara Hoberock, "State Won't Fight Same-Sex Adoption Ruling," *Tulsa World*, August 17, 2007, p. A9.

7. *Hicklin v. Orbeck*, 437 U.S. 518 (1978).

8. *Sweeny v. Woodall*, 344 U.S. 86 (1953).

9. Marlise Simons, "France Won't Extradite American Convicted of Murder," *New York Times*, December 5, 1997, p. A9.

10. Patricia S. Florestano, "Past and Present Utilization of Interstate Compacts in the United States," *Publius* 24 (Fall 1994), 13–26.

11. A good discussion of the constitutional position of local governments is in York Willbern, *The Withering Away of the City* (Bloomington: Indiana University Press, 1971). For more on the structure and theory of federalism, see Thomas R. Dye, *American Federalism: Competition among Governments* (Lexington, MA: Lexington Books, 1990), chap. 1; and Martha Derthick, "Up-to-Date in Kansas City: Reflections on American Federalism" (the 1992 John Gaus Lecture), *PS: Political Science & Politics* 25 (December 1992), 671–75.

12. For a good treatment of the contrast between national political stability and social instability, see Samuel P. Huntington, *Political Order in Changing Societies* (New Haven, CT: Yale University Press, 1968), chap. 2.

13. *McCulloch v. Maryland*, 4 Wheaton 316 (1819).

14. *Gibbons v. Ogden*, 9 Wheaton 1 (1824).

15. The Sherman Antitrust Act, adopted in 1890, for example, was enacted not to restrict commerce, but rather to protect it from monopolies, or trusts, in order to prevent unfair trade practices and to enable the market again to become self-regulating. Moreover, the Supreme Court sought to uphold liberty of contract to protect businesses. For example, in *Lochner v. New York*, 198 U.S. 45 (1905), the Court invalidated a New York law regulating the sanitary conditions and hours of labor of bakers on the grounds that the law interfered with liberty of contract.

16. The key case in this process of expanding the power of the national government is generally considered to be *NLRB v. Jones & Laughlin Steel Corporation*, 301 U.S.

1 (1937), in which the Supreme Court approved federal regulation of the workplace and thereby virtually eliminated interstate commerce as a limit on the national government's power.

17. *United States v. Darby Lumber* Co., 312 U.S. 100 (1941).

18. W. John Moore, "Pleading the 10th," *National Journal*, July 29, 1995, p. 1940.

19. *United States v. Lopez*, 115 S.Ct. 1624 (1995).

20. *Printz v. United States*, 117 S.Ct. 2365 (1997).

21. *Seminole Indian Tribe v. Florida*, 116 S.Ct. 1114 (1996).

22. See the poll reported in Guy Gugliotta, "Scaling Down the American Dream," *Washington Post*, April 19, 1995, p. A21. See also Richard Cole, John Kincaid, and Alejandro Rodriguez, "Public Opinion on Federalism and Federal Political Culture in Canada, Mexico and the United States, 2004," *Publius: The Journal of Federalism* 34, no. 3 (2004), 201–21, http://publius.oxfordjournals.org/cgi/reprint/34/3/201 (accessed 2/12/08).

23. Kenneth T. Palmer, "The Evolution of Grant Policies," in *The Changing Politics of Federal Grants*, ed. Lawrence D. Brown, James W. Fossett, and Kenneth T. Palmer (Washington, DC: Brookings Institution Press, 1984), 15.

24. Palmer, "The Evolution of Grant Policies," 6.

25. Morton Grozdins, *The American System*, ed. Daniel J. Elazar (Chicago: Rand McNally, 1966).

26. See Terry Sanford, *Storm over the States* (New York: McGraw-Hill, 1967).

27. James L. Sundquist with David W. Davis, *Making Federalism Work* (Washington, DC: Brookings Institution Press, 1969), 271.George Wallace was mistrusted by the architects of the War on Poverty because he was a strong proponent of racial segregation and "states' rights."

28. See Don Kettl, *The Regulation of American Federalism* (Baton Rouge: Louisiana State University Press, 1983).

29. Cindy Skrzycki, "Trial Lawyers on the Offensive in Fight against Preemptive Rules," *Washington Post*, September 11, 2007, p. D2.

30. Skrzycki, "Trial Lawyers."

31. *Wyeth v. Levine*, 555 U.S. _____ (2009).

32. Philip Rucker, "Obama Curtails Bush's Policy of 'Preemption,'" *Washington Post, May 22, 2009, p. A3.*

33. See U.S. Advisory Commission on Intergovernmental Relations, *Federal Regulation of State and Local Governments: The Mixed Record of the 1980s* (Washington, DC: Advisory Commission on Intergovernmental Relations, July 1993).

34. U.S. Advisory Commission on Intergovernmental Relations, *Federal Regulation of State and Local Governments*, iii.

35. Shailagh Murray, "States Resist Medicaid Growth: Governors Fear for Their Budgets," *Washington Post*, October 5, 2009, p.

36. Quoted in Timothy Conlon, *New Federalism: Intergovernmental Reform from Nixon to Reagan* (Washington, DC: Brookings Institution Press, 1988), 25.

37. For the emergence of complaints about federal categorical grants, see Palmer, "The Evolution of Grant Policies," 17–18. On the governors' efforts to gain more control over federal grants after the 1994 congressional elections, see Dan Balz, "GOP Governors Eager to Do Things Their Way," *Washington Post*, November 22, 1994, p. A4.

38. U.S. Advisory Commission on Intergovernmental Relations, *Federal Regulation of State and Local Governments*.

39. For an assessment of the achievements of the 104th and 105th Congresses, see Timothy Conlan, *From New Federalism to Devolution: Twenty-Five Years of Intergovernmental Reform* (Washington, DC: Brookings Institution Press, 1998).

40. Robert Frank, "Proposed Block Grants Seen Unlikely to Cure Management Problems," *Wall Street Journal*, May 1, 1995, p. 1.

41. Sarah Kershaw, "U.S. Rule Limits Emergency Care for Immigrants," *New York Times*, Sepember 22, 2007, p. A1.

42. U.S. Committee on Federalism and National Purpose, *To Form a More Perfect Union* (Washington, DC: National Conference on Social Welfare, 1985). See also the discussion in Paul E. Peterson, *The Price of Federalism* (Washington, DC: Brooking Institution Press, 1995), esp. chap. 8.

43. Malcolm Gladwell, "In States' Experiments, a Cutting Contest," *New York Times*, March 10, 1995, p. 6.

44. The phrase *laboratories of democracy* was coined by Supreme Court Justice Louis Brandeis in his dissenting opinion in *New State Ice Co. v. Liebman*, 285 U.S. 262 (1932).

45. "Motor Vehicle Fatalities in 1996 Were 12 Percent Higher on Interstates, Freeways in 12 States that Raised Speed Limits," Insurance Institute for Highway Safety, press release, October 10, 1997.

46. Adam Nagourney, "G.O.P. Right Is Splintered on Schiavo Intervention," *New York Times*, March 23, 2005, p. A14.

47. National Conference of State Legislatures, "State Laws Related to Immigrants and Immigration, January 1 – June 30, 2009," www.ncsl.org/default.aspx?tabid=18030, (accessed 10/16/09).

48. David Nasaw, "Toughest US Sheriff Loses Power to Arrest Illegal Immigrants: Stripping of Federal Duties Political Move, Says Officer: Female Chain Gangs among Criticized Tactics," *The Guardian*, October 10, 2009, p. 27; Anna Gorman, "ICE-Local Alliance to Stay; but the Immigration Enforcement Will Be Subject to More Federal Oversight, Officials Say," *Los Angeles Times*, October 17, 2009, p. A16.

49. Kate Phillips, "South Carolina Governor Rejects Stimulus Money," *New York Times*, March 20, 2009, http://thecaucus.blogs.nytimes.com/2009/03/20/round-2-omb-rejects-sc-governors-stimulus-plan/ (accessed 10/06/09).

50. Robert Pear and J. David Goodman, "Governors' Fight over Stimulus May Define G.O.P.," *New York Times*, February 22, 2009, http://www.nytimes.com/2009/02/23/us/politics/23governors.html (accessed 10/07/09).

51. The White House, Office of the Press Secretary, Memorandum for the Heads of Executive Departments and Agencies, Subject: Preemption, May 20, 2009, http://theusconstituion.org/blog.history/wp-content/uploads/2009/05/obama-preemption-memo-5202009.pdf (accessed 10/17/09).

52. This was a comment from Walter E. Dellinger, President Clinton's acting solicitor general. Linda Greenhouse, "Will the Court Reassert National Authority?" *New York Times*, September 30, 2001, sect. 4, p. 14.

53. The Pew Research Center for People and the Press, "Budget Woes Take Tool on Views of State Governments," August 11, 2009, http://people-press.org/report/534/government-favoribility (accessed 10/17/09).

Chapter 4

1. Alexander Hamilton, James Madison, and John Jay, *The Federalist Papers*, ed. Clinton Rossiter (New York: New American Library, 1961), No. 84, 513.

2. Rossiter, ed., *The Federalist Papers*, No. 84, 513.

3. Clinton Rossiter, *1787: The Grand Convention* (New York: Norton, 1987), 302.

4. Rossiter, *1787*, 303. Rossiter also reports that "in 1941 the States of Connecticut, Massachusetts and Georgia celebrated the sesquicentennial of the Bill of Rights by giving their hitherto withheld and unneeded assent."

5. *Barron v. Baltimore*, 7 Peters 243, 246 (1833).

6. The Fourteenth Amendment also seems designed to introduce civil rights. The final clause of the all-important Section 1 provides that no state can "deny to any person within its jurisdiction the equal protection of the laws." It is not unreasonable to conclude that the purpose of this provision was to obligate the state governments as well as the national government to take positive actions to protect citizens from arbitrary and discriminatory actions, at least those based on race. This will be explored in Chapter 5.

7. For example, *The Slaughterhouse Cases*, 16 Wallace 36 (1883).

8. *Chicago, Burlington and Quincy Railroad Company v. Chicago*, 166 U.S. 226 (1897).

9. *Gitlow v. New York*, 268 U.S. 652 (1925).

10. *Near v. Minnesota*, 283 U.S. 697 (1931); *Hague v. C.I.O.*, 307 U.S. 496 (1939).

11. *Palko v. Connecticut*, 302 U.S. 319 (1937).

12. All of these were implicitly included in the *Palko* case as "not incorporated" into the Fourteenth Amendment as limitations on the powers of the states.

13. There is one interesting exception, which involves the Sixth Amendment right to public trial. In the 1948 case *In re Oliver*, 33 U.S. 257, the right to the public trial was, in effect, incorporated as part of the Fourteenth Amendment. However, the issue in that case was put more generally as "due process," and public trial itself was not actually mentioned in so many words. Later opinions, such as *Duncan v. Louisiana*, 391 U.S. 145 (1968), cited the *Oliver* case as the precedent for more explicit incorporation of public trials as part of the Fourteenth Amendment.

14. *District of Columbia v. Heller*, 07-290 (2008).

15. *Abington School District v. Schempp*, 374 U.S. 203 (1963).

16. *Engel v. Vitale*, 370 U.S. 421 (1962).

17. *Wallace v. Jaffree*, 472 U.S. 38 (1985).

18. *Lynch v. Donnelly*, 465 U.S. 668 (1984).

19. *Lemon v. Kurtzman*, 403 U.S. 602 (1971). The *Lemon* test is still good law, but as recently as the 1994 Court term, four justices have urged that the *Lemon* test be abandoned. Here is a settled area of law that may soon become unsettled.

20. *Rosenberger v. Rector and Visitors of the University of Virginia*, 115 S.Ct. 2510 (1995).

21. *Van Orden v. Perry*, 545 U.S. 677 (2005).

22. *McCreary v. ACLU*, 545 U.S. 844 (2005).

23. *West Virginia State Board of Education v. Barnette*, 319 U.S. 624 (1943). The case it reversed was *Minersville School District v. Gobitus*, 310 U.S. 586 (1940).

24. *Employment Division, Department of Human Resources of Oregon v. Smith*, 494 U.S. 872 (1990).

25. *City of Boerne v. Flores*, 117 S.Ct. 293 (1996).

26. *Abrams v. U.S.*, 250 U.S. 616 (1919).

27. *U.S. v. Carolene Products Company*, 304 U.S. 144 (1938), note 4. This footnote is one of the Court's most important doctrines. See Alfred H. Kelly, Winfred A. Harbison, and Herman Belz, *The American Constitution: Its Origins and Development*, 7th ed. (New York: Norton, 1991), vol. 2, 519–23.

28. *Schenk v. U.S.*, 249 U.S. 47 (1919).

29. *Brandenburg v. Ohio*, 395 U.S. 444 (1969).

30. *McConnell v. FEC*, 124 S.Ct. 34 (2003).

31. *Federal Election Commission v. Wisconsin Right to Life*, No. 06-969 (2007).

32. *Davis v. Federal Election Commission*, 07-320 (2008).

33. *Stromberg v. California*, 283 U.S. 359 (1931).

34. *Texas v. Johnson*, 488 U.S. 884 (1989).

35. *United States v. Eichman*, 496 U.S. 310 (1990).

36. Lizette Alvarez, "Measure to Ban Flag Burning Falls 4 Votes Short in the Senate," *New York Times*, March 30, 2000, p. A24; Adam Clymer, "House, in Ritual Vote, Opposes Flag Burning," *New York Times*, July 18, 2001, p. A20.

37. *Virginia v. Black*, 528 U.S. 343 (2003).

38. For a good general discussion of speech plus, see Louis Fisher, *American Constitutional Law* (New York:

McGraw-Hill, 1990), 544–46. The case upholding the buffer zone against the abortion protesters is *Madsen v. Women's Health Center*, 114 S.Ct. 2516 (1994).

39. *Rumsfeld v. FAIR*, No. 04-11152 (2006).
40. *Near v. Minnesota*, 283 U.S. 697 (1931).
41. *New York Times v. U.S.*, 403 U.S. 731 (1971).
42. *Branzburg v. Hayes*, 408 U.S. 656 (1972).
43. *New York Times v. Sullivan*, 376 U.S. 254 (1964).
44. *Hustler Magazine v. Falwell*, 108 S.Ct. 876 (1988).
45. See *Zeran v. America Online*, 129 F3d 327 (4th Cir. 1977).
46. *Roth v. U.S.*, 354 U.S. 476 (1957).
47. Concurring opinion in *Jacobellis v. Ohio*, 378 U.S. 184 (1964).
48. *Miller v. California*, 413 U.S. 15 (1973).
49. *Reno v. American Civil Liberties Union*, 117 S.Ct. 2329 (1997).
50. *U.S. v. American Library Association*, 539 U.S. 194 (2003).
51. *U.S. v. Williams*, 06-694 (2008).
52. *Chaplinsky v. State of New Hampshire*, 315 U.S. 568 (1942).
53. *Dennis v. United States*, 341 U.S. 494 (1951), which upheld the infamous Smith Act of 1940, which provided criminal penalties for those who "willfully and knowingly conspire to teach and advocate the forceful and violent overthrow and destruction of the government."
54. *Bethel School District No. 403 v. Fraser*, 478 U.S. 675 (1986).
55. *Hazelwood School District v. Kuhlmeier*, 108 S. Ct. 562 (1988).
56. *Morse v. Frederick*, No. 06-278 (2007).
57. *Meritor Savings Bank v. Vinson*, 477 U.S. 57 (1986).
58. *R.A.V. v. City of St. Paul*, 506 U.S. 377 (1992).
59. *Capital Broadcasting Company v. Acting Attorney General*, 405 U.S. 1000 (1972).
60. *Board of Trustees of the State University of New York v. Fox*, 109 S.Ct. 3028 (1989).
61. *City Council v. Taxpayers for Vincent*, 466 U.S. 789 (1984).
62. *Posadas de Puerto Rico Associates v. Tourism Company of Puerto Rico*, 479 U.S. 328 (1986).
63. Fisher, *American Constitutional Law*, 546.
64. *Bigelow v. Virginia*, 421 U.S. 809 (1975).
65. *Virginia State Board of Pharmacy v. Virginia Citizens Consumer Council*, 425 U.S. 748 (1976). Later cases restored the rights of lawyers to advertise their services.
66. *44 Liquormart, Inc. and Peoples Super Liquor Stores Inc., Petitioners v. Rhode Island and Rhode Island Liquor Stores Association*, 116 S.Ct. 1495 (1996).
67. *Lorillard Tobacco v. Reilly*, 121 S.Ct. 2404 (2001).
68. *Presser v. Illinois*, 116 U.S. 252 (1886).
69. *District of Columbia v. Heller*, No. 07-290 (2008).
70. *In re Winship*, 397 U.S. 361 (1970). An outstanding treatment of due process in issues involving the Fourth through Seventh Amendments will be found in Fisher, *American Constitutional Law*, chap. 13.
71. *Horton v. California*, 496 U.S. 128 (1990).
72. *McDonald v. Chicago*, 08-1521 (2010).
73. *Mapp v. Ohio*, 367 U.S. 643 (1961). Although Ms. Mapp went free in this case, she was later convicted in New York on narcotics trafficking charges and served nine years of a twenty-year sentence.
74. For a good discussion of the issue, see Fisher, *American Constitutional Law*, 884–89.
75. *U.S. v. Grubbs*, No. 04-1414 (2006).
76. *National Treasury Employees Union v. Von Raab*, 39 U.S. 656 (1989).
77. *Skinner v. Railroad Labor Executives Association*, 489 U.S. 602 (1989).
78. *Vernonia School District 47J v. Acton*, 115 S.Ct. 2386 (1985).
79. *Chandler et al. v. Miller, Governor of Georgia et al.*, 117 S.Ct. 1295 (1997).
80. *Indianapolis v. Edmund*, 531 U.S. 32 (2000), 121 S.Ct. 447 (2000).
81. *Brendlin v. California*, 06-8120 (2007).
82. *Ferguson v. Charleston*, 121 S.Ct. 1281 (2001).
83. *Kyllo v. U.S.*, 121 S.Ct. 2038 (2001).
84. *Safford Unified School District No. 1 v. No. Redding*, 08-479 (2009).
85. Corwin and Peltason, *Understanding the Constitution* (New York: Holt, 1967), 286.
86. *Miranda v. Arizona*, 348 U.S. 436 (1966).
87. *Berman v. Parker*, 348 U.S. 26 (1954). For a thorough analysis of the case see Benjamin Ginsberg, "*Berman v. Parker*: Congress, the Court, and the Public Purpose," *Polity* 4 (1971): 48–75. For a later application of the case that suggests that "just compensation"—defined as something approximating market value—is about all a property owner can hope for protection against a public taking of property, see Theodore Lowi et al., *Poliscide; Big Government, Big Science, Lilliputian Politics*, 2nd ed. (Lanham, MD: University Press of America, 1990), 267–70.
88. *Kelo v. City of New London*, 545 U.S. 469 (2005).
89. *Gideon v. Wainwright*, 372 U.S. 335 (1963). For a full account of the story of the trial and release of Clarence Earl Gideon, see Anthony Lewis, *Gideon's Trumpet* (New York: Random House, 1964). See also David O'Brien, *Storm Center*, 2nd ed. (New York: Norton, 1990).
90. *Wiggins v. Smith*, 123 S.Ct. 2527 (2003).
91. For further discussion of these issues, see Corwin and Peltason, *Understanding the Constitution*, 319–23.
92. *U.S. v. Gonzalez-Lopez*, No. 05-352 (2006).
93. *Furman v. Georgia*, 408 U.S. 238 (1972).
94. *Gregg v. Georgia*, 428 U.S. 153 (1976).
95. *Kennedy v. Louisiana*, No. 07–343 (2008).

96. *Snyder v. Louisiana*, No. 06–10119 (2008).

97. *Medellin v. Texas*, No. 06–984 (2008).

98. *Baze v. Rees*, 553 U.S. 35 (2008).

99. *Olmstead v. U.S.*, 227 U.S. 438 (1928). See also David M. O'Brien, *Constitutional Law and Politics*, 6th ed. (New York: Norton, 2005), vol. 1, 76–84.

100. *West Virginia State Board of Education v. Barnette*, 319 U.S. 624 (1943).

101. *NAACP v. Alabama ex rel. Patterson*, 357 U.S. 447 (1958).

102. *Griswold v. Connecticut*, 381 U.S. 479 (1965).

103. *Griswold v. Connecticut*, concurring opinion. In 1972, the Court extended the privacy right to unmarried women: *Eisenstadt v. Baird*, 405 U.S. 438 (1972).

104. *Roe v. Wade*, 410 U.S. 113 (1973).

105. *Webster v. Reproductive Health Services*, 109 S.Ct. 3040 (1989), which upheld a Missouri law that restricted the use of public medical facilities for abortion. The decision opened the way for other states to limit the availability of abortion.

106. *Planned Parenthood of Southeastern Pennsylvania v. Casey*, 112 S.Ct. 2791 (1992).

107. *Stenberg v. Carhart*, 120 S.Ct. 2597 (2000).

108. *Ayotte v. Planned Parenthood*, No. 546 U.S. 320 (2006).

109. *Gonzales v. Carhart*, No. 05-380 (2007).

110. *Bowers v. Hardwick*, 478 U.S. 186 (1986).

111. The dissenters were quoting an earlier case, *Olmstead v. United States*, 27 U.S. 438 (1928), to emphasize the nature of their disagreement with the majority in the *Bowers* case.

112. *Lawrence v. Texas*, 123 S.Ct. 2472 (2003).

113. It is worth recalling here the provision of the Ninth Amendment: "The enumeration in the Constitution, of certain rights, shall not be construed to deny or disparage others retained by the people."

114. *Gonzales v. Oregon*, No. 04-623 (2006).

115. *Lawrence v. Texas*, 539 U.S. 558 (2003).

116. In the 1965 case of *Griswald v. Connecticut*, 381 U.S. 479 (1965) the Supreme Court asserted that the Constitution created a "zone of privacy" for individuals. Since that decision, the Court has been attempting to explain what that zone includes and does not include.

117. *Gonzales v. Oregon*, 546 U.S. 243 (2006).

118. *Hamdi v. Rumsfeld*, 542 U.S. 507 (2004).

119. *Hamdan v. Rumsfeld*, No. 05-184 (2006).

120. *ACLU v. NSA*, 06-2095 (6th Cir. 2007).

Chapter 5

1. Paula Baker, "The Domestication of Politics: Women and American Political Society, 1780–1920," *American Historical Review* 89 (June 1984), 620–47.

2. Oscar Handlin, *America—A History* (New York: Holt, Rinehart & Winston, 1968), 474.

3. *Dred Scott v. Sandford*, 19 Howard 393 (1857).

4. August Meier and Elliot Rudwick, *From Plantation to Ghetto* (New York: Hill and Wang, 1976), 184–88.

5. Jill Dupont, "Susan B. Anthony," New York Notes (Albany: New York State Commission on the Bicentennial of the U.S. Constitution, 1988), 3.

6. *Plessy v. Ferguson*, 163 U.S. 537 (1896).

7. Dupont, "Susan B. Anthony," 4.

8. The prospect of a Fair Employment Practices law tied to the commerce power produced the Dixiecrat break with the Democratic Party in 1948. The Democratic Party organization of the States of the Old Confederacy seceded from the national party and nominated its own candidate, the then-Democratic governor of South Carolina, Strom Thurmond, who later became a Republican senator. This almost cost President Truman the election.

9. This was based on the provision in Article VI of the Constitution that "all treaties made, . . . under the Authority of the United States," shall be the "supreme Law of the Land." The committee recognized that if the U.S. Senate ratified the Human Rights Covenant of the United Nations—a treaty—then that power could be used as the constitutional umbrella for effective civil rights legislation. The Supreme Court had recognized in *Missouri v. Holland*, 252 U.S. 416 (1920), that a treaty could enlarge federal power at the expense of the states.

10. *Missouri ex rel. Gaines v. Canada*, 305 U.S. 337 (1938).

11. *Sweatt v. Painter*, 339 U.S. 629 (1950).

12. *Smith v. Allwright*, 321 U.S. 649 (1944).

13. *Shelley v. Kraemer*, 334 U.S. 1 (1948).

14. Kermit L. Hall, *The Magic Mirror: Law in American History* (New York: Oxford University Press, 1989), 322–24. See also Richard Kluger, *Simple Justice* (New York: Random House, Vintage Edition, 1977), 530–37.

15. The District of Columbia case came up too, but since the District of Columbia is not a state, this case did not directly involve the Fourteenth Amendment and its "equal protection" clause. It confronted the Court on the same grounds, however—that segregation is inherently unequal. Its victory in effect was "incorporation in reverse," with equal protection moving from the Fourteenth Amendment to become part of the Bill of Rights. See *Bolling v. Sharpe*, 347 U.S. 497 (1954).

16. *Brown v. Board of Education of Topeka, Kansas*, 347 U.S. 483 (1954).

17. The Supreme Court first declared that race was a suspect classification requiring strict scrutiny in the decision *Korematsu v. United States*, 323 U.S. 214 (1944). In this case, the Court upheld President Roosevelt's executive order of 1941 allowing the military to exclude persons of Japanese ancestry from the West Coast and to place them in internment camps. It is one of the few cases in which classification based on race survived strict scrutiny.

18. The two most important cases were *Cooper v. Aaron*, 358 U.S. 1 (1958), which required Little Rock, Arkansas, to desegregate; and *Griffin v. Prince Edward County School Board*, 377 U.S. 218 (1964), which forced all the schools of that Virginia county to reopen after five years of closing to avoid desegregation.

19. In *Cooper v. Aaron*, the Supreme Court ordered immediate compliance with the lower court's desegregation order and went beyond that with a stern warning that it is "emphatically the province and duty of the judicial department to say what the law is."

20. *Shuttlesworth v. Birmingham Board of Education*, 358 U.S. 101 (1958), upheld a "pupil placement" plan purporting to assign pupils on various bases, with no mention of race. This case interpreted *Brown* to mean that school districts must stop explicit racial discrimination but were under no obligation to take positive steps to desegregate. For a while black parents were doomed to case-by-case approaches.

21. For good treatments of this long stretch of the struggle of the federal courts to integrate the schools, see Paul Brest and Sanford Levinson, *Processes of Constitutional Decision-Making: Cases and Materials*, 2nd ed. (Boston: Little, Brown, 1983), 471–80; and Alfred Kelly et al., *The American Constitution: Its Origins and Development*, 6th ed. (New York: Norton, 1983), 610–16.

22. Pierre Thomas, "Denny's to Settle Bias Cases," *Washington Post*, May 24, 1994, p. A1.

23. See Hamil Harris, "For Blacks, Cabs Can Be Hard to Get," *Washington Post*, July 21, 1994, p. J1.

24. For a thorough analysis of the Office for Civil Rights, see Jeremy Rabkin, "Office for Civil Rights," in *The Politics of Regulation*, ed. James Q. Wilson (New York: Basic Books, 1980).

25. This was an accepted way of using quotas or ratios to determine statistically that blacks or other minorities were being excluded from schools or jobs, and then on the basis of that statistical evidence to authorize the Justice Department to bring suits in individual cases and in class action suits as well. In most segregated situations outside the South, it is virtually impossible to identify and document an intent to discriminate.

26. *Swann v. Charlotte-Mecklenburg Board of Education*, 402 U.S. 1 (1971).

27. *Milliken v. Bradley*, 418 U.S. 717 (1974).

28. For a good evaluation of the Boston effort, see Gary Orfield, *Must We Bus? Segregated Schools and National Policy* (Washington: Brookings Institution, 1978), 144–46. See also Bob Woodward and Scott Armstrong, *The Brethren: Inside the Supreme Court* (New York: Simon & Schuster, 1979), 426–27; and J. Anthony Lukas, *Common Ground* (New York: Random House, 1986).

29. *Board of Education v. Dowell*, 498 U.S. 237 (1991).

30. *Missouri v. Jenkins*, 115 S.Ct. 2038 (1995).

31. John A. Powell, "Segregated Schools Ruling Not All Bad: In Rejecting Seattle's Integration Bid, Top Court Majority Also Held that Avoiding Racial Isolation Is a Legitimate Public Goal," *Newsday*, July 16, 2007, p. A33.

32. See especially *Katzenbach v. McClung*, 379 U.S. 294 (1964). Almost immediately after passage of the Civil Rights Act of 1964, a case was brought challenging the validity of Title II, which covered discrimination in public accommodations. Ollie's Barbecue was a neighborhood restaurant in Birmingham, Alabama. It was located eleven blocks away from an interstate highway and even farther from railroad and bus stations. Its table service was for whites only; there was only a take-out service for blacks. The Supreme Court agreed that Ollie's was strictly an intrastate restaurant, but since a substantial proportion of its food and other supplies were bought from companies outside the state of Alabama, there was a sufficient connection to interstate commerce; therefore, racial discrimination at such restaurants would "impose commercial burdens of national magnitude upon interstate commerce." Although this case involved Title II, it had direct bearing on the constitutionality of Title VII.

33. *Griggs v. Duke Power Company*, 401 U.S. 24 (1971). See also Allan Sindler, *Bakke, DeFunis, and Minority Admissions* (New York: Longman, 1978), 180–89.

34. For a good treatment of these issues, see Charles O. Gregory and Harold A. Katz, *Labor and the Law* (New York: Norton, 1979), chap. 17.

35. In 1970, this act was amended to outlaw for five years literacy tests as a condition for voting in all states.

36. Joint Center for Political Studies, *Black Elected Officials: A National Roster—1988* (Washington, DC: Joint Center for Political Studies Press, 1988), 9–10. For a comprehensive analysis and evaluation of the Voting Rights Act, see Bernard Grofman and Chandler Davidson, eds., *Controversies in Minority Voting: The Voting Rights Act in Perspective* (Washington, DC: Brookings Institution Press, 1992).

37. Ford Fessenden, "Ballots Cast by Blacks and Older Voters Were Tossed in Far Greater Numbers," *New York Times*, November 12, 2001, p. A17.

38. See Douglas S. Massey and Nancy A. Denton, *American Apartheid: Segregation and the Making of the Underclass* (Cambridge, MA: Harvard University Press, 1993), chap. 7.

39. Reuters, "Countrywide Sued in Race Bias Case," *Los Angeles Times*, July 13, 2007, p. C2.

40. Michael Powell, "Bank Accused of Pushing Mortgage Deals on Blacks," *New York Times*, June 6, 2009; Office of the Illinois Attorney General, "Madigan Sues Wells Fargo for Discriminatory and Deceptive Mortgage Lending Practices, Press Release July 31, 2009," www.illinoisattorneygeneral.gov/pressroom/2009_07/20090731.html (accessed 10/23/09).

41. See Jane J. Mansbridge, *Why We Lost the ERA* (Chicago: University of Chicago Press, 1986); and Gilbert Steiner, *Constitutional Inequality* (Washington, DC: Brookings Institution Press, 1985).

42. See *Frontiero v. Richardson*, 411 U.S. 677 (1973).

43. See *Craig v. Boren*, 423 U.S. 1047 (1976).

44. *Franklin v. Gwinnett County Public Schools*, 503 U.S. 60 (1992).

45. Jennifer Halperin, "Women Step Up to Bat," *Illinois Issues* 21 (September 1995), 11–14.

46. Joan Biskupic and David Nakamura, "Court Won't Review Sports Equity Ruling," *Washington Post*, April 22, 1997, p. A1.

47. *U.S. v. Virginia*, 116 S.Ct. 2264 (1996).

48. Judith Havemann, "Two Women Quit Citadel over Alleged Harassment," *Washington Post*, January 13, 1997, p. A1.

49. *Meritor Savings Bank v. Vinson*, 477 U.S. 57 (1986). See also Gwendolyn Mink, *Hostile Environment—The Political Betrayal of Sexually Harassed Women* (Ithaca, NY: Cornell University Press, 2000), 28–32.

50. *Harris v. Forklift Systems, Inc.*, 510 U.S. 17 (1993).

51. *Burlington Industries v. Ellerth*, 118 S.Ct. 2257 (1998); *Faragher v. City of Boca Raton*, 118 S.Ct. 2275 (1998).

52. New Mexico had a different history because not many Anglos settled there initially. ("Anglo" is the term for a non-Hispanic white, generally of European background.) Mexican Americans had considerable power in territorial legislatures between 1865 and 1912. See Lawrence H. Fuchs, *The American Kaleidoscope* (Hanover, NH: University Press of New England, 1990), 239–40.

53. *Salvatierra v. Del Rio Independent School District*, 1931 (Texas).

54. David Montgomery, "A First Class Civil Rights Lesson," *Washington Post*, October 9, 2007, p. C01; *Mendez v. Westminster School District, et al.*, 64 F. Supp. 544 (S.D. Cal. 1946), 64 F. Supp. 544 (D.C.CAL. 1946), http://w3.uchastings.edu/wingate/Mendez%20v.htm (accessed 3/28/08).

55. On La Raza Unida Party, see "La Raza Unida Party and the Chicano Student Movement in California," in *Latinos in the American Political System*, ed. F. Chris Garcia (Notre Dame, IN: University of Notre Dame Press, 1988), 213–35.

56. Dick Kirschten, "Not Black and White," *National Journal*, March 2, 1991, p. 497.

57. Krissah Thompson, "Justice Department to Address Backlog of Civil Rights Complaints," September 25, 2009, www.washingtonpost.com/wp-dyn/content/article/2009/09/25/AR2009092502151.html?nav=emailpage (accessed 10/27/09).

58. Anna Gorman, "ICE-Local Alliance to Stay; but Immigration Enforcement Will Be Subject to More Federal Oversight, Officials Say," *Los Angeles Times*, October 17, 2009, p. 16.

59. *United States v. Wong Kim Ark*, 169 U.S. 649 (1898).

60. *Korematsu v. United States*, 323 U.S. 214 (1944).

61. Children of the Camps, http://pbs.org/childofcamp/history/civilact.html (accessed 2/17/08).

62. *Lau v. Nichols*, 414 U.S. 563 (1974).

63. Not all Indian tribes agreed with this, including the Navajos. See Ronald Takaki, *A Different Mirror: A History of Multicultural America* (Boston: Little, Brown: 1993), 238–45.

64. On the resurgence of Indian political activity, see Stephen Cornell, *The Return of the Native: American Indian Political Resurgence* (New York: Oxford University Press, 1990); and Dee Brown, *Bury My Heart at Wounded Knee* (New York: Holt, 1971).

65. See the discussion in Robert A. Katzmann, *Institutional Disability: The Saga of Transportation Policy for the Disabled* (Washington, DC: Brookings Institution Press, 1986).

66. For example, after pressure from the Justice Department, one of the nation's largest rental-car companies agreed to make special hand controls available to any customer requesting them. See "Avis Agrees to Equip Cars for Disabled," *Los Angeles Times*, September 2, 1994, p. D1.

67. The case and the interview with Stephen Bokat were reported in Margaret Warner, "Expanding Coverage," *The News-Hour with Jim Lehrer*, July 1, 1998, www.pbs.org/newshour/bb/law/jan-june98/hiv_6-30.html (accessed 2/18/08).

68. Supreme Court of the United States, *Gross v. FBL Financial Service, Inc.*, No. 08-411, www.supremecourtus.gov/opinions/08pdf/08-441.pdf (accessed 10/22/09).

69. *Bowers v. Hardwick*, 478 U.S. 186 (1986).

70. Quoted in Joan Biskupic, "Gay Rights Activists Seek a Supreme Court Test Case," *Washington Post*, December 19, 1993, p. A1.

71. *Romer v. Evans*, 116 S.Ct. 1620 (1996).

72. *Lawrence v. Texas*, 123 S.Ct. 2472 (2003).

73. From Lyndon B. Johnson, *The Vantage Point* (New York: Holt, Rinehart, and Winston, 1971), 166.

74. The Department of Health, Education, and Welfare (HEW) was the cabinet department charged with administering most federal social programs. In 1980, when education programs were transferred to the newly created Department of Education, HEW was renamed the Department of Health and Human Services.

75. *Regents of the University of California v. Bakke*, 438 U.S. 265 (1978).

76. See, for example, *United Steelworkers v. Weber*, 443 U.S. 193 (1979); and *Fullilove v. Klutznick*, 100 S.Ct. 2758 (1980).

77. *Ward's Cove v. Atonio*, 109 S.Ct. 2115 (1989).

78. *Adarand Constructors v. Pena*, 115 S.Ct. 2097 (1995).

79. *Gratz v. Bollinger*, 123 S.Ct. 2411 (2003).

80. *Grutter v. Bollinger*, 123 S.Ct. 2325 (2003).

81. Michael A. Fletcher, "Opponents of Affirmative Action Heartened by Court Decision," *Washington Post*, April 13, 1997, p. A21.

82. See Sam Howe Verhovek, "Houston Vote Underlined Complexity of Rights Issue," *New York Times*, November 6, 1997, p. A1.

83. CNN/Opinion Research Corporation, "CNN/Opinion Research Corporation Poll, January 12–15, 2009," www.pollingreport.com/race.htm (accessed 10/23/09).

84. Frank Newport, "Little 'Obama Effect' on Views about Race Relations; Attitudes toward Race Not Significantly Improved from Previous Years," October 29, 2009, www.gallup.com/poll/123944/Little-Obama-Effect-Views-Race-Relations.aspx (accessed 10/30/09).

85. There are still many genuine racists in America, but with the exception of a lunatic fringe, made up of neo-Nazis and members of the Ku Klux Klan, most racists are too ashamed or embarrassed to take part in normal political discourse. They are not included in either category here.

86. *Slaughterhouse Cases*, 16 Wallace 36 (1873).

87. See Paul M. Sniderman and Edward G. Carmines, *Reaching beyond Race* (Cambridge, MA: Harvard University Press, 1997).

Chapter 6

1. Carol Glynn et al., *Public Opinion*, 2nd ed. (Boulder, CO: Westview, 2004), 293.

2. For a discussion of the political beliefs of Americans, see Harry Holloway and John George, *Public Opinion* (New York: St. Martin's, 1986). See also Paul R. Abramson, *Political Attitudes in America* (San Francisco: Freeman, 1983).

3. See Paul M. Sniderman and Edward G. Carmines, *Reaching beyond Race* (Cambridge, MA: Harvard University Press, 1997).

4. See Angus Campbell et al., *The American Voter* (New York: Wiley, 1960), 147.

5. CNN Poll, 2009.

6. CNN Poll, 2009.

7. CNN Poll, 2009.

8. CBS News/New York Times Poll, 2008.

9. Donald Green, Bradley Palmquist, and Eric Schickler, *Partisan Hearts and Minds: Political Parties and the Social Identities of Voters* (New Haven, CT: Yale University Press, 2002).

10. David S. Broder, "Partisan Gap Is at a High, Poll Finds," *Washington Post*, November 9, 2003, p. A6.

11. Pamela Johnston Conover, "The Role of Social Groups in Political Thinking," *British Journal of Political Science* 18 (1988), 51–78.

12. See Michael C. Dawson, "Structure and Ideology: The Shaping of Black Opinion," paper presented at the annual meeting of the Midwest Political Science Association, Chicago, Illinois, April 7–9, 1995. See also Michael C. Dawson, *Behind the Mule: Race, Class, and African American Politics* (Princeton, NJ: Princeton University Press, 1994).

13. Elisabeth Noelle-Neumann, *The Spiral of Silence* (Chicago: University of Chicago Press, 1984).

14. O. R. Holsti, "A Widening Gap between the Military and Society? Some Evidence, 1976–1996," *International Security* 23 (Winter 1998–1999), 5–42.

15. Michael X. Delli Carpini and Scott Keeter, *What Americans Know about Politics and Why It Matters* (New Haven, CT: Yale University Press, 1996).

16. For a discussion of the role of information in democratic politics, see Arthur Lupia and Matthew D. McCubbins, *The Democratic Dilemma: Can Citizens Learn What They Need to Know?* (New York: Cambridge University Press, 1998).

17. Larry M. Bartels, "Homer Gets a Tax Cut: Inequality and Public Policy in the American Mind," paper prepared for presentation at the annual meeting of the American Political Science Association, Philadelphia, August 2003.

18. Sniderman and Carmines, *Reaching beyond Race*, chap. 4.

19. Benjamin Ginsberg, *The American Lie: Government by the People and Other Political Fables* (Boulder, CO: Paradigm, 2007).

20. Gerald F. Seib and Michael K. Frisby, "Selling Sacrifice," *Wall Street Journal*, February 5, 1993, p. 1.

21. Joshua Green, "The Other War Room," *Washington Monthly*, April 2002.

22. Peter Marks, "Adept in Politics and Advertising, 4 Women Shape a Campaign," *New York Times*, November 11, 2001, p. B6.

23. See Gillian Peele, *Revival and Reaction* (Oxford, UK: Clarendon, 1985). Also see Connie Paige, *The Right-to-Lifers* (New York: Summit, 1983).

24. See David Vogel, "The Power of Business in America: A Reappraisal," *British Journal of Political Science* 13 (January 1983), 19–44.

25. See David Vogel, "The Public Interest Movement and the American Reform Tradition," *Political Science Quarterly* 96 (Winter 1980), 607–27.

26. Jason DeParle, "The Clinton Welfare Bill Begins Trek in Congress," *New York Times*, July 15, 1994, p. 1.

27. Joe Queenan, "Birth of a Notion," *Washington Post*, September 20, 1992, p. C1.

28. John Zaller, *The Nature and Origins of Mass Opinion* (New York: Cambridge University Press, 1992).

29. See Shanto Iyengar, *Is Anyone Responsible? How Television Frames Political Issues* (Chicago: University of Chicago Press, 1991); and Shanto Iyengar, *Do the Media Govern?* (Thousand Oaks, CA: Sage, 1997).

30. Herbert Asher, *Polling and the Public* (Washington, DC: CQ Press, 2001), 64.

31. Anna Greenberg and Michael Bocian, "Uncertainty in Internet-Based Polling," paper presented at the Annual Meeting of the American Association of Public Opinion Research, 2000.

32. Carl Cannon, "A Pox on Both Our Parties," in *The Enduring Debate*, ed. David C. Canon et al. (New York: Norton, 2000), 389.

33. John Goyder, Keith Warriner, and Susan Miller, "Evaluating Socio-economic Status Bias in Survey Nonresponse," *Journal of Official Statistics* 18, no. 1 (2002).

34. Michael Kagay and Janet Elder, "Numbers Are No Problem for Pollsters, Words Are," *New York Times*, August 9, 1992, p. E6.

35. "Dial S for Smear," *Memphis Commercial Appeal*, September 22, 1996, p. 6B.

36. Amy Keller, "Subcommittee Launches Investigation of Push Polls," *Roll Call*, October 3, 1996, p. 1.

37. For a discussion of the growing difficulty of persuading people to respond to surveys, see John Brehm, *Phantom Respondents* (Ann Arbor: University of Michigan Press, 1993).

38. For an excellent and reflective discussion by a journalist, see Richard Morin, "Clinton Slide in Survey Shows Perils of Polling," *Washington Post*, August 29, 1992, p. A6.

39. See Michael Traugott, "The Impact of Media Polls on the Public," in *Media Polls in American Politics*, ed. Thomas E. Mann and Eary Orren (Washington, DC: Brookings Institution Press, 1992), 125–49.

40. Christopher Wlezien and Stuart Soroka, "The Relationship between Public Opinion and Policy," in Russell Dalton and Hans-Dieter Klingemann, eds., *Oxford Handbook of Political Behavior* (New York: Oxford, 2009), 799–817.

41. John Kingdon, *Agendas, Attitudes and Public Policy*, 2nd ed. (New York: Longman, 2003).

Chapter 7

1. UPI.com, "*Stars & Stripes* Reporter Barred from Mosul," June 24, 2009, www.upi.com/Top_News/2009/06/24/Stars-Stripes-reporter-barred-from-Mosul/UPI.

2. Dan Baltz and Anne E. Kornblut, "Public Voice Adds Edge to Debate," *Washington Post*, July 24, 2007, p. 1.

3. Jose Antonio Vargas, "For Candidates, Web Is Power and Poison," *Washington Post*, November 8, 2007, p. A6.

4. Amy Schatz, "BO, UR So Gr8: How a Young Tech Entrepreneur Translated Barack Obama into the Idiom of Facebook," *Wall Street Journal*, May 26, 2007, p. 1.

5. Samantha M. Shapiro, "The Dean Connection," *New York Times Magazine*, December 7, 2003, p. 58.

6. Amy Schatz, "Local Politics, Web Money," *Wall Street Journal*, September 28, 2007, p. A6.

7. Leslie Wayne, "A Fund-Raising Rainmaker Arises Online," *New York Times*, November 29, 2007, p. A22.

8. June Kronholz and Amy Schatz, "How Conservatives Enhanced Online Voice," *Wall Street Journal*, July 3, 2007, p. A5.

9. David Perlmutter, "Photojournalism in Crisis," *Editor and Publisher*, August 2006, www.editorandpublisher.com/eandp/columns/shoptalk_display.jsp?vnu_content_id=1003019475.

10. *Red Lion Broadcasting Company v. FCC*, 395 U.S. 367 (1969).

11. U.S. Census Bureau, *Statistical Abstract of the United States: 2007* (Washington, DC: U.S. Government Printing Office, 2007); "How Much Information? 2003," www.2.sims.berkeley.edu/research/projects/how-much-info-2003/broadcast.htm (accessed 2/20/08).

12. For a criticism of the increasing consolidation of the media, see the essays in Patricia Aufderheide et al., *Conglomerates and the Media* (New York: New Press, 1997).

13. See Ben Bagdikian, *The New Media Monopoly* (Boston: Beacon Press, 2004).

14. See Benjamin Ginsberg, *The Captive Public* (New York: Basic Books, 1986).

15. Pew Research Center for the People and the Press, May 2004.

16. University of Connecticut, Department of Public Policy, May 2005.

17. Katherine Q. Seelye, "Citizen-Journalism Project Gains a Voice in the Campaign," *New York Times*, July 25, 2008, p. A14.

18. *New York Times v. U.S.*, 403 U.S. 713 (1971).

19. Michael Massing, "The Press: The Enemy Within," *New York Review of Books*, December 15, 2005, p. 6.

20. See Tom Burnes, "The Organization of Public Opinion," in *Mass Communication and Society*, ed. James Curran (Beverly Hills, CA: Sage, 1979), 44–230. See also David Altheide, *Creating Reality* (Beverly Hills, CA: Sage, 1976).

21. David J. Garrow, *Protest at Selma: Martin Luther King, Jr., and the Voting Rights Act of 1965* (New Haven, CT: Yale University Press, 2001).

22. See Todd Gitlin, *The Whole World Is Watching* (Berkeley: University of California Press, 1980).

23. Katherine Q. Seelye, "Obama Plays Convincing Obama in a Skit Mocking Clinton," *New York Times*, November 5, 2007, p. A17.

24. See Martin Linsky, *Impact: How the Press Affects Federal Policymaking* (New York: Norton, 1986).

Chapter 8

1. Douglas R. Hess and Jody Herman, "Representational Bias in the 2008 Electorate, November 2009", www.projectvote.org/reports-on-the-electorate-/440.html (accessed 11/21/09).

2. Joanne Laucius, "Vote or Die?" *Ottawa Citizen*, November 4, 2004, p. A8.

3. The OnLine News Hour, Generation Next: Speak Up Be Heard, "Iraq, Economy Weigh on Minds of Young Voters," August 31, 2007, www.pbs.org/newshour/generation-next/demographic/youthvote_08-31.html (accessed 2/21/08).

4. For a discussion of the decline of voting turnout over time, see Ruy A. Teixeira, *The Disappearing American Voter* (Washington, DC: Brookings Institution Press, 1992). On the 1994 elections, see Paul Taylor, "Behind the Broom of '94: Wealthier, Educated Voters," *Washington Post*, June 8, 1995, p. A12.

5. Sidney Verba, Kay Lehman Schlozman, and Henry E. Brady, *Voice and Equality: Civic Voluntarism in American Politics* (Cambridge, MA: Harvard University Press, 1995), chap. 3, for kinds of participation, and pp. 66–67 for prevalence of local activity.

6. For a discussion of citizen lobbying, see Jeffrey M. Berry, *The New Liberalism: The Rising Power of Citizen Groups* (Washington, DC: Brookings Institution Press, 1999).

7. Laurie Davies, "25 Years of Saving Lives, 1980–2005," www.madd.org/getattachment/48e81e1b-df43-4f31-b9al-d94d5b940e62/MADD-25-Years-of-Saving-Lives.aspx (accessed 12/6/09).

8. Nina Bernstein, "In the Streets, Suddenly, An Immigrant Groundswell," *New York Times*, March 27, 2006, p. 14.

9. Emma Brown, James Hohmann, and Perry Bacon, Jr., "Lashing Out at the Capitol Tens of Thousands Protest Obama Initiatives and Government Spending," *Washington Post*, September 13, 2009, www.washingtonpost.com/wp-dyn/content/article/2009/09/12/AR2009091200971.html?sid=ST2009091201255 (accessed 12/6/09).

10. The American National Election Studies (ANES), "American National Election Study, 2008: Pre- and Post-Election Survey" [Computer file], ICPSR25383-v1, Ann Arbor, MI: Inter-university Consortium for Political and Social Research [distributor], 2009-06-10. doi:10.3886/ICPSR25383 (accessed 12/4/09).

11. Michael McDonald, "Voter Turnout," *United States Election Project*, http://elections.gmu.edu/voter_turnout.htm (accessed 11/20/09).

12. Douglas R. Hess and Jody Herman, "Representational Bias in the 2008 Electorate," November 2009, www.projectvote.org/reports-on-the-electorate-/440.html (accessed 11/21/09).

13. Robert Jackman, "Political Institutions and Voter Turnout in the Democracies," *American Political Science Review* 81 (June 1987): 420.

14. Aaron Smith, "The Internet's Role in Campaign 2008," Washington, DC: Pew Research Center, 2009, www.pewinternet.org/~/media//Files/Reports/2009/The_Internets_Role_in_Campaign_2008.pdf, pp. 3–4. (accessed 3/5/10).

15. Aaron Smith, "The Internet's Role in Campaign 2008," Washington, DC: Pew Research Center, 2009, www.pewinternet.org/~/media//Files/Reports/2009/The_Internets_Role_in_Campaign_2008.pdf, pp. 10–11. (accessed 3/5/10).

16. Aaron Smith, Kay Lehman Schlozman, Sidney Verba, and Henry Brady, "The Internet and Civic Engagement," Washington, DC: Pew Research Center, 2009, pp. 3–5, 54, 58, www.pewinternet.org/~/media//Files/Reports/2009/The%20Internet%20and%20Civic%20Engagement.pdf, p. 4.

17. Smith et al., "The Internet and Civic Engagement," p. 56. (accessed 3/5/10).

18. See William Julius Wilson, *The Truly Disadvantaged: The Inner City, the Underclass, and Public Policy* (Chicago: University of Chicago Press, 1987); and Douglas Massey and Nancy Denton, *American Apartheid: Segregation and the Making of the American Underclass* (Cambridge, MA: Harvard University Press, 1993).

19. See Michael C. Dawson, *Behind the Mule: Race and Class in African-American Politics* (Princeton, NJ: Princeton University Press, 1994), chaps. 5 and 6.

20. Dawson, *Behind the Mule.*

21. U.S. Census Bureau, "Resident Population by Race, Hispanic Origin Status, and Age—Projections," www.census.gov/compendia/statab/cats/population/estimates_and_projections_by_age_sex_raceethnicity.html (accessed 11/25/09).

22. Douglas R. Hess and Jody Herman, "Representational Bias in the 2008 Electorate, November 2009," www.projectvote.org/reports-on-the-electorate-/440.html (accessed 11/21/09).

23. Center for Health Policy, University of New Mexico, "New Survey Shows Overwhelming Support Among Latinos for Health Care Reform that Includes Public Option," November 30, 2009, http://healthpolicy.unm.edu/resources/new-survey-shows-overwhelming-support-among-latinos-health-care-reform-includes-public-opt (accessed 12/1/09).

24. Liz Sidoti, "Keeping Latino Support a Big Challenge for Obama," *Associated Press*, November 29, 2009, www.chron.com/disp/story.mpl/nation/6743401.html (accessed 11/29/09).

25. U.S. Census Bureau "Resident Population by Race, Hispanic Origin Status, and Age—Projections," www.census.gov/compendia/statab/cats/population/estimates_and_projections_by_age_sex_raceethnicity.html (accessed 11/24/09).

26. U.S. Census Bureau, "Reported Voting and Registration by Race, Hispanic Origin, Sex, and Age Groups: November 1964 to 2008"; "Reported Voting and Registration by Region, Educational Attainment, and Labor Force: November 1964 to 2008" CNN National Exit Poll 2008, www.cnn.com/ELECTION/2008/results/polls/#USP00p1 (accessed 11/22/09).

27. Anne E. Kornblut, "Bush Plan to Win over Democratic Voters Lags," *Boston Globe* (April 27, 2003), p. A1.

28. CNN.com, "America Votes, 2006."

29. Ronald Brownstein, "Response to Terror: The Times Poll," *Los Angeles Times*, November 15, 2001, p. A1.

30. Dan Balz and Jon Cohen, "Majority in Poll Favor Deadline for Iraq Pullout," *Washington Post*, February 27, 2007, p. A1.

31. Gallup Poll, January 2003.

32. Center for American Women and Politics, "Gender Gap in 2004 Presidential Race is Widespread" (November 10, 2004), www.cawp.rutgers.edu/Facts/Elections/GG2004widespread.pdf (accessed 2/22/08).

33. National Conference of State Legislatures, "Women in State Legislatures: 2009 Legislative Session," www.ncsl.org/default.aspx?tabid=15398 (accessed 11/25/09).

34. Kira Sanbonmatsu, "Political Parties and the Recruitment of Women to State Legislatures," *Journal of Politics* 64, no. 3 (August 2002), 791–809; Jennifer L Lawless and Richard L. Fox, *Why Are Women Still Not Running for Public Office?* Washington, DC: Brookings Institution (May 2008).

35. Center for American Women and Politics, "The Impact of Women in Public Office: Findings at a Glance" (New Brunswick, NJ: Rutgers University, n.d.).

36. Paul Taylor, Rich Morin, D'Vera Cohn, April Clark, and Wendy Wang, "A Paradox in Public Attitudes: Men or Women: Who's the Better Leader?" (Pew Research Center, August 25, 2008), p. 25, http://pewsocialtrends.org/assets/pdf/gender-leadership.pdf (accessed 12/6/09).

Rating the Genders

Are men or women in public office better at . . .

	Men %	Women %	Same %	DK/Ref. %
Standing up for what they believe	16	23	57	4
Keeping government honest	10	34	51	5
Working out compromise	16	42	39	3
Dealing with crime and public safety	42	12	44	2
Dealing with education and health care	7	52	40	1
Representing interests of people like you	18	28	50	4
Dealing with national security and defense	54	7	36	3

37. *Engel v. Vitale*, 370 U.S. 421 (1962); *Abington School District v. Schempp*, 374 U.S. 203 (1963); *Roe v. Wade*, 410 U.S. 113 (1973).

38. Laurie Goodstein, "Bush's Charity Plan Is Raising Concerns for Religious Right," *New York Times*, March 3, 2001, p. A1.

39. Emily Hoban Kirby and Kei Kawashima-Ginsberg, "The Youth Vote in 2008," Center for Information and Research on Civic Learning and Engagement, August 17, 2009, www.civicyouth.org/?page_id=241 (accessed 11/25/09).

40. Michael DeCourcy Hinds, "Youth Vote 2000: They'd Rather Volunteer," *Carnegie Reporter* 1, no. 2 (Spring 2001): 2.

41. Kristen Oshyn and Tova Andrea Wang, "Issue Brief: Youth Vote 2008," (Century Foundation), www.tcf.org/publications/electionreform/youthvote.pdf (accessed 2/21/08).

42. Kirby and Kei Kawashima-Ginsberg, "The Youth Vote in 2008," *The Center for Information & Research on Civic Learning & Engagement*, August 17, 2009, www.civicyouth.org/?page_id=241 (accessed 11/25/09).

43. CNN National Exit Poll 2008, www.cnn.com/ELECTION/2008/results/polls/#USP00p1 (accessed 11/22/2009).

44. Emily Hoban Kirby, Karlo Barrios Marcelo, and Kei Kawashima-Ginsberg "Volunteering and the College Experience," Center for Information & Research on Civic Learning & Engagement, August 2009, www.civicyouth.org/?page_id=237 (accessed 11/25/09).

45. The Center for Information & Research on Civic Learning & Engagement, "Millennials Talk Politics: A Study of College Student Political Engagement," 2007, www.civicyouth.org/?page_id=250 (accessed 11/29/09).

46. U.S. Census Bureau, "Statistical Abstract of the United States: 2008," Table 404: Voting-Age Population, Percent Reporting Registered, and Voted: 1994 to 2006.

47. CNN National Exit Poll 2008, www.cnn.com/ELECTION/2008/results/polls/#USP00p1 (accessed 11/22/09).

48. See Richard A. Brody, "The Puzzle of Political Participation in America," in *The New American Political System*, ed. Anthony King (Washington, DC: American Enterprise Institute, 1978), chap. 8.

49. On the nineteenth century, see Michael E. McGerr, *The Decline of Popular Politics: The American North, 1865–1928* (New York: Oxford University Press, 1986).

50. Verba, Schlozman, and Brady, *Voice and Equality*.

51. See Alexis de Tocqueville, *Democracy in America* (New York: Vintage, 1945).

52. Robert D. Putnam, "Bowling Alone: America's Declining Social Capital," *Journal of Democracy* 6, no. 1 (January 1995): 65–78.

53. On television see Robert D. Putnam, "Tuning In, Tuning Out: The Strange Disappearance of Social Capital in America," *PS: Political Science and Politics* 28, no. 4 (December 1995): 664–83; for a reply see Pippa Norris, "Does Television Erode Social Capital? A Reply to Putnam," *PS: Political Science and Politics* 29, no. 3 (September 1996): 474–80.

54. Michael Schudson, "What If Civic Life Didn't Die?" *American Prospect* 25 (March–April 1996): 17–20.

55. Steven J. Rosenstone and John Mark Hansen, *Mobilization, Participation, and Democracy in America*, (New York: Macmillan Pub. Co.; Toronto: Maxwell Macmillan Canada; New York: Maxwell Macmillan International, c1993), 59.

56. Robert A. Jackson, Robert D. Brown, and Gerald C. Wright, "Registration, Turnout and the Electoral Representativeness of U.S. State Electorates," *American Politics Quarterly* 26, no. 3 (July 1998): 259–87. See also, Benjamin Highton, "Easy Registration and Voter Turnout," *Journal of Politics* 59, no. 2 (April 1997): 565–87.

57. Connie Cass, "'Motor Voter' Impact Slight," *Chattanooga News-Free Press*, June 20, 1997, p. A5. On the need to motivate voters see Marshall Ganz, "Motor Voter or Motivated Voter?" *American Prospect*, no. 28 (September–October 1996): 41–49. On the hopes for Motor Voter, see Frances Fox Piven and Richard A. Cloward, "Northern Bourbons: A Preliminary Report on the National Voter Registration Act," *PS: Political Science and Politics* 29, no. 1 (March 1996): 39–42. On turnout in the 1996 election, see Barbara Vobejda, "Just under Half of Possible Voters Went to the Polls," *Washington Post*, November 7, 1996, p. A3.

58. The data in this paragraph are drawn from The Sentencing Project and Human Rights Watch, "Losing the Vote: The Impact of Felony Disfranchisement Laws in the United States" (October 1998), www.sentencingproject.org/tmp/File/FVR/fd_losingthevote.pdf (accessed 2/22/08).

59. Sentencing Project, "Expanding the Vote: State Felony Disenfranchisement Reform, 1997–2008," September 25, 2008, www.sentencingproject.org/detail/news.cfm?news_id=492 (accessed 11/30/09).

60. Ryan S. King, "Expanding the Vote: State Felony Disenfranchisement Reform, 1997–2008" (Sentencing Project, September 2008), www.sentencingproject.org/doc/publications/fd_statedisenfranchisement.pdf; (accessed 12/5/09).

61. Chris Uggen and Jeffrey Manza, "Democratic Contraction: Political Consequences of Felon Disenfranchisement in the United States," *American Sociological Review* 2002 67, no. 6: 777–803.

62. Michael McDonald, "2008 Early Voting Statistics," *United States Election Project*, http://elections.gmu.edu/early vote 2008.html (accessed 11/20/09).

63. Democracy Corps, "The 2008 Early Vote," January 13, 2009, www.democracycorps.com/strategy/2009/01/the-2008-electorate/?section=Analysis (accessed 12/5/09).

64. "Voting by Mail and Turnout: A Replication and Extension," Early Voting Information Center, www.earlyvoting.net/blog/node/155 (accessed 12/5/09); Paul Gronke, Eva Galanes-Rosenbaum, and Peter Miller, "Early Voting and Turnout," *PS: Political Science and Politics* 40, no.4 (October 2007), 639–45.

65. Lawrence Bobo and Franklin D. Gilliam, "Race, Sociopolitical Participation, and Black Empowerment," *American Political Science Review* 24, no. 2 (June 1990): 377–93.

66. Rosenstone and Hansen, Mobilization, Participation, and Democracy in America, 59.

67. Alan S. Gerber and Donald P. Green, "The Effects of Canvassing, Telephone Calls, and Direct Mail on Voter Turnout: A Field Experiment," The American Political Science Review 94, no. 3 (September 2000): 660.

68. Donald P. Green and Alan S. Gerber, "Getting Out the Youth Vote: Results from Randomized Field Experiments," December 29, 2001, pp. 26–27, www.youngvoterstrategies.org (accessed 3/8/08).

69. Student PIRGs New Voter Project, "Text Reminders Increase Primary Youth Turnout," October 2008, www.newvotersproject.org/research/text-messaging (accessed 11/30/09).

70. Erik Austin and Jerome Chubb, *Political Facts of the United States since 1789* (New York: Columbia University Press, 1986), 378–79.

71. Kenneth N. Weine, "Campaigns without a Human Face," *Washington Post*, October 27, 1996, p. C1; see also Margaret Weir and Marshall Ganz, "Reconnecting People and Politics," in *The New Majority: Toward Popular Progressive Politics*, ed. Stanley B. Greenberg and Theda Skocpol, (New Haven, CT: Yale University Press, 1997), 149–71.

72. Douglas R. Hess and Jody Herman, "Representational Bias in the 2008 Electorate, November 2009," www.projectvote.org/reports-on-the-electorate-/440.html, p. 25, (accessed 12/5/09).

73. *Buckley v. Valeo*, 424 U.S. 1 (1976).

74. See Christopher Lasch, *The Revolt of the Elites and the Betrayal of American Democracy* (New York: Norton, 1995). The idea of the "secession of the rich" comes from Robert Reich, *The Work of Nations* (New York: Knopf, 1991), chaps. 23 and 24.

Chapter 9

1. See Matthew Crenson and Benjamin Ginsberg, *Downsizing Democracy* (Baltimore, MD: Johns Hopkins University Press, 2002).

2. See Morris Fiorina, "Parties and Partisanship: A Forty Year Retrospective," *Political Behavior* 24, no. 2 (June 2002): 93–115.

3. Benjamin Ginsberg, *The Consequences of Consent* (New York: Random House, 1982), chap. 4.

4. For a discussion of third parties in the United States, see Daniel Mazmanian, *Third Parties in Presidential Election* (Washington, DC: Brookings Institution Press, 1974).

5. Alex Isenstadt, "Tea Party Candidates Falling Short," *Politico* March 7, 2010, www.politico.com/news/stories/0310/34041.html (accessed 3/11/10).

6. See Maurice Duverger, *Political Parties* (New York: Wiley, 1954).

7. Glen Justice, "F.E.C. Declines to Curb Independent Fund Raisers," *New York Times*, May 14, 2004, p. A16.

8. Jim Rutenberg and David D. Kirkpatrick, "A New Channel for Soft Money Appears in Race," *New York Times*, November 12, 2007, p. A1.

9. See Harold Gosnell, *Machine Politics Chicago Model*, rev. ed. (Chicago: University of Chicago Press, 1968).

10. For a useful discussion, see John Bibby and Thomas Holbrook, "Parties and Elections," in *Politics in the American States*, ed. Virginia Gray and Herbert Jacob (Washington, DC: Congressional Quarterly Press, 1996), 78–121.

11. Kyle L. Saunders and Alan I. Abramowitz, "Ideological Realignment and Active Partisans in the American Electorate," *American Politics Research* 32 (May 2004): 285–309.

12. John C. Green, "Religion and the Presidential Vote: A Tale of Two Gaps" (Pew Forum on Religion and Public Life, August, 21, 2007), www.pewforum.org/docs/?DocID=240 (accessed 2/24/08).

13. Christopher Shea, "Who Are You Calling Working Class?" *Boston Globe*, February 12, 2006, www.boston.com/news/globe/ideas/articles/2006/02/12/who_are_you_calling_working_class/ (accessed 2/24/08).

14. For an excellent analysis of the parties' role in recruitment, see Paul Herrnson, *Congressional Elections: Campaigning at Home and in Washington* (Washington, DC: Congressional Quarterly Press, 1995).

15. Daniel Galvin, *Presidential Party Building: Dwight D. Eisenhower to George W. Bush*. Princeton N.J.: Princeton University Press, 2009.

16. Duverger, *Political Parties*, 426.

17. Duverger, *Political Parties*, chap. 1.

18. Stanley Kelley, Jr., Richard E. Ayres, and William Bowen, "Registration and Voting: Putting First Things First," *American Political Science Review* 61 (June 1967): 359–70.

19. David H. Fischer, *The Revolution of American Conservatism* (New York: Harper & Row, 1965), 93.

20. Fischer, *The Revolution of American Conservatism*, 109.

21. Henry Jones Ford, *The Rise and Growth of American Politics* (1898 reprint; New York: Da Capo Press, 1967 edition), chap. 9.

22. Ford, *The Rise and Growth of American Politics*, 125.

23. Ford, *The Rise and Growth of American Politics*, 125.

24. Ford, *The Rise and Growth of American Politics*, 126.

25. Walter Dean Burnham, "The End of American Party Politics, 1969", *Transaction* no. 7 (Dec.), 12–22.

26. Raymond J. La Raja, "Political Parties in the Era of Soft Money," in *The Parties Respond: Changes in American Parties and Campaigns*, 4th ed., ed. Sandy L. Maisel (Boulder, CO: Westview Press, 2002), p 163–88.

27. On the limited polarization among ordinary voters, see Morris P. Fiorina, with Samuel J. Abrams and Jeremy C. Pope, *Culture War? The Myth of a Polarized America* (New York: Pearson Longman, 2004); on growing partisan attachment among a subset of voters, see Alan Abramowitz and Kyle Saunders, "Why Can't We Just Get Along? The Reality of a Polarized America," *The Forum* 3, no. 2 (2005), p. 1-22.

Chapter 10

1. *League of United Latin American Citizens v. Wilson*, CV-94-7569 (C.D. Calif. 1995).

2. *Gray v. Sanders*, 372 U.S. 368 (1963); *Wesberry v. Sanders*, 376 U.S. 1 (1964); *Reynolds v. Sims*, 377 U.S. 533 (1964).

3. *Thornburg v. Gingles*, 478 U.S. 613 (1986).

4. *Shaw v. Reno*, 509 U.S. 113 (1993).

5. State legislatures determine the system by which electors are selected. Almost all states use this "winner-take-all" system. Maine and Nebraska, however, provide that one electoral vote goes to the winner in each congressional district and two electoral votes go to the winner statewide.

6. Stephen Ansolabehere and James Snyder, "Campaign War Chests and Congressional Elections," *Business and Politics* 2 (2000), 9–34.

7. Gary W. Cox and Eric Magar, "How Much Is Majority Status in the U.S. Congress Worth?" *American Political Science Review* 93 (1999), 299–309.

8. Howard Kurtz, "Presidential Ad Wars Heat Up," *Washington Post*, September 20, 2007, p. A4.

9. Amy Schatz, "BO,URSoGr8," *Wall Street Journal*, May 26, 2007.

10. M. Ostrogorski, *Democracy and the Organization of Political Parties* (New York: Macmillan, 1902).

11. Timothy Clark, "The RNC Prospers, the DNC Struggles as They Face the 1980 Election," *National Journal*, October 27, 1980, 1619.

12. For discussions of the consequences, see Thomas Edsall, *The New Politics of Inequality* (New York: Norton, 1984). Also see Thomas Edsall, "Both Parties Get the Company's Money—But the Boss Backs the GOP," *Washington Post*, National Weekly Edition, September 16, 1986, p. 14; and Benjamin Ginsberg, "Money and Power: The New Political Economy of American Elections," in *The Political Economy*, ed. Thomas Ferguson and Joel Rogers (Armonk, NY: M. E. Sharpe, 1984).

13. Leslie Wayne, "A Fund-Raising Rainmaker Arises Online," *New York Times*, November 29, 2007, p. A22.

14. Peter Baker, "Obama Strains to Get Liberals Back Into Fold: Urges His Base to Put Aside Hard Feelings," *New York Times*, October 6, 2010, p. 1.

15. No. 08-205 (2010).

16. Dan Eggen and T. W. Farnam, "Super PACs Alter Campaign," *Washington Post*, September 28, 2010, 1.

17. Brody Mullins and Danny Yadron, "GOP Groups Launch Massive Ad Blitz: Alliance Spends $50 Million on Competitive House Races Where Democrats Have Moore Money Now," *The Wall Street Journal*, October 13, 2010, A4.

18. Tom Curry, "An Older, More Conservative Electorate," November 3, 2010.

19. *New York Times*, November 3, 2010, P8.

20. Michael Luo and Jeff Zeleny, "Straining to Reach Money Goal, Obama Presses Donors" *New York Times*, September 9, 2008, p. 1.

Chapter 11

1. Andrew Zajac, "How Health Lobbyists Influenced Reform Bill." *Chicago Tribune*, December 20, 2009, http://archives.chicagotribune.com/2009/dec/20/health/chi-health-lobbyists_bddec20.

2. Clinton Rossiter, ed., *The Federalist Papers* (New York: New American Library, 1961), No. 10, p. 83.

3. Rossiter, ed., *Federalist Papers*, No. 10.

4. The best statement of the pluralist view is in David Truman, *The Governmental Process* (New York: Knopf, 1951), chap. 2.

5. Betsy Wagner and David Bowermaster, "B.S. Economics," *Washington Monthly*, November 1992, 19–21.

6. Truman, *The Governmental Process*.

7. Mancur Olson, *The Logic of Collective Action* (Cambridge, MA: Harvard University Press, 1965).

8. Timothy Penny and Steven Schier, *Payment Due: A Nation in Debt, a Generation in Trouble* (Boulder, CO: Westview, 1996), 64–65.

9. Kay Lehman Schlozman and John T. Tierney, *Organized Interests and American Democracy* (New York: Harper & Row, 1986), 60.

10. John Herbers, "Special Interests Gaining Power as Voter Disillusionment Grows," *New York Times*, November 14, 1978.

11. Erika Falk, Erin Grizard, and Gordon McDonald, "Legislative Issue Advertising in the 108th Congress: Pluralism or Peril?" *Harvard International Journal of Press/Politics* 11, no. 4 (Fall 2006), 148–64, http://hij.sagepub.com/cgi/reprint/11/4/148 (accessed 3/2/08).

12. Jeffrey Birnbaum, "The Road to Riches Is Called K Street," *Washington Post*, June 22, 2005, p. 1.

13. For discussions of lobbying, see Allan J. Cigler and Burdett A. Loomis, eds., *Interest Group Politics* (Washington, DC: Congressional Quarterly Press, 1983). See also Jeffrey M. Berry, *Lobbying for the People* (Princeton, NJ: Princeton University Press, 1977).

14. "The Swarming Lobbyists," *Time*, August 7, 1978, p. 15.

15. See Frank Baumgartner and Beth Leech, *Basic Interests* (Princeton, NJ: Princeton University Press, 1998).

16. "Top Lobbyists: Hired Guns," *The Hill*, May 14, 2009, p. 1.

17. Eliza Carney, "Cleaning House," *National Journal*, January 28, 2006, p. 36.

18. Brody Mullins, "Growing Role for Lobbyists: Raising Funds for Lawmakers," *Wall Street Journal*, January 27, 2006, p. 1.

19. Jonathan Weisman and Charles H. Babcock, "K Street's New Ways Spawn More Pork," *Washington Post*, January 27, 2006, p. 1.

20. Daniel Franklin, "Tommy Boggs and the Death of Health Care Reform," *Washington Monthly*, April 1995, 36.

21. Marie Jojnacki, "Interest Groups' Decisions to Join Alliances or Work Alone," *American Journal of Political Science* 41 (1997), 61–87; Kevin W. Hula, *Lobbying Together: Interest Groups Coalitions in Legislative Politics* (Washington, DC: Georgetown University Press, 1999).

22. Peter H. Stone, "Follow the Leaders," *National Journal*, June 24, 1995, p. 1641.

23. "The Microsoft Playbook: A Report from Common Cause," www.commoncause.org, September 25, 2000.

24. Michael Barbaro, "A New Weapon for Wal-Mart: A War Room," *New York Times*, November 1, 2005, p. 1.

25. *The Washington Times*, May 7, 2009, www.washingtontimes.com/news/2009/may/07/obamas-lobbyists.

26. John P. Heinz et al., *The Hollow Core: Private Interests in National Policy Making* (Cambridge, MA: Harvard University Press, 1993).

27. For an excellent discussion of the political origins of the Administrative Procedure Act, see Martin Shapiro, "APA: Past, Present, Future," 72 *Virginia Law Review* 377 (March 1986), 447–92.

28. David Kirkpatrick, "Congress Finds Ways of Avoiding Lobbyist Limits," *Washington Post*, February 11, 2007, p. 1.

29. *Roe v. Wade*, 93 S.Ct. 705 (1973).

30. *Webster v. Reproductive Health Services*, 109 S.Ct. 3040 (1989).

31. *Brown v. Board of Education of Topeka, Kansas*, 74 S.Ct. 686 (1954).

32. E. Pendleton Herring, *Group Representation before Congress* (New York: McGraw-Hill, 1936).

33. Michael Weisskopf, "Energized by Pulpit or Passion, the Public Is Calling," *Washington Post*, February 1, 1993, p. 1.

34. Julia Preston, "Grass Roots Roared and Immigration Bill Collapsed," *New York Times*, June 10, 2007, p. 1.

35. Richard L. Burke, "Religious-Right Candidates Gain as GOP Turnout Rises," *New York Times*, November 12, 1994, p. 10.

36. Elisabeth R. Gerber, *The Populist Paradox* (Princeton, NJ: Princeton University Press, 1999).

37. Rossiter, ed., *The Federalist Papers*, No. 10.

38. Olson, *The Logic of Collective Action*.

Chapter 12

1. Kathy Chu, "Obama Signs into Law Credit Card Reform," *USA Today*, May 22, 2009, www.usatoday.com/money/perfi/credit/2009-05-21-obama-credit-card-reform-law_N.htm (accessed 1/30/10).

2. Tamar Lewin, "House Passes Bill to Expand College Aid," *New York Times*, September 17, 2009, p. A15.

3. Mildred Amer and Jennifer E. Manning, *Membership of the 11th Congress: A Profile*, Congressional Research Service 7-5700, December 31, 2008, p. 5, http://assets.openers.com/rpts/R40086_20081231.pdf (assessed 1/31/10).

4. Mildred Amer and Jennifer E. Manning, *Membership of the 11th Congress: A Profile*, Congressional Research Service 7-5700, December 31, 2008, p. 2, http://assets.openers.com/rpts/R40086_20081231.pdf (accessed 1/31/10).

5. Mildred Amer and Jennifer E. Manning, *Membership of the 11th Congress: A Profile*, Congressional Research Service 7-5700, December 31, 2008, p. 3, http://assets.openers.com/rpts/R40086_20081231.pdf (accessed 1/31/10).

6. For a discussion, see Benjamin Ginsberg, *The Consequences of Consent* (New York: Random House, 1982), chap. 1.

7. For some interesting empirical evidence, see Angus Campbell, Philip Converse, Warren Miller, and Donald Stokes, *Elections and the Political Order* (New York: Wiley, 1966), chap. 11.

8. Emily Yehle, "CMF Says New Technology Can Solve Workload Issues," *Roll Call*, December 15, 2008, www.allbusiness.com/government/elections-politics-lobbying/12216448-1.html (accessed 1/31/10).

9. Normal J. Ornstein, Thomas E. Mann, and Michael J. Malbin, *Vital Statistics on Congress 2008* (Washington, DC: Brookings Instruction, 2009), 111–12.

10. See Linda Fowler and Robert McClure, *Political Ambition: Who Decides to Run for Congress* (New Haven, CT: Yale University Press, 1989); and Alan Ehrenhalt, *The United States of Ambition: Politicians, Power, and the Pursuit of Office* (New York: Three Rivers Press, 1992).

11. Barbara Palmer and Denise Simon, *Breaking the Political Glass Ceiling: Women and Congressional Elections*, 2nd ed. (new York: Routledge, 2008); Jennifer L. Lawless and Kathryn Pearson, "The Primary Reason for Women's Underrepresentation? Reevaluating the Conventional Wisdom," *Journal of Politics*, 70 (2008) 67–82.

12. Michael Leahy, "House Rules," *Washington Post*, June 10, 2007, p. W12.

13. See Burrell, *A Woman's Place Is in the House*; and David Broder, "Key to Women's Political Parity: Running," *Washington Post*, September 8, 1994, p. A17.

14. Dan Balz, "Dodd, Dorgan, and Ritter to Retire as Democrats Face a Difficult Mid-Term Year," *Washington Post*, January 7, 2010.

15. Damien Cave, "Recession Slows Population Rise across Sunbelt," *New York Times*, December 23, 2009, p. A1.

16. Bernie Becker, "Reapportionment Roundup," *New York Times*, December 24, 2009, http://thecaucus.blogs.nytimes.com/2009/12/24/reapoortionment-roundup/ (accessed 1/31/10).

17. "Did Redistricting Sink the Democrats?" *National Journal*, December 17, 1994, p. 2984.

18. *Miller v. Johnson*, 115 S.Ct. 2475 (1995).

19. Tom Hamburger and Richard Simon, "Everybody Will Know if It's Pork," *Los Angeles Times*, January 6, 2007, p. A1.

20. David Clarke, "Earmarks: Here to Stay or Facing Extinction." *Congressional Quarterly Weekly*, March 16, 2009, p. 613; Jared Allen, "Lawmakers Pushing for Earmark Reform Think Obama Boosted Their Chances," *The Hill*, January 30, 2010, http://thehill.com/homenews/house/78869-lawmakers-think-obama-boosted-earmark-reform- (accessed 1/31/10).

21. Timothy Eagan, "Built with Steel, Perhaps, but Greased with Pork," *New York Times*, April 10, 2004, p. A1.

22. Congressman Pete Stark, "Constituent Services: FederalGrants," www.house.gov/stark/webarchives/Stark%20Web%20Page/services/grants.html (accessed 3/5/08).

23. Kelly McCormack, "Private Bills," *The Hill*, May 9, 2007, http://thehill.com/cover-stories/private-bills-2007-05-08.html (accessed 3/20/08).

24. Richard Fenno, Jr., *Home Style: House Members in Their Districts* (Boston: Little, Brown, 1978).

25. Carl Hulse, "In Conference: Process Undone by Partisanship," *New York Times*, September 26, 2007, p. A1.

26. Derek Willis, "Republicans Mix It Up When Assigning House Chairmen for the 108th," *Congressional Quarterly Weekly*, January 11, 2003, p. 89.

27. Rebecca Kimitch, "CQ Guide to the Committees: Democrats Opt to Spread the Power," *Congressional Quarterly Weekly*, April 16, 2007, p. 1080.

28. Richard E. Cohen, "Crackup of the Committees," *National Journal*, July 31, 1999, pp. 2210–16.

29. David W. Rhode, "Committees and Policy Formulation," in *Institutions of American Democracy: The Legislative Branch*, ed. Paul J. Quirk and Sarah A. Binder (New York: Oxford University Press, 2005), 201–23.

30. CNN Fact Check, "Senate Cloture Votes," February 3, 2010, http://politicalticker.blogs.cnn.com/2010/02/03/cnn-fact-check-senate-cloture-votes/?fbid=PBasffbGtrY (accessed 2/5/10).

31. See Robert Pear, "Senator X Kills Measure on Anonymity," *New York Times*, November 11, 1997, p. 12.

32. Jonathan Weisman, "House Votes 411–18 to Pass Ethics Overhaul," *Washington Post*, August 1, 2007, p. A1.

33. Kate Phillips and Jeff Zeleny, "White House Blasts Shelby Hold on Nominees," *New York Times*, February 5, 2010, http://thecaucus.blogs.nytimes.com/2010/02/05/white-house-blasts-shelby-hold-on-nominees/ (accessed 2/5/10).

34. Carl Hulse and David M. Herszenhorn, "Defiant House Rejects Huge Bailout; Next Step is Uncertain," New York Times, September 29, 2008, www.nytimes.com/2008/09/30/business/30cong.html?pagewanted=1&_r=1 (accessed 02/04/2010); Reuters. "House Passes

Bailout, Focus Shifts to Fallout," October 3, 2008, www.reuters .com/article/idUSTRE49267J20081003 (accessed 2/04/10).

35. See John W. Kingdon, *Congressmen's Voting Decisions* (New York: Harper & Row, 1973), chap. 3; and R. Douglas Arnold, *The Logic of Congressional Action* (New Haven, CT: Yale University Press, 1990).

36. Jane Fritsch, "The Grass Roots, Just a Free Phone Call Away," *New York Times*, June 23, 1995, p. A1.

37. Robert Pear, "In House, Many Spoke with One Voice: Lobbyists,'" *New York Times*, November 14, 2009, p. A1.

38. Eliza Newlin Carney, "For Ethics Hawks, Congress Could Be Next," *National Journal Online*, February 17, 2009, www.nationaljournal.com/njonline/rg_20090217_2426 .php (accessed 2/5/10).

39. Holly Idelson, "Signs Point to Greater Loyalty on Both Sides of the Aisle," *Congressional Quarterly Weekly Report*, December 19, 1992, p. 3849.

40. "GOP Leadership PACs' Fundraising Far Outstrips 1997–98," *Congressional Quarterly Weekly Report*, August 15, 1999, p. 1991.

41. Kimitch, "CQ Guide to the Committees," p. 1080.

42. Leahy, "House Rules," p. W12.

43. James J. Kilpatrick, "Don't Overlook Corn for Porn Plot," *Chicago Sun-Times*, January 3, 1992, p. 23.

44. Dennis McDougal, "Cattle Are Bargaining Chip of the NEA," *Los Angeles Times*, November 2, 1991, p. F1.

45. Susan Milligan, "Congress Reduces Its Oversight Role; Since Clinton, a Change in Focus," *Boston Globe*, November 20, 2005, p. A1; Bill Shaikin, "Clemens Is Star Attraction at Hearing," *Lost Angeles Times*, February 12, 2008, p. D1.

46. Elizabeth Williamson, "Revival of Oversight Role Sought; Congress Hires More Investigators, Plans Subpeonas," *Washington Post*, April 25, 2007, p. A1.

47. Thomas E. Mann, Molly Reynolds, and Peter Hoey, "A New, Improved Congress?" *New York Times*, August 26, 2007, p. 11.

48. Peter Grier, "Financial Crisis Inquiry Commission: Top Bankers Contrite, Sort Of," *Christian Science Monitor*, January 13, 2010, www.csmonitor.com/USA/Politics/ 2010/0113/Financial-Crisis-Inquiry-Commission-Top-bankers-contrite-sort-of (accessed 2/5/10).

49. *United States v. Pink*, 315 U.S. 203 (1942). For a good discussion of the problem, see James W. Davis, *The American Presidency* (New York: Harper & Row, 1987), chap. 8.

50. Carroll J. Doherty, "Impeachment: How It Would Work," *Congressional Quarterly Weekly Report*, January 31, 1998, p. 222.

51. See Kenneth A. Shepsle, "Representation and Governance: The Great Legislative Trade-off," *Political Science Quarterly* 103, no. 3 (1988), 461–84.

52. John R. Hibbing and Elizabeth Theiss-Morse, *Congress as Public Enemy: Public Attitudes toward American Political Institutions* (New York: Cambridge University Press, 1996), 105.

Chapter 13

1. "The Cover-Up Continues," *New York Times*, October 26, 2009, p. A20.

2. *In re Neagle*, 135 U.S. 1 (1890).

3. James G. Randall, *Constitutional Problems under Lincoln* (New York: Appleton, 1926), chap. 1.

4. Edward S. Corwin, *The President: Office and Powers*, 4th rev. ed. (New York: New York University Press, 1957), 229.

5. These statutes are contained mainly in Title 10 of the United States Code, Sections 331, 332, and 333.

6. The best study covering all aspects of the domestic use of the military is that of Adam Yarmolinsky, *The Military Establishment* (New York: Harper & Row, 1971). Probably the most famous instance of a president's unilateral use of the power to protect a state "against domestic violence" was in dealing with the Pullman Strike of 1894. The famous Supreme Court case that ensued was *In re Debs*, 158 U.S. 564 (1895).

7. Josh Gerstein, "Bush Pardons Few in Final Hours," *Politico.com*, January 18, 2009, http://dyn.politico.com/ printstory.cfm?uuid=EC742C8A-18FE-70B2-A869 DC74EA110133 (accessed 6/10/10).

8. In *United States v. Pink*, 315 U.S. 203 (1942), the Supreme Court confirmed that an executive agreement is the legal equivalent of a treaty, despite the absence of Senate approval. This case approved the executive agreement that was used to establish diplomatic relations with the Soviet Union in 1933. An executive agreement, not a treaty, was used in 1940 to exchange "fifty over-age destroyers" for ninety-nine-year leases on some important military bases.

9. A third source of presidential power is implied from the provision for "faithful execution of the laws." This is the president's power to impound funds—that is, to refuse to spend money Congress has appropriated for certain purposes. One author referred to this as a "retroactive veto power" (Robert E. Goosetree, "The Power of the President to Impound Appropriated Funds," *American University Law Review*, January 1962). This impoundment power was used freely and to considerable effect by many modern presidents, and Congress occasionally delegated such power to the president by statute. But in reaction to the Watergate scandal, Congress adopted the Budget and Impoundment Control Act of 1974 and designed this act to circumscribe the president's ability to impound funds by requiring that the president must spend all appropriated funds unless both houses of Congress consent to an impoundment within forty-five days of a presidential request. Therefore, since 1974, the use of impoundment has declined significantly. Presidents have had either to bite their tongues and accept unwanted appropriations or to revert to the older and more dependable but politically limited method of vetoing the entire bill.

10. For a different perspective, see William F. Grover, *The President as Prisoner: A Structural Critique of the Carter and Reagan Years* (Albany: State University of New York Press, 1988).

11. For more on the veto, see Chapter 13 and Robert J. Spitzer, *The Presidential Veto: Touchstone of the American Presidency* (Albany: State University of New York Press, 1989).

12. Dan Eggen, "Bush Announces Veto of Waterboarding Ban," *WashingtonPost.com*, March 8, 2008, www.washingtonpost.com/wp-dyn/content/article/2008/03/08AR2008030800304.html (accessed 6/10/10).

13. For a good review of President Clinton's legislative leadership in the first session of his last Congress, see *Congressional Quarterly Weekly*, November 13, 1999, especially the cover story by Andrew Taylor, "Clinton Gives Republicans a Gentler Year-End Beating," pp. 2698–2700.

14. Kenneth F. Warren, *Administrative Law*, 3rd ed. (Upper Saddle River, NJ: Prentice-Hall, 1996), 250.

15. Theodore J. Lowi, *The End of Liberalism*, 2nd ed. (New York: Norton, 1979), 117–18.

16. *J. W. Hampton & Co. v. U.S.*, 276 U.S. 394 (1928).

17. 48 Stat. 200.

18. David Schoenbrod, *Power without Responsibility: How Congress Abuses the People through Delegation* (New Haven, CT: Yale University Press, 1993), 49–50.

19. Lowi, *The End of Liberalism*, 117.

20. Adam Clymer, "The Transition: Push for Diversity May Cause Reversal on Interior Secretary," *New York Times*, December 23, 1992, p. 1.

21. A substantial portion of this section is taken from Theodore J. Lowi, *The Personal President* (Ithaca, NY: Cornell University Press, 1985), 141–50.

22. All the figures since 1967, and probably 1957, are understated, because additional White House staff members were on "detail" service from the military and other departments (some secretly assigned) and are not counted here because they were not on the White House payroll.

23. The actual number is difficult to estimate because, as with White House staff, some EOP personnel, especially in national security work, are detailed to EOP from outside agencies.

24. Article I, Section 3, provides that "The Vice-President . . . shall be President of the Senate, but shall have no Vote, unless they be equally divided." This is the only vote the vice president is allowed.

25. David Ignatius, "A Skeptical Biden's Role," *RealClearPolitics.com*, November 26, 2009, www.realclearpolitics.com/articles/2009/11/26/a_skeptical_bidens_role_99320.html (accessed 5/12/09).

26. Samuel Kernell, *Going Public: New Strategies of Presidential Leadership*, 3rd ed. (Washington, DC: Congressional Quarterly Press, 1997); also, Jeffrey K. Tulis, *The Rhetorical Presidency* (Princeton, NJ: Princeton University Press, 1987).

27. Tulis, *The Rhetorical Presidency*, 91.

28. Sidney M. Milkis, *The President and the Parties* (New York: Oxford, 1993), 97.

29. James MacGregor Burns, *Roosevelt: The Lion and the Fox* (New York: Harcourt, Brace, 1956), 317.

30. Burns, *Roosevelt*, 317.

31. Kernell, *Going Public*, 79.

32. Tulis, *The Rhetorical Presidency*, 161.

33. Lowi, *The Personal President*.

34. Lowi, *The Personal President*, 11.

35. Harold W. Stanley and Richard G. Niemi, *Vital Statistics on American Politics, 2001–2002* (Washington, DC: Congressional Quarterly Press, 2001), 250–51.

36. Milkis, *The President and the Parties*, 128.

37. Milkis, *The President and the Parties*, 160.

38. The classic critique of this process is Theodore J. Lowi, *The End of Liberalism* (New York: Norton, 1969).

39. Kenneth Culp Davis, *Administrative Law Treatise* (St. Paul: West Publishing, 1958), 9.

40. For example, Douglas W. Kmiec, "Expanding Power," in *The Rule of Law in the Wake of Clinton*, ed. Roger Pilon (Washington, DC: Cato Institute Press, 2000), 47–68.

41. Presidential Memorandum on Regulatory Review, January 30, 2009, www.gpoaccess.gov/predocs/2009/DCPD-200900287.pdf (accessed 2/9/09).

42. A complete inventory is provided in Harold C. Relyea, "Presidential Directives: Background and Review," Congressional Research Service Report 98–611 (Washington, DC: Library of Congress, November 9, 2001).

43. Terry M. Moe and William G. Howell, "The Presidential Power of Unilateral Action," *Journal of Law, Economics and Organization*, 15, no. 1 (January 1999), 133–34.

44. Moe and Howell, "The Presidential Power of Unilateral Action," 164.

45. *Youngstown Sheet & Tube Co. v. Sawyer*, 346 U.S. 579 (1952).

46. Todd Gaziano, "The New 'Massive Resistance,'" *Policy Review* (May–June 1998), 283.

47. Mark Killenback, "A Matter of Mere Approval: The Role of the President in the Creation of Legislative History," 48 *University of Arkansas Law Review* 239 (1995).

48. Philip Cooper, *By Order of the President* (Lawrence Kansas: University Press of Kansas, 2002), p.201.

49. Edward S. Corwin, *The President: Office and Powers*, 4th rev.ed. (New York: New York University Press, 1957), p. 283.

50. Cooper, p. 201.

51. Cooper, p. 203.

52. Cooper, p. 216.

53. Peter Baker, "Obama Is Making Plans to Use Executive Power For Action on Several Fronts," *New York Times*, Feb. 13, 2010, p. A12.

54. Baker, p. A12.

55. Alexander Hamilton, James Madison, and John Jay, *The Federalist Papers*, ed. Clinton Rossiter (New York: New American Library, 1961), No. 70, 423–30.

56. Terry Moe, "The Presidency and the Bureaucracy: The Presidential Advantage," in *The Presidency and the Political System*, ed Michael Nelson (Washington, DC: Congressional Quarterly Press, 2002), 416–20.

Chapter 14

1. John B. Judis, "The Quiet Revolution," *New Republic*, February 1, 2010, www.tnr.com/article/politics/the-quiet-revolution (accessed 2/2/10).

2. "Obama's Health Care Speech to Congress," *New York Times*, September 9, 2009, www.nytimes.com/2009/09/10/us/politics/10obama.text.html (accessed 2/10/10).

3. U.S. Census Bureau, "Federal Civilian Employment and Annual Payroll by Branch: 1970–2008," *Statistical Abstract of the United States 2010*, Table 484, www.census.gov/compendia/statab/2010edition.html (accessed 02/10/2010); U.S. Census Bureau, "Department of Defense Personnel: 1960–2008," *Statistical Abstract of the United States 2010*, Table 498, www.census.gov/compendia/statab/2010edition.html (accessed 2/10/10).

4. U.S. Census Bureau, "Table 450. All Governments—Employment and Payroll by Function: 2007," *Statistical Abstract of the United States 2010*, Table 484, www.census.gov/compendia/statab/2010edition.html (accessed 2/21/10).

5. Arnold Brecht and Comstock Glaser, *The Art and Techniques of Administration in German Ministries* (Cambridge, MA: Harvard University Press, 1940), 6.

6. Linda Greenhouse, "Justices Say E.P.A. Has Power to Act on Harmful Gases," *New York Times*, April 3, 2007, www.nytimes.com/2007/04/03/washington/03scotus.html?ex=1333339200&en=e0d0a1497263d879&ei=5124&partner=permalink&exprod=permalink(accessed 2/15/10).

7. Environmental Protection Agency, "Endangerment and Cause or Contribute Findings for Greenhouse Cases under Section 202(a) of the Clean Air Act," epa.gov/climatechange/endangerment.html (accessed 2/16/10).

8. Environmental Protection Agency, "Regulations and Standards: Vehicles/Engines," www.epa.gov/oms/climate/regulations.htm (accessed 2/16/10).

9. John B. Judis, "The Quiet Revolution," *New Republic*, February 1, 2010, www.tnr.com/article/politics/the-quiet-revolution (accessed 2/2/10).

10. Greg Gardner, "U.S. Probes Toyota Recall, Could Levy $16.4M Fine if Carmaker Acted too Slowly," *Detroit Free Press*, www.freep.com/article/20100216/BUSINESS01/100216030/1318/U.S.-probes-Toyota-recall-could-levy-16.4M-fine-if-carmaker-acted-too-slowly (accessed 2/16/10).

11. Gary Bryner, Bureaucratic Discretion (New York: Pergamon, 1987).

12. This account is drawn from Alan Stone, *How America Got On-Line: Politics, Markets, and the Revolution in Telecommunications* (Armonk, NY: M. E. Sharpe, 1997), 184–87.

13. There are historical reasons that American Cabinet-level administrators are called "secretaries." During the Second Continental Congress and the subsequent confederal government, standing committees were formed to deal with executive functions related to foreign affairs, military and maritime issues, and public financing. The heads of those committees were called "secretaries" because their primary task was to handle all correspondence and documentation related to their areas of responsibility.

14. David Johnston, "Bush Intervened in Dispute over N.S.A. Eavesdropping," *New York Times*, May 16, 2007, p. A1; Scott Shane, David Johnston, and James Risen, "Secret U.S. Endorsement of Severe Interrogations," *New York Times*, October 4, 2007, p. A1.

15. Rob Margetta, "Homeland Security for Hire," *Congressional Quarterly Weekly*, November 12, 2007, pp. 3392–99, http://library.cqpress.com/cqweekly/weeklyreport110-000002625610 (accessed 11/14/07).

16. U.S. Department of State, "Department Organization Chart," www.state.gov/r/pa/ei/rls/dos/99494.htm (accessed 2/16/10).

17. For more detail, consult John E. Harr, *The Professional Diplomat* (Princeton, NJ: Princeton University Press, 1972), 11; and Nicholas Horrock, "The CIA Has Neighbors in the 'Intelligence Community,'" *New York Times*, June 29, 1975, sec. 4, p. 2. See also Morton H. Halperin and Priscilla Clapp, with Arnold Kanter, *Bureaucratic Politics and Foreign Policy*, 2nd ed. (Washington, DC: Brookings Institution Press, 2007).

18. *The 9/11 Commission Report: Final Report of the National Commission on Terrorist Attacks upon the United States* (New York: Norton, 2004).

19. Daniel Patrick Moynihan, "The Culture of Secrecy," *Public Interest* (Summer 1997) 55–71.

20. OpenTheGovernment.org, "Secrecy Report Card 09: Indicators of Secrecy in the Federal Government," p. 2, www.openthegovernment.org/otg/SecrecyRC_2009.pdf (accessed 2/25/10).

21. Charlie Savage, "Obama Curbs Secrecy of Classified Documents," *New York Times*, December 30, 2009, p. A19.

22. See Paul Peterson, *The Price of Federalism* (Washington, DC: Brookings Institution Press, 1995) for a recent argument that "redistribution" is the distinctive function of the national government in the American federal system.

23. U.S. Department of the Treasury, "The Debt to the Penny and Who Holds It." www.treasurydirect.gov/NP/BPDLogin?application=np (accessed 2/18/10).

24. For an excellent political analysis of the Fed, see Donald Kettl, *Leadership at the Fed* (New Haven, CT: Yale University Press, 1986).

25. Sewell Chan, "Agreement Is Near on New Overseer of Banking Risks," *New York Times*, February 17, 2010, www.nytimes.com/2010/02/18/business/18regulate.html (accessed 2/18/10).

26. George E. Berkley, *The Craft of Public Administration* (Boston: Allyn & Bacon, 1975), 417 (emphasis added).

27. OMB Watch, "IRS Gets Serious about Tax Enforcement," November 24, 2009. www.ombwatch.org/node/10583 (accessed 2/18/10).

28. Eric Schmitt, "Washington Talk: No $435 Hammers, but Questions," *New York Times*, October 23, 1990, p. A16.

29. Vice President Gore's National Partnership for Reinventing Government, "Appendix F, History of the National Partnership for Reinventing Government Accomplishments, 1993–2000, A Summary," http://govinfo.library.unt.edu/npr/whoweare/appendixf.html (accessed 3/28/08).

30. Public Law 101–510, Title XXIX, Sections 2,901 and 2,902 of Part A (Defense Base Closure and Realignment Commission).

31. John Herbst, "Guiding Principles for Stabilization and Reconstruction: A Strategic Roadmap for Peace," *Dipnote: U.S. Department of State Official Blog*, October 7, 2009, http://blogs.state.gov/index.php/entries/strategic_roadmap_for_peace/ (accessed 2/18/10).

32. Paul C. Light, "The New True Size of Government," Organizational Performance Initiative, Research Brief no. 2, p. 8, Wagner School of Public Service, New York University, http://wagner.nyu.edu/performance/files/True_Size.pdf (accessed 3/11/08).

33. Joe Davidson, "OMB Moves to Cut Outside Contractors," *Washington Post*, July 29, 2009, www.washingtonpost.com/wp-dyn/content/article/2009/07/28/AR2009072802812.html (accessed 2/18/10).

34. Scott Shane and Ron Nixon, "In Washington, Contractors Take on Biggest Role Ever," *New York Times*, February 4, 2007, p. A1.

35. Shane and Nixon, "In Washington, Contractors Take on Biggest Role Ever."

36. Matt Kelly, "GAO challenges $150B Contract Awarded By Army," *USA Today*, November 30, 2007, p. 5A.

37. Congressional Research Service, "The Department of Defense's Use of Private Contractors in Iraq and Afghanistan: Background, Analysis, and Options for Congress," September 29, 2009, fpc.state.gov/documents/organization/130803.pdf (accessed 2/18/10).

38. Committee on Oversight and Government Reform, Hearings on Blackwater USA, preliminary transcript, October 2, 2007, http://oversight.house.gov/documents/20071127131151.pdf (accessed 3/10/08).

39. Committee on Oversight and Government Reform, Hearings on Blackwater USA.

40. Shane and Nixon, "In Washington, Contractors Take on Biggest Role Ever."

41. Shane and Nixon, "In Washington, Contractors Take on Biggest Role Ever."

42. General Accountability Office, *Federal Contractors: Better Performance Information Needed to Support Agency Contract Award Decisions*, April 2009, GAO-09-374; www.gao.gov/new.items/d09374.pdf (accessed 2/26/10).

43. Neil Gordon, "Move Over FCMD, Make Way for FAPIIS," Project on Government Oversight, pogoblog.typepad.com/pogo/2009/09/move-over-fcmd-make-way-for-fapiis.html (accessed 2/26/10).

44. Dan Egan, "Democrats Proposing New Limits on Corporate Campaign Donations," *Boston Globe*, February 12, 2010, www.boston.com/news/nation/washington/articles/2010/02/12/democrats proposing new limits on corporate campaign donations/ (accessed 2/27/10).

45. Joe Davidson, "OMB Moves to Cut Outside Contractors," *Washington Post*, July 29, 2009, www.washingtonpost.com/wp-dyn/content/article/2009/07/28/AR2009072802812.html (accessed 2/18/10).

46. Alexander Hamilton, James Madison, and John Jay, *The Federalist Papers*, ed. Clinton Rossiter (New York: New American Library, 1961), No. 51, 322.

47. The title of this section was inspired by Peri Arnold *Making the Managerial Presidency* (Princeton, NJ: Princeton University Press, 1986).

48. See Richard Nathan, *The Plot that Failed: Nixon and the Administrative Presidency* (New York: Wiley, 1975), 68–76.

49. For more details and evaluations, see David Rosenbloom, *Public Administration* (New York: Random House, 1986), 186–221; Charles H. Levine with the assistance of Rosslyn S. Kleeman, *The Quiet Crisis of the Civil Service. The Federal Personnel System at the Crossroads* (Washington, DC: National Academy of Public Administration, 1986).

50. Lester Salamon and Alan Abramson, "Governance: The Politics of Retrenchment," in *The Reagan Recors*, ed. John Palmer and Isabel Sawhill (Cambridge, MA: Ballinger, 1984), 40.

51. Colin Campbell, "The White House and the Presidency under the 'Let's Deal' President," in *The Bush Presidency. First Appraisals*, ed. Colin Campbell and Bert A. Rockman (Chatham, NJ: Chatham House, 1991), 185–222.

52. See John Micklethwait, "Managing to Look Attractive," *New Statesman* 125, November 8, 1996, p. 24.

53. Quoted in I. M. Destler, "Reagan and the World: An 'Awesome some Stubborness,'" in *The Reagan Legacy: Promise and Performance*, ed. Charles O. Jones (Chatham, NJ: Chatham House, 1988), 244, 257. The source of the quote is *Report of the President's Special Review Board* (Washington, DC: US. Government Printing Office, 1987).

54. Thomas E. Mann and Norman J. Ornstein. *The Broken Branch: How Congress Is Failing America and How to Get It Back on Track* (New York Oxford University Press 2006), 155.

55. The Office of Technology Assessment (OTA) was a fourth research agency serving Congress until 1995. It was one of the first agencies scheduled for elimination by the 104th Congress. Until 1983, Congress had still another tool of legislative oversight: the legislative veto. Each agency operating under such provisions was obliged to submit to Congress every proposed decision or rule, which would then lie before both chambers for thirty to sixty days. If Congress took no action by one-house or two-house resolution explicitly to veto the proposed measure during the prescribed period, it became law. The legislative veto was declared unconstitutional by the Supreme Court in 1983 on the grounds that it violated the separation of powers—the resolutions Congress passed to exercise its veto were not subject to presidential veto, as required by the Constitution. See *Immigration and Naturalization Service v. Chadha*, 462 U.S. 919 (1983).

Chapter 15

1. *Morse v. Frederick*, No. 06–278 (2007).

2. Charles Lane, "Court Backs School on Speech Curbs," *Washington Post*, June 26, 2007, p. A6.

3. U.S. Bureau of the Census, *Statistical Abstract of the United States* (Washington, DC: Government Printing Office, 2008).

4. Michael A. Fletcher, "Obama Criticized as Too Cautions on Judicial Posts," *Washington Post*, October 15, 2009, www.washingtonpost.com/wp-dyn/content/article/2009/10/15/AR2009101504083.html (accessed 3/1/10).

5. Peter Wallsten and Richard Simon, "Sotomayor Nomination Splits GOP," *Los Angeles Times*, May 27, 2009, http://articles.latimes.com/2009/may/27/nation/na-court-access27 (accessed 3/1/10).

6. *Marbury v. Madison*, 1 Cr. 137 (1803).

7. *Clinton v. City of New York*, 55 U.S.L.W. 4543 (1998).

8. *Federal Election Commission v. Wisconsin Right to Life*, No. 09–969 (2007).

9. This review power was affirmed by the Supreme Court in *Martin v. Hunter's Lessee*, 1 Wheat. 304 (1816).

10. *Brown v. Board of Education*, 347 U.S. 483 (1954); *Loving v. Virginia*, 388 U.S. 1 (1967).

11. *Griswold v. Connecticut*, 381 U.S. 479 (1965).

12. *Brandenburg v. Ohio*, 395 U.S. 444 (1969).

13. See Theodore J. Lowi, *The End of Liberalism*, 2nd ed. (New York: Norton, 1979); also, David Schoenbrod, *Power without Responsibility: How Congress Abuses the People through Delegation* (New Haven, CT: Yale University Press, 1993).

14. Kenneth Culp Davis, *Discretionary Justice* (Baton Rouge: Louisiana State University Press, 1969), 15–21.

15. Emergency Price Control Act, 56 Stat. 23 (January 30, 1942).

16. *Hamdi v. Rumsfeld*, 2004 Westlaw 1431951.

17. Charles Lane, "Justices Back Detainee Access to U.S. Courts," *Washington Post*, June 29, 2004, p. 1.

18. *Shelley v. Kraemer*, 334 U.S. 1 (1948).

19. *Burlington Northern v. White*, No. 05–259 (2006).

20. *Engel v. Vitale*, 370 U.S. 421 (1962); *Gideon v. Wainwright*, 372 U.S. 335 (1963); *Escobedo v. Illinois*, 378 U.S. 478 (1964); and *Miranda v. Arizona*, 384 U.S. 436 (1966).

21. *Baker v. Carr*, 369 U.S. 186 (1962).

22. Walter F. Murphy, "The Supreme Court of the United States," in *Encyclopedia of the American Judicial System*, ed. Robert J. Janosik (New York: Scribner's, 1987).

23. 200 U.S. 321 (2009).

24. Robert Scigliano, *The Supreme Court and the Presidency* (New York: Free Press, 1971), 162. For an interesting critique of the solicitor general's role during the Reagan administration, see Lincoln Caplan, "Annals of the Law," *New Yorker*, August 17, 1987, pp. 30–62.

25. Edward Lazarus, *Closed Chambers* (New York: Times Books, 1998), 6.

26. *Hopwood v. State of Texas*, 78 F3d 932 (Fifth Circuit, 1996).

27. *Gratz v. Bollinger*, 123 S.Ct. 2411 (2003).

28. *Jacobs v. Independent School District No. 625*, 99-CV-542 (D. Minn., filed April 6, 1999).

29. *NAACP v. Button*, 371 U.S. 415 (1963). The quotation is from the opinion in this case.

30. *Smith v. Allwright*, 321 U.S. 649 (1994).

31. *Griswold v. Connecticut*, 381 U.S. 479 (1965).

32. R. W. Apple, Jr., "A Divided Government Remains, and with It the Prospect of Further Combat," *New York Times*, November 7, 1996, p. B6.

33. For limits on judicial power, see Alexander Bickel, *The Least Dangerous Branch* (Indianapolis: Bobbs-Merrill, 1962).

34. *Worcester v. Georgia*, 6 Pet. 515 (1832).

35. *Immigration and Naturalization Service v. Chadha*, 462 U.S. 919 (1983).

36. See Walter Murphy, *Congress and the Court* (Chicago: University of Chicago Press, 1962).

37. Robert Dahl, "The Supreme Court and National Policy Making," *Journal of Public Law* 6 (1958), 279.

38. Martin Shapiro, "The Supreme Court: From Warren to Burger," in *The New American Political System*, ed. Anthony King (Washington, DC: American Enterprise Institute, 1978).

39. *Citizens to Preserve Overton Park v. Volpe*, 401 U.S. 402 (1971).

40. Toni Locy, "Bracing for Health Care's Caseload," *Washington Post*, August 22, 1994, p. A15.

41. See "Developments in the Law—Class Actions," *Harvard Law Review* 89 (1976), 1318.

42. *In re Agent Orange Product Liability Litigation*, 100 F.R.D. 718 (D.C.N.Y. 1983).

43. See Donald Horowitz, *The Courts and Social Policy* (Washington, DC: Brookings Institution Press, 1977).

44. *Moran v. McDonough*, 540 F2d 527 (1 Cir., 1976; *cert. denied*, 429 U.S. 1042 [1977]).

45. Alexander Hamilton, James Madison, and John Jay, *The Federalist Papers*, ed. Clinton Rossiter (New York: New American Library, 1961), No. 10, 78.

Chapter 16

1. Robert Nozick, *Anarchy, State and Utopia* (New York: Basic Books, 1974; reprint, Oxford: Blackwell, 2003).

2. Compare with Gabriel Kolko, *The Triumph of Conservatism* (New York: Free Press, 1963), chap. 6.

3. Bureau of Economic Analysis, "Percent Change from Preceding Period in Real Gross Domestic Product," www.bea.gov/national/nipaweb/SelectTable.asp?Popular=Y (accessed 3/5/10).

4. See David M. Hart, *Forged Consensus: Science, Technology and Economic Policy in the United States, 1921–1953* (Princeton, NJ: Princeton University Press, 1998).

5. See Margaret Weir, *Politics and Jobs: The Boundaries of Employment Policy in the United States* (Princeton, NJ: Princeton University Press, 1992).

6. David Leonhardt, "Judging Stimulus by Jobs Data Reveals Success," *New York Times*, February 16, 2010, www.nytimes.com/2010/02/17/business/economy/17leonhardt.html?hp (accessed 3/6/10).

7. Ben Pershing, "House Passes $15 Billion Jobs Bill," *Washington Post*, March 5, 2010, www.washingtonpost.com/wp-dyn/content/article/2010/03/04/AR2010030402757.html (accessed 3/5/10).

8. Bradford DeLong, "America's Only Peacetime Inflation: The 1970s" (University of California at Berkeley and National Bureau of Economic Research, December 19, 1995), www.j-bradford-delong.net/pdf_files/Peacetime_Inflation.pdf (accessed 3/18/08).

9. The act of 1955 officially designated the interstate highways as the National System of Interstate and Defense Highways. It was indirectly a major part of President Dwight Eisenhower's defense program. But it was just as obviously a "pork barrel" policy as any rivers and harbors legislation.

10. The members were AMD, Digital, Hewlett-Packard, Intel, IBM, Lucent, Motorola, National Semiconductor, Rockwell, and Texas Instruments.

11. U.S. Department of Defense Small Business Innovation Research and Small Business Technology Transfer Programs, www.acq.osd.mil/osbp/sbir/ (accessed 3/7/10).

12. U.S. Consumer Product Safety Commission, *2009 Annual Performance and Accountability Report*, www.cpsc.gov/about/budperf.html (accessed 3/7/10).

13. For a good summary of Keynes's ideas see Robert Lekachman, *The Age of Keynes* (New York: McGraw-Hill, 1966).

14. Kevin G. Hall, "Bernanke to Stay on Greenspan Path, But Not All the Way," *Seattle Times*, November 16, 2005, p. C1.

15. The Federal Reserve Board, *Intended Federal Funds Rate, 1990 to Present*, www.federalreserve.gov/fomc/fundsrate.htm (accessed 3/8/10).

16. As a rule of thumb, in a growing economy where there is demand for credit, and assuming a reserve requirement of 20 percent, a deposit of $100 will create nearly $500 of new credit. This is called the "multiplier effect," because the bank can lend out $80 of the original $100 deposit to a new borrower; that becomes another $80 deposit, 20 percent of which ($64) can be lent to another borrower, and so on until the original $100 grows to approximately $500 of new credit.

17. Good treatments of the Federal Reserve System and monetary policy can be found in Donald Kettl, *Leadership at the Fed* (New Haven: Yale University Press, 1986); and Albert T. Sommers, *The U.S. Economy Demystified* (Lexington, MA: Lexington Books, 1988), especially chap. 5.

18. Majority Staff of the Joint Economic Committee, Senator Charles E. Schumer, Chairman Rep. Carolyn B. Maloney, Vice Chair, *The Subprime Lending Crisis: The Economic Impact on Wealth, Property Values and Tax Revenues, and How We Got Here*, Report and Recommendations, October 2007, p. 1, http://jec.senate.gov/index.cfm?FuseAction=Files.View&FileStore_id=148eaf7c-ee62-42f0-b215-006db6a11d65 (accessed 5/8/08).

19. Steven R. Weisman, "Bernanke Faces Bear Stearns Queries," *New York Times*, April 2, 2008, p. C1.

20. John Ydstie, "Federal Reserve Mulls Its Role One Year after Crisis," National Public Radio, September 14, 2009, www.npr.org/templates/story/story.php?storyId=112767144 (accessed 3/8/10).

21. Sewell Chan, "Agreement Is Near on New Overseer of Banking Risks," *New York Times*, February 17, 2010, www.nytimes.com/2010/02/18/business/18regulate.html (accessed 2/18/10).

22. Executive Office of the President of the United States, GPO Access, "Budget of the United States Government: Historical Tables Fiscal Year 2009," Table 2.2—Percentage Composition of Receipts by Source: 1934–2013, http://origin.www.gpoaccess.gov/usbudget/fy09/hist.html (accessed 5/9/08).

23. For a systematic account of the role of government in providing incentives and inducements to business, see C. E. Lindblom, *Politics and Markets* (New York: Basic Books, 1977), chap. 13. For a detailed account of the dramatic Reagan tax cuts and reforms, see Jeffrey Birnbaum and

Alan Murray, *Showdown at Gucci Gulch: Lawmakers, Lobbyists, and the Unlikely Triumph of Tax Reform* (New York: Random House, 1987).

24. For further background, see David E. Rosenbaum, "Cutting the Deficit Overshadows Clinton's Promise to Cut Taxes," *New York Times*, January 12, 1993, p. A1; and "Clinton Weighing Freeze or New Tax on Social Security," *New York Times*, January 31, 1993, p. A1.

25. Center on Budget and Policy Priorities, "Tax Cuts, Myths and Realities," November 16, 2007, www.cbpp.org/9-27-06tax.htm (accessed 3/20/08).

26. Jay Heflin, "House Dems Want Bush Tax Cuts to Expire, but Say It's Tough Sell," *The Hill*, 02/08/10, http://thehill.com/homenews/house/80133-democrats-supporting-ending-tax-cut-but-see-it-as-tough-sell (accessed 3/8/10).

27. Andrew Taylor, "With Half-Trillion in Red Ink, U.S. Inc. Looks Bad on Paper," *Congressional Quarterly Weekly*, January 17, 2004, p. 132.

28. Adam Levine, "Senate Rejects Additional F-22 Funding," *CNN Politics*, July 21, 2009, www.cnn.com/2009/POLITICS/07/21/senate.f22/index.html (accessed 3/8/10).

29. For an account of the relationship between mechanization and law, see Lawrence Friedman, *A History of American Law* (New York: Simon & Schuster, 1973), 409–29.

30. The *Federal Register* is the daily publication of all official acts of Congress, the president, and the administrative agencies. A law or executive order is not legally binding until it is published in the *Federal Register*.

31. New York Times, "Times Topics: Financial Regulatory Reform," http://topics.nytimes.com/topics/reference/timestopics/subjects/c/credit_crisis/financial_regulatory reform/index.html (accessed 3/7/10).

32. Sewell Chan, "Democrats Push Ahead on Finance Bill," *New York Times*, March 11, 2010, www.nytimes.com/2010/03/12/business/12regulate.html (accessed 3/11/10).

33. *Cato Handbook for Policymakers*, 7th ed. (Washington, DC: Cato Institute, 2009), p. 281, www.cato.org/pubs/handbook/hb111/hb111-26.pdf (accessed 3/19/10).

34. James Dao, "The Nation; Big Bucks Trip Up the Lean New Army," *New York Times*, February 10, 2002, sec. 4, p. 5.

35. See Samuel P. Hays, *Beauty, Health, and Permanence: Environmental Politics in the United States, 1955–1985* (Cambridge: Cambridge University Press, 1987).

36. Jonathan Harr, *A Civil Action* (New York: Vintage, 1996).

37. Pew Center on Global Climate Change, "Climate Change 101: The Science and Impacts," www.pewclimate.org/docUploads/101_Science_Impacts.pdf (accessed 3/21/08).

38. See the discussion in Peter R. Orszag, "Issues in Climate Change," Congressional Budget Office, November 16, 2007, www.cbo.gov/ftpdocs/88xx/doc8819/11-16-ClimateChangeConf.pdf (accessed 3/21/08).

39. Energy Information Administration, "Greenhouse Gases, Climate Change, and Energy," www.eia.doe.gov/oiaf/1605/ggccebro/chapter1.html (accessed 3/21/08).

40. John M. Broder and Marjorie Connelly, "Public Says Warming Is a Problem, But Remains Split on Response," *New York Times*, April 27, 2007, p. 20.

41. Juliet Eilperin and David A. Fahrenthold. "Harsh winter a sign of disruptive climate change, report says," *Washington Post*, January 28. 2010, www.washingtonpost.com/wp-dyn/content/article/2010/01/28/AR2010012800041.html (accessed 3/8/10).

42. Broder and Connelly, "Public Says Warming Is a Problem."

43. Survey by Cable News Network, conducted by Opinion Research Corporation, November 2–November 4, 2007 and based on telephone interviews with a national adult sample of 1,024. [USORC.110707.R05L]

44. Peter Baker, "In Bush's Final Year, the Agenda Gets Greener," *Washington Post*, December 29, 2007, p. A1.

45. Associated Press, "Obama Proposes Agency on Climate Change," February 8, 2010, www.cbsnews.com/stories/2010/02/08/tech/main6186608.shtml (accessed 3/8/10).

46. Broder and Connelly, "Public Says Warming Is a Problem."

47. Environmental Defense Fund, "Top Firms Call for Climate Action," www.edf.org/article.cfm?contentID=5828&bclid=CJjkwl_p-5ACFSoWiQodHGVGhA (accessed 3/21/08).

48. Juliet Eilperin and Steven Mufson, "Senators to Propose Abandoning Cap-and-Trade," *Washington Post*, February 27, 2010, www.washingtonpost.com/wp-dyn/content/article/2010/02/26/AR2010022606084.html?hpid=topnews (accessed 3/5/10).

49. The White House, "Energy and the Environment," www.whitehouse.gov/the-press-office/remarks-president-state-union-address; The White House, "Remarks by the President in the State of the Union Address," January 27, 2010, www.whitehouse.gov/issues/energy-and-environment (accessed 3/8/10).

50. Thomas L. Friedman, "The Power of Green," *New York Times*, April 15, 2007.

51. Orszag, "Issues in Climate Change."

52. Joe Palca, "California Turns to Holland for Flood Expertise," National Public Radio, January 14, 2008. www.npr.org/templates/story/story.php?storyId=18080442 (accessed 3/21/08).

53. Roger Pielke, Jr., Gwyn Prins, Steve Rayner, and Daniel Sarewitz, "Climate Change 2007: Lifting the Taboo on Adaptation," *Nature*, February 8, 2007, pp. 597–98.

54. Megan Garvey, "Company Town; SAG Says Canada Film Policies Illegal, Seeks Federal Inquiry," *Los Angeles Times*, August 22, 2001, part 3, p. 5.

55. David H. Autor, Lawrence F. Katz, and Melissa S. Kearney, "The Polarization of the U.S. Labor Market," *American Economic Review* 96, no. 2, (May 2006): 189–94 (6).

56. Thomas Piketty and Emmanuel Saez credit the progressive income tax with reducing income inequality in the

United States since the 1930s. See their argument in "Income Inequality in the United States, 1913–1998," *Quarterly Journal of Economics* 118, no. 1 (February 2003): 1–39.

57. Tax Policy Center, Table T06-0279 Combined Effect of the 2001–2006 Tax Cuts, Distribution of Federal Tax Change by Cash Income Percentile, 2006, November 13, 2006, www.taxpolicycenter.org/numbers/displayatab .cfm?DocID=1361 (accessed 3/22/08).

58. Robert H. Frank, *Falling Behind: How Rising Inequality Harms the Middle Class* (Berkeley: University of California Press, 2007).

59. For a classic statement, see Milton Friedman and Rose Friedman, *Free to Choose* (New York: Harvest Books, 1990). See also Bruce Bartlett, "Is Income Inequality Really a Problem?" *New York Times*, January 24, 2007, http://bartlett.blogs.nytimes.com/2007/01/24/is-income-inequality-really-a-problem/ (accessed 3/22/08).

60. David Sanger, David Herszenhorn, and Bill Vlasic, "Bush Aids Detroit, but Hard Choices Await Obama," *New York Times*, December 19, 2008, www.nytimes .com/2008/12/20/business/20auto.html? r=3&hp (accessed 3/7/10).

61. David Shepardson, "Obama Administration Predicts $30B Loss on Auto Bailout," *Detroit News*, December 8, 2009, http://detnews.com/article/20091208/ AUTO01/912080414/Obama-administration-predicts-$30B-loss-on-auto-bailout (accessed 3/7/10).

62. *New York Times*, "Times Topics: Car Allowance Rebate System (Cash for Clunkers)," http://topics.nytimes .com/topics/reference/timestopics/subjects/c/cash for clunkers/index.html (accessed 3/7/10).

63. Matthew Ericson, Elaine He, and Amy Schoenfeld, "Tracking the $700 Billion Bailout," *New York Times*, http://projects.nytimes.com/creditcrisis/recipients/ table (accessed 3/7/10).

64. *New York Times*. "Times Topics: Economic Stimulus," http://topics.nytimes.com/top/reference/timestopics/ subjects/u/united states economy/economic stimulus/ index.html (accessed 3/7/10).

65. U.S. Department of Labor, Bureau of Labor Statistics, "Table A-1, Employment Status of the Civilian Population by Sex and Age," www.bls.gov/news.release/ empsit.t01.htm (accessed 3/20/10).

66. *New York Times*, "Times Topics: Economic Stimulus," http://topics.nytimes.com/top/reference/timestopics/ subjects/u/united states economy/economic stimulus/ index.html (accessed 3/7/10).

67. Office of Management and Budget, "Federal Debt at the End of the Year, 1946–2015," *The Budget for Fiscal Year 2011, Historical Tables*, www.whitehouse.gov/omb/ budget/Historicals/ (accessed 3/7/10).

68. Jackie Calmes, "Party Gridlock in Washington Feeds Fear of a Debt Crisis," *New York Times*, February 16, 2010, www.nytimes.com/2010/02/17/business/ economy/17gridlock.html?pagewanted=1 (accessed 3/7/10).

69. Calmes, "Party Gridlock in Washington Feeds Fear of a Debt Crisis."

70. David Cho and Brady Dennis, "Financial System Reforms Won't Wait," *Washington Post*, March 12, 2010, p. All (accessed 3/12/10).

Chapter 17

1. A good source of pre-1930s welfare history is James T. Patterson, *America's Struggle against Poverty, 1900–1994* (Cambridge, MA: Harvard University Press, 1994), chap. 2.

2. Quoted in Patterson, *America's Struggle against Poverty*, 26.

3. Patterson, *America's Struggle against Poverty*, 26.

4. Patterson, *America's Struggle against Poverty*, 27.

5. This figure is based on a WPA study by Ann E. Geddes, reported in Merle Fainsod et al., *Government and the American Economy*, 3rd ed. (New York: Norton, 1959), 769.

6. Social Security Online, "Contribution and Benefit Base," www.socialsecurity.gov/OACT/COLA/cbb.html (accessed 4/22/10).

7. Edward J. Harpham, "Fiscal Crisis and the Politics of Social Security Reform," in *The Attack on the Welfare State*, eds. Anthony Champagne and Edward Harpham (Prospect Heights, IL: Waveland, 1984), 13.

8. Liz Schott and Zachary Levinson, *TANF Benefits Are Low and Have Not Kept Pace with Inflation* (Washington, DC: Center on Budget and Policy Priorities) November 24, 2008, www.cbpp.org/pdf/11-24-08tanf.pdf (accessed 3/11/10).

9. U.S. Department of Health and Social Services, Administration for Children and Families, LIHEAP Clearinghouse, 2010 HHS Poverty Guidelines, liheap.ncat.org/ profiles/povertytables/FY2010/popstate.htm (accessed 3/11/10).

10. *Goldberg v. Kelly*, 397 U.S. 254 (1970).

11. Henry J. Kaiser Family Foundation, Statehealthfacts. org, "Distribution of Medicaid Payments by Enrollment Group (in millions), FY2005," www.statehealthfacts .org/comparetable.jsp?ind=182&cat=4 (accessed 4/9/08).

12. See Martin Gilens, *Why Americans Hate Welfare* (Chicago: University of Chicago Press, 1999), chaps. 3, 4.

13. Gilens, *Why Americans Hate Welfare*.

14. Center for Law and Social Policy, "Analysis of Fiscal Year 2006 TANF and MOE Spending by States," http:// clasp.org/WelfarePolicy/pdf/map100907us.pdf (accessed 4/9/08).

15. See the discussion of the law and the data presented in House Ways and Means Committee Print, WMCP: 106-14, 2000 Green Book, Section 7, Temporary Assistance for Needy Families (TANF), http://frwebgate. access.gpo.gov/cgi-bin/useftp.cgi?IPaddress=162.140.64 .181&filename=wm014_07.wais&directory=/data/wais/ data/106_green_book (accessed 3/26/08); Rebecca M.

Blank, "Evaluating Welfare Reform in the United States," *Journal of Economic Literature* 40 (December 2002): 1105–66.

16. Robert Pear, "House Democrats Propose Making the '96 Welfare Law an Antipoverty Weapon," *New York Times*, January 24, 2002, p. A22.

17. Robin Toner, "Welfare Chief Is Hoping to Promote Marriage," *New York Times*, February 19, 2002, p. A1.

18. LaDonna Pavetti and Dottie Rosenbaum, *Creating a Safety Net that Works When the Economy Doesn't: The Role of the Food Stamps and TANF Programs* (Washington, DC: Center on Budget and Policy Priorities), February 25, 2010, www.cbpp.org/cms/index.cfm?fa=view&id=3096 (accessed 3/12/10).

19. Data for 2010 are estimates. Office of Management and Budget, The President's Budget, Historical Tables, Table 2.2, Percentage Composition of Receipts by Source: 1934–2015; Table 8.3, Percentage Distribution of Outlays by Budget Enforcement Act Category: 1962–2015, www.whitehouse.gov/omb/budget/Historicals/ (accessed 3/12/10).

20. President's Commission to Strengthen Social Security, "Strengthening Social Security and Creating Personal Wealth for All Americans," December 21, 2001, 5, www.csss.gov/reports/Final_report.pdf (accessed 3/26/08).

21. President's Commission to Strengthen Social Security, "Strengthening Social Security."

22. Alicia H. Munnell, "Are the Social Security Trust Funds Meaningful?" Center for Retirement Research, Boston College, May 2005, no. 30, p. 4, http://crr.bc.edu/images/stories/Briefs/ib_30.pdf (accessed 3/25/08); see also Social Security Online, Summary of P.L. 98-21, (H.R. 1900) Social Security Amendments of 1983—Signed on April 20, 1983, www.ssa.gov/history/1983amend.html (accessed 3/25/08).

23. Christian E. Weller, "Undermining Social Security with Private Accounts," Economic Policy Institute Issue Brief, December 11, 2001, www.epi.org/content.cfm/issuebriefs_ib172 (accessed 3/26/08); Robert Greenstein, "Social Security Commission Proposals Contain Serious Weaknesses but May Improve the Debate in an Important Respect," Center on Budget and Policy Priorities, December 26, 2001, www.centeronbudget.org/12-11-01socsec.htm (accessed 3/26/08).

24. Quoted in Jill Quadragno, "Social Security Policy and the Entitlement Debate," in *Social Policy and the Conservative Agenda*, eds. Clarence Y. H. Lo and Michael Schwartz (Malden, MA: Blackwell, 1998), 111.

25. There were a couple of minor precedents. One was the Smith-Hughes Act of 1917, which made federal funds available to the states for vocational education at the elementary and secondary levels. Second, the Lanham Act of 1940 made federal funds available to schools in "federally impacted areas," that is, areas with an unusually large number of government employees and/or where the local tax base was reduced by large amounts of government-owned property.

26. Office of Management and Budget, *Budget of the United States Government, Fiscal Year 1982* (Washington, DC: Government Printing Office, 1981), 427.

27. Sam Dillon, "Obama Proposes Sweeping Change in Education Law," *New York Times*, March 14, 2010, p. A1.

28. For an analysis of employment and training initiatives since the 1930s, see Margaret Weir, *Politics and Jobs* (Princeton, NJ: Princeton University Press, 1992).

29. On CETA, see Donald C. Baumer and Carl E. Van Horn, *The Politics of Unemployment* (Washington, DC: Congressional Quarterly Press, 1985).

30. Morton Keller, *Affairs of State: Public Life in Nineteenth Century America* (Cambridge, MA: Belknap Press, 1977), 500.

31. Office of Management and Budget, "Historical Tables, Budget of the United States Government, Fiscal Year 2011," Table 16.1—Outlays for Health Programs: 1962–2015, www.gpoaccess.gov/usbudget/fy11/pdf/hist.pdf (accessed 3/14/10); Henry J. Kaiser Family Foundation HIV/AIDS Policy Fact Sheet (March 2008), www.kff.org/hivaids/upload/7029_07.pdf (accessed 3/13/10).

32. For a description of the 2008 candidates' statements on health care, see "The Front Runners," *Washingtonpost.com*, http://projects.washingtonpost.com/2008-presidential-candidates/ (accessed 1/4/08); see also Atul Gawande, "The Obama Health Plan," *New York Times*, May 31, 2007, p. A19.

33. John E. Schwarz, *America's Hidden Success*, 2nd ed. (New York: Norton, 1988), 41–42.

34. U.S. Census Bureau Current Population Survey, Annual Social and Economic (ASEC) Supplement, "POV01: Age and Sex of All People, Family Members and Unrelated Individuals Iterated by Income-to-Poverty Ratio and Race: 2008," www.census.gov/hhes/www/cpstables/032009/pov/new01_100_01.htm (accessed 3/14/10).

35. See, for example, Theodore R. Marmor, Jerry L. Mashaw, and Philip L. Harvey, *America's Misunderstood Welfare State* (New York: Basic Books, 1990), 156.

36. Carmen DeNavas-Walt, Bernadette D. Proctor, and Jessica C. Smith, *Income, Poverty, and Health Insurance Coverage in the United States: 2008*, Table 1, Income and Earnings Summary Measures by Selected Characteristics: 2007 and 2008 (Washington, DC: U.S. Government Printing Office, 2009), p. 6, www.census.gov/prod/2009pubs/p60-236.pdf (accessed 3/14/10).

37. Burdett A. Loomis and Allan J. Cigler, "Introduction: The Changing Nature of Interest Group Politics," in *Interest Group Politics*, 4th ed., eds. Burdett A. Loomis and Allan J. Cigler (Washington, DC: Congressional Quarterly Press, 1995), 12.

38. See Senator Bob Kerrey's remarks quoted in David S. Broder, "Deficit Doomsday," *Washington Post*, August 7, 1994, p. C9.

39. Christopher Howard, *The Hidden Welfare State: Tax Expenditures and Social Policy in the United States* (Princeton, NJ: Princeton University Press, 1999); Jacob S. Hacker, *The Divided Welfare State: The Battle over Public and Private Benefits in the United States* (New York: Cambridge University Press, 2002).

40. Thomas L. Hungerford, "Tax Expenditures: Trends and Critiques," Congressional Research Service, September 13, 2006, http://assets.opencrs.com/rpts/RL33641_20060913 .pdf (accessed 3/25/08).

41. Raymond Hernandez, "Federal Welfare Overhaul Allows Albany to Shift Money Elsewhere," *New York Times*, April 23, 2000, p.1.

42. Frances Fox Piven and Richard Cloward, *Poor People's Movements* (New York: Pantheon, 1977), chap. 5.

43. U.S. Census Bureau, Current Population Survey, Annual Social and Economic (ASEC) Supplement, "POV01: Age and Sex of All People, Family Members and Unrelated Individuals Iterated by Income-to-Poverty Ratio and Race: 2008," www.census.gov/hhes/www/cpstables/032009/ pov/new01_100_01.htm (accessed 3/14/10).

44. DeNavas-Walt et al, *Income, Poverty, and Health Insurance Coverage*, Table 1, p. 6, www.census.gov/prod/ 2009pubs/p60-236.pdf (accessed 3/14/10).

45. See for example, Sharon Hayes, *Flat Broke with Children: Women in the Age of Welfare Reform* (New York: Oxford University Press, 2004).

46. For an argument that children should be given the vote, see Paul E. Peterson, "An Immodest Proposal," *Daedalus* 121 (Fall 1992): 151–74.

47. On the relationship between education and democracy in the United States, see Ira Katznelson and Margaret Weir, *Schooling for All: Race, Class, and the Democratic Ideal* (New York: Basic Books, 1985).

48. See L. Free and Hadley Cantril, *The Political Beliefs of Americans* (New York: Simon & Schuster, 1968).

49. See Fay Lomax Cook and Edith Barrett, *Support for the American Welfare State* (New York: Columbia University Press, 1992); and Hugh Heclo, "The Political Foundations of Antipoverty Policy," in *Fighting Poverty: What Works and What Doesn't*, eds. Sheldon H. Danziger and Daniel H. Weinberg (Cambridge, MA: Harvard University Press, 1986), 312–40.

Chapter 18

1. Geoffrey Perret, *A Country Made by War* (New York: Random House, 1989), 558.

2. Alexis de Tocqueville, *Democracy in America*., trans. Phillips Bradley, 2 vols. (1835; New York: Vintage, 1945), I, 243.

3. Rupert Smith, *The Utility of Force: The Art of War in the Modern World* (New York: Vintage, 2008).

4. D. Robert Worley, *Shaping U.S. Military Forces: Revolution or Relevance in a Post-Cold War World* (Westport, CT: Praeger Security International, 2006).

5. This was done quietly in an amendment to the Internal Revenue Service Reform Act (PL 105–206), June 22, 1998. But it was not accomplished easily. See Bob Gravely, "Normal Trade with China Wins Approval," *Congressional Quarterly Weekly Report*, July 25, 1998; and Richard Dunham, "MFN by any other name is . . . NTR?," Business Week online news flash, June 19, 1997.

6. Eduardo Porter, "True or False: Outsourcing Is a Crisis," *New York Times*, June 19, 2005, sec. 3, p. 4.

7. Deborah McGregor, "Democrats Set Trail Alight with Attacks on Free Trade," *Financial Times*, February 4, 2004, p. 9.

8. Matthew Crenson and Benjamin Ginsberg, *Presidential Power: Unchecked and Unbalanced* (New York: Norton, 2007).

9. Benjamin Ginsberg, *The American Lie: Government by the People and Other Political Fables* (Boulder, CO: Paradigm, 2007).

10. Paul R. Pillar, *Terrorism and American Foreign Policy* (Washington, DC: Brookings Institution Press, 2003).

11. Raymond A. Bauer, Ithiel de Sola Pool, and Lewis Anthony Dexter, *American Business and Public Policy: The Politics of Foreign Trade*, 2nd ed. (Chicago: Aldine-Atherton, 1972).

12. For a good treatment of this in regard to Irish Catholics and Catholics in general, see Timothy Byrnes, *Catholic Bishops and American Politics* (Princeton, NJ: Princeton University Press, 1991). For a (controversial) discussion of the role of Jewish groups, see John J. Mearsheimer and Stephen M. Walt, *The Israel Lobby and U.S. Foreign Policy* (New York: Farrar, Straus and Giroux, 2007).

13. This felicitous term is from David R. Mayhew, *Congress: The Electoral Connection* (New Haven: Yale University Press, 1974).

14. John H. Aldrich, *Why Parties? The Origin and Transformation of Political Parties in America* (Chicago: University of Chicago Press, 1995), 278.

15. A very good brief outline of the centrality of the president in foreign policy is found in Paul E. Peterson, "The President's Dominance in Foreign Policy Making," *Political Science Quarterly* 109 (Summer 1994): 215–34.

16. One confirmation of this is found in Theodore Lowi, *The End of Liberalism: The Second Republic of the United States*, 2nd ed. (New York: Norton, 1979), 127–30; another is found in Stephen Krasner, "Are Bureaucracies Important?" *Foreign Policy* 7 (Summer 1972): 159–79. However, it should be noted that Krasner was writing his article in disagreement with Graham T. Allison, "Conceptual Models and the Cu-ban Missile Crisis," American Political Science Review 63, no. 3 (September 1969): 689–718.

17. Peterson, "The President's Dominance in Foreign Policy Making," 232.

18. Hans Morgenthau, *Politics among Nations*, 2nd ed. (New York: Knopf, 1956), 505.

19. See Theodore Lowi, *The Personal President: Power Invested, Promise Unfulfilled* (Ithaca, NY: Cornell University Press, 1985), 167–69.

20. "IMF: Sleeve-Rolling Time," *Economist*, May 2, 1992, pp. 98–99.

21. James Dao and Patrick E. Tyler, "U.S. Says Military Strikes Are Just a Part of Big Plan," *The Alliance*, September 27, 2001; and Joseph Kahn, "A Nation Challenged: Global Dollars," *New York Times*, September 20, 2001, p. B1.

22. Turkey was desperate for help to extricate its economy from its worst recession since 1945. The Afghanistan crisis was going to hurt Turkey all the more; its strategic location helped its case with IMF. "Official Says Turkey Is Advancing in Drive for I.M.F. Financing," *New York Times*, October 6, 2001, p. A7.

23. George Quester, *The Continuing Problem of International Politics* (Hinsdale, IL: Dryden Press, 1974), 229.

Chapter 19

1. Molly Ivins quoted in Jon Thurber, "Obituaries; Bob Bullock; Colorful Longtime Politician in Texas," *Los Angeles Times*, June 20, 1999.

2. Alan Rosenthal, "On Analyzing States," in *The Political Life of the American States*, ed. Alan Rosenthal and Maureen Moakley (New York: Praeger, 1984), 11–12.

3. Daniel Elazar, *American Federalism: A View from the States*, 2nd ed. (New York: Crowell, 1971), 84–126. See also John Kincaid, "Introduction," in *Political Culture, Public Policy and the American States*, ed. John Kincaid (Philadelphia: Center for the Study of Federalism, Institute for the Study of Human Issues, 1982), 1–24.

4. Rosenthal, 13.

5. See Dallas Morning News, *Texas Almanac* 2010–2011 (Dallas: Dallas Morning News, 2010), 395, 396.

6. The following is drawn from Dallas Morning News, *Texas Almanac 2000–2001* (Dallas: Dallas Morning News, 1999), 55–58.

7. See Dallas Morning News, *Texas Almanac 2000–2001*, 62; Ogallala Aquifer, http://ogallala.tamu.edu/economics.php (accessed 3/28/08).

8. See Joseph A. Schumpeter, *Capitalism, Socialism, and Democracy*, 3rd ed. (New York: Harper & Brothers, 1950), chap. 6.

9. The following is drawn from Karen Gerhardt Britton, Fred C. Elliott, and E. A. Miller, "Cotton Culture," *The Handbook of Texas Online*, www.tshaonline.org/handbook/online/articles/CC/afc3.html (accessed 3/28/08).

10. See Dallas Morning News, *Texas Almanac 2000–2001*, 51.

11. *Texas Almanac 2000–2001*, 567–68.

12. See "Ranching" in *The Handbook of Texas Online*, www.tshaonline.org/handbook/online/articles/RR/azr2.html (accessed 3/28/08).

13. Dallas Morning News, *Texas Almanac 2010–2011*, 673–85.

14. The following is drawn from Mary G. Ramos, "Oil and Texas: A Cultural History," Dallas Morning News, *Texas Almanac 2000–2001*, 29–35; and Roger M. Olien, "Oil and Gas Industry," *The Handbook of Texas Online*, www.tshaonline.org/handbook/online/articles/OO/doogz.html (accessed 3/28/08).

15. Ramos, 31.

16. Olien, "Oil and Gas Industry."

17. Texas State Comptroller, www.window.state.tx.us/taxbud/revenue_hist.html#2008.

18. UTIMCO 2009 Annual Report, Fund Management Overview, http://www.utimco.org/funds/allfunds/2009annual/ar_fund_mgmt.asp (accessed 7/7/10).

19. The following is drawn from Anthony Champagne and Edward J. Harpham, "The Changing Political Economy of Texas," in *Texas Politics: A Reader*, 2nd ed., ed. Anthony Champagne and Edward J. Harpham (New York: Norton, 1998), 4–6. Production figures are drawn from Dallas Morning News, *Texas Almanac 1994–95* (Dallas: Belo, 1993); and John Sharp, *Forces of Change: Shaping the Future of Texas* (Austin: Texas Comptroller of Public Accounts, 1993).

20. *Texas Almanac 2010–2011*, 603.

21. Anil Kumar, "Did NAFTA Spur Texas Exports?" *Southwest Economy* 2 (March–April 2006), www.dallasfed.org/research/swe/2006/swe0602b.html (accessed 3/28/08); and U.S. Department of Labor Employment & Training Administration, "Trade Adjustment Assistance: Number of Certified Workers by State," www.doleta.gov/tradeact/workermap.cfm (accessed 6/4/08).

22. Texas Economy Online Report from the Office of the Governor, www.texaswideopenforbusiness.com (accessed 7/7/10).

23. Daniel Gross, posted Monday, April 19, 2010, "Lone Star: Why Texas Is Doing So Much Better than the Rest of the Nation," www.slate.com/id/2250999 (accessed 7/7/10).

24. Bruce Wright, "Weathering the Storm," *Fiscal Notes*, March 2009 at www.window.state.tx.us/comptrol/fnotes/fn0903/economy.html; D'Ann Petersen and Laila Assanie, "Texas Dodges Worst of Foreclosure Wars," Federal Reserve of Dallas, http://www.dallasfed.org/research/swe/2009/swe0904c.cfm (accessed 7/7/10).

25. Federal Reserve Bank of Dallas, *Texas Leading Economic Indicators*, May 2010.

26. See "Estimated Population by Year for Texas, 1980–94," www.txsdc.tamu.edu/txnypop.html (accessed 3/28/08).

27. *Texas Almanac 2007–2008*, 411.

28. See Arnoldo De León, "Mexican Americans," *The Handbook of Texas Online*, www.tshaonline.org/handbook/online/articles/MM/pqmue.html (accessed 3/28/08).

29. Pew Hispanic Center, "A Statistical Portrait of Hispanics at Mid-Decade" (September 2006), http://pewhispanic.org/reports/middecade/ (accessed 3/28/08).

30. www.naleo.org/downloads/NALEO_LEH_2008_final.pdf08postELEC-PROFILE.pdf. (accessed 11/4/10).

31. See W. Marvin Dulaney, "African Americans," *The Handbook of Texas Online*, www.tshaonline.org/handbook/online/articles/AA/pkaan.html (accessed 3/28/08); and Chandler Davidson, "African Americans and Politics," *The Handbook of Texas Online*, www.tshaonline.org/handbook/online/articles/AA/wmafr.html (accessed 3/28/08).

32. U.S. Census Bureau, "Texas," www.quickfacts.census.gov/qfd/states/48000.htm (accessed 11/4/10).

33. Bruce H. Webster, Jr., and Alemayehu Bishaw, "Income, Earnings, and Poverty Data from the 2006 American Community Survey" (American Community Survey Reports, U.S. Census Bureau, August 2007), www.census.gov/prod/2007pubs/acs-08.pdf (accessed 3/28/08); U.S. Census Bureau, *Poverty 2007 and 2008 American Community Surveys* (September 2009), www.census.gov/prod/2009pubs/acsbr08-1.pdf (accessed 7/7/10).

34. The following is based on David G. McComb, "Urbanization," *The Handbook of Texas Online*, www.tshaonline.org/handbook/online/articles/UU/hyunw.html (accessed 3/28/08).

35. The following is drawn from David G. McComb, "Houston, Texas," *The Handbook of Texas Online*, www.tshaonline.org/handbook/online/articles/HH/hdh3.html (accessed 3/28/08).

36. Estimates are drawn from U.S. Census Bureau, American Community Survey 2006–2008, www.census.gov/prod/2009pubs/acsbr08-1.pdf (accessed 7/7/10).

37. The following is drawn from Jackie McElhaney and Michael V. Hazel, "Dallas, Texas," *The Handbook of Texas Online*, www.tshaonline.org/handbook/online/articles/DD/hddl.html (accessed 3/28/08).

38. The following is drawn from Janet Schmelzer, "Fort Worth, Texas," *The Handbook of Texas Online*, www.tshaonline.org/handbook/online/articles/FF/hdfl.html (accessed 3/28/08).

39. The following is drawn from T. R. Fehrenbach, "San Antonio, Texas," *The Handbook of Texas Online*, www.tshaonline.org/handbook/online/articles/SS/hds2.html (accessed 3/28/08).

40. Estimates are drawn from U.S. Census Bureau, American Community Survey 2006–2008, www.census.gov/prod/2009pubs/acsbr08-1.pdf (accessed 7/7/10).

Chapter 20

1. The following is drawn from Proposition 10, Deleting Constitutional References to County Office of inspector of Hides and Animals, www.hro.house.state.tx.us/focus prop80–10.pdf (accessed 3/31/08); Eric Aasen, "Round 'Em Up: Hide Inspectors Abolished," *Dallas Morning News*, November 8, 2007; John Council, "Richmond Lawyer Has Personal Stake in Hide Inspector Position," *Texas Lawyer*, November 2, 2007; Mark Lisheron, "Prop 10. Would Abolish Office That No One Holds," *Austin American-Statesman*, October 15, 2007.

2. See Dick Smith, "Inspector of Hides and Animals," *The Handbook of Texas Online*, www.tshaonline.org/handbook/online/articles/II/mbil.html (accessed 3/31/08).

3. Donald E. Chipman, "Spanish Texas," *The Handbook of Texas Online*, www.tshaonline.org/handbook/-online/articles/SS/npsl.html (accessed 3/31/08); Donald E. Chipman, *Spanish Texas, 1519–1821* (Austin: University of Texas Press, 1992).

4. S. S. McKay, "Constitution of 1824," *The Handbook of Texas Online*, www.tshaonline.org/handbook/online/articles/CC/ngc2.html (accessed 3/31/08).

5. S. S. McKay, "Constitution of Coahuila and Texas," *The Handbook of Texas Online*, www.tshaonline.org/handbook/online/articles/CC/ngcl.html (accessed 3/31/08).

6. See Ralph W. Steen, "Convention of 1836," *The Handbook of Texas Online*, www.tshaonline.org/handbook/online/articles/CC/mjc12.html (accessed 3/31/08).

7. The following is drawn from Joe E. Ericson, "Constitution of the Republic of Texas," *The Handbook of Texas Online*, www.tshaonline.org/handbook/online/articles/CC/mhcl.html (accessed 3/31/08).

8. Randolph B. Campbell, "Slavery," *The Handbook of Texas Online*, www.tshaonline.org/handbook/online/articles/SS/ypsl.html (accessed 3/31/08).

9. For a brief summary of the war, see Eugene C. Barker and James W. Pohl, "Texas Revolution," *The Handbook of Texas Online*, www.tshaonline.org/handbook/online/articles/TT/qdtl.html (accessed 3/31/08).

10. S. S. McKay, "Constitution of 1845," *The Handbook of Texas Online*, www.tshaonline.org/handbook/online/articles/CC/mhc3.html (accessed 3/31/08).

11. The Texas Ordinance of Secession (February 2, 1861), www.lsjunction.com/docs/secession.htm (accessed 3/31/08).

12. See Walter L. Buenger, "Secession Convention," *The Handbook of Texas Online*, www.tshaonline.org/handbook/online/articles/SS/mjsl.html (accessed 3/31/08); Walter L. Buenger, *Secession and the Union in Texas* (Austin: University of Texas Press, 1984).

13. See Claude Elliott, "Constitutional Convention of 1866," *The Handbook of Texas Online*, www.tshaonline

.org/handbook/online/articles/CC/mjc3.html (accessed 3/31/08); S. McKay, "Constitution of 1866," *The Handbook of Texas Online*, www.tshaonline.org/handbook/online/articles/CC/mhc5.html (accessed 3/31/08); Charles W. Ramsdell, *Reconstruction in Texas* (New York: Columbia University Press, 1970).

14. See S. S. McKay, "Constitution of 1869," *The Handbook of Texas Online*, www.tshaonline.org/handbook/online/articles/CC/mhc6.html (accessed 3/31/08); Ramsdell, *Reconstruction in Texas.*

15. See John Walker Mauer, "Constitution Proposed in 1874," *The Handbook of Texas Online*, www.tshaonline.org/handbook/online/articles/CC/mhcl2.html (accessed 3/31/08); John Walker Mauer, "State Constitutions in a Time of Crisis: The Case of the Texas Constitution of 1876," *Texas Law Review* 68 (June 1990).

16. For a further discussion, see George D. Braden et al., *The Constitution of the State of Texas: An Annotated and Comparative Analysis* (Austin: University of Texas Press, 1977), 707–10, www.sll.state.tx.us/const/braden.html (accessed 3/31/08).

17. See Sam Kinch, Jr., "Sharpstown Stock-Fraud Scandal," *The Handbook of Texas Online*, www.tshaonline.org/handbook/online/articles/SS/mqsl.html (accessed 3/31/08); Charles Deaton, *The Year They Threw the Rascals Out* (Austin: Shoal Creek, 1973).

18. Angela Shah, "Both Sides Claim Victory in Approval of Lawsuit Caps," *Dallas Morning News*, September 15, 2003, pp. 1A, 10A.

19. Terry Maxon, "Prop. 12 Battle Was Costliest Yet," *Dallas Morning News*, January 19, 2004, p. 2D.

20. John Council, "Power and the Prize," *Texas Lawyer*, June 16, 2003, pp. 1, 22.

Chapter 21

1. Jeffrey M. Jones, "Special Report: Many States Shift Democratic During 2005," *The Gallup Poll*, January 23, 2006, www.gallup.com/poll/21004/Special-Report-Many-States-Shift-Democratic-During-2005.aspx (accessed 4/7/08).

2. Use of party affiliation as an ideological cue is discussed in Philip L. Dubois, *From Ballot to Bench* (Austin: University of Texas Press, 1980).

3. Quoted in Chandler Davidson, *Race and Class in Texas Politics* (Princeton, NJ: Princeton University Press, 1990), 198.

4. Davidson, *Race and Class in Texas Politics*, 24–25.

5. Jones, "Special Report: Many States Shift Democratic During 2005."

6. Pew Research Center for the People and the Press, "Fewer Voters Identify as Republicans," March 20, 2008.

7. Gallup, "Party ID: Despite GOP Gains, Most States Remain Blue," February 1, 2010.

8. James R. Soukup, Clifton McClesky, and Harry Holloway, *Party and Factional Division in Texas* (Austin: University of Texas Press, 1964), 22.

9. Wayne Slater, "Strayhorn Gets Democratic Cash," *Dallas Morning News*, January 26, 2006, pp. 1A, 17A.

10. Pete Slover, "Independents' Day is a Bid for the Ballot," *Dallas Morning News*, March 8, 2006, p. 14A.

11. Robert T. Garrett, "2 Major GOP Donors Show Rift in Party," *Dallas Morning News*, February 3, 2006, p. 2A.

12. Robert T. Garrett, "PAC's Late Aid Altered Races," *Dallas Morning News*, March 10, 2006, pp. 1A, 16A.

13. Terri Langford, "District Judge Fends off Democratic Rival's Challenge," *Dallas Morning News*, November 9, 2000.

14. Anthony Champagne and Greg Thielemann, "Awareness of Trial Court Judges," *Judicature* 75 (1991): 271–72.

15. Anthony Champagne, "The Selection and Retention of Judges in Texas," *Southwestern Law Journal* 40 (1986): 80.

16. The lone Democratic survivor, Ron Chapman, became an appellate judge. Democratic judges who did not switch to the Republican Party were defeated.

17. Langford, "District Judge Fends off Democratic Rival's Challenge."

18. Joe Holley, "Are Texas' Hispanics Ready to Go Democrat?" *Houston Chronicle*, April 3, 2010.

19. In 1994, it was estimated that there were between 420,000 and 460,000 illegal immigrants in Texas. Many of those illegal immigrants were Hispanic. See Leon F. Bouvier and John L. Martin, "Shaping Texas: The Effects of Immigration, 1970–2020," Center for Immigration Studies, April 1995, www.cis.org/articles/1995/texas.html (accessed 4/7/08). The Federation for American Immigration Reform cites the Immigration and Naturalization Service for a January 2000 estimate that there were 1,041,000 illegal immigrants then in Texas. See their report, "Texas: Illegal Aliens," www.fairus.org/site/PageServier?pagename=research_researchable (accessed 4/7/08). An April 2006 study by the Pew Hispanic Center estimated that between 1.4 and 1.6 million unauthorized individuals were living in Texas. Pew Hispanic Center, "Estimates of the Unauthorized Migrant Population for States Based on the March 2006 CPS, Fact Sheet: April 26, 2006," http://pewhispanic.org/files/factsheets/17.pdf (accessed 4/7/08).

20. Holley, "Are Texas' Hispanics Ready to Go Democrat?"

21. Texas Secretary of State, "Turnout and Voter Registration Figures, 1970–Current," www.sos.state.tx/elections/historical/70-92.shtml (accessed 4/7/08). Dallas and Harris counties have more voting precincts than are found in the entire state of New Hampshire.

22. Sam Acheson, *Joe Bailey: The Last Democrat* (New York: Macmillan, 1932), 354.

23. Joe Robert Baulch, "James B. Wells: State Economic and Political Leader" (Ph.D. dissertation, Texas Tech University, 1974), 358–59.
24. Sue Tolleson-Rinehart and Jeanie R. Stanley, *Claytie and the Lady* (Austin: University of Texas Press, 1994), 18–19.
25. O. Douglas Weeks, "The Texas-Mexican and the Politics of South Texas 34," *American Political Science Review* (1930): 625–26; Anthony Champagne, "John Nance Garner," in *Masters of the House*, ed. Roger H. Davidson, Susan Webb Hammond, and Raymond W. Smock (Boulder, CO: Westview, 1998), 145–80.
26. *U.S. v. Texas*, 384 U.S. 155 (1966).
27. *Beare v. Smith*, 321 F. Supp. 1100 (1971).
28. *Kramer v. Union Free School District No. 15*, 395 U.S. 621 (1969); *Hill v. Stone*, 421 U.S. 289 (1975).
29. *Dunn v. Blumstein*, 405 U.S. 330 (1972).
30. *Newberry v. United States*, 256 U.S. 232 (1921).
31. *Nixon v. Herndon*, 273 U.S. 536 (1927).
32. *Nixon v. Condon*, 286 U.S. 73 (1932).
33. *Grovey v. Townsend*, 295 U.S. 45 (1935).
34. *Smith v. Allwright*, 321 U.S. 649 (1944).
35. *Terry v. Adams*, 345 U.S. 461 (1953).
36. www.sos.state.tx.us/elections/historical/70-92.shtml (accessed 11/4/10).
37. The motor voter law is a federal statute that requires states to allow voter registration when individuals apply for or renew their driver's licenses.
38. Ibid.
39. Thomas R. Patterson, *The American Democracy* (New York: McGraw Hill, 1999), 188.
40. Susan Combs, Texas Comptroller of Public Accounts, "Texas Where We Stand: Education," Window on State Government, undated.
41. Texas Performance Review, "Challenging the Status Quo: Toward Smaller, Smarter Government," vol. 1.
42. Center for Public Policy Priorities, "Census Data Shows Only Beginning of Texans' Growing Need," September 29, 2009.
43. For this classic in campaign mistakes, see the October 2002 issue of *Texas Monthly* magazine. An example of the negative impact of the ad can be found in a front-page article, Wayne Slater and Pete Slover, "Dewhurst Campaign Ad: The Flag Is Ours, But What's with the German Officer?" *Dallas Morning News*, October 26, 2001.
44. Candidates in Texas Supreme Court races are affected by "friends and neighbors" voting, whereby voters tend to cast ballots for candidates from their home county or from neighboring counties. See Gregory Thielemann, "Local Advantage in Campaign Financing: Friends, Neighbors, and Their Money in Texas Supreme Court Elections," *Journal of Politics* 55 (1993): 472–78.
45. Roy A. Schotland, "Campaign Finance in Judicial Elections," *Loyola of Los Angeles Law Review*, (2001), 1508–12.

Chapter 22

1. 545 U.S. 469.
2. James W. Lamare, *Texas Politics: Economics, Power and Policy*, 3rd ed. (St. Paul: West, 1988), 82.
3. Kenneth R. Mladenka and Kim Quaile Hill, *Texas Government: Politics and Economics* (Belmont, CA: Wadsworth, 1986), 80–82.
4. Kristen Mack, "New Lawmakers Learn to Juggle Hectic Lives; Everybody—Lobbyists, Family—Wants a Moment of Their Time," *Houston Chronicle*, February 6, 2005, p. 1B.
5. Texans for Public Justice, "Power Surge: TXU's Patronage Grid Plugs All but Seven Lawmakers," Lobby Watch, March 1, 2007.
6. Steve McGonigle, "For Perry, Big Game Means Big Business—Trucking Lobby Paid for Governor's Private Jet to Rose Bowl," *Dallas Morning News*, December 12, 2006.
7. Emily Ramshaw and Marcus Funk, "For Some Dallas-area Legislators, Donations Fund the Good Life," *Dallas Morning News*, February 1, 2009.
8. Texas for Public Justice, "Ten New Lawmaker Retreads Merge into the 2009 Lobby," Lobby Watch, May 20, 2009.
9. Texans for Public Justice, "Ten New Lawmakers."
10. Texas Ethics Commission, 2009 Lobby Lists (2009).
11. Texas Ethics Commission.
12. Texans for Public Justice, "Austin's Oldest Profession" (2008).
13. Texans for Public Justice, "Austin's Oldest Profession."
14. Texans for Public Justice, "Texas Revolvers: Public Officials Recast as Hired Guns" (1999).
15. Texans for Public Justice, "Special-Interests Spend Up to $180 Million on Lobby Services in 1999 Legislative Session," May 24, 1999.
16. Texans for Public Justice, "Money in Politex" (2008).
17. Anthony Champagne, Campaign Contributions in Texas Supreme Court Races," *Crime, Law & Social Change* 17 (1992); 91–106.
18. Texas for Public Justice, "Texans for Lawsuit Reform Sustains Pricey Primary Hits," Lobby Watch, March 5, 2010; Julian Aguilar, "Primary Color: HD-43, *The Texas Tribune*, February 26, 2010.
19. National Institute on Money in State Politics.
20. Texans for Public Justice, "Interested Parties" (2009).
21. Mack, "New Lawmakers Learn to Juggle Hectic Lives."
22. Texans for Public Justice, "Texans for Lawsuit Reform."
23. Texans for Public Justice, "Operation Vouchsafe: Dr. Leininger Injects $5 Million into Election; Many Candidates Fail on His Life Support," Lobby Watch, n.d.

24. Emily Ramshaw, "Fighting for Fair Warning—Man Who Lost Wife, Kids in Blaze Seeks Visual Smoke Alarms for Deaf," *Dallas Morning News*, April 17, 2009; "Tragedy Leads to Improved Fire Safety in Texas," National Association of the Deaf, July 1, 2009.

Chapter 23

1. The above is drawn from S. C. Gwynne, "Tom Craddick. How Did Tom Craddick Become the Most Powerful Speaker Ever—and the Most Powerful Texan Today? Let Us Count the Ways," *Texas Monthly*, February 2005, www.texasmonthly.com; R. G. Ratcliffe and Gary Scharrer, "Craddick Safe as Session Ends, but '08 Race Is Ahead," *Houston Chronicle*, May 28, 2007, www.chron.com; Dan Collins, "Chaos in Texas House over Speaker Fight," CBSNEWS, May 26, 2007, www.cbsnews.com; Karen Brooks and Christy Hoppe, "Craddick Quits House Speaker's Race; Straus Poised to Take Over," *Dallas Morning News*, January 5, 2009; Karen Brooks, "GOP Bloc Backs Joe Straus to Topple House Speaker Tom Craddick," *Dallas Morning News*, January 3, 2009.
2. *Dallas Morning News*, "Senate Gives Tentative OK to Guns on Campuses," May 20, 2009.
3. Ann Marie Kilday, "Equal Measure," *Dallas Morning News*, May 24, 2001, p. 31A.
4. Anthony Champagne and Rick Collis, "Texas," in *The Political Life of the American States*, ed. Alan Rosenthal and Maureen Moakley (New York: Praeger, 1984), 138.
5. Kelley Shannon, "Doctor Twice Honored by the Texas Legislature Registered as Sex Offender," *Sulphur Springs News-Telegram*, June 22, 2007, p. 1.
6. Frank M. Stewart, "Impeachment in Texas," *American Political Science Review* 24, no. 3 (August 1930): 652–58; George D. Braden et al., *The Constitution of the State Texas: An Annotated and Comparative Analysis* (Austin University of Texas Press, 1977), 707–18.
7. Texas Legislature, Legislative Statistics, 4-20-2010.
8. Lisa Falkenberg, "Texas Lawmakers Scramble to Finish Last-Minute Bills," *Dallas Morning News*, March 10, 2001, p. 38A.
9. Steve Bickerstaff, *Lines in the Sand: Congressional Redistricting in Texas and the Downfall of Tom DeLay* (Austin University of Texas Press, 2007), 242–43.
10. Office of Governor Rick Perry, "Press Release," June 19, 2009.
11. Karen Brooks, "Craddick's Win May Cost Him," *Dallas Morning News*, May 27, 2007, p. 1.
12. Karen Brooks, "In 1877, Lawmakers Ran Republican Out of the Chair," *Dallas Morning News*, May 27, 2007, p. 26A.
13. John W. Gonzalez, "Texas Legislature; Jobs Well Done; Laney, Lauded for Maintaining Order and Fairness, Ends 3rd Term as Speaker," *Houston Chronicle*, June 6, 1999, p. State 1.
14. Vince Leibowitz, "Texas Senate Republicans Trying to Dump Two-Thirds Voting Rule," *Capitol Annex*, January 14, 1009.
15. Terrence Stutz, "Texas Senate at Odds over Voter ID Legislation, Two-Thirds Rule," *Dallas Morning News*, January 14, 2009.
16. *Baker v. Carr*, U.S. 186 (1962); *Reynolds v. Sims*, 377 U.S. 533 (1964).
17. *Wesberry v. Sanders*, 376 U.S. 1 (1964).
18. Sam Attlesey, "Panel OKs Map Favoring GOP," *Dallas Morning News*, December 7, 2001.
19. The above is drawn from Sam Attlesey, "Taking Stock of the Fallout from Redistricting," *Dallas Morning News*, December 11, 2001; Terrance Stutz, "GOP Expecting to Grab the House," *Dallas Morning News*, January 3, 2002; Sam Attlesey, "Before Election, House Democrats Seeing Losses," *Dallas Morning News*, December 11, 2001.
20. Medill School of Journalism, "On the Docket: League of United Latin American Citizens, Travis County, *Jackson, Eddie and GI Forum of Texas v. Perry, Rick (Texas Gov.).*"
21. State Appellants' Brief in the Supreme Court of the United States, *LULAC v. Perry.*
22. Medill School of Journalism, "On the Docket."
23. Appellants' Brief on the Merits, *LULAC v. Perry*, www.tlc.state.tx.us/redist/pdf/05-204_Appellants.pdf (accessed 4/10/08).
24. See, generally, Bickerstaff, *Lines in the Sand.*

Chapter 24

1. The next two paragraphs rely on James C. McKinley, Jr. "Re-elected Texas Governor Sounding Like a Candidate." *The New York Times*. November 5, 2010: A18.
2. See the discussion of gubernatorial power in Cheryl D. Young and John J. Hindera, "The Texas Governor: Weak or Strong?" in *Texas Politics: A Reader*, ed. Anthony Champagne and Edward J. Harpham (New York: Norton, 1998), 53.
3. Sam Kinch, in *Government by Consent—Texas, A Telecourse* (Dallas: Dallas County Community College District, 1990).
4. Brian McCall, *The Power of the Texas Governor: Connally to Bush* (Austin: University of Texas Press, 2009).
5. Kinch, *Government.*
6. Polly Ross Hughes, "Farewell to a Yalie, Howdy to an Aggie," *Houston Chronicle*, December 14, 2000, p. 1A.
7. Hughes, p. 26A.
8. George Kuempel, "The Tab Texas Taxpayers Are Picking up for Security Protection," *Dallas Morning News*, February 2, 2000, p. 25A.

9. William P. Hobby, in *Government by Consent*.

10. Christy Hoppe, "Lt. Gov. Rick Perry, Honoring the Economic Generators of Texas Tourism," *Dallas Morning News*, February 28, 2000, p. 13A.

11. Hoppe, "Lt. Gov. Rick Perry."

12. Young and Hindera, 62.

13. Richard Whittaker, "Gov. Perry's Ham-Fisted Veto Pen Strikes Again," *Austin Chronicle*, June 22, 2007.

14. Office of Governor Rick Perry, "Governor Perry Signs State Budget That Reduces GR by $1.6 Billion," Press Release, June 19, 2009.

15. Texas Legislative Library, Special Sessions of the Texas Legislature (2010).

16. Young and Hindera, 61.

17. Young and Hindera, 61.

18. The above discussion was taken from Jim Yardley, "Public Lives; This Texan, Too, Has a Lot Riding on Bush's Campaign," *New York Times*, October 7, 2000, p. 9; and Kathy Walt, "Texas Legislature; Jobs Well Done; Senators Give Perry High Marks after Starting out with Low Expectation," *Houston Chronicle*, June 6, 1999, p. State 1.

19. Jim Yardley, "Public Lives; A Power in Texas Governing Finds Fault in Texas Politics," *New York Times*, June 9, 2001, p. A7.

20. Texas General Land Office, "About the Land Office."

21. Christy Hoppe, "Perry's Appointees Give Him Unprecedented Hold on Texas—Longest-Serving Governor Spreads Pro-Business View," *Dallas Morning News*, December 19, 2008.

22. Christy Hoppe, "Perry Ousts Officials before Arson Hearing—He's Assailed as New Chair Delays Session on Flawed Case That Led to Execution," *Dallas Morning News*, October 1, 2009.

23. William McKenzie, "Rich Perry's Curious Ways—Governor's Strongman Tactics Are Hard to Comprehend amid a Heated Campaign, says William McKenzie," *Dallas Morning News*, October 20, 2009.

24. Terrence Stutz, "Senate Rejects Perry Appointee to Parole Board—Activist Faulted on Credentials; Governor Stands by Nominee," *Dallas Morning News*, May 14, 2009.

25. Texas Department of Insurance, "Texas Department of Insurance History."

26. Bill Peacock, "Policy Perspective: Is the Free Market Working for the Texas Homeowners' Insurance Market?" Texas Public Policy Foundation, February 28, 2006.

27. Terrence Stutz, "State Farm Stiff-Arming Regulators," *Dallas Morning News*, April 14, 2010.

28. Terrence Stutz, "Legal Tactics Stall Insurance Reform," DallasNews.com, September 16, 2007.

29. Russell Shorto, "How Christian Were the Founders?" *New York Times*, February 14, 2010; Terrence Stutz, "Debate Continues over Social Studies," *Dallas Morning News*, March 11, 2010.

Chapter 25

1. Ralph Blumenthal, "Texas Judge Draws Outery for Allowing an Execution," *New York Times*, October 25, 2007; Christy Hoppe, "Criminal Appeals Court Creates Emergency Filing System." DallasNews.com. November 6, 2007; "Texas Judge Fosters Tough-on-Crime Reputation," MSNBC, October 23, 2007; State Commission on Judicial Conduct, Special Master's Findings of Fact, In Re: Honorable Sharon Keller, Presiding Judge of the Texas Court of Criminal Appeals, January 20, 2010.

2. Texas Office of Court Administration, "Activity Report for Justice Courts, September 1, 2008 to August 31, 2009."

3. Barbara Kirby, "Neighborhood Justice: Campaign Funding and Texas Justice of the Peace Courts," paper presented at the annual meeting of the Southern Political Science Association, New Orleans, Louisiana, January 3, 2007.

4. Ed Housewright. "Emotional Issues, Historical Pedigree," *Dallas Morning News*, April 9, 2001, p. 10A.

5. Texas Office of Court Administration, "Activity Report for Municipal Courts, September 1, 2008 to August 31, 2009."

6. Texas Office of Court Administration. "Activity Report for Municipal Courts, September 1, 2008 to August 31, 2009."

7. Thomas Petzinger, Jr., *Oil and Honor: The Texaco-Pennzoil Wars* (New York: Putnam, 1987).

8. Task Force on Indigent Defense, "Evidence for the Feasibility of Public Defender Offices in Texas."

9. Mary Alice Robbins. "West Texas Plans Public Defender Office for Capital Cases," *Texas Lawyer*, August 20, 2007, pp. 1, 19. "New Public defender for capital cases," Tex Part Blog, October 16, 2007.

10. Ken Anderson, *Crime in Texas* (Austin: University of Texas Press, 1997), 40.

11. Anderson, 44. Nationally, 95 percent of felonies are plea-bargained.

12. Of the seventy-nine judicial appointments made by Governor William Clements, only six were either African American or Hispanic. In contrast, one-third of Governor Ann Richards's judicial appointees were minorities. See Michael Totty, "Is This Any Way to Choose a Judge?" *Wall Street Journal*, August 3, 1994, pp. T1, T4.

13. Texas Office of Court Administration, "Profile of Appellate and Trial Judges as of September 1, 2009."

14. Anthony Champagne, "The Selection and Retention of Judges in Texas," *Southwestern Law Journal* 4 (1986), 78–79.

15. Texans for Public Justice, "Payola Justice: How Texas Supreme Court Justices Raise Money from Court Litigants."

16. Texans for Public Justice. "Judging Texas Justice in the Court of Opinion."

17. L. Douglas Kiel, Carole Funk, and Anthony Champagne, "Two-party Competition and Trial Court Elections in Texas," *Judicature* 77 (1994), 291.

18. Linda Campbell, "'H' as in Herasimchuk," *Fort Worth Star-Telegram*, December 6, 2001.

19. Anthony Champagne and Greg Thielemann, "Awareness of Trial Court Judges," *Judicature* 74 (1991), 271–76.

20. Mary Flood and Brian Rogers, "Why Some Harris County Judges Lost Not Entirely Clear," *Houston Chronicle*, November 6, 2008.

21. Elliott Slotnik, "Gender, Affirmative Action, and Recruitment to the Federal Bench," *Golden Gate University Law Review* 14 (1984), 524.

22. Texas Office of Court Administration, Profile of Appellate and Trial Judges as of September 1, 2009.

23. Barbara L. Graham, "Toward an Understanding of Judicial Diversity in American Courts," *Michigan Journal of Race and Law* 10 (2004), 178.

24. One report is that 90 percent of African American voters and 60 to 79 percent of Hispanic voters vote Democratic. See Ronald W. Chapman, "Judicial Roulette: Alternatives to Single-Member Districts as a Legal and Political Solution to Voting-Rights Challenges to At-Large Judicial Elections," *SMU Law Review* 48 (1995), 182.

25. The trial court opinion was unpublished.

26. *League of United Latin American Citizens v. Clements*, 902 F2d 293 (1990), and *League of United Latin American Citizens v. Clements*, 914 F2d 620 (1990).

27. *Houston Lawyers' Association v. Attorney General of Texas*, 501 U.S. 419 (1991).

28. *League of United Latin American Citizens Council v. Clements*, 999 F2d 831 (1993).

29. Rodney Ellis, "Supreme Court Ruling Mocks Civil Rights," *Dallas Morning News*, January 28, 1994, p. 25A.

30. David Godbey, "People, Not Courts, Should Determine System," *Dallas Morning News*, January 28, 1994, p. 25A.

31. A discussion of the Bullock plan and the politics surrounding it is in Anthony Champagne, "Judicial Selection in Texas," *Texas Politics: A Reader*, 2nd ed., ed. Anthony Champagne and Edward J. Harpham (New York: Norton, 1998), 99–103.

32. Godbey, "People, Not Courts, Should Determine System," p. 25A.

33. Susan Carbon and Larry Berkson, *Judicial Retention Elections in the United States* (Chicago: American Judicature Society, 1980), 21.

34. A discussion of these general systems of selection is found in Champagne, "Judicial Selection in Texas," pp. 88–104.

35. Daniel Becker and Malia Reddick, *Judicial Selection Reform: Examples from Six States* (Chicago: American Judicature Society, 2003), 1–10.

36. Bill Jeffreys, "Death, Simplified," *Texas Lawyer*, October 23, 2000, p. 1.

37. Pete Slover, "Attorney's Inexperience No Barrier," *Dallas Morning News*, September 11, 2000, p. 12A.

38. Texas Department of Criminal Justice, "Death Row Information."

39. Texas Department of Criminal Justice, "Death Row Information."

40. Texas Department of Criminal Justice, "Death Row Information."

41. Texas Department of Criminal Justice, "Executions, December 7, 1982 through March 16, 2010"; Texas Department of Criminal Justice, "Gender and Racial Statistics of Death Row Offenders," *McClesky v. Kemp* 481 U.S. 279 (1987).

42. Erica C. Barnett, "No Sunshine on Clemency," *Austin Chronicle*, January 1, 1999.

43. "Gov. Perry Commutes Sentences of Man Scheduled to Die Thursday," abc 13, August 30, 2007.

44. The Pew Center on the States, Prison Count 2010 (March 2010) p. 7.

45. The Innocence Project of Texas, "Facts on Post-Conviction DNA Exonerations."

46. "DNA Proving to Cut Both Ways on Death Penalty," *Dallas Morning News*, January 14, 2006, 10A.

47. See Nate Blakeslee, *Tulia: Race, Cocaine, and Corruption in a Small Texas Town* (New York: Public Affairs, 2005).

48. Paul Duggan, "'Sheetrock Scandal' Hits Dallas Police," *Washington Post*, January 18, 2002, p. 12.

49. Michael Hall, "Why Can't Steven Phillips Get a DNA Test?" *Texas Monthly*, January 2006.

50. The Innocence Project of Texas, "Texas Exonerations."

51. Radley Balke, "The 250th DNA Exoneration," *Reason*, February 4, 2010.

52. Steve McGonigle, "Righting Wrongs," *Dallas Morning News*, January 22, 2007, p. 1; Jennifer Emily, "DA: Man Didn't Do '82 Rape," *Dallas Morning News*, September 17, 2007, p. 1B.

53. David Grann, "Trial by Fire," *The New Yorker*, September 7, 2009.

54. Jeff Carleton, "Cameron Todd Willingham: Texas Governor Dismisses 3 Commission Members Just 48 Hours before Arson Review," *Huffington Post*, September 30, 2009.

55. Jeff Blackburn, "Dog Scent Lineups: A Junk Science Injustice," a special report by the Innocence Project of Texas, September 21, 2009.

56. Phil Hardberger, "Juries under Siege," *St. Mary's Law Journal* 30 (1998), pp. 6–7.

57. "High Court Voting Patterns," *Texas Lawyer*, September 6, 1999, p. 5.

58. David A. Anderson, "Judicial Tort Reform in Texas," *Review of Litigation* 26, no. 1 (Winter 2007), 7.

Chapter 26

1. This discussion of the office of constable is taken from Ed Timms and Kevin Krause, "Constables' Tickets Collect Funds, Critics," *Dallas Morning News*, October 25, 2009; Kevin Krause, "Commissioners OK Hiring Own Lawyer," *Dallas Morning News*, September 30, 2009; Kevin Krause, "Towed Cars Remain on Road to Nowhere," *Dallas Morning News*, September 18, 2009; Ed Timms and Kevin Krause, "Constables' Mission Has Changed," *Dallas Morning News*, October 26, 2009.

2. This discussion of the Hill corruption case in from Gromer Jeffers, Jr., "Political Star Tainted by Liabilities—Dallas: Hill's Successes Slowed by Sanctions, FBI Investigation," *Dallas Morning News*, July 23, 2005; Jason Trahan, Hill's Trial Opens Today—Third Corruption Case Involving a Councilman Is Wide in Scope," *Dallas Morning News*, June 29, 2009; Jason Trahan and Diane Jennings, "Three Sentenced in 'Betrayal of Our City,'" *Dallas Morning News*, February 27, 2010.

3. Dallas Morning News, *Texas Almanac 2009–2010* (Dallas: Dallas Morning News, 2008), p. 500; U.S. Census Bureau, *Lists & Structure of Government*.

4. The two states that don't use countries as units of local government are Connecticut and Rhode Island. See Richard L. Cole and Delbert A. Taebel, *Texas: Politics and Public Policy* (Fort Worth: Harcourt Brace Jovanovich, 1987), 151.

5. Texas Association of Counties, "About Counties: County Government."

6. Ibid.

7. Cole and Taebel, *Texas Politics and Public Policy*, 152.

8. *Avery v. Midland County*, 88 S. Ct 1114 (1968).

9. Anthony Champagne and Rick Collis, "Texas," in *The Political Life of the American States*, ed. Alan Rosenthal and Maureen Moakley (Washington, DC: Congressional Quarterly Press, 1984), 140.

10. Texas State Data Center.

11. Brenda Rodriguez, "Loving and Losing in West Texas," *Dallas Morning News*, March 14, 2001, p. 21A

12. Russell Gold, "Counties Struggle with High Cost of Prosecuting Death-Penalty Cases," *Wall Street Journal*, January 9, 2002, p. B1.

13. "Capital Trial Could Be Costly for Franklin Co.," *Sulphur Springs News-Telegram*, June 27, 2007, p. 4.

14. Adam M. Gershowitz, "Statewide Capital Punishment: The Case for Eliminating Counties' Role in the Death Penalty," 63 *Vanderbilt Law Review* (2010), pp. 8–9.

15. Cole and Taebel, *Texas: Politics and Public Policy*, 155.

16. Texas Commission on Jail Standards, "Jail Population Report," February 1, 2010.

17. "Knock! Knock! Smith County Sheriff's Office Goes Armored," *County Magazine*, July/August 1997.

18. Article XI, Section 5, of the Texas Constitution is concerned with home rule. For a further discussion of home rule in Texas see Terrell Blodgett. *Texas Home Rule Charters* (Austin: Texas Municipal League, 1994); Terrell Blodgett, "Home Rule Charters," *The Handbook of Texas Online*, www.tshaonline.org/handbook/online/articles/HH/mvhek.html (accessed 4/17/08).

19. Correspondence with Terrell Blodgett, Wednesday, February 3, 2000; 2009–2010 Texas Almanac, pp. 500–510.

20. The following is drawn from Bradley R. Rice, "Commission Form of City Government," *The Handbook of Texas Online*.

21. Dallas Morning News, *Texas Almanac* 1996–97 (Dallas: Dallas Morning News, 1995), 513.

22. Correspondence with Terrell Blodgett, Wednesday, February 3, 2000.

23. For a further discussion, see Terrell Blodgett, "Council-Manager Form of City Government," *The Handbook of Texas Online*. Blodgett, *Texas Home Rule Charters*.

24. For a history of the Office of Controller in Houston, see "Office History."

25. Jack C. Plano and Milton Greenberg. *The American Political Dictionary*, 10th ed. (Fort Worth: Harcourt, Brace, 1997).

26. *Texas Almanac and State Industrial Guide*, 2000–2001 (Dallas: Dallas Morning News, I.P 1999), 533. *Statistical Abstract of the United States* (Washington, DC: Bureau of the Census, 1998), 496.

27. Brooks Egerton and Reese Dunklin, "Government by Developer," *Dallas Morning News*, June 10, 2001, p. 1A.

28. Peggy Heinkel-Wolfe, "Developers Still Using Renters to Create Special Tax Districts," *Dallas Morning News*, November 1, 2006, p. 1B.

29. Sara C. Galvan, "Wrestling with MUDs to pin Down the Truth about Special Districts," 75 *Fordham Law Review* (2007), pp. 3041–80.

30. Jim Getz, "Pickens Seeks Local Help to Deliver Water, Power," *Dallas Morning News*, September 1, 2007, p. 1A; Jim Getz, "Kaufman Says No to Water Plan," *Dallas Morning News*. September 5, 2007, p. 1B.

31. See Texas Association of Regional Councils, "About TARC."

Chapter 27

1. The following is drawn from Brandon Formby, "Schools Wrestling with Policies under New Religious Liberties Act," *Dallas Morning News*, August 27, 2007; Jenny Lacoste-Caputo, "Law on Religion in School Spurs Fear," *San Antonio Express-News*, July 25, 2007; Kelly Coghlan, "Religion Gets Equal Treatment," *Dallas Morning News*, September 6, 2007; Karen Brooks, "One State under

God," *Dallas Morning News*, April 22, 2007; Wendy Gragg, "New State Law on Religious Expression in Schools Draws Mixed Reactions," *Waco Tribune-Herald*, August 9, 2007. The text of HB 3678 is available at www.capitol.state.tx.us/tlodocs/80R/billtext/html/HB03678F.htm (accessed 4/21/08).

2. See Texas Association of School Boards, "Legal Notes: An Open Mike."

3. Tax Foundation, 2009, Facts and Figures Mid-Year Update (2009), 3, 23. Other ranking information is available from Lisele Zavala, Revenue Estimate Division, Texas Comptroller of Public Accounts. See also tax burden rankings provided by the Tax Foundation at www.taxfoundation.org.

4. The above data on Texas is from the Tax Foundation, 2009, Facts and Figures Mid-Year Update (2009), 7.

5. See Bernard L. Weinstein, "Taxes in Texas," in *Texas Politics: A Reader* ed. Anthony Champagne and Edward J. Harpham (New York: Norton, 1998), chap. 12.

6. The following discussion is drawn from Texas Legislative Budget Board, *Texas Facts Book* (Austin: State of Texas, 1998).

7. For a discussion of the budgetary process, see Texas Comptroller of Public Accounts, *Disturbing the Peace*, Appendix I (Austin: State of Texas, 1996), www.window.state.tx.us/tpr/tpr4/vol1/v13app12.html (accessed 4/21/08).

8. For a discussion of these issues, see Weinstein, "Taxes in Texas."

9. See Kim Quaile Hill and Kenneth R. Mladenka, *Texas Government* (Belmont, CA: Wadsworth, 1993), 269–70; James MacGregor Burns et al., *Government by the People: Texas Version* (Englewood Cliffs: Prentice Hall, 1995), 746–48.

10. Texas Lottery Commission, Demographic Survey of Texas Lottery Players 2009, December 1, 2009, 11.

11. *Texas Almanac 2008–2009* (Dallas: Dallas Morning News, 2007), 497.

12. Texas Lottery Commission, Demographic Survey of Texas Lottery Players 2009, December 1, 2009, 11.

13. See James LeBas, "Who Wants to Be a Billionaire? Texas Spending Tobacco Money on Health Care, Endowments," Texas Comptroller of Public Accounts, *Fiscal Notes* (January 2000).

14. The following is drawn largely from Robert T. Garrett, "Many Texas politicians, including Perry and White, talk little of $21 billion budget gap." *Dallas Morning News*, September 12, 2010; Robert T. Garrett, "Budget likely to cut deep." *Dallas Morning News*, October 24, 2010; Emily Ramshaw, "Legislators Consider Medicaid Withdrawl." *Texas Tribune* for *New York Times*, November 7, 2010.

15. Harry Mika and Lawrence J. Redlinger, "Crime and Correction," in *Texas at the Crossroads*, ed. Anthony Cham-

pagne and Edward J. Harpham (College Station: Texas A&M University Press, 1987), 245–46.

16. Mika and Redlinger, "Crime and Correction," 245–46.

17. *Ruiz v. Estelle*, 503 F. Supp. 1265 (1980).

18. Mika and Redlinger, "Crime and Correction," 247.

19. Texas Department of Criminal Justice, "Fiscal Year 2006 Statistical Report, Demographic Highlights—August 31, 2006, TDCJ On Hand," p. 1, www.tdcj.state.tx.us/publications/executive/FY_2006_Statistical_Report.pdf (accessed 4/21/08).

20. Texas Department of Criminal Justice, "Fiscal Year 2004 Statistical Summary," December 2004. See also Pew Center on the States, "Public Safety Performance Project, Work in the States: Texas" www.pewcenteronthestates.org/uploadedFiles/Texas.pdf (accesssed 4/21/08).

21. Texas Department of Criminal Justice, "Fiscal Year 2005 Operating Budget and Fiscal Years 2006–2007 Legislative Apropriations Request," August 23, 2004, www.tdcj.state.tx.us/Publications/Finance/LAR-FY2006-7-Short.pdf (accessed 4/21/08).

22. See Associated Texans against Crime, Annual Report, 1998.

23. Marc A. Levin, 2009–2010 Legislators Guide to the Issues (November, 2008), 1.

24. See Associated Texans against Crime, Annual Report, 1998.

25. Texas Department of Criminal Justice, "Fiscal Year 2008 Statistics"; Mika and Redlinger, "Crime and Correction," 245.

26. Texas Department of Criminal Justice, "Fiscal Year 2008 Statistics"; Mika and Redlinger, "Crime and Correction," 245.

27. See Associated Texans against Crime, Annual Report, 1998.

28. Texas Department of Criminal Justice, Fiscal Year 2006 Statistical Summary, December 2006.

29. Texas Department of Criminal Justice, Fiscal Year 2008 Statistical Summary, December 2008.

30. Mika and Redlinger, "Crime and Correction," 245.

31. U.S. Department of Justice, Bureau of Justice Statistics Bulletin, Prisoners in 2008, December, 2009, Table 10.

32. Scott Morgan and Kathleen O'Leary Morgan, eds., *Crime State Rankings 2009* xxi. (Washington, DC: Congressional Quarterly Press, 2009).

33. U.S. Department of Justice, Bureau of Justice Statistics Bulletin, Prisoners in 2008, December, 2009, Table 10.

34. Texas Department of Criminal Justice Fiscal Year 2008 Statistical Summary, December 2008.

35. L. Tucker Gibson, Jr., and Clay Robinson, *Government and Politics in the Lone Star State*, 2nd ed. (Upper Saddle River, NJ: Prentice Hall, 1995).

36. Marc A. Levin, *2009–2010 Legislators Guide to the Issues* 1. (Washington, DC: Congressional Quarterly Press, 2009).

37. For a discussion of the history of public education in Texas from which the following is drawn, see Max Berger and Lee Wilborn, "Education," *The Texas Handbook Online*, www.tshaonline.org/handbook/online/articles/EE/khel.html (accessed 4/21/08); Dallas Morning News, "Public Schools," *Texas Almanac 2000–2001*, Millennium Edition (Dallas: Dallas Morning News, 1999), 533–34.

38. See Lewis B. Cooper, *The Permanent School Fund of Texas* (Fort Worth: Texas State Teachers Association, 1934); Michael E. McClellan, "Permanent School Fund," *The Handbook of Texas Online*, www.tshaonline.org/handbook/online/articles/PP/khpl.html (accessed 4/21/08).

39. See Oscar Mauzy, "Gilmer-Aikin Laws," *The Handbook of Texas Online*, www.tshaonline.org/handbook/online/articles/GG/mlgl.html (accessed 4/21/08); Dick Smith and Richard Allen Burns, "Texas Education Agency," *The Handbook of Texas Online*, www.tshaonline.org/handbook/online/articles/TT/met2.html (accessed 4/21/08); Berger and Wilborn, "Education."

40. See Anna Victoria Wilson, "Education for African Americans," *The Handbook of Texas Online*, www.tshaonline.org/handbook/online/articles/EE/kde2.html (accessed 4/21/08).

41. Arnoldo De León and Robert A. Calvert, "Segregation," *The Handbook of Texas Online*, www.tshaonline.org/handbook/online/articles/SS/pksl.html (accessed 4/21/08).

42. The following discussion of the *Rodriguez* and *Edgewood* cases is drawn from Legislative Budget Board Staff, "Financing Public Education in Texas: Kindergarten through Grade 12," *Legislative Handbook* (February 1999); Berger and Wilborn, "Education"; Cynthia E. Orozco, *"Rodríguez v. San Antonio ISD,"* The Handbook of Texas Online, www.tshaonline.org/handbook/online/articles/RR/jrrht.html (accessed 4/21/08); Teresa Palomo Acosta, *"Edgewood ISD v. Kirby,"* The Handbook of Texas Online, www.tshaonline.org/handbook/online/articles/EE/jre2.html (accessed 4/21/08).

43. See Legislative Budget Board Staff, "Financing Public Education in Texas: Kindergarten through Grade 12," *Legislative Handbook* (February 1999), 26–27.

44. See Texas House of Representatives, House Research Organization, "Focus Report: Schools and Taxes," May 25, 2007, www.house.state.tx.us/featured/schools&taxes79–13.pdf (accessed 4/21/08); Jason Embry, "Session Ends with Property Tax Cut," *Austin American-Statesman*, May 26, 2006.

45. See Clark D. Thomas, "Education Reform in Texas," in *Texas Politics*, ed. Champagne and Harpham, chap 13.

46. National Commission on Excellence in Education, *A Nation at Risk: The Imperative for Educational Reform* (Washington DC: Department of Education, 1983).

47. See Thomas, "Education Reform in Texas," 218.

48. See Thomas, "Education Reform in Texas," 221.

49. See Thomas, "Education Reform in Texas," 231; Dallas Morning News, "Public Schools," *Texas Almanac 2000–2001*, Millennium Edition (Dallas: Dallas Morning News, 1999), 533. See also Terrence Stutz, "State's List Cites Sub-par Schools in Transfer Plan," *Dallas Morning News*, December 24, 1999, p. 1.

50. Commonwealth Foundation, Texas Fact Book (2009), p. 19; College Board, Mean 2009 SAT Scores by State; College Board, 2009 College-Bound Seniors Total Group Profile Report (2009), 3.

51. See Joshua Benton, "Legislators Left Unanswered Questions on New State Tests," *Dallas Morning News*, June 11, 2007, p. B1.

52. Health and Human Services, Medicaid Enrollment by Month; U.S. Census Bureau, 2007 American Community Survey.

53. Center for Public Policy Priorities, Policy Point, Policy 101, September, 2009.

54. The following is drawn from Edward J. Harpham, "Welfare Reform and the New Paternalism in Texas," in *Texas Politics*, ed. Champagne and Harpham, chap. 14.

55. See Vivian Elizabeth Smyrl, "Texas Department of Human Services," *The Handbook of Texas Online*, www.tshaonline.org/handbook/online/articles/TT/mct6.html (accessed 4/23/08).

56. Harpham, "Welfare Reform and the New Paternalism in Texas," 238.

57. See Smyrl, "Texas Department of Human Services."

58. See Charles Murray, *Losing Ground* (New York: Basic Books, 1984).

59. For a discussion of these programs, see Lawrence Mead, *The New Politics of Poverty: The Nonworking Poor in America* (New York: Basic Books, 1992).

60. The following paragraphs are drawn from Harpham, "Welfare Reform and the New Paternalism in Texas," 244–47.

61. See Texas Health and Human Services Commission, "Temporary Assistance for Needy Families (TANF): Frequently Asked Questions," www.hhsc.state.tx.us/programs/TexasWorks/TANF-FAQ.html (accessed 4/23/08).

62. See Texas Workforce Investment Council, "Issues in Welfare to Work: A State of the Workforce Report on State Issues Arising from TANF Reauthorization," December 2006, p. 11, www.governor.state.tx.us/divisions/twic/files/wfwissues.pdf (accessed 4/23/08). Texas Health and Human Services Commission, Texas TANF and SNAP Enrollment Statistics, 3/2010. www.hhsc.state.tx.us. (accessed 4/23/10).

63. Texas Workforce, "Welfare Reform Initiatives, 2005," www.twc.state.tx.us/welref/wrabout.html (accessed 4/23/08).

answer key

Chapter 1
1. d
2. b
3. a
4. d
5. c
6. b
7. b
8. b
9. d
10. a
11. c
12. d
13. d
14. a
15. d

Chapter 2
1. d
2. b
3. b
4. c
5. c
6. c
7. a
8. d
9. b
10. d
11. d
12. a
13. d
14. a
15. b

Chapter 3
1. b
2. c
3. b

4. a
5. a
6. c
7. c
8. b
9. b
10. a
11. d
12. b
13. c
14. d
15. d

Chapter 4
1. a
2. c
3. d
4. d
5. a
6. a
7. d
8. b
9. d
10. b
11. a
12. a
13. c
14. a
15. c

Chapter 5
1. b
2. d
3. a
4. a
5. b
6. b
7. c

8. d
9. b
10. d
11. a
12. d
13. d
14. a
15. b

Chapter 6
1. c
2. a
3. d
4. d
5. c
6. d
7. b
8. c
9. d
10. b
11. b
12. a
13. a
14. b
15. d

Chapter 7
1. b
2. c
3. b
4. c
5. b
6. a
7. d
8. a
9. b
10. a
11. b

12. d
13. a
14. b
15. b

Chapter 8
1. d
2. d
3. a
4. c
5. d
6. a
7. b
8. b
9. d
10. c
11. c
12. d
13. c
14. a
15. d

Chapter 9
1. a
2. c
3. c
4. d
5. c
6. a
7. d
8. c
9. a
10. c
11. b
12. a
13. b
14. d
15. d

Chapter 10
1. b
2. a
3. b
4. c
5. c
6. b
7. c
8. a
9. b
10. d
11. d
12. a
13. b
14. b
15. a

Chapter 11
1. a
2. a
3. d
4. c
5. a
6. b
7. a
8. c
9. a
10. d
11. d
12. b
13. a
14. d
15. a

Chapter 12
1. c
2. a
3. c

4. b
5. a
6. a
7. a
8. a
9. c
10. a
11. d
12. c
13. a
14. a
15. b

Chapter 13
1. b
2. b
3. b
4. d
5. a
6. c
7. b
8. a
9. c
10. a
11. c
12. b
13. b
14. a
15. c

Chapter 14
1. b
2. a
3. c
4. d
5. b
6. a
7. c
8. d
9. b
10. d
11. c
12. a
13. a
14. c
15. c

Chapter 15
1. a
2. b
3. a
4. a
5. c
6. d

7. a
8. c
9. b
10. c
11. d
12. a
13. b
14. c
15. c

Chapter 16
1. a
2. b
3. b
4. b
5. b
6. a
7. b
8. d
9. c
10. b
11. d
12. a
13. c
14. a
15. c

Chapter 17
1. c
2. c
3. c
4. c
5. d
6. a
7. b
8. a
9. c
10. c
11. a
12. c
13. d
14. d
15. b

Chapter 18
1. b
2. c
3. a
4. a
5. d
6. c
7. b
8. b
9. d

10. a
11. a
12. c
13. a
14. b
15. d

Chapter 19
1. b
2. a
3. c
4. d
5. b
6. b
7. d
8. b
9. a
10. d
11. c
12. b
13. c
14. a
15. a

Chapter 20
1. b
2. c
3. d
4. c
5. d
6. c
7. a
8. d
9. d
10. c
11. a
12. a
13. c
14. d
15. d

Chapter 21
1. b
2. a
3. a
4. d
5. d
6. a
7. d
8. c
9. c
10. c
11. b

12. a
13. a
14. a
15. d

Chapter 22
1. d
2. d
3. b
4. a
5. c
6. d
7. d
8. d
9. a
10. d
11. c
12. a
13. a
14. d
15. c

Chapter 23
1. a
2. d
3. a
4. b
5. c
6. a
7. b
8. b
9. d
10. c
11. a
12. a
13. d
14. d
15. c

Chapter 24
1. d
2. c
3. d
4. a
5. c
6. a
7. a
8. c
9. c
10. d
11. d
12. c
13. a

14. d
15. d

Chapter 25
1. c
2. d
3. c
4. b
5. a
6. b
7. d
8. d
9. c
10. d
11. d
12. a
13. a
14. d
15. c

Chapter 26
1. b
2. c
3. d
4. c
5. c
6. a
7. b
8. b
9. d
10. d
11. a
12. a
13. c
14. a
15. b

Chapter 27
1. b
2. a
3. d
4. b
5. d
6. d
7. c
8. a
9. b
10. a
11. c
12. b
13. b
14. a
15. b

photo credits

394: AP Photo; 396: AP Photo/Denis Paquin;; 385: AP Photo/Rob Carr; 387: Jim Wilson/The New York Times/Redux; 389: AP Photo/Rogelio V. Solis. **Chapter 11:** 400: AP Photo/Ann Heisenfelt; 403: The Granger Collection, New York; 404: Zunique/Newscom; 406: Chip Somodevilla/Getty Images; 407: Bettmann/CORBIS; 410: AP Photo/Patricia McDonnell; 415: Corbis; 416: AP Photo/Richmond Times-Dispatch, Bob Brown; 417: Ron Sachs/Pool/CNP/Corbis; 418: AP Photo/U.S. Attorney's office; 420: AP Photo/J. Scott Applewhite; 422: AP Photo/Rick Bowmer; 429: AP Photo/Jean-Marc Bouju; 430: AFP/Getty Images. **Chapter 12:** 434: Ron Sachs/CNP/Corbis; 438: Bettmann/Corbis; 439: Alex Wong/Getty Images; 443: Chris Gardner/epa/Corbis; 450: Olivier Douliery/ABACAUSA/Newscom; 452: AP Photo/Tanya Makeyeva, UNHCR Pool; 456: Zuma Press/Newscom; 460: Benjamin J. Myers/Corbis; 462: Photo by Jay Tinker/Courtesy of Maryland Society for Sight, founded in 1909 with the mission of saving sight; 464: AP Photo/Susan Walsh; 467: Aristide Economopoulos/Star Ledger/Corbis; 468: AP Photo/The Indianapolis Star, Charlie Nye; 470: AP Photo/Dennis Cook; 471: Getty Images; 473: AP Photo/APTN; 474: Courtesy of Armenian Assembly of America. **Chapter 13:** 480: Larry Downing/Reuters/Corbis; 483: The Granger Collection, New York; 485: AFP/Getty Images; 487: Larry Downing/Reuters/Corbis; 488: Pete Souza/Corbis; 490: AP Photo/Susan Walsh; 491: Pierre Manevy/Hulton Archive/Getty Images; 501: AP Photo/Christina Jamison/NBC NewsWire; 502: JASON REED/Reuters/Corbis; 503: Dana Edelson/NBCU Photo Bank; 506: Bettmann/Corbis; 508: AP Photo; 513: AP Photo/Kathy Willens; 514: Rafael Suanes/MCT /Landov. **Chapter 14:** 520: ERIK S. LESSER/epa/Corbis; 527: Everett Kennedy Brown/epa/Corbis; 533 (left): AP Photo/Debra Reid; 533 (right); AP Photo/Fort Collins Coloradoan, V. Richard Haro; 536: Everett Collection/20th Century Fox Film Corp. All rights reserved; 540: Stephen Crowley/The New York Times/Redux; 543: Matthew Cavanaugh/epa/Corbis; 544: CBS/Courtesy Everett Collection; 546: AP Photo/Richard Drew; 548: Scott Peterson/Getty Images; 552: Scott Peterson/Getty Images; 554: Ron Sachs/CNP/Corbis; 556: Michael Reynolds/epa/Corbis; 557: Jeff Greenberg / Alamy. **Chapter 15:** 562: J. Scott Applewhite/Pool/CNP/Corbis; 565: AP Photo/Dennis Cook; 571 (left): AP Photo/Ken Heinen; 571 (right): AP Photo/Pablo Martinez Monsivais; 574: Steve Petteway, Collection of the Supreme Court of the United States; 575: Bettmann/Corbis; 578: AP Photo; 579: AP Photo/Susan Walsh; 582: AP Photo/Thomas Cain; 587: Nicholas Kamm/AFP/Getty Images; 590: Collection of the Supreme Court of the United States, photo by: Steve Petteway; 593: AP Photo/Shawn Baldwin; 595: AP Photo/J. Scott Applewhite; 596: Chris Graythen/Getty Images. **Chapter 16:** 602: Reuters/Jim Young; 605: AP Photo/Jason DeCrow; 606: The Granger Collection, New York; 607: Harald Sund/Getty Images; 610: AP / Marcio Jose Sanchez; 611: Bettmann/Corbis; 613 (left): The Granger Collection, New York; 613 (right): Bettmann/Corbis; 614: Bettmann/Corbis; 616: North Wind Picture Archives/Alamy; 617: Bettmann/Corbis; 619: Scull/BloombergNews/Landov; 630: AP Photo; 631: Paramount Classics/Photofest; 632: Jeff and Meggan Haller/Keyhole Photo/Corbis; 634: Casper Christoffersen/epa/Corbis; 638: Uriel Sinai/Getty Images; 640: Daily News; 645: Steve Liss//Time Life Pictures/Getty Images. **Chapter 17:** 650: AP Photo/Kennell Krista/SIPA; 653: Chicago Historical Society; 654: AP Photo; 656: AP Photo/Toby Talbot; 663: AP Photo/Eric Draper; 665: Chip Somodevilla/Getty Images; 668: David Hoffman Photo Library/Alamy; 669: AP Photo/Dima Gavrysh; 671: Leon/Retna Ltd./Corbis; 673: AP Photo/Matt Rourke; 674: AP Photo/Denis Paquin; 676 (left): AP Photo; 676 (right): AP Photo/Dawn Villella; 679: Seth Wenig/Star Ledger/Corbis. **Chapter 18:** 684: AP Photo/Charles Dharapak; 687: AP Photo/David Duprey; 689: Bettmann/CORBIS; 691: AP Photo/Rahmat Gul; 69: Ryan Pyle/Corbis; 694: AP/KEYSTONE/Martial Trezzini; 696: Darcy Padilla/Redux; 697: Brooks Kraft/Corbis; 698: AP Photo/Manuel Balce Ceneta; 701: Mandel Ngan/AFP/Getty Images; 704: AP Photo/Atef Safadi, Pool; 706: AP Photo; 707: Paramount Pictures/The Kobal Collection/Vaughan, Stephen; 711: Reuters/Corbis; 715: Somodevilla/Getty Images. **Chapter 19:** 720: Bo Zaunders/Corbis; 723: DAEMMRICH BOB/CORBIS SYGMA; 725: Karl Stolleis/Getty Images; 728: Ted Spiegel/Corbis; 730: Joseph Scherschel/Time & Life Pictures/Getty Images; 732: Bettmann/Corbis; 734: Ed Lallo/Bloomberg/Getty Images; 735: Bettmann/Corbis; 736: Marjorie Kamys Cotera/Daemmrich Photography; 738: From the Collections of the Texas Memorial Museum, The University of Texas at Austin; 740: AP Photo; 741: AP Photo; 749: Robert W. Ginn/Alamy; 750: Jensen Walker/Getty Images. **Chapter 20:** 754: Austin American-Statesman/WPN; 759: Library of Congress; 760: Courtesy Texas State Library and Archives Commission; 762: Bettmann/Corbis; 764: Bettmann/Corbis; 766: Courtesy Texas State Library and Archives Commission; 767: Courtesy Texas State Library and Archives Commission; 776: Courtesy Bob Taylor; 778: AP Photo; 782: AP Photo/Harry Cabluck. **Chapter 21:** 786: AP Photo/Louis DeLuca, Pool; 789: AP Photo/David J. Phillip; 793: Al Fenn//Time Life Pictures/Getty Images; 795: Erich Schlegel/Dallas Morning News/Corbis; 798: AP Photo/Harry Cabluck; 802: Adam Lotia; 804: Time & Life Pictures/Getty Images; 808: Bob Daemmrich/Corbis. **Chapter 22:** 816: AP Photo/Harry Cabluck; 819: Sargent: © 2002 The Austin American Statesmen. Reprinted with permission of Universal Press Syndicate. All rights reserved; 823: AP Photo/Harry Cabluck; 829: AP Photo/Harry Cabluck; 830: Bob Daemmrich/Bob Daemmrich Photography, Inc./Corbis; 831: AP Photo/ Henry Cabluck. **Chapter 23:** 834: Bob Daemmrich; 837: AP Photo/Harry Cabluck; 838: Bob Daemmrich/Corbis; 850: Bob Daemmrich; 851: AP Photo/Jack Plunkett; 852: AP Photo/Eric Gay; 854: Bob Daemmrich; 857: AP Photo/Ron Heflin; 858: AP Photo/Harry Cabluck. **Chapter 24:** 862: AP Photo/ Reed Saxon; 866: PAUL BUCK/AFP/Getty Images; 868: Tom Pennington/Getty Images; 871: Bob Daemmrich/Corbis; 873: Mark Wilson/Getty Images; 878: AP Photo/Harry Cabluck; 880: AP Photo/Harry Cabluck; 884: Courtesy Alcoholic Beverage Commission; 887: Marjorie Kamys Cotera; 889: AP Photo/Harry Cabluck. **Chapter 25:** 892: Hooman Hedayati /www.texasabolition.org; 895: Bob Daemmrich/Corbis; 898: AP Photo/Joe Mitchell; 900: AP Photo/Tony Gutierrez; 902: Sargent: © 2001 & 2002 The Austin American Statesman. Reprinted with permission of Universal Press Syndicate. All rights reserved; 911: AP Photo/ The Global News Henry Bargas; 914: ANDY RAIN/epa/Corbis; 915: Reuters/Landov; 918: Lara Solt/Dallas Morning News/Corbis. **Chapter 26:** 924: David Woo/Dallas Morning News; 929: AP Photo/Harry Cabluck; 931: Bob Daemmrich; 932: AP Photo/J. Scott Applewhite; 934: AP Photo/David J. Phillip; 937: North Wind Picture Archive; 938: Courtesy of the Office of Mayor Annise Parker; 939: AP Photo/ Ben Fredman, Pool; 940: AP Photo/San Antonio Express-News John Davenport; 941: Bob Owen, Express-News/Zuma Press; 944: Charles O'Rear/Corbis. **Chapter 27:** 950: Michael Ainsworth/Dallas Morning News/Corbis; 953: AP Photo/Harry Cabluck; 954: Spencer Platt/Getty Images; 961: AP Photo/Harry Cabluck; 970: AP Photo; 972: AP Photo/Harry Cabluck; 974: Marjorie Kamys Cotera; 976: Corbis; 979: AP Photo.

index

Page numbers in *italics* refer to tables, figures, and photos.

executive orders by, 511
foreign policy and, 593, 697
gay rights and, 183
health care reform and, 502, 669–70
housing and, 672
impeachment and, 80, 253, 462, 473
job training advocated by, 666–67
Lewinsky affair and, 250, 253, 473
media and, 250, 251, 253, 257, *261*, 262, 506, *508*
military actions of, 487
Northern Ireland peace efforts and, 705
NPR of, 501, *544*, 545–46
policy initiatives of, *228*
polling used by, 219, *219*
public appearances of, 506, *508*
regulatory review by, 509
signing statements by, 512
smaller government proclaimed by, 523
trade policy and, 692
welfare reform and, 660, 980
White House staff of, 499
Clinton, Hillary Rodham, 10, 123, 181, 218, 257, 258–60, 286–87, 291, *329*, 358, 359, 365, 366, 370, 376, 466, *704*, 705
in elections of 2000, 502
media and, 237–38
as secretary of state, 502
in 2008 election primaries, 377–79, *377*, 382
closed caucuses, 359
closed primaries, 349, 801
closed rule, 459
cloture, 459–60
Club for Growth, 209
CNN (Cable News Network), 125, 239, *242*, 247, 263, 394
Coalition for Affordable and Reliable Energy, 423
Coast Guard, U.S., 489, *520*, 537
coattail effect, 353
Coca-Cola, 638
Cochran, Cathy, 906
Coke, Richard, 766
COLAs (cost of living adjustments), 656, 657
Colbert, Stephen, 365
Colbert Report, The, 12, 263
Cold War, 107, 128, 217, 501, 546, 548, 549, 629, 689–90, *689*, 710–11
Coleman, Norm, 225
collective bargaining, 87
collective goods, 407
collective security, 710–12
College Cost Reduction and Access Act, 429, 474
Colorado, 296, 968
anti-gay rights amendment in, 184
political culture of, 723
Combs, Susan, *953*
Comedy Central, 209
Comercia Bank, *725*
comity clause, 53, 81
commander in chief, 486
commerce clause, 85, 87, 88
Commerce Department, U.S., 489, *498*, 542, 545, 632, 692, 736
"commercial republic," 82
commercial speech, 129–30
Commission on Civil Rights, U.S., 170
Commission on Wartime Contracting, 551

committee markup sessions, 457
Committee on Administrative Management, 553
Committee on Oversight and Government Reform, 556
Committee on Standards of Official Conduct, 456
committees, congressional, 337, 425, 450, 452–55, *453*
assignments to, 467
conference, 454, 461
deliberation in, 457–59
joint, 454
oversight by, 555–59
select, 453–54
standing, 452
Committee to Protect America's Health Care, 423
Common Cause, 220, 405, 412, 822
Commonwealth Edison, 416
Communications Decency Act (CDA) (1996), 127, 246
community college districts, 942
Community Reinvestment Act (CRA) (1977), 171
community service, 290
"Compassionate Conservative," 212
complaint, in civil law, 899
Comprehensive Employment and Training Act (CETA) (1973), 666
Compromise of 1850, 763
Compromise of 1877, 156
comptroller of public accounts, Texas, 772, 849, 875, 881–83, 889, 954, 955
computers, hacking into, 688
concurrent powers, 78
concurrent resolutions, 842
Confederacy, 764–65, 807, 927
confederation, 42, 758
conference:
congressional, 449
Supreme Court and, 589
Conference Board, 374
conference committees, 454, 461, 847
Congress, Texas, *see* House of Representatives, Texas; Senate, Texas
Congress, U.S., 434–79, 977, 981
African Americans in, 439, *439*, *440*, *441*
agent role of members of, 439–42
base-closings and, 546
and Bill of Rights, 66, 113–14
block grants from, 97–99
budget process and, 624–25, *626*
and bureaucracy, 523, 526
campaign expenditures by members of, *357*, 389
caucuses in, 449, 456–57
celebrity witnesses and, 464
civil rights and, 162–64, 168, 170
constituencies of, 440–42, 462, 475–76
in Constitution, 50–53, 55, 56, 130, 483, 513–16, 758
death penalty and, 138
decision-making process in, 462–69
delegate vs. trustee representation in, 475
delegation of powers by, 482, 496–97
democracy and, 473–76
diversity in members of, *441*
elections of, 442–47
electoral college and, 353–55

ERA in, 172
executive agencies established by, 531
and financial reform, 628
flag burning and, *123*, 124
floor access in, 467, *467*
foreign policy role of, 470, 513, 548, 687, 697, 699–701
grants-in-aid and, 94
handgun regulation by, 88
health care legislation and, 308, *400*, 401–2, 410, *410*
and health care reform, 495
immigration and, 19, 20
influences on, 469, 475–76
Internet speech and, 127
in iron triangle, 418, *419*, *534*
judicial legislation of, 592–97
judicial review of, 576
labor and, 627
Latinos in, 439, *440*, *441*
lawmaking rules in, 457–62, *458*
leadership PACs and, 466
lobbying of, 413–16, *414*, 418
logrolling in, 468–69
military role of, 488
minimum wage and, 642
national bank and, 85
national security vs. domestic policy in, 470
"necessary and proper clause" and, 758
non-legislative powers of, 469–73
occupational backgrounds of members of, 439, *441*
organization of, 449–57
oversight in, 471–72
parties in, 334, 342–43, 450–51, 465–69, *466*, *468*
party leadership in, 449–51, *450*
permanent committees of, *453*
presidents' relations with, 337, 469, 483–86, 492–95, *505*, 513
re-election to, 443–45
reform of, 475
and regulations on contractors, 551–52
and regulatory review, 509
representation in, 437–49, *449*
Republicans' 1995 takeover of, 95, 98, 316, 336, 337, 428, 467
responsible bureaucracy and, 555–59
same-sex marriage and, 79
seniority system in, 337, 342, 454
and size of Supreme Court, 571–72, 594
social composition of, 439
sociological vs. agency representation in, 438–42
staff system in, 455–56
standing committees in, 452
subcommittees in, 455
terrorism and, 4
Texas statehood approved by, 763
2008 Democratic gains in, 376
under Articles of Confederation, 42–44
unfunded mandates and, 96–97
and war on terror, 470
war powers of, 699–700
whip system in, 467–68
women in, 286, *286*, *438*, 439, *440*, *441*, *450*
see also committees, congressional; *specific issues and legislation*
Congressional Black Caucus, *439*, 456

General Agreement on Tariffs and Trade (GATT), 491, 692
general bills, 842
General Dynamics, 748
general election, 364–71, 802, 867, 868
General Land Office (GLO), Texas, 772, 875, 880, *880*
General Motors (GM), 640
general purpose governments, 927
General Revenue Fund, Texas, 955
General Services Administration, 489–90, 551
Genêt, Edmond, 490
Geneva Conventions, 537
Genoa, Italy, 702
Gensemer, Thomas, 371
geography, population and, *17*
George III, King of England, 217
Georgia, 594
  gerrymandering in, *352*
  political culture of, 724
  slaves in, 48
  sodomy laws in, 143
  voting rights in, *169*
Gerber, Alan, 296–97
Gerbner, George, 536
Gere, Richard, 425
German Americans, *738*, 749
Germany, 29, 63, 668, 711
  Nazi, 688, 689
Gerry, Elbridge, 351, *351*
gerrymandering, 170, 351, *351*, 446–47, 858
get-out-the-vote campaigns, 298–99
Getty Oil Company, 900
Gibbons v. Ogden, 85
GI Bill of Rights (1944), 664
Gideon, Clarence Earl, 137
Gideon v. Wainwright, 137, 580
GI Forum, 176
Gilens, Martin, 660
Gilmer-Aikin Laws, 968–69
Gingrich, Newt, 454, 465
Ginsburg, Ruth Bader, 176, *572*, 590, *590*, 593
Gitlin, Todd, 707
Giuliani, Rudy, 359, *377*
Glasscock County, Tex., 932
globalism, 686
globalization:
  economic policy and, 692–93
  interest groups and, 406
global warming, 630, 631–32
GMAC, 640
GNP (Gross National Product), 607
Godbey, David, 909–10, 911
Goldberg, Arthur, 141
Goldberg v. Kelly, 658
Goldwater, Barry, 227, 316, 366
Gonzales, Alberto, *471*, 537
Gonzales v. Carhart, 141
Gonzales v. Oregon, 144, 593
Gonzalez, Henry B., 741
Gonzalez, Raul, 906
GOP (Grand Old Party), 314, 316
  see also Republican Party
Gore, Al, 296, *320*, *544*, 545–46, 631, *631*
  Clinton and, 501
  in elections of 2000, 12, *226*, 260, 355
  media and, 12, 260
government, 13–16
  authoritarian, 13

constitutional, 13–14
dependence on, 3–4, 5
divided, 317, 353
economy and, 605–17
effectiveness of, 70
expanding participation in, 15
expansion of, 214, 411–12
forms of, 13–14
limited, 13–15, 25, 59–60, 767–68
media and, 239–49
parties and, 334–37, 789–90
privatization of, 547–52, *550*
public opinion as influence on, 230–32
republican, 770
in shaping of public opinion, *218*, 219
size and scope of, 5
totalitarian, 14–15
trust in, 5–8, *7*, *9*, 106–7
  see also economic policy; federalism; national government
Government Accountability Office (GAO), 177, 456, 551, 558
government corporations, 531
governor, Texas, 859, 865–75
  appointment powers of, 871–72
  bills and, 847–48, 849
  budgetary power of, 872
  campaigning for, 867–68
  clemency power of, 874–75, 915–16
  compensation and salary of, 870
  executive powers of, 871–73, 888–89
  impeachment of, *see* impeachment
  judicial power of, 874–75
  legislative powers of, 873–74, 888–89
  limited powers of, *862*, 865–66, 870, 875–77, 888–89
  message power of, 849, 873–74
  military power of, 872, *873*
  off-year elections for, 867
  patronage powers of, 871–72
  in plural executive, 875–77, 882, 888–89
  police power of, 872–73
  protection of, 870
  qualifications for, 866
  special sessions called by, 849, 874
  staff of, 870–71
  State of the State speeches of, 849
  succession of, 870
  term lengths of, 866–67
  veto power of, 847–48, *848*, 849, 874
  women as, 866
  see also specific governors
Governor's Task Force on Homeland Security, 812
Grand Coulee Dam, *607*
grand juries, 134, 900–901
Grange Movement, 729, 767, 820
grants, federal, 91–93, *92*, 97–98
  block, 97–99
grants-in-aid, 91–92, 94, *94*
Grassfire.org, 423
grassroots mobilization, 422–23, 463
Gratz v. Bollinger, *187*, 188
Gravel, Mike, 378
Gray v. Sanders, 351
Great Britain, 63, 217, 276, 369, 668, 688, 712
Great Compromise, 45–48, 50
Great Depression, 5, 26, 90–91, *91*, 292, 314, 412, 547, 609, 637, 653, *654*, 655, 666, 672, 729, 736, 977

Great Recession, *see* financial crisis of 2008–2009
Great Society, 666
Green, Donald, 296–97
Green, Gene, 448
greenhouse gases, 527, 631–35
green jobs, 667
Green Party, 319, 320, *320*, 321
"greens," 702
Greensboro, N.C., lunch counter sit-in in, *150*, 151
Greenspan, Alan, 555, 618
green technologies, 635–36
Grenada, 487
Griswold, Estelle, 140–41
Griswold, Roger, 61
Griswold v. Connecticut, 140–41, 577
Grokster, 587
Gross Domestic Product (GDP), 607, *608*, 641
groups and interests, 400–433, *400*, *403*, 475–76, *701*
  access gained by, 301, 418–20
  in American Revolution, 39
  benefits of membership in, 408–10, *409*
  benefits to lawmakers provided by, 822–23, 824–25
  campaign activism by, 426, 428
  celebrities and, 425
  characteristics of members of, 410–11
  character of, 403–4
  in congressional decision-making, 463, 465
  courts used by, 420–21
  definition of, 403
  democracy and, 430–31
  economic policy and, 641–42
  electoral politics used by, 423–28
  foreign policy role of, 701–2
  "free rider" problem in, 407–8
  going public by, 421–23
  as influences on values, 202–7
  liberal, 220
  litigation by, 420–21
  media and, 256
  New Politics movement, 412, 421
  organization components in, 405–10
  pluralism, 16, 403
  political action committees and, 423–28
  political mobilization and, 297–98, 299, 301
  political parties and, 327–30, 332, 342
  proliferation of, 411–12
  protests and demonstrations by, 422, *422*
  in shaping of public opinion, 220–21, *221*
  strategies of, 413–29
  unrepresented, 405
  see also lobbying
Grovey v. Townsend, 805
Grozdins, Morton, 93
Grutter v. Bollinger, *187*, 188
Guadalupe Hidalgo, Treaty of, 176
Guantánamo Bay:
  military prison at, 144, 146, 511, *565*, 714–15
  naval base at, 579
Gulf of Mexico, 2010 oil spill in, 257, *460*, 482, *520*, 632
Gulf of Tonkin Resolution (1964), *485*
Gulf Oil, 731

laws passed by, 74, 75–76
numbers of, *81*
obligations of, to other states, 78–81
regulation and, 77–78, 82–84
traditional system of, *83*
trust in, 106–7
State Board of Education (SBOE), Texas, 876, 886–87, *887*, 969, 974
State Children's Health Insurance Program (SCHIP), 99, 100, 547, *659*, 668, 670
State Commission on Judicial Conduct, Texas, 781
state constitutions, functions of, 757–58, 795–96
see also Constitution of 1876, Texas; constitutions, Texas
State Department, U.S., 252, *498*, 537–39, 548, 696, 698, 699, 705, 710
State Depository Board, Texas, 881
State Farm, 885
"State of the Union" address, 492
of 2010, 448, 460
State Preservation Board, Texas, 871
State Seed and Plant Board, Texas, 883
state sovereignty, 89
states' rights, 87–88, *90, 100,* 101, *101*
and discrimination against African Americans, 87, *88,* 93
in Texas Constitution of 1861, 765
state supreme courts, 566
Statue of Liberty, 158, *271*
"steak men," 825
Steele, Michael, 324
Stein, Bob, 800
stem cell research, 511
Stenberg v. Carhart, 141
Sterling County, Tex., 932
Stern, Howard, 246, *246*
Stevens, John Paul, 127, 575, 917
Stevens, Ted, 448
Stevenson, Adlai, *227,* 792
Stevenson, Coke, 866–67
Stewart, Jon, 12, 263
Stewart, Potter, 127
stimulus bill, *see* American Recovery and Reinvestment Act (2009)
stock market, *639*
Stone, Harlan Fiske, 87, 590
straight-ticket voting, 353
"strategic reassurance," 181
Straus, Joe, 836, *850,* 852, *852,* 859
Strauss, Annette, 906
Strayhorn, Carole Keeton, 795–96, 810, 876, 882, 889
Streamcast, 587
"strict construction," 67
strict scrutiny, 121, 161
Strine, Harry, 464
Student Aid and Fiscal Responsibility Act (2009), 435–36
Student Nonviolent Coordinating Committee, 162, *164,* 280
subsidies, 628–29, 694
automobile, 640
suburbanization, 744
Sudan, *701,* 712, 715
suffrage, 274
see also voting rights
Sugar Act (1764), 39
suicide, doctor-assisted, 96, 143, 144
see also assisted suicide issue
Sundquist, James, 93
Sun Oil, 732

Sunset Advisory Commission (SAC), 888
Sunset Review Act (Texas) (1975), 841, 882, 888
Sunshine, Ken, 764
Sunstein, Cass, 335
Sununu, John, 376
superdelegates, 363
in elections of 2008, 378–79
supervisory powers, 843
Supplemental Security Income (SSI), 657, *659,* 978
supply-side economics, 617, 623
supremacy clause, 51, 54, 59, 77, 576, 757
Supreme Court, Texas, 760, 765, 766, 774, 795, 828, 830, 868, *871,* 895, *895, 896,* 899, *900,* 904–5, *911,* 920–21
cost of campaigning for, 902, 904–5
on education, 972–73
and elections of 1988, 920
eligibility requirements for, 895
tone of civil cases set by, 920–21
tort law and, 920, 921
Supreme Court, U.S., 28, *86,* 87–90, 94–97, *95, 96,* 251, 283, 324, 367, 564, *565,* 568–72, *575,* 579, *584,* 818, 893–94, 909
abortion and, 141, 220, 420, 591
activism and restraint on, 591
affirmative action and, 186–87, 188, 586, 588
appointments to, 572–75, *572*
assisted suicide and, 102–3, 593
on campaign finance, 301, 391
child labor and, 87
civil liberties and, 112, 540
civil rights and, 157
conferencing in, 589
Congress and size of, 571–72, 594
in Constitution, 53, 570–72, 576–77, 581
constitutional amendment and, 67
death penalty and, 138–40, 915, 931
decisions of, 511
defendants' rights and, 132–33, 580–81
digital media and, 587
disabled and, 182
dissenting opinions in, 590
on education, 580, 586, 588, 742, 971
and elections of 2000, *578*
on electoral districts, 351–52, *352,* 447, 581, 855, 858, *858*
employment discrimination and, 168
on entitlements, 658
ERA and, 64–65
and expansion of national government, 85–90, 101–2
explanations of decisions of, 590–92
free speech and, 121–30, *129,* 242
future of civil liberties in, 144
gambling and, 182
gay rights and, 143, 183–84
gender discrimination and, 174–76
ideology in, 591–92
and incorporation of Bill of Rights, 113–17
intellectual property and, 587
international law and, 593
and interracial marriage, 79
on interstate commerce, 85–86
judicial interpretation and, 67
judicial review by, 53, 67, 575–92
law clerks to, 585–86
lobbying for access to, 586–90
opinion writing by, 589–90
oral argument in, 588–90
original jurisdiction in, 567, 570, 581

path of cases of, 582, *583*
political ideology and, 591–92
on presidential power, 482, *491,* 497
procedures of, 588–90, *589*
religious freedom and, 118–21, 140, 580, 595
on restrictive covenants, 580
rules of access to, 581–82
on school prayer, 118, 287, 580
segregation and, 87, 159–63, 166–67, 591, 969
sexual harassment and, 174–75
sodomy laws and, 143
Ten Commandments and, 120
on Texas county system, 928
on Texas elections, 804–5
voting rights and, 742
writs of, 582–84
Sutherland, Kiefer, 536
Sweatt v. Painter, 742
Swift Vote Veterans for Truth, *393*
Swiss banks, 544
Switzerland, 668

TABC (Texas Alcoholic Beverage Commission), 883, *884*
Taliban, 488, 495, 578, 579, 708
talk radio, 240, 243, 247, 248
talk shows, *261*
TANF (Temporary Assistance to Needy Families), 532, 656–57, *657, 659,* 661, 676–77, 678, 954, 980
Target, 416
tariffs and duties, 39–40, 82, 312, 314, 497, 543, 621, 692–93, 694
TARP (Troubled Asset Relief Program), 472, *543,* 556
Tarrant County, Tex., 912, 931
Tauzin, Billy, 416
taxation and revenue, Texas, 724, 733, 881, 928, 953–62, *953, 954*
budget and, *see* budget, budget process, Texas
constitutional provisions on, 773–74, 953–55
dedicated funds in, 954
expenditures and, 960–61, *962*
federal matching funds in, 958
income tax issue and, 958
inheritance, 957–58
Legislative Budget Board and, 955
low-tax state image and, 953
school districts and, 940–42
special districts and, 942
specific taxes in, 956–57, *956*
state lottery in, 958, 960, *961*
tobacco settlement in, 960
2010 budget crisis and, 961
taxes, taxation, 621–23, *622,* 640, 641
American Revolution and, 39–40
in Constitution, 52
cuts in, 218, *228,* 610, 616, 617, 621, 623, 640, 642, *644*
economic equality and, 30
federal, *960*
income, 39, 543–44, 621–23, *622,* 773–74, 958
inflation and, 611–12
loopholes in, 622
oil, *954*
poll, 169, 176, 275, 293, 741, 742, 793, 803–4, *804*
progressive, 621, 623, 958

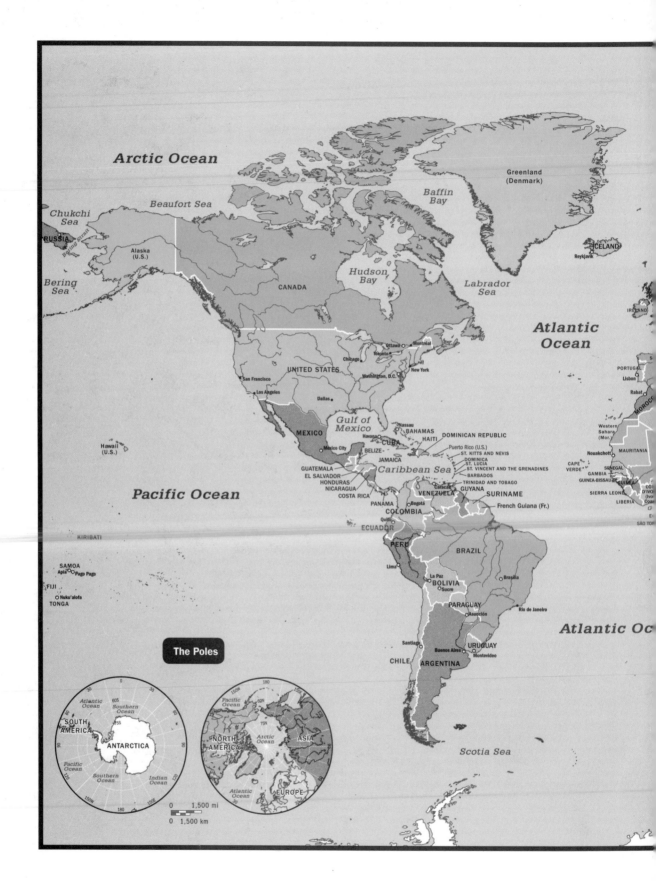

Arctic Ocean

Chukchi
Sea

RUSSIA

Bering
Sea

Beaufort Sea

Alaska
(U.S.)

CANADA

Hudson
Bay

Baffin
Bay

Greenland
(Denmark)

Labrador
Sea

ICELAND

Reykjavik

IRELAND

Atlantic
Ocean

PORTUGAL
Lisbon

Rabat
MOROCCO

Ottawa   Montreal
Toronto
Chicago
Washington, D.C.   New York

UNITED STATES

San Francisco
Los Angeles
Dallas

Hawaii
(U.S.)

MEXICO

Gulf of
Mexico

Mexico City

Nassau
BAHAMAS
Havana   CUBA
HAITI
DOMINICAN REPUBLIC
Puerto Rico (U.S.)
ST. KITTS AND NEVIS
DOMINICA
ST. LUCIA
ST. VINCENT AND THE GRENADINES
BARBADOS
TRINIDAD AND TOBAGO

BELIZE
JAMAICA

Western
Sahara
(Mor.)

Nouakchott   MAURITANIA

CAPE
VERDE   SENEGAL
GAMBIA
GUINEA-BISSAU   GUINEA
SIERRA LEONE   CÔTE
D'IVOIRE
(Ivory
Coast)
LIBERIA

SÃO TOM

Pacific Ocean

GUATEMALA
EL SALVADOR
HONDURAS
NICARAGUA
COSTA RICA

PANAMA

Caribbean Sea

Caracas
VENEZUELA   GUYANA
SURINAME
French Guiana (Fr.)

Bogotá
COLOMBIA
Quito
ECUADOR

KIRIBATI

SAMOA
Apia   Pago Pago
FIJI
Nuku'alofa
TONGA

PERU

Lima

BRAZIL

La Paz
BOLIVIA
Sucre

Brasília

PARAGUAY

Asunción

Rio de Janeiro

Atlantic Oc

Santiago

Buenos Aires
Montevideo

URUGUAY

CHILE   ARGENTINA

Scotia Sea

The Poles

ANTARCTICA

Atlantic
Ocean
Southern
Ocean
SOUTH
AMERICA
Pacific
Ocean
Southern
Ocean
Indian
Ocean

Pacific
Ocean
NORTH
AMERICA
Arctic
Ocean
ASIA
Atlantic
Ocean
EUROPE

0   1,500 mi
0   1,500 km